D1714907

THE THREE YUGOSLAVIAS

THE
THREE
YUGOSLAVIAS

State-Building and Legitimation, 1918–2005

Sabrina P. Ramet

Woodrow Wilson Center Press
Washington, D.C.

Indiana University Press
Bloomington and Indianapolis

EDITORIAL OFFICES
Woodrow Wilson Center Press
One Woodrow Wilson Plaza
1300 Pennsylvania Avenue, N.W.
Washington, D.C. 20004-3027
Telephone 202-691-4029
www.wilsoncenter.org

ORDER FROM
Indiana University Press
601 North Morton Street
Bloomington, IN 47404-3797
Telephone 800-842-6796
Fax 812-855-7931
iuporder@indiana.edu
http://iupress.indiana.edu

Printed in the United States of America
on acid-free paper ∞

9 8 7 6 5 4 3 2 1

Library of Congress Cataloging-in-Publication Data

Ramet, Sabrina P., 1949–
    The three Yugoslavias : state-building and legitimation, 1918–2005
/ Sabrina P. Ramet.
        p.   cm.
    Includes bibliographical references and index.
    ISBN 0-253-34656-8 (cloth : alk. paper)
    1. Yugoslavia—History—20th century.   2. Yugoslavia—Politics
and government.   3. Yugoslav War, 1991–1995.   4. Yugoslavia—
Ethnic relations.   5. Nationalism—Yugoslavia.   6. Former Yugoslav
republics—History.   I. Title.
DR1282.R36   2005
320.949709′04—dc22
                                                                2005027387

To Ola Listhaug, in friendship

When we contemplate this display of passions and the consequences of their violence, the unreason which is associated not only with them, but even—rather we might say especially—with good *designs and righteous aims; when we see arising therefrom the evil, the vice, the ruin, that has befallen the most flourishing kingdoms which the mind of man ever created, we can hardly avoid being filled with sorrow at this universal taint of corruption. And since this decay is not the work of mere nature, but of human will, our reflections may well lead us to a moral sadness.*

—G. W. F. Hegel, *Reason in History,* translated by Robert S. Hartman

Contents

Maps

Tables

Preface and Acknowledgments

This book was originally conceived as a third edition of my earlier book, *Nationalism and Federalism in Yugoslavia*, which went through two editions (Indiana University Press, 1984 and 1992). I began work on it in 1996, but gradually it became clear that much of the book would be changed, and that much would be added to the story. Of the 14 chapters which constituted the second edition of *Nationalism and Federalism,* only 6 chapters and parts of a seventh remain, and even they are considerably overhauled and enriched by research conducted since 1992. Thirteen of the chapters in this present book are, thus, entirely new, as is the title. From the very start I jettisoned the theoretical structure which framed the earlier book, in order to raise what seem to be more important questions about what constitutes strength or weakness in state systems and what constitutes legitimacy. I wanted, in particular, to examine the question as to why the Yugoslavs (as the citizens of both the Kingdom of Yugoslavia, 1929–1941, and of the Socialist Federated Republic of Yugoslavia, 1946–1991, were officially called) repeatedly failed to create a stable state. That this result should be traced to factors other than mere ethnic diversity should be obvious to anyone with even the most superficial acquaintance with the experiences of Great Britain, Spain, Switzerland, Canada, and other multiethnic or multicultural systems which have already established their credentials through sheer longevity. But if multiethnicity should not be seen as the vortex driving states toward collapse, then should one look to failures in institutions or in the fashioning of civic culture or to economic injustices or to some other variables, or perhaps to several of these, for the answer? Although I have chosen to place my emphasis on the failure to create a legitimate and functional system, a system respecting human rights and the rule of law, inter alia, it seems to me that the failures in regard to civic culture and economic injustice, and, for that matter, problems related to *procedural illegitimacy* are by no means irrelevant to the outcome. And, to underline the obvious, such failures are always the failures of identifiable human actors and should not be attributed to agentless forces. This book represents, thus, simultaneously an affirmation of certain elements of continuity in my thinking and evidence of a certain growth or development in my understanding.

Be that as it may, this book, partly old, mostly new, is clearly an outgrowth of that earlier volume. As such, it still owes much to the support extended to me by the Fulbright-Hayes program during the 1979–1980 academic year (which I spent in Belgrade) and by the American Council of Learned Societies during the summer of 1982 (when I conducted interviews in Belgrade, Zagreb, Ljubljana, and Sarajevo). The International Research and Exchanges Board (IREX) has also graciously assisted me over the years, funding short-term visits to the Yugoslav area, so that I might conduct research interviews: in 1989 (Belgrade, Zagreb, Ljubljana, Sarajevo, Skopje), in 1992 (Ljubljana), in 1995 (Skopje, Tetovo), and in 1997 (Zagreb). I also conducted interviews in the region in 1987, 1999, and 2004: the 1987 trip took me to Belgrade, Zagreb, and Ljubljana, the 1999 trip brought me to Ljubljana, as part of the University of Washington— University of Ljubljana faculty exchange program, and in 2004 I had the occasion to undertake a few interviews in Belgrade, Novi Sad, and Sarajevo, thanks to the support of the Department of Sociology and Political Science of the Norwegian University of Science & Technology and of the Peace Research Institute of Oslo (PRIO). I am grateful to all of these agencies for facilitating my research over the years.

I am also indebted to the Slavic Research Center at Hokkaido University, where I spent the 1993–94 academic year as a Foreign Visiting Fellow. The reading completed there is reflected in these pages. I am also grateful for the opportunity to spend the 2000–2001 academic year at the Woodrow Wilson International Center for Scholars in Washington, D.C. During that academic year I had the opportunity to make use of the holdings of the National Archives II, in College Park, Maryland, and to enjoy the intellectually stimulating company of Marty Sletzinger, head of the East European Studies Program at the Wilson Center, Martha Merritt, Aleksa Djilas, Sharon Wolchik, and others. Immediately after my term at the Wilson Center had ended, I spent nine weeks in Zagreb, Croatia, thanks to a generous grant from IREX. During the time I spent in Zagreb, I devoted my energies to trudging through various police reports from 1929–1939 on file at the Croatian State Archives. Archivists Mirjana, Dunja, Dorotea, and Boris were especially helpful during the weeks I spent at the archives. I took advantage of a subsequent trip to Zagreb in March 2002 to use materials at the Croatian National and University Library (*Nacionalna i Sveučilišna Knjižnica*). In researching this book, I also had the occasion to make use of the Svetozar Marković University Library in Belgrade, the National Library of Serbia (in Belgrade), the University Research Library of UCLA, the Suzzallo & Allen Library of the University of Washington, the Widener Library of Harvard University, the John M. Olin Library of Cornell University, the John P. Robarts Library of the University of Toronto, and the University Library of the Norwegian University of Science & Technology (NTNU).

Publication of this volume was facilitated by a generous publication subsidy from the Centre for the Study of Civil War of the Peace Research Institute in Oslo (PRIO). In addition, thanks to the generosity of Ola Listhaug and PRIO's Centre for the Study for Civil War, a special symposium was held on 9 January 2004 in order to afford me the opportunity to obtain critical feedback on the manuscript before going to press. Thomas Emmert, Marko Attila Hoare, Matjaž Klemenčič, Greg Reichberg, and Jim Sadkovich took part in this event, sharing their insights with me and generously offering suggestions for improvement. Various other scholars/friends have graciously taken time to read through one or more chapters and to give me valuable feedback. In alphabetical order, I would like to acknowledge here: Ante Čuvalo, Vlasta Jalušič, Roman Kuhar, Tonči Kuzmanić, Zlatko Matijević, György Péteri, Lea Plut-Pregelj, Vladimir Pregelj, Rudi Rizman, Pablo Valverde, and a kind gentleman living in Los Angeles who has preferred to retain anonymity. I am also grateful to Aleš Gabrič, Roman Kuhar, and Božo Repe for helpful comments on an oral presentation of a portion of chapter 19, to Janet Spikes and Dagne Gizaw, the librarians at the Wilson Center, for their help with many aspects of the research of this volume, and to Joe Brinley, director of the Wilson Center Press, for catching certain infelicities in the text. During 1978–1980 I studied Serbo-Croatian, as the language was then called, though some people now deny that there was ever any language known by this name. Thanks to my study of this disputed language, I have been able to read Serbian- and Croatian-language materials published during the years 1923–1940, Serbo-Croatian materials published during the years 1945–1991, and materials published since 1991 in Serbian, Croatian, Bosnian, and Montenegrin. Although I am also comfortable reading German and Italian, in addition to my native English, and am beginning to become comfortable reading the Scandinavian languages, I wanted to be able to access material published in other languages. Thanks to the generosity of the Wilson Center, which hired research assistants to work in Slovenian and French materials, and to the HMJ School of International Studies at the University of Washington, which hired a research assistant to work in Macedonian materials, I have been able to take advantage, indirectly, of materials published in these other languages. I am grateful to Thomas Greene, who read the Macedonian and Bulgarian materials cited in the text, to Tamara Kotar, who read most of the Slovenian materials cited in the text, and to Tiziana Stella, who read the Italian materials cited in chapters 4 and 5 and all of the French materials cited in the text. Special thanks are also owed to Marijan Gubić, who helped me to find rare books and who, after I thought I had exhausted all possibilities, was repeatedly able to locate copies of books I needed for my work on this volume, and to Vjeran Pavlaković, who, over the course of a two-year period, sent me enough clippings from the Croatian press to fill a large clipping file. I am also grateful to Millie Kahn for her hard work during the page proof stage and to Bill Nelson for providing the maps used in this book.

I am also grateful to archivists Amy Schmidt and Lewis Holland for their invaluable assistance in the use of the National Archives in College Park, Maryland, to Rosemary Lyon, Sabina A. M. Crisen, Meredith L. Knepp, Rosita Hickman, Sean McQuitty, Ben Amini, and Lindsay Collins of the Wilson Center for assistance in various regards, and to my editors Janet Rabinowitch and Joe Brinley for their enthusiasm for this project, their patience, and their wise counsel. The generous counsel of friends, who have alerted me to important literature and who have in other ways helped me to avoid error, should also be acknowledged. Among these friends I wish to acknowledge especially Ivo Banac, Norman Cigar, and Jim Sadkovich, whose own works have set a high standard for the field.

The work on this book at the Wilson Center involved nine months' separation from my spouse, Christine Hassenstab. As rich and as rewarding as the program at the Wilson Center was, the separation from Chris was not always easy, even with monthly visits. I am therefore all the more grateful to her for her enthusiastic support for my research and her understanding.

An extract from chapter 2 (the section dealing with the Concordat) was first published in *Bulletin of the Association for Croatian Studies* (2002). A portion of chapter 5 was published, in an earlier version, under the title "Gradualism in International Confrontation: The Soviet-Yugoslav Crisis of 1947–51," in the *Ukrainian Quarterly,* vol. 44, no. 3–4 (Fall–Winter 1988). A portion of chapter 10 was published, in an earlier version, under the title "Problems of Albanian Nationalism in Yugoslavia," in *Orbis,* vol. 25, no. 2 (Summer 1981). Chapter 12 was published, in an earlier version, under the title "Serbia's Slobodan Milošević: A Profile," in *Orbis,* vol. 35, no. 1 (Winter 1991). Chapter 17 was first published, in an earlier version, under the title "The Third Yugoslavia, 1992–2001," as *East European Studies Occasional Paper No. 66* by the Woodrow Wilson International Center for Scholars, July 2001, which drew, in part, as this incarnation does, upon a section of my book *Balkan Babel: The Disintegration of Yugoslavia from the Death of Tito to the Fall of Milošević,* 4th ed. (Boulder, Colo.: Westview Press, 2002). I am grateful to these journals and publishers for permission to reuse this material. An extract from chapter 18 was published under the title "KFOR's Record in Kosovo," in Sabina Crisen (ed.), *NATO Enlargement and Peacekeeping: Journeys to Where?* (Washington, D.C.: East European Studies, Woodrow Wilson International Center for Scholars, 2001). An extract from the section dealing with Slovenia, in chapter 19, was first published in *EES News* (May–June 2001), a publication of the East European Studies Program of the Woodrow Wilson International Center for Scholars.

I worked on this book under unusual circumstances, moving 12 times in the course of work on this project. In 1997 I moved to Bergen, Norway, for nearly three months, returning to Seattle in June of that year. The following March Chris and I put most of our possessions in storage and moved to Kyoto, where we spent nine months, so that we could teach at Ritsumeikan University, Kyoto's most illustrious university. After our return to the U.S., we lived briefly in Seattle before purchasing a home in Lynnwood. In September 2000, I moved to the Washington, D.C., area in connection with my affiliation with the Wilson Center, returning to Lynnwood at the end of May. I transferred to Zagreb in early June 2001, returning to Lynnwood in the first half of August. After two weeks in Lynnwood, I flew to Norway, taking up residence in Ranheim, where Chris joined me a month later. At the end of the year, Chris and I moved from Ranheim, on the outskirts of Trondheim, to Byåsen, a district just outside the center of Trondheim. In August 2002, we moved yet again, taking up residence in Hundhamaren, a small town just outside Trondheim. That adds up to a dozen moves in six years—an average of one move every six months. Somehow, through it all, I have managed to keep the materials relating to this project organized and accessible—no small feat, I think.

Sabrina P. Ramet
Trondheim, Norway

Abbreviations and Acronyms Used in the Text

ANLA Albanian National Liberation Army

AVNOJ Antifašističko Vijeće Narodnog Oslobodjenja Jugoslavije (the Antifascist Council of the People's Liberation of Yugoslavia)

CC Central Committee

CPA Communist Party of Albania

CPY Communist Party of Yugoslavia

DOS Democratic Opposition of Serbia

DS Demokratska stranka (Democratic Party, the party headed by Zoran Djindjić until March 2003, and since then by Boris Tadić)

DSS Demokratska stranka Srbije (Democratic Party of Serbia, headed by Vojislav Koštunica)

ELAS Greek National Liberation Army (*Ellinikós Laikós Apeleftheorotikós Stratós*)

FADURK Federal Fund for the Accelerated Development of the Underdeveloped Republics and Kosovo

FRY Federal Republic of Yugoslavia (1992–2003)

GRECO Groupe d'Etats contre la corruption (Group of States against corruption)

HDZ Hrvatska demokratska zajednica (Croatian Democratic Community, the party founded by Franjo Tudjman in 1989)

HIP Hrvatski identitet i prosperitet (Croatian Identity and Prosperity, the party founded by Miroslav Tudjman, Franjo Tudjman's son)

HOS Hrvatske Oružane Snage (Croatian Armed Forces, established by the Croatian Party of Right in 1991)

HPSS Hrvatska pučka seljačka stranka (Croatian People's Peasant Party, the party founded by the brothers Antun and Stjepan Radić in 1905; later renamed the HRSS)

HRSS Hrvatska republikanska seljačka stranka (Croatian Republican Peasant Party, as the HPSS was renamed in December 1920; later renamed the HSS)

HSS Hrvatska seljačka stranka (Croatian Peasant Party, as the HPSS/HRSS was renamed in 1925)

HV Hrvatska Vojska (Croatian Army)

HVO Hrvatsko Vijeće Obrane (Croatian Defense Council)

HZ Hrvatska zajednica (Croatian Community, a political party formed in July 1919 through the fusion of the Starčević Party of Right and the Progressive Democratic Party)

ICTY International War Crimes Tribunal for the former Yugoslavia

IFOR Implementation Force (in Bosnia-Herzegovina)

IMRO-DPMNU Internal Macedonian Revolutionary Organization—Democratic Party for Macedonian National Unity

JNA Jugoslovenska Narodna Armija (Yugoslav People's Army)

KFOR Kosovo Protection Force

KGB Soviet secret police

KKE Greek Communist Party (*Kommounistiko Komma tis Elladas*)

KLA Kosova Liberation Army

KOS Kontra-obavještajna služba (Counterintelligence Service, the secret service of the JNA)

LCY League of Communists of Yugoslavia

LNC Levicija Nacional Çlirimtarë (National Liberation Movement [of Albania], established by the Albanian communists at Peza in September 1942)

LRDG Long Range Desert Group (of the British Army, in World War Two)

MBO Muslim Bosniak Organization (the party founded by Adil Zulfikarpašić)

MUP Ministarstvo Unutrašnjih Poslova (Ministry of Internal Affairs)

NOB Narodnooslobodilačka borba (People's Liberation Struggle)

NOR Narodnooslobodilački rat (People's Liberation War)

NS New Slovenia

OSS Office of Strategic Services, an American agency headed by General William J. Donovan

OZNA Odeljenje za zaštitu naroda (Department for the Protection of the People—the original name for the Yugoslav communist secret police). *See also* UDBa

SANU Srpska Akademija Nauka i Umjetnosti (Serbian Academy of Sciences and Art)

SAWPY Socialist Alliance of Working People of Yugoslavia

SDA Stranka Demokratske Akcije (Party of Democratic Action, Alija Izetbegović's party)

SDB Služba Državne Bezbednosti (State Security Service)

SDS Srpska Demokratska Stranka (Serbian Democratic Party, Radovan Karadžić's party)

SEED Support for East European Democracy

SFOR Stabilization Force (in Bosnia-Herzegovina)

SFRY Socialist Federated Republic of Yugoslavia

SIV Savezno izvršno vijeće (Federal Executive Council)

SPO Srpski pokret obnove (Serbian Renewal Movement, led by Vuk Drašković)

SPS Socijalistička partija Srbije (Socialist Party of Serbia, established by Slobodan Milošević, on the framework of the old League of Communists of Serbia)

SRS Srpska radikalna stranka (Serbian Radical Party, established by Vojislav Šešelj)

SUBNOR Savez Udruženja boraca NOR-a (League of Associations of Veterans of the People's Liberation War)

UDBa Uprava državne bezbednosti (State Security Administration, i.e., the secret police). *See also* OZNA

UNCRO United Nations Confidence Restoration Operation in Croatia (as UNPROFOR's contingent in Croatia was renamed in 1995)

UNMIK United Nations Interim Administration Mission in Kosovo

UNPROFOR United Nations Protection Force (the UN "peacekeeping" contingent sent to Croatia and Bosnia in 1992). *See also* UNCRO

UNRRA United Nations Rescue and Relief Agency

ZAVNO-BiH Zemaljsko antifašističko vijeće narodnog oslobodjenje Bosne i Hercegovine (Country Anti-fascist Council of the People's Liberation of Bosnia and Herzegovina)

Glossary

Anti-bureaucratic Revolution a slogan used by Milošević and his coterie in the years 1988–90, as a code for the overthrow of duly elected governments in other republics

Brotherhood and Unity the normative principle declaring all peoples of socialist Yugoslavia "brothers" and urging them to desist from internecine fighting, operationalized in socialist governance through the use of the "ethnic key," the principle of routine rotation of cadres, and the prohibition on party members to criticize the members or branch party organizations of other nationalities or their policies

Conservative, in reference to communists preferring administrative measures to consultative approaches, and preferring firm party control of the political and economic machinery, as well as of the media, to solutions which would allow some form of devolution

Democracy a system based on multi-candidate elections, an uncensored press, and the separation of powers, with an informed public and campaign funding from public coffers

Ethnic key the principle establishing ethnic quotas for positions of responsibility on the basis of approximate proportionality to population

Liberal (a) anyone who supports the rule of law, respect for individual rights, tolerance, respect for the harm principle, equality, and neutrality of the state in matters of religion; and (b) (among communists) anyone who supports loose party supervision of the political and economic machinery, supports limited press freedom, and prefers solutions which would allow some form of devolution of control

Modern, Efficacious State another slogan used by Milošević and his coterie in the years 1988–1991, as a code for a centralized state

Nationalism chauvinism centered on the Nation, usually defined as a collectivity of people sharing a common language and a common history, and manifesting itself in the denial of individual rights when they obstruct the realization of nationalist goals

Nonalignment the principle of avoidance of affiliation with either the Soviet bloc or the Atlantic Alliance, while affirming an active presence in foreign policy, through the Nonaligned Movement

Quisling Vidkun Quisling, a Norwegian who collaborated with the Nazis during World War Two and who headed a collaborationist government under Nazi auspices; and, by extension and general convention, anyone who collaborated with the Nazis during World War Two and who headed a collaborationist government under Nazi auspices—such as Milan Nedić in Serbia

Self-management a system whereby workers are represented in elected workers' councils, which take decisions affecting the operations of the plants in which they function

Skupština Assembly (as in federal *Skupština*)

Sporazum the agreement concluded in 1939 between Vladko Maček and Dragiša Cvetković, establishing an autonomous banovina of Croatia

Ustaša the Croatian fascist movement which dominated Croatia in the years 1941–1945 (also used as an adjective to refer to that movement)

Ustaše members of the *Ustaša* movement

Map 1. Administrative Borders of Yugoslavia, 1929

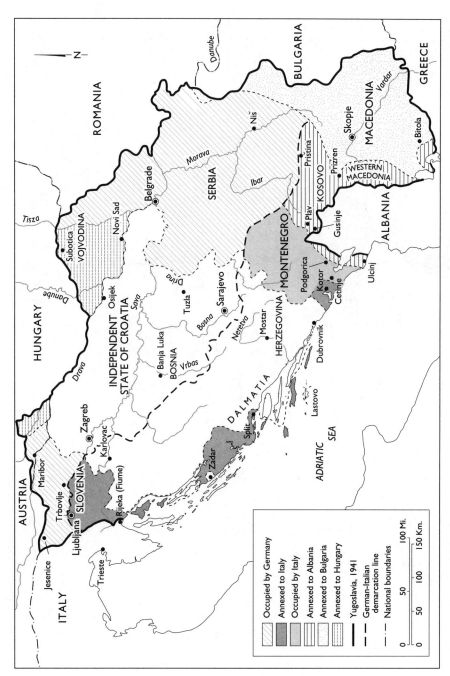

Map 2. The Partition of Yugoslavia, 1941

Legend:
- Occupied by Germany
- Annexed to Italy
- Occupied by Italy
- Annexed to Albania
- Annexed to Bulgaria
- Annexed to Hungary
- Yugoslavia, 1941
- German-Italian demarcation line
- National boundaries

0   50   100 Mi.
0   50   100   150 Km.

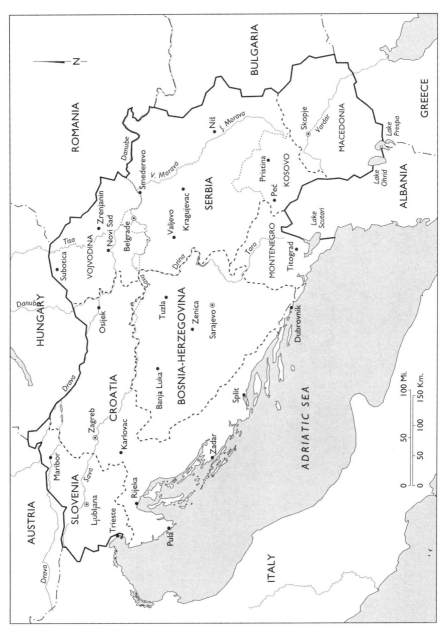

Map 3. The Socialist Federated Republic of Yugoslavia

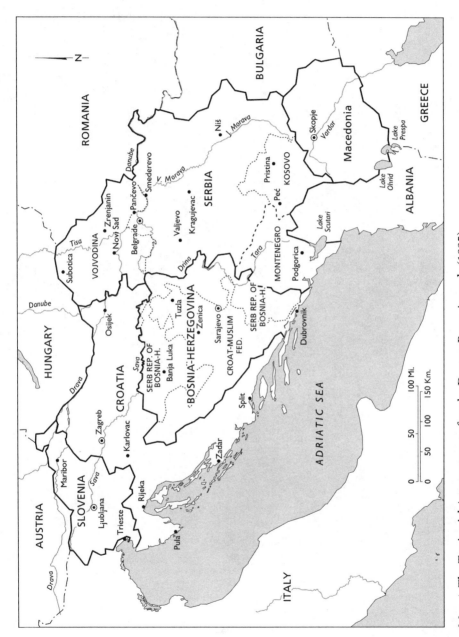

Map 4. The Territorial Arrangement after the Dayton Peace Accords (1995)

THE THREE YUGOSLAVIAS

Introduction

I

Yugoslavia exploded onto the front pages of world newspapers in the early 1990s, with stories about the gouging of eyes, the mutilation of genitals, massacres, and the expulsions of civilians from their villages. The war of 1991–1995, herein called the War of Yugoslav Succession, gave the peoples of Yugoslavia, and especially the Serbs, a bad name in the West and revived calls, in some quarters, to abandon the name "Balkan" altogether, on the argument that the very name "Balkan" had become so closely associated with bloodletting that it could no longer be considered a neutral term appropriate for designating any geographic zone.

It was not always this way. Yugoslavia was a crisis-ridden state in all three of its incarnations—the interwar kingdom (1918–1941, but only called "Yugoslavia" after 1929), communist Yugoslavia (1945–1991), and the rump Yugoslav state set up by Slobodan Milošević (1992–2003). Yet in spite of this state of permanent crisis, the country enjoyed a certain prestige in the Tito era (1945–1980), when Marshal Josip Broz Tito defied the Soviets and helped to establish the nonaligned movement, bringing together states which did not want to align themselves with either the Soviet Union or the United States. Ruling first as prime minister and later as president of the republic, Tito fashioned a system of workers' councils called "self-management," in which—it was claimed—workers managed their own factories and enterprises, and in the 1960s and 1970s delegations came to Yugoslavia from all over the world to study self-management and see what lessons they could learn from it. Yugoslav self-management, in short, was seen as a model for the world to study and perhaps emulate.

In spite of that, and in spite of the democratic trappings of all three Yugoslavias, the country never had what could be considered a normal, stable democracy—although Slovenia, largely escaping from the war, quickly succeeded in this after the country broke up in 1991. The interwar kingdom was undermined by the disinclination of the leading Serbian politicians, until 1939, to engage in political compromise, by the proliferation of armed militias inspired by xenophobia, and by widespread political and economic corruption, among other things, leading to a sense of constant crisis. Communist Yugoslavia was subverted by the party's inability to transform itself into a democratic player (as per the Hungarian and Polish examples), by the evaporation in the years after Tito's death of such support for the system as there had been, by economic deterioration (which drove people onto the streets in protest), and

1

by the federal system itself, which divided power in the name of unity in a self-contradictory formula which drew the fault lines along which the country would later break up. And "third Yugoslavia," as Milošević's Federal Republic of Yugoslavia has often been called, succumbed to the self-destructive policies of aggression and deficit spending on which the Milošević regime had tried to establish itself.

Although there was no Yugoslavia before the 20th century, the history of the "Yugo-slavs" (or South Slavs) may be traced to the 6th century, when Slavic tribes settled in the area which would later become Yugoslavia. Originally polytheist, the South Slavs gradually converted to Christianity, with large numbers of conversions in the eighth and ninth centuries. Slovenes, Croats, Bosnians, and Serbs can all look back to medieval states. The Slovenes initially called their state Carantania. Eventually, local dynasties declined, and by 1460, the Habsburg dynasty, based in Vienna, had established its control over all Slovene lands.[1] Croatia gained its independence (from Frankish overlords) in 878 and enjoyed an early highpoint during the reign of King Tomislav (ca. 910–928), but lost its independence in 1097, when Koloman, the Hungarian king, defeated the Croatian king on the field of battle, subsequently taking the crown of Croatia for himself.[2] According to Mitja Velikonja, the first mention of a political formation in the territory of what came to be called Bosnia after 958 can be dated to the late 700s. After the Hungarian absorption of Croatia, Hungary gained sway over Bosnia too, appointing its governor (*ban*). It was during the era of Ban Kulin (1180–1204) that medieval Bosnia enjoyed what has come down as its "golden age." Controversies concerning the religion practiced in Bosnia led to military intervention by Hungarian forces in the early 13th century, but after the Mongol sacking of Budapest in 1241, Bosnia was able to revive, and in the 14th century, Tvrtko I of Bosnia (ban, 1353–1377; king of Rascia and Bosnia, 1377–1391; and king of Croatia and Dalmatia after 1390) defeated the Hungarians and built up Bosnia to its greatest extent.[3] And finally, the Serbs formed a state in the early 9th century but came under Bulgarian rule soon thereafter; they reasserted themselves in the late 12th century, when Stefan Nemanja rallied the Serbs and defeated Byzantine and Bulgarian armies. The medieval Serbian state reached its zenith in the 14th century, during the reign of Tsar Dušan the Mighty ("Emperor of Serbia and Greece," 1346–1355), who repeatedly emerged victorious in battle and who issued an important law code in 1349. He died in 1355, while leading an army against Constantinople.[4]

In the course of the 14th and 15th centuries, the Ottoman Empire took control of Serbia and Bosnia, even pushing into Croatia. Hungary also lost its independence and was partitioned in three. The crown of the Kingdom of Hungary passed into Habsburg hands in 1526 and, with it, the crown of the Kingdom of Croatia. For about four centuries (1459–1878 in the case of Serbia, 1463–1878 in the case of Bosnia, and 1481–1878 in the case of Herzegovina), the Balkan peninsula was under Ottoman rule or suzerainty, which treated Muslims and non-Muslims differently. It was only in the context of the Napoleonic wars that things began to change dramatically. Napoleon's sponsorship of an "Illyrian" state, consisting of much of present-day Slovenia and Croatia, provided a strong encouragement to the development of national feeling among the people in those regions, while the outbreak of a rebellion among Serbs in 1804, led by Djordje Petrović ("Karadjordje"), marked the beginning of the Serbs' march to independence. The Illyrian episode in particular encouraged ideas about a South Slav, or Yugoslav, state, and "Yugoslavism" gained some articulate advocates in the course of the 19th century—most prominently, Josip Juraj Strossmayer, the bishop of Djakovo. It would take another continental war—the "Great War" of 1914–1918—to break up the Habsburg and Ottoman empires and to create conditions in which the Kingdom of Serbs, Croats, and Slovenes—as the interwar kingdom was first called—could emerge.

This was an inauspicious time for the establishment of new states, insofar as the liberal ideas of the Enlightenment were being challenged by two authoritarian ideologies—communism and fascism. The latter, which viewed democratic culture as decadent and sought to realize a spiritual renewal through a cult of heroism and the glorification of wars of conquest, was especially influential in East-Central Europe.[5] While Norway (which regained its full independence only in 1905) and Finland (independent only since 1918) provided models of what newly independent countries in Europe could achieve in terms of building legitimate political institutions, such models were scarcely relevant in Yugoslavia, where the Radical Party and Democratic Party set up a system which discriminated against non-Serbs. Discontent was rife among non-Serbs, who made up more than 60% of the population—especially among Croats, Macedonians, Vojvodina's Hungarians, and Kosovo's Albanians. Such a system could only be maintained by force, and the proliferation of semi-legal militias such as ORJUNA (Organization of Yugoslav Nationalists) and SRNAO (Serbian National Youth) provided the muscle to maintain this dysfunctional system for an unstable decade. In June 1928, the popular Croatian leader Stjepan Radić was shot on the floor of the Assembly; he later died of his wounds. Then, in January 1929, King Aleksandar declared a royal dictatorship and imposed a constitution of his own design on the country in 1931, having decided that the various political parties were incapable of behaving responsibly. The dictatorship was widely unpopular. Some Croats had had enough and left the country to form the Ustaša movement. In 1934, a Macedonian militant, working together with members of the Ustaša, gunned down King Aleksandar on the occasion of his visit to Marseilles. In fact, the Croats, in general, never reconciled themselves to a centralized system and would have preferred a federalized system or possibly a system modeled on post-1867 Austria-Hungary. Finally, in August 1939, a historic *Sporazum* (agreement) was signed, which granted the Croats a significant amount of autonomy within a designated area called the "Banovina of Croatia." Meanwhile, after Hitler's election as German chancellor in 1932 and seizure of unconstitutional power in 1933, Germany undertook an active policy of drawing East-Central Europe into its orbit, using foreign trade and German diasporas as instruments of influence.[6] Yugoslavia, like other countries in the area, soon found itself in a position of partial economic dependence on its German trading partner.

The *Sporazum,* signed on the eve of World War Two, was a case of "too little, too late." It was too little because it addressed the wishes of Croats, but not those of Slovenes, Bosnian Muslims, Macedonians, Kosovar Albanians, or, for that matter, Serbs. It was too late because by then the resentments of Serb hegemony among the Croats and Bosniaks had reached the boiling point. Besides, fascist movements had emerged among the Croats (the Ustaša, led by Ante Pavelić) and among the Serbs (the Zbor, led by Dimitrije Ljotić), and the former, in particular, would play an important role in the Nazi-sponsored carving up of Yugoslavia in April 1941, when the war reached the country. Then, in response to the Axis occupation of Yugoslavia, 1941–1945, two important resistance movements emerged: the Chetniks, led by Draža Mihailović, most of whose adherents were Serbs, and the Partisans, led by Josip Broz Tito, whose ranks were more diverse. Both began as resistance movements, but, as will be documented in chapter 4, the Chetniks soon slid into collaboration with the Axis powers, with the Nazi-sponsored occupation regime in Serbia, and even with the fascist regime of Ante Pavelić in Croatia. It was the Partisans who carried out the most sustained anti-Axis resistance and who, by 1943, had gained the confidence of the British government.

As the war ended, many supporters of the occupation regimes or of Mihailović's Chetniks fled the country. Some of the prewar politicians tried to rebuild their party organizations and to reenter political life, but the communists stifled them and established a one-party state.[7] During the years 1945–1948, the Tito regime did its best to emulate Stalin's example and introduced many features of the Soviet system including Pioneer organizations for youngsters,[8] agricultural collectivization, five-year plans, socialist realism in music and film, and censorship of the mass media. Resistance to collectivization in the countryside was sustained, and Tito eventually retreated and allowed private farming to continue. In the meantime, Tito refused to subordinate Yugoslavia to Stalin's control, resulting in Yugoslavia's expulsion from the Cominform, the imposition of an economic embargo by Stalin, and the launching of preparations for an armed invasion of Yugoslavia by Soviet bloc forces. The plan to invade Yugoslavia was abandoned at the last minute, when the U.S. showed resolve in Korea; to Stalin's mind, Korea was marginal and Yugoslavia strategically valuable, and he calculated that if the U.S. would send in an expeditionary force to fight the North Koreans, it would surely do likewise in Yugoslavia in the event of Soviet invasion there.

At first, the economic embargo hit Yugoslavia very hard, but then the U.S. entered into the picture, offering first economic assistance and trade and then also military assistance. During the years 1952–1962, Yugoslavia's economic growth rate was one of the fastest in the world.[9] This was also the period in which the slogan "brotherhood and unity," which had been used during the war, was refined into a central pillar of the system, and in which nonalignment and self-management were developed as the central principles of foreign policy and domestic policy, respectively. By 1962, however, economic problems forced the authorities to rethink their approach, and their response was to adopt a major reform package which introduced a mixed system called "market socialism." In 1963, the constitution of 1946, which had been massively amended via the Basic Law of 1953, was finally replaced with a new constitution, which was itself subjected to extensive revision almost immediately. Aleksandar Ranković, Tito's vice president, had done his best to assure Serb predominance in the administrative apparatuses in Croatia, Bosnia, and Kosovo, even though Serbs were in the minority in these areas, and to fight the movement for reform; but in 1966, Tito dismissed Ranković from his posts in a move which was welcomed by more liberal communists. Indeed, by the late 1960s, Yugoslavia seemed to be on its way to something comparable to the "socialism with a human face" attempted by Alexander Dubćek in Czechoslovakia, i.e., to a liberal form of communism enjoying considerable popular support.[10] The Yugoslav economy was also once more on the upswing, thanks in no small measure to the development of the tourist industry along Croatia's Dalmatian coast. In Serbia, party leaders Latinka Perović and Marko Nikezić earned respect by repudiating the sort of policies associated with Ranković and treating the other peoples of Yugoslavia as equal partners. In Croatia, however, party leaders Miko Tripalo and Savka Dabćević-Kućar, though hugely popular, were unable to distance themselves from nationalist currents which Tito considered threatening to his system. Tito's response was to fire liberal party leaders not only in Croatia but also in Slovenia, Macedonia, and Serbia. The dismissal of Perović and Nikezić was one of the most fateful errors committed by Tito.

In spite of that, and in spite of the incipient economic damage wrought by the sharp rise in oil prices in 1974, the late 1970s were a kind of "golden age" for Tito-era Yugoslavia in terms of general economic well-being and culture. There were fears even at high levels that the Soviets might use Tito's death as a pretext for invasion, but when Tito finally passed away in May 1980, after lying in a coma for four months, there was no invasion, and Tito's heirs were able to effect a smooth transition, operating under the banner of collective leadership.

On the political level, the collective leadership fashioned by Tito loudly insisted on its determination to follow Tito's path, but it proved unable to prevent a loosening of the system for at least four reasons. First, without Tito, the League of Communists of Yugoslavia lacked an ultimate arbiter and was therefore tangibly weaker than before. The divided party leadership could not assert itself because, in many cases, "the will of the party" could not even be determined. Second, important power centers within the party wanted change (albeit change disguised as continuity) and pressed for a measure of relaxation. Such relaxation as did take place probably exceeded the limits of what these party "liberals" had in mind, since a retrenchment which was set in motion in the summer of 1982 met no serious overt resistance within that party. Third, the tangible economic deterioration that began in 1979 threw the entire system into disarray, and numerous officials blamed the distribution of power between the federal government and the federal units for the country's economic problems. Although some suggested that the country suffered from too much decentralization, others took the opposite tack and argued that only extensive decentralization had enabled Yugoslavia to function even as well as it had. And fourth, the explosion of violence in Kosovo in April 1981, when discontented Albanians burned cars and attacked Serbs, produced a nationalist backlash throughout Serbia. Kosovo was placed under military occupation, and the episode reopened the question of the utility of federalism as a solution for interethnic tensions and distrust.

These sundry problems gradually sapped the political capacity of the system, and by 1989, Slovenia was talking of secession, Serbia was trying to eliminate its autonomous provinces, and the Serbian minority in Croatia was becoming restive. Free elections in Slovenia and Croatia in spring 1990 brought noncommunist governments to power in those republics, and by the end of the year, Bosnia's communists had been swept out of power and replaced by an unstable coalition among three ethnic parties, representing respectively Serbs, Croats, and Bosnian Muslims, while in Macedonia the local communists entered into a coalition with non-communist parties. In Serbia and Montenegro, by contrast, local communists retained power by embracing nationalist programs; in Serbia that meant committing to a program of annexing portions of Croatia and Bosnia. In the course of 1990, tensions escalated, culminating in the outbreak of war in June 1991. After four years of fighting, more than 200,000 persons were dead, Bosnia was divided, and Serbia had become a pariah state. The war also disseminated nationalism of the most xenophobic brand, and, at this writing, the largest party in the Serbian Assembly is the extreme nationalist Serbian Radical Party.

II

This book is conceived as a *thematic history,* which differs from a general history in the sense that whereas a general history aspires to cover everything which the author considers important in the history of a country, a thematic history covers only those developments which are important to the theme of the work. The themes of this work are political legitimacy, political development, and nationalism. That said, I have chosen to interpret these themes rather broadly, thus including some discussion of foreign policy, where this seemed essential. The book is driven by a specific view of the question of legitimacy, which is outlined in chapter 1. Since chapter 1 is heavily theoretical, readers interested only in the history of Yugoslavia but not in the more theoretical discussion may safely skip this chapter if they wish; the ideas developed there are, in any case, implicit in the chapters which follow.

The longest chapters in the book are those devoted to the two major wars which shook Yugoslavia—World War Two (known in communist times as the National Liberation War) and the second phase (in Bosnia) of the War of Yugoslav Succession. There are two chapters devoted to the interwar era, with the declaration of the royal dictatorship in 1929 serving to mark the break between the two chapters. Seven chapters (chapters 5–11) are devoted to the 46-year-long communist era, with two chapters (12, 13) devoted to the breakdown of the system and the drift toward war. The War of Yugoslav Succession takes up two chapters, with chapter 14 covering military and diplomatic developments in 1991 (that is, as related to the fighting in Slovenia and Croatia), and chapter 15 covering the war from January 1992 to October 1995. Chapter 16 looks at postwar Bosnia, and chapter 17 traces the story of the "Third Yugoslavia" from 1992 to 2005 (including developments in Kosovo preceding and during NATO's air campaign), while chapters 18 and 19 discuss developments in postcampaign Kosovo and, in comparative perspective, post-1990 Slovenia, Macedonia, and Croatia. A short conclusion summarizes the themes and findings of this volume.

One of the unfortunate delusions which has taken hold among some people, since the War of Yugoslav Succession broke out, is one which would endeavor to trace the Yugoslav meltdown to "ancient hatreds." If by "ancient" one means before the fall of Rome, then the notion is utterly absurd, since the Slavs had not even settled in the Balkan peninsula at that time. But even if one takes a less literal reading, the notion even of "very old" hatreds still has problems. In fact, the region probably had more cooperative ties than conflicts prior to the founding of the state in 1918, and there were no special "hatreds" prior to that time. More particularly, the problems which Yugoslavs experienced may be said to have begun with the Vidovdan constitution of 28 June 1921, which did not enjoy broad support. In particular, the Croatian Republican Peasant Party, by far the most popular party among Croats, rejected the constitution as unfair to Croats. The authorities in Belgrade also adopted policies which discriminated against the Albanians of Kosovo and against Macedonians. The reason that the government had to sign the *Sporazum* in 1939 was because its effort, over the previous two decades, to ignore Croatian preferences had failed to produce a stable formula for the state.

The relationship between the Serbs and the Albanians in Kosovo may be a special case. But even here, much depends on whether one thinks of the Serb perspective or of the Albanian perspective. Serb complaints about suffering at the hands of Albanians began in the late 19th century—for the sake of convenience, we may say "after 1878." From the Albanian point of view, the problems began in 1913 when the Serbs ignored the borders proclaimed by the newly independent Albanian state and sent in an army to occupy Kosovo.

The interwar kingdom was undermined by a proliferation of organized militias acting outside the law, by an unequal treatment of the constituent peoples of the kingdom, by significant levels of corruption, by the preemptive incarceration of leading figures in the political opposition, and by other actions for which leading figures in the kingdom's political establishment may be held responsible. In other words, the problems of the kingdom were the responsibility of identifiable actors, rather than the result of blind historical forces. But these problems in turn sowed deep resentments which flared during World War Two, taking the form of massive intercommunal violence. That said, it is important to avoid the error of equating the Croatian fascist regime of Ante Pavelić with the Serbian occupation regime of Milan Nedić. These regimes were not, as I emphasize in chapter 4, either moral or functional equivalents. The Pavelić regime in Croatia was more brutal than the Nedić regime in Serbia and also enjoyed more autonomy than did the Nedić regime. But while Nedić was less brutal than Pavelić, he was no less a collaborator than Pavelić; indeed, because of his lesser autonomy, he was more effectively subordinated to the Nazi occupation authorities. Dimitrije Ljotić, a Serb fascist who headed the fascist movement called Zbor, admired the Nazi system and collaborated with the Nazis, as did also Kosta Pećanac, a prominent Chetnik leader.[11] Moreover, as already suggested, Draža Mihailović entered into open collaboration with fascist Italy and cooperated with the Germans on certain occasions as well. Mihailović was quite open about the fact that he regarded the anti-Axis Partisans, rather than the Axis occupation forces, as his principal foe.

The war left just over one million Yugoslavs dead—not the 1.7 million as estimated by some observers. In fact, the figure of 1.7 million was generated hastily after World War Two as the basis for German reparations, so there was every incentive to estimate high. Some extraordinary estimates have been made concerning the number of persons to have been killed at Jasenovac, but more scholarly analyses estimate that between 50,000 and 100,000 persons lost their lives at Jasenovac.[12]

World War Two left the country devastated and drained, and the task of rebuilding was ineluctable. Still, in the early years, remnants of the Ustaše and the Chetniks held out against the new communist authorities, fighting a small-scale rearguard guerrilla war for a few years. Tito, who had gained enormous prestige in the West as a result of the operations of the Partisans, played a key role in launching the Nonalignment Movement in the early 1950s and tried to use this, together with his concept of self-management (embodied, above all, in a network of workers' councils) and the not entirely vague notion of "brotherhood and unity" to forge a basis for the legitimation of his system. To enforce "brotherhood and unity" among the country's diverse peoples, Tito introduced a quota system according to which a certain number of positions would be reserved for the members of each nationality group. In spite of this, Serbs and Montenegrins held a significantly larger number of high positions in the army—a fact usually traced to the fact that they were the first to join the Partisan movement in large numbers. Given efforts to develop loyalty to the Yugoslav state (as well as to the communist system), it was not unexpected that some people began to demand the right to declare themselves as "Yugoslavs" on the census forms—a right originally not recognized. Once this was granted, the number of self-declared Yugoslavs grew steadily, reaching a high of 1.2 million persons, or about 5.4% of the population, in the 1981 census. Many, but not all, of these were the offspring of ethnically mixed marriages. The Yugoslav communists used various devices to try to promote "brotherhood and unity," and the policy was reflected even in the cultural sphere. The federal system itself was a product of the desire to accommodate the desire for self-government on the part of the diverse nationality groups.

But the communist system proved to be politically and economically inefficient, and ultimately unstable. By the early 1980s, it was clearly in decay. The questions were how rapid would the system decay and what would be the outcomes? Given other leaders, given consensual patterns of compromise, it is conceivable that the country could have found a peaceful path to democratization. Culpability for the eventual Yugoslav meltdown must be shared by those responsible for setting up the communist system in the first place, by those who, in the course of the 1980s, failed to agree on measures to take the country down a peaceful, democratic path, and by those who took the decision for war. As has been documented, among other places, in the diary of Borisav Jović, when it comes to the war of 1991–1995, this was planned, above all, by Slobodan Milošević, Borisav Jović, and other members of the Serbian leadership, working together with Radovan Karadžić, Veljko Kadijević, Milan Martić, Milan Babić, and others, and working through various channels identified in the text. They were able to succeed both because of their use of the media to sow hatreds and resentments, and because the decay of the system had reached an advanced state. Specifically, SFRY (Socialist Federated Republic of Yugoslavia) institutions were already in an advanced state of decay by March 1991: many federal employees were as much as three months behind in their salaries; some agencies of the federal government had been shut down for lack of funds; the army had failed to deliver its annual report to the federal Assembly as required by law in 1990; and Slobodan Milošević, head of the Serbian party, was violating a number of constitutional provisions and laws.[13] Thus, the SFRY was already dying.

Milošević and his colleague, Borisav Jović, had begun active preparations for war in 1990, and the conflict in fact began in March 1991. Some observers have speculated that Slovenia and Croatia could have reversed the direction in which things were moving simply by staying in the federation. Given that the SFRY had largely decayed, that Serbia had been stockpiling arms while the Yugoslav Army had (illegally) confiscated most of the arms held by the Croatian territorial militia and some of the arms held by the Slovenian territorial militia, and that the media had stoked up resentments, fears, and hatreds among the peoples of Yugoslavia, it would have been enough of an accomplishment to stop the slide to war—to have resuscitated Yugoslavia would have taken a miracle. Yet if anyone could have stopped the slide to war in early 1991, it would have been the

U.S. and the European Union (EU); but this would have required a clear, firm, and convincing response.

It was Germany and Austria which had the most realistic assessments at the time, with Austria taking the lead in advocating Western diplomatic recognition of the newly independent republics of Slovenia and Croatia. Germany held back initially, and its government's early pronouncements during June and early July 1991 were indistinguishable from what was being said by other Western governments. But as the fighting escalated, the German government became convinced that Yugoslavia had died and that refusing to recognize that fact would serve no useful purpose. By mid-December 1991, the rest of the European Community (EC) had come around to the Germans' point of view.[14] Less than three weeks after the EC announced its intention to recognize Slovenia and Croatia in the new year, a ceasefire was signed between the Serbian insurgents and Croatian government forces, and a United Nations peacekeeping force was sent in.

When serious fighting broke out in Bosnia-Herzegovina in April 1992, it originally assumed the form of a war between Serbian forces and non-Serb forces. By the end of the year, fighting had also broken out between Croatian forces and Muslim forces, converting the war into a complicated three-sided conflict, in which each side was engaged in both conflictual and collaborative relations with each of the other sides. During the war, the American media portrayed the Croatian side as exclusively responsible for the fighting between Croats and Muslims. More recently, there have been scholarly arguments that it was, in fact, the Muslim/Bosniak side which bore the greater responsibility for the outbreak of fighting between these two sides.[15] The position taken in this book is that the conflict was overdetermined and that, given the distrust which had developed among Croats during 1991, when Bosnian president Alija Izetbegović did nothing to prevent Yugoslav Army troops from moving across Bosnia into Croatia, and given the natural antagonism between rival military forces operating within the same area, it would have taken more wisdom than was available to prevent fighting from breaking out between the two sides.

III

The philosophical and political suppositions which I make in undertaking this history are "classical liberal" in nature, which means, among other things, that I believe that such things as the rule of law, recognition of individual rights, toleration, and equality are not only morally superior to tyranny, the suppression of individual rights, bigotry, and the unequal treatment of persons of different nationality, confession, gender, or sexual orientation, but are also politically more expedient. The liberal project is, moreover, an important component in what constitutes a legitimate, and hence stable, state. In so saying, I am suggesting that values are not simply a matter of preferences and cannot be relativized away by arguing that whatever any society wants is fine for that society; on the contrary, the values which become prevalent in a society, and the nature of the values which a state embodies, have direct consequences for the path which that state and society traverse. In the case of Yugoslavia, the dominant values under-pinnng each of the three Yugoslavias were values hostile to the liberal project and, ultimately, conducive to instability and decay.

CHAPTER 1

A Theory of System Legitimacy

Yugoslavia failed as a state several times over. There were the grand failures of 1928–1929, 1990–1991, and 2000, and there were crises which signaled somewhat less grand failures of particular political formulae, as in 1931 (when King Aleksandar was constrained to abandon open dictatorship and declare a constitution), 1939 (when Belgrade political circles felt constrained to concede wide-ranging autonomy to the Croats), 1966 (when Tito fired secret police chief Ranković and reversed his hard-line course), and 1971–1973 (when Tito removed liberals from office in Slovenia, Croatia, Serbia, and Macedonia and reversed his brief experiment with headlong liberalization). Yugoslavia was, thus, unstable, but it was not just unstable. There was, on the contrary, a deeper crisis which ran through Yugoslav history in 1918–2004, a permanent crisis rooted in its elites' failure to resolve the dual challenges of state-building and legitimation.

By placing state-building and legitimation at the center of focus, I am suggesting that these twin tasks enjoy a certain primacy in politics; but to say as much does not predetermine how one will approach the subject. Leaving aside nonliberal and illiberal approaches, there are, one may say, four major strands of the liberal tradition which vie for favor: classical universalism (my own position, with its roots in the thinking of Locke and Kant and finding expression more recently in the writings of Charles Beitz and John Finnis, but able to trace its prehistory back to St. Thomas Aquinas); liberal realism or conventionalism (with its roots in the nonliberal Hobbes and finding expression more recently in the writings of Samuel P. Huntington); consequentialism (with its roots in the writings of Jeremy Bentham and John Stuart Mill and finding expression more recently in the writings of Russell Hardin and L. W. Sumner); and communitarianism (a more recent theory, advocated by Amitai Etzioni and Michael Sandel, among others).[1] Briefly stated, where universalists argue that human rights enjoy priority over the claims of sovereignty,[2] emphasize that systems depend for their survival on their ability (and the ability of their societies) to sustain cultures supportive of the systems in question, and view the failure to build legitimate institutions and changes in the moral consensus as the best predictors of system change, realists (conventionalists) insist that human rights be treated as the internal affair of each "sovereign" government, emphasize that systems depend for their survival on their ability to develop and maintain strong political institutions, ignore or dismiss changes in moral consensus, and see the strength of both participatory and coercive institutions as a better predictor of system survival than questions of legitimacy or illegitimacy (including the pervasiveness of violations of human rights).[3] For universalists, nationalism is a problematic force, because it focuses on the needs and interests of one community, subordinating, sometimes with horrific exaggeration, the interests of other communities to the interests of their own community. Consequentialists, as their self-designation suggests, want to emphasize the consequences of the actions of both individuals and governments in assessing moral worth, but what is striking is that consequentialists "tend to view government as a [potential] facilitator of the pursuit of *individual interests,* rather than as either an absolute enforcer of Order or the vehicle for maximizing either the common good or justice."[4] Because of their emphasis on actual results, consequentialists are inclined to take the results of government policies as determinative of system legitimacy and as a predictor of system or government endurance. In the argument between universalists and realists concerning the standing of human rights, as against the claims of sovereignty, consequentialists tend to draw closer to the universalists. Finally, communitarians reject the contemporary liberal supposition of what Sandel calls "the unencumbered (or voluntarist) conception of the self."[5] They also challenge the universalist conception of universally valid moral norms and standards and stress their view "that social goods have different meanings for different communities."[6] This does not induce communitarians to embrace complete normlessness, however. On the contrary, "[u]nlike relativists, who think that people's values are so different that there is no sense in talking about common values, communitarians believe that certain types of value[s] have stood the test of time across different cultural variations."[7] This means that for communitarians it requires particular care to assess what principles should be taken as truly universal and what should be seen as cultural products. The communitarian emphasis on national boundaries may also lead to a rehabilitation of nationalism and the apotheosis of the principle of national self-determination. David Miller has pointed out, in this spirit, that "[t]he duties we owe to our fellow-nationals are different from, and more extensive than, the duties we owe to human beings as such." He calls this position "ethical particularism" and claims that solidarity based on common nationality is appropriate for mobile societies, where other ties (clan, village) have broken down. He also draws the corollary that it is functional for societies to organize school curricula in such a way as to build and reinforce awareness of local/national history, culture, traditions, and accomplishments.[8] Finally, communitarians are also concerned about predatory capitalism's "cancerous effects on community life," viewing consumerism and "market individualism" as the instruments of this calamity.[9]

These alternative theories are not just the stuff of classes in political philosophy. They are also the currency of lively debates, in which both prognoses of likely futures and policy recommendations hang in the balance. Where the writing of history is concerned, the questions one asks, and even more the selection of which events are germane to "the story," together with the answers one provides, reflect one's assumptions concerning the central questions in political theory. In adopting the universalist paradigm, rather than some other paradigm, I am proceeding on the assumption that system stability depends upon system legitimacy and the further assumption that, whatever permutations may result from cultural variation, there are principles which a state cannot violate without sacrificing its legitimacy—in other words, that legitimacy cannot be turned into a purely subjective affair. There are those who dispute both suppositions, as will be noted below.

Following Kant,[10] I understand the challenge of state-building (in the contemporary era) as involving the establishment of a representative government which respects the primacy of law and safeguards the rights, freedoms, and equality of its subjects. That said, the task of state-building will not be understood here in the narrow sense, à la Hobbes, as confined to the mere establishment of civil order, but rather in a broader sense of entailing, specifically, the task of building a *legitimate* state, not just any state at all.[11] This is why Kant writes that "in objective or theoretical terms, there is no conflict whatsoever between morality and politics," or again, that "a true system of politics cannot therefore take a single step without first paying tribute to morality."[12] It is in this same spirit, again, that Hume tells us that "the principal object of government is to constrain men to observe the laws of nature [i.e., Natural Law],"[13] and that Plato urges, in *The Laws*, that good government must, in the first place, codify and adhere to the moral law, educating people in the Natural Law rather than catering to prejudices.[14] Or again, one may consult Jean Bodin (1530–1596), who urges that the authority of the sovereign be understood to be limited by Natural Law, Divine Law, international law, and the laws of the realm.[15] The notion that repressive rulers, who have committed grievous violations of any of the aforementioned bodies of law, could still lay claim to *sovereignty*, would have struck Bodin as completely self-contradictory. The moral law has, however, not been understood in the same way over time. Equality, a value common in many societies today, albeit understood in different ways in different sectors of society, was considered heinous in centuries past (indeed, pleas on its behalf were included on the 19th-century papal "Syllabus of Errors").[16] Thus, what should be seen as "objectively" moral and immoral is always *as understood by the majority of people at the given time and place.* As a result, the boundaries of the moral law may change over time. St. Thomas Aquinas (1225?–1274) put it this way in his *Summa theologiae:*

The natural law can be understood to be changed in two ways. In one way, by addition; and in this sense nothing prohibits the natural law from being changed, for many things advantageous to human life have been added over and above the natural law, both by the Divine law and by human laws. In another way, a change in the natural law can be understood to occur by subtraction, so that what was formerly according to the natural law ceases to be part of the natural law.[17]

But this does not mean that there is no limit to the changes which may affect the moral law, much less that the moral law vanishes down the rabbit hole of pure subjectivity. Aquinas himself notes that "the natural law is entirely immutable as to its first principles . . . it may nonetheless be changed in some particular instance and in a few cases." Indeed, he adds, people may become corrupted and lose sight of certain principles of natural law, so that positive law may need to supply a "correction."[18] Thus, even though Aquinas considers the "first principles" of natural law to be immutable, he allows that the practical application of these principles and the expostulation of secondary principles must inevitably depend upon their interpretation in specific historical contexts.

Richard Hooker, a "pre-liberal" thinker, and some of the most prominent early liberals, among them John Locke (1632–1704) and Jean-Jacques Rousseau (1712–1778), developed their theories on the foundation of a theory of Natural Law.[19] There is, thus, a potential compatibility between Natural Law and the liberal tradition; for "Natural Law liberals," the principles of tolerance and respect for the harm principle loom large (with "the harm principle" defined as the injunction not to harm other living beings, except in defense of life or property, and using only so much force as is necessary to effect such defense[20]). "Natural Law liberals" are, thus, likely to agree with Finnis that "[i]nciting hatred amongst sections of the community is not merely an injury to the rights of those hated; it threatens everyone in the community with a future of violence and of other violations of right, and this threat is itself an injury to the common good and is reasonably referred to as a violation of public order."[21]

But not all Natural Law theorists are liberals. Robert P. George, for example, even while placing Natural Law on his escutcheon, argues forcefully against both tolerance and the harm principle, urging that government may use legislation and organs of repression to enforce a specific vision of morality *narrower* than that defined by tolerance and the harm principle.[22] In another context, George joins co-author Christopher Wolfe in urging that considerations of the precepts of Natural Law (as they understand these precepts) lead them to conclude that "opposition to homosexual and other nonmarital sex acts may be based on moral insight, not mere prejudice."[23] My own position is that in marshaling Natural Law *against* the liberal project, Robert George is relying on a plausible but atavistic, controversial, and ultimately wrong-headed understanding of Natural Law.

A Few Words about Objectivity

The *Cassell Pocket English Dictionary* defines *objectivity* as "the tendency to give priority to what is objective; the theory that stresses objective reality," and *objective* as "actual, real, substantive; as distinct from the subjective [and hence] uninfluenced by emotion, impulse, prejudice etc." For Rawls, objectivity is associated with "a public framework of thought sufficient for the concept of judgment to apply and for conclusions to be reached on the basis of reasons and evidence after discussion and due reflection."[24]

For the purposes of this work, however, I shall mean the following in using the terms *objective* and *objectivity* viz., I shall consider that a value or statement has objective validity when (1) the analyst affirming the value or making the given statement has not allowed personal interest to affect his or her judgment; (2) the analyst can provide reasons for her or his conclusion, sufficient to persuade others that the conclusion (value, statement, etc.) is reasonable and plausible; (3) the analyst can provide reasons for excluding other conclusions and explanations sufficient to persuade others that these conclusions are reasonable and plausible; (4) the conclusion can be integrated into or reconciled with a broader theory or conception; and (5) it is not possible to identify errors in logic or in the arguments made in support of the conclusion. If any of these conditions should not hold, then we shall consider that the given conclusion, value, or statement is subjective in nature or flawed by errors in logic, or both. To call a statement objective, then, is not the same as claiming that it is true. But to say that it is objective *is* to claim that it is reasonable for someone to treat that statement as "provisionally true"—until a better statement comes along.

Underpinning this chapter, and indeed this volume, are claims made about values. Specifically, I argue that the classical liberal values may be treated as objective goods, as objectively easier to defend than their opposites, and as objectively better suited to guaranteeing political stability precisely because they are generally accepted as proper. That is to say, I consider that it would be an easy matter to provide reasons for thinking that the rule of law, respect for human rights on the part of a regime, tolerance, and respect for the harm principle (defined above) are generally more acceptable to people and more conducive to political stability than arbitrary rule by a despot, disregard for human rights, widespread bigotry, and the widespread infliction of harm by organized paramilitary groups—not only because these latter elements hurt people and offend our sensibility, but also because they strike most of us as contrary to what is rationally defensible.

In claiming "objective" validity for certain values, thus, I shall mean that these values (1) do not result in the personal enrichment of persons advocating them, (2) can be reasonably defended as capable of eliciting greater support over the long term and more conducive to political stability over the long term than their alternatives, (3) can be integrated into a broader theory of politics, and (4) do not stand in obvious contradiction with each other; and I shall also mean (5) that a reasonable argument can be made that other values, such as security, if given paramount importance resulting in the demotion of any of the liberal values, will lead to results quite different from what the majority of people would freely choose.

In spite of a superficial resemblance to Rawls's theory, my own approach is *not* constructivist, at least not in Rawls's sense. On the contrary, the approach I am taking here is closer in spirit to that of Immanuel Kant (1724–1804) and to that of Lawrence Kohlberg (d. 1987),[25] in that I stress the criterion of universalizability.

Sovereignty and Legitimacy

For the purposes of this book, I shall use the term *sovereignty* in a very specific way. It will be necessary, therefore, to define some terms before proceeding.

Definition 1: By **authority** we shall mean legitimate power (and hence, by political authority we shall mean legitimate political power).

It might be objected that not all authority is political; but by the same virtue, not all power is political.

Definition 2: By **sovereignty** we shall mean supreme political authority within a territorially defined area.

Quite often people use the term "sovereign state" to indicate that a state has obtained widespread diplomatic recognition (sometimes called "external sovereignty"). This usage does not reflect the way in which I choose to use the term in this book (a choice which has roots in Bodin's theory); I am talking about the sovereign power-holder and thus am concerned with sovereignty as a potential aspect of government (which is sometimes called "internal sovereignty").[26] The definitions I provide are stipulative and intended to make the argument which follows intelligible.

To continue: in the traditional view, then, the notion of legitimacy was inseparable from that of morality and embraced notions of justice. In the latter sense, Marx too was "traditional" in his understanding of legitimacy, up to a point. Though he endeavored to avoid placing absolute value even on proletarian rule and was pointedly vague as to whether "communism" was an endpoint or merely as much as one could foresee from the vantage point of the mid-19th century, he clearly felt that not only certain kinds of politics, but also certain economic systems, could be characterized as more, or less, legitimate.

The 20th century has seen a revolution in thinking about the concept of legitimacy, in which much of its earlier significance has been simply abandoned. This revolution began with Max Weber who sought, *inter alia*, to suggest that even regimes founded on nothing more than the charisma of a self-promoting leader could count as "legitimate." This seemed to refer legitimacy to public enthusiasm or emotion. Not only that, but legitimacy came to be seen, in the literature produced in the 1950s–1970s, as, in the first place, *subjective*. Ted Robert Gurr, for instance, declares systems "*legitimate* to the extent that their citizens regard them as proper and deserving of support,"[27] while Seymour Martin Lipset has suggested that "[l]egitimacy involves the capacity of the system to engender and maintain the belief that the existing political institutions are the most appropriate ones for the society."[28] Pushing subjectivism to its logical extreme, Lipset therefore concludes that a state with "appropriate" institutions should be counted as "legitimate" even if those very institutions are used to persecute and oppress large sectors of the population.[29] This is not a merely abstract question, as the example of communist Czechoslovakia makes clear. Here, constitutional guarantees read like textbook examples of democratic rights, the laws offered nominal protections to people, and the assembly was elected in popular elections; the problem was that the regime did not respect its own constitution or follow its own laws—giving rise to the Charter 77 dissident group, which demanded that the regime respect its own constitution and laws. Clearly, Václav Havel and other dissidents associated with Charter 77 did not consider the Czechoslovak state to be "legitimate," in spite of its "appropriate" institutions. The reason is that political legitimacy cannot be reduced to mere institutions.

Peter Stillman offers a variation on this theme by making system legitimacy relative to the value patterns found in a given society, so that what is legitimate in one society (for example, limited monarchy, capital punishment, the welfare state) may not be considered legitimate in another society.[30] What Stillman is surely *not* arguing, however, is that there are no practices which would be considered legitimate or illegitimate across all societies. Someone wishing to argue that, for example, there are no universally valid human rights should be able to point to at least one society where the torture of children is considered a legitimate "local tradition." But such a notion is remote from the intentions of either Stillman or Gurr.

But some writers continue to trip over the concept, because they cannot figure out how public opinion can be relevant to questions of legitimacy unless it is reduced to mere opinion, i.e., unless legitimacy is taken to mean absolutely anything. This is, however, a false dilemma, as is aptly shown by Rodney Barker, who, for his part, endeavors to square the circle by arguing that

legitimacy is precisely the belief in the rightfulness of a state, in its authority to issue commands, so that those commands are obeyed not simply out of fear or self-interest, but because they are believed in some sense to have moral authority, because subjects believe that they ought to obey.[31]

Richard Merelman's construal of a given government as legitimate to the extent that it "is viewed [by its citizens] as morally proper for a society" is close to Barker's approach in spirit.[32] Insofar as a given society is characterized by some common notions about morality (even if only minimal ones), held by the majority of persons living in that society, we may agree with Andreas Hasenclever in understanding morality as a *social institution*.[33]

Moreover, John Schaar, contrasting traditional understandings of legitimacy, which emphasized notions of morality or law, with more recent definitions, which refer legitimacy to people's subjective beliefs and opinions, has warned that the newer definitions, which stripped out the moral dimension and the economic sphere alike, may be too narrow. Such an approach, Schaar warns, risks reducing the assessment of legitimacy to the mere gauging of public opinion, which in turn, Schaar continues, may render the assessment of legitimacy hostage to the efficacy of the given system's propaganda.[34]

Aside from traditional, law-based notions of legitimacy and more recent construals of legitimacy in terms of subjective perceptions, James Fishkin notes the existence of three further understandings of legitimacy and legitimation.[35] The first of these emphasizes *procedural principles* such as majority rule or consensual decision making. John Rawls, for example, lays great stress on this point in his *Political Liberalism*. In his words,

democratic decisions and laws are legitimate, not because they are just but because they are legitimately enacted in accordance with an accepted legitimate democratic procedure. It is of great importance that the constitution specifying the procedure be sufficiently just, even though not perfectly just, as no human institution can be that. But it may not be just and still be legitimate, provided that it is sufficiently just in view of the circumstances and social conditions. A legitimate procedure gives rise to legitimate laws and policies.[36]

The second of these understandings refers legitimacy to *structural principles*, such as equality or utilitarianism, according to Fishkin. Here one may recall Carl von Rotteck's essay "Gleichheit" (1838), in which he tied system legitimacy firmly to the maintenance of civic *and economic* equality among the system's citizens, concluding that the existence of pervasive civic or economic inequalities may undermine system legitimacy.[37] And the third alternative approach refers legitimacy to *absolute rights principles*, as, for example, per Robert Nozick. Fishkin explains that these principles "prescribe that a person must *never* experience consequences (or consequences brought about in certain ways) that would violate his [or her] rights."[38] But, according to Fishkin, under Nozick's theory, there is no obligation to help those in distress, whether individuals or nations, while majority rule (following the most widely accepted procedural principle) could legitimate tyrannical systems.[39] Fishkin also rejects structural principles, believing that they too could be used to "legitimate" tyranny.[40] Having rejected the three "alternative" approaches, Fishkin declines to embrace either the traditional-absolutist approach or the subjectivist-relativist approach and, instead, elevates the harm principle to place of honor, prioritizing the avoidance of tyranny. Still, the council "Do no harm" does not, in itself, provide any injunction of "Do good to others." It certainly does not lead us to Mill's admonition, "the most important point of excellence which any form of government can possess is to promote the virtue and intelligence of the people themselves."[41]

A Theory of Legitimacy

The theory I shall propose hereunder represents a synthesis of universalist, constructivist, and procedural approaches. I believe that structural approaches may be treated as a particular adaptation of the universalist approach, while the absolute rights approach, at least as summarized by Fishkin, seems to me too one-sided, forgetting that respect for the rights of individuals must be balanced by respect for the rights of the society as a whole. System legitimacy, accordingly, will be seen as having objective (in the sense in which I have defined *objective*), procedural, and subjective components. In the present day and in most countries, a system is seen as legitimate in the objective sense to the degree that the government protects human rights, including but not limited to freedom of association and freedom of the press, ensures citizens' access on an equal basis to quality education, work commensurate with qualifications, and salary commensurate with work, and fosters the moral excellence of its citizens. It is important to keep the line of causality clear. To believe that it is the moral excellence of the broad mass of a society which enables its people to erect a legitimate system is to construe the system as a "perfect moral commonwealth," which, as I have noted elsewhere, operates according to a logic opposite to that of the liberal project.[42] But, as Kant warns, "we cannot expect [people's] moral attitudes to produce a good political constitution; on the contrary, it is only through the latter that the people can be expected to attain a good level of moral culture."[43] The so-called "civic culture," to use the expression popularized by Gabriel Almond and Sidney Verba 40 years ago,[44] does not just spring forth out of nowhere; it is nurtured by institutions.[45]

In the Yugoslav case, even in the interwar years (1918–1941), however, even though the discourse was different from what one encounters in Western Europe today, for example, the citizens of the Yugoslav kingdom were angered by police beatings, by the muzzling of the press, by the suppression of existing associations, and by discriminatory practices in education, promotion, and taxation—to be detailed in chapters 2 and 3.[46]

A system is *procedurally* (or *juridically)* legitimate to the extent to which it functions in harmony with its own constitution and laws, which of necessity entails the rule of law. This, in turn, entails that all laws and codes be published and available to the public, that there be no consciously adopted contradictions between precepts in one legal statute and those in another, that the laws be applied to all inhabitants equally, and that officeholders obey the laws of the land and be themselves subject to the law.

Finally, a system is *subjectively* legitimate to the extent that its citizens *believe* that it is objectively and procedurally legitimate. In other words, subjective legitimacy is merely a filter through which given criteria (possibly of an objective nature) and procedural legitimacy are apprehended. Subjective legitimacy has nothing to do with prosperity or specific policy measures, still less to do with the popularity or lack thereof of one or another officeholder, though, of course, the perceived illegitimacy of a ruler may be a major factor in his or her unpopularity.[47]

Returning to what I have chosen to call *objective* measures of legitimacy, I propose that this may be seen as consisting of three strands: moral legitimacy (in which universalism, with its notion of morally grounded rights and duties and of the fundamental morality of humans, may lay claim to legitimacy), political legitimacy (with two alternative legitimate schemes: hereditary monarchy and representative government), and economic legitimacy (in which—in the contemporary setting—neither the unfettered tyranny of the market nor the unbridled tyranny of the state may be allowed to be legitimate). At the center of this triad is Natural Law, which as per Aquinas may be understood as the modal understanding of morality in a society and which provides the measure for legitimacy in all three aspects. Those who wish to deny that there are any absolute (i.e., inalienable) rights or any intrinsic duties or any necessity for the government to assure a minimal level of subsistence for legal residents willing to work and for pensioners always begin by attacking the notion that one can identify any standards which may be represented as universally reasonable, i.e., as reasonable in any national context, whether that might be freedom of speech or a national health program or free public education through university. Their position goes far beyond mere cultural relativism (the acknowledgment that there are different customs and traditions to be found across the globe) but sinks deep into what Habermas has called "metaethical skepticism." This position leads its adherents into an anomalous situation in which, as Habermas notes, these skeptics "cannot explain what they are trying to explain, namely, everyday moral practices, which would break down if the participants thought that their moral disputes did not have any cognitive content."[48]

In objective terms, a system is *politically legitimate* when its officeholders obtain office according to legally prescribed procedures which are widely accepted in the society. The door to subjective reductionism is not cracked open as far as one might at first suppose, insofar as there are historically only three methods by which officeholders have assumed political office: election (representative government), hereditary succession in a royal dynasty (hereditary monarchy) which might operate in consultation with representative assemblies of one form or another, and claim to personal divinity or to divine designation (both claims having been widespread in the ancient world and having arguably some reflection in the writings of Sir Robert Filmer (1588–1653) but now generally invoked only by parties seeking to impose religious repression in their societies). With the possible exception of papal election in the Vatican as an instance of divine sanction, only election (ideally by popular vote) and hereditary succession in a royal dynasty still qualify at present as legitimate methodologies of political succession. Other methodologies, such as coups d'état, designation within a one-party system, imposition by foreign armies, internal subversion, lottery, and qualifying tests, have not been seen as legitimate, albeit for different reasons.

In the case of royal Yugoslavia, there was, to be sure, a royal dynasty in place, operating according to the rule of primo geniture. But the Karadjordjević dynasty was specifically a *Serbian* dynasty, and for many non-Serbs (perhaps especially Albanians, Slovenes, Croats, and members of the local Italian, German, and Hungarian minority groups) that meant a *foreign* dynasty. Insofar as a foreign dynasty can aspire to legitimacy only if it can come to be seen as impartial, and insofar as the Serbian character of the dynasty meant that it was, for the most part, viewed as partial to Serbs, the Karadjordjević dynasty cannot be considered to have functioned as an unproblematic legitimating factor in royal Yugoslavia.

Where socialist Yugoslavia is concerned, the Communist Party of Yugoslavia (CPY) moved quickly and decisively to suffocate rival political parties and never allowed free elections to take place—i.e., at least not until 1990. The communist system was based on party control of elections, appointments, media, and economic life. Political succession was determined within party channels and was not open to free electoral challenge.

And in the post-1990 Yugoslav successor states, as will be seen in chapters 17 and 19, free and fair elections were regularized quickly in Slovenia and Macedonia while, in Croatia and Serbia, presidents Franjo Tudjman and Slobodan Milošević used various dubious means to subvert the political process. Within Croatia, however, the political opposition continued to fight a rearguard defense against Tudjman's HDZ (Hrvatska demokratska zajednica) in the Sabor (the Croatian Assembly), in the mayoral race in Zagreb, and in regional elections and assemblies (especially in Istria), while, in Serbia, the Skupština (the Assembly) was turned into a largely docile instrument of Milošević, driving the opposition to resort to street protests to voice their displeasure with regime policies. With the death of President Tudjman in December 1999, Croatia rapidly transformed itself into a vigorous parliamentary democracy, repudiating the state-sponsored nationalism of the Tudjman years. In the Federal Republic of Yugoslavia (FRY), by contrast, the forced resignation of Milošević on 5 October 2000 left Serbia and Montenegro in a highly ambiguous state, while nationalism continued to be viewed as a suitable medium for political discourse.

Democracy (representative government) may be described in terms of a syndrome, consisting of

Multi-candidate elections
Uncensored press
Separation of powers
Informed public
Campaign funding from public coffers

The first three should require no comment. As for the last two: To the extent that the public is uninformed or ill-informed or misinformed, the public cannot be effective in advocating its own interests, or even in voting for those candidates who will best serve the public interest. Campaign funding from public coffers is necessary because, where private donations are allowed to fund electoral campaigns, democracy is quickly subverted and transmogrified into plutocracy. This last factor has come into focus only since the subversion of American democracy which began roughly speaking in 1980. In interwar Yugoslavia, the utility of the first four factors would have been generally understood. The foregoing may be stated more formally as follows:

Definition 3: A **representative democracy** is a system based on multi-candidate elections, an uncensored press, and the separation of powers, with an informed public (and campaign funding from public coffers).

But this formal definition tells us only about the form of a representative government, not about its spirit. When I say this, I am thinking of Yves Simon's explanation in *Philosophy of Democratic Government,* where he summarizes alternative ways of thinking about the way in which democratic government would actually function. One theory, developed and advocated by Paul-Louis Courier, a latter-day admirer of Voltaire, holds that "government is like a coach-driver, hired and paid by those whom he drives."[49] Known as the "coach-driver theory," this theory seeks to reduce democratic government to the blind executor of the wishes of the people. An alternative theory, known as the "transmission theory" has been credited to St. Thomas Aquinas and holds that the authority originally vested in the people is transferred to government by virtue of its establishment and that government, therefore, can genuinely claim to embody popular sovereignty.[50] Aquinas's great commentator, Cajetan—Thomas de Vio Cardinalis Caietanus—who lived and worked in the early 16th century, developed this theory further, urging that "royal power, by natural law, resides primarily in the people," with the consequence that "civil society can depose a tyrannical ruler."[51] Francisco Suarez, the distinguished Spanish philosopher, took this theory to its logical conclusion, declaring that only democracy was "natural" and that monarchical and aristocratic systems could be legitimately established only by the consent of the people, i.e., by democratic means.[52]

Simon rejects the "coach-driver" theory, arguing that "there cannot be democratic government when the very essence of government [deliberation and decision making] is negated." Yet Simon also emphasizes that the "transmission theory" was not intended by its originators to justify only democratic government; it was, and is, intended to justify government by consent—which includes democratic government as one possible form. Because democracy involves, in Simon's view, the incomplete transmission of sovereignty to the government, "the people retains the character of a deliberating assembly."[53] And this, in turn, serves to reemphasize the importance, in a democracy, that the citizens be well informed and that they possess what Jean Bethke Elshtain has called "democratic dispositions"—viz., "a preparedness to work with others different from oneself toward shared ends; a combination of strong convictions with a readiness to compromise in the recognition that one can't always get everything one wants; and a sense of individuality and a commitment to civic goods that are not the possession of one person or of one group alone."[54]

In "objective" terms, a system is *economically legitimate* when it safeguards both the short-term and long-term interests of the public and aspires to something which might be understood as social justice. Such a system must find a middle path between the laissez-faire favored by the political right and the "bolshevik" policy of seizing the assets of private individuals, for example. It must therefore safeguard private property and free enterprise, while at the same time establishing checks on the rapacity of the well-to-do. Such a system will also endeavor to counter the natural tendency of plant owners to exploit employees and customers alike and to disregard the environmental damage their factories perpetrate, by establishing some minimal standards for wages and plant safety, by enforcing minimal standards for environmental safeguards and for the quality of products of all kinds, and by imposing a system of taxation under which excessive income is taxed away. Such a system is commonly called social democracy; out of deference to Popes Leo XIII, John XXIII, and John Paul II, who have championed these principles in their encyclicals *Rerum novarum* (1891), *Mater et magistra* (1961), *Sollicitudo rei socialis* (1988), and *Centissimus annus* (1991), even if without any desire to be associated with the secular model of social democracy, I will call this system *solidarism*.

Neither capitalism nor state socialism (the economic system of communism) may be considered (fully) legitimate; both result in the suffocation of basic human liberties, and as Hume wrote in 1739, "nothing is more essential to public interest than the preservation of public liberty."[55] And notice, too, that Hume writes of *public* liberty, not of the liberty of business tycoons, corporate magnates, and real estate developers who want to chew up what little unspoiled land remains on this planet.

Royal Yugoslavia was, of course, a fledgling capitalist state, in many ways more pre-capitalist (agrarian-based) than capitalist, though developing in line with the rules of the capitalist marketplace. Titoist Yugoslavia professed to offer a unique economic model, self-managing socialism, and even criticized the Soviet Union for its state socialism ("state capitalism," in the Yugoslav communist code). But ultimately, as Milovan Djilas pointed out in various books,[56] socialist Yugoslavia generated at the most a variation on the state socialist model, and at any rate, the Yugoslav economic model, with its rigid limits on free enterprise, was remote from the principles of solidarism.

Since 1990, the Yugoslav successor states have jettisoned self-managing socialism. Slovenia has come closest to embracing a system in which some principles of social democracy are honored,[57] while Croatia under Tudjman, Serbia under Milošević, Macedonia under Kiro Gligorov, and Bosnia, whether during the war years or after, combined capitalism with elements of kleptocracy, in which local favored elites operated in illegal channels.

Finally, a system is seen as *morally legitimate* to the extent to which the government behaves in accordance with generally accepted moral precepts (e.g., the prescription that people treat each other with respect, or the proscription of torture), and the concomitant principle that moral notions which have been strenuously disputed for 2,000 years or more (such as is the case with abortion) ought not to be regulated by government. The principles of individual rights and equality were articulated only in the 17th century; before then there was little awareness that these principles had any special claim to validity. The principle of tolerance, discerned by Kant and Mill as essential to protect individual rights and equality, initially gained acceptance only within the limited domain of religion; later, other dimensions of tolerance gained acceptance among intellectuals in the course of the 19th century, and after World War Two, gradually the principles of ethnic, racial, and sexual tolerance gained widespread acceptance in Western Europe and Canada and partial acceptance in the United States. These values, thus, reflect Aquinas's principle that it is possible to add to the Natural Law and, thus, that the scope of natural rights may expand over time. But it is impossible to name a civilization in which rule of law was not presumed: indeed, the ancient civilizations of Babylonia and Egypt were famed for honoring this principle, as were the Roman Empire and the Byzantine Empire later. The harm principle, likewise, was embodied in the so-called Code of Hammurabi ("an eye for an eye, a tooth for a tooth"), and indeed, the entire notion of retributive justice, which has been the cornerstone of legal and penal systems throughout recorded history, is rooted in an explicit or implicit endorsement of the harm principle. Thus, only two central values of liberalism seem to have been transhistorically valid—i.e., treated as objective standards in all societies, at all times—*rule of law* and *respect for the harm principle,* by which is meant that no one has the right to harm another person intentionally, whether physically, verbally, or financially, except for the purpose of protecting the innocent (whether oneself or someone else), and that, even in conditions of the defense of the innocent, the harm inflicted should not exceed what is necessary for the purpose of an effective defense; as already noted, however, the harm principle is generally understood to entail the notion of retributive justice, so that the state's authority to inflict punishment is seen not as an exception to the harm principle, but as its ultimate guarantee. Beginning with St. Thomas Aquinas and accelerating with the writings and activity of John Locke, Algernon

Sydney (1622–1683), Immanuel Kant, and John Stuart Mill (1806–1873)—among others—a tectonic shift in the moral landscape occurred, as a result of which a set of values developed, which have come to be widely regarded as legitimate, at least in liberal circles. This set of values constitutes what may be called the liberal project and embraces the following key elements:

Rule of law
Individual rights and duties
Tolerance
Harm principle, respect for
Equality
Neutrality of the state in matters of religion.

This may be stated in formal terms:

Definition 4: **A liberal system** is a system based on the rule of law, respect for individual rights, tolerance, respect for the harm principle, equality (whether interpreted narrowly or broadly), and neutrality of the state in matters of religion.

By equality I shall mean (1) that all citizens are equal before the law, (2) that there is no discrimination, either by the government or by other institutions, agencies, or businesses operating within the society, on the basis of ethnicity, religion, gender, sexual orientation, class of origin, or residence, (3) that citizens compete for work on the basis of qualifications, with pay commensurate with seniority, performance, and overall merit (i.e., equal pay for equal work), and (4) that citizens willing to work and pensioners be assured of a certain minimal standard of living, to be determined in the national legislature. The other four elements in the liberal project require no further elaboration.

While only rule of law and the harm principle have been recognized as valid in all human societies, both the concept of individual rights and duties and the value of tolerance have acquired widespread acceptance in the years since World War Two, to the extent that they have become truly universal values. The philosophical-political revolution achieved by the Enlightenment had, as regards these two values, the character of a scientific breakthrough, a discovery of principles conducive to social harmony, human cooperation, and political stability. A close reading of Bodin's *Six Books* and of Locke's *Letters concerning Toleration* makes clear that their priorities were social harmony and political stability, to which ends toleration and the recognition of individual rights were thought to be conducive.[58]

Equality and neutrality of the state in matters of religion are also clearly *not* transhistorical, but again, both are clearly functional, given certain conditions. The value of equality is critical to the liberal project and, where the public is mobilized into politics, may be ineluctable. But history has shown that social harmony and human cooperation can be founded also on principles of extreme inequality, especially when large portions of the population live a marginal existence. As for the confessional neutrality of the state, this is a contingent value, arising and proving its utility precisely in conditions of confessional hetero-geneity. In religiously homogeneous societies of the past, state neutrality would have seemed as odd as putting salt in coffee.

Liberal Values in the Yugoslav Context

All six "liberal" values were already in circulation by 1918, and one or more of them were championed, in interwar Yugoslavia, by such persons as Dragoljub Jovanović, Jaša Prodanović, and Stjepan Radić. It requires no special effort to demonstrate that the highly discriminatory practices of interwar Yugoslavia made a mockery of all six elements in the liberal project,[59] and that these illib-eral practices were deeply resented by the victims of such discrimination. Again, in socialist Yugoslavia, the system fell short in terms of rule of law, respect for individual rights and duties, and respect for the harm principle. The record in the other three areas was more complex. Where tolerance is concerned, the communists always preached *bratstvo i jedinstvo* (brotherhood and unity) and imposed a stricture that public figures were allowed, at most, to criticize the shortcomings of their own nationality and their own republic, but not the shortcomings of other nationalities and republics. But intolerance raised its ugly head from time to time (as will be documented, for example, in chapters 8, 10, and 12), and the party tended to give tolerance a repressive cast. Equality was, in some ways, the best protected of these principles, and women benefited from the honor paid to the principle of "equal pay for equal work"; the sticking point was that women did not enjoy equal access to equal work.[60] National groups were protected under the so-called "ethnic key," which prescribed fixed percent-ages of offices to be allocated to the members of each nationality group. But whatever one makes of the relationship of the "ethnic key" to the principle of equality, it is fact that the "ethnic key" stirred up resentment among major national groups of the Socialist Federated Republic of Yugoslavia (SFRY).

And finally, where neutrality of the state in matters of religion is concerned, the Yugoslav communists always professed to observe a strict neutrality vis-à-vis the country's sundry religious communities, but the state's high level of interest in religion, manifested in its maintenance of three distinct bureaucracies for managing the religious communities (within the state bureaucracy, the party bureaucracy, and the machinery of the Socialist Alliance of Working People of Yugoslavia, or SAWPY), dictated that neutrality would remain an elusive virtue. Ranković's protection of the Serbian Orthodox Church from Macedonian auto-cephalists would not normally be considered an example of "neutrality," any more than Belgrade's active promotion of Macedonian ecclesiastical auto-cephaly after the fall of Ranković would be.[61] Or again, the state's obstruction, in the years up to 1987, of Orthodox initiatives to build new church facilities, or of Catholic initiatives to build anything other than grand church facilities,[62] would not normally be considered neutral. And again, there were the incessant press campaigns against the major Christian Churches and the Islamic community alike, in which certain clerics were invariably portrayed as "reactionary." To harness the state media to attack religious bodies in print cannot be considered "neutral."

Since 1990, the greatest challenge to the liberal project, as I have defined it, has come from nationalists. Where nationalism has been the weakest (Slovenia, especially), progress toward the realization of the liberal project has come the farthest. Where nationalism has been strong, hostility toward basic liberal principles has likewise been strong. For the purposes of this book, the following definition will be useful:

Definition 5: **Nationalism** will be defined as an orientation which holds that there are national rights, that among these are the rights to establish a national state in which members of the titular nation are privileged in certain ways, that all members of the nation have the right to live in the national state, that contiguous territories in which members of the nation live should ideally be attached to the national state, and that the foregoing national "rights" take precedence, always and everywhere, over individual rights, whether the individual rights of members of the nation or those of members of other nations.

Under this definition, Dobrica Ćosić, Franjo Tudjman, and Vojislav Šešelj would qualify as nationalists, while Slobodan Milošević certainly appealed to nationalist sentiments. While Alija Izetbegović, elected president of Bosnia-Herzegovina in 1990, cannot be accused of having promoted nationalism as such, his early pamphlet, "The Islamic Declaration," for which he stood trial in 1983, played its part in fanning interconfessional intolerance, in spite of his alleged good wishes to the contrary. Izetbegović put it this way in "The Islamic Declaration":

The first and foremost conclusion is always the incompatibility of Islam and non-Islamic systems. There can be neither peace nor coexistence between the Islamic faith and non-Islamic social and political institutions. . . . In its assertion of the right to organize its own world, Islam clearly excluded any foreign ideology on its territory from the right or possibility of action. There is, moreover, no such thing as "the secular principle" [i.e., no such thing as neutrality of the state in matters of religion], and the state should be the expression of and [provide] support for the moral precepts of religion.[63]

Izetbegović lived to regret his authorship of the declaration and, belatedly, came to realize that Muslim extremism was also a danger for Bosnia.[64]

But if religious bigotry and nationalism are inimical to the liberal project, then, in combination, within the context of a multi-confessional, multi-ethnic society operating under an illegitimate system, they introduce a particularly toxic poison. Take, for example, the following statement by Bosnian Croat leader Mate Boban: "The Serbs are our brothers in Christ, but the Muslims are nothing to us, apart from the fact that for hundreds of years they raped our mothers and sisters."[65] The statement is a classic example of nationalist bigotry: the right to be treated with respect is reduced, by Boban, to an entitlement based on religious affiliation, human dignity and human rights as such are denied, tolerance is scorned, and an inequality based on religion is implicitly embraced as the operative political formula.

Some brilliant writers have argued that there is something one might call "liberal nationalism," or perhaps "civic nationalism."[66] Much as I respect the meticulous scholarship of their advocates, it seems to me that these concepts suggest, respectively, that liberalism might be reconciled with favoritism toward members of one's own national group or that civic-mindedness is somehow part of the same set in which chauvinistic bigotry is to be found. I am not convinced that this is the best way in which to categorize and conceptualize these unlike phenomena. I would suggest, rather, that we understand nationalism as a phenomenon which subordinates the authentic rights of individuals and of the community as a whole (regardless of the nationality of individual members) to the spurious "rights" of one or another nation, attacks tolerance and equality head-on, and provides an ideological foundation for justifying violations of the harm principle, where members of other nations are concerned. In this regard, it is fundamentally at war with the moral universalism of the liberal project. Indeed, nationalism (thus defined) can only be "justified" on the basis of a *limited* moral consequentialism (limited to what is good for "*our* nation") or nihilism.[67]

In so saying, I do not by any means wish to imply that love of one's homeland or interest in one's own nation's history and culture should be avoided or even annihilated. But these sentiments may be more suitably subsumed under the rubric of civic-mindedness[68] or caring for one's community or, possibly, to use Kant's term, patriotism.[69] Thus, although my position is distinct from that of David Miller, my critique of nationalism is by no means directed against his defense of cultural protectionism, much less against his realization that cultural bonds can help to build civic consciousness. But whereas civic-mindedness is oriented to the needs, interests, culture, and history of the community and society in which one lives, taking into account all its diverse members, nationalism is specifically oriented to the needs, interests, culture, and history of one national group. This is an essential difference.

Propositions

In the remaining pages of this chapter, I should like to present a few propositions and corollaries which may be helpful in approaching the text which follows:

Proposition 1: System legitimacy embraces political, economic, and moral factors; illegitimacy in any one of these spheres will tend to erode legitimate practices in the other spheres, unless effectively countered.

Proposition 2: The internal and external behaviors of illegitimate states differ from the internal and external behaviors of legitimate systems.

Corollary 2a: Illegitimate rulers tend to create mythologies to justify their holding power; such mythologies often portray the (illegitimate) ruler as the nation's champion against certain specified enemies and conspiracies.

Corollary 2b: Insofar as illegitimate systems do not respect human rights, they tend to adopt policies threatening to neighboring states.

Proposition 1 suggests that the three spheres in which the relative legitimacy of a system may be measured are interrelated, while proposition 2 and corollary 2b take their cue from Hannah Arendt's observations about the nature of totalitarianism.[70] Historically, political "realists" have tended to downplay the difference that lack of legitimacy makes; this was, for example, the mistake made by British prime minister Neville Chamberlain in his dealings with Hitler in 1938, and it was the error made by a later British prime minister, John Major, in his dealings with Milošević in the first half of the 1990s (though he was not alone in this error).

Proposition 3: Stable equilibrium in a political system hinges on that system's legitimacy.

Corollary 3a: Only a legitimate system can enjoy stable equilibrium.

Corollary 3b: The more illegitimate a system, the more unstable is its equilibrium.

Proposition 4: An unstable equilibrium is no guarantee of transformation toward legitimate politics; an unstable equilibrium provides incessant pressure for change.

Corollary 4a: Incessant pressure for change creates an atmosphere of crisis.

Corollary 4b: One illegitimate system may be replaced by another, whether of a different political type or of the same type.

***Definition 6:* Crisis** may be defined as a collective consensus that the status quo is untenable.

Proposition 5: Illegitimate systems cannot allow the introduction of legitimate or semi-legitimate institutions or practices, without exposing themselves to decay and ruination.

Propositions 3–5 and their corollaries deal with the vulnerability of illegitimate systems to decay and collapse. The connection between system illegitimacy and vulnerability to decay is well known. Seymour Martin Lipset, for example, writes that "the stability of a given democratic system"—and, I would add, of *any* system—depends, inter alia, "upon the effectiveness and legitimacy of the political system."[71] Or again, Ekkehart Krippendorff links the stability and durability of political systems to their legitimacy. He adds, further, that to the extent that the proportion of active citizens is greater in the ranks of the supporters of the ruling party or coalition than in the opposition, legitimacy and stability are fostered, while, to the extent that the ranks of the opposition may count a larger contingent of active citizens, legitimacy and stability are eroded.[72]

Proposition 6: The greater the sense of crisis, the more vulnerable the system is to collapse.

Proposition 7: The more illegitimate the system is, the more likely it is that people will organize to overthrow it.

Definition 7: Political legitimacy may be defined as the presence of a broad consensus on the rules of the political game, especially on the rules of political succession.

Proposition 8: The greater the correlation between political-programmatic preferences and ethnic affiliation, the greater the ethnic polarization.

> *Corollary 8a:* When, in a multi-ethnic state, there is no consensus on the political rules of the game, and different political-programmatic preferences are highly correlated with ethnic affiliation, the system remains in a state of intense crisis.
>
> *Corollary 8b:* Crisis is associated with vulnerability to and openness to wholesale change.

Propositions 6–8, with corollaries, emphasize the role of popular discontent, including ethnically associated discontent, in provoking system crisis and system decay. Proposition 6 connects with the writings of Ted Robert Gurr, Crane Brinton, and James C. Davies,[73] while proposition 7 follows closely Ronald Rogowski's suggestion that "the more serious the loss of legitimacy . . . in a given society, the more likely is overt action against the existing government."[74] Corollary 8b mirrors Lipset's observation that "A crisis of legitimacy is a crisis of change." Lipset adds, further, that "[a]fter a new social structure is established, if the new system is unable to sustain the expectations of major groups (on the grounds of 'effectiveness') for a long enough period to develop legitimacy upon the new basis, a new crisis may develop."[75]

Proposition 9: The wider the gap between rich and poor, the greater the pressure on the system to assure a basic standard of living at the lower end of the scale.

Proposition 10: The more educated the population, the less the tolerance of wide gaps between the rich and the poor.

Proposition 11: The greater the correlation between economic class and ethnic affiliation, the greater the potential for ethnic mobilization.

> *Corollary 11a:* The greater the sense of discriminatory injustice on the part of one or more ethnic/nationality groups, the greater the erosion of system legitimacy.
>
> *Corollary 11b:* The greater the sense of economic discrimination along eth-

nic lines, the greater the proclivity of members of the victimized group(s) to resort to violence.

And, as Gurr has warned, "If discontent is widespread in a society, anomie (normlessness) common, and political violence frequent, there is a tendency for attitudes of expectancy of violence to be converted into norms justifying violence."[76]

And legitimation has its symbols:

Definition 8: **Legitimating symbols** are symbols used by an institution in order to contribute to its own legitimation.

Proposition 12: The lower the consensus on symbols of legitimation, the greater the awareness of the problematic nature of the system.

Proposition 13: The greater the awareness of the problematic nature of the system, the greater and the more widespread the willingness to oppose the system.

Proposition 14: The greater the tendency of different ethnic/nationality groups to have *competing* legitimation symbols, the greater the ethnic polarization and the less the legitimacy of the system.

Throughout this chapter, it has been clear that the existence of diverse nationality groups can create fault lines along which fissures may occur, so that, in this and other ways, multi-ethnicity affects the tasks of state-building and legitimation. As John Stuart Mill wrote 140 years ago,

in a country made up of different nationalities . . . [t]he influences which form opinions and decide political acts are different in the different sections of the country. An altogether different set of leaders have the confidence of one part of the country and of another. The same books, newspapers, pamphlets, speeches, do not reach them. One section does not know what opinions, or what instigations, are circulating in another. The same incidents, the same acts, the same system of government, affect them in different ways; and each fears more injury to itself from the other nationalities than from the common arbiter, the state [provided that the state is not seen as being dominated by one or another nationality group]. Their mutual antipathies are generally much stronger than jealousy of the government.[77]

On the other hand, multi-ethnicity need not constitute an absolute impediment on the road toward legitimate government, legitimate economies, and the diffusion of moral univeralist (liberal) norms. It may even contribute to breaking down stereotypes and narrow provincialism. At any rate, multi-ethnicity is an important part of the socio-political landscape in which systems operate and inevitably affects the way in which crises in illegitimate systems are played out.

CHAPTER 2

The First Yugoslavia, Part 1: The Kingdom of Serbs, Croats, and Slovenes, 1918–1929

> Inequality is everywhere at the bottom of faction, for, in general, faction arises from men's striving for what is equal.
>
> —Aristotle, *Politics*, V, i

The founding of new states is generally fraught with risk. Quite apart from the possibility of challenges to the borders of a new state or the potential presence of internal resistance movements or, again, the need to establish trade connections capable of sustaining the new state, there are also questions concerning the state itself as the symbol of the collective identity of its inhabitants and its claim to legitimacy. As Peter Burgess has noted, "it is implicitly understood that any state foundation is based on a *principle* which guarantees the legitimacy of the state—in other words, a principle independent of time and space, a principle which extends beyond the concrete context in which the state was grounded."[1] There is, however, nothing to guarantee that such principles as may be invoked are either grounded on legitimate philosophical presuppositions or adequate to the task of state-building. In the Yugoslav context, the principle invoked was the (bogus[2]) principle of national self-determination then in vogue in diplomatic circles. Poland was to be resurrected as the national state of the Poles (though the Russo-Polish war resulted in the incorporation of large areas inhabited by Ukrainians and Belarusians, to say nothing of Jews and Lithuanians, into Poland). Hungary was to be a national state of the Hungarians. An expanded Romania was understood as the national

35

state of the Romanians. Czechoslovakia was explained as the national state of the "Czechoslovaks" (an artificial construction, to be sure). Finland, Estonia, Latvia, Lithuania, Ukraine, and others were recognized as new "national" states, while Albania and Bulgaria were confirmed likewise on the nationality principle, even if lands inhabited by their co-nationals ended up under foreign rule. And the Kingdom of Serbs, Croats, and Slovenes was justified on the argument that Serbs, Croats, and Slovenes were but three "tribes" of a single, "tri-named" nation. There were three chief problems with this logic, however: first, Serbs, Croats, and Slovenes did not share a common recollection of the past as per the concept of Ernest Renan; second, Croatia, Serbia, and, for that matter, Montenegro looked to different state traditions, the Albanians of Kosovo and the Macedonians identified with neighboring states, and the Croats and Serbs at least came into the kingdom with rather different political expectations; and third, the principle of national self-determination stood on shaky philosophical foundations, in that it could not explain why the empirical fact of language difference generated a normative imperative that a state be constituted to coincide with linguistic frontiers. Philosophers are fond of asserting that "you cannot derive an 'ought' from an 'is.'"[3] And yet, this is what the advocates of national (linguistic) self-determination set out to do. The principle was, of course, often justified as a logical extension of the democratic principle. But this derivation, based on a dubious application of the doctrine of popular sovereignty (which fails to acknowledge that government is the receptacle and agency of sovereignty[4]), wants to see nationalism as a respectable partner for liberal democracy when, in fact, "[n]ationalism threatens liberal democratic political principles and practices primarily by the way in which it connects political rights and privileges to relatively exclusive understandings of cultural community."[5] But if the new kingdom was to have any claim to a "democratic" consensus, then surely a referendum should have been organized in its various regions (Slovenia, Croatia, Macedonia, etc.) in which people should have been asked to vote on three separate questions: the union itself, the question of whether to accept the (Serbian) Karadjordjević dynasty as the new Yugoslav dynasty, and the nature of the constitutional framework to be drawn up (federal vs. unitary). Indeed, as of 1918, Croatian peasant leader Stjepan Radić (1871–1928), while not irrevocably opposed to union with Serbia, insisted at a minimum on the preservation of Croatian autonomy within a federally organized state and rejected the notion of monarchy in principle.[6] It is no doubt because of difficulties in reaching consensus on such questions that, in new states generally, there is a tendency, as Clifford Geertz has observed, toward the intensification of "group tensions within the society by raising settled cultural forms out of their particular contexts, expanding them into general allegiances, and politicizing them."[7] Moreover, when economic inequalities are correlated with group boundaries, the potential for inter-group resentment and distrust is significantly increased. State illegitimacy, economic inequality among the component peoples of the state, and the subscription of the state's several peoples to alternative histories and symbols are a deadly mix, and any state would be hard put to build a sense of community in such conditions (as per propositions 3, 11, 12, and 14 in the previous chapter). Add to this mix the phenomenon of *ethnic politics,* in which each component national group (in this case, Serbs, Croats, Slovenes, Bosnian Muslims, et al.) looked to "its own" political party or parties, so that one could safely assume that, for the most part, only Croats joined the Croatian Peasant Party, only Slovenes joined the Slovene People's Party, only Serbs joined the (Serbian) Radical Party, and only Muslims joined the Yugoslav Muslim Organization (JMO), and in which a "loyal Croat" was expected to vote for Radić, a "loyal Slovene" to vote for Anton Korošec, leader of the Slovene People's Party, and a "loyal Muslim" to vote for JMO leader Mehmed Spaho, and destabilization, if not collapse, must be seen as sown into the very fabric of state. What needs to be emphasized is that it is not the multi-ethnic composition of a state which is destabilizing, but ethnic politics, defined here as the alignment of ethnic cleavages with political cleavages. Thus, had the Yugoslav kingdom succeeded in its later effort (in the 1930s) to overcome nationality divisions by creating a political party which could appeal to all national groups, an important vulnerability of the system would have been overcome. As it was, the Axis powers, upon attacking Yugoslavia in April 1941, found it easy and convenient to divide the state into quisling national states, giving rise to quisling regimes in Serbia and Croatia, and expanded Hungarian, Albanian, and Bulgarian states.

The component peoples of the Kingdom of Serbs, Croats, and Slovenes came into the kingdom with rather different expectations and for different reasons. For the Serbs, the new kingdom was the fulfillment of the 19th-century dream of unifying all Serbs in one state and of Serbian expansion to the Adriatic, the "Greater Serbia" envisioned by Ilija Garašanin in his so-called *Načertanije* of 1844.[8] (As John Lampe has noted, Garašanin used the language of romantic nationalism in urging Serbian expansion into Bosnia-Herzegovina, Montene-gro, Macedonia, Kosovo, and the area which today constitutes northern Albania. Garašanin thus anticipated the eventual collapse of the Ottoman Empire and wanted to preempt any possible Russian or Austrian moves into the South Slav areas then under Ottoman rule.[9]) The Serbian politicians took their privileged place for granted, and took it for granted as well that the capital of the new state would be in Belgrade and that the Serbian Karadjordjević dynasty would be the dynasty of the new state; for the most part, they aspired to nothing less than political, economic, and cultural hegemony within the new state and saw strict centralism as a "logical" solution. The Croats and Slovenes, by contrast, looked to the kingdom to protect them from further territorial losses to Italy, which had been promised Istria, Friuli, and Dalmatia under the so-called London Agree-ment of 1915[10] and whose appetite might well grow larger if opportunity pre-sented itself. The Croats and Slovenes hoped, moreover, for a federal constitu-tion but lost a key champion of South Slav federalism with the death, in 1917, of Frano Supilo, a member of the London-based Yugoslav Committee, who had insisted that the Kingdom of Croatia-Slavonia-Dalmatia be accorded equal diplomatic status with the Kingdom of Serbia and that the two unite on the basis of parity within a federal system. Serbian troops entered Montenegro toward the end of 1918, and in their wake, a body calling itself the Central Executive Committee for the Unification of Serbia and Montenegro emerged. Ignoring the Montenegrin king, government, and parliament, as well as Montenegro's constitution, the committee proceeded to set up a body of 165 persons dubbed the "Grand National Assembly." Lacking either legal status or control of Cetinje, which was at the time the capital of Montenegro and a stronghold of those loyal to the legal government of Montenegro, this conjured "Assembly" met instead in Podgorica and, albeit not without some internal dissension, voted to depose King Nikola and merge Montenegro with Serbia.[11] After Montenegrin union with Serbia was proclaimed, an armed uprising broke out in Montenegro.[12] In Vojvodina and Kosovo, where there were large enclaves of Hungarians and Albanians (Albanians constituting the majority of the population of Kosovo even then), diplomats might have insisted on a referendum, but instead, to borrow the phrase Radić used in referring to some of his fellow Croats, they were acting "like drunken geese in a fog,"[13] happily unaware that their actions might have consequences which they themselves would not have desired. In Bosnia-Herzegovina, Muslims and Croats cooperated and, in August 1911, merged the leaderships of their political parties; but where the Muslims and Croats hoped for an autonomous status for Bosnia within the then-existing Austro-Hungarian Empire, local Serbs, who constituted about 43% of the population of Bosnia-Herzegovina in 1910, stayed outside the coalition. When the Habsburg Empire disintegrated and plans to constitute the South Slav state quickened, Muslim politicians pressed for autonomy for Bosnia-Herzegovina.[14] This was not to be.

In fact, not only did Serb politicians not respect the autonomist aspirations expressed by Croats and Bosnian Muslims (Bosniaks) at the time they joined the kingdom, but they did not even share the leading political offices on a remotely equal basis. At the time of unification, Serbs constituted about 40% of the population. And yet the prime minister's job went to Serbs for 264 of the 268 months that the interwar kingdom lasted (going to a Slovene for the other four months), the ministry of the army and navy was run by Serbs for all 268 months, the minister of internal affairs was a Serb for 240 out of 268 months, the minister of foreign affairs was a Serb for 247 months, and the minister of justice was a Serb for 237 of those months. As Mark Thompson has noted, "Serbia never intended to enter the new state on terms of equality. . . . Equality was unthinkable."[15] But even if one were to give the regime the benefit of the doubt, for the sake of argument, and assume that Serbs may have had greater administrative experience than Slovenes and Croats (a highly dubious proposition, to be sure), one should nonetheless have to concede that the policy of monopolizing the top posts in the country for Serbs was, at a minimum, politically insensitive, likely to give provocation, and short-sighted. The birth of the Kingdom of Serbs, Croats, and Slovenes was, thus, as inauspicious as any, and the prospects for the kingdom's success were, given the attitude of the leading Serbian politicians, bleak.

The Gestation and Birth of Yugoslavia

During the 19th century and early 20th century, four alternative understandings of nation were developed among Croats and Serbs. The first of these, developed by Serbian orthographer Vuk Karadžić (1787–1864), looked to language as the foundation of nation; it followed, in his view, that if a common orthography could be developed for Serbs and Croats, then, to the extent that they adopted this common form, they would be (or become) one nation.[16] Josip Juraj Strossmayer (1815–1905), appointed bishop of Djakovo in 1849, saw religion as the critical variable; committed to the "Illyrian" program of Yugoslav unification, Strossmayer felt that the confessional divide between Serbs and Croats was a potential obstacle and therefore applied himself toward achieving a religious reconciliation between the two peoples.[17] For Ante Starčević (1823–1896), founder of the Croatian Party of Right, by contrast, neither language nor religion was determinative of nation; looking instead to Croatian state right, established through various compacts and charters over the centuries, Starčević could cite the examples of France and England in support of his contention that the state could create the nation. Starčević, thus, "was interested in building up a state of equal citizens (a "citizens' state") and not in constructing an exclusivist ideology on the basis of either national or religious homogeneity."[18]

Understandings of nation which emphasize language, religion, or state are all, at least potentially, embracive, rather than exclusive. One can learn a new language and raise one's children speaking it; one can adopt a new religion; one can assume the citizenship of a new country and give the new state one's loyalty. However, a fourth strand of nationalism also emerged, stressing blood and race. On the Croatian side, this may be traced to the activity of Josip Frank (1844–1911), who succeeded Starčević as head of the Croatian Party of Right only to split it in two through his distinctly anti-Serbian orientation.[19] The writings of Ivo Pilar, an officer in the Austro-Hungarian Army, emphasized racial traits and endeavored to "prove" that Croats were racially distinct from Serbs.[20] Among Serbs, Orthodox theologian Žarko Gavrilović developed what was roughly a Serbian counterpart in the 1930s, stressing blood, religion, and state tradition, with undercurrents of messianic pan-Slavism. That Gavrilovic's formula had an intolerant aspect was clear from his stress on the purity of the Orthodox Church, "whose authentic sources have been obscured by the Roman Catholicism and Protestantism of the West."[21]

In the 19th century, Serbia, like Greece, Bulgaria, Romania, and Albania, had a vision of national expansion—a "Great Idea," as the Greeks would call it. This expansionism was driven, in the first place, by the desire to obtain ports on the Adriatic and on the Aegean (with Salonika/Thessaloniki as the target port on the Aegean coast) and to build up national power but was legitimated by variants of pan-Slavism. The absorption of Croatia and Bosnia-Herzegovina, as spelled out in the *Načertanije*, was only one vision entertained by Belgrade in those years. Another vision riveted on a drive to the south, entailing unification with Bulgaria and the annexation of Macedonia. Much of Macedonia, together with Kosovo-Metohija or Kosmet (as the Serbs call Kosovo), was annexed by Serbia in the course of the Balkan Wars of 1912–1913. Soon after the outbreak of World War One, the Serbian National Assembly, meeting in Niš, declared that Serbia's goal in the war was "the liberation and unification of all of our unliberated brothers."[22]

But the Slovenes and Croats had their own history of enthusiasm for a Yugoslav state. In Croatia, Ljudevit Gaj (1809–1872), publicist and journalist, did much to popularize the "Illyrian" (i.e., Yugoslav) idea, supporting Vuk Karadžić's call for a unified orthography for all South Slavs, though Gaj proposed that the Latin alphabet would serve best.[23] Among Slovenes, during the revolutionary turmoil of 1848, there had, moreover, been calls for the creation of a Yugoslav federation, consisting of Slovenia, Croatia, and Vojvodina.

As national consciousness grew among the South Slavs of the Habsburg Empire, "Yugoslav" champions at first looked to a reorganization of the Austro-Hungarian Empire and the creation of a South Slav state *within* the empire. This project, called "trialism" because of its advocacy of the creation of a third fully self-governing unit under the Habsburg scepter, gathered steam almost as soon as Hungary gained its autonomy under the *Ausgleich* (compromise) of 1867. The following year brought the Hungarian-Croatian *Nagodba*, which promised a measure of autonomy to Croatia. Then, in 1870 in Ljubljana, a Yugoslav Congress was calling for the reorganization of Austria-Hungary on a trialist basis. This "Yugoslav" orientation spread to Catholic circles as well. For example, in December 1912, the Catholic newspaper *Riječke Novine* recommended that its readers work for "the national unity of Slovenes, Croats, and Serbs."[24]

In May 1917, in what proved to be a false start, 33 deputies of the Yugoslav deputies' club in the Vienna parliament, proposed the unification of Slovenes, Croats, and Serbs of the Habsburg Empire in an "independent state body" under the scepter of the Habsburg-Lorraine dynasty. Within Croatia (whose deputies were represented in the Budapest parliament, not in Vienna), the Starčević Party of Right was the first party to declare its support for the program spelled out in the May Declaration, while the Croatian Party of Right (HSP) –Frankists (the party shaped by Josip Frank), while not endorsing it as such, promised not to interfere with the efforts of the signatories. The May Declaration also won some lukewarm support from Stjepan Radić, who had joined his brother Antun in forming the Croatian People's Peasant Party (Hrvatska pučka seljačka stranka, or HPSS) in December 1904, but who was still far from being as influential in Croatian political circles as he would later become. Antun Bauer, the Catholic archbishop of Zagreb, and authoritative figures among the Bosnian Franciscans also declared their support for the May Declaration. But among the Bosniaks (Muslims of Bosnia) and Serbs, the response was less enthusiastic. Safvet-beg Bašagić, president of the local assembly, and Šerif Arnautović, one of the leaders of the United Muslim Organizations, developed an alternative idea and suggested, in a memorandum submitted to the Austrian Kaiser, that Bosnia-Herzegovina be attached to Hungary but with local autonomy.[25] Bosnian Serbs, by contrast, were "reserved" in their comments on the declaration, while Serbs in Croatia let it be known that they were opposed to the solution outlined in the May Declaration.[26] Nor were all Catholics uniformly in favor of it. Dr. Janez Evangelist Krek, a Roman Catholic priest and deputy in the local Carniola (Krain) Assembly, specifically wanted to see the future Yugoslav state constructed *outside* any Habsburg framework. In his view, the state should be a constitutional monarchy, in which the monarch should not have any legislative powers.[27]

The May Declaration continued to be actively discussed for a little over a year. In May 1918, Antun Mahnič,[28] bishop of Krk, began writing a series of newspaper articles defending the program of the May Declaration. Mahnič took the establishment of some sort of South Slav state for granted and was concerned mainly to defend the principle of ethnic and confessional cohabitation. For Mahnič,

Serbs live with us and among us. Serbdom is a fact. . . . What is . . . better for Croats and Catholics—to declare a war to the finish against Serbdom, or to try to reach a friendly modus vivendi with them? . . . Serbs are not Catholics, but they are nonetheless Christians; . . . Serbs are our . . . brothers by blood and by language.[29]

But Mahnič's efforts, like those of other apologists of the Declaration, were cut short by a decision by imperial authorities on 12 May 1918 to ban any agitation in favor of the May Declaration.

In the meantime, the Yugoslav Committee, a group of intellectuals and political activists from the Habsburg Empire who professed to represent the interests of South Slavs living in that empire but at least some of whose expenses were underwritten by the Serbian government-in-exile,[30] agitated in Allied capitals for Yugoslav unification. In spite of Belgrade's involvement in launching and defraying the costs of the Yugoslav Committee, major differences of opinion arose between the two sides. The Serbian government preferred to regard the Yugoslav Committee as a body subordinate to its own needs, indeed in its service, but as early as the second half of 1915, Frano Supilo, arguably the committee's most distinguished member, urged that the future Yugoslav state adopt a federal system with five constituent units: Serbia in its borders of 1913 (i.e., including Macedonia and Kosovo-Metohija) together with Vojvodina, Croatia (including Slavonia and Dalmatia), Slovenia, Bosnia-Herzegovina, and Montenegro. But in May 1917, Nikola Pašić, Serbia's prime minister, arranged for conversations between representatives of the Serbian government and of the Yugoslav Committee. Supilo was suspicious of Pašić, whom he regarded as a sly champion of Greater Serbian hegemonism, and warned his colleagues on the committee that the issue of Serbian pretensions needed to be addressed; and, in fact, from the earliest days of the war, Pašić envisioned that, in the event of Yugoslav unification, administration and policy-making power would be centralized in Belgrade.[31] However, the other members of the committee were concerned about Italy's territorial appetite (being aware of the "secret" London protocol in which Istria, along with almost a third of what is today Slovenia, half of Dalmatia, and also some islands, had been promised to Rome). They were therefore eager to reach a preliminary agreement with the Serbian government and accepted the invitation. When he heard this, Supilo resigned from the committee; he died later that same year.

Members of the Yugoslav Committee came to Korfu in mid-June 1917, for the historic meeting with the Serbian government. The two sides met for 28 plenary sessions over a period of 35 days, but the differences between them immediately became apparent.[32] Finally, on 20 July 1917, the two sides agreed on a joint declaration which represented a compromise on both sides. Ante Trumbić, president of the Yugoslav Committee and the future first foreign minister of the Kingdom of Serbs, Croats, and Slovenes, signed on behalf of the committee, with Nikola Pašić signing in the name of the Serbian government. The Korfu Declaration affirmed that Serbs, Croats, and Slovenes were one, "tri-named" people, that the Karadjordjević dynasty would be the ruling house in the new state, which would, however, be organized on a constitutional and parliamentary basis, and that the postwar government would respect the equality of religion and alphabets, as well as voting rights, etc. The key question as to whether the future state would be centralized or federal was, however, not addressed.[33] In January 1918, Trumbić advanced a proposal that a Yugoslav assembly be summoned in Paris or London, composed of representatives of the Serbian government and of the Yugoslav Committee and functioning as a provisional representative body, but Pašić refused to go along with the idea because he understood that the intent was to use this representative body as a provisional government, thereby compromising Serbia's military and diplomatic advantage.

In the second half of 1918, the military situation changed dramatically, with the Central Powers suffering reverses on the frontlines, and with mutinies in the Habsburg Army and wholesale desertions. Political structures and boundaries had suddenly become very fluid. On 5–6 October 1918, representatives of the Croatian, Slovenian, and Serbian parties operating within the Habsburg lands established the National Council of the Slovenes, Croats, and Serbs, committing themselves to work for full independence. In these circumstances, in October 1918, Kaiser Karl belatedly declared his intention to reorganize the empire as a federal state, in which the South Slavs would have their own federal unit. But the announcement came too late. On 16 October 1918, the National Council declined the Kaiser's offer and, two days later, declared itself the "central organ" of a new state, the State of Slovenes, Croats, and Serbs, embracing Slovenia, Croatia-Slavonia, Dalmatia, and Bosnia-Herzegovina. On 29 October, the Croatian Sabor (Assembly), which had yet to act on this issue, declared the severance of all political ties with Austria-Hungary and the formal establishment of the State of Slovenes, Croats, and Serbs. Korošec, the SLS (Slovenian People's Party) leader, was elected president, while Dr. Ante Pavelić (the dentist), president of the Starčević Party of Right, and Svetozar Pribićević (1875–1936), the leading figure among the Serbs of Croatia and president of the Croat-Serb coalition, were elected vice presidents.

This act created a new legal situation in which, at least in theory, the South Slavs of the now-deceased Habsburg Empire should have been in a better position vis-à-vis the Kingdom of Serbia than they had been when they were being represented only by the ad hoc and entirely unofficial Yugoslav Committee. On 6–9 November 1918, representatives of the Serbian government, the National Council, the Yugoslav Committee, and the Serbian opposition conducted negotiations in Geneva. The two bodies representing Habsburg-area South Slavs hoped to hammer out a declaration in which the Serbian side would forswear the "unitarist" concept of unification. Nikola Pašić was, indeed, induced to sign a declaration along those lines, but no sooner was he back in Belgrade than the regent extracted his resignation from office, thereby annulling Serbia's adherence to the declaration.[34] The new Serbian government now declined to confirm the Geneva declaration and proceeded along a line directly antithetical to it. For the National Council, this was a dramatic setback.

Meanwhile, the newborn State of Slovenes, Croats, and Serbs was facing unrest in the countryside, revolutionary tremors, and the threat of an Italian military incursion. As early as 4 November, the National Council appealed to Vojvoda[35] Stepa Stepanović, commander of the Second Serbian Army, to bring his troops into Bosnia-Herzegovina to maintain order; the first Serbian units entered Sarajevo two days later.[36] By mid-November, the Italian Army was pushing into Istria, replacing local administrative organs and introducing Italian law, and advancing into Carniola; on 17 November, Italian troops entered Rijeka (already known in Italian as Fiume) and were also threatening other parts of Dalmatia. A large Italian force was also descending on Ljubljana, apparently intending to occupy it. The Italians were prevented from taking Ljubljana by the resolute action of Lt. Col. Stevan Švabić, commander of the city defenses, who ordered his troops to open fire on the Italians, and by a Serbian battalion consisting of Austro-Hungarian prisoners of war.[37] The National Council appealed to the international community for assistance, but none was forthcoming—except potentially from Serbia. Under these circumstances, the National Council selected a committee of 28 persons to travel to Belgrade and arrange for unification urgently. To be sure, the delegation had been instructed to press for a federal system,[38] but once in Belgrade, the delegation, feeling under a lot of pressure both from the Serbs and from the threat posed by Italy and perhaps influenced by the sense of momentum created by the votes by the assemblies in Vojvodina on 25 November and Montenegro on 26 November to join Serbia,[39] abandoned these instructions. On 1 December 1918, the delegation addressed an appeal to Crown Prince Aleksandar, regent for the ailing King

Petar I, asking him to assume power in a unified state; nothing was said now about federation. The king accepted, and with this, the Kingdom of Serbs, Croats, and Slovenes, as the country would be called until 1929, was born. With this, Italian military advances came to a halt.[40]

The Politics of "No Consensus"

In ignoring its instructions, the National Council's delegation had exceeded its mandate; strictly speaking, the unification proclaimed in Belgrade on 1 December stood, therefore, on dubious legal grounds. But, for all that, the story of the Kingdom of Serbs, Croats, and Slovenes (hereafter, the Kingdom of SHS) might have been a happier one, had it been possible to reach a consensus on the basic principles of state and to hammer out a constitution which would have satisfied the basic expectations of the principal national groups. In writing this, I am suggesting that deterministic and fatalistic accounts of the interwar period proceed as if human agency made no difference in what happened in the interwar kingdom; on the contrary, I argue, the failures of the interwar kingdom were the result of decisions taken by identifiable political figures.

Although the Serbs were by far the most numerous group in the kingdom, they were themselves a minority. Even combined with the Montenegrins, not all of whom considered themselves "Serbs," the Serbs amounted to less than 40% of the total population. The national diversity of the kingdom is shown in Table 2.1. Where the Albanians are concerned, the figure provided is open to dispute. The official census figure for 1921 set the number of Albanians in the Kingdom of SHS at 439,657, slightly less than the figure in the table provided by the noted Serbian historian Petranović. On the other hand, Antonio Baldacci, an Italian specialist on Kosovo, estimated the number of Albanians living in the kingdom at 700,000 at the time.[41] Be that as it may, at the dawn of the new kingdom there were ideological divisions in all regions of the country, with clericals contesting with liberals in Slovenia and Croatia, monarchists challenging republicans in Serbia, secular peasant parties in Croatia and Serbia offering alternatives, communists and social democrats in all parts of the country, and alternative political currents among the Muslims of the country. As of 1918, in spite of the inauspicious beginning, the development of an "ethnic politics" syndrome was not inexorable destiny.

As early as November 1918, before the act of unification had been taken, Stjepan Radić, president of the Croatian People's Peasant Party (HPSS, or hereafter, Croatian Peasant Party), offered his plan for a confederal state, with representatives from Serbia, Croatia, and Slovenia constituting an executive triumvirate. In his plan, the legislature would have carried over the name "National Council" and would have consisted of 10 deputies each from Croatia, Serbia, and Slovenia, four deputies from Bosnia-Herzegovina, and two deputies each from Dalmatia, Montenegro, Istria, and Vojvodina. Six of these units—all

Table 2.1. The National Composition of the Kingdom of Serbs, Croats, and Slovenes (1918)

		% of total
Serbs & Montenegrins	4,704,876	38.8
Croats	2,889,102	23.9
Slovenes	1,023,588	8.5
Muslims	759,656	6.3
Macedonians	630,000	5.3
Germans	512,207	4.3
Albanians	483,871	4.0
Magyars	472,079	3.9
Romanians	183,563	1.6
Turks	143,453	1.2
Italians	11,630	0.1
Others Slavs[a]	198,857	1.6
Others	42,756	0.3

Source: Branko Petranović, *Istorija Jugoslavije, 1918–1988*, Vol. 1: *Kraljevina Jugoslavija, 1914–1941* (Belgrade: Nolit, 1988), p. 32; and Dušan Bilandžić, *Hrvatska moderna povijest* (Zagreb: Golden Marketing, 1999), p. 86.

a. Czechs, Slovaks, Bulgarians, Russians, Ukrainians, Ruthenes

except Istria and Montenegro—would have had their own provincial parliaments and their own autonomous administrations. Istria and Montenegro, though sending delegates to the National Council, would have been administratively incorporated into Croatia and Serbia respectively.[42] On the Serbian side, Stojan Protić, a leading figure in the (Serbian) National Radical Party (hereafter, Radical Party) and the country's first prime minister, saw positive value in the preservation of the cultural and national diversity of the kingdom's peoples and, while not advocating a federal solution as such, favored the decentralization of state administrative functions to historically defined provinces, which would enjoy legislative and executive responsibilities, with their own assemblies and provincial governments. Protić actually prepared his own draft constitution, which was designed as a compromise between pure centralists such as Pribićević and (con)federalists such as Radić. Protić envisioned that the decentralized state could consist of the following provinces: Serbia; Old Serbia with Macedonia; Croatia and Slavonia, with Rijeka (Fiume); Istria and Medjimurje; Bosnia; Montenegro and Herzegovina; Boka Kotorska and Primorje; Dalmatia; Srem and Bačka; Banat; and Slovenia.[43]

Negotiations between representatives of the National Council and the Serbian government, concerning the formation of a common, transitional government began on 11 December, and on 20 December 1918 the composition of the new government was announced. The principal political actors in Serbia, Croatia, and Slovenia had previously agreed that Nikola Pašić, the erstwhile prime minister of Serbia, should be entrusted with the post of prime minister in the first government, but Prince Aleksandar, acting as regent for the ailing King Petar I, showed his contempt for the parties by entrusting Protić, who had been representing the Kingdom of SHS at the Paris peace talks, with the job.[44] Although Serbs amounted to less than 40% of the population of the kingdom, 13 of the 20 ministers constituting the first cabinet (65%) were Serbs, with four Croats, two Slovenes, and one Bosniak completing the lineup. Korošec became deputy prime minister, Trumbić became foreign minister, Pribićević became minister of internal affairs, and Ljubomir Davidović, president of the Democratic Party, a party which was committed to a centralist program and viewed Croats and Slovenes as branches of the Serbian nation, became minister of education.

The prince-regent followed this up with another action which showed contempt for the political parties. Where the proclamation of 1 December, issued by the regent himself, had promised that the provisional parliament would be constituted "by agreement between the National Council in Zagreb and the representative of the people of the Kingdom of Serbia,"[45] the list of candidates for the first parliament was, in fact, drawn up by the regent's minister, Albert Kramer (leader of the Slovenian "liberals" and a close collaborator of Pribićević's), on authorization from the regent. The provisional parliament had the following composition: 84 deputies from Serbia (including Macedonia and Kosovo), 62 deputies from Croatia-Slavonia, 42 from Bosnia-Herzegovina, 32 from Slovenia, 24 from Vojvodina, 12 from Dalmatia, 12 from Montenegro, and four from Istria. Even here, there were problems: among the 42 deputies from Bosnia-Herzegovina, only 11 were Bosniaks, while the JMO felt that there should have been 15 Bosniaks in the provisional parliament.[46] The fact that the JMO was concerned about the ethnicity of the deputies was already a small sign of incipient ethnic mobilization, a preliminary stage which can lead to "ethnic politics."

Meanwhile, the new Kingdom of SHS was engulfed in widespread turmoil and violence. During the winter of 1918–1919, there were revolutionary tremors and acts of sedition in Osijek, Našice, Maribor, Varaždin, Subotica, and other towns.[47] A 20,000-strong National Guard was mobilized specifically to put down unrest in Vojvodina in 1919, inspired by the short-lived Soviet republic established in neighboring Hungary by Béla Kun, and in Bosnia-Herzegovina authorities took into custody about 3,000 activists in workers' organizations.[48]

In Macedonia, pro-Bulgarian sentiment was widespread, and there was little support among the Macedonians for the Belgrade regime.[49] Macedonia had been annexed by force of arms during the Balkan Wars of 1912–1913, and now, after the end of World War One, resistance to Belgrade was resurfacing. The authorities responded by forbidding the use of the Macedonian language and by mandating 20-year terms at hard labor for those convicted of involvement in anti-state organizations. Perhaps as many as 324 advocates of a Greater Bulgaria were murdered in Macedonia in the years 1918–1924, while up to 47 persons simply disappeared.[50] Some 50,000 Serbian Army troops and police were stationed in "southern Serbia," as Macedonia was called in Belgrade. Serbian *četas* (armed bands) were organized (such as that led by Jovan Babunski) and terrorized the region. These Chetniks had orders to kill local resistance leaders and to recruit the local population "into forced labor for the army."[51] On 24 September 1920 came the passage of the Regulation for the Settlement of the New Southern Regions, designed to encourage Serb "colonists" to settle in Macedonia and Kosovo. By the end of 1928, a total of 63,939 hectares of land had been distributed to 6,377 "colonist" families. The former exarchate schools (schools which had been operated by the exarchate of the Bulgarian Orthodox Church) were shut down (130 of them in the 1922–1923 academic year alone), and teachers deemed unreliable were dismissed. History textbooks were revised to prove that Macedonia's history was conjoined with Serbia's, and schoolchildren were taught to speak Serbian.[52] Macedonians were forced to Serbianize their family names. Bulgarian clubs and societies were suppressed. As many as 2,900 persons were apprehended for political reasons during the years 1918–1924, according to a pro-Bulgarian source.[53] The Macedonians fought back, with resistance carried out chiefly by the Internal Macedonian Revolutionary Organization (IMRO),[54] which maintained bases in Pirin Macedonia (western Bulgaria) and built up an army of 9,100 men by 1923. The Serbian authorities replied with terror. For example, in March 1923, all males from Garvan (Radoviš) were murdered. The Association against Bulgarian Bandits, launched in 1922 and based in Štip, was led by Kosta Pećanac and Ilija Trifunović-Lune and acquired notoriety for the arbitrary terrorization of Macedonians.[55]

In Montenegro, after the shotgun marriage of Montenegro and Serbia,[56] civil war broke out between the widely popular pro-independence "greens" and the less popular but better armed pro-Serbian "whites." Loyalists held onto Cetinje, Rijeka Crnojevića, and Virpazar for a while but were repelled when they tried to establish their control of Nikšić. Paramilitary units organized by the unionists joined Serbian troops in mounting a siege of Cetinje. Stiff Montenegrin resistance to union continued until 1924, with atrocities committed on both sides. The death in exile of Montenegro's King Nikola on 1 March 1921 was dispiriting to the loyalists, and upon the death of Queen Milena two years later those exiles who had remained committed to the cause of Montenegrin independence dispersed.[57] The resistance was motivated not by loyalty to the Petrović-Njegoš dynasty but by anger at what the greens considered to be discriminatory treatment by the Serbs. While most greens would have preferred independence, they were prepared to accept union with Serbia, provided that Montenegrins were accorded full equality as citizens of the new state.[58] Meanwhile, negotiations were underway between the Montenegrin patriarchate and the Holy Synod of the Serbian Orthodox Church regarding unification; these negotiations were concluded in March 1920, when it was announced that the de facto autocephalous Montenegrin Orthodox Church, which had been administered by the metropolitan of Cetinje, would be integrated into the structure of the Serbian Church. The unification was solemnly proclaimed on 12 September 1920, bringing some 600 places of worship under the jurisdiction of the Serbian Orthodox Patriarchate in Belgrade.[59] The unification was accomplished canonically but would later be recalled with bitterness by Montenegrin greens.

In Kosovo, relations between local Albanians and Serbs had been deteriorating at least since 1878. According to Serbian sources, about 150,000 Serbs were driven out of Kosovo by Albanians in the years 1876–1912.[60] As in the case of Macedonia, Kosovo had come under Serbian rule as a result of the force of arms, and the local population was not reconciled to rule from Belgrade. In November 1918, local Albanians formed the Committee for the National Defense of Kosovë (popularly known as the Kosovë Committee), which supported the resistance movement. The Albanian fighters were known as *kaçaks* (from the Turkish *kaçaklar* = outlaws). Perhaps the most famous *kaçak* leader was Azem Bejta (1889–1924), who as of spring 1919 had about 10,000 men under his command.[61] As early as October 1918, some Serbian soldiers in Kosovo sought revenge for the attacks the Serbian Army had suffered at the hands of Albanians during its retreat in 1915, which had been, in turn, a revenge for the repressive treatment which Serbian authorities had meted out to Albanians after the Serbian conquest of the province in 1912, which had included the forced conversion of Albanians to Orthodoxy.[62] The authorities replied with counterforce, and during 1918 and 1919 the Serbian Army was repeatedly deployed to suppress uprisings on the part of Albanians. There were reports of massacres of Albanians by the Serbian Army in and around Podgor Metohijski (near Peć), in Rožaj (in the Sandžak), in the Djakovica region, in the Rugovo Gorge, and in the Plav and Gusinje districts.[63] Pećanac's Chetniks were also given free rein in Kosovo. The Kosovë Committee became involved in arms trafficking and established connections with discontents among the Macedonians and Croats (especially émigré Frankists), as well as with the Italians. The *kaçaks* bombed government buildings, attacked trains, and rustled cattle during the years 1918–1924; moreover, as Banac notes, the Albanians had no trouble obtaining firearms, since corrupt Serbian officials were more than happy to profit from the insurgency and sell the Albanians weapons from the Serbian Army's stock.[64]

Meanwhile, the authorities in Belgrade shut down all Albanian-language schools in Kosovo, shunting Albanian schoolchildren and adolescents into Serbian schools. Later, the authorities decided that educating the Albanians was contrary to the interests of state and applied pressure to keep the Albanians out of the state schools altogether. The Albanians were allowed, however, to obtain basic Islamic religious instruction in "Turkish schools," but the Albanians, in due course, succeeded in converting these "Turkish schools" into "formidable centers of underground national education and opposition activity."[65]

As early as 24 September 1920, a decree on the colonization of the "southern regions" of the kingdom was issued, laying the legal groundwork for the transfer to Serb and Montenegrin "colonists" of land confiscated from local Albanians. By 1938, according to Miranda Vickers, some 10,877 Serb and Montenegrin families were brought to Kosovo and settled on 120,672 hectares of land.[66]

In Bosnia-Herzegovina, there was no equivalent to the resistance being waged in Macedonia and Kosovo. But there was widespread violence all the same. In the first months of 1919, Bosnian Serbs repeatedly attacked Muslims across Bosnia, setting their homes on fire, seizing their land, and shouting at them to "go back" to Asia.[67] Just in the months through July 1919, some 4,281 Muslim farmers were driven from their land, losing 400,072 hectares of land to Serbs. Even Stepa Stepanović, commanding the Second Serbian Army, was unable to put a stop to the violence. Altogether, between December 1918 and September 1920, about 2,000 Muslims were killed by local Serbs. There were also persecutions of Bosniaks in the Sandžak, a strip of land which had been separated from Bosnia-Herzegovina in 1878 but garrisoned by Austrian troops until 1909. The bloodletting and persecutions continued through 1924, in November of which year about 2,000 armed Montenegrins descended on Šahoviće and Pavino Polje, killing about 600 Bosnian Muslim men, women, and children. By July 1926, about 500 Bosniak village cooperatives had been burned to the ground. Some of the violence had a class nature, with Serbian peasants seizing land from Muslim estate-owners. But Muslim peasants were also targeted, because they were Muslims. Most of Serbia's troops had had "no experience of living among Muslims, and had been brought up to think of Muslims as such almost as mythical symbols of the enemies of Serbia."[68] In addition, such sentiments were reportedly fanned by the Serbian boulevard press.[69] This was not the case with Bosnian Serb villagers, however, "who had lived at peace with their Muslim neighbours for forty years or more."[70]

The land reform was pushed through with uncharacteristic haste, being proclaimed already in February 1919. Some 66.9% of the land affected was in Bosnia-Herzegovina; with this framing, the land reform obtained high priority in Belgrade, as it could serve to destroy the power of the Bosniaks as such. But the regime undertook to pay 255,000,000 dinars in compensation per a period of 40 years, at an interest rate of 6%. Since the payments were, in fact, only started in 1936, they were supposed to be completed by 1975. By 1941, when the spread of World War Two to Yugoslavia interrupted and ended all such payments, only 10% of the projected remittances had been made.[71]

In Croatia, shortly after the unified kingdom was proclaimed, there were anti-monarchy, pro-republic protests on Zagreb's main square (Jelačić Square); these protests were brutally suppressed. Then, on 10 December 1918, a Serbian military mission arrived in Zagreb with the assignment to reorganize the military forces in Croatia, disbanding the existing regiments and replacing them with new structures integrated into the Royal Army of the Kingdom. This was done with considerable speed.[72] Violence swept the Croatian countryside in 1918–1919. Some of this had an inter-ethnic character, but this was usually subsidiary to the class nature of the turmoil, in which peasants felt at liberty to loot shops, plunder large estates, and generally run amuck. In early February, the HPSS leadership drafted a petition to the Paris peace conference, asking for international support for a "neutral Croat peasant republic"; within six weeks, 115,167 signatures had been collected in support of this petition. While this petition campaign was underway, a mob of pro-government students attacked Radić's bookshop in Zagreb on 9 March, causing much damage. Radić himself was arrested on 25 March 1919, for his role in drafting and circulating the petition.[73] Numerous other leading figures in Radić's party were also taken into custody at this time, and public rallies on the part of the HPSS were banned. Radić himself would remain incarcerated for nearly a year. In September 1920, renewed violence flared up in the Croatian countryside, sparked by the Royal Army's branding of draft animals—an undertaking intended to designate which animals were fit to be drafted for military service and which were not. This came against a background of various economic and other grievances nurtured by the peasants. Now, pushed over the edge by the branding of their animals, Croatian peasants seized control of Čazma, a small town east of Zagreb, on the night of 4 September 1920. The following day, the peasants seized Vojni Križ, and from there, the insurgency spread in a southeasterly direction, toward Kutina. At Bregi, some 2,000 insurgents took control, detaining the gendarmes. From there, about 600 peasants marched on Dugo Selo, taking control for a few hours. The authorities restored order before the end of the month but, in the wake of the rebellion, sought to downplay the genuine grievances of the peasants and to attribute the uprising, rather, to Bolshevik influences among the peasantry.[74]

Later, under the rubric of "agrarian reform," the regime deprived Churches, schools, hospitals, and libraries in Croatia of lands which had been granted to these institutions in perpetuity by the Austro-Hungarian government, shut down a number of departments in the University of Zagreb, and shipped large quantities of books from Croatia to Belgrade on the argument that they were no longer needed in Croatia![75]

In Slovenia, by contrast, developments took a different course. Here General Rudolf Maister (1874–1934), a major in the Austro-Hungarian Army until promoted to the rank of general in the chaotic days of November 1918, assumed command of Maribor and organized Slovenes from the disintegrating Austro-Hungarian Army into a 4,000-strong force (with 200 officers) and marched them into Carinthia and Styria, in hopes of annexing these regions to Slovenia. The Austrian Army fought back, but in May 1919, Maister succeeded in blocking the Austrian counteroffensive.[76] Under the Treaty of Saint Germain, signed with Austria on 10 September 1919, it was agreed that a plebiscite would be organized in the Klagenfurt basin, the disputed frontier region between Austria and the kingdom. On 10 October 1920, the plebiscite was held: 22,052 of those voting opted for Austria, with only 15,279 expressing a preference to join the Kingdom of SHS. Among those voting for union with Austria were many local Slovenes. After the plebiscite, relations between the Serbian bloc in the government and the Slovenian People's Party (SLS) worsened, with each side blaming the other for the large number of Slovenes who voted to join Austria rather than the kingdom.[77] Yet the plebiscite contributed to a sense that the border was just and that people had been allowed to make their own decision. There were no plebiscites held in Kosovo or Montenegro or Macedonia or, for that matter, Vojvodina, in spite of complaints on both sides, manifested, at one point, in the organization of the short-lived *Baranjska republika* by Serbs on the Hungarian side of the border.

At the same time, even though Slovenia was free of the kind of violence and turmoil which plagued other parts of the country in the 1920s, the Slovenes were not enthusiastic about being submerged in a Serbian ocean. Korošec, by far the most influential Slovenian politician in the entire interwar era (1918–1941), specifically wanted to see a provision for provincial autonomy added to the constitution. During the first parliamentary election campaign, his SLS campaigned as an antagonist of centralism, championing autonomy for Slovenia, and pressed for the establishment of a regional parliament in Ljubljana; later the Slovenian People's Party abandoned these proposals.

And finally, in Vojvodina, where, prior to World War One, there had been large estates owned by Hungarians and prosperous farms owned by Serbs and Germans, after the war the Belgrade regime confiscated many of the Hungarian estates and turned the land over exclusively to Serbs, leaving local Hungarian peasants landless. Belgrade turned some of the land over to Serb "colonists" who were invited to come to Vojvodina to take up residence. The authorities also closed all Hungarian-language schools, both at the primary and at the secondary level,[78] in spite of the fact that there were nearly half a million Hungarians living in Vojvodina, many of them concentrated in villages and towns near the new border with Hungary. Later, after the assassination of King Aleksandar in 1934, the government used the assassination as a pretext to expel a large number of Hungarians from the country (even though the Hungarians of Vojvodina had absolutely nothing to do with the killing).[79]

From the Provisional Parliament to the Constituent Assembly

Even before work on the constitution began, there were already signs of trouble ahead. To begin with, the semi-official doctrine of the "tri-named people" and its practical corollary that the official language was "Serbo-Croato-Slovenian"[80] —in practice, Serbian—not only relegated Croatian and Slovenian language and culture to a secondary status, but effectively denied the distinct culture of the Bosniaks and the distinct nationality and language of the people of Macedonia. One of the first acts of the new government (in December 1918) was to declare the equality of the Cyrillic and Latin alphabets, but it soon developed that Cyrillic predominated in official documents and communications generated in the central government. In spite of this ideology, however, the Slovenes maintained their own language, writing it, as ever, in the Latin alphabet. The doctrine of the "tri-named people" was imported into the educational system. Although the curricula and textbooks were not standardized, the first postwar edition of the fourth-grade reader for Serbian schools, prepared by Ljubomir Protić and Vladimir Stojanović, advised young (Serbian) readers that "The Slovenes are only another name for our nation," and that the Slovenian language was "really only a dialect of the beautiful Serbian language."[81] In the 1926 edition of the widely used reader, Serbian schoolchildren were given to understand that Serbian shepherds were grazing their flocks in Dalmatia while singing old Serbian folk songs.[82]

On the administrative front, in spite of the priority given by prominent Slovenes, Croats, and Bosnians to obtaining guarantees of provincial autonomy, the central government moved in precisely the opposite direction. Immediately after 1 December, Pribićević, in his capacity as minister of the interior, asked the provincial governments of Croatia, Slavonia, and Dalmatia to submit their resignations. The provincial government for Croatia and Slavonia did so on 28 December, and a new government was appointed on 15 February 1919. But this was not merely a question of a change of personnel. On the contrary, in the interval between his acceptance of the provincial governments' resignations and his appointment of new incumbents, Regent Aleksandar eliminated a large number of commissions and bureaus in the provincial government. In fact, out of 11 departments in the provincial government for Croatia and Slavonia in 1918, eight were eliminated by the king at this time.[83] Belgrade authorities also severely reduced the competency and powers of the Croatian ban (governor). Later, on 30 November 1920, a royal edict dissolved the Croatian Sabor, stripping Croatia of a vital factor and symbol of its statehood. Since the state constitution was still being debated, this move was of dubious legality and was, in any event, sharply condemned in Croatian political circles. But Pribićević, one of the dominant voices in the Serbian choir in the early years of the kingdom, was convinced "that only strict centralization could secure the position of Serbs in Croatia."[84] It was in Zagreb that the greatest resistance to centralization was mounted; but it was a lost cause: the central government simply took over the functions which had been performed by the provincial authorities, shutting their offices down, one by one. This process, completed only in 1928, inflamed disorders and turmoil in many Croatian towns.

But in the dispute over centralization, the constitutional debate had the potential to play a critical role. As the provisional parliament began its work (on 1 March 1919), it became apparent that there were four alternative orientations concerning the constitution: the Democratic Party (of Davidović and Pribićević) and, after its founding in October of that year, the Agrarian Union favored centralized administration and subscribed, at this time, to the notion of a "tri-named nation," although this was not the center of gravity where the Agrarian Union was concerned; the Radical Party (of Pašić and Protić) also favored centralized administration but thought at the time that the three titular nations should have the possibility of continuing their national and cultural development; the Republican Party (a Serbian party headed by Jaša Prodanović, which found its strongest support not in Serbia but in Montenegro and southeastern Macedonia) believed that the Serbs, Croats, and Slovenes were well on the way to national "amalgamation" but favored a decentralized republic on the Girondist model; and the Slovenian People's Party, the Croatian Peasant Party, Croatian Community, and Montenegrin federalists were convinced that the constituent national groups were distinct and favored one or another alternative to centralism (whether confederalism or federalism or some form of decentralization).[85] Protić, although a Radical, was closer to the last of these groups. The communist party, just organizing itself in 1919, started out favorably disposed toward a unified Yugoslav state and, out of deep political conviction, favored centralism but felt that the issue of nationality was secondary to issues of class. The Agrarian Union was likewise oriented to class divisions and wanted to see the creation of a peasant state on the principle of agricultural cooperatives, demanding the overthrow of the capitalist state. There were also deep differences of opinion over the monarchy, with the Radicals and Democrats most devoted to the Serbian monarchy, and the Croatian Peasant Party, the communists, and Prodanović's Republicans among the most anti-monarchical in persuasion.

The provisional parliament sat in session until 22 October 1920. Its primary task was to prepare elections to a Constituent Assembly, which would be authorized to draw up the constitution for the country. Since the parliament was tasked to define who could and could not vote, there were inevitably bitter debates over the question of women's suffrage. In fact, Crown Prince Aleksandar had issued a decree on 15 May 1920, establishing universal adult suffrage in *local* elections; the decree inflamed passions on both sides. Prodanović, leader of the Republican Party, was one of the more outspoken supporters of the extension of suffrage to women. The Social Democrats also favored general female suffrage.[86] Among other parties, the attitude ranged from the polite but politically meaningless respect offered, for example, by Korošec's SLS and Radić's HPSS to the outright opposition to women's suffrage on the part of the Radical Party,[87] whose most vocal speakers made the argument that it made no sense to grant women the right to vote as long as women did not enjoy equality of pay and inheritance; the Radicals also argued that women were "not prepared" to make their own decisions, adding that granting women the right to vote would result in the breakup of marriages. The Croatian Community (Hrvatska zajednica, or HZ, created in July 1919 through the fusion of the Starčević Party of Right[88] and the Progressive Party of Right) also declared itself against women's suffrage. And there were controversies, too, over the scope of any such suffrage—for example, should the vote be limited to financially independent women? The Republican Party favored a trial period, during which only women who lived in the larger cities and unmarried women in the villages would be allowed to vote.[89]

The strongest party in the provisional parliament was the Democratic Party, and it seemed for a while that that party might swing the Assembly in the direction of expanding the suffrage to women. The Democrats had already declared themselves in favor of female suffrage toward the end of 1919, and in mid-1920, Ivan Palaček, a Democratic deputy, affirmed that his party supported the extension of the right to vote to all women, on the same basis as for men. But the Democratic Party did not embrace the cause as its own, and on 17 February 1921, the Crown Prince bowed to the pressure and withdrew the decree he had issued the previous May. Ultimately, Yugoslav women were not granted the right to vote until 1945. The law on elections to the Constituent Assembly was passed on 7 September 1920, with elections scheduled for 28 November 1920.

Of 2,480,623 eligible voters, 1,607,625, or 64.95%, actually voted, with the lowest turnouts in Serbia (56.33%) and Macedonia (55%). As a result of these elections, the Democratic and Radical Parties emerged as the major power brokers in the Constituent Assembly, which was convened on 12 December 1920 with an effective parity between Democrats and Radicals (see Table 2.2). Clerical circles had hoped that the Croatian People's Party (HPS) would emerge as the dominant political force among Croats, while the HSP (Frankist), heir to the tradition of Josip Frank, considered itself the mouthpiece for Croatian nationalism. But it was the Croatian People's Peasant Party (the HPSS), Radić's party, which emerged as the strongest contender for Croatian votes. There were two principal reasons for this result: the fact that Croatia (and for that matter, the kingdom as a whole) was overwhelmingly rural, and the fact that Radić—much more than the leaders of the competing Croatian parties—understood the concerns of the peasantry and made their concerns *his* concerns. Insofar as Radić was also convinced that the interests of Croatia's peasants would best be served if Croatia could retain its autonomy and insofar as the Belgrade regime repeatedly incarcerated Radić, thereby bestowing on him the glow of a martyr for Croatia, his peasant party came to be seen as Croatia's most effective guardian and Radić as a kind of guardian angel for the entire Croatian nation. This, in turn, explains why the Croat national movement of the interwar period developed within the framework of this agrarian populist party.

Controversy flared immediately, when the newly elected deputies were asked to swear an oath of allegiance to the king. Seven of the nine parties represented in the Assembly (all except the Democrats and the Radicals) objected that the swearing of the oath implied that the king stood somehow above the Assembly, and that the Assembly was therefore not fully sovereign.[90] An even more vital controversy had to do with the procedure for voting. The Korfu Declaration had foreseen some form of qualified majority voting in the Constituent Assembly, though the Croatian Peasant Party hoped that the interests of the regions would be taken into account—in effect that the constitution would be adopted through some form of consensus—what the communists would later call "the harmonization of viewpoints." When it was decided that the constitution would be adopted by simple majority vote, the Croats felt betrayed, and on 8 December, addressing a throng of 100,000 supporters, Radić announced that the Croatian Peasant Party was changing its name to the Croatian *Republican* Peasants'

**Table 2.2. Results of the Elections to the Assembly
(12 December 1920)**

	Seats in the Assembly
Democratic Party	92
Radical Party	91
Communist Party	58[a]
HPSS–HRSS	50
Agrarian Union	39
SLS & HPS	27
JMO	24
Social Democrats	10
Džemijet[b]	8
Croatian Bondsmen's Party	7
HZ	4
Republican Party	3
HSP	2
Others	4
TOTAL	419

Source: Branislav Gligorijević, *Parlament i političke stranke u Jugoslaviji, 1919–1929* (Belgrade: Narodna knjiga, 1979), p. 89; and Ivo Banac, *The National Question in Yugoslavia: Origins, History, Politics* (Ithaca, N.Y.: Cornell University Press, 1984), pp. 394–395.

a. Later the number of seats for the Communist Party dropped to 57, after one mandate was canceled.

b. Džemijet was the party defending Islamic interests in Macedonia and Kosovo. The Turkish spelling is Cemiyet; the Albanian spelling is Xhemijet. I am using the Serbian spelling in the text.

Party (HRSS[91])—a transparent challenge to the Serbian monarchy—and that the deputies of this party, bearing in mind what they considered an unacceptable rule for voting on the constitution, would boycott the work of the Constituent Assembly. The communists, likewise angered by both the oath to the king and the decision to allow the constitution to be adopted by a simple majority, ostentatiously walked out of the Assembly on 22 December.[92] There was also controversy over voting procedures. A new set of procedures was drawn up and submitted to the Assembly for its approval on 25 January 1921, but the most important articles, which the anti-monarchist parties had denounced as "reactionary," remained unchanged. These revised procedures were adopted by majority vote on 28 January, in spite of opposition from the CPY (the Communist Party of Yugoslavia), the Slovenian People's Party, and the Croatian Community. Meanwhile, the committee charged with formulating a draft constitution had been presented with a number of constitutional drafts, including drafts submitted by Radić and Protić. In this regard, 23 December 1920 was a critical day, for it was then that the deputies of the Radical Party met to discuss their position on the form of the state. Some of the deputies present favored the decentralist draft prepared by Radical former prime minister Protić. Others saw it as an acceptable fallback position. But Pašić, who was an ideological kin to then-prime minister Milenko Vesnić and who served as prime minister from 1 January to 26 March 1921, was dead set against any concession to decentralization in any form and insisted on collaborating with the inflexibly centralist Democratic Party to draft the country's constitution.

Both the CPY and the Croatian (Republican) Peasant Party were profoundly dismayed by the direction in which things were moving, but when the communists suggested that the two parties might make a common front and develop a joint strategy, Radić's party rebuffed the communist overture. Instead, on 11 February 1921, the Croatian (Republican) Peasant Party leadership sent Regent Aleksandar a memorandum asking the prince not to force Croatia to accept the status quo and insisting on Croatia's right to "a completely unlimited right of national self-determination."[93] Indeed, Radić did not want to close the door to possible cooperation with the regent and therefore tried, through an emissary in Belgrade, to obtain concessions to his party's point of view. But the Serbian bloc—the Radical and Democratic parties—hoped to reach an agreement which would satisfy both their own agendas and that of the regent, without needing to accommodate Croatian and Slovenian interests,[94] and the bloc looked rather to the JMO and Džemijet to provide the extra votes the bloc needed in order to pass the constitution.

For the JMO, however, the draft constitution was problematic. The JMO was loath to see a centralized administration, and in a session in January 1921, that party's Central Committee decided that it would enter into only those coalitions in which "all three tribes of our undivided nation" were included.[95] On 15 March 1921, the Serbian bloc reached an agreement with the JMO by agreeing to include in the constitution guarantees that Bosnia-Herzegovina would remain an administrative unit within its given borders and that religious equality would be respected, and by guaranteeing the autonomy of religious education and of the Shari'at courts. The Serbian bloc also agreed to assure the former feudal landlords of financial compensation for lands confiscated (to the sum of 305 million dinars) and promised that Muslims would be better represented in the provincial government in Sarajevo. In exchange for these pledges from the ruling coalition, the JMO agreed to vote for the government draft. The JMO now joined the government coalition, receiving two cabinet seats: Mehmet Spaho became minister of industry and commerce, and Hamdija Karamehmedović became minister of national health. According to Imamović, the government did not, in fact, keep most of the promises it made to the JMO,[96] and in the short run, the JMO's pact with the Serbian bloc provoked a bitter reaction on the part of some opposition parties, such as the Agrarian Union, whose leaders saw their own goals in agrarian reform sacrificed.

In courting Džemijet, the Radical Party was encumbered by the threat by

Democratic deputies from Macedonia (numbering 18, or six more than Džemijet had to offer) to leave the party's parliamentary club if Džemijet's demands for protection for Muslim landowners in Macedonia were accommodated. As a result, the Democratic Party threw its weight against Džemijet, and Džemijet, in turn, gravitated toward the opposition. On 27 June 1921, however, the ruling coalition reached a compromise with Džemijet, assuring the protection of the former feudal land barons in "South Serbia"; this was to take the form of financial compensation and a guaranteed minimum amount of land for the former estate owners in Macedonia, Kosovo, and the Sandžak. With this agreement in their pocket, the Radical-Democratic coalition put the constitution to a vote the following day, 28 June, celebrated in Serbia as St. Vitus Day (Vidovdan, in Serbian). The constitution was supported by all 89 Democratic deputies present, all 87 Radicals present, 23 JMO deputies, 11 Džemijet deputies, all 10 deputies of the Bondsmen's Party, three deputies of the Agrarian Union, and Spasoje Piletić. Voting against the constitution were 21 deputies of the Agrarian Union, both Socialist deputies, all seven Social Democrats, and all three Republicans, as well as Ante Trumbić and Momčilo Ivanić. Absent on the day of the vote were all 58 communist deputies (who had decided on 11 June to boycott further work of the Constituent Assembly, all 52 deputies of the Croatian (Republican) Peasant Party, all 11 deputies of the People's Club, all 27 deputies of the Yugoslav Club (dominated by the Slovenian People's Party or SLS), five members of the Agrarian Union, one JMO deputy, one Agrarian deputy, and the Liberal Party's only deputy in the Assembly. The final tally was 223 in favor, 35 against, and 158 absent (most of them boycotting in protest). Because of the date on which it was passed, the constitution has come down as the "Vidovdan constitution." The constitution could not have been passed without the support of the Muslim deputies of the JMO and the Džemijet; if they had repudiated the draft constitution, Pašić would have needed to find an alternative strategy, and the resulting constitution would probably have been different.

The Question of Croatia

The unification of the Kingdom of SHS had been proclaimed on the strength of the assent of a delegation which chose to ignore binding instructions from the National Council, and the constitution had been passed without the participation of Croatia's most significant political party and without taking into consideration the demand registered by Croatia's most vocal politicians that Croatia be granted autonomy within the kingdom, preferably on a confederal or federal basis. These problems rendered the kingdom *subjectively* illegitimate in the eyes of most Croats. In addition, actions already taken by the government would soon allow outside observers to conclude that the state was deficient in terms of rule of law, respect for the equality of all of its peoples, and neutrality in sacerdotal matters, as well as disrespectful of individual rights, involved in the organization of paramilitary forces functioning outside the framework of the state, and engaged in widespread corruption—in other words, that the new state was *objectively* illegitimate, in the sense intended in chapter 1.

In August 1920, Milorad Drašković, an Independent Radical, was named minister of internal affairs. One of his first acts was to cancel the communists' recent electoral victory in Belgrade, by which the communists had expected to take over the administration of the city; this followed a similar act by the Croatian ban, in which the communists had been denied their victories in several Croatian district governments. Subsequently, in May 1921, Minister Drašković ordered the Croatian regional government to ban all Croatian (Republican) Peasant Party rallies temporarily.[97] On 29 June 1921 a young communist named Spasoje Stejić threw a bomb at the royal cavalcade. Although the assassination attempt failed in its object, it sparked angry physical attacks on communist deputies in the halls of the Assembly. Less than a month later, there was a second such attempt—this time on the life of Minister Drašković. Drašković was killed, and six persons were arrested. When their trial finally began, on 6 October 1921, the prosecution concentrated on arguing that the accused persons had been in close contact with the communist party leadership and that, therefore, the CPY as such was implicated in the assassination.[98]

.· The Radical-Democratic coalition had already shown its hostility to the communists and now used the assassination to push through a proclamation (*Obznana*) banning all communist activity and propaganda. Subsequently, on 1 August 1921, the authorities also passed the Law on the Protection of Public Order and the State, stripping the communist deputies in the Assembly of their parliamentary immunity. Nedim Šarac notes that this law, proposed by the coalition government of Radicals, Democrats, the JMO, and the Bondsmen's Party,

> by making it possible to pronounce the death sentence for political transgressions and by nullifying the mandates of duly elected deputies, by annulling freedom of assembly and of the confession of one's political convictions [and] by dismissing people from public service because of their philosophical convictions, and so forth, negated the basic principles of bourgeois democracy and parliamentarism, created a precedent for similar ambushes and persecutions in the future, [and] in reality legalized the political repression of any opponents of the regime to whom subversive intentions were attributed.[99]

That this law could be applied against the Croatian (Republican) Peasant Party, an avowedly anti-monarchist party which continued to reject the Vidovdan constitution as illegitimate, was obvious enough.

The Organization of Yugoslav Nationalists (ORJUNA[100]) was established in Split by the royal administrator for Croatia in 1921 and operated under the umbrella of Pribićević's wing of the Democratic Party (which would separate from the party and establish itself as the Independent Democratic Party in 1924). Funded by the provincial government,[101] ORJUNA was a paramilitary organization, designed for extralegal actions against communists, Croatian separatists, and other persons deemed threatening to the state. Its special units, known as Action Groups, numbered about 10,000 troops by 1925 and conducted military exercises under the mottoes "Victory or Death" and "Whoever is not with us, is against us!"[102] As Avakumović and Čulinović have both noted, ORJUNA had several characteristics typical of a fascist organization, including the glorification of violence and an organizational structure similar to that of Italian fascism, complete with *vodja* (the leader).[103] Devoted to the centralist model, ORJUNA members felt an especial antipathy for federalist (or confederalist) minded persons but were also known to attack those they considered chauvinists regardless of nationality.[104]

The following year saw the virtually simultaneous formation of parallel terrorist organizations by the Serbs and Croats, respectively. The Serbian organization was known as the Serbian National Youth (SRNAO[105]) and was inspired by the notion that ORJUNA was not "Serbian" enough. Close to the Radical Party as well as to the king, its stated goals included "the extermination of all anti-state and anti-national elements."[106] Its Croatian counterpart was the Croatian National Youth (HANAO[107]), which was established as a response to ORJUNA. Both SRNAO and HANAO, like ORJUNA, reflected fascist influence in their organizational structures and ideology; all three of them were prone to engage in physical violence against their opponents. SRNAO was especially given to anti-Muslim sentiments and, in 1927, instigated an attempt on the life of JMO president Mehmed Spaho, who was serving as a cabinet minister at the time.[108]

In addition to the army, the kingdom had also established already a 10,000-strong gendarmerie, which expanded until it counted 60,000 gendarmes by the beginning of the 1930s.[109] The extralegal ORJUNA gave the regime raw power, while the purposes of SRNAO, some of whose activists went into the Radical Party,[110] overlapped with those of the regime to a considerable extent. But even this was not enough. The Chetnik movement, in its "modern" incarnation, could be dated to 1903, when the Serbian military organized a special training program for those prepared to carry out terrorist operations in Macedonia. The Chetniks continued to function throughout the interwar years, though the movement split in 1924. The leader of one of these Chetnik factions, "the Union of Serbian Chetniks—for the King and the Homeland," was Puniša Račić who, in June 1928, would gun down five deputies in the Assembly, including Stjepan Radić and his nephew, Pavle. The "Petar Mrkonjić" Association of Serbian Chetniks built up a network across Bosnia-Herzegovina during the 1920s, maintaining close relations with SRNAO: both organizations were ill disposed toward all opposition parties, including the Agrarian Union—in the case of the Agrarian Union, because of that party's significant following among Bosnian Serbs.[111]

The Croatian (Republican) Peasant Party parliamentary club had already drawn up a memorandum addressed to the international and domestic public, accusing Serbian politicians of the Radical and Democratic parties of pursuing assimilatory cultural and administrative policies "the main and obvious goal of which is, purely and simply, to annihilate the ethnic nation of Croatia."[112] Within the Democratic Party, however, Pribićević denied that there was any problem where Croatia was concerned. But the Democratic Party was deeply factionalized, with Pribićević's group increasingly being challenged by a group loyal to the more liberal Ljubomir Davidović. Moreover, while the HSP–Frankists (HSP–F) wanted to resolve the question of Croatian self-rule on the international level, Radić's HRSS felt that it was best to try to obtain satisfaction within the framework of the kingdom. In early October 1922, representatives of the Croatian bloc (the HRSS, the HZ, and the HSP–F) and the Democratic Party opened discussions concerning collaboration to bring down the existing coalition and to replace it with a new coalition in which representatives of the Croatian bloc would receive three ministries. On 18 November 1922, the HSP–F leadership broke off its participation in these talks; thereupon, Radić, who was already upset with the HSP–F because of its connections with Croatian émigré circles, saw to it that that party was expelled from the Croatian bloc (on 25 November 1922).[113]

Immediately after that, the rump Croatian bloc outlined its conditions for an agreement, stressing that the new government be formed on the basis of an agreement with Croats and undertake to effect changes in the provincial administration in Croatia, Dalmatia, and Bosnia-Herzegovina. On 29 November, Davidović, speaking on behalf of the left wing of the Democratic Party, answered that he and his colleagues accepted the Croatian conditions in principle, but that the Croats needed to end their boycott of the Assembly first, before any concrete step could be taken. Davidović drew up a joint statement for representatives of the Croatian bloc to sign, in which the Croats would agree to return to the Assembly even before new elections would be called. But the Croatian bloc hesitated, replying on 1 December that, insofar as there was still a parliamentary majority supporting the existing government, the most reliable method for assuring the desired changes was to continue opposition outside the Assembly. In fact, Prime Minister Pašić resigned three days later, but not before he had warned his allies that a Democratic–HRSS coalition might repeal the Law on the Protection of Public Order and the State, thereby allowing the communists to reclaim their seats.

Meanwhile, Davidović's openness to turning to the extraparliamentary opposition had exacerbated the not-so-latent disagreements within the Democratic Party. Pribićević and his sympathizers sharply condemned Davidović's overture to the Croats and reiterated their commitment to the Vidovdan constitution. The president of the Assembly, Edo Lukinić, suggested to Aleksandar, who had been confirmed as king after the death of his father in August 1921, that he invite one of the leaders of the Democratic Party to form a new government. Instead, however, the king asked Pašić to form a new government and to call new elections. Pašić now formed a minority government and called new elections for 18 March 1923. The Radical Party used the police to intimidate and rough up the Democrats. Moreover, the Democrats were so divided that, in nine electoral districts in Serbia, they had nominated two rival lists, while in one district, there were four alternative "Democratic" lists. The result was a major setback for the Democrats, who emerged with less than half the number of seats in the Assembly that the Radicals won. The results of the election are shown in Table 2.3. Although the Radicals emerged as the most powerful party in the Assembly, they did not have enough seats to support a narrowly based government. But for Radić's HRSS, now the second largest party in the Assembly, the elections represented a major advance and seemed to provide the party with the political resources to work toward achieving equality and autonomy for Croatia.

Immediately after the elections, the HRSS deputies to the Assembly adopted a resolution demanding that the Radicals and other Serbian political figures recognize the Croats' "complete and unlimited right of national self-determination."[114] At this point, however, the HRSS's strategy was to "encircle" Serbia, by building bridges with political parties in Slovenia, Bosnia-Herzegovina, Montenegro, Macedonia (i.e., Džemijet), and Vojvodina. The first manifestation of this was the creation of the "Federalist bloc," bringing together the HRSS, the JMO, and the "Yugoslav Club" (the SLS and other clerical parties). But the Slovenian clericals were playing a double game; even though it joined the Federalist bloc, Korošec's SLS was careful not to burn bridges with Pašić. Where the JMO was concerned, that party's engagement in collaboration with Radić's Croatian party inflamed some Muslim critics, who claimed that "Islam and Catholicism cannot go together, because Catholicism is conquest-oriented and intolerant, while Orthodoxy is a Slavic religion, peace-loving and inactive. Accordingly, Islam is freer and more comfortable when it cooperates with Orthodoxy than when it [attempts to form a partnership] with Catholicism."[115]

The Federalist bloc undertook to try to reach an agreement with the Radical

Table 2.3. Results of the Elections to the Assembly (18 March 1923)

	Votes	%	Seats
Radical Party	562,213	25.8	108
HRSS	473,333	21.8	70
Democratic Party	400,342	18.49	51
Slovenian People's Party	139,171	6.4	24
JMO	112,171	5.1	18
Džemijet	71,453	4.4	14
Agrarian Union	164,602	7.6	11
German Party	43,415	1.99	8
Others	182,362[a]	8.42	8

Sources: Branislav Gligorijević, *Parlament i političke stranke u Jugoslaviji 1919–1929* (Belgrade: Narodna knjiga, 1979), p. 150; and Mark Biondich, *Stjepan Radić, the Croat Peasant Party, and the Politics of Mass Mobilization, 1904–1928* (Toronto: University of Toronto Press, 2000), p. 188.

a. Estimate calculated from the percentage for "Others"

Party, and already in April 1923 HRSS delegates held talks with leading figures of the Radical Party in Belgrade. These talks were continued in Zagreb on 12–13 April 1923. The Federalist bloc had two demands: first, the removal of the provincial administrations in Croatia, Slovenia, Bosnia-Herzegovina, and Vojvodina, and their replacement by new administrations to be appointed in agreement with the "Federalists"; and second, the cancellation of plans to divide the country into smaller administrative districts (33 total), which would mean an end to such provincial power as there still was. Pašić agreed to these two conditions in an agreement known as the "Markov protocol"; in exchange for this expression of his good intentions, Pašić obtained the assent from the Federalist bloc not to prevent him from forming a homogeneous government. Radić agreed that the deputies of the SLS and the JMO, together with the three deputies of the Bunjevačko-šokačka Party, would enter the Assembly.

But neither King Aleksandar nor Prime Minister Pašić was interested in honoring these promises, and once Pašić's minority government was secure, "the Radical Party no longer had any reasons to engage in maneuvers with the Federalist bloc."[116] Now the Pašić government banned a public meeting which the HRSS had scheduled for 24 June 1923. With this, Pašić terminated the pragmatic partnership, and relations between the Federalist bloc and the Radicals deteriorated. On 14 July—the anniversary of the French Revolution—Radić delivered a fiery public speech, in which he said that Croatia was imprisoned in a "Serbian bastille."[117] The government now charged that, in this speech, Radić had used insulting language, and ordered his parliamentary immunity lifted and his arrest. Radić, however, managed to slip out of the country on 21 July without a passport and made his way to London. Immediately after this, the HRSS leadership publicly distanced itself from an offer of cooperation from HANAO, which had been looking to the HRSS for support for its violent actions.[118] On the contrary, the HRSS leadership declared that it was determined to pursue its objectives "without any hatred for the Serbian people."[119]

Meanwhile, the government interpreted Radić's rather innocent and politically barren sojourn in London as involving anti-state conspiracy. After several fruitless months in London, Radić transferred to Vienna at the end of December 1923. Fearful that he would be arrested if he attempted to return to the kingdom, Radić decided to lead his party, for the time being, from Vienna. Radić still hoped for a confederalist solution and, in spring 1924, was hoping to put together a conference of disaffected nationality groups of Europe but was prevented from doing so by the vigilant police of Vienna.[120] While the Croatian party leader was out of the country, the Pašić government finally completed the dismantlement of the provincial governments for whose survival the HRSS, the SLS, and the JMO had been fighting, and implemented the system of 33 administrative districts; it was also—no doubt coincidentally—while Radić was out of the country that Belgrade signed a pact with Rome in January 1924, confirming Belgrade's recognition of Italy's annexation of Fiume (Rijeka).

Radić and other HRSS leaders now concluded that there might be something to be gained from a partial lifting of the party's boycott of the Assembly. The HRSS agreed to contribute to the desired result by sending just enough of its deputies to the Assembly to assure that Pašić would lose a vote of no confidence. The Agrarian Union, though not part of the opposition bloc, was likewise hostile to the Radical government, and the opposition Federalist bloc could count on Agrarian support. On 8 February 1924, Vladko Maček (1879–1964) and Juraj Krnjević took along 50 duly authorized HRSS deputies to Belgrade and presented them to the Assembly for verification. But upon their arrival, they were informed that they did not enjoy the right to vote in the Assembly until "verification" of their credentials had been completed. Optimistically, on 2 March, the HRSS confirmed that it would work with the SLS and JMO to bring down the Radical government, and on 7 March, the three parties signed an agreement to coordinate their work. The Radical regime, however, held up such verification, and even as late as 30 March, when the budget came up for a vote, 41 HRSS deputies had still not been "verified" and were, accordingly, prevented from voting. On 12 April 1924, 157 deputies associated with the opposition held a joint conference, adopting a resolution in which they condemned the delay in approving HRSS mandates as a violation of parliamentary procedure tantamount to "an open trampling on the constitution."[121]

By this point, even Džemijet, whose leaders had extracted concessions from the Radical Party the previous December in exchange for its support, was wavering in its attitude toward the Radical regime. In the meantime, the Democratic Party had now split, with Pribićević and his adherents forming their own Independent Democratic Party and joining the Pašić government on 27 March, while Davidović had begun cooperating with the HRSS. The Pašić-Pribićević government (known colloquially as the "P-P" government) constituted itself as "the National bloc." And while the king gave out signals that he was not a priori against the opposition, provided that the opposition supported the monarchy, the HRSS issued a statement on 1 May 1924, reiterating its commitment to a republican form of government. Finally, on 27 May, the last of the HRSS mandates were approved, after nearly 16 weeks! Immediately after that, the king dismissed the Assembly, "thereby rendering it impossible for the opposition to use its majority to vote no-confidence [in the government]."[122]

Eleven days later, on 7 June, Radić left Vienna and went to Moscow, where, on 1 July, he made the HRSS a member of the Bolshevik-sponsored Peasant International (Krestintern). Whether Radić was naïve, as Matkovič suggests,[123] or perhaps saw some reason to think that the Soviet Union, then still very much a pariah in the international community, could somehow help his cause, what is clear is that, in spite of Radić's pains to stress that he was not accepting any of the usual conditions for affiliation and that he was not altering the party's statutes or orientation in the slightest regard, the adherence of the HRSS to the Krestintern would later provide the regime with a justification to move against the Croatian party. Radić's trip to Moscow was, thus, a political miscalculation, which served to convince many Serbs that he was not to be trusted. In the short run, after Pašić's resignation on 17 July 1924, the king entrusted the prime ministership to Davidović, who in turn resigned in mid-October, having been brought down by maneuvers on the part of the Radical Party. After an abortive effort by Kosta Timotijević (Democrat) to form a government, the king once more turned to Pašić on 6 November, authorizing the resilient ideologue to dissolve the Assembly and call new elections for 8 February 1925. In the meantime, Radić had returned to the country on 11 August, proceeding to make himself unpopular by referring to General Stevan Hadžić, the minister of defense, as a "political idiot," to Pašić as a "criminal," and to Pribićević and his adherents as "vermin." Yet, in the same speech in which he cast these aspersions on some of the country's most visible personalities, Radić also underlined that he was prepared to recognize the Karadjordjević dynasty and to make other concessions in order to reach an agreement with the Radical Party.[124]

Back in the saddle again, the Pašić government did its best to stir up fears, both at home and in west European capitals, of communist subversion via Radić as well as of the danger of Soviet expansionism. In this way, Radić's ill-conceived essentially empty gesture of protest in Moscow was manipulated to translate the HRSS's advocacy of Croatian interests into treason. Then, on 19 December 1924, the newspaper *Reč*, the official organ of Pribićević's Independent Democratic Party, published a fabricated document which was purported to be the text of an agreement between Radić and the president of the Comintern, in which Radić supposedly accepted the 21 conditions for affiliation with the Comintern; there was no date, and some of the signatures were illegible.[125] The executive committee of the Comintern immediately issued a statement denying the authenticity of the document as well as of any kind of agreement, characterizing the falsification as a "crude provocation." The general secretary of the Krestintern also issued a statement, noting that the HRSS had not altered a single article in its program upon affiliating and adding that Radić's party had no connections with the Comintern. The government paid no particular attention to these denials, however, and instead, on 23 December 1924, accepted the proposal of Minister of Internal Affairs Božidar Maksimović that the HRSS be banned, under the provisions of the Law on the Protection of Public Order and the State. In asking for this decision, Maksimović argued that that party had assumed a communist and anti-state character.[126] What followed was that the government banned any activities on the part of Croatia's most popular party; the application of the law to the HRSS, in turn, laid the basis for criminal proceedings against HRSS leaders. Radić and other leading figures in the party (including Maček and the Košutić brothers) were arrested and put in prison, but the Zagreb court rejected a motion by the public prosecutor to put the entire leadership of the Croatian party on trial and ordered the release of all HRSS leaders being held in custody—except for Radić. But no sooner were Maček and the others released from custody than they were rearrested, at the exit from the jail, and interned in police barracks on charges of having organized armed units to be used against the police and army for the purpose of enabling the HRSS, allegedly, to take power.[127] In this way, the HRSS was effectively prevented from engaging in any activity during the election campaign. The regime hoped that this would finish off the HRSS.

Throughout these years, Macedonian political aspirations were frustrated. There were efforts in 1924 and 1925 to obtain permission to post a "Macedonian list" in the parliamentary elections, but the regime firmly rejected the initiative. Even so, notions about establishing a Macedonian party lingered on as late as 1928. During the same time frame, the idea of annexation to Bulgaria lost ground in Macedonia, and people began to think of themselves simply as Macedonians.[128]

Turning Point

Although the HRSS was prevented from campaigning, the law did not provide a basis for suspending the party's candidate lists. In other words, the HRSS could not engage in any electoral campaigning, but people could vote for HRSS candidates all the same. The SLS, moreover, campaigned on an autonomist program and continued to demand a revision of the constitution; on the other hand, the SLS adopted a highly critical stance vis-à-vis the HRSS. The JMO also continued to plead for an autonomist restructuring of the state, and party leader Spaho even bravely declared himself open to cooperation with the HRSS after the elections. The JMO was, in fact, subjected to various repressive measures during the election campaign, as was the Agrarian Union, in spite of the fact that the latter party attracted exclusively Serbian voters; the problem with the Agrarian Union, of course, was twofold: first, it was not nationalist; second, and more particularly, it was not in coalition with the Radical Party. Purivatra notes that SRNAO and the "Petar Mrkonjić" Association of Serbian Chetniks were used to intimidate and terrorize the opposition during these elections.[129] The government allowed itself to gloat, much like the king of Spain in 1588, when he sent the doomed Spanish Armada to teach the English a lesson; it was even being helped in Radić's own backyard by the HSP–F, which tried to use the ban on the HRSS for its own purposes, accusing Radić of having placed his party "at the service of Moscow" and parading its credentials as Croatia's "oldest" and "purest" party.[130]

Some 2,177,051 persons voted on 8 February, representing 73.7% of the 2,852,907 registered eligible voters.[131] The results confirmed the ever-stronger position of the Radical Party among Serbs, as well as the resilience of the HRSS among Croats, even under conditions of considerable adversity. In Serbia, the Radical Party captured 297,065 votes (55.2%), winning 49 seats in the Assembly; the Democratic Party (Davidović) retained 150,264 votes (27.0%), capturing 18 seats; and the Agrarian Union attracted 9.7% of the vote, to capture Serbia's last remaining seat. In Macedonia/Kosmet/Sandžak, the Radical Party also finished in first place. In Montenegro, however, the Montenegrin Federalist

Party (25.7% of the vote) had now emerged as the strongest party, albeit by a small margin, climbing up from its third-place finish two years earlier.

But the Radical Party and the king were dealt a more serious setback in Croatia, where the HRSS, sharing a common list with the Croatian Community, boosted its vote tally from 367,846 in 1923 to 376,414 now; in percentage terms, this translated into a small decline (slipping from 65.9% of the vote in 1923 to 60.9% in 1925). In Dalmatia, on the other hand, the HRSS more than doubled its vote tally, from 27,688 in 1923 to 66,133, strengthening its proportional presence from 26.4% to 48.7%. With this, the HRSS retained 67 seats in the Assembly (counting three seats picked up in Slovenia), only three fewer than in the previous Assembly—a dramatic testament to the party's credibility among Croats, given that the party had been prevented from campaigning. In Slovenia, the SLS continued to dominate the political landscape, winning 105,304 votes, or 56.3% of the total, with the HRSS coming in second place, with 16,424 votes or 8.8% of the vote.

In the overall tally, the Radical Party captured 143 seats, the HRSS finished second with 67 seats, the Democratic Party third with 37, the SLS 21, the Independent Democrats (Pribićević's party) 21, the JMO 15, the German Party five, the Agrarian Union three, and the Montenegrin Federalists three. These results confirmed that, with the passage of time, ever larger percentages of Serbs were voting Radical, while the SLS and the Montenegrin Federalists continued to strengthen their own positions.

In spite of this electoral success, the HRSS leaders remained, for the time being, behind bars. There was talk now of a total boycott of the Assembly by all opposition parties, unless the HRSS leaders were released. The HRSS also tried to make itself a more acceptable partner for the Radical Party by abandoning its demand for a confederal or federal system, offering instead that some form of local self-government would be sufficient. Moreover, in a joint statement with other opposition parties, the HRSS specifically ruled out any cooperation with communists or other revolutionaries. In spite of this, the Radicals remained deeply hostile toward the HRSS and used their effective control of the verification committee to vote to cancel the HRSS's 67 mandates, on the argument that the Croatian party was a party given to "notorious communist and anti-state" conspiracy.[132] With controversy over the HRSS continuing, Stjepan Radić, still sitting in prison, penned a letter for his nephew, Pavle, who was himself a deputy, to read to the Assembly on 27 March 1925. In the letter, Radić declared that his party accepted the Vidovdan constitution and the Karadjordjević dynasty and emphasized his party's loyalty and commitment not to do damage to the unity of the state. This speech made a profound impression on all present, and a new proposal was at once developed: to cancel the mandates of "only" six HRSS deputies (S. Radić, Maček, and four others), approving the rest. The president of the verification committee was quite prepared to accept this "compromise." In the meantime, investigating authorities proved unable to gather evidence on the basis of which to prosecute Stjepan Radić. Furthermore, had the authorities brought Radić to trial, regardless of the nature of the charges or of the documentation, he would have emerged as "a national hero," as L. Marković, president of the polling commission, warned Pašić in a letter of 1 June 1925.[133] Moreover, the HRSS now dropped the word "republican" from its name, as a token of good faith. Henceforth, the party would be known simply as the Hrvatska seljačka stranka (HSS, or Croatian Peasant Party). Radić remained in prison for the time being, but channels of friendly communication had been opened. On 22 April, Radić was visited in prison by an emissary from King Aleksandar; Radić used the occasion to pass along a message to the king that he was renouncing any thought of autonomy for Croatia.[134]

After all of its machinations, the Radical Party had suffered a major blow to its prestige and credibility; its readiness to use the police and the judiciary to destroy a rival party with whom it did not want to negotiate did not suggest vast respect for the democratic process. But for all that, the Radical Party was still the strongest party in the parliament, and now, given the resilience of the HSS, the latter was a logical partner for the Radicals. On 2 July 1925, the two parties initiated negotiations concerning political collaboration. The negotiations continued until 14 July, when the two sides signed an agreement to form a coalition government, in the process violating their obligations toward their respective bloc partners. The agreement had the potential to be a turning point for the kingdom. And insofar as the leading Serbian and Croatian parties had renounced their erstwhile positions of uncompromising hostility, there seemed to be some chance to save the day. The challenge was to put the state on more legitimate footing before it would be struck by the next crisis.

The HSS in Government

Radić's deal with the Devil was deeply disturbing to many HSS deputies. What was worse, perhaps, was that the Radicals retained the most important ministerial portfolios and allowed the Croats to take responsibility only for agrarian reform, post and telegraph, commerce and industry, and forests and mines. Radić was released from prison the day that the coalition government was formed (18 July 1925) and joined the government on 17 November 1925, assuming the post of minister of education. But in spite of all the mutual congratulation and joint self-promotion, and in spite of the fact that the coalition even survived Pašić's death in 1926, the two sides remained poles apart. Radić may have accepted the constitution, but only with an eye to changing it—the goal remained the same, only the path had been altered. Moreover, even though he and his party associates were prepared to concede that Serbs and Croats were "ethnically and linguistically" one people, they continued to underline that their respective political cultures were entirely different.[135] Hence, to the charge registered by some in 1925 that Radić had "capitulated" to the Radicals, one might reply, yes, he capitulated, but only in form, not in substance. What Radić hoped to achieve within the government was to begin to reconstruct the Kingdom of SHS as a "peasants' state," hence, perhaps, as a "peasant Kingdom." To his mind that meant providing protection of the peasants' economic interests, peasant participation in the organs of local administration, and the reform of education;[136] given the last of these concerns, Radić's control of the portfolio for education was a strategic coup. Pašić did not see the situation that way. In Pašić's mind, what had occurred in spring 1925 was that his old nemesis had given up the fight and had given the Radical Party carte blanche. When that proved not to be the case, tensions emerged within this unlikely coalition, and Radić complained that all of his party's policy proposals were being blocked.

Less than a year after the formation of the Radical-Peasant coalition, Pašić's son, Rade, was implicated in a corruption scandal, which flared up after the publication of an article in the Belgrade daily newspaper, *Novosti*, on 22 February. It soon came out that the prime minister and several of his cabinet ministers (from the Radical Party) were also implicated in the affair,[137] and in early April 1926, Nikola Pašić resigned as head of the government, under considerable pressure from the opposition as well as from Radić, who was still serving at the time as minister of education. Fellow Radical Nikola Uzunović took his place as prime minister. By the end of the year, the elder Pašić, who had continued to think of a return to power, was dead, and the Radical Party he had led for so long was increasingly fractured. But Pašić's influence lingered after his death, with "pašićites" engaged in a contest of wills with a rival group led by Velimir Vukićević. In these conditions, with the Radical Party torn apart by internal struggles, it was decided to readmit to the party those who had left (or had been excluded) earlier, such as the Independent Radicals led first by Protić and later by Nastas Petrović.

The HSS was also riven by fractures, these being more specifically the product of the agreement with the Radical Party. The first fraction to revolt was a group of five deputies led by Stjepan Buć, who constituted their own list, "Republican Freedom," under the slogan "The leader has capitulated, but the army remains and has not surrendered."[138] In October 1925, this group constituted itself as a separate party, the Croatian Republican Peasant Union. A second fracture occurred when two HSS deputies, followed by several more, defected to a group of five HZ deputies headed by Ivan Lorković, at one time leader of the Progressive Democratic Party, and Ante Trumbić. This group of discontents proceeded to create the Croatian Federal Party, accusing the HSS of having betrayed its own program. As its name suggests, the Croatian Federal Party was committed to a federal program.

A third fracture came from the right, when eight deputies, led by Nikola Nikić, broke away while the HSS was still negotiating with the Radicals. Nikić's group eventually numbered 30 deputies who were prepared to come to their own agreement with Pašić. On 17 April 1926, after Pašić's resignation, they actually broke away from the HSS parliamentary club and formed their own club; this was at a time when there were strains between the Radicals and the HSS.

But just five days later, they dissolved their new club and returned to their original political home. The story of this group was not over, however, and already the following month there were problems of insubordination on Nikić's part, with Nikić entering into side negotiations with the Radicals concerning his group's representation in the government. Radić successfully blocked that development (see below) and now saw to it that Nikić was excluded from the party (on 7 July), and Nikić, in turn, supported by a few adherents, set up his own deputies' club on 12 July 1926.[139]

In the meantime, in the wake of the "Rade Pašić affair," the Assembly took up the issue of corruption in high circles. The HSS joined the opposition now in demanding that the government appoint a committee to investigate the extent of corruption and report back after two months. The Radical Party wanted the committee to have six months to do its research and did not want the committee to report anything to the Assembly. The Radicals' proposal was put to a vote and was defeated by a vote of 150 to 127. Uzunović accordingly resigned, having served barely five weeks as prime minister. Uzunović was, however, given a chance to put together a second government, and it was at this point that he threatened to bring Nikić into the government unless Radić made concessions. Radić did so. Nikić was excluded from the government, and in turn, the HSS agreed to accept a modified version of the Radicals' proposal for dealing with corruption: the committee would have six months to complete its investigation but would then report its findings to the Assembly. Uzunović resigned for a second time on 7 December 1926. Less than three weeks later, however, the HSS and the Radicals had agreed on their fifth coalition government, even though, as Gligorijević notes, "the differences between them had not been eliminated."[140] The Radical Party had had the upper hand in May, but in December, the HSS was in a stronger position, and Pavle Radić and August Košutić, persons close to Stjepan Radić, entered the government.

In January 1927, there were district elections. The Radicals used their control of the Ministry of Internal Affairs and the police to obstruct electioneering on the part of the HSS. This obstructionism was especially intense in Bosnia and Vojvodina. This provoked a response from the HSS parliamentary club which, at a meeting on 23 January 1927, accused Prime Minister Uzunović and cabinet ministers Milan Srškić (the minister of justice) and Maksimović of gross violations of the laws and of the constitution. This attack effectively ended two years of coalition between the HSS and the Radicals.

The sixth Uzunović government was formed on 1 February 1927, in coalition with the SLS, the HSS dissident group associated with Nikić, and a Radical dissident group associated with Velimir Vukićević. In the interrogations in the Assembly in connection with HSS charges of police persecution and harassment, Maksimović rather spectacularly admitted the truth of all the charges, explaining that, in the case of Vojvodina, the Radicals preferred to see the locals identify themselves as Šokci and Bunjevci, rather than as Croats. The HSS, now in opposition, also continued to press for a frank discussion of corruption, but here the government succeeded in stifling debate on this subject, first by allowing the investigative committee to take eight months (instead of six) to complete its report and then by postponing a reading of the report, so that it was never brought before the Assembly at all! Finally, in April 1927, King Aleksandar removed the sitting government and turned to the Vukićević fraction to form a new government, without the main Radical Party. Vukićević and his fraction returned to the Radical Party now and on 17 April formed a government in coalition with a faction of the Democratic Party, led by Vojislav Marinković.

Vukićević as Prime Minister

Since the Vukićević fraction had complained loudly about corruption, the government it formed seemed generally more acceptable. It also tried to deal with the pitiful backlog in legislation. During 1926, some 60 bills had been submitted from the floor of the Assembly, but not a single one had been adopted. Indeed, in all of 1926, the Assembly took decisions on only 29 issues, and 22 of these involved the ratification of international conventions. And the few bills passed in the first months of the Uzunović government had all been prepared earlier. The Vukićević government, by contrast, tried to set a new course, by passing the various laws which were needed. But the selection of Vukićević, who had been on the margins of the party and who, at the time he was appointed prime minister, could only count about 10 persons loyal to him, aroused much petty jealousy within the Radical Party, especially on the part of Uzunović, who felt that he should have been retained in power.[141] Eventually Vukićević reached an agreement with Uzunović's group, though the "pašićites," led since Pašić's death by Aca Stanojević and Marko Trifković, remained estranged.

Vukićević's strategy was to isolate the Croatian Peasant Party, and this could be best effected by creating a broad alliance, bringing the SLS and the JMO into the government. The JMO entered the Vukićević government,[142] but the agreement signed between Korošec and Vukićević in Bled on 10 July specified that the SLS would enter the government only after new elections were held. In fact, these had been scheduled for 11 September 1927. But the HSS had a new and "prettier" face, campaigning not as the advocate of specifically Croatian interests, but as the defender of the king, the constitution, and legality! Moreover, looking to the Democratic Party and the Agrarian Union as potential allies, Radić decided against fielding HSS candidates in Serbia and Macedonia, and instead, the HSS appealed to voters in those regions to support the candidates of those two parties. The results (shown in Table 2.4) recorded an erosion in the strength of the Radical Party, which lost about 100,000 votes and dropped from 143 seats won in 1925 to 112 in 1927. The HSS also declined in strength, though not as seriously as the Radicals, dropping from 67 to 61 seats, probably through the loss of support among Croats unforgiving of Radić's pact with Pašić. The big gainers were the Democratic Party, which staged a dramatic recovery, boosting

Table 2.4. Results of the Elections to the Assembly (11 September 1927)

	Votes	%	Seats
Radical Party	742,111	31.9	112
Democratic Party	386,656	16.6	61
HSS	368,320	15.8	61
Independent Democrats	204,350	8.7	22
SLS	139,611	6.0	21
JMO	129,676	5.6	18
Agrarian Union	147,822	6.4	9
German Party	36,228	1.6	6
Communists	43,114	1.9	0
Others	127,977[a]	5.5	5

Sources: Branislav Gligorijević, *Parlament i političke stranke u Jugoslaviji, 1919–1929* (Belgrade: Narodna knjiga, 1979), pp. 237–242; and Mark Biondich, *Stjepan Radić, the Croat Peasant Party, and the Politics of Mass Mobilization, 1904–1928* (Toronto: University of Toronto Press, 2000), p. 224.

a. Approximate figure: exact figure not available

its strength in the Assembly from 37 deputies to 61, while the JMO also strengthened its position slightly, placing an additional three deputies in the parliament.

After the elections, Radić developed the idea of forming a stable parliamentary bloc to be called the Democratic-Peasant Union. This bloc would consist of the HSS, the Democratic Party, the JMO, Pribićević's Independent Democrats, and the Agrarian Union. Altogether, this bloc controlled 170 of the 307 seats in the Assembly. On 22 October 1927, leading figures in the HSS, Independent Democratic Party, and Agrarian Union sent a formal proposal to this effect to the other two parties.[143] While they were waiting for the Democrats and JMO to consider this proposal, the HSS and Independent Democrats decided to create their own Peasant-Democratic Coalition (SDK[144]). The SDK program included calls for protecting the constitutional order and for carrying out social and economic reforms, with an emphasis on ending the unequal taxation system.[145] But this first step actually complicated the project of moving forward toward a broad coalition, by defining the program of the apparent nucleus. In the meantime, on 26 October, representatives of the HSS brought charges of electoral terror on the part of the Vukićević government before the Assembly. The HSS and the Agrarians hoped that the Democrats would support them against Vukićević, but the Democrats calculated what they thought would best serve their short-term interests and supported Vukićević, voting to throw out the charges.[146]

Again, on 4 November 1927, HSS deputies submitted a request that the government place a discussion of a law on direct taxation on the Assembly's agenda within three days. The Radicals themselves had included this issue in their electoral program, and the Democratic Party, JMO, and SLS had all campaigned on the platform of giving this issue high priority. Now, however, that there was a concrete proposal on the table, these three parties voted against it. These same parties also voted against a legislative proposal to cancel the debts of farmers.

In the meantime, the Radicals, Democrats, and JMO had formed a coalition, which controlled 190 seats out of the 307 in the Assembly—later to be joined by the SLS, which thereby chose party interests over programmatic goals, abandoning its call for Slovenian autonomy, even though it had long seen that as the precondition for the realization of a series of programmatic goals. But in February 1928, the Democratic ministers resigned from the cabinet, bringing the Vukićević government down.

Shootings in the Assembly

The SDK's demands for participation in any government were, by contrast, largely programmatic: a more equal participation of the nationality groups in the state administration, an improvement of the economic conditions in the *prečanski* districts (i.e., districts north of the Danube), more equal taxation, an expansion of local administrative autonomy at the county and district levels, the equal participation of Croats and Slovenes in state institutions including the National Bank and diplomatic service, and changes in the larger counties in Croatia, Slavonia, Dalmatia, and Bosnia-Herzegovina.[147]

The SDK controlled 83 seats in the Assembly and now insisted that Radić be given a chance to form a government. On 9 February 1928, the king gave Radić his chance, but Vukićević, who had been making overtures to Radić on the eve of his fall from office, immediately indicated that the Radical Party would not participate in any coalition with Radić unless the Radicals could name the prime minister and fill the most important ministries from its own ranks. In spite of the apparent strength of the opposition in the Assembly, Radić was unable to form a government and, on 19 February, in growing frustration, even suggested to the king that he appoint a general to run the government. HSP–F leader Ante Pavelić (the lawyer)—a political figure with increasingly obvious radical right proclivities—commented that this proposal brought "shame to the Croatian people."[148] Four days later, Vukićević was once more entrusted with the task of forming a government.

During the succeeding weeks there were renewed battles over the unequal tax system as well as over charges brought against two former ministers and one sitting minister by SDK deputies. The latter served as a vehicle for a broader verbal assault on the government, disintegrating into fisticuffs in the Assembly itself on 28 February 1928. Rather than listen to what the opposition had to say, the president of the Assembly repeatedly had Radić and other opposition figures removed from the hall. On 3 March 1928, deputies of the SDK proposed that a committee of 15 persons be appointed to determine who had started the brawling on 28 February; the ruling coalition rejected this proposal out of hand. By now, the atmosphere in the Assembly was increasingly nasty, with the nationalist press only contributing to the heating of tempers.

Politika, the influential Belgrade daily newspaper, was under the editorial direction of Milan Gavrilović, a prominent member of the Agrarian Union.[149] *Politika, Samouprava* [Self-administration], the news organ of the Radical Party, and *Jedinstvo* [Unity], a Belgrade paper subsidized by Prime Minister Vukićević, contributed to the souring atmosphere by demonizing Croatian politicians and calling for the murder of leading figures in the opposition, including Radić.[150] Then, on 19 June 1928, *Politika* ran an article calling for Radić's murder, attributing to the Croatian leader statements he did not make. Meanwhile, Puniša Račić, a Radical deputy, who "had just been charged with dishonest appropriation of lands in south Serbia [i.e., Macedonia],"[151] was engaging in raucous exchanges with Radić and other HSS deputies on the floor of the Assembly. In the course of these exchanges, Račić and fellow Radical deputy Toma Popović warned that there would be no peace until Radić had been murdered! On the following day, several HSS deputies, fearing the worst, pleaded with Radić not to attend the Assembly session that day—a plea seconded by Sekula Drljević, a Montenegrin Federalist. But Radić was not to be restrained. "I am like a solder in war, in the trenches," he told Drljević. "I am waging a struggle for the rights of the Croatian peasant people. Either I come out of the trenches as the victor, or they shall deliver my dead body to the Croatian people."[152]

Radić attended the session on 20 June 1928. The atmosphere in the Assembly that day was electrified. Radić was quieter than usual—out of caution. But then Ivan Pernar, an HSS deputy, returned to the question of Račić's corruption. Stijepo Perić, president of the Assembly, declared the debate closed, but immediately reversed himself to allow Račić to take the floor. But instead of answering the charges, Račić pulled out a revolver and shot five HSS deputies. Pavle Radić and Djuro Basariček died on the spot. Ivan Pernar and Ivan Grandja were wounded but later recovered. Stjepan Radić was seriously wounded in the stomach. The shooting had the appearance of a spontaneous outburst, but according to Kulundžić, it was "ordered [from above], organized, and staged."[153] The assassin turned himself in several hours later; he was never brought to trial.

Less than an hour after the news reached Zagreb, some 19,000 persons gathered on Jelačić Square, "demanding that the Croatian parliament be convoked for the purpose of demanding separation 'from bloody Serbia.'"[154] In Belgrade, the government issued a decree, forbidding newspapers from publishing articles which might present the news about the shooting in such a way as to stir up inter-ethnic hatreds—a measure aimed, rather transparently, at Croatian newspapers.[155] Meanwhile, in Zagreb, angry HSS adherents went on a rampage the following day, raiding the Café Corse, a club frequented by Serb politicians, attacking those they found there. At the end of the ensuing violence and disorder, three more persons lay dead, 40 had been wounded, and 180 persons had been arrested.[156] Later, on 4 August, Josip Sunić, a member of the HSP–F's youth organization, assassinated the editor of *Jedinstvo*, which had called for the killing of Radić and Pribićević.

On 4 July 1928, in the immediate aftermath of the shootings, the Vukićević government stepped down. The king's first reaction was to ask Aca Stanojević to form the next government, but Stanojević suggested that he and the king ask for a meeting with Radić in the hospital. Radić angrily refused to receive Stanojević, who then stepped aside. The king now offered the prime ministership to Radić, but the latter declined, suggesting that the Assembly be dissolved and new elections held. He further suggested that the king form a caretaker government from representatives of the opposition. The king ignored these suggestions from Radić and, instead, took up the suggestion Radić had made in February, offering the prime ministership to a general—in fact, to the very man whom Radić had characterized as a "political idiot" three years earlier, General Stevan Hadžić.[157] The general did not get anywhere, however, and eventually, the out-going four-party coalition formed a new government, with Anton Korošec, leader of the Slovenian People's Party, as the prime minister.

The Korošec government announced an ambitious legislative program, advertising its intention to pass laws on peasant credits, on the liquidation of feudal relations, on local administration, etc. In fact, these various bills had been ready for a long time but had been stuck in committees. On 19 October 1928, exasperated at the endless delays in getting legislation to the floor, deputies of the Agrarian Union submitted a resolution which would have required that all bills, whether submitted by the government or by the opposition, be scheduled for discussion in the Assembly and for a vote. The government refused to allow this proposal, however. The opposition made another attempt the following month, prioritizing the draft law on the cancellation of peasant debts; but this effort likewise ran aground, with the government parties justifying further delay by claiming that the draft bill was "long and complicated."[158]

In the meantime, Radić passed away on 8 August 1928. Huge crowds turned out for his funeral in Zagreb four days later. There were, at this time, many public displays of collective grief across Croatia and Bosnia-Herzegovina. On 13 August, Vladko Maček was elected to succeed Radić as president of the HSS. Maček was not as charismatic or as mercurial as Radić, but time would prove that he was a more cautious and more capable leader.

After the shootings in the Assembly, King Aleksandar saw only two possibilities: either that he introduce a royal dictatorship or that he allow Slovenia, Croatia, and perhaps other parts of the country to separate. The king specifically rejected any notion of federalization but, according to one version, offered Radić, Maček, and Pribićević the option of "amputation"—an option they allegedly rejected because they feared that the surgeon-king might well intend, in that eventuality, to annex a large part of Croatia to an enlarged Serbia.[159] But in the meantime, the SDK leadership, meeting in Zagreb on 1 August, had passed a resolution breaking off relations with parties based in Serbia and declaring that the coalition no longer recognized the Kingdom of SHS! This signified that the HSS, now seconded by the Independent Democrats, was returning to its earlier advocacy of a republic. As for the parties in Serbia, Maček told a journalist for *Vreme* in November 1928, "I have said several times already, that we cannot talk with the Belgrade parties, because these are not parties in the sense of European democracy. All those parties, as they call themselves, have only one point in their program, and that point is—power!"[160]

In the meantime, the king had decided on taking power into his own hands, but he needed to go through the motions of consulting with the country's most prominent politicians. On 4 and 5 January 1929, the king consulted with all the party leaders, including Maček, and on 6 January 1929, the king annulled the constitution, dissolved the Assembly, banned all political parties, and named a new government (headed by General Petar Živković) which, on 3 October 1929, changed the name of the country to the Kingdom of Yugoslavia. The king explained that the June assassinations had shaken people's faith in the institutions and that it had become impossible for the leading political actors to come to an agreement. "Our supreme ideal is to safeguard the unity of our people and of the state," said the king in a manifesto he released to the public on the day he introduced the royal dictatorship. "This duty is imposed on us by our responsibility vis-à-vis the nation and vis-à-vis history, by our love for the Motherland, and by the sacred debt of honor that we owe to the innumerable victims who have sacrificed their lives for this ideal."[161]

Radić had feared for the worst. "I am, like all of us Slavs, an optimist," Radić had said in 1927, "but there is so much evil among us, that there will be a catastrophe one day. . . . Our state is not fulfilling that which was expected from it."[162] What had been expected was that the state would bring together the peoples of the Kingdom of SHS on the basis of consensus, mutual understanding, mutual trust, and equality. Instead, in spite of friendly intentions at the outset, the peoples of the kingdom never reached a consensus, never understood each other, were separated by walls of distrust, and were unequal in civic terms, in terms of language use, in terms of cultural policy, in terms of personnel recruitment, in terms of taxation, and in other regards as well. What had been expected was that Regent-King Aleksandar would be a monarch for all of the people; yet he worked in collusion with Serbian politicians, often keeping the same people in office even after they had lost the confidence of the Assembly. What had been expected was that the rule of law and the spirit of fairness would prevail. But instead, the leading parties in the state showed contempt for the very laws they themselves had passed, lined their pockets with illicitly obtained funds, and acted variously in a spirit of self-interest or in a spirit of revenge, suffocating all non-Serbs of the kingdom, but perhaps especially the Albanians, the Macedonians, and the Croats of the kingdom.

There are many reasons why the Vidovdan constitution failed. One could, for example, mention that illiteracy was high in most parts of the country, with

Slovenia standing as an exception with the lowest rate (8.8% illiteracy in 1921), but with rates of 23.3% illiteracy in Vojvodina, 32.3% in Croatia-Slavonia, 49.5% in Dalmatia, 65.4% in Serbia, 67% in Montenegro, 80.5% in Bosnia-Herzegovina, and 83.4% in Macedonia.[163] With such high rates of illiteracy, most people's information—and especially in the southern regions of the country—was limited to what they could hear at political rallies or learn by word of mouth. In such a society, the tendency to vote for "one's own," rather than for the party advocating the best social and economic program, would be reinforced.

Or again, one could note that, in the interwar period, the kingdom was the second most indebted country in Europe (after Greece); the kingdom's public debt stood at 25 billion dinars in 1925, rising to 45 billion dinars by 1937. Moreover, as of 1921, there were only 1,831 factories in the entire country, with 75% of the population employed in the agricultural sector.[164] This made for an economically troubled country, and in classical democratic theory, economic problems are generally thought to present a serious challenge to any ambitions to establish or even maintain a democracy.

But the foregoing problems might have been overcome, had it not been for other problems, which made a decisive contribution to the failure of the Vidovdan constitution. Many of these problems can be summed up in one sentence: the Vidovdan system was objectively illegitimate, in that it failed to establish the rule of law, to protect individual rights, to build an atmosphere of tolerance and fair play, to support real equality, and to guarantee the neutrality of the state in matters relating to religion, language, and national culture; it may be doubted whether confessional neutrality could have been achieved in the kingdom at a time when most of the states in East Central and Southeastern Europe were confessional states, but, be that as it may, Orthodox establishmentarianism in the confessionally heterogeneous kingdom stirred resentment among Catholics especially and proved to be a factor for instability. The ethnic politics syndrome which developed was the by-product and reflection of this underlying problem of system illegitimacy and dysfunctionality. Or, to put it another way, the national question was not a cause of the dysfunctionality of the system; on the contrary, it was the dysfunctionality of the system which generated the national question.

But the system need not have been born dysfunctional. On the contrary, this was the result of the policies adopted, in the first place, by Nikola Pašić, supported in the early years by Davidović and Pribićević, and by King Aleksandar. In their view, the Kingdom of Serbs, Croats, and Slovenes represented an expansion of the Kingdom of Serbia, and it was therefore, in their view, "logical" that Serbs controlled the levers of power. Insofar as Slovenes, Croats, Bosniaks, and the Albanians of Kosovo did not share this view of the state, resentments were bound to develop and conflicts came about as the direct result of the strategy of Serb hegemonism. Stjepan Radić certainly miscalculated the effects of his famous trip to Moscow and was not known for tact and fine etiquette in characterizing the work of ministers he did not respect. But it would be a serious mistake to blame Radić for the fact that the Vidovdan constitution collapsed. A constitution achieved by consensus and perceived as serving the interests of all of the country's peoples, at least to some degree, should have been able to weather even the assassination of Radić; the problem, to repeat, was that the constitution had been designed to serve a particular interpretation of *Serbian* national interests, and not the interests of the several peoples of the kingdom.

CHAPTER 3

The First Yugoslavia, Part 2: The Kingdom of Yugoslavia, 1929–1941

> If injustice invariably implants hatred, whether among groups of free men or [among] slaves, will it not cause them to hate and injure each other, making it impossible for them to cooperate in common enterprises?
>
> —Plato, *The Republic,* Book I

In proclaiming a royal dictatorship, King Aleksandar served notice that, in his mind, the existing parties and structures could not be rendered functional. He did not trace their dysfunctionality, however, to the failure of the major actors in the system to reach a consensus on the most fundamental questions or to the failure of the regime to respect human rights (most obviously in Kosovo and Macedonia) or to the fact that the very constitution had been adopted in a manner which, some believed, violated the spirit of the Korfu Declaration. Had the king traced the Vidovdan system's dysfunctionality to these anterior factors, he might not have acted as he did. Yet, ironically, the harsh dictatorship which he established *did* bring the Radicals, Democrats, SLS, HSS, and JMO together —but in opposition to him and to the dictatorship itself!

Nor was his river-based administrative overhaul of the country any more successful. Regardless of what Serbian nationalists would claim in the 1990s, Slovenia, Croatia, Bosnia-Herzegovina, Montenegro, and even, though less obviously, Macedonia *did* have historically established boundaries to which many locals were attached. When the king advised them that they should henceforth think of themselves as living, not in Croatia or Serbia or Bosnia, but in

Sava or Drina or Drava or Zeta (provinces named for rivers), people felt deprived of their birthright. To some extent, of course, the king enjoyed the halo of royal authority, although the excesses of his regime demonstrated that it was a regime based on violence. But having made violence part of the fabric of state, he was not able to monopolize it and was felled by an assassin's bullet in 1934. After that, his successor, Prince Paul, acting as head of a three-man regency for an underage king, charted a new course; the other two regents were Radenko Stanković and Ivo Perović.

The Kingdom of Rivers

The dictatorship was months in the planning. Before proclaiming his dictatorship, King Aleksandar assured himself of the understanding of the ruling establishments in key Allied countries, especially France, firmed up his support among certain key political figures, among them Anton Korošec, and obtained the pre-approval of the economic establishment in Croatia.[1] The meetings with various party leaders during 3–5 January 1929 were purely pro forma, designed to convince the leaders that they had been consulted, the public that the king had acted after listening to all voices and considering all options, and everyone concerned that the king was acting selflessly. Nor was it likely that the sixth of January—Orthodox Christmas Eve—had been chosen arbitrarily as the date on which to strike.

After the proclamation of what came to be known as "the Sixth of January Dictatorship," the king appointed General Petar Živković to serve as prime Minster. Korošec joined the government, as did Slavko Švrljuga, vice president of the Association of Croatian Industrialists and a prominent critic of the late Stjepan Radić. Even Vlatko Maček, though remaining in opposition, had positive things to say about this ultima ratio in his first public statement after the proclamation. But the king had resolved on force now, and this was manifested by the suppression of nationally oriented organizations, such as the athletic associations, teachers' societies, and even singing clubs, and their replacement by "Yugoslav" organizations and by the active repression of the opposition.[2]

The arrests of influential opposition leaders began in April 1929. The first to be arrested and imprisoned was Dragoljub Jovanović, leader of the left wing of the Agrarian Union and a professor at the University of Belgrade. Charged with having expressed anti-state opinions in a lecture to a student organization, he spent half a year in detention before a court finally cleared him of the charges in November 1929.[3] In the meantime, in May 1929, Svetozar Pribićević was arrested and interned in the village of Brus near Kopaonik. Later that year, after police apprehended several youth on charges of having prepared to assassinate members of a royal deputation, Maček was arrested and accused of complicity in the plot. All of the accused were found guilty, except for Maček, who was acquitted for lack of evidence connecting him with the case. Josip Predavec, a close confidant of Radić's and one of the HSS vice presidents, was also arrested in December 1929, indicted on political charges, and handed a two-and-a-half-year sentence, later extended by two and a half months. Eventually even Korošec would find himself behind bars, as would scores of communists and communist sympathizers, rounded up and brought before the Tribunal for the Protection of the State in the years 1929–1932. During 1929 and 1930 alone, the Tribunal conducted 36 trials involving 357 communists; other communists were murdered or were alleged to have committed suicide after being taken into custody.[4] Meanwhile, after proclaiming his dictatorship, the king enacted a new legal code, reduced regional differences in taxation, established a Yugoslav Agrarian Bank, and purged the bureaucracy to clean up the worst cases of corruption. In March 1929, the king ordered four ministries (for postal affairs, religious affairs, agrarian reform, and public health) shut down and their responsibilities transferred to other agencies and ministries, as a cost-cutting measure; on 18 April 1929, a law was issued imposing strict censorship on all newspapers.[5] That same month, the king pensioned off about 50 former prime ministers, cabinet ministers, and state secretaries, together with 35 generals. More ominously, the regime "organized terrorist bands, composed for the most part of members of the police,"[6] for the purpose of dealing with dissidents.

On 3 October 1929, the Kingdom of the Serbs, Croats, and Slovenes was officially renamed the Kingdom of Yugoslavia. Where Nikola Pašić had insisted on preserving the name *Serbia,* King Aleksandar sought to promote and safeguard the political-bureaucratic dominance of the Serbian bourgeoisie under the *Yugoslav* rubric. It was at this time that the king introduced a new administrative system in which the new borders cut across the pre-war national-political provincial borders, with the new units named for rivers. The new units were: Dunav (Danube), with its seat in Novi Sad; Sava, with its seat in Zagreb; Vrbas, with its seat in Banja Luka; Drina, with its seat in Sarajevo; Zeta, with its seat in Cetinje; Vardar, with its seat in Skopje; Morava, with its seat in Niš; Primorje, with its seat in Split; and Drava, with its seat in Ljubljana. Belgrade and environs had a special status. Serbia (including "southern Serbia") was divided among the Drina, Dunav, Morava, Vardar, and Zeta banovinas, while Bosnia-Herzegovina was divided among four banovinas. Sava and Primorje accounted for most of what had historically been Croatia. In the king's mind, the new administrative system was designed to foster even greater centralization and to sap people's attachment to their historic regions. Indeed, under a 1929 decree, the public display of "tribal" (*plemenski*), i.e., national, standards and colors was strictly prohibited.[7]

The royal dictatorship was characterized by a high level of surveillance. In the Sava banovina, the state police maintained close surveillance over the movements of Dr. Ante Trumbić, Dr. Vlatko Maček, Dr. Milan Šuflaj (Šufflay), and Marija Radić (Stjepan's widow), recording their comings and goings and the amount of time they spent visiting each other and others.[8] Later, after the assassination of Šufflay in February 1931,[9] the police added Dr. Ivan Pernar to the list of politically active Croats whose movements should be monitored. A combination of fear and opportunism worked to deplete the ranks of the opposition. Where the HSS was concerned, the party's leadership was badly shaken after Maček's arrest in December 1929, and Dragutin Karlo Kovačević, one of four vice presidents of the HSS, joined the Živković government in early 1930. In spring 1930, while Maček was still in detention, another four HSS figures, who had served as deputies in the Assembly, defected to the regime.[10]

The kingdom was affected, of course, by the world economic depression. Foreign capital vanished, Belgrade cut back on financial assistance to the periphery, and "[i]n 1931 Croatia suffered a catastrophic financial crash after more than eighty years of almost unbroken economic growth and development."[11] The HSS leadership concluded that the dictatorship would not be changed soon and therefore decided to strengthen its presence abroad. Thus, in August 1929, August Košutić, another HSS vice president and Radić's son-in-law, slipped out of the country and went to Italy; Juraj Krnjević, the general secretary of the HSS, followed soon after, taking refuge in Hungary.

The Ustaša Movement

The Croatian Right Republican Youth (*Hrvatska pravaška republikanska omladina*, or, hereafter, Croatian Youth), organized in 1926 under the wings of the HSP–F, provided organizational support for Ante Pavelić (1889–1959), who was elected to serve as deputy in the regional assembly in Zagreb in February 1927. At its second congress (in September 1928), the Croatian Youth passed a resolution demanding the reestablishment of an (independent) Croatian state and provided for the establishment of terrorist groups to work toward this objective.[12] Immediately after this Croatian Youth congress, the illegal terrorist organization *Hrvatski domobran* (Croatian Homeland Defender) was set up; this organization joined the Croatian Youth in organizing demonstrations in Zagreb on 1 December 1928, which finished with fierce battles with the police.

After the proclamation of the royal dictatorship, Pavelić fled the country during the night of 19 January, crossing into Austria. After a brief sojourn in Vienna, Pavelić moved to Hungary and from there traveled to Sofia, receiving a big welcome in Bulgaria from the leader of IMRO, Ivan "Vančo" Mihajlov. Before the end of the year, Pavelić had made his way to Italy, where Mussolini, the Italian strongman, was disposed to view Croatian separatism with favor. Although Maček and Pavelić had been in charge of rival party organizations, the dictatorship brought them together temporarily. Thus, after going to Czechoslovakia for medical treatments in October 1930, Maček stopped over in Vienna and Salzburg on his return trip, in order to meet with Pavelić, Košutić, and Krnjević. These conversations dealt with questions of cooperative action.[13] Indeed, during the years 1929–1932, Maček was seriously considering the separatist option, and Košutić made frequent visits to Italy during 1929–1932 in order to confer with Pavelić.[14]

The formal establishment of the *Ustaša* (Insurgent) organization took about two years. The name *Ustaša* first appeared in April 1931, when the organization's name was announced as the *Ustaša—hrvatska revolucionarna organizacija* (Insurgent—Croatian Revolutionary Organization). In 1933, the name was changed to the *Ustaški pokret* (*Ustaša* movement). During these years, the Italian government provided subsidies to Pavelić, allowing him to establish military training camps for *Ustaša* recruits.[15] Although ideological development was not a strong point in the *Ustaša* movement, the *Ustaša* shared such prototypically fascist characteristics as the glorification of violence, the cult of the leader, the hearkening back to pristine glories in the past, the urge to fulfill its desire for "repristination," and the belief that national rebirth could only be achieved through some form of "cleansing," i.e., genocide.[16] Rejecting the Illyrian (Yugoslav) tradition, the *Ustaša* tried to construe Ante Starčević as a progenitor of nationalist-inspired Croatian separatism; in fact, as Jelić-Butić notes, the *Ustaša* misappropriated and abused Starčević's legacy.[17]

The movement's principal base of activity in the early 1930s was in Italy, where, by 1934, there were about 560 active members. Hungary was also an important base for the *Ustaša*. Hungary was, of course, aflame with irredentist resentment after the punitive Treaty of Trianon, and as early as 1932, Hungarian authorities were reported to be preparing their military forces to retake those parts of Yugoslavia which had been Hungarian until after World War One, waiting for the day when civil war would break out in the kingdom.[18] There were also *Ustaša* groups in Germany (Berlin), Austria (Vienna), and Belgium, as well as in North and South America. As of 1930, Ignac Domitrović, Gašo Balenović, Gustav Perčec (general secretary of the HSP–F), and Josip Metzger (a Hungarian intelligence officer) were actively organizing Croatian émigrés in towns along the border with the kingdom, though after the attempt on King Aleksandar's life in December 1933, the Italians took some steps to curtail *Ustaša* activity in Dalmatia, and the Hungarians curtailed *Ustaša* activity in the frontier zone.[19]

In September 1932, the *Ustaša* organized a raid into the Lika region. Although the raid did not spark a general insurrection, there were clashes not only in the Lika region, near Gospić, but also in Slavonia, south of Osijek, and in Dalmatia. The Belgrade government rushed 400 gendarmes to the Lika region in order to stamp out the disorders. But the *Ustaša* raiders held their positions and even succeeded in blowing up four gendarme barracks in northern Dalmatia; by mid-October, the government had dispatched another 1,000 gendarmes to the trouble spots.[20] Eventually the raid was suppressed. The *Ustaša* had shown its ability to cause disruption, but also its inability to overthrow the regime. In July 1933, the *Ustaša* conducted another operation, destroying some sections of railroad tracks, but especially after the failure of the Lika raid, the *Ustaša* pinned its hopes above all on assassination, rather than insurrection. Thus, in October

1932, the Ministry of Internal Affairs (*Ministarstvo unutrašnjih poslova,* or MUP) in Belgrade received information that fascist circles in Trieste were preparing to make an attempt on the king's life, in the event that he would visit Split.[21] Later, at the end of November 1932, it was reported that the *Ustaša* had smuggled two bombs and three revolvers into the country in order to assassi- nate the king on the occasion of his visit to Zagreb on 1 December 1932.[22]

The King's New Clothes and the "Lemonade Declaration"

The naked dictatorship was not working as King Aleksandar had hoped. The royal dictatorship was not making any headway against unemployment, by con- trast with fascist Italy and Nazi Germany. The Serbian civic opposition had retreated into passivity and, for the most part, was not prepared to support the king's methods. The Democratic Party, once a mainstay of a unitary system under the Karadjordjević dynasty, was no longer in the king's court. Indeed, by spring 1929, there were two viewpoints within the Democratic Party: (1) that the monarchy be abolished, a republic proclaimed, and an agreement reached with the HSS; and (2) that parliamentarism be restored and considerable autonomy granted to seven or eight units: Slovenia, Croatia-Slavonia, Dalmatia, Vojvodina, Bosnia-Herzegovina, Serbia, Macedonia, and possibly also Mon- tenegro.[23] Moreover, the excesses of the Sixth of January Dictatorship were increasingly being criticized abroad, including in high circles in France; this crit- icism, which became voluble in the second half of 1930, reached a crescendo after the assassination of the widely respected scholar Šufflay in February 1931, when Albert Einstein and Thomas Mann, among others, raised their voices in protest.[24] Finally, in summer 1931, in an effort to broaden the base of his regime's support, King Aleksandar opened negotiations with Serbian Radical Party leaders Aca Stanojević and Miloš Trifunović, as well as with SLS leader Korošec. The king now repeated the mistake he and Pašić had made in 1921— of ignoring the Croats. In September 1931, the king issued a new constitution, introducing a bicameral legislature but retaining the administrative division of the country introduced two years earlier. This constitution proclaimed its adherence to the principle of the separation of powers, but in practice, all authority and power were concentrated in the king's hands; interestingly enough, the 1931 constitution neither established one Church as the state Church nor proclaimed the principle of the separation of Church and state. The constitution also proclaimed freedom of the press and of assembly, but other legislative acts rendered the guarantee of press freedom null and void, while the government reserved to itself the right to constrict freedom of assembly at its discretion.[25] Student demonstrations in Belgrade during October and Novem- ber 1931, organized on the initiative of the communist party, were the first pub- lic protest against the royal dictatorship after the issuance of what came to be known locally as "the imposed constitution." Students at the universities of

Ljubljana and Zagreb also staged anti-regime demonstrations, and student unrest continued into 1932, with renewed student demonstrations in Zagreb in January and March, and in Belgrade in April 1932. In Zagreb, anti-regime students unfurled the (banned) Croatian national colors, clashing with local pro-regime students. There were also anti-regime demonstrations in May 1932 in Montenegro (in Nikšić and Cetinje) and in the Bosanska Krajina, while in Slovenia, the celebration of Korošec's 60th birthday on 12 May 1932, organized by local SLS figures, took on the character of an anti-regime demonstration in some localities.[26] At the same time, denunciations of the new constitution circulated underground.[27]

With the passage of the new constitution, the regime needed a political party to carry out its program. The result was the creation of the Yugoslav Radical Peasant Democracy, forerunner to the Yugoslav National Party (*Jugoslovenska narodna stranka,* or JNS) and to the Yugoslav Radical Community (*Jugoslovenska radikalna zajednica*). Veterans of the Radical Party and the Democratic Party—men such as Nikola Uzunović, Božidar Maksimović, Milan Srškić, Vojislav Marinković, and Kosta Kumanudi—joined the regime party, assuming prominent roles.

The parliament now consisted of a popularly elected lower house (the National Assembly) and a partly elected upper house (the Senate). Under the law concerning the election of the deputies to the Assembly (10 September 1931) and the law concerning candidate lists (7 September 1931), deputies could be elected only on the basis of country-wide lists; this spelled an end to the dominance of regionally based, ethnically or confessionally oriented parties but, in the conditions created by the king, reinforced the position of the regime party. Where the Senate was concerned, half of the senators were picked by the king outright, and half of them were elected. But even the elected senators were not elected by the citizens directly. Rather, they were elected by an electoral commission composed of Assembly deputies, councilors, and district presidents—all of them, people under the king's thumb.

The first elections to the new Assembly were set for 8 November 1931, with the parliament scheduled to open on 7 December 1931. Prior to the elections, the leaders of five political parties—Spaho (JMO), Stanojević (Radicals), Davidović (Democrats), Joca Jovanović (Agrarians), and Korošec (SLS)—issued a joint statement, assessing that the new constitution had made it impossible for people to vote for the candidates of their choice. They therefore decided to boycott the elections, in order to signal their complete rejection of the existing order. But when Maček contacted them about issuing a joint condemnation of the regime, Stanojević drafted a wishy-washy text, which he offered for general subscription. Maček forwarded Stanojević's draft to Pribićević, who was in Prague by then; Pribićević wrote back to dismiss the draft as a "lemonade declaration."[28] The HSS and SDK were not prepared to engage in what they considered to be a watered-down protest. All the same, the HSS decided to join the other opposition parties in boycotting the elections. As a result, there was only one list of candidates presented to the voters: the regime list. No more than 30% of the electorate could be bothered to cast their ballots for the unopposed slate.[29] The Yugoslav Radical Peasant Democracy was formed via the deputies' club which was set up once the parliament was reconstituted. On 27 January 1932, the Senate and Assembly gave their approval, after the fact, to the king's proclamation of the royal dictatorship on 6 January 1929. In so doing, the two houses of parliament agreed "that it was the right and duty of his Majesty as supreme guardian of the greatest interests of the Yugoslav people to lead the country out of chaos, [and] that the dictatorship was the only *legal* way to [effect] the political regeneration of the country."[30]

In mid-January 1932, Davidović sent Maček and Stanojević the text of a draft resolution which his party had prepared together with the Agrarian Union; Davidović hoped that all the opposition parties might support this resolution. Maček found it unsatisfactory, and the resolution died a quiet death. But contacts among the opposition parties continued all the same. In May 1932, for example, Jovan Radonić and Ž. Tajsić, two members of the leadership of the Radical Party, came to Zagreb to meet with Maček. Radonić and Tajsić told Maček that their party, while still opposed to federalization, was now prepared to discuss "Serb-Croat dualism" (on the Austro-Hungarian model).[31] Maček neither embraced this concept nor rejected it. Maček was also visited by leading figures from the Democratic Party, the Agrarian Union, and the JMO. Meanwhile, Pribićević was coming around to the conclusion that federalism was the best solution, urging that it should involve extensive devolution to the constituent federal units.

In late January 1933, the newspaper *Le petit parisien* published an interview with the HSS leader, in which Maček was reported to have declared that, even after 14 years of living in the same state, Serbs and Croats still inhabited "two different worlds."[32] When the journalist interviewing Maček asked what the Croatian party leader thought could be done about this, Maček responded that the two peoples should separate as much as possible. The publication of these statements was received very badly in ruling circles in Belgrade. But immediately after this, Srdjan Budisavljević (SDK) sent a letter to leading figures in the Radical and Democratic parties and the Agrarian Union, indicating that Maček was prepared to negotiate with them and that "the Serbian opposition parties needed to come out with a program which would show that aside from the regime, there also existed a democratic Serbia."[33] This note from Budisavljević made a very positive impression on Serb opposition figures.

It was, however, about this time that the regime decided to arrest Maček once again, hoping to use judicial means to remove him from political life permanently. Thus Maček was arrested on 31 January 1933. An investigation was conducted, and after a month, charges were brought before the Tribunal for the Protection of the State. The key evidence against Maček was the "Zagreb points" (*Zagrebačke punktacije*), drafted by Trumbić and signed by various figures from both the HSS and the SDS, including Maček, in November 1932. Among other things, the *punktacije* charged that the state was committed to the principle of Serbian hegemony and that it had "destroyed our [i.e., Croatian] moral values and our progressive institutions as well as our traditions. . . . Considering these disastrous experiences, we have arrived at the inevitable conclusion that we must go back to the starting-point of 1918."[34] In spite of its call for a return to the "starting-point," however, the *punktacije* continued to look to a solution within the framework of Yugoslavia. But, for the authorities, Maček was a threat, above all because he effectively rallied Croats behind a common program. For a dictatorship, the point is not whether an opposition leader is Croat or Serb or Albanian, but whether that leader is effective and whether he can be bought off. If he is effective and cannot be bought off, he is a threat. Maček was convicted of violating the law on the security of the state and convicted, on 30 April 1933, to three years in prison and taken to Srijemska Mitrovica.[35] Meanwhile, the "Zagreb points" inspired a series of copycat *punktacije*, issued in Sarajevo (by the JMO leadership), in Ljubljana, and even in Novi Sad.

While in prison, Maček turned the management of the HSS over to Predavec, who had only recently been released from prison himself. But on 14 July 1933, Predavec was brutally murdered by Tomo Koščec, a resident of Dugo Selo, on instructions from the regime.[36] During these years, political violence and political trials became commonplace. In April 1931, for example, 14 Croats were put on trial in Belgrade on charges of collaboration with Pavelić and Perčec in setting up a secessionist organization in Croatia and of having imported explosives from Hungary; 13 of the accused were convicted. The following month, a separate trial began in Zagreb for 23 young men accused of complicity in the murder (in March 1929) of Toni Schlegel, a close confidant of the king and editor of a Zagreb newspaper. In June 1932, a conspiracy was discovered in Maribor, leading to the arrest and trial of nine officers and three NCOs of the 45th Infantry and 32nd Artillery Regiments; the accused were charged with having plotted to overthrow the legal order and with having relied on Soviet assistance to bring this about. Pernar and five other members of the HSS were put on trial in March 1933, in a trial not connected directly with the trial of Maček. According to the indictment, they had distributed propaganda urging sympathizers to work "for the overthrow of the present regime, to resist the authorities by force, and to kill 10 Serbs for every Croat peasant killed."[37] Discontent was so rife in the Sava banovina (Croatia) that by 1933 it had become the scene of extensive civil strife. The regime struck back with a series of assassinations. In addition to Šufflay and Predavec, there was also an attempt on the life of Mile Budak, a lawyer and Croatian political activist, who subsequently went into exile in early 1933, becoming an important *Ustaša* leader.[38]

Nor was discontent a monopoly of the Croats. A draft proposal prepared in the winter of 1931–1932 by Korošec and supported by Serbian opposition figures called for the division of the state into six administrative units: Slovenia, Croatia, Bosnia-Herzegovina, Vojvodina, Serbia, and Montenegro.[39] Under this concept, Macedonia was to have been included within Serbia. There were also persistent autonomist pressures in Vojvodina (as well as evidence of separatism among the region's Hungarian minority[40]). D. Bošković and R. Djermanović, leading opposition figures in Vojvodina, were strongly in favor of Vojvodina's being established as an autonomous federal unit in any future federation—a notion to which, however, there continued to be strong opposition from some of the more prominent Radical and Democratic party leaders. The aforementioned "Novi Sad *punktacije*"—adopted toward the end of 1932—noted that there was deep discontent with the regime throughout Vojvodina and criticized the post-September regime for "total incomprehension of the specific circumstances and needs of individual provinces." In January 1933, representatives of opposition groups in Vojvodina formed the Committee to Carry out the Novi Sad *punktacije*, which in turn distributed the full text of the "punktacije" to the leaders of all opposition parties, proposing that a meeting would be held to discuss these ideas. Soon after this initiative was taken, however, some of the authors of the "Novi Sad *punktacije*" were taken into custody by the police. As for the *punktacije*, this initiative died when leading figures in the Serbian opposition parties refused to accept it as the basis for any discussions.[41]

Moreover, the Agrarian Union had been gravitating for some time toward opposition, and after the imposition of the royal dictatorship, Dragoljub Jovanović, the aforementioned leader of the Agrarian Union's left wing, was steadfast in opposition. Jovanović became involved in the illegal publication and distribution of an underground newspaper, *Zemljoradničke novine*, as well as anti-regime leaflets. On 2 May 1932, 43 prominent Left Agrarians, including Jovanović, took part in a conference in Kragujevac; it was the largest meeting of opposition politicians since 6 January 1929. The police intervened, apprehending Jovanović and 11 others, who were put on trial on charges of having held an illegal meeting. The accused based their defense on the argument that they were not anti-state but merely favored a federal arrangement for the state. Jovanović would be (re)incarcerated for a year, with three other persons receiving lighter sentences.[42] The *Times*'s optimistic declaration (in June 1932) that a general consensus had been reached in Yugoslavia on the need to reorganize the system along federal lines notwithstanding,[43] the advocacy of political change remained a political crime.

Serbia's second major political trial of the 1930s took place in November 1933, involving persons from the Democratic Party and the Agrarian Union. They were charged with having written and distributed anti-regime leaflets (in which they had demanded civil liberties and ethnic equality, among other things). This was preceded by the trial of a group of SLS members in early March 1933 and the trial, in Banja Luka, of Branko Čubrilović, one of the most distinguished members of the Agrarian Union, in May 1933.[44]

Meanwhile, at the time when Maček's trial was still underway (March 1933), the Democrats proposed that opposition leaders in Belgrade issue a joint condemnation of the regime. A committee was then formed of representatives of the Radical and Democratic parties and the Agrarian Union; the intention was both to protest the trial of Maček and to issue a joint condemnation of the regime more generally. Ljubomir Davidović and J. Jovanović signed the proposed text at once (which had been prepared by Milan Stojadinović, Milan Grol, and Milan Gavrilović), but, on the Radical side, neither Trifunović nor Stanojević would sign it. Trifunović now wrote up a counter-proposal, removing any references to the trial of Maček. The Radical leaders also objected to the insistence on the part of the Democrats and the Agrarians that the eventual statement be released not only to the domestic public, but also abroad. But in spite of all of this squabbling, at the end of April 1933, the three Serbian parties managed to issue a joint protest of the regime's persecution of Maček—a protest which, nonetheless, differed in content from the abortive draft of 19 March. Finally, in May 1933, the three Serbian opposition parties agreed on a formulation for a joint statement, committing themselves to struggle for the restoration of free parliamentarism and civic liberties, and for the reform of the constitutional order on the basis of an agreement to be reached among Serbs, Croats, and Slovenes.[45]

The Croatian Resistance to October 1934

General Živković remained prime minister until 4 April 1932. It was during his term of office that, on 7 November 1929, a chapter of the Chetnik organization, "For King and Fatherland—Petar Mrkonjić," was established in Sunj; subsequently, a second chapter was set up in Orahovica (20 km. west of Našice). Also in 1929, a chapter of the Association of Serbian Chetniks for King and Fatherland was established in Rajić, in the Jasenovac district (*općina*).[46] The expanded edition of the rules for Chetniks had been published in Belgrade in 1928; these rules were self-consciously adopted by the Supreme Council ("Vrhovna Uprava") of the organization on 28 June 1928, replacing those passed on 3 April 1924.[47] The Chetnik organization remained a nationalist-chauvinist organization, and the establishment of branches in Croatia was, therefore, a dangerous development. It was only somewhat later, specifically in May 1934, however, that Serb students from Croatia at the University of Zagreb launched a Chetnik bulletin called *Student*. The first issue (a three-page typed leaflet) defined *Chetnik* rather broadly, to include anyone defending Yugoslavs from foreign and internal enemies, and called for the "spiritual unification" of Yugoslavs and the radical "cleansing" of every "foreign and anational element," among other things.[48] Živković was succeeded by Vojislav Marinković, whose own term of office was cut short when, in a speech he presented to a party conference in Niš in May, he conceded that the national problem remained unresolved. This concession angered some old-style unitarists who now would not rest until he was out of office. Milan Srškic, who was possibly Marinković's loudest critic, became prime minister after Marinković's resignation. Srškić lasted somewhat longer in office, resigning on 27 January 1934, after two terms as prime minister. Srškić, in turn, was succeeded by Nikola Uzunović, well known for his Serbian hegemonic orientation,[49] who served in office until 20 December 1934.

Srškić, an ideological kin to Uzunović, adopted a "no nonsense" attitude toward Croatian advocates of federalism and believed that the best way to combat federalist and separatist ideas alike was through repression.[50] Indeed, upon assuming office, Srškić sent instructions to the Ministry of Internal Affairs insisting on a strict application of the law on the protection of public security. It was during his term of office that Maček was arrested for the second time, tried, and imprisoned. Srškić also believed that the regime should continue to draw most of its staff from the Serbian and Montenegrin populations. As of 1932, when Serbs and Montenegrins in combination accounted for about 39% of the population, they accounted for 89% of the staff at the Ministry of Internal Affairs, 85% of the staff at the Ministry of Justice, 90% at the Ministry of Social Policy and National Health, 96% at the Ministry of Education, and so forth.[51]

By 1932, thanks to the consistently nonconsensual approach taken by Belgrade, separatism in Croatia was clearly on the upswing. Separatist sentiment was rising among students ranging from middle school to the university.[52] In November 1932, for example, a student association called the Central Representative Student Organization was established at the University of Zagreb, on the initiative of the former rector, Dr. Josip Belobrk; the organization was inspired by Frankist ideas and was said, by MUP, to have an "anti-Yugoslav" character.[53] But separatist sentiment was not confined to the student population; on the contrary, it was manifested both in the cities and in the countryside.[54] In Crkvenica, for example, there were clashes between police and local citizens on 30 April 1932, leaving some persons wounded and resulting in multiple arrests.[55] On 26 May 1932, there were major demonstrations in Split when expectant crowds, looking forward to Dr. Maček's arrival by train, learned that the authorities had prevented Maček from coming; the people marched through the town calling for an independent Croatia.[56] But the most serious unrest in the first half of 1932 affected Ludbreg county in April, when local peasants from six villages hoisted the Croatian colors and swore to continue to fight against the authorities with whatever weapons they had on hand, including axes and knives, until they had realized their ambition to self-government.[57]

Meanwhile, the *Ustaša* continued to hatch regicidal plots. *Grič*, an *Ustaša* periodical named for a hill in Zagreb, boasted openly, in summer 1932, of the movement's determination to gun down King Aleksandar:

Down in Niš where life is gay
They'll shoot you down on any day.
Račić, villain—he's the one
Who shot five bullets from his gun.
Stjepan, Pavle, Djuro—dead,
But there's no price on Puniša's head.
Oh Croatia, mother dear

You suffer and you live in fear.
Hey, you Serbs, we'll make you pay.
Time will show what comes your way.
"Beloved" Aleksandar King
In mourning do the Croats sing.
Aleksandar, just you wait.
Time for you to meet your fate![58]

The *Ustaša* saw an opportunity to realize these fantasies in December 1933, when the king was scheduled to visit Zagreb, and contracted Petar Oreb and Josip Begović to do the job. The police learned of the plot in advance, however, and when the would-be assassins lost their nerve at the last minute, the police apprehended them before they could do any damage.[59] Afterward, the regime, wanting to exact retribution, had "approximately 100 persons . . . executed . . . , most of them having been picked out of the population at random and not necessarily having had anything to do with the attempted assassination or [even] with the *Ustaša* movement."[60]

Eugen Kvaternik, one of the leading figures in the *Ustaša,* now developed a plan to kill the king not in Yugoslavia but in France, where the king was planning an official visit in October 1934. Kvaternik prepared two teams of assassins, the first of which would attempt to kill the king in Marseilles upon his arrival on 9 October, the second of which would be waiting in Paris to make a second attempt, in the event that the first attempt failed.[61] The assassination was prepared in collaboration with the IMRO. Ironically, the French police received an anonymous tip about the assassination plans three days in advance, but were unequal to the task of preventing the plot from coming to fruition. Aside from the king, three other persons died as a result of the shootings in Marseilles, one of them being French foreign minister Louis Barthou. But if the *Ustaše* imagined that the regicide would encourage Croats to rise up against the Serb-dominated government, they were very much mistaken. On the contrary, in spite of everything, royalty still had its allure, its magic, and the king, uniquely among Serb politicians, enjoyed a mystique among Croats, who mourned his passing in bitterness.[62] In Zagreb, for instance, "nationally oriented" students expressed their grief at the assassination of the king and declared their intention to organize a meeting at the university at which they would condemn the assassination and affirm their complete loyalty to Yugoslavia.[63]

The assassination may have been carried out by an IMRO agent,[64] but evidence connecting the *Ustaša* to the murder quickly accumulated. When two suspects arrested on the French-German border revealed "that the murder had been organized by a terrorist band based on Hungarian soil,"[65] Yugoslav attention turned to the *Ustaša* training camp at Janka puszta in Hungary. As already mentioned, the Yugoslav regime now forced thousands of Hungarians to leave Yugoslavia,[66] and, in mid-November, sent a demarche to Budapest, charging that Hungarian authorities had assigned Hungarian officers to train *Ustaša* recruits at Janka puszta, provided *Ustaša* operatives with fake identification, and paid for the agents involved in the assassination to stay at the plushest hotels in Marseilles.[67]

Pavelić had hoped that the regicide would cause Yugoslavia to unravel. But instead, Hungary and Italy took steps to restrict the *Ustaša,* which thereupon went into a decline. The Italians expelled some *Ustaše* and interned the rest of them on the small island of Lipari, off the coast of Sicily, and even promised the Yugoslav government to liquidate the organization altogether. "By early 1935," as Sadkovich writes, "as the echoes of Marseilles died away, it seemed that the assassinations had dealt a mortal blow not to Yugoslavia, but to the *Ustaša* themselves."[68]

From Jevtić to Stojadinović

The Marinković-Srškić-Uzunović group had enjoyed King Aleksandar's trust. But Prince Paul, the king's cousin, who now assumed the role of regent on behalf of the underage King Petar II (age 11 as of the end of 1934), found his political views better reflected in the thinking of Bogoljub Jevtić, then foreign minister. Within the government, there had been growing signs of distrust between the Marinković-Srškić-Uzunović group and Jevtić even before Marseilles, and there were rumors that Jevtić had pretensions to the prime minister's job. In mid-December 1934, after a factious session of the cabinet, Jevtić and D. Kojić submitted their resignations. Prime Minister Uzunović did not consider it necessary to dismiss the entire cabinet, let alone to call new elections. But Prince Paul had a different opinion and demanded that the entire government resign. Once Uzunović had resigned, Prince Paul asked Jevtić to form the next government. This signified the end of the political careers of Marinković, Srškić, and Uzunović, as well as most of the other members of the outgoing cabinet. One of the first acts of the Jevtić government (taken within its first week in office) was to grant amnesty to Maček and release him from prison. In Croatia, Maček was given an ecstatic welcome.[69]

During the days following Uzunović's forced resignation, Prince Paul and Jevtić held consultations with a number of figures from the opposition, as well as with personalities who had been playing roles in the government. Jevtić wanted to reach agreements with the Radicals (of the executive committee), with Korošec, and with Spaho, and indicated that parliamentary elections would be announced shortly. But Jevtić was unable to reach an agreement with any of these political actors. When he announced his cabinet, it included only three persons carried over from the outgoing government: Jevtić himself, as prime minister and foreign minister; Petar Živković, as minister of the army and navy; and D. Kojić, as minister of justice. All the others were "new" and included, among others, Milan Stojadinović, a member of the Radical Party leadership associated with the executive committee, as minister of finance, and

Dragutin Janković, formerly of the Agrarian Union, as minister of agriculture. Jevtić's cabinet also included three Croats: M. Vrbanić, M. Kožulj, and Lj. Auer. Elections were scheduled for 5 May 1935.

The elections of 1935 marked a turning point in interwar Yugoslav history, insofar as the HSS now found itself in a broadly based coalition with the Democrats, the Agrarians, and the JMO. This broad coalition put up a list called the "United Opposition list," headed by Maček. The Radicals and the SLS stayed out of the coalition, preferring to keep channels open with Jevtić, though the SLS eventually decided to boycott the elections. Jevtić, following the tradition established in Belgrade, ran a dirty campaign, using the organs of power to harass the opposition and used the press and radio to attack and run down the leadership of the United Opposition; needless to say, the opposition was not afforded the opportunity to reply in the state-controlled media.[70] But Maček's followers were also reported to be resorting to illegal methods to maximize their votes. In Slavonska Požega, Maček's sympathizers were reported to have attacked six peasants who favored Jevtić's list.[71] There were also physical attacks on candidates on Jevtić's list, e.g., Dr. Nikola Badovinac of Ribnik (on 19 March 1935).[72] In Vukovar, the terror carried out by Maček's adherents reached a high level of intensity, and some locals were allegedly afraid to vote against Maček.[73] The terror reached its crescendo on election day, and in some districts, the terror continued even after the elections.[74]

Many Croatian peasants became convinced during the campaign that once the elections were behind them, Croatia would become independent.[75] In some localities, people spoke openly how, after 5 May, Maček would "assume full power in a free Croatia" and change the entire bureaucratic apparatus, alleging further that Croatia would be placed under international protection, while it prepared for full independence.[76] Rumors also circulated that, after the elections, the Third Reich and the English (!) would come to Maček's assistance so that he might set up an independent Croatia, which would then enter into friendly relations with Hungary. Other rumors were circulated to the effect that all of Serbia supported Maček, and even that the Serbs would recognize Maček's "right" to set up an independent Croatia.[77]

Of the 3,908,313 registered voters, some 2,880,964 (or 73.7%) actually voted. The official results assigned 1,746,982 votes (60.6%) to Jevtić's list, 1,076,345 votes (37.4%) to the opposition list headed by Vlatko Maček, 33,549 votes (1.16%) to a maverick list headed by Božidar Maksimović, and 24,088 votes (0.84%) to a list headed by Serbian fascist Dimitrije Ljotić. But under the provisions of the election law of 24 March 1933, the government list was awarded 40% of the mandates immediately, even before the tally of the votes, with the remaining seats to be allocated according to the vote.[78] Thus, in the final tally, of the 370 seats in the Assembly, 303 were awarded to Jevtić's list, and 67 were awarded to Maček's list. But although there had been violations on both sides, foreign observers concluded that, on balance, the published results probably underestimated the actual votes won by the opposition. The fact that, in many localities in Croatia, the authorities actually arrested the election monitors contributed to this general impression.[79] In disgust, the SDK (HSS and SDS) decided to boycott the Assembly; subsequently, the Democrats and Agrarians agreed to join the SDK in its boycott. A joint declaration dated 30 May 1935, signed by Davidović, J. Jovanović, Maček, and V. Vilder (on behalf of Pribićević), charged electoral fraud and characterized Jevtić's government as "a continuation of the erstwhile dictatorial regime."[80] It was, thus, quite apparent that the Jevtić government would lack credibility and in consequence, Prince Paul decided to ask Jevtić to resign. He considered two potential candidates: Petar Živković, who had already served as prime minister, and Milan Stojadinović, the capable and ambitious minister of finance. The nod finally went to Stojadinović, who put together a coalition with Korošec and Spaho on 25 June 1935.

The Struggle for the Concordat

King Aleksandar had aspired to regulate not only the political life of the country but also its religious life. His incorporation of the Montenegrin Orthodox Church into the regular structures of the Serbian patriarchate in 1920 was one manifestation of this aspiration. The king's revocation, in 1930, of the statute for the autonomous administration of Islamic religious and vakuf-mearif affairs for Bosnia-Herzegovina, which had been issued during the era of Habsburg rule (1909), was another. In the latter case, the king even ordered the Reis-ul-ulema to move his seat from Sarajevo to Belgrade. The sitting reis-ul-ulema refused and resigned in protest, allowing the king to appoint Ibrahim Maglajlić, a pro-regime Muslim politician, to fill the vacancy.[81]

The Catholic Church was, however, harder to bring under regime influence and control. So, failing to exert influence, the regime opted for a strategy of trying to erode its influence. Accordingly, the regime supported Orthodox proselytization in Catholic areas, used the press to attack the Vatican for being pro-fascist (at a time when the Belgrade regime was taking on various characteristics of fascism itself), and even endeavored to promote the Old Catholic Church, a rival Church body which had arisen when a number of Catholics refused to accept the proclamation of the doctrine of papal infallibility at the First Vatican Council, in hopes of eroding Roman Catholic strength.[82] Confessional discrimination was also reflected in the allocations of subsidies from the budget of the Ministry of Faiths. Although Catholics accounted for 39.3% of the kingdom's population in 1921, with Orthodox believers accounting for 46.7%,[83] the Ministry of Faiths allocated (in its 1921 budget) 141,246,426 K. for the Orthodox against a paltry 10,903,993 for the Catholic Church. The figures remained about the same in 1922: 161,601,026 K. for the Orthodox Church, 13,855,268 K. for the Catholic Church. In spite of a partial correction in subsequent years, the imbalance and discrimination continued (e.g., in 1923–1924: 45,057,037 dinars for the Orthodox Church, 18,015,769 for the Catholic Church).[84]

Educational policy in the 1920s and 1930s was driven by the objective of making Serbdom the cultural core of all of Yugoslav society; accordingly, schoolbooks played up Serbian monasteries in Dalmatia, while brazenly ignoring the historic role played by Catholic monasteries in Croatia and Dalmatia.[85] Ante Ciliga, at one time a major figure in the CPY, reflected on this dynamic much later. In his view,

What is least understood is that [in the interwar kingdom] war was being waged against the Catholic Church and in favor of the Serb Orthodox Church at the same time. The Catholic Church accepted loyally the new state, departing from its universalistic idea in the hope of assuring the rapprochement of the two Christian Churches. The Orthodox Church, unfortunately, followed the opposite path, desiring [to use] the new State as a point of departure "to create first a national Catholic Church," that is, separated from the Roman Pontiff, in order in the second phase to unite it to the Orthodox Church. So it came to the singular fact that a state, where almost half of the population was Catholic, did not permit the construction of [a] Catholic Cathedral in Belgrade, as was said, "in order not to break the Orthodox appearance of the city."[86]

Strikingly, the official organ of the Serbian Orthodox Church wrote explicitly that what it wanted to achieve was "the victory of Serbian Orthodoxy" throughout the country.[87]

The Catholic Church fought back. In January 1933, for example, Archbishop Antun Bauer of Zagreb circulated a pastoral letter denouncing the regime; among the problems he cited were interference by the government to prevent clergy from teaching in the schools and anti-Catholic activities on the part of the Yugoslav "Falcons" (an athletic-patriotic organization). Later, in summer 1934, a new Croatian Union was established under the patronage of Bauer's co-adjutor and successor-designate, the young Alojzije Stepinac. With a starting capital of 40 million dinars and some 500 members, the organization promised to be, in the words of a police report, "a strong clerical peasant organization" which could be put to use for political purposes.[88]

But the torrent of abuse to which the Serbian Orthodox Church subjected the Catholic Church antedated these later developments. As early as 1931, *Vesnik srpske crkve,* the official organ of the Orthodox Priests' Association, charged that

The Catholic Church is an inquisitorial organization. Every century of the development of the western Church is but one character in the abominable inscription, *ferro igneque*—with sword and fire. The sorrowful inscription is not to be found only in Dante's hell ["ye who enter, leave all hope behind"]. The Catholic Church watches the tribulations of the Russian Church with a perfidious kind of satanic sadism. She [the Catholic Church] is [the embodiment of] a Luciferian Latin spirit. The weird spirit of the Anti-Christ is embodied in her. Her interpretation of the Holy Gospel is mefistophelian. . . . She is full of apostasy, theomachy, and pornocracy. She is the hotbed of all revolutions, of all atheist movements. Atheism, communism, and every kind of impiety are more respectable than Catholicism.[89]

Or again, *Glasnik,* the official organ of the Serbian Orthodox patriarchate in Belgrade, in a 1932 issue, wrote:

The Roman Catholic Church threatens the sovereignty of our state and because of that it is necessary to call for self-defense. The Roman Catholic Church, and thus also Roman Catholics, threaten the peaceful development of the citizens of our state, and protection against them is therefore necessary.[90]

The point, as *Glasnik* noted, was that all Catholics should "liberate themselves from Roman parasitism."[91] In fact, under the constant pressure, some Catholics did convert to Orthodoxy, with the result that, in the years 1921–1931, the proportion of Catholics declined from 39.3% to 37.4% while that of the Orthodox increased from 46.7% to 48.7%.[92] According to Rogošić, more than 100,000 Croatian Catholics converted to Orthodoxy in 1935 alone; Rogošić attributes that result to the various forms of pressure brought to bear on Catholics.[93]

From the Catholic viewpoint, the solution was to obtain a concordat with the state, guaranteeing the rights of the Catholic Church and of Catholics and providing some legal protection against the Orthodox Church. At the time of unification, the status of the Catholic Church was, at least formally, regulated by four separate concordats: that of 18 August 1855, signed with Emperor Franz Josef for Slovenia, Croatia, and Vojvodina; that of 8 July 1881, regulating the Church's status in Bosnia-Herzegovina; that of 18 August 1886, concluded between the Holy See and the Principality of Montenegro; and a fourth, signed on 24 April 1914, between the Holy See and the Kingdom of Serbia. But there were differences from one concordat to the other, and with the establishment of the kingdom, the Holy See considered it essential to sign a concordat with the new state authorities in order to assure a standard system throughout the country.

The Catholic Church's desire for a concordat never became a cause for the HSS. Radić himself was tenaciously opposed to the signing of any concordat with the Vatican, while Maček considered it a matter of indifference. For Dr. Korošec, however, the concordat was of vital interest, and Korošec devoted some of his energy to pressing for full freedom for the Catholic lay organization Catholic Action. But the issue became, in spite of the HSS's low level of interest, a major political controversy, reaching a climax during Stojadinović's prime ministership.

The negotiations concerning the concordat lasted very long, partly because neither side entirely trusted the other. A commission was formed already on 24 July 1922 to prepare a draft concordat, and initially, the commission included a significant number of Catholics. Then the Holy Synod of the Serbian Orthodox Church asked to have one of its own clergy named to the commission.[94] The first draft was finalized in 1923; a second draft followed in 1925; a third draft was ready by 1931; finally, the fourth draft was signed in Rome on 25 July 1935, a month after Stojadinović had become prime minister. The bill would become law only after it had been reviewed and approved by both houses of parliament.

Stojadinović knew from his contacts within the Orthodox hierarchy that there was considerable vacillation among the bishops in regard to the concordat; in fact, Patriarch Varnava allegedly saw nothing wrong with the concordat at first.[95] The Serbian Orthodox leadership subsequently spelled out its views on the subject, for the government's benefit, on two occasions: on 13 September 1935, when Patriarch Varnava visited Stojadinović, and on 5 December 1935, when the Holy Synod sent a memorandum to the prime minister. One of the provisions which particularly inflamed anti-concordat sentiment was the guarantee that the Catholic Church would enjoy complete freedom "to carry out its mission."[96] The concordat also provided that Catholic matrimony would be recognized under civil law.

The Holy Synod of the Serbian Orthodox Church was not the only source of opposition to the concordat. Dr. Ivan Ribar, a Roman Catholic, presented a highly critical report concerning the document at a session of the Juridical Chamber on 30 December 1936, commenting on the legal aspects of its provisions. Ribar's report was subsequently published in a law journal, but the Stojadinović government, which was backing the concordat, saw to it that the offending issue of the journal was banned. Ribar was, in fact, excommunicated from the Church because of his opposition to Catholic Action, which, he believed, would serve to strengthen fascist currents in Yugoslavia.[97] The public prosecutor in Zagreb banned Sima Simić's book *Jugoslavija i Vatikan,* while his counterpart in Belgrade banned Marko Cemović's brochure, *Konkordat izmedju Sv. Stolice i Kraljevine Jugoslavije.* These bans were a sure sign of the acrimony increasingly associated with the controversy, as well as of attendant political sensitivities. But of all the various brochures written against the concordat, none caused as much displeasure in Stojadinović's cabinet as *Primedbe i prigovori na projekt Konkordata,* published anonymously, which included what was purported to be the authentic text of the document together with a point by point critique of its provisions; the authorities established soon enough, however, that the author was Bishop Platon.[98] The controversy held up the legislative review of the bill implementing the concordat.

In November 1936, representatives of the Vatican paid a visit to Stojadinović to request that the bill be brought before the Assembly without further delay. Immediately following this meeting, Stojadinović submitted the concordat bill to the Assembly for its review. On 5 December 1936, Metropolitan Gavrilo Dozić of Montenegro-Primorje and Bishops Nikolaj Velimirović and Irinej Ćirić visited the prime minister to acquaint him with the Holy Synod's by now well-known views concerning the concordat.[99] The following month, a special session of the Holy Synod was convened in order to discuss the concordat. The Holy Synod alleged that under the concordat, the Catholic Church "would recover estates secularized in the eighteenth century or would be indemnified for their loss . . . , although the Orthodox Church, which suffered greater losses than the Roman Catholic Church, has no claim for compensation."[100] The Holy Synod also charged that Catholic Action, as an organization based on confessional affiliation, was contrary to the constitution of 1931. In response to the Holy Synod's charges that the measure was discriminatory, the government decided in early July 1937 to add a supplementary clause to the bill, extending to all other religious associations the same prerogatives and concessions which were being guaranteed to the Catholic Church.[101] This measure was intended to conciliate Serb Orthodox opinion. On 7 July, Prime Minister Stojadinović met with deputies of the Yugoslav Radical Community (JRZ) and members of the concordat commission to assure them that there was nothing in the bill which was prejudicial to the equality of the Orthodox Church.[102]

In the meantime, Patriarch Varnava had become seriously ill in early June and was confined to his bed. The patriarch's illness and the fate of the concordat became eerily intertwined, as Orthodox believers told themselves that he was dying because of the concordat. In mid-July, as tensions in Belgrade heated up, the parliamentary commission for the review of the concordat met and voted, 11 to 10, to accept the law and to recommend it to the Assembly.[103] On 19 July, there were fierce debates in the Assembly. Outside, Serb Orthodox believers tried to march through the city; the believers ignored police orders to disperse, and the authorities called for reinforcements. The believers marched for about a quarter of a mile when four trucks of police arrived. The police charged, using rubber truncheons and rifle butts, and knocked the bishop of Šabac senseless.[104] While this was happening outside, an opposition deputy rushed into the Assembly, shouting, "The police are killing people in the streets!"[105] These words provoked general chaos and fistfights in the Assembly, between government deputies and opposition deputies. Later that evening, a carload of priests drove through the town, the sacerdotal passengers shouting, "The police have killed our Bishop!"[106] Meanwhile, after the violent incidents of that day, the city government of Belgrade banned all public meetings and processions until 1 August 1937. In spite of the ban, noisy demonstrations continued in Belgrade through the night.

On the following day, Orthodox churches throughout Yugoslavia hung out black flags, to protest what the patriarchate was increasingly choosing to construe as an assault on Orthodox belief. In this atmosphere, the Assembly session scheduled for 20 July was postponed until 8 A.M. on 21 July. When the Assembly reconvened, Kosta Kumanudi (JNS) warned that the concordat would release the Catholic Church from any form of state supervision, grant Catholic priests privileges, allow the Catholic Church to build an "unlimited" number of schools and seminaries, and render the Catholic Church in Yugoslavia legally independent.[107] On 23 July, the Assembly passed the concordat bill by a vote of 167 to 127, in spite of ecclesiastical threats to excommunicate any deputy voting for the bill. But instead of forwarding the bill to the Senate, Stojadinović announced that he would delay the legislative process in order to try to mend fences with the Serbian Orthodox Church.[108] This announcement unleashed pandemonium in the Assembly, with opponents cheering the news and supporters shouting loud curses. That same night, Patriarch Varnava passed away.

The Serbian Orthodox Church now excommunicated all the ministers who had supported the concordat, except for the minister of the army and navy,[109] along with all the deputies who voted for the measure. Within a matter of days, one deputy discovered that this meant that he could not obtain a Church wedding for his daughter. Only in October did the locum tenens, Patriarch Dositej, begin the process of rehabilitating the "delinquent" ministers and deputies.[110] On 28 January 1938, the Holy Synod wrote to Stojadinović to seek assurance that the concordat had been "definitively removed" from the Senate's agenda. In a letter of reply dated 1 February, Stojadinović noted that he had removed from office certain ministers to whom the Holy Synod most strenuously objected. The Holy Synod in reply demanded that persons removed from office because of opposition to the concordat be restored to their positions, that indemnities be paid to them and their families, that fines levied against individual priests and believers in connection with the disturbances in front of the synodal church be reimbursed, and that all police and judicial procedures against the Serbian Church be terminated immediately. With small modifications, the Stojadinović government accepted all of these conditions.[111]

With this, the Serbian Orthodox Church had triumphed over the government. The Church had defeated any prospect of the government establishing confessional equality. It had promoted intolerance against the Catholic Church and used the threat and execution of excommunication to impose its agenda. As Stella Alexander writes, after the collapse of the concordat bill, "it was now clear to [the country's Catholic bishops] . . . that the government lacked the power to ensure real equality, either theoretically or in practice, between the two religious confessions."[112] The Catholic Church now felt deeply estranged from the Kingdom of Yugoslavia, which it viewed, for good reason, as the agency of a hostile Orthodox Church. This should be kept in mind in assessing the initial reaction of Archbishop Stepinac in 1941 to the proclamation of a Croatian state independent of Belgrade.

Serbian Plans for Kosovo

The same chauvinism which manifested itself in the confessional sphere, in the Serbian Church's war against the concordat, was also manifested in the sphere of inter-ethnic relations. The most extreme case of ethnic chauvinism in interwar Yugoslavia was, without a doubt, the attitude and policies of the Belgrade politicians vis-à-vis the Albanians of Kosovo. Some of this had to do with associations with the 14th-century Serbian Kingdom of Tsar Dušan the Mighty, of which Kosovo had constituted a central part; but the "Greater Serbian" project articulated by Ilija Garašanin, Vuk Stefanović Karadžić, Vladimir Karić, and others, and embraced by Nikola Pašić and, for that matter, King Aleksandar, was the more immediate and more powerful influence here. The memories of the sufferings experienced at the hands of Albanians in the years after 1878 and again during World War One reinforced Serb attitudes by contributing a sense of resentment and self-righteousness.

The underlying notion was twofold: first, that the Kingdom was a kingdom of and for Slavs, and that the Albanians were therefore unwelcome guests; and second, that Serbian history and culture should provide the "core" around which a new "Yugoslav" identity would be constructed. The notion that Albanian heroes and traditions could somehow be assimilated into this Serbian "core" was inconceivable to Serb and Albanian alike.

The main axle of Belgrade's policy wagon was the "land reform" in Kosovo, which would, in Belgrade's plans, remove "unwanted" Albanians and replace them with Serbs and Montenegrins. Already in the first years after World War One, the government undertook to reward Serbian and Montenegrin volunteers in war by assigning them parcels of land, without payment to the land's previous owners, in Vojvodina, Kosovo, and Macedonia; these were three to five hectares in size and were awarded as a sign of "state and national recognition."[113] These areas were targeted because they had significant Hungarian, Albanian, and Bulgarian irredenta, and Belgrade wanted to dilute the non-Serb communities in these lands. In the years 1918–1941, about 45,000 Albanians fled the country, as a result of Serb pressure, their places being taken by about 60,000 Serbs.[114] According to Ivo Banac, the authorities confiscated 154,287 acres of land from the Albanians by the end of 1940, making 57,704 acres available to Slav "colonists."[115] The Radical Party organized terrorist groups to rough up the Albanians and convince them that there was no life for them in Serbia. Belgrade authorities hoped that the harsh conditions they created for the Albanians would induce many of them to leave; some did so, usually taking refuge in Turkey.

The government scarcely needed Professor Vaso Čubrilović's frenetic memorandum calling for "brute force" against the Albanians[116] to remain committed to the goal of expelling the Albanians. On 11 July 1938, Belgrade signed an accord with Ankara, under which the Turkish government agreed to take in 40,000 Albanian families (roughly 200,000 Albanians) during the years 1939–1944.[117] Some Albanians were, in fact, deported to Turkey, where the authorities settled them primarily in the interior of the country; others ended up in Albania or in Arab countries. But budgetary problems together with the outbreak of war at the end of 1939 resulted in this program never being carried to fruition. Still, according to official Yugoslav government figures, 19,279 Albanians were settled in Turkey during the years 1927–1939, with an additional 4,322 being moved to Albania.[118] The remaining roughly 20,000 Albanians fleeing Kosovo went to other destinations.

Croatian Resistance, October 1934–February 1939

Milan Stojadinović took office as prime minister in June 1935, remaining in office until 4 February 1939. He was, by a wide margin, interwar Yugoslavia's longest-serving prime minister. Upon taking office, Stojadinović enjoyed an enviable reputation as an efficient economic manager, an opponent of authoritarianism, and a supporter of parliamentarism. Indeed, after he took office, the political atmosphere *did* become freer in some ways, and the press was a major beneficiary of this new climate. Stojadinović was also regarded as impressed with the importance of finding a solution to Croatian discontent. Indeed, in an early address to the Assembly on 1 July 1935, Stojadinvić declared, "I believe that in the entire country we shall create such an atmosphere of mutual trust, in which it will be nonetheless easier to resolve the Croatian question, which today looks so difficult."[119] Time would show that these exquisite phrases were only political prattle.

Meanwhile, in December 1934—in a dangerous development—three Serb fascist groupings merged under the name "Zbor" (the Gathering), electing Dimitrije Ljotić, a religious ultra-conservative and anti-Semite,[120] as its president. Ljotić, a member of the patriarchal council of the Serbian Orthodox Church and a friend of Bishop Velimirović, had urged the king in June 1931 to restructure the Yugoslav political system on the Italian fascist model[121]—a proposal which the King had rejected—but Ljotić remained committed to fascist ideas. At the same time, police continued to harass Croatian peasants.

As early as 1932–1933, adherents of the HSS had set up illegal paramilitary organizations in Donja Stubica, Čazma, Garešnica, and Koprivnica. Subsequently, in spring 1935, even before the 5 May elections, the HSS leadership took remedial action to respond to Chetnik and police harassments, setting up certain illegal self-defense organizations in the Zagreb district.[122] HSS members also began to set up branches of these organizations in other large towns in the Sava banovina.[123] The atmosphere in the Croatian countryside was increasingly tense; in September 1935, for example, the Ministry of Internal Affairs in Belgrade advised authorities in Sava banovina that it was aware that "sundry false and alarming" rumors were spreading across Croatian villages.[124] The aforementioned self-defense organizations presaged the creation in early 1936, on Maček's instructions, of a more formal organization called Croatian Peasant Defense (HSZ[125]). Based in the villages, the HSZ consisted of military formations and engaged in military drills and exercises. The authorities viewed the HSZ as the embryo for the construction of a Croatian army which, with the help of Croatian émigrés, could bring about Croatia's secession; HSS representatives admitted the existence of the Croatian Peasant Defense but insisted that its purpose was limited to self-defense against Chetniks and communists.[126] Later that year, a second illegal organization, Peasant Economic Unity (SGS[127]), was established in the Croatian area; local authorities had the same fears about the SGS's purposes as they had about the HSZ.[128]

In fact, there is some evidence that Maček's followers expected a solution of the Croatian question very soon, and that such a solution would take the form of Croatian independence.[129] Indeed, in the village of Bistričko Podgorje in the county of Marija Bistrica, peasants set up what they called the "Croatian Army" (*Hrvatska vojska*) in June 1936; they justified this step by claiming that "you cannot get anywhere with the Serbs."[130] Similarly, in Vrapče, a "Croatian People's Army" (*Hrvatska narodna vojska*) was organized about the same time, registering 60 members aged 25–40.[131]

The main assignment of the HSZ in the short term was, in fact, to protect the villages from the Chetniks, other anti-Croat paramilitary formations, and, allegedly, the communists. The HSZ was especially concerned to prevent arson, the poisoning of water in the wells, and other similar actions.[132] In spite of the return of some *Ustaše* to Croatia, after their post-Marseilles expulsion from Italy, in HSZ military exercises conducted in more than a dozen villages across Pregrada county over a three-day period beginning on 30 October 1937, participants sang songs identifying themselves as "Maček's guard," not Pavelić's![133] In fact, the HSZ was not merely designed to defend the peasants, it was also designed to shore up and reinforce Maček's authority in the countryside, where it was increasingly being challenged by Pavelić. Indeed, by late 1937, the growing rivalry between Maček and Pavelić was reflected ever more clearly at the grassroots level, where Pavelić and his collaborators maintained a presence and endeavored to set up *Ustaša* branches, contrary to the wishes of Maček and his confidants.[134]

In some places (e.g., Sisak county), pressure by state authorities, including legal sanctions against local HSZ functionaries, resulted in a complete stagnation in the local organization, with some chapters going into decline.[135] But in spite of some successes in this regard, the regime ultimately failed in its effort to undermine the organization, which continued to spread. The HSZ had some success in obtaining weaponry, and by late 1938, Maček's office included a department for military affairs (*odeljenje za vojne poslove*). HSZ forces had even obtained uniforms, by then, including caps with the Croatian coat of arms. Maček was, however, playing a double game, prepared to settle issues diplomatically if possible, militarily if necessary. His flexibility extended even to his choice of foreign partners. Indeed, *Hrvatski list*, an émigré Croatian periodical published in South America, carried a statement attributed to Maček in its 23 March 1939 issue—that is, several months *before* Maček reached his historic agreement with Cvetković—to the effect that the Croats had to obtain self-rule and that it was a matter of indifference whether this goal was achieved with the help of Western democracies or with the assistance of the Third Reich.[136]

Stojadinović–Mussolini–Hitler

Stojadinović, like other heads of government in Central and Eastern Europe at the time, found himself faced with three rival poles: the Anglo-French pole, the Third Reich, and Stalinist Russia. Fascist Italy gained importance in Stojadinović's calculations because of its proximity to the Kingdom. In fact, in November 1932—some two and a half years before Stojadinović would become prime minister—Mussolini had come close to invading Yugoslavia and setting up the

Ustaša in control of a satellite Croatia. He had even started to amass troops on the border. But Yugoslav intelligence operatives learned of these plans, and King Aleksandar warned Mussolini that if Italian forces attacked, he would take the question before the League of Nations.[137] Although Mussolini backed off, he kept the *Ustaša* in reserve. Things changed after the assassination of the king, as already noted; but with the accession of Stojadinović to the leadership post in Belgrade, relations with Rome became positively comradely. Count Galeazzo Ciano was very impressed with Stojadinović and recorded in his diary, "Stojadinović is a fascist. If he is not entirely open about it, he is nonetheless a fascist in his concept of the authority of the party, [and] he is certainly so with regard to his conception of the authority of the state and with regard to life [in general]."[138] And there were at least some of the trappings of fascism: fascist-style uniforms with green shirts, speeches interrupted by crowds chanting, "Leader, Leader!"

But Stojadinović also offered substance. When fascist Italy attacked Abyssinia in 1935 and Emperor Haile Selassie brought his case to the League of Nations, the League imposed economic sanctions. Stojadinović then saw to it that Yugoslavia supplied Italy with goods covered by the sanctions. Again, when civil war broke out in Spain in 1936, with Germany and Italy backing the fascist insurrection led by General Francisco Franco, Stojadinović supported the fascist side and even ordered his police to arrest persons thought to be attempting to exit the country for purposes of fighting on the side of the republic. And again, when German troops marched into Austria in March 1938, Stojadinović treated it as a routine matter. Later, when Czechoslovak president Eduard Beneš came to Belgrade to seek the support of Prince Paul and Stojadinović in the face of pressures from the Third Reich, the Yugoslavs kept their Czechoslovak guest at arm's length.[139]

Economically, Yugoslavia was also drifting into the arms of Germany and Italy. Yugoslavia was becoming steadily more dependent on Germany for both imports and export markets. In fact, Belgrade was eager for alternatives, and on several occasions, the Yugoslavs approached the British and asked for an increase in trade with Britain in order to reduce the country's growing dependence on the German market. But the Yugoslavs were consistently rebuffed by the British. Nazi Germany used a system of "clearing accounts" to develop trade, in essence a kind of semi-barter system in which credits were transferred back and forth in "payment" for goods shipped. This system of "clearing accounts" was the key to Germany's sudden and dramatic economic recovery under the Nazis; but the Central and East European states also benefited. But Germany frequently took goods purchased through "clearing accounts" and resold them for hard currency, often undercutting the world price. This practice resulted in Yugoslavia's losing non-German markets, reinforcing and deepening Yugoslavia's dependence on its German trade connection.[140]

In 1936, Stojadinović's government persuaded the British to increase their purchases of Yugoslav goods, but the amount of increase was not enough to make a significant difference. The following year brought the trade pact with Italy (and Italy's agreement to cut off all assistance to the *Ustaša*). In October 1938, Walter Funk, the *Reichsminister* for economic affairs, came to Belgrade to offer that Germany could purchase 50% of Yugoslavia's exports and assist in developing ore extraction. The Yugoslavs refused. Konstantin Baron von Neurath renewed the offer later in the year, but again the Yugoslavs refused. But when Belgrade once more contacted Whitehall to ask for a boost in Anglo-Yugoslav trade, the British government again declined, since it would have entailed the provision of government subsidies which the British government felt it could not afford.[141] Yugoslavia was sliding, in spite of itself, into the Axis embrace.

For the Croats, this reorientation on the part of the Belgrade government was of the essence. If Belgrade tied its interests to Germany and Italy, then the Croats should, of necessity, look to England and France for support—an unlikely strategy given the sentimental affection which the latter two states felt for "plucky Serbia" after its performance during the Great War. But if, on the other hand, Belgrade were to reorient itself in an alliance with Britain and France, then the Croats could look to Germany and Italy, more natural partners for secession given their shared revisionism.

The Fall of Stojadinović and the Cvetković-Maček "Sporazum"

The elections of 11 December 1938 were called by Stojadinović at the insistence of Prince Paul, before the Assembly had reached the end of its four-year mandate. As before, there was a United Opposition list headed by Maček, but this time Maček's list enjoyed even broader support than previously. Of the 4,080,286 eligible voters (in a total population of 13,934,038), 3,039,041 persons actually voted, or 74.48% of those eligible to do so. Stojadinović's list was said to have obtained 1,643,783 votes (54.09%) vs. 1,364,524 votes for Maček's list (44.9%) and 30,734 votes (1.01%) for Ljotić's list. Under the electoral rules which, as already mentioned, assigned some 40% of the seats to the government list in advance, the government list was awarded 306 seats out of a total of 373; the remaining 67 seats went to the United Opposition. Thus, for example, in Primorje, even though Maček's list attracted 78.80% of the vote, the opposition was awarded only 10 seats in the Assembly; Stojadinović's list, which had won a mere 20.06% of the vote, was awarded 14 seats representing Primorje. This pattern was repeated in variations throughout the country. In Drina banovina, the opposition won more than 40% of the vote but was awarded 13% of the seats; in Sava banovina, the opposition garnered 82.57% of the vote, but was granted 31 out of the 76 seats representing that province, or 40.79% of the seats; in Vrbas, the opposition took 49% of the vote and received 23% of the seats; in Drava banovina, the opposition list attracted more than 20% of the vote but all 29 seats representing Drava were assigned to Stojadinović's list.[142]

Stojadinović appreciated that the overwhelming vote for the opposition in Primorje and Sava reflected deep and widespread discontent with the regime in those regions. Thus, soon after the elections, the reelected prime minister called a meeting of Serb ministers in his government (including Milan Ačimović) to develop a strategy to counter Maček's all-too-evident strength.[143] Stojadinović also resented the fact that Korošec's SLS had so totally outstripped the government party (the JRZ) in Slovenia and plotted to exact Korošec's resignation from the cabinet. But Stojadinović, aware that Korošec had the prince's ear, blundered. He calculated that having the wily Slovene appointed president of the Senate would remove him from an effective policy-making position, but he failed to appreciate the importance of the role played by the president of the Senate in advising the prince.[144] Stojadinović would soon regret having unnecessarily alienated Korošec.

Meanwhile, there was a general understanding that a resolution of what had come to be called "the Croatian question" was long overdue. Already in the first days after the elections, two cabinet ministers from Croatia, Marko Kožul and Mile Miškulin, proposed that the constitution be revised with an eye to resolving this issue. The prince himself assigned the highest priority to this question but was aware that Maček was demanding Stojadinović's removal as a precondition for any negotiations.[145] Then, on 3 February 1939, Bogoljub Kujundžić, minister of forests and mines, gave a speech in the parliament, boasting that the Serbs were "superior" to Croats and Slovenes and casting aspersions on the Croats in general and on the HSS in particular.[146] That same night, at the urging of Korošec, five cabinet ministers resigned; Prince Paul refused to allow Stojadinović to appoint a new cabinet, bringing about Stojadinović's fall. The prime ministership was now entrusted to Dragiša Cvetković (Radical), erstwhile minister of social policy and public health in the Korošec government of 1928 and also minister in both Stojadinović cabinets. Cvetković was convinced that only direct negotiations with the HSS could bring a satisfactory resolution of "the Croatian question."

The first Cvetković government lasted from 5 February to 26 August 1939. Cvetković's highest priority was to reach an agreement with the HSS, and to that end, he undertook negotiations with the Croatian leader soon after taking office. Maček, however, was keeping his options open and, even while conducting direct negotiations with Cvetković, was carrying on discussions with the Italian government, through intermediaries.[147] First, a mysterious gentleman named Count Josip Bombelles turned up in Rome, introducing himself as an envoy from Maček and alluding to the "impossibility" that any accord with the Serbs might be reached; he seemed receptive to the suggestion by Galeazzo Ciano, Italy's foreign minister, that Croatia be separated from Belgrade and linked to Italy through a personal (dynastic) union. Less than two weeks later (on 20 March 1939), Amadeo Carnelutti, an Italian from Croatia and member of the HSS, arrived in Rome and contacted the Italian foreign minister. Carnelutti spoke of the possibility of an uprising by Croats within six months, in which case they would look to Italy for assistance. Carnelutti took it for granted that this would result in a "personal union" joining Croatia and Italy.[148]

As Maček and Cvetković began their talks, Maček pressed for the reorganization of the country on a federal basis, with seven federal units: (1) Slovenia, (2) Croatia, (3) Dalmatia, (4) Bosnia-Herzegovina, (5) Serbia (including Kosovo), (6) Vojvodina, and (7) Macedonia and Montenegro.[149] But this was more than Cvetković was prepared to accept. As a fallback position, however, Maček was prepared to settle, for the interim, for a dualist formula, on the model of Austria-Hungary. It was on the basis of this compromise that, in the course of meetings held 2–4 April 1939, Maček and Cvetković came to an agreement. The basic idea was to join the banovinas of Sava and Primorje, to form a new banovina of Croatia, adding to it some territory from other banovinas. There were some disputes about the Bosanska krajina and parts of Srijem, but it was decided to resolve these disagreements by holding plebiscites in the disputed areas. The text of their *sporazum* (agreement) was confirmed on 27 April 1939. But the prince vetoed the agreement, maintaining that the notion of holding plebiscites was problematic. Matković speculates that this may have been merely an excuse and that, more likely, the general staff may have objected to the notion that one of the banovinas would come to enjoy a special status in Yugoslavia.[150] It is also well known that many Serbian politicians, both in the JRZ and in the opposition parties, were opposed to any enhancement of Croatia's position. With the prince's veto, the Cvetković-Maček talks were adjourned.

Maček now resumed contacts with Italian foreign minister Ciano, who, in his diary, records that Maček was prepared to cede territory to Italy and accept a joint foreign ministry and joint ministry of war with Rome in exchange for Italian support for this truncated independence for Croatia. On 26 May 1939, Carnelutti met with Ciano again and told the Italian foreign minister that Maček was prepared to commit himself to preparing an uprising within four to six weeks.[151] (Presumably, Maček considered the HSZ adequate to the task of staging an uprising.) But Maček declined to sign the transcript of these talks and, shortly thereafter, resumed his talks with Cvetković. The two men met in mid-July and again in mid-August, drawing up a revised text, in which there would no longer be any call for plebiscites. The prince received Maček and Cvetković in a private audience in Brdo kod Kranja on 24 August 1939, on which occasion the prince accepted the proposed text, with or without the assent of the general staff. Two days later, the *sporazum* was signed. Thereupon, Cvetković resigned, in order to create an opportunity to restructure the government; the prince once more asked Cvetković to form the government, and Maček now came in as deputy prime minister. The cabinet included five HSS ministers and one minister from the Independent Democrats:

Vlatko Maček (HSS), deputy prime minister
Juraj Šutej (HSS), minister of finance

Josip Torbar (HSS), minister of post and telegraph
Ivan Andres (HSS), minister of commerce and industry
Bariša Smoljan (HSS), minister without portfolio
Srdjan Budisavljević (SDS), minister of social policy.
General Milan Nedić became minister of the army and navy.

Under the ordinance concerning the Banovina of Croatia, the territory of the new banovina was said to consist of the territories previously constituting the banovinas of Sava and Primorje, together with the districts of Dubrovnik, Šid, Ilok, Brčko, Gradačac, Derventa, Travnik, and Fojnica; in comparison with Croatian boundaries in the Habsburg empire, this new Croatia lost part of Srijem as well as Boka Kotorska and the immediate area to the south of it, but added Medjimurje, Kastav, and portions of the historic province of Bosnia-Herzegovina (mostly those areas inhabited by Croats).[152] The ordinance also created the office of ban (governor) and entrusted the ban (Ivan Šubašić) and the Croatian Sabor (Assembly) with responsibilities in eleven policy spheres, for which corresponding ministries were established, including for internal affairs, education, judiciary, industry and trade, and finances. In the text of the *sporazum*, it was emphasized that the agreement was of a "temporary" nature, and the signatories seem to have thought in terms of using it as a first step toward the eventual federalization of the country.

Whether because it did not go far enough (taking into account also the interests of the country's other national groups) or because it came so late in the life of the Kingdom of Yugoslavia or because of the economically strained circumstances prevailing in Yugoslavia or because of the stresses induced by the war or because fundamental disagreements between different groups still existed or perhaps because of all of these things, the *sporazum* did not result in the spread of feelings of general contentment. Already at the time of its signing, the *sporazum* provoked sharp reactions from leaders of the Serbian opposition parties (the Radicals and the Democrats). The Democrats, now being led by Milan Grol, simultaneously condemned the agreement and demanded that the Serbs be granted their own banovina—in effect, that the principle of the *sporazum* be taken as the basis for a revised formula more favorable to Serbian interests. Within less than a year, some Serb politicians were demanding that the banovinas of Vrbas, Drina, Dunav, Morava, Zeta, and Vardar be combined to form a Serbian mega-banovina;[153] this banovina would have corresponded roughly to the present Republic of Serbia (including Kosovo and Vojvodina) together with Montenegro, Macedonia, and parts of Bosnia-Herzegovina. The Radical Party, restrained at first, later issued a pamphlet (in spring 1940) in which it claimed "that the *sporazum* threatened the interests of the entire country."[154] Stojadinović also came out against the *sporazum* and, together with some 80 deputies and 20 senators, established a new party, the Serbian Radical Party. Dragoljub Jovanović, unlike most other Serbs associated with the United Opposition, welcomed the *sporazum*, as the culmination of a long struggle on the part of Croats, but he noted, at the same time, that there remained a "Serbian question" which needed to be addressed.

The Slovenes, with their Drava banovina, were reasonably content with the situation. But Vojvodinan autonomists led by Dušan Bošković, a Pančevo attorney, remained unsatisfied; in Bosnia-Herzegovina, the Bosniak public was shocked by the agreement, and there were many public meetings held in various parts of Bosnia-Herzegovina in which, among other things, the necessity of organizing the Bosniak community was stressed. On 24 November 1939, for example, a meeting of representatives of various social, political, and religious institutions was held in Sarajevo, demanding the establishment of an "autonomous unit of Bosnia-Herzegovina within its historic borders."[155] The JMO leadership was angered that it had not been included in the Maček-Cvetković talks, and Džafer Kulenović (1891–1956), who took over as president of the JMO in June 1939, after the death of Spaho, soon identified himself with demands for the establishment of a banovina of Bosnia-Herzegovina. *Muslimanska svijest*, the organ of Gajret, the pro-Serb cultural association in Bosnia-Herzegovina, declared directly: "Our thesis is that the return of Bosnia-Herzegovina to its historic borders and the autonomy of these lands constitute a precondition for a just solution of the relations between Croats and Serbs."[156]

As early as October 1939, Orthodox and Muslims held a meeting in Banja Luka and discussed what steps needed to be taken in order to retrieve the land which had been transferred to the Banovina of Croatia. Indeed, Bosnian Serbs and Bosniaks alike were bitter about the *sporazum*. On 20 November, citizens in Tuzla formed an "action committee" to work for Bosnian autonomy and subsequently issued a brochure on the subject of autonomy. On 25 November, Muslims in Travnik held a public meeting and unanimously supported the resolution adopted the previous day in Sarajevo. Two further meetings held in Sarajevo at the end of the year, attended by Kulenović, served to launch the movement for Bosnian autonomy.[157] Even the Muslim branch[158] of the HSS, set up in 1936, supported Bosnian autonomy.

The *sporazum* also divided Croats, with the more nationalist-oriented Croats rejecting the agreement as a "capitulation." The *Ustaše* had been opposed to the entire notion of Maček's negotiating with the Serbs in the first place,[159] but raged against Maček's "sellout" of Croats, as they viewed the agreement. Anti-Serbian incidents proliferated across the Croatian banovina, while, in June 1940, a Croatian National-Socialist Party was established in Zagreb. The Cvetković-Maček government turned to repressive measures, taking a large number of communists into custody in mid-December 1939. Earlier that year, the coalition government had established several concentration camps—in Bileća, Kerestinec, and elsewhere.[160] Add to the foregoing expressions of discontent, the numerous demonstrations and protest meetings in autumn 1939—prompted by economic malaise and probably instigated by the communists—including one in Zagreb in which some 15,000 persons took part and a massive anti-regime demonstration in Belgrade in mid-December,[161] and one could diagnose the system as unstable and vulnerable.

The Crash

The First Yugoslavia was heading toward crash and breakup as a result of a combination of at least three factors: (1) widespread discontent among all peoples of the country, (2) the worsening international situation, in which Yugoslavia found itself torn between two warring blocs, and (3) the failure among the country's leading politicians to reach a consensus on a formula for the creation of a legitimate system. What the Cvetković-Maček government wanted most, where the war was concerned, was to be allowed to remain neutral. Within this context, Yugoslavia moved gradually closer to France in the period September 1939–May 1940. Prince Paul even tried to persuade the French of the importance of a preemptive Allied occupation of Salonika in order to keep the Italians out.[162] But in the early months of 1940, Mussolini became increasingly impatient to grab portions Dalmatia and Croatia, as well as some Adriatic islands, though, at this stage, he was restrained by Berlin, which, in March 1940, flatly ordered him to stay out of Yugoslavia. Meanwhile, that same month, as rumors of a combined Italian invasion and *Ustaša* uprising were in the air, the Yugoslav government instructed its ambassador to Turkey to approach the Soviet ambassador to Turkey and propose economic relations and also impress on Russia the danger of Italian expansionism. The Soviets were receptive, agreed with the Yugoslav assessment of Italy, and signed three economic agreements with the Yugoslavs on 11 May 1940. On 24 June 1940, Yugoslavia and the Soviet Union established diplomatic relations, and in the wake of this development, a military attaché was assigned to the Yugoslav embassy in Moscow.[163]

The Germans were not at all pleased about Yugoslav overtures to France and the Soviet Union and, in the course of November 1940, joined Italy in trying to lure Belgrade into signing the Tripartite Pact (as the Axis Pact linking Germany, Italy, and Japan was formally termed). In exchange for that, they promised to guarantee Yugoslavia's borders and even to assign Salonika and its hinterland to Belgrade's control. On 6 December 1940, Belgrade turned down a German request for about a thousand trucks to cross Yugoslav territory to reinforce the Italian troops in Albania. Meanwhile, Hungary and Romania had signed onto the Tripartite Pact in November, while Bulgaria did so (without conditions) on 1 March 1941. In preparation for an assault against Greece, German troops moved into Romania in the first week of January 1941 and into Bulgaria on 2 March. Prince Paul met with Hitler on the latter's request on 4 March, at which time the German führer pressured the prince to follow the example of his neighbors and join the Axis, again offering Salonika as a bait. Upon his return to Belgrade, Prince Paul called a meeting of the Crown Council (Cvetković, Maček, Foreign Minister Aleksandar Cincar-Marković, General Petar Pešić, co-regents

Radenko Stanković and Ivo Perović, and Fran Kulovec) and informed its members of Hitler's demand. Although those present had different points of view about the situation, they eventually agreed to sign the pact on three conditions: (1) that the sovereignty and territorial integrity of Yugoslavia be respected, (2) that Yugoslavia would not be obligated to provide military assistance to the Axis or to allow the Axis to transport troops and war materiel across its territory, and (3) that it be guaranteed the annexation of Salonika and its hinterland after the war.[164] After some hesitation in connection with the second condition, Hitler agreed to these conditions, the first and third of which he had already offered on his own initiative anyway. The Yugoslav government then agreed to sign the pact, though three ministers—Branko Čubrilović, Mihajlo Konstantinović, and Srdjan Budisavljević—resigned from the government in protest. Prince Paul was well aware of the widespread, though by no means universal, anti-Axis sentiment in the country and said that if he signed the pact, he would be overthrown or pushed out of the government within six months at the most.[165] Even so, he was prepared to sign the pact, in order to save the country from war.

The Yugoslavs signed the pact on 25 March in the Belvedere palace in Vienna. The next day, angry Yugoslavs marched through the streets of Belgrade shouting "Bolje grob nego rob, bolje rat nego pakt!" [Better the grave than to be a slave, better the war than the pact!] On 27 March 1941, at 2:15 A.M., a group of army officers led by Air Force general Bora Mirković overthrew the government, declared the still-underage King Petar II to be "of age," and put together a new government. The coup excited ephemeral jubilation in Belgrade. General Dušan Simović, also of the Air Force, took the post of prime minister and named Maček to serve as one of two deputy prime ministers, though without first consulting with the Croatian leader. The coup—executed at British instigation and involving British intelligence operatives—was apparently not well thought out and should probably be viewed largely as the expression of outrage at the accession to the Axis Pact, though Milazzo is not alone in thinking that Serbian opposition to the concessions made to the Croats via the *Sporazum* may have been a motivating factor, too.[166] Be that as it may, anti-Axis outrage did not translate into a policy reversal, and the new government immediately reassured Hitler that it intended to honor its "commitments" under the Axis Pact.[167]

Back in Berlin, the irascible Hitler was in no mood to listen to reassurances from Belgrade. The mere fact that the coup *seemed* in some way to have had an anti-Axis orientation was enough to change Hitler's plans. Hitler now decided to postpone his invasion of Russia, in order to teach the Yugoslavs a lesson. To Hitler's mind, the Yugoslav state should be demolished permanently; one of the keys to achieving that end was the establishment of an "independent" Croatia under Axis influence, more or less on the Slovak model. At the end of March and beginning of April, German agents in Zagreb made contact with Maček, who had not yet returned to Belgrade to join the Simović government. The Germans were impressed by Maček's widespread popularity among Croats, by his control of the HSZ paramilitary forces, and by the credibility he had won through his association with the Cvetković government; they tried to persuade Maček to proclaim Croatian independence and invite German troops to come to Croatia's assistance. In return, the Germans would recognize Maček as the head of the Croatian satellite government. Maček, however, refused to cooperate with the Germans and instead, on 3 April, left Zagreb for Belgrade to take up his duties as deputy prime minister, though he knew that the Simović government would be shortlived.[168]

On 6 April 1941, German and Italian troops crossed the Yugoslav borders; on the same day, the German *Luftwaffe* began a bombardment of Belgrade. Maček returned to Zagreb on 8 April, by which time the Germans had already decided to bring Pavelić out of cold storage and use him as their agent in Croatia. Maček issued an ambiguous and largely noncommittal statement, which has been widely misinterpreted, on 10 April—the day that German troops entered Zagreb —telling Croats,

the greatest possible misfortune that can occur to a nation has struck us—war. This evil can be mitigated only if we remain united and disciplined. . . . I shall remain among you and will share with you the good and the evil. . . . At this moment, I ask from you order and discipline, regardless of whether you are in the forces or at home.[169]

Two days later, the first German forces reached Belgrade. On 14 April, the Royal Yugoslav Army received orders to desist from further resistance. The king and his family fled to Greece; they later joined several of his ministers in London, where they set up a government-in-exile. On 17 April, General Danilo Kalafatović signed the act of surrender on behalf of the Yugoslav government and army. In the brief conflict, the Germans had taken about 350,000 Yugoslav soldiers prisoner; the Royal Yugoslav Army's arsenal also fell into German hands.[170]

With this, the first Yugoslavia came to an end. Neither its birth nor its death was the product of consensus, and neither the Vidovdan constitution nor the royal constitution of 1931 was ever accepted as legitimate by a sufficiently broad spectrum of the population to enable the system to stabilize itself. Meanwhile, as the HSS, JMO, and SLS increasingly became identified with the Croatian, Bosniak, and Slovene peoples, and with the Radical Party and Democratic Party permanently viewed as Serbian parties, interparty differences increasingly took on the character of inter-ethnic differences. In this way, system illegitimacy and dysfunctionality generated what came to be called "the national question," and resentments between ethnic groups, of which there was for all practical purposes no memory of any prior to 1878 and which had, in any event, been unremarkable even in the years 1878–1918 (except arguably in the case of Serb-Albanian frictions), had steadily intensified in depth and fury to the point where it was possible for Serbs and Croats alike to scandalize even the Nazis by their wartime excesses.

CHAPTER 4

World War Two and the Partisan Struggle, 1941–1945

T he Axis invasion resulted in the partition of Yugoslavia. Germany annexed Lower Styria and Upper Carniola (from Slovenia) outright, including the towns of Maribor and Bled, while Italy occupied Lower Carniola, including Ljubljana. Croatia, set up as a supposedly independent state, was augmented by the addition of Bosnia-Herzegovina but at the same time was compelled to cede portions of Dalmatia, along with some Adriatic islands, to Italy. Hungary received Bačka (western Vojvodina) and Baranja, while Bulgaria was allowed to occupy most of Vardar Macedonia. Italian-occupied Albania was augmented by the incorporation of Kosovo and the Albanian-inhabited areas of western Macedonia, and Italy also occupied Montenegro. German troops took direct control of the Banat (the area east of the Tisa River and north of the Danube, in the northeast corner of Yugoslavia); they also retained control in areas around Mitrovica (in Kosovo), including the rich Trepča mines, which the Germans valued for their iron ore.[1] What was left of the country was set up as a rump Serbian state, of which General Milan Nedić, the erstwhile minister of the army and navy, became prime minister in August 1941.

In conditions of the collapse of the Yugoslav state, armed groups appeared, for the most part formed by officers of the former Yugoslav Army. Later, the Partisan movement, led by Josip Broz Tito (1892–1980), was created on the initiative of the Communist Party of Yugoslavia. The communist-led Partisans understood their anti-Axis resistance to be inextricably connected with communist social revolution, while the Chetniks, who collaborated with the Italian fascists extensively and, on a more limited basis, also with the German occupation authorities, sought to realize a Serbian nationalist program which involved the removal of most non-Serbs from the lands to be included in the projected Greater Serbian state.[2]

Deportations and liquidations of Jews and Roma took place throughout occupied Yugoslavia. The Germans, acting on their notions of race, planned to deport up to 260,000 Slovenes from the portion of Slovenia which they occupied;[3] they were to move into areas of Croatia, from which a corresponding number of Serbs were to be expelled to Serbia. In fact, the number of Slovenes deported from the German occupation zone totaled "only" about 55,000.[4] An estimated 120,000 Serbs were deported from the Independent State of Croatia (NDH) to German-occupied Serbia, among them many priests, while, in addition, an estimated 300,000 Serbs fled from the NDH by 1943.[5] In addition, more than 300,000 Serbs were massacred by the Ustaše. In Kosovo, between 70,000 and 100,000 Serbs were either transferred to concentration camps in Priština and Mitrovica or expelled to Serbia, in order to effect the Albanianization of the province.[6] In Croatia, Kosovo, and Macedonia, local populations initially welcomed the new authorities, feeling that anything would be better than the chauvinism, corruption, administrative hegemonism, and exploitation which they had experienced at the hands of Serbian politicians during the interwar years. It was not long before the populations in all three areas recoiled at the excesses of the governing authorities and turned to the resistance.

Where legitimate government would be founded on a formula embracing rule of law, guarantees for individual rights, tolerance, respect for the harm principle, civic equality, and neutrality of the state in matters of religion, fascism promulgated a system based on the superiority of the leader over the law, collective rights, intolerance of designated "outgroups," the infliction of harm on members of designated "outgroups," and the glorification of violence, civic inequality based on racial (and, in the case of the NDH, also religious) grounds, and the manipulation of religion to serve the purposes of state. Fascism, in other words, must be understood as the rejection of the entire liberal project and as an illegitimate system par excellence.

Fascist Croatia

From time to time there have been efforts by Croatian nationalists either to whitewash the NDH or to construe the Serbian collaborationist state of World War Two as morally and functionally equivalent to the NDH. Both of these theses must be rejected. The NDH was not the functional equivalent of the Serbian collaborationist state because the Ustaše enjoyed tangibly more autonomy; for example, while the Croatian fascists operated the concentration camps within the NDH, the camps set up in occupied Serbia were operated by the Germans themselves. Nor were wartime Croatia and Serbia morally equivalent. Although innocent people were put to death in both places, the Ustaša movement was founded on the principles of racialism and intolerance, while the foremost principle inspiring the Nedić regime was the instinct for survival. It is not without significance that the eleventh principle of the Ustaša program, drawn up in 1933 and confirmed as an operational guide for the new state in April 1941, declared that "In state and national affairs in the Independent State of Croatia nobody can participate in political decision-making who is not by origin and blood a member of the Croatian nation."[7] Finally, any notion that the NDH could be seen as an embodiment of the Croatian desire for independence, as suggested by Franjo Tudjman, who would be elected president of Croatia in 1990, must be rejected as absurd, since fascism enslaves the societies in which it establishes its control, and slavery cannot be interpreted as "independence" nor even as the realization of a long struggle for a national state; on the contrary, fascism extinguishes hope and crushes the spirit. While occupied Serbia, with Milan Nedić as the head of government, certainly committed atrocities, the Ustaša authorities in the NDH were decidedly more brutal.

The establishment of the NDH was proclaimed in the afternoon of 10 April 1941 in a radio broadcast by Slavko Kvaternik, a week before the Yugoslav Army surrendered. Pavelić was in Rome at the time but arrived in Karlovac in the evening of 13 April, accompanied by about 250–400 Ustaše. In Karlovac, Pavelić met with SS regiment commander Edmund von Veesenmayer, who had been appointed by Reichs foreign minister Joachim von Ribbentrop to oversee the establishment of a separate Croatian state. Pavelić immediately assured the German envoy that he had no intention of pursuing an independent foreign policy, adding that the Croats were not Slavs at all, but Slavophone Germans![8] The plan had been for the Axis to extend diplomatic recognition to the NDH on 13 April, but this was delayed while Pavelić confirmed the territorial cessions to Italy upon which he had previously agreed. On 15 April 1941, Pavelić arrived in Zagreb; on the same day, Germany and Italy extended diplomatic recognition to the NDH, two days before the unconditional surrender of the Yugoslav Army. The lands ceded to Italy embraced 5,400 square kilometers with 380,000 inhabitants (consisting roughly of 280,000 Croats, 90,000 Serbs, 5,000 Italians, and 5,000 members of other nationalities[9]). Although the NDH authorities were permitted to annex Bosnia-Herzegovina, their desire to annex also the Sandžak of Novi Pazar ran aground as a result of Italian opposition, while Croatia consented, on 10 July, to the annexation of Medjimurje by Hungary. The population of the NDH was approximately 6 million and consisted of about 3 million Croats, almost 2 million Serbs, between 500,000 and 800,000 Bosnian Muslims, 140,000 *Volksdeutsche,* 70,000 Hungarians, 35–36,000 Jews, and about 150,000 members of other nationality groups (including Slovenes, Czechs, Slovaks, and Ukrainians).[10]

In the succeeding days, Ustaša groups around the country established control at the local level; in Split and Gospić, the Ustaše established their control as early as 10 April and, in the latter town, immediately commenced to arrest and terrorize local Serbs.[11] "There is no doubt," says Sundhaussen, "that the largest portion of the Croatian population (especially in the cities) welcomed the establishment of the state with enthusiasm or at least receptivity," at least initially.[12] Already by the end of April, members of the right wing of the Croatian Peasant Party (HSS) joined the Ustaša movement; the Croatian Peasant Defense (HSZ), the armed militia of the HSS, placed itself at the service of the new authorities and "performed important services at the time of the establishment of the new regime, through the protection of objects, the disarmament of units of the Yugoslav Army, etc."[13] At the beginning of June 1941, however, the Croatian Peasant Defense was disarmed and dissolved, evidently because the Ustaša leadership felt that they could not rely on the loyalty of these units. Maček's albeit ambiguous proclamation calling on Croats to obey the new authorities played a role in encouraging almost all village mayors to cooperate with the new regime; the majority of town councils as well as many party functionaries in local HSS organizations in the vicinity of Zagreb also made declarations of loyalty to the new Ustaša regime after 10 April. Indeed, Maček's passive attitude proved to be shortsighted, in that it contributed to the collapse of the Croatian Peasant Party as well as to the fact that Croats did not join the resistance in large numbers until 1942.

In the meantime, the Ustaše set up a government, with the following composition: Ante Pavelić, *Poglavnik;* Slavko Kvaternik, deputy *Poglavnik,* commander of the army, and minister of the Croatian National Guard; Osman Kulenović, vice president; Andrija Artuković, minister of internal affairs; Mile Budak, minister of religious affairs and education; Mladen Lorković, foreign minister; Mirko Puk, minister of justice; Ivan Petrić, minister of health; Lovro Sušić, minister of national economy; Ivica Frković, minister of forestry and mineral resources; and Milovan Žanić, minister of legislative commission. Džafer Kulenović, the erstwhile head of the JMO, later joined the government as vice premier. Other high-ranking ministers in the government included Eugen Kvaternik, Jozo Dumandžić, Ismet ef. Muftić, Marko Veršić, and Jure Vranešić.[14] The NDH passed restrictive racial legislation on 30 April, setting up its first concentration camp in Drnje on the grounds of the "Danica" factory about the same time.[15] Additional concentration camps were also set up at this time at Jadovno, Slano, and Metajna on the island of Pag, though these would be shut down in mid-August 1941. Other camps were set up at Kerestinec (in the vicinity of Zagreb), Lepoglava, Jastrebarsko (for the internment of children), Djakovo, Loborgrad, and elsewhere, as well as a camp at Tenje near Osijek, designated for the internment of Jews exclusively. The most ill-famed camps established by the NDH were those at Jasenovac and Stara Gradiška; between 50,000 and 100,000 persons were liquidated at Jasenovac alone.[16] Although, as already noted, there were concentration camps elsewhere in Croatia as well as in Serbia, "nowhere was the torture comparable to Jasenovac," according to Žerjavić.[17]

The Ustaše targeted Serbs, Jews, and Roma for liquidation. Budak has famously been quoted as having declared that the NDH would liquidate one-third of its Serbian population, expel another third, and Croatize the remaining third. Whether the quotation is historically accurate or not, it captures the spirit of Ustaša policy vis-à-vis the Serbs. As for the Jews, Artuković declared, just 11 days after the establishment of the NDH, that the government would "soon solve the Jewish question in the same way in which the German government has solved it."[18] By December 1941, the Ustaša regime had reduced the number of Jews from 35,000 to about 12,000, according to figures cited by Bilandžić.[19] Most Croatian Roma lost their lives at Jasenovac during 1941–1942.

On 4 May 1941, the regime established the Directorate of Public Order and Security as a department of the Ministry of the Interior. Eugen Kvaternik headed the directorate for its first 18 months. On 17 May, the regime issued a law on courts martial, laying a legal basis for punishing persons in unlawful possession of firearms. Pavelić set up two military organizations—the Ustaša Militia and the Bodyguard—which were operationally independent of the Ministry of War and responsible only to Pavelić. They were, accordingly, outside the law and immune to prosecution, much like the *oprichnina* of Russian tsar Ivan the Terrible.[20] On 4 June, the government barred Jews from participation in any social, sporting, or cultural organizations in Croatia.[21] A decree issued on 8 July granted the Ministry of Finance and the Ministry of Industry and Trade the authority to nationalize private banks when it was deemed to serve the national interest. In the meantime, following the examples set by Nazi Germany and Fascist Italy, the regime set up the Ustaša Youth Organization and the Ustaša Women's Organization.[22] The purpose of the latter organization was to encourage Croatian women to participate in charitable and social work and to educate them to be good mothers and housewives.[23] In January 1942, the Croatian state assembly (Sabor) was belatedly reestablished by order of Ante Pavelić, to be composed of all surviving deputies from the last Croatian Sabor of 1918, all surviving Croatian Peasant Party deputies to the Yugoslav Skupština elected in 1938, all surviving members of the Council of the former Croatian Party of Right elected in 1919, adjutants and commissions in the Main Ustaša House of the Croatian Ustaša liberation movement, and two representatives of the German national minority.[24]

Ustaša Ideology

The NDH tried to portray itself as an organic part of Croatian culture and history, rather than as representing and effecting a dramatic rupture with the past. Accordingly, the Ustaše tried to lay claim to the legacy of the Radić brothers, setting aside 11 June, the birthday of Ante Radić, as a special day of commemoration.[25] Even greater emphasis was placed on asserting the Ustaša movement's alleged compatibility with the views of Ante Starčević, with plans being drawn up to erect monuments to the renowned Croatian liberal in Zagreb and Banja Luka.[26] In so doing, the Ustaše falsified Starčević's legacy, denying that the 19th-century liberal had ever believed in human equality, ignoring his championing of women's equality, and endeavoring to portray him as an prototypical racist.[27] Similarly, Dr. Milan Šufflay (1879–1931) was recalled and celebrated; Croatia, Šufflay was reported to have said, had been "one of the strongest ramparts of Western civilization for many centuries" but had lost its connection with the West and even its humanity because of its union with Serbia during the years 1918–1941.[28]

The regime promoted "traditional" models of gender behavior: women were supposed to bear children and care for the men, while the men were supposed to display stereotypical "manly" virtues.[29] But women and men alike were expected to recognize that they had no rights save those recognized by the state since, as the regime news organ *Hrvatski narod* put it in 1942, "Neither the individual nor the group is comprehensible outside the framework of the state."[30] The party organ Ustaša amplified this, revealing the totalitarian spirit of the new system: "In the Ustaša Croatian state, which the Poglavnik and his ustaše set up, one must think Ustaša-style *[ustaški]*, speak Ustaša-style, and—what is most important—work Ustaša-style. In other words, all of life in the Independent State of Croatia must have Ustaša content."[31] Not surprisingly, the regime revealed a new concept—"Ustaša music."[32] The regime also attended to the language, passing a law regulating the orthography and "purity" of the Croatian language on 14 August 1941. The use of the Cyrillic alphabet was banned as early as 25 April 1941, and efforts were made to root out words viewed as Serbisms.[33] This linguistic policy was closely related to Pavelić's insistence that Croats were not Slavs and therefore had no connection with the Serbs whatsoever. But the Ustaša program called for the eradication not only of Serbs and Jews and Roma, but also of Croats and Muslims found guilty of "un-Croatian behavior."[34] Non-Ustaša Croats who expressed alternative political viewpoints were, for example, at risk of being shot.

The Ustaša movement was driven by a deep antipathy to Serbs and Serbdom, and Ustaša leaders repeatedly asserted that Croats and Serbs were separated by an unbridgeable cultural gulf. Marshal Kvaternik, for example, declared that "The Serb is an oriental, the purest child of the oriental philosophy and mode of living . . . who is always contrary to the life of the occidental people to which the Croat also belongs."[35]

For the Ustaše, religion and nationality were closely linked; Catholicism and Islam were declared to be the national religions of the Croatian people, while Orthodoxy was initially described as inherently incompatible with the Croatian state project. Indeed, one of the first decrees issued was a decree of 30 April 1941 on the protection of Aryan blood, which forbade marriage between Croats and "non-Aryans." Starčević's idea that the Bosnian Muslims were the "purest" Croats was resurrected, and Muslims were given permission to build mosques in Zagreb and elsewhere in the country.[36] As early as 3 May 1941, a law concerning religious conversions was passed, in order to pressure Serbs into converting to Catholicism and thereby, so the regime thought, into accepting Croatian nationality; in mid-July, an ordinance was issued banning the use of the expression "Serbian Orthodox faith," which was described as "no longer compatible with the new state order," and mandating the expression "Greek-Eastern faith" as the approved substitute.[37] Protestants were guaranteed full equality under the laws of the NDH, but there were reports, all the same, of discrimination at the local level.[38] As for the Old Catholic Church—the religious association of those Catholics who, at the time of the First Vatican Council (1869–1870), had refused to accept the doctrine of papal infallibility—this organization was banned within the first 10 months of the NDH's existence.[39] But where the Serbs, Jews, and Roma were concerned, the repression was fierce. In Lika, Kordun, and Banija alone, some 172 Orthodox places of worship were closed, plundered, or destroyed, and countless Orthodox priests disappeared into the Croatian prison camp system, many of them never to reemerge.[40] Moreover, the forced religious conversions, which were promoted as offering a chance for Serbs to survive, became extremely controversial, and eventually the regime felt constrained to allow the establishment of a *Croatian* Orthodox Church. This body was not recognized by the Ecumenical Patriarchate in Istanbul, however.

Genocidal Policies

All told, about 623,000 persons were killed in the territory of the NDH in the years 1941–45 (counting both civilian and combatant casualties). Of this number, 307,000 were Serbs; 255,000 were Croats.[41] The policies of the Ustaše were genocidal in intent and in execution. Of the 35–36,000 Jews living on the territory of the NDH, about 28,000 either perished locally or ended up in German concentration camps; 4,000 or more succeeded in emigrating, many of them as a result of assistance from the Italian forces.[42]

As early as 17 April 1941, the NDH issued a decree on the defense of the people and the state, thereby laying the groundwork for the subsequent terror. In addition to the Office for Public Order and Security, Pavelić also set up the *Ustaška nadzorna služba* (Ustaša supervisory service, or UNS);[43] the 3rd Division of the UNS was known as the Ustaša Defense and, together with the Office for Public Order and Security, was responsible for killing those deemed "undesirable."[44] On 27–28 April, the Ustaše committed their first mass atrocity, killing 196 Serbian men at Grudovac, near Bjelovar (80 kilometers east of Zagreb). On 11–12 May, there was a mass execution of about 300 Serbs in Glina, and there were further massacres in Herzegovina and elsewhere in June. Meanwhile, the incarceration of Serbs began with those who had played a role in the political life of the Kingdom of Yugoslavia; these Serbs were invariably described in the NDH press as "Chetniks."[45] Maček, in spite of his encouragement to Croats to obey the NDH authorities, was not trusted by the Ustaše, who interned him in the Jasenovac concentration camp for five months, before transferring him to house arrest at his domicile near Zagreb.

On 25 June 1941, some 260 Serbs were massacred at several locations, while an additional 280 Serbs were killed by the Ustaše near Metković. Killings continued at Čapljina, Knin, Prisoj, Suvaj, Slunj, Polača, Bihać, Bosanska Krupa, Cazin, Sanski Most, Prijedor, and Bosanski Novi. The terror was intended, in part, to induce survivors to flee to Serbia. While the killings continued, the NDH passed a law on 7 June requiring all Serb families who had settled in Croatia after 1 January 1900 and their descendants to register with local authorities within 10 days or be subject to arrest as prisoners of war.[46]

In early June, in conversations with German representatives, Slavko Kvaternik and Mladen Lorković agreed to accept a portion of the population being expelled from the German zone of occupied Slovenia, and in exchange the NDH would be entitled to expel an equal number of Serbs to German-occupied Serbia. It was agreed that 179,000 Slovenes and 179,000 Serbs would be involved in this "swap." The Slovenes were mostly sent to Bosnia, with a smaller number being settled in northern Croatia. But the resettlement of Serbs from the NDH was not organized according to plan, because of lack of adequate means to accomplish the resettlement and because it had quickly become difficult to contain the violence, which was, in any event, stimulated by Ustaša propaganda. The mass incarcerations of Serbs, massacres of civilians, forced emigration of Serbs, and also murders of targeted individuals during the period April–August 1941 reached such a frenzy that the German authorities concluded that these policies were destabilizing. Insofar as this was fueling armed resistance, the Germans counseled a change of policy and urged the *Poglavnik* to guarantee basic civil rights to Serbs, including the right to work, and urged that the regime create a special Orthodox Church separate from Belgrade for local Serbs, who still numbered more than 1,500,000.[47]

Fascism, Forced Conversions, and the Role of the Catholic Church

Two popes presided over the Catholic Church during the fascist era: Pope Pius XI (1857–1939; pope, 1922–1939) and Pope Pius XII (1876–1958; pope, 1939–1958). There has never been any controversy concerning the attitude of Pius XI (born Ambrogio Achille Ratti) toward fascism. Already in 1931, in his pastoral letter *Non abbiamo bisogno*, Pius XI denounced the fascist doctrine that the individual existed to serve the state, rather than the other way around.[48] Six years later, the pope issued his encyclical, *Mit brennender Sorge* [With burning concern], denouncing Nazi excesses. Drafted for the most part by Michael Cardinal Faulhaber, the archbishop of Munich, and by Eugenio Pacelli, the future Pope Pius XII, the encyclical was issued in German because it was addressed to the German people and regime. Alluding to the Natural Law, described as inscribed in people's hearts, the encyclical accused the Nazi regime of departing from Natural Law, i.e., of acting immorally.[49] The encyclical also declared:

Whoever raises race or nation or state or state form or the agents of state authority or other values of human communal life—which, within the terrestrial order, have an essential and honorable place—to the highest norm for all, taking it out of the merely temporal scale of values to turn it into a religious value, making it the object of idolatry, inverts and adulterates the God-created and divinely ordained scheme of things.[50]

So upset were the Nazis over this encyclical, which was being read in Germany's Catholic churches over consecutive Sundays, that they tried to pressure the Church into withdrawing the encyclical. The Church refused to budge and, indeed, in response to a note from Reichskirchenminister Kerrl, the archbishop of Breslau wrote to underline the Church's unity on the question of Naziism and to note that the Catholic press had been persecuted by the Nazis, Catholic schools had been repeatedly "violated," freedom of speech and assembly had been destroyed, and public expressions of Catholic life had become all but impossible.[51]

Pope Pius XII was elected to the Holy Office on the eve of World War Two. Within a matter of months of his assumption of office, he issued his first encyclical letter (*Summi Pontificatus,* 20 October 1939), in which he criticized anti-Semitism, described the idolatry of the state as damaging to international law, and condemned "state-worship" which, he said, "brings fatal consequences to the internal life of a society and . . . is equally disastrous to the relations of peoples with one another."[52] In that same encyclical, the pope "single[d] out, as the fountainhead . . . from which the evils of the modern state derive their origin," the tendency to set aside, neglect, subvert, and repudiate the moral law, with damaging consequences for "the mutual relations of race with race, of country with country."[53] Although it has become fashionable in recent years for critics of Pius to allege that the references in *Summi Pontificatus* were too vague to be intelligible, the Nazis thought that the references were all too clear and banned its distribution in the Third Reich.[54] Indeed, the Gestapo also prohibited any discussion of the encyclical in the press, including in the Church press.[55] In his Christmas message for 1939, the pope specifically condemned the Nazi aggression in Poland and the Soviet aggression in Finland, and, two years later, condemned prejudice based on linguistic, cultural, and racial grounds[56]— again a criticism which could only have been directed against the Axis. In a subsequent radio broadcast (on Christmas Eve, 1942), Pius XII denounced "the theory which claims for a particular nation, or race, or class, a juridical instinct against whose law and command there is no appeal," and stressed that the role of the state was to protect society in all its variety, not to dominate it.[57] The engagement of the pope in resisting Naziism and fascism went beyond rhetoric and also included concrete actions so that, after the war, Pius XII was credited with having saved the lives of many Jews.[58] While it is, thus, historically inaccurate to accuse Pope Pius XII of "silence" in the face of Nazi atrocities and misleading to suggest that he was inactive, the Holy See did not share its extensive intelligence concerning death camps and other atrocities with the Allies, even after any conceivable doubts had evaporated.[59] Eugenio Orsenigo, the papal nuncio in Berlin, also played a subversive role by preventing information about the Nazi mobile killing squads—information drawn up by Bishop Konrad Preysing of Berlin—from reaching the Holy See and by criticizing Bishop Clemens August von Galen when the latter publicly upbraided the Nazis for their program of euthanasia.[60] On the other hand, in addition to condemning Nazi idolatry of the state repeatedly, in January 1940 the pope "issued instructions for Vatican Radio to reveal 'the dreadful cruelties of [the] uncivilized tyranny' the Nazis were inflicting on Jewish and Catholic Poles." Taking stock of the evidence, David Dalin concludes that "the best historical evidence now confirms both that Pius XII was not silent and that almost no one at the time thought him so."[61] It is often forgotten that of the 44 speeches which Pacelli, then papal nuncio, gave in Germany between 1917 and 1929, 40 of them condemned one or another aspect of Nazi ideology. Furthermore, it would be erroneous to look only to papal encyclicals and speeches to document the pope's concern about mass murder. For example, in assessing the engagement of the Holy See, it is surely not irrelevant that in January 1942 Vatican Radio broadcast a graphic report concerning German atrocities in Poland.[62] Again, it is not irrelevant that the Nazis were hatching plans to kidnap Pius and that Pius knew of these plans, or that German Führer Adolf Hitler had been thundering about his intentions to send troops into the Vatican in order to "pack up that whole whoring rabble" of cardinals. And finally, it is not irrelevant that while approximately 80% of European Jews were annihilated during the years of the Holocaust, an estimated 80% of Italy's Jews were saved.[63]

Where Croatia is concerned, controversy has centered on the role played by Archbishop Alojzije Stepinac of Zagreb (1898–1960) and that played by the Franciscans. Whatever the latter may have done by way of joining the Ustaša movement and executing its policies, they did not enjoy the support of the Vatican or of their own superiors. On the contrary, at a meeting of Franciscan provincials in Zagreb on 10–12 June 1941, an order was issued barring any Franciscan from joining the Ustaša. The order added, "Franciscans must not take part in the persecution of Serbs and Jews, in the confiscation of their personal possessions and land, [or] in the banishment of Serbs to Serbia and resettling of Croats in places vacated by Serbs. . . . Wherever the occasion arises, Franciscans should protect Serbs and Jews both from the populace and [from the] State authorities. . . . Franciscans must not take part in [the] forcible and mass conversion of Orthodox believers to the Catholic faith."[64] The directive was issued precisely because a certain number of Franciscans in Bosnia-Herzegovina and southern Dalmatia (not to mention other Catholic priests) had already joined the Ustaša movement before April 1941.[65] The most notorious Franciscan was, without question, Father Tomislav Filipović aka Miroslav Majstorović, who was expelled from the Franciscan Order on 28 April 1942, after his superiors learned that he had been accompanying the Ustaše in attacks on Serbs in the vicinity of Banja Luka.[66] He subsequently served as commander of the Jasenovac camp for about a year and admitted, in the course of his trial in summer 1945, that he had personally killed about 100 persons.[67] But Filipović was not alone in this. Among those Catholic priests who became Ustaša functionaries, in some cases with high rank, one may mention Božidar Bralo (from Sarajevo), Petar Berković (from Drniš), Ilija Tomas (from Klepce near Čapljina), Dragutin Kamber (from Doboj), Radoslav Glavaš (a Franciscan at Široki brijeg), and Vilim Cecelj (from Zagreb). Among Catholic priests to take part in massacres one may mention Srećko Perić, Ivan Hrstić, Josip Matijević, Stanko Milanović, Josip Bekman, Petar Pavić, Zvonimir Brekalo, Cvitan Čulina, Josip Vukelić, and Josip Bujanović, while Ivan Guberina, a professor of theology, chastised Croats who protested against Ustaša atrocities, calling them "spiritual dwarfs."[68] But, according to Ćiril Petešić, the majority of the Catholic clergy in the territory of Yugoslavia were opposed to Axis occupation, and within the NDH, those clergy who embraced Ustaša ideology were, in fact, in the minority (and consisted, for the most part, of younger clergy).[69] Indeed, some of the older clergy in Croatia continued to be Yugoslav-oriented. Some Catholic priests even joined the communist-led Partisans, in spite of their atheist ideology. Among the Catholic clergy to join the Partisans, the most prominent was Monsignor. Svetozar Rittig, pastor at St. Mark's in Zagreb; others included Fathers Jože Lampret, Franc Šmon, Matija Medvešek, Stanko Strašek, Srećko Štifanić, Zvonimir Brumnić, Josip Pavlišić, and, among the Franciscans, Father Jozo Markušić.[70]

Among the Catholic prelates, Archbishop Ivan Šarić (1871–1960) of Sarajevo and Bishop Josip Garić (1870–1946) of Banja Luka sympathized with the Ustaša regime, though the latter was evidently upset about the use of force to effect conversions and wrote to Stepinac about this on 4 November 1941,[71] while Bishop Kvirin Klement Bonefačić of Split, Bishop Miho Pušić of Hvar, Bishop Josip Srebrnić of Krk, Bishop Viktor Burić of Senj, and Bishop Antun Akšamović of Djakovo all made positive statements in public about the NDH;[72] Archbishop Stepinac of Zagreb, in spite of his initial enthusiasm for the idea of a separate Croatian state, did not make such statements and joined Bishop Alojzije Mišić of Mostar in railing against Ustaša oppression of Serbs as early as 1941.[73] In early July 1941, Archbishop Stepinac wrote a letter of protest to the *Poglavnik* and "sent Canon Dr. Pavao Lončar to verbally protest the government's actions. Pavelić immediately had Lončar arrested, tried, and sentenced to death for insulting him and making anti-ustaša pronouncements," though the sentence was commuted to 20 years' imprisonment.[74] The Ustaše reciprocated Stepinac's hostility, characterizing him as a "Serbophile."[75] On 26 October 1941, Stepinac delivered a bold sermon (on the feast of Christ the King), accusing the Ustaše of "poisoning the minds of people to such an extent that I could say that hate has become the chief motivating factor of all human activities," and urging his listeners to love "all men without difference."[76] In March 1942, Stepinac received reports that Croatian Jews would shortly be handed over to the Nazis and immediately wrote to Interior Minister Artuković to protest against this "unlawful attack on citizens who are not personally guilty of anything."[77] Stepinac also spoke out publicly against Ustaša atrocities and implored the *Poglavnik* privately to end the depredations against Serbs, Jews, and Roma.[78] He specifically denounced the Jasenovac camp in a letter to Pavelić on 24 February 1943, but the forced conversions being promoted by the Ustaše as a way of "Croatizing" Serbs proved more vexing for the Church.[79] Stepinac, like other prelates, denounced the use of coercion in promoting the conversions of Orthodox believers to the Catholic faith but at the same time realized that such conversions could save lives. Moreover, the entire subject of forced conversions had a particular edge for Catholic prelates in the 1940s, because, at that time, it was the teaching of the Catholic Church that only baptized Catholics could go to heaven. It was in this spirit that a leaflet circulating in the diocese of Djakovo encouraged "inhabitants of Greek-eastern faith" to accept Catholicism so that they might thereby "ensure the salvation of your immortal souls according to the holy exhortation of our Saviour Jesus Christ."[80]

The Ustaše had no intention of allowing the Church to review applications for conversion according to canon law. The whole thrust of the policy was political, and indeed, the authorities sought to limit the conversion option to poor peasants and the less well educated, and to insist that converts join the Latin-rite *Roman* Catholic Church, rather than the Eastern-rite *Greek* Catholic Church. Moreover, while Stepinac and other bishops protested against both regime infringement of the Church's jurisdiction and the regime's anti-Serb and anti-Jewish policies, Vatican, Italian, and British sources confirm that some priests were taking part in Ustaša atrocities against Serbs, with the worst violence being committed in Bosnia-Herzegovina.[81] Moreover, once the massacres of Serbs began, Catholic clergy and lay activists often defended the conversions by asserting that it offered the best chance for Serbs to save their own lives. That the situation presented Catholic hierarchs with a moral dilemma should be recognized.

The Vatican became involved in the controversy concerning forced conversions, opposing the NDH pressure to force converts into the Latin rite and directing instead that "where there are already parishes of the Greek Catholic rite, let the non-Catholics who wish to be converted be directed to those parishes. It is recognized that if the non-Catholics do not wish or are not able to keep their Oriental rite, they may choose the Latin rite."[82] Although the Vatican did let it be known that it preferred that a "more cautious" approach to conversions be adopted, in which coercion would be absent, it did not actually protest against the forced conversions. Locally, however, Bishop Mišić was perhaps the most eloquent on this subject, protesting, on 7 November 1941, that NDH authorities

have abused their positions, exploited the worst instincts of the masses and the weakest side of human nature, with the result that a reign of terror has come to pass. And there is nowhere a remedy for it. Men are captured like animals. They are slaughtered, murdered; living men are thrown off cliffs. The underprefect in Mostar, Mr. Bajić, a Mohammedan, has stated . . . that at Ljubinje, in a single day, 700 schismatics were thrown into their graves. From Mostar and from Čapljina a train took six carloads of mothers, young girls, and children ten years of age to the station at Šurmanci. There they were made to get off the train, were led up to the mountains, and the mothers together with their children were thrown alive off steep precipices. In the parish of Klepci 700 schismatics from the surrounding villages were murdered. Must I continue this enumeration? In the town of Mostar itself, they have been bound by the hundreds, taken in wagons outside the town, and there shot down like animals.[83]

The Serbs had three alternatives: flee to Serbia, convert to Catholicism, or join the growing resistance movement. As a result, in many parts of the NDH, Serbs abandoned their villages, took to the hills, and spontaneously organized armed *čete* on a local basis.[84] Mišić wrote to Stepinac to register his outrage at the use of force to bring about conversions; so did Pavao Butorac, the bishop of Kotor and apostolic administrator of the diocese of Dubrovnik, who expressed his concern that the forced conversions could have a "catastrophic" impact on the reputation of the Catholic Church.[85]

The Catholic Church hierarchy in Croatia dealt with the issue of forced conversions, if anything, with greater clarity and resolution than had been displayed by the Vatican. From the beginning, the Croatian hierarchy took the position that conversions should be encouraged only when application for rebaptism was the result of genuine conviction, and on 19 October 1941, Archbishop Stepinac sent around a memorandum concerning conversions, reemphasizing that it was impermissible to use force to achieve conversions but also noting that no one was entitled to obstruct genuinely felt conversions.[86] In a resolution issued by the Episcopal Conference, chaired by Archbishop Stepinac, at the end of a conference in Zagreb on 17–18 November 1941, the Croatian bishops declared, inter alia, that:

1. The Conference considers it a *dogmatic principle* that the solution of all questions pertaining to the conversion of Orthodox persons to the Catholic religion is *exclusively* within the province of the hierarchy of the Catholic Church, which alone, according to Divine Law and canonical regulations, has the right to lay down rules and regulations; and, as a result, all outside action on this matter is excluded.

2. For this reason, no one, with the exception of the hierarchy of the Catholic Church, has the right to appoint "missionaries" to take charge of the conversion of Orthodox persons to the Catholic Church. Any missionary of this kind must receive his mission and the jurisdiction for his spiritual work from the Ordinary of the place where he is active. It is, consequently, *contrary to dogma and to canonical regulations* that "missionaries" receive their mission, unknown to the Ordinary of the place where they work, from the commissioners of communes, representatives of the civil authority, Ustashi officials of the Religious Section of the Department of Reconstruction, or from any civil authority whatsoever. . . .

4. The Catholic Church can recognize as valid only those conversions which have been or will be carried out according to these *dogmatic principles. . . .*

8. Only those may be received into the Catholic Church who are converted *without any constraint, completely free, led by an interior conviction of the truth*

of the Catholic faith, and who have entirely fulfilled ecclesiastical regulations. . . .

10. The Bishops' Committee for Conversions will organize courses for priests
    who take charge of conversions to Catholicism. They will receive in these
    courses practical and theoretical instructions for their work.
11. It is necessary to create among the Orthodox inhabitants a psychological
    basis for conversion. Toward this end they shall not only be promised but
    actually be guaranteed all civil rights, especially personal freedom and the
    right to hold property. All proceedings contrary to law in regard to Ortho-
    dox persons shall be strictly forbidden and they shall be penalized as other
    citizens through due process of law. And, most important, all private actions
    in destroying the churches and chapels of the Orthodox or the stealing of
    their property should be severely punished.[87]

In the wake of this resolution, the Croatian hierarchy established a committee of
three bishops, headed by Stepinac, to deal with issues relating to Orthodox conversions. Even though the committee hoped to enforce canon law, in defiance of
Ustaša policies, the mere existence of the committee indicated, in Tomasevich's
view, "that the Church was willing to cooperate with the regime's policy of conversions, provided that canonical rules were safeguarded."[88] Indeed, some Catholic
priests decided to tie their fortunes with those of the NDH, throwing canon law
to the winds, and defied their own bishops in participating in forced conversions;
all told, with or without the cooperation of the hierarchy, an estimated 244,000
Orthodox Serbs were rebaptized as Catholics during the years 1941–1945.[89]

Moreover, people came to the archbishop to plead with him to relax his stricture, spelled out in *Katolički list* already in May 1941, that conversions would be
encouraged only in the case of a free and sincere choice based on conviction,
arguing that, superficial or not, conversions to Catholicism could save lives.
Finally, responding to these pressures, Archbishop Stepinac issued a circular letter on 2 March 1942, to the effect "that other motives [i.e., other than convic-
tion], as long as they were honorable, should not prevent the people from being
received into the Catholic Church. He stressed that the converts could return to
their own faith once the danger was over."[90] The following month, however, the
bogus Croatian Orthodox Church was established, and the regime began extending citizenship to those Orthodox believers who affiliated themselves with this
new institution.[91] Father Germogen, a defrocked Russian Orthodox clergyman,
was named metropolitan of Zagreb and head of the Croatian Orthodox Church.

For its part, the NDH justified itself not so much on the basis of the conversion of Catholics to Orthodoxy in the Kingdom of Yugoslavia (described in
chapter 3) but rather on the basis of the thesis advanced by Reverend Krunoslav
Draganović that many Catholics, especially in southern Herzegovina, had converted to Orthodoxy in the course of the sixteenth and seventeenth centuries
and that, therefore, the mass conversions being promoted by the regime could
be construed as a "return" by locals to the faith of their forefathers.[92]

Stepinac worked quietly to obtain the release of Orthodox prisoners from detention and has been credited with having arranged for some Serbs and Jews to be hidden from the Ustaše. He publicly reprimanded the regime for its racial laws and appealed to the regime to moderate its policies. Stepinac's anti-racist sermons of July and October 1943 were read by priests from pulpits across Croatia and so angered German occupation authorities that 31 Catholic priests were immediately arrested in retribution, and some of his sermons were transcribed and read over Partisan radio. Michael Phayer, a cautious critic of Pope Pius XII, writes of Stepinac: "No leader of a national Church ever spoke about genocide as pointedly as Stepinac. His words were courageous and principled."[93]

But criticism of Stepinac has persisted. Communist accusations that the archbishop "collaborated" with the NDH go too far.[94] But consider the following: Stepinac, in a letter to Pavelić, dated 21 July 1941 (three weeks after some 2,500 Jews had been deported from Zagreb to death camps in and around Gospić), asked that the deportees be allowed to settle their affairs before being deported, that they not be packed into overcrowded wagons, that they be given enough food and provided with adequate medicine during their incarceration, and that their families be allowed to send them food. Commenting on this letter, historian Ivo Goldstein suggests that Stepinac was missing the point here and that "it had to have been clear to everyone in those days, including to those much less educated and less well-informed than Stepinac, what was happening to the deportees, because already by then Jews had been executed as hostages by decisions of military courts."[95] On the other hand, it is an easy matter to find both private communications and public sermons in which Stepinac condemned the policies of the NDH, indeed beginning early in the war. In late May 1941, for example, Stepinac wrote to Minister Andrija Artuković to ask that laws discriminating against Jews, Serbs, and others be administered in such a way as to respect the individual "personality and human dignity," though, of course, it could be noted that the whole problem with discrimination is that it does not respect human dignity.[96] But Stepinac delivered one of his sharpest sermons on 24 May 1942, at a time when many people still expected the Axis to win the war. Speaking on that day before thousands of Catholics, Stepinac declared:

All races and nations were created in the image of God; . . . therefore the Church criticized in the past and does so in the present all deeds of injustice or violence, perpetrated in the name of class, race or nationality. It is forbidden to exterminate Gypsies and Jews because they are *said* to belong to an inferior race.[97]

According to Goldstein, Stepinac was not a war criminal but a controversial figure who seems to have wanted to square discrimination with respect for human dignity, as if these were compatible.[98] Stepinac was, in fact, pleased that the Ustaše had banned pornography and swearing and had even forbidden abortion on pain of capital punishment. Moreover, even while respecting canon law, the archbishop of Zagreb agreed with the Ustaša tenet that Croats and Serbs were separated by a formidable cultural gulf. Writing in his diary in spring 1941,

Stepinac had this to say: "All in all, Croats and Serbs are two worlds . . . which will never draw together except by a miracle of God. Schism [i.e., Orthodoxy] is the greatest curse of Europe, almost worse than Protestantism. There is no morality in it, no principles, no truth, no justice, no honesty."[99]

Relations with the Axis

Although Pavelić assumed control of Croatia thanks to Italian sponsorship, these erstwhile partners soon became estranged, both because the Croatian side resented the cession of portions of Dalmatia to Italy and because the Italians, alarmed by the chaos produced by Ustaša persecutions, felt constrained to take on greater responsibilities in attempting to maintain order and gravitated into collaborative arrangements, first with local Serbian noncommunist leaders and, eventually, with the main body of the Chetnik movement itself.[100] This developed in spite of the fact that Pavelić and Mussolini had agreed in May 1941 to a customs union and in spite of the fact that, in a token of Croatian-Italian unity, the Duke of Spoleto had been designated King of Croatia—though the new "king" never even visited Croatia.[101]

Split became a center of anti-fascist sentiment, and between September and October 1941 about 10 Italian functionaries were assassinated in that city. Stepinac criticized the transfer of Croatian coastline to Italy, as did likewise Bishop Josip Srebrnić of Krk. Pavelić also faced stiff criticism in the Croatian state assembly for having ceded Dalmatia to Italy, and in December 1941, there were anti-Italian demonstrations on the streets of Zagreb; on 25 December 1941 there was a "mass for Dalmatia" in downtown Zagreb, followed by a spontaneous anti-Italian demonstration on Zagreb's main square.[102]

As Italian influence ebbed, German influence in the NDH grew. The Germans had two priorities in Croatia: a secure rail connection through the country to destinations further to the southeast, and the exploitation of Croatia's mineral wealth, especially bauxite and iron ore. At first, the Germans had intended to withdraw their forces from Croatia as soon after the proclamation of the NDH as feasible. But even before the end of April 1941, the Germans reconsidered, deciding to maintain a military presence in "their" half of Croatia, in order to protect the aforementioned objects. The Germans kept many of their agreements with the NDH secret, making public only the treaty of frontiers, the agreement on the use of Croatian labor in Germany, and the agreement on the settlement of Slovenes on Croatian territory.[103] But the Germans were dismayed by the "problematic" relationship between the Ustaša Militia and the army, while General Edmund Glaise von Horstenau (1882–1946), an ex-imperial Austrian general staff officer appointed as general-plenipotentiary representing the *Wehrmacht* in the NDH, was appalled by the savagery of the Ustaše, and protested both publicly and privately.[104] Indeed, Glaise von Horstenau played a unique role in this equation, passing along a list of war criminals to the Allies (with Stepinac's help) and offering advice to Mladen Lorković and

Ante Vokić in summer 1944 when they plotted to introduce a HSS government and pressed Pavelić to resign.[105]

A strange triangular relationship developed among these nominal allies.[106] The Germans supported the NDH against the Chetniks and against the Partisans. The Italians supported the Chetniks against the NDH and the Partisans. The Chetniks collaborated with the Germans and the Ustaše against the Partisans, beginning in 1942; toward the end of April 1942, specifically, Ustaša representatives reached an agreement with Uroš Drenović, commander of Chetnik groups in the vicinity of Mrkonjić Grad, for cooperation against the Partisans. About two weeks later, Ustaša and Chetnik representatives met in Knin, where the former proposed an agreement for "full cooperation." By mid-June 1942, the NDH authorities had established cooperation with the following Chetnik leaders: Mano Rokvić (Drvar, Bosanski Petrovac), Branko Bogunović (Bosansko Grahovo), Stevo Radjenović (Srb), and Momčilo Djujić (Strmica). Since the cooperation between the NDH and the Chetniks was based only on their common fear of the Partisans, relations between these putative allies were always characterized by distrust and uncertainty.[107]

Occupied Serbia

In setting the boundaries for Serbia, Adolf Hitler was driven by a burning hatred of Serbia which may have gone back to his earlier involvement in the Habsburg Army.[108] Be that as it may, the rump Serbian state formed in April 1941 returned Serbia to its borders of 1912, with a population of about 3,810,000. Less than 10% of this total lived in the Belgrade area.[109] Initially, the Germans set up a so-called government of commissars, headed by Milan Aćimović, who also took the post of minister of internal affairs, having served in this capacity in Stojadinović's government). General Milan Nedić (1877–1946) was first mentioned as a candidate to head the collaborationist state on 14 July 1941. German preference for the non-fascist Nedić reflected a general preference on Berlin's part to attempt to engage more or less legitimate local leaders to serve as their quislings (see glossary), wherever possible (and hence, the effort to recruit Maček in Croatia). Dimitrije Ljotić, leader of the fascist Zbor movement, and Aćimović both supported Nedić's candidacy for the post of prime minister. Interestingly enough, Nedić was under house arrest until the end of July 1941.

There was tangible support for collaboration among prominent Serbs. Thus, on 13 August, 545 Serbs, including three Serbian Orthodox bishops, four archpriests, and at least 81 professors at the University of Belgrade, signed an "Appeal to the Serbian Nation," calling on Serbs to collaborate with the Axis and "to thwart the infernal intentions of the communist criminals."[110] When the appeal was issued, the Serbian Bar Association (in Belgrade) adopted a resolution in support of it, by unanimous vote. Offered the post of prime minister by the German occupation authorities, Nedić informed General Heinrich Danckelmann, military governor of Serbia from August to November 1941, that he had nine conditions which had to be satisfied if he was to accept the post: enhanced competence, an armed force, the release from internment of the sick and the aged, an enlargement of Serbian borders, a reduction in anti-Serb discrimination in Croatia, summoning of the political (advisory) council, German assistance in the fight against the communists where needed, repression only of the guilty, and the retention of Serbian national emblems. These conditions, to which the Germans agreed, were only ever partly respected.[111] But Nedić now took office as prime minister on 29 August 1941; in this capacity, he enjoyed the support of a portion of the officer corps, officials, and the general population, as well as of the Serbian intelligentsia. A quisling government was now set up, consisting of the following ministers: Milan Nedić, prime minister; Milan Aćimović, minister of internal affairs; Čedomir Marjanović, minister of justice; Miloš Trivunac, minister of education; Mihailo Oljćan, minister of the economy; Miloš Radosavljević, minister of agriculture; Ognjen Kuzmanović, minister of construction; Josif Kostić, minister of transportation and minister of postal affairs and telegraph; Panta Draškić, minister of labor; Ljubiša Mikić, minister of finance; Jovan Mijušković, minister of health and social policy; and Momčilo Janković, minister without portfolio.[112] Significantly, there was no minister of foreign affairs. Three of these ministers (Nedić, Kostić, and Draškić) had attained the rank of general in the kingdom.

Nedić apparently "entertained illusions that, with the formation of his cabinet, Serbia would obtain some kind of 'autonomy.'"[113] On 2 September 1941, Nedić spelled out his program in a "declaration," promising, among other things, to put together a Serbian army and to smash the communist-led liberation forces, using his own resources. Nedić felt that if he succeeded in suppressing Partisan activity in Serbia, the Germans would become more solicitous of Serbian interests, and that the Serbs might even obtain territorial concessions enlarging their domain. Nedić wanted to ingratiate himself with the Germans, but he also wanted to portray himself as an authentic Serbian patriot, consciously modeling himself on the French collaborator Marshal Petain.[114] Thus, Nedić, aspiring to convey the impression of loyalty to King Petar II, hung a portrait of the king in his office and ordained that police recruits swear an oath to Petar II.[115] But Nedić's competence remained strictly circumscribed; indeed, his government had a largely "formal character," being for the most part restricted to ratifying decisions made previously by German authorities. The German military administration in Serbia was formidable, with a staff of 700 officers.[116] Already by September 1941, rump Serbia had had to take in some 20,000 persons expelled from Bulgarian-occupied Macedonia, 37,000 from Hungarian-occupied Bačka, and 104,000 from Croatia.[117] The Serbian State Guard was established by Nedić in March 1942, with German support; in October 1943, the State Guard and Border Guard were placed under the operational control of the SS. The State Guard was employed in executing captured Partisans.

Even before Nedić assumed the prime ministership, orders were given for all of Belgrade's 12,000 Jews to report to the occupation authorities; 9,145 of them did so. On 14 May 1941, Jews were removed from any and all official posts, Jewish-owned land was confiscated, Jewish "work teams" were set up, Jewish physicians were forbidden to treat *Volksdeutscher* patients, and Jews were forbidden to visit restaurants, movie houses, or theaters, to be employed in Aryan-owned enterprises, or to ride the streetcar, except in the caboose. Between the end of April and mid-June 1941, all able-bodied Jewish males between the ages of 14 and 60 and all able-bodied Jewish females between the ages of 16 and 60 were inducted into forced labor brigades; in Belgrade, between 3,500 and 4,000 Jews were assigned to clear up the rubble resulting from the recent German air campaign.[118]

Concentration Camps in Serbia

Soon after capturing Belgrade, German authorities established concentration camps in Serbia for the purpose of incarcerating, torturing, and annihilating Jews, anti-fascists, and other persons deemed "unworthy of life." Among the camps were the Banjica and Sajmište camps near Belgrade, the Topovska Šupa camp in Belgrade (where Jewish men were incarcerated), and camps near Niš and Šabac. These were operated by the German occupation authorities. By the end of 1941, about 2,000 to 3,000 prisoners had been interned at Banjica. Before arriving at the camp, prisoners would spend several days in Gestapo and Special Police prisons, where they would be beaten and tortured; by the time they were transferred from these detention centers to the concentration camps, some of the prisoners had already been seriously mutilated. The rules of conduct at Nazi-run concentration camps "strictly prohibited singing, loud talk, conversations on political subjects, possession of writing paper, pen or pencil or any other personal belongings." Infraction of any of these rules could mean execution. Prisoners at the Banjica camp were continually beaten and otherwise maltreated by the camp staff. In spite of this, imprisoned Partisans set a courageous example by singing Partisan songs, shouting their support for Tito and Stalin, and arranging for impromptu lectures, discussions, one-act plays, recitals, and even folk song and dance performances. The first mass execution at Banjica camp took place on 17 December 1941, when 170 prisoners were shot. Altogether, some 3,849 persons were killed at Banjica (3,420 males and 429 females).[119]

Better known is the Sajmište camp, established on 28 October 1941 on the grounds formerly used by the Belgrade fair, by order of the German military governor of Serbia, which remained in operation until July 1944, when it was evacuated. Between December 1941 and May 1942, about 7,000 Jews were exterminated at Sajmište. According to the State War Crimes Commission, about 40,000 persons were killed at Sajmište, though this figure must be treated with some caution.[120] By the end of 1943, when the certainty of Nazi defeat was clear to all concerned, the Nazis made some effort to expunge the evidence of their crimes by burning camp records, cremating corpses, and destroying other evidence. But the evidence was too widespread to be destroyed totally. It has been estimated that some 120,000 persons were interned in concentration camps in Serbia, among whom 50,000 persons were killed; another 50,000 persons were deported to Germany or other Axis-occupied countries.[121]

National Ideology and Clericalism

Unlike Pavelić, General Nedić did not attempt to portray his rump state as the fulfillment of Serbian national aspirations. More realistically, he conceded, in a speech presented on 2 September 1941,

Today the Serbian nation is living through its most difficult days since it came to these Balkan lands. In April of this year we lost our freedom and our state, and now we are facing the danger of national extinction. . . . I came into the government to save the people, to keep them from destroying each other. . . . Solely solidarity saves the Serbs. What can we do now? Nothing. We only hurt ourselves. We are a grain of sand in the agitated global sea. Today the greatest powers on earth are settling accounts. In that we can neither help nor obstruct.[122]

On the other hand, although born in tragedy, the rump Serbian state could, in Nedić's view, effect the return of the Serbian people to their roots. Nedić shared with the fascists an emphasis on the peasantry as the foundation of state, a preference for a strong leader (to include a dynastic monarchy, where Serbia was concerned), an idealization of the past, and a claim that the (Serbian) people, restored to their pristine state, would once more display a natural feeling for justice.[123] For Nedić and his coterie, World War Two figured as "a duel between materialism and idealism, . . . a struggle between plutocratic-bolshevik destructive internationalism and the healthy nationalism of social constructivism."[124] And even while mourning the loss of national freedom, Nedić counseled against armed resistance, which he said would only cause suffering and hardship for Serbs, advising members of the resistance to lay down their arms in exchange for amnesty, and hailed the arrival of a "new era," declaring that there could be no return to the ways of prewar society.[125] Whitehall, Nedić claimed, spoke with a "Satanic voice," Draža Mihailović (1893–1946) was an English agent, and Yugoslavia would have done better to have stuck with the Tripartite Pact.[126] Nor was there, in his eyes, anything inspiring or even respectable in Western democracy, which he described as "the [political] world of capitalism and false democracy, a world which created the monied aristocracy and the indigent working class."[127]

The strain of nationalism promulgated in Nedić's Serbia was colored by anti-Semitism; indeed, the municipal government of wartime Belgrade included a Section for Jewish Questions, which participated in implementing the anti-Jewish measures dictated by the Gestapo.[128] The collaborationist press of Nedić's Serbia played its part, too, painting the Jews as "ancient enemies" of the Serbs, as did the Holy Synod of the Serbian Orthodox Church, which publicly supported Nedić and proclaimed its loyalty to the occupation forces.[129] In November 1941, Father Dušan Popović, a Serbian Orthodox priest, delivered an anti-Semitic sermon in Belgrade, while *Obnova,* about the same time, published an anti-Semitic diatribe, claiming that "no matter how much a Jew feigns having integrated with the people in whose midst he lives, even if he has changed faith, he remains first of all and above all a Jew!"[130]

Dimitrije Ljotić, the Serbian fascist who had established his Zbor movement in 1934 and initiated collaboration with the Nazis the following year, had been advocating the extermination of the Jews for a number of years. More ominously, "[p]rominent Serbian Orthodox clergy, too, publicly supported the persecution of the Jews."[131] Two prominent Orthodox churchmen spent the war years in internment. The first of these was Patriarch Gavrilo Dožić, who had publicly opposed Yugoslavia's adherence to the Tripartite Pact and who was interned, by the Germans, first in the Rakovica Monastery and then in the Vojlovica Monastery near Pančevo in the Banat; he spent the final months of the war interned in the Dachau concentration camp.[132] The other prominent Orthodox clergyman interned by the Germans was Bishop Nikolaj Velimirović, bishop of Žiča. Ill-disposed toward the Nazis, Velimirović was nonetheless positively disposed toward Ljotić's Zbor movement, though apparently because of Ljotić's religious conservatism rather than because of his fascism.[133] In the patriarch's absence, Metropolitan Josif, who had been expelled from Bulgarian-occupied Skopje, administered the Serbian Church. Josif and the Holy Synod collaborated with the Germans, at least in part in the hope of getting the Germans to pressure the Croatian regime into easing its oppression of its Serbian population. Most of the Serbian Orthodox clergy sympathized with the Serb nationalist Chetniks, however, with Reverend Momčilo Djurić rising to become the most important Chetnik *vojvod* (duke) in northern Dalmatia and western Bosnia, and Reverend Savo Božić assuming the command of a Chetnik grouping in northeastern Bosnia.[134]

Contacts with the Chetniks

The beginnings of collaboration between Mihailović's Chetniks and the collaborationist government of Milan Nedić may be traced to September 1941, when Mihailović entered into secret negotiations with the quisling Serbian government. Indeed, on or about 15 October, Colonel Milorad Popović, acting on behalf of Nedić, brought Mihailović some 500,000 dinars (in addition to an equivalent sum which had been paid on 4 October) in order to win the Chetnik leader over to collaboration. Subsequently, on 26 October 1941, Popović delivered an additional 2,500,000 dinars to Mihailović.[135] Acting in the name of the Nedić government, Aćimović served as the key liaison between the Germans and Mihailović.[136] By mid-November 1941, Mihailović had placed 2,000 of his men under the direct command of General Nedić, and a few days later these Chetniks joined the Germans in a military operation against the Partisans.[137] The Nedić government filtered some of its arms to the Chetniks and, in the later stage of the war, "authorized the transfer of money to the Chetniks from the Serbian National Bank."[138] Indeed, a U.S. Office of Strategic Services (OSS) report prepared in April 1944 "suggested that the general [Mihailović] should be viewed in the same light as Nedić, Ljotić, and the Bulgarian occupation forces."[139]

The Neubacher Plan

Hermann Neubacher, special envoy and the Third Reich's roving troubleshooter in southeast Europe, arrived in Belgrade in late summer 1943, with responsibility for coordinating local policies with the needs of the German Foreign Ministry in Serbia, the Banat, Macedonia, Kosovo, Montenegro, the Sandžak, and Romania. He immediately undertook a critical review of German occupation policy, which he believed had failed to achieve its objectives, concluding that the system of punitive reprisals, under which the Germans killed 100 locals for every German soldier or functionary killed, was only counterproductive.[140] (The victims were typically either local villagers who had harbored members of the resistance or Jews and suspected communists detained as hostages precisely for the purpose of use in such "reprisals."[141]) In October 1943, he submitted a proposal to Reichs foreign minister von Ribbentrop, asking for some changes to Germany's policy vis-à-vis Serbia, including an exceptional revision of borders. Specifically, Neubacher sought (1) to return to Serbian control Montenegro and that part of the Sandžak which had been assigned to Montenegro, (2) to install General Nedić as president of the resulting Great Serbian federation, (3) to allow autonomous administration in Montenegro, (4) to reopen the University of Belgrade and abolish German supervision of national cultural institutions, and (5) to reduce the size and purview of the German military administration, at the same time allowing the federal government to exercise executive power, inter alia through its own gendarmerie.[142] In agreement with Nedić, Neubacher also sought to obtain the release of Patriarch Gavrilo and Bishop Nikolaj Velimirović, who had been interned in the Banat since 1941. Neubacher easily obtained permission to reopen the University of Belgrade and to free the Serbian cultural institutions from supervision by organs of the military administration, but although von Ribbentrop listened to Neubacher's proposals, he was unenthusiastic about them, presenting them to the Führer only after a delay. Neubacher's proposals died on Hitler's desk.[143] Neubacher was, however, able to bring an end to the erstwhile system of reprisals and henceforth had to approve every recourse to the execution of hostages.

Neubacher continued to play an active role, however. He had already begun to fight against Ustaša persecutions of the Serbs in Croatia, with the result that the NDH regime soon referred to the German diplomat as "enemy of the state no. 1."[144] Neubacher also arranged, in autumn 1943, for the release from prison of Chetnik commander Pavle Djurišić and won him over to collaboration; Djurišić now received arms, ammunition, and other supplies from the Germans and returned to Montenegro in November 1943 to fight the Partisans.[145] Toward the end of 1943, the Germans signed an agreement with the Chetniks headed by Major Vojislav Lukačević for military collaboration in the Sandžak, and subsequently, on 29 November 1943, Captain Nikola Kalabić and Colonel Jevrem Simić—the latter, an inspector on Mihailović's staff—signed an agreement suspending hostilities in the districts of Umka, Vračar, Grocka, Podunavlje, Kosmaj, Mladenovac, Oplenac, Lepenica, Kragujevac, Gruža, Kačer, and Kolubara.[146] By this point, Nedić feared that the Germans were embracing the Chetniks as their primary proxies in Serbia, and when the Chetniks murdered his deputy minister of internal affairs, Ceka Djordjević, in March 1944, Nedić co-opted a prominent Chetnik to take his place, hoping in this way to defuse some of the rivalry.[147] The Nedić government lasted until the beginning of October 1944, when Nedić and his government ministers were evacuated from Belgrade to Austria. American military authorities extradited him to Yugoslavia after the war, however, so that he might serve as a witness in trials being conducted in Belgrade. The Americans believed that they had an understanding that Nedić would be returned to them so that he might be tried by the Allies. The Yugoslav authorities, however, refused to return him to Allied hands, and on 4 February 1946 Nedić fell (or was pushed) from a window in a Belgrade hospital to his death.[148]

Other Occupation Zones

In addition to the NDH and the German occupation zone in Serbia, there were five other occupation zones carved out of the defunct Kingdom of Yugoslavia: Slovenia, divided between the Germans and the Italians until the Italian capitulation in September 1943; the Hungarian occupation zone in Bačka, Baranja, and Prekmurje; the Banat and a strip of land in northern Kosovo, administered directly by the Germans themselves; the Bulgarian occupation zone in Macedonia and portions of southern Serbia; and the Italian occupation zone, embracing Dalmatia, Montenegro, parts of the Sandžak, and most of Kosovo. In all of these sectors, national homogenization was considered a desirable end, to be achieved by forcible measures of expulsion, resettlement, terror, and linguistic assimilation. These will be discussed in seriatim.

Occupied Slovenia

In fact, the Axis partitioned Slovenia into three sectors: the Germans took the largest part, in the north, covering 10,261 square kilometers, with 798,700 inhabitants; the Italians took control in a sector in the south, covering 4,551 square kilometers, with 336,279 inhabitants; and the Hungarians annexed the Prekmurje region in the east, covering 998 square kilometers, with 102,867 inhabitants.[149] The German sector included the valuable coal mines of the Sava basin. The Germans intended to annex their sector of Slovenia to the Reich and, given their racialist presuppositions, considered Germanization central to this project. As early as 12 April 1941, Reinhard Heydrich, chief of the Reich Security Police and Security Service, who was responsible for German population policies in Lower Styria (the eastern half of the German occupation zone in Slovenia), set up the Staff for the Resettlement of the Population. What the Germans hoped to do was to expel between 220,000 and 260,000 Slovenes to Croatia or Serbia (especially intellectuals), to bring in *Volksdeutsche* from the Italian sector of Slovenia (lower Carniola), from the Südtirol, and from east and southeast Europe, and to Germanize those Slovenes allowed to remain.[150] The Germans planned to bring in a total of more than 80,000 ethnic Germans to take the place of the expelled Slovenes and to complete the cultural and linguistic Germanization of the remaining Slovenes within three to five years. The use of the Slovenian language in public was prohibited by the Germans, who converted the schools over to using German as the language of instruction. The Germans also shut down the libraries, confiscating some items for libraries in the Reich and burning the rest of the collections. The Slovenian-language press was also banned. Slovenes were obliged to use German spellings of their family names and to adopt Germanized forms of their given names. The Germans also brought in their own administrators, allowing Slovenes to serve as mayors only where no Germans (or Austrians) were available. To account for the "Germanizability" of some Slovenes, the Nazis concocted the *Windisch* theory, which held that some of the Slovenes were really "Wends," i.e., a distinct Germanic people, who had adopted Slovenian as their language. The theory had no scientific basis but was designed to provide an ideological underpinning for the policy of Germanization.[151]

Between 6 June and 10 July 1941, a total of 6,720 Slovenes were sent to Serbia and 397 priests to Croatia; by late September the total number of Slovenes expelled had reached 17,317. But the expulsions provoked widespread anger, and armed uprisings organized by the communist-led Partisans created complications for the Germans and induced Heinrich Himmler to reduce the targets for the subsequent wave of expulsions from 145,000 to 65,000.[152] By the summer of 1942, the Germans had given up plans to expel Slovenes from their own country; by that point, barely 1,000 *Volksdeutsche* and South Tyroleans had been brought into the German sector.[153] In the course of the war, the Germans expelled about 80,300 Slovenes or about one-third of the number originally planned.[154]

The Italians introduced a milder occupation than the Nazis and tried to win over Slovenes. Thus, the Italians allowed Slovenian cultural institutions and associations to continue to function, left Slovenes in administrative and judicial posts, and allowed both Slovenian and Italian to be used as official languages. The Italians set up a Milizia volontaria anticomunista (MVAC) for Slovenes open to collaboration; as of the end of 1942, MVAC had about 6,000 men under arms. MVAC forces have come down in communist historiography as "the White Guard."[155] The Hungarians were harsher than the Italians but milder than the Germans; there were, for example, no efforts to expel large numbers of Slovenes from Prekmurje, and the Slovenian language continued to be allowed in public by Hungarian occupation authorities.

After the war, the communists tried to weaken public support for the Catholic Church by putting the bishop of Ljubljana, Dr. Gregorij Rožman, on trial in absentia in August 1946, on charges of treason and collaboration with the authorities and convicted him. Tamara Griesser-Pečar, co-author of a study of the trial of Rožman, disputes the communist charges.[156] She notes that on the day the occupation began, Rožman had the Church's secret archives burned, rather than seeing them fall into Axis hands, that the Nazis persecuted the Slovenian Church, and that he informed Pope Pius XII in May 1942 of the Italian occupation authorities' "harsh measures against opposition activists."[157] Rožman repeatedly spoke out against the terror unleashed by the Axis occupation forces against the civilian population. On the other hand, he was criticized even at the time of failing to speak out against the deportations of Slovenes.[158]

When Italy capitulated in September 1943, the Germans assumed control in lower Carniola (which the Italians had called the Province of Ljubljana). On 20 September 1943, General Leon Rupnik assumed the presidency at the head of a Slovenian administration in the Province of Ljubljana. Since the interests of the Slovenian anti-revolutionary camp coincided, in the short term at least, with those of the Germans, a Slovenian Homeguard (*Domobranska legija*) was set up already on 23 September 1943, carrying over veterans from the MVAC alongside new volunteers and recruits. The *Domobranci* numbered about 13,000 and were the largest Slovenian armed collaborationist formation.[159]

The Hungarian Occupation Zone

On 10 April 1941, the same day as the proclamation of the NDH, Hungarian regent Miklós Horthy issued a declaration alleging that, given the collapse of Yugoslavia, Hungary was obliged to take steps to assure the welfare of those lands which it had lost after 1918. The Hungarian occupation of Baranja and Bačka began in the morning of 11 April with the deployment of 80,000 troops. The Hungarians met with no resistance; on the contrary, the local *Volksdeutsche* minority, which was overwhelmingly pro-Nazi, had already organized a militia and quickly disarmed some 90,000 Yugoslav troops. In spite of the lack of resistance, however, the Hungarian troops killed about 3,500 civilians in episodes of "wild shooting" which also struck local Germans.[160]

The 1931 census had recorded a total population of 873,742 inhabitants in Bačka and Baranja. Of these, 305,917 were Serbs or Croats, 283,114 were Hungarians, 185,458 were Germans, and the remaining 99,253 belonged to other national groups (chiefly Slovaks, Ukrainians, Russians, and Gypsies). The Hungarian occupation authorities quickly established who were newcomers to the region (i.e., who had moved to the area after 1918, as part of Belgrade's program of Serbianization); within two weeks, some 10,000 persons were expelled to

Serbia, Croatia, and Montenegro. Another 35,000 Serbs were later sent to Serbia in secret, while yet another 12,000 Serbs were incarcerated in Hungarian concentration camps from which they too were eventually transshipped to Serbia.[161] Some 15,593 Hungarians were settled in the occupation zone, moving into the houses of Serbs being expelled.[162] These measures were accompanied by systematic processes of Magyarization, involving the terrorization of the local Serbs and discrimination against local Serbs and Croats. As elsewhere, the schools were employed to achieve linguistic (and, it was hoped, ethnic) conversion. Only German schools were exempted from the rule otherwise enforced that all instruction should be in Hungarian.[163] The Hungarian authorities also almost totally suppressed publishing activity in Serbo-Croatian, excluded educated Serbs and Croats from employment appropriate to their educational preparation, and confiscated assets which had belonged to the Yugoslav state.

Many Germans of Bačka belonged to the local *Kulturbund* which, since 1939, had been dominated by local Nazis. When the Axis attacked, the leadership of the *Kulturbund,* which by then embraced 95% of Germans living in Bačka, advised its members not to respond to the Belgrade government's call for national defense. Leaders of the *Kulturbund* hoped for the creation of a Danubian German autonomous province within Hungary, to which other areas inhabited by Germans might be attached.[164] These hopes conflicted, of course, with Budapest's own plans and were therefore never fulfilled.

The occupation of Bačka and Baranja lasted until late 1944; the German evacuation of the region, including of the local *Volksdeutsche,* began in early October of that year. About 60,000–70,000 Germans were successfully evacuated from Bačka; an additional 30,000–40,000 Germans from Bačka were serving in the *Wehrmacht* at the time.[165] The Hungarians were pushed out of Medjimurje and Prekmurje only in the last weeks of the war, in spring 1945.

The Banat

That portion of Vojvodina bounded by the River Tisza in the west and by the Danube River in the south and bordering on Romania to the east is known as the Banat. The area had been promised to the Hungarians by Berlin, together with Bačka and Baranja, but on the eve of the Axis invasion, the Romanian government let it be known that it would view any Hungarian occupation of the Banat as a hostile act. As a result, Berlin decided to assume direct control of the economically important region. The Banat had some 640,000 inhabitants at the time, consisting of 280,000 Serbs, 130,000 Germans, 90,000 Hungarians, 65,000 Romanians, 15,000 Slovaks, and 60,000 members of other nationalities, according to a 1941 German estimate.[166] Direct German control of the Banat satisfied the local German minority and assured Germany of access to the ample agricultural produce of the region. On the other hand, the aforementioned aspiration of Yugoslav Germans (spread over Bačka, Baranja, Srijem, Slavonia, and parts of Slovenia) to have their own distinct political unit was not satisfied.

The Bulgarian Occupation Zone

Bulgaria, tied to the Kingdom of Yugoslavia by alliance, did not participate in the first wave of the Axis invasion, though it did encourage pro-Bulgarian Macedonians to take initiatives. The Bulgarian government was aware that some Macedonians wanted independence, not union with Bulgaria, and did what it could to encourage the unionists. On 15 April 1941, Bulgaria broke off diplomatic relations with Yugoslavia on the apparently specious argument that Yugoslav soldiers had made unprovoked attacks on Bulgarian border posts and that Bulgarian towns had been attacked by Yugoslav aircraft.[167] Three days later, after the surrender of the Yugoslav Army, Tsar Boris of Bulgaria came to Vienna for a meeting with Hitler, at which the borders of the Bulgarian occupation zone were set. The following day, 19 April 1941, Bulgarian troops entered Skopje. The Bulgarians occupied most of Macedonia, as well as portions of Serbia and Kosovo, which the Bulgarian government said were inhabited by "Morava Valley Bulgarians."

At first, Macedonians gave German and Bulgarian troops a warm welcome. But the Bulgarian troops behaved like conquerors rather than liberators, alienating the local population. Perhaps even more important in terms of alienating the locals were the Bulgarian policies of sending corrupt and incompetent officials to administer the region and of Bulgarianization in general.[168] The Bulgarianization campaign was intended to promote Bulgarian national feeling among the Macedonians and concentrated on the educational system, from elementary school to the university. Where instruction had been in Serbian during the interwar years, schools were now established with Bulgarian as the language of instruction, using Bulgarian textbooks; teachers were sent to Macedonia from Bulgaria and treated Macedonian as a (substandard) dialect of the Bulgarian language. The Bulgarians also paid attention to the Church, expelling Josip Cvijović, the metropolitan of Skopje, and two other bishops, as well as other Serbian clergy, replacing them with Bulgarians. The Bulgarian Army also demolished some historical monuments associated with Serbian national history.[169] The Bulgarian occupation regime integrated Macedonia directly into the Bulgarian state, banned the local press, and set up youth organizations inspired by fascistic ideas.[170]

The Bulgarian occupation zone also included the Ohrid region, where a large number of Albanians lived. But whatever might be said in favor of the Bulgarian treatment of Macedonians, by contrast with the treatment typically meted out to locals in other occupation zones, the treatment of local Albanians was "uniformly harsh," culminating in the Bulgarian decision to drive the Albanians out of their sector.[171]

In spite of the alienation of the local population, armed resistance among the Macedonians developed slowly. The main reason for this was the Bulgarian Communist Party's insistence that working for the integration of the Macedonian population into Bulgarian culture should enjoy higher priority than fighting occupation forces. The local Macedonian communist leadership followed the lead of their Bulgarian comrades until the Central Committee of the Communist Party of Yugoslavia (CC CPY) finally sent Dragan Pavlović and Lazar Koliševski to remove the existing communist leadership and installed a new team, headed by Koliševski.[172] But the Macedonian resistance remained weak until early 1943, when, at the end of February, Tito dispatched Svetozar Vukmanović-Tempo, a Montenegrin communist familiar with Macedonia, to take command locally. Vukmanović-Tempo made a decisive difference by transferring "the center of operations from the strongly occupied eastern portion of Macedonia to the western area near the Albanian border, establish[ing] a working relationship with the Albanian and Greek Communist partisans, and reorganiz[ing] the partisan units to take full advantage of the growing popular discontent."[173] The Bulgarian occupation of Macedonia lasted until early September 1944.

The Italian Occupation Zone—Montenegro, Kosovo

The Italian occupation zone in the Balkans embraced Dalmatia, Albania, Kosovo, and Montenegro. Initially, both Italian and German forces participated in the invasion of Montenegro, but the Germans soon withdrew, leaving the Italians to set up an occupation regime. On 28 April, Count Serafino Mazzolini was appointed as civil commissioner to take charge of civil affairs in Italian-occupied Montenegro. Local anti-Serbian separatists seemed to be favorably disposed toward the Italians, and at first the Italian regime was lenient.[174] But the Italian transfer of hitherto Montenegrin territory along Lake Scutari and elsewhere to the enlarged Albanian state that the Italians were setting up stirred resentment among locals, especially when some 5,000 Montenegrins were expelled from Kosovo (and Vojvodina) and arrived in Montenegro. The territories lost to Kosovo had more than merely symbolic value; the loss of those lands cost Montenegro its only food-surplus zone and a valuable salt-producing facility.[175]

An Italian plan to install Prince Mihajlo Petrović-Njegoš, a grandson of the late King Nikola of Montenegro, on the Montenegrin throne ran aground when the prince declined the throne. By this point, there was general insurgency, to which the Italians responded forcefully. In July 1941, Mazzolini was recalled to Rome, and General Alessandro Pirzio Biroli, erstwhile commander of Italian forces in Albania, was appointed military governor of Albania. He remained in that post until 1 July 1943, when General Curio Barbasetti assumed the post of military governor. When Italy surrendered, German forces assumed control of those parts of Montenegro not controlled by the Partisans, and named Major General Wilhelm Keiper to take command of the region.

In Kosovo, the dynamics were very different. When the German 60th Motorized Infantry Division, commanded by Colonel-General von Mackensen, rolled into Kosovo in April 1941, as the spearhead of the Axis occupation of the province, local Albanians hailed the Germans as liberators. Kosovo was, in fact, partitioned in three: the Germans occupied the northern strip including the

Trepča mines, which produced lead, zinc, iron ore, and silver; then there was the aforementioned sector occupied by Bulgaria; the largest portion of Kosovo, however, was attached to Italian-occupied Albania. Interestingly enough, the Germans initially set up "a model occupation regime," at least as far as local Albanians were concerned, according to Bernd Fischer. General Eberhard signed agreements with local Albanian leaders establishing a self-governing council and granting the Albanians more autonomy than their compatriots were enjoying in Italian-occupied Albania. The German occupation was sufficiently lenient that the Italians complained that the German sector could become a focal point for anti-Italian activity.[176]

As in Slovenia, the Italians were solicitous of the local culture. The Italian occupation authorities organized Albanian-language education and allowed the Albanian flag to be flown throughout Kosovo. Altogether, Italian authorities established 173 elementary schools using Albanian as the language of instruction and, in February 1942, assigned Albanian citizenship to inhabitants of Kosovo. Large numbers of Serbs were killed across Kosovo or deported to camps in Albania beginning in 1942. Local Albanians saw an opportunity to take their revenge upon their Serbian neighbors for the sufferings they had endured over the previous two decades; Albanians attacked the Serb colonists, burning perhaps as many as 30,000 houses belonging to Serb and Montenegrin settlers. During 1943–1944, Serbian residents of Kosovo fled in terror, taking refuge in Montenegro and Serbia or in Orthodox monasteries in Kosovo itself. By German estimates, some 40,000 Serbs and Montenegrins were driven from their homes in Kosovo between November 1943 and February 1944 alone. The occupation forces hunted down the fugitives and interned those they captured in camps in Albania and Italy.[177] Altogether, in the course of World War Two, an estimated 10,000 Serbs and Montenegrins lost their lives in Kosovo, most of them killed by Albanian collaborationist forces.[178] Meanwhile, with Italian encouragement, as many as 72,000 Albanians from Albania were settled (or resettled) in Kosovo.[179]

The population of Kosovo in 1939 was 645,017, among whom 65.6% were Albanians or other non-Slavs; among the remainder (Slavs), 9.2% were "new settlers" brought to the area in the interwar years.[180] Aside from the collaborationists, there were two other important groups among the Albanians: the communists, who began to organize themselves in November 1941 with assistance from the CPY, and liberal nationalists who were opposed to communism and who, in November 1942, formed a group called the Balli Kombëtar (National Front). The Balli Kombëtar elected the elderly Mithat Frashëri, a former diplomat, as its leader. The organization's initial central committee included moderates, but they were quickly taken into custody by the Italians; those who were elected in their stead were older, more conservative, and more inclined to collaboration with occupation forces. Among this latter group, Rexhep Mitrovica would be chosen, late in the war, to head a collaborationist government under German sponsorship. The Balli Kombëtar wanted to come out of the war with an enlarged Albania which would include Kosovo/a, i.e., within its occupation borders. It engaged in some limited resistance but on the whole preferred to adopt a more passive posture, deferring an active recourse to arms to the inevitable showdown with the communists.[181] The German occupation lasted until the end of 1944, with battles flaring between Germans and the communist-led Partisan forces in October and November 1944.

The Resistance, June–December 1941

At the time of the surrender of the Yugoslav Army to the Axis in mid-April 1941, many Serbian detachments refused to capitulate and retreated to the hills. Since the army high command had surrendered, there was at first no one in a position of clear authority over these diverse and small bands of soldiers. The Chetnik tradition of paramilitary activity, maintained during the interwar years, had an impact on developments in the wake of the Axis invasion, with outrage at German and Ustaša atrocities quickly attracting recruits to the Chetnik banner. The most prominent Chetnik leader at the time was the aging Kosta Pećanac, whose priority never lay in resistance and who came to an arrangement with Nedić already in August 1941.[182] Colonel Draža Mihailović, a rival Chetnik leader, called his movement the Ravna Gora movement, naming it for the town where he had his headquarters, and in early September 1941, he established radio contact with the British.

Meanwhile, immediately after the Axis invasion, the communists had begun preparatory work for launching an uprising, though they delayed action until orders came down from Moscow. On the day that Nazi Germany began its attack on the Soviet Union, 22 June 1941, orders went out from the Comintern to all communist parties to come to the Soviet Union's aid. The following day, the CPY made its decision to launch an uprising in Serbia. Those taking part in the meeting of the Serbian provincial committee of the CPY were Aleksandar Ranković (1909–1982), Spasenija Babović, Djuro Strugar, Moma Marković, Ivo Lola Ribar, Blagoje Nešković, Vukica Mitrović, Mirko Tomić, Miloš Matijević, Ljubinka Milosavljević, Vasilije Buha, and Milovan Djilas (1911–1995). The communists put together its Supreme Staff of the National Liberation Partisan Units of Yugoslavia on 27 June 1941, electing to this body Josip Broz Tito, chair; Milovan Djilas, Edvard Kardelj (1910–1979), Ivan Milutinović, Aleksandar Ranković, Rade Končar, F. Leskošek, Sreten Žujović (1899–1976), Ivo Lola Ribar, and Svetozar Vukmanović-Tempo.[183] On 4 July 1941, this body issued a formal order to launch the anti-fascist resistance. At this point, there were probably only about 2,000 communists in rump Serbia, about one-third of them in the Belgrade area.[184]

In spite of that, in July 1941 alone, there were 220 acts of sabotage carried out by resistance forces in Serbia. Meanwhile, a spontaneous uprising began in Montenegro on 13 July 1941. Initially, the communist-led Partisans in Serbia concentrated their attacks on gendarme stations and the communications network, rather than on German garrisons. These raids had a tangible disruptive effect on occupation forces, and by August the rebellion had spread over all of western Serbia. The Partisans were able to capture the town of Užice in western Serbia in September, pushing out the German occupation troops and enthusiastically declaring the establishment of the Užice Republic. The Partisans began to set up an alternative administrative structure in Užice, at the center of which were councils of national liberation. At the start of the uprising, the Partisans had had only 20,000 antiquated firearms, about 500 automatic weapons, and five artillery pieces. But with the capture of Užice, the Partisans came into possession of a munitions factory and were able to manufacture weapons and ammunition for themselves until the factory blew up on 21 November 1941.[185] The Partisans were forced to abandon Užice on 29 November 1941 by the German 113th, 342nd, and 717th Infantry Divisions.[186]

Some Chetnik leaders entered into collaborative arrangements with the Partisans and conducted joint operations against the occupation authorities. Among those Chetnik leaders who collaborated with the Partisans against the Germans at this time were Pop Vlada Zečević (an Orthodox priest), Lieutenant Ratko Martinović, and Captain Dragoslav Račić (the son of Stjepan Radić's assassin), who was leader of the Cer Chetniks. During September and most of October, Račić's Chetniks and local Partisans conducted joint operations, capturing a number of German troops. When the Germans launched a counterattack against these formations, however, Račić retreated, with about 1,500 Chetniks and a few thousand Partisans.[187]

While some Chetnik officers, such as those mentioned above as well as Artillery General Ljubo Novaković, staged an abortive action in late September with about 3,000 underarmed men, some armed with only picks and scythes, Mihailović was already advocating the postponement of military action against the Germans. Under the pressure of events, however, Mihailović and his staff met with Partisan representatives in mid-August and again in early September, without producing any results. Tito and Mihailović met for the first time on 19 September 1941 at Struganik; on this occasion, Tito offered Mihailović the post of chief-of-staff at joint headquarters in exchange for the merger of their units. This meeting came three days after Field Marshal Wilhelm Keitel, chief of the High Command of the German Armed Forces, issued his ill-famed directive, instructing German forces to execute 50–100 hostages for every German soldier killed; General Franz Böhme, German commander in Serbia, announced that this directive would be given the most draconian implementation, i.e., 100 locals to be executed for every German killed (and 50 for every German wounded). According to Roberts, this directive was weighing on Mihailović's mind when he met with Tito at Struganik, and he apparently refused to consider any military action against the Germans at the time, for fear of provoking reprisals, though he promised that his Chetniks would not attack Partisan formations. But the promise was disingenuous, given that Mihailović was simultaneously negotiating with Nedić, and Tito was apparently aware of Mihailović's duplicitous game. In spite of this, one final effort at forging a common front against the occupation was undertaken on 20 October 1941, when Tito proposed a 12-point program, offering it to Mihailović as a potential basis for cooperation. The two men met on 26 October 1941, in the vicinity of Mihailović's headquarters, but Mihailović rejected the principal points in Tito's proposal (establishment of a common headquarters, combined military action against the Germans and the quisling formations, establishment of a combined staff for the supply of troops, and the organization of a system of local administration in the form of national liberation committees). In the morning of 2 November 1941, Mihailović's Chetniks attacked Partisan headquarters in Užice. The attack was repulsed, and in a counterattack on the following day, the Partisans dislodged the Chetniks from the city of Požega. The Chetniks lost 1,000 men in these two battles, as well as a considerable quantity of weaponry.[188] On 18 November 1941, Mihailović accepted a truce offer from Tito, but renewed efforts to agree on a common front made no progress.

The Partisans' activity quickly assumed such proportions that the Germans felt compelled, at the beginning of August 1941, to ask the Oberkommando der Wehrmacht, or OKW, (in vain, as it turned out) for reinforcements. By October, the Germans were increasingly impatient with Partisan sabotage and raids and threatened to execute anyone assisting the Partisans in any way, including by providing information, assisting with transport, helping to set up blockades, and assisting with sabotage.[189] There was an anti-fascist uprising in the Macedonian town of Drama and its vicinity on 28 September 1941. Led by communists, the insurgents liberated about 30 villages and destroyed a bridge in Angista before the Germans were able to suppress the uprising.[190] There were also spontaneous stirrings among the Albanians, who began to organize resistance by autumn 1941; one of the best known Albanian resistance leaders was Muharem Bajraktari. Interestingly enough, by spring 1942, at least some Albanian resistance forces were cooperating with Chetnik leader Draža Mihailović.[191]

The German attack on Užice left the Partisans with 1,415 dead, 80 wounded, and 718 captured, against *Wehrmacht* casualties of 11 dead and 35 wounded.[192] When Užice fell to the Germans, the Partisans fled, for the most part, to Croatia or to Italian-occupied Montenegro. Only one Partisan company remained in Serbia. The fall of Užice was a heavy blow to the Partisans.

Mihailović had already established friendly relations with the Nedić regime and turned to the Germans directly, asking them for munitions in order to fight the communists. In reply, General Böhme informed Mihailović that the Germans were quite capable of suppressing the communist insurrection without any assistance and demanded Mihailović's unconditional surrender! The German forces were also brought against Mihailović, attacking his headquarters at Ravna Gora; on 7 December 1941, the 342nd Infantry Division was hurled against Ravna Gora, killing 10 Chetniks, taking 390 prisoners, and pushing the rest out. The result was a military debacle for the Chetniks. Ironically, King Petar II, sitting in exile in London and apparently not yet informed of this military reverse, chose precisely that day to promote Mihailović to brigadier-general and to name him commander of the Yugoslav Home Army. But as Manoschek reports, from that point forward, Mihailović's Chetniks barely maintained any presence in Serbia; some of his adherents joined the Nedić formations and even carried out small acts of sabotage, but after December, the center of Chetnik activity moved to the NDH.

The Chetniks

Both the Chetniks' political program and the extent of their collaboration have been amply, even voluminously, documented; it is more than a bit disappointing, thus, that people can still be found who believe that the Chetniks were doing anything besides attempting to realize a vision of an ethnically homogeneous Greater Serbian state, which they intended to advance, in the short run, by a policy of collaboration with Axis forces. The Chetniks collaborated extensively and systematically with the Italian occupation forces until the Italian capitulation in September 1943, and beginning in 1944, portions of the Chetnik movement of Draža Mihailović collaborated openly with the Germans and Ustaša forces in Serbia and Croatia.[193] Moreover, as already mentioned, the Chetniks loyal to Kosta Pećanac collaborated with the Germans from early in the war.

The Chetnik Organization was inspired by anti-democratic, anti-liberal, and anti-communist ideas and was prepared to allow, at most, that (some) Slovenes and Croats might live alongside Serbs in a postwar Serb-ruled state. Stevan Moljević, as a member of the Executive Council of the Chetnik Central National Committee (formed at Ravna Gora in August 1941), was a close adviser to Mihailović. At the end of June 1941, Moljević drew up a program for a Greater Serbia, demanding that Serbia enjoy an access to the Adriatic Sea and calling for the incorporation into Serbia of Macedonia, Montenegro, Herzegovina, Dubrovnik and its vicinity, northern Albania and portions of Bulgaria, Vrbas, northern Dalmatia, the Serbian part of Lika, Kordun, Banija, part of Slavonia, etc.[194] In a Chetnik directive issued on 20 December 1941, the goal of the movement was specified as the creation of a Greater Serbia, embracing also Macedonia, Montenegro, Bosnia-Herzegovina, and Vojvodina, all of which would need to be "cleansed" of non-Serbs; specifically, this meant that the local Croatian and Muslim populations would have to be driven out of Bosnia-Herzegovina, and the Muslims also out of the Sandžak.[195] Among the cities to be incorporated into Greater Serbia were Zadar, Vukovar, Osijek, and even the Romanian town of Timișoara. According to Walter Manoschek, "the Chetniks planned to expel more than 2.6 million Yugoslavs of other nationalities from Serbia after the war and to resettle 1.3 million Serbs from non-Serbian parts of Yugoslavia in Serbia, so that Greater Serbia would constitute about two-thirds of the population and territory of [the new] Yugoslavia."[196] Within the framework of a plan drawn up by the Chetnik National Committee in summer 1941, only about 200,000 Croats would have been allowed to remain in Greater Serbia.[197]

For the Chetniks, the war provided an excellent opportunity to begin to put their program into effect, and between autumn 1942 and spring 1943, the Chetniks carried out slaughters of Croatian civilians in a wave of terror across Dalmatia. Chetnik leader Petar Baćović boasted at the time, "Our Chetniks killed all men 15 years of age or older. . . . Seventeen villages were burned to the ground."[198] During this period, some 5,500 Chetniks joined the Italian forces in an offensive directed at Partisans and pushing in the direction of Prozor. But, to the dismay of General Mario Roatta of Italy, these Chetnik forces repeatedly took time off from the operation to swoop into villages along the way, in order to butcher Muslim and Croat civilians; Roatta, commander of the Italian Second Army, protested these "massive slaughters" and threatened to cut off Italian supplies and money if Chetnik depredations against noncombatant civilians did not end. Nor was the Chetnik terror limited to non-Serbs; on the contrary, the Chetniks also terrorized those Serbs who were opposed to the Chetnik program.[199] This prompted the CP provincial committee for Dalmatia to send a report to the Central Committee of the Croatian Communist Party, noting: "The Chetniks are carrying out fearful terror even against the Orthodox population. They plunder, arrest, kill, and incarcerate massive numbers of people into their concentration camp in [the town of] Kosovo (near Knin), which people have called a second Jasenovac."[200] According to Vladimir Žerjavić, the Chetniks killed about 65,000 Croat and Muslim civilians in the NDH. The Chetniks completely destroyed 300 villages and small towns in the NDH, as well as a large number of mosques and Catholic churches.[201] Some Muslims reacted by joining the 13th SS Division "Handžar" (Dagger) or "Jure Frančetić's Black Legion, the Ustaša unit that crushed the rebellion in Eastern Bosnia in the spring of 1942."[202] Others joined the Partisans, and by the end of 1944, Muslim troops of the "Handžar" Division were crossing over to Partisan ranks.

The Chetniks wanted to "win," and their notion of winning involved not merely the removal of the Axis occupation forces but also the establishment of a largely homogeneous Greater Serbian national state founded on traditional patriarchal values and infused with an authoritarian spirit.[203] Since the Chetniks pinned their hopes on an Allied victory (specifically on an Allied naval landing), which, in their view, would drive out the Axis forces, they believed that their interests were best served by avoiding unnecessary provocation to the Axis. Other factors entered into the calculation too, including the need for reliable sources of weapons (which they succeeded in obtaining from both the Allies and the Axis, until the beginning of 1944, when the British reassessed the policy of supplying the Chetniks and withdrew their mission from Chetnik headquarters in May 1944), and the occasional impulse to try to impress the Americans and the British with violent attacks on Axis forces and acts of sabotage. The ruse—for that is what it became—was remarkably successful, at least for a while.

The Chetniks did, for all that, engage in acts of resistance, especially in the months up to November 1941. But the impulse to collaborate developed quite independently among various Chetnik groups. In Montenegro, for example, when, the communists gained the ascendancy after the temporarily successful uprising of July 1941, General A. Pirzio Biroli, the Italian military governor of Montenegro, aware of Chetnik hostility toward the Partisans, offered to leave the Chetnik forces in the countryside alone, if they reciprocated. Thus began Italian-Chetnik collaboration in Montenegro.[204] In the NDH, local Chetnik leaders Momčilo Djujić and Stevo Radjenović made contact with the Italians by early summer 1941, seeking an end to the persecution of Serbs, the possibility for Serb refugees to return in safety to their homes, and the rescinding of a decree authorizing the confiscation of Serb-owned property. The Italians accepted these demands, believing that such measures would win the Chetniks over to a collaborative arrangement and take the wind out of the communist insurrection, allowing also the restoration of rail traffic along the disrupted Split-Karlovac line.[205] In this connection, Dobroslav Jevdjević, a leading Chetnik in the interwar kingdom, met in early October 1941 with Italian captain Angelo de Matteis, chief of the information division of the Sixth Army Corps. Soon thereafter, Ilija Trifunović-Birčanin, already a prominent Chetnik before the war, arrived in Split, meeting with de Matteis and Jevdjević on 20 October; they came to an agreement.[206] Meanwhile, negotiations with the Nedić government, described above, were also underway about the same time, driven by the Chetniks' hunger for weapons.

But by its very nature, the Chetnik movement was polycephalous. Thus, even while some Chetnik leaders entered into collaborative relations with the Italians and with the Nedić government, others—for example, those in Bosanska Krajina—"avoided any cooperation with the occupation regime."[207] Moreover, even where local Chetniks did collaborate, they did so on their own terms, not necessarily accommodating their activity to the priorities of their arms suppliers. Given the disunity and pervasive opportunism of the Chetnik movement, the German efforts during 1941–1942 to smash the Chetniks were not necessarily illogical. But even as the Chetnik organization in Serbia atrophied, it gained a new center of gravity in western Yugoslavia in the course of 1942.

The Italians wanted to extend their sphere of influence in Croatia and to pacify the rebellion and, perhaps giving in to wishful thinking, "tended to see the Chetniks as a fairly well-coordinated movement which was ready to join the Axis powers and the Serb collaborators in a struggle aimed exclusively at the Partisan rebellion."[208] In January 1942, General Renzo Dalmazzo, commander of the Italian Sixth Army Corps, met with Radjenović, Trifunović-Birčanin, Jevdjević, and Major Jezdimir Dangić, a free agent whose small force had carried out some sorties against NDH troops, hoping to use the Chetniks in a joint operation against the Partisans.[209] For the time being, however, the Germans vetoed any use of the Chetniks in such a capacity. In spite of that, the Nevesinje Chetniks were working together with the Italians in anti-Partisan operations as early as April 1942. Indeed, by mid-1942, the Italians had acquired a vested interest in arming and using the Chetniks against the Partisans. In addition to the aforementioned Chetnik collaborators, one should also mention Pop Djujić, an Orthodox priest in his late 30s, who led an armed band of about 3,000 men and who was, by mid-April, launching anti-Partisan raids in coordination with the Italians. By early summer, the Italians were arming and supplying about 10,000 "legal" Chetniks in the Italian zone in the NDH.[210]

Mihailović was aware of and condoned the collaborationist arrangements into which Jevdjević and Trifunović-Birčanin entered. Meanwhile, the NDH government had already initiated talks with Chetnik groups in Herzegovina and was open to expanding cooperative links with the Chetniks against the shared communist foe. On 19 June 1942, Zagreb and the Italian high command agreed to set up a Voluntary Anti-Communist Militia (MVAC) into which Chetnik volunteers would enter. The agreement reached in Zagreb foresaw that these de facto reorganized Chetnik units would be under the firm control of the Ustaše and the Italians. Mihailović himself was drawn into this collaborative web, and by late August, he was sanctioning the use of his units in an anti-Partisan campaign with Ustaša and Italian troops.[211] Yet even here, as Matteo Milazzo notes, "in these parts of Yugoslavia, formally attached to Croatia and occupied successively by *Ustaše* and Italians, the Chetnik groups were motivated far more by intense hatred for the Croats and Muslims than by anti-Partisan sentiments."[212] Chetnik savagery toward civilians alienated potential recruits, thereby undermining any potential there might have been for the Chetnik movement to expand its membership.

In August 1942, the Chetniks carried out a sabotage operation at the Germans' expense—the price Mihailović had to pay for the delivery of heavy explosives from the British. The Germans responded by rounding up various Chetnik officers as well as those Chetniks who had infiltrated Nedić's administration. The Germans wanted to finish off the Chetniks, but meanwhile, several of Roatta's divisions were to be transferred to North Africa to face the Allied invasion. Under the circumstances, Roatta contacted Jevdjević in November and legalized an additional 3,000 Chetniks. The Chetniks were also given authorization to operate throughout eastern Herzegovina. Thus, by the end of 1942, Chetnik-Italian collaboration had become routine, while in Serbia, the Chetniks had become convinced that they "could survive only if they refrained from all anti-German activity."[213]

At this time, Serbs comprised not only the overwhelming majority of the Chetniks, but also the clear majority of the Partisan resistance. But while the Partisans continued to woo Croats and Muslims to join the resistance, the Chetniks, through their rampages against Croat and Muslim civilians, seemed to be doing everything they could to alienate non-Serbs. The Chetniks were, at the time, full of confidence, with Chetnik conferences at the end of 1942 committing themselves to extend a "Chetnik dictatorship" to "half of Albania, all of Bulgaria, half of Hungary, and Rumania up to the oil reserves."[214] Mihailović even mused, at this time, about extending "Greater Yugoslavia" as far as the Black Sea!

Any doubt which might have remained in anyone's mind as to whether the situation within the lands which had been Yugoslavia could be characterized at all as a civil war, or concerning the willingness of the Chetniks to collaborate with Axis forces in order to fight the Partisans, were laid to rest in February 1943, when the Chetniks joined German and Italian forces in the so-called Fourth Offensive (Operation *Weiss*) against the Partisans. (Curiously, although the Italians and the Chetniks collaborated hand in glove, the Germans remained deeply suspicious and even tried to turn the Italians against their Chetnik allies![215] Indeed, in the third and final phase of this offensive, the Germans had foreseen that the Italians would move against the 20,000 Chetniks in Montenegro and Herzegovina, but the Italians simply refused to carry out this plan.[216]) The Fourth Offensive fizzled out, with the Partisans maintaining the upper hand over their adversaries. Indeed, in the course of this offensive, the Partisans captured most of the Chetnik strongholds around Knin and dealt the Chetniks a blow from which the Serb nationalists never recovered. Moreover, the Partisan seizure of Prozor in mid-February gave them an infusion of Italian arms, enabling them to attack Mihailović's forces in Herzegovina.

In the meantime, Mihailović had given a speech in the village of Donje Lipovo in Montenegro in which, according to a report which Colonel S. W. Bailey sent to Whitehall, he described the Serb nation as "friendless," accused the British of "pressing them to engage in operations without any intention of helping them, either now or in the future," complained that King Petar and his government had been reduced to the status of prisoners of the British government, and added—in what may have been a whine—that "as long as the Italians comprised his only adequate source of help generally, nothing the Allies could do would force him to alter his attitude towards them."[217]

Bailey's report angered the British government, which replied with a note to Prime Minister Slobodan Jovanović (of the government-in-exile), signed by Churchill, criticizing Mihailović's speech and warning that the British government might revise its policy of favoring his forces. Indeed, in May 1943, the British sent their first mission to the Partisans; the mission included Major William D. Jones, Captain A. D. N. Hunter, and radio operator Ronald Jephson, who were joined, on 28 May, by Captain F. W. Deakin and Captain W. F. Stuart, a Canadian officer fluent in Serbo-Croatian. The first airdrop of military supplies to the Partisans followed on 25 June. For the time being, the British were supplying both the Chetniks and the Partisans. But by September, SIS (Britain's Secret Intelligence Service) had "concluded that Mihailović had failed in the crucial matter of persuading Serbs and Croats to fight side by side." Evidence also emerged, in the form of an enigma decrypt, of Mihailović's collaboration with Nedić—evidence which was considered damning in British eyes. By November, British assistance to the Chetniks had ended.[218] From that point, the

Partisans were the exclusive beneficiaries of British military assistance on the Yugoslav front.

Meanwhile, on 19 May 1943, Hitler sent a teletyped message to Mussolini repeating his determination to destroy all Yugoslav fighting forces, whether Chetniks or Partisans. Mussolini replied, on 22 May 1943:

In consequence of these accords [concluded with von Ribbentrop in February], the Italian side immediately suspended all further distribution of arms; the resupply of munitions was reduced to the minimum and elements of the formations were purged to reduce their cohesion gradually. Thus, without delay, measures were taken to weaken and reduce these formations. . . . The proof of the above is furnished by the fact that, unlike in the past, the Chetnik formations are besieged by Partisan attacks. Though fighting resolutely, they have not been able to carry out an effective resistance and have been in the process of rapid dissolution.[219]

In this letter, Mussolini also complained that the Germans had launched their "Fifth Offensive" against the Chetniks and Partisans (on 15 May) without even notifying his government; in fact, this was because the Germans did not trust the Italians. The "Fifth Offensive" (Operation *Schwarz*) targeted Montenegro. The Germans apprehended a number of Chetniks, provoking protests from the Italians, but failed to locate any large body of Chetniks. Meanwhile, the Chetnik leadership in Montenegro broke up in the face of this new offensive, with a large number of Montenegrin Chetniks joining the Partisans at this time.[220]

The prevalent disposition among the Chetniks remained one of collaboration with the Axis, but on Romanija Mountain, pro-Partisan Chetniks fought against the Axis. Among those Chetniks who were collaborating with the Italians, German hostility was increasingly creating problems. Pop Djujić, for example, was fighting against the Bosnian Partisans all summer long but was faced with the German demand (to the Italians) that all the Dinaric Chetniks be disarmed forthwith. Djujić pleaded his case with the Italians, and in early June, General Mario Robotti was able to convince Colonel-General Alexander Löhr, the chief of German Army Group E, to allow that Djujić's forces be disarmed over a period of months, rather than all at once. The Italians were also constrained to reduce their food supplies to the Dinaric Chetniks. Under these circumstances, a tangible component of Djujić's forces defected to the Partisans at this time. [221]

On 25 July 1943, Mussolini was ousted. In anticipation of Italian capitulation, Mihailović issued orders that attacks on Second Army garrisons be prepared; these garrisons held the promise of substantial supplies of arms which could, if they fell into Chetnik hands, revive the Chetnik war effort, or so Mihailović calculated. But the Chetniks were in no position to undertake any such action, and when Italy capitulated on 8 September, the Allies ordered the Italians to surrender their weapons to the Partisans, not the Chetniks. Of the 16 Italian divisions stationed in Yugoslavia at the time, all but two surrendered their arms to the Partisans.[222]

The Partisans

The Partisans differed from the Chetniks in a number of key respects: to begin with, the Partisans were unified under a central command, were anti-national-ist and offered a truly "Yugoslav" vision, in which all peoples were promised equality, and encouraged women to play an active role in the resistance.[223] By the time that the war broke out, the Yugoslav communists "had built up a secret party organization with 12,000 members"—some of them with combat experi-ence from having fought in the Spanish Civil War—and this gave the commu-nist-led Partisans an important boost.[224] Moreover, unlike the Chetniks, whose efforts at social transformation were limited to killing off Croat and Muslim civilians, the Partisans aspired to bring about a social revolution in those areas which they liberated, setting up a hierarchy of people's liberation committees in the areas they liberated from Axis control.[225] And finally, as already noted, they were prepared to fight the Axis immediately, rather than waiting for the war to enter its final phase. In spite of that, there were efforts undertaken by the Parti-sans from time to time to reach some sort of limited understanding with the Nazis—for the last time on 25 March 1943—but Hitler had no interest in any such understanding, reportedly shouting on that occasion, "One does not nego-tiate with rebels—rebels must be shot!"[226]

Tito as Leader

The leader of the Partisans, Josip Broz, was born in the village of Kumrovec on the Slovene-Croat border in 1892. Half Slovene and half Croat, he served in the Austro-Hungarian Army in World War One, spending more than a year in a POW hospital in Russia and later in a prison camp before escaping. Instead of returning immediately to his native country, however, Broz stayed in Russia until 1920, joining the communist party in 1919. In 1924, he was elected to a lower-level post in the by-then illegal communist party organization in Yugo-slavia and in 1928 became head of the Zagreb party organization. He subse-quently spent time in Yugoslav prisons because of his work as a communist. He was in Moscow in 1934–1936, working in the Comintern and learning Russian in the process. Broz used a number of aliases in the years before he took over in Yugoslavia (being known to Stalin, for example, as "Walter"), but in 1934 he took the alias "Tito" and this name stuck. Various rumors circulated about the origin of this name, with some insisting that it was an acronym for *Tajna Inter-nacionalna Teroristička Organizacija* (secret international terrorist organiza-tion). In 1937 he became general secretary of the CPY.[227]

Tito was a natural leader whose very presence seemed to command respect and deference. A man of vast parade, he did not like to be crossed. Although determined to be his own boss, he listened to the advice and counsel of subor-dinates, indulged a certain amount of criticism, and, until the final decade of his life, tended to surround himself with persons holding to quite different points of view. In spite of this, Tito could come across as a rather pedantic schoolmaster at times. For example, in his letter dismissing Milovan Djilas from the command of Partisan forces in Montenegro in 1941, Tito wrote:

It was not incorrect to start an uprising [in Montenegro], but it was incorrect to start that uprising without political operations from below. It was incorrect for you to separate the Partisan struggle from the people's uprising. It was incorrect that right from the start you created armies and fronts, instead of adopting the Partisan method of warfare. Your basic error is not a premature popular uprising, but your military strategy. Your frontal struggle forced you into a frontal withdrawal; it was pointless to expect that you would be able to put up strong resistance to a much stronger enemy by a frontal defense. Furthermore, it was incorrect for you to dismiss the armed masses instead of breaking up large units into smaller Partisan detachments and carrying on a continuous Partisan war. It was incorrect to call the National Liberation Struggle an antifascist revolution.[228]

But this sharp reprimand did not signify the end of Djilas's communist career; indeed, he was immediately entrusted by Tito with the editorship of the party newspaper, *Borba*—a critical job, for which Tito apparently thought Djilas would have more talent.

The Partisans and the Allies

As Kardelj notes in his reminiscences, the Western governments tried repeatedly during 1941 and 1942 to persuade the Partisans and the Chetniks to mend their fences and to forge a common front against the Axis occupation. Indeed, in November 1941, the British government, at the behest of the Yugoslav government-in-exile, had asked Moscow to intercede with Tito to persuade him to accept Mihailović as commander-in-chief of Yugoslav resistance forces; but Tito refused to consider this demand.[229] Meanwhile, as Djilas recalls, the truces arranged between the Partisans and the Chetniks were repeatedly violated by the Chetniks—in the first instance (in October 1941) when the Chetniks killed a local Partisan commander and, after a second apparent rapprochement, in the second instance (in November 1941) when Chetnik forces, acting on orders from Mihailović's staff, massacred some 30 Partisan adherents, most of them girls and wounded persons.[230] But even after the final rupture between Tito and Mihailović, there continued to be coordination between Partisans and Chetniks in eastern Bosnia for a while.

On 21 December 1941 (Stalin's birthday), the Partisans established the First Proletarian Brigade; Koča Popović (1908–1993), a veteran of the Spanish Civil War, was named commander of this brigade. Stalin, however, was not pleased with this "birthday present," since he feared that it could complicate his relations with Britain and the United States. Moreover, in the short run, this incipient sovietization damaged the Partisans' reputation, while contributing to a massive increase in the number of Serbian peasants joining the Chetniks. In response to the loss of Užice, Tito and the First Proletarian Brigade pushed south toward

Foča, which they captured from the Chetniks, establishing their new headquarters there (25 January–10 May 1942). On 1 March 1942, Tito created the Second Proletarian Brigade. But on 15 April, a combined German-Italian-Ustaša-Chetnik counteroffensive (the "Third Enemy Offensive") put serious pressure on the Partisans, who were forced to abandon their recent conquests and to begin their "Long March" to safety in western Bosnia, begun on 23 June 1942. In 1941, the Partisans had had some 55,000 fighters in Serbia and Montenegro, but barely 4,500 Partisans escaped to Bosnia.[231]

But this setback, as serious as it was, did not result in a halt to Partisan attacks on Axis and collaborationist forces. In July 1942, the Second Proletarian Brigade moved on Kupres and, with the assistance of local Partisans, seized control of a group of villages populated by Catholics. Then, during the night of 4 August 1942, the Partisans attacked the town of Livno and, by morning, held the entire town except for one building where Ustaša forces continued to hold out. Later that year—in November 1942—some 68 delegates handpicked by the CPY assembled in the town of Bihać in northwestern Bosnia and constituted themselves as the Anti-Fascist Council of the National Liberation of Yugoslavia (AVNOJ).[232]

As a communist, Tito had hoped for military assistance from the Soviet Union. As early as 31 July 1941, Tito sent a message to Bulgarian communist leader Georgi Dimitrov (1882–1949), who had taken up temporary residence in Moscow in order to serve as head of the Comintern, asking him to relay to the Soviets a request that they send the Partisans in Serbia "arms, ammunition, and several military specialists." But the Soviets did not think that they could spare anything, and on 26 September, after making some effort on Tito's behalf, Dimitrov was constrained to advise Tito that he and his Partisans would have to rely on their own resources. In spite of this early rebuff, however, there was an encouraging sign in October 1941, when the acting head of Soviet General Staff Intelligence wrote to the Executive Committee of the Comintern to request that Tito be asked to identify possible landing sites for supply planes. The Partisans replied that they were in control of three good airfields (Arilje near Užice, Užička Požega, and Sokolac, about 40 kilometers from Sarajevo), but they were to be disappointed, as nothing was sent from the Soviet Union at this time.[233] By the latter half of 1942, the center of Partisan activity had shifted to Croatia, though Partisan ranks were still composed predominantly of Serbs. As the war continued, ever greater numbers of Croats joined the Partisans, so that by the end of 1944, Croats accounted for 60.4% of Partisan forces in Croatia, with Serbs accounting for 28.6%, Muslims for 2.8%, and members of other nationalities for the remaining 8.2%.[234] In Bosnia-Herzegovina, assigned to the NDH, Serbs were again the first to rally in large numbers to the Partisan banner.[235] As of May 1944 (according to what Tito told the London *Times*), the national composition of the Partisan Army in Yugoslavia as a whole was 44% Serb, 30% Croat, 10% Slovene, 5% Montenegrin, 2.5% Macedonian, and 2.5% Bosnian Muslim.[236]

The Partisans in Macedonia

In Macedonia, by contrast, the Partisan movement scarcely got off the ground, and there was little evidence of an armed uprising. On the other hand, the Bulgarian occupation authorities were able to put together eight *četas* (armed bands), comprising about 200 Chetnik fighters in all. At least part of the problem on the Partisan side apparently was that the Bulgarian communists refused to make a common front with the Yugoslav Partisans. Tsola Dragoicheva, a prominent Bulgarian communist, summarized the Bulgarian communist viewpoint in her memoirs, claiming that the Macedonians simply did not want to be reabsorbed back into any kind of Yugoslavia and therefore refused to have anything to do with the Partisans, who were committed to establishing their authority over all regions which had been part of the Kingdom of Yugoslavia (plus additional lands).[237] Vukmanović-Tempo, the Yugoslav Partisan dispatched to Macedonia by the CC CPY and the Partisan Supreme Command in order to organize Partisan resistance, gives a different account. According to him, he encountered an enthusiastic response, but with only 10 members of the (communist) Regional Committee and local committees still at liberty—the rest having been incarcerated—the situation could only be described as difficult. And this was why cooperation on the part of the Bulgarian communists was so important. But the Bulgarian comrades had their own agenda and, in 1943, explicitly raised the question of the possibility of the post-war absorption of Macedonia into Bulgaria. The Partisans did especially well recruiting among the younger generation of Macedonians, who had grown up in the Kingdom of Yugoslavia, but Tempo himself admits that among the Macedonian population at large, there were also Bulgarophiles and even some Grecophiles.[238] But by 8 August 1943, Tempo was able to report some progress to the Central Committee: "A new militancy has seized the Macedonian people," he reported,

The unification of the Macedonian masses and their involvement in the national liberation struggle is gathering momentum. . . . Countless conferences and meetings in all the villages [of Macedonia] show that these are no longer little bands of comitadijis, but real partisan units. Our units have become steeled in battle and surrender to the enemy and flight to the towns, which were a regular phenomenon earlier, are becoming increasingly rare.[239]

The Partisans articulated the slogan of Macedonian unification (i.e., to include "Pirin Macedonia," which had been part of Bulgaria since the establishment of the Bulgarian state and "Aegean Macedonia," which had been annexed by Greece) for the first time in early October 1943, and this goal was mentioned in a Central Committee letter of 6 December 1943. It was with an eye toward the realization of this goal that Tempo initiated talks with the Bulgarian CP representative in Skopje and subsequently with a representative of the Greek Communist Party (KKE).[240] Quite consistently, Tempo carried his recruitment efforts across the border into Greece, where he apparently had some success, leading to some nasty exchanges between the Yugoslav and Greek communist parties and to the demand, by ELAS (the Greek National Liberation Army) that the newly organized Macedonian Partisan units be disarmed.[241] The Macedonians refused, however, and crossed into Yugoslav territory.

As the Partisans expanded their sphere in western Macedonia, SS headquarters dispatched a plenipotentiary to meet with Ivan Mihajlov, the head of IMRO, who had been serving as an adviser to Pavelić in Zagreb in order to persuade him to organize volunteer units to operate primarily in Greek Macedonia under SS command. Later, as the Axis continued to lose ground, German authorities decided to send Mihajlov to Skopje to proclaim the establishment of an "independent" Macedonia, as an alternative to assigning the area to Bulgaria.[242] But Tito's Partisans (or, more formally, the Anti-Fascist Council for the People's Liberation of Macedonia) had already declared the foundation of the "second Ilinden" on 2 August 1944. Mihajlov's arrival in Skopje a month later came too late to make any difference, and by 6 September, this farcical attempt by the Nazis had collapsed in disarray.[243]

The Partisans in Occupied Kosovo

As of mid-1941, there was no Albanian communist party, though there were groups of communists. But in November 1941, two Yugoslav communist emissaries, Miladin Popović and Dušan Mugoša, met with representatives of three Albanian communist groups in Tirana; at the end of six days, the 15 communists in attendance established a unified Albanian communist party and elected a provisional central committee of seven at its head.[244] Enver Hoxha (1908–1985) became general secretary of the new party. Nine months later came the formation of the Partisan-led National Liberation Council in Albania, and in April 1943, Svetozar Vukmanović-Tempo arrived in Kosovo as representative of the CC CPY and of the Partisan Supreme Command. Tempo's assignment was to organize the resistance in Kosovo and to assume command of Partisan detachments in that region. Tempo visited Hoxha on three occasions in the course of 1943, reaching an agreement on the formation of a Balkan general staff. Albanian Partisans carried out small-scale guerrilla actions during 1943, destroying large quantities of ammunition buried at Trepča, sabotaging electric power stations, and cutting telephone lines along the roads from Prizren to Djakovica and Uroševac. Meanwhile, Serbs and Montenegrins continued to flee from Kosovo until early 1944; altogether at least 10,000 Slav families fled, mostly to Serbia, their places being taken by Albanian "colonists" from the poorer areas of northern Albania.[245]

The CPY had endorsed the notion of assigning Kosovo to Albania on two previous occasions—in 1928, before Tito was head of the party, and again in 1940, at the party congress in Zagreb, by which time Tito was general secretary of the party. But the CPY now backed away from its earlier posture and, in September 1943, sent a letter to the CC of the Albanian Labor Party emphasizing that Kosovo's Albanians would enjoy full freedom in post-war communist

Yugoslavia. Trouble was, thus, already brewing. It exploded with full force in the village of Bujan at the end of 1943 when 49 communists from Albania and Kosovo (43 Albanians, three Serbs, and three Montenegrins) met for the soon-to-be-famous "Bujan conference" (31 December 1943–2 January 1944). Rejecting the decision of the second session of AVNOJ held in November, the Bujan conference adopted a resolution declaring, inter alia: "Kosovo is an area mostly inhabited by the Shqiptar [i.e., Albanian] people, who have always wished to become united with Shqipni [Albania]. We, therefore, feel it our duty to point to the road that is to be followed by the Shqiptar people in the realization of their wishes."[246] There was, to be sure, some sentiment in the CPY at the time in favor of assigning Kosovo to Albania, according to Branko Petranović, but only on the assumption that Albania itself would be included within Yugoslavia as one of seven republics. The Politburo of the CC CPY declared the Bujan resolution null and void; indeed, Tito himself, in a letter to Tempo (dated 6 December 1943), had already characterized the demand to include Kosovo in Albania as "reactionary."[247]

In October 1944, the German Army began retreating through Kosovo; fierce battles between the Germans and the Partisans continued for about six weeks during October–November. After the Germans had been driven out, Tito ordered the collection of weapons in Kosovo and the arrest of prominent Albanians. The order was not well received and, combined with the passions felt about Kosovo, inflamed an insurrection. On 2 December 1944, anti-communist Albanians from the Drenica region attacked the Trepča mining complex and other targets; numbering at most 2,000 men, these anti-communists held off a Partisan force of about 30,000 troops for two months.[248] Now, "an armed uprising of massive proportions broke out in Kosovo."[249] The goal of the uprising, led by the Balli Kombëtar (which had around 9,000 men under arms at the time), was to defend the enlarged and ethnically purged Albania created during the Axis occupation and to resist incorporation into communist Yugoslavia. But the uprising may also have been provoked by violent Yugoslav Partisan reprisals conducted against many Albanians, justified on the grounds that they had collaborated with the Axis during the war years but more likely inspired, at least among Serbs in Partisan ranks, by a desire for revenge for the sufferings inflicted on local Serbs by the Albanians during the war.[250] It was only in July 1945 that the Yugoslav Partisans were able to put down the uprising and establish their undisputed control of Kosovo.

After the Italian Capitulation

On 8 September 1943, Italy surrendered unconditionally, and on 13 October, the new Italian government in Rome declared war on Germany. In the meantime, Mussolini was freed from prison by the Germans and installed at the head of a German puppet regime in the German-occupied part of Italy in the north. The surrender of Italian arms to the Partisans has already been mentioned. Before Italy's capitulation, some 1,000 Italian soldiers had deserted to the Partisans; after the capitulation, about 40,000 more went over to Tito's forces.[251] The Partisans moved resolutely and, within a few days of the Italian capitulation, had seized control of almost all of the Dalmatian coast, including the larger islands. On 15 September, the Partisans audaciously pushed into Italy, occupying Istria and the mountainous region between Trieste and Austria. As Partisan strength grew, those Germans who had been arguing all along for accepting the Chetniks (who still had as many as 30,000 to 40,000 men under arms as late as September 1944[252]) as partners of convenience against the Partisans finally prevailed, and the Chetniks became collaborators directly with the Germans. On 19 November 1943, the first nonaggression pact between German forces and Chetniks was signed, with other similar pacts with individual Chetnik commanders following in the wake of this agreement. Among those Chetnik commanders to sign agreements with the Germans at this time were Nikola Kalabić, Dragutin Keserović, and Voja Lukačević.[253]

AVNOJ Declares a Provisional Government

Meanwhile, AVNOJ held its second session at Jajce, in Bosnia, on 29 November 1943, electing a 67-member "presidency" and declaring the establishment of a nine-member National Committee of Liberation (five members of which were communists) as a de facto provisional government.[254] AVNOJ also promised to constitute Yugoslavia as a federation, based on the national principle. By this point, the Partisans controlled about 130,000 square kilometers, or more than half of Yugoslavia, with an estimated 5 million inhabitants.[255] Stalin, fearing that the actions at Jajce might provoke Western wrath, scolded the Yugoslav communists for their impetuosity.[256] But the West was focusing on winning the war and was scarcely about to get into arguments with Tito about the future. Thus, on 2 December 1943, General Dwight D. Eisenhower, commander-in-chief of Allied Forces (North Africa), was instructed to furnish the Partisans with such arms, clothing, food, medicines, equipment, and other supplies as they might require. The British were also thinking pragmatically. For example, that same month Ralph Stevenson sent a telegram from Cairo to the British Foreign Office urging, "Our policy must be based on three new factors: [1] The Partisans will be the rulers of Yugoslavia. [2] They are of such value to us militarily that we must back them to the full, subordinating political considerations to military. [3] It is extremely doubtful whether we can any longer regard the Monarchy as a unifying element in Yugoslavia."[257]

On 4 January 1944, Radio Free Yugoslavia reported that Tito's forces were fighting their way into Banja Luka (population 18,000, at the time) and had already captured the town hall and the prison. Meanwhile, officers of the Royal

Yugoslav Army stationed in the Middle East started a movement to transfer their allegiance to Tito; 17 officers and a large number of conscripts had already done so before the end of the first week of January.[258] From then until after the end of the war, thousands of Chetniks crossed over into Partisan ranks; for the most part, these defections were motivated by opportunistic considerations and not by ideological conversion.[259]

The Chetniks' collaboration with the Axis now bore its inevitable fruit. In February 1944, after Mihailović's forces had failed to blow up certain key bridges spanning the Morava and Ibar Rivers, as demanded by the British, Whitehall decided to withdraw its remaining liaison officers from Chetnik headquarters and to cease supplying Chetnik forces. Only now, on 23 February 1944, did the Soviets belatedly send a military mission to the Partisans. A month later, the British put pressure on King Petar to dismiss Mihailović and to replace the government-in-exile with a three-member committee. On 12 April 1944, Churchill suggested to King Petar that he ask Ivan Šubašić (1892–1955), governor of Croatia at the time of the German invasion and living in the U.S. since 1941, to become prime minister. The king complied, and Šubašić was appointed prime minister on 1 June 1944. Šubašić met with Tito two weeks later and reached an agreement under which the prime minister recognized the decisions of the second AVNOJ congress (in November 1943) as valid, together with the institutions it had set up, and agreed that a united (i.e., coalition) government would be formed, composed of the National Liberation Committee and elements from the government-in-exile who were not hostile to the communists.[260]

The Germans' seventh and last offensive against the Partisans was directed against Tito's headquarters, but by June 1944, it had lost its steam. With the Germans in decline, Mihailović's arms supplies were limited and drying up. On 12 September 1944, King Petar read a statement over the radio (broadcast from London) calling on all Yugoslavs to unite under Tito's leadership and declaring all who failed to do so "traitors."[261] This broadcast had an immediate and thoroughly demoralizing effect on Mihailović's forces, many of whom now simply left his command. On 29 September, Tito met with Stalin in Moscow, and they agreed that Soviet troops, being sent to Yugoslavia to assist the Partisans, would leave Yugoslavia as soon as the Germans had been driven out, surrendering command to Yugoslav civilian authorities. On 20 October 1944, the Russians and the Partisans entered Belgrade, and the Šubašić-Tito negotiations could now be resumed in Belgrade, yielding a draft agreement by 1 November.[262] Under this agreement, the coalition government would consist of 12 members from the National Liberation Committee and six members from the Royal Government; Šubašić himself would become foreign minister in the first postwar government. Tito, of course, became prime minister. Given that neither the king nor Šubašić had any military force to use as a bargaining chip, this outcome can only be explained as a calculated move on Tito's part to maintain Western good will.

Partisan Policies in the Vojvodina and Austrian Carinthia

On 21 November 1944, the presidency of AVNOJ declared members of the "Swabian" (German) minority in Yugoslavia to be collectively guilty and hostile to the country and interned those Germans living in areas already under communist control. Of the roughly half a million Germans living in Yugoslavia prior to 1944, about 240,000 were evacuated before the arrival of the Red Army; about 50,000 died in communist-run concentration camps, with an additional 15,000 dying at the hands of the Partisans; and about 150,000 were deported to the USSR to work at forced labor.[263] Additional numbers were deported. The new authorities issued a decree dispossessing the Germans of all their property, and at the beginning of 1945, the houses confiscated from the Germans (mostly in Vojvodina) were given to new settlers from the southern regions of the country, mostly Montenegro and Bosnia; altogether about 60,000 families moved to Vojvodina and Slavonia as a result of these expropriations. By the time of the 1948 census, only 55,337 Germans remained in all of Yugoslavia.[264]

Meanwhile, the Partisans pressed onward, liberating Karlovac and Varaždin on 7 May 1945 and Zagreb on 8 May. By this point, the Partisan Army numbered 800,000 officers and recruits—a massive force—facing only about 150,000 NDH troops and at most 400,000 German troops.[265] But Tito did not stop at the former borders of the kingdom; instead he pushed into Austrian Kärnten (Carinthia), awakening dreams of a "Greater Slovenia."[266] The Allies were opposed to Tito's apparent territorial grab but wanted to avoid provoking hostilities with his forces. On 17 May 1945, Field Marshal Sir Harold Alexander reported to the Combined Chiefs of Staff that the Yugoslavs "are endeavouring to set up their own government, and have posted proclamations, are looting shops and houses and maltreating local inhabitants."[267] Three days later, Field Marshal Alexander wrote again to report that the buildup of Yugoslav forces in Kärnten was continuing; indeed, since 16 May, more than 16,000 Yugoslav troops had moved into the area of Klagenfurt-Volkermarkt-Dravograd; fearing hostilities with the Yugoslavs, Alexander took preparatory steps for the possible evacuation of all British and American personnel, including the United Nations Rescue and Relief Agency (UNRRA), from Yugoslavia at short notice.[268] The Allies asked Tito to withdraw his forces from portions of Austria and Istria, but Tito was not inclined to cooperate. Thus, on 21 May 1945, the Combined Chiefs of Staff sent this advisory to Field Marshal Alexander and General Eisenhower:

> In connection with the problem of occupying Venezia Giulia and portions of Austria, Marshal Tito's reply to our proposals is unsatisfactory, and he is being urged to reconsider his decision. Meanwhile, Field Marshal Alexander is directed, with maximum practicable assistance from General Eisenhower, immediately to reinforce his forces in the disputed areas so that our preponderance of force in those areas and the firmness of our intentions will be clearly apparent to the Yugoslavs.[269]

By 21 May, Tito had "issued orders for a general withdrawal of all Jugoslav forces" from Kärnten. But Field Marshal Alexander remained cautious, insofar as the

Yugoslavs had been circulating pamphlets claiming that Bleiburg, Villach, Klagenfurt, and even Graz would soon be incorporated into socialist Yugoslavia.[270]

Massacres at Bleiburg and Kočevje

As the Partisans swept to victory throughout Yugoslavia, various anti-communist forces fled the country with their families—some of them finding their way to Italy, Spain, Argentina, Venezuela, the United States, Canada, Australia, or other locations. Among those fleeing from Slovenia was the bishop of Ljubljana, Gregorij Rožman, who left Slovenia on 5 May, accompanied by General Rupnik and Dr. Janez Kraljić.[271] More than 60,000 Chetniks and Croatian troops and dependents had crossed into Austria by mid-May and had surrendered to Field Marshal Alexander. But for reasons which continue to be the subject of controversy, the British disarmed them and sent these refugees back to Yugoslavia, turning them over to the Partisans. The Partisans massacred them at Bleiburg, Kočevje, and elsewhere. Altogether, between 20,000 and 30,000 Serb Chetniks and Slovene Home Guards as well as 36,000 Croats and 5,000 Muslims were slaughtered by the Partisans at this time.[272]

A young Partisan who participated in the massacres at Kočevje (in Slovenia) but who later defected wrote down his recollections in 1953, noting that those who had participated in the exterminations were treated as "heroes" and rewarded:

On Sunday morning at seven o'clock, the "exterminator company" left by train for a vacation at Lake Bled. I didn't know this at the time, but learned it only much later when these killers rejoined their old companies, which had been sent to Macedonia in the meantime. They told me that as a reward for the massacres they had committed at Kočevje they had received twelve days' vacation on the island of Bled, where they were lodged in a former luxury hotel. They received good food, went swimming, had sail boats at their disposal and saw plays performed for their special benefit every evening by a group of amateur actors provided by the Headquarters of their Division (the Twenty-Sixth Dalmatian Division). In addition, all of the "exterminators" received two or three decorations from the Tito Government, along with gold watches, cameras and other presents of value.[273]

Some of the "exterminators" later suffered nervous breakdowns or impotence, or became drug addicts, being especially inclined to become addicted to morphine and cocaine. After the mass executions were completed, the areas were dynamited to fill in the mouths of the caves and cover the pits. Young larch trees were then planted. Today, at Kočevje, the larch trees sway in beguiling innocence, as if nothing at all had happened there.

The Numbers Game

For socialist Yugoslavia, the tabulation of the number of war-related deaths had direct financial relevance, since that figure would constitute one of the factors in establishing the level of reparations to be paid by Germany to the Yugoslav state. Already in May 1945, Marshal Tito declared, in a public speech, that Yugoslavia had lost some 1,700,000 of its citizens in the war. Given Tito's position and power, this figure was inevitably treated as authoritative. Thus, in August 1945, Mitar Bakić set the total at 1,685,000—a figure only trivially divergent from Tito's—and in late 1945, the Yugoslav Reparations Commission transmitted the figure of 1,706,000 to the Inter-Allied Reparations Agency in Paris.[274] Thus, in March 1947, when a 24-year-old sophomore at the Institute of Statistics in Belgrade named Vladeta Vučković received orders to calculate the number of war victims in Yugoslavia, he knew already what the "correct" answer was. Vučković duly provided scientific reasoning to justify estimating the *net demographic loss* at 1.7 million, but this estimate included those who had died of typhoid fever, those who had emigrated, and the impact of the war on natality.[275] Vučković did not intend for his estimate to be used as a calculation of the number of war casualties as such. But *Borba* quickly cited his work as constituting documentation that 1.7 million Yugoslavs had lost their lives in the course of the war.

More recent calculations by Croatian demographer Vladimir Žerjavić have shown that the number of persons to die in Yugoslavia as a result of combat operations or war crimes was closer to 1,027,000. According to Žerjavić, more than half of these—some 530,000—were Serbs, of whom 307,000 died in the NDH, where most of the fighting took place; about 192,000 were Croats (of whom 184,000 lost their lives in the NDH), and 103,000 were Muslims (about 80,000 of them perishing in the NDH).[276] Population losses due to reduced natality have been estimated at between 326,000 and 338,000, while the demographic loss due to emigration (up to the March 1948 census) has been estimated at about 660,000 by both Serbian demographer Bogoljub Kočović and Žerjavić.[277] The large numbers of Germans fleeing Yugoslavia have already been mentioned. Members of other nationalities fled as well. The figure of more than a million dead is already horrific. Subsequent claims that 700,000 Serbs died at Jasenovac alone make a mockery of the sufferings of all of Yugoslavia's peoples and reduce the tabulation of the dead to absurdity.

Without exception, the occupation forces and quisling regimes in the Yugoslav area, as well as the Chetniks, wanted in the first place to engineer ethnically (and, in some cases, also confessionally) homogeneous spheres from which non-ethnics were to be "cleansed"; in the NDH, occupied Slovenia, Bačka and Baranja, and Macedonia, there were also efforts to assimilate those deemed assimilable. This ethno-chauvinist (i.e., fascist) orientation was perhaps the most obvious among the German occupation authorities in Slovenia, the Ustaše, and the Chetniks, but it was also characteristic of other zones in occupied Yugoslavia.

The quest for national unity and the belief that unity requires homogeneity laid the foundation for pervasive lawlessness on the part of fascists (including

Nazis). Fascists believe they are furthering a higher good, a collective good sanctioned by science or history or race or, in some cases, religion, a collective and ethnic good which stands above the law. This is why, as Hannah Arendt writes, fascism, as a species of totalitarianism, "does not replace one set of laws with another, does not establish its own *consensus iuris,* does not create, by one revolution, a new form of legality. Its defiance of all, even its own positive laws, implies that it believes it can do without any *consensus iuris* what[so]ever." Instead of respect for the law, fascism substitutes terror, so that terror becomes "the very essence of its form of government."[278] But terror, in turn, does not build a community as such. Instead, society is transformed, reconstituted on the basis of hatred and fear. In such conditions, only those who reject fascism from root to stem and take up arms against it can be free. Only those who reject the fascist (and also post-modern) conceit that chauvinism can sometimes be functional, even positive, can contribute to the consolidation of legitimate and stable government.[279]

World War Two in Yugoslavia has come down as the National Liberation War. That war demolished the kingdom and its advocates, demolished the Chetnik and Ustaša movements, and put the communists in power, endowing them with short-term legitimation based on their heroic struggle against Naziism and fascism. The war also de-legitimated radical right ideology, but at the cost of immense suffering and tragedy. And finally, the war scarred a generation and left the country with a huge reservoir of sorrow which could be tapped, at any point, for political purposes.

CHAPTER 5

Happy Comrades? Tito, Stalin, and the Birth of the Second Yugoslavia, 1945–1951

The communists were well aware that the "first Yugoslavia" had proven dysfunctional. In their assessment, this was due to the nature of exploitative capitalism and to the failure of the regime to accommodate Croatian, Bosnian, Slovenian, and Montenegrin demands for federalism, Vojvodinan autonomism, and the legitimate demands of Macedonians and Albanians for education in their own languages and support for their distinctive cultures. The failure of the first Yugoslavia was *not* due, in communist thinking, to the effort to lay the foundations of state by fiat rather than by consensus; consensus, thought the communists, much as Pašić and King Aleksandar had thought earlier, could be built up after the fact.

One problem, as the communists saw it, was that the old political parties from before the war were resurrecting themselves and clearly intended to play a role in shaping postwar Yugoslavia. In order to establish their organizational monopoly, therefore, the communists had to smash the incipient pluralism; to accomplish this, they were prepared to use the instruments at their disposal, including extralegal ones.

But there was a second problem which absorbed the communists already during the last two years of the war, viz., which regions to establish as constituent republics in the socialist federation being erected and where to draw the boundaries between the republics. No one doubted but that Slovenia, Croatia, Serbia, and Macedonia would be established as constituent republics, but there were doubts and disagreements concerning the fate of Bosnia-Herzegovina, Vojvodina, and Kosovo, and to a lesser extent also concerning the borders of

Croatia, Montenegro, and the Sandžak. Already in November 1942, AVNOJ, meeting for its first session, promised to establish Bosnia-Herzegovina as a separate autonomous zone, more or less within its historic borders (which, in practice, meant the borders established in 1878, when the Sandžak was separated from Bosnia-Herzegovina). But in the course of summer 1943, there were lively discussions in the Bosnian party organization concerning the future of the region. Bosnian Serbs were not keen on the idea of a separate Bosnian unit and would ideally have liked to see Bosnia attached to Serbia. There was also a question as to whether to establish Bosnia as a republic, with the same status as Slovenia, Croatia, Serbia, Macedonia, (and Montenegro), or whether it should have a lower status, as an autonomous province. This question was resolved at AVNOJ's second session (November 1943), in favor of full republic status for Bosnia.[1] The Sandžak was divided between Serbia and Montenegro. Where Vojvodina was concerned, there was a general understanding that, given the region's long-standing autonomism, some form of autonomy was essential; the question as to whether to attach Vojvodina as an autonomous province to Serbia or to Croatia might seem a bit artificial, given the strong Serbian demographic presence, but the resolution of this question was deferred until 6 April 1945.[2] At that point, eastern Srem, historically the easternmost district of Croatia, was assigned to Vojvodina, because of the local Serb majority. Croatia also lost a sliver of territory in the south to Montenegro. But with those two exceptions, Croatia's postwar boundaries followed historical precedent. Thus, most of Croatia's border with Slovenia can be dated back to the Middle Ages, while the border separating Croatia and Bosnia closely followed the line of demarcation drawn by the Ottomans at the end of the 17th century.[3] Far more vexing was the debate concerning Kosovo. Among those Albanians who were prepared to work within the Yugoslav framework there was virtual unanimity that Kosovo should enjoy status as a republic; but Serbs, both locally and in Serbia proper, were firmly opposed, and Tito, fearful of alienating Serbs, indeed of losing the support of those Serbs who had only recently left Chetnik ranks, decided to square the circle by granting Kosovo status as an "autonomous region"—considered to involve a status lower than Vojvodina (an "autonomous province")—but placing the region firmly within Serbia's jurisdiction.[4] The assignment of Kosovo to Serbia would not have stood the test of a local referendum and was therefore viewed as a concession to Serbian sensibilities; to balance this, the Tito regime made an important concession to local Albanians, by ruling that Serbian "colonists" who had come to Kosovo in the interwar years but who had been expelled during the war would not be allowed to return to their homes; the authorities also turned a blind eye toward those Albanians who had come to Kosovo during the years that the Italians occupied the area.[5] Macedonia provoked less debate, though even here the border drawn between Macedonia and Serbia left the Monastery of Prohor Pchinski, a historic ecclesiastical site of great value to Macedonians, outside their republic. But as regards Macedonia, the communists were concerned from the beginning to establish that Macedonians were *not* just Bulgarians. To do this, they set about engineering differences. A Commission for Language and Orthography, consisting of philologists, writers, military personnel, party officials, and educators, began work in summer 1944 and, after rejecting two drafts, finally issued a new alphabet and orthography on 3 May 1945, drawing upon both Serbian and Bulgarian to fashion a new language.[6] Although the engineering of a language may seem strange to some readers, it is worth keeping in mind that other languages, such as Norwegian and the American form of English, also had a similar injection of engineering assistance.

Delegitimating the Opposition

Throughout East Central Europe, the communists liquidated opponents; some, such as Jan Masaryk in Czechoslovakia, Nikola Petkov and Archimandrites Paladi of Vidin, Ireney of Sofia, and Nahum of Rousee, in Bulgaria, were prominent, while others, such as most of the 2,800 anti-communists executed in the Polish penal system between 1944 and 1956 were not.[7] Communists staged show trials of uncooperative prelates (e.g., of Archbishop Mindszenty in Hungary, Archbishop Beran in Czechoslovakia, Archbishops Wyszyński and Kaczmarek in Poland, and several Orthodox bishops in Albania, as in the case of Yugoslavia's Archbishop Stepinac) and the dethroned heads of quisling regimes (Monsignor Tiso in Slovakia, Marshal Antonescu in Romania; in Yugoslavia, that role being played by Mihailović), defamed noncommunist politicians—such as "Gemeto" (as Georgii M. Dimitrov,[8] the leader of the Bulgarian Agrarian National Union, or BANU, was called) and Romanian Peasant Party leader Iuliu Maniu, as well as Milan Grol (1886–1952) in Yugoslavia—pushed out the kings (in Romania and Bulgaria, as in Yugoslavia), suffocated the free press, and crushed political pluralism and parliamentary life. In this respect, Yugoslavia's communists followed the pattern.

There were two hugely symbolic trials in Yugoslavia held within the first year and a half after the war ended: the June–July 1946 trial of Chetnik leader Draža Mihailović and the September–October 1946 trial of Zagreb's Archbishop Alojzije Stepinac. Although there were additional (and differing) reasons for putting these two men on trial, there was one reason which underlay both trials: by putting these figures on trial, the Serbian national and Croatian national projects could be effectively delegitimated and champions of Serbian or Croatian national states silenced. The trial of the Zagreb archbishop followed a general pattern in the region of putting Catholic prelates on trial, and the reasons which motivated communists to stage such trials elsewhere were also pertinent where Stepinac was concerned. But in the case of Stepinac, there was an additional motivation, viz., the archbishop figured as a stand-in for the absent Maček, who, as head of the Croatian Peasant Party, much more aptly embodied and symbolized the Croatian national project, even though, from exile, Maček sent out signals of willingness to cooperate with Serbian noncommunist politicians in making a common front against the communists.[9]

The Trial of Draža Mihailović

It was not possible to apprehend Mihailović immediately, but as early as July 1945, Yugoslav communist authorities captured Colonel Dragutin Keserović, commander of one of Mihailović's corps in Serbia; Keserović's detachment had 9,000 men.[10] Meanwhile, Mihailović's force continued to atrophy. Finally, on 13 March 1946, making use of a ruse, communist authorities were able to capture Mihailović and 11 of his followers.[11] As the communists prepared to put Mihailović on trial, Vladko Maček, by that point in exile in Paris, issued a statement condemning the planned trial.[12] When the Chetnik leader's trial began on 10 June 1946, Mihailović appeared to have been weakened by torture. Mihailović was charged with having collaborated with German and Italian occupation forces, as well as with the Nedić regime, with having fought against the Partisans, and with having committed various war crimes. He was put on trial with Stevan Moljević and 22 other persons—13 of them also in the hands of the authorities and the other 10 (in exile) being tried in absentia.[13] Mihailović defended himself by insisting that he did not collaborate personally with occupation forces and that he was not in control of those Chetnik commanders who did so. He also denied that he had collaborated with the Nedić regime in any way or that he had reached an accord with Nedić.[14] He also claimed that he did not know at the time that Chetnik commanders Rade Korda, Petar Baćović, and Pavle Djurišić were taking part in the German "Third Offensive" against the Partisans.[15] In spite of the hard work of two very capable defense attorneys, the accused were found guilty, and on 15 July 1946, the court sentenced Mihailović and 10 others to death; the remainder were sentenced to prison terms ranging from 6 to 20 years, except for a single 18-month sentence. Two days later, Mihailović was executed.

The Trial of Archbishop Alojzije Stepinac

Stepinac was a different case. Initially, the communists courted him and tried to win him over to collaboration. Tito hoped that Stepinac would break ties with the Vatican, establish an autocephalous Croatian Catholic Church (as opposed to the Roman Catholic Church in Croatia), and agree to work within the framework set by the communist party.[16] This course was not without its advocates; in Slovenia, for instance, Dr. Metod Mikuš, a well-known Partisan priest, was advocating the establishment of a Slovenian Catholic Church divorced from Rome.[17] But not only did Stepinac refuse any such collaboration, but he also joined his fellow bishops in criticizing the communist law on agrarian reform, condemning press censorship, and demanding the return of confiscated property to the Church and complete freedom for Church activities.[18] It was for these reasons that the communists decided that Stepinac had to be tried and incarcerated, though, of course, they could not put him on trial for refusal to become a marionette of the communist regime; hence, the communists, having made use of his anti-Ustaša sermons during the war, now portrayed him as having been an active supporter of the Ustaša regime.

Stepinac was arrested on 18 September 1946, a year after the episcopal conference over which he presided had issued the criticisms and demands outlined above and, in a curious jurisprudential innovation, added him to a trial already underway, involving 15 persons accused of war crimes.[19] The trial ended on 11 October, when the court found 13 of the defendants, including the archbishop, guilty of the charges brought against them. In the court's verdict, published in *Vjesnik* on 13 October 1946, Archbishop Stepinac was found guilty of having visited Slavko Kvaternik on 12 April 1941 to congratulate him on the establishment of the NDH (Independent State of Croatia), of having lent his authority to the forced conversions of Serbs, of having functioned as the supreme chaplain in Pavelić's army, of having called on Croats in Germany, in his Christmas message of 18 December 1941, to work hard, and of having plotted, after the war, to overthrow the communist regime.[20] Stepinac was sentenced to 16 years at hard labor, which was immediately commuted to incarceration; in 1951, he was released from prison and transferred to house arrest in his hometown of Krašic, near Karlovac. In political terms, the trial and imprisonment of Stepinac can only be seen as a disaster, at least in the long run: the case only deepened the antipathy which many Croats already felt toward the communists and, in any event, gave Croats a symbolic martyr. Later, in the 1970s and 1980s, Franjo Kuharić, who was by then the incumbent archbishop of Zagreb, used annual commemorations of Stepinac to drive home the point that, in the eyes of Croatian Catholics, Stepinac was no fascist sympathizer but a genuine hero, if not a saint.[21]

Crushing Democracy

The Tito-Šubašić agreement of 1 November 1944 had provided that the new postwar government would issue a declaration guaranteeing democratic liberties, personal freedom, freedom of speech, assembly, and religion, and a free press.[22] Indeed, during 1944, Tito repeatedly reassured the Allies that he had no intention of introducing a communist system in Yugoslavia and was, on the contrary, committed to the principles of pluralist democracy.[23] But as early as January 1945, even before the war had ended, Tito was already shifting his emphasis and, in a speech delivered at the end of that month, declared:

I am not in principle against parties because democracy also presupposes the freedom to express one's principles and one's ideas. But to create parties for the sake of parties, now, when all of us, as one, must direct all of our strength in the direction of driving the occupying forces from our country, when the homeland has been razed to the ground, when we have nothing but our awareness and our hands . . . we have no time for that now. And here is a popular movement [the communist-controlled People's Liberation Front]. Everyone can be in it—both Communists and those who were democrats and radicals, etc., whatever they were called before. This movement is the force, the only force which now can lead our country out of this horror and misery and bring it complete freedom.[24]

In February 1945, representatives of the government-in-exile as well as some politicians who had been living in exile during the war years came to Belgrade; among them was Milan Grol, president of the Democratic Party, whom the British favored for the post of deputy prime minister in a new, unified government. On 7 March, the formation of a coalition government was announced. Tito came in as prime minister with Grol as his deputy and Šubašić as foreign minister. The cabinet also included additional noncommunists, specifically Juraj Šutej (1889–1976), one of the founders of the HSS in Bosnia-Herzegovina, as well as Sava Kosanović (Independent Democrat), Frane Frol (HSS), E. Kocbek (Christian Socialist), and Jaša Prodanović (Republican). At the same time, representatives of the Democratic Party, the Agrarian Union, the Croatian Republican Peasant Party, the People's Peasant Party, the Yugoslav Republican Party, and the Socialist Party, as well as individuals not associated with any parties, were admitted into AVNOJ.

But controversy soon flared over the election law and over the composition of AVNOJ, with Grol criticizing the draft election law as undemocratic and demanding an expansion of AVNOJ.[25] Grol and former Serbian Radical Party leader Miloš Trifunović planned to put up a joint opposition slate at the elections, but as the election got underway the communists campaigned under the slogan "Ballots for Tito, bullets for Grol!" Grol's most potent weapon was his newspaper, *Demokratija,* but unidentified hoodlums, evidently acting at communist instigation, attacked the paper's vendors and burned the paper in the streets of Belgrade. By August, Grol's patience had run out, and he resigned as deputy prime minister; in his letter of resignation Grol protested the regime's undemocratic methods, especially the use of terror and the role of OZNA, the secret police. Grol and Trifunović also decided to boycott the elections. No one else joined Grol in resigning at this time, however; indeed, the Republican Party, the Croatian Republican Peasant Party, and the Independent Democratic Party went out of their way to accommodate the communists, stressing the similarity in their party programs.[26] But two months later, Šubašić and Šutej also resigned, citing Tito's failure to honor his agreements with the former. On 20 October 1945, a fresh newspaper, *Narodni glas,* commenced publication; the publisher was none other than Marija Radić, Stjepan's widow, and the first issue carried an article explaining why the opposition was boycotting the forthcoming elections. The prosecutor's office in Zagreb immediately banned the paper, and the local printers, responding to the vote of the communist-controlled printers' union, refused to print further issues.[27] According to the official results, candidates of the communist-controlled Popular Front captured 81.53% of the vote in the elections conducted on 11 November, with 18.47% of voters casting their ballots for the opposition, even though the opposition had not offered a list of candidates.[28] On 13 November, two days after the boycotted elections gave the communist Front candidates just over 80% of the vote, a bomb destroyed Marija Radić's stationery shop.[29] On 29 November 1945, on the second anniversary of AVNOJ's historic second session at Jajce, the Constituent Assembly declared Yugoslavia a republic and reprimanded King Petar for his alleged support of Chetnik collaboration.

Even as communist authorities put discontents, including those among the clergy and the students, on trial, Edvard Kardelj told the People's Assembly in December 1945, "democratic rights are not something absolutely valid for all times."[30] Unrest was widespread in many parts of the country in the latter months of 1945, with *Križari* ("Crusaders," composed of former members of the armed forces of the NDH) and Chetniks undertaking small-scale operations against limited targets. Among the anti-communist guerrillas, morale remained high for the time being, with persistent rumors to the effect that an Allied intervention in Yugoslavia was "imminent" and that a new government-in-exile, headed by King Petar and Vladko Maček, was preparing a coup in Belgrade to overthrow Tito.[31]

But the CPY, led by Tito, proceeded to build communism, step by step, setting up the various mass organizations, such as the Pioneer Organization,[32] building up the party-controlled press as an instrument of socialization, molding the film industry to suit its purposes, fostering a cult of Tito, and organizing volunteer labor brigades, both for economic reasons and for the purpose of fostering "the political, ideological, professional, and cultural education of youth."[33] On 31 January 1946, the regime promulgated a new constitution for the country. Closely modeled on the constitution adopted by the Soviet Union in 1936, the Yugoslav constitution guaranteed various freedoms, including the inviolability of one's home and the right to private property, to freedom of speech and religion, and to organize diverse political parties—at least nominally. The reality was that certain clauses in the constitution served to secure a dictatorship by the communist party. One curious reflection of the party's "meta-legal" or even "supra-constitutional" status was that, while certain noncommunist parties were being allowed to register with the authorities as a precondition for their being allowed to function, the CPY was not, itself, registered![34] Still, as late as May 1946, Jaša Prodanović, head of the Republican Party in the National Front and, by then, deputy prime minister, told officials at the U.S. Embassy in Belgrade that he was satisfied with the participation accorded to noncommunist parties in the Front in preparing legislation and claimed that these noncommunist parties had helped to shape the agrarian law, softening some of its provisions.[35]

In late December 1946, the aforementioned Miloš Trifunović (age 74), who had briefly served as prime minister of the Yugoslav government-in-exile (June–

August 1943), was brought to trial, together with seven others, on charges of having supplied military and political information to the American Embassy in Belgrade. On 6 January, death sentences were handed down for three of the accused; Trifunović was given an 8-year prison term.[36] Other political opponents were also put on trial about this time, including Boris Furlan, a Slovene progressive, and Franjo Gaži and Tomo Jančiković, members of the Croatian Republican Peasant Party. Some judges were reluctant, however, to subordinate legal ethics to communist political objectives. The code words for a commitment to uphold the law were "political immaturity." Thus, in February 1947, *Vjesnik*, the news organ of the Croatian communist organization, complained that

The greatest negative characteristic of the people's courts is the lack of political maturity of a large number of judges. The majority of judges taken over from the former legal organization show political immaturity, lack of knowledge of the essential changes in the organization of our State authority and of the fundamental changes in our political, social and economic structure. Many judges continue today to live isolated from social and political development.[37]

Communist figures such as Edvard Kardelj, Miloš Minić, and Miloš Žanić argued that legal training was less important than "correct" political attitudes, while representatives of the Public Prosecutor's Office publicly underlined "the necessity of *full* cooperation between the judges and the Public Prosecutor." The public prosecutor went on to threaten that judges "who think differently from the people . . . will not be able to remain as judges."[38]

    In the Constituent Assembly, noncommunist deputies had hoped, at a minimum, that they might be able to speak freely in this forum. But from the very beginning, communist deputies made a practice of shouting, whistling, and otherwise making a disturbance when opposition deputies offered ideas which departed from the communist party program. Opposition deputies were also subjected to verbal attacks and threats.[39]

    The case of Dragoljub Jovanović, the erstwhile leader of the Left Agrarians in the kingdom and now general-secretary of the People's Peasant Party, is illuminating. The freethinking Jovanović, who was not prepared to sit quietly while basic democratic freedoms were subverted and demolished, repeatedly spoke out. His courage was repeatedly put to the test. In July 1946, as a direct result of his comments in the People's Assembly of Serbia, Jovanović was expelled from that body. The following month, the Law Faculty of the University of Belgrade stripped Jovanović of his rank as honorary professor "because of unscientific and anti-people's statements in his lectures."[40] Subsequently, in October 1946, he was expelled from his own increasingly docile party, though he remained, for the time being, a member of the federal People's Assembly. Then, in March 1947, during a joint session of the Assembly attended by Tito, Jovanović delivered a speech criticizing some aspects of the proposed budget, emphasizing the amount being allocated to the defense ministry (which he considered excessive).

Reactions to his speech ranged from "suppressed applause" to shouts of "Kill him!"[41] Not much later, after a presidium vote had stripped him of his parliamentary immunity, Dragoljub Jovanović was arrested on charges of espionage for unnamed foreign interests.[42] On the following day, *Republika,* the news organ of the Republican Party, published an editorial by Prodanović concerning freedom of speech, asking how freedom is advanced if people's elected representatives "are prevented from expressing their opinions and convictions in Parliament."[43]

By the time his public trial opened in Belgrade on 1 October 1947, Jovanović had been charged, together with co-defendant Franjo Gaži, a member of the HSS, with having sought to overthrow the regime, in collaboration with the British intelligence service. On 7 October, Jovanović was sentenced to nine years at hard labor and loss of political and civil rights, as well as his government pension, for an additional three years; Gaži was given five years at hard labor.[44] Released from incarceration at hard labor in 1955 or 1956, Jovanović was assigned to a road gang in the vicinity of Belgrade, thus being forced to continue to do hard labor.[45]

The trials continued into 1948. In February 1948, Tomi Jančiković, a leading figure in Maček's HSS, was convicted of membership in a supposed "Maček Center" which, according to the indictment, had been devoting itself to plotting the assassination of Yugoslav communist officials.[46] Then, in April, there were two trials in Ljubljana. In the first, 12 persons were charged with having operated a "spy center" and of having maintained contact with intelligence services in Switzerland and Italy. The second trial opened eight days later, involving 15 defendants charged with sabotage and the disclosure of secret economic information to foreign agencies. In this second Slovene trial, all of the accused pleaded guilty and even asked the court to impose severe sentences.[47] And in June 1948, Dr. Ivo Tartaglia, a committed anti-fascist and one of the most prominent political personalities in Dalmatia in the interwar years, who had served, at one time, as *ban* (governor) of the Primorska banovina, was put on trial in Split, together with several other persons. Tartaglia, who had opposed Mussolini during the war, was now accused of having expressed pro-Mussolini sentiments and of having "worked right up to the capitulation of Yugoslavia on the systematic strangling of every democratic movement of the people, at the same time endeavoring to carry out such an economic policy which placed the economy of former Yugoslavia in full dependence on foreign imperialistic powers and foreign capital."[48] Tartaglia was sentenced to seven years at hard labor, the loss of civic rights for an additional two years, and the confiscation of all of his property.

One by one, the independent party newspapers were shut down. *Narodni glas,* as already mentioned, lasted for only one issue; *Demokratija,* the news organ of Milan Grol's Democratic Party, was the next to go. *Republika* and *Slobodni dom,* the news organ of the Croatian Republican Peasant Party, lasted somewhat longer, but only at the cost of losing their character as party organs.

Both of these papers continued to be published long after the demise of their supposed sponsoring organizations—*Republika* continuing to appear until 1956 and *Slobodni dom* until 1963. In the meantime, addressing the Second Congress of the People's Front in September 1947, Tito pronounced a death sentence on political pluralism in Yugoslavia. "All of the pre-war bourgeois parties have been discredited and have lost the right to speak on behalf of the people today," Tito told those assembled. "They have shown that they are incapable of running the country, that in the new social order their existence is not justified and that it [pluralism] has become superfluous."[49]

Dreams of "Greater Yugoslavia"

Tito's territorial pretensions matched his sense of his own grandeur. In Tito's imagination at the time, the Italian province of Venezia Giulia as well as Gorizia and the port city of Trieste, Pirin Macedonia (in Bulgaria), Aegean Macedonia (in Greece), all of Albania, and at least a part of Austrian Carinthia should all fall to Yugoslav control. These ambitions complicated Tito's relations with both Britain and the United States, on the one hand, and the Soviet Union, on the other.

Ambitions in Italy and Austria

As early as November 1943, the Partisans proclaimed the annexation of Venezia Giulia including the city of Trieste, though they were in no position to act on that proclamation at the time; the Allies refused to recognize this, however. When Churchill met with the Partisan leader in Italy in August 1944, he informed Tito of the Allies' intentions regarding Istria and underlined the importance which the Allies attached to their retention of control of the port city of Trieste. In spite of that, when German forces completed their withdrawal from the Yugoslav area in the early months of 1945, the Partisans pushed into Istria and threatened Trieste itself. By 1 May 1945, the Yugoslav Partisans had entered Trieste and began taking brutal measures in an effort to get control of the city. The following day New Zealand troops under the command of General Freyberg took possession of the dock area in Trieste. For a while, Tito continued to demand Allied recognition of his "right" to annex Trieste, declaring his intention to establish the city and its hinterland as a seventh republic in the Yugoslav federation. But Churchill refused to accommodate Tito, and on 9 June 1945, giving in to a virtual ultimatum, Yugoslav troops withdrew behind the "Morgan Line," leaving the city of Trieste in Allied hands.[50] About the same time, Tito pulled his troops out of Austria—again, as a result of Western pressure. But in a speech delivered in Celje (Slovenia) on 1 June 1945, Tito left no doubt concerning his intentions. "We have liberated Trieste, Austria, and Carinthia," he told his listeners. "We have liberated Carinthia but international conditions were such that we had to leave it temporarily. *Carinthia is ours and we shall fight for it.*[51]

Thus, Tito continued to engage in diplomatic maneuvers designed to give him portions of Italy and Austria. Indeed, by November 1946, the Yugoslav government was demanding the cession of Burgenland in eastern Austria, the acquisition of which would have given Yugoslavia, in the boundaries which Tito demanded, a common frontier with Czechoslovakia.[52] Meanwhile, the Yugoslavs continued to press their claims to Trieste and its surrounding area. On 1 July 1946, the Allies declared Trieste a "free territory," conceding to Yugoslavia the land east of the "French line" (i.e., up to the edge of the city). For the time being, the Soviets backed Yugoslav claims, but by the time of Kardelj's visit to Moscow in 1947, Stalin had cooled toward the Yugoslavs and declined to press Belgrade's case. Subsequently, in 1948, the U.S., Britain, and France issued a "tripartite declaration" indicating their intention to restore the entire area of the "free territory of Trieste" to Italian sovereignty.[53] Much later, in October 1954, under the impact of the Soviet-Yugoslav rift and Yugoslavia's temporary gravitation toward NATO, Belgrade signed the Memorandum of Understanding with representatives of Whitehall and Washington, renouncing its claims in Trieste and Venezia Giulia.

The Greek Civil War

As early as 1942, armed resistance groups had appeared in the Greek mountains, offering resistance to Axis occupation. The first such group was the Greek National Liberation Army (*Ellinikós Laikós Apeleftheorotikós Stratós*—ELAS), under the control of the communist National Liberation Front (*Ethnikón Apeleftheoretikón Métopon*—EAM). Like their Yugoslav cousins, the Greek communists viewed their resistance as constituting the first stage in the social revolution they wished to bring about, and accordingly they set up a youth movement, a cooperative society, a secret police, a civil guard, and a trade union organization. They also collaborated with Macedonian communists, who had their own National Liberation Front (*Naroden Osloboditelen Front*, or NOF).[54] Altogether, by the end of the civil war, the communists fielded about 35,000 troops in the war—14,000 of them Macedonians and the remainder Greeks.[55]

After the end of World War Two and the expulsion of the Germans from Greece, a noncommunist government was set up under G. Papandreou, with Allied backing. But communist guerrillas continued to fight—only now against Papandreou's government. Tito was determined to assure the victory of the communists in Greece—in spite of Churchill's clearly demonstrated determination to keep Greece in the Western camp—and provided significant assistance to the communist guerrillas, sending them arms and financial assistance, dispatching General Vladimir Dapčević and other military experts to train their fighters, and allowing them to use Yugoslav terrain as a safe haven from which to make attacks against Greek government targets.[56] Although communist Albania and Bulgaria also provided some support to the Greek communist rebels, Yugoslav support was more extensive and lasted longer; it also brought Tito into direct conflict with Stalin, who did not want to stir up unnecessary problems with Britain and the United States. In exchange for Yugoslav assistance, the KKE (*Kommounistiko Komma tis Elladas,* i.e., the Greek Communist Party) promised to cede Aegean Macedonia to Yugoslavia, assuming that it emerged victorious from the struggle.[57] Even after the passage of UN resolutions condemning its involvement in the Greek Civil War, the Yugoslav government continued to assist the Greek communists. The alliance between the KKE and the NOF was an unstable one, however, marred "by deep-seated mutual distrust and animosity."[58] The nub of the problem was that the Greek communists resented the Macedonians' aspiration toward national unification, even while the Macedonians bore the brunt of the fighting.

But it was specifically the expulsion of Yugoslavia from the Soviet-controlled Cominform (Communist Information Bureau) in June 1948 which prompted Belgrade to reassess its attitude toward the KKE. But, ironically, the KKE also provoked the Yugoslav reassessment insofar as it immediately took Moscow's side in the dispute, in spite of the fact that Moscow was not providing any form of assistance to their struggle! The principal reason for this self-destructive decision on the part of the KKE was apparently that Nikos Zachariades, the general secretary of the KKE, was a slavish follower of Stalin and could not imagine taking a position against the Soviet "Generalisimo."[59] But there was a second factor which entered into Belgrade's calculations, viz., Western offers of sizeable credits in the event that Yugoslavia closed its border with Greece. Tito, in desperate need of cash, readily agreed to this condition and, in July 1949, kept his promise, terminating his assistance to the KKE and scuttling his hopes of annexing Aegean Macedonia.

Aspirations in Albania and Bulgaria

Meanwhile, elsewhere in the Balkans, Tito was dreaming of drawing not only Albania and Bulgaria but also Romania into a federal union of which he would be president. Discussions concerning the incorporation of Albania and Bulgaria into an expanded Yugoslav state began already during World War Two, with Stalin himself proposing the establishment of a federation uniting Bulgaria and Yugoslavia in conversations with Tito in autumn 1944. Indeed, talks for this purpose were initiated in late December of that year. But it quickly became apparent that the Yugoslavs and the Bulgarians had different concepts concerning this prospective federation, with the Yugoslav communists thinking in terms of adding Bulgaria as the seventh republic, and the Bulgarians thinking rather in terms of Bulgaria having equal weight with Yugoslavia; Stalin, taking the Bulgarian side in this dispute, even cited the Austro-Hungarian "dual monarchy" as a potential model for a Bulgaro-Yugoslav union.[60]

The Yugoslav-Bulgarian negotiations dragged on for a few years, but in late July 1947, Tito and Dimitrov met in Bled for historic talks, which culminated in an agreement signed on 1 August. The Bulgarian side agreed to accept teachers from Yugoslav Macedonia and allow them to handle the instruction of school-children in Bulgarian-controlled Pirin Macedonia, but the question of the union of Pirin with the Macedonian Republic was deferred. Moreover, although the two sides agreed in principle to establish a federation, they still had not agreed on the formula for such union. In the meantime, the Yugoslav government renounced any claim to war reparations from Bulgaria.[61] In the third week of August 1947, the Yugoslav government dispatched a delegation to Sofia to carry out the interstate agreements; as part of these agreements, the Bulgarian government allowed the opening of schools in Pirin Macedonia with Macedonian as the language of instruction. About this time, the newspaper *Pirinsko delo*, published in Macedonian, began to circulate in western Bulgaria, and on 7 November 1947, on the thirtieth anniversary of the October Revolution, a Macedonian national theater was opened in Bulgaria.[62]

As these processes were underway, the Yugoslavs received a cable from Moscow asking the Central Committee to dispatch one of its members to the Kremlin so that Yugoslavia and the Soviet Union could "reconcile" their policies toward Albania. Milovan Djilas, Koča Popović (1908–1992), and Mijalko Todorović set out for Moscow on 8 January 1948 "buoyant and full of hope," according to Djilas.[63] It was during this visit that Stalin told the Yugoslavs to "swallow" Albania as soon as possible. But the discussions dragged on, with huge breaks between sessions, so that Djilas, Popović, and Todorović started to visit museums and theaters in order to kill time. Eventually, Popović returned to Yugoslavia, but Edvard Kardelj and Croatian communist leader Vladimir Bakarić (1912–1983) arrived on 8 February. Tito had been invited as well, but, distrusting Stalin, he had declined the invitation on the spurious grounds that he was ill. In the meantime, *Pravda*, Stalin's obedient mouthpiece, had expressed reservations about the notion of a Yugoslav-Bulgarian union, criticizing Dimitrov by name.[64] In the evening of 10 February 1948, Stalin and Soviet foreign minister Vyacheslav Molotov (1890–1986) received the Yugoslavs together with a high-ranking Bulgarian delegation and proceeded to browbeat their guests. In the course of the meeting, Stalin both advocated and condemned the proposed Yugoslav-Bulgarian union, but it was not Stalin's intention to urge either course of action where the union was concerned: Stalin's purpose was specifically to browbeat the Yugoslavs and Bulgarians into submission, repeatedly insisting that all decisions be cleared with him in advance. The Yugoslavs, seeing how servile the Bulgarian communists were becoming vis-à-vis the Kremlin, now backed away from the planned unification; they also shelved plans to annex Albania.

The Soviet-Yugoslav Split

The Soviet-Yugoslav rift, which broke into the open in early summer 1948, had various roots, including disagreements concerning the Partisans' political decisions during World War Two, Yugoslav meddling in the Greek Civil War, Soviet refusal to back Yugoslav claims in Carinthia, Soviet abandonment of Yugoslavia in its demands for territorial concessions in Venezia Giulia and Gorizia, arguments in connection with Bulgaria and Albania, and, beginning immediately after the war, Soviet efforts to recruit agents within the Yugoslav party, government apparatus, and secret police. But the principal point of dispute was that Tito, unlike communist leaders in Bulgaria, Poland, Hungary, and Czechoslovakia, insisted on being his own boss. As already suggested, Stalin wanted the Yugoslavs to be his subordinates; the Yugoslavs, for their part, believed that they could be Stalin's *allies*. Thus, at least until the conflict exploded into the open in June 1948, the Yugoslavs worked hard at being Stalin's "best comrades." In this spirit, as parts of Yugoslavia faced starvation in 1945, holding on only thanks to a steady flow of food assistance from UNRRA (the United Nations Rescue and Relief Agency), the Yugoslavs devoted tangibly more space in the press to praising the Soviets for the much smaller quantities of food being sent from those quarters.[65]

But problems could not always be hidden either. Already on 27 May 1945, Tito delivered a defiant speech in Ljubljana. Angry at the Soviets for not backing his pretensions in Carinthia and Venezia Giulia and resentful of incipient Soviet efforts to impose their domination on the CPY, Tito told his audience,

Our goal is that every man be the master in his own house. We are not going to pay the balance on others' accounts, we are not going to serve as pocket money in anyone's currency exchange, we are not going to allow ourselves to become entangled in political spheres of interest. Why should it be held against our peoples that they want to be completely independent? And why should that autonomy be restricted, or the subject of dispute? We will not be dependent on anyone ever again.[66]

Moscow protested this speech—not to the Yugoslav government, however, but rather to the CC CPY. The protest, delivered to Kardelj in early June, said inter alia, "We regard the speech by Comrade Tito as an unfriendly attack on the Soviet Union. . . . Tell Comrade Tito that if he should mount such an attack one more time on the Soviet Union, we will be compelled to answer him in the press and to disavow him."[67]

Although most Western observers either did not take any notice of the rising tensions between the Soviet Union and Yugoslavia or dismissed them as tricks aimed at Western audiences, Cavendish W. Cannon, assigned to the U.S. Embassy in Belgrade, understood from relatively early that these tensions could flare into a full-scale conflict and, in September 1947, informed the Department of State that the Tito regime had staked out an independent position in foreign policy and predicted that the regime "may well some day conflict with Soviet purpose."[68]

Other Frictions

In addition to the aforementioned points of contention, sharp frictions were also aroused by Soviet insistence that the Yugoslav Army be reorganized on the

Soviet model[69] and by the so-called joint enterprises, which the Yugoslavs considered tools of Soviet penetration and domination; among the top leaders, only Andrija Hebrang (1899–1948) and Sreten Žujović (1899–1976) made no criticisms of the joint enterprises. Hebrang had crossed swords with Tito already during the National Liberation Struggle, when, as secretary of the Croatian Communist Party, he had repeatedly made decisions autonomously and tried to maximize the autonomy of Croatian party and state institutions.[70] As a result, he was removed from his power base in Croatia and appointed minister of industry and chair of the Federal Planning Commission after the war. Subsequently in April 1946, Hebrang was expelled from the party politburo. Now, as frictions developed between Moscow and Belgrade, Hebrang joined Žujović in taking Moscow's side. Thus, for example, when a letter arrived from the Kremlin, dated 27 March 1948, in which Djilas, Kidrič, Ranković, and Vukmanović-Tempo were criticized by name as "dubious" Marxists, only Žujović spoke in favor of Moscow. By exempting Tito and Kardelj from criticism, Moscow hoped to lull them into purging those named as "dubious," thereby initiating the process of splitting and whittling down the party. But Tito saw through this tactic and held fast.

The Soviets were, in fact, maintaining close contact with Hebrang and Žujović and instructed them in early 1948 to see to Tito's removal from office; apparently the Soviets hoped to see Žujović become general secretary of the CPY with Hebrang assuming the post of prime minister.[71] In March or April 1948, the Kremlin gave orders to Ivan Krajačić, chief of the Croatian secret police, to shoot Tito; instead of carrying out these orders, however, Krajačić informed Tito and provided him with a list of all Yugoslavs working for the Soviet secret police—among them Hebrang and Žujović.[72] Hebrang was placed under house arrest in early April.[73] The Yugoslav communists had scarcely replied to the first Soviet letter when a second letter arrived, dated 4 May. Some 31 pages long, this letter now named Tito and Kardelj as the principal heretics, while defending Hebrang and Žujović and urging the CPY to take its "case" to the Cominform. The CPY responded on 9 May 1948 by expelling Hebrang and Žujović from the Central Committee and from the party. On 19 May, an advance invitation, signed by M. A. Suslov, was delivered to Tito, inviting him to attend a special session of the Cominform to be devoted to Yugoslavia's "errant" ways. The CC CPY rejected the invitation unanimously at a plenary session the following day. This was followed by a third letter from Stalin, now addressed to Tito and Hebrang. The Cominform's official invitation to the Yugoslavs to attend the planned meeting arrived on 19 June; Tito once more declined. Stalin was ready for his showdown with Tito, threatening that he would wag his little finger, and there would be no more Tito.

The Cominform meeting was held on 28 June 1948—on the triple anniversary of the Battle of Kosovo (1389), the assassination of Archduke Franz Ferdinand (1914), and the adoption of the Vidovdan constitution (1921). The date was no coincidence; Stalin chose the date in order to add poignancy to the ritual of drumming the Yugoslavs out of the international communist movement. Meeting in Bucharest, the Cominform wasted no time in adopting the prepared text of a resolution. In this resolution, the Soviet bloc accused the Yugoslav communist leaders of having pursued an anti-Soviet policy, of having defamed Soviet military specialists, of having lapsed into "Trotskyism," of having carried out "an erroneous policy in the villages, ignoring class differentiation in [the] villages and considering the individual peasantry as [a] class entity, contrary to Marxist-Leninist teachings," and of having elevated the Popular Front to a position of authority *over* the communist party. The resolution also called on Yugoslav communists whose primary loyalty was to the Kremlin "to force their present leaders to an open and honest recognition of their mistakes and to order them to . . . return to internationalism."[74] This was followed by the rupture of economic ties between the Soviet bloc and Yugoslavia and, on 18 August, by yet another bullying note from the Soviets, who reiterated their criticisms of the allegedly "Trotskyist" nature of the Yugoslav regime. After the Cominform's expulsion of Yugoslavia, Yugoslav army generals Branko Petričević and Vladimir Dapčević sided with Moscow. But as Belgrade clamped down on the dissent, a certain number of Soviet sympathizers flew across the border to Hungary, Romania, or Bulgaria; General Arso Jovanović, chief-of-staff of the Partisan Army and another Soviet sympathizer, joined Petričević and Dapčević in attempting on 13 August to cross into Romania. Jovanović was shot on the spot, while Dapčević and Petričević, deputy head of political administration in the Yugoslav Army, were apprehended and eventually sentenced to 20 years at hard labor.[75] In the meantime, at the Fifth Party Congress (convened toward the end of the year),Tito devoted a large part of his opening speech to underlining his country's loyalty to the USSR, and at the end of his speech there were cries of "Tito! Stalin!"[76] Within party echelons, Tito was quite frank about the repugnance he felt for Stalin. But it was too early to be completely frank with the rank and file; indoctrinated for years to believe that Stalin was all-wise and all-good, the rank and file needed to be weaned more gradually from psychological dependence on Stalin.

In fact, many Yugoslavs refused to break with Stalin; for them there could only be one path to communism, and if Tito was not on that path, then Tito was indeed a heretic. These "Cominformists," as they came to be called in official Yugoslav jargon, variously fled (in some cases to operate émigré newspapers or to attempt to stage armed provocations from across the borders) or remained in the country, where they were hunted down by Ranković's secret police. According to official figures provided to the Sixth Party Congress (1952) by Ranković, some 11,128 alleged Cominformists had been "penalized by summary administrative procedure" by then, with an additional 2,572 persons sentenced by civilians or military courts for pro-Cominform activities.[77] The actual figure may, however, be slightly higher. According to Radovan Radonjić, there were 55,663 certified Cominformists, of whom 16,288 were arrested or sentenced. Of the 16,288 arrested and convicted Cominformists, 7,235 (44.42%) were Serbs and

3,439 (21.13%) were Montenegrins; only 436 (2.68%) were Albanians. According to Ivo Banac, Cominformist tendencies were overrepresented among Montenegrins, Bulgarians, Italians, and Czechs, and "underrepresented" among Slovenes, Hungarians, Albanians, and Croats.[78] Convicted Cominformists were incarcerated at Goli Otok, Lepoglava, or other prisons and were subjected to prolonged and intense psychological harassment.

Of the 55,663 Cominformists identified by Radonjić—i.e., counting both those convicted and those who escaped arrest—28,661 (or 51.49%) were found in Serbia, while Serbs predominated among Cominformists in Bosnia-Herzegovina, Vojvodina, and Kosovo and constituted an important segment of Croatian Cominformist ranks.[79] One may speculate that at least a portion of the Serb Cominformists consisted of those Chetniks who had come over to the Partisans late in the war, who perhaps were taking Stalin's side more out of continued hostility toward Tito than out of any real affection for Stalin. Be that as it may, Cominformist sentiment instigated outright rebellion in Montenegro in a series of waves.

Mobile UDB-a forces suppressed the strongest outbreaks during the summer and autumn of 1948. The following year the security units of Komnen Cerović destroyed the Cominformist strongholds in the Montenegrin portion of the Sandžak. Rebellions also broke out in the Zeta valley, between Nikšić and Titograd, the capital of Montenegro; most party members there sided with the insurgents and fought alongside them. The participation of leading Cominformists from other areas—such as Miloš Stojaković, former forestry minister in Bosnia-Herzegovina—indicates that some *ibeovci* [i.e., Cominformists] thought of Montenegro as a possible base area from which partisan warfare could spread to the other republics, especially Bosnia-Herzegovina and eventually Serbia.[80]

To Invade or Not to Invade

In the period June 1948–mid-1949, the Kremlin hoped that Yugoslav Communists, trained for decades to assume Stalin's infallibility, would revolt against Tito.[81] Hundreds of Yugoslav citizens were already in the USSR, and a large number of these were now recruited into armed units being formed and trained in the USSR. They were subsequently infiltrated back into Yugoslavia, where they attempted to stir up rebellion.[82] In Bucharest, for example, about 200 defectors from Yugoslavia received training in espionage and sabotage beginning in 1949 and were subsequently parachuted back into their country of origin.[83] According to Krzavac and Marković, "more than 700 émigrés were infiltrated [into Yugoslavia] across the frontiers, with arms, mines, leaflets, [on] spying and terrorist assignments. Around 160 were captured, and forty were killed in direct conflict with [Yugoslav] security organs."[84] Anti-Tito émigrés were also given funding to publish and distribute propaganda. In Moscow, for instance, they were allowed to broadcast programs on Radio Moscow, and in Prague, Cominformists published the newspaper *Nova Borba* and maintained close contact with Bedrich Geminder, head of the Foreign Section of the Czechoslovak CP.

Yugoslav Cominformists also established three International Brigades, stationed in Hungary, Romania, and Bulgaria, the last of which included 6,000 "volunteers" from the German Democratic Republic. Belgrade sources estimate that there were some 3,500 Cominformist émigrés at the time. In addition, there were hundreds, if not thousands, of disaffected Yugoslavs who had remained in Yugoslavia. Cominformist insurgency began in summer and autumn 1948, and although most intense in Montenegro, it affected also Slovenia, Croatia, and Bosnia-Herzegovina, where, in May 1950, army units rose up in Cominformist mutiny. [85]

Beginning in autumn 1949, the Soviets refused to have any official or even private contacts with the Yugoslavs; from 1949 to 1953, the only exception was the exchange of protest notes.[86] The Soviets obviously hoped that the domestic insurgents could either overthrow Tito single-handedly or create enough political disorder to facilitate a Soviet intervention. As early as 7 November 1948, Foreign Minister Molotov, in a speech commemorating the October Revolution, called on the Yugoslav people to overthrow Tito, and a year and a half later (6 May 1950), Nikolai Bulganin declared in Prague, "We believe it will not be long before [the Yugoslav people] achieve victory over the Tito-Ranković clique."[87]

In communications dated 6 July 1948 and 11 June 1949, the Yugoslav government sought to recall its citizens studying in civilian and military schools in the USSR and protested Soviet failure, even after repeated requests, to permit the repatriation of Yugoslav children in the USSR. The Yugoslav government also protested that the USSR was nurturing anti-Tito exiles. The Kremlin replied on 31 May 1949, asserting its right "to receive and give shelter to the Yugoslav patriot-exiles, persecuted by the Yugoslav anti-democratic regime for their democratic and socialist convictions."[88] As a secret Cominformist directive of 1951 makes clear, the Kremlin looked to the domestic Cominformists to build up an alternative organizational apparatus and considered that the timetable for takeover would depend on the relative success in organization building.[89] But by the end of summer 1949, Ranković's secret police had by and large broken the back of the domestic Cominformist dissent.[90] Hence, if Stalin was to stay in the game, he had to escalate.

The escalation came in September 1949, when the Soviet government declared itself "released" from any obligation under its 1945 Treaty of Friendship with Yugoslavia, citing the "evidence" produced at the trial of László Rajk in Hungary. Shortly before Molotov's ultimatum, intelligence sources had revealed the formation of special armed groups for the projected invasion of Yugoslavia, ascertaining that some seven motorized divisions were close to Yugoslav borders.[91] Between 1945 and 1948, the Hungarian Army, for example, had been allowed to fall into a state of decrepitude. Within three months of the expulsion of Yugoslavia from the Cominform, however, the Hungarian armed forces began to be rejuvenated, a political officer system was introduced along with party cells and anti-Titoist indoctrination, the army's strength was beefed up, and Hungarian production of war materiel was stepped up. In September 1948, the Hungarian Army consisted of a paltry two undermanned rifle divisions plus one engineering division. By summer of 1950, it counted nine infantry divisions, three engineering divisions, one chemical division, one horse cavalry division, one signal regiment, one communication brigade, and three heavy armored regiments. Béla Király, an eyewitness, recalls having seen the "feverish modernization" of airfields and the construction of new ones, whose immediate purpose was to provide air bases for assault against Yugoslavia.[92] Arms industries were quickly developed, rail lines with strategic value were upgraded, and the highway system was developed with military needs foremost among the considerations. Throughout 1950 and early 1951, there were repeated war games and military maneuvers designed to practice for invasion. By then, armed strength levels in Hungary, Romania, and Bulgaria were two to three and a half times the levels permitted by the Paris Peace Treaty. Table 5.1 shows strength levels in 1951.

In early June 1950, the highest echelons in the Hungarian Army were arrested and variously executed or imprisoned; military illiterates were named to replace them, with the effect that actual operational control passed clearly into the hands of Soviet "advisors."[93] This was a clear signal that the Kremlin considered the preparations for invasion complete and that the assault would come shortly. Mátyás Rákosi, the Hungarian party leader, expecting that Yugoslavia would be broken up, evidently hoped to annex Croatia to Hungary, thereby reclaiming the Habsburg patrimony.[94]

On 25 June 1950, news came that North Korea had launched an offensive against South Korea. Király believes that this was timed to precede the invasion of Yugoslavia by a few months.[95] But whether it was so timed or not is inessential to the argument. The point is that Yugoslavia had been in contact with the Americans since early 1948, had signed a foreign trade agreement with a U.S. company as early as April 1949, and, under the Yugoslav Emergency Act of 1950, had obtained $50 million from the U.S., in addition to $26.5 million in previously authorized agricultural goods. The Americans sent boatloads of sugar, wheat, and flour, agreed to send tanks, heavy artillery, and fighter aircraft, and

Table 5.1. Military Forces in the Balkans, Summer 1951

	# of troops permitted under peace treaty	Actual # of troops	Total # of divisions	# of divisions oriented toward Yugoslavia
Hungary	70,000	200,000	13	7
Romania	138,000	290,000	19	9
Bulgaria	65,000	220,000	18	8

Source: Vladimir Dedijer (ed.), *Dokumenti 1948,* vol. 3 (Belgrade: Rad, 1979), p. 332.

offered equipment to outfit heavy armaments factories; these factories were now built in Bosnia and western Serbia.[96] When Stalin considered the firm American response in Korea and saw the increasing favor with which the U.S. regarded Tito, he shelved the projected invasion. Yet even now, Yugoslavia's worries were not over. In early August 1950, Bulgarian authorities started removing and interning many families from villages along the Yugoslav frontier in the northwestern tip of Bulgaria, evacuating the villages of Rakovica, Kakres, Aleksandrov, Kapetanovac, Sardev, Jesnjinac, Kobilje, Dragovac, and Lesikac.[97] It was hard to avoid interpreting these evacuations as anything but continued preparations for a possible invasion.

Under the circumstances, Tito wanted to obtain as firm a guarantee of Western support as possible. U.S. secretary of state Dean Acheson offered an unambiguous guarantee of protection in February 1951 when, in response to a question about U.S. willingness to defend Yugoslavia if it were subjected to a military assault, the secretary declared that the U.S. attitude could be inferred from its response to the military aggression on the Korean peninsula.[98] But even several months after invasion had most likely ceased to be on the agenda, Tito told foreign journalists at a press conference in Brdo (Slovenia), August 1951, that the danger of a Soviet invasion of Yugoslavia was greater than ever and declined to exclude the possibility that an American military mission might be invited to Yugoslavia, noting that U.S.–Yugoslav negotiations about military instruction were in progress.[99] Tito was probably genuinely worried, given a series of border incidents along Yugoslavia's borders with Hungary, Romania, Bulgaria, and Albania over the months April–September 1951 and the Czechoslovak government's noisy closure of its consulate in Zagreb in May of that year.[100] On 14 November 1951, finally, the U.S. and Yugoslavia signed an agreement on military assistance to strengthen Yugoslav defense capability, and an American military assistance advisory group was established in Belgrade.[101] Large-scale military maneuvers had been staged in Bulgaria in September–October 1950 (with the participation of Soviet generals and other officers), in Hungary in January 1951, and in Hungary again in September 1951.[102] After the establishment of the American advisory group in Belgrade, the military maneuvers by bloc states came to an end, and the East bloc armies were once more reduced in size.

Impact of the Rift on Yugoslav Foreign Relations

As early as 3 September 1948, Secretary of State Acheson and British deputy foreign secretary Hector McNeil advised Moscow that an attack on Yugoslavia would have "serious" consequences. A new tone crept into Yugoslav rhetoric. Tito, for example, in an address to the AFŽ (Anti-Fascist Women) Third Congress on 29 October 1950, thanked the U.S. for having provided the bulk of the $430,000,000 in UNRRA aid after World War Two and made other pro-American and pro-Western allusions, referring, for example, to the "progressive leaders" in the West.[103] By 1950, the Yugoslav government, having abandoned the

Greek communist guerrillas, was seeking to normalize its relations with the Greek government.[104]

Tito's gravitation to the West survived Stalin's death in March 1953, and in May 1954, Tito told Cyrus L. Sulzberger, in an interview published in *Borba*, that he was interested in "direct military association with leading NATO powers, [and] indirect cooperation with NATO through [the] Ankara agreement."[105] The following month, Tito paid a state visit to Athens, and in August Yugoslavia signed the Balkan Pact with Greece and Turkey, establishing a combined General Staff and some institutions for cooperation in nonmilitary spheres. The pact's ill-named Permanent Council met the following February, but soon after the Balkan Pact withered away, partly under the impact of the Soviet-Yugoslav rapprochement which began in May of that year, but also as a result of the estrangement between Greece and Turkey over Cyprus. By 1960, the Balkan Pact was officially declared dead, even as Yugoslavia raised the question of a revision of its borders with Greece.[106]

Impact of the Rift on Yugoslav Domestic Politics

In late November 1950 came the dramatic release of Sreten Žujović from prison. According to the party organ, *Borba*, Žujović had recanted his previous views and had admitted that he had felt that Yugoslavia should and would be annexed to the Soviet Union.[107] He was lucky. Hebrang died in prison, allegedly from suicide, while many other alleged Cominformists—some of them guilty of nothing more than competing for the fancy of a woman being eyed by a local communist—would serve out long terms before being released, only to find, not surprisingly, their families gone, their careers ruined, their lives wrecked.

But in the wake of Yugoslavia's expulsion from the Cominform, Kardelj, Djilas, and others had begun to rethink not only the ideological premises of their own system but also their relationship to the Soviet Union. As early as the Fifth Congress of the CPY, Kardelj declared authoritatively that "the forms of expression of [the] dictatorship of the proletariat . . . are not and cannot be the same in all countries and conditions."[108] Subsequently, the Yugoslavs came to the conclusion that the Soviet Union had erred in failing to push forward with the devolution of authority to workers' councils and organs of direct people's authority. This meant that the Soviets had not taken the steps necessary to assure the inception of the process of the withering away of the state, a process prescribed by Friedrich Engels and endorsed by V. I. Lenin. Kardelj made the question of the withering away of the state a major theme for his address to the Skupština in May 1949 and, two years later, avowed that "the state in the Soviet Union and in the lands with Cominform governments is not a state in the Marxist or Leninist sense, namely a state which is so organized that it can gradually wither away."[109] Rodoljub Čolaković, another senior Yugoslav leader, went even further, warning, in 1952, that Soviet neglect of the dangers coming from the state apparatus risked the burgeoning of that apparatus "into a machine of

force and coercion over society."[110] As late as February 1953, in a major theoretical address, Kardelj told the Fourth Congress of the People's Front (in Belgrade) that, in the Soviet Union

the state-capitalist forms represent the result of the degeneration of the proletarian revolution, that is, a completely reactionary product of the bureaucratic caste, which had
gradually wrested power from the hands of the working class. . . . [T]he degeneration of
the Soviet Revolution is due to the fact that bureaucratism—insufficiently controlled by
the political consciousness and actions of the working class—has strengthened the necessary transitional state-capitalist forms instead of eliminating them, and has subsequently developed them even further and has finally transformed them into the only
existing social relations, protected with all the means of coercion.[111]

That this critique entailed, of necessity, institutional adaptation within Yugoslavia was abundantly clear; the nature of this response is, however, the subject
of the next chapter.

The clash between Stalin and Tito assumed an ideological dimension from
the beginning, with Stalin denying Tito's communist credentials, and Tito in
turn affirming them. At first Tito and his comrades did not deny Stalin's communist credentials; later, after they discovered that Stalin was actually running
a state capitalist system, they did. But the clash between these two illegitimate
systems had a further ideological impact, viz., it gave the Titoist system an aura
of quasi-legitimacy, upon which Tito would wisely build. Tito, perhaps more
than any other East European communist leader, appreciated that legitimation
was indeed the central challenge which a communist system confronts.

CHAPTER 6

Dreaming a New Dream, 1950–1962

To turn an illegitimate system into even a quasi-legitimate system may seem, to some, rather like transforming a frog into a prince. So how did Tito accomplish this bit of magic? Already in the late 1940s, the reemergence of various noncommunist, anti-fascist parties forced Tito and his circle to prioritize the challenge of legitimation. To meet this challenge, the Tito regime invoked the mythology of the Partisan war, with its legitimating symbols of heroic resistance and its allegedly revolutionary character. Edvard Kardelj, then foreign minister, put the case in these terms in a speech delivered in 1951: "Our people's authority arose from the revolution. In the course of a revolution, the people's will can find its full expression and that is the reason why democracy and revolutionary dictatorship mean the same thing."[1] The People's Liberation Struggle (or NOB) had not been only a triumph of anti-fascist resistance, however. It had also born witness to inter-ethnic cooperation or, as the Partisans would have it, the brotherhood and unity of Yugoslav peoples under a communist banner. In this way, the first component of the legitimating triad (brotherhood and unity, self-management, nonalignment) was born. One could fairly describe this as the "moral" component of the triad.

The schism with the Cominform forced the Tito regime to distinguish its political and economic formula from that of the Soviets. The invention of workers' self-management in 1950 was the regime's answer. The formula of self-management was simultaneously economic (in the sense that it created a category of rather nebulously defined "social property" and assigned workers certain administrative prerogatives within their places of work) and political (in the sense that self-management was seen, from the beginning, as an instrument for effecting a movement in the direction of the ultimate withering away of the state[2] and insofar as the entire political system came to be characterized as a "self-managing socialist system").

The third leg in the triad—nonalignment—emerged in the mid-1950s, as Tito collaborated with Third World leaders, such as Egypt's Gamal abd al-Nasir and India's Jawaharlal Nehru, to develop a nonaligned movement in which member states would abjure both the passive role of unaligned or neutral states and any affiliation with either the Soviet bloc or the American-sponsored Atlantic Alliance. Yugoslavia's membership—indeed, leadership role—in the nonaligned movement was designed to legitimate Yugoslavia's foreign policy (specifically, its refusal to subordinate its foreign policy to Kremlin coordination) and to demonstrate that Yugoslav foreign policy was fundamentally progressive.

Taken in sum, these programmatic components struck many observers as amounting to a new vision of politics, a new dream; and at the height of the Titoist experiment, delegations from all over the world would visit Yugoslavia to study self-management and see what might be applicable in their own countries.

But in addition to the Cominformist challenge discussed in the previous chapter, there were three additional areas in which the communists confronted vexing problems. The first was that Ustaša and Chetnik activities continued until the mid-1950s, a full decade after Tito's communists declared their victory over those elements. The second was that, among the peasants, collectivization was actively resisted; as noted in the previous chapter, the series of harvest failures compelled Yugoslavia to turn to Britain and the U.S. for emergency food deliveries. These harvest failures signaled the failure of the collectivization drive, ultimately compelling the authorities to permit the dismantlement of most of the agricultural cooperatives. And third, within the party, there were repeated efforts variously to soften party discipline or to devolve administrative authority from the party to various sectors in the society or to circumvent party discipline or to deflect the party toward a more "liberal" course. These sundry efforts were characterized by the party as "anarcho-liberalism." The most stinging critique of the system in this regard came from Milovan Djilas who, in a series of articles for *Borba* in late 1953 and early 1954, accused the CPY leadership of establishing itself as a new elite and demanded a comprehensive liberalization of the system. These three points are considered immediately below, followed by sections on the failure of collectivization, the war against organized religion, the Soviet-Yugoslav rapprochement of 1955, controversies surrounding the Hungarian revolution in October 1956 and the League of Communists of Yugoslavia (LCY) Seventh Congress in April 1958, and the growing pressures for change accumulating over the years 1959–1962.

Disgruntled Émigrés, Fascists in the Hills

As Tito's forces swept northward across Croatia and Slovenia and into Carinthia in 1945, many Ustaša and Chetnik elements fled to Austria and Italy. Pavelić himself was in Salzburg briefly after the war before transferring secretly first to Florence and then to Rome, where he was given shelter by the Vatican. According to *Borba*, Pavelić also stayed for a while at Gandolfo Castle, the papal summer residence, before emigrating to Montevideo, with the assistance of the Vatican. He later settled in Argentina.[3] Nor was Vatican assistance limited to the former *Poglavnik*'s case. As of 1947, a number of prominent Ustaše were living in Rome, benefiting from the protection of the Church. According to a report filed by an American special agent, nine former ministers of the NDH were living at the time on the premises of the Monastery of San Girolamo in Rome, including Vjekoslav Vrančić, former deputy foreign minister; Dragutin Toth, former minister of the Croatian State Treasury; and Mile Starčević, former minister of education.[4] Eventually, with the help of the Vatican, most of the Ustaše, who had eluded capture by Tito's forces, succeeded in emigrating to South America.

Others—both Ustaše and Chetniks—remained in Austria for the interim, though many of the Ustaše later resettled in the United States, Canada, Australia, and Argentina, establishing the Hrvatski Narodni Odbor (Croatian National Committee) as their political front organization.[5] The Chetniks also dispersed, some of them ending up in the United States.[6] Meanwhile, among the Croatian émigrés in Austria after the end of World War Two there were two orientations: the Ustaša current and the HSS current, whose adherents had emigrated not because of war crimes but because of their opposition to communism. Some of the Ustaše in Austria were personally loyal to Pavelić and refused to consider collaboration with any other Croatian political grouping. But there were also Ustaše who were open to collaboration with the HSS. Maček's people, on the other hand, were not interested in collaboration with the Ustaše but were open to collaboration, up to a point, with émigré Slovenes and Serbs. There were also HSS adherents who rejected any notion of cooperation with Slovenes and Serbs, however; these Croats looked to Juraj Krnjević for leadership, rather than to Maček.[7] At the same time, members of Mihailović's Ravna Gora Movement continued to generate Chetnik propaganda and to protest local Ustaša activities.

The Ustaše and Chetniks held out hope, for some years, that the U.S. would bankroll their return to Yugoslavia. Already in 1947, Dr. Petar Prokop, a well-known Ustaša, met with four American special agents in order to solicit financial and moral support for his rump Ustaša organization, which was dreaming of overthrowing the Tito regime. The organization, headquartered in the British zone of occupation in Austria, included both former Ustaša and former Domobran elements. Significantly, although based in Austria, the organization claimed that the bulk of its membership had remained in Croatia.[8] In November 1947, Ustaša activity in the American zone of occupation in Germany was first noticed.[9]

Dragomir Ostrić made a similar appeal for American assistance, presenting himself at the U.S. Embassy in Madrid in December 1950, on which occasion he claimed to represent a group of Yugoslav émigrés in Spain having contact with some 15,000 battle-worthy anti-communist Yugoslavs across Europe, including 5,000 in the United Kingdom, 5,000 in Germany, and 5,000 in other West European countries.[10]

Among disaffected Yugoslav émigrés, Milivoje Šokić earned a certain notoriety in U.S. policy-making circles for his ambitious schemes. In May 1950, Šokić and 37 other Yugoslav émigrés in the U.S., Canada, the United Kingdom, France, and Argentina were said to be assembling an opposition organization which already had at least three trusted contacts in each of 67 cities across Yugoslavia.[11] In June 1952, Šokić turned up in Libya and presented himself to the American Embassy in Tripoli and to the American Consulate in Benghazi, talking about salvaging sunken vessels off Libya's coast for scrap, obtaining an exclusive concession to market Coca-Cola in Libya, and establishing the National Bank of Libya and about having the backing of the Chase National Bank for the creation of a Balkan army to receive commando training in Cyrenaica; he wanted American support.[12] Bolard More, the American consul in Benghazi, reported to the Department of State that he found conversations with Šokić to be "vague" and "exasperating," concluding that he was "a man of talk and projects with no very clear view of how to put them into action."[13]

Among Yugoslav émigrés, probably no one commanded as much respect as Vladko Maček, the Croatian Peasant Party leader who had refused Hitler's offer to establish him as president of a quisling Croat state. By 1952, Maček, who had for a while nurtured hopes of seeing the emergence of a *democratic* Croat state, had given up notions of Croatian independence and was seeking to build bridges with anti-communist Serbian exile groups in opposition to the communist regime in Belgrade. In this spirit, the new party program for the HSS, adopted in 1952, said that there were "no insoluble differences between Serbs and Croats."[14]

The Yugoslav secret police proved effective in rooting out the small networks of anti-communist political discontents. In February 1950, for example, 15 members of an underground opposition group calling itself the Union of Yugoslav Nations, were put on trial in Belgrade. They were found guilty of having sought to overthrow the communist regime and reestablish the Kingdom of Serbs, Croats, and Slovenes and given sentences ranging from two years at "corrective" labor to 20 years at hard labor.[15] Eleven months later, another 16 persons (Chetnik in orientation) were put on trial in Belgrade on charges of conspiracy to overthrow the government and restore King Petar. Among the accused were General Mica Stefanović, former commander of the royal Yugoslav police, Kosta Kumanudi, minister of the interior in the interwar cabinet, and Velimir Popović, speaker of parliament and minister of finance in royal

Yugoslavia.[16] Prosecutors alleged that the conspirators had been assisted by French military intelligence operatives and that some of the accused had been instructed by persons connected with the U.S. Army, Trieste. All 16 were convicted; 15 of them received long prison terms, while the 16th was sentenced to death.[17] Six of the convicted had been members of the wartime Chetnik organization.[18] Shortly thereafter, Andre (or Andrei) Kocebu, formerly an officer in the Royal Yugoslav Army, was arrested and put on trial, after he had organized armed bands in Macedonia to fight the communist regime.[19] A confidential report dated 12 January 1951 claimed that there were, at the time, still four to five Chetnik "brigades" operating in the back woods of Yugoslavia, each brigade consisting of about 400 men. These groups stayed close to the borders of Hungary, Romania, Bulgaria, and Albania, and in the forests of Montenegro, attacking Yugoslav troops and police, firing on communist party meetings, and raiding police buildings.[20] One of these brigades (operating in Montenegro) was being led by Dragutin Stanislav, who had served as an officer with the Chetniks during World War Two, though the identity of the overall leader of the Chetniks was not known. Small groups of Chetniks continued to operate in the mountains and forests between Kalinovik and Trnovo as late as November 1952.[21] Trials of wartime Chetniks and Ustaše continued until 1957.[22]

Contacts between local citizens and unfriendly émigré organizations continued even longer. In early January 1958, for example, Yugoslav police arrested Milan Žujović, a law professor at the University of Belgrade, on suspicion of maintaining contact with émigré Chetnik organizations. His arrest followed the arrests, the previous month, of Professor Dragoslav Stranjaković (a member of the theological faculty at the University of Belgrade), Bogdan Krekić (a labor leader before the war), Aleksandar "Aca" Pavlović (a Belgrade lawyer and, during World War Two, a member of the Chetnik political committee), and Myrgud Sambek [sic] (a Yugoslav working as a translator at the U.S. Embassy). Stranjaković, Krekić, and Pavlović, like Žujović, were arrested, because, as a regime spokesperson put it, they were "well-known collaborators and Chetnik leaders" who had been trying to continue their political activity, seeking Chetnik support abroad.[23] Brought to trial on charges of plotting to overthrow the regime, Krekić, Pavlović, and Žujović were found guilty, in spite of claims by the accused that their alleged conspiracy had amounted to no more than vague grumblings "over cups of coffee," and sent to prison.[24] Pavlovic's admission that the accused favored "peaceful and democratic change" in Yugoslavia scarcely seemed compatible with the prosecution's characterization of their views.[25]

Discontent among the Croats also continued. On 31 March 1959, a trial opened in the Bosnian town of Zenica of 11 persons accused, under Article 117 of the penal code, with conspiracy against the state. They were said to have received assistance "from abroad" and to have been recruiting members into an underground organization inspired by the ideas of the wartime NDH.[26] Scarcely nine months later, another 16 Croats, with a Franciscan monk (Monsignor Jerak) as chief defendant, were brought to trial for "having maintained contact with Croatian émigré circles and having committed other offenses such as writing letters to Radio Madrid, keeping in touch with the Ustaša émigré center in Rome, sending information for use in propaganda broadcasts, and endeavoring to establish an underground organization."[27] After nearly two weeks of hearings, in which the Roman Catholic Church was characterized as inspiring Croatian separatism, the 16 were convicted of anti-state conspiracy. Monsignor Jerak received the harshest sentence—15 years in prison.[28]

Moreover, as Tito and his ministers knew, those actively engaged in political opposition were only the tip of an iceberg of discontent. In summer 1950, it was reported that many people in Yugoslavia were opposed to the regime and "bitterly hate[d] Tito and his entire government."[29] Tito drew the appropriate conclusions and traveled around Belgrade under heavy guard.

So intense and so widespread was opposition to the communist regime in these years that, as the authorities themselves conceded, there was a high percentage of "no" votes in the elections of 26 March 1950 in certain rural areas in Serbia, Croatia, Slovenia, and Vojvodina—in some cases as much as 35%.[30] Overall, negative votes represented 13.1% of the tally in Vojvodina, 7.7% of the vote in Serbia proper (i.e., not counting Vojvodina and Kosovo), 6.2% in Kosovo, and 4.0% in Slovenia in 1950. Although the proportion of negative votes generally declined in parliamentary elections held the following year, in Slovenia the proportion of negative votes actually increased in 1951—to 7.6%.[31]

From Workers' Councils to the Djilas Affair

The first public enunciation of the doctrine of workers' self-management came on 26 June 1950, with Tito's address to the Skupština, introducing a law establishing workers' councils. Although the communist party–state apparatus remained in command of the economy and continued to draw up plan targets, the law reinforced some tendencies toward administrative devolution. Indeed, that same year the republics were entrusted with a large share of the administrative responsibilities hitherto reserved to the central government, e.g., the supervision of electric power, mines, agriculture, forestry, light industry, and public works. In Belgrade, the federal departments were now said to have been replaced by "coordination councils."[32] On 1 February 1951, the Yugoslav government announced the abolition of the Federal State Control Commission, an economic regulatory body, and instructed the republics to abolish the counterparts to this body at their level. The functions which had been entrusted to these commissions were now transferred to "higher economic associations" to be governed by workers' councils.[33] The Yugoslavs talked of dismantling the state as such, in favor of free associations of workers. A speech by Boris Kidrič, president of the Economic Council, captures the mood of that day very well. "We actually are carrying out the withering away of the state," Kidrič told the Association of Economists of Serbia in April 1951,

We really are switching over to a system of free association under direct producers . . . and we are carrying out [this] plan under special circumstances . . . of . . . unheard of economic pressure from the Eastern imperialist bloc. . . .

We have a very bad remnant of Soviet practice, the so-called theory of generalizing at all costs and glorifying every positive occurrence . . . [which] represents a bit of danger now . . . when we are in the process of transforming the state into [the] general property of the people.[34]

Further reorganization of the economic branches of both the federal and the republican governments was undertaken in mid-1952 in the direction of greater decentralization; at least 20 important officials and 5,000 minor officials were reassigned to new posts at this time, contributing to "an almost uniform confusion . . . among Belgrade officials."[35]

A pivotal event at this time was the Sixth Party Congress, held in Zagreb in November 1952. In the lead-up to the Congress, there were signs of serious differences of opinion within the CPY Politburo concerning the desired pace of socio-economic transformation. Djilas, Moša Pijade, and possibly Nešković were said to favor a fast tempo of decentralization, the control of industry by labor, less bureaucracy, and an expanded role for workers' councils. Kardelj, Ranković, Ivan Gošnjak, and Kidrič favored a slower pace of development. At the time, Tito was rumored—correctly, as it turned out—to be leaning toward the latter group.[36]

Djilas, then deputy chair of the Federal Executive Council, was at the height of his power and was chosen to draft the resolution to be adopted at the forthcoming party congress. Djilas, whose maverick tendencies had been evident to an external observer as early as 1944,[37] gave an early indication of his policy preferences in March 1952, when he penned an article for the party daily, *Borba*, warning,

it seems to me very dangerous for our democratic development if, in the struggle against reactionary bourgeois intriguers, against the backwardness of some individual priests, etc., we would come forward with [a] campaign and administrative measures, and not mostly and exclusively (when it is not a question of evident breaking of the law) with ideological, educational, and similar measures. A campaign and administrative conduct could make us only retrogress, . . . and strengthen bureaucracy both in the Party and outside of it and . . . hinder our democratic development.[38]

When the Sixth Congress finally convened on 2 November 1952 (after a short postponement from 19 October), the CPY was, in a symbolically laden move, renamed the League of Communists of Yugoslavia (LCY),[39] while the party Politburo was renamed the Executive Committee. The Congress called for communists to struggle against both bureaucratism and bourgeois notions (i.e., against both left-wing and right-wing deviations from the party line) but placed stress on the notion that the party should and would "wither away."

In the wake of the Sixth Congress, party functionaries enthusiastically set about to realize the "withering away of the state" by dissolving party cells (these being replaced by territorial organizations) and slashing the number of professional party functionaries down to 369 by March 1954.[40] It was still under the influence of the spirit of the Sixth Party Congress that the Yugoslavs adopted the Basic Law of 1953, which nullified large parts of the 1946 constitution and substituted various new provisions; so extensive were the changes introduced by this "law" that it came to be viewed as the "second" postwar constitution. While this 1953 document did not recognize the individual rights normally assured in liberal systems as such, it provided for the "free association of working people," "personal freedom and other rights of man," and "the right to work."[41] The new constitution further encouraged hopes of greater internal democracy. Not all party officials welcomed these developments, which, in any event, revived problems of internal party discipline. Accordingly, on 16–17 June 1953, the party Central Committee met on the island of Brioni in order to quash the tendencies toward internal democratization which had been set in motion in Zagreb the previous autumn and to counter "negative" trends in the press, in economic management, and in the religious sphere.[42]

The Sixth Party Congress had also unleashed hopes for change among those sympathetic to traditional parliamentary democracy.[43] In mid-summer 1953, *Komunist* published a CC letter to basic organizations of the party, emphasizing the importance that party elders attached to the rooting out of "bourgeois-anarchist conceptions of freedom and democracy."[44] In its campaign against Western ideas, the LCY now imposed stricter controls on the media. In Ljubljana, Rudi Janhuba, former Yugoslav press attaché in Rome, was named "responsible editor" (*odgovorni urednik*) of *Slovenski Poročevalec*. As a member of the CC of LC Slovenia, Janhuba was also entrusted with broad authority to discipline the Slovenian press; using his control of workers' councils at the Slovene printing presses, he brought a second local daily, *Dnevnik*, under his control as well, becoming the responsible editor of that newspaper, too. Before the end of the summer, Janhuba had also asserted control over the Slovenian edition of *Borba*, and in the last week of September 1953, after some further machinations, Janhuba became responsible editor also for *PP* (*Petkov Poročevalec*), transforming it into a duller weekly newspaper called *TT* (*Tedenska Tribuna*, or Weekly Tribune), which figured now as the weekly edition of *Slovenski Poročevalec*. Both *Dnevnik* and *PP* had displayed unmistakable signs of editorial independence up to now, and their takeover by Janhuba signified the extirpation of their independent lines.[45]

If the Brioni line was intended as a corrective to the Zagreb line, for which, as already mentioned, Djilas shared personal responsibility, Djilas found himself unable to go along with the Brioni conclusions. Djilas continued to think hard about issues of party and state development; in October 1953, with Tito's encouragement, Djilas began to put those thoughts on paper, publishing them in a series of articles appearing in *Borba*, In one article, Djilas reviewed the argument that "enemies" of socialism should be denied civic rights, pointing to elements of self-contradiction in the socialist line. A further article, published in

Borba on 29 November 1953, saw Djilas arguing for an aspiration toward *democracy* and making it sufficiently clear that he did not mean "*socialist* democracy." In the course of December, Djilas carried his thoughts to their logical conclusion, embracing what, to Tito and his inner circle, inevitably seemed like outright heresy. In one of his December articles, for example, he called for complete freedom of thought, while in another (published on 31 December), he criticized "the security service as a law [un]to itself and an instrument for imposing the authority of the Party, regardless of the interests and rights of the people."[46] In that latter article, Djilas conceded that a vigorous "class struggle" had been necessary as long as the bourgeoisie still had some power, but warned that to continue the tactics of the class struggle once the bourgeoisie had been defeated was "to deviate into bureaucratism," urging that UDBa and the regular police "rid themselves of Party interference."[47] Elsewhere, Djilas advanced the argument "that the once-revolutionary LCY leadership was degenerating into a self-serving bureaucratic caste," advocating a radical reorganization of the League of Communists and the abolition of the communist youth and trade union organizations.[48]

Djilas's articles kindled considerable excitement in certain circles, especially in Slovenia and Croatia, but to a lesser extent elsewhere as well. In Zenica, Bosnia, for example, locals received Djilas's articles as "rays of light and strong beams of sunshine which lighten up our lives."[49] By the end of December, Kardelj was at work on a report concerning Djilas, to be presented at a CC plenary session. Word quickly got out that Tito had become displeased with Djilas's articles, and, significantly, at a New Year's Eve celebration in Ljubljana attended by Tito, Kardelj, Boris Ziherl (a Slovenian member of the CC LCY), and others, a well-known Yugoslav comedian performed a burlesque around Djilas's articles—something he would not have dared to do had Djilas still been in favor.[50] As if his *Borba* articles had not been enough, Djilas had sealed his fate with the publication of an article in the journal *Nova misao* in which, inter alia, he criticized the wives of prominent politicians for ostracizing the wife of General Peko Dapčević, a close friend of Djilas's; the *Nova misao* article evidently infuriated Tito. Meanwhile, Djilas's last article for *Borba* appeared on 7 January 1954, under the headline "Revolution." In this article, Djilas urged,

Today Revolution is reform, peaceful progress. Today it is nonsense to struggle for power in a revolutionary form, not only because it is unrealistic, but [also] because it is counter-revolutionary. . . . The soul of the Revolution can be preserved only in real freedom, because it was carried out by free men, for freedom, and in the name of freedom.

Three days later, *Borba* published a formal disavowal of Djilas's series of articles, which was now characterized as "contrary to the opinions of all other members of the Executive Committee."[51]

A plenary session of the Central Committee was convened at 3 P.M. on 16 January to consider the Djilas case; members of the committee debated deep into the night, reconvening at 9 A.M. the following day. One after another, the party elders took the podium to denounce Djilas. Moša Pijade accused Djilas of "vast conceit," for example, while Aleš Bebler, undersecretary of state for foreign affairs, said that Djilas's office had "gone to his head," adding that he had urged Djilas to "come down off your pedestal." Miha Marinko, the Slovenian prime minister, declared that he was unable to regard Djilas as a true communist.[52] Kardelj accused Djilas of wanting to see the party transformed into "some kind of debating club," using the vocabulary once employed by Lenin to disparage pleas for internal party democracy.[53] Even Tito lashed out against Djilas, whom he accused of resurrecting Bernsteinian revisionism, i.e., social democratic notions.[54] Of the senior party officials, only Gošnjak and Bakarić—the latter rightly regarded as a moderate liberal—declined to speak; the only figure actually to defend Djilas at the plenum was Tito's official biographer, Vladimir Dedijer.

Djilas remained defiant, even telling the Central Committee that he continued to be convinced of the truth of his ideas, admitting only that it had been an error not to have consulted with party executives before publishing his ruminations. Indeed, when Vukmanović-Tempo attempted to read a litany of accusations against Djilas, Djilas repeatedly interrupted Vukmanović, until the latter gave up, and a recess was called. All the same, the CC adopted a resolution on 17 January 1954, charging that Djilas's ideas were "basically contrary to the political line adopted at the VI [party] Congress."[55] Djilas was deprived of all party functions and strongly reprimanded; Dedijer was censured for having defended Djilas. Now, in the wake of the January plenum, 23 persons were expelled from the party in connection with the Djilas case, while another 20 were disciplined.[56] Dušan Diminić, editor of *Naprijed,* a Zagreb weekly, who had been openly enthusiastic about Djilas's ideas, was formally condemned on 23 January; shortly thereafter, his paper was shut down because of "financial difficulties" (a euphemism for the party's withdrawal of funding).[57] At post-affair congresses of the republican parties, the Macedonian and Serbian CCs largely ignored the Djilas affair, but the Slovenian and Croatian congresses, especially the latter, devoted considerable energy to attacking Djilas's ideas.[58] In Bosnia-Herzegovina, a relatively large number of party members were expelled from party ranks in connection with the Djilas affair.[59]

There was an interesting postscript to Djilas's challenge. Namely, in 1957, Vladimir Bakarić, president of the Croatian People's Sabor and, since November 1952, member of the Executive Committee of the CC LCY, spoke out against some of Tito's political plans and let it be known that he favored a more "moderate" line, similar to what he had been fostering in Croatia. As a result, Bakarić was for a while largely "exiled from public life, in spite of his high positions, and was [for some months] not even mentioned in the press."[60] Bakarić's limited championing of a more liberal line confirmed that there continued to be reservations about the conservative line taken by the LCY in the 1950s. Beyond that, the Djilas affair brought home the impatience of the regime with sustained criticism and the depths of popular discontent with communist rule, especially in Slovenia and Croatia.

The Failure of Collectivization

If Djilas's criticisms drew up, at the elite level, a tally of the legitimation problems of the regime, the widespread discontent, and even disorders, among the peasantry documented the peasants' complete and total rejection of the communist economic system which, to their mind, was completely illegitimate.

Yugoslavia's communist elite came to power with the notion that the political recipe for communism entailed, of necessity, agricultural collectivization. Moreover, following the Soviets in this regard, the Yugoslavs believed that, up to a point, large agricultural cooperatives were a "higher" form of agricultural organization than small cooperatives; this was the reason why the average number of households per cooperative swelled from 50 in 1949 to 200 in 1950. As of 1948, there were only 1,318 agricultural cooperatives in Yugoslavia, embracing some 60,158 households. But in 1949, a concerted effort was made to drive the peasants into cooperatives, with violence, intimidation, high delivery quotas, and cuts in supplies of seed and fertilizer figuring among the instruments employed to achieve this end. By the fourth quarter of 1949, the number of cooperatives had risen to 6,625; and in 1950, this figure reached 6,968, involving 418,659 households.[61] Until 1949, the peasants had fought back with such tactics of soft resistance as "foot-dragging, false compliance, feigned ignorance, pilfering, smuggling, arson, slander, and other surreptitious actions."[62] But as the party pressure increased, so too did peasant resistance. In some cases, local communist officials were murdered or wounded by angry peasants; in other cases, peasants used a combination of social ostracism and rumormongering about the evils of collectivization in order to fight the cooperative movement. In Trebinje, peasants being pressured to join the local cooperative fought back by slaughtering 50,000 sheep. Then, in early May 1950, disgruntled peasants joined discontented veterans in staging an armed insurrection in the Cazin region in the northwest corner of Bosnia-Herzegovina. The peasants severed telephone lines, disarmed local police, and carried their revolt to a total of five villages. The authorities sent in the army to crush the revolt, arresting and executing the three ringleaders. There were also peasant disorders at this time at Furjan, where groups of peasants shouted royalist slogans and attacked a militia station.[63]

All told, the combination of bad harvests and peasant resistance placed the government under stress, and on 27 September 1950, the authorities ordered a 10% reduction in bread rations, reduced maize quotas for peasant harvests, and encouraged the selective slaughter of livestock in order to conserve feed.[64] That same month, the Machine Tractor Stations were dissolved and the machinery under their control transferred directly to the cooperatives. The following year, on 14 January, the Yugoslav government passed a decree lowering the prices of foodstuffs for urban dwellers (hardest hit by the previous summer's drought) and reducing the prices of some consumer goods (such as soap). The peasants stood to benefit the least from this decree, however.[65] Subsequently, the federal government lifted some of its controls on the peasants as to their sale of their produce, abolishing the compulsory annual levy of the bulk of their meat, milk, potatoes, beans, hay, and straw.[66]

Although nearly half a million peasant households had been brought into the cooperative farm system by June 1951, some 2.5 million peasant households remained outside the system.[67] But livestock production in 1951 remained below prewar levels, and a severe drought in summer 1952 hit corn, sugar beets, sunflowers, and potatoes especially hard, resulting in harvest losses estimated at $100 billion, or 15% of the national income.[68] The regime was forced to retreat, which it did on 30 March 1953, with the issuance of a decree authorizing peasants to leave the cooperative, taking their land, livestock, and farm implements with them. By May 1953, the total number of cooperatives had dipped to 4,821, or just over two-thirds of the level reached in 1950; the cooperatives accounted at the time for 19.6% of arable land.[69] As the cooperative system gradually dissolved, the regime tried to shore it up by setting a limit of 10 hectares (about 25 acres) for a private farm.

But the peasants continued to abandon the cooperatives, and by September 1953, only 2,000 remained. In a speech delivered at the end of that month, Tito said that it had been a mistake to introduce collectivization so quickly and confessed that it would take more than a few years to change the way people thought about such things. Although the LCY had abandoned forcible collectivization, the party still nurtured hopes, for a while at least, that it could promote the *voluntary* formation of agricultural cooperatives.[70] This proved to be a pipe dream.

The War against Organized Religion

One should not underestimate the depth of communist hostility toward organized religion, and perhaps especially toward the Roman Catholic Church, which the communist regime viewed, not entirely without reason, as having had some sympathies for the Ustaše. Thus, the trial and imprisonment of Zagreb's Archbishop Stepinac was only a beginning. Over the succeeding months and years, there were repeated arrests and trials of clergy, physical attacks on clergymen, seizures of Church publications which offended the regime in one or another way, and a steady barrage of propaganda depicting the clergy, especially the Catholic clergy, as backward, primitive, and reactionary.

For the communists, it was not merely because of cooperative links between certain Catholic clergy and the Ustaše; after all, some Catholic clergy had taken the side of the Partisans in the NOB.[71] It was also because the Catholic clergy proved harder to bring around, harder—if one will—to "tame." Be that as it may, arrests of Catholic clergy continued into the 1950s. In December 1949, for example, Monsignor Janez Janko, vicar-general of the Belgrade Diocese, was detained on charges of black marketing and of hiding fugitives from the law.[72] In March 1950, Reverend Jako Vresk was condemned to death, while three other priests were given prison sentences ranging from 6 to 15 years.[73] That same month, Reverend Andrija Majić was taken into custody by the secret police and imprisoned.[74] According to Vatican sources, some 300 Catholic priests were sitting in prison awaiting trial on alleged political offenses as of September 1950; that figure did not include those already convicted and sentenced. The result was that many Catholic parishes were left priestless.[75]

From late 1950 to the end of 1951, there was a relaxation in the CPY's policies vis-à-vis the Catholic Church, indeed, vis-à-vis all religious associations in the country. Already in the summer of 1950, the Roman Catholic Church was allowed to consecrate a bishop—the first such consecration since World War Two—and later, Bishop Petar Čule of Mostar, imprisoned for an 11-year term in July 1948 on charges of having succored anti-Partisan Ustaše bands in his diocese during World War Two, was released and sent to live in the town of his birth.[76] About this time, Belgrade offered Archbishop Stepinac his freedom, provided only that he agree to leave Yugoslavia forever; the archbishop declined the offer.

But early in 1952, the party decided to end this liberalization and stirred up fresh press campaigns against Roman Catholic and Muslim clerics, though not against prelates or clergy of the Serbian Orthodox Church. The campaign was generally understood to be designed, in the first place, to shake party members out of the somnolent "petit bourgeois" attitudes and behaviors into which they had slid, renewing their militancy by attacking clergy as a foil for the "bourgeois" ideas they represented.[77] Thus, in January 1952, a crowd of 150 persons threw gasoline on Monsignor Anton Vouk, Catholic archbishop of Ljubljana; as a result, the bishop had to be hospitalized. Radio Belgrade appeared to legitimate the attack, which took place within a few days of the sentencing of a Slovenian priest on charges of wartime collaboration with the occupation forces, by tracing it to popular anger at "the treacherous activities of some priests in this district."[78] In this connection, the trial of Father Carlo Gnidovec and two other Slovene Catholic priests in September 1952, on charges of having organized anti-Partisan Home Guard units in 1942, is also worth mentioning. The trial lasted just four days, resulting in the conviction of all of the accused; Gnidovec received a commuted death sentence, while his two alleged collaborators were given prison terms of 12 years each.[79]

In the meantime, Archbishop Stepinac had been released from prison on condition that he remain in his hometown of Krasić. Not quite a year later (on 29 November 1952), Pope Pius XII named 24 bishops to the College of Cardinals, among them Stepinac. Two weeks later, Belgrade testily broke off diplomatic relations with the Holy See, at the same time complaining of alleged Catholic involvement in anti-Yugoslav organizations and activities abroad.[80]

Where the Serbian Orthodox Church was concerned, the death of Patriarch Gavrilo (Dozic) on 7 May 1950 gave the regime an opportunity to press for a more cooperative successor. The favorite among members of the Holy Synod was Metropolitan Arsenije (Bradvarević) of Montenegro, known to be even less inclined to compromise with the authorities than Gavrilo had been. The authorities preferred 60-year-old Bishop Vikentije (Prodanov), regarded as a "fellow traveler" and thought to be a heavy drinker.[81] The authorities took Metropolitan Arsenije into custody and prepared to put him on trial. The metropolitan's sudden unavailability to serve in the position of patriarch undoubtedly weighed on the minds of the members of the Holy Synod, who now approved Vikentije as patriarch by a vote of 33 to 25.[82] But Arsenije remained a rallying point for Orthodox clergy opposed to too close an association with the communists, and in May 1952, *Borba* published an article condemning unnamed priests who were sympathetic to Metropolitan Arsenije and "hostile" to the regime, alleging that they were "obstructing the work of the Association of Orthodox Priests in Montenegro."[83] Metropolitan Arsenije himself was eventually put on trial after a long delay and was sentenced, in July 1954, to eleven and a half years at hard labor on several charges, including conspiracy to overthrow the communist government and restore the monarchy, the propagation of religious hatred, and calling Tito a "dictator." In fact, no real evidence was presented to suggest that Metropolitan Arsenije was guilty of anything along the lines of anti-state conspiracy. The real reason for pressing forward with his trial after Vikentije was safely ensconced as patriarch was that Arsenije had fought relentlessly against ecclesiastical recognition of the state-sponsored priests' associations and had resisted all efforts to bring the Orthodox Church and the state to some agreement.[84]

A similar fate befell Vojislav Varnava Nastić, officiating Serbian Orthodox vicar of Sarajevo, sentenced to 11 years at hard labor in March 1948, on a charge of conspiracy against the state, and Archbishop Josef (Cvijovic), the former metropolitan of Skopje, who, at age 73, was taken into custody for his opposition to Vikentije and forced into retirement.[85] Nastić, a tough anti-communist, was offered his freedom in July 1951 on the condition that he resign as officiating vicar and retire to a monastery; Nastić refused. Meanwhile, Patriarch Vikentije lived up to regime expectations, proclaiming in 1950 that "Full religious freedom prevails all over the country," and alleging that at least some of the roughly 60 Orthodox priests then behind bars had engaged in political activities unacceptable to the regime.[86]

The Islamic community was the weakest of the three major religious communities and the most pliable. Islamic elders offered no effective resistance when the authorities banned the Dervish orders and the *takiyyas* in 1952 and pushed forward with a program to promote the unveiling of women. That same year, *Borba* sought to stir up anti-Islamic sentiment by complaining about an alleged recrudescence of medieval Islamic practices, including the alleged sale of supposedly miraculous cures by local Muslim elders.[87]

The constant drum beating by the regime press about the allegedly wicked, collaborationist, superstition-mongering, reactionary, and self-serving clergy of all three faiths brought a sector of the population to a state of anti-religious frenzy, and many clergymen were beaten up by mobs. In late August 1953, a series of hostile demonstrations against the Roman Catholic Bishop of Banja Luka, Dr. Josip Celik, finally compelled the cleric to leave his diocese. There were four other, similar incidents that month, involving Catholic, Orthodox, and Islamic clerics—all of these cases in Bosnia-Herzegovina.[88] The situation was clearly getting out of hand, and besides, the anti-religious pogroms made for bad press for the Yugoslav communist regime in Western capitals, to which Tito was by now looking for economic, diplomatic, and military support. Hence, in an election speech in Ruma (in Vojvodina) on 27 September 1953, Tito urged citizens to stop the "lawless" assaults on clergy, at the same time blaming "bitter memories" of the wartime behavior of some clerics for the violence.[89]

All in all, however, the anti-religious drive had proven more successful than the collectivization campaign. The Orthodox Church and the Islamic community had been brought to heel, while the Catholic Church's most visible symbol of anti-communist resistance, Alojzije Cardinal Stepinac, had been tarred with charges of collaboration, removed to his native village, and effectively neutralized. By 1958, to the Vatican's displeasure, many Catholic clergy, including several prelates, were going to the polls and voting—in essence, validating the political credentials of the communist regime.[90] On the other hand, among religious believers, the anti-religious campaign was the ultimate proof of the illegitimacy of the regime.

Although Tito's speech in Ruma certainly signaled the end of a phase in LCY religious policy, it did not mean an end of Church-state friction, by any means. In mid-May 1955, for example, communist authorities ordered the closure of the Roman Catholic high school and the classical high school in Rijeka; this action came in the wake of a trial involving five members of the two Church-run educational institutions, in which Josip Kaps, prefect of the theological school, and the other four accused were found guilty of "hostile activities" against the state and imprisoned for terms ranging from one to six years.[91] Moreover, authorities continued to view clergy with suspicion and to see the Catholic Church, in particular, as a "menace."[92]

Soviet-Yugoslav Relations and Yugoslav Ideological Development

Although Stalin gave up his plans to invade Yugoslavia upon seeing the firm response of the U.S. to the outbreak of war on the Korean peninsula in early 1950, he did not give up hopes that Tito might be removed from power. The repeated incidents along Yugoslavia's frontiers with Hungary, Romania, and

Bulgaria, which continued even after invasion plans had been called off, were a clear sign of continued Cominform hostility to the Tito regime.[93] But more pointedly, Stalin planned to have a Kremlin agent named Iosif Romualdovich Grigulevich (code name: "Max"), who was serving as Costa Rica's ambassador to Yugoslavia, assassinate President Tito by shooting him or using lethal bacteria or a poisoned jewel box.[94] Lavrenti Beria, KGB chief and interior minister, prepared these three alternative scenarios and submitted a top secret report on preparations for the assassination to Stalin in 1952. The plan had not yet been activated when Stalin died; with his death, the plan, code-named "scavenger," was scrapped.[95] But with the death of Stalin on 5 March 1953, relations between Moscow and Belgrade improved. The New Course inaugurated by the Kremlin leaders in summer 1953 included promises of increases in consumer goods, an easing of collectivization pressures, relaxation in policy in the religious sphere and in the cultural sector, and a less confrontational foreign policy. Already in the spring of 1953, Soviet leaders began to woo Tito, though they nurtured hopes at first that they could coax Tito into coming to Moscow for the intended reconciliation.[96] Tito was not prepared to take this dramatic step, however, and instead, in May 1955, Khrushchev led a delegation to Belgrade to express his regrets for the souring of relations during the period 1948–1953, which the Soviet leader blamed, rather improbably, on "Beria, Abakumov and others— recently exposed enemies of the people,"[97] carefully avoiding assigning any blame either to Stalin or to any members of the post-Stalin collective leadership. More significantly, Khrushchev declared Soviet acceptance, already in his speech at Belgrade Airport, of Yugoslavia's right to maintain friendly relations with Western states. The two sides devoted a week to discussions, during which time Khrushchev reportedly behaved badly, abusing alcohol, singing popular songs boisterously, and even flirting shamelessly with Tito's wife, Jovanka.[98] But for all that, the two sides reached an agreement on 2 June, signing a declaration of friendship and cooperation containing a seven-point program embracing respect for the sovereignty, independence, and equality of all socialist states, acceptance of the principle of peaceful coexistence between blocs, acceptance of the principle of non-interference in each other's internal affairs "because questions of internal organization, or difference in social systems and of different forms of Socialist development, are solely the concern of the individual countries," affirmation of the desire to further reciprocal economic cooperation, assistance through UN bodies to underdeveloped countries, the elimination of propaganda and disinformation or other kinds of conduct which might foster distrust, and condemnation of all aggression and all attempts to realize political or economic domination.[99] Underpinning these seven points was the concession, by the Soviets, that there could be more than one strategy adopted in building socialism. This declaration, which came to be known as the Belgrade Declaration, would be regularly cited by socialist Yugoslavia in all future meetings with Soviet representatives as the basis for their relations.

The West tried to offset the dramatic impact of the Soviet-Yugoslav reconciliation by issuing a communiqué, jointly with the Yugoslav government, at the end of June, reaffirming Western commitment to Yugoslav independence.[100] But there was no mistaking the fact that the Soviet-Yugoslav relationship had changed decisively, at least for the short term. Already in February 1956, it was reported that a group of Soviet technicians would be coming to Yugoslavia to help to set up new factories.[101] The Twentieth Congress of the Communist Party of the Soviet Union (CPSU), in February 1956, at which Khrushchev blasted Stalin in the course of a lengthy "secret speech," impressed Yugoslav politicians favorably, and in June 1956, Tito visited Khrushchev in Moscow; the two leaders, and their wives, seemed to be the best of friends, and Tito's brand of socialism seemed to have been fully endorsed by the Kremlin leadership. Significantly, an interparty agreement between the CPSU and the LCY was signed in Moscow on 20 June, confirming that the 2 June 1955 Belgrade Declaration would be the basis for future cooperation, and providing for the development of interparty ties, to include "mutual study." At the same time, the 1956 agreement also underlined, in a pointed concession to the Yugoslavs, that "the roads and conditions of socialist development are different in different countries" and that "any tendency of imposing one's own views in determining the roads and forms of socialist development [is] alien to both sides."[102]

The Soviet-Yugoslav reconciliation probably encouraged those in Eastern Europe who were impatient for ideological de-Stalinization to be translated into practical policy. Riots in Poznań in June 1956 were followed by an escalation of demands for change in Poland and in Hungary. In September 1956, the CPSU sent a warning around to its fraternal parties underlining that they should not consider themselves at liberty to follow the Yugoslav example, and drawing attention, in particular, to the allegedly pro-Western elements in Yugoslav foreign policy.[103] On 19 September 1956, Khrushchev came to Yugoslavia for private discussions with Tito; subsequently, Yugoslav newspapers reported that serious ideological differences had surfaced during their conversations.[104] By early October, the Polish communists were publicly singing the praises of the Yugoslavs, even as they pressed for the restoration of Władysław Gomułka to the first secretaryship of the Polish United Workers' Party (PUWP).[105] Then, in mid-October, a five-member Hungarian party delegation, headed by party secretary Ernő Gerő, arrived in Belgrade, where the Hungarians announced that the liberally inclined Imre Nagy, who had jousted with then-party General Secretary Mátyás Rakosi in the period 1953–1955 before being ejected from the Hungarian communist party, had been readmitted to the party.[106] Subsequently, Nagy was appointed prime minister of Hungary, even as socialism itself came under threat from what communists would call "the Hungarian Counter-revolution." Tito was, by his own admission, concerned about developments in Hungary and therefore welcomed Soviet intervention as the "lesser evil," though he drew a distinction between the first (muddled) Soviet intervention, which occurred before the uprising in Hungary had (in Tito's mind) assumed a decidedly anti-socialist cast and which he therefore described as "absolutely wrong," and the second (effective) Soviet intervention, which he said had been "necessary" if "chaos, a civil war, a counterrevolution and a new world war" were to be avoided.[107] Tito posed as a defiant rebel, but according to what Dedijer told Eric Bourne of the *Christian Science Monitor* at the time, many communists in Zagreb, especially the younger ones, were embarrassed about Tito's response to the developments in Hungary.[108]

The Soviets replied two weeks later in an article in the party daily, *Pravda*, insisting that the victory of world communism required the unity and solidarity of all socialist states and alleging that "Tito's speech [in Pula] contains, along with correct judgments on the Hungarian events, judgments which cannot but evoke legitimate objections."[109] But Soviet objections were rejected by the Yugoslav communists. Edvard Kardelj gave the official Yugoslav rendering of the Hungarian events and the lessons to be drawn from them in a speech to the federal Skupština on 6 December, advising the deputies that socialism "must be liberated from bureaucratic brakes and be able to develop by its [own] internal experience," adding that "socialism nowadays does not need empty eulogies of what has been done in a Socialist country and among Socialist countries."[110] For the next six months, relations between Moscow and Belgrade were frosty. But in May 1957, Moscow ordered a halt to its anti-Yugoslav press campaign, and the two sides tried to rebuild bridges. About this time, Milovan Djilas's book *The New Class,* with its devastating critique of communism, was published by a New York publishing house. *Borba* (11 August 1957) commented that Djilas was "demoralized and insane," adding that his book was allegedly "written in the language and psychology of Goebbels' propaganda."[111] The authorities quickly banned the importation and distribution of Djilas's book and sentenced Djilas, who had already been serving a three-year prison sentence since the previous December, to an additional seven years' imprisonment plus five years' deprivation of civil rights.[112] (In fact, Djilas was released on probation on 20 January 1961, after serving four years and two months of his ten-year sentence.)[113] By this point, Yugoslav delegates were already looking ahead to the Seventh Party Congress, scheduled to be held in Ljubljana. Strikingly, in spite of the harsh treatment meted out to Djilas, the draft party program, published in Yugoslavia in March 1958, would contain a number of ideas which seemed to owe much to Djilas's inspiration.

This draft program provoked a sharp response from the Soviets, who charged that it contained "many theses that clearly depart from the theory and practice of Marxism-Leninism."[114] A follow-up article, published in *Pravda*, complained that the Yugoslav leaders were putting the Soviet Union "on the same level with the imperialist powers," that the Yugoslavs rejected the two-camp theory of international politics still "commonly recognized by Communists in every country," that the Yugoslavs were too eager to affirm "that there could be no infallible judge who could decide what was right and what was wrong in matters of ideology"—a formulation rather obviously aimed at the Kremlin—and that the Yugoslav leaders were contrasting the development of socialist democracy with the development of the socialist state.[115] The Yugoslav reply came a week later, when *Borba* accused *Pravda* of obscurantism, in having failed to reprint even one sentence from the Yugoslav draft program, and of "malicious . . . distortions and vilifications."[116]

The crossfire between the Soviet and Yugoslav party organs scarcely conveyed the real importance of the draft program, however, which was the boldest ideological challenge presented to the Soviets by any ruling communist party up to then. Among other things, the party program, which had something of the character of a manifesto, declared that socialism could not be homogeneous and that, unavoidably, there would be different paths to socialism. The Yugoslavs also repeated their old refrain criticizing bureaucratism and "stateism" and offering their own experiences as a guide for those wishing to construct socialism. But the program also contained a warning:

Anti-socialist forces will with more or less frequency appear in our development for some time to come. It would be most dangerous for the success of the Communist activity to believe that, in comparison with past difficulties, our present or future difficulties are or will be smaller. We have surmounted many past difficulties through constant struggle and unity of our ranks, incessant activity, dynamism in work, continuous overcoming of all that is antiquated, irrepressible striving for all that is better and more progressive, sharp vigilance against all that is negative, criticism of our own weaknesses and relentless struggle against conservatism and stagnation in ideas. These qualities must be nurtured in the future, too, and transmitted to younger generations. Weakening of a critical attitude toward one's own work, toward negative phenomena in our development, toward manifestations that obstruct that development, will create a favorable ground for the growth and activity of anti-socialist forces.[117]

Pressures for Change, 1957–1961

The maintenance and enforcement of internal party discipline had been a problem all along, as the Djilas case illustrates.[118] Indeed, Djilas continued to haunt the Yugoslav political landscape, even from the political wilderness. The publication of *The New Class* in August 1957 sent renewed shock waves through the LCY. But there were also problems at the grass roots. At the end of February 1958, a letter was drawn up at the highest level and sent to all party organizations, taking communist officials to task for corruption, unwarranted privileges, and "strong localist tendencies, coupled with tendencies to neglect and overlook the interests of the community as a whole."[119] According to *The Times* of London, the letter came in response to "the recently vigorously expressed resentment of industrial workers at the glaring discrepancies between their wage packets and conditions and salaries, and bonuses pocketed by managers, officials, and many white-collar workers."[120] This letter, signed by the party Executive Committee, warned that if the situation were not corrected "in good time and with due firmness . . . [it] might weaken and hold up further successes in our internal political development, and . . . harm the international prestige of Yugoslavia . . . as a Socialist country."[121] Opportunism, bureaucratism, the inappropriate suppression of criticism, favoritism, irregularities in the payment of wages, and the growth of privilege among LCY apparatchiki sounded, up to a point, like a paraphrase of Djilas's *The New Class*. At the same time, the letter also criticized "petit-bourgeois and anarchistic conceptions of democracy," using the well-known code for demands for liberalization and pluralization.

The fallout from the letter was rather dramatic. There was a "rash of expulsions" from the party, accompanied by public self-criticisms, the surrender of fancy cars by some party figures, the ejection of some apparatchiki from luxury apartments, and the opening up of funds which had been "stashed away for questionable purposes."[122] In the wake of the Seventh Party Congress, the party center took a more energetic role than it had in the years between the Sixth and Seventh congresses in advising local party functionaries on appropriate behavior. There were also changes made in the structure of the party secretariat and the establishment of special secretariats for organizational-political work, ideological matters, and cadres. These were headed, respectively, by Aleksandar Ranković, Petar Stambolić (who was also president of the Skupština), and Veljko Zeković. The Socialist Alliance of Working People of Yugoslavia also set up a number of new commissions, designed to tighten party discipline, while eliminating the SAWPY commission on work in the villages.

These moves set the tone for the next two to three years. In mid-November 1959, for instance, President Tito presented a speech to the party Central Committee underlining the need, in his view, to "tighten party discipline and restore centralism to all party activity."[123] As if in illustration of the breakdown of party discipline and coordination, Tito rebuked several previous speakers at the CC session for having allegedly glossed over shortcomings, and he charged that communist directors in industry and economic enterprises were acting in a "high-handed" fashion, retaining undue privileges and thereby alienating ordinary workers. Tito also accused communist managers of adopting an excessively "liberal attitude" in dealings with foreign partners.

In 1960, Ranković assumed the post of secretary general of the Socialist Alliance. Ranković was still serving as minister of internal affairs, head of the party's organizational-political secretariat, and head of UDBa (the State Security Administration, or secret police). Then, at the Fifth Congress of the Socialist Alliance held in Belgrade in April 1960, questions were raised about the future of the LCY, alongside speculations that the latter might be "swallowed" up by the Socialist Alliance. In a controversial speech to the congress on 19 April, Cvijetin Mijatović, editor of *Komunist* and a prominent member of the LC Bosnia-Herzegovina, urged that many of the functions hitherto exercised by the party should be transferred to the Socialist Alliance. The full text of Mijatović's speech was published in *Komunist* on 21 April, after two bowdlerized versions had been distributed to those attending the congress. Kardelj, in his address to the same congress, impressed upon his listeners the need for a new constitution.[124]

Yugoslavia's leaders appeared to be vacillating between decentralization and recentralization and were quite clearly alert to the advantages and drawbacks of both of these options. But when they spoke of decentralization, they had in mind a devolution of administrative responsibility and the surrendering of some tasks to local leaders or party organizations, rather than the withdrawal of the party from real authority. This was why the party repeatedly attacked "petit-bourgeois and anarchist" concepts of democracy. But by 1959 pressure was building for a more coherent codification of constitutional principles than what had been provided, in a quilt work fashion, by the 1953 Basic Law. Work began already that year on an entirely new constitution, which was supposed to be ready by 1962. By 1961, pressure was also building for a reform of the economic system, and it became increasingly apparent that only a radical reform would begin to address the problems mounting in the economic sector. These pressures—for political-constitutional reform and for economic reform—would merge into a single, mutually reinforcing reform movement. Moreover, as party leaders bearing the banner of "reform" started blaming "bureaucratic conceptions and bureaucratic praxis" for the country's economic woes, it became increasingly clear that Yugoslavia was about to cross the ideological Rubicon.[125] The economic reform of 1961–1965, the constitution of 1963, and the Eighth Party Congress of 1964 would prove to be landmarks in this new direction.

CHAPTER 7

The Reform Crisis, 1962–1970

If, as has been suggested, an illegitimate system is inherently unstable, then reform will inevitably seem to be the solution to the elites in power, insofar as they do not want to lose their privileged position. "Reform" in an illegitimate system is designed, in a word, to obtain the benefits of political legitimacy, without yielding the substance of political legitimacy. Once that is grasped, the entire notion of "reform" in an illegitimate system is understood to be doomed from the beginning. It is not that "reform" cannot improve the situation; of course it can. It is not that persons who have previously suffered discrimination cannot achieve some degree of equality under such "reform"; of course they can. It is not that a "reformed" illegitimate system cannot extend its lifespan in this manner; of course it can. What such "reform" cannot do, however, is what it is intended to do, viz., to obtain the full benefits of political legitimacy within the framework of an illegitimate system.

At the dawn of the 1960s, Yugoslavia was run by a small circle of functionaries. Aside from President Tito, this circle included Aleksandar Ranković (a Serb), minister of internal affairs until 1963, who became vice president of the SFRY in 1963; Edvard Kardelj (a Slovene), vice chair of the Federal Executive Council, president of the Committee for Legislation and the Building of People's Power, chief architect of the social system, and former foreign minister; Mijalko Todorović (a Serbian liberal), who exercised leading authority in the economic sphere after 1958; Svetozar Vukmanović-Tempo (a Montenegrin), president of the Yugoslav Labor Union; Ivan Gošnjak (a Croat), state secretary for people's defense; and Koča Popović (a Serb), foreign minister. To this group, one might add the names of Vladimir Bakarić (a Croat), secretary of the League of Communists of Croatia, and Petar Stambolić, a senior figure in the Serbian party apparatus. Although Bakarić eschewed removal to the center, he was nonetheless a senior figure in the party and played a larger role than other regional barons. Although these figures presented a unified front to the outside world, they were torn by serious internal differences. Kardelj, in particular, was by now the leading advocate of political reform, and under his influence, the federal Skupština (Assembly) passed a series of laws in March 1961, setting up, at the same time, joint commissions of representatives of several federal bodies to carry out reforms in the economic sector.[1]

In mid-March 1962, the executive bureau of the LCY Central Committee held a closed session to discuss the political directions of the system. The session saw sharp political conflicts but ultimately produced a decision to take concrete steps to address certain problems and shortcomings. Among these problems were localism, chauvinism, and national particularism.[2] The session unleashed an ideological-political campaign against these and other problems, and party members were placed on "alert." On 6 May 1962, Tito delivered an important address in Split, highlighting the dangers associated with localism and telling his audience that there was a real danger that each republic was just out for itself, ignoring the interests of the Yugoslav community as a whole.[3] Subsequently, in an effort to curb growing polycentrism in Slovenia, Macedonia, and Croatia, Tito adopted disciplinary measures against republican politicians at an LCY Executive Committee session on 14–16 May 1962.[4] But the session did not solve the problem; on the contrary, the conflicts only intensified.

The importance of this early evidence of internationality and interrepublican frictions cannot be overemphasized since it gives the lie to claims by later advocates of recentralization that these problems were "created" by decentralization. On the contrary, decentralization was undertaken in order to address this issue, and in this regard, decentralization was partially successful, prolonging the life of an illegitimate system while allowing its more basic problems to fester below the surface.

The adoption of postwar Yugoslavia's third constitution in 1963 was an important step in the direction of political decentralization, whereby the status and prerogatives of the six republics were enhanced. At the same time, under the 1963 constitution, Kosovo-Metohija (Kosmet) was elevated from a "region" (the status it had obtained in 1946) to a "province" on an equal par with Vojvodina. The new constitution enshrined the right of the republics (though not of the provinces) to leave the Yugoslav federation, prescribed that all federal laws and acts were to be published in the country's four official languages (Serbo-Croatian, Croato-Serbian, Slovenian, and Macedonian), and restructured the federal Skupština into a five-chamber body, with its deputies elected through indirect elections (replacing the direct electoral system used hitherto). The 1963 constitution also gave the executive councils in the republics a new freedom vis-à-vis the Federal Executive Council.[5] And under the new constitution, the Muslims, hitherto not officially recognized as culturally distinct (so that Muslims had had a choice, on the census, among the possibilities of registering as "Muslim Serbs," "Muslim Croats," or "Muslims with undetermined nationality"), were now raised to the rank of an "ethnic group" (a status recognized semi-officially on the 1961 census forms). The constitution also reflected a repudiation of any policy of homogenization (even though not all party leaders were yet reconciled to this policy line). Hence, in the context of discussions of the draft constitution, Edvard Kardelj told a joint meeting of the federal Skupština and the Federal Committee of SAWPY on 20 September 1962: "our Federation is not a frame for making some new Yugoslav nation, or a frame for the kind of national integration [of] which various advocates of hegemonism or denationalizing terror have been daydreaming."[6]

Liberals, Conservatives, and Economics

During the period 1957–1961, the rate of investment remained a robust 30% of GNP on the average, and the GNP grew at an average annual rate of more than 12%. Personal consumption rose an average of 10% per year in this period, while agricultural output increased about 40% during 1957–1961 over the previous five-year-plan period. This result was achieved in spite of a bad harvest in 1960, which forced Yugoslavia to import wheat from the U.S.[7] As of 1961, Yugoslavia undertook a reform of foreign exchange, aimed at permitting its accession into GATT (General Agreement on Tariffs and Trade) and its fuller integration into the world market. This was but a straw in the wind, however.

On 8 April 1962, the Skupština listened as a sobering picture of the Yugoslav economy was presented. Mijalko Todorović, who presented the report, noted that imports were rising, while production and exports were declining, and called for austerity measures.[8] Step by step, through a series of ad hoc adjustments to the economic administrative mechanism, the reform initiative blossomed, by 1965, into a full-fledged assault on economic inefficiency, unprofitable enterprises, inflationary development, and distorted prices. "Centrally planned investment [had become] impossible in Yugoslavia because it was no longer possible to agree politically about such planning."[9] The alternative concept was to reduce the role of the federal government, scrap central planning, and allow greater say in economic planning and administration to the local decision makers, that is, the republics and provinces, the *opštinas*, and enterprises. The chief beneficiaries of this devolution were, in the short term, the republics, and in the longer term, the provinces of Kosovo and Vojvodina.

The motivations for the reform were, at first, purely economic. The overriding issue was that of efficiency, and partisans of all sides addressed this key issue, marshaling pertinent economic arguments. The debate quickly took on an ideological character, however, when the loose alliance of party liberals, technocrats, and enterprise managers met more ideologically doctrinaire opponents, who appealed as much to socialist values as to economic criteria. Liberals considered it "an illusion [to think] that it is possible to build socialism in an autarkic fashion."[10] Some even dared to summon Adam Smith in defense of the proposition that every nation and every republic should produce whatever goods and services it can produce best and most cheaply and should import whatever it cannot produce well, cheaply, or efficiently.[11] Moreover, as opinions hardened on each side, the controversy surrounding the reform took on interrepublican characteristics. As Kardelj noted at the time, the less developed republics (Bosnia-Herzegovina, Montenegro, and Macedonia) wanted to maximize the assistance they received and therefore preferred to see a centralized economic system, while Croatia and Slovenia championed decentralization and the marketization of the economy, with profit operating as the dominant economic criterion for investment; according to Kardelj, a "third, hegemonic orientation found its advocates in Serbia."[12]

The Eighth Congress of the LCY, held in December 1964, had the task of assuaging the surfacing tensions in interrepublican relations. The Eighth Congress was the occasion for the first open discussion of the national question and for a somewhat nebulously worded agreement to undertake economic reform. The Croats began to argue the case for economic "optimalization," that is, the use of profit criteria in investment, and questioned the lack of circumspection with which the General Investment Fund (GIF) resources had been funneled into the south. Drawing on support from Slovenia and (perhaps surprisingly) Macedonia, the Croats achieved a partial victory at this congress. But the consensus reached was flimsy and even superficial, since, in practice, rival and contradictory economic orientations were incorporated into the resolutions adopted at the Eighth Congress.[13] The reform and the subsequent political devolution, along with the resultant institutional configuration of Yugoslavia, were, to a considerable extent, the handiwork of the liberal wing of the party, whose advocates won them by wrenching control of the system from the more doctrinaire old-style "conservatives." In time, however, the liberals lost the reins of power to a coalition of new-style conservatives and party centrists.

The Yugoslavs in power from 1971 to 1980 did not refer to themselves as "conservatives" any more than they called themselves "unitarists" (a term of abuse in socialist Yugoslavia from at least the mid-1960s). The regime had a tendency occasionally to concatenate the label "liberal" with another one—normally considered unrelated in Western thought—namely, "anarchist." This produced the hybrid "anarcho-liberalism." Although in Western usage anarchists are usually considered to have occupied a niche far to the left in the political spectrum, historically (though their successors of sorts, the libertarians, advocate what at first sight may appear to be similar anti-state positions in order to maximize the freedom of the rich and the super-rich), the Tito-era communists condemned "anarcho-liberals" for right-wing deviationism. "Anarcho-liberals" were said to favor the establishment of a multiparty system (though anarchists, of course, propose to do away with all government and, hence, all political parties) and were said to be hostile to self-management on principle.

A related difficulty is that the meaning assigned by Yugoslav communists to the word *liberal* was fluid. In 1970 and 1971, the term was generally applied to the programmatic current represented by Croats Miko Tripalo and Savka Dabčević-Kučar, Slovene Stane Kavčič, and Macedonians Krste Crvenkovski and Slavko Milosavlevski, as well as by Serbs Marko Nikezić and Mirko Čanadanović. It was considered respectable at that time to be "liberal," and such liberalism distinguished its adherents from the more centralistically oriented line which "conservatives" had favored. By the late 1970s, however, the term *liberal* was more often applied to dissident intellectuals such as Ljubomir Tadić and Milovan Djilas. The identification of liberalism with dissent was obvious from the title of the two-volume work *Liberalism from Djilas to Today* [*Liberalizam od Djilasa do danas*]. By the time of the Twelfth Party Congress (in June 1982), liberalism had once again become a respectable, even fashionable, epithet, and a leading figure in the Bosnian party told me, two weeks after the congress, that "*we liberals* won a great victory at the Twelfth Party Congress."

Every selection of terminology involves a compromise. Some terms may be more precise but suffer from unfavorable political overtones. Other terms may be more neutral but also less precise. Neologisms have the advantage of affording the possibility of avoiding unwanted associations but have the disadvantage of exoticism. I have decided to follow the common practice adopted by most of the leading historians of Yugoslavia and use the terms *liberal* and *conservative* to designate the two principal political currents within the LCY in the 1960s–1980s, realizing that these terms may call forth associations entirely irrelevant to the Yugoslav context.

By "liberal" in the Yugoslav context, I mean someone who favors the reduction of central party control and less party supervision of society. By "conservative" in the Yugoslav context, I mean someone who favors strong central party control and tight party supervision of society. These respective orientations tended to be associated with other policy preferences, as the record will show, including in the economic sphere. Not all party officials fell neatly into one of these two categories, however. In addition to these two groups, there was a fluid group of "brokers" who adopted a flexible attitude, emphasizing loyalty to Tito. Vladimir Bakarić and Petar Stambolić were prominent "brokers." In practice, though, the brokers were usually closer to the conservatives than to the liberals, though most brokers, Tito included, identified with the liberals during the 1966–1971 period. What should be stressed is that there were liberals and conservatives in the party organizations of every republic, though not in equal measure; as a result, the conflict had both an intra-republican dimension and, during such periods when liberals dominated some party organizations and conservatives others, also an interrepublican dimension. This scheme is broadly relevant for the period 1962–1987, with much more muted conflicts before 1962 and a transformation of the entire political landscape after 1987.

As in any society, Yugoslavia embraced a variety of interests and orientations, with certain groups placing their emphasis on one policy sphere, other groups on other policy spheres, and with various positions being possible. The two dominant issues at that time were (1) centralism vs. decentralism, and (2) liberalization vs. retrenchment in economic policy (or in the media, though economic liberals tended to be liberal on media policy and vice versa). That said, one could begin to assay the potential complexity of the policy landscape by identifying four possible combinations: liberal decentralism, liberal centralism, conservative decentralism, and conservative centralism. Later, in the early 1980s, it would indeed be possible to identify specific groups associated with each of these four orientations.[14] But one would have to strain to identify more than a few, if any, liberal centralists or conservative decentralists in the late 1960s and early 1970s. The reason for this is quite elementary: in those years, the center (the central party apparatus) had been conservative, and those pursuing a liberal agenda looked to decentralization to give them the maneuvering room in which to liberalize policies; moreover, there were powerful forces pushing in the direction of political polarization, so that, within the party, two vocal blocs confronted each other, with Tito-loyalists offering a kind of "nonpolitical" alternative, in which loyalty to Tito was emphasized over particular policy preferences.[15]

Economic Reform as a Stimulus of System Change

Prior to 1963, Yugoslavia was a centralized state with a federal veneer. After 1963, however, changes began to take place in the behavior of the republics, changes which bubbled up from the realm of economics into the political world and impelled ultimate institutional overhaul. By 1971, various observers, both Yugoslav and American, believed that decentralization had gone so far that Yugoslavia was on the verge of reconstituting itself as a confederation. The economic reform, by unleashing certain political forces, proved a stimulus for system change.

The years immediately prior to the economic reform of 1965 were riddled with difficulties. Industrial plants had often been built more for political—that is, cosmetic or palliative—reasons than with an eye to economic rationality, and inventories of unwanted goods were rising. Unused capacities in industrial production were accompanied by the unprofitable records of many "political factories." All this was aggravated by growing inflationary pressure and by perennial balance-of-payments deficits.[16] When the economic reform began, it was conceived, as such things usually are, as a simple adjustment to enable the existing system to function more smoothly. Its origins were piecemeal adjustments which prompted further adjustments. Three reform measures were introduced in 1961: opening the Yugoslav economy to the world market, reorganizing the financial markets, and relaxing wage controls. "The reform measures were, however, insufficiently prepared and hastily implemented," as a World Bank report notes.[17] Economic problems continued to mount, with inflation quickening after 1962, and they compelled a major reexamination of the premises of the system.

Between 1964 and 1965, a series of policy decisions were made which reflected the outlook of the economic liberals, that is, of the system's discontents. Among the chief elements of this reform were:

- the transfer of considerable responsibility for administration of the economy from the federal government to the republics;
- the repudiation of the concept of regional autarkic development (the concept that *every* Yugoslav republic should be self-supporting);
- the adoption of a more realistic exchange rate, permitting greater participation by Yugoslavia in world trade;
- the complete revision of price ratios, marked by steep hikes in the prices of raw materials, agricultural goods, and certain other commodities and services;
- the aggrandizement of the role of banks and economic enterprises (susceptible to republican pressure and manipulation), at the expense of the federal government; and
- the abolition of the federally controlled General Investment Fund (GIF).

The reform had an unmistakable devolutionary character: its main features were the strengthening of the role of the republics (and enterprises) at the expense of the center (the federal government and the Belgrade banking monopoly); this, in turn, shifted part of the onus of legitimation to the republics. But by turning the resources of the defunct GIF over to the large central banks, the reformers failed to carry the reform through to its logical conclusion. Thus, they aggravated certain latent antagonisms in the system, stimulating a growing conflict between the central banks, insurance companies, and foreign trade organizations on the one side and their republic counterparts on the other. This conflict increasingly took on political overtones and in time assumed nationalist garb as a conflict between the conservatives gathered around the assimilationist Ranković and the reformist currents which were gaining strength, in the first place, in Slovenia and Croatia, which were championed initially by the anti-assimilationist Kardelj.[18]

As Crane Brinton has noted in his classic study of revolution, collective cognitive dissonance sets in not during a period of sustained oppression or exploitation but, rather, as a formerly oppressive or exploitative regime begins to reform itself.[19] Once given better conditions, citizen-subjects inevitably ask why conditions could not have been better *sooner* and why they could not be *better yet*. In Yugoslavia, repression had been perceived in regional terms, and, therefore, the heightened consciousness produced by the relaxation of federal control was also framed in regional-ethnic terms. Cognitive dissonance was experienced at the level of the republic, i.e., as Croatian cognitive dissonance or Macedonian cognitive dissonance, for example; it was not experienced as *Yugoslav* cognitive dissonance, which is to say that difficulties and discontent tended to divide the Yugoslav community, rather than to unite it. Miko Tripalo, then a member of the Executive Council of the presidency of the LCY, recognized this when he told *Borba* in 1970 that "nationalism of all sorts is one of the negative reactions to unitarism. Its essence is *etatism,* but at the level of the republic."[20]

The crisis which would unfold in the years 1967–1971 was, in fact, revolutionary in character and signaled the surfacing of long-repressed resentments. It was natural, therefore, that this sentiment should carry over into the political realm, so that Croats, perceiving themselves to be economically exploited, should champion not only further economic liberalization but also political reform. Some Yugoslavs recognized this tendency quite early; shortly after the fall of Ranković (in July 1966); one disgruntled conservative pointed to the futility of trying to contain reform in the economic sphere.

Politicization of the Reform

If the recession which struck Yugoslavia in 1961–1962 served as a spur to economic reform, it was also the irritant which inflamed Yugoslav politics. Slovenes and Croats argued that central planning was no longer relevant to their level of development. But the Yugoslav south lagged considerably behind this standard, and some argued that the use of a centralized mechanism to distribute resources was still a boon to the less developed parts of the country. The northerners complained that gross investment figures disguised the true advantage enjoyed by the south, since large sums had to be spent in the north for the maintenance and replacement of existing equipment, while the admittedly lower gross amounts for the south could largely be funneled into new projects and direct expansion. The southerners replied that development of the south was the most rational strategy over the long run, because the mineral wealth and other natural resources were concentrated there, and it would be cheaper to process natural resources in the south than to transport them elsewhere.[21] Kosta Mihailović, for instance, in a 1962 article for *Ekonomist,* claimed that the eastern republics (the "Danubian zone") were more suitable targets for Yugoslav investment, that that region was economically more dynamic, and that for the next 30 years it would not be necessary to build *anything* on the Adriatic coast![22] But, as Deborah Milenkovitch has pointed out, "few really believed that rapid development of the less developed regions was also a maximum growth policy for the nation, and fewer still believed that their rapid development was economically more beneficial to the already advanced areas than an equivalent amount of investment in the advanced areas would have been."[23] The northerners complained of excessive waste in southern investment and noted the higher marginal capital coefficients (i.e., the greater investment necessary to produce a given income) and the lower labor efficiency prevailing in the underdeveloped areas.[24]

Šime Djodan, then a prominent Croatian economist, outlined three alternative models of economic development applicable to a country with heterogeneously developed zones: accelerated development of the underdeveloped areas to equalize all areas, concentration on further development of the better developed areas, and development according to the principle of economic rationality. We have already seen that the first approach was associated with the so-called Danubian concept of development and that the third model was espoused by advocates of the "Adriatic concept." Conservatives like Stipe Šuvar unfairly attempted to identify the liberals with the second model. But, in fact, there was another faction, small and not very vocal, that believed the second model to be a suitable framework. This faction espoused a "Slovenian concept" which called for the intensification of investment in the most advanced areas: not surprisingly, advocates of the "Slovenian concept" tended to be Slovenes.[25]

Under the third ("Adriatic") model, optimal economic results were the guiding criterion; for example, it would favor development of nonferrous metallurgy in Serbia, Kosovo, and Macedonia, and of aluminum, bauxite, and hydroelectric industries in Croatia and Bosnia. In a key argument, Djodan claimed that the less developed republics suffered as much from the errors of the Danubian concept as did the Adriatic republics. If the development of Slovenia, Croatia, and the province of Vojvodina had not been hindered by advocates of the Danubian concept, he argued, "the development of the underdeveloped districts would be a far more tractable problem today than it is."[26] Unfortunately, charged the Croatian liberal critics, Yugoslavia had operated on the basis of the first model. Too many factories had been built in the south without economic justification—and the phenomenon of the "political factories" was said to be worst in Bosnia-Herzegovina and the province of Kosovo.[27] Djodan, like many other Croats at that time, concluded that "if one considers regional development on the territory of Yugoslavia as a whole over the preceding period, one must confess that it was understood as the development of the insufficiently developed regions."[28] Some demanded that a federally appointed agency be created to supervise investments in the south and assure that funds were sensibly spent. (Djodan's arguments will be taken up at greater length in the following chapter, in the context of the Djodan-Šuvar debate.)

The LCY tried to hold the line against the growing criticism. Answering the charge that northern money was being squandered on the construction of "political factories" in the south, Kardelj asked a Slovenian audience,

But is it really true that there are no irrational investments in Slovenia and Croatia? I will not cite instances of such failures and misses, because you yourselves know them well, but I would pose the following question: what would be the reaction in Slovenia if someone were to demand that predetermined federal organs should evaluate the rationality of Slovenian investments and the economic policies of the organs of the republic of Slovenia? There is no doubt that such a demand would be bitterly repulsed and that it would be viewed as an attack on the independence of the Slovenian nation. I think that such a reaction would be legitimate. Is it not clear, then, that the same things cannot be measured with different measures? And is it not clear that the use of such different criteria [for Slovenia and Croatia on the one hand, and for the underdeveloped republics on the other] would lead not only to the undermining of the equality of the Yugoslav peoples, but also—in that event—to the economic and political dependence of the economically less developed nations and republics on the more developed?[29]

But the underdeveloped republics showed no sign of catching up with the developed republics, and thus it could be (and was) convincingly argued that, if equalization was indeed the aim, a new approach was necessary.

These arguments, and the presence of liberals like Crvenkovski in the Macedonian leadership and of others potentially sympathetic to overtures from Slovenia and Croatia in the other underdeveloped areas, converted this rich-poor debate, which might have produced a simple economic polarization under other circumstances, into a political question. It provided the basis for a broad liberal coalition. Bakarić was instrumental in bringing about a change in Croatian tactics, designed to appeal to the non-Serbian underdeveloped areas. The Croats actively began to woo the south, and as early as 1961, Croats began to talk of de-etatization rather than decentralization. Evidently, Bakarić indeed believed that the underdeveloped areas could profit economically from decentralization and de-etatization; he was staunchly anti-nationalist and consistently opposed to expressions of ethnic particularism, especially in his native Croatia.[30]

The liberals, who had taken up the banner of decentralization, and the conservatives, led by Ranković and seeking, as ever, to keep the central party apparatus as strong as possible, began to look around for allies. The liberals' identification with Croatian-Slovenian interests and conservativism's association with the interests of the Serbian republic became a complicating factor. Macedonia and Croatia both had a stake in federalism and had resisted suggestions made in the early 1950s, during the Yugoslavism campaign, that nominal federalism be dumped and replaced by open unitarism.[31] Croatian and Macedonian elites, both motivated by the desire to maximize their own autonomy, reached a working understanding. Ranković and his allies concentrated on courting Bosnia-Herzegovina and Montenegro and had some success with Montenegro: in December 1963, the party leaderships in Serbia and Montenegro announced the integration of their respective industries; cooperation in communications, foreign trade, and long-term joint planning; and the conclusion of an agreement to complete the Belgrade-Bar railway. In the course of 1964 and 1965, the Serbian and Montenegrin parties signed additional protocols for economic and cultural cooperation.[32] These actions collectively constituted the domestic equivalent of a treaty. They also signified the abandonment of any pretense to neutrality on the part of the Serbs. (It might be recalled, in this connection, that Šuvar, among others, had at one time claimed that the Serbs were uniquely "internationalistic," i.e., culturally neutral, and that Serbs were ready to become "Yugoslavs.") The Serbo-Montenegrin protocols and Serbian wooing of Bosnia-Herzegovina signaled an effort on the part of conservatives based in Serbia to put together a conservative bloc. But the situation rapidly became more complex. A stable national-liberal coalition began to take shape, composed of Slovenia, Croatia, and Macedonia, with Vojvodina as a kind of associate partner.[33]

This national-liberal coalition, applying pressure both through its representatives in Belgrade and through vigorous self-assertion within the areas of its collective geographic jurisdiction, was able to push the reform forward between 1965 and 1966, dramatically reducing the prerogatives of the federal government in the economic sector. Federal subsidies to industry were slashed—a clear victory for Croatia and Slovenia and an unmistakable setback for the conservatives. Profitability began the chief criterion for the allocation of resources. The market reform of 1965 effectively ended the golden age of "political factories," and central investment planning was abandoned. Yet the Serbs were not unconditional losers in this round of battle; they continued to dominate the national banks since the reforms were not inimical to Belgrade's larger corporations. Moreover, the distinction between advocacy of pluralistic decision making through syndicalist mechanisms and decision making along territorial/ethnic lines was blurred by the temporary alliance of proponents of both approaches in the fight against "unitarism."[34] At the same time, concern over the slide toward some sort of political pluralism was growing among conservative Serbs. They were sensitive to accusations of Serbian hegemony and harbored lingering resentment against the Croats for the establishment of an independent Croatia in World War Two and the concomitant Ustaša massacres of Serbs.

Passage of the reform did not, therefore, signify the end of the issue. For one thing, the Macedonian League of Communists (LCM) was internally divided. Many in the LCM were as bitterly opposed as their colleagues in the LC Serbia to the decision, taken at the Third Plenum of the CC LCY in early March 1966, to reduce federal investment, support economic reform, and permit enterprises to invest throughout Yugoslavia. For another thing, the conservatives, still in control of many of the levers of command, were sabotaging the reform through a combination of perverse implementation of policies in such a way as to undermine their intended function, sly subversion, and outright noncompliance. The Serbian party was taking a hard line. Men like Jovan Veselinov and Vojin Lukić, both party secretaries and the latter a close confidant of Ranković, were determined to block devolution and reform to the furthest possible extent. Ranković, as head of the state security service, had carved out a small empire for himself and had long opposed Kardelj's increasingly more liberal, polycentric visions with his own neo-Stalinist doctrinaire views.

In March 1966, *Komunist* reported discussions (of 10 March) "of a markedly political character" between representatives of the executive committees of the party central committees of Macedonia and Serbia. Though the parties met in part to explore the possibilities for widening bilateral interrepublican cooperation in the fields of economics and culture, the contacts also represented an effort to dampen lingering Macedonian suspicions that the LC Serbia might still be inspired by Greater Serbian chauvinism (of the sort which had labeled

Macedonians "south Serbs" during the interwar period). The Serb discussants hoped to lure Macedonia away from the liberal fold and back into the conservative orbit.[35] This gambit failed, however, as Macedonia clung fast to its coalition with Slovenia and Croatia.

The Fall of Ranković

In 1959, there was an attempt on Kardelj's life. Kardelj was seriously wounded but survived. Although nothing was proven, Kardelj's wife, Pepca, let it be known that she blamed the leading Serbs in the party, that is, Ranković, for the assassination attempt.[36] Her suspicion makes clear the depth of enmity existing between the two men by this time. They were not merely rivals—they were deadly enemies. The incident was passed over but not forgotten. Meanwhile, Ranković was making enemies in other ways. His use of methods of intimidation and his surveillance of leading party functionaries, including the collection of intimate details of their lives, angered many.[37] Allegedly, Ranković had even bugged Tito's bedroom. Kardelj and his liberal allies prepared the field of battle in early 1965, when they obtained the reassignment of Ranković's loyal ally, Vojin Lukić, who was now moved from his post as federal secretary for internal affairs to a less sensitive job as organizational secretary of the Serbian party.[38] By spring 1966, the liberal bloc had finally persuaded Tito that Ranković had to go. The final decision seems to have been made suddenly, and the "investigation" of Ranković was rushed through in order to deny him any possibility to respond.

Only on 16 June 1966 was a special commission appointed by the executive bureau of the CC LCY, with the task of preparing the case against Ranković. The commission was chaired by Krste Crvenkovski of Macedonia. Its other members were Blažo Jovanović, Djuro Pucar, Dobrivoje Radosavljević, and, most interestingly, Miko Tripalo (of Croatia) and France Popit (of Slovenia). The commission worked in secret, with the responsibility for producing a full report within six days. Although not members of the commission, the powers behind this commission were Kardelj, Bakarić, and Petar Stambolić. They would be among the chief beneficiaries, ultimately, of Ranković's removal. Crvenkovski and Tripalo would also soon show liberal colors. Ranković was kept in the dark about the commission's work until the last minute and only received the documentation amassed against him on the eve of the Brioni plenum, at the same time that this documentation was also made available to the other delegates invited to the meeting.[39]

At the 1 July 1966 session, Tito accused Ranković of deviating from party policy as early as 1964, of forming a political clique with the objective of taking power, and of authorizing illegal wiretaps on himself, Kardelj, and other comrades.[40] Ranković and his adherents were specifically accused of "dragging their feet in carrying out the decisions of the Eighth Congress—in fact, they have as much as completely forgotten about the decisions altogether."[41] Ranković was further accused of equating UDBa's authority with that of the Central Committee of the LCY, thereby subverting the supposed hierarchy and converting UDBa into an instrument of his own personal power.[42] Ranković was stripped of his posts and expelled from the Central Committee. His deputy, Svetislav Stefanović, was likewise stripped of his posts and expelled from the party, as was Vojin Lukić.[43] Many Serbs reacted to Ranković's ouster as though the Serbian nation itself had been defeated. *Borba* (15 September 1966) cited lamentations that LCY policy had become anti-Serb and that the Serbs no longer had anyone to defend their interests. UDBa itself was shaken up, and many key security personnel were transferred to large trading corporations in Belgrade.

Although Ranković's fall in July 1966 essentially ended the crisis, there was an interesting sequel. The provincial committee of Kosovo was angered by the revelations of UDBa misconduct and by the "gentleness" with which Ranković was being coddled. Alienated from its former "protector," the Kosovo party organization demanded Ranković's expulsion from the LCY itself—a demand seconded by the central committees of the LC Montenegro, LC Bosnia-Herzegovina, and LC Macedonia and passed by the Fifth Plenum on 10 April 1967. The composition of the committee which had prepared Ranković's fall had been distinctly interrepublican, including Crvenkovski from Macedonia, Pucar from Bosnia, and Radosavljević from Montenegro, as well as the aforementioned members from Croatia and Slovenia; thus, although the regional party organizations in the underdeveloped republics clearly sensed which way the wind was blowing, it is likely that their alienation from Ranković and from the conservative platform was genuine. The fall of Ranković, thus, also signaled the establishment of a broadly based liberal coalition, with shades of an anti-Serbian orientation.

Ascendancy of the National-Liberal Coalition

At this juncture, there were three obvious alternative paths of development: recentralization, further devolution culminating in the transformation of Yugoslavia into a loose confederation, and shoring up of the status quo on the basis of interrepublican consensus. Such consensus was lacking. Throughout this period, the liberal coalition (Croatia-Slovenia-Macedonia) concentrated on further decentralization and "democratization" of both the LCY and society as such. A key issue was federal control of the greater part of earned foreign currency. In championing the federalist principle, the Croatian party was supported by the Slovenes, who had common economic interests and favored currency reforms; by the Macedonians, fearful, above all, of a revival of Serbian chauvinism; and even by some members of the new Serbian leadership, who were hostile to centralism. There was some support for centralism throughout the less developed regions, but all of these areas, especially Macedonia, saw the

Serbian republic as minatory to the autonomy of the other republics. Serbia, it was thought, viewed its own interests as tantamount to the interests of the whole and tended to benefit disproportionately from centralism.

After Ranković's resignation from his posts, Koča Popović (who had served as foreign minister in 1963–1965) was elected vice president (in Ranković's place), Mijalko Todorović took Ranković's slot as secretary of the CC, and Milentije Popović inherited Ranković's position as a member of the Executive Council; all three replacements were Serbs, thus giving the lie to the notion that the removal of Ranković was some sort of anti-Serbian ploy. In addition, Todorović was appointed to chair a commission charged with making radical recommendations for the overhaul of the LCY. Early in October 1966, the party Fifth Plenum reviewed and accepted the Todorović Commission's recommendations, thereby abolishing the party secretariat, reducing the party Executive Committee to purely administrative functions, barring members of the Executive Committee from holding other executive posts, and reducing the size of the Executive Committee to just 11 members.[44]

Throughout 1967 and 1968, there was considerable furor over whether republican delegates to the Chamber of Nationalities ought to be free to act on their own opinions (thus allowing for compromise with opponents and a possible failure to assure the interests of their respective republics) or whether delegates ought to be bound by an "imperative mandate" to observe the strictures and instructions of their republics. In vain, Miloš Žanko, a Croatian representative in the chamber and vice president of the federal Skupština, urged deputies to transcend the parochial interests of their respective republics and to adopt policy stances consonant with the interests of Yugoslavia as a whole. Žanko was reported to have said that "deputies in the Assembly [must] make decisions according to their own convictions.... No deputy is answerable only to his own [republic]. Every deputy is answerable to all the peoples of our country."[45] For this, and for openly criticizing the laxity of Zagreb in dealing with Croatian nationalism, Žanko was recalled by the Croatian party and relieved of his posts.

This was a period of liberal ascendancy, which reached its high-water mark in the summer of 1971 (i.e., after the liberal coalition had fallen apart) with the passage of a series of amendments to the constitution. Together, these amendments amounted to the reconstitution of Yugoslavia as a confederative republic. Throughout this period (and especially in the years immediately prior to the fall of Ranković), there was a tendency for liberals to identify centralism with Greater Serbian assimilationism, resulting in the translation of a dispute about political legitimacy into an inter-ethnic political battle.

This was also a period in which various circles indulged in what, under the circumstances, can only be judged to have been idle fantasies. Stevan Vračar, for example, seeing in the breath of liberalism an opportunity to dismantle the dictatorial superstructure altogether, openly advocated the installation of a two-party system in Yugoslavia, his only proviso being that both parties be committed to socialism—a notion Crvenkovski was said to have favored.[46] Certain unnamed individuals allegedly tried to seize control of SAWPY in order to use it as the nucleus for an opposition party parallel to the LCY.[47] Milosavlevski, in a 1966 article for *Gledišta,* urged that SAWPY be empowered to reach its own conclusions independent of LCY direction and even to differ with the LCY over policy matters.[48]

Not even the LCY appeared, at first, to be immune to the reformist contagion. A commission was set up as early as September 1966 to consider the possibility of a reorganization of the LCY throughout the country, with the Macedonians perhaps in the forefront of the campaign. Even the official party journal, *Socijalizam,* published an article by Tomislav Čokrevski in October 1967 which argued that the Leninist conception of democratic centralism had been devised to meet the needs of an underground party in tsarist Russia and that the Yugoslav party organization had to reflect changed historical and social conditions.[49] Party reform appeared, for a while, to be a logical extension of the reform, and indeed, party structure was reorganized in October 1966. It soon became clear that what the reformers wanted was no less than the complete and official federalization of the party. The LCY could not be satisfied with the faithful representation of the "general interest" of the working class, the reformers argued. According to Stojan Tomić, a high-ranking party member in the LC Bosnia, "the League of Communists must also realize partial interests," and accordingly, the LC Bosnia was obliged to represent specifically Bosnian interests just as the LC Macedonia ought to represent specifically Macedonian interests.[50] Tomić added the understandable qualification that the "partial interests" of the republics should not be pursued at the expense of the general interest of Yugoslavia. Seeking to strengthen the ability of the republican parties to defend precisely such partial interests, Macedonian Mito Hadži Vasilev tried to obtain for the republican parties a veto power over the decisions of federal party organs. In a daringly blunt repudiation of the concept of democratic centralism, Vasilev argued that "no majority, no matter how overwhelming, can, in and of itself, justify a decision—we say within the League of Communists of Yugoslavia—when it is clear that even a single republican organization cannot accept and implement this decision."[51] That this demand was no idiosyncratic fluke was clear from its subsequent reiteration at the Fifth Congress of the LC Macedonia (Skopje, 18–20 November 1968), when Milosavlevski unreservedly came out in favor of the extension of federalism to all political sectors, including the LCY. Among the Montenegrins, the anti-centralist faction also appeared to be ascendant in the post-Ranković phase. Budislav Soškić, candidate member of the LCY presidium representing Montenegro, fully expressed the waxing federal spirit when he declared, in December 1968, that the republican party organizations were no mere "transmission belts" for LCY policy.[52]

This anti-Leninist talk elicited resistance from those unwilling to equate party democratization and party federalization. Dragomir Drašković, denouncing such talk of federalization on behalf of the Serbs, declared that communism must be proletarian, not national, in content and that proletarian interests would only be diluted, fractionalized, and prejudiced by allowing the ethnic factor into the political calculus in this respect.[53] The issue was still a live one when the Ninth Congress of the LCY met in March 1969, and the participants carried the debate into the halls of that congress.[54] Yet, while the liberal coalition showed itself to be all for democratization of the party as long as this strengthened the autonomy of the republic organizations, once that process threatened to factionalize the republic party organizations, the coalition resurrected the old doctrine of democratic centralism. Neither side, thus, challenged democratic centralism per se; the dispute raged over its appropriate application. While the Ninth Congress ended up being purposefully vague in some of its resolutions, republic party congresses were empowered to select members of the LCY presidium and to draw up their own party statutes. The more active role which the liberal coalition was claiming for the republic party organizations was accorded a degree of legitimacy when the Ninth Congress resolved that "instead of binding them in a centralized fashion, the League of Communists of Yugoslavia realizes a creative ideopolitical synthesis of the conceptions, opinions, activities, and initiatives of the Leagues of Communists of the socialist republics."[55] Although Aleksandar Fira, then a professor at the University of Novi Sad, fired back that "the League of Communists is not a league of leagues of communists, but a league of communists of Yugoslavia," the tethers seemed to be slackening, the transformation was complete, and the movement for economic reform had been metamorphosed into a movement for political reform.[56]

Disintegration of the Coalition

The Ninth Congress was perhaps the highpoint of the liberal coalition. Within a few months, the Slovenes became enraged at their coalition partners for pusillanimous support or outright desertion on an issue of vital importance to the Republic of Slovenia, the Croatian and Macedonian parties were engaged in open polemics, and the coalition drifted apart.

The Third Session of the LCY presidency, held on 29 May 1969, just two months after the Ninth Party Congress, signaled the first crack in the liberal coalition. The session highlighted the inner tension in the alliance of actors with divergent interests. Serbian liberal Mijalko Todorović had already thrown the issue into relief by venting his concern over expressions of exclusivist nationalism in the publications of Matica Hrvatska (the Croatian Cultural Society). More potent yet was Crvenkovski's denunciation of Croatian economic nationalism as a kind of separatism. Crvenkovski called for a retreat from economic decentralization, arguing that the persistence of Yugoslavia's economic woes was due to the inadequate integration of the Yugoslav economy. Tripalo, speaking on behalf of the Croatian party, rejected Crvenkovski's analysis and insisted that economic troubles could best be cured by more thorough decentralization.[57]

The strains in the alliance were subsequently exacerbated by the Slovenian road affair, during which alliance partners Croatia and Macedonia declined to share the cuts in funding for highway construction, which Slovenia was expected to shoulder alone. Generally, by the time a foreign credit or foreign aid package was formally tendered to Yugoslavia, the republics had already agreed on the disbursement and disposal of the funds, and project work could therefore proceed without further discussion. In the summer of 1969, however, after the World Bank had announced the award of extensive credits to Yugoslavia for structural development, including road construction, the Yugoslav Federal Executive Council (SIV) revised its project package, provoking a sharp Slovenian reaction. The project for which Yugoslavia had sought World Bank assistance was originally supposed to include road links with Austria, which the World Bank deemed to be a particularly wise investment in view of the potential for developing the tourist industry in the northeast. But after the award had been made, SIV decided to shelve construction on the Postojna-Razdrto and Hoce Lovec roads temporarily, in order to apply the funds designated for that stretch of road against work in other republics. The decision sent shock waves through Slovenia, and citizens of that republic convened meetings to protest the decision. Some Slovenes surmised that a Serb-Croat deal had been concluded at their expense. The Slovenian executive council took up the issue on 31 July and issued an acerbic protest, insisting that the project was of "extraordinary significance."[58] The executive council declared that the project, as originally conceived, would have provided for the optimal road connection between Yugoslavia and the West and requested that the project be restored to the agenda. The following day, the secretariat of the CC of the LC Slovenia, chaired by Andrej Marinc, convened again to consider SIV's road decision. The Slovenes complained that the decision was contrary to the spirit of the Ninth Congress insofar as the decision had been made unilaterally, without any consultation with the republic. Indeed, the Slovenes had not even been told that SIV would take up the question of the road project and the bank loan at its July meeting. The Slovenian central committee warned of negative consequences for relations between the republics and the federal government if this decision was not reversed and once more asked the Federal Executive Council to reconsider.[59]

The move was unprecedented. As Bilandžić has noted, this was the first time that a republic had dared to remonstrate against a federal decision.[60] Croatia quickly lent its support to the Slovenes, despite the Slovenes' heated allegation of a deal between Serbia and Croatia. Not so sympathetic were the Serbs, whose condemnation of the Slovenian protests came as a surprise to no one. The harshness of Crvenkovski's castigation of the Slovenes for "republican egoism" and weakness of Yugoslav socialist patriotism was unexpected and produced another fissure in the liberal coalition.[61] Then, on 4 August, there was a meeting of the presidium of the Slovenian parliament, attended by Sergej Kraigher and Stane Kavčič, among others; this body raised the stakes by asking awkward questions about Slovenia's constitutional status, about the ways in which Slovenia's economic needs were being met within the federation, and about the need to "resolve" the question of democracy in the political system.[62] The Federal Executive Council responded, finally, on 7 August, when it sharply upbraided the Slovenes—embittering them—and adamantly refused to revise the new disbursement schedule. The secretariat of the CC LC Slovenia was still discussing the "road affair," as it came to be called, at its meetings of 25–26 August 1969, but there was nothing more to be done. Still, Slovenian tempers had become so inflamed that France Popit, president of the LC Slovenia, felt compelled to explain that Slovenia had no intention of seceding from the Yugoslav federation—a sure sign that the subject had been broached unofficially.[63]

The project, as it was finally carried out, involved the following sections: (1) in Croatia, a highway from Zagreb to Karlovac with access roads in Zagreb and Karlovac, which accounted for 34% of project costs; (2) in Slovenia, a highway from Vrhnika to Postojna, which accounted for 54% of project costs; and (3) in Macedonia, a highway from Gostivar to Kicevo, which accounted for 12% of project costs. Thus, although the losers in their struggle with the Federal Executive Council, the Slovenes still garnered the lion's share of the loan. Ironically, the Croatian and Slovenian roads, segments of the international highway system which had been expected to see considerable use, actually had less traffic than anticipated, largely because they were operated as toll roads. The Macedonian highway, however, which replaced a low-grade, mountainous road, experienced greater traffic than anticipated. (By way of a footnote to this episode, it should be noted that the Slovenes did obtain credit support for the two outstanding stretches of highway under a World Bank loan contracted on 18 June 1971 [the "Fifth Highway Project"], which were completed by the end of 1977.)[64]

Thus, in terms of what roads were ultimately constructed, the crisis had no effect whatsoever. But it had momentous ramifications in the political system in two respects: (1) it changed expectations of republic behavior and, despite Belgrade's sharp condemnation, set a precedent which expanded the realm of allowable action, and (2) by stirring Slovenian resentment against the Croats and pitting the Macedonians against the Slovenes, it effectively shattered the erstwhile trilateral coalition. After the Slovenian road affair, the Slovenian leadership became increasingly tepid in its support of Croatian demands for reform, even if their interests were similar. The liberal coalition had become a Croatian-Macedonian alliance, and that nexus was itself increasingly strained.

There were other changes in republican (and provincial) orientations. Vojvodina, which had been associated with Croatian and Slovenian demands for further decentralization of the banking system and reform of the foreign currency exchange systems, began to back off in mid-1969. Montenegro—as we shall see in the following chapter—steadily took on a more clearly anti-Serbian, if not exactly pro-Croatian, hue. And Croatia, shorn of support to the north and east, began actively courting Kosovo.

The Slovenes had been more or less cowed by the response to their own half-conscious bending of the rules of the system. The Croatian leadership, however, set out to change those rules. Tripalo, already at the head of this movement, published an article in *Socijalizam* in November 1969, in which he cautioned:

Social praxis, events, and experiences since the Fourth Plenum of the central committee of the LCY up to now clearly show that our system cannot work without a reorganization of the League of Communists. . . . The League of Communists cannot realize its vanguard role if it plays the lackey of corporate management or some sort of propaganda machine for higher organs of power and representative bodies. But, in the same way, the League of Communists must have the powers to resist demagogic, *petit bourgeois,* and primitive conceptions of one section of the working class and of working people in general.[65]

At the Tenth Session of the Croatian central committee, amid criticisms of unitarism—which was said to underestimate the seriousness of the national question—the Croats launched a campaign aimed at further devolution of authority to the republics.[66] The Croats became the primary advocates for adoption of the principle of unanimity in decision making in governmental and party organs. They inherited the task which the Macedonians had earlier pursued with such vigor and which the Slovenes had given up after the road crisis. In this they were successful, moreover, and in April 1970, the LCY party presidium accepted the principle of unanimity in decision making, effectively granting the coalition's demand for a veto power.

CHAPTER 8

The Rise and Fall of Yugoslav Liberalism, 1967–1973

The rift between party liberals and party conservatives widened in the 1960s, as liberals gained footholds in the party leaderships in Slovenia, Croatia, Serbia, and Macedonia. In each of these cases, ousted party conservatives remained in the respective central committee, but in each of these cases, it was liberals who, by the late 1960s, were in the key leadership positions and in control of the policy agendas in the given republic. The result was the adoption of policies inspired by notions of tolerance for cultural and literary activities supportive of the development of national consciousness, a softening of censorship in the media, a softening of policies vis-à-vis religious associations, and noninterference in the affairs of other republics (a notion which, in the Serbian party, represented a complete break with the policy orientation of the fallen Aleksandar Ranković and his hangers-on).

At least some of the liberals—Miko Tripalo in Croatia and Stane Kavčič in Slovenia certainly—came to power because they were trusted protégés of Kardelj and Bakarić, the leading "liberals" up to then. But the liberal leaderships of Slovenia and Croatia quickly proved to be more liberal—and, in the Croatian case, also much more sympathetic to nationalism—than their sponsors and eventually lost their trust and support. Once the liberals had lost the trust of Kardelj, Bakarić, and, above all, Tito, their fall from power was only a matter of time.

227

Economic Exploitation

The economic reform of the mid-1960s has come down, in historical memory, as a partial success. After all, it made possible the economic boom of the late 1970s. But in the short run, the reform engendered disappointment. Economic growth slowed from 9.7% annually in the prereform period (1954–1965) to 6.0% annually in the immediate post-reform period (1966–1970). The rate of increase of employment also slowed—from 5.9% annually in the earlier period to 1.0% in the subsequent period. At the same time, however, labor productivity rose measurably.[1]

In Croatia, the economic reform was disappointing. Croats found their expectations often unfulfilled, and in some cases, their economic position actually deteriorated. A leading Croatian economist claimed, further, that economic resources and credits were more concentrated in Belgrade after the reform than before.[2] The reform had been forged by the forces of devolution but seemed only to have served to further advance the centralization of resources. Even four years after the reform, Belgrade's banks had a stranglehold on the Yugoslav economy, controlling more than half of the total credits and some 81.5% of foreign credits. As of 1969, according to a Croatian economist, Croatia brought in about 50% of all foreign capital but controlled—between Zagreb, Split, and Rijeka—scarcely more than 15% of total credits. Belgrade's foreign trade companies, moreover, were said to enjoy a virtual monopoly, garnering 77.1% of Yugoslav income in this sector, with Ljubljana accounting for most of the rest (19.4%) and Zagreb for a mere 2.4%.[3]

In September and November of 1971, *Hrvatski tjednik,* the weekly newspaper of the Croatian cultural society Matica Hrvatska, published a series of articles which gave detailed information about the secret contents of the so-called Green Book (*Analyses of the Conditions of Crediting the Hotel-Touristic Organizations in the Coastal Region of Croatia*). The book showed how Belgrade's banks had monopolized credit in Dalmatia and squeezed out the indigenous Croatian banks. Belgrade export firms were also exploiting Croatia unfairly, *Hrvatski tjednik* charged. For instance, Progress, a trade corporation in Belgrade, illegitimately reaped huge profits at Croatia's expense throughout 1971 by the sale of ships earmarked for the Croatian merchant fleet, using, as a cover, fictitious companies registered in Liberia and Luxembourg.[4] It was bad enough that the Serbs were penetrating the Croatian hotel industry; worse yet was the Croats' growing perception that their resources were being drained away by Serbia. Thus, during the 1965–1969 period, the very time when investments in the Croatian hotel and tourist industry began to climb at a fast pace, profitability slumped: the reason, charged *Hrvatski tjednik,* was Serbian manipulation of investment credits and terms.[5] In some of the most controversial cases, Serbian corporations allegedly applied political pressure in order to obtain long-term agreements of a colonial character. In other cases, bribery may have been involved. Generalexport, for instance, whose main offices were in Belgrade, secured 10-year agreements with Croatian hotels in Jelsa and Primošten and a 20-year agreement with a hotel in Cavtat. According to *Hrvatski tjednik,* Generalexport obtained these agreements through political pressure and, though putting up only 10% of the capital in each case, assured itself of the legal right to lay claim to at least 50% of the foreign currency earnings of the enterprises in question. It also established "service committees" that exercised wide authority in the management of the hotels without being bound by explicit regulations. In every case, Generalexport was assured a fixed dividend even if the enterprise went into the red. Nor was this an isolated case. Belgrade's Jugoslovenska Poljoprivredna Bank similarly extracted foreign currency privileges as terms of agreement with the Veruda enterprise in Pula and the Plava laguna enterprise in Porec.[6]

It was impossible to divorce economics from politics because it seemed clear to an increasing number of Croats not only that they were being exploited but also that they were being exploited *as Croats.* The Croats noted that Generalexport, the same Belgrade company which was knee-deep in the Croatian hotel industry, "was permitted to set up its own airline long before permission for a Croatian airline was granted."[7] Since this was Serbia's second airline, the Croats concluded that Generalexport benefited from a pro-Serb prejudice among the Serb-dominated federal bureaucracy. More disturbing to Croats was Šime Djodan's argument that Croatia had been forced to accept a deficit in trade with every other republic in the Yugoslav federation, even while netting a sizeable surplus in foreign trade.[8] Djodan, an economist by training and a leading Croatian nationalist, identified Croatia's interests with liberalism and associated Yugoslav conservatives, insofar as they were partial to centralism, with "opposition to self-management."[9] He also criticized Belgrade for an iniquitous economic policy vis-à-vis Bosnia-Herzegovina, Croatia, Slovenia, and Vojvodina and for an inefficiency which undermined whatever benefits might have accrued to Macedonia or Kosovo. After the fall of the triumvirate of Miko Tripalo, Savka Dabčević-Kučar, and Pero Pirker, Djodan would be arrested and jailed. He was unable to publish anything after that for some 20 years.

Cultural and Demographic Threat

It is a well-known constant of social psychology that perception of a threat incites collective affectivity and stimulates recourse to countervailing action. There is no surer way to rally any group around a flag than to convince its members that they are menaced by some other group and that their most cherished values are endangered. Threat perception may, thus, be manipulated. In the Croatian case, however, it seems not to have been manipulated: those nationalists who anxiously warned Croats of impending Serbianization were convinced that the threat was real.

The Serbian threat was thought to take four forms: the use of textbooks to suppress Croatian national sentiment, the Serbianization of the Croatian language, the demographic displacement of Croats by Serbs, and the encouragement of Dalmatian sentiment in order to split Croatia in two. It is interesting that these four phenomena should have been read by the overwhelming majority of Croats as symptoms of a Serbian threat. Population movements can, after all, be explained as strictly economic phenomena, and linguistic homogenization is a typical epiphenomenon of modernization. Even the stirrings of Dalmatian regional identity might have been interpreted as a genuine manifestation of endogenous currents. The public did not, however, view these developments as isolated features, and increasingly the talk was of Croatia's need to defend itself.

Anti-Croatian Manipulations in Textbooks

As Ante Čuvalo has pointed out in his vivid account of the Croatian national movement 1966–1972, textbooks in use in Croatian schools devoted more attention to literature produced by writers from other nations in Yugoslavia than to Croatian literature. The use of the words *Croatia* and *Croatian* was also minimized, although the adjective *Serbian* occurred at least 30 times in one of the chapters of the textbook on literature in use in Croatia. Scholars who dared to use the adjective *Croatian* in their writings "were regarded as anti-Yugoslav nationalists and chauvinists," according to Čuvalo.[10]

Vlatko Paletić, writing in *Hrvatski tjednik,* complained further that important artifacts of Croatia's cultural heritage were being represented as the work of Serbs,[11] while certain textbooks distinguished among Dalmatia, Slavonia, and Croatia, as if Dalmatia and Slavonia were not parts of Croatia. Croats did not fail to notice that textbooks did not treat Serbia or Macedonia or Slovenia, for that matter, in this way.

Linguistic Homogenization and Its Foes

In December 1954, the cultural associations of those federal units in which Serbo-Croatian was the lingua franca had convened in Novi Sad in order to make arrangements for collaboration on the creation of a common orthography for the entire country and to produce a definitive Serbo-Croatian dictionary. Although an official document dating from 1945 had seemed to accord distinct status to Serbian and Croatian (or Serbo-Croatian and Croato-Serbian, as they were sometimes called), Matica Srpska, the Serbian cultural association, had succeeded in persuading the other associations that creation of a unified standard dictionary and orthography was in the best interests of Serbs, Croats, Bosniak Muslims, and Montenegrins alike.[12]

When the first two volumes of this dictionary were finally published in 1967, however, they inflamed the informed Croatian public. Common Croatian vocabulary and expressions were either excluded or relegated to the status of a local dialect; everywhere the Serbian variant was presented as the standard, the Croatian as the deviation. This consistency was more remarkable insofar as a certain Dr. Miloš S. Moskovljević had been reprimanded the previous year for putting out an allegedly chauvinistic dictionary which had no entry for *Hrvat* (Croat), though *Srbin* (Serb) and related words (e.g., *Srbovati*, to act like a real Serb) were well represented. Croatian linguists in Zagreb severely criticized the orientation of the new dictionary and issued a declaration of protest in the 17 March edition of the Zagreb newspaper *Telegram*. This "Declaration concerning the Characterization and Status of the Croatian Literary Language" demanded that Croatian and Serbian be considered two distinct languages and that recognition of this fact be incorporated into a reformulated Article 131 of the constitution, so that all laws and treaties would have to be published in four languages instead of three (i.e., Serbian, Croatian, Slovenian, and Macedonian, instead of Serbo-Croatian, Slovenian, and Macedonian). The declaration continued by demanding "that civil servants, teachers, and officials, without regard to their place of origin, use in their official functions the literary language of the area in which they are working."[13] This last clause was unmistakably aimed at the large number of Serbian bureaucrats who were working in Croatia, and the entire declaration had an overtly anti-Serbian tone. Inevitably, the declaration aroused Serbian tempers and elicited an angry rebuttal from a group of Serbian writers only two days later.[14] This exchange signaled the beginning of a four-year period of heightened Croatian nationalism, which has come to be called "the Croatian spring." The issuance of this declaration set communist nerves on edge, and there were various ritual denunciations of the declaration, meetings of communist functionaries devoted to the document, and expulsions from the LCY of those responsible for the declaration.[15] The following month, Miloš Žanko, vice president of the Croatian Sabor, contributed to an escalation of tensions by denouncing fellow CC members Franjo Tudjman, then director of Zagreb's Institute for the History of the Workers' Movement, and Večeslav Holjevac, president of Matica Iseljenika, for having allowed "the occurrence in their respective organizations of . . . numerous chauvinist[ic] and nationalist outbursts." According to Žanko, Tudjman had consciously hired persons of known nationalist orientation, including some persons who had served time in prison for "activity hostile to the state."[16] The party became concerned about the increasing fireworks in discussions about language, nationalism, and related themes and was having to devote ever more time to these subjects.

The March declaration did not, however, resolve the immediate issue. Throughout the late 1960s, the cultural associations Matica Hrvatska and Matica Srpska engaged in protracted discussions about the cooperative project. The central committees of the communist parties of Croatia, Serbia, Bosnia-Herzegovina, and Montenegro also conducted lengthy joint discussions concerning language policy.[17] Failing to obtain satisfaction in a joint enterprise, the Croats set about compiling a new Croatian orthography and dictionary and began to "purify" Croatian of Serbian "infiltration." Challenged by skeptics, Ljudevit Jonke, president of Matica Hrvatska, wrote in *Kritika* (1968) that the *Broz-Iveković Dictionary of the Croatian Language*, first published in 1901 but still generally considered authoritative in 1968, actually relied heavily on Serbian materials and cited Serbian roots as the sources of 90% of its words—an unacceptable device, according to Jonke.[18] Serbian recalcitrance and Croatian discontent finally prompted Matica Hrvatska to unilaterally withdraw from the joint project on 22 November 1970. Matica Hrvatska declared, on that occasion, that it saw no point in further cooperation in the writing of a Serbian dictionary. Matica Hrvatska's position had been stiffened by Matica Srpska's adamant insistence that Croatian was only a dialect of Serbian (as opposed to suggesting that Serbian and Croatian were equal variants of a common Serbo-Croatian language). But when the Croats went their own way, the Serbs loudly protested. In January 1971, Matica Srprska objected that "The mechanical division of this language, which results from their [Matica Hrvatska's] . . . decisions, is not only scientifically ungrounded but also unjust to our two republics as well as to the Croats in S.R. Serbia and the Serbs in S.R. Croatia."[19]

At approximately the same time, Matica Hrvatska issued another proclamation, declaring that the Novi Sad agreement was "null and void" from the beginning and condemning Matica Srpska's endeavors to systematically suppress the Croatian language. Professor Jonke was able to obtain an interview with *Komunist* and stated simply, "Matica Srpska says that we have a single uniform language, and we say that that is not the case. . . . it is one language, but it is not uniform."[20] Whatever conciliation may have seemed to be implied in Jonke's concession that Serbian and Croatian were "one language," the lines of battle were nonetheless drawn. In autumn 1971, the publication of the Croatian Orthography (*Hrvatski pravopis*) with a new dictionary of the "Croatian language" precipitated Serbian condemnations. *NIN* warned that the publication would exacerbate the growing ethnic tensions between Croats and Serbs, not help to heal them.[21]

Threat of Demographic Displacement

Croatia's population was proportionately older than that of any other republic except Slovenia. The Croatian mortality rate of 11.6 per 1,000 was second only to Vojvodina's rate of 11.8 per 1,000, and its birth rate (in 1972) was the third lowest, behind Vojvodina and Serbia proper.[22] Later, in the period between the 1971 and 1981 censuses, Croatia recorded the lowest birth rate (3.3%) of all the Yugoslav federal units—lower than Vojvodina's 3.8% (second place) and far below Kosovo's 27.4%.[23]

In this context, the large emigration of Croatian workers to Western Europe, which had formerly been construed as an economic opportunity, was suddenly interpreted, at least in some quarters, in darker colors—indeed, as serving to move able-bodied Croats out of the country, so that Serbs could take their places. An official Yugoslav source recorded that 9.6% of the Croatian labor force was employed abroad in 1971—the highest proportion of all the federal units, and significantly higher than the Yugoslav average of 6.6%. Bosnia was a close second with 9.2% of its labor force employed as Gastarbeiter, but Serbia and Slovenia were far behind with rates of 3.7% and 5.4%, respectively.[24] Djodan claimed that more than half of Yugoslavia's émigré workers in 1968 were ethnic Croats and that Croats' net rate of emigration more than canceled out the rate of increase in the Croatian population.[25] Sociologist M. Rendulić, addressing a 1971 conference in Zagreb on "Population, Emigration, and Employment," warned that the rate of natural increase in Croatia was declining and gradually approaching zero.[26] These projections and forebodings were perhaps borne out by the results of the 1981 census, which showed that the number of Croats living in Croatia actually decreased from 3,513,647 in 1971 to 3,454,661 in 1981, while the number of Croats living in Yugoslavia as a whole declined from 4,526,782 to 4,428,135 during the same period.[27]

This situation was compounded by another variable—the increasing influx of Serbs into Croatia. These Serbian immigrants were believed to be taking the places relinquished by the Croatian Gastarbeiter. As early as 1967—the same year in which the *Telegram* declaration was published—a certain Minić addressed an open letter to Miko Tripalo, secretary of the LCC. "We want you to prevent any more Serbs from moving into Croatia," he said plainly. "They are already talking of a Serbia [extending] all the way to Omiš. The Croatian nation will not pardon you!"[28] Simultaneously, concerned Croats organized to "reclaim" immigrants of earlier centuries who had hitherto been written off as Serbian. The immigrants were recast (as they had been during the war) as "Orthodox Croats," thus confounding the traditional shibboleth that a Croat is a Catholic and a Serb is an Orthodox.

The Campaign to Split Off Dalmatia

As early as the end of the 18th century, when I. Kreljanović published his book *Dalmacija autonomna*, there was an articulate coterie of Slavs who viewed Dalmatia as distinct from the rest of Croatia. "Autonomists" were fond of emphasizing the Mediterranean, even Italian, character of the Dalmatian culture and people. During the 19th century, autonomism found followers chiefly among the wealthier families of Dalmatia—merchants, entrepreneurs, bankers, and landowners—and the notion, which originally had a largely cultural hue, took on political overtones. In *Ai Dalmati* (1861), N. Tommaseo, a Dalmatian of Italian extraction, opposed the unification of Dalmatia with the rest of Croatia. He argued that the Dalmatian name was older than the Croatian and that Dalmatian culture was of a higher level, with dialect and customs that differed from those of other Croats. Hence, Dalmatian autonomists were pleased with the outcome of the Austro-Hungarian *Ausgleich* of 1867, because Dalmatia was allotted to Austria, although the rest of Croatia fell to Hungary.[29]

Most early Dalmatian autonomists were foreigners "together with a handful of native renegades schooled in Italy and Vienna," as one Croatian nationalist put it. The Dalmatian idea did not clash with the Croatian idea in an organic sense but, on the contrary, fed Italian irredentism as it was manifested during and after World War One. With the establishment of the Kingdom of Serbs, Croats, and Slovenes in 1918, however, Dalmatian consciousness came to be seen in a new light. Nikola Pašić, the prime minister of Serbia and later of Yugoslavia, had claimed in a 1914 telegram that "Dalmatia wants to be annexed to Serbia—that is its ideal, that is what its interests require, and it is the longstanding drive of the Serbo-Croatian nation."[30] The concept is scarcely surprising, since it is well known that Pašić and his cohorts believed that Croats, Slovenes, and Macedonians were all in fact Serbs (the "tri-named people") and that they all spoke dialects of Serbo-Croatian. Pašić's separate reference to Dalmatia is interesting, for it is suggestive of what proved to be regime policy until the Maček-Cvetković *Sporazum,* viz., to divide the Croats into as many parts as possible and attempt to make those divisions permanent by cultivating and encouraging the development of local identity among Dalmatians, Istrians, Slavonians, Kordunians, and so forth.

As the 1970s began, Serbian interest in Dalmatia was more openly expressed. The Serbian Orthodox Church, for one, published a book entitled *Serbs and Orthodoxy in Dalmatia and Dubrovnik (Srbi i pravoslavlje u Dalmaciji i Dubrovniku)* in 1971.[31] *Srbi u prošlosti,* a book written by Josip Potkozarac and published by a Smederevo publishing house in 1969, was belatedly banned by civil authorities in 1970 for its alleged effort to prove that the populations of Dalmatia, Bosnia, and other regions were purely Serbian and that "the borders of Serbia extend from Djevdjelija to Split."[32] During 1971, a ring of Serbian nationalists which included Slobodan Subotić and Radisav Mičić printed and distributed pamphlets which called for the immediate organization of autonomous Serbian provinces in Dalmatia and elsewhere in Croatia and for the subsequent removal of these areas from Croatia.[33] Croats thus had reason to believe that Dalmatian autonomism was reviving in the 1960s, and Serbian involvement in this phenomenon was evident.[34]

The Dalmatians continue, to be sure, to view themselves as distinct from other Croats—but in most cases this feeling is as harmless as the Texan's pride in being Texan. But the Croatian central committee took pains to make it absolutely clear that in its view no province in Croatia had any ethnic or historical basis for seeking autonomous status nor had it the right to do so.[35] Dalmatian autonomism could lay no claim to any kind of legitimacy, because it was nothing less than "treason" against the Croatian nation.[36]

The Croatian Backlash

Threatened, as they saw it, with the suppression of their language, the obliteration of their people, and the usurpation of their land, the Croats reacted in fear.

They began to look for institutional-legal measures to safeguard the Croatian nation from the Serbs. The argument made was that "the Croatian nation will cease to be manipulated and exploited only if it realizes its statehood, that it will be truly equal only insofar as it attains its sovereignty. If that is not achieved, then it will [continue to] serve as a plaything for other actors."[37]

Early in 1969, Petar Šegedin, president of the Croatian Literary Society, wrote an article for *Kolo* (the bimonthly journal published by Matica Hrvatska) that spelled out Croatian grievances in detail. Among other things, he complained that Croatian interests were systematically subordinated to Serbian interests, that the Croatian people were being unfairly equated with the Ustaše, and that the regime in Belgrade was pursuing a policy aimed at assimilating Croatia, so that any sense of Croatian distinctiveness would disappear.[38] One policy which troubled culturally conscious Croats was the promotion of Serbian conventions as the standard (albeit written in the Latin alphabet), and a reaction developed against this policy, with the revival of some linguistic archaicisms and the active promotion of Croatian conventions in preference to Serbian conventions for use in Croatia. At the same time, a meeting of teachers and textbook writers demanded the revision of school history books to give greater emphasis to specifically Croatian achievements and called for devoting two-thirds of the time allotted to history lessons to Croatian culture and history.[39] Matica Hrvatska, whose championing of the Croatian language had made it the darling of Croatia, became the focal point of the nationalist revival. Had a free election been held in Croatia in 1969 or 1970, Šime Djodan, himself closely affiliated with Matica Hrvatska, would indisputably have been elected to high office.

But the Croatian leadership was internally divided, and those leaders who were unfavorably disposed toward these developments attempted to abort the Croatian revival and to resist demands for greater autonomy. In a series of articles for *Borba* (14–20 February 1969), Miloš Žanko, the prominent Croatian conservative, attacked the nationalistically inclined *Hrvatski književni list* (Croatian Literary Gazette). Immediately thereafter, the Third Plenum of the Central Committee of the LCC (21 February 1969) roundly condemned the gazette for its nationalist orientation and put it on "probation." The Zagreb city council of the League of Communists, still in the hands of the conservatives, likewise took the newspaper to task.[40] Within a matter of weeks, *Hrvatski književni list* was silenced, and nationalist elements in the Emigrant Society (Matica Iseljenika) and the Institute for the History of the Workers' Movement were neutralized. But that act scarcely deprived the nationalists of a forum, and *Studentski list, Hrvatsko sveučilište, Kritika, Kolo, Dubrovnik,* and *Vidik* continued to espouse nationalist viewpoints. Two periodicals catering to the youth, *Tlo* and *Omladinski tjednik,* also joined the nationalist ranks, and *Hrvatski gospodarski glasnik* adopted a nationalist stance in May 1971. In April 1971, Matica Hrvatska inaugurated *Hrvatski tjednik,* whose reportage far surpassed that of *Hrvatski književni list* in the radicalism of its approach. Its subscription list quickly outstripped all competitors, *Vjesnik* included. Even *Vjesnik* and Radio-Television

Zagreb, though formally the organs of the SAWP of Croatia, began to show signs of deviating from the LCY line.[41] Little surprise, then, that the suppression of *Hrvatski književni list* met with a welter of open criticism. In November 1969, *Borba,* unnerved by the continued criticism of this and other policies emanating from *Kolo, Kritika,* and *Dubrovnik,* warned that "there is a system to all this [nationalistic] lunacy."[42]

The Turning Point

Until the end of 1969, the Croatian party leadership had not taken a clear stand on the nationalist revival, principally because neither of its two principal factions had been able to get the upper hand. Žanko, who was at that time vice president of the federal Skupština, publicly attacked Petar Šegedin, Šime Djodan, Vlado Gotovac, Marko Veselica, and others, and charged that exclusivist nationalism was on the rise in Croatia.[43] He exhorted delegates of the Chamber of Republics and Provinces to keep the interests of the entire Yugoslav community uppermost in their minds and to subordinate Croatian interests to those of the entire community.[44] In so doing, he may have deepened the polarization in the Croatian party; at any rate, a counterattack was not long in coming. This took place at the Tenth Plenum of the CC of the LCC (15–17 January 1970), on which occasion LCC president Savka Dabčević-Kučar herself led the attack on Žanko. She claimed that the struggle against unitarism and the struggle against nationalism were two sides of the same coin, but that because of the influence of demented "unitarists" such as Žanko, the LCC had devoted its energies exclusively to the struggle against nationalism. She concluded that far from concentrating on problems of nationalism, the Croatian party organization would have to devote greater attention to combating unitarism. Dabčević-Kučar interpreted Žanko's behavior as a species of disloyalty, betraying an intention to topple the republican leadership and necessarily implying a readiness to mobilize intervening forces from outside the republic in order to achieve that end.[45] The LCC rebuffed Žanko for anti-party views, stripped him of his posts, and attested that "the struggle against nationalism cannot be waged from unitarist battlements."[46] From this point on, the Croatian party leadership drew steadily closer to the ideology of Matica Hrvatska and the nationalists. An internal alliance was being forged to replace the moribund interrepublican alliance with Slovenia, Vojvodina, and Macedonia. The Tenth Plenum was a turning point in another sense: it was the first time that a republican central committee had rendered an assessment of problems of issues relating to nationalism independently of central party organs. The republican leadership was coming into its own.

A new mood prevailed, a sense that the tide had been turned and that the conservatives were on the defensive. Two manifestations of this mood were a seminar held in Zagreb the following month on the theme "Socialism and the National Question" and a large symposium in Krapinske Toplice in March focusing on "The Relation of Class and Nation in Contemporary Socialism." Participants at the latter event displayed a candor which would have been unthinkable a few years earlier. Most significant, this symposium all but ratified nationalism as a legitimate ideology. One of those in attendance, Professor Zdenko Roter of Ljubljana, was most explicit on this score, avowing that "it is necessary to accept nationalism as a positive phenomenon that makes possible the creativity and faster integration of a nation."[47] Others, including Esad Ćimić, echoed his sentiments. Anton Marušić went still further, portraying nationalism as a presupposition of democratic society and opposing national- ism to totalitarianism. More important still, the leadership identified itself with these currents. Tripalo remarked that "It would be good if we could disabuse ourselves of the habit of using the term "nationalism" only in a pejorative sense, for . . . nationalism can have various contents. I think that nationalism is our foe only when it develops into chauvinism."[48]

The Croatian revival reclaimed the heroes of the past. Croats began reexam- ining their history, searching for "lost heroes" who had been swept under the carpet by the communist regime. Stjepan Radić, founder of the Croatian Peas- ant Party, became overnight the most popular (albeit deceased) politician in Croatia, with Miko Tripalo, the engaging secretary of the LCC Central Com- mittee, in second place, and Tito, possibly, a distant third.[49] In August 1971, the culture committee of the presidency of the League of Students of Croatia put up a commemorative plaque in honor of Radić on the facade of the Zagreb house in which he had lived and died. Subsequently, a statue of Radić (Yugoslavia's first) was unveiled in Metković, and there was even talk of erecting a monument to Radić in Zagreb.[50] The coastal town of Šibenik, swept along by the euphoria, canceled plans to erect a monument to the victims of fascism and decided to construct instead a statue of the Croatian king, Petar Krešimir IV.[51]

More daring were efforts to rehabilitate a 19th-century Croatian military governor, Josip Jelačić, and restore him to the Valhalla of Croatian gods and heroes. Marx had savagely condemned Jelačić for his "reactionary" support of the Austrian Kaiser in the suppression of the "progressive" Hungarian rebellion of 1848–1849, and the CPY had manifestly identified itself with Marx's censure by renaming Zagreb's Jelačić Square (*Trg Jelačića*) the "Square of the Republic" (*Trg Republike*). Nevertheless, in the spring of 1971, Zvonimir Kulundžić demanded that the LCY admit that it had erred in debunking Jelačić and called on the party to erect a public statue to Jelačić, "the symbol of old Zagreb."[52] The subsequent wave of letters to the editor of *Hrvatski tjednik* suggested broad sup- port and enthusiasm for the proposal. The entire atmosphere changed—almost overnight. As Miko Tripalo recalled much later, "the whole political life, which had been closed to the public, now opened up and people started to speak their minds, both about the way things were then and about how things had been in the past."[53]

During Croatia's flourishing national exultation, the (officially proscribed) traditional patriotic songs of the Croatian homeland were revived and could often be heard publicly in Croatia's restaurants. Vice Vukov became Croatia's most popular singer in the course of 1971, and also its most controversial.[54] His specialty was songs of Croatia, and at least two of his concerts were banned by a nervous regime fearful of nationalist outbursts.

Now, Matica Hrvatska began to discuss Serbian influences on the Croatian language. In June 1971, Matica Hrvatska organized an open meeting to discuss the *Zadar Review (Zadarska revija)*. The discussion became intense and bitter, with Matica Hrvatska complaining that the *Review*'s language was "impure," a concatenation created by the contributions of a staff drawn not merely from Croatia but from various parts of the country.[55] Matica Hrvatska also pressured Yugoslav Railways, objecting that its exclusive use of the ekavian variant (Serbian) was prejudicial to the Croatian language. Under additional pressure applied by Zagreb, Yugoslav Railways agreed that by 1 September 1971, all railway notices, schedules, and forms would be printed in the ijekavian variant (Croatian) as well.[56] *Hrvatski tjednik,* always in the midst of the fray, complained that the buses servicing the Zagreb airport were marked "Jugoslovenski Aerotransport"—correct Serbian—rather than "Jugoslavenski Aerotransport" —correct Croatian.[57] *Hrvatski tjednik* even initiated a column devoted to distinguishing correct Croatian from common Serbian infiltrations. There was a new mood in Croatia—a belief that anything was possible—and the team of Dabčević-Kučar and Tripalo, firmly in the saddle, was riding the crest of the wave. But they had not solved the problem of how to reconcile Croatian nationalism with the imperatives of coalition politics.

Revision of Croatia's Constitution

Throughout the gathering maelstrom, the Serbs living in Croatia—who comprised some 15% of the republic's population—occupied a unique and rather precarious niche. Their economic interests were inseparable from the interests of the Croatian republic, and they were represented in the federal Skupština by the delegation from Croatia. Moreover, most of these Serbs spoke ijekavian or a mixture of ijekavian and ekavian, not the pure ekavian of their kin in SR Serbia. But in the ever more polarized atmosphere of the time, Serbs of Croatia identified with fellow Serbs in Serbia and started to affect ekavian speech. There was also a growing controversy surrounding the status of the Serbs in Croatia and the impact of heightened Croatian national consciousness on their rights of national self-expression.

Inevitably, there were currents which gave the nationalist awakening the most negative interpretation possible. Before the end of the year, *Hrvatski tjednik* found it necessary to warn of the development of a campaign "to convince the Serbs in Croatia of two big lies": that the aesthetic self-development of Croatia serves the exclusive purpose of setting Croatian apart from Serbian and that by means of this "artificial, exclusivist, anti-Serbian language and orthography, the Croats mean to oppress the Serbs in Croatia." But the explanation that the Croats were only embarking on "the elimination of what was by coercion and pressure forced on the Croatian language" failed to assuage fears on the part of Croatia's Serb community, who looked for allies among Croatian conservatives and initiated a campaign to incorporate co-sovereignty for Serbs in the Croatian constitution.[58]

Professor Mihailo Djurić, a member of the law faculty in Belgrade, told a colloquium at the law school in March 1971 that Croatia's Serbs needed special constitutional guarantees to safeguard their rights of national self-expression.[59] Djurić zeroed in on the opening paragraphs of the Croatian constitution. Article 1 in the 1963 version read, "The Socialist Republic of Croatia is the socialist democratic state community of the Croatian nation (*narod*), established on the power of the working people and self-management." This article was preceded by an apparently innocuous section of "general principles" which began, "The Croatian nation, in harmony with its historical aspirations, proceeding from the right of self-determination, including also the right of secession, in common struggle with the other nations of Yugoslavia . . . united with the other nations of Yugoslavia in a federal republic of free and equal nations and nationalities."[60] Djurić believed that this signified that the Serbs were excluded from participation in the "socialist democratic community" and denied explicit credit for their role in the "common struggle." He therefore proposed to rectify these oversights by inserting, after the words "in harmony with its historical aspirations," the signal phase "*in common struggle with the Serbian nation and the nationalities in Croatia,*" and by defining the republic of Croatia as "the sovereign national state of the Croatian nation, *the state of the Serbian nation in Croatia,* and the state of the nationalities that live in it."[61] The insertions made explicit the rights of the Serbs in Croatia, but they also compromised the national status of the Croatian republic. Djurić's intervention was not welcome to the LCY establishment, however, and he was put in prison as a result.[62]

In the meantime, Matica Hrvatska immediately sprang forward with a detailed critique of the draft amendment urged by Djurić, rejecting the notion that it was at all appropriate to refer to Croatia as "a state of the Serbian nation."[63] *Hrvatski tjednik* dredged up a 15-year-old statement by jurist Jovan Stefanović to the effect that it would be erroneous to conclude, on the basis of "the regulation . . . regarding the equality of Serbs in Croatia, . . . that NR [*narodna republika*] Croatia is the republic of Croats and Serbs. It is the republic of the Croatian nation."[64] The paper complained that Djurić's draft would have reduced Croatia to a quasi-federation of nationalities.

The effect of this confrontation was electric: all Croatia was fired into a state of excited agitation, and support for the concept of the Croatian national state became a fundamental test of republican and ethnic loyalty. One disconcerted reader of *Hrvatski tjednik* expressed his wonderment that the "unitarists" and Serbophiles had not yet proposed renaming the republic "Serbo-Croatia" (*Srbo-Hrvatska*).[65] Consistent application of the principle implied in the draft amendment would have required redefining Macedonia as the state of the Macedonians, Albanians, Turks, and Bulgarians; Serbia as the state of Serbs, Albanians, Hungarians, Croats [found in the largest numbers in the Vojvodina], Roma, and others; Montenegro as the state of the Montenegrins, Albanians, Muslims, and Serbs; and so on.

Matica Hrvatska countered with its own draft of Amendment 1 for Croatia's constitution, emphasizing Croatia's character as the national state of the Croats, while declaring the full civic equality of all citizens living in the republic.[66] However popular its version may have been with the majority of Croats, more conservative members of the LCC together with some of those sympathetic to the concept of defining Croatia as a national state felt that Matica Hrvatska had gone too far. Party organs reacted vehemently to Matica Hrvatska's draft amendment, while the Zagreb daily newspaper *Vjesnik* defended the notion of adding explicit reference to the Serbs in the constitution.[67] It quickly became obvious, if it had not been clear from the beginning, that Matica Hrvatska's draft was incapable of passage. In its 5 November 1971 issue, *Hrvatski tjednik* extended an olive branch, offering a compromise formulation in which the order of fundamental principles was changed and in which there would be an explicit mention of Serbs in Article 3, where Croatia would be characterized as the "homeland of all its citizens, Croats, Serbs in Croatia, and the members of other nations and nationalities who inhabit it."[68] Matica Hrvatska had lost this round, however, and the official governmental draft amendments were ultimately passed. Hence, from that point until the Croatian constitutional amendments of 1990, "the Socialist Republic of Croatia [was] the national state of the Croatian nation, the state of the Serbian nation in Croatia, and the state of the nationalities inhabiting it."[69]

Nationalist and Liberal Echoes in Other Republics

Every republic and autonomous province was struck by nationalist outbursts in these years, and among all the non-Serbian nationalities, there were strong anti-Serbian feelings. The fall of Ranković had been a cathartic catalyst because, by branding this prominent Serb as arch-villain, the party legitimated the release of pent-up frustrations even as it made their expression more practical. Nationalist discontent was most visible in Croatia and Kosovo, followed, in declining intensity, by Serbia, Montenegro, Bosnia-Herzegovina, Macedonia, Slovenia, and Vojvodina. In some places, for instance, ethnocentric behavior on the part of Serbian bureaucrats provided a stimulus for remonstration. There were hints of this even in Vojvodina, where the so-called Rehák affair signaled the beginning of a breakdown in the Serbian-Hungarian equilibrium. László Rehák, an active member of the LCY, had complained in the Serbian republic Assembly (in 1967) that the University of Novi Sad was dragging its feet in setting up the approved Hungarian Studies Institute; in response, the Serbian press hauled him over the coals for "nationalism" and mobilized forces sufficient to block his election as vice president of the executive council of SR (Socialist Republic of) Serbia. Though in some ways the most pacific of Yugoslavia's minorities, the Hungarians of Vojvodina were ruffled by this development and affected by the train of events in Croatia. In an article for *Uj Symposion* (Novi Sad, August 1971), Sándor Rosza, a student at the University of Novi Sad, charged that Hungarians were victims of overt discrimination and that shopkeepers in Novi Sad were loath to speak Hungarian. Rosza's charges reached the absurd degree of portraying the Hungarians as the "niggers" of Yugoslavia, and the regime reacted swiftly and vengefully. Rosza lost his scholarship and his post as Hungarian-language program coordinator of the Novi Sad Youth Council and was sentenced to three years of strict imprisonment. Oto Tolnak was fired from the editorship of *Uj Symposion* and sentenced to one year in prison. Finally, *Uj Symposion,* under a new editor, had to print an apology for having permitted the publication of the offending article in the first place.[70] Nor was this an isolated instance. Indeed, as early as 1968, Dobrica Ćosić had cautioned the Fourteenth Plenary Session of the central committee of the LC Serbia that the problem of Hungarian nationalism in Vojvodina ought not be underestimated.

A far more serious flare-up of nationalism occurred in Montenegro, where, during this period, the anti-Serbian faction temporarily prevailed over its pro-Serbian colleagues. The latter group had traditionally been inclined to stress the close kinship, if not outright identity, of Montenegrins and Serbs; the former, in affirming the distinctiveness of the Montenegrin nation, made hostility to Serbia the core of its program. The Montenegrin Literary Society, following in Matica Hrvatska's footsteps, became embroiled in various nationalist disputes, and the review *Ovdje* and the journal *Stvaranje* provided forums for nationalist discontent. Certain problems were revived and reexamined with great interest, including the ethnogenesis and formation of the Montenegrin nation (a politically sensitive subject even in the 21st century), the relation of the Montenegrin nation to the Serbian nation, the relationship of a possible Montenegrin variant to Serbo-Croatian (or Croato-Serbian), and various issues regarding the content of textbooks in Montenegro.

But unlike Croatia, where officialdom represented the only stronghold for pockets of conservatives, in Montenegro the pro-Serb faction had deep social roots and recourse to alternative institutions. Forcefully resisting Montenegrin nationalist currents, a Serbian Orthodox Church symposium, meeting at Karadjordjevo in the spring of 1970, alleged that the so-called Montenegrins had been forced to identify themselves as Montenegrins but were, in essence, Serbs.[71] But when Patriarch German began a speech shortly thereafter by saying, "We Serbs—of course, I believe that Montenegrins are also Serbs,"[72] even the conservatives were dismayed. *NIN* sprang to the attack and upbraided the patriarch for the "negation of the national sovereignty of a certain nation," a stance which, said *NIN,* derived from the tenet held by "certain elements" in the Serbian Orthodox Church that ethnic affiliation is only *artificially* distinguished from confessional affiliation.[73]

Nationalism even made certain inroads in Slovenia, though the Slovenes, lacking any tradition as a separate state, were somewhat more disposed to moderation. All the same, the pattern was a familiar one. A prominent Slovenian writer and chairman of the League of Yugoslav Writers voiced an early protest, complaining in February 1967 that Slovenian resources had been siphoned off to build up the south and that this policy was contrary to Slovenian interests in both the long and the short run. Another Slovenian novelist, Marjan Rožanc, received a six-month prison term in October 1967 for having written an article for the Slovenian-language journal *Most* (which appeared in Trieste), in which he described the Slovenian nation as a sacrificial offering on the altar of Yugoslavism.[74] Such sentiments spread to the general public of Slovenia, and there were reports of Slovenian workers noisily protesting the showing of films with Serbo-Croatian subtitles.[75] During this time, Stane Kavčič, head of the Slovenian government in 1970–1971, tried to wrest as much political autonomy for Slovenia as possible, gave preference to the construction of transportation links with the north and west rather than with Zagreb and Belgrade, and allied himself with liberals in Croatia. Kavčič was opposed in Ljubljana by Sergej Kraigher and France Popit (the latter, president of the League of Communists of Slovenia), both hostile to massive decentralization.[76] Although Kavčič himself clearly opposed secession, Mitja Ribičič, a member of the Slovenian party's executive committee, warned in 1967 of an incipient frondescence of separatist sentiment in Slovenia.[77] Alojz Vindiš later claimed that certain groups in Slovenia took advantage of the uncertainties of the early 1970s to coquette with the idea of Slovenian secession from Yugoslavia, allegedly envisioning the establishment of an independent neutral state based on the Swiss model and oriented to the West.[78]

Nationalist chauvinism also affected Serbs at this time, even though, paradoxically, they often said that they were immune to chauvinism. Yet as early as February 1966—that is, even before the fall of Ranković—*Komunist* had charged that "some members of the LC Serbia have not studied the materials of the Eighth Congress of the LCY and the Fifth Congress of the LCS, in which all the aspects and problems of interethnic relations in our socialist community are treated very clearly and openly." They continued to act, *Komunist* observed, as if they were a special caste whose voice had a certain priority.[79]

Croatian nationalism had flared in reaction to the hegemonistic posture adopted by the Serbian and Montenegrin parties, the Serb communists within Croatia, and Ranković's people in general. But Croatian Serbs were not disposed to a posture of contrition and asserted themselves against their Croatian neighbors. Serb nationalism among Serbs of Croatia grew, drawing energy also from the traditional, religiously derived distrust which Croatia's Serbs had long felt toward their Croatian cousins.[80] Prosvjeta, the Serbian cultural society in Croatia which had been created in 1944, started to change its character around 1969 and became a stronghold for Serbian nationalists and a forum for former Chetniks. Exploiting this institutional base, Croatia's Serbian nationalists sought in 1970 to create a Serbian autonomous province within Croatia and demanded the establishment of a separate network of special Serbian schools; those further to the right even broached the idea of seceding from SR Croatia and attaching themselves to SR Serbia.[81] In one of its last meetings in 1971, the executive committee of Prosvjeta demanded (1) that Croatian and Serbian be recognized as official languages of SR Croatia and that all republican legislative acts be published both in Croatian and in Cyrillic-Serbian; (2) that a Chamber for Interethnic Relations be formed within the framework of the Croatian Sabor (Assembly), with the delegates from each national group chosen exclusively by the members of that group; and (3) that this chamber play a deciding role in all questions relevant to the equality of nationalities and that its decisions require the assent of *all* delegations.[82] What would have been the reaction in Serbia if the Croats of Vojvodina had made the equivalent demand?

Symptomatic of the same syndrome, experimentation with semi-free elections in 1967 and 1969 led in Serbia to the election of opposition nationalists to the federal Assembly. Nationalism animated a large portion of the Serbian population, from the peasantry to those on the rungs of power. Thus, in a story recounted by Carl Gustav Ströhm, Slobodan Penezić-Krčun, Ranković's onetime deputy, even sought to pay Tito a compliment by saying that he had only one shortcoming—he was not a Serb![83]

All of the regional parties—whether one thinks of Slovenia or Croatia or Bosnia or Serbia or Montenegro or Macedonia—were internally divided, and typically the two chief political camps were liberals and conservatives. (This picture had rather specific local nuances in Bosnia and Montenegro.) In Serbia, the party was temporarily under the leadership of Marko Nikezić and Latinka Perović. As leading representatives of the liberal wing of the party, they wanted to reach a modus vivendi with their Croatian counterparts and lay a foundation for the system to move beyond inter-ethnic antagonisms and to achieve some measure of internal stability. This ambition brought them into conflict with conservatives in the party.

The Serbian Liberals

Aleksandar Ranković was not the only powerful Serbian conservative to lose office in the summer of 1966. Others fired at the time included his deputy, Stevislav Stefanović, and important republic-level figures Vojin Lukić and Životija Srba-Savić. The longtime head of the Serbian party, Jovan Veselinov, was also retired at that time. The leadership which took the reins in Serbia in September 1966 included Mijalko Todorović and Milentije Popović on the federal level and Dobrivoje Radosavljević, Miloš Minić, and Stevan Doronjski at the republic level. However, this leadership, though committed to political and economic liberalization, lacked a power base at lower levels in the party and soon ran into trouble.[84] In 1967, the party rebuked Partisan hero Svetozar Vukmanovič for his criticism of structural reforms to the LCY and censured federal deputy Radivoje Jovanovič for his outspoken opposition to certain proposed economic reforms, for which Jovanovič was denounced as a Serbian "nationalist."[85] Jovanovič was described as a member of the anti-reform "political underground" in Serbia and had won office by running as an "independent" candidate against the party's officially sponsored candidate, in April 1967, during the LCY's brief experiment with multi-candidate elections.[86]

For a year and a half after the fall of Rankovič and his associates, the Serbian party remained severely fractured to the point of being unable to maintain minimal internal party discipline, with serious departures from policy occurring both in some smaller towns in southern Serbia and in Belgrade. Then, in late November 1968, a new Serbian party leadership was elected at the Sixth Congress of the LC Serbia. Marko Nikezič, who had served as foreign minister of the SFRY, was now elected president of the League of Communists of Serbia, while Latinka Perovič, a young and urbane intellectual, came out of an academic setting to become secretary of the LC Serbia. The Sixth Congress also saw a lot of young blood entering into the party leadership, with 95% of the Congress's 690 delegates attending a party congress for the first time.[87] Together Nikezič and Perovič took Serbian policy in a new direction, emphasizing industrial development and, in 1971, courageously defending the Croatian liberal leadership from Tito's criticisms.[88] They adopted a strict principle of noninterference in the affairs of other republics, limiting their critical attention to critiquing Serbian nationalism and Serbian hegemonic tendencies within Yugoslavia.[89] Ironically, one of Nikezič's first acts as president of the Serbian party, in November 1968, was to approve the use of deadly force by local police in order to suppress the Albanian riots. The Albanians were exerting pressure at the time to see Kosovo elevated to the level of a republic equal with Serbia, but the Serbian party, meeting in February 1969 to consider this request, turned it down. On the other hand, Nikezič, Perovič, and Predrag Ajtič defended the provinces' constitutionally anchored autonomy against demands registered by Draža Markovič, by then president of the republic Assembly of Serbia, that their newly won autonomy be curtailed.[90]

The Serbian liberals wanted to see the development of a market economy—a priority which inevitably set them on a confrontation course with the more doctrinaire Tito. They also wanted to abandon the earlier Serbian course of confrontation with other republics and to take their republic into genuine cooperation with the others. Nikezič, in particular, felt that nationalist posturing could only be self-destructive. "We cannot expect unity within the country," he said, "if the feeling continues that Serbs are the foundation for Yugoslavia. . . . If Yugoslavia is necessary, then it is necessary for all, and not just Serbs."[91] But if this orientation seemed to bring the Nikezič-Perovič team into harmony with Tito's post-1966 policy line, there were disagreements between the Serbian liberals and Tito quite apart from economic strategy. In March 1971, for example, at a high-level meeting, Tito and Nikezič engaged in verbal dueling, in which Nikezič complained that Tito was treating Serbia as the "black sheep" of the Yugoslav flock, with Tito accusing Nikezič of leading a smear campaign against him, against the constitution, even against the communist system.[92] Draža Marković had opposed the election of Marko Nikezič to the Serbian party leadership in the first place and, according to a rising star in the LCY, was constantly feeding Tito information that Nikezič and Perovič were against him.[93] Later, in November 1971, when Tito was seriously considering dumping the Serbian liberal team, he contacted Marković (who had enjoyed some credibility with the liberals at one time[94]) and invited him to come to his villa at Karadjordjevo for talks. Word of the meeting was leaked to Nikezič and Perovič, and the internal rift between liberals and conservatives within the Serbian party deepened.[95]

Slovenian Liberalism

The five dominant Slovenian voices in the late 1960s and early 1970s were those of Edvard Kardelj, Stane Dolanc, France Popit, Sergei Kraigher, and Kraigher's brilliant understudy, Stane Kavčič, the last of whom was elected chair of the executive council of Slovenia in May 1967 (as successor to Janko Smole). Popit and Kavčič proved to be natural foes, with Popit articulating a more conservative line, and Kavčič advocating a more liberal line. As Kavčič staked out his own position, supported among others by the young Milan Kučan, who would be elected president of Slovenia two decades later, Kardelj developed second thoughts about Kavčič. Kardelj felt that Kavčič was taking too much into his own hands and building up cliques loyal to him personally. Kardelj remained close to Kraigher, who was likewise becoming alienated from Kavčič. Popit joined Tito in advising Kavčič that they had confidence that, with their help, Kavčič could overcome his "weaknesses."[96] Dolanc, at that time executive secretary of the LCY Presidium, would later announce his intention to introduce a Yugoslav variant of the Chinese cultural revolution in the country; Kavčič considered Dolanc to be a died-in-the-wool Stalinist.[97] In spite of Slovenes' complaints that they were being asked to contribute to the federal budget at a level far out of proportion to their population size, Kavčič won Tito's respect during his first 18 months in office, and at the beginning of 1969, Tito would even offer Kavčič the post of chair of the Federal Executive Council.[98] Kavčič declined.

It was at this time, in the aftermath of the Soviet invasion of Czechoslovakia in August 1968—which the Yugoslav leadership sharply denounced[99]—that the Yugoslavs developed their concept of people's territorial defense, basically endeavoring to adapt their Partisan experience in World War Two to a possible confrontation with Soviet armed forces. There were discussions within Slovenia about defense plans to be developed at the republic level, and Slovenian political leaders allegedly entered into contacts with French army representatives with the objective of purchasing French weaponry for use in Slovenian territorial defense.[100]

While his liberal counterparts in Croatia and Serbia were taking laissez-faire literally, thinking increasingly within the framework of their own republics only, Stane Kavčič continued to think on an all-Yugoslav level and was convinced of the need to negotiate an agreement among the republics, on the basis of which they could move toward a market economy and a more democratic system.[101] But the "road affair" was a turning point of sorts. Slovenia's claims as regards funding for highway construction engendered negative reactions in many other parts of Yugoslavia, especially in Macedonia.[102] The "road affair" also contributed to undermining the Slovenian liberals in Tito's eyes, as the Yugoslav leader began to conclude that liberalism lent itself inevitably to national egoism. Moreover, the "road affair" fit a pattern established earlier in which Slovenian liberals expressed concern lest Slovenes be underrepresented in the Yugoslav diplomatic corps, demanded increase use of the Slovenian language on the television and radio as well as in the debates of the federal Skupština, and pleaded for greater use of Slovenian in court proceedings and official federal documents.[103]

Slovenia's experiences in these years illustrated as well as any republic the depth of internal division between liberals and conservatives. In essence, the liberals had taken control of some of the leading posts, but they had not taken control of the party apparatus as such, and indeed had no hope of doing so insofar as Tito never, in fact, converted to the liberal camp; he tolerated the liberals' political experimentation for as long as he thought it might strengthen the country's socialist system; once he concluded that the liberals were weakening socialism and undermining the unity of Yugoslavia, he turned against them. In Slovenia, the "road affair" already began the process of undermining Kavčič's position, but the clash between liberals and conservatives came to a head only in late spring and summer 1971, during debates over the two official Slovenian candidates for the newly established presidency of the SFRY, Mitja Ribičič and Marko Bulc. Instead of simply endorsing the party's choices—the "correct" response—certain communal councils and city party organizations proposed one or another alternative candidate, whether Kavčič or Dolanc or Ivan Dolničar or someone else. In spite of all the clamor, however, in the end Ribičič and Bulc were elected, to no one's surprise.[104]

Liberal Echoes in Macedonia

There were also echoes of this liberal current in Macedonia, where liberal-minded Krste Crvenkovski dominated the republic's politics for a number of years. Crvenkovski was elected chair of the CC LC Macedonia in July 1963. It was Crvenkovski who headed the committee which investigated violations of party discipline by Ranković and UDBa, filing the report which catapulted Ranković out of office.[105] By contrast with their counterparts in Slovenia, Serbia, and Croatia, Macedonia's liberals did not have an articulate program of economic liberalization, but they were convinced advocates of a democratization of political life. In Macedonia as elsewhere, the party was divided between a liberal faction and a conservative faction, but perhaps more than elsewhere, there was a clear generational divide associated with the ideological division.[106] Liberals Crvenkovski and Slavko Milosavlevski represented the younger generation, while Lazar Koliševski, who had dominated Macedonian politics before Crvenkovski came to power and who would once more dominate Macedonian politics after Crvenkovski's removal from power in 1972, was a member of an older and more conservative generation. In 1968, the Macedonian liberal leadership plucked Kiro Gligorov, a member of the CC LCY with economic expertise, to represent Macedonia in the LCY Presidium.[107] Rather significantly, it was during the liberals' brief rule that demands were raised that Macedonia's border with Serbia be "corrected" to Macedonia's advantage. There were also complaints raised at this time that the Macedonian language was underutilized in official settings; Macedonian and Slovenian complaints on this score led to an announcement in January 1967 "that all documents sent to the Federal Assembly would be in Slovenian and Macedonian as well as Serbo-Croatian, and that Assembly debates would be simultaneously translated into all three languages."[108]

The Battle at the Center

After the passage of some 19 amendments to the federal constitution during 1967–1968, trimming the prerogatives of the federal government, enhancing the status and powers of the republics, and granting the autonomous provinces near parity with the republics, a movement emerged to transform the federal government itself into an interrepublican agency. The chief advocates of this movement were Stane Kavčič, Slavko Milosavlevski, and Miko Tripalo, and the means of transformation were to be the network of interrepublican committees which had finally been established in mid-1971, after a lot of discussion. One of the movement's more alacritous adherents, the young Dražen Budiša, even suggested redesignating Yugoslavia the "League of Yugoslav Socialist Self-Managing Republics" as an explicit token of the system's imminent metamorphosis into a confederation.[109]

Although part of a package of 23 more amendments passed on 30 June 1971, stripping the federal government of most of its remaining prerogatives (limiting its powers to foreign affairs, defense, foreign trade, and the common currency, and guaranteeing a common tariff system and the free flow of goods throughout the country), the committees themselves seem to have been conceived in a spirit of experimentation.[110] Amendment 33, adopted at this time, specified that economic questions of general interest were to be resolved through direct consultation with deputies of the republics. This was the legal foundation for the committees. In the last week of June 1971, Djemal Bijedič was asked to form a new government, and it fell to his administration to inaugurate the new committee system. By the end of August, the newly constituted Federal Executive Council (SIV) had managed to set up most of the working bodies and had announced its determination to complete all appointments to the nascent interrepublican committees by 2 September.

Five interrepublican committees were created to monitor the following areas: developmental policy, the monetary system, foreign trade and hard currency, the market, and finance. Each committee would consist of nine members, one from each federal unit and a chairman selected by SIV from among its own ranks. They were authorized to consider any questions lying within their jurisdiction either at the request of SIV or on their own initiative, even if their involvement was not technically and specifically prescribed by the constitution. At the time of the committees' birth, their creators argued that they would quicken the legislative process without impinging on the jurisdiction of SIV or of the federal Skupština. The committees were to render their evaluations to SIV and to the executive councils of the federal units. But the positions of an interrepublican committee could be overruled only if SIV could obtain the specific assent of the executive councils of the republics and provinces (Article 12). This meant that the new committees would become the ultimate repository of power where economics was concerned.

The interrepublican committees proved very efficient. At the time the committees were set up, there were some 124 questions of interrepublican importance which had not been resolved, even after months of debate. The committees disposed of all these questions within five months—92 of them in the committees themselves, 32 in the Coordination Commission which had been established as a kind of supervisory board over them. Satisfied with what was at least partly his handiwork, Bijedić told the Twenty-eighth Session of the presidency of the LCY, "I am convinced that, in our phase of development, we could not discover and pass decisions so quickly without accommodation via the committees and Coordination Commission."[111] Dragutin Kosovac, president of the executive council of Bosnia-Herzegovina and ipso facto a member of the Coordination Commission, was even more rhapsodic and raved that the interrepublican committees had assured "the most rational decisions and these, in essence, represent the optimal interest of the whole."[112]

So smoothly did the committees do their work that other organs of decision making found themselves sidelined. Even the Federal Executive Council's meetings merely ratified the decisions and conclusions of the Coordination Commission, now alternatively dubbed the "Supreme Interrepublican Committee" or the "Super-Government" (*super-vlada*).[113] The confederal character of this institution was unmistakable. Yet the system's proponents looked forward to the further expansion of the powers of the new committees. Ksente Bogoev, president of the executive council of Macedonia, even suggested expanding the scope of the interrepublican committees, proposing that questions arising in the spheres of education, science, culture, and health also be turned over to the committees for resolution.[114]

The Croatian Liberals' Last Stand

The various factions in the Yugoslav debate over the federalization of the LCY—democratizers, liberals, nationalists, humanists, and conservatives—had their counterparts within the League of Communists of Croatia (LCC). There were the "liberals," such as Savka Dabčević-Kučar, Miko Tripalo, and their coterie, together with technocrats and other economic reformers; the "nationalists," such as Šime Djodan, Marko Veselica, and the exploding membership of Matica Hrvatska; and the band of centralist-humanists known as the "Praxis group," who were hostile to any species of nationalism or autonomism. In addition to these three groups were the conservatives, including such persons as Miloš Žanko (by now discredited), Stipe Šuvar, Veljko Rus, Dušan Dragosavac, Jure Bilič, J. Radojčević, and Milutin Baltič (Radojčević, Dragosavac, and Baltič were Serbs, while Šuvar, and Bilič were Croats; Rus, whose confidence in self-management was legendary, was a Slovene).

But the liberal-nationalist alliance seemed to have been consolidated by early 1971. Specifically, in February of that year, conservative members of the LCC executive committee demanded that resolute action be taken against Matica Hrvatska, Dabčević-Kučar, and Pirker; but liberal loyalists Tripalo, Dragutin Haramija, Ivan Šibl, Marko Koprtla, and Srečko Bijelič (president of the city conference of the LC of Zagreb) blocked this initiative. Encouraged by this development and other signs of liberal strength, *Omladinski tjednik* and *Hrvatski tjednik* floated the idea of convoking an extraordinary session of the LCC, hoping to further strengthen the hands of the liberals.

Conservative strength was, however, scarcely spent, and the anti-nationalist factions in the Croatian party scored a victory on 23 July, when they succeeded in having Šime Djodan and Marko Veselica expelled from the party as "ringleaders" of ethnocentric turmoil. This decision was made by the presidency of the city conference of the LC Zagreb where, Bijelič notwithstanding, the conservatives still had strength. But this victory was an isolated triumph, for the strength of the liberal-national coalition was not yet spent. Bakarič, no conservative but no nationalist either, was retired to the backbenches. Membership in Matica Hrvatska soared to 41,000 members in 55 branches by November 1971 (up from 2,323 members in 30 branches in November 1970).[115]

During the summer of 1971, the periodicals of Belgrade and Zagreb engaged in polemics over a series of incidents and provocations, many of which were undoubtedly blown out of proportion if not essentially fabricated. The most celebrated of these incidents was probably the "Podravska Slatina" affair, a story which broke on 11 May 1971, when Belgrade's *Politika* reported obstructive activities by members of Matica Hrvatska on their way to a society meeting. The article portrayed the members as anti-Yugoslav Croatian nationalists—they were said to have been flying Croatian colors only, lacking the red star, on their car antennae (an allegation they denied)—and accused them of trying to break up a meeting of old partisans in the town of Podravska Slatina in Slavonia. The article was immediately lambasted by Croatia's *Glas Slavonije* (13 May), which described the *Politika* article as "fabricated disinformation" which distorted an insignificant non-event so as to make it appear to *Politika'* s Serbian readers that the Croats were getting completely out of control. Yet the *Politika* version was also picked up by *Komunist, Vjesnik,* and *Večernje novosti,* a Belgrade tabloid. By the following day (14 May), *Glas Slavonije* was nervously drawing the conclusion that *Politika*'s provocation had been designed to undermine Matica Hrvatska's prestige and legitimacy, throttle the reform movement, and abort passage of the constitutional amendments by portraying their chief exponents (the Croats) as nationalistic zealots.[116] The central committee of the LCC appointed an investigative commission to look into the various allegations pertaining to the Podravska Slatina affair. After two weeks the commission concluded (on 30 May) "that there had been no provocation of the meeting of partisans on the part of [Matica Hrvatska]" and that claims that the Matica cars had been flying Croatian, not Yugoslav, colors were groundless.[117] As the summer drew on, Matica Hrvatska became convinced that there was a determined campaign to paint it "as a nationalistic, even chauvinistic, organization"—a conviction which only deepened when, immediately after the Brioni meeting, party conservatives demanded that the organization be put in a straightjacket.[118]

In this politically fluid situation, the Croatian conservatives employed any and all available means in their struggle for control of the Croatian party. Ironically, they found natural allies in the so-called humanists of the Praxis group, who felt an ideologically rooted antipathy toward decentralization, nationalism, and even federalism (which the humanists reviled as an unnecessary compromise with the principle of political unity). When the Sisak district court banned the May–August 1971 issue of *Praxis* because of an article by Milan Kangrga which contained, among other things, "the most searing indictment hitherto printed in *Praxis* of the rising nationalist movement in Yugoslavia (and especially in Croatia), linking it intimately with the efforts of a new middle class to consolidate its position," the conservatives took the issue to the republic's Supreme Court.[119] Both sides in the contest knew exactly how *Praxis* figured in the struggle. While the conservatives did not sympathize with that publication's notions of "democratization," they were pleased that the Croatian Supreme Court overturned the ban which had been issued by the Sisak court.[120]

By that point, the Serbs were putting pressure on Tito to curb the Croatian liberals,[121] and Tito himself was watching developments in Croatia with increasing concern. Already in May 1971, Tito admitted, in a speech in Labin, that the LCY had lost control of part of the media.[122] Then, in July, he traveled to Zagreb to talk with Croatia's leadership. At a closed meeting, Tito revealed his misgivings that Croatia was sliding back to the atmosphere of the interwar era and expressed concern that the republic leadership was losing control of the situation. "Are we going to have 1941 all over again?" Tito asked. "That would be a catastrophe." Of special concern to Tito was the growing cult of Stjepan Radić. "Radić's organization was a kulak organization," Tito snapped. "He hated communists and did not represent the interests of the working class. We offered to cooperate with him, but he didn't want to have anything to do with us."[123] Tito also criticized efforts to bring back Jelačić's statue, calling Jelačić a reactionary and condemning him for having helped suppress Lajos Kossuth's "progressive" revolution; indeed, Tito stated firmly that he would not permit any monument to Jelačić on the Trg Republike (Zagreb's main square, casually referred to by Zagrebers, even during communist times, as the "Trg Jelačića"). Tito even offered to make Tripalo prime minister of Yugoslavia in order to get him out of Croatia and away from the Croatian nationalists. But Tripalo declined. Tito remained the ultimate arbiter in interrepublican and—so it seemed—intrarepublic affairs as well; when he brought the full force of his power to bear, a republic leadership had to yield ground, at least temporarily. But since Tito was increasingly considering that Yugoslav stability was best guaranteed when Yugoslavia operated as a "self-regulating" system of broadly autonomous federal units, the republics, in practice, perceived his interventions as setting the limits of legitimate activity rather than as aborting independent decision making.

Hence, the response of Croatia's "national communists" to Tito's 4 July lecture was not to cave in but to conclude that Tito was "poorly informed" and that it was necessary "to select proper representatives of the Croatian nation who will converse with Comrade Tito." The Zadar district (*općina*) committee of the LCC circulated a letter among the presidency of the CC LCC and all regional political organizations; the letter called into question the loyalty and political reliability of Baltić, Dilić, Dragosavac, Ema Derosi-Bjelajac, and Radojcević (all Croatian conservatives) because of their efforts to obstruct the liberals' control of the channels of political communication.[124] The conservatives had to be neutralized, and Tito had to be wooed and convinced that, far from being a "key problem," as he had claimed, Croatia was politically sound. This the Croatian liberal leadership managed to do by mid-September in a carefully orchestrated reception for Tito in Zagreb. Tito made an about-face and told his Zagreb audience on 14 September, "I have been able to convince myself [on this visit] just how absurd certain stories about Croatia are—that there is no unity here, that people here think differently, that chauvinism blossoms and thrives here. None of that is true."[125]

Croatian nationalists now took a dangerous turn, however, riveting their attention on ethnically mixed Bosnia to the south. In the gathering storm, it was inevitable that Croatian eyes should turn to Bosnia—a territory which many Croats continued to believe was rightfully theirs. This territory had been a part of Croatia during World War Two, and some 20% of its population consisted of ethnic Croats. By now it had been openly admitted that, under Ranković, the state security apparatus had systematically persecuted Croats in Bosnia.[126] Matica Hrvatska claimed that Croats were still being denied their rights in Bosnia and other republics and, therefore, sought to set up branches in Bosnia and Vojvodina to cater to the needs of Croats in those areas. Viewing this as a kind of cultural imperialism, however, neither Bosnia nor Vojvodina would permit it.[127] Bakarić's earlier charge that Matica Hrvatska was comporting itself as a shadow government was proving accurate.[128] Meanwhile—so claimed *Oslobodjenje*—Ante Paradžik, president of the League of Students of Croatia (LSC), along with other members of the LSC leadership, was traveling around parts of Herzegovina, organizing student meetings and attempting to court support for the recently expelled Veselica and Djodan.[129]

In November 1971, *Hrvatski tjednik* added fuel to the fire by publishing statistics on the ethnic affiliation of members of elite bodies in Bosnia-Herzegovina. The paper charged that Croats were systematically underrepresented at all except the highest levels of republic administration, where they enjoyed pro forma proportional parity. Under the 1961 census—then the most recent set of population statistics available—the population of Bosnia consisted of 42.9% Serbs, 25.7% Muslims, 21.7% Croats, and 9.7% other nationalities. Yet Croats made up only 11.1% of the Higher Economic Court of Bosnia, 16.6% of the justices on that republic's Constitutional Court, 7.6% of the staff of the public prosecutor's office, 12.5% of the undersecretaries, 15.3% of the chiefs of Bosnia's inspectorates, and 17.8% of the staff of the Ministry of Internal Affairs of Bosnia-Herzegovina. All presiding members in the judicial branch were Serbs, as was the republic's secretary for national defense. And though the Croats were generously represented among republic secretaries and their assistants, no republic secretary of Croatian nationality sat on the executive council (although four Serbian secretaries and one Muslim secretary were on the council), and there were no Croats in the republic's Ministry for People's Defense. The trend penetrated into the media as well, where Croats constituted only 17% of the editorial board of *Oslobodjenje* and had only one of the six seats on the Board of Documentation. The general director of Radio-Television Sarajevo, the director of Sarajevo Television, the editor and director of *Odjek,* the director of the National Library of Bosnia-Herzegovina, and the president of the Bosnian Academy of Arts and Sciences were all Serbs, and the director of Sarajevo Radio, the director of *Zadruga,* and the editors of *Život, Izraz,* and *Pregled* were all Muslims. The only important positions held by Croats in the media were the directorship of joint services of Radio-Television Sarajevo and the editorship of television programming—both clearly subordinate. The pattern was replicated in the structure of the bank directorates where, of 32 directors, directorate chiefs, and division chiefs, only three were Croats. The pattern even extended to the composition of the League of Communists of Bosnia-Herzegovina (LC BiH), where the Serbs were clearly overrepresented and the Croats drastically underrepresented. Citing 1966 figures, *Hrvatski tjednik* claimed that the LC BiH consisted of 57.14% Serbs, 26.30% Muslims, and 12.05% Croats.[130] While these imbalances were probably connected with the fact that the Serbs were the first to join the Partisans in large numbers in World War Two and had therefore enjoyed a "head start" in terms of obtaining positions of responsibility, Croats looked at the raw numbers and, in many cases, felt that they were the victims of discrimination.

But waving aside Croatian objections that they were underrepresented in the Bosnian political structure, Hamdija Pozderac, member of the presidency of the CC LCY and a prominent Bosnian politician, replied facilely that "no one is responsible for his work only 'to some nation of his' but rather to the working class and to all the peoples and nationalities in our self-managing socialist community."[131] In fact, the proportion of Croats in the Bosnian party declined steadily in the late 1960s and early 1970s, and even the somewhat higher tally recorded for 1981 (12.27%) was still drastically lower than the proportion of the Bosnian population which Croats comprised—18.38% in 1981.[132] Gradually Croatian nationalists became convinced that the only solution was to incorporate the "expatriate" Croats into an expanded Croatian republic. Therefore, they demanded the attachment of the western part of Bosnia-Herzegovina to Croatia. Ironically, Serbian nationalists responded to this not by aligning themselves with Bosnia in a show of solidarity but rather by claiming the southeastern sections of Bosnia-Herzegovina for themselves.[133] This syndrome held lessons for the future.

The LCC had had good relations with the parties of Slovenia and Macedonia as long as Croatia was perceived to be "playing by the rules of the game." Indeed, in the 1970–1971 period, the Croats went to great lengths to establish a special relationship with the provincial party leadership in Kosovo. This included the stimulation of historical research designed to reveal and emphasize traditional historical links between parts of Croatia and the Kosovo region. These efforts bore some fruit, and on the occasion of one particular visit to Kosovo, Croatia's Dabčević-Kučar was welcomed as a queen by enthusiastic Kosovars. A certain solidarity also developed of its own accord between Croatian and Kosovar Albanian students. This spontaneous and natural solidarity, rooted in common resentment of the Serbs, was brought out, for instance, at a dinner for delegations from student organizations from all parts of Yugoslavia which convened in conjunction with a student conference in Ljubljana (13–14 May 1971). When certain students tactlessly began singing nostalgic songs about Ranković, the Croatian and Kosovar students predictably arose and left together.[134] Yet ultimately, by their excessive demands and intransigence, the Croatian leadership frightened other republic leaderships, especially the party leadership in Bosnia. In spite of that, Crvenkovski of Macedonia and Kavčič of Slovenia remained political allies with the Tripalo/Dabčević-Kučar leadership.

Although the Nikezič/Perović leadership in Serbia was broadly sympathetic to the Croatian leadership's call for more liberal politics and more liberal media, it did not support the reforms in the banking, foreign trade, and foreign currency systems being demanded by the Croatian leadership; nor did the leaderships of Kosovo, Montenegro, or Bosnia-Herzegovina. Friction between the Croatian and Serbian party leaderships over economic questions became so grave that, at a meeting in Brioni in April 1971, the Slovenian and Bosnian representatives urged a public airing of their differences. But the Croats were giving such stress to their economic desiderata that they could no longer see the Serbian liberals as potential partners and increasingly dismissed as "central-ists" all those who opposed the decentralizing economic reforms they were demanding.

On 5 November 1971, the CC LCC heard a report from party president Dabčević-Kučar on Croatia's foreign currency earnings, economic grievances, and economic woes in general. The Croatian government took a strong stand on increased retention of foreign currency earnings—a stand which was, at first, backed by the Slovenian party. Matica Hrvatska, of course, played an instru-mental role in propelling the Croatian leadership further to the right. In an arti-cle which appeared in Matica Hrvatska's journal, *Kritika*, Petar Šegedin, presi-dent of the Croatian Writers' Association, repeated that Croatian policy must be predicated on self-interest and *not* on the interests of Yugoslavia as a whole.[135] Matica Hrvatska then called for use of Croatian as the language of command for military units stationed in Croatia, or, alternatively, if Serbian was retained as the language of command for the army, the establishment of Croatian as the language of command for the navy (on the grounds that 90% of the Yugoslav navy operated in Croatian waters). By the summer of 1971, Matica Hrvatska had lent its voice to demands for the enlargement of Croatian territory at the expense of both Herzegovina and Montenegro and had begun to mobilize eth-nic Croats in both Bosnia and Vojvodina.[136] By failing to suppress Matica Hrvatska at this juncture, the Croatian party leaders lost their chance to save themselves. By threatening the territorial integrity of Bosnia-Herzegovina and alienating Serbia (by their unfriendly attitude toward Serbs residing in Croatia), the Croatian party leaders violated the most basic presuppositions of the sys-tem. The only question was whether this would ultimately be understood, by party elders, to be a Croatian problem or a broader problem involving both lib-erals and nationalists. Time would prove that Tito and his closest allies were concluding that the problem was broader in scope.

Nor could there any longer be any doubt as to the ideological coloration of the Croatian troika: at the Twentieth Plenum of the CC LCC (13–14 May 1971), Miko Tripalo openly identified with the Croatian national movement led by Matica Hrvatska and *Hrvatski tjednik*. The intense and broadly based popular-ity which this generated for the troika would be confirmed later when the August 1972 funeral for the former secretary of the Croatian party's central committee, Pero Pirker, prompted a massive demonstration by more than 100,000 supporters.

The Croats began to press their demands with determination. Not only should the foreign currency retention system be renegotiated so that Croatia might retain a larger chunk of its earnings, but it was even suggested that a sep-arate Croatian currency be created. Not only was the Croatian district of the JNA (Yugoslav People's Army) to become, in effect, a Croatian army, but also the Supreme Headquarters of the People's Navy should be relocated to Split. Not only was there a need to further decentralize and reform the banking system, but Croatia should also have its own Croatian national bank with a governor appointed by the republic leadership and empowered to negotiate foreign loans independently. Not only was republic statehood to be "more precisely" defined, but also—more concretely—the Croatian national Sabor was to be recognized as the highest organ of power in Croatia (relegating the LCC, thus, to second place at best).[137] Economist Hrvoje Sošič demanded that Croatia be represented in the United Nations.[138] Vladimir Loknar lodged a demand for the passage of an endogenous Croatian legal code. Others clamored for the printing of Croatian postage stamps.[139] Ultimately, the nationalist group gathered around Matica Hrvatska explicitly raised the cry for complete Croatian independence: secession was fast becoming mainstream political sentiment in Croatia.[140] In ethnically heterogeneous communities, friction between Croats and Serbs became commonplace, and there were reports that in some communities residents were "arming themselves in anticipation of a physical showdown."[141]

Ironically, despite their huge popularity and the symbolic leadership of both the mass movement and the LCC, the national troika (Tripalo, Dabčević-Kučar, and Pirker) actually controlled neither. The popular movement, under the guidance of Matica Hrvatska, was antipathetic toward the key desiderata of the entrenched conservative faction in the LCC. The troika was thus confronted with an ineluctable choice between (1) allying with Matica Hrvatska against the conservatives and gambling that Tito's confidence could be retained and that the conservatives could be outmaneuvered, and (2) seeking a compromise with the conservatives and moving to bridle Matica Hrvatska. But the latter option was unpalatable now because the liberals and the conservatives were separated by an unbridgeable gulf of distrust and because the liberals and the nationalists continued to share a number of common positions, especially where economic complaints were concerned. When Dabčević-Kučar addressed the Twenty-second Session of the CC LCC on 5 November, it was abundantly clear that the choice had been confronted and the dilemma decisively resolved in favor of the national mass movement.

Collapse of the House of Cards

The Croatian conservatives were gathering their forces, planning how best to administer the coup de grace to the liberal troika. Moreover, by late 1971, the aging political moderate Bakarič was once more engaging himself and, in late October, journeyed to Sarajevo, looking for support against Tripalo and Dabčević-Kučar. Bakarič hoped to escalate the intra-Croatian party contest to the federal level in order to defeat the coalition of Croatian liberals and nationalists there. Branko Mikulič, a Bosnian Croat and president of the Bosnian party, was sensitive to the nationalist propaganda washing over from Croatia and was receptive to Bakarič's wooing. Almost at the same time, Tito, closeted with Yugoslav army leaders at a secret meeting in Bugojno, Bosnia, was being shown "suppressed TV [news]reels of Croatian Communist mass meetings, with only Croatian flags [missing the Communist red star] and with national-ist and anti-Tito slogans, songs, shouts and signs."[142] Unnerved by the obvious exacerbation of the intraparty conflict, Tripalo made a show of force, telling a gathering in Vela Luka at the end of November, "The policy we are pursuing in Croatia cannot be changed. Our opponents think that that policy can be changed by replacing a few leaders. In order to achieve that [objective], it would be necessary to replace thousands of leaders in Croatia. . . . We have taken our fate in our hands and we will keep it in our hands."[143] Ultimately, time would show that Tito would make use of his own recipe to change policy in Croatia and was quite prepared to dismiss thousands of Croats from office.

The public did not know—even though Matica Hrvatska and the student leaders apparently did—that the party conservatives in Croatia had undertaken a concerted effort to enlist Tito's support in bottling the liberals.[144] At this point, the Croatian Students' Union, in a dramatic gambit designed to demon-strate support for the troika and outbid the conservatives, organized a massive strike in support of the liberal leadership, hoping to undermine the conserva-tive move by making it clear that the conservatives lacked a popular base. Some 3,000 students met in Zagreb on 22 November 1971 and unanimously voted to begin a strike at 9 A.M. the following day to protest the federal regulations gov-erning hard currency, banking, and commerce.[145] At Paradžik's prompting, the union also endorsed most of the various linguistic, military, and political demands outlined above.[146] Interestingly, representatives of the Native Mace-donian Students Club and of the Native Club of Kosovar Students, who were present at the meeting, firmly supported the Croatian students.

The following day, student meetings were held at many university depart-ments in Zagreb and strike committees were formed. At 7 P.M., a plenum of the Croatian Students' Union unanimously passed a resolution calling for a strike at all institutions of higher education in Croatia, and faculty deans, meeting in Zagreb, expressed solidarity with the students. Two months earlier, the student pro-rector, Ivan Zvonimir Čičak, had advised this very tactic when, on the occa-sion of the 100th anniversary of the birth of Stjepan Radić, he had told a uni-versity crowd that "students must be prepared to demonstrate, rebel, and strike, because their youth and their radicalism are the only guarantee to their nation for a better and brighter future."[147] Although the liberal establishment in the LCC felt that the strike was "premature," it did not want to risk estrangement from the mass movement by distancing itself from the strike, and therefore the group lent its support to the students.[148] Dabčević-Kučar commented, "I am deeply convinced that the motives of the greatest portion of the students who have undertaken this strike were positive and well-meaning and progressive."[149]

On 25 November, the League of Students of Split convened an emergency plenum and enthusiastically endorsed the resolutions passed by the students in Zagreb. In Rijeka, students began circulating a petition for use of a chamber in which to convene a similar meeting. In Dubrovnik, the presidency of the Dubrovnik Student Union came out in support of the Zagreb resolutions.

Within a matter of days, at least 30,000 university students across Croatia were on strike. By the beginning of December, students at the Zagreb law school had demanded the expulsion of all "unitarists" from the LCC, specifically naming Dušan Dragosavac (a CC secretary) and Bilič (president of the Croatian Sabor), along with Baltič, Ema Derossi-Bjelajac, and Čedo Grbič.[150]

Until the autumn of 1971, Tito had hoped that it would be possible to effect a compromise with the forces in power in Croatia and to let things develop more or less on their own. If the suppressed newsreel footage was not enough, the student strike helped to convince Tito that compromise was impossible.[151] Liberalization, decentralization, and appeasement of Croatia had only fed the Croats' ever-increasing hunger for autonomy. Indeed, military intelligence later uncovered evidence that some of the party leaders had been in contact with Croatian Ustaša émigré groups in West Germany.[152] Before taking action, however, Tito contacted officials in Washington, D.C., to obtain a "green light" from the Americans to remove the Croatian liberals from their posts.[153] The U.S. did not object, and Tito briefly considered sending troops into Croatia; eventually, he decided to simply decapitate the Croatian party leadership. On 1 December, Tito convened a joint meeting of the party presidia of the LCY and the LCC at Karadjordjevo, Vojvodina. On this occasion, the famous Twenty-first Session of the LCY presidium, it became obvious just how isolated the Croatia liberal leadership had become. Croatian conservatives led the charge, supported by a coalition of party elders from Serbia proper, Vojvodina, and Montenegro. Representatives of Bosnia, Slovenia, and even Kosovo also criticized the waxing exclusivist nationalism in Croatia and called for stern measures to combat it.[154] Latinka Perovič, the liberal Serbian leader and Serbia's spokesperson at the session, declared that "Yugoslavia will emerge from this crisis only if nationalism is *wiped out* in every constituent national group."[155] Only the Macedonian representative, Angel Čemerski, showed any readiness to treat the Croatian liberals mildly. The Croatian leaders were treated to a tongue-lashing for "unhealthy liberalism," nonchalance with respect to counterrevolutionary groups, and the (mis)use of student groups to advance their political aims. The Croats were told to put their house in order, but given the denunciation of the policy pursued by the liberal troika, the Twenty-first Session could only strengthen the hands of the conservatives on the Croatian central committee.

In spite of this, there was a scurry of activity designed to avert the inevitable. At a meeting of the city conference of the LC of Zagreb on 4 December, immediately after the Twenty-first Session of the LCY presidency, conference president Srečko Bijelič omitted any mention of "nationalism" or "counterrevolutionary activity" in discussing the session's resolutions and employed only bland and ambiguous references to "anti-self-management" and "anti-democratic forces." He proposed the relatively mild remedy of meeting with representatives of Matica Hrvatska in order to sort things out.[156] Mirko Dragovič and Pero Kriste, chair and deputy chair, respectively, of the LCC interdistrict conference for Dalmatia, made an attempt to stem the tide unleashed by the Twenty-first

258 *The Rise and Fall of Yugoslav Liberalism*

Session. Kriste, after a hastily arranged meeting with Tripalo, assembled a number of political functionaries in Dubrovnik, told them that it seemed the Croatian leadership might be changed, blamed the forthcoming changes on the fact that Tito was "probably poorly informed" about the situation in Croatia, urged the mobilization of strong support for the troika, and suggested convoking an extraordinary congress in order to underline that support. Simultaneously, Dragovič invited various leaders from Zadar (Šarič, Pera, Zanki, and Festini) to Hotel Solaris on the outskirts of Šibenik, where he also warned that Tito was poorly informed, the state security apparatus was behind the uproar, and the Croatian leadership required rescue. *Vjesnik* (6 December 1971) reported that working collectives and local assemblies in Croatia were voicing their implicit faith in and strong support of the troika. At the Twenty-first Session of the LCY presidency (9 December), Dabčevič-Kučar defended herself and claimed that she and her cohorts would faithfully undertake such actions as were necessary *in the spirit of the Twenty-first Session.*[157]

Meanwhile, the Croatian conservatives demanded that they be provided a copy of the stenographic record of the Twenty-first Session (held 1–2 December). The liberal troika, still formally holding the reins, tried to submit only an edited transcript. Finally, on 12 December, the house of cards collapsed. Tripalo, Dabčevič-Kučar, Pirker, and Marko Koprtla, hitherto a member of the executive committee, resigned their posts under pressure. Milka Planinc, who would later serve as Yugoslav prime minister in 1982–1986, was at this point entrusted with the reins of the Croatian party. In protest of Tripalo's resignation, 500 student militants demonstrated for four days in downtown Zagreb and demanded the creation of a separate Croatian state—a response which only served to further incriminate Tripalo and strengthen Tito's hand. Helmeted riot police were sent in to occupy strategic points in Zagreb, while helicopters surveyed the streets from above. If necessary, the army was prepared to move in. A follow-up conference to the Twenty-first Session declared that "nationalism has become . . . the focal point for everything in our society that is reactionary, anti-socialist and anti-democratic, bureaucratic, and Stalinist."[158]

In the aftermath of the crisis, literally tens of thousands of members were expelled from the Croatian party, most for failure to toe the party line. In the higher echelons of political authority, 741 persons were stripped of their posts and expelled from the party, another 280 party members were compelled to resign their posts, and yet another 131 Croatian functionaries were merely demoted. Of this total, the greatest number were to be found in Osijek, Zagreb, and Split (in that order).[159] Others—Djodan, Čičak, Marko Veselica, Hrvoje Sošič, Franjo Tudjman (the JNA general-turned-historian), and Gotovac, editor of *Hrvatski tjednik,* were sentenced to long prison terms.[160] Party conservatives clamored for a major show trial, with Tudjman as the principal defendant, in which the "Croatian Spring" would be demonized, but Tito would not hear of such a trial.[161] The conservatives did not forget about Tudjman, however, and within a few months of Tito's death, Tudjman and three other Croatian nationalists were arrested, tried, and put back in prison. Altogether some 200–300 persons were imprisoned for political reasons in Croatia in the wake of the fall of Tripalo and Dabčević-Kučar; thousands more were held administratively (without formal charges) for two to three months.[162] Matica Hrvatska was shut down, and its 14 periodical publications (including the popular *Hrvatski tjednik* and *Kolo*) were put out of business. *Tlo* survived only a few months longer—long enough to publish four issues in 1972. *Dubrovnik* was placed under provisional ban. Within two weeks, the party removed the director of Radio Dubrovnik and the editors of *Vjesnik, Vjesnik u srijedu, Vidici, Pitanja, Tlo, Jež,* and *Omladinski tjednik,* and the staff of Radio Pula was obliged to engage in self-criticism. Wayward student publications in other republics were also "cleansed": the editors of *Student* (Belgrade), *Bota ë Re* (Kosovo), and a Macedonian student newspaper were replaced, and the editor of the Ljubljana student newspaper *Tribuna* was reprimanded. On 8 May 1972, the Twenty-eighth Session of the League of Communists of Croatia, meeting in Zagreb, adopted a resolution expelling Dabčević-Kučar, Tripalo, Pirker, and Koprtla from the party. The backlash continued through 1972, reaching a climax in October and November of that year, with the continued purge of writers, filmmakers, university professors, and former liberal leaders.[163] The Roman Catholic Church also came under press attack during 1973 for alleged nationalism.

At the same time, however, Tito moved to undercut the popular bases of the Croatian nationalists by granting many of the nationalist demands. Thus, export firms were allowed to retain 20% of foreign exchange earnings instead of 7 to 12% as previously, and tourist enterprises were permitted to retain 45% of their earnings, instead of 12%.[164] In addition, the dinar was devalued (by 18.7%) for the second time in a year, boosting the value of Croatia's foreign currency earnings and complicating the importation of goods and materials into less developed areas in Serbia, Montenegro, and Macedonia. Belgrade was even willing to concede that, in a sense, Croatia *had* been exploited; it admitted that Croatia's contribution to the federal budget had been proportionately the largest. *Ekonomska politika* noted that whereas, in 1970, Slovenia had freely disposed of 62.2% of its social product, Serbia 59.2%, Bosnia 62.1%, Montenegro 60.1%, Macedonia 59.2%, Vojvodina 59.0%, and Kosovo 59.7%, Croatia disposed of only 58.3% of its own income—the lowest figure among the eight regions comprising the Yugoslav federation.[165]

The Yugoslav federation had, to be sure, weathered the crisis—but not without demonstrating the flimsiness of system support founded only on groups' perceived self-interest. With federal lines drawn to coincide, for the most part, with the boundaries of nationality groups and with political competition largely limited to interrepublican negotiation, competition inevitably took the form of inter-ethnic disputes.

Twenty-four years later, by which time Franjo Tudjman had become president of an independent Croatia in which, inter alia, such diverse Croats as Jelačič, Budak, Stepinac, and Andrija Hebrang—all of them condemned to oblivion under Tito (Stepinac the least successfully)—were rehabilitated in one way or the other, a prestigious Zagreb publisher brought out a gorgeous volume devoted to the history of Zagreb, offering the following summary of the collapse of the liberal-nationalist experiment in Croatia in 1971:

> In the summer and autumn of 1971 the pressure of all those opposed to change inten-sified coming from the political leaders in Belgrade, Ljubljana and other republican centres as well as the Zagreb (communist) dogmatists and (Yugoslav and Greater Ser-bian) unitarists around Vladimir Bakarić. These had the support of the officer corps of the Yugoslav army who accused some outstanding party leaders in Croatia of support-ing the "nationalistic separatism" of the Croatian masses. . . .
>
> The reformists now found themselves caught in the cross-fire of attack from the Bel-grade Yugocommunists, Greater Serbians—and their own extreme nationalists, who operated on the margins of the Croatian national movement. In line with a century-long tradition a segment of Croatian lower-middle-class extremists (never fully aware of the scope of the Croatian idea) pursued their own narrow interests even at the cost of compromising the movement by . . . e.g., selling symbols of the tragic period of Ustasha terror of 1941–1945 in the streets and squares of Zagreb. This was simply play-ing into the hands of the enemies of Croatia.[166]

If the foregoing interpretation has any importance, it is in its construal of the dismissal of the Croatian liberal leadership as a tragedy for Croatia—a construal which has been widely shared by Croats in the wake of December 1971 and down to today. But if this verdict summarizes the way in which some Croats have come to interpret the events of 1971, it is nonetheless not the only inter-pretation which one may find, whether in Croatia or outside Croatia.

The Purge of the Liberals Continues

In January 1972, the LCY adopted an "action program," committing itself to a continued struggle against nationalism and technocratism, understood as the political and economic faces of the "liberal" program. As far as Tito was con-cerned, the situation in Slovenia, Macedonia, and especially Serbia remained unsatisfactory. In October 1972, Tito met with the political leadership of Serbia, accusing the Serbian leaders of insubordination and of unsocialist economics. Soon after this meeting, Nikezić and Perović, together with Bora Pavlović, sec-retary of the Belgrade city committee of the LCY, submitted their resignations. That same month, Stane Kavčič was forced out of office, his removal having been engineered by ideological foe France Popit. In Macedonia, Crvenkovski and his closest loyalists were dismissed from office.

At the same time that the liberals were slipping from power, the interrepub-lican committee system, a by-product of the liberal ascendancy, became the tar-get of conservative ire. The committees had been conceived, from the begin-ning, as a kind of experiment. But though the liberals and those who favored decentralization of the decision-making process claimed that the experiment had proven a success in that it had speeded legislation and further devolution, the conservatives condemned it as a failure, complaining that it had fundamentally altered the way in which the legislative process took place. Some critics charged that the interrepublican committees were behaving as if they constituted a shadow government, usurping the real power in the system, and that the federation was about to be swallowed up by an explicitly confederal body. The Coordination Commission was repeatedly charged with bypassing regular government channels. Kavčič tried to defend the interrepublican committee system, at least as long as he was in power.[167] But before the end of 1972, the committees were in retreat. First the Interrepublican Committee for Developmental Policy was abolished, its functions transferred to the Federal Committee for Social Planning; then the other interrepublican committees were, shortly thereafter, significantly downgraded. Under the 1974 constitution, they were transformed into service committees for the Chamber of Republics and Provinces (CRP). But under the revamped system, legislation would henceforth no longer start in the interrepublican committees but rather in the CRP, with the committees serving largely to smooth out the edges. Once the fulcrum of decision making, the committees were now a mere cog in the legislative machine. Ironically, at the end of 1978, the Federal Committee for Social Planning was abolished, and its functions were restored to a resurrected Interrepublican Committee for Social Planning and Development, restoring the original constellation of five committees.

The entire period of the liberal heyday may be viewed as one in which the political actors were testing the limits of legitimate behavior and, in some cases, attempting to transcend them. Had the liberals succeeded, Yugoslavia would have been put on a new foundation. "The Croatian Spring was not about separatism," Latinka Perović told me in 2004.

It was about reform of the system. We [Nikezić and I] were ready for dialogue with the Croats. We wanted the Croats to state their views in federal forums. . . . The conservatives were worried that we would find a modus vivendi with the Croatian liberals and that's why we were removed from power.[168]

Even before the liberals were removed from power, however, they found themselves blocked within the system and, in these circumstances, turned to noncommunist liberals and local nationalists for allies. It was a problematic alliance and put the Croatian leadership, on occasion, at odds with Tito—for example, on 20 April 1971 when Dabčević-Kučar refused Tito's request to have Šegedin, Veselica, Budiša, Čičak, and Djodan arrested.[169] This alliance also marked a return to the ethnic politics of the interwar years. The major difference was that in the SFRY, ethnic politics was played out within the framework of a one-party system; but it was the federal system itself, which the communists had developed in order to "tame the beast," which provided the setting within which ethnic politics could develop. With one exception, every political figure in the country was apt to be viewed as a "foreigner" ("not one of us") in another part of the country. The one exception was Tito, and Tito was entering the last decade of his life.

CHAPTER 9

Controversies in the Economic Sector, 1965–1990

It is a well-known constant of political life that even slight differences in interregional economic standards may awaken sharp feelings of resentment which catalyze, where they coincide with ethnic divisions, surges of nationalism. Jealousy kindles collective affectivity and ethnocentric behavior, resulting in violence and sometimes even civil war. In Western analyses, however, economic differences accentuate but do not themselves generate nationalist feelings. Leninism pushes the analysis one step further and claims that all nationalism has its wellsprings in oppression, exploitation, and inequality: liquidate the bourgeoisie and eliminate economic inequality among national groups, and nationalist attachments will lose their hold. The infusion of tangible economic aid and the application of large doses of industrialization should, accordingly, have offered the prospect of alleviating Serb-Albanian tensions in Kosovo.[1] Indeed, the policy of aid to the underdeveloped regions of Yugoslavia was viewed by the Tito regime and the Titoists who ruled Yugoslavia after his death from 1980 to 1987 as the key to eliminating the nationalities question altogether. Alternatively, the failure to ease interregional economic inequalities, it was argued, "would threaten the integrity of the Yugoslav community and throw into question the common interests of all its regions and nationalities."[2] Inter-ethnic relations are colored by economic differentials, and inter-ethnic harmony is incapable of realization in the presence of collective cognitive dissonance. None of the republican leaderships challenged this principle.

Conflict of Interest

So deep were the divisions in Yugoslav society in 1945 that the Communist Party had little with which to hold the country together except the Partisan myth, promises of future cornucopia, and coercive force. The break with the Cominform certainly helped in this respect, for even anti-communists rallied to Tito rather than risk further Sovietization. But the promises remained important. The regime had pledged, for example, to intensify industrialization—a clearly perceived need—and to level interregional economic disparities. This was to be done by funneling a disproportionate amount of new investments into the poorer regions of the south.

This early period was, of course, also the period of the Stalin model—with or without Stalin—and the decision to emphasize heavy industry naturally gave preference to the southern regions which were rich in such basic raw materials as minerals and energy sources. Kosovo in particular is rich in minerals, with its mines at Trepča alone producing, at one time, 25% of Europe's lead and 13% of Europe's zinc.[3] Bosnia-Herzegovina has important reserves of coal, iron ore, and lumber, and sizeable potential sources of hydroelectric power. Thus, it made good economic sense to locate heavy industry in the south. But as Kardelj himself noted in 1960, the overall effect of this was "to contribute indirectly to the rise in national income in other regions with developed manufacturing by supplying them with raw materials from less developed areas."[4] Slovenia, Croatia, and the Belgrade environs—and, to a lesser extent, Vojvodina—continued to be preferentially favored with the development of light and consumer industries. Understandably, politicians in the underdeveloped republics saw parallels to the classic model of imperialism. In addition, income differentials were widening. Macedonian per capita income, for instance, dipped from 31% below the national average in 1947 to 36% below the average in 1963, while during the same period the average per capita income in Slovenia soared from 62% above the national average to almost twice the national average.[5]

Yet the more advanced republics were also dissatisfied. In addition to investments in raw material extraction and processing, the south was also the recipient of certain investments demonstratively made on political rather than economic grounds. Croatia and Slovenia were particularly irked by the duplication of industries already flourishing in their own republics. Furthermore, these new industries often proved glaringly inefficient. Thus, with the shift of the center of steel production from Slovenia to Bosnia, it became cheaper to import steel than to produce it in Yugoslavia. The market reform of 1965 "revealed that 600,000 industrial workers, nearly half the industrial labor force, were employed in enterprises that operated at a loss."[6] Croatia's share in the total Yugoslav industrial potential dropped from 33% in 1925 to 29% in 1946 and plunged to 19% in 1965.[7] Of course, since Croatia's industry was expanding during this period and since percentages reflect a relationship to a greater whole, these figures do not necessarily mean that Croatia was being "oppressed"; the important point is that many people thought that the figures did mean just that. Croatian scholars like Šime Djodan and Marko Veselica lashed out at the alleged exploitation of Croatia (and Slovenia). Djodan, who was later imprisoned, often hinted at secession. The Croats did not deny that Croatia had made progress under communism, but they adamantly maintained that progress would have been far greater had the Croatian economy not been "milked" to succor the less developed republics.

As early as 1957, Bosnia's share in industrial investment began to slip as investment in heavy industry (and, more particularly, in raw materials extraction) reached the saturation point. Bosnia's share of federal investment funds had declined from 19.4% under the first five-year plan to 12.6% under the second. Serbia's share, meantime, jumped from 31.3% to 41.7%—the only increase among the six republics. Serbia was now garnering between 50% and 60% of all new investments in metalwork, machine-building, nonferrous metallurgy, and chemical industries. These facts convinced Joseph Bombelles that it was no longer possible to "speak of a conscious government policy of aiding underdeveloped republics after 1956. Rather, the western republics were now supposed to subsidize the eastern republics without regard to the level of development."[8] The entire system of investments was overhauled in the 1965 reforms (as discussed in detail in chapter 6), with profitability elevated to a priority concern. The central government ceased to channel funds to the south under a planned system, and despite continued payments of subsidies to certain industries and the invocation of "special case" tax considerations for investments in the south, the reform generally favored the developed regions.

Aid for the Underdeveloped Regions

There are two basic strategies of directed economic development: (1) *sector* development, emphasizing the optimal development of each sector of the economy, with a view to the well-being of the entire country; and (2) *regional* development, treating each of a plurality of regional units as a discrete subject of policy and giving rise to tendencies toward autarky. Although the former strategy has the advantage by utilitarian calculations, it confronts the difficulty, in multi-ethnic environments, of alienating entire nationality groups. Thus, it was the latter orientation which found expression in the policy decisions taken in early postwar Yugoslavia, the assumption being that equality could not be differentiated from uniformity. Yet, although the first (abortive) five-year plan (1947–1951) and the tenuous period of the one-year plans (1953–1956) showed some attention to the need to develop the southern regions of Yugoslavia, the Cominform blockade and Soviet economic embargo dealt a severe blow to Yugoslavia's early developmental ambitions. It was not until 1957, with the adoption of the second five-year plan, that a coherent policy of stimulating the development of the underdeveloped regions of the south could be said to have existed.[9] The policy of guaranteed investments in the underdeveloped regions was introduced then, with the result that investments all too often were funneled into unprofitable prestige projects (the so-called political factories) rather than into rationally conceived objects. A further difficulty in the early period was that only a republic could be classified as developed or underdeveloped—and was so considered in its entirety. As a result, Kosovo was treated as a developed region (within SR Serbia) until 1957, when Bosnia, which had hitherto enjoyed preferential treatment as an officially "underdeveloped" republic, was abruptly dropped from the roster.

The Croats, plagued with their own pockets of poverty, particularly (at that time) Dalmatia, pressed the argument that the classification of entire federal units as either "developed" or "underdeveloped" was senseless, since every republic had underdeveloped zones. In 1961, the Croats, reinforced by Bosnian disgruntlement with the status quo, won their point. Portions of Croatia (Dalmatia, Lika, Banija, and Kordun), together with the southern and southwestern districts of Serbia and most of Bosnia-Herzegovina, were added to the roster of underdeveloped areas and were made the beneficiaries of special federal treatment.[10] At the same time, the system of guaranteed investments was transformed into a system of specialized funds.

But, even if this overall policy represented an advance over the more or less overtly exploitative policy of the interwar regime, it was flawed not only by repeated instances of mismanagement (resulting in the creation of factories which operated at a loss), but also by a systematic bias which, ironically, reinforced the traditional cleavage. Although light industry, even where traditional branches have been concerned, would have yielded "incomparably better results" than heavy industry in terms of impact on local income and employment, postwar economic planning emphasized investment in heavy industry in the south, thus encouraging interregional polarization.[11] Just as important, if not in fact the central reason for the failure to narrow the developmental gap between the Yugoslav north and south, was the sheer inadequacy of investment in the South. In fact, over the 1947–1962 period, per capita investment in Macedonia and Kosovo—the most seriously afflicted regions at that time—was well below the Yugoslav average. Not surprisingly, these federal units grew restive, and in the course of a drawn-out public debate over the proposed (reworked) seven-year plan for the 1964–1970 period, various voices challenged the premises on which the old developmental policy had been based. For example, Kiril Miljovski, a Macedonian economist, objected that

In the proposed texts [of the 1964–1970 seven-year plan] there are plenty of measures, methods, instruments—in a word, techniques of financing. . . . Interest-free credits, credits at special rates of interest, allocated credits, renunciation of annuities, budgetary grants—all of this is very interesting, but entirely ineffective as long as it is not laid down by what deadline the relationship between the developed and underdeveloped regions must be placed on an economically and socially rational basis, what rates of growth must be assured in order to guarantee the desired rates of growth. . . . The weaknesses which we have noted thus far are not the weaknesses of financing but rather the consequences of a lack of a clear conception of time-limits, rates of growth, and the volume of investments [needed] in the insufficiently developed regions.[12]

So ineffective had federal policy been, Miljovski complained, that between 1959 and 1962 unemployment in Macedonia increased by 85% (reaching an unemployment rate of 18% in 1962), and the Republic Commission for Employment anticipated a continued worsening of the situation.

The Widening Gap

By the early 1960s, it was clear that the policy of attempting to accelerate development of the underdeveloped regions through unregulated federal grants had failed. In 1961, party politicians began to discuss the possibility of introducing a special fund to accelerate development in poorer regions. By the time this fund was introduced in its present form, however, the 1965 reforms had already been put into effect—which brought to a crashing close any immediate prospects for the continued spread of light industry to the south. Although figures fluctuate from year to year, the overall trend between 1953 and 1971 was for the underdeveloped regions to be outpaced by the developed areas in the north. Thus, per capita income in the underdeveloped regions, taken as a whole, was 65% of per capita income in the developed regions in 1953; by 1971, that share had shrunk to 50% of the northern level. The biggest decline was registered by Bosnia, which in 1953 had enjoyed per capita incomes averaging 74% of the rate in the developed republics, but which, by 1971, retained a rate of only 53%. The situation in Kosovo, by this measure, was nothing short of desperate: from 42% of the developed average in 1953, Kosovo's average shriveled to a meager 28%. Macedonia's figure sank from 60% to 56%, while Montenegro's slipped only two points from an initial average of 60%.[13] As is suggested by these figures, Montenegro and Macedonia had succeeded in maintaining developmental paces significantly stronger than those of Kosovo and Bosnia-Herzegovina. In fact, despite a certain advantage initially enjoyed by Bosnia in its possession of a number of industrial plants installed under the Habsburgs, Bosnia had failed, until the mid-1970s, to achieve an economic growth rate at all commensurate with the rest of Yugoslavia. Of course, in different degrees, each republic replicates the overall pattern and has below-average sectors. In Macedonia, for example, the communes of Debar, Kičevo, Brod, Kriva Palanka, and Kratovo are sufficiently behind the rest of the republic to warrant special assistance.

Yet, from 1947 to 1966 and again throughout the 1971–1975 period, the underdeveloped republics and Kosovo recorded faster economic growth rates than those prevailing in the north. The 1971–1975 growth rates are contrasted with the 1966–1970 rates in Table 9.1. Even within the south there was a narrowing of the range of growth rates. Montenegro's industrial production, which, in the 1947–1974 period, grew at a rate of 14.1% per annum, climbed

Table 9.1. Economic Growth Rates in Yugoslavia (1966–1975)

(in Percentages)

	1966–1970		1971–1975	
	A	**B**	**A**	**B**
Yugoslavia	18.1	14.6	5.5	15.9
Underdeveloped republics and Kosovo	14.9	14.1	26.9	27.3
Developed areas	19.4	14.7	25.0	25.5

A = *Annual growth rate of investment in fixed assets*
B = *Annual growth rate of gross material product*

Source: Milivoje Vujačić, "Investment, 1966–1975," *Yugoslav Survey* 18, no. 2 (May 1977): 61–62.

only 10.1% per annum in the 1974–1977 period.[14] For Macedonia, by contrast, 1977 showed exceptional growth, especially in heavy industry. *Nova Makedonija* (Skopje) reported that Macedonian industry grew 52.1% in iron ore industry, 47.2% in electrical machinery and appliances, 43.5% in the processing of non-ferrous metals, 36.6% in the production of base chemicals, 31.6% in paper processing, 27.8% in electrical industry, 24.7% in ferrous metallurgy, and 21.3% in the production of animal feed.[15] Moreover, the federal budget for 1978 nearly doubled the amount of money being turned over to the three underdeveloped republics and Kosovo under the rubric of general supplemental funds. Certainly, investment was disproportionately heavy in the less developed regions. On a pessimistic note, however, Ksente Bogoev, a Macedonian economist, calculated that the less developed regions were capable of absorbing investment at a rate of only 50% of what would have been required if they were to have had any chance of catching up with the more developed northern republics.[16] As Ragnar Nurkse has observed, "economic progress is not a spontaneous or automatic affair. On the contrary, it is evident that there are automatic forces within the system tending to keep it moored to a given level,"[17] the chief of which is the tendency of capital to seek short-term investments and to gravitate toward extraction industries—with the consequent problems of achieving balanced growth. The result is that underdeveloped regions find it impossible to replicate the pattern of development set by the industrialized regions. The trick—to set a society on a developmental trajectory—has historically tended to have required a "kick-start" by the government, even (as is usually forgotten) in the American case, where the construction of the railroads was funded by large infusions of money from the U.S. Treasury.

If instead of looking at the growth of investment, we observe the republics' shares of total investment, a very different picture emerges. This positive trend toward equalization disappears (see Table 9.2). By this measure, Kosovo and Macedonia showed the least progress and are therefore grouped together. This measure reveals that Croatia and Slovenia were indeed the chief beneficiaries of

Table 9.2. Share of Republics and Autonomous Provinces in Total Investments in Fixed Assets (1966–1975)

(at Current Prices in Percentages)

	1966	1969	1972	1975
A	60.2	65.0	61.1	63.0
B	35.8	37.6	37.7	43.7
C	31.1	26.5	30.0	28.4
D	14.1	11.0	10.3	9.5

A = *developed republics (Slovenia, Croatia, Vojvodina, Serbia proper)*
B = *Slovenia and Croatia only*
C = *underdeveloped republics and provinces (Bosnia-Herzegovina, Kosovo,*
    Macedonia, Montenegro)
D = *Kosovo and Macedonia only*

Source: Calculated by the author from data given in Milivoje Vujačić, "Investment, 1966–1975," *Yugoslav Survey* 18, no. 2 (May 1977): 63.

the 1965 reforms and that the underdeveloped sector as a whole stagnated. The only (albeit, partial) exception was Bosnia, which showed some signs of gradually pulling itself out of the abyss. But even in Bosnia, economic progress tended to be centered in the cities, while the countryside lagged behind.

The gap which separated the developed from the underdeveloped regions might be illustrated by various other indicators, such as the numbers of vocational and technical schools, cinemas, televisions, and so on. Croatia and Slovenia constituted 29% of the total population, and yet these two republics had, in 1972, 44% of the newspapers (11 of Yugoslavia's 25 dailies were published in either Croatian or Slovenian) and 46% of the radio stations. Kosovo, the most deprived of the federal units, had almost 7% of the population, but only 4.9% of the vocational-technical schools, 2.7% of the cinemas, one Albanian-language daily, and two radio stations (out of 174 in Yugoslavia).[18] Kosovo also remained far behind in per capita television ownership.

At the same time, poverty tends to be associated with ignorance of or hostility toward contraceptive devices, and the poor, accordingly, tend to reproduce faster than those in more developed areas, while, among Albanians, large families were prized. Table 9.3 shows the rates of increase, by republic, between the 1961 and 1981 censuses. Those in the most underdeveloped regions were increasing the fastest—the Macedonians by one and a half times the national average, and the Albanians by almost three times the national average. As a consequence of their higher birth rates, the Albanians and Macedonians also had the largest households—6.61 and 4.68 persons per family, respectively, in 1971, against a Yugoslav average of 3.80 and a low of 3.18 in Vojvodina (3.34 in Slovenia).[19] Unemployment was highest in these areas, skilled labor the scarcest. Illit-

Table 9.3. Population Growth by Republic (1961–1981)
(in Percentages)

	1961–1971	1971–1981
YUGOSLAVIA	10.0	9.2
Kosovo	25.4	27.5
Macedonia	15.8	16.1
Bosnia-Herzegovina	13.2	10.1
Montenegro	11.7	10.1
Serbia proper	8.3	8.4
Slovenia	8.1	9.5
Croatia	6.1	4.0
Vojvodina	5.0	3.9

Sources: Nicholas R. Lang, "The Dialectics of Decentralization," *World Politics* 27, no. 3 (April 195): 322; and Slobodan Stanković, "Yugoslavia's Census—Final Results," *Radio Free Europe Research,* 10 March 1982, p. 2.

eracy was highest in these areas, especially in Kosovo, where 36% of the Albanian population admitted to being illiterate in 1971.[20]

A related problem was the lower labor efficiency in the underdeveloped republics—rates which, as proportions of the Yugoslav average, actually declined. The lesser efficiency of labor was partly a reflection of lower overall educational attainment and partly the result of cultural differences, and is, to a significant extent, a concomitant part of the underdevelopment syndrome. Lower labor efficiency also figured as a contributory factor to the lesser efficiency of investments in the southern regions, though the structure of the economy (e.g., fewer manufacturing industries) also had a hand in producing the higher capital coefficients of the south.

Not only was the south poor in infrastructure, but it also suffered from too large a proportion of capital-intensive industry in comparison with the northern republics, which had developed labor-intensive industry already in Habsburg times. Unemployment, thus, remained a constant problem throughout the 1965–1980 period, especially in Macedonia and Kosovo. In 1970, for instance, there were 31 Slovenes seeking work for every 1,000 Slovenes employed and 49 Croats out of work for every 1,000 employed Croats—the comparable figures for other nationalities were 73 Bosnians, 74 Vojvodinans, 77 Montenegrins, 97 Serbs, 216 Macedonians, and 310 Kosovars. The Yugoslav average was 83 unemployed for every 1,000 working.[21]

An *Ekonomska politika* report of April 1980 chronicled this situation and found that the four officially "underdeveloped" federal units accounted for a smaller portion of the Yugoslav social product in 1978 than they had in 1947—21.6% in 1978 as opposed to 23.5% in 1947.[22] During 1947–1978 average annual growth rates were smaller in the underdeveloped republics than in the developed republics, with the inevitable result that the developmental gap continued to widen—a fact noted with concern in the less developed regions.[23]

Macedonia

Of all the underdeveloped republics, Macedonia derived the greatest portion of its income (72.4% of the total of its industrially derived social product) from light industry (as of 1977)—a statistic which pointed to an unmistakable transformation in Macedonian industry in the postwar era. Of those employed in Macedonian industry, 82.9% were in light industry, and only 17.1% in heavy industry. The largest sectors in the Macedonian economy were metallurgy, textiles, and tobacco. In Macedonia, as elsewhere, development was uneven, and the republic continued to register a number of especially underdeveloped districts, which received additional assistance from a special republican fund established to supplement the federal program. These pockets of poverty, inhabited by 30% of the republic's population, accounted for only 18.6% of total fixed investments in 1980 and only 17.5% of the social product of the republic.[24]

Aside from the problem of the underdevelopment of the economic infrastructure, Macedonia was also challenged by a scarcity of trained personnel. In 1971, for example, 25% of Macedonian adults had three years or less of grade school education, and another 45% had only 4–7 years of grade school.

Because of these and other factors, between 1975 and 1986 Macedonia's economic position relative to the Yugoslav average declined steadily. In 1975, Macedonia's social product per worker was 86% of the Yugoslav average. This slipped to 83% in 1980, 73% in 1985, and 70% in 1986.[25] As of 1987, Macedonia's unemployment rate stood at 26.7%—the second highest in the country (after Kosovo's).[26]

Bosnia-Herzegovina

In 1947, three-quarters of Bosnia's population depended on agriculture, only 14% were employed in industry, and 14% were unemployed. There were only 1,781 kilometers of railway lines, mostly narrow gauge, and no modern roads. Only one-fifth of all homes even had electricity. Yet, because Bosnia was classified as "developed" for much of the postwar period, it experienced only a 4.2% average annual growth rate in per capita income for 1952–1968—the lowest rate of all of Yugoslavia's federal units, and significantly less than the 6.4% Yugoslav average.[27] And while the rural population of Yugoslavia declined 4% during the years 1961–1968, in Bosnia the rural population increased 8% during the same period. In spite of that, the urban population of Bosnia tallied a proportional increase, rising from 14% in 1948 to 28% of the republic's population by 1971. The figure for those employed in agriculture declined from 77% in 1948 to 40% in 1971. In education, Bosnia lagged behind Macedonia: in 1971, less than 25% of the population had completed seven years of grade school and only 1% had completed university training. In addition, of the three-fourths with only grade school education, more than a third (36.2%) had completed no more than three years.[28]

Bosnia's proportion of gross investments declined from 18.3% in the 1953–1956 period to 12.9% in the 1957–1960 period and was reduced to 12.4% in the 1961–1964 period. Bosnia's national income was 20% below the Yugoslav average in 1947 and sagged to 27% below in 1960, to 34% below in 1964, and to 38% below average in 1967.[29] Only in the 1970s was this slippage finally checked. During the 1971–1975 medium-term plan, the republic's growth rate finally surpassed the Yugoslav average,[30] and in the course of the 1976–1980 period, the rate of growth of the Bosnian economy exceeded its rate of growth during any of the three previous five-year plans. Despite that improvement, there was no narrowing of the developmental gap between Bosnia and the Yugoslav economic average during this period.[31]

Bosnia's "ace in the hole" was its raw wealth, particularly its energy resources. Bosnia accounted for 81% of known Yugoslav iron ore reserves, 20% of its coal, 28% of its hydroelectric potential, and 30% of its lumber. Notching a 6% rise in the production of electric energy and coal from 1979 to 1980, Bosnia recorded production of 11.18 billion kilowatts of electric energy and 13.8 million tons of coal—enough to satisfy the energy needs not only of Bosnia but of other republics as well. Unfortunately, however, shortages of extractive equipment and fluctuations in the quality of the ore deposits hindered full exploitation of Bosnia's coal reserves.[32]

Like Macedonia, Bosnia had its own pockets of poverty. At the time of the passage of the republic's 1966–1970 five-year plan, 77 of the republic's 106 *općinas* were classified as especially underdeveloped and therefore eligible for additional help at the republic level. By the end of that five-year plan, only 48 *općinas* continued to be identified as especially backward. At that time, these districts covered 42.9% of the territory of the republic and included 38.5% of the republic's population, but they accounted for only 18.9% of the annual income of the republic—which means that the average per capita income in these areas was less than half the republican average and only 31% of the Yugoslav average.[33] Although the Bosnians chalked up some progress in these parts, certain districts remained mired in poverty. Thus, a 1980 study prepared by the Bosnian Economic Bureau in Tuzla indicated that in the republic's three poorest communes (Tuzla, Banovići, and Lukavac) the overall economic situation and the unemployment problem were on a par with conditions in Kosovo.[34] In the years 1981–1987, Bosnia expanded its work force 3.6% (against a Yugoslav average of 2.4%). In spite of this, unemployment in the republic remained a troubling 22.7% in 1987.[35]

Montenegro

The rugged mountainous terrain which enabled the Montenegrins to resist Turkish encroachment for centuries has proven less amenable to development.

Roads and railways were long in coming; the land is largely ill-suited to farming. The latter disability notwithstanding, 72% of Montenegro's population was engaged in agriculture in 1948.

After the war, developmental efforts focused on exploitation of Montenegro's metallurgical resources. The republic maintained an average annual growth rate of 6.4% between 1947 and 1974, while Montenegrin industry grew 14.1% annually. Thus, industry, which had represented only 5.8% of the Montenegrin economy in 1947, climbed to 32.6% in 1974, employing 41.5% of the republic's workforce. Simultaneously, the proportion of those employed in agriculture shrank to 27% in 1978.[36] Yet these impressive results were somewhat compromised by the failure to produce developmental depth. With 70% of its economy in capital-intensive basic industry (as of the late 1970s), Montenegro has had real problems. Its economy was excessively oriented toward the exploitation of its mineral wealth. Montenegro's rate of capital formation, moreover, was the second lowest of Yugoslavia's federal units, undercut only by Kosovo. Added to this was the inability of the Montenegrin economy to keep pace with projected rates of growth: between 1976 and 1978, Montenegrin industry grew by 13.1%—impressive enough, but well below plan.[37]

One of Montenegro's biggest problems, at least until the 1970s, was the serious lack of transport infrastructure, with the result that Montenegro was less well integrated with the rest of the country than, for example, Croatia or Serbia. The Belgrade-Bar railway (completed in 1976) represented a decisive step toward overcoming this isolation. Montenegro's development was, however, set back by several years by the devastating earthquake of April 1979, which cost the republic more than 50 billion dinars in damage.

In the years 1981–1987, the Montenegrin labor force grew 4.0%. But unemployment still stood at 23.4% in 1987.[38] In 1989, average income in Montenegro was only 48% of Slovenian earnings—and reportedly insufficient to maintain a minimal standard of living.[39] The average monthly salary in September 1990 was $400—which was $70 less than the Yugoslav average. One out of every five Montenegrins lived below the poverty line, and as of 1989, one out of every ten workers in Montenegro was employed at a firm facing imminent bankruptcy.

Kosovo

Kosovo was, by all measures, the poorest, most backward region in the SFRY. It had the highest rates of unemployment, the lowest levels of literacy and educational attainment, the highest birthrates, the worst roads, the least infrastructure, the least developed plumbing and electricity services, and, until the early 1970s, the slowest-growing economy. As of 1939, there had been only 24 industrial plants in all of Kosovo, mostly saw mills, carding mills, and small electric power plants; these were either destroyed or damaged during World War Two, leaving the province essentially without functioning industries at war's end.[40] Despite this consistent and unmistakable picture of underdevelopment, Kosovo was excluded, between 1947 and 1955—as already noted—from special treatment as an underdeveloped region. Only in 1955 was Kosmet (Kosovo) finally classified as "underdeveloped" for funding purposes, and there was talk of "substantial investment funds" to be funneled into the province.[41] Even after it became eligible for special federal grants, however, Kosovo still had to deal with the highest capital coefficients in the country and with problems of poor management. For these and other reasons related to the underdevelopment syndrome, Kosovo registered the slowest rate of growth in social product of all the republics and provinces over the period 1948–1972.[42] Broken down into five-year periods, it is clear that, in the years prior to 1972, Kosovo experienced its most impressive growth in the mid-1950s and again in the mid-1960s. Impressive as these figures may seem, two things should be noted. First, Kosovo's growth throughout this period remained below the Yugoslav average. Excluding the earliest postwar period, when Yugoslavia's economy was perilously unstable, one finds that whereas Kosovo's social product grew at an average annual rate of 7.4% (calculated in 1966 prices), the average annual growth rate for the Yugoslav economy as a whole during this period was 7.7%.[43] Thus, Kosovo could scarcely be said to be "catching up." Second, its growth took place mainly in heavy industry, with only 12.4% for agriculture, 8.9% for transport development, and 11.1% for non-economic projects. Most of the investments in this last category, moreover, had the character of building infrastructure, such as sewers and water lines, schools and hospitals, and residences. All told, about 85% of all industrial projects undertaken in Kosovo in the years 1947–1970 were in heavy industry.

In the period 1971–1975, Kosovo experienced the fastest economic growth rate among the republics and provinces. During this period, industrial production in Kosovo grew at a rate of 11.6% per year (as compared to a Yugoslav average of 8.2% per year), and annual provincial agricultural production increased 30% during 1971–1975.[44] Kosovo's social product increased at a rate of 7.3% annually. Between 1970 and 1975, the number of physicians in Kosovo doubled. Whereas there were only 2,712 cars registered in Kosovo in 1966, there were 34,311 in 1976. At the same time, 1,504 kilometers of new roads were laid, of which 1,007 kilometers were asphalt.[45] The employment roster expanded some 7% in this time frame, even as the share of agriculture in Kosovar employment fell to 45% in 1975. Yet, despite all this, Mahmut Bakalli, president of the provincial committee of the LC Kosovo, could complain in 1976 that Kosovo was relatively more backward than it had been five years earlier. The key measures corroborated Bakalli's claim. In 1947, for instance, Kosovo's per capita social product stood at 49.3% of the Yugoslav average; by 1970, however, Kosovo's share had shrunk to 34.1%. In 1975, Kosovo tallied no more than 33.4%, and by 1976, this figure had slipped even further, to 32.2%. In part, of course, this measure reflected Kosovo's exploding population, half of which was then of school age or younger. Again, Kosovo's share in Yugoslavia's total fixed investments actually dropped from 3.7% during the 1966–1970 period to 3.5% for the 1971–1975 period.[46]

Trends were not much better in the period 1976–1985; economic progress was being made in absolute terms, but in relative terms, the province continued to slide backward. During the 1986–1990 plan period, Kosovo received 48.1% of the funds being disbursed by the Fund for the Accelerated Development of the Underdeveloped Republics and Kosovo (FADURK). In spite of this, progress, in relative terms, was imperceptible. A large portion of Kosovo's 406.5 thousand hectares of arable land was, in any event, not being put to use, and mining-related enterprises (coal, lead, zinc, nickel, etc.) were operating well below capacity. The same was true for other sectors of the Kosovar economy. Meanwhile, Kosovo's birthrate—the highest in Europe—caused the population of the province to double in just three years (1981–1984). By 1990, Kosovo had 140,000 jobless people, with young people accounting for 70% of the unemployed.[47]

Pockets of Underdevelopment in Other Republics

As already noted, in the years prior to 1989, Yugoslavia classified various regions as "underdeveloped" for purposes of allocating developmental funds. But except for the brief period between 1961 and 1964, Yugoslavia reserved the "underdeveloped" classification in federal aid for entire republics and provinces. As ought to be clear from the foregoing discussion, those republics and province so identified (Bosnia, Macedonia, Montenegro, and Kosovo) lagged behind the others in economic development. Yet there were pockets of relative backwardness in *every* republic and autonomous province. For this reason, the 1963 federal constitution called on each republic and autonomous province to set up a republic Fund for the Economic Development of Underdeveloped Districts (FREDUD), mirroring the federal fund at the level of the republic.

Establishment of FADURK

By 1964, everyone had become disgruntled with the existing system for financing economic development. The underdeveloped republics complained that the amounts tendered were insufficient. The developed republics complained that, owing to mismanagement and poor use of funds, their contributions were being squandered. These currents came to a head at the Eighth Party Congress, which decreed that drastic organizational changes be made in the manner in which aid was funneled to the underdeveloped zones. With the bankruptcy of the centralized system of economic stimulation openly admitted, it was decided to establish a new office to coordinate developmental efforts. Finally, in February 1965, the federal Assembly passed a bill creating the federal Fund for the Accelerated Development of the Underdeveloped Republics and Kosovo

(FADURK), to be operated by a 13-member board of directors (one per socialist republic and seven appointed by the Skupština). The fund was to be financed by a 1.85% tax on the social product, to be paid by all republics and provinces.[48] It was decided to treat only entire republics and provinces as "underdeveloped" for FADURK purposes, and Bosnia, Macedonia, Montenegro, and Kosovo were declared eligible for assistance under the new program. A large portion of these funds would take the form of credits to be repaid at a low rate of interest. Controversies soon arose over the distribution of FADURK funds, however, with Bosnia seeking a larger slice of the 1966–1970 pie than it ultimately obtained, for example.[49] Kosovo's representatives complained that they were having to devote some three-quarters of the provincial budget to service previous loans, and that the province was thus trapped in a vicious circle of inescapable indebtedness. In December 1969, Kosovo submitted an official request to the Federal Executive Council and the federal Skupština, asking to be absolved of all debts incurred through acceptance of FADURK credits over the 1966–1970 period and asked that subsequent credits be extended on an interest-free basis.[50] Kosovo also wanted direct representation on FADURK's board of directors.

Kosovo's demands created a minor crisis, especially since certain parties among the developed republics were becoming impatient with the entire concept of aiding the south. They were raising the embarrassing question of how much longer the underdeveloped republics and Kosovo would continue to receive special treatment and even broached the idea of liquidating FADURK altogether. The developed republics tended to view the program not as an investment but as charity. Hence, as Kosta Mihailović, a noted Serbian economist, observed at the time, "the thesis that the development of the underdeveloped regions is also in the interest of the developed regions, and accordingly in the interest of the entire economy, is more often than not accepted as an [empty] slogan rather than as the truth."[51]

In the end, Kosovo was granted two of its three demands. All credits extended during 1966–1970 were written off as grants, and two members were added to the board of directors, permitting both Kosovo and Vojvodina to be directly represented.[52] After 1970, the underdeveloped republics enjoyed repayment schedules of only 15 years, at an annual interest rate of 4%. An exception was made for Kosovo, however, which was allowed a repayment term of 19 years at an annual interest rate of 3%.

Continuing Disputes over Fund Criteria

With the 1974 constitution, the republics and provinces alike were defined as "federal units"—in a move which inflamed tempers in Serbia, since the redefinition gave the status of Kosovo and Vojvodina an explicit anchor in federal law. In 1976, a new law regulating FADURK was drawn up. The new statute converted FADURK into an interrepublican agency and replaced the 15-member board of directors with an eight-member board—one delegate from each federal unit. The amount of the contribution drawn from the basic organizations of associated labor was raised to 1.97% of the social product. This was to be divided as follows: of the resources represented by a 1.77% levy on the social product, Bosnia would receive 34%, Macedonia 24%, Montenegro 12%, and Kosovo 30%; a 0.17% levy would be reserved entirely for Kosovo; and a 0.03% levy would finance construction of the Ibar-Lepenac irrigation project in Kosovo.[53]

The 1976–1980 social plan stipulated that the economic growth rate of the underdeveloped regions *as a whole* should exceed the average Yugoslav rate by 20–25% and reiterated that "the policy of the accelerated development of the economically insufficiently developed republics and Kosovo has especial meaning for the further advancement of inter-ethnic relations and for the consolidation of the unity of the working class."[54] At the same time, it was increasingly recognized that the operative definition of "underdevelopment" as simply *a developmental level below the Yugoslav average* was becoming less relevant as that average improved. That is to say, the inequalities might well remain, but to interpret those inequalities as symptoms of underdevelopment could not be justified on a priori grounds. Hence, the social plan for the period 1976–1980 called on the federal units to agree by the end of 1978 on new criteria for classifying their developmental levels.

The program had, in fact, been plagued from the beginning by the absence of hard and fast criteria. When the issue came up in 1971, the republics proved unable to reach an agreement, and disbursement under the 1971–1975 plan period began while negotiations regarding criteria were still being carried on. The so-called Law regarding Criteria of Disbursement was finally passed in November 1972, but this law did not in fact establish criteria of disbursement—it merely determined the allocations. This situation was perhaps not intolerable at that time, but by 1978, the growing conviction that at least two of the underdeveloped republics were no longer disadvantaged made the resolution of the issue a more burning need. Meanwhile, even as this debate continued, the Croats demanded that FADURK be disbanded and replaced by an informal pool of work organizations in which cross-regional, inter-enterprise investment would produce development on the basis of mutual profitability, while the Slovenes urged that FADURK concentrate, in the future, on facilitating the investment in the less developed areas by enterprises based in more developed republics.[55] The Slovenes also proposed a set of criteria which would have left only Kosovo as eligible for low-interest credits.

Even though it seemed unlikely that the Slovenian proposal would be accepted, rumors spread that both Macedonia and Bosnia would be reclassified as "developed" after 1980.[56] The Macedonians anxiously made it known that they would not be able to meet planned targets or maintain a satisfactory rate of growth in the 1980–1990 period solely on the basis of their own financial resources.[57] Likewise concerned lest it be dropped from the ranks of FADURK recipients, Bosnia invited the Slovenian executive council to send a delegation to Sarajevo and endeavored to evoke some sympathy among the Slovenes for Bosnia's situation.[58] The Bosnians also courted Croatia, entertaining a high-ranking Croatian delegation in May 1980.[59] The deadline for setting the program criteria was pushed back three times, and still the republics were unable to agree. Finally, in July 1980, a compromise guaranteed eligibility for the same four federal units until 1985, while the deputies continued to seek agreement on new criteria.[60]

Actually, by this time it was generally agreed that neither Macedonia nor Bosnia-Herzegovina would require federal assistance after 1985, and FADURK's projected outlay was already being cut back for the 1981–1985 period from 76 billion dinars to 41 billion dinars. Outside Kosovo there were complaints heard that the province was being turned into a showcase. But the underdeveloped republics insisted that the projected outlay was entirely inadequate, and eventually, the FADURK purse for 1981–1985 was set at 80 billion dinars. But there were genuine worries throughout the country when, in 1980, the Yugoslav standard of living declined for the first time in decades. In spite of that, and in spite of the growing economic problems plaguing Yugoslavia during the 1980s, the prospects of the underdeveloped republics (aside from Kosovo) seemed to be fair to good, from a purely economic standpoint, at least until the mid-1980s, and perhaps until the outbreak of war in 1991 and the accompanying economic crash. Yet, viewed in relative terms—that is, from the standpoint of a comparison with the more developed parts of the country—their prospects, except possibly in the case of Bosnia, were never anything other than hopeless. As a report submitted to the World Bank in 1975 noted, Yugoslavia's regional economic problem was "not a problem of economic stagnation in the less developed republics . . . [but] one of increasing regional differences between developed and less developed republics despite rapid growth in both."[61]

Final Battles over FADURK

There were repeated efforts over the years to obtain the abolition of FADURK—naturally, on the part of Slovenia and Croatia. During 1985 and 1986, the republics were much divided over the criteria for disbursement but finally, in April 1986, agreed on the criteria for the 1986–1990 period. Yet, despite the investment of $10.5 billion of FADURK money from 1965 to 1988, Macedonia, Montenegro, and Kosovo were unable to narrow the developmental gap. In Montenegro and Kosovo, per capita social product declined relative to the Yugoslav average from 1970 to 1986, while in Macedonia it was more or less stagnant.[62]

In January 1990, the Slovenian government (still controlled by the communists) proposed that it reduce its contribution to FADURK by about half. The Belgrade daily *Politika* attacked this decision, and Fund Director Momčilo

Čemović used the army daily *Narodna armija* as the vehicle for an interview in which he called the Slovenian move a contravention of federal law.[63] In February 1990, the board of FADURK failed to reach agreement on a financial plan for 1990 when the Slovenian delegation, angered by the Serbian economic blockade of Slovenian goods (which had been imposed in December 1989), refused to cooperate. Since the fund depended on Slovenia and Croatia for 45% of its financial means, Slovenian noncooperation was a serious blow. In March 1990, the Federal Executive Council ordered the finance ministry to freeze Slovenian accounts until the republic resumed payments to FADURK.[64] But with the entire country poised, by 1990, on the brink of a choice between transformation into a confederation, dissolution of the federation, and war, this position could not be maintained. In the first week of July 1990, the Croatian Sabor, now controlled by Tudjman's HDZ, announced that Croatia was going to stop making payments to FADURK. Two weeks later, the Federal Executive Council announced that FADURK would cease all activity by the end of the year and that it would be replaced by a development bank which would operate according to market principles.[65] One Macedonian intellectual, contemplating this and other developments, bemoaned the fact that (in his view) Macedonia was ending up in the most difficult straits of any of the republics, and he commented, "Probably it's because we Macedonians are [still] on the margins of 'the broad Yugoslav public,' just as, by the way, Yugoslavia is on the margins of the world public."[66]

Controversies over Road and Railway Construction

The 1965 reforms had considerable fallout in all sectors of the economy. Among the results was the decision to devolve major responsibilities for public works and construction to the republics. Thus, in 1967, the republics were given almost total control over the planning, routing, contracting, construction, maintenance, and financing of public roads within their respective territories. Republican and regional funds were now the primary source of funding for road construction and maintenance. Certain projects, however, particularly those connecting major cities in different republics, could obtain support from federal funds, army funds, the World Bank, other foreign sources (channeled through Belgrade), and, for those eligible, the funds for underdeveloped areas.

Socialist Yugoslavia was long plagued by a deficient transport system and only in the 1980s began to reach the point at which the country could be said to be integrated by a workable system of roads, railways, and airports, even if most of the roads were narrow, and air connections were, in many cases, rather irregular and often operating with long delays. As of 1966, Yugoslavia had the fifth sparsest network of roads in Europe, after Norway, Sweden, Finland, and Albania. Proportional to population density, however, only Albania fell behind Yugoslavia. Some regions were markedly less developed in this respect in 1945. Montenegro, for instance, had 0.7 kilometers of hard surface roads per 1,000 square kilometers in 1945, as compared with 80.9 kilometers per 1,000 square kilometers in 1974. But even in the developed areas there were problems. Of 54,180 miles of classified roads in 1968, just over 20% were paved. Most of the rest were gravel or packed-dirt roads. But the Yugoslavs maintained a steady pace of road construction, tripling the net length of modern paved roads in less than ten years, from 12,950 kilometers in 1965 to 35,380 kilometers in 1974.[67]

Side by side with the development of roads, the Yugoslavs were updating and extending their rail lines. Here a crucial problem was antiquated tracks and stock. Much of the rail system consisted of narrow-gauge tracks, capable of carrying only half the weight that standard gauge could bear. In addition, only 24% of the standard gauge lines were adequate for speeds over 80 kilometers per hour in 1966, and only 33% could handle loads of more than 18 tons per axle. This meant that freight cars were compelled to run below capacity. At that time, moreover, about half of the locomotives and passenger and freight cars were more than 40 years old. Add to this the fact that 70% of rail traffic was concentrated on 30% of the trackage, and it is apparent that the system was not only technically deficient but also had a warped spatial distribution that was completely inadequate for the needs of the country as a whole.[68]

Rail construction was inseparable from republic competition in the development of seaports. In 1945, there were rail connections to only four Yugoslav ports: Rijeka, in the north; historic Dubrovnik; Split; and nearby Šibenik. Yet reconstruction of these ports, badly damaged during World War Two, proceeded at a slow pace. The Germans had destroyed more than 80% of the port facilities at Rijeka when they had withdrawn from Yugoslavia, and about 20 years later, Rijeka's capacity still had not been restored to 1913 levels, although traffic had passed the 1913 mark in 1950.[69] Rijeka and Split remained major ports for Yugoslav traffic. Šibenik, however, was long neglected as a recipient of investments. Work on a new terminal for handling phosphate finally began at the port of Šibenik on 27 November 1979.[70] In contrast, money was poured into Koper (in Slovenia), Bar (in Montenegro), and Ploče (in Croatia, but built by Bosnian authorities, with Slovenian money, as the logical outlet for their goods). The waxing interport rivalry had an interrepublican character from the beginning. Rijeka, Koper, and Ploče—each backed by a different republic—competed for preponderance as the network terminal for Yugoslavia. Attempts to reach an agreement on a coordinated program of port development, such as a meeting of port representatives convened in 1974, repeatedly fell through. Rijeka argued that investment should be funneled into the port with the highest profitability of traffic—a self-serving argument, in fact. Koper and Ploče argued that each zone should have a port to serve its own hinterland, thus cutting transport costs. According to one Yugoslav economic analyst, however, there was no economic justification for massive investment in all three, because there would not be enough cargo in the foreseeable future to occupy even one port at full capacity.[71] Yet Rijeka would not, in fact, have been able to handle demand single-handedly; Croatia's Pula and Slovenia's Koper were the obvious alternative Istrian ports. The Slovenes, however, controlled the access routes to Pula and, taking advantage of the decentralization of authority for railway tariffs in 1966, introduced certain disproportionate tariffs for railway freight headed for Rovinj and Pula, in order to give Koper a competitive edge. The result was that Pula, though enjoying certain advantages of infrastructure and an excellent natural harbor and actually being connected by a shorter route to both Ljubljana and Zagreb, became less attractive from a financial viewpoint.[72]

Interport competition for funding was intense, and Rijeka, for one, insisted that without financing from the federal government, necessary modernization of its port facilities would be impossible.[73] Yet even when funds had been allocated, the ports had to struggle to ensure that the funds were made available. Thus, for instance, a delegate from Split complained in 1978 that although the 1976–1980 plan had authorized the expenditure of 20 million dinars for technical research preparatory to reconstruction of the Split-Knin railway under the 1981–1985 plan, nothing had in fact been done. He added that almost nothing had been done to improve Split's rail connections since the war.[74]

The most controversial port development project, however, was the development of Bar. Isolated and far from the major industrial centers of the north, the port could only be made feasible if a rail connection were built. The Croats protested loudly that the money could be better spent improving facilities at Split, Šibenik, or even Zadar, all of which were located in southern Croatia, along the Dalmatian coast. The ports of Rijeka and Ploče both tried to block pursuit of the Belgrade-Bar project because they feared that development of the port of Bar and its connection by rail with Belgrade would pose a dangerous threat to their business.[75] Serbian, Kosovar, and Macedonian interests, however, lent strong support to the Montenegrins, which resulted in approval of Yugoslavia's most expensive marine project since the war. The railway itself stretches for 296 miles and was completed only in 1976, after the blasting of some 50 miles of tunnels.[76] The railroad, some 13 years in the works, was the object of repeated Croatian complaints. From the Croatian standpoint, the development of the port of Bar was politically motivated; the Serbs and Montenegrins wanted to have their own port, said the Croats, and avoid having to deal with Croatia. Bar certainly relieved Rijeka of some of its congestion, but, perhaps more important, it also helped to open part of the south to foreign trade. In a country riddled by mountain ranges, the Belgrade-Bar railway and the development of the port of Bar also linked the eastern two-fifths of the country with the rest of the economy. On the other hand, it was no secret that the idea for the Belgrade-Bar railway had originated with the Serbian and Montenegrin parties, and not with the federal government. But after 1966, in spite of opposition from Slovenia, Croatia, and Bosnia, some 85% of the cost of the construction of the Belgrade-Bar railway would be paid out of federal coffers.[77]

Controversies over the "Brotherhood and Unity" highway were another occasion for interrepublican rivalry to express itself. Some 1,200 kilometers of highway in the E-70 and E-75 sections of the international network in Yugo-slavia needed reconstruction or widening as of 1975, and under the Social Agreement for 1976–1980, Slovenia, Croatia, Vojvodina, Serbia, and Macedonia had agreed to complete fixed lengths of road construction. By April 1980, how-ever, only Serbia and Macedonia had met their quotas, Croatia was close, hav-ing completed 137 out of a planned 148 kilometers of road work, while neither Slovenia nor Vojvodina had even begun work on their assigned quotas. Slove-nia, in particular, had possessed funds for the work but had chosen to allocate them to the improvement of a network of regional roads within the republic and to the modernization of certain sections of highway other than parts of E-70, in a classic case of self-interest. Keti Comovska, deputy chair of the federal Committee for Transportation and Communication, claimed that the Slovenian move would result in *irredeemable* losses for the federation.[78] As for Vojvodina, it was only in the summer of 1982 that the Vojvodinans began work on a 17-kilometer stretch of highway, but even then it was not the 30-kilometer stretch which had been promised for early 1982.

Freed from political constraint, the federal units pursued their own individ-ual interests—consistently and as a matter of policy. They could not entirely trust each other and certainly did not wish to defer to each other's judgment—as was demonstrated by the constant demands for the establishment of control commissions to verify the rationality of investments in the south. The units were motivated by exclusive interests, and they would pursue exclusive interests whenever they could. The trick of Yugoslav federalism—not accomplished, in the event—had to be to accomplish the Madisonian feat and so arrange the political order that the outcome of interrepublican debate would be the same as it would have been had the republics been seeking the Yugoslav general interest.

Stabilizing the Economy, 1984–1990

At one time it was axiomatic that the more developed republics favored eco-nomic liberalization and that the less developed republics favored economic centralism and the maintenance of centrally controlled state funding. By the mid-1980s, however, first Slovenia, then Croatia, and finally economic liberals in all of the republics came around to the idea that the return to private enter-prise was necessary and inevitable if there was to be any substantial economic recovery. The Yugoslav economy, which had seemed promising and even resilient in the mid-1970s, was in deep trouble by the late 1980s. The foreign debt had reached about $20 billion by 1988, the inflation rate was accelerating out of control, and the social product was declining about 1–1.5% annually.[79] Wracked with problems of economic insolvency, foreign debt, unemployment, and inflation, the Yugoslav economy was further strained, in 1987, by an espe-cially widespread rash of strikes, some of them protesting a national wage freeze decreed by federal prime minister Branko Mikulić.[80] There were large-scale protests by thousands of workers in Skopje in November 1987 and in Belgrade in October 1988, protesting low wages.[81] Conditions became so bad that on 20 August 1989, some 30,000 citizens—mostly local Montenegrins—demonstrated in Nikšić to protest their hunger and poverty.[82]

The Mikulić government, which had sworn to fight inflation, made no headway whatsoever. By October 1987, inflation hit 200%. It would eventually rise to 893.8% by August 1989.[83] The massive report on economic stabilization produced by the Kraigher Commission in 1986 had proven barren. Slovenia and Croatia, in particular, resented Mikulić's lame efforts to deal with the economic problems and in May 1988 requested a vote of no confidence in the federal Skupština. But the two houses of the legislature voted down the Slovenian-Croatian motion by margins of 64–23 and 125–64.[84] Mikulić stayed in office but gradually converted to advocacy of market reform; this was to cost him his support among those who favored strong state intervention in the economy.

On 12 December 1988, Oskar Kovač, an economics professor of the University of Belgrade who had been serving in Mikulić's cabinet, resigned his portfolio (relations with the EEC and EFTA), accusing Mikulić of failing to honor a promise he had made to the IMF (International Monetary Fund) to keep interest rates higher than the rate of inflation. Two weeks later, *Borba* published an article demanding that Mikulić resign. Four days later, on 30 December, Mikulić resigned—a year and a half before the expiration of his four-year term. Mikulić had been brought down not by the pro-reform republics, Slovenia and Croatia, but by Serbian leader Milošević, who was steadfastly opposed to any movement in the direction of a market economy and whose preferred economic model was state capitalism. Mikulić had remained secure in office as long as he advocated administrative interventions à la state capitalism. When he belatedly converted to a reform orientation in the second half of 1988, Milošević turned against him. Milošević had his way with Mikulić but was less successful in influencing the choice of a successor. Milošević wanted to install his loyal acolyte, Borisav Jović, in the post, but his candidacy was supported only by Serbia and Montenegro. Defense Minister Kadijević, concerned lest a reformist get the job and proceed to slash the army's budget, nominated Milošević to assume the prime ministership (a nomination quickly seconded by Milošević's enemy, Šuvar, who was eager to strip the Serbian leader of his power base); but Milošević was scarcely interested in assuming a position with such narrowly economic responsibilities.[85] Finally, the nod went to Ante Marković, hitherto prime minister of Croatia. The preferred candidate of Slovenia and Croatia, Marković had proven reformist credentials. Marković gradually put together a program aimed at curbing inflation (he had brought it down to about 5% by early 1990, although it later once more climbed to unmanageable levels). But when Marković presented his program to the respective republic assembles in December 1989, Serbia and Vojvodina rejected it, the former claiming that "the implementation of this program would impose the greatest burden on the most endangered strata of the population."[86] All the other republics gave their approval, although

Kosovo's assembly noted some objections to the program and indicated that its delegation in the Skupština would try to obtain some adjustments.[87]

Pressure for privatization can be traced to mid-1986, when Judge Čedo Grbić daringly spoke in favor of private enterprise. But the drive for reprivatization gathered steam only in 1988, when it became legitimate for the communists themselves to sing the praises of private enterprise. Yugoslavia's first private factory was set up in April 1986, in a village just outside Maribor. Two years later, the Croatian Sabor approved a widening of possibilities for private initiative in tourism.[88] Also in 1988, a private stock exchange was established in Ljubljana. By September 1990, more than 30,000 private companies were operating in Yugoslavia.[89]

In late 1988 (while Mikulić was still prime minister), a series of measures were adopted which changed procedures in management and in the selection of managers, enabled foreigners to set up economic enterprises in Yugoslavia, and expanded the maximum size allowed for private farms.[90] By June 1989, *Borba* was calling reprivatization "the last chance for socialism"—a claim not without irony.[91] And with the election of noncommunist governments in Slovenia, Croatia, Macedonia, and Bosnia in 1990, the process of reprivatization quickened.

CHAPTER 10

Nationalist Tensions, 1968–1990

I f the nationalist euphoria of 1969–1971 demonstrated anything, it was that, maxims of socialist unity notwithstanding, building a sense of community was going to be more complicated than Yugoslavia's communists had anticipated; to their disappointment, localism could still be mobilized around national symbols, national history, and the defense of one's language and of one's people from perceived threats. Tito and his associates believed that by demonizing nationalism, they could persuade people to cease to make local interests and local identity their primary focus and that people would then shift their primary loyalty to socialist Yugoslavia. This was a mistaken strategy, and Tito and his supporters reinforced resentments which, within the context of the decentralized system, would be experienced as collective sufferings of the nation.

By the end of the 1970s, Bosnia-Herzegovina and Kosovo had become the loci of new ethnocentric malaises. Indeed, the Muslim question and the persistence of separatist sentiment among Kosovo's Albanians were, by the mid-1980s, the chief axes of nationalist disequilibrium in the country. But by the end of the 1980s, under the pressure of the disintegration of the system, nationalism was stirring among the members of every nationality.

The Muslim Question

In the early postwar period, the Muslims were viewed as the least "national" of Yugoslavia's peoples, even as potentially anational (if they did not identify themselves as either Serbs or Croats). Some party conservatives viewed the Muslims as the anational core around which the new Yugoslav nation would be formed. No one dared suggest that the Muslims might themselves have a claim to recognition as a nationality group. Ranković, who covertly admired Soviet nationalities policy and favored emulation of Russification, was openly against the notion of Muslim particularity and denied the existence of, or the possibility of, a Muslim nation. Throughout this period, antagonistic groups advanced rival theories about the origins of the Bosnian Muslims. The best known in the West is the now largely discredited Bogomil theory.[1] The variant expostulated by Croatian nationalists held that certain groups of ethnic Croats embraced a Manichean religion known as Bogomilism, were thereafter persecuted by both the Catholic and Orthodox Churches, and converted en masse to Islam when the comparatively liberal-minded Turks subsequently conquered the region.[2] This theory (which would be favored by Croatian president Tudjman[3]) contends that the Muslims are "Islamic Croats" and describes Bosnia-Herzegovina as the Croatian hinterland. An alternative theory, espoused by some Serbs and Serbophiles, holds that the Muslims are, in fact, Serbian settlers from the time of the Turkish occupation who abandoned Orthodoxy and adopted Islam. This theory adds, for good measure, that some Serbian immigrants in the 16th and 17th centuries converted to Catholicism, so that many of today's Croats in Bosnia are Serbs by origin.[4] Radovan Karadžić, leader of the Bosnian Serbs during the bloody conflict of the first half of the 1990s, held to the theory that Bosnia's Muslims were Islamicized Serbs.[5] By 1971, the Serbianists in the LCY had, for the time being, been squeezed out of positions of power.

In time, a third theory was advanced by Muslim nationalists, who argued for a Turkish origin and traced their antecedents to immigration from Anatolia. This theory contests the customary belief that the Bogomil sect was a spin-off from Christianity and contends that the Bogomils were a non-Christian sect whose doctrines were related to Islam (or, alternatively, to Zoroastrianism). According to this theory, the only thing Slavic about the Bosnian Muslims is their language, which they absorbed from the indigenous population.[6]

Secret police chief Ranković, whose repressive Serbianization policies, in the postwar years to 1966, were concentrated in Kosovo, Vojvodina, and Bosnia-Herzegovina (i.e., against the Albanians, the Hungarians, and the Muslims), subscribed to the second theory, i.e., to the notion of a Serbian origin for the Muslims. During the period of his ascendancy, Ranković and his coterie emphasized Yugoslav unity and attempted to suppress any acknowledgment or discussion of ethnic particularities. Thus, not until the Eighth Congress in 1964—that is, after the expiration of 24 years—was the subject of Muslim nationality reopened by Yugoslav communists.[7]

The fall of Ranković was not merely a victory for the Croats or the decentralists, nor even "merely" for the forces of reform: it was a victory for Yugoslavia's Muslims. Within five years of the defeat of Ranković, the status of the Muslims was significantly enhanced on a number of levels. To begin with, shortly after Ranković's expulsion from the party, Tito made an ex cathedra declaration that the national identity and national specificity of the Muslims must be recognized—a pronouncement which made possible the recognition of the Muslims as a sixth Yugoslav nationality. Tito also endorsed the concept of *organic Yugoslavism* (*organsko Jugoslovenstvo*), a harmonious symbiosis between national specificity and affective attachment to the Yugoslav federal community (as opposed to the concept of *integral Yugoslavism* endorsed by Ranković, under which national specificity and affective attachment to Yugoslavia were seen as antagonistic). Tito's endorsement of all three theories of Muslim ethnogenesis must be seen as an effort to deny exclusive legitimacy to any one theory and to close the debate once and for all.

Yet there continued to be uncertainties about the Muslims, centering especially on the relationship of Islam to their national identity. Many continued to doubt, in particular, whether the Muslims could lay claim to being more than a distinct cultural community. Though the "Bosniaks" were recognized as an "ethnic group" (but not a "nationality") in 1961, and despite the fact that the Fourth Congress of the Bosnian party had, in 1964, assured these "Bosniaks" of their right of self-determination, it was not conceded that the Bosnian Muslims were as fully "national" as the Serbs or Croats. R. V. Burks credits Muhamed Filipović, a professor at Sarajevo, with having been the first (in 1967) to articulate the Muslim claim to separate national status.[8] Filipović's claim was politically premature, and he was summarily expelled from the party. But just a few months later—in February 1968—the central committee of the League of Communists of Bosnia-Herzegovina resolved, at its Eighteenth Session, that "experience has shown the damage of various forms of pressure and insistence, in the earlier period, that Muslims declare themselves ethnically to be Serbs or Croats because, as was demonstrated still earlier and as contemporary socialist experience continues to show, the Muslims are a separate nation."[9] This proclamation provoked certain groups in other republics, and at the Fourteenth Session of the central committee of the LC of Serbia (May 1968), historian Jovan Marjanović, supported by novelist Dobrica Ćosić, declared that "the proclamation of a Muslim nation is senseless" and sought to obtain a resolution that would prevent the category "Muslim" (in the national sense) from appearing on the next census forms. The resolution failed to find support, however, and the majority condemned Marjanović and Ćosić for their views, expelling them from the party.[10] The Fifth Congress of the LC Bosnia-Herzegovina (9–11 January 1969) capped the process of recognition of the Muslim nation by formally endorsing its complete equality with the other Yugoslav nationalities.[11]

The final token of the coming of age of the Muslim nationality was its formal recognition on the 1971 census forms. In the 1948 census, Bosnia's Muslims had had only three options: "Serb-Muslim," "Croat-Muslim," and "ethnically undeclared Muslim." "Muslim" continued to be treated as a matter of religious preference rather than ethnicity in the 1953 census, but the category "Yugoslav, ethnically undeclared" was introduced. It is now more or less acknowledged that the overwhelming majority of such "Yugoslavs, ethnically undeclared" were Muslims. Whereas the original census report listed 998,698 "Yugoslavs, ethnically declared," the 1979 edition of *Statistički godnišnjak* lists that same figure for "Muslims in the national sense" for 1953. Even in the 1961 census, when the category "Yugoslav in the national sense" was incorporated into the census, the Muslims were still more or less ignored; most of the reporting "Yugoslavs" were once again Muslims. The 1971 census was the first in which "Muslim" was treated as a fully recognized nationality (see Table 10.1). As it turned out, the non-Muslim nationalities of Bosnia-Herzegovina, i.e., the Croats and Serbs, felt threatened by the recognition of a third major grouping, while the Muslims were eager to legitimate the fruit of a long campaign. The 1971 census thus witnessed considerable nationalist agitation in Bosnia, as some groups pressured citizens to declare themselves "Muslims in the national sense," while others pressured them to declare themselves "Yugoslavs, ethnically undeclared."[12]

A coalition of conservatives and other forces who felt they stood to lose by the introduction of the new ethno-national category attempted to restrict the Muslim category to the republic of Bosnia-Herzegovina and the Sandžak region of Serbia.[13] This ostensible compromise was clearly a rearguard reaction, a device to block full recognition of the Muslim nationality, by linking it with republican citizenship. The move failed, and the party presidium, echoed by the leading body of the Socialist Alliance of Working People of Yugoslavia, declared that the Muslims constituted a national group on a par with Serbs, Croats, Slovenes, Macedonians, and Montenegrins. As a result, ethnic Muslims could be found in every Yugoslav federal unit (see table 10.2).

Table 10.1. Major Nationality Groups in Bosnia-Herzegovina, 1948–1981

	1948	1953	1961	1971	1981
TOTAL	2,565,277	2,847,790	3,277,935	3,746,111	4,124,008
Serbs	1,136,116	1,264,372	1,406,053	1,393,148	1,320,644
Of whom,					
Serb-Muslims	71,991	—	—	—	—
Croats	614,123	654,229	711,660	772,491	758,136
Of whom,					
Croat-Muslims	25,295	—	—	—	—
Muslims, ethnically					
undeclared	788,403	—	—	—	—
"Yugoslavs"	—	891,800	275,883	43,796	326,280
Muslims, in the					
ethnic sense	—	—	842,247	1,482,430	1,629,924

Sources: "Staat und Nationalität in Jugoslawien," *Wissenschaftlicher Dienst Südosteuropa* 19, no. 8 (August 1970): 114; *Statistički godišnjak Jugoslavije 1979* (Belgrade: Savezni zavod za statistiku, July 1979), p. 413; and Tanjug, 16 February 1982, in FBIS, *Daily Report* (Eastern Europe), 17 February 1982.

**Table 10.2. Distribution of Ethnic Muslims
in Yugoslavia, 1981**

Bosnia	1,630,033
Serbia proper	151,674
Montenegro	78,080
Kosovo	58,562
Macedonia	39,513
Croatia	23,740
Slovenia	13,425
Vojvodina	4,930

Source: Statistički godišnjak Jugoslavije 1989 (Belgrade: Savezni Zavod za Statistiku, 1989), p. 453.

In the latter half of January 1971, immediately after the census, the Muslim question fueled a dramatic interrepublican confrontation and underlined the fragility of interethnic harmony. Esad Ćimić, a professor at the University of Sarajevo, sparked controversy when, in the course of a program broadcast over Sarajevo television, he opined that Yugoslavia's Muslims were "a national hybrid" and not a nationality, because it was "too late for them to be a people (*narod*) and too early for them to be nation (*nacija*)."[14] Although he did not exclude the possibility that they might have certain characteristic features of nationality, at the same time he questioned whether those who declared themselves "Muslims in a national sense" were in fact doing so under duress.

Shortly thereafter, the executive committee of the Socialist Alliance of Working People of Bosnia-Herzegovina (SAWP B-H) issued a sharp condemnation of Ćimić's opinions. Atif Purivatra, president of SAWP B-H's Commission for Interethnic Relations, said that Ćimić's sentiments were at odds with LCY policy in the area of inter-ethnic relations and denounced the recently touted designation "Bosniak." The label was unacceptable, he said, because it was a denial of specificity and a negation of the Serbian, Croatian, and Muslim national feeling within the Bosnian republic. Nationality, Purivatra went on, cannot be determined only on the basis of the individual's group consciousness, i.e., on the basis of his ethnic self-identification. Accordingly, any suggestion that the Muslims were in some way "second-rate," "incompletely developed," or "immature" was not only demeaning but historically inaccurate.[15]

Though one might argue that Purivatra's comments were in a sense defensive, they incited the Macedonians and ignited a polemical exchange between Macedonia and Bosnia-Herzegovina over the status of the Muslims. The Macedonian party was sensitive to waxing Muslim nationalism because, though the majority of Macedonians are Orthodox—to the extent that Orthodoxy is identified with Macedonianness much as Catholicism is identified with Croatianness, the alleged Orthodoxy of certain pockets of Croats notwithstanding—a certain segment of Macedonian-speaking citizens were, and are, Muslim. The LC Macedonia insisted that "Muslims who speak Macedonian *are* Macedonian" and that they were, as they viewed themselves, "Macedonians of Islamic faith." *Nova Makedonija,* the official organ of the Macedonian communist party, worriedly warned that "the thesis about Muslims of Slavic origin in Macedonia, as parts of a nascent Muslim nation, conceals an immediate threat of the reawakening of an old hegemonism vis-à-vis Macedonian nationality, history, and culture."[16] *Nova Makedonija's* reference to "Muslim hegemonism" naturally rankled the Bosnian party, and polemics ensued between the Macedonian and Bosnian parties, with even the provincial party organization in Kosovo joining in the dispute. This was followed by an article in *Kritika,* in which Vladimir Blašković, a professor of economics at the University of Zagreb, questioned the degree to which the Bosnian Muslims had developed a distinct ethnic consciousness. His skepticism could only signify de facto support for a claim presented by Vječeslav Holjevac that Slavic Muslims are Croats.[17] Shaken by the renewed challenge to the claims of Muslim nationalists, Branko Mikulić, president of the central committee of the LC B-H, nervously warned that such opinions undermined the equal status of the Muslim nationality with the other Yugoslav nationalities and thereby threatened the delicate balance achieved in Bosnia.

The squabble was clearly getting out of hand. Most interesting in all this ruckus was that the position advanced by each republic—whether Bosnia, Macedonia, Croatia, or Kosovo—was the theory most appropriate to its own conditions. Each unit attempted to impose its own theory on the others, even though that theory was only appropriate to its own republic. Bosnia wanted religiocultural heritage accepted as a sufficient basis for national identity. Macedonia wanted to emphasize language and ethnic descent; Croatia, chiefly ethnic descent. Kosovo, finally, with its mixed population of Muslims of Albanian, Turkish, and Macedonian descent, preferred to articulate what superficially appeared to be the most open-minded approach.

Eventually, the Serbian party lent oblique support to the Bosnia-Kosovo coalition when Latinka Perović, secretary of the central committee of the LC Serbia, declared it a matter of LCY policy that all people in Yugoslavia must be free to determine their own ethnic or national affiliation. This vaguely formulated declaration amounted to a reprimand of Macedonia and Croatia and succeeded in bringing this particular episode to a close. Ironically, Professor Ćimić, whose opinions on the subject had sparked the controversy, eventually declared himself a Croat and moved to Zadar.

The Kosovar-Macedonian quarrel over Muslim nationality resurfaced 10 years later in the months preceding the 1981 census, when a Macedonian historian, Nijazi Limanovi, published a 23-installment study, in the Skopje daily *Večer* (25 September–21 October 1980), on "Islamism in Macedonia." He argued that the Albanians of Kosovo were utilizing Islam in a strategy to de-Macedonize Macedonia. Limanovi's conclusion was that there were some 50,000 Muslim

Macedonians in Macedonia who had previously reported themselves to be Albanians, Muslims, or even Serbs, and that, in the forthcoming census, they should declare themselves to be Muslim Macedonians. Ali Hadri, a Kosovar historian, shot back in the Priština daily *Rilindja,* accusing Limanovi of being "maliciously disposed toward the Albanian nation."[18] Hadri remonstrated against Limanovi's attempt to fix the Macedonian label on this group of 50,000 and asserted that, on the contrary, ethnic identity was a matter of individual determination—a right guaranteed by the Yugoslav constitution.

Having emerged victorious both in the 1971 controversy over Macedonian Muslims and in the debate surrounding the 1971 census, Muslim nationalists gained confidence and began to agitate for redesignating Bosnia a "Muslim Republic" in the same way that Serbia was defined, at the time, as the "Republic of the Serbs" and Macedonia as the "Republic of the Macedonians" and presaging the affirmation of Muslim nationalism in the republic two decades later.[19] Under the 1974 constitutional order, however, the Serbian constitution declared that the "Socialist Republic of Serbia is the state of the Serbian nation and of sections of other nations and nationalities who live . . . in it," and Montenegro's constitution allowed that "the Socialist Republic of Montenegro is the state of the Montenegrin nation and of members of other nations and nationalities who live in it"—both thus listing only one titular nationality. But the Bosnian constitution of 1974 asserted that "the Socialist Republic of Bosnia-Herzegovina is a socialist democratic state and a socialist self-managing democratic community of the working people, citizens, and nations of Bosnia-Herzegovina— Muslims, Serbs, and Croats—and of members of other nations and nationalities living in it." Croatia and Macedonia were, for their part, described as "national states" (as opposed to "citizens' states"), while the Socialist Republic of Slovenia was said to be "a state based on the sovereignty of the Slovene nation and the people of Slovenia."[20] The Muslim nationalists wanted the Bosnian constitution to read something like, "the Socialist Republic of Bosnia-Herzegovina is a state based on the sovereignty of the Muslim nation; it is the national state of the Muslim nation, and the state of the members of the Serbian and Croatian nations who live in it, as well as of the members of other nations and nationalities who live in it." The distinction between "national state" and "state" was drawn in the Croatian constitution and implied a somewhat higher status for the possessors of the "national state."

About the same time that agitation for a Muslim republic began, certain Bosnian linguists started toying with the idea that Bosanski, the language of the Muslims, should be recognized as a distinct language.[21] By 1972–1973, the party had concluded that increasing Muslim ethnic consciousness was potentially threatening, and in 1972, two leading Muslim politicians—Avdo Humo and Osman Karabegović—were dismissed from their posts for alleged Muslim "exclusivism" and "nationalism." The following year, 1973, the earliest warnings were sounded about "pan-Islamism" in Bosnia and about Muslim nationalists' aspirations toward "supremacy" in Bosnia.[22] Muslim nationalism, the party admonished, was no special case but was just as "dangerous" as Serbian or Croa-tian nationalism.[23] In a four-part article for *Oslobodjenje* (19–22 February 1974), Aziz Hadžihasanović warned of the misconception that Muslim nation-alism, unlike Serbian and Croatian nationalism, was somehow "naïve, harmless, . . . on another political plane." That was sheer "confusion," charged Hadžihasanović, for Muslim nationalism, even when wearing a "red veil," was a breeding ground for "antisocialist forces."[24] Hadžihasanović also condemned efforts to identify everything positive in Bosnian culture with the Islamic legacy. The Muslim clergy, the *ulema,* had become increasingly active spokesmen for Muslim ethnic interests and had repeatedly sought permission to establish cul-tural institutions to stimulate Muslim communal identity. Even before the cen-sus, *Preporod* (15 June 1970), the official organ of the Islamic community of Bosnia, had complained that "in an organizational sense we still exist only as an Islamic community. Neither as Muslims in the ethnic sense nor as Muslims in the religious sense do we have any specific institutions through which we might develop our Islamic and Muslim activity, other than the existing institutions and organs of the Islamic community."[25] Later, nationally conscious Muslims renewed efforts to found autonomous cultural institutions. Citing the existence of Matica Hrvatska and Matica Srpska, Muslim nationalists demanded the establishment of a Matica Muslimanska and the organization of Muslim cul-tural-artistic societies. But the LCY consistently blocked such endeavors, calling them efforts to obtain a "privileged status" and to establish a power base from which to pursue a policy of "discrimination against the other religions."[26]

In the late 1960s and early 1970s, attendance at Muslim religious services in Yugoslavia seemed to be in decline, and some mosques drew only meager atten-dance. But this situation changed in the late 1970s, when a new generation, edu-cated to think of the Bosnian Muslims as a national group and encouraged by contacts with a renascent Middle East, began to look to Islam as a basis for polit-ical mobilization. In April 1983, Yugoslav authorities became increasingly con-cerned about the whole notion of an ethnic identity rooted primarily in religion and, in April 1983, arrested 11 persons, including two imams, and put them on trial on charges of having criticized Yugoslav nationalities policy as aimed at the Serbianization of the Muslims, plotted to eliminate the Serbian and Croatian populations in Bosnia-Herzegovina, and manipulated the religious feelings of others in an effort to mobilize support for a militant Islam. After a month-long trial, they were ultimately sentenced to prison for terms averaging more than eight years but were amnestied at the end of 1988.[27] Among those sentenced was Alija Izetbegović, whom the authorities had previously incarcerated for Islamic fundamentalism in 1946.[28]

Certain of the Bosnian *ulema* tried to draw a line between "positive political activity" and "negative political activity" on the part of religious organizations and thus to claim for the Islamic community a legitimate role in the political constellation. This has often been combined with a desire to stress that religion is, after all, the source of Muslim "ethnicity." But the LCY, which feared the identification of religion and nationality, wanted to have it both ways: viz., to derive a new nationality from a religion but yet to deny that derivation and suppress demands based on it.

The rising tide of Muslim nationalism in Yugoslavia probably owed more to indigenous factors than to any influence from abroad. The nationalist renaissance of the 1969–1971 period was, in particular, an important stimulus of Muslim nationalism, insofar as Croatian and Serbian calls for the annexation to their respective republics of all or part of Bosnia provided the sort of cultural threat which so quickly inflames ethnic sensitivities. At any event, Muslim nationalism in Yugoslavia predated the worldwide Islamic revival by several years.

It is somewhat ironic that Tito, in one of his last public addresses (25 November 1979), should have claimed that "the nations of Bosnia-Herzegovina can be proud of their successes . . . because they have succeeded in outgrowing mutual conflicts and frictions among nationalities."[29] There was a degree of stability, of course, but all of the nationality groups in Bosnia could imagine other scenarios (e.g., proclamation of a Muslim republic, annexation of Bosnia by Croatia, annexation of Bosnia by Serbia, etc.), one or more of which appeared more palatable to certain people than the status quo. Edvard Kardelj once wrote that "a nation does not arise by chance, and when it does arise, it must doubtless have a social function."[30] As for this functional view of nationality, it might be argued that the Bosnian Muslims served to keep the Croats and Serbs from destroying each other. Such, at least, seemed to be the view of the LCY, even if it feared the growth of rampant nationalism.

Albanian Nationalism in Kosovo

The Albanian striving for republic status (if not for secession) impacted the federation for at least six reasons: (1) it directly affected relations between Kosovo on the one hand and Serbia, Macedonia, and Montenegro on the other (since Kosovo was, for much of the 20th century, dominated by Serbs and since many Albanians had been living in Macedonia and southern Montenegro); (2) Albanian agitation for republic status for Kosovo—the central force for upgrading the autonomous provinces—had an impact on the interrepublican balance of power; (3) the nationalism of one group inevitably had (and has) an incendiary effect on the others; (4) the threat of secession was a matter of concern not merely to the federation as a whole but also to its several parts; (5) Kosovo was the ultimate test of the Titoists' Marxist premise that economic equality causes nationalist temper to abate; and (6) continued Albanian discontent directly challenged the purported legitimacy of the state. The last census taken in the SFRY (1991) recorded the presence of 1,596,072 Albanians in Kosovo and about 427,000 Albanians in western Macedonia. A small group of Albanians could also be found in Montenegro along the frontier with Albania.

As early as May 1945, Djoko Pajković, secretary of the district committee of

Kosmet (as Kosovo was then called) warned that if the communists repeated the error of the interwar kingdom by assigning leadership positions in Kosovo predominantly to Serbs and Montenegrins, the local Albanians would revolt.[31] But this warning fell on deaf ears, and Serbs and Montenegrins were overwhelmingly dominant in the leadership, as well as in the state security forces and the regular police. As of 1956, Serbs accounted for some 23.5% of the province's population but made up 58.3% of the members of the security forces and 60.8% of the regular police. Montenegrins accounted for only 3.9% of the local population, but fully 28.3% of security forces were Montenegrins, alongside 7.9% of regular police. By contrast, Albanians, who already numbered 64.9% of the population, accounted for only 13.3% of security police and 31.3% of regular police.[32]

Tension between Serbs and Albanians in Kosovo ran high in the 1950s, and the provincial police often terrorized the local population. In July 1956, several ethnic Albanians were tried in Prizren on charges of espionage (for Albania) and subversion. They were convicted and given prison terms ranging from 3 to 12 years. In the course of the proceedings, testimony was presented implicating several leading functionaries—specifically, Mehmet Hodža, provincial deputy in the Serbian Assembly; Fadilj Hodža, member of the executive council of Kosovo-Metohija; Seho Hasani, provincial deputy in the Serbian Assembly; Čamilja Šarko, former deputy in the Serbian Assembly; Ismet Saćiri, member of the executive council of Kosovo-Metohija; Dževet Hamža, provincial deputy in the federal Assembly; Avdi Bakalli, former committee secretary; and Saiti Bakalli, functionary of the District People's Committee. All were said to have engaged in espionage for the Albanian secret service. Obviously, testimony to this effect was troubling to local Albanian communists, and already in 1956, the district assembly of Kosmet allegedly decided to collect all the materials and documentation related to the Prizren trial and destroy them. They subsequently declared that the entire affair had been an anti-Albanian machination on the part of the UDBa (the secret police, controlled by Ranković).[33] In fact, far from having sympathies for Enver Hoxha, most of Kosovo's Albanians recoiled at the mere thought of having to live under his rule; indeed, in the four and a half years following Yugoslavia's expulsion from the Cominform, some 6,000 Albanians fled from Albania into Yugoslavia.[34]

Aleksandar Ranković, the head of the secret police, deeply distrusted non-Serbs in general and Albanians in particular. He believed that surveillance was the best method for ruling Kosovo. As early as the winter of 1956, UDBa undertook to confiscate the weapons of the Albanian population of Kosovo—an undertaking which provoked resistance and resulted in the deaths of a number of Albanians before an estimated 9,000 firearms were confiscated.[35] There were some 300 trials of Kosovar Albanians during the period March 1961 to March 1962, on charges of espionage, political diversion, subversion, irredentism, and gunrunning.[36] But the disruption of the political equilibrium in Kosovo is normally traced to 1966, when revelations of Serbian dominance of the governmental, party, and security apparatus in Kosovo inflamed resentment among the Kosovar Albanians.

As late as 1971, 36% of Kosovo's Albanians were officially illiterate. Since statistics failed to distinguish between formal literacy and working literacy, however, the actual level of illiteracy among the Albanians at any given time was much worse than the statistics indicated.[37] There were, furthermore, enduring problems of infrastructure: as late as the 1974–1975 school year, for example, 564 Kosovar towns and villages lacked elementary schools, and many were hampered by the lack of good roads to bus children.

As Ranković's power base eroded and the nature of his practices in Kosovo came to light, the demand for reform became irresistible. The Sixth Session (1966) of the Serbian party's central committee (CC) issued a condemnation of "certain sections of the State Security Apparatus," i.e., Ranković's domain, for discriminatory and illegal practices "entirely contrary to the LCY program and the Yugoslav constitution," especially vis-à-vis the Albanians. The subsequent Fourth Plenum of the CC of the LCY, reviewing conditions in Kosovo, amplified this judgment and warned of Greater Serbian tendencies within the ranks of the League of Communists. The consensus was that Greater Serbian nationalism was a stimulus to Greater Albanian separatism and, therefore, had to be systematically expunged.[38] Albanian separatism was identified as a problem at this time, even though Kosovo had not yet been shaken by ethnic riots.

These conclusions were echoed by the provincial committee of the central committee of the Kosovar branch of the LCY at its Seventh Session of that year. Excoriating "Greater Serbian chauvinistic tendencies," the provincial committee warned that "every nationalism . . . represents a menace to LCY policy. . . . Communists must be alert to the man and active in the struggle against all nationalist deviations."[39] By then, Ranković had slipped from power, and command of the security forces in Kosovo had been turned over to Albanian cadres. Subsequently, the Albanians were also granted permission to celebrate the 500th anniversary of the death of the Albanian national hero Skanderbeg. But Serbs were still far more likely than Albanians to find employment in the party/governmental apparatus, and the Tenth Session of the LC of Kosovo (1967) paid particular attention to the ethnic structure of employment in the province.

In February 1968, those Albanians who had been convicted in the Prizren trial of 1956 were rehabilitated on the grounds that the security apparatus under Ranković had rigged the proceedings, fabricated evidence, and bribed witnesses.[40] On the urging of Kosovar Albanians Mahmut Bakalli and Salih Nuši, the LCY agreed in the spring of 1968 to substitute the neutral term *Albanians* (Albanci) for the term *Shiptar* (Šiptar), which the Albanians considered pejorative, but which had hitherto been standard vocabulary in official as well as unofficial business. In April 1968, Mehmet Hoxha, a hero of the Partisan war, told a session of SAWP-Serbia that if 370,000 Montenegrins were entitled to their own republic, then the 1.2 million Albanians then living in Kosovo were likewise entitled to a republic.

In summer 1968, the Commission for Constitutional Questions met. It consisted of delegates from all the chambers of the federal Skupština. Their meetings were accompanied by public discussions through the country. In Djakovica and Peć, local communists criticized the draft drawn up by the Provincial Committee for Constitutional Questions and demanded that Kosovo be reconstituted as a republic. But this demand was not confined to local committees; it was, in fact, a sentiment shared by many Albanian communists in Kosovo. The Albanian-language daily *Rilindja* reflected this broad sentiment by urging the same thing in an August 1968 editorial. But the provincial party apparatus itself shied away from this and pushed, instead, for an "enrichment" of the prerogatives of the province.[41]

At the plenum of the CC of the LC Serbia, held in early November 1968 (i.e., just before the 1968 Kosovo riots), it was finally proposed that the designations of the party organizations of the autonomous provinces be changed: henceforth, the League of Communists of Serbia for Vojvodina would be simply the League of Communists of Vojvodina, and the League of Communists of Serbia for Kosovo and Metohija would be simply the League of Communists of Kosovo-Metohija. The Sixth Congress of the LC Serbia (mid-November 1968) authorized the provincial party organizations to pass their own statutes. The Albanian component was immediately strengthened in the Kosovar party organization (though it must be admitted that Albanians and Hungarians were still significantly underrepresented in the respective party organizations of Kosovo and Vojvodina).

There were signs of steady deterioration in Serbian-Albanian relations as 1967 drew on, including sporadic eruptions of inter-ethnic violence.[42] By October 1968, reports surfaced of anti-Serbian demonstrations in Suva Reka, Prizren, and Peć. Participants were said to number only a "couple of hundred," and officials tried to peg the blame on "foreign [i.e., Albanian] intelligence services."[43] Officials failed to assuage Albanian discontent, and tension mounted. On 27 November, the eve of Albanian National Independence Day, Kosovar Liberation Day, and the anniversary of the proclamation of the Yugoslav federal state—all celebrated, by an ironic twist of fate, on 29 November—"Kosmet" (Kosovo-Metonija) exploded in violence. Demonstrators numbering in the hundreds smashed windows and overturned cars in Priština, and the anti-Serbian demonstrations quickly spread to other towns in Kosovo, leaving 37 injured (among them, 13 police) and one dead. There were reports that some rioters demanded annexation by Albania and that riotous crowds could be heard chanting "Long live Enver Hoxha!"[44] The protestors drew up a list of demands which included dropping "Metohija" (a Serbian word) from the official name of the region, its redesignation as a republic, the extension of the right of self-determination to Kosovo (the right of a republic but not of an autonomous province), and the establishment of an independent university in Priština. At the same time, the disturbances spread to the Macedonian cities of Gostivar and Tetovo, both with large Albanian populations.

The League of Communists responded swiftly and decisively. The ringleaders of the apparently well-organized demonstrations received jail terms of up to five years, and those held chiefly responsible for the unrest in Macedonia received sentences of up to seven years. Another 44 persons in Kosovo received jail terms of up to 30 days. By mid-March, moreover, at least 52 LCY members had been expelled from the party for participation in or support of the demonstrations (27 in Macedonia, 25 in Kosovo).[45] In the "postmortem" analysis which followed these disturbances, Veli Deva, president of the party Regional Committee of Kosovo, admitted that there were discontents among both Albanian and Slavic inhabitants of Kosmet, while Latinka Perović, the newly elected secretary of the LC Serbia, agreed with a pre-disturbance report by Deva which had linked inter-ethnic problems with economic dissatisfaction.[46]

The federal government was not prepared to indulge in the partition of Serbia; nevertheless, ameliorative measures had to be taken. The demand for republic status was flatly turned down. But Kosovo and Vojvodina were granted some of the prerogatives of republics, and the modifier "socialist" was appended to their official designations (hence, the Socialist Autonomous Province of Kosovo). In December, in another concession to the Albanians, Kosovo-Metohija was redesignated simply Kosovo, dropping the purely Serbian "Metohija," and the Kosovars were also granted permission to fly the Albanian flag beneath the Yugoslav one. Furthermore, even while jailing 30 of the leading Albanian agitators for extended periods, Belgrade took steps to improve the economic situation in Kosovo and to promote more Albanians to positions of authority. In 1969, Kosovo was granted a new "Constitutional Law" which, inter alia, authorized the provincial Assembly to draft and pass laws (instead of the "decrees" which it had previously been authorized to issue *on the basis of Serbian laws)* and created the Supreme Court of Kosovo (thus granting the province a prerogative which Vojvodina had enjoyed since the adoption of the 1946 constitution).[47] Finally, there followed the creation of an independent University of Priština in 1969 and the rapid Albanianization of both faculty and student body in what had hitherto been a branch of the University of Belgrade.

Although this poured oil on the waters of discontent and eased federal regime–Albanian minority relations, Serbian-Albanian relations within Kosovo remained tense. For the Serbs, the demographic threat in Kosovo had long seemed poignant, mainly because the Serbs thought of Kosovo as the heart of the medieval Serbian kingdom. It was, moreover, at Kosovo Polje (the Field of the Blackbirds) that the Serbian Army of Tsar Lazar clashed with Ottoman forces in 1389, and the battlefield has retained great patriotic value for the Serbs. The region, however, was and is overwhelmingly inhabited by Albanians, who had by far the highest birth rate of all of Yugoslavia's peoples. As a result of the turmoil, moreover, Albanian and Serbian neighbors became openly hostile, and the university polarized along ethnic lines: the result—as revealed in March 1969—was that thousands of Serbs and Montenegrins streamed out of Kosovo, most of them professionals and specialists with higher education. Even the dead were not immune to the ethnic hatred, as Albanians broke up Serbian and Montenegrin gravestones in Kosovo. Meanwhile, relations between Albanians and Macedonians remained tense, as the first of some 100 accused instigators was sentenced to seven years at hard labor on 15 March 1969.

Obviously, the Kosovo question remained—and, at this writing, still remains—unresolved. It is worth noting, at the same time, that recurrent problems in Kosovo have manifested some of the same characteristics which marked the Croatian crisis. First, there were instances of anomic and collective violence manifested in the demonstrations of 1968, the mutual incitement of the two national groups, and the Serbian exodus itself. Second, there was strong evidence that members of the local nationality were not prepared to organize in defense of their aspirations: in 1975, for example, four Yugoslav citizens of Albanian nationality were imprisoned for plotting the secession of Kosovo and its attachment to Albania.[48] Third, conflict in Kosovo, as in Croatia, was transmuted to the elite level: thus, at the Twenty-ninth Plenum of the Kosovo party organization in June 1971, Serbs and Montenegrins exchanged broadsides with Albanian delegates over questions of rights for the Serbian minority in Kosovo and alleged separatist plots. Finally, the Kosovo case exemplifies conflict accommodation as it was practiced in communist Yugoslavia: jail the troublemakers but grant their nondisintegrative demands.

Albanian gains in Kosovo, though modest, excited a Serbian backlash. Serbs became apprehensive at Albanian inroads, dreaded the transfer of any property from Serb to Albanian, and agitatedly spoke of "losing" Kosovo. Shortly after the 1971 census, a number of periodicals began to question the validity of the Kosovo count and to spread the idea that Albanians there had pressured the indigenous Slavs to declare themselves Albanians. Stane Stanić, writing in the Belgrade weekly *NIN* in August 1971, followed this tack, adding that the Albanians were also exerting unrelenting pressure on Serbian and Montenegrin inhabitants to leave Kosovo. Stanić concluded that the census results were unreliable, and that the Slavic proportion had been seriously underestimated.[49] As the Albanian component of the central committee of the LC Kosovo edged upward from 61.7% (in 1973) to 62.5% (in 1974) and the Albanians registered small gains in governmental employment, local Serbs clamored that the status quo in Kosovar employment and political representation was entirely satisfactory and opposed any further changes in the ethnic structure of the civil service in Kosovo. Yet the Albanians tallied some 73.7% of the province's population in 1971—they accounted for 77.5% in 1981—and they were demanding equivalent representation.[50]

Nebi Gasi, chair of Kosovo's Commission for Interethnic Relations, told a Belgrade audience in 1977 that although 8% of the Albanians in Kosovo had jobs in the social sector, 17% of the Serbs and 20% of the Montenegrins in Kosovo were employed in the social sector. This reflected the fact that of the 128,000 Kosovars employed in the social sector at the end of 1974, 58.2% were

Albanians, 31% were Serbs, 5.7% were Montenegrins, and 5% were members of other nationality groups.[51] By 1978, however, Albanians accounted for 83% of Kosovars employed in the social sector, with Serbs numbering only 9.3%. By 1980, Albanians constituted fully 92% of those employed in the social sector, with Serbs dramatically underrepresented at a mere 5%.[52]

During the 1970–1971 period, when political controls were loosened, chauvinist outbursts became more frequent and more open, in Kosovo as elsewhere. The Istok region of Kosovo was identified at this time as a particular trouble spot. With anti-Serbian sentiment sweeping through Croatia and Kosovo, Mujo Krasnići, a Kosovar student, told a receptive Croatian audience in Zagreb that the Albanians were the "original" Kosovars, that the Slavs were "guests," and that the people of Kosovo wanted their own socialist republic.[53] In mid-December 1971, at the same time as Croatian students at the University of Zagreb were bringing matters in Croatia to a head, Albanian students clashed with Slavic students (mostly Serbian and Macedonian) at the University of Priština. In a stormy session of the provincial committee of the LC Kosovo, committee member Jovo Sotra observed that Albanian separatist nationalism was the principal source of instability in the province.[54]

Inter-ethnic tension remained high in Kosovo over the years, and distrust between the Slavs and the local Albanians ran deep, even before Milošević set in motion a series of harsh policies in the winter of 1988–1989. Indeed, the heavily Albanianized security forces enjoyed only a brief respite between 1969 and 1973, when Albanian separatists launched their first large-scale propaganda offensive since the demonstrations of November 1968. Yugoslav security forces discovered evidence of an underground separatist organization known as the Revolutionary Movement of United Albania, led by Adem Demaĉi, but were unable to uproot it. This group, together with the so-called Marxist-Leninist Communist Party of Albanians of Yugoslavia, which may have enjoyed Albania's support, undertook what the regime labeled "serious propaganda actions" in 1973–1975. The group called for the secession of Kosovo and those parts of Macedonia and Montenegro inhabited by Albanians and the creation of a Greater Albania which would have been specifically anti-Serbian in orientation. This "Marxist-Leninist" party was apparently uncovered by Yugoslav security organs in early 1975. Another underground group, similar in nature and dubbed the National Liberation Movement of Kosovo, was discovered shortly thereafter. Two of its leading members, both students at the University of Priština and both in their mid-20s, were given lengthy prison sentences. Five more groups, operating in Priština and Uroševac, were discovered in the course of 1979 and 1980. Security organs turned up still another such group early in 1981, which, according to Franjo Herljević, minister of internal affairs, had been operating in conjunction with the pro-Albanian "Red Front" organization.[55]

There were reports of student demonstrations in Priština in December 1974 in which more than 100 ethnic Albanians were said to have been arrested. There were other telltale signs of trouble in the 1970s. In fact, between 1974 and the beginning of 1981, the state security service arrested more than 600 Kosovars for Albanian separatism.[56]

At the same time, organized Albanian separatism was spreading to neighboring Macedonia, where Yugoslav security organs reportedly uncovered and suppressed two illegal Albanian separatist organizations between 1978 and 1981. The situation was complicated by another factor, however. The increasingly Albanian-dominated provincial leadership in Kosovo was loath to allow Serbian involvement in anti-separatist efforts, partly because of a natural sympathy with the province's Albanian population and partly because of a fear that the problems might incite the leadership of the Serbian republic to retract some of the political powers which the Kosovar party had—sometimes unconstitutionally—acquired. The provincial leadership engaged in a massive cover-up, the scale of which was appreciated only after the province erupted in violence in the spring of 1981. Certainly, the LCY was well aware that trouble was brewing in Kosovo. The arrests of several hundred Albanian nationalists in 1979, on charges of distributing subversive material, and a telltale eruption of ethnic turmoil in Kosovo in May 1980 were powerful reminders that the festering discontent retained political significance. State security organs were placed in a state of alert in the months following Tito's demise. As early as 1977, in fact, Kardelj had warned his colleagues that if the party failed to adopt a resolute policy which would narrow the economic gap and tranquilize inter-ethnic tensions in the province, Kosovo would explode in violence. But Belgrade had only sketchy information about the Albanian separatist movement; the Kosovar ministry of the interior, which was well informed about the strength and doings of at least some of the underground organizations, was withholding its intelligence from the capital.[57] Thus, although Albanian-language *Rilindja* warned (in 1975) of persistent problems with Albanian separatist groups, the Kosovar leadership, when dealing with the Belgrade media, was far less open.[58] In 1975, for instance, Mahmut Bakalli told a Tanjug reporter that inter-ethnic relations in Kosovo were "good, because there is a good degree of brotherhood and unity and of trust between nations and nationalities living here."[59] Again, in 1980, Bakalli, the leading Kosovar politician at the time, would tell *Politika* that "the efforts of enemies have not found wide support among the Albanian masses . . . [which] shows that the devotion of the Albanians to Tito's Yugoslavia is durable and indestructible."[60]

But the information problem involved not merely the Serbia-Kosovo relationship; it was, in fact, also an internal problem within Kosovo itself. As Živorad Igić noted in an article which appeared in *Obeležja*, the Kosovar party theoretical organ, in 1979, the district committees in the province were routinely withholding information from the provincial committee. In addition, the growing tendency to publish internal information in Kosovo in Albanian only tended to leave local Serbs ignorant of important aspects of basic issues.[61]

In February 1981, on the eve of a new eruption of ethnically inspired tumult, both *Komunist* and *Politika* warned of simmering discontent in the province, the latter adding that "antisocialist forces" continued to organize hostile provocations in various parts of Kosovo.[62] In spite of this, and in spite of the evident latent instability in the province, few observers were prepared for the vehemence of the nationalistically colored riots which shook the province in March and April 1981. In fact, when some 2,000 Albanian students at the University of Priština went on a rampage on 11 March, officials initially denied any ethnic link and claimed that the riot had been sparked by dissatisfaction with bad cooking in the university cafeteria. The mere fact that the riots lasted two days, producing 13 injuries, suggested that more than bad food was involved.[63]

Further demonstrations by Prizren students on 25 March and by University of Priština students on 26 March resulted in 35 injuries (23 demonstrators and 12 police) and 21 arrests. Demonstrations followed in Obilić on 31 March. Subsequently, on 1 April, violent riots broke out at the University of Priština (whose full-time student body numbered 37,000 at the time). Beginning with marauding protesters who smashed factory equipment and shop windows and set trucks on fire, tensions quickly escalated into open street battles, in which some rioters used kindergarten-aged children as shields against police.[64] Miners from the nearby coal mine and workers from the electric power station in the neighboring town of Obilić joined the students as disorder spread to Podujevo, Leposlavic, Vučiturn, Vitina, and Glogovac. By 3 April, the strife had spread to Kosovska Mitrovica and Uroševac. Hardly any municipality in Kosovo abstained from the violence. Many of the demonstrators—said to have numbered between 10,000 and 20,000—were armed, and in the ensuing clashes with the riot police, perhaps as many as 1,000 persons were killed and about 1,000 persons injured, many of them by firearms.[65] The revolutionary overtones of the Albanian riots were unmistakable. Rioters demanded either republican status for Kosovo or outright secession. In the official viewpoint, these amounted to the same thing.[66] The regime rushed in tanks and armored personnel carriers, imposed a curfew throughout the province, cut off telephone connections with the rest of Yugoslavia, and established control points on all roads into Priština. Commandos and soldiers armed with machine guns moved in to patrol the streets, and helicopters hovered overhead. Some two dozen ringleaders were incarcerated immediately, and a state of emergency was declared.[67] On 5 April, Priština's factories were reopened, though a ban on public meetings remained in effect. Only on 8 April did the Yugoslav authorities finally lift the nighttime curfew.

But pacification failed, as local Albanians continued to scrawl anti-Serbian and anti-Yugoslav graffiti on public walls, to distribute insurrectionary pamphlets, and to disrupt instruction in schools. Trains were derailed, and the power station in Kosovo Polje, the furniture factory in Uroševac, and numerous other installations and buildings suffered varying degrees of damage in a rash of unexplained fires. Further strife flared up in Istok on the night of 30 April and at the University of Priština on 12 May.[68] Eventually, the schools, closed once and reopened two weeks later, were closed for a second time, and the school year was declared over. *Borba* openly asked why the University of Priština had been encouraged to grow so large, when it was inconceivable that its graduates could find jobs commensurate with their training and ambitions. Meanwhile, the unrest spread to Montenegro, where *Borba* reported the perpetration of "incidents" by the local Albanian minority in the capital city of Titograd and the scrawling of anti-Tito slogans on shop windows. In January 1982, it was revealed that Albanian nationalists were active in the Bar commune.[69]

In Macedonia, which had endured prolonged Albanian unrest 13 years earlier, there were initially no hints of turmoil. Officials did charge, however, that Albanian nationalists, including Muslim clergy of Albanian extraction, had exerted pressure on Macedonian Roma and Turks and on Muslim Macedonians, during the census taken early that year, to declare themselves Albanians.[70] The apparent calm notwithstanding, the Macedonian security apparatus was put on high alert. By the end of May, reports surfaced that local Albanians were distributing insurrectionary and irredentist literature, writing revolutionary slogans in public places, and engaging in various acts of desecration. These activities, which were especially serious in the Ohrid and Tetovo districts, prompted Yugoslav authorities to tighten security in Tetovo and the surrounding area in early July. By mid-July, manifestations of Albanian nationalism in the Tetovo region were said to be escalating. Skopje was rocked by "organized enemy manifestations" involving ethnic Albanians early in July. Moreover, hostile Albanian activities, such as sloganeering, were still reported in the Tetovo region in late August.[71] Even Serbia-proper had problems, with Albanian nationalists making their presence felt in the communes of Bujanovac, Preševo, and Medvedja in southern Serbia.[72]

Arson, sabotage, terrorism, and pamphleteering became, overnight, a way of life in Kosovo. Some 680 fires, attributed to arson, caused damage estimated at 70 million dinars between 1980 and 1981.[73] There were again violent demonstrations in July 1981 in Djakovica, in January 1982 at the University of Priština, in February and March 1982 in Priština and Suva Reka, and in April 1982 in Uroševac. Three bombs were set off in downtown Priština between October and November 1982, the third exploding in the immediate vicinity of the headquarters of the party provincial committee. Hundreds of demonstrators clashed with security police in the February and March riots, leaving numerous injured. As 1982 drew to a close, the situation was still said to be "deteriorating," with the authorities unable to guarantee public safety or the security of property.[74]

Mahmut Bakalli resigned his post as provincial party chief, admitting to the futility of past policy in Kosovo and confessing that he had attempted to sweep problems under the rug. In April 1983, he was belatedly expelled from the party. By late July 1982, some 1,000 LCK members had been expelled from the party, at least some for having participated in the 1981 riots. Several basic organizations of the LCK were simply dissolved outright. More than 700 Albanians had, by this time, been put behind bars.[75] Even the party-controlled press had proven unreliable. The 1 April issue of *Fjalja,* an Albanian-language periodical, was suppressed for nationalistically provocative material, and *Obeležja* itself, the Kosovar party's Serbo-Croatian theoretical journal, was said to be treading a fine line.[76] Yet resistance to Belgrade's policy ran so deep that, even two years later, at a session on 6 June 1983, the Provincial Committee for Information revealed that the reportage in the province's Albanian-language daily, *Rilindja,* regularly differed from that in its Serbo-Croatian daily, *Jedinstvo.* Specifically, *Rilindja* was said to be allowing "alien positions" to infiltrate its pages.[77]

The LCY Central Committee convened on 7 May and reprimanded the Kosovar party organization for serious "weaknesses."[78] A series of purges followed. Among those dismissed were Mahmut Bakalli (he subsequently resigned his membership in the CC LC Serbia and was replaced as president of the Kosovo party's provincial committee by his predecessor, Veli Deva); assembly president Dušan Ristić (replaced by Ilija Vakić); SAP (Socialist Autonomous Province) premier Bahri Orući; Priština television station director Fahredin Ginga; Radio Priština director Šaban Hiseni; University of Priština rector Gazmend Zajmi; and both the secretary for internal affairs (Mustafa Šefedini) and the undersecretary for internal affairs (Ismail Bajrami). Six of the 19 members of the provincial committee presidium were expelled. Three persons were dropped from the executive council. The editors of the radio and television stations in Priština were fired, as were more than 200 faculty members at the University of Priština.[79]

A state of siege prevailed in the province, with 30,000 troops and police— many of them sent from Croatia and Slovenia—patrolling the province. All incoming and outgoing traffic was scrupulously checked, and the movement of outsiders into the province was largely proscribed. Belgrade hastened to ban textbooks imported from Albania, which were now discovered to have incendiary overtones, and undertook to translate the more "reliable" Serbian textbooks into Albanian for the use of Kosovo's Albanian students.[80] Party spokespersons also began to express misgivings about the radical devolution of authority to the autonomous provinces, arguing that they should coordinate their policies more closely with the Serbian republic and that some of the prerogatives they enjoyed in practice had no constitutional basis. Understandably, members of the Vojvodinan party, uncompromised in this debate, expressed strong opposition to suggestions that the prerogatives of the autonomous provinces be curtailed.[81]

The 1981 riots were a rude awakening insofar as they signified the repudiation of more than 10 years of intense efforts to accelerate development in this economically backward region. They bore witness to the depth of local discontent and demonstrated the primacy of ethnic community in conditions of unequal deprivation. That the rioters had shown some separatist sympathies certainly troubled Belgrade. Rumors circulated, moreover, that at least some of the Albanian separatist groups had formed guerrilla units in the backcountry of Kosovo—an allegation quickly denied by Yugoslav authorities and evidently without foundation.[82]

The incipient revolt in Kosovo drove additional Kosovar Montenegrins and Serbs out of Kosovo, sparked a nationalist backlash among Macedonians and Serbs, and triggered the proliferation of nationalist excesses throughout the other seven federal units.

The 1981 census had already shown an absolute decline in the Serbian and Montenegrin populations of Kosovo, even as the Albanians threatened to over-take the Slovenes as Yugoslavia's fourth largest nation (see Table 10.3). There were 18,172 fewer Serbs in 1981 than in 1971, while the number of Montene-grins decreased by 4,680. As a result of the post-April turmoil, in which Alban-ian residents frequently "targeted" local Slavs, there was a renewed exodus of Serbs and Montenegrins from Kosovo. By one estimate, some 10,000 Serbs and Montenegrins left Kosovo between April and the end of October 1981.[83] Most of the out-migrants fled to Serbia, often to Belgrade, bearing tales of Albanian excesses.

This exodus only served to reinforce a Serbian nationalist backlash, aggra-vating a problem to which the party had to devote increased attention in subse-

Table 10.3. Population of Yugoslavia by Nationality Group, 1981

Nationality	Number	Percent
Serbs	8,136,578	36.3
Croats	4,428,135	19.7
Muslims	2,000,034	8.9
Slovenes	1,753,605	7.8
Albanians	1,731,252	7.7
Macedonians	1,341,420	6.0
"Yugoslavs"	1,216,463	5.4
Montenegrins	577,298	2.6
Hungarians	426,865	1.9
Roma/Gypsies	148,604	0.7
Turks	101,328	0.5
Slovaks	80,300	0.4
Romanians	54,721	0.2
Bulgarians	36,642	0.2
Vlahs	32,071	0.1
Ruthenes	23,320	0.1
Czechs	19,609	0.1
Italians	15,116	0.1
Ukrainians	12,716	0.1
Undeclared	46,716	0.2
TOTAL (including other categories not listed above)	22,418,331	100.0

Source: Statistički kalendar Jugoslavije 1982 (Belgrade: Savezni zavod za statistiku, February 1982), p. 37.

quent years. It was just three years earlier, at the Fifteenth Session of the CC of the LC Serbia (19 April 1978) that various speakers inveighed against a renaissance of Serbian ethnocentric chauvinism. Incensed by the anti-Serbian edge to these latest Albanian riots, Serbs began to speak openly of the "good old days" when Ranković had been in charge of the security apparatus and claimed that it was time to put the Albanians of Kosovo in their place once and for all. Indeed, Ranković became, overnight, a hero of Serbs. Simultaneously, Serbs and Macedonians began boycotting Albanian shops and bakeries, cutting sales, in some cases, by as much as 85%.[84] There were even demands by Serbs that the autonomous province of Kosovo be abolished altogether—an alternative which party officials quickly labeled "unacceptable." A similar syndrome developed in Macedonia, where Macedonians started ostracizing Albanian neighbors, acquaintances, and former friends. At the same time, the Albanians of Kosovo found considerable sympathy among the Hungarians of Vojvodina.[85]

Throughout the 1980s, various underground organizations of Albanians were uncovered in Kosovo, and their members were prosecuted.[86] Between April 1981 and September 1987, criminal charges were brought against 5,200 Kosovar Albanians, according to official figures. In the Yugoslav Army alone, some 216 illegal organizations were discovered in those years, with some 1,435 members of Albanian nationality.[87] Some 1,800 (1,600 of them Albanians) were expelled from the Kosovo party organization. And in June 1987, the LCY Central Committee convened a special two-day session to review the situation in Kosovo, describing it as "the most difficult crisis in the history of new Yugoslavia."[88] The session devoted special attention to the out-migration of Serbs and Montenegrins from the province, which had already reduced the Slavic population in the province by 22,000. By September 1988, this figure would reach 30,000.[89] The session concluded that LCY policy until then had been essentially nugatory and gave impetus to discussions about how to halt the out-migration of Serbs and Montenegrins from Kosovo. In November 1987, a program was agreed upon to deal with that issue.[90]

The Belgrade media (especially television and periodicals such as *Duga* and *Reporter*) began to give play to stories about Albanian atrocities against Serbs. Meanwhile, the Serbs who had left Kosovo, including some who had left for economic reasons, began to talk of their own alleged sufferings and to demand special benefits in Kosovo in terms of housing and job placement. By 1986, Serbia (especially Belgrade) was aflame with nationalism. Overnight it became fashionable for Serbs to proclaim their devotion to the Serbian Orthodox Church, which presented itself as the guardian of the Serbian people and culture.[91]

In October 1986, members of the Serbian Academy of Sciences and Art drew up a 70-page "Memorandum" bewailing Serbia's fate in communist Yugoslavia and accusing Tito and Kardelj of having conspired to "destroy Serbia." Vuk Drašković, a Serbian novelist who would found a Serbian nationalist party three years later, addressed an appeal to the Association of Hebrew Writers in Tel-Aviv, proposing a "blood brotherhood" between Serbs and Jews. In Drašković's view, "We Serbs are a lost unhappy tribe of Israel."[92] Eight months later, the Serbian Association of Writers issued its own appeal, accusing responsible government organs of covering up the true situation in Kosovo and of ignoring the plight of local Serbs.[93] Serbs complained that Albanians dominated various sectors of Kosovar society, such as Priština television, and the press became awash with poems devoted to the sufferings of Serbs in Kosovo.[94] While Kosovar Albanians continued to demand republic status, Serbs began to talk increasingly of the need to whittle down the prerogatives of the provincial party apparatus.

As long as Ivan Stambolić headed the Serbian party apparatus, little was done to change the situation in Kosovo in any direction, and party organs repeated vapid and vacuous phrases about the situation improving and being under control. But in late 1987, Stambolić was ousted by his erstwhile understudy, Slobodan Milošević, and the entire political picture changed overnight. (Slobodan Milošević's rise to power is discussed in more detail in chapter 12.) Milošević's adherents were angered by the steady decline in the number of Serbs and Montenegrins in the province. In 1953, these two groups combined had accounted for some 27.9% of the provincial population. This figure had steadily dropped— to 20.9% in 1971, 14.9% in 1981, and finally to 10% in 1987.[95]

Having told the Yugoslav public for years that the situation in Kosovo was being normalized, the Serbian party, now controlled by unabashed nationalists, announced that, in fact, the complete opposite was the case. Thus, Petar Gračanin, president of the Serbian presidency, declared at a joint session of the Serbian presidency and the Serbian LC central committee presidium in September 1988,

In all essential respects the political and security situation in Kosovo is getting significantly worse. In the past month, since the 16th LCY central committee plenum, several incidents have occurred which constitute an extremely serious warning about the negative tendencies of the continuing aggressive activity of Albanian nationalism and separatism which, if it is not ended urgently and in a radical way, will have wider and tragic consequences.[96]

The new Serbian leadership staged large-scale "spontaneous" demonstrations by Serbs and Montenegrins, to which the Albanians replied with equally large demonstrations. On 18 November 1988, in particular, some 100,000 ethnic Albanians marched through Priština in what was described as the biggest protest by Albanians in Kosovo since 1981.[97] Shortly after that protest, provincial officials in Kosovo banned any further public meetings in a vain effort to contain overt expressions of discontent.

As we shall see in chapter 12, tensions in Kosovo provided the grist for Milovević's rise to power in Serbia, provoked a dramatic showdown between Slovenia and Serbia over the place of the autonomous provinces in the federation, provided the backdrop for a general deterioration in relations between Serbia and the other republics, and fueled rising Serbian nationalism, which in turn infected Serbs in Croatia, leading to renewed difficulties in Croatia. These tensions also reflected the fact that, as far as both Albanians and Serbs were concerned, neither the purposes nor the policies of the regime in Kosovo were legitimate.

The Croatian Question

The purge of the Zagreb troika and the closing of Matica Hrvatska could not liquidate Croatian nationalism: it only drove it underground. The Croatian press again became, at least until the last year of Tito's reign, relatively timid about such sensitive questions as the interests of the republic and the nature of Croatian nationalism. The charismatic and popular leaders were purged and driven out of politics. They were replaced by mediocre, if pragmatic, bureaucrats who were unpopular with the people. Only one institution was available to champion Croatian national interests until 1989—the Croatian Catholic Church. Whatever it might do to Matica Hrvatska, the regime dared not suppress the Church.

According to Šime Djodan, thousands of Croats were punished in one way or another. He estimates that 50,000 members of the LC Croatia lost their party cards, 12,000 enterprise directors and engineers were fired, 2,000–5,000 persons were imprisoned, 50,000 students were identified as "class enemies" and thus had a permanent blemish entered on their records which would obstruct career advancement. In addition, 270 partisan officers were expelled from the party or punished in other ways, 18 generals were punished, and 14 national heroes (including some of the aforementioned generals) were likewise punished. These sweeping penalties sowed deep bitterness among Croats. When I met Djodan in 1989, he drew attention to the fact that shortly after the purge of the Croatian liberals, Tito was decorated, by Moscow, with the Order of Lenin.[98]

Of those Croats who received prison sentences, many were brought to Stara Gradiška, an antiquated prison known for its poor conditions and callous treatment of prisoners. Among its inmates were Croatian economists Marko Veselica and Šime Djodan, who became so seriously ill while in prison that they were finally released: they were not, however, able to find work for some time (in Djodan's case, until 1982). Neither they nor Franjo Tudjman, a Croatian historian who had earned a Ph.D. at the Zadar branch of the University of Zagreb, who was sentenced to a two-year prison term in 1972, and who was likewise unemployed, was allowed to publish in Yugoslavia. *Vjesnik* reported that some 5,806 indictments for political crimes were handed down between January 1972 and March 1973; 44% of these involved Croats, though their republic represented only 21% of the total Yugoslav population. Bosnia, with 19% of the Yugoslav population, accounted nonetheless for another 27% of these indictments, and many of those were no doubt Bosnian Croats.[99] Party conservatives quickly quashed almost all the forums in which the nationalists had been able to publish their views, including *Tlo, Kolo, Kritika, Hrvatski književni list,* and *Stu-*

dentski list. The prestigious Croatian magazine *Encyclopaedia Moderna,* however, which was somewhat independent in its editorial policy, continued to be published until 1974, allowing articles of liberal inspiration into its pages.

Deprived of any input into the politics of the society, nationalistically inclined Croats often "dropped out" altogether, adopting a forced apathy. In the rural regions of Croatia, anti-Serbian feelings became more intense than ever, and certain towns, particularly Zadar, were said to display a defiant mood.[100] Fifteen Croats—among them three professors, a building technician, and a "distinguished member" of the Communist Party—were taken into custody in July 1974. After three months of interrogation, a four-month trial ensued in which the 15, together with Pavle Perović, a 22-year-old philosophy student who had managed to escape to West Germany, were accused of having organized a terrorist organization known as the Hrvatska Oslobodilačka Revolucionarna Armija (Croatian Liberation Revolutionary Army). Perović denied that there had been any such organization or that the group had any armaments whatsoever but admitted that he and the other defendants were Croatian nationalists. Another 15 Zagrebers were brought to trial in 1976 for allegedly having planned to assassinate President Tito. The 15 appealed their convictions, and in the retrials, two of the accused complained of having been tortured and harassed by the police while in custody. In the end, the court reduced their sentences to 15 years at hard labor.

Rumored attempts to rehabilitate the fallen troika and reinstate its members in the party inevitably failed, and the expression of sympathy for their program remained totally taboo. One Croatian farmer, Josip Cesarec, who ignored this taboo and praised the troika in public, was said to have been given a four-year prison term in 1980. After Tito's passing, some thought it might be possible to obtain a certain degree of liberalization, and, accordingly, in a petition sent to the federal Skupština and to the party presidium, 45 Croatian intellectuals sought a general amnesty for all political prisoners. The petition, drawn up and submitted in November 1980, was signed, among others, by the former rector of Zagreb University, Ivan Supek, by novelists Vlado Gotovac (restricted to Zagreb for having spread "hostile propaganda") and Zlatko Tomičić, by former partisan colonel Franjo Tudjman (who had risen to the rank of major-general after the war), and by bygone student leaders.[101]

Temporarily freed from jail, Gotovac told a foreign journalist in 1978, "We could be put in jail again at any moment, under any pretense, although we have not done anything."[102] By the end of 1980, both Gotovac and Tudjman were once again taken to court. The charge this time was spreading anti-Yugoslav propaganda, specifically by complaining, in interviews given to Western correspondents over the years 1977–1980, that the Croatian people continued to be politically, economically, and culturally oppressed in socialist Yugoslavia. Tudjman had gone so far as to provide Peter Miroshnikoff, a correspondent for ARD (a German news agency), with up-to-date statistics showing that the Serbs continued to dominate both the Croatian Communist Party and the officer corps of the JNA within Croatia. The timing of their arrest may have had more to do with Tito's disappearance from the scene than with these interviews, however. Reportedly, Planinc and other Croatian conservatives had wanted to put Tudjman on trial after the quashing of the liberal troika, using a script which would have cast Tudjman as the "mastermind" behind the Croatian Spring, but Tito had vetoed this scenario.[103] Now that Tito was dead, the conservatives dusted off the decade-old script, "updating" it with references to Tudjman's (and Gotovac's) more recent activities.[104] Tudjman's claim that Serbs were disproportionately overrepresented in the Croatian party and in the officers corps, however, was not disputed; *NIN*, in fact, admitted in 1980 that Serbs constituted 24% of the Croatian party and a majority of the Croatian police force, even though only 14% of Croatia's inhabitants were Serbs at that time.[105] On 20 February 1981, Tudjman was found guilty of having engaged in hostile propaganda and sentenced to three years in prison. He was released early, after having served almost two years, because of illness.[106] Gotovac and former student leader Dobroslav Paraga, also identified with the Croatian mass movement, went to prison for "anti-state activity," and the sickly Marko Veselica, arrested in the early spring of 1981, likewise charged with spreading hostile propaganda, eventually received a sentence of 11 years' imprisonment.[107]

There was a certain irony in the fact that, having repudiated the Novi Sad agreement and having produced a separate Croatian orthography in the early 1970s, the Croats should have been forced subsequently to accept a new orthography based on the defunct Novi Sad agreement. This new Croatian orthography, the work of Vladimir Anić and Josip Silić, appeared in mid-1980. Work had begun on the project in 1976, on assignment from the Croatian Commission for Language Questions. In an interview with *NIN*, Anić admitted that because the language of the Croats, Serbs, Muslims, and Montenegrins was a single language, he and his collaborators had consulted the incomplete Novi Sad orthography whenever possible.[108]

As a result of the purge of the Croatian liberals and the suppression of Matica Hrvatska, the Catholic Church became the leading advocate of disaffected Croats, a role not altogether different from that acquired by the Church in Poland. Several, if not most, of the Croatian upper clergy sympathized with all the traditional Croatian nationalist desiderata.[109] Tellingly, although the Belgrade regime asked the Vatican and Croatian bishops to condemn the terrorist attacks being carried out by Croatian exile groups in the years 1968–1972, no ecclesiastical leader ever issued a public condemnation of the terrorism.[110] But the Church was prepared to defend the human rights of local citizens. Specifically, Archbishop Franjo Kuharić of Zagreb openly took up Paraga's cause in his Christmas sermon in 1980.[111] Later, Jožo Zovko, the parish priest of Medjugorje in Herzegovina, went to prison for three and a half years, after telling his parishioners that they had been "enslaved for forty years" and that it was time to "remove the chains, [and] untie the knots."[112] Not sporadic misdemeanors on the part of isolated clergymen, however, but systematic Church insistence on the legitimacy of its public role disquieted the LCY since it did not recognize the legitimacy of such a role for the Church. "A depoliticized Church does not bother the state," wrote Todo Kurtović, the chair of SAWPY in 1978, "but the identification of religion and nationality in our conditions is sheer politicization—it is an undiluted clerical act. . . . It cannot be viewed as anything but a political act when someone claims . . . that no one can be a good Croat unless he is a good Catholic."[113] Monsignor Franjo Kuharić, archbishop of Zagreb, was guilty of this cardinal sin of "politicization," and Milka Planinc, Dabčević-Kučar's successor as president of the Croatian party, denounced the archbishop in July 1977 for using "the pulpit to appear as the protector of the Croatian nation."[114] Although relations between the Slovenian Catholic Church and the regime were reasonably amicable in these years, the same could not be said for relations between the Croatian Catholic Church and the regime. The difference was that the former had been uninvolved in Slovenian nationalist currents (which, in any event, seemed far less potent and thus less threatening at the time), while the Croatian Catholic Church continued to act out the role of institutional bulwark against Serbianization.

Although the communists could not close down the Church as they did Matica Hrvatska, the clergy enjoyed no immunity from prosecution. There continued to be reports of arrests and sentences for nationalistic clergy. In May 1980, to cite one instance, two young Croatian Franciscan monks were sent to jail: one for five years, for writing a poem treating the "oppression of the Croatian people," the other for five and a half years, for possessing a copy of his fellow friar's poem and a Croatian flag which lacked the communist red star.[115] As 1981 opened, the regime, shaken by the Church's renewed confidence in defending human and national rights in Yugoslavia, initiated a ferocious and slanderous anti-clerical campaign in the media, which did not stop short of identifying the archbishop of Zagreb as a fascist sympathizer.[116] Yet in February 1981, when the archbishop celebrated a commemorative mass for Cardinal Stepinac, vilified by the communists as a wartime collaborator, several thousand Croats jammed into the cathedral in a show of solidarity and defiance of the regime.

Later, in spring 1985, there were trials in Zagreb and Varaždin of alleged terrorists, said to have been members of an organization called the Croatian Fighting Unit and to have maintained contact with hostile Croatian exiles in West Germany. Stjepan Deglin was identified as the leader of the Varaždin group. The trials produced allegations of distribution of propaganda and the massing of weapons and incendiary devices. Members of a third alleged Ustaša group were put on trial about the same time in Osijek. These trials resulted ultimately in sentences of up to 15 years in prison.[117]

Shortly after this, the party weekly *Komunist* published an article by Franjo Butorac, party secretary in Rijeka, complaining of the infiltration of purely Croatian words into Croatian schoolbooks and media (replacing words shared with Serbian). The purpose of this "strategy," according to Butorac, was "to indoctrinate young Croats with the spirit of nationalism."[118] Despite the fact that some of Croatia's most prominent nationalists were being shuttled in and out of prison, Butorac argued that "the nationalists defeated in 1971 are mostly operating legally today, using means to push the ideas defeated in 1971: they are exceptionally well organized and linked, and are acting deliberately and 'for the long [haul]', and they are doing so in a particularly sensitive sphere—language and education."[119] The article sparked polemics in the Croatian Sabor and gave rise to a flood of letters to *Komunist* alleging that there was linguistic nationalism in Croatia. But when one of the chiefs of Školska Knjiga, the Zagreb publishing house responsible for most of the textbooks being attacked in *Komunist*, tried to contact the authors of the letters, he found that all the names and addresses were fake. He surmised that the letter campaign had figured as part of a "wider political game."[120]

The "Croatian question" had a particular edge because of the presence, in the republic, of several hundred thousand Serbs, accounting for about 12% of the republic's population in 1981. The number of Serbs residing in Croatia 1948–2001 is shown in Table 10.4.

The Serbs came to Croatia in Habsburg times beginning in the early 16th century, when the Austrian dynasty invited Serbs to settle along the border and serve as border guards, fighting the Ottoman Turks when necessary. In exchange for this service, they were granted small tracts of land and paid a state salary. The Military Frontier (*Militärgrenze* in German, *Vojna Krajina* in Serbo-Croatian) was established in the 1520s by Kaiser Ferdinand I, with military colonists (in practice, Serbs) exempted from the usual manorial obligations. They were promised freedom of worship, allowed to elected their own magistrates, and separated from civil Croatia.[121] This pattern resulted in Croatian Serbs abandoning agriculture, and when some of them returned to farming decades later, not surprisingly, they were far less skilled at it than the Croats. The Vojna Krajina was abolished only in 1881, in the wake of the 1878 Treaty of Berlin, which

Table 10.4. Total Residents and Serbs Living in Croatia, 1948–2001

	Total	Serbs
1948	3,756,807	543,795
1953	3,918,817	588,411
1961	4,159,696	624,985
1971	4,426,221	626,789
1981	4,601,469	531,502
1991	4,784,265	581,000[1]
2001	4,437,460	201,000–300,000[1]

Sources: NIN, no. 2018 (3 September 1989): 28 June 2001, p. 3; *Večernji list,* 18 June 2002, at www.vecernji-list.hr; and *Agence France-Presse,* 23 June 2002, at www.reliefweb.int.

1. Approximate figures: exact figures not available

sanctioned Austro-Hungarian occupation of Bosnia-Herzegovina, pushing the border with the Ottoman Empire back. After the Old Empire collapsed, they joined the Yugoslav Army or took employment in the police force, the post office, the railways, and the administration. Already beginning in 1861, pupils in Croatian elementary schools were exposed to the Cyrillic alphabet from the second grade on,[122] and in the Kingdom of Serbs, Croats, and Slovenes, Croatian pupils continued to be exposed to Cyrillic alongside their native Latin alphabet; but in 1941 the Ustaše banned the Cyrillic alphabet in the areas under their control. During World War Two, Croatian Serbs responded enthusiastically to Tito's call, as noted in chapter 4, and about 50% of Tito's recruits in Croatia were Serbs. After the war, many Croatian Serbs remained in the army and many joined UDBa (the secret police).[123] After the war, the communists allowed Croat schools to switch to teaching only the Latin alphabet, although Croatia's Serbs preferred to use Cyrillic.

In late 1942, Moša Pijade, one of the partisans' "Big Five," had proposed that a Serbian autonomous province be established in Croatia after the war. But Tito vetoed the proposal at once.[124] Yet the idea of some form of autonomy for Croatian Serbs never died and resurfaced in 1971, during the Croatian Spring. But to Serbian demands for autonomy or, alternatively, for state support for special Serbian cultural societies, Croats generally replied that there were also pockets of Croats in Vojvodina and Bosnia-Herzegovina, and yet no one talked of Croatian autonomous provinces in those federal units—not, that is, until 1990.[125] Thus, neither the Croats nor the Serbs of Croatia considered the political status quo legitimate.

The Slovenian Syndrome

For the first three decades of postwar Slovene history, the Catholic Church was arguably the most important thorn in the side of the Slovenian communist establishment. In April 1967, for example, the CC LC Slovenia held its Seventh Plenum and adopted a resolution calling on its members to be more resolute in the fight against "the remnants of reactionary bourgeois clericalism" and characterizing the Church as seeking to revive the spirit of the wartime (collaborationist) Home Guard.[126] A follow-up resolution a year later only restated the party's long-standing line on religion, criticizing any tendencies toward the politicization of religion.[127]

Sometime in the early 1980s, or perhaps even in the late 1970s, intellectuals and cultural elites in Slovenia began to stir. An adumbration of things to come came in May 1982 with the launching of the critical magazine *Nova revija*. Beginning with its first issue, *Nova revija* took up controversial subjects and provided a forum for an open discussion of issues. In 1985, for example, *Nova revija* devoted some of its pages to a frank discussion of the case of Stane Kavčič, including his forced resignation from the Slovenian government in 1972.[128]

Igor Torkar's novel, *Umiranje na obroke* (Dying in Installments), published in 1983, breached a previous taboo by taking as its theme the Stalinist trials in Slovenia in the late 1940s.

Punk music emerged in Slovenia toward the end of the 1970s, setting in motion a ripple of social repercussions. The prohibition of a concert by Peter Lovšin's Pankrti (The Bastards) in 1977 sent a clear signal that officialdom was not inclined to treat punk as an innocent affair. Then, on 1 June 1980, came the founding, in Trbovlje, of Laibach, an alternative music group, whose members attired themselves in uniforms which looked all too reminiscent of those of the Nazi Third Reich. Laibach was mounting an obvious provocation, but there was, all the same, some uncertainty at first as to the precise intentions of Laibach's blending of political and aesthetic imagery. In 1983, Laibach affiliated itself with the Irwin artistic collective and the Scipion Našice Sisters Theater (later forming the core of the Neue Slowenische Kunst (NSK) arts collective). That same year, on 6 March, Laibach put on an exhibition at Zagreb's Prošireni Mediji Gallery, but the exhibition was shut down by the management after four days, when Laibach refused to take down some exhibits which the management found unacceptable.[129] At first, Slovenian authorities were nervous about the group's ostensibly "fascist" bent and banned its performances in Slovenia. Later, the authorities relaxed, and Laibach became part of the established cultural landscape of Slovenia. Moreover, although Laibach was the best-known artistic product from Slovenia internationally, the city of Ljubljana generated a cultural efflorescence of alternative art, literature, drama, and music, especially popular music, in the 1980s, in which the rock group Borghesia, the Anna Monro Theater (launched in 1981), the Helios Theater, the Glej Theater, the Ljubljana Dance Theater, the Slovene Youth Theater, and other initiatives all played vital roles.[130]

Then there was the Alternative Movement, which is to say, the network of pacifist, environmentalist, feminist, gay rights, and other alternative groups, which emerged at the beginning of the 1980s and established a public presence. Magnus, the local gay rights group, formed in 1985 and at once began staging annual gay rights festivals in Ljubljana. The youth magazine *Mladina*, the student newspaper *Katedra*, and the independent Radio Student also provided increasingly independent outlets for the exchange of views. Radio Student had been established in 1969 on a student initiative and granted a license to operate, albeit reluctantly, by the authorities, to whom the alternative of denying the students' application seemed like the riskier course. The final component of the "Slovenian syndrome," a sympathetic communist leadership, was achieved in April 1986, when Milan Kučan, a 45-year-old member of the liberal wing of the LC Slovenia, was elected Slovenian party chief, ending the long reign of the relatively more dogmatic Tito-loyalist, France Popit.

In February 1987, the aforementioned *Nova revija* brought out a special issue (issue number 57) devoted to the "Slovenian national program," which included, among other things, a protest against the second-class status of the Slovenian language in Yugoslavia. The issue was quickly subjected to attack in other republics in Yugoslavia, where some people expressed concern that the Slovenes were sliding in the direction of secessionism.[131] Belatedly, the federal prosecutor Miloš Bakić contacted the Slovenian state prosecutor on 18 January 1988 (after Stambolić had been edged out of power in Belgrade and Milošević had consolidated his power within the Serbian party apparatus) and demanded that criminal proceedings be initiated against those responsible for issue number 57, on the grounds that the issue involved "the crime of hostile propaganda."[132] But the Slovenian state prosecutor rejected Bakic's arguments and refused to undertake legal proceedings. This was only one of a growing number of incidents in which Slovenes came to see themselves as being at odds with Belgrade over fundamental issues.

Meanwhile, the Yugoslav Army did not like what was happening in Slovenia. In particular, the army took umbrage at the publication in the daily newspaper *Delo* of critical reports concerning an arms-peddling visit by Defense Minister Branko Mamula to Ethiopa in February 1988 and at the publication in *Mladina* on 12 February of a particularly critical article about the military, in which the construction of a luxurious villa for the army commander-in-chief was discussed in negative terms. Shortly thereafter, the federal prosecutor tried to file an indictment against *Mladina,* but the growing institutional confusion within the SFRY and lack of cooperation between the Slovenes and the federal authorities resulted in this procedure being aborted.

On 25 March 1988, at a session of the Military Council, an advisory body to the federal presidency, it was decided to appoint General Svetozar Višnjić, then commander of the Ljubljana Military District, to contact the Slovenian minister of internal affairs, Tomaž Ertl, in order to discuss with him remedies for the "counterrevolutionary activity" taking place in Slovenia.[133] Višnjić met with Ertl on 26 March, in the presence of Kučan and Stane Dolanc, then Slovenia's representative in the Yugoslav state presidency; he advised that it might be "necessary" to arrest some Slovenian intellectuals and said that the army was prepared to extend its "assistance" to the Slovenian government. On 29 March, select members CC LCY met in secret with representatives of the army to discuss the case of *Mladina* and Slovenian liberalism more generally. At this meeting, Kučan protested vociferously against proposals to arrest prominent liberals in his republic. The meeting was taped, and Sergeant Major Ivan Borštner stole the tape and turned it over to *Mladina* for its use. Psychologist Vlado Miheljak "used the transcript as a basis for his article, 'The night of long knives,'" which was published under a pseudonym.[134] Consultations between the heads and other representatives of the Republic Secretariat for Internal Affairs and the Ljubljana Military District had already begun, and at one point, the central committee of the LC Slovenia held a secret meeting at which it attempted to refute the Military Council's accusations, but soon rumors were circulating in Ljubljana to the effect that the army was preparing a coup in Slovenia. Then, on 27 April 1988, state security police broke into the premises of Mikro Ada at Cankarjeva Street 10 and confiscated a tape recording of the 72nd session of the CC LCY; this tape would later figure as evidence in the military trial of "the Four."[135] Undaunted, *Mladina* proceeded with the publication, in May, of "documented evidence of JNA preparations to arrest large numbers of Slovenian liberals and thereby put the lid on Slovenian democratization."[136] *Mladina* was preparing yet another article on the subject of the army when, on 31 May, *Mladina*'s Janez Janša and Borštner were taken into custody; David Tasić, a journalist working for *Mladina*, was arrested on 4 June, while editor Franci Zavrl, named as the fourth suspect in the case, temporarily eluded the authorities by taking flight to a nearby hospital. On the same day that Janša and Borštner were arrested, the LCY presidency issued a rather unbelievable statement to the effect that "rumors of alleged preparations for a military coup in the Republic of Slovenia last March are absolutely groundless and represent a political intrigue."[137] In the meantime, Stane Dolanc and Milan Kučan had succeeded in thwarting the plan.

The army now put Janša, Borštner, Tasić, and Zavrl ("the Four") on trial, staging the trial in Ljubljana but conducting it in Serbo-Croatian, outraging Slovenes, who considered the use of Serbo-Croatian to be a violation of their sovereignty. The trial sent political shock waves through Slovenia. The four accused became national heroes overnight, and in Ljubljana, crowds of 10,000 to 20,000 regularly convened, day after day, for the duration of the trial. The trial came to be seen in national-patriotic terms, as Slovenes turned out for the demonstrations waving the Slovenian flag and singing nationalistic Slovenian songs. Folk musicians accompanied the singing and played well-known Slovenian marches.[138] The demonstrations took on the character of a vigil. The Catholic Church called for the release of the accused and conducted an all-night prayer vigil on 18 July. The Slovenian communist authorities objected vociferously to the trial, and when an extralegal Committee for the Protection of Human Rights began functioning (and signing up tens of thousands of sympathizers), the authorities entered into direct and supportive contact with the committee, even declaring their views identical with those of the committee.[139]

The trial was bad enough in and of itself, as far as Slovenes were concerned, and anti-military sentiment now ran in high fever. Anti-military graffiti adorned public walls in Ljubljana, in open expression of this tide.[140] But as already mentioned, the entire affair was aggravated by the army's decision to conduct the trial—being held in Ljubljana—in Serbo-Croatian. The party leadership in Slovenia took the matter to the Yugoslav presidency, which ruled that the use of Serbo-Croatian in the Ljubljana military court was not unconstitutional—that is, that Slovenian law did not apply to the Yugoslav military. It was a straight line from this ruling to Slovenia's 1990 declaration that its own legislation took priority over federal law. The Slovenian party leadership, of course, appealed the presidency's decision, but in vain. Milan Kučan commented bitterly that "Slovenes cannot regard as their own any state that does not secure the use of their mother tongue and its equality, and in which the freedom, sovereignty, and equality of the Slovene people [are] not guaranteed."[141] Finally, on 27 July, the court found the four guilty and sentenced them to prison terms of four years (Borštner), one and a half years (Janša and Zavrl), and five months (Tasić).

The trial had mobilized the Slovenian public, inflamed Slovenian exclusivism, provoked the creation of a human rights committee, and legitimated dissent. An opinion poll conducted in July 1988 found that 63% of Slovenes favored independence for their republic.[142] In the wake of the trial, a series of political initiatives was undertaken, giving birth to the Social Democratic Alliance of Slovenia, the Slovenian Democratic Union, the Slovenian Christian Socialist Movement, and the Green Party.

The Slovenian party also began to speak a new political language. Already in June 1988, Kučan underlined the right of Slovenes to legislate for their own republic.[143] Then, in December 1988, Kučan introduced an entirely new element into the discourse, when, in an article penned for the party weekly, *Komunist*, he underlined that Slovenia retained the right of secession.[144] Republic leaders had not broached this subject in 20 years. There was no immediate follow-up to this, but then, in September 1989, Vladimir Rabzelj, a Slovenian lawyer, wrote an article for *Mladina* urging the secession of Slovenia and Croatia from the Yugoslav federation and the creation of a Slovenian-Croatian confederation.[145]

Mazes in Montenegro

Montenegro is a special case. Unlike the other nationalisms of Yugoslavia, Montenegrin nationalism comes in two variants—an anti-Serbian and a pro-Serbian variant—and there were (and are) Montenegrins adhering to each. Anti-Serbian nationalism followed the model of nationalism in the other republics, with the refinement that some scholars have argued that Montenegrins are not Slavs at all but descend, allegedly, from originally non-Slavic stock, only accepting Serbo-Croatian as their indigenous language somewhat later.[146] Anti-Serbian nationalists typically wanted, in the 1970s and 1980s, to maximize the sovereignty and juridical autonomy of the Montenegrin republic and were highly distrustful of Serbs. This distrust increased after Milošević took power in Serbia.

Pro-Serbian Montenegrin nationalists perhaps should be called simply Serbian nationalists, since the argument they make is that Montenegrins are merely one tribe of the Serbian nation and that Montenegrins and Serbs have the same ethnogenesis, the same culture, and—allowing, of course, for the refinement of the independent Principality of Montenegro, which existed until 1918—in some "larger" sense, the same history.[147] Serbian nationalists in Montenegro complained that the "artificial" resurrection of a separate Montenegro by the communists after World War Two was no more than a ploy to weaken Serbia.

Until the mid-1970s, the cultural infrastructure in Montenegro was weak. Only at that time were the University of Titograd and the Montenegrin Academy of Sciences founded. And only then was there a tangible development of

Montenegrin media (including local television) and local scientific, cultural, and research institutes. That is to say, the institutional prerequisites for the development of an articulate Montenegrin culture and identity were long in coming. By the mid-1980s, however, Montenegro was becoming sharply polarized between anti-Serbian and pro-Serbian nationalists, resulting in a worsening of the political climate among Montenegrins.[148]

In 1990, a new People's Party was established in Montenegro. Its president (Novak Kilibarda) argued that Montenegro and Serbia were two Serbian states and that Montenegrins should be encouraged to think of themselves as Serbs. Although Kilibarda allowed that Montenegrins should have their own state, he also told a public gathering in July 1990 that in the event of the disintegration of Yugoslavia—a prospect increasingly on people's minds from 1988 on—Montenegro and Serbia should be united as a single Serbian state.[149] A movement for the unification of Serbia and Montenegro was, in fact, set up, and a petition to that effect was circulated, gathering more than 10,000 signatures from "citizens *of Serbia* and Montenegro."

These Serbophile currents in turn provoked fear and anxiety among many Montenegrins, and one highly placed Montenegrin official claimed, in August 1990, that anti-Serbian sentiment in Montenegro had never been as strong.[150] A new Party of Socialists came into being in Montenegro and quickly issued a public warning of the threat of "Greater Serbian pretensions to the territory of the state of Montenegro."[151]

Macedonians and Macedonianism

Perhaps nowhere in the SFRY was the dependence of the state system on a specific hermeneutics of national identity more clearly manifested than in Macedonia. Here, in a region inhabited by persons who might easily have been taken for Bulgarophones,[152] and who had been subjected to a vigorous campaign of Serbianization during the interwar years, Tito and his cohorts set out, as has already been noted, to fashion a distinctive Macedonian national identity. In so doing, Tito set his ship of state on a collision course with Bulgaria's communists, redefined the identity of Slavophones in northern Greece (and therefore also an important dimension of Yugoslav-Greek relations), and, with the establishment of the Macedonian Orthodox Church in 1967, underlined his rejection of the interwar Serb nationalist line which had defined Macedonians as "south Serbs," a line which continues to inspire some Serb Orthodox clerics to this day. Within this context, it is understandable that Macedonians have, from time to time, displayed symptoms of collective *Angst* at being surrounded by potentially hostile or "hungry" neighbors.[153] It is perhaps not irrelevant either that, leaving aside ethnically fractured Bosnia, in no other republic did the titular nationality constitute a smaller proportion of the local population (see the figures in Table 10.5).

Table 10.5. Population of Yugoslavia by Republic and Autonomous Province, 1981

	Number of inhabitants in thousands	Percentage of largest nationality
YUGOSLAVIA	22,418	N/A
Republic		
Bosnia-Herzegovina	4,128	39.5[1]
Croatia	4,582	75.4
Macedonia	1,921	66.7
Montenegro	585	68.2
Serbia	5,673	85.7
Slovenia	1,887	90.1
Autonomous Province		
Kosovo	1,595	76.9[2]
Vojvodina	2,029	54.6[3]

Notes
1. Muslims
2. Albanians
3. Serbs

Sources: Statistički kalendar Jugoslavije 1982 (Belgrade: Savezni zavod za statistiku, February 1982), p. 33; and author's calculations from *NIN*, no. 1626 (28 February 1982): 19–20.

This vulnerability to collective *Angst,* built into the tenuous foundation of Macedonian national identity, combined with the region's geostrategic situation, also colored relations between Macedonians and Albanians within the Socialist Republic of Macedonia. Certainly, collective *Angst* played a smaller role in the relative overrepresentation of ethnic Macedonians in the membership of the LC Macedonia than did differences in the nationality structure of cities and countryside within the republic. But it has influenced the local party's responses to local Albanian complaints and agitation. During the lifespan of the SFRY, for example, Macedonian authorities remained steadfastly opposed to any creation of a Republic of Kosovo, fearing that such a republic would also lay claim to territories in the western part of Macedonia, where many Albanians live. And after the April 1981 riots in Kosovo, Macedonian authorities authorized a revision of syllabi and textbooks, in a move intended to counter the spread of ethnic nationalism among Albanians of Macedonia, and increased the number of hours of instruction in Macedonian in Albanian-language schools.[154]

"Counter-revolutionary" activities inspired by Albanian irredentism were said to be increasing as of 1983–1984. Albanian popular songs with "nationalistic or national-romantic" content infiltrated the programs of the Albanian-language service broadcast by Radio Skopje. There were also reports (in 1986) that large numbers of Macedonian Albanians were obtaining religious instruction in

Islamic countries—a development which communist authorities feared would erode the effectiveness of their own secular socialization programs. Moreover, in 1987, a Tanjug report revealed that some Albanian pupils were unable to follow classes conducted in Macedonian.[155] All of these were disquieting to Macedonian authorities.

Skopje was also concerned about demographic trends, in that the birthrate among Albanians was tangibly higher than that among Macedonians. In January 1988, the Albanian news agency ATA accused the government in Skopje of having prepared a package of measures allegedly designed to reduce the birthrate among the Albanians. The measures included a provision to eliminate state coverage of medical care for any children beyond the first two.[156] Azem Vllasi, then president of the Provincial Committee of the LC Kosovo, criticized Macedonia's policies vis-à-vis its Albanians, provoking a sharply worded response in the Macedonian Assembly.

In 1988, tensions reached the breaking point. There were demonstrations by young Albanians in Kumanovo in August and in Gostivar in October of that year. Demonstrators claimed that Macedonian authorities were not safeguarding the rights guaranteed to ethnic Albanians under the 1974 federal constitution. Ultimately, 20 of the demonstrators were sent to prison for terms of up to 11 years.

In 1989, as the Yugoslav system disintegrated, the Macedonian government amended the republic's constitution. Where the constitution had previously defined the Macedonian republic as "a state of the Macedonian people and the Albanian and Turkish minorities," the amended constitution referred to it as "the national state of the Macedonian people."[157] In the process, Macedonianism was raised from the official *national* ideology for the Macedonian people to the official *state* ideology of the Macedonian republic.

The Serbian "Awakening"

From the standpoint of contemporary Serbian nationalist ideology, the years 1966–1980 were years of deprivation and repression. Nikezić and Perović, the two non-nationalist liberals of the late 1960s and early 1970s, were now reviled, Tito demonized, the 1974 constitution condemned (among other things for Article 3, in which "the two autonomous provinces were listed, together with the republics, as constituent parts of Yugoslavia" rather than merely as units within the Republic of Serbia),[158] and the LCY system recalled as a kind of anti-Serbian conspiracy. According to this point of view, the years 1980–1986—sparked by Tito's death in May 1980 and the Albanian demonstrations in April 1981—were years of reawakening. This "reawakening," achieved with the drafting of the aforementioned "Memorandum of the Serbian Academy of Science and Arts" in 1985 (leaked in 1986), was adopted as the basis for programmatic policy as a result of Milošević's conquest of power in Serbia in 1987. Continuing the time line, one might describe the years 1987–1995 as constituting a period of aggressive Serbian nationalism in service to the idea of a Greater Serbia (to be built at the expense of Croats and Bosnian Muslims), and the years 1995–2000 as years of bitterness and growing resentment both of Milošević's kleptocratic regime and, simultaneously if inconsistently, of perceived enemies on Serbia's flanks as well as on farther shores.

An "awakening" always signifies a change of perspective, and no one can doubt but that the "Memorandum," drafted after a steady stream of horror stories over a five-year period about the treatment of Serbs in Kosovo, signified just such a change in perspective. The Memorandum was the collaborative product of a number of persons. The most important figures in this collaboration were novelist Antonije Isaković, historian Vasilje Krestić, economist Kosta Mihajlović, and former *Praxis* collaborator Mihajlo Marković, though others, such as Radovan Samardžić, Pavle Ivić, Dušan Kanazir, Miloš Macura, Dejan Medaković, Miroslav Pantić, Nikola Pantić, Ljubiša Rakić, Miomir Vukobratović, Ivan Maksimović, Stojan Celić, and Nikola Čobeljić took part in the writing of the Memorandum.[159] Dobrica Ćosić, widely regarded as the "father" of the Memorandum, did not participate in its writing, although he and former *Praxis* collaborator Ljubomir Tadić participated in some of the discussions of the Memorandum.[160] Ostensibly still in "draft" form, the Memorandum first reached the Yugoslav public on 24–25 September 1986, when the Belgrade daily newspaper *Večernje novosti* published extracts of the leaked and allegedly unfinished Memorandum. The document shocked Yugoslavs, though in different ways. The general tone of the document was accusatory; the picture it painted was conspiratorial. According to the Memorandum, Serbs were underrepresented on the LCY Central Committee, Serbia had been "unjustifiably" held back in the first five-year plan, and Serbian voters counted for less than voters in other republics. Developments in Kosovo were summarized as tantamount to "the physical, political, legal, and cultural genocide of the Serbian people in Kosovo and Metohija," while the Memorandum held that "except for the period of the existence of the NDH, Serbs in Croatia were never so endangered as they are today." The assignment of largely Albanian Kosovo and ethnically mixed Vojvodina to Serbian jurisdiction, in spite of Tito's wartime pledge to Enver Hoxha to allow the former region to be conjoined with Albania and in spite of the fact that Vojvodina had never been part of any historic Serbian state, was turned on its head and portrayed as a dual blow *against* Serbian sovereignty. To the authors of the Memorandum, the assignment of Kosovo and Vojvodina to Serbia as respectively autonomous region and autonomous province seemed best understood as the "division" of the Serbian republic in three; this "curse" was specifically linked with the constitution of 1974, insofar as that document confirmed and deepened the autonomy of the provinces.[161] Toward the end of the text came the following breathtaking charge:

Under the influence of the ruling ideology, the cultural heritage of the Serbian people is being alienated, usurped, invalidated, neglected, or wasted; their language is being suppressed and the Cyrillic alphabet is vanishing. . . . No other Yugoslav nation has been so rudely denied its cultural and spiritual integrity as the Serbian people. No literary and artistic heritage has been so routed, pillaged, and plundered as the Serbian one.[162]

The Memorandum broke every rule in the proverbial rule book of post-Tito Titoism. The publication of this inflammatory document in a major daily newspaper brought it to a mass public. Among Serbs, the Memorandum connected with latent and not-so-latent nationalist stirrings; among non-Serbs, to the extent that there was any reaction, it tended to be one of consternation. The LCY took a hard line against this overt rehabilitation of nationalism. Ivan Stambolić, president of Serbia, and Dragiša Pavlović, Belgrade party chief, loudly denounced the document. Slobodan Milošević, secretary of the LC Serbia, however, maintained an inscrutable silence, at least in public. Milošević did authorize the publication, in *Politika,* of the text of a speech delivered by his close friend, Dušan Mitević, Belgrade TV chief, which was sharply critical of the Memorandum.[163] And speaking on his own authority, Milošević told a small group of secret police, at a closed meeting held shortly after the publication of the Memorandum,

The appearance of the Memorandum of the Serbian Academy of Arts and Sciences represents nothing else but the darkest nationalism. It means the liquidation of the current socialist system of our country, that is the disintegration after which there is no survival for any nation or nationality. . . . Tito's policy of brotherhood and unity . . . is the only basis on which Yugoslavia's survival can be secured.[164]

About the same time, Sarajevo psychiatrist Dr. Radovan Karadžić, the future leader of the Serbian Democratic Party in Bosnia who, at the time, was reportedly best known for having made some suggestions about food labeling, offered his observation, "Bolshevism is bad, but nationalism is even worse."[165] Thus, ironically, as of 1986, the two figures who would later organize and lead the campaign for a Greater Serbia were distancing themselves from the very nationalism which they would later embrace. Their conversion was fired by hunger for power—that intoxicating elixir which imbues the otherwise shabby morbidities of collective self-glorification with a beguiling allure and seductive appeal.

Vojislav Šešelj, later leader of the Serbian Radical Party and self-styled Chetnik "Duke," on the other hand, was in prison at the time, after he had been convicted in 1985 of producing a nationalistic map in which Serbia was depicted with enlarged borders (above all at Bosnia's expense).[166] Interestingly enough, Amnesty International adopted the imprisoned chauvinist as a "prisoner of conscience."

Much of the anger and resentment associated with post–World War Two Serbian nationalism was fired by perceived losses in Kosovo. In April 1967, for example, Bishop Pavle of Raška-Prizren diocese (and current Serbian Orthodox Patriarch) expressed anxiety over the out-migration of Serbs from the province during the previous year; in a strange twist, the bishop accused former interior minister Ranković of having orchestrated the migration of Serbs in order to have arguments he could use against the province's Albanians! Ten years later, Bishop Pavle returned to this theme, noting that over a period of 20 years, the number of houses owned by Serbs in Podujevo had declined from more than 1,000 to barely 350. While the bishop conceded that Serbs often left in order to find better work or in order to place their children in higher-quality schools elsewhere, he also claimed that local Albanians had been exerting "organized pressure on our people" to leave the province.[167] Allegations of such pressure eventually spawned allegations of "genocide," said to be perpetrated by Kosovo's Albanians.

Serbian intellectuals began their defection from Titoist orthodoxy soon after Tito's death, typically taking a nationalist tack. Vladimir Dedijer, Tito's official biographer, put the first crack in the dam with a kind of "anti-biography" entitled *Novi prilozi za biografiju Josipa Broza Tita* [New Contributions to the Biography of Josip Broz Tito]. Published in 1981, the book "demythologized the late dictator and portrayed him as a lecher and schemer, dissembler and master of craftiness, bon vivant and tyrant, charismatic leader and pacesetter in 'excessive retortion' (Dedijer's euphemism for the execution of 'enemies')." In a survey of Yugoslav historiography originally published in the *American Historical Review,* Ivo Banac described Dedijer's *Novi prilozi* as an "ungraceful book, a cabbage head on a makeshift body, full of unrelated provocations, including Dedijer's obsession with 'revolutionary suicides.'"[168]

Although *Novi prilozi* provoked widespread criticism, it also opened the gates to a new revisionism in Serbian historiography. Branko Petranović's *Revolucija i kontrarevolucija u Jugoslaviji, 1941–1945* [Revolution and Counter-Revolution in Yugoslavia, 1941–1945], published in 1983, broke a major taboo by lauding executed Chetnik leader Draža Mihailović as an important "anti-fascist." That same year Vladimir Terzić's *Slom kraljevine Jugoslavije 1941* was published in Belgrade, attributing the speedy defeat of the Yugoslav Army in 1941 to alleged treason on the part of Croatian leaders such as Maček. Also in 1983, Vasilije Krestić published his *Srpsko-hrvatski odnosi i jugoslovenska ideja* [Serb-Croat Relations and the Yugoslav Idea] in which he interpreted "Yugoslavism" as a cover for Croatian hegemony over Serbs, Slovenes, and other peoples of the country. Three years later, Krestić would publish an even more troubling article, in which he claimed that Croats have a centuries-old "tradition" of genocide.[169]

It was in the context of this transmogrified intellectual milieu that, in May 1985—at their annual convention—members of the Serbian Academy of Sciences and Art decided to establish a committee to draft a statement on the situation in Yugoslavia. The result was the ill-famed, brooding Memorandum, which riveted on sundry alleged despoliations of the Serbs and demonized the Croats and Kosovar Albanians. But as Susan Woodward has noted, "the claim by Serbian nationalists in the 1980s in Kosovo and Croatia that Serbs were, or were threatened with becoming, victims of genocide was absurd."[170] But the systematic construction of Serbs as victims of genocide prepared Serbs to take revenge in "like manner" against their presumed persecutors. In this way, mythologies of genocide may engender *actual* genocide.[171]

This chapter has highlighted the phenomenon of nationalism among seven constituent peoples of the SFRY—Muslims, Albanians, Croats, Slovenes, Montenegrins, Macedonians, and Serbs. Nationalism, which derives its strength from perceived wrongs to the nation, which is to say from the perception of political illegitimacy, is a kind of political fuel. And as fuel, it can power different engines, driving in different directions. At various times, scholars, politicians, and polemicists have linked nationalism to fascism or democracy or political atavism—and perhaps to other things as well. But none of these linkages are automatic. They are only *possible* linkages. But in the context of socialist Yugoslavia, which is also to say, in the context of communist one-party rule, this fuel powered a specific engine, namely, the engine of republic etatism, with differences in the degree of liberalization playing a catalyzing role as well. Hence, as Slovenian journalist Miha Kovač told the *New Left Review* in 1988,

the nationalisms or local interests of Yugoslavia's six republics and two autonomous provinces became a kind of surrogate for all other political identities. You could be active within the existing political structure only on the basis of defending the interests of your republic or province. . . . Thus the system that had supposedly emerged through the defeat of Croat and other nationalisms turned out to be itself most conducive to nationalism. Nationalism is produced within the very structure of the [socialist] Yugoslav system.[172]

CHAPTER 11

A Crisis of Legitimacy, 1974–1989

The late 1970s were, in Yugoslav terms, a kind of "golden age." The Tito regime had had ever less need to resort to force in order to assert and maintain its authority, the oil price shock of 1973–1974 had not yet made its full impact, there was a degree of freedom of the press, and, in general, the people of the SFRY lived better than they had for many years. And yet, the equilibrium was unstable, both because of the incipient economic decay and because there were too many attempts to "square the circle" (for example, by substituting regional pluralization for authentic pluralization, by pushing for "democratization" of the party without accepting party democracy as such, and by seeking to achieve brotherhood and unity without depoliticizing ethnicity). And, as was noted in proposition 4 (chapter 1), while "an unstable equilibrium provides incessant pressure for change," an "unstable equilibrium is no guarantee of transformation toward legitimate politics." On the contrary, it is often easier for one illegitimate system to melt into another than it is for a legitimate system to spring forth from the entrails of a dying illegitimate system.

But, Golden Age or not, there was already a sense of crisis in the air, a sense, at times, even of foreboding, and that very sense of crisis rendered the system more vulnerable to collapse (proposition 6). As we have seen, crisis may be understood as "a collective consensus that the status quo is untenable" (definition 1). Hence, the pressure for change could only become ever greater, ever more irresistible, as that consensus spread among the public and officeholders alike. In the Yugoslav case, this growing consensus was manifested in the first place in interviews published in *Duga* and *Intervju*, two influential Belgrade weekly magazines, and in the weekly Zagreb magazine *Start*. In these interviews, the reader could find that even members of the political elite had become alienated from the system in which they had been active participants, and that they did not expect the system to continue as it had.

From the Constitution to "Democracy and Socialism"

The Constitutional Commission of the SFRY agreed on the text of the preliminary draft constitution on 21 May 1973; on 7 June, the draft was accepted by the Chamber of Nationalities and submitted to the public for discussion. After the conclusion of public discussion, the Constitutional Commission met and prepared the final draft, which was completed on 8 January 1974. The constitution was presented to the Chamber of Nationalities on 22 January 1974 and promulgated on 21 February. It was Yugoslavia's fourth postwar constitution and, at the time, the longest constitution in the world. At the same time, it was, according to Gisbert Flanz, "probably one of the least legalistic and most emphatically ideological and programmatic documents among the contemporary constitutions of the countries of the world."[1] With detailed provisions, among other things, for citizens' rights to a clean environment, it was also, very much, a constitution which sought to address the concerns of the late 20th century.

The constitution also introduced some new concepts, perhaps most prominent of which was designating both the republics and provinces "federal units"; with this redesignation, the source of authority for the provinces seemed to be moved from the Republic of Serbia to the federation itself.[2] The republics were defined explicitly as states (in Article 3), while the provinces, though not defined in this way, were nonetheless granted "equality with the republics at the level of the common state . . . [so that effectively] every republic or province enjoyed a veto right in practically all affairs of any importance."[3] The provinces were further protected by a guarantee that their borders could not be altered without their consent (Article 5) and by the provision (in Article 296) that the delegations sent by the provinces to the Chamber of Republics and Provinces (which replaced the Chamber of Nationalities) should represent the stands of their respective Assemblies, and not those of the Assembly of Serbia;[4] in this way, the Autonomous Provinces were, once again, given political equivalence with the constituent republics. Important circles within the LC Serbia viewed these constitutional innovations with great displeasure, holding that they effectively reduced the territorial extension of the Republic of Serbia by granting the autonomous provinces full equivalence with the republics; they vowed, secretly, to revise or overthrow the constitution as soon as they could. The JNA shared the Serbian leadership's displeasure with the 1974 constitution,[5] and, in 1977, the Serbian leadership drew up a so-called *Blue Book,* spelling out its objections to the constitution.

The 1974 constitution sought simultaneously to strengthen the authoritarian power of the LCY and to confirm the devolution of power to the republics. It carried this to the extent of guaranteeing, in the preamble, the right of every *nation* of Yugoslavia to self-determination, even to the point of secession, though these rights were qualified in Article 5, where it was noted that "The frontiers of the Socialist Federal Republic of Yugoslavia may not be altered without the consent of all [the] Republics and Autonomous Provinces."[6] Strikingly, the constitution did not set forth any procedures whereby the people of Yugoslavia might exercise this nominal right, suggesting that it was not intended that anyone actually exercise that right. The constitution (Article 247) guaranteed each nationality the right to set up organizations to protect and develop its national culture—a guarantee which would be put to the test by the founders of the "Zora Society" in summer 1989.

The 1974 constitution scrapped the pentacameral legislative system set up in 1963 and restored a bicameral structure (with a 220-member Federal Chamber operating alongside the 88-member Chamber of Republics and Provinces). Under the new constitutional framework, a collective presidency was also created, composed of nine members: one from each federal unit plus Tito, who presided over this body while simultaneously holding the post of president of the Republic. It was specified that after Tito's passing, the collective presidency would continue to operate on the basis of a rotating chair, with the post of president of the Republic to be buried with Tito.

The late 1970s saw also the promulgation of the Basic Law on Associated Labor (in 1976) and the publication of Edvard Kardelj's major doctrinal tract, *Democracy and Socialism*, in 1978.[7] Kardelj's book was published the following year in English translation and contained some interesting arguments. Among other things, Kardelj abandoned the Marxist-Leninist concept that a socialist regime could build a system which would freeze out unwelcome change; on the contrary, he argued that any system would always be exposed to the challenges of further transformation, coming from both within and without, embraced the notion that few political systems are pure systems (e.g., pure socialist systems or pure bourgeois democracies), mixing elements of different systems, and accepted the rather non-Marxist premise that there could be "non-antagonistic conflicts" in Yugoslav society, conflicts which cannot be reduced to a supposed clash between the general (proletarian) interest of the society and the interests of bourgeois remnants (as classical Stalinism liked to put it).[8] Along these lines, Kardelj wrote,

> There is no denying that in our society, too, such contradictory interests are possible, [which] . . . cannot be resolved either through self-management channels or through state coercion. Such contradictions include, for instance, differences in interests between the developed and underdeveloped parts of the country, different conditions of income earning resulting from the different organic composition of the factors of production . . . etc.[9]

Looking ahead, Kardelj situated himself, as he had all along, at the center of the political spectrum, criticizing simultaneously two alternative currents: those who wanted to reduce the LCY to a mere ideological-propaganda machine (reviving the ideas of Milovan Djilas) and those who wanted the LCY to assume a monopolistic control of society and to emasculate self-management (championed by circles that were, in effect, probably more conservative than Ranković had ever been). Later, toward the end of his book, Kardelj warned, "Historical processes have never taken place by inertia. There have always been certain ideological and political forces which shaped and mobilized social consciousness and, by pointing the way to the future, fought for progress."[10] While optimistic on the surface, this statement contained the implicit warning against tendencies which would endeavor to push the country either toward bourgeois democracy or toward repressive authoritarianism.

Life without Tito

As Dušan Bilandžić has perceptively noted, three developments were occurring at the transition from the late 1970s to the early 1980s which ultimately shook the foundations of the Yugoslav socialist state and stirred pressure for system transformation. These were the deaths of the founders—Kardelj (in 1979) and Tito (in 1980)—the deep economic crisis, which began to command attention already in 1979 and which saw inflation rising to 30% by 1983, by which point the national debt had climbed to $20 billion;[11] and the eruption of ethnic tensions in Kosovo in April 1981.[12] Two further problems emerged at the same time: the exacerbation of divisions within the party after Tito's death in May 1980, and a riveting of attention, at first obliquely but increasingly in explicit terms, on the problem of legitimation itself.[13]

In December 1979 Tito developed a blood clot in one of his arteries of his left leg and was hospitalized in Ljubljana. When the operation proved unsuccessful, gangrene set in, and doctors amputated the leg. At first Tito seemed to revive, but then he slid into a coma. For four months, Tito lay in a coma, while the newspapers issued daily reports about his health, usually describing his condition as "stable, but unchanged." The mood in the country was sober; one small sign of this came from Radio B, a popular station in Belgrade which usually played lively pop and rock hits, but which now played, for months on end, calm, tranquil music reminiscent of the music of Mantovani. Many Yugoslavs, especially young people, started to gather at railroad stations and other public places to sing the patriotic song "Jugoslavijo" and the old Partisan song "Druže Tito, mi ti se kunemo da sa tvoga puta ne skrenemo" ("Comrade Tito, we pledge to you that we shall not deviate from your path"). The country pulled together in a show of unity. I was in Belgrade (and briefly also in Dubrovnik) at the time, and I remember vividly both people's desire to deny that the end was near and the widespread and genuine grief—perhaps fueled by uncertainty—which overcame Yugoslavs when, on 4 May 1980, he finally passed away. Tito's funeral, attended by a huge number of foreign dignitaries, was the occasion for a final farewell to a leader who had ruled the country for so long that an entire generation had no memory of having lived under any other government. Every periodical published in Yugoslavia marked the occasion by issuing a special issue honoring the deceased president, including *Žena* (a monthly journal devoted to the advancement of women's social position), *Bazar* (a family and fashion magazine), *Radio amatir* (a magazine oriented to radio amateurs), and the local magazine for stamp collectors. Even *Zum Reporter,* a magazine known for its photo spreads of naked women, its sexual advice column, and its constant reports of scandals and alleged scandals, devoted an issue to Tito, placing Tito's picture in the centerfold where, in other issues, a photo of a naked woman was to be found.

For several months after Tito's death, local newspapers continued to publish large photos of him visiting foreign lands, shaking hands with prominent foreign leaders, giving speeches, inspecting factories—and that, on an almost daily basis, conveying the illusion that perhaps he wasn't really dead after all. Indeed, since, at his last reelection, he had been elected "president without limitation of mandate," that very formula could be read to imply that even his death did not end his presidency—and, for that matter, it was only a cumbersome collective leadership that replaced him. Meanwhile, public speeches were replete with death-denying slogans such as "After Tito—Tito!" and "We are Tito's, Tito is ours!"

But in spite of the careful preparations for political life after Tito, the preexisting problems, which even Tito had proven unable to solve[14]—indeed, some of them, such as the country's growing indebtedness, were products of his own handiwork—exerted ever greater pressure on the system. Moreover, as the 1980s wore on, it became clear that the fragmentation of power engineered by Tito's quasi-confederal but one-party framework was producing institutional weakness and political chaos. Chaos, of course, creates maneuvering room and uncertainty—which gives one a sense of freedom. And this inevitably opened the door to greater political participation by large numbers of citizens.

The League of Communists of Yugoslavia convoked its first post-Tito congress in Belgrade from 26 June to 29 June 1982. The league had weathered the initial post-Tito transition and could congratulate itself on the stability of the system of collective decision making it had set up in the late 1970s. Yet, for a variety of reasons, the Twelfth Party Congress also became an arena for voicing various complaints and proposals, both by liberals and by conservatives. To begin with, the party was starting to become troubled about the country's deteriorating economic situation, the growing Serb-Albanian frictions in Kosovo, spiraling nationalism (in reaction to Kosovo and to the Serbian nationalist backlash) throughout the other federal units, and a growing crisis of confidence rooted in popular despair about the party's ability to cope with the situation effectively. Although the institutions were functioning much as they had for years, there was a groundswell of criticism (both in party forums and in the press) of some of the pillars of Yugoslav stability. As early as June 1973, the presidium of the LCY Central Committee released a document which admitted that, in 23 years of "self-management," workers' self-management had not been implemented in its intended form. In the months after Tito's death, various party spokespersons charged that self-management had been "neglected," that it existed "only on paper," that workers' councils were regularly circumvented and forced to acquiesce in decisions made elsewhere, and that no large enterprises had ever introduced self-management per se.[15] Others charged that the interrepublican committees, which had been created through legislation passed in 1971, had been working inefficiently and that the state presidency was increasingly intruding into the legitimate domain of the Federal Executive Council and the Skupština.[16] Not even Tito was spared criticism. First, Bosnian general Boško Siljegović accused Tito (in May 1981) of having made "great errors" in policy toward Kosovo; then poet Gojko Djogo (who would later affiliate himself with Karadžić's Serb nationalist program in Bosnia) referred to Tito as "the rat from Dedinje" in a collection of poems published by the Belgrade publishing house "Prosveta." Djogo was jailed for that offense in September 1981. Even the party was taken to task. *Danas* dourly charged that the Eleventh Party Congress (1978) had failed to accomplish anything at all and that its resolutions for decisive action had never been translated into policy.[17] Similarly, in February 1982, the Commission for the Development of the Political System of LC Serbia sharply rejected the draft political report, complaining that its authors had tried to cover up serious weaknesses in the party and that they had blithely described party efficacy in superlatives, even though the Kosovo problem remained unresolved.[18]

As the Twelfth Party Congress approached, centralists began to clamor for withdrawal of power from the federal units and the reinstitution of a strong center and openly fretted about what they termed the de facto federalization of the party. Throughout the summer of 1981, Serbian and Bosnian centralists blasted what they called "unacceptable tendencies toward the federalization or even confederalization" of the party.[19] They urged that the autonomy of the regional party organizations of Kosovo and Vojvodina be reduced; that much greater coordination among the republics be required in education, transport, price policy, supplies, and other areas; that federal agencies be given an increased role in supervising this coordination; and that general party discipline be tightened.

Liberals, rallying around the banner of decentralization, responded by proposing (in late 1981) that Central Committee members be made responsible to the republican organs that elected them rather than to the committee itself[20]—a move which would have constituted an unmistakable step toward de jure federalization of the party—and also urged that the powers of the LCY presidium be scaled down.[21] When they followed these proposals with an endorsement of a statute change retaining the principle of democratic centralism within the regional party organizations of the federal units but abandoning it at the level of the central party apparatus, party conservatives feared that the federalization program would mean the destruction of the party altogether.[22] The conservative-dominated Montenegrin Central Committee shot back, in November 1981, with a suggestion that republican party organizations be stripped of their power to elect members of the LCY Central Committee and be allowed only to nominate candidates for selection by the Yugoslav party congress.[23] Other conservative circles went so far as to demand that the statutes of the regional parties be abolished and that those bodies be governed by the statute of the LCY.[24] Conservatives in the Croatian, Vojvodinan, and Serbian regional parties added fuel to the fire by demanding the imposition of standard mandates throughout the system—a proposal which excited considerable remonstration from the maverick Slovenes as well as from the JNA party organization, which was an important player, in its own right, in the post-Tito system.[25] Indeed, by 1981—in the wake of the Albanian demonstrations in Kosovo—the Croatian party leadership was already betraying concerns that the country was about to witness an eruption of Serbian nationalism.[26]

On 24–26 December 1981, the Central Committee of the Serbian party met in Belgrade to discuss inter-ethnic relations within Serbia. Only a portion of the record was ever published; the most negative and most pessimistic assessments were not shared with the public. CC members attending this session complained that Serbia did not have a unified constitutional order. There were also lamentations that Serbia was being transformed into a federation and that Kosovo and Vojvodina were behaving like republics. Draža Marković, then one of the leading figures in the Serbian party, addressed the session and, in the course of his speech, stated that Yugoslavia consisted of five "peoples"—ignoring the Muslims (Bosniaks), who had been officially recognized as a "people" in 1968. The session sent shock waves through the country, alarming, perhaps especially, the leadership of Bosnia-Herzegovina, which feared that the session would be destabilizing in its effects, threatening the position of the autonomous provinces.[27]

On the eve of the congress, the conservatively inclined party organ *Komunist* groaned volubly that, under the spell of ethnocentric nationalism and burdened by "the inertia of the unsurmounted bourgeois history of Yugoslavia" and an "irrational fixation" on the interests of their respective groups, the Yugoslav federation was dissolving into congeries of bickering regional organizations.[28] A small conservative minority from Belgrade tried, at the Twelfth Party Congress, to replace the territorial organization of the party (the basis of the quasi-federal character of the LCY) with a production principle whereby the party would have been structured according to branches of manufacture, but this was roundly rejected.[29] In September 1982, Mitja Ribičič, the newly elected chair of the party presidium, charged (at the Third Party Plenum) that "much has to be changed" and, in particular, that the various regional leaders should agree, or be compelled to agree, on general policy guidelines for the federation as a whole. But within the party the differences were, if anything, getting deeper. This was amply revealed immediately after the Twelfth Party Congress, when the Serbian party refused to accept the results of the 30 June vote in which Draža Marković had failed to obtain the two-thirds vote of the CC needed to confirm his appointment to the LCY presidium. Petar Stambolić, at that time president of the state presidency (i.e., of the presidential council) of Yugoslavia, took the podium and charged that Marković was the victim of "a big game" being played at Serbia's expense, while Radenko Puzović, a member of the CC LCY from Serbia, threatened that Serbia's representatives might resign from the Central Committee as a bloc unless Marković was endorsed. Such a move would have meant the collapse of the LCY. Finally, at the insistence of the Serbs present at the 30 June session, the non-Serbs agreed to hold a second vote and now approved Marković's appointment to the presidium. But, as Dizdarević notes in his memoirs, this forced reversal, within two hours, badly damaged the CC's prestige. It also damaged the prestige of the Serbian party among the other republic party organizations. On the following day, Mitja Ribičič, the newly elected chair of the party presidium, noted that what had happened on 30 June was without precedent in postwar Yugoslavia and warned that if such behavior continued, Yugoslavia would be thrust "not merely into political crisis, but into complete chaos."[30]

Meanwhile, the broader political debate continued. Najdan Pašić, a leading party theorist, proposed the establishment of a special commission, the Commission to Study the Problems of the Functioning of the Political System, and urged that the powers and jurisdiction of the federal units be tangibly curtailed. Predictably, Pašić's proposal met with mixed response. In March 1983, the Tanjug news agency issued a report on the conclusions of the Skupština's working group on federal relations. The report criticized the federal units for autarkic behavior, charged that the republics were engaging in active dialogue only in the context of federal organs, and complained of inconsistencies, weaknesses, and deviations from the constitution.[31] This kind of institutional disarray was typified by the continued resistance by Vojvodina and Kosovo to efforts by the Republic of Serbia to reduce their prerogatives. In January 1983, for instance, the two autonomous provinces refused to allow Serbian government representatives to be present during their talks with Milka Planinc, chair of the Federal Executive Council, and other federal officials.

As the party gradually came to grips with the scope of the challenge with which it was confronted, it set up two commissions to study the economic and political crises, respectively, and to recommend appropriate strategies for dealing with them. The economic commission, chaired by Slovene Sergej Kraigher, delivered its report in April 1982. But interrepublican differences assured that no effective action would be taken to adopt and apply the recommendations contained in the Kraigher report.[32] The political commission, chaired by Serb Tihomir Vlaškalić, president of the Federal Social Council for Questions of the Social System, delivered its report in December 1985. The report's starting point was that republican autonomy was a given—but that meant the Vlaškalić commission continued to operate within the framework of a unit veto system and inevitably evoked criticism from centralist-minded would-be reformers.[33]

From the death of Tito in 1980 until the rise of Slobodan Milošević in 1987, the regional party organizations were factionalized along the following lines (defined by the dual issues of liberalization versus retrenchment and recentralization versus preservation of the decentralized system): liberal recentralizers were dominant in the Serbian party, conservative recentralizers were dominant in the Bosnian and Montenegrin parties, liberal decentralists in the Slovenian and Vojvodinan parties, and conservative decentralists in the Croatian, Macedonian, and Kosovar party organizations.[34]

Defense of the decentralized system was especially important for the autonomous provinces, Kosovo and Vojvodina, which had the most to lose from any move toward recentralization. Serbia, by contrast, jealously eyeing the two provinces, felt it had the most to gain. Hence, in October 1984, the Serbian party issued a draft reform program calling for, among other things, the strengthening of the federal government and the curtailment of the jurisdiction and prerogatives of the autonomous provinces in particular.[35] Slovenia and Croatia quickly came to the defense of the embattled provincial party organizations, and a Slovenian-Serbian clash at the Fourteenth Plenum of the Central Committee in October 1984 served as a dress rehearsal for the playing out of more serious Slovenian-Serbian tensions in 1989.

But by 1986, with the deepening crisis and a growing—if transitory—consensus that Yugoslavia's troubles were somehow associated with its quasi-confederal framework, the Slovenian party had become isolated in its defense of the status quo. Typical of the mood was a statement made by Montenegrin Vidoje Žarković, rotating president of the LCY Central Committee presidium, in September 1985. Žarković blasted what he called "polycentric etatism" as the chief cause of the country's problems. In his view,

polycentric etatism is the major cause of [our] economic crisis, technological stagnation, and our financial dependence on foreign countries. . . . In the past and current year, we have witnessed serious problems concerning decision making in the federation, particularly agreement-seeking between the republics and provinces. Many difficulties, manifested in the process of coordination, for instance in the SFRJ Assembly, have been not only the result of objective circumstances, but largely the expression of the etatization of relations both in the republics and provinces and in the federation. It is unacceptable to give instructions to delegations and often to delegates in the SFRJ Assembly's chambers about how long they should discuss specific standpoints, and when and to what extent they should give in and hence, satisfy even the most trivial interests of their republic or province.[36]

The provincial party organizations were intimidated and temporarily passive, while both the Macedonian and the Croatian party organizations—though dominated by persons sympathetic to a decentralized system—had agreed to work toward constitutional reform, the purpose of which was no less than the reconsolidation of a strong central government. The tide, thus, seemed to be turning against the decentralists. And eventually (in 1988), pressured from various sides, the Slovenian Assembly even gave its preliminary approval to a set of draft amendments to the SFRY constitution, amendments which would have had serious consequences for the autonomy of the republics.[37]

But in 1987, there was a political coup in the Serbian party apparatus, which now came under the control of the ambitious Slobodan Milošević, who was prepared to play the nationalist card. As will be discussed in the next chapter, Milošević's centralist program ultimately pushed too far, evoking resistance and resulting, in time, in a complete turn in the tide, with sentiment for confederalization growing steadily throughout 1989 and 1990.

The Quest for Reform, 1981–1987

The political debate opened virtually as soon as Tito was buried.[38] In the years 1981–1983, the debate focused on reforming existing institutions, on making the existing system function effectively, on averting crisis, on reform. In the years 1984–1987, by which time there was a general consensus that the system was in crisis, the debate focused on many substantive changes in the system, possibly to include amendments to the constitution or even the writing of an entirely fresh constitution. In the earlier phase, much of the debate was couched in language referring to the need for the "democratization" of the party and political institutions. In both phases, the issues of decentralism versus recentralization and liberalization versus retrenchment dominated the agenda. Since there was entrenched opposition to any given combination (liberal-recentralization, conservative-decentralization, etc.), motion toward change appeared to be ruled out—at least as long as those elites were in power.

Much of the debate was carried out in code. For example, in the years 1981–1986, recentralizers often presented themselves as guardians of Tito's legacy (this would change after Milošević came to power in Serbia), making it appear that the decentralists wanted to loosen the system further. But at this stage, the decentralists were fighting a purely defensive battle; they, too, claimed to be protecting Tito's legacy. The decentralists would switch to the offense only in 1989.

A book by political scientist Jovan Mirić, published in 1984 and excerpted in *Borba* in four installments, raised the political temperature by arguing that under the system established by the constitution of 1974, the federation lacked sovereignty and derived it only from the autonomous sovereignty of the republics. Mirić considered this a weakness and criticized, in particular, the republics' enjoyment of a veto over any important decisions.[39] Many in the party, however, feared at that time that any tinkering with the system would unleash unpredictable pressures for change, and for several years they held to a strict defense of the constitutional order.[40] Between this fear and the incompatibility of the sides to the debate, reform was impossible. Slovenia and Croatia feared any move that might curtail their autonomy, and when, in 1985, the federal government introduced a bill, at the prompting of the International Monetary Fund and the World Bank, which would have obliged enterprises to surrender their foreign currency earnings to the national bank in Belgrade, Slovenia and Croatia blocked the bill and succeeded in scuttling it.[41]

By 1984, it was pretty clear that some changes to the constitution were needed—even if the allies could not agree on what kind of changes. Changes to the republic constitutions were made in Bosnia, Croatia, and Montenegro, while in Serbia, the pressure for change to the republic's constitution could be traced back to 1981, if not back to 1974.[42] The mood in Serbia was changing, becoming more assertive, as evinced at the funeral of former vice president and Minister of Internal Affairs Aleksandar Ranković in August 1983. Attended by thousands of people, the funeral figured as a cathartic moment for those Serbs who looked back with nostalgia to the days when Ranković had played a role in framing internal policies.[43]

Some people once again raised the issue of having multi-candidate elections. But since the LCY was not prepared to countenance the establishment of a second party, any choice of candidates would inevitably have to be drawn from a purely communist slate. As for this adapted form of pluralism, Dragoslav ("Draža") Marković, a member of the LCY Central Committee Presidium from 1981 to 1985, asked what was the point of having a choice of candidates when all the candidates would be drawn from the same party anyway? Marković felt that such a system could at the most encourage "factionalism" within the party.[44] Parallel to these discussions were discussions about the reform and reorganization of the party and its umbrella organization, the Socialist Alliance of Working People of Yugoslavia (SAWPY). The same issues of recentralization versus decentralism and liberalization versus retrenchment could be seen in this arena, too: hence demands that the powers of the LCY Central Committee be dramatically enhanced, that a tighter (and smaller) politburo be created to take over work assigned to the 23-member party presidium, that a single LCY statute be adopted without the possibility of separate statutes for the republic and provincial party organizations, and so forth.[45] Meanwhile, economic crisis was fueling institutional disintegration. Already in summer 1986, *Narodna armija* expressed concerns about the "disintegration and fragmentation of basic organizations" and alleged that the procedures for reaching consensus were leading only to policy fragmentation.[46]

The Thirteenth Party Congress (25–28 June 1986) was billed as a "congress of the strengthening of socialist self-management, a congress of the strengthening of the unity of the country and of the LCY in the struggle against waxing etatism."[47] But despite such proclamations and associated efforts to put some meat on the principle of democratic centralism, *Borba* soon declared the congress a failure, noting that the federalization of the party was continuing and deepening, despite vows to halt and reverse the process.[48]

Increasingly, the federal party structures proved themselves inadequate to the task of bringing the federal units together; policy making at the federal level ground almost to a halt. Between June 1986 and June 1988, the SFRY presidency adopted 322 acts and resolutions, concerning specific policy questions; but most of them were never carried out, never respected. Only those resolutions dealing with military and security affairs were ever carried out.[49] As for SAWPY, there

were those who wanted to loosen its ties to the party and enhance its independence and those who wanted to increase the LCY's role in SAWPY's activity.
By 1987, the latter had asserted a transitory dominance, and over the 12-month
period beginning in July 1987, steps in this direction were taken.[50] Finally, there
were occasional voices like that of Branko Horvat, who advocated the adoption
of a partyless form of socialism.[51] Although this idea was by and large rejected,
it still had its advocates even in 1987.[52]

By 1986, the collective state presidency had agreed to authorize the preparation of amendments to the federal constitution. On 20 October, the Constitutional Commission of the federal Skupština met and appointed a coordinating
group headed by Hamdija Pozderac to prepare specific proposals. Among the
issues the coordinating group was to consider were questions of property ownership, federal relations, the unity of the Yugoslav market, the planning system,
and the relationship of the autonomous provinces to the Republic of Serbia.
Then, in the course of 1987, it came to light that the agro-firm Agrokomerc,
headed by the popular Fikret Abdić and headquartered in Velika Kladuša on the
border with Croatia, had been issuing uncovered promissory notes worth more
than a trillion Yugoslav dinars as collateral, in order to obtain bank loans to
cover losses. All told, Agrokomerc, which employed some 13,500 persons, had
managed to borrow funds from 63 banks in all. When the news broke, Abdić,
who had just been elected to the federal Skupština, was expelled from the Central Committee of the LC Bosnia-Herzegovina, and Hamdija Pozderac had to
resign all his posts, among other reasons because his brother had been involved
in covering up Agrokomerc's financial improprieties; the prestige of the Sarajevo government in general was seriously tarnished.[53]

Meanwhile, on 21 January 1987, the coordinating group finished its preliminary work, and the state presidency submitted its proposal for what it considered the "minimal" changes necessary for the constitutional system to continue
to function. These included, above all, proposals to create a unified legal system;
to bring the railroad, postal, and telephone systems under central authority; and
to tighten the unity of the Yugoslav economy—at the expense of the economic
sovereignty of the individual republics. "All in all," *NIN* wrote at the time, "the
presidency evidently considers that the rights and duties of the federation must
be widened through the constitutional changes." [54] The Serbian government
quickly applauded the presidency's proposals and declared them capable of
leading the way out of the crisis.[55] But in Slovenia, the general reaction was outrage. Addressing a five-hour public forum organized by the Slovenian Writers'
Association on 17 March, sociologist Dimitrij Rupel (later to become Slovenian
foreign minister) exclaimed,

To my great surprise, I discovered that the proposal for changes in the Constitution follows word for word, so to say, the requests of the "Memorandum" [of the Serbian Academy of Sciences and Art in 1986] for unified technological systems such as the railroad
systems, the post, telegraph, and telephone system, energy system, and so forth. . . . Of
course, the worst is the request for a unified legal system which in fact suits those who

claim that liberal-nationalist and other hostile elements have been tolerated too much in some parts of the country and that, for instance, this system should be simplified so that Draconian sentences such as those pronounced in Kosovo, are pronounced in Slovenia too.[56]

Ciril Ribičič, a leading member of the Central Committee of the Slovenian party, professor of constitutional law at the University of Ljubljana, and son of Mitja Ribičič, rebutted the Serbian argument that the recentralizing measures were necessary to deal with the country's problems. On the contrary, Ribičič told the weekly magazine *Danas* in a July 1987 interview,

I am convinced that our problems would be much smaller, and the present debate calmer and more even-tempered, if the Federation had less authority in the domain of economic relations and if it did not interfere so much in the laws of the market as it is doing at present.[57]

The stage was thus set for the fiercer Slovenian-Serbian polemics which erupted in 1989.

The Battle Escalates, 1987–1989

If the years 1981–1983 saw a denial of crisis and an effort to reform the existing system and 1983–1987 saw an admission of crisis and an elevation of reform efforts to the constitutional plane, the years 1987–1989 were characterized by the revival and proliferation of (virulent) nationalism in Serbia (provoking fears among Croats, Bosniaks, Macedonians, and Albanians alike), a growing criticism of Tito (emanating above all from Serbia) and of the "AVNOJ-system" generally, and a transformation of the two sides to the debate. The recentralizers had hitherto operated within the ideological framework of the old Titoist system and hence saw recentralization in supranational terms. With the arrival of Slobodan Milošević on the Serbian political scene, however, recentralization became associated with Serbian nationalism and Serbian interests ("strong Serbia, strong Yugoslavia," as Milošević put it). Reacting to this, the decentralists, who had hitherto largely defended the existing division of powers, became confederalists and now sought to expand the prerogatives of the republics even further, to reduce the financial obligations of their republics to the federation, and, ultimately, to transform the country into a de jure confederation.

By this point, the constitutional debate revolved around five key issues:

(1) change in the status of the autonomous provinces;
(2) change in the structure of the federal Skupština;
(3) the nature of the procedure whereby members of a proposed Chamber of Citizens would be elected;
(4) asymmetric or symmetric federation; and
(5) change in the role of the LCY in the federation.[58]

The Serbian party was responsible for putting the first three items on the agenda, the Slovenian party was responsible for the fourth item, and the fifth emerged naturally as a by-product of the crisis of legitimacy. In a nutshell, the Serbian party wanted to erode the autonomy of the autonomous provinces and to strengthen the federal center, and it saw a restructuring of the federal Skupština as a means of achieving the latter.

At first, other republics registered their hostility to Serbian intentions vis-à-vis the provinces. But eventually, one by one—with the exception of Slovenia—they came around to the view that this was an internal matter for the Serbian republic, in spite of the elevation of the provinces to the status of "federal units" in the 1974 constitution. In August 1988, for example, the presidium of the Bosnian LC Central Committee discussed Serbia's proposed constitutional changes and gave its endorsement.[59] In Slovenia, however, there was less sympathy for Serbia's point of view. Ciril Ribičič articulated the Slovenian position that any change in the status of the autonomous provinces was not merely a matter for Serbia to decide but was, in fact, a question for all of Yugoslavia.[60]

But the question of change in the structure of the federal Skupština was viewed negatively not just by Slovenia but by other republics as well. Serbia wanted to replace the bicameral arrangement (Chamber of Republics and Provinces, Federal Chamber) with a tricameral arrangement (Chamber of Republics and Provinces, Chamber of Citizens, Chamber of Associated Labor). And whereas under the existing framework, the deputies of the chambers were selected by the assemblies of the respective republics and provinces, with equal numbers from each republic being elected to each chamber (and with lesser but equally empowered numbers from each autonomous province), the Serbian party wanted to have the delegates to the Chamber of Citizens represent citizens proportionally—a model which would have favored the Serbian nation. Although the proportional model appears natural to Americans, it was a politically charged proposal in the Yugoslav context—one which was aimed specifically at undercutting the quasi-confederal element in the system. Only Montenegro supported Serbia on this issue. Slovenia, Croatia, and Bosnia adamantly opposed it.[61] Macedonia, by contrast, took the cautious position that no change should be made until more serious study could be conducted.[62]

The Chamber of Associated Labor was, further, a Serbian proposal, while both Slovenia and Croatia opposed it because they feared that the new chamber was designed in part to increase the state's role in the economy. Slovenia and Croatia, for their part, wanted to see a diminution in the role of the state in the economy. Serbia was not alone in wanting the federation to have a role in the economy; this proposal was also supported by Macedonia, Montenegro, and Kosovo. Bosnia was a more complex case, however. Economics has often been secondary to politics in ethnically troubled Bosnia. Bosnian Serbs, for example, have often endorsed Serbian proposals only because they were Serbian. Bosnian

Croats and Muslims tended to oppose Serbian proposals for the same reason. At another level, Serbia sought to have members of the SFRY presidency elected by the federal Skupština rather than by the respective republic or provincial assemblies. Bosnia and Montenegro supported the Serbian proposal, while Slovenia, Croatia, Vojvodina, and Kosovo were opposed.[63]

Eventually, in August 1988, the draft amendments to the constitution were published with the idea that they would be discussed and refined and eventually passed.[64] In Slovenia and Croatia, however, these amendments ran into trouble immediately. And in Slovenia, they stimulated ideas of confederation and asymmetric federation. The latter notion held that federal units in a federation do not have to enjoy the same autonomy and prerogatives; these may be tailored to circumstances and needs. This allowed Slovenes to think in terms of their obtaining additional prerogatives *even if the other republics did not want such prerogatives for themselves.*[65] The resulting system could, for example, take the form of a federation within a confederation, with Slovenia having a confederal link with a Yugoslav federation which united the rest of the country. The asymmetric idea enjoyed only a limited life span, however—scarcely much more than a year. By the end of 1989, Slovenes were becoming less interested in asymmetric federation and more interested in confederation, and the atmosphere became steadily more polarized.

In this context, interrepublican clashes over the federal budget acquired a new intensity. In July 1989, the Federal Executive Council proposed a formula under which the republics would pay the federation an additional 61 trillion dinars in order to balance the 1989 federal budget. Only Slovenia and Croatia supported the council's proposal. Montenegro and Bosnia sought to reduce their payments, while Serbia and Montenegro claimed that their allocation from the federal budget would be "unjustifiably reduced" under the proposed distribution arrangement.[66]

There was also a growing realization that Yugoslavia's problems were not different from those of other communist systems in Eastern Europe (except, of course, in regard to the national question, but even here, the national question derived its urgency from the political dynamics which obtained in an illegitimate system). Like the other countries of the region, Yugoslavia's various economic reforms had never been carried through "to the limit," with the result, as author Marijan Korošić put it, that Yugoslavia was constantly forced to adjust and readjust the system. Korošić argued, in fact, that the 1974 constitution was prolonging the Yugoslav crisis and had to be abandoned.[67]

Given all of the aforementioned issues, it will be apparent why the constitutional debate excited widespread interest among the educated public, and why arguments for republic self-determination inevitably led to reconsideration of the parameters of popular self-determination, especially in the form of a multiparty parliamentary system. This broader debate in turn exerted pressure on the party's debate and eventually forced the party to rethink its premises.

An Extraordinary Congress?

By mid-1988, many communists started talking about an extraordinary congress as a way of dealing with the gathering crisis. Slobodan Milošević, as head of the Serbian party, pushed hard for such a congress. The initial impetus for the congress came, in fact, from the Serbian and Vojvodinan party organizations and won early support in Montenegro. But at first, the Slovenian and Croatian parties resisted, fearing that the convocation of an extraordinary congress could be a prelude to the invocation of "special measures" both within the party and in Yugoslavia as a whole. Miloš Prošenc of Slovenia argued that convocation of an extraordinary congress would evoke a state of political "psychosis." Nor was the Bosnian party entirely enthusiastic about the prospect of an extraordinary congress. Speaking to a session of the LCY Central Committee on 19 April 1989, Nijaz Skenderagić of Bosnia came out against the congress, commenting that "certain leaderships and leaders behave like arsonists rather than fire-fighters."[68]

Eventually, however, the various republic organizations agreed to hold the Fourteenth (Extraordinary) Congress in December 1989—a date later postponed until January 1990. The congress was supposed to tackle three issues: reform of the constitutional system, economic reform, and transformation of the LCY.[69] Some people pinned great hopes on the congress, but as the date drew nearer, the prospects for its success grew steadily dimmer. Indeed, the Fourteenth Extraordinary Congress would prove to be the party's swan song.

CHAPTER 12

Hail Caesar! The Rise
of Slobodan Milošević

Hail Caesar! We who are about to die salute you!
—Gladiators' oath, in ancient Rome

Until 1987, it seemed conceivable that Yugoslavia could continue to muddle along—agreeing on long-term programs of stabilization but failing to carry them out, fretting about ethnic violence in Kosovo but being content with containing rather than defusing it, groping its way toward pluralism slowly if persistently.[1] Yugoslavia's regional elites, governing the eight federal units (six republics and two autonomous provinces, all of them defined as "federal units" in the 1974 constitution), continued to quarrel about the fundamental choices in future development. Yet, as long as they quarreled, they were at least talking to each other, and that signaled a degree of consent on the rules of the game. Then, in late 1987, the entire political game was changed overnight. Slobodan Milošević, a former banker, succeeded in deposing his erstwhile mentor, Ivan Stambolić, and in establishing himself as the unrivaled boss in the republic of Serbia. From that bastion, Milošević started to rewrite the rules of the game and, in so doing, dramatically sharpened the growing crisis in Yugoslavia, forcing it to a head.

Since 1974, there had been little overt challenge, until Milošević came along, to the principle that the two autonomous provinces—Kosovo and Vojvodina, both of which lay within the juridical frontiers of the Republic of Serbia—should enjoy de facto parity with the six constituent republics which made up the Socialist Federated Republic of Yugoslavia. Like the republics, the two autonomous provinces enjoyed wide-ranging autonomy and even conducted foreign economic relations independently of the federal government. Milošević was determined to end this.

Before Milošević, there had been a strong tendency to channel power through institutional channels—chiefly the republic party organizations and republic governments. Milošević would turn to mobs and orchestrated protests to marshal and apply power. Before Milošević, there had been a string of "faceless bureaucrats" who, after the death of President Josip Broz Tito in May 1980, seemed determined to prevent the rise of a "new Tito." But Milošević's followers evidently thought of him as a new Tito—or even better—and marched down the streets, bearing his portrait and singing songs in his honor. Before Milošević, the communist party—able to agree on little else—agreed all the same that any resurgence of nationalism would destabilize the system and promote serious political change. The party leaders, therefore, repeatedly reminded each other that "every nationalism is dangerous" and refused to legitimize *any* nationalism. Milošević changed that from the start, openly embracing both Serbian nationalism and Serbian Orthodoxy (the "Serbian" religion). For the first time since the communists had taken power, the Serbian Orthodox Church found itself coddled by the communists.[2] These changes had a powerful effect on the system and pushed it toward a showdown. In the gathering crisis, Milošević's Serbia was initially challenged by Slovenia and Croatia and, as the months unfolded, seemed to wax in strength, only to find itself increasingly isolated.

From Bureaucrat to Politician

In his early months in power, Milošević championed what he called the "anti-bureaucratic revolution," adopting a strategy well known to American politicians who want to paint themselves as "outsiders" and as being "against big government." But Milošević himself was nurtured in the economic bureaucracy and had risen through its ranks.

Born in Požarevac, Serbia, on 29 August 1941, Milošević joined the Communist Party at age 18. He was actively involved in party politics (as chair of the university's party ideological committee) while studying at the University of Belgrade, from which he graduated in 1964 with a degree in law. He took a post in economic management within the party hierarchy, and in 1968 was named to an executive position in the state-owned Tehnogas company; one of his colleagues there was none other than Ivan Stambolić, his later mentor and eventual rival in the Serbian party apparatus. In 1973, Milošević became general director of Tehnogas and, five years later, took the highly visible post of president of Beobanka (Belgrade Bank). In that capacity, he visited the United States several times and, over the years, polished his English. It was not until 1984, however, that Milošević entered politics, when he became head of the Belgrade city committee. He was 43 years old at the time.

Meanwhile, Ivan Stambolić, his former colleague at Tehnogas, had become chair of the Central Committee (CC) of the Serbian party in April 1984. Milošević seemed, at the time, to be a loyal standard-bearer for Stambolić, and there were no detectable differences in their statements on policy matters. Stambolić and Milošević seemed as close as brothers; each served as "best man" at the other's wedding. But it was noticed that at a meeting of the Serbian CC sometime in 1985, Milošević was the only speaker to address the meeting in emotional tones, and the only speaker to be given a passionate applause.[3] Later—in May 1986—Stambolić vacated his position as chair of the CC LC Serbia in order to become president of the Socialist Republic of Serbia. With his blessing, Milošević succeeded him as chair of the Serbian party.

Even at that stage there were signs of a waxing Serbian nationalist backlash in reaction to the repeated Albanian riots in Kosovo and the mass exodus of Serbs and Montenegrins from the province, not to mention the dramatic petitions presented by Kosovar Serbs to the federal authorities in 1982, 1985, and 1986.[4] As early as 1983, in an overt expression of nostalgia for the "good old days," some 100,000 people showed up for the funeral of Aleksandar Ranković. The Memorandum (discussed in chapter 10) thus played to a receptive audience. Even Stambolić found that he had to pay at least lip service to the demands of Serbian nationalism. In his report to the Tenth Congress of the Serbian party (26 May 1986), Stambolić endorsed the Serbian nationalist position that the federal constitution of 1974 was contrary to the interests of Serbs, although he also warned that "certain individuals" were "coquetting" with Serbian nationalism.[5] Stambolić straddled the fence.

Not so Milošević—and gradually differences emerged between the two men. Then, on 24 April 1987, an event occurred which had a profound effect on Milošević. The situation in Kosovo seemed to be deteriorating again, and a meeting of 300 party delegates was called in Kosovo Polje, a suburb of Priština. As head of the Serbian party, Milošević went there to attend the meeting; most of the 300 delegates were, however, ethnic Albanians. When the meeting began, some 15,000 Serbs and Montenegrins—mostly locals but also a few who had come to Kosovo for this purpose—tried to force their way into the hall. The meeting was supposed to be closed. So police blocked their way and started to beat them back with clubs, while the Serbs seized rocks from the bed of a truck which had been conveniently parked in the vicinity and started hurling them at the police. Then Milošević raised his hands, signaling to the police to let the Serbs through, and told the Serbs, "No one should beat you, no one should beat you."[6] These words assured Milošević of a place in Serbian mythology. Milošević stayed in the building until dawn—nearly 14 hours—listening to hundreds of Serbs tell him of their troubles and blame the Albanian leaders of the provincial government for allowing the situation to deteriorate. He emerged from that night a changed man. As a Serbian journalist who had known Milošević for years put it, "After that night, suddenly there was a psychological change in him. All at once, he discovered he had this power over people."[7] The April meeting was presented as if it had been entirely spontaneous. In fact, this was not so, as the parked truck, laden with rocks, suggested.[8]

Milošević's words, "No one should beat you," were repeated over and over again on the television, sending shock waves through Yugoslav society. Within the Republic of Serbia, many functionaries, whether in the press or in political positions, especially in the provinces, who owed their positions to Ivan Stambolić, now drew closer to Milošević, sensing that his star was ascendant. Indeed, with Draža Marković and Petar Stambolić in retirement, there was perhaps only one political figure in Serbia with sufficient prestige to challenge Milošević—that was General Nikola Ljubičić, the People's Hero, minister of national defense, and member of the Yugoslav presidency. But Ljubičić, widely regarded as a principled Titoist having no patience for nationalist manipulations, proved to be entirely opportunistic and gave his support, as he had done consistently in all previous political battles, to the stronger contestant; as the battle between Milošević and the younger Stambolić emerged, Ljubičić threw his stock in with Milošević.[9]

Less than five months after Milošević's visit to Kosovo, on 3 September, Aziz Kelmendi, a 19-year-old Albanian recruit, opened fire in the Paraćin barracks in central Serbia, killing four of his fellow recruits in their sleep (two Bosnian Muslims, one Serb, and one Croat) and wounding five others. Kelmendi was found dead half a mile away; his death was declared a suicide. In spite of the fact that non-Serbs predominated among those killed by Kelmendi, the Belgrade media interpreted the event as an Albanian assault on Serbia. Hence, when the funeral was held for Kelmendi's Serbian victim, about 20,000 Serbs turned out, in a demonstration of national solidarity. As Milošević's adherents drummed up hysteria and hatred of Albanians, Belgrade party chief Pavlović tried to warn his countrymen that Milošević was taking Serbia down the road to disaster by convening a press conference at which he criticized the Serbian party boss. But Milošević already had some key media under his wing, and two days later, the tabloid daily *Politika ekspres* published a fierce attack on Pavlović, penned by Milošević's wife, Mirjana ("Mira") Marković, which accused Pavlović of undermining Serbian and Yugoslav unity.[10] A few days later, the CC LC Serbia convened for its fateful Eighth Plenum (23–24 September 1987). Milošević had put Pavlović's insubordination on the agenda, and Milošević's supporters quickly made mincemeat of the brave Belgrade party chief. Then, Milošević turned on Stambolić, stripping him of his power. Stambolić remained nominal president of Serbia until 14 December, when he was dismissed from office. Milošević would not assume the post of Serbian president until two and a half years later, in May 1989.

The upper echelons in the JNA were troubled by Milošević's *putsch*. Branko Mamula, who served as SRFY minister of defense from May 1982 to May 1988, recalled later that

Some of the leading personalities from the previous leadership of Serbia—Ivan Stambolić and Radiša Gačić, for example—came to us frightened and demoralized and asked
us to protect them if it came to persecution and physical threats.[11]

Mamula recalled that he told them that he did not expect anything illegal, let
alone threats to people's lives. But all the same, Mamula and other figures in the
defense establishment contacted the leaderships of Slovenia, Croatia, and
Bosnia-Herzegovina to see if they could agree to treat Milošević's *putsch* as illegal and adopt remedial measures. These leaders were too self-absorbed at the
time to want to worry about what *might* be the significance of developments in
Serbia. There were also allegations that Zdravko Mustać, head of the federal
State Security Service, had persuaded the Croatian leadership to accept the
results of the Eighth Session of the Serbian party.[12]

Mamula and his deputy, Veljko Kadijević, independently contacted Lazar
Mojsov (of Macedonia) and Boško Krunić (of Vojvodina) in a vain attempt to
bring the question of Milošević's *putsch* before the CC LCY. Krunić, however,
who was serving at the time as chair of the party presidium, actually thought
that Milošević might be preferable to Stambolić, insofar as the latter had made
clear his desire to see the autonomous provinces lose their autonomy.[13] Finding
no support for any remedy anywhere in the country, Mamula and his associates
concluded that there was nothing to be done about the Eighth Session of the LC
Serbia.

With Stambolić ejected from power, Milošević began to put a new program
into effect. Whereas Stambolić had carefully balanced his speeches with veiled
self-contradictions and obscure summons to action which would not be carried
out, Milošević spoke simply and directly and outlined a program he intended, in
fact, to carry out. The program involved four overlapping stages, but these stages
entailed mutually incompatible prerequisites, so that the program appeared
doomed from the start.

The *first stage* in his program entailed establishing his full control in Serbia.
To do so, he felt he needed a pliant press. He therefore fired a number of editors
and journalists at the prestigious "Politika" publishing house. The daily papers
Politika and *Politika ekspres* and the weekly magazines *Duga* and *NIN* became
mouthpieces of Milošević. He also reached out for an alliance with the Serbian
Orthodox Church, giving the Church a new prominence and dignity in social
life. Through the Church, Milošević tapped one of the primordial wellsprings of
Serbian nationalism. Through publications and displays and public events, Serbian society now began to revive memories of its past—especially of the Battle
of Kosovo, at which the Serbian Army of Tsar Lazar had been beaten by the
Ottoman Army in 1389. This battle, which symbolically captures the essence of
the tragedy of Serbia's conquest and occupation by the Ottoman Empire, has
figured prominently in Serbian mythologizing of Kosovo—though the Albanians constituted about 90% of the province's population by the late 1980s. In
June 1989, Milošević joined Serbian Orthodox Church dignitaries in a joint

commemoration of the battle: it was nothing less than a celebration of Serbian nationalism. A year later, on 15 June 1990, Milošević received a delegation of the Serbian Orthodox Church Synod to work out remaining problems in the Church-state relationship in Serbia.[14]

This first stage necessarily entailed the development of a localized "cult of the personality"—the first in socialist Yugoslavia since the death of Tito. It was nothing to see shops and vendors and restaurants displaying photo portraits of Milošević in the front windows. At a more fundamental level, it became impossible for Serbs to criticize Milošević publicly and retain jobs of any importance. Many Serbs were buoyed by an intoxicating senses of Serbian pride, as "Comrade Slobo" began to promote criticism of Tito for having weakened Serbia. Among the alleged anti-Serbian acts said to have been committed by Tito: the removal of large amounts of Serbian industry to new locations in Croatia and elsewhere in the late 1940s and early 1950s;[15] the expansion of the prerogatives and powers of the autonomous provinces, especially after 1968; and the federal constitution itself. Some Serbs told foreigners that they had never been free under Tito but were, with "Slobo" at the helm, "completely free as never before." Other Serbs quietly fretted, as did growing numbers of non-Serbs, that Milošević was patterning himself not merely after Tito, but after Stalin!

Since 1980, 4 May had been observed solemnly each year as a day on which to honor Tito, and in May 1988, Tanjug still commemorated Tito as one of "the great men of the twentieth century."[16] Two years later, the anniversary of Tito's death was marked by a protest march by 2,000 young Serbian nationalists, who shouted anti-Tito chants, destroyed street signs with Tito's name, and demanded that Tito's body be taken out of Belgrade and moved to Croatia.[17] About this time, a group called the Democratic Peasant Ecological Party of Yugoslavia sent a letter to the federal Skupština accusing Tito and Peko Dapčević "of causing the mass killing of children from Serbia who, on orders of the Yugoslav Supreme Command, were sent to the Srem and other fronts during the Second World War, although they were not yet of age to serve in the army."[18] Shortly thereafter, Tito's likeness was removed from the covers of first-grade textbooks in Serbia and replaced by the likeness of Vuk Karadžić, the 19th-century Serbian orthographer.[19]

Supporters of the Titoist line, such as Petar Stambolić, Dragoslav Marković, Miloš Minić, Tihomir Vlaškalić, and Fadilj Hodža, were criticized openly now, while the demand was heard for the posthumous reopening of the question of Ranković's expulsion from the party in September 1966. The aforementioned Marković, at one time president of the federal Skupština, replied to attacks on his good name in a lengthy letter to the LCY Central Committee in September 1988, in which he accused Milošević of mendacious misrepresentations of his record and of stoking inter-ethnic hatreds in order to build his power base.[20]

The *second stage* of Milošević's program involved the establishment of Serbian control over its autonomous provinces and the subversion of Montenegro in order to bring it under the control of pro-Milošević forces. To accomplish this, Milošević proposed to mobilize Serbian and Montenegrin citizens and take politics "to the streets." This stage was aptly captured in the slogan "strong Serbia, strong Yugoslavia." This slogan appealed to many Serbs, but it was deeply alienating to Croats, Slovenes, Macedonians, and Bosnian Muslims, as well as to Kosovo's Albanians, all of whom remembered what Serbian hegemony had meant for them in the interwar kingdom and who likewise remembered the hegemonic aspects of some of Ranković's policies.

With the successful accomplishment of the tasks of the second stage, Milošević hoped, in the *third stage,* to bring down the constitution of 1974, tightening up the federation and reducing the powers of the six constituent republics. There was some support among Serbs for this ambition, since many Serbs, including some at high levels, had resented that constitution above all because of its recognition and consolidation of the expansion of the rights of the autonomous provinces which had begun soon after the disturbances of November 1968. Indeed, "[a]s early as 1975, the Serbian party leadership had made its first attempt to trim back the extensive powers ceded to the provinces." A "Blue Book" made its appearance about that time, which explored the jurisdictional disputes between Serbia and its provinces and advocated rectification to Serbia's advantage. Later, after the Kosovo riots of 1981, a working group was established under the chairmanship of Professor Radoslav Ratković of the University of Belgrade, which "reached the conclusion that Serbia had become steadily more "federalized" ever since 1974." As a first step toward regaining control of the provinces, the Serbian party had demanded that it be allowed to control the flow of its economic assistance to Kosovo, rather than channeling it through the federal fund for the underdeveloped regions. At the time, "the Serbian proposals encountered open opposition in both autonomous provinces," and the Serbian effort to revise the 1974 constitutional order was blocked.[21] But Milošević now took up this cause and made it his own, and he found a way to ram through at least some of the changes which had been demanded by key figures in Belgrade.

And in the *fourth stage,* Milošević promised a reform of the by-then unified system, claiming to favor the marketization of the economy and the controlled democratization of internal party life, but stopping short of the political repluralization of society. What Milošević understood by "controlled democratization" was never entirely clear, but the stress was clearly on *control* rather than *democratization.* Milošević's repeated allusions to the need for democracy and for a free market economy won him respect in the West, particularly in the United States, at first, where it was noted with approval that Milošević looked to South Korea as a kind of model. And at that point, he won some support at home because of his reputation as a technocrat. But in the long run, he looked to political strategies, rather than economic ones, to legitimate his authority and gained a reputation as a Serbian nationalist. This image gradually eclipsed his earlier technocrat image. Moreover, in his bid to use his power base in Serbia to establish his personal political primacy within the SFRY as a whole, Milošević did not shrink from brazen violations of the laws of the land.[22]

The First Stage: Building Strength in Serbia

Milošević once boasted that he had brought Serbia "strong arm" rule (*čvrsta ruka*).[23] His rule was also one continuous celebration of Serbia—indeed, that was the foundation and source of his strength. Milošević appealed to the passions, not to the intellect; he talked of Serbia's place in the world, of struggle, of enemies, of solutions. The spirit of his appeal is captured in the following excerpt from a speech he delivered at an outdoor meeting at the confluence of the Sava and Danube rivers in Belgrade, on 19 November 1988:

This is no time for sorrow; it is a time for struggle. *(indistinct shouting)* This awareness captured Serbia last summer and this awareness has turned into a material force that will stop the terror in Kosovo and unite Serbia. *(indistinct shouting)* This is a process which no longer can be stopped by any force, a process in the face of which all fear is weak. People will even consent to live in poverty but they will not consent to live without freedom, at least not the people gathered here and the people in Serbia, to whom I myself belong and therefore I know that they can only live in freedom and in no other way. *(indistinct shouting)* Both the Turkish and the German invaders know that these people win their battles for freedom.

We entered both world wars with nothing but the conviction that we would fight for freedom, and we won both wars. *(cheers)* Now we have the unified LC stances on Kosovo and we shall implement them energetically to the very end. *(chanting: "Yugoslavia.")*

We shall win the battle for Kosovo regardless of the obstacles facing us inside and outside the country. *(cheers)*. . . . We shall win despite the fact that Serbia's enemies outside the country are plotting against it, along with those in[side] the country. *(cheers)* We tell them that we enter every battle *(Milošević is interrupted by cheers)* with the aim of winning it. *(cheers)*

We have never waged unjust and dishonest battles that would be to the detriment of other peoples. *(shouts of: "that is right")* The people, all citizens regardless of their nationality and profession, are at the head of this battle for Kosovo. And there is no battle in the world that the people have lost. *(shouts of "that is right")* The leadership has little choice there: It shall either head the people and listen to their voice, or time will push it aside. *(cheers)*.[24]

Milošević owed his rise, above all, to the growing Serbian bitterness about the demographic changes in Kosovo and Serbian fears that the province would be "lost." Milošević's style was populist—building popular trust in him personally rather than trust in the political institutions. This aspect of his power was repeatedly demonstrated—for example, in October 1988, when 6,000 angry demonstrators peacefully dispersed moments after Milošević drove up in his car and told them that he would take up their complaints personally. Other Yugo-slav politicians (outside Serbia) began to compare him to Mussolini.[25]

Milošević stoked the fires of Serbian nationalism, and in the resultant atmos-phere, strange things happened. Calls for the posthumous rehabilitation of Aleksandar Ranković have already been noted.[26] Serbs also began talking about a Vatican-Comintern conspiracy and tried to vilify the Catholic Church—the cultural champion of the Serbs' arch-rivals, the Croats. Thus, in 1987, a Belgrade publisher brought out a book which attempted to link the Vatican with the mis-deeds of the Ustaše, and in November 1988, the Serbian Academy of Sciences ordered a scientific meeting on the theme "Jasenovac, 1945–1988," in order to keep alive Serbian resentments of the liquidations of Serbs at the wartime con-centration camp at Jasenovac.[27] There were also reports that Serbs were reor-ganizing Chetnik formations, that these Chetniks were holding demonstrations in traditional insignia and flowing beards, and that Serbian demonstrators in Montenegro were heard chanting, "Long live King Petar!" and "We want the Russians!"[28] Meanwhile, the Serbian Orthodox Church, which had grown accustomed to being treated like an unwelcome stepchild, suddenly found itself lauded and feted in the Serbian press, and its priests, inspired with a new confi-dence, began to take part in nationalist demonstrations and to fantasize about a restoration of the ecclesiastical status quo ante. In fact, many Serbian Orthodox bishops and priests welcomed Milošević's expansionist project. They also wel-comed his legitimation of Serbian nationalism and his reopening of "unre-solved" historical questions. Indeed, on three occasions (May 1990, December 1990, and May 1991), the Serbian Orthodox Church demanded that the state authorize the disinterment of the final remains of persons thrown into caves during World War Two, so that their skeletal remains might be reinterred with proper ceremony. That any such ceremony would stir up bitterness and resent-ment over past suffering was clear to all concerned. It was, further, not without significance that Patriarch Pavle chose to open the regular meeting of the Church Sabor, scheduled for 9–24 May 1991, not in Belgrade, as would have been customary, but in Jasenovac, where he celebrated a holy liturgy commem-orating the 50th anniversary of the suffering of the Serbian people in wartime Croatia. But among Croats, this liturgical offensive was seen as reopening old wounds.[29]

Milošević's style of rule sometimes exploited the Serbian party apparatus as an instrument of power, and, at other times, simply bypassed it. Not without reason did he confess to a French journalist in July 1989 that he was hostile to a multi-party system and actually preferred "a system without parties."[30] In a nonparty system, the people place their trust directly in the leader, who there-fore embodies the will of the people. The formula seemed to work. Said Budimir Kostić, president of the Serbian Investment Bank: "Milošević has [in mid-1989] full support in Serbia, from the peasants to the Academy of Science. He'd get 90 percent of the vote in any election."[31]

The Second Stage: Conquering the Provinces

From early on, Milošević's supporters began saying that Serbia was a second-class republic and that the prerogatives enjoyed by the autonomous provinces of Kosovo and Vojvodina were extraconstitutional. Central to Milošević's program was the "reconquest" of these provinces. To realize this program in Kosovo, the Committee for the Protection of Kosovo Serbs and Montenegrins was set up, under Milošević's wing, in 1988. Between 9 July and 4 September 1988, the committee organized 11 rallies, involving up to 160,000 persons at a time, and by spring 1989, had organized almost 100 protest demonstrations, involving a cumulative total of some 5 million people, or an average of 50,000 participants per demonstration. This committee was a key instrument in Milošević's drive for power. Chair of this committee was Miroslav Šolević, who expressed the committee's philosophy quite simply when he told Radio Zagreb, "If we don't get our rights, we will take up arms."[32] Another important member of the committee was Mića Sparavalo, at one time a lieutenant to UDBa chief Ranković.

On 3 July 1988, the weekly magazine *NIN* published an interview with Milošević, in which the Serbian party leader accused the leaders of Vojvodina and Kosovo of plotting to separate their provinces from Serbia's jurisdiction altogether. The party leadership of Vojvodina reacted immediately, publicly rejecting Milošević's accusation.[33] Less than a week after the publication of Milošević's interview—on 9 July 1988—a seven-hour demonstration took place in Novi Sad, Vojvodina's capital city, in which about 500 Kosovar Serbs were joined by several thousand local Serbs. The demonstrators shouted slogans against Vojvodina's alleged "separatism" and called the province's leaders "traitors." Vojvodina's leaders stood their ground. Three days later, on 12 July, Raif Dizdarević, president of the SFRY presidency, presented a report to the party presidium in an effort to alert that body to the threat posed by such meetings and to try to engage that body in constructive prophylactic action.[34] Vojvodina's leaders met on 15 July and accused Milošević of making a grab for power. Three days later, at a closed session of the 23-member federal party presidium, Vojvodina's leaders demanded that Milošević be fired.[35] But Milošević was able to ride out this challenge, painting these mob demonstrations ("meetings" as the Serbian political jargon of the day had it) as sublime embodiments of democracy. Meanwhile, Milošević kept up the pressure, and in late September, a joint meeting of the Vojvodina presidency and the Vojvodina party leadership released a communiqué warning that "an attack unprecedented in the post–World War II history of Vojvodina has been launched at this province."[36]

On 21 July 1988, members of the SFRY presidency held a meeting with the party and state leaders of Serbia, headed by Slobodan Milošević, and the presidents of the provincial presidencies. In conversation some years later, Dizdarević told me that the presidency was, at the time, already paralyzed. "We could sit and discuss an issue for seven hours," he told me, "and not reach any conclusion."[37] Dizdarević, as president of the presidency, noted that the escalation of tensions was accompanied by ever more aggressive attacks on the legacy of anti-fascist struggle, and thus on the mythology of the party itself. But at the very time that the presidency was meeting with Serbian leaders to warn them of the dangers in staging nationalistic mass meetings, the Committee for Protests and Solidarity with Kosovar Serbs and Montenegrins, headed by Miroslav Šolević, was making preparations for the departure of Serbs and Montenegrins from Kosovo to Pančevo, where they intended to hold another inflammatory "meeting of solidarity" to undermine the Vojvodinan leadership. At a pause in the session, Dizdarević pulled aside Petar Gračanin, president of the Serbian presidency, and Milošević and pressured them to prevent the planned meeting in Pančevo from taking place. Milošević promised to do so, and later, when the session resumed, informed those present that he had, during the break, dispatched a group of emissaries to Kosovo to see that the meeting in Pančevo was called off. It was an empty promise, however, and the gathering in Pančevo went forward, with the participation of about 10,000 persons.[38]

The situation took a turn for the worse in August 1988, when public meetings shook Pančevo, Titograd, Kolašin, Novi Vrbas, Srpski Miletić, and other towns in Serbia, Vojvodina, and Montenegro. Among the slogans shouted by participants were "Give us arms!" "We want weapons!" "Long live Serbia—death to Albanians!" and "Montenegro is Serbia!" Dizdarević would later claim that he had evidence that Šolević's committee, which was behind these disturbances, was doing Milošević's bidding.[39]

Meanwhile, Milošević also set in motion efforts to destabilize Montenegro and Bosnia, with the aim of installing his followers in power in those republics, too. An early move came on 20 August 1988, when his action committee organized a protest involving 30,000 people in the Montenegrin capital of Titograd.[40] Further protests followed on 18 September (50,000 persons in Nikšić) and 7 October (in Titograd). The latter demonstrations initially shook the confidence of the republic leadership, which briefly considered bowing to the protesters' demands that the leadership resign. Instead, the Montenegrin leaders sent club-wielding police to disperse the crowd. Later, to appease them, the local politicians gave the workers wage increases of up to 30%.

At the end of August and beginning of September, the party leaders of Bosnia-Herzegovina, Croatia, Vojvodina, and Kosovo issued sharp condemnations of the mass meetings. The Slovenian leadership registered a mild criticism; the leadership of Montenegro offered a watered-down "compromise"; and the Macedonian leadership kept silent. A meeting of the SFRY presidency in mid-September heard warnings that Yugoslavia's very survival was at stake. General Nikola Ljubičić, who had served as SFRY minister of defense for 12 years before being elected president of the Serbian presidency in 1982 and later member of the SFRY presidency in 1984, met with Milošević in September to express his own personal fears for the future.[41]

But all such cautions and warnings were to no avail, and on 6 October 1988,

Milošević mobilized some 100,000 supporters on the streets of Novi Sad. They carried portraits of Milošević, Tito, Lenin, and Lola Ribar; at that time, Milošević had not yet begun to distance himself in symbolic terms from Tito, let alone to associate himself with Chetnik leader Draža Mihailović.[42] This time the pressure was too much for the local communist leaders to resist; the entire leadership of Vojvodina resigned, including provincial party chief Milovan Šogorov and provincial president Nandor Major. Further resignations were tendered in the cities and local communities of Vojvodina.[43] In their places, Milošević installed his own people: in particular, Nedeljko Sipovac became party chief in Vojvodina, while Mihalj Kertes took over the presidency.

In emotional terms, Vojvodina was only a dress rehearsal for Kosovo—the real jewel in the Serbian crown, despite its extreme poverty. Further rallies in Belgrade, Smederevo, and various cities throughout Serbia, as well as a march of 17,000 Serbs and Montenegrins through the streets of Priština on 9 August 1988 (by coincidence, Milošević's birthday), helped prepare the way for a takeover in the largely Albanian-populated province as well. Already in May 1988, Azem Vllasi had been forced out of his post as chair of the party leadership in Kosovo. Kaqusha Jashiri, a 42-year-old civil engineer turned trade union functionary, was installed in his place. But if politicians in Belgrade thought that the half-Montenegrin Jashari (on her mother's side) would be more "cooperative," they were to be sadly disappointed, as Jashari took up the defense of Kosovo's autonomy along the same lines as Vllasi had done.[44] Meanwhile, local Serbs, backed by Milošević, escalated their challenge to the constitutional order in Kosovo. On 11 June 1988, the draft of a new Serbian constitution was published, with articles assigning defense and security within the provinces unambiguously to Belgrade. Moreover, as Šolević's newly established committee proceeded with meetings directed toward applying mass pressure on the existing constitutional system, Deputy Defense Minister Stane Brovet (a Slovene) signaled the army's sympathy for these meetings in late September, telling an audience of army officers that

> there were three kinds of meetings: first, hostile meetings, including those critical of the army; second, meetings having socio-economic roots, reflecting the difficult economic situation; and third, meetings in which people, especially Serbs and Montenegrins, tried to secure their rights within the system. One could not condemn meetings of this third kind [he felt].[45]

These developments were deeply unsettling to non-Serbs, and at the Seventeenth Plenary Session of the CC LCY, held 17–20 October 1988, there were tough words for Milošević, as Šuvar rallied the opposition to Milošević's destabilizing campaign. But Milošević used the occasion to reply to his critics, characterizing the outgoing provincial leadership in Vojvodina as "counterrevolutionary" and distancing himself from Serbian nationalist rhetoric which, he claimed, figured only marginally in the "meetings."[46] At the same time, Milošević had soothing words for his critics, assuring them that "Serbia does not have pretensions to the territory of other republics, but it has pretensions [only] to the territory of its own republic."[47] In other words, if the other republics allowed Milošević to annihilate the autonomy of the two provinces, he and other Serbs would be fully satisfied, and Yugoslavia could get back to "normal." The other republics accepted this assurance at face value and stepped aside as Milošević resumed his pressure on the leadership in Priština, ignoring Jashari's warning, in the pages of *Nedeljna borba* in early October, about the dangers associated with the way Belgrade was manipulating Serbian nationalism.[48]

In November 1988, Ekrem Arifi and some other outspoken allies of Jashari and Vllasi were forced to resign. By January 1989, Jashari herself had been forced out of power, and police chief Rahman Morina, a Milošević protégé, was elected president of the party presidium in Kosovo. The following month, the Serbian parliament unanimously approved a package of amendments which effectively snuffed out the autonomy of the two provinces. On 24 March 1989, the deputies to the provincial parliament, having been visited by the police on the eve of the vote, timidly and obediently voted to approve the amendments; of the 187 deputies present, only 10 voted to reject the amendments.[49] With this, Kosovo was shorn of its autonomy. Meanwhile, on 2 March, Vllasi, the former provincial party president, and two leading figures in the Trepča mines were arrested, in connection with a hunger strike which some 1,500 miners had conducted briefly in protest of the removal of Jashari and of pressures on the province's autonomy. Vllasi was put on trial on charges of organizing Albanian unrest between November 1988 and March 1989, only to be acquitted in April 1990.[50] Milošević also pledged to construct some 2,000 new dwellings in Kosovo by 1993 for the use of Serbian families who should decide to return to the province, funding the construction almost entirely out of federal funds.[51]

On 10 January 1989, there was renewed unrest in Titograd, Montenegro's capital. Božina Ivanović, president of the presidency in Montenegro, telephoned Dizdarević and told him that the situation in her republic was "alarming." By 11 a.m., some 15,000 persons were on the streets, supporting a list of exclusively political demands prepared in advance.[52] The protests continued the following day; by the afternoon of 11 January, there were some 50,000 protesters on the streets, and Montenegrin functionaries feared that the number could double. Finally, on the afternoon of the second day of protests, the entire Montenegrin collective presidency resigned, along with Montenegro's delegates in the federal party presidium (Marko Orlandić, Vidoje Žarković, and Slobodan Filipović) and its member in the federal collective presidency (Veselin Djuranović).[53] They were replaced by supporters of Milošević. Serbian nationalists had long tended to regard Montenegrins merely as coastal Serbs, and scholars had argued back and forth throughout the 1970s and 1980s about whether Montenegrins came from the same ethnic stock as Serbs. This controversy was now revived with a vengeance, as pro-Serbian Montenegrins urged the annexation of Montenegro to the Republic of Serbia.[54]

By early 1989, Milošević seemed to be in a strong position. He controlled Serbia, Kosovo, and Vojvodina outright. He had installed his people in Montene-gro. Macedonia was, for the time being, allied with Milošević. And Milošević had quietly sent agents of the Serbian security service into Bosnia in order to gather intelligence and subvert the republic from within—although this did not come to light until October 1989.[55] In fact, the Serbian security service had been especially active in Srebrenica and Bratunac, two towns in eastern Bosnia close to the border with Serbia; insofar as this had not been cleared with the Sarajevo government, this activity was completely illegal.[56] A confident Milošević now assumed the post of state president of Serbia on 8 May, sanctioned by a unani-mous open vote.[57] Meanwhile, having destroyed the autonomy of the provinces, Milošević nonetheless was able to pocket the provinces' representatives in the collective presidency, representatives allocated on the presumption of the provinces' autonomy. Only later (in 1991) did the Croatian delegation object, in the federal Skupština, that "if Serbia did not recognize the Assembly of Kosovo or the presidency of Kosovo, [and] if by its own constitution, it had eliminated the autonomy of Kosovo, then it could not 'in the name of Kosovo' send anyone from Kosovo to the presidency."[58] But by that point federal structures were in an advanced state of decay, the LCY had disappeared from the political land-scape, and the other republics seemed to have little or no leverage any longer against the "Serbian bloc."

The Third Stage: Bringing Down the Constitution

As early as 1988, Milošević's moves had stirred federal party president Stipe Šuvar to defend the constitutional status quo against the revisionist Milošević. Šuvar had, for years, figured as a centralist and had, therefore, long been more popular in Serbia than in his native Croatia.[59] But now Šuvar criticized Milošević's use of street demonstrations. On 19–20 January 1989, the new pro-Milošević leadership of Vojvodina held an extraordinary conference of the LC Vojvodina at which there were sharp attacks on Šuvar, together with demands that he be dismissed from office. Milošević, in turn, accused Šuvar of opposing the people's will, and at a stormy session of the Central Committee on 30 Janu-ary 1989, various Serbian leaders called for Šuvar's resignation. Šuvar suddenly became the rallying point for anti-Milošević sentiment, and former critics of Šuvar now became his loudest advocates. Milošević tried to orchestrate Šuvar's removal from office before the expiration of his term in May 1989, but failed, and Šuvar served out his term. Meanwhile, on 26 January 1989, the SFRY pres-idency was informed that the party organization of the city of Belgrade was preparing to stage demonstrations once the scheduled plenum of the CC began, in order to bring force to the demand that the entire membership of the CC LCY resign from office. General Kadijević, who had taken over duties as minis-ter of defense in May 1988, told state president Dizdarević that he had reliable information that in some factories there were preparations to bring factory workers onto the streets during the time the plenum was in session.[60]

Having identified himself for three years with the slogan "strong Serbia, strong Yugoslavia"—a slogan which had endeared him to Serbs but alienated non-Serbs—Milošević tried, in the course of 1989, to repackage himself in order to complete his program. He therefore tried to identify himself with what he called the "anti-bureaucratic revolution." He also talked of the need to build a "modern, efficient, stable state"—by which he meant a centralized state.[61] But Milošević's efforts to mobilize the Serbian population in Bosnia only consolidated the anti-Serbian solidarity between Bosnian Croats and Bosnian Muslims, and the more the Belgrade media harped on "the alleged imperilment of Serbs in Bosnia-Herzegovina,"[62] the more the Bosnian communist leadership (voted out of power in 1990) tended to look to Slovenia and Croatia for allies against Milošević.

In Macedonia, moreover, locals were becoming increasingly agitated already in early 1989 by the proliferation in that republic of slogans, graffiti, and songs glorifying Serbian leader Milošević.[63] In fact, the Macedonians were already upset that Milošević was refusing to discuss an adjustment of the Serbian-Macedonian border since the border drawn after World War Two had placed the Monastery of Prohor Pčinski, dear to Macedonian Orthodox believers, on the Serbian side of the border. Then Milošević proposed a law to allow Serbs who had land titles from the interwar period to reclaim their land. The measure was designed to provide a legal basis for large numbers of Serbs to move to Kosovo, but it also threatened to dislocate Macedonians. Relations between the two republics, accordingly, soured. And subsequently, Milošević introduced a proposal to declare 1 December—the day on which the establishment of the Kingdom of Serbs, Croats, and Slovenes had been proclaimed in 1918—a national holiday. But any celebration of the old Kingdom inevitably hurt Macedonian sensitivities, since they recalled that the old Kingdom had called them "south Serbs" and had denied them any cultural or educational guarantees.

As for Slovenia and Croatia, they were, by the latter part of 1989, rapidly moving from a defense of the quasi-confederal status quo to advocacy of a multi-party system and full-fledged confederalization of Yugoslavia. Already in February 1989, the Croatian Writers' Association was openly calling on Milošević to resign from office.[64] In the meantime, Milošević had suffered two setbacks (in addition to his failure to remove Šuvar from office). The first was the aforementioned acquittal of Vllasi on 24 April 1990, the third anniversary of Milošević's historic visit to Kosovo. The second was the installation (already in 1988) of Croat Ante Marković as prime minister, instead of Borisav Jović, Milošević's preferred candidate for the post.[65] By June 1990, moreover, Marković was found, by pollsters, to be the most popular politician in the country—with growing support even in Milošević's Serbian backyard.[66] Then, in mid-June 1990, a remarkable political inversion occurred: some 30,000 Serbs marched through Belgrade carrying Serbian flags with the old (precommunist) Serbian insignia, chanting "Down with communism!" and bearing pictures of Milošević, with a black "X" across his face and the slogan written above, "We don't want another dictator!"[67]

The Consequences of Repluralization

Beginning in 1988, independent political parties started to form in Yugoslavia. By early 1990, there were 86 of them, including six in Serbia. In Croatia, retired General Franjo Tudjman formed a political party with a vaguely eclectic program, calling it the Croatian Democratic Community (HDZ, from the Croatian *Hrvatska Demokratska Zajednica*).[68] In January 1990, the Slovenian party severed its links with the LCY. Free elections were scheduled to be held in Slovenia and Croatia in spring. In April, the anti-communist "Demos" coalition won 55% of the vote in Slovenia; Lojze Peterle, a Christian Democrat, became prime minister. Milan Kučan, the outgoing head of the LC Slovenia, won 44% of the vote in the first round of the presidential elections and captured 58% in the second round (defeating runner-up Jože Pučnik) to become Slovenia's first "postcommunist" president. In Croatia, the reformed communist party, the Party of Democratic Change (SDP) headed by Ivica Račan, was widely expected to win the elections; Račan himself was confident of victory until the very eve of the elections and saw to it that the apportionment of seats in the Sabor would give a disproportionate advantage to the party gaining the largest number of votes. But the rising tide of Serbian nationalism, both within Serbia and among the Serbs of Croatia, produced a backlash among Croats, who streamed to Tudjman's banner. The Croatian elections involved two rounds—on 22–23 April and 6–7 May 1990—and brought the HDZ 42% of the votes. Because of the stipulations in the electoral law, this gave the HDZ 58.62% of the seats in the Chamber of Districts, 67.5% of the votes in the Socio-Political Chamber, and 51.88% of the seats in the Chamber of Associated Labor (see Table 12.1).[69]

The new noncommunist governments of Slovenia and Croatia immediately removed the red star from their flags, and the Slovenian parliament shortly issued a somewhat ambiguous declaration of "sovereignty" (not independence), explaining that Slovenian law overrode federal law, and that the latter would apply only when it was consistent with Slovenian law.[70] The Croatian Sabor likewise declared the Republic of Croatia "sovereign." One of Croatian president Tudjman's earliest decisions was to take actions to change the proportion of Serbs in the Croatian police force. Although Serbs constituted about 12% of the population, they made up about 75% of the police force of Croatia. Tudjman authorized the firing of Serbs from the police and their replacement by Croats; by November 1992, Serbs constituted only 28% of the force. Some Serbs were pushed out of the force, others left in protest of the Croatian government's decision to remove the red star from the insignia on the police uniform, and still

Table 12.1. Distribution of Seats in the Croatian Sabor, as a Result of the 1990 Elections

	Number of seats
Croatian Democratic Community (HDZ)	193
Party for Democratic Change (SDP)	81
Others	91

Source: Paul Garde, *Život i smrt Jugoslavije,* trans. from French by Živan Filippi (Zagreb: Ceres, 1996), p. 274.

others left in order to join the insurgent forces being organized among Croatian Serbs.[71]

Tanjug, the Yugoslav news agency, was by that point embattled, as Milošević gradually inserted more and more of his people into positions at the agency. Risto Lazarev, a ruggedly independent and politically astute veteran journalist from Macedonia, was director-general of Tanjug at the time and did his best to block Milošević's moves, staying on even after the war had begun. But in February 1992 he was dismissed from that post, on the argument that a Macedonian could not be the head of a Serbian news agency.[72] In the meantime, seeing which way the wind was blowing, the new HDZ-controlled Croatian government set up its own news agency (the Hrvatska Informativna Novinska Agencija, or HINA). On 1 August, Bosnia-Herzegovina declared itself a "sovereign and democratic state."[73] These declarations prepared the way for possible declarations of withdrawal from the Yugoslav federation.

About the same time, the Bosnian government announced that it would hold multi-party elections on 18 November. Alija Izetbegović's Party of Democratic Action (SDA, from the Bosnian *Stranka za Demokratsku Akciju*) swept the Muslim vote for the parliamentary elections, winning 86 seats, alongside 72 for the Serbian Democratic Party, 44 for the Bosnian branch of the HDZ, 14 for the reformed communists, and 12 for a reform party created by Ante Marković.[74] Izetbegović won 40% of the popular vote among Muslim candidates, eight percentage points behind the popular Fikret Abdić; but as per a pre-election arrangement, Izetbegović became president of the Bosnian state presidium. The small Democratic Socialist Alliance, led by Mirko Pejanović, a Bosnian Serb of anti-nationalist persuasion, was marginalized. But even before the elections, Pejanović met with Karadžić to warn him that his advocacy of the formation of municipal organizations based on the national concept, in effect declaring certain towns and areas to be Serb, "would lead sooner or later to conflict between the Bosnian nations." But now, in the wake of the elections, as Pejanović has noted, the three nationalist parties, in spite of their earlier professions of readiness to cooperate, drifted steadily further apart.[75]

Macedonia had already scheduled elections for that month, in which the nationalist-oriented IMRO-DPMNU won the largest number of seats (see Table 12.2). When the first-place IMRO-DPMNU failed to form a government, how-

Table 12.2. Distribution of Seats in the Macedonian Assembly, as a Result of the 1990 Elections

	Number of seats
IMRO–DPMNU	37
Social Democratic Party (former communists)	31
Party of Democratic Prosperity (Albanian)	25
Reform Party (led by Ante Marković)	18
Others	8

Source: Paul Garde, *Život i smrt Jugoslavije,* trans. from French by Živan Filippi (Zagreb: Ceres, 1996), p. 286.

ever, a coalition involving the Social Democratic Party (former communists), the Party of Democratic Progress (an Albanian party), and the small Liberal Party was formed, with Branko Crvenkovski as prime minister. The highly popular Kiro Gligorov, a 73-year-old veteran of the Partisan war, who had had a long career in politics and administration before retiring in 1978, came out of retirement to run for the presidency of Macedonia. And in Montenegro, the government amended the republic constitution in order to lay a legal basis for holding multi-party elections. Montenegro's communists swept to victory, winning 83 of the 125 seats in the Assembly, while their candidate for president of the republic, Momir Bulatović, garnered 77% of the vote.[76] Even the Serbian leadership was eventually forced, reluctantly, to agree to promise a multi-party system.

Meanwhile, Milošević was faced with new competition for the Serbian "nationalist" vote. Two new parties, set up between 1990 and early 1991, were expressly nationalist in character—one ostensibly monarchist and one crypto-fascist. The former traced its origins to the founding of the Serbian National Renewal (SNO) on 6 January 1990; the SNO was an outgrowth of the Saint Sava Society, set up by Vuk Drašković in Nova Pazova earlier. But SNO president Mirko Jović, a local café owner, and SNO vice president Drašković fell out, and Drašković left the party on 10 March, taking his adherents with him. Four days later, he merged his faction with Vojislav Šešelj's Serbian Freedom Movement (SSP), to form the Serbian Renewal Movement (SPO) on 14 March 1990.[77] This organization called for a restoration of the Serbian Karadjordjević dynasty at the head of a Greater Serbia, which would include the territories of Serbia (including Vojvodina and Kosovo), Montenegro, and Macedonia, as well as those regions in Bosnia and Croatia (such as Knin and parts of Dalmatia) which had heavy concentrations of Serbs. In keeping with the restorationist inspiration of this program, the SPO also promised that "the state institution[s], the economy, education, the army, [the position of] the Church, and foreign policy would be restored in the form corresponding to the period [of the interwar Kingdom]."[78]

But Šešelj, in turn, quarreled with Drašković. The bone of contention was Siniša Kovačević's play "Saint Sava," which Šešelj considered offensive; Šešelj told Drašković that he wanted to disrupt the play, but Drašković thought that "a theatre is not a place for shouting and howling."[79] Thereupon, Šešelj left the SPO (on 31 May). Šešelj, whose family origins lay in eastern Herzegovina and who had earned a doctorate in 1979 with a dissertation titled "The Essence of Fascism and Militarism," organized his own party, the Serbian Chetnik Movement (SČP) on 18 June 1990, which was denied official registration, however, on the grounds of its overt identification with Mihailović's wartime Chetniks. Later, on 23 February 1991, through a merger of the SČP with the National Radical Party (NRS), the Serbian Radical Party was formed, with Šešelj as party president and Tomislav Nikolić, hitherto associated with the NRS, as vice president. The Serbian Radical Party oriented itself as a neo-fascist party with maximalist territorial ambitions for Serbian expansion.[80]

In the meantime, Milošević, who had hitherto declared confederalization "unacceptable," had to concede, by late June 1990, that this solution had become a very real possibility; indeed, it was probably the one route whereby Yugoslavia might have survived. But in this context, Milošević added, ominously, that in the event that Yugoslavia became a confederation, the external borders of Serbia would be an "open question."[81] Even more ominously, the draft of the new constitution of the Republic of Serbia gave the president of Serbia an unusual new prerogative—the power to declare war and conclude peace. This, of course, presumed the creation of an independent Serbian Army, as Macedonian politicians were quick to note.[82] Just as obviously, this new prerogative was a dangerous escalation in a country which had been abuzz for about three years with rumors of impending civil war.

Sliding toward Catastrophe

Milošević had a profound effect on developments in Yugoslavia. His concerted campaign to refashion Yugoslavia along centralist lines and to erode the two autonomous provinces provoked a powerful anti-Serbian reaction throughout the rest of the country, a reaction that wedded pro-democracy sentiment to pro-confederation sentiment in Slovenia and Croatia. In what appeared to be a last-ditch effort to consolidate at least his minimal program, Milošević staged a referendum on 1 July 1990, asking Serbian voters to endorse constitutional changes which would virtually eliminate any vestige of provincial autonomy. The supposedly docile Kosovo Assembly replied the following day by declaring Kosovo a republic, independent from Serbia, though still a constituent part of the Yugoslav federation.[83]

The Serbian parliament replied by suspending the provincial assembly and the provincial executive council and assuming full and direct control of the province. Serbian authorities dismissed the editors of Kosovo's principal Albanian-language newspapers, as well as the station managers of radio and television stations. Albanian-language broadcasts ceased. Police even occupied the offices of the Kosovo Writers' Association, which had become politicized. When *Rilindja*, the Priština daily, nonetheless continued to criticize Serbian policy, Milošević closed the paper down as well. On 4 September, Albanians observed a 24-hour general strike, virtually shutting down the province. Meanwhile, some 111 members of Kosovo's dissolved assembly—representing about two-thirds of the body's membership—met clandestinely and drew up an alternative constitution for Kosovo which spelled out Kosovo's rights as a republic within the Yugoslav federation (or confederation) and designated Albanian as the official language of the Republic of Kosovo.[84] Milošević replied by ordering the arrest of the deputies to Kosovo's now-banned assembly.

The new governments of Slovenia and Croatia declared themselves ready for immediate negotiations on the transformation of Yugoslavia into a confederation.[85] But Yugoslavia was distinctly unstable, and the lame-duck governments of Macedonia and Bosnia were not really in a position to negotiate something so fundamental as the confederalization of the country, while the governments of Serbia and Montenegro were completely opposed to any such notion, which ran counter to their own preferred solution.

With the federal government in decay, the republics drifting apart, the sense of community seriously eroded, cultural and political ties reduced to their lowest levels since 1945, Kosovo operating under conditions of *apartheid,* and Serbia and Slovenia granting themselves the supreme authority in matters of defense and security, thus denying the authority of the federal government, Yugoslavia seemed ripe for violent disintegration.[86] As bad as the situation in Kosovo was, however, and in spite of the fact that Kosovo became an issue between Slovenia and Serbia in the course of 1989, thus contributing to the inflammation of interrepublican relations broadly, the most dangerous flashpoint in Yugoslavia at the time was the Serbian region in Croatia. And under Milošević's influence, Croatia's Serbs started to press demands, calling for "political autonomy" and insisting that if Yugoslavia were to become a full-fledged confederation, Serbs would have the "right" to create an autonomous province within Croatia.[87] In summer 1989, there had been an abortive effort to set up an autonomous Serbian cultural society (the "Zora Society") in the Knin region of Croatia: Croatia's communist authorities had immediately banned the organization and jailed its chief organizer, Jovan Opačić.[88] When the Serbian Writers' Association sprang to Opačić's defense and took up the cause of political autonomy for Croatia's Serbs,[89] Croatian authorities blasted the association for seeking to change Croatia's borders and to destabilize the republic altogether.[90] In August 1990, following the election of Tudjman's noncommunist government in Croatia, leaders of Croatia's Serbian community pledged to seek territorial-political autonomy—a solution unacceptable to either the Croatian people or the Croatian government. But Jovan Rašković, president of the Serbian Democratic Party, recruited for this position by his fellow psychiatrist Radovan

Karadžić, declared, "If the Croatian people want their own state, then the Serbs will decide their own fate."[91] Rašković added that if Croatia seceded from Yugoslavia, Croatia's Serbs would try to attach their areas to Serbia.

In mid-August, Croatian Serbs conducted a referendum on autonomy within Croatia, defying a ban by Zagreb authorities. There were maneuvers by armored vehicles of the Croatian police, and meanwhile, hundreds of Serbs, armed with AK-47 rifles and pistols, sealed the roads to Knin, felling trees to block entry. Federal army units were also sent into the Knin region, contributing to the tension.[92] Meanwhile, *Politika* blasted Croatian president Tudjman simultaneously for trying to restore the Ustaše and for copying Tito and pledged the support of Belgrade Serbs for the Serbian minority in Croatia.[93] These developments were clearly encouraged by Milošević's policies.

Officially, 756,781 Serbs took part in the 9 August–2 September referendum. Of this total, it was reported, 756,549 voted for Serbian autonomy, 172 voted against, and 60 ballots were invalid. On 1 October 1990, the Serb National Council in Croatia declared the autonomy of areas in Croatia inhabited primarily by Serbs.[94] With this move, civil order broke down in Croatia. The Croatian Ministry of Internal Affairs, meanwhile, decided to confiscate the weapons of local militias, which is to say, to disarm Serbian civilians. The Serbs, who were already receiving arms transfusions from the JNA, resisted, raiding at least one police station, burglarizing gun shops, and erecting barricades around Knin and other municipalities.[95] Railway lines to Knin were also cut. Meanwhile, Serbs in Belgrade gathered in front of the Parliament building, shouting, "We want arms" and "Let's go to Croatia!"[96] A similar rally took place in Zagreb. The individual republics' ever-greater assertion of control over their own military districts seemed to prefigure eventual warfare. In mid-October, the Slovenian prime minister, Lojze Peterle, even suggested that Slovenia would welcome an international peacekeeping force if the situation deteriorated any further.

Milošević was a catalyst for crisis; his campaigns forced things to a head. But the processes which unfolded had deep roots, and pressure for repluralization and confederalization had been building for some two decades.[97] Indeed, the demand for the restoration of political pluralism had never vanished, as the discussion in chapters 5–8 made clear; the illegitimacy of socialist Yugoslavia's one-party system left the system vulnerable and in a state of perpetual crisis. Milošević talked a great deal about democracy and free enterprise (though, in fact, his policies were directed toward the transformation of the Serbian economy along kleptocratic state capitalist lines[98]), but he was driven by a hunger for power and prepared to take the country to war in order to realize his ambitions.

In his dialogue *Gorgias,* written possibly in 385 BCE, Plato (via Socrates) argued that the effect of bad government was to make people "less moral" and "wilder,"[99] so that bad government—which is to say also illegitimate government, as the most glaring manifestation of "bad government"—pushes the society in the direction of violence, stirring up conflicts which naïve observers take to be "ancient." The Titoist system, which tried to find some quasi-legitimation in memories of the Partisan struggle, kept alive the mythologies of World War Two, in the process slowing the healing process from all the bitterness stirred up during the years 1941–1945. But if Tito's system contributed to making people "wilder" in this way, it also had some countervailing energies, which worked in the opposite direction. With Milošević at the head of the Serbian party, however, there was a powerful agent pushing consciously in the direction of making Serbs "wild." This was palpably dangerous.

There are at least two great questions which one may pose at this point. First, why did Milošević succeed in his unconstitutional and illegal campaign to seize control not only of Serbia but also of Montenegro, Kosovo, and Vojvodina? And second, was the system in fact destroyed by Milošević and his cohorts, or did they merely finish off a system already in an advanced state of decay, in which, as Obrad Kesić put it, there were various "crises . . . many of which could have proven fatal for Yugoslavia if all the right circumstances [had been] in place."[100] To answer these questions it is necessary to reiterate that Serbian nationalism was revived in the 1980s as the expression of collectively experienced victimization, in which the system's infrastructure, framework, policies, or responses were seen as illegitimate, taking the form of chauvinism and being reflected in a heightened readiness to perpetrate violence against group outsiders. Thus, it was precisely the illegitimacy of the Titoist and post-Titoist system which allowed collective resentments to fester and which enabled Milošević to play the nationalist card. The system did not collapse in 1971 or in 1981, rather obviously, because not "all the right circumstances" were present at those earlier times. But by the time Milošević came to power, four conditions had changed, thereby rendering this illegitimate system especially vulnerable to collapse: the serious deterioration of the economy, with rising indebtedness, rising unemployment, and rising rates of inflation; the repeated violations of the harm principle between ethnic communities, with verbal attacks becoming commonplace, thereby undermining the sense of a Yugoslav community as such; the rapid withering away of federal authority after Tito's death; and an inability of key political figures such as Stipe Šuvar (chair of the party presidium) and Stane Dolanc (member of the collective presidency) to realize that Milošević's ambitions were not limited to the autonomous provinces, and a lack of will on the part of various figures, both within Serbia and elsewhere in socialist Yugoslavia, to mount a serious effort to stop Milošević in his tracks. These four conditions were "the right circumstances" in which a power-hungry politician could bring the system down. Had the leading politicians in Slovenia, Croatia, Bosnia-Herzegovina, and Macedonia understood the situation earlier and had they reacted decisively and cooperatively, it is conceivable that history might have unfolded along different lines.

CHAPTER 13

The Road to War

The year 1989 was a turning point in the evolution of Yugoslav politics. Several factors entered into this. First, as already discussed, the party apparatus started crumbling at a fast pace, from the bottom up. Citizens stopped going to meetings, local committees stopped functioning and closed up, party members returned their party cards, and the party's "reach" steadily shrank. Second, inflation was soaring at 800–900% most of the year, and topped 1,000% by the end of the year. This had a tremendous impact on people's mood, attitudes, and behavior at all levels—including politics. Third, the national question, which had seemed to be under control in the late 1970s and still roughly manageable in the first half of the 1980s, had clearly reemerged as a powerful force in the course of the latter half of the 1980s—that, to some extent, as a product of Milošević's program and strategy. Fourth, in Kosovo in particular, after the Serbian annexation of the province in March 1989, extinguishing most of the province's juridical prerogatives, the Kosovo question alone became vastly more serious, as Serb-Albanian tensions took a turn for the worse. Fifth, the continuing constitutional debate contributed to a sense that change was not only necessary but inevitable. And sixth, the changes sweeping through other parts of Eastern Europe—in particular, Poland and Hungary, but eventually also East Germany and Czechoslovakia—helped redouble Yugoslavs' growing impatience with their system, as they saw their neighbors make their first steps toward democratization. As a result, by 1989, the system had lost its earlier resilience and had become, in fact, quite fragile. There was a growing sense that it was breathing its last breath.

Slovenia versus Serbia

As of 1989, the Serbian party was advocating that the federation be restructured in such a way as to incorporate the principle "one person, one vote" while insisting that in Kosovo, the interests of 10% of the population took precedence over those of the other 90%. And after the Opačić affair in Croatia, the Belgrade regime began advocating the right of the Serbian minority in Croatia (12.2% of Croatia's population) to enjoy an autonomous region, even though Serbs already had a republic of their own and even though Belgrade was, at the same time, denying that the Albanians had any right even to autonomy in Kosovo, let alone to their own republic.

Slovenia's view of the situation was radically different from Serbia's, and already in 1988, serious polemics divided the two leaderships. In early autumn 1988, the Serbian leadership approached the Slovenian leadership and asked for the latter's support for the proposed amendments to the Serbian constitution. The Slovenian leadership, however, refused, saying that this would amount to interference in Serbia's internal affairs.[1] This might have sufficed for Belgrade, as a token of Slovenian disinterest in the provinces, but in the closing months of 1988, Slovenian-Serbian relations soured. Milošević's political ambitions and program were increasingly unsettling to the Slovenes. "This Stalinist concept of 'democratic centralism' unavoidably leads to extolling the central figure [as] a living god," Slovenia's president, Janez Stanovnik, said of Serbia in a 1988 interview. "When you start worshipping a leader, you no longer have a population that is able to act democratically."[2] Slovenia's leaders accused Serbia's of "Stalinism," and Serbia's leaders accused Slovenia's of "betrayal." Hostility bred distrust, and by mid-October 1988, the two leaderships were no longer on speaking terms. On 16 November, the SFRY presidency intervened in the dispute and urged the leaderships of Slovenia and Serbia to meet.[3] But nothing came of this initiative. On the contrary, Serbs started boycotting Slovenian products. Belgrade citizens also started withdrawing their savings from the Bank of Ljubljana. And the director of the Jugoexport work organization threatened to terminate joint ventures with some 88 Slovenian partners.[4]

At this stage, the writers' associations of Slovenia and Serbia played a key role. In late February 1989, when Albanian miners at the Trepča mine in Kosovo went on strike, the Slovenian Writers' Association held a public meeting at Cankarjev Dom (Cankar Hall) in Ljubljana, criticizing the stationing of some 15,000 army troops in Kosovo[5] and the implementation of extraordinary measures, and expressing sympathy with the miners. On 28 February, there were massive, organized protest meetings across Serbia and Montenegro to protest the Slovenian protest. Eventually there were about a million persons on the streets of Belgrade alone, expressing their anger against the Slovenes.[6] Also on 28 February, the Serbian Writers' Association broke off relations with the Slovenian Writers' Association. In the telegram sent to Ljubljana, the Serbian association accused the Slovenian association "of betraying the traditional, historic, and predestined friendship between our two nations."[7] The Slovenian association refused to believe that the rupture was permanent, and when, in April 1989, a meeting of the Association of Writers of Yugoslavia was held, Rudi Šeligo, president of the Slovenian association, attended. At the meeting Šeligo tried to persuade that body to issue a criticism of Serbian policy in Kosovo—but this was blocked. So immediately after the meeting, the Slovenian association decided that it had nothing further to expect from that body and ended all practical cooperation with it. The Slovenian association continued to have good relations with its sister organizations in Croatia, Bosnia, and Macedonia, however.[8]

Developments in Kosovo were also prompting a politicization of the Catholic Church, and in early March 1999, immediately after the arrest of Azem Vllasi, the executive committee of the Episcopal Conference of Yugoslavia issued a statement calling for respect for human rights. The Catholic Commission for Justice and Peace issued a similar statement.[9]

In Slovenia, people started to manufacture and distribute Star of David badges, with the legend "Kosovo"—a gesture which infuriated Serbs. The mass demonstrations by Milošević supporters that had shaken the regional governments in Novi Sad, Pristina, and Titograd were condemned by SAWP-Slovenia as injurious to democracy.[10]

During May and June 1989, various Slovenian organizations issued statements of solidarity with the Albanians of Kosovo, while a war of words raged between the leaderships of Slovenia and Serbia. Repeated Slovenian initiatives to open a dialogue were rebuffed by Milošević. After a speech at Novi Sad on 23 May, in which the Serbian party boss called Slovenia a "lackey" of Western Europe and called into question its right to speak out on Kosovo,[11] the presidency of Slovenia sent a letter to the Serbian presidency, declaring, among other things,

The Socialist Republic of Slovenia is a sovereign state of the Slovene people who, of their own free will and on the basis of their right to self-determination, have decided to live together with other peoples and nationalities of Yugoslavia in a democratic, federally organized socialist community. Therefore, it has the right and the responsibility to adopt positions and to make judgments freely and autonomously, even on the content of our joint life and our joint future, for these are parts of the joint fate of every people in a joint motherland, including the situation in Kosovo.[12]

Subsequently, in early July, the central committee of LC Slovenia issued a major programmatic statement which codified the republic's newly discovered claim to self-determination. Recalling that while still underground, Slovenian communists had, in 1923, underlined Slovenes' right of self-determination, the central committee declared that

The right of a people to self-determination is comprehensive, lasting, and inalienable. With this right, the sovereign Slovene people, together with the two nationalities and all the other citizens of the Socialist Republic of Slovenia, ensure their independent political status and their comprehensive economic, social, and cultural development.[13]

Croatia's leadership contacted Slovenia's to express solidarity, while Montenegro's leadership faithfully followed the Serbian lead. Bosnia's leadership tried to find a middle ground but warned that the Slovenian-Serbian dispute was injurious to Yugoslavia.[14]

Then in September 1989, the Republic of Slovenia published a series of controversial draft amendments to its constitution. These included a clear assertion of the right of secession, the declaration that only the Slovenian Assembly could introduce a state of emergency in Slovenia, and the proscription of the deployment of military forces in Slovenia, except by the agreement of the Slovenian Assembly.[15] The significance of these amendments was patently clear, and the Serbian press noisily attacked the amendments as "destabilizing."[16] The amendments were passed in October all the same.

About this time, Šolević's committee declared its intention to hold a protest rally in Ljubljana on 1 December. The committee planned to mobilize some 30,000–40,000 Serbs and Montenegrins from Serbia and Kosovo and supposedly inform Slovenes about the "real" situation in Kosovo. There were also implied threats to destabilize Slovenia. The Slovenian government asked the SFRY presidency to ban the proposed meeting, but the Yugoslav presidency refused. *Delo* wrote,

In the Slovenian view, . . . the announced march would de facto be an act of civil war, because the people of one sovereign state would march against the legal and legitimate representatives of another state. The federal organs, from the state presidency and the Assembly to the government and the defense ministry, are obliged, in conformity with their constitutional and legal powers, to prevent such an intention in advance; if they do not prevent it, the question of the "purpose" of Yugoslavia arises at once.[17]

The Croatian Sabor expressed its solidarity with the Slovenian Assembly and demanded that federal organs prevent the meeting from taking place.[18] The Slovenian government then issued its own ban. And when the Serbian committee tried to proceed anyway, the Slovenian and Croatian railway unions stopped the trains carrying the would-be protesters and turned them back.[19]

Enraged, the Republic Conference of SAWP-Serbia cut its ties with SAWP-Slovenia, in a move the Croatian Socialist Alliance immediately condemned as "one of the most dangerous steps toward [the] disintegration of Yugoslavia," lending its firm support to Slovenia.[20] The Serbian Socialist Alliance did not stop there, however, but called on Serbian enterprises to take "revenge" by cutting all cooperative links with Slovenia. Within two weeks, Serbian enterprises had canceled business contracts with some 98 Slovenian enterprises, affecting deliveries and commerce in all branches of the economy.[21] A week later, some 329 Serbian enterprises had severed business relations with Slovenian firms.[22] The rupture was, in economic terms, an act of war.

Two months later, the Slovenian Assembly replied. It cut off payments to

FADURK that would have been payable to the now no-longer-autonomous Kosovo, reduced its contribution to the federal budget by 15% (the amount it estimated was being siphoned to assist the Serbian economy), and declared that Slovenia would immediately stop payments to Vojvodina and Serbia in connection with rehabilitation after damage caused to agriculture and settlements in Vojvodina (by hail, in 1987) and Serbia (by flooding, in 1988).[23]

A Wildfire of Nationalism

Yugoslavia was now swept by a wildfire of nationalism. Everywhere one turned, there were intolerant actions, strangely impassioned rhetoric, discrimination, wanton violence, ethnic reprisals. The new mood was struck at an Extraordinary Assembly of the Serbian Association of Writers on 4 March 1989, to which gathering, association president Matija Bečković made his now-famous declaration that "There is so much Serbian blood [which has been shed in Kosovo] and so many sacred relics that Kosovo will remain Serbian land, even if not a single Serb remains there."[24] Pathos, it seems, should count for more than democracy; relics may outvote citizens.

Bosnia became a political battleground. The marketplace was full of confirmable rumors about incidents between local Serbs and Croats, or between Serbs and Muslims, and as 1989 wore on, Bosnian officials began to admit that inter-ethnic troubles were becoming serious. Serbs and Croats alike began to revive arguments that Bosnia's Muslim nation was only a political construct, and the Bosnian leadership confessed that it was worried that this notion could encourage ambitions to redraw the boundaries of Serbia and/or Croatia, at Bosnia's expense.[25] Even in Montenegro, there were currents favoring the dismantling of Bosnia.[26] The founding of a local branch of the new Serbian Democratic Party, in Trebinje (Herzegovina) in July 1990, could scarcely be reassuring to the Croats and Muslims of Bosnia.[27] In March 1990, as Serbian and Croatian irredentism gathered steam, the three chambers of the Bosnian Republic Assembly met in joint session and denounced tendencies to redraw the map.[28] That did not prevent Serbian president Milošević and Croatian president Tudjman from explicitly alluding to possible border revisions at Bosnia's expense, however.[29] By midsummer, there were skirmishes between Serbs and Muslims, and the former were said to be organizing armed militias.

In fact, Serbian domination of Bosnia-Herzegovina remained considerable. In the Bosnian Ministry for People's Defense, for example, 63.2% of the 28 active officers on the staff were Serbs, compared with 10.5% Yugoslavs, 10.5% Croats, 7.9% Muslims, and 5.3% Montenegrins. Among the nine Bosnian functionaries working in the federal Ministry for Internal Affairs, all nine were Serbs. Or again, among the 1,770 persons employed in the federal Ministry of Foreign Affairs at the time, only 23 were Muslims, indicating a representation of 1.5%— far below the 8% of the Yugoslav population that they constituted.[30]

In Macedonia, too, there were grave warnings that a revival of, in this case, Macedonian nationalism was destroying inter-ethnic harmony in the republic and destabilizing it politically.[31] Those warnings notwithstanding, on 17 May 1989, the Macedonian Assembly adopted an amendment rewriting Article 1 of the constitution of Macedonia. In the new version, the article proclaimed Macedonia "the national state of the Macedonian people," dropping any reference to the Albanian and Turkish national groups.[32] In Vojvodina, the chief issue was—and, at this writing, remains—the autonomist striving of local Serbs, who did not want to be dominated by Belgrade.[33] But even here, the founding of a Democratic Union of Croats in Vojvodina in July 1990 was accompanied by complaints that Croats in the Republic of Serbia lacked their own schools, cultural-artistic societies, television, and media and by pledges to work for the creation of a Croatian autonomous region in Vojvodina or Serbia-proper.[34] The move mirrored earlier demands by Croatian Serbs and figured—at least symbolically—as a kind of reply to Serbian irredentism in Croatia.

In southern Serbia, Muslims of the Sandžak of Novi Pazar began demanding "cultural autonomy" and created the Sandžak Party of Democratic Action to promote their cause.

And then there was Croatia—the vortex of nationalism in the late 1960s and early 1970s and ostensibly dormant through much of the late 1970s and early 1980s.[35] Croatian nationalism rebounded suddenly, in the course of 1989, and seems to have been triggered to a considerable extent by aggressive Serbian behavior. There were, altogether, three chief sparks that contributed to the rekindling of Croatian nationalism.

First, after a few years during which attacks on the Croats had died down, the Serbian press renewed the attack in late 1988 and early 1989, once again talking about the Ustase, the concentration camp at Jasenovac, everlasting Croatian guilt for what fascism had done to Croats and Serbs alike, and the alleged support of the Catholic Church for genocide.[36] Disgusted by the continued misrepresentation, the Catholic Church replied, finally, by publishing the transcript of the Vatican's directives to clergy in the Independent State of Croatia, dated 24 July 1941: the letter had explicitly ordered the Franciscans to desist from taking part in any forced conversions of Orthodox Serbs, from any persecution of Serbs, and from participation or membership in the Ustaše movement.[37]

Second, on 27 July 1989, the Italian magazine *Il Tempo* published the text of an interview with Serbian writer Dobrica Ćosić, which seemed to Croats to open up the question of reassigning Istria, Zadar, and the Adriatic islands to another republic—that is, of taking them away from Croatia.[38] The political fallout from this interview was enormous. For a few weeks, Croats could talk of little else, and the issue was discussed and rediscussed in the Croatian and Serbian press throughout the late summer. Local municipalities throughout Croatia met and issued condemnations of Ćosić, day after day.[39] The Association of Historical Societies of Croatia sent letters of protest to the Serbian Academy of Sciences and Art and to the Serbian Association of Writers.[40] Moreover, the

Croatian authorities claimed to see an emerging pattern, aimed at the destabilization of Croatia.[41]

And third, the mobilization of Croatia's Serbian minority, briefly described in the preceding chapter, frightened and enraged Croats at the same time. The Split weekly newspaper *Nedjeljna Dalmacija* echoed widespread Croatian sentiment in seeing in developments in Knin a first step in the direction of breaking up Croatia and annexing large portions of it to a "Greater Serbia."[42] Meanwhile, clergy of the Serbian Orthodox Church in Croatia complained of growing intolerance toward the Orthodox faith,[43] while the Serbian Orthodox news organ *Pravoslavlje* complained of discrimination, published statistics showing a decline in the number of Orthodox facilities in Croatia between 1932 and 1988, and registered a number of demands designed to change the situation to their satisfaction.[44]

The new mood in Croatia was well symbolized by the decision, in September 1989, to restore the statue of 19th-century governor Josip Jelačić to Zagreb's main square, thus finally satisfying one of the demands of 1971.[45] About the same time, the Croatian town of Zirje unveiled a bust of Jerko Sizgorić, one of the organizers of the sailors' revolt against the Austro-Hungarian monarchy in 1918.[46]

There were repeated warnings that inter-ethnic relations in Croatia were rapidly deteriorating. One sign of this was the renewed eruption of inter-ethnic violence at sporting events.[47] As of summer 1990, there were reports that Serbs were boarding trains in Croatia in order to beat up Croatian passengers.

The Army Debates

For years, Western observers speculated about a possible military intervention in Yugoslav politics. But with perhaps the sole exception of the 1988 conspiracy against Slovenian liberalism (detailed in chapter 10)—which was, in any case, scotched—the Yugoslav People's Army (JNA) did little except talk—until April 1990, when, at a session of the War Council held in Belgrade, JNA leaders adopted a program for the disarmament of the territorial militias (TOs), justifying this decision by characterizing the political changes affecting Slovenia and Croatia as "counterrevolutionary."[48] Generally speaking, the JNA's primary concern had been to assure itself of the lion's share of the federal budget. In 1989, for example, the Yugoslav Armed Forces were allocated some 57% of the federal budget.[49] Understandably, with such a favorable distribution of resources, the military tended to be enthusiastic about maintaining the status quo. After all, if a multi-party system were introduced—who knows?—there might be a more far-reaching debate about military expenditures. The ruling party might not be as sympathetic to military spending as the communists were.

There were other reasons for the military's conservatism, though. The fact that 60–70% of the general staff consisted of Serbs and Montenegrins had something to do with it.[50] Then again, the army was obliged, by the constitution of 1974, to defend the constitutional system, and that tended to reinforce its tendency to oppose political change and to stress the importance of fidelity to the principles of AVNOJ.[51] But there was more than conservatism at work in the military's attitude toward the growing crisis. Toward the end of 1989, Colonel Milan Damjanović, a member of the cabinet of ministers, told Admiral Branko Mamula that Veljko Kadijević (defense minister since May 1988) and Milošević had taken a joint vacation that year and that, in the course of their vacation, they had agreed to engage the JNA politically and militarily in an attempt at resolving the Yugoslav crisis. Still, the JNA was not ideologically homogeneous. Within the JNA's party organization there were, as of the beginning of 1990, two principal opinion groupings: the "progressives," gathered around Admiral Simić, who were endeavoring to come to their own assessment as to how to respond to the breakdown of the socialist system, and the "dogmatic camp," whose members were working hand-in-glove with Milošević.[52]

As the state formula continued to break down in 1989 and as nationalism reared its head, the military and the JNA party organization expressed concern. The military took the position that while reform was necessary, multi-party democracy was out of the question, and that the LCY should remain the pivot of any process of democratization.[53] The dangers of "bureaucratic nationalism" became a constant theme of military spokespersons, who thought in terms of restoring "the unity of the LCY and its leadership, as well as the full affirmation of Yugoslavia as an equal, socialist community of all nations and nationalities." In the military's view—as expressed in September 1989—"the League of Communists must continue to be the leading ideopolitical force in society."[54]

When Slovenia adopted its controversial constitutional amendments in October 1989, there were rumors once again that the military would somehow intervene. There is no evidence that the military contemplated such a move at that point, however, although Assistant Defense Minister Lieutenant General Simeon Bunčić let it be known that the military was opposed to the amendments since the exercise of the right of secession "would prevent the army from doing its duty as guardian of the country's territorial integrity." That literal-minded answer concealed the military's real reasons for opposition to Slovenian self-determination, which had more to do with conservatism, communist dogmatism, and Kadijević's agreement with Milošević to support Serbian interests than any fixation on carrying out specific guidelines to the end of time.

Time after time, the military reiterated its opposition to a multi-party system. In late October 1989, for example, Bunčić told a television audience,

We favor political pluralism, but not of the multiparty type. The introduction of a multiparty system would imply the depoliticization of the JNA, which would then lose its popular character, and have to become a professional, mercenary, apolitical army in the service of whichever party was in power. . . . [And consequently,] the LCY organization in the JNA, which numbers almost 80,000 [members], would also have to cease to exist.[55]

Despite its opposition to Slovenia's amendments, the military also criticized Serbia's economic blockade of Slovenia as "inappropriate" in view of the political and economic consequences it was having. But by December 1989, as the pressure for repluralization gathered momentum, the military was sounding more flexible. For instance, Major General Ivo Tominč, assistant commander of the Fifth Military District for Political and Legal Activities, told a press conference that month that the JNA would not interfere in developments, would not slow down democratic change, and would adjust to all changes in the political system.[56]

Yet in May 1990, a month after free elections in Slovenia ended communist power in that republic, the JNA began confiscating weapons from the Slovenian Territorial Defense (TO) forces, taking them to unknown locations. News of these illegal confiscations provoked deep consternation in Slovenian policy-making circles, where the JNA move was characterized as "theft." General Ivan Hočevar, commander of the Slovenian TO and a native Slovene, stood by the JNA decision, which he tried to excuse as a "safety measure." The Slovenian presidency in turn sent a telegram on 19 May ordering local TO forces to resist any further confiscations. Ultimately, the Slovenes were able to hold onto most of their weapons in 12 municipal TO headquarters, but in just two days, the JNA had succeeded in confiscating more than 70% of Slovenian TO arms and equipment.[57]

In Croatia, facing no organized resistance, the JNA disarmed the territorial militias quickly, very soon after the electoral victory of Tudjman and the HDZ. The result was that "the incoming government found itself with no armed force capable of acting independently of the JNA, except the police" and with "no more than 15,000 rifles" in their arsenal.[58] It was a pitifully modest force with which to defend itself against the growing threat posed by Greater Serbian pretensions.

Meanwhile, voices were raised calling for a constitutional redefinition of the JNA's role in society. In July 1990, for example, the (noncommunist) presidency of the Republic of Croatia pledged to push for the complete depoliticization of the army (including the dismantlement of its party organizations and the constitutional provision tying the military to the defense of socialism).[59] Earlier, in January 1990, the new Democratic Party (in Montenegro) had demanded that party organizations in the army and police be abolished immediately. The Montenegrin party added that the generals "should particularly not be allowed to threaten us with the use of arms, which are not their property, in order to defend socialism, which is also not their property, from us democrats—as if we care about it at all."[60] This was an augur of things to come.

The Collapse of the Party

In December 1989, on the eve of the Fourteenth (Extraordinary) Congress, Slovenian party leader Milan Kučan warned that the country was on the brink of civil war.[61] Some people pinned hopes for a solution on the congress, and the draft program published in advance of the congress seemed serious about finding a way out: it promised free multi-party elections, freedom of speech, guarantees for other human rights, and efforts to obtain entry into the European Economic Community. But when the congress was convened on 23 January 1990, the Slovenian party pushed for reforms more extensive than at least some of the other republic party organizations were prepared to embrace. Some 458 amendments to the party resolution had been proposed, but the congress quickly descended into polemics. Every one of the Slovenes' proposed amendments was rejected, however, thanks to the monolithic opposition of the Serbian and Montenegrin delegations. The congress appeared deadlocked, and in frustration and protest, the Slovenian delegation walked out that same day. Milošević wanted the congress to continue, but then the Croatian delegation followed the Slovenes, causing the entire congress to fall apart. The "Congress of Salvation" ended in complete fiasco. Twelve days later, the Slovenian party pulled out of the League of Communists of Yugoslavia, shattering the remaining superficial semblance of unity. The Slovenian communists renamed their party the Party of Democratic Renewal.

The Slovenian party did not stop there but proposed that the entire LCY be disbanded, that all its officers resign, and that the new organizations be created with new political programs, new organizational structures, new methods of decision making, and a new recruitment and promotion policy.[62] In Slovenia and Croatia, the Socialist Alliance reorganized itself as an independent Socialist Party, while in Serbia, it merged with the LC Serbia to form a new Socialist Party of Serbia. Unlike the LC organizations, these new parties were not united in any way at an all-Yugoslav level. By this point, it was not entirely clear whether Yugoslavia even existed any longer in any meaningful sense. "This is a strange state," Kosta Ćavoški, of the Serbian Democratic Party, conceded. "We have to conduct our internal relations like other countries conduct international affairs."[63]

Chaos or Fragmentation

The restructuring (or rebirth) of a society is preceded by the death of its previous incarnation. That death is accompanied by uncertainty, depression, groping, and fear—in a word, by trauma. It is also the catalyst of creative energy, which sparks the search for a new social order, which in turn makes restructuring possible. In multi-ethnic Yugoslavia, restructuring inevitably meant change in the way the nationality groups structured their relations.

The signs of the approaching death of the self-managing socialist system could be read several years in advance of its final arrival. Writing in 1985, I observed that there had been a subtle but significant change in Yugoslav consciousness and behavior over the preceding years. The earlier confidence and self-congratulation had given way to "pessimism, gloom, resignation, escapism of various kinds," and an inward-looking quest for meanings which I call "apocalypse culture." This syndrome is associated with normlessness and anomie, deriving from social decay and the deep collective insecurity to which it gives rise. "Apocalypse culture" is characterized by an "openness to radically new formulas [which] springs from the sense—whether a belief or (as more usually) merely a mood—that the system in question has arrived at a historical turning point, that it is, so to speak, the 'end of time.'" [64] Yugoslavia began to shift into an apocalyptic stage as a result of the various developments noted in chapter 10. Doubts about the workability of the system came to the surface within a matter of weeks after Tito's death and gathered intensity over time.[65] Dire predictions and catastrophic visions, symptomatic of the psychology of the transitional phase associated with apocalypse culture, could be heard from time to time. Particularly striking were the comments made by Slovene Franc Šetinc on the occasion of his resignation from the LCY presidium in 1989: "In my [letter of] resignation," he told the presidium,

I drew attention to the madness which is pushing us toward the abyss in front of our very eyes. There is a great danger that our constitutional system may be carried away with the tide. . . . I have warned of the dramatic situation, the destructive lava which has spread over a large part of the country. It concerns the future of the SFRJ and in this respect, the last hour is striking when we must sober up.[66]

But if social pressure produces creativity and the anxiety which undermines dogmatism and stimulates receptivity to new ideas, the weakening of the party under pressure created conditions in which political debate became steadily more and more open, involving ever larger numbers of people in political activity, whether legal, semi-legal, or technically illegal. In these conditions, independent organizations sprouted, developed, and, as already noted in the preceding chapter, grew into political parties. Concomitant with that, the proclamation of "full sovereignty" by Slovenia, Croatia, and Bosnia rewrote the rules of the game at the structural level as well;[67] there were also rumors at the time about the potential creation of a Slovenian-Croatian confederation.[68] In 1988 and 1989, Serbs continued to denounce confederalization as impractical, unwieldy, and unrealizable.[69] By mid-1990, complete confederalization appeared inevitable and was, in large part, already accomplished. Given Serbian consent, it is possible that a formal confederal solution could have been stabilized. Given Serbian opposition, confederalization could only figure as a prelude to complete disintegration.

Meanwhile, the social fabric was coming apart as tensions between Croatia's Serbs and Croats escalated. Serbs in Knin erected the first barricades, launching a quiet rebellion against Zagreb. On 10 September, President Tudjman met with Croatian defense minister Martin Špegelj and Croatia's prime minister, Josip Manolić, to review the security situation in the republic. The consensus was that the situation was deteriorating from day to day. The three drew up a plan for restoring Croatian authority in the Knin region but faced the difficulty that the

JNA had confiscated the weaponry which had been assigned to the Croatian TO. The solution was to find an external supplier which could compensate Croatia for the loss of its arsenal.[70] On 5 October, Špegelj traveled with Croatian foreign minister Zdravko Mršić to Hungary, in order to purchase arms. Meanwhile, civil order continued to disintegrate in the Serbian-populated areas in Croatia, as local Serbs armed themselves, forming underground militias. Some of these were said to be calling themselves "Chetniks," after the Serbian nationalist formations of World War Two. But in violation of both the constitutional-legal order and the federal principle, Milošević had ordered "the establishment . . . , training, equipping, and funding of paramilitary units within Croatia, which were subordinate to JNA command and which were intended to play a role in the military occupation of portions of Croatia."[71] Milošević diverted money from federal coffers to finance these Serb paramilitary units, and the JNA began shipping arms (under a ruse) to these units in October 1990; cargo trains bearing arms were unexpectedly routed through Knin and made lengthy unscheduled stops there, while local Serbs relieved the trains of their cargo.[72] Local Serbs also raided gun shops and police stations in several locations and felled trees to erect natural barricades. In some cases, Territorial Defense forces of the Republic of Croatia were "used to provide rebel Serbs with a military structure and weaponry, and this occurred long before the outbreak of open conflict."[73] JNA instructors arrived in Croatia to train local Serbs to fight against their Croatian neighbors. Croatian Serbs also established their own "police force."[74] Both in Belgrade and in Knin, Serbs talked of detaching the Serb-populated regions in Croatia and attaching them to Serbia. The Croatian government in turn placed republic military formations under its own authority[75]—a move taken earlier by Slovenia—and set up a special "Croatian Guard," consisting of about 4,000 troops. As these developments undermined stability in Croatia, there were serious clashes between Serbs and Muslims in Bosnia and in the Sandžak of Novi Pazar (in southern Serbia).[76]

As early as January 1990, work had begun on what would have been Yugoslavia's fifth postwar constitution. Yet, in an ominous portent, Borisav Jović, the president of the SFRY presidency from May 1990 to May 1991, and Milošević took aside Janez Drnovšek, then member of the SFRY presidency, in August 1990 to inform him that they would not object if Slovenia were to disassociate from the rest of Yugoslavia![77] Under the constitutional amendments passed by Slovenia the previous year, reinforced by a decision of Slovenia's presidential council on 17 July 1990, the Slovenian Territorial Defense forces were under Slovenian command. At the end of September, Slovenian authorities dismissed General Hočevar from the command of the Slovenian TO and appointed, in his stead, Reserve Major Janez Slapar. The JNA protested loudly, and during the night of 4 October 1990, 16 military police entered the former headquarters building of the Slovenian TO in downtown Ljubljana and took control of it. But the Slovenian authorities had, in fact, abandoned the building the day before, so that Defense Minister Janša was able to remark, to a crowd which had gathered the next day to protest this action, that since the building was the property of the JNA, its police could stay there as long as they liked.[78] It was in this tense atmosphere that Slovenia, which for the time being remained open to an alternative solution (other than outright secession), joined Croatia, on 10 October, in submitting a joint proposal for the confederalization of the SFRY.[79] The proposal was discussed in the chambers of the SFRY presidency, where Jović argued heatedly against any notion of confederation. Since Milošević by then controlled the votes of Montenegro, Kosovo, and Vojvodina, and since Bosnia and Macedonia were disinclined to support a confederal notion, Slovenia and Croatia stood alone at this critical juncture. On 16 October, Jović proposed to the presidency that he would present to the federal Assembly not the Slovenian-Croatian proposal but an alternative, diametrically opposed, Serbian proposal, which had been drawn up in response to the Slovenian-Croatian initiative. Drnovšek strenuously objected, arguing that if the Assembly were to be asked to review the Serbian proposal, it should also have the opportunity to review the proposal which his republic had prepared in collaboration with Croatia.[80] In the midst of this increasingly heated row, the Croatian government removed its representative, Stipe Šuvar, from the SFRY presidency, replacing him with Stipe Mesić, the erstwhile prime minister of Croatia and an HDZ member at the time. Since the vice presidency of the presidency had been assigned to Croatia, Mesić would now become vice president of the SFRY presidency. Jović, however, objected to this new development and demanded that Mesić's nomination be submitted to the Skupština for approval. But as Viktor Meier notes, Jović's argument on this score was fundamentally flawed because "according to Article 321 [of the 1974 constitution] the members of the highest organ of state were 'elected' exclusively in the republics they were to represent and only 'announced' by the federal parliament."[81] Mesić was finally seated, but Jović refused to forward the Slovenian-Croatian proposal to the Assembly, and further discussions proved to be entirely fruitless. Later, Zdravko Tomac, who served as deputy prime minister in the Croatian Government of National Unity from August 1991 to June 1992, would recall that Edvard Kardelj had told him, in the course of a conversation in 1967, that in his view, only a confederal solution could preserve Yugoslavia.[82]

With the failure of the endeavor to confederalize the state, Slovenia and Croatia effectively gave up on Yugoslavia and began to make preparations for eventual independence. In Slovenia, privately printed "lipa" banknotes came to be accepted as negotiable currency in a number of Slovenian shops and restaurants, and in October 1990, the Slovenian government set an important precedent by opening its first diplomatic mission abroad (in Brussels). The following month, Kadijević summoned a group of JNA generals to meet in conference in Belgrade and Niš and told them that, in his view, the JNA was the last bulwark of socialism in Eastern Europe. "The ideas of socialism . . . belong to the future," he told the assembled generals. "The experience of developed countries confirms that [socialism] is one of the greatest achievements of contemporary civilization."[83] On 4 November, an "army party" was established in Belgrade, with the involvement of Mira Marković, wife of Slobodan Milošević, under the name "League of Communists—Movement for Yugoslavia."

About this time, Croatia, Slovenia, Vojvodina, and Kosovo began withholding tax payments from the federal government.[84] As a result, by late November, income into the federal treasury had shrunk to only about one-third of what had been budgeted, and federal officials described the situation as "extremely serious."[85] This already grave economic situation was compounded when, in the course of some secret meetings arranged by Milošević the following month, the Yugoslav National Bank granted the Republic of Serbia a "loan" for 28 billion dinars, or about 2 billion DM. The money was used to pay off the debts of some Serbian enterprises and to purchase hard currency for Serbian reserves, but it effectively broke the back of Prime Minister Ante Marković's economic reform efforts. As the deal became public, non-Serbs were enraged, feeling that, for so large a transfer of funds, they should at least have been consulted. Representatives of Slovenia and Croatia met in early January 1991 and agreed that they would not recognize any new financial obligations (including foreign loans) assumed by the federation after 28 December, the day on which the Serbian parliament had approved the loan.[86] Insofar as no government can continue to function when it loses control of its own finances and when its own constituent parts no longer recognize their financial obligations, the Serbian bank loan was the economic death knell for socialist Yugoslavia.

The lines of confrontation were clearly drawn. On the one side, Slovenia and Croatia, having failed to bring the other republics around to a consensus on a new confederal structure modeled on the European Community, were preparing for secession. On the other side, Serbia and the JNA rejected any confederal principle and insisted on the necessity of reintegrating the country firmly under Serbian hegemony, which Milošević and his adherents called a "modern, efficacious federation." The army, additionally, wanted to restore communism throughout the country.[87]

On 3 December 1990 came a demand from General Kadijević that Slovenia and Croatia disarm their Territorial Defense forces. If the two republics refused to comply, Kadijević warned, the army would use force to effect the desired result. The Slovenes and Croats held fast, calling up reservists, placing their units on high alert, and bracing for invasion.[88] The ministers of defense and interior from Slovenia and Croatia convened an urgent meeting in the border town of Mokrice and agreed to coordinate defense and security.[89] Although the two sides agreed that an attack on either republic would be considered an attack on both, nothing came of this agreement, however; indeed, when, on 22 June 1991, Slovenian president Kučan asked Croatian president Tudjman to take actions to obstruct the passage of JNA forces through Croatian territory to Slovenia, Tudjman declined to offer any explicit assurances.[90] Thus, the JNA, during its brief combat in Slovenia, was able to move its forces across Croatian territory with impunity.

Already in November 1990, the Slovenes and Croats had been ordered to dismantle their "paramilitary forces," even though the JNA was at the same time building up paramilitary formations among the Serbs of Croatia. That same month, Jović and Kadijević met to discuss the possible arrest of Croatian defense minister Špegelj.[91] Later, on 9 January 1991, Jović went to the SFRY presidency to seek a confirmation of this order. The Serbian bloc (Serbia, Kosovo, Vojvodina, and Montenegro) was one vote short of having a majority in this body, but Bogić Bogićević, the Bosnian representative, provided the critical fifth vote, enabling the presidency to apply pressure on Slovenia and Croatia. Bogićević, a man of considerable integrity who agonized over his every vote, later "retracted" his vote, but by then the damage had been done.[92] The state presidency handed down a deadline of midnight, 19 January 1991, for Slovenian and Croatian compliance. Although he voted against the "compromise" decision, Mesić had succeeded in inserting the word "illegal" into the resolution, so that only "illegal paramilitaries" should be disarmed. This qualification allowed the government in Zagreb to insist that the resolution applied only to the insurgent Serb militias in the Krajina and not to the units set up by the government itself, least of all to the regular police.[93]

The Defense Ministry, by now increasingly in Milošević's corner, was not impressed with the logic of this argument and threatened to mobilize troops in the event that Croatia did not disband its forces and surrender Špegelj to federal military authorities. To say that tensions were running high would be to put it mildly. Already on 22 January, Presidents Kučan and Tudjman met for talks and agreed that, in the event of JNA intervention against either republic, both would cease all financial contributions to the federal budget, immediately declare independence, and contact the U.N. Security Council. Three days later, as an expanded session of the SFRY presidency opened, Belgrade television broadcast a film titled "The truth about the arming of terrorist formations of the HDZ in Croatia," showing Špegelj talking openly about Croatia's arms-smuggling operations which he was organizing (importing weaponry from Hungary) and issuing threats of reprisals against JNA officers and their families in the event the JNA were to make an offensive move against Croatia.[94] Croatian TV immediately denounced the film as a fabric of lies.

That same evening, Tudjman met with members of the SFRY presidency, Prime Minister Marković, and high officers of the JNA in an effort to avert bloodshed. At the end of this meeting, which lasted deep into the night, the storm clouds seemed to have cleared. Jović, then president of the SFRY presidency, tried to win approval in the presidency for a crackdown in Croatia but was unable to muster a majority for this move. Tudjman took some of the wind out of Serbian sails by agreeing to call off the mobilization of reserve units (some 20,000 strong), but no weapons were surrendered.[95] For his part, General Kadijević agreed to call off the military alert at army bases in Croatia and not to interfere in Croatian internal affairs. Tudjman declined to disband any of the units, however, or to turn over any of their weaponry to the army. The crisis had hardly passed, however, for Yugoslav troop movements continued in the Zagreb environs.[96] Meanwhile, Yugoslav military police arrested various persons in Croatia, including members of the ruling HDZ.[97] Then, on 30 January, Kadijević ordered the arrest of Špegelj, on allegations that he had made preparations for armed insurrection in Croatia. But Croatian authorities refused to turn over Špegelj, who went into hiding. Jović threatened to use armed force to assure the apprehension of the Croatian defense minister. Tudjman, in turn, promised to employ force to prevent the arrest. By the end of January 1991, political talks between Croatian and federal leaders had broken down, with Croatia's Tudjman refusing to take part in any further meetings at which any JNA representative would be present. Finally, on 8 February, the Republic of Slovenia declared that it had given up on Yugoslavia and would formally secede from the federation before the end of the month. The Slovenian prime minister added that Slovenia would annul all federal laws on 20 February.[98] Slovenia was not, however, logistically in a position to secede quite so quickly, and the "deadline" was later extended to 26 June.

What was evident as of early 1991—though it had surely been obvious by summer 1989, if not earlier—was that the old Titoist program to defuse the nationalities problem, a problem which had been created by the illegitimate politics of the interwar kingdom and powerfully reinforced by the sanguinary fratricidal conflict of 1941–1945, and to fashion a "subjectively legitimate" state had completely failed. The question is why.

Theorists partial to notions of "subjective legitimacy" assure us that if people just believe that a state is legitimate, then it is, and that even the most tyrannical state can, therefore, become "legitimate" if its propaganda is good enough. This analysis is misguided. Rather than endeavoring to dissolve legitimacy into mere subjective self-delusions, we should instead understand that legitimacy, as I argued in chapter 1, has an objective core and content, even if subjectively interpreted and perceived. The existence of international covenants such as the Universal Declaration of Human Rights, and the very wording of the American Declaration of Independence, provide testimony to the fact that many people have been convinced that there are some objective criteria which a system must meet if it may be considered legitimate. Or, to put it crassly, a system which engages in mass murder, for example, cannot be considered "legitimate," no matter how good its propaganda.

This provides a clue as to the first, and most fundamental, failure of the Titoist experiment. The Titoist solution did not embrace moral universalism but instead appealed to a confused version of secular theocracy.[99] Because theocracy, whether in a religious variant (and there are many religious variants, and not just one, as at least one author supposes) or in a secular variant, is essentially illegitimate, it cannot survive, and will inevitably decay—unless that decay can be halted by a timely and proactive promotion of universalist values.

Second, the Titoist solution did not embrace political pluralism either. Instead, Titoism tried to substitute regional pluralization (decentralization to regional communist elites) for real political pluralism (which would have entailed the establishment of multi-party democracy). But insofar as this regional pluralization operated within a federal structure founded on differences of nationality, it was apt, in conditions of political illegitimacy and economic deterioration, to reinforce nationalism, an orientation at odds with universalist values and, therefore, likewise incompatible with legitimate politics.

Third, the Titoist economic system, while avoiding the pitfalls of monopoly capitalism, slipped into a chaotic version of socialism, which proved to be likewise illegitimate. Indeed, the Titoist economic program failed even to achieve its more limited goal of equalizing economic levels across the republics and provinces. On the contrary, under self-managing socialism, the economic gap steadily widened, with the results already described in preceding chapters. Thus, the Titoist experiment was objectively illegitimate at all three levels and therefore could not succeed. And if the Titoist experiment could not succeed, then nor could its sundry policies.

By the late 1980s, as both political life and economic life disintegrated, the Titoist experiment was also increasingly seen by the Yugoslav population to be illegitimate. That is to say, the system was not merely *objectively* illegitimate, but also *subjectively* understood to be illegitimate. As this understanding took hold and as the illegitimate structures of state sank into paralysis in the wake of Tito's death, consensus grew that the system was in crisis. Yet ultimately, in spite of all of this, it took the rise of Slobodan Milošević in Serbia, supported by persons such as Jović, Kadijević, Šolević, and others, to bring the country from a state of confused paralysis to the brink of fratricidal war. Franjo Tudjman, for all of his insensitivity to Serb complaints, was at the most playing a reactive role in 1990; he became complicitous in the approaching war in March 1991, when he met with Milošević at Karadjordjevo and tried to persuade Milošević to agree to Croatia's annexation of portions of Bosnia-Herzegovina.[100] Thus, while the SFRY was doomed, by its illegitimacy, to fail as a political experiment, the country was *not* preordained to fall apart or to go to war. It took the combination of system illegitimacy, dysfunctional federalism, economic deterioration, and the mobilization of Serbian nationalism by Milošević and his coterie to take the country down the road to war.

CHAPTER 14

The War of Yugoslav Succession, Phase 1 (1991)

B y the end of January 1991, efforts to find a formula which could avert war
seemed increasingly forlorn. Some three years of officially sponsored hate
propaganda in Serbia (and 10 years of unofficial hate propaganda, if one
dates the Serbian backlash to the April 1981 riots) and eight months of officially
sponsored, but somewhat milder, hate propaganda in Croatia were having their
effect. And, for some Yugoslavs, the point of no return had already been passed.
Warnings about "civil war" had been in the air since at least 1983,[1] but when the
war finally broke out, it took the form—at least in part, in Croatia and Bosnia—
of a premeditated Serbian insurgency. In these two republics, it was the Serbs
who first armed themselves and formed paramilitary militias; it was the Serbs
who turned their backs already on the lame duck communist governments, subsequently rejecting the legitimately elected governments of Tudjman and
Izetbegović; it was the Serbs who first set up illegal militias and who initiated
hostilities in both republics. It is, of course, true that Tudjman embraced some
illiberal policies immediately after being elected president of Croatia and that
Izetbegović had been accused, by the communists, of Islamic fundamentalism.
But Serb demonization of Croatia and Croats *preceded* Tudjman's election, having been initiated long before there was any thought of having free elections at
all in Croatia. The cranking up of the anti-Croatian campaign in the Serbian
media may be dated to early 1989, though the anti-Albanian and anti-Slovenian
media campaigns had been set in motion in Serbia even earlier.[2] This campaign
was reflected at the same time in a "verbal war" between some Croatian newspapers and Croatian Serb newspapers; it had erupted by the beginning of 1989

382   *The War of Yugoslav Succession, 1991*

and was contributing to an escalation of inter-ethnic tensions in that republic.[3] Likewise in Bosnia, rumors about Muslim physicians harming Serb children preceded Izetbegović's election; moreover, the establishment of Serb autonomous zones in that republic (in September 1991), the secret order issued by Milošević (in January 1992) to transfer JNA officers born in Bosnia back to their republic of birth, in preparation for reassigning them to a new Bosnian Serb army, and the declaration of the secession of the "Serbian Republic of Bosnia-Herzegovina" from BiH on 9 January 1992 all preceded the referendum of 29 February–1 March 1992 which Karadžić's people would later cite in justification of their preparations for war.

Serbia Decides on War

According to Zdravko Tomac, contingency plans for an armed insurrection by Serbs living in Croatia had been drawn up even before the 14th Extraordinary LCY Congress of January 1990.[4] As early as 13 February 1990, Milošević, Jović, and Kadijević had talked about the coming war. Jović still wanted, at the time, to do what was necessary to avoid war, but Milošević confidently predicted that there would be a war in which the peoples of Yugoslavia would be pitted against each other, while Kadijević expressed his determination to see to it that the Serbs would win.[5] Significantly, this conversation took place at a time when Ivica Račan, the anti-nationalist candidate for the Croatian presidency, still expected to defeat Tudjman.[6] A month later, on 4 March, a mass meeting of Serbs took place on Petrova Gora in the former Vojna Krajina; the meeting expressed "support for Milošević's policy of restoring Serbian hegemony wherever Serbs lived outside Serbia proper."[7] Račan had wanted to prevent the meeting from taking place, but he was not able to convince other key officials in Croatia, including in the Sabor and the Executive Council, of the need to do so.[8] Under the motto "all Serbs should live in one state," Milošević was preparing Serbs for an expansionist war. On 28 June 1990, Milošević told Jović that he wanted to drive Slovenia and Croatia out of Yugoslavia, keeping the other republics in union with Serbia and annexing Serb-inhabited areas which were juridically parts of Croatia.[9]

The Serbian secret service (SDB) was put to work to prepare the ground logistically. The SDB established contact with General Andrija Biorčević, commander of the Novi Sad Corps, and Colonel Ratko Mladić, commander of the Knin garrison, and clandestine operations began. Two high-ranking SDB agents, Frano ("Frenki") Simatović and Radovan ("Badža") Stojčić made frequent visits to Knin during 1990 to help to organize the SDS and its military arm and to distribute weapons. Other key SDB agents working among Croatian Serbs at this time were Dragan Filipović, Mile Radonić, and Jovica Stanišić.[10] In mid-August 1990, Croatian Serbs erected barricades across Croatian highways, initiating a revolt against Zagreb. On 21 December, Serbs in Knin issued a declaration, proclaiming the establishment of the Serb Autonomous Oblast of Krajina, adopting a statute five days later. Two further Serb autonomous zones were proclaimed in Western Slavonia and Eastern Slavonia. Serb paramilitary militias were set up illegally. The JNA sent trainloads of weapons to these militias, often under the cover of darkness, and JNA instructors showed up in the Krajina to train the militias for warfare against their Croatian neighbors. Contacts between Knin and Belgrade during 1990 were intense, with Milošević appointing the commanders of the Serbian Army of the Republic of the Serbian Krajina—the Srpska Vojska Krajine (SVK)—and providing financial support.[11] Milošević even assigned JNA officers to assume command in the eventual Croatian Serb army; altogether some 13,000 Yugoslav Army officers would serve in the SVK and in the Bosnian Serb Army (the VRS).[12] Subsequently, on 28 February 1991, three months before the Croatian referendum on disassociation and four months before Croatia officially withdrew from the collapsing SFRY, the Croatian Serbs declared their secession from Croatia.[13] Milošević kept in close contact with Croatian Serb leader Milan Babić, reportedly meeting with Babić 25 times between October 1990 and December 1991.[14]

It was not enough, however, as far as Milošević and Jović were concerned, for the Serb militias to be armed. It was also important that the Croatian authorities be disarmed, as far as possible. It was with this objective in mind that, as already discussed, as early as 17 May 1990, less than a month after the first free elections in Croatia since World War Two, the army leadership confiscated the weaponry of the territorial defense (TO) forces in Slovenia, Croatia, and Bosnia-Herzegovina. Tudjman had not even been sworn in as president of Croatia at the time.[15] In Slovenia, thanks to the quick-wittedness of Defense Minister Janša, President Kučan, and others, a portion of the TO weaponry was retained, but in Croatia, the confiscation was complete, leaving Croatia defenseless. The importance of this confiscation or of its timing should not be underestimated. It was, according to Davorin Rudolf, who served briefly as Croatian foreign minister in 1991, a precondition for the Serbian insurrection and JNA assault against Croatia,[16] while its timing—before the Croatian-Slovenian joint proposal for confederalization and before the summit discussions held in the early months of 1991—confirms that the Milošević regime was, by spring 1990, already making plans for war against Croatia and Bosnia-Herzegovina. These intentions are also confirmed in the memoirs of Borisav Jović.[17]

Milošević's preparations for war were comprehensive and included the vilification of Albanians, Croats, Muslims, and Slovenes in the Serbian media (together with "documentaries" about Ustaša massacres of Serbs, while Chetnik and Nedićite atrocities against non-Serbs during World War Two were conveniently forgotten), the clandestine importation of weaponry from the moribund Soviet Union, and constitutional changes designed to give the president of Serbia, one of the SFRY's constituent republics, the authority of a head of state. Specifically, the constitution of the Republic of Serbia, adopted on 28 September 1990, empowered the president of Serbia to "command the armed forces in peace and in war, [and to] order general and limited mobilization."[18] This clause was completely illegal under the federal constitution then supposedly in force.

Tensions continued to rise throughout the country, but perhaps especially in Croatia, where violence flared in Pakrac in February, when local Serbs, led by Milan Babić and Milan Martić, their political and military leaders, seized control of the police station and the municipal building. Over the next weeks, local Croatian officials were subjected to a campaign of vilification and intimidation. Then Tudjman authorized a counterstrike, and a force of 200 men trained in anti-terrorist operations entered Pakrac on 2 March 1991 at 4:30 A.M., arresting some 180 insurgents and restoring Croatian authority. Although there were no deaths or injuries, Borisav Jović supported Defense Minister Kadijević's request to dispatch the army to the scene. By the time JNA tanks arrived in Pakrac, Croatian special forces had taken control of the town, but the arrival of the JNA forces encouraged Serb insurgents to open fire on the town from the hills, and fighting ensued. After talks between Colonel Vasiljević and Stipe Mesić, Croatia's representative in the SFRY presidency, Croatian police were allowed to reestablish control of the town. Pakrac was the first skirmish in what would, by July, become a full-fledged war between Croats and Serbs.

Yet Serbs were by no means unanimous in support of war. Anti-Milošević demonstrations broke out in Belgrade on 9 March 1991, involving up to 70,000 anti-war protesters, who demanded that the country be pulled back from the brink.[19] However, these protests barely ruffled the Serbian leader, whose friend Jović arranged for the presidency to authorize the dispatch of JNA tanks and troops to suppress the demonstrations. Several thousand riot policemen were rushed to downtown Belgrade, while crowds fought back by overturning buses and trams and attacking police with pavement slabs, rocks, and metal pipes. Demonstrators shouted "Slobo killer," "Arrest Slobo," and "Slobo-Saddam," drawing an explicit comparison between the Serbian leader and Iraqi president Saddam Hussein. By 13 March, at least two people had been killed and some 636 protesters had been detained.[20] Thousands of anti-war protesters continued to assemble on the streets of Belgrade for several days, singing "Give Peace a Chance" and registering their opposition to the growing war mania in their republic and throughout the SFRY. A few days later, the SFRY presidency met for an interrupted session on 12, 14, and 15 March. Instead of meeting at the federal building, presidency members were removed to the headquarters of the General Staff, where General Kadijević demanded that the collective presidency proclaim a state of emergency throughout the country, put the army in a state of combat readiness, grant the army special police powers, and declare the abolition of all legislative acts deemed incompatible with the federal constitution.[21] Although the Serbian and Slovenian constitutions were the most flagrantly incompatible with the federal constitution, the proposal was transparently aimed at Croatia. Only the four members of the "Serbian bloc" (i.e., Jović and the delegates from Kosovo, Vojvodina, and Montenegro) supported Kadijević's proposal, which died on the table. The presidency was in recess the next day, for reasons not clarified at the time. It turned out later that Kadijević and Jović flew to Moscow on 13 March for talks with Minister of War Dimitry Yazov. Although these talks were shrouded in secrecy, Mesić has speculated that these talks may have been intended to coordinate simultaneous *putsches* in the Soviet Union and Yugoslavia.[22] Kadijević and Jović were back in Belgrade for the resumption of the talks the following day. Angry exchanges punctuated the sessions of 14 and 15 March, with Kadijević issuing dark threats against Slovenia and Croatia. On 14 March, Milošević and Jović sought a revote in the presidency, but the Kosovar delegate, Riza Sapunxhiu, joined Mesić, Drnovšek, Bogićević, and Vasil Tupurkovski in voting against the proposal. The evening of 15 March, at Milošević's insistence, Jović resigned as chair of the SFRY presidency and declared that he was leaving the SFRY presidency as well. Nenad Bucin, the delegate from Montenegro, now also submitted his resignation from the presidency.[23] Mesić thought that this meant that he, as vice chair, should succeed to the chair early. Drnovšek and Prime Minister Ante Marković supported Mesić, but on the following day Milošević went on television to announce that the Republic of Serbia would no longer "recognize" the state presidency. Meanwhile, before Mesić was even able to convene a session under his chairmanship, Jović, having indulged in the questionable act of resigning, now declared on the basis of nobody knew what that his resignation was not final until the Serbian parliament accepted it. On Milošević's instructions, the parliament refused to accept Jović's resignation, and Jović then returned to his post. With this, Milošević's strange gambit came to an end, and the collective presidency hobbled along for a few more months.[24] Apparently, Milošević had hoped to create an "institutional vacuum" in which the army could carry out a *putsch,* but he abandoned this concept when Mesić showed himself prepared to step into the breach.[25]

At the height of this gambit, Vuk Drašković, president of the opposition Serbian Renewal Movement (SPO), declared, "This despotic, tyrannical, one-sided, one-legged, one-eyed regime cannot have any friend left in the world."[26] "Serbia," Drašković told some 30,000 opposition protesters two weeks later, "does not want Bolshevism. . . . Serbia wants democracy."[27] These latter comments were made at a rally held on 27 March to commemorate the fiftieth anniversary of the Belgrade protests at which Serbs had declared themselves ready to go to war rather than to become slaves. In those days, Drašković seemed to provide the principal alternative "voice" in Serbia. It was, thus, not without interest that, in mid-April 1991, Drašković proposed the widespread cantonization of Yugoslavia, giving autonomy to Istria and Dubrovnik, both parts of Croatia, as well as to the Albanian-inhabited parts of western Macedonia, and dividing Bosnia into Croatian, Serbian, and Muslim cantons. Drašković also thought that if Croatia seceded, it would end up "without the parts inhabited by Serbs but with western Hercegovina and part of Kupres" annexed to it. He does not seem to have thought that Serbia might be cantonized, for example, by granting autonomy to Kosovo or Vojvodina or the Sandžak. By May, moreover, the SPO leader, who had called Tudjman and his associates "sensible men" the previous month,[28] was denouncing the Croatian leadership as "fascist" and calling for the army to intervene in Croatia for the purpose of restoring "order."[29] Indeed, Drašković wanted to see the establishment of a government of national "salvation" which would undertake serious preparations for war with Croatia.[30] Later, after war had broken out, Drašković was explicitly nationalist, putting forward a fantasy map of the region in which large parts of Croatia would be annexed to Serbia, Dubrovnik would be stripped away from Croatia and set up as a city-state, and Croatia would be partially compensated with the assignment of Croat-inhabited areas of BiH.[31]

A Last Chance for Peace?

It was in these conditions that the presidents of the six republics were trying to conduct talks about the future of the country. There was an atmosphere of psychosis in the country, and it became increasingly impossible to tell which fears were rational and which were not. Thus, when President Tudjman and other Croatian leaders departed for a summit meeting in Belgrade the night of 25 January 1991, there were fears in Croatia that Tudjman would be gunned down in Belgrade just as Stjepan Radić had been nearly 63 years earlier.[32] As for the summit meetings themselves, they never stood a chance. At one such summit meeting, held in Sarajevo on 22 February, Bosnian president Alija Izetbegović proposed that the six republics agree to an asymmetric federation in which Serbia and Montenegro could enjoy a tight federation, Slovenia and Croatia could be associated with that federation on a confederal basis, and Macedonia and Bosnia-Herzegovina (BiH) could enjoy an intermediate level of association. There was no serious discussion of this proposal. On the contrary, on 25 March 1991, Croatian president Tudjman met with Serbian president Milošević at Karadjordjevo to discuss the partition of BiH. The seriousness of this discussion is revealed in the fact that the two republics subsequently sent teams of experts to work out the details.[33] In spite of this "collaboration" between the Croatian and Serbian leaders, Serb insurgents seized a police station at Plitvice National Park in Croatia at the end of the month, sparking conflict between the insurgents and the Croatian police. In response, the JNA moved in units to separate the two sides and served the Croats with an ultimatum compelling authorities in Zagreb to pull out the special police forces which had been rushed to the park.[34]

Within Croatia there were moderates, such as Davorin Rudolf, who worked earnestly for peace, hoping to head off what could only prove a tragedy for all sides. There were also radicals such as Gojko Šušak, who, according to Laura Silber and Allan Little, "did what they could to provoke conflict."[35] In an eerie episode, Šušak (a close adviser of Tudjman's who would later become Croatian minister of defense) allegedly arranged for the murder of pacifist Josip Reihl-Kir, the Osijek police chief who was working to build trust between Croats and Croatian Serbs. The silencing of this voice for moderation (on 1 July 1991) ended inter-ethnic negotiations in the key district of Osijek and accelerated the slide toward intercommunal violence.[36]

The mood turned ugly with fear, hatred, and intense preoccupation with the need to prepare for a showdown spreading through much of the country, so that it was strange to hear some foreign observers dismissing fears of intercommunal conflict as overdrawn. Within the country, there was no underestimation of the dangers, however. Janez Drnovšek, Slovenia's delegate to the SFRY presidency, for example, warned explicitly that "the possibility of civil war in Yugoslavia cannot be excluded if mutual pressures and threats against negotiations on the future of the country continue."[37] No party to the gathering conflict was prepared to pull back and examine its own conscience—least of all those who were contributing the most to the escalation of tensions. That the populations were being mobilized along ethnic lines was also palpably evident. In May, there were clashes in the village of Borovo Selo in eastern Slavonia, leaving more than 30 persons dead, among them 12 Croatian policemen. A JNA unit was sent to the area and established a buffer zone between the armed Serbs and the Croatian police.[38] Now Serb nationalists in Belgrade demanded arms to defend their fellow Serbs living in Croatia. *NIN,* the weekly Belgrade newsmagazine, approached a group of Yugoslav intellectuals, including Drago Roksandić, Darko Bekić, and Alija Hodžić, with the question Is civil war unavoidable? Lazar Stojanović, the first respondent in *NIN'* s roundtable, replied that civil war had already begun in Yugoslavia, while Slobodan Rakitić felt that the emerging conflict between Serbs and Croats should not be called a civil war but would be a war, pure and simple.[39]

In mid-May 1991, a very strange drama was played out. According to the rules established for the SFRY presidency, the chairmanship was supposed to rotate each year according to an agreed formula. Under this scheme, Jović, the Serbian delegate, was supposed to step down on 15 May, yielding the chairmanship to Stipe Mesić, the Croatian delegate. However, instead of stepping down, Jović mobilized the "Serbian bloc" to obstruct the rotation, justifying his action by declaring that his republic could not support the emplacement of a president who was committed to a program of dismemberment of the country. What should have been a routine rotation was blocked by a vote of 4 to 4, with the Slovenian, Macedonian, and Bosnian delegates supporting Mesić. Slovenian president Milan Kučan described this move as "a camouflaged coup d'etat" perpetrated by Serbian authorities,[40] while Mesić himself warned that unless the situation were resolved soon, Croatia would be left with no option but to secede. At the same time, army units were ordered to move into eastern Croatia where conflict had broken out between Serbs and Croats.[41]

Mesić's succession had been blocked by virtue of the fact that the delegates nominally representing Kosovo and Vojvodina had, in fact, been appointed by

Milošević and confirmed by the Serbian Assembly, even though Kosovo and Vojvodina had been granted representation on the SFRY presidency only on the presumption that they were autonomous units and that their delegates would be appointed by their own assemblies. This was a point not lost on Mesić, who had tried earlier to bring the question of the provincial delegates before the Constitutional Court.[42] But the Kosovar delegate, Sapunxhiu, had shown unwelcome independence in the past, noting in March, for example, that "what was going on in Kosovo had nothing to do with the constitution."[43] Now, on 16 May, the Serbian authorities took care of this loose end, removing Sapunxhiu and appointing the more compliant Sejdo Bajramović to take his place. Meanwhile, Serbian radicals Vojislav Šešelj and Mirko Jović shamelessly organized "anti-Mesić" demonstrations in front of the Skupština building, while Serbian deputy Milan Paroški publicly denounced Mesić as a "terrorist," suggesting that Mesić should be arrested rather than installed as chair of the SFRY presidency.[44]

By the time the six republic presidents met in Stojčevac near Sarajevo on 6 June, there was little prospect that the clock could be turned back. All the same, Bosnian president Izetbegović joined Macedonian president Gligorov in proposing that Yugoslavia be transformed into a union of states, virtually a confederation (reviving, in effect, the Slovenian-Croatian proposal of October 1990). Janez Drnovšek immediately endorsed the concept, which his republic had supported already in October of the previous year. More surprisingly, Milošević's adviser described the proposal as "a step forward."[45] The Izetbegović-Gligorov initiative also won praise from the European Community. But Milošević and Tudjman were not interested in their initiative, and when the six reassembled in Split on 12 June, the Serbian and Croatian leaders tried to steer the conversation around to a tripartite division of BiH. There was one final summit meeting, held in Belgrade on 19 June, on which occasion Tudjman expressly rejected the Izetbegović-Gligorov proposal. When U.S. secretary of state James Baker came to Belgrade on 23 June, Izetbegović took him aside and tried to impress upon the American diplomat the desperation of the situation and the need for resolute American mediation. As Izetbegović notes with disappointment in his memoirs, there was no response on the part of the United States.

Rival Claims to Legitimacy and Alternative Perceptions

The withering away of the believability of the SFRY's bases for claiming legitimacy—self-management, nonalignment, brotherhood and unity, and, in a historical sense, the Partisan struggle—preceded and underpinned the withering away of the socialist state itself. As the old socialist myths and doctrines lost their hold on people, new leaders made appeals to alternative notions. The loudest appeals—hence also the best known—were the nationalist appeals registered by Milošević's Socialist Party together with the intellectuals associated with SANU in Serbia and those advanced by Tudjman's HDZ in Croatia. By contrast, in neither Slovenia nor Macedonia was nationalism the dominant theme of discourse, even though resentment against the JNA for holding a trial in Serbo-Croatian in Ljubljana in 1988 played its part in stirring Slovenian anger against the JNA and Serbia. In Bosnia-Herzegovina, by contrast, only the Serbs united early behind a single faction (Karadžić's). Among Bosnian Croats, there were important differences of opinion between those Croats gathered around Stjepan Kljuić, who wanted to work within the framework of a united BiH in cooperation with the Muslims, and those gathered around Mate Boban and Dalibor Brozović, who wanted to amputate Croatian-inhabited portions of BiH and attach them to Croatia.[46] And among Muslims, there were three alternative notions, advocated respectively by Alija Izetbegović, Adil Zulfikarpašić, and Fikret Abdić. Where Izetbegović tried to be all things to all men, presenting himself as a devout Muslim to certain audiences and as a champion of tolerance and secular liberal democracy to other audiences, Zulfikarpašić and Abdić were more clearly secular in orientation.

Verbal attacks on Tito, to whom Milošević now referred exclusively as "Broz," became commonplace in Serbia, where Šešelj's Serbian Radical Party, at the time still unregistered, threatened to tear down the memorial to Yugoslavia's long-time president and dig up his remains.[47] Belgrade's Marshal Tito Road was renamed Serbian Rulers' Street, and Belgrade's cosmopolitanism and relative sophistication were derided and attacked. At the same time, Milošević began to rehabilitate the Chetnik movement of World War Two, while Tudjman undertook a partial rehabilitation of the Ustaša and the NDH—an undertaking which created some problems. Milošević even erected a monument to Chetnik leader Draža Mihailović (in 1992),[48] while the Tudjman regime renamed streets in honor of Mile Budak (the minister of religious affairs and education in the NDH but said to have been an accomplished writer in his own right). It is scarcely irrelevant that Serbia's two most influential novelists—Dobrica Ćosić and Vuk Drašković—were both well known for their intolerant nationalism. Drašković, in his two-volume novel *Molitva* [The Prayer], wrote, "Christ was crucified for three hours only, but some nations [such as the Serbs] never descend from the cross."[49] Meanwhile, Milošević adopted the slogan "all Serbs must live in one state" as a programmatic principle, in spite of the corollary implications that non-Serbs living in areas inhabited by Serbs must be either subjected to Serb domination or expelled.

In Croatia, the proliferation of rehabilitations—ranging from Starčević to Hebrang to Stepinac to Ban Josip Jelačić, the military governor of Croatia who had helped Kaiser Franz Josef to push back Hungarian rebels in 1848–1849—even while continuing to honor Tito and Bishop of Djakovo Strossmayer, served notice that the regime was adopting an eclectic nationalism in which there was little ideological content besides the embrace of Croatian history and territorial irredentism. Robert Hutchings, who served as director for European affairs at the National Security Council in 1989–1992, described Croatian president Tudjman as "a romantic lost in dreams of a glorious Croatian past that never was."[50]

Even more than Milošević, Tudjman thought in terms of a nationally homogeneous homeland, and in 1991, he championed what he called the "humanitarian moving of peoples"—in essence, large-scale population transfers for the purpose of creating ethnically homogeneous states.[51] Notions of inter-ethnic tolerance, individual rights, equality, and multi-culturalism were as foreign to Tudjman and Šušak as they were to Milošević and Šešelj.

There is also a direct correlation between nationalist intolerance and the proclivity toward violence against the members of other national groups. Hence, too, the rehabilitation of historical figures who gained notoriety through the advocacy or practice of intolerance plays a dangerous role in catapulting a community toward intercommunal violence. The war which flared in 1991 cannot be reduced to mere economic deterioration, let alone to primordial factors; on the contrary, it was consciously planned, prepared, and ignited in service of a Greater Serbian nationalist program. Tudjman's not insignificant contribution was to embrace a program of ethnic nationalism and to try to collaborate with Milošević at Bosnia's expense, rather than to make common cause with the Bosnian leadership in defense of the rights of people to live in their own homes and in defense of existing borders. But Tudjman was elected, in the first place, because his brand of eclectic nationalism was welcomed by Croats who rejected Ivica Račan's more cautious approach and who saw in Tudjman the best defense against Milošević.

The years 1988–1991 saw a steady escalation of fear and resentment throughout the country. Where Serbs and Croats are concerned, it is striking that among both groups there were resentments at being treated as second-class citizens and fears of each other's leaders. Croatian Serbs resented, in particular, the fact that they had been denied administrative autonomy and, after the election of Tudjman, were angered by Tudjman's firing of Serbs from the police force, by his plans to restore the kuna as Croatia's currency, and by the Tudjman government's selective reinterpretation of the NDH. They also claimed that the checkerboard emblem (the *šahovica*), used continuously throughout Croatian history, including during the socialist era, as the central feature of the Croatian coat of arms, had been associated only with the NDH and ignored the fact that the configuration of red and white squares differed from the arrangement on the NDH coat of arms and preserved the arrangement used in socialist times.[52] How many Serbs were actually ignorant concerning the Croatian coat of arms is hard to say, but the vast majority of Western journalists knew nothing about this and took the Croatian Serb claim at face value. In the Serbian media generally, Tudjman was cast as "Pavelić revividus" and in Serbia, the impression was taking hold that Tudjman was a dangerous lunatic and troublemaker. Serb nationalists considered the famous "meetings" organized by Šolević's committee to have been legitimate affirmations of popular power and believed that, if Croatia were to declare its independence, then Serbs of Croatia should enjoy the right to secede from Croatia and choose their own political destiny. The recourse to arms, therefore, seemed to many Serbs of Croatia to be a logical necessity and an act of defense. These were, however, only tendencies existing alongside other tendencies. In Croatia, there were Serbs, such as those associated with Milorad Pupovac, who were committed to a strategy of negotiation with the new Croatian authorities and who abjured the recourse to arms. In Serbia, there were likewise liberal Serbs, such as the brave pacifists associated with Women in Black, who refused to fight nationalism with nationalism and who remained committed to the principles of liberal democracy.

The same range of opinion and perceptions could also be found among Croats, among whom one could find both liberals and nationalists, as well as very traditional Catholics, and even a small number of anarchists. Strikingly, research conducted by Ivan Grdešić has shown that 42% of votes cast for Tudjman and the HDZ in 1990 came from persons who subscribed to intolerant views associated with the radical right.[53] For these and many other Croats, there was deep anger over the fallout from Tito's purge in December 1971 and after; many Croat professionals had seen their careers destroyed at that time and resented the overrepresentation of Serbs in the Communist Party of Croatia and in the Croatian police forces in the communist era. Croatian newspapers had provided little coverage of developments in Kosovo, with the result that ordinary Croats typically had little idea as to why Serbs were becoming agitated about the situation there. What Croats had read and heard about Milošević convinced them that the Serbian leader was extremely dangerous, while Serbian nationalist "meetings" were viewed as subversive. As support for Croatian independence grew, Croats took the view that Serbs already had their republic, recalled that there were Croats living in the Vojvodina who, nonetheless, did not think of seceding from Serbia, and therefore denied that Serbs living in Croatia enjoyed any right of secession from Croatia. To the Croatian public, the arming of the Serbs did not appear defensive in nature but seemed to figure as the first step in preparing for a war of Serbian expansionism at Croatia's expense.

In spite of all of this, however, there were long-established patterns of ethnic cohabitation in communities across Croatia, and inter-ethnic trust did not vanish overnight. In the initial phase of the conflict, the critical antagonism was not so much between Serbs and Croats as between families which had lived in the same town for centuries (*starosedioci)* and those who had assumed their present places of residence after 1945 (*došljaci).* It was Serbian *došljaci,* the newcomers, who were the most susceptible to Serbian propaganda and who, among those living in Croatia, first rallied to the Serb nationalist banner. In Vukovar, Serb *došljaci* attacked not only local Croats, but also Serb *starosedioci,* while Croats who fled the fighting in that city often gave their house keys "not to the local Croatian police, whom they did not know, but to their Serbian neighbors."[54] The war, thus, not only disrupted traditional patterns but figured, in part, as the mobilization of those who were not integrated into the multi-cultural life of the cities against urban multi-culturalism. This also suggests why citizens living in ethnically homogeneous villages were particularly receptive to mobilization for the upcoming war.

War in Slovenia

On 24 January 1991, Kučan and Milošević met in private to discuss the breakup of the country. Milošević assured Kučan that Belgrade had no pretensions toward Slovenian territory and would not try to keep Slovenia within Yugoslavia. Kučan, in turn, assured Milošević of his understanding for the Serbian desire to unite all Serbs, provided that the members of other national groups were not hurt. Both men understood their conversation to amount to an agreement on Slovenia's peaceful disassociation from the Yugoslav federation.[55]

At the same time, the Slovenes were also coordinating with the Croats. On 15 June 1991, for instance, the two sides agreed that Croatia would proclaim its independence on 25 June, and that Slovenia would follow with its own declaration of independence on the following day. A week later, Kučan came to Zagreb with France Bučar, president of the Slovenian Assembly, for final pre-independence consultation with the Croatian government; on that occasion it was decided that the two republics, Slovenia and Croatia, would proclaim independence on the same day, i.e., 25 June 1991.[56] Throughout the spring, the Slovenes made defense preparations, fortifying the existing state borders and setting up 22 border control points along the border with Croatia. The Slovenes also drew up mobilization plans and prepared barricades.[57]

The timing was by no means arbitrary. Until 21 June, the Slovenes had barely 23,000 rifles, with inadequate ammunition, and just over 1,000 light anti-tank weapons. The Slovenian arsenal also contained some light cannon but little else which could be used in defense against aerial assault. Only on 21 June did an impatiently awaited shipment of 5,000 automatic rifles, five million rounds of ammunition, more than 1,000 anti-tank weapons, and a few dozen Strela 2M anti-aircraft missile systems arrive.[58] That same day, however, federal air traffic control closed Brnik airport (just outside Ljubljana), as six MI-8 helicopters landed there to enforce the closure. But Kadijević, who was apparently ignorant of the Kučan-Milošević understanding and who, in any case, still wanted to defend the unity of Yugoslavia, was aware that the Slovenes had intended to declare independence on 26 June but did not learn until the last minute that the declaration had been advanced to 25 June.[59] But, by then, contingency preparations had already been made for JNA intervention on 27 June.[60]

It was in the middle of these active preparations for independence that American president George Bush dispatched Secretary of State James Baker to Belgrade at the eleventh hour. Baker arrived in Belgrade on 21 June, just five days before the publicly announced Slovenian-Croatian deadline, and had few ideas to offer except to suggest that while the U.S. wanted to see Yugoslavia remain united, democracy was more important than unity, and to advise the leaders of Yugoslavia's republics to "negotiate," as if the negotiations over the past year and a half had not reached a complete dead-end. Baker was heavily dependent upon notes from his press secretary and was apparently unaware that he was simultaneously endorsing the Slovenian-Croatian position (by calling for "the devolution of additional authority, responsibility, and sovereignty to the republics of Yugoslavia"[61]) and giving encouragement to Milošević and the JNA to attack Croatia (by promising that the U.S. would not recognize the independence of either Slovenia or Croatia).[62] President Kučan told me in 1999 that he tried to tell Baker that it was far too late to call off the transition to independence, but that Baker did not want to listen.[63]

When Slovenia declared its independence on 25 June 1991 and moved to take control of border checkpoints, the SFRY presidency, which had sole authority to decide on the use of the military, was not functioning, because of the Serbian bloc's refusal to confirm Mesić as president. On 24 June, Milan Pavić, the former chair of the economic chamber of the SFRY, paid a surprise visit to former defense minister Branko Mamula, to inquire as to whether he thought that the army was prepared to move into Slovenia on the joint authorization of the Federal Executive Council (i.e., Prime Minister Ante Marković) and the Ministry of Defense (i.e., Veljko Kadijević). Pavić was, in fact, delivering the inquiry on Marković's behalf and at his request.[64] Mamula favored the idea and relayed it to Kadijević in person, who readily agreed to this proposal, confirming his agreement in a telephone call to Marković in Mamula's presence that same day.

The Constitutional Act on the Independence and Sovereignty of the Republic of Slovenia was duly passed on 25 June, but not unanimously, since some of the deputies feared that Slovenia would be crushed.[65] On the following day, the Federal Executive Council, which was not authorized by the constitution to deal with problems of state borders, declared that the Slovenian and Croatian proclamations of independence were "illegal." Milošević, for his part, was opposed to the use of the JNA in Slovenia, according to Branko Mamula, or even to any effort to secure the northern and western borders of Croatia; Milošević's priority was to redraw the borders so that the Serbs of Croatia would be included within an expanded Serbian state.[66] But Marković had neither formal nor de facto authority with the army; and Kadijević, for one, did not even like Marković. The military response to the secession of Slovenia may be seen, thus, as the product of strategic momentum rather than as part of a conscious design: Milošević and Jović were interested in annexing large portions of Croatia and Bosnia-Herzegovina to an expanded Serbian state, and their plans had been directed toward preparing for military action directed toward achieving those objectives; but even if Milošević and Jović had no territorial ambitions in Slovenia, Milošević certainly appreciated that the army's deployment against newly independent Slovenia set a precedent which could be applied, later, in Croatia and Bosnia.[67]

At 1:15 A.M. on 27 June, JNA units crossed the border at Metlika. Orders were also given for the first armored battalion to leave its barracks and surround Brnik airport, which, though closed, was not under JNA control. The Slovenes were, however, able to prevent the battalion from taking control of Brnik and, later that morning, stopped a tank column from Varaždin at the bridge near

Ormož. Helicopter assaults also began, but the Slovenes shot down several of them, completely destroying two helicopters. Intelligence was poor; at one point, for example, Slovenian defense minister Janša had to call his father-in-law by phone in order to find out what he could see of JNA positions from his window. Lacking radar equipment, the Slovenes had to rely on intercepting radio communications between JNA air command and JNA flight crews in order to have some forewarning of aerial attacks.[68]

At the time, the Slovenes regarded Austria (not Germany) as their chief ally. Some of this had to do with the fact that Austrian foreign minister Alois Mock was exceptionally well informed about Yugoslav developments and had strong sympathy for the Slovenian position; the rapport which developed between Mock and his Slovenian counterpart, Dimitrij Rupel, was also important in this regard. Early on the morning of 27 June, as JNA tanks rolled across Slovenia, Rupel drove to the Austrian consulate in the Slovenian capital and rang the bell. There was no answer. Rupel could see the Austrians inside their offices and continued to ring the bell for half an hour. But the Austrians were too petrified to be capable of a response and left Rupel outside. There was a second factor which was probably relevant: as Rupel told me, the Austrian consul in Ljubljana was a socialist and did not share Mock's sympathies for an independent Slovenia.[69]

The Slovenes had hoped for some assistance from Croatia. At a minimum, the Slovenes had hoped that the Croats would undertake some measures to obstruct the movement of JNA troops from barracks located in Croatia into Slovenia; the Croats, however, were not prepared to get involved at this point.[70] Although the Croatian leadership was divided between the "pro-actives," who wanted to move rapidly to place the JNA barracks in Croatia under siege and endeavor to seize their arms, and the "passives," who considered such an idea completely reckless and wanted to adopt a more passive strategy, there was a general consensus among the leadership in Zagreb that Croatia was militarily unprepared to involve itself in the defense of Slovenia.[71] Croatian defense minister Špegelj, who may be counted among the "pro-actives," maintained private contact with Janša, and the two exchanged information during the seven-day war in Slovenia. Tudjman, a "passive" for purposes of this issue, was not unaware of the threat to Croatia but had been promised by Milošević, Jović, and Kadijević that Croatia would not be attacked, provided only that it stayed out of the fighting in Slovenia. Tudjman hoped that somehow this promise would be kept.[72]

Beginning already in January 1991, at the time of the weapons crisis, Špegelj argued tenaciously that the sooner the JNA barracks were placed under siege the better. Špegelj, who served as Croatia's first minister of defense until he was fired by Tudjman on 15 June 1991, argued that, as of early 1991, it would take the JNA two months to mobilize its forces. After his dismissal and appointment as commander of the Croatian National Guard, Špegelj presented a siege plan to Tudjman and to Prime Minister Manolić (in July 1991); in his view, "the conditions for a complete defeat of the aggressor had been created and there exist very strong military arguments that this could have been accomplished by the second half of 1992 at the latest (to include not only Croatia but also the defense and complete liberation of Bosnia-Herzegovina, naturally in agreement with its legal leadership [i.e., the Izetbegović government] and in alliance with its legal defense forces."[73] If this had been done consistently, this strategy would have included cutting off electricity and water and also blockading the 15 barracks in and around Zagreb, including those in the vicinity of residential areas.[74] There were legitimate grounds to fear that this could have led to fighting on the streets of Zagreb (and other large cities).[75]

On 27 June, Prime Minister Lojze Peterle received a telegram from General Konrad Kolšek, commander of the Fifth Army District. In this communication, Kolšek warned Peterle that the Fifth Army District had "been ordered to take control of all border crossings" and that the army was prepared to use force to carry out the order. As the JNA made its initial thrusts, the Slovenes received reports of movements by the Italian Army, while Italian navy assault ships were assembled in Italy's northern Adriatic ports.[76] The Austrian Army and NATO command in Naples were also on high alert.

The army launched a second offensive against Slovenia, and on 29 June, Marko Negovanović, commander of JNA counterintelligence, issued an ultimatum to the Slovenian government, over Belgrade television, calling on Slovenia to capitulate by 9 A.M. the following day. Instead of surrendering, however, the Slovenes put the JNA barracks under siege, blockading them and cutting off their water and electricity. Here and there were reports of individual JNA soldiers defecting (especially Croatian and Albanian recruits) or surrendering to the Slovenes.[77] The JNA did not lack the resources to crush the Slovenes; what was lacking was the will, though some JNA commanders, including JNA chief of staff General Blagoje Adžić, appeared to be resolved on suppressing Slovenian independence by force, as was Kadijević. But on 30 June, at a session of the Council for the Defense of the Constitution, Borisav Jović told the army generals that the federal Assembly should recognize Slovenian independence and that the JNA should prepare to withdraw from Slovenia. There was stunned silence after Jović's admonition, which in effect signaled the end of the JNA mission in Slovenia.[78] Janša reports that, after this, Kadijević became "totally irrational" while Mesić and Macedonian delegate Vasil Tupurkovski, his informants concerning military deliberations in Belgrade, "did not even want to mention the state Blagoje Adžić was in." By 2 July, the Slovenes had the upper hand and, that same day, declared a unilateral ceasefire. During the following night, skirmishes continued, however, especially in the Stajerska region. There was renewed fighting at Radenci, Kog, and Gornja Radgona the morning of 3 July, but by this point, the Slovenes had taken control of all border posts, and in the view of Defense Minister Janša, "the rest of the armoured columns no longer presented a threat."[79]

That same day (3 July), in a massive display of force, a lengthy column including 180 tanks, other heavy armor, and thousands of troops, left barracks in Belgrade and moved westward, ignoring appeals for restraint from the not-yet-installed SFRY president, Stipe Mesić. Soon after leaving Belgrade, the column split into three branches. One of them crossed into Croatia, a second moved to a position in Vojvodina, near the Hungarian border, and the third unit moved southward, entering Bosnia-Herzegovina.[80] It was quite apparent, from their positioning, that these troops were not being mobilized for action in Slovenia, but for action in Croatia and Bosnia-Herzegovina. Indeed, by 5 July, JNA troops in Slovenia had returned to their barracks, and a tenuous peace was holding. By this point, the Slovenes had captured more than 2,000 JNA troops.[81]

Even now, General Adžić remained committed to a "Yugoslav" solution. As he told officers at the military academy in Belgrade on 5 July, "a Greater Serbia is not a realistic option and cannot be realized without a catastrophe. This is why the battle for Yugoslavia is the only solution and the one giving Serbs a chance to preserve their rights."[82] But the European Community had sent mediators to the region already on 28 June and, by 7 July, had convened a conference at Brioni for the purpose of "resolving" the crisis. Viktor Meier, the distinguished foreign correspondent for the *Frankfurter Allgemeine,* notes, "The fact that it did not occur to the three EC foreign ministers even to come to Ljubljana, even though Slovenia was a combatant, was itself a bad sign. As a result of this, Slovenian President Kučan and Foreign Minister Rupel had to travel to Zagreb taking irregular by-ways, and at risk to their lives."[83] Rupel recounted the experience for my benefit in 1999:

That [ride] was terrifying. The main road was controlled by the Army. It was occupied territory. There is one very narrow road which our people controlled along the River Sava, and we drove during the night. There was enough space for one car only [on the road], and we were driving 100 miles an hour. Later, on the way back, we made a terrible mistake.[84]

That mistake might have cost them dearly. But in the meantime, Dutch foreign minister Hans van den Broek chaired the Brioni meeting, in which Kučan, Tudjman, and Jović took part. The "solution" dictated[85] by van den Broek involved a three-month moratorium on the further implementation of the declarations of independence, the withdrawal of JNA troops in Slovenia and Croatia to their barracks, the de-activation of Slovenian forces, acceptance of Slovenian control of all Slovenian border crossings, provided only that all customs revenues be turned over to the SFRY federal reserves, and the confirmation of Stipe Mesić as president of the SFRY presidency. In other words, the EC solution was to perpetuate an illusion for three months, viz., the illusion that the SFRY still existed. Under the provisions of the Brioni Moratorium, Slovenia and Croatia were barred from passing a defense law or establishing an army. Croatia got around the moratorium by building up its defense system within the framework of the Ministry of the Interior and the police.[86] But Croatia was experiencing difficulties in obtaining heavy weaponry even before the imposition of the UN arms embargo (imposed, ironically, at Belgrade's request).

It was precisely the perpetuation of this illusion which allowed Drnovšek and Mesić to continue to sit on SFRY presidency meetings, at least for a while, and which, in September, would allow the UN Security Council to agree, at Milošević's suggestion, to impose an international arms embargo against all the republics of the defunct SFRY. On 18 July, in a separate development, the SFRY presidency agreed to pull all JNA troops out of Slovenia by 18 October, though this deadline was later extended to 26 October.[87] Interestingly, Mesić opposed the decision to pull JNA troops out of Slovenia, because he was aware that they could then be used in Croatia.[88]

The three-month moratorium consigned Slovenia and Croatia to a kind of political limbo, in which they were not exactly reincorporated into the SFRY, but at the same time, they were not recognized as independent and therefore not permitted to set up the diplomatic infrastructure necessary for an independent state. During this period, rumors continued to fly, alleging, for example, that the JNA planned to renew the fight for Slovenia. But van den Broek left Brioni with a feeling of cautious optimism, allowing himself to declare, upon his return to Amsterdam, "We have the feeling that we have prevented a great volcanic eruption."[89]

In the meantime, the Macedonian Assembly had taken up the question of Macedonia's secession on 26 June, at which time representatives of the IMRO-Democratic Party for Macedonian National Unity urged the immediate proclamation of independence. Other Macedonian parties urged restraint, and the Assembly adopted a "wait and see" strategy.[90] Macedonian Kiro Gligorov cautiously told the Turkish daily *Hurriyet* on 30 June, "Macedonia will remain faithful to Yugoslavia and will not follow the example of Slovenia and Croatia."[91] But events were moving rapidly, and by 6 July the political wind was shifting: on that day, the Macedonian Assembly decided that "if no agreement can be reached in a peaceful and democratic way on a union of sovereign states on Yugoslav territory, the government must put before the assembly a constitutional law whereby the Republic of Macedonia, as an independent and sovereign state, will assume and carry out its sovereign rights."[92]

The War Spreads to Croatia

Although one can quite properly date the outbreak of the war for Croatia to the Serbian revolt in Knin from 17 August 1990 or from 3 March 1991, when Jović, as president of the SFRY presidency, approved Kadijević's request for authorization to send the army into Pakrac, or from the events in Plitvice on 31 March, or perhaps from the clashes in Borovo Selo on 2 May 1991, the JNA war against Croatia, in the proper sense of the word, began on 3 July 1991, with the occupation of the Baranja region of eastern Slavonia.[93] Montenegro entered into the war against Croatia only later, in the night of 23 September, by participating in an attack on the Dubrovnik littoral.

Kadijević, the defense minister of a country which no longer existed, saw the JNA's main task in the first phase of the war in terms of "protect[ing] the Serbian people in Croatia so that all districts with a majority Serbian population would be liberated in every regard from the presence of the Croatian army and Croatian authority."[94] Thus, although Kadijević still saw himself as loyal to the defunct SFRY, his formulation of the army's task already suggested that he was prepared to put the military forces under his authority at the disposal of the Serbian leader, whose commitment was to build a "Greater Serbia."

Tudjman, however, had been lulled into complacency as a result of his meeting with Milošević in March and indulged in unwarranted optimism.[95] "Croatia is not Slovenia," he said in mid-July. "We will not allow the army to become involved in the battle. Our path to freedom is different."[96] Even at the end of July, by which point the war was clearly spreading to Croatia, General Špegelj, on paying a visit to Tudjman, found the Croatian president relaxing with a game of tennis in an atmosphere "as if there had been 1,000 years of peace."[97] But as the fighting in Croatia heated up, Bosnian president Izetbegović expressed the view that the fighting in Croatia "had nothing to do with Bosnia".[98] Izetbegović thought he could reach an agreement with the JNA guaranteeing its neutrality and reach some sort of "understanding" with local Serbs while still proceeding on the road to Bosnian independence.

In the course of July, clashes between Serbian irregulars and the Croatian militia escalated in the "Krajina" and in Slavonia. On 10 July, in a feeble effort to draw the Serbian insurgents back to the negotiating table, Croatian authorities repeated their guarantee of equal rights and their promise of full cultural autonomy to the Serb minority living within Croatia's borders.[99] Self-styled Chetniks, sporting long beards, traditional Serbian shepherds' caps, and royalist badges, staged rallies in the mountains of Ravna Gora, chanting "We want war!" and recalling the "glories" of the earlier Chetnik massacres of Croats and Muslims. Amply equipped with heavy artillery and backed by the Serbian-led JNA, they struck at various targets, including Vinkovci and Vukovar in eastern Slavonia, Glina, Banja, Tenja, Petrinja, and Osijek. Serbian forces also attacked exclusively Magyar villages (such as the village of Korogy)[100] and the exclusively Czech village of Ivanovo Selo.[101] A few soldiers deserted from the JNA almost immediately,[102] and in Belgrade there were a few scattered anti-war demonstrations by students and opposition forces. But these protests were ineffectual. Meanwhile, within a matter of weeks, some 40,000 volunteers joined the Serbian Guard organized under the auspices of the Serbian Renewal Movement (SPO). Additional numbers volunteered to join Vojislav Šešelj's Chetnik movement and other paramilitary units. Of special interest here was Tanjug's 2 July announcement that the League of Communists–Movement for Yugoslavia (the communist party organization set up within the army, with the involvement of Mira Marković) was organizing guerrilla units of the People's Front of Yugoslavia and signing up volunteers.[103] The Croatian government claimed that the JNA was assisting the insurgents. The army denied these allegations and said that it was only trying to keep the warring sides apart.

War spread rapidly, as Serbian forces laid siege to key Croatian cities. Vukovar, 150 miles east of Zagreb, was bombarded and placed under siege. Although seriously outgunned, Croatian forces in Vukovar held out for 86 days, claiming, on 19 September, to have destroyed 60 Serbian tanks and to have killed 800 Serbian soldiers.[104] As the siege of Vukovar continued, rumors spread that the Croatian government had written off Vukovar, in order to give Croats a "martyr-city." Zdravko Tomac, who served as deputy prime minister in the Croatian Government of Democratic Unity from August 1991 to June 1992, denies the charge and claims that, on the contrary, the Croatian government was doing everything it could for the defenders of Vukovar—flying in medicines and ammunition and authorizing several attempts by Croatian forces to break through Serbian lines and relieve the siege of the city.[105] On the other hand, according to General Anton Tus, who was at the time the Croatian Army's chief-of-staff, Croatian military forces could have swept into Vukovar and ended the siege as of 13 October 1991 but for Tudjman's personal intervention. Tudjman's explanation, according to the general, was that the European Community was pressuring him to demur from any military response to the siege of Vukovar, allegedly because Doctors without Borders wanted to send a humanitarian convoy to that city.[106] By the time the convoy had come and gone, the military situation on the ground had changed.

By the end of the first week in October, after two months of heavy fighting, Serbian irregulars and the JNA controlled the center of Vukovar, but Croatian forces continued to hold onto the western part of the city. Finally, on 18 November, as the defenders ran low on ammunition, Serbian forces overran the remainder of the battered city, massacring some of the survivors (including wounded persons) who did not manage to escape and removing eight truckloads of art from the city museum. The art ended up in the Museum of Novi Sad and in the Belgrade Museum of Art and would not be returned until December 2001.[107] On the Croation side, some 2,800 persons lost their lives in the siege, while quite apart from its casualties and loss of equipment, the JNA emerged from the siege of Vukovar "exhausted" and psychologically drained.[108] The Yugoslav Army was recruiting students from the University of Belgrade and other young men by force, according to Aleksandar Fira, a former president of the SFRY Constitutional Court.[109] There were also serious problems of desertion.[110] And further, there was also a problem with distrust felt by Serb recruits toward non-Serbian officers still in the JNA. Indeed, Croatian authorities had been doing their best to encourage officers and enlisted men from the JNA to defect to Croatia's side. and according to Tomac, some 17,000 did so within a matter of a few months.[111] In September 1991, Kadijević came to Jović, worried that the army would lose its campaign against Croatia unless mobilization efforts were intensified. Still nervous a month later, Kadijević asked the government to call up 30,000 reservists. Ten days later, having already received half of that number, he returned to ask for 250,000![112]

Meanwhile, the war continued. The Slavonian capital of Osijek (24 miles northwest of Vukovar), which had been part of Croatia for more than a thousand years, was shelled by Serbian forces; the newspaper of the Serbian Orthodox Church, *Pravoslavlje,* gave its blessing to the campaign in a lengthy article on "the contribution of the Serbian Orthodox Church to the development of the culture of the city of Osijek."[113] The Serbian Orthodox Church also published a series of articles on "the massacres of the Serbian people" in Croatia during World War Two,[114] as well as a number of articles about Serbian sufferings at the Ustaša concentration camp at Jasenovac;[115] an article also recalled the attacks endured by the Serbian Orthodox Church in Croatia during World War Two.[116] The Serbian Orthodox Church seemed to bless the campaign as a "holy war."[117] Meanwhile, the Croatian weekly *Danas* published material from British archives to the effect that Tito's Partisans had liquidated large numbers of Catholic priests immediately after the war, including (according to the translation published in *Danas)* "the entire Catholic clergy" in "occupied Herzegovina."[118]

Now, half a century after that earlier conflict, nonstrategic sites in Croatia were being targeted by Serb forces, including hospitals, a veterinary station, schools, churches, a Franciscan monastery, and many of Croatia's historical and cultural landmarks.[119] A *New York Times* editorial said that "calculated assaults" had already destroyed 116 churches, castles, and other historic monuments as of 22 September, including the great dome of St. Jacob's Cathedral in Šibenik, the castle and museum in Vukovar, the historic center of Karlovac, and a number of baroque buildings in Varaždin.[120] At the same time, Ilija Kojić, minister of the territorial defense of the Serbian Autonomous Region of Slavonia, Baranja, and Western Srem, claimed that "members of the [Croatian] Ministry of Internal Affairs and other Croatian storm troopers [had] attacked all [the] Serbian villages in this region. These villages are: Pačetin, Bršadin, Trpinja, Borovo Selo, Tenja, and Bogota."[121] There were also credible reports of atrocities committed by both sides against civilian populations.[122]

Croatia was, in fact, seriously short of weapons, and authorities felt the need to remove World War Two–vintage weapons from museum cases and from film studios in order to equip their forces.[123] In Slavonia, Croatian forces had only two mortars at their disposal, and periodically moved them around by jeep in order to fool the Serbs into thinking that the Croats were better armed than they were.[124] Then, in Slavonski Brod, Croatian forces successfully attacked a train transporting JNA weaponry from Slovenia; the Croats thereby obtained their first anti-aircraft and anti-tank weapons, their first artillery pieces, and more mortars. This capture was one of a number of important turning points for the Croatian cause. But in mid-September, the JNA imposed a naval blockade of Croatia's coast and launched aerial attacks on the Croatian capital of Zagreb. At this point, Prime Minister Franjo Gregurić proposed that General Špegelj's plan be put belatedly into action. The government accepted this proposal and imposed a blockade on 33 large JNA garrisons across their territory, cutting off food supplies, water, and electricity. One by one, these garrisons surrendered, allowing the Croats to confiscate JNA equipment. Now, the JNA began shelling the outskirts of the walled city of Dubrovnik, long a favorite destination for Western tourists, while the Belgrade weekly magazine *Intervju* published an interview with academician Miroslav Pantić demanding that Dubrovnik and its surrounding area be set up as an "independent" republic.[125] While the inhabitants of Dubrovnik dug in to resist the JNA attack, the Serbian propaganda machine accused the Croats of attacking the city themselves![126] The prime minister of the government of Serbia even sent a letter to the Croatian government on 5 October expressing his hope that the Croats would "make every effort to prevent your armed forces [from] destroying Dubrovnik," and pledging that "the Yugoslav People's Army and Territorial Defence will spare no effort to protect this historical city."[127] As of early October, Sisak, Šibenik, and Zadar were also besieged, and Serbian forces were within 20 kilometers (12 miles) of Zagreb. Slobodan Milošević, speaking in English at one of a number of "peace conferences" called by the European Community, said, "Serbs in Croatia are not attacking anybody. They are purely defending themselves."[128] When Tudjman's Presidential Office was rocketed, nearly killing the Croatian president, the Serbian government issued a statement holding Croatian forces responsible for the rocket attack; Zdravko Tomac recalls that Serbian leaders even claimed that Tudjman had tried to kill himself "in order to smear Serbia's reputation."[129]

The International Dimension

When Croatia and Slovenia first declared their independence and violence broke out, various countries repudiated the seceding republics and endorsed the continued existence of a unified Yugoslav state—among them, the United States, the Soviet Union, China, Britain, France, Sweden, Denmark, Italy, Greece, Romania, Poland, and (cautiously) Hungary. The governments of Austria and Germany, pressured by populations long accustomed to vacationing along the Dalmatian coast and, partly for that reason, broadly sympathetic to Croatian and Slovenian aspirations, nonetheless held back from recognizing the breakaway republics. The Serbian press expressed misgivings about German intentions, referring to alleged dangers of a "Fourth Reich."[130] At the same time, Milan Drećun, a military-political commentator for the army newspaper *Narodna armija,* accused Austria and Germany of supplying sophisticated anti-tank and anti-aircraft weaponry to Croatia.[131] For his part, Croatian foreign minister Separović indicated, in an interview with Austrian television on 12 August, that Croatia looked to Austria and Germany to lead the way in extending diplomatic recognition to Croatia.[132]

Albania and Hungary accused the Yugoslav Air Force of having violated their airspace, and both countries took military precautions lest the fighting spill across their borders. Hungary's precautions focused on defense of its air-space.[133] The Albanian president placed Albania's army in a state of alert as early as the beginning of July.[134] Bulgaria issued a statement to the effect that the Bulgarian Army would not threaten "Yugoslav" security,[135] but also intimated that it was prepared to recognize an independent Macedonian state—which it did on 15 January 1992. Bulgaria was, however, afraid of being drawn into the conflict and was among the first countries to declare neutrality in the Yugoslav fighting.[136]

As for the Western powers, they were distinguished by a marked reluctance to get involved.[137] Even so, the European Community's General Council met in Brussels on 25 July 1991, as the violence in Croatia escalated, and condemned the bloodshed. Hans-Dietrich Genscher, then German foreign minister, recalled later that the session "appealed to the Collective Presidency in Belgrade to encourage an immediate truce and to begin negotiations on the future of Yugoslavia's peoples . . . [and] reaffirmed our earlier statement that any change of internal and external borders of the country achieved by force was unacceptable."[138] Given that the collective presidency had become completely dysfunctional, unable even to agree where to meet (in Brioni or in Belgrade), there was little to expect from that body.

The Bush administration, by contrast, scarcely even noticed what was happening in the Yugoslav lands. On 1 August 1991, the American president visited Ukraine, where he tried to dissuade locals from pursuing a course of independence, warning them, "Americans will not support those who seek independence in order to replace a far-off tyranny with a local despotism. They will not aid those who promote a suicidal nationalism based upon ethnic hatred."[139] Although aimed at Ukrainian separatism, the speech also reflected Bush's thinking about the breakup of multi-ethnic states more generally; in addition, Bush was known to believe that supporting the breakup of Yugoslavia could send the "wrong message" to the non-Russian republics of the dying USSR.

The August putsch in the Soviet Union was welcomed in Belgrade, for two reasons. First, for the roughly 10 days that the putsch lasted, Western attention was almost totally riveted on Moscow—and hence, not on developments on the ground in Croatia. Second, Milošević felt ideologically comfortable with the putschists, both because they were communists (and hence hostile to notions of privatization[140]) and because they were markedly anti-Western and hence, he calculated, more likely to assist his campaign in Croatia. But the putsch fell through, and by mid-October, the U.S. State Department signaled a reorientation in American policy by issuing a statement supporting the principle of (national) self-determination.[141] Since the Americans were not, in fact, supporting this principle for the peoples of Bosnia, it is clear that, in spite of such rhetoric, what they actually favored was the principle of *uti possidetis*, which holds that when complex states break up, internal administrative borders become international borders.

By this point, Peter Lord Carrington, a retired British diplomat who had been working as chairman of Christie's, the London auction house, had been brought out of semi-retirement and put in charge of a peace conference which began in The Hague on 7 September. Lord Carrington was convinced that he needed the "carrot" of international recognition to persuade the republics to cooperate in the conference, and was therefore hostile to any notion of recognizing any of the successor states until a peace accord had been signed.[142] But by this point, the German government had become convinced that only the internationalization of the crisis, via recognition, could hold any hope of dampening the violence and bringing the combatants to the negotiating table. By September, French president François Mitterand agreed, as did British prime minister John Major by December.[143]

In early October, Javier Pérez de Cuéllar, who was nearing the end of his decade-long term as UN secretary-general (from 1982 to December 1991), appointed Cyrus Vance, the former U.S. secretary of state, to serve as his personal envoy to Yugoslavia. During the period 11–18 October 1991, Vance met with the presidents of the republics, the members of the collective presidency, the Yugoslav prime minister, and the federal defense minister (General Kadijević), among others. Vance's objective was to win support for the notion of a settlement based on three principles: a loose association of sovereign or independent republics, adequate protections for ethnic minorities, and no unilateral (i.e., forceful) changes in borders. Five of the six republic presidents agreed to these principles; Milošević did not. However, Croatian president Tudjman admitted to Vance that he hoped to annex portions of Bosnia-Herzegovina to Croatia. Upon his return to New York, Vance apprised Pérez de Cuéllar that time was running out and that if an agreement could not be reached quickly, the fighting would likely escalate.[144]

By early autumn, the entire EC had endorsed the principle that the Yugoslav republics had a right to independence. In a 23 October draft paper to be discussed at the European Conference, there was a call for Serbia to restore the autonomy of Kosovo and Vojvodina, though this clause disappeared from the draft of 4 November. On 27 October, the EC foreign ministers issued a collective condemnation of Yugoslav Army attacks on Croatia's cities and, on the following day, ruled out any unilateral changes of borders. On 27 November, in an address to the *Bundestag*, German chancellor Helmut Kohl set a date for German recognition of Slovenia and Croatia—24 December 1991. Although much would later be made of this "unilateral" move by the German chancellor, the date was in fact two weeks *later* than a deadline suggested by van den Broek.[145] On 7 December, the Badinter Commission, headed by a French diplomat, submitted its expected evaluation of the candidates for recognition: the commission found that the SFRY was in the process of dissolution and that the international community therefore ought not block efforts on the part of the successor republics to make their own way. The commission recommended immediate recognition of Slovenia and Macedonia, and recognition of Croatia upon the passage of legal acts to guarantee the rights of the Serb minority—a stipulation with which the Republic of Croatia quickly complied. On 16 December 1991, the EC foreign ministers met and agreed to recognize the independence of all Yugoslav republics asserting their independence, on or after 15 January 1992. Genscher addressed the meeting to raise the issue of Germany's announcing recognition by 24 December but implementing it only after 15 January; none of the EC foreign ministers objected.[146] True to its word, the German government did not take up diplomatic relations until after 15 January, when the EC presidency announced the recognition of Slovenia and Croatia. Lord Carrington was unable to reconcile himself to this development, and he and others began to criticize Germany for its role. Among the charges hurled at Germany were that it had plotted to break up Yugoslavia from the beginning, that it was primarily responsible for the outbreak of the conflict in the first place, that it had acted "unilaterally" in extending formal recognition on 24 December, that it had "forced" its hapless EC partners to accept its wishes against their better judgment, that Germany was pro-Croat because of the Nazi-Ustaša connection of more than half a century earlier, and that Germany was bent on building a sphere of influence in the Balkans at the expense of other more deserving powers. These and other Germanophobic charges are preposterous and cannot be substantiated.[147] Certainly, had the EC decision to extend recognition been exacerbatory, then one would not have expected a truce to be signed at the beginning of January 1992, temporarily ending (most of) the fighting in Croatia.

Dissension within the Republics

As serious as the Serbian assault on Croatia was, a number of observers expressed fear that if the conflict spread to Bosnia-Herzegovina, the result would be a Balkan Armageddon.[148] Cantonization was being discussed actively at the time, but the population of Bosnia-Herzegovina was so intermixed that it would have been impossible to draw a line dividing people into homogeneous cantons or states without voluntary—or more likely, involuntary—population transfers. Yet, by spring 1991, the Bosnian-based Serbian Democratic Party was appealing to the principle of self-determination and actively promoting the secession of those parts of Bosnia-Herzegovina bordering on Croatia and advocating their union with Serbian-held sections in Croatia to form a new "Krajina" Republic.[149] Meanwhile, the Croatian Party of Right (headed by Dobroslav Paraga) demanded that all of Bosnia be annexed to Croatia.[150] Croatian president Tudjman, whose March 1991 meeting with Milošević had not yet become public knowledge, was nonetheless repeatedly making allusions to the possibility of changing Bosnia's borders, apparently unaware of the damage that he was doing to the Croatian diplomatic and war effort.

In Slovenia, Croatia, Serbia, Macedonia, Montenegro, and Bosnia-Herzegovina, fissures appeared within the elite establishments, and internal dissension grew. It would be misleading to portray the situation as if politically unified republics were engaged in controversy and debate only with each other. On the contrary, not one of the republics was able, as of October 1991, to achieve internal consensus.

The divisions within Bosnia, including among the Muslims themselves, have already been traced. It should, perhaps, be emphasized that among the Bosnian Croats there were differences between those who supported the idea of a united, independent Bosnia and those who favored the partition of Bosnia, annexing Croat-inhabited areas to Croatia, while among Serbs, there were not only nationalists of the Karadžić stripe but also those who were hostile to nationalist appeals and were prepared to fight for the government headed by Izetbegović.

In Croatia, part of the controversy arose from differences of opinion as to what policy should be adopted vis-à-vis the Serbs of Croatia. In late July, for example, Zvonimir Lerotić, a political scientist and close adviser of Tudjman's, said that Croatia's Serbs would soon be offered political and territorial autonomy.[151] Less than two weeks later, however, Zvonimir Separović, Croatia's foreign minister, was reported to have said that Croatian Serbs were being offered only cultural autonomy and "local self-management."[152] At the same time, the Zagreb daily *Večernji list* wrote that granting "autonomy" (presumably political autonomy was meant) would not alleviate problems; *Večernji list* argued that some people wanted to destabilize Croatia and were not interested in compromises.[153]

But there were broader issues dividing Croatian politicians. Some favored negotiations, whereas others preferred a hard line of "no compromise" and opposed any negotiation with the Serbs. Opposition extended even into the ranks of Tudjman's party, and in June 1991, three high-ranking members were expelled from that party.[154] On 31 July, leaders of eight opposition parties in Croatia joined in accusing the HDZ of having "considerably contributed to the difficult political and security situation in Croatia." Opposition leaders said that the "postponement of democracy" in Croatia was unacceptable and demanded that the powers of the president be curtailed and that the use of "various influential parastate organs" be curbed.[155]

In Macedonia, there were signs of alarm in August, when Ljupčo Popovski (of the Social Democratic Alliance of Macedonia and a member of the Assembly of that republic) accused unnamed persons of having committed "high treason" by "selling" Macedonia to Serbia in secret talks. The Social Democrats demanded that the guilty persons be named, arrested, and tried on charges of treason. They also accused Macedonian President Gligorov and Assembly president Andov of "turning Macedonia into a Serbian protectorate."[156]

At the same time, there were signs of distrust, or fear, of other republics. *Nova Makedonija*, the Skopje daily, described a proposal outlined by Serbian president Milošević in mid-August as "a hegemonistic stand" said to reflect "a desire for a greater Serbia";[157] yet, the following day, *Nova Makedonija* also expressed its disapproval of Croatian authorities, whom it characterized as "war-mongers." The Macedonian daily also criticized a view commonly expressed both in Yugoslavia and by Yugoslavs abroad at the time—that Milošević and Tudjman shared exclusive responsibility for the crisis. *Nova Makedonija* underlined that other people had also made their contribution to the escalation of tensions.[158]

A small reflection of internal divisions in Macedonia came on 22 August, when Macedonian prime minister Nikola Kljusev reportedly dismissed the republic's defense minister, Risto Damjanovski, ostensibly because of the latter's opposition to demands that Macedonian conscripts in the JNA should serve in Macedonia—and although, given the republic's steady gravitation toward independence and the consequent implication that this issue would resolve itself in time, it is difficult to imagine that no more than this was involved. In fact, a vague statement from Kljusev was reported, with words to the effect that Damjanovski had "lately worked in contravention of the positions taken by the Macedonian government."[159]

In Serbia, too, there were pressures and fissures. In mid-October, the *Financial Times* reported that Belgrade was gripped by "an atmosphere of desperation" as oil suppliers dwindled, the money supply soared beyond the government's capacity to back it, and people expressed concern about an accelerating slide toward widespread poverty.[160] In this climate, criticism of the government inevitably surfaced, and divisions came into public view. The most extreme position among the Serbs, at the time, was that taken by Vojislav Šešelj, leader of the Serbian Radical Party, who suggested, in an interview for *Der Spiegel,* that Croatia be whittled down to just a few square miles—in his words, "[t]o as much as one can see from the tower of the cathedral in Zagreb."[161] At the other end of the Serbian political spectrum one could find small groups of convinced liberals, pacifists, and feminists, clustered in organizations such as the aforementioned Women in Black.[162] Often highly articulate, they lacked a strong power base with which to challenge the regime. As for the better-known opposition figures—such as Vuk Drašković and Zoran Djindjić—they tended to endorse nationalist demands for territorial expansion, though Drašković would convert to an anti-war position by spring 1993.[163] Vesna Pešić was an important exception among opposition politicians, but her Civic Alliance remained on the margins even of opposition currents.

As for Milošević himself, he held to the notion that the interrepublican borders which had been set nearly half a century earlier and which had, in any case, closely followed historic borders, especially in the case of Slovenia, Croatia, and Bosnia-Herzegovina, could be revised. In August 1991, he set forth a preliminary plan for redrawing these borders, only to find that some of the other republics were not willing to discuss his suggestions seriously.[164] The federally oriented newspaper *Borba* also expressed its reservations about these ideas.[165]

In the course of summer 1991, various Serbian critics of Milošević raised their voices in protest. In July, the leaders of Serbia's principal opposition parties united in demanding changes in the government of Serbia, to include creating a government of "national unity," replacing Milošević with a "noncommunist," and appointing the majority of the ministers of the new government from outside the ranks of Milošević's Serbian Socialist Party.[166] Although Milošević ignored these demands, *NIN* opined that time was on the side of the opposition. Less than two weeks later, Vuk Drašković, the leader of the Serbian Renewal Movement, told the Austrian magazine *Profil* that "Serbs and Croats should rise against the dictatorial regimes in their republics."[167] But in another context, Drašković agreed with Šešelj that the western border of Serbia should be drawn along the line determined by Karlobag, Karlovac, and Virovitica.[168]

Serbian writer Borislav Mijalović Mihiz also criticized Milošević. Setting forth his ideas in a *Proposition for Reflections, in Ten Points,* Mihiz declared his belief that Yugoslavia could not be revived or sustained. He therefore called on Serbs to set aside their self-ascribed reputation as "the guardians" of Yugoslavia, to recognize the independence of Slovenia, and to accept the legitimacy of Croatia's claim to independence, conditional upon Croatia's recognition of the right of Serb-populated districts to decide freely with which state they wished to be affiliated.[169]

There was, thus, a wide spectrum of political opinion in Serbia, just as there was in Bosnia, Croatia, Macedonia, and—even though I have not discussed them here—the other republics as well. The various opinion groupings held different views about the interests of their respective republics, as well as about the appropriate policies, strategies, and instrumentalities to be adopted. Commenting on Serbia, the Swiss newspaper *Neue Zürcher Zeitung* claimed that local opposition to Milošević was placed at a disadvantage: "Every criticism of Milošević or the army is portrayed as treason or as an attempt, at a time of highest danger, to split the Serbian nation."[170]

Escalation and Truce

Four months after its outbreak in late June 1991, the War of Yugoslav Succession showed no signs of abating. By that point, there had been unconfirmed reports that the Yugoslav air force had used napalm against the Croats,[171] claims by Serbs that Croatian president Tudjman was trying to develop a nuclear option, and open discussion in the Serbian press about the possibility of an air strike against Slovenia's nuclear power plant at Krško (*NIN* cited the precedent of Israel's strike against Iraq's French-built nuclear power plant). [172] Large numbers of ethnic Croats from Canada, the United States, Australia, and various European countries were returning to Croatia to fight for their homeland.[173] By late September, some 232,412 Croatian citizens had reportedly been driven from their homes. Of this number, 106,000 refugees were said to have fled to other locations in Croatia, 60,000 (chiefly Serbs) to locations in Serbia, about 30,000 to Hungary, and some 3,500 to Germany.[174]

Up to that point, despite the "disassociation" of Slovenia and Croatia, the increasingly impotent eight-person collective presidency had continued to exist

—at least in theory. But on 3 October, the four pro-Serbian delegates (representing Serbia, Montenegro, Kosovo, and Vojvodina) expelled the delegates from the other four republics and elected Montenegrin delegate Branko Kostić president of the collective presidency. This produced the ironic result that Slovenia and Croatia, which had declared their separation from Yugoslavia, wanted nonetheless to keep their representatives in the presidency, while Serbia and Montenegro, which did not recognize the separation of Croatia, at least not within the borders it had had up to then, refused to allow either the Slovenian or the Croatian delegate in that body. Macedonia and Bosnia joined Slovenia and Croatia in condemning the Serbian move, which they termed a "putsch."[175] The U.S. State Department also issued a statement characterizing this development as "a clear attempt by Serbia and Montenegro to seize control of the federal government." The State Department added, "In such circumstances, the United States does not accept that this rump group legitimately speaks for Yugoslavia."[176] One of the first acts of the "rump" presidency was to praise the work of the JNA up to then. In the wake of this development, Defense Minister Kadijević pledged "to force the 'neo-fascist leadership' [of Croatia] to its knees . . . [and called upon] all 'patriots' to defend their country against the threat of 'fascism.'"[177]

In early October, according to Zdravko Tomac, Croatian intelligence services intercepted a communication originating at Supreme Headquarters in Belgrade: it was an order "for an all-out attack on Croatia, which was intended to break Croatia politically and economically, and compel it to capitulate and stay in Milošević's Yugoslavia, [and which] outlined in detail attacks on industrial facilities, with the aim of causing an ecological catastrophe." The Croatian cabinet considered the U.S., Britain, and France to be inflexibly attached to the illusion of Yugoslav territorial integrity and therefore decided to appeal to the Russians to intercede with the Serbs. Late in the night of 6 October, the Croats contacted Consul-General Nikolai Girenko in a state of high agitation, and Girenko telephoned Gorbachev, waking him out of his slumber. Gorbachev in turn telephoned Kadijević, rousing him from his nocturnal respite and advising the general against rash and totalistic military moves.[178] The following day, the Yugoslav Army fired a missile at Tudjman's office. Milošević had supported Gorbachev's opponents in August; by firing at Tudjman, Milošević served notice that he was not about to take orders from the lame-duck president in the Kremlin.

A series of ceasefires brokered by the European Community fell through. The eighth such ceasefire, negotiated on 9 October, was violated within a few hours, when the JNA and Croatian units resumed the exchange of artillery fire. The following day, Germany's Martin Bangemann, vice president of the EC Commission, called for Bonn to extend diplomatic recognition to Slovenia and Croatia without any further delay. His initiative seemed to be ignored, but it reflected the increasingly frantic fears among some Western diplomats about the dangers which this war held. At the same time, Dutch Foreign Minister van den Broek announced that after five hours of discussions with Presidents Milošević and Tudjman and Defense Minister Kadijević, all present had agreed that all units of the JNA would be withdrawn from Croatia within a month. The following day, however, the Defense Ministry indicated that it considered the agreement nonbinding and null because it had not been officially signed.[179] By then, the Yugoslav Army was building bunkers and digging trenches in Croatia, to defend areas which they had captured—specifically, the Knin littoral, Kordun, Banija, Baranja, and the Papuk Mountain range.[180]

The JNA continued its campaign against Croatia, sending its air force on bombing missions against the Croatian towns of Osijek, Nova Gradiška, Ogulin, Otačac, Gospić, and Pakrac. At the same time, the JNA tightened its siege of the Croatian port city of Dubrovnik by mounting an amphibious assault to seize a beachhead and then capturing several coastal villages to establish a base of operation three miles from Dubrovnik. Dubrovnik was also said to have been subjected to aerial bombardment.[181] On 15 October, the Yugoslav Army pushed into the town of Cavtat, south of Dubrovnik. Ninety percent of Dubrovnik's 60,000 inhabitants were Croats, so that any Serbian claims based on ethnic criteria were entirely spurious. In response to the siege of the walled city, the U.S. State Department issued a protest on 24 October 1991.

The Hague peace conference (which had convened on 7 September) came up with a confederal package ("the Carrington Plan") in early October, apparently taking over the now-obsolete ideas proposed nearly two years earlier by Slovenia and Croatia and, when Milošević rejected that plan, offered a slightly revised peace package on 25 October. But Milošević rejected this proposal as well. This second proposal would have entailed the demilitarization of all ethnic enclaves and guarantees of autonomy for Kosovo and Vojvodina. Milošević said the proposed changes would have "opened the way to new instability and tension."[182] In August, Croatian president Tudjman had told a German journalist that he was not prepared to surrender any of Croatia's territory to Serbia.[183] The tenth ceasefire was announced on 19 October, and after more than a week of nonobservance, the European Community belatedly announced that this latest ceasefire had collapsed. "Ceasefire agreements have been violated by all parties," the European Community noted in a public statement. "But recent Yugoslav Army attacks are out of all proportion to any noncompliance by Croatia."[184]

On the face of it, Croatia looked more vulnerable than ever and on all fronts. With an estimated 30% of its territory controlled by Serb insurgents and the Yugoslav Army, Croatia had been thrust onto the defensive, with Eastern Slavonia apparently exposed to further inroads, Dubrovnik under siege, and Serb forces entrenched in Petrinja, about 30 miles from Zagreb. In some places in Dalmatia, the area under the control of the Croatian Army was reduced to a depth of no more than a few hundred meters. But Croatia's military capability had changed dramatically in the three months since General Anton Tus's appointment (in August 1991) as chief-of-staff of Croatia's armed forces. To begin with, a number of important barracks had surrendered to the Croats, most notably those in Rijeka and Delnice, and in late September, Tudjman claimed that Croatian forces had taken possession of some 70 JNA installations, grabbing a rich cornucopia of arms and ammunition. Moreover, General Tus, as Silber and Little note,

had turned a rag-bag chaotic assembly of volunteers and reserve policemen into a disciplined fighting force. When he had taken command, the Croatian armed forces consisted of a National Guard of four brigades, together with a large reserve police force. By October, Tus had assembled all available forces into a system of thirty-five brigades. . . . By December, he claimed to have 250,000 fighting men under arms, organized, across the republic, in sixty brigades.[185]

Milošević thought he would "quit"—at least on the Croatian front—while he was ahead, and in late November, he agreed that international peacekeepers would be deployed in Croatia. The deployment seemed to offer the prospect of freezing the partition of Croatia into Serb and Croat sectors. The internationalization of the crisis, most visibly manifested in the belated announcement by the EC member states in mid-December of the imminent recognition of Slovenia and Croatia, also affected Milošević's calculations. The Serbian leader joined his Croatian counterpart in accepting a ceasefire plan prepared by UN mediator Cyrus Vance, which called for freezing the front lines in place and the dispatch of about 14,000 peacekeeping troops to the area. Milan Babić, the leader of the Krajina Serbs, did not want to accept the plan until Belgrade's leaders threatened to replace him; at that point, Babić signed on the dotted line. But Milošević was not inclined to forgive Babić's insubordination and, shortly thereafter, arranged for the Krajina Assembly to replace the annoying dentist with the more compliant Goran Hadžić, who had been working as a storeroom clerk.[186] By 2 January 1992, all relevant parties had signed the truce, and UN peacekeepers were on their way to take up positions in Croatia, separating the two sides. The arrival of the UN troops gave the Serb occupation a measure of international legitimation, but it also muted the fighting in Croatia for more than three years.

Between 6,000 and 10,000 persons were dead, more than 400,000 persons were homeless, 40% of Croatia's industrial plant had been destroyed, gross industrial production was down 28.5% in 1991, and tourism, a mainstay of the Croatian economy, had fallen by more than 80% in 1991.[187] Net income declined, unemployment rose, and inflation in Croatia stood at 123% for the year as a whole.

The war caused deep suffering among all the peoples inhabiting Croatia and also affected the inhabitants of Serbia, both directly (through casualties and flights to foreign countries) and indirectly (chiefly through the distortion of economic life). Scholars wrote papers demonstrating that the war had been "avoidable"[188] but often neglected to add that it had also been "stoppable" from the beginning, had there only been resolve in Western capitals.[189]

Definition 6 (in chapter 1) defined *crisis* as "a collective consensus that the status quo is untenable." Or, to put it differently, people behave as if there were a crisis when they believe that there is a crisis, and that in turns consists in the apprehension that the situation has become unacceptable. There was a general consensus on that point in the early months of 1991: indeed, it was the only important point on which the leaderships of all six Yugoslav republics agreed. Corollary 8b specified that "crisis is associated with vulnerability to and openness to wholesale change." Why this should be so should be apparent from definition 6. But implicit in this is also the notion that crisis may open the doors to rapid change, with unpredictable consequences. Legitimate systems may, of course, experience crises, but illegitimate systems are crisis-prone, as has already been noted, and moreover, are apt to suffer crises more bitterly.

The record of the events of 1987–1991 also confirms the greater proclivity of multi-ethnic systems, *where the "different ethnic/nationality groups . . . have competing legitimation symbols,"* to ethnic polarization (proposition 14).

Finally, the record of 1991 confirms what was already stated in proposition 2, viz., that "the internal and external behaviors of illegitimate states differ from the internal and external behaviors of legitimate systems." The tragedy of the West was to have forgotten this simple rule in dealing with Milošević—for a long, long time. In this sense, Tomac's comparison of U.S. president Bush's handling of Milošević with Neville Chamberlain's handling of Hitler in 1938[190] is to the point: both men chose to treat a morally decrepit head of state as if he were a legitimate ruler, or perhaps, as if there were no difference between legitimate politics and illegitimate politics.

CHAPTER 15

The War of Yugoslav Succession, Phase 2 (1992–1995)

> Come on now, lads, the time is here
> to leave behind those we hold dear.
> There's no more time for love or prattle,
> Time instead to head to battle.[1]
> —Chetnik song

A s early as 1984, Zachary Irwin, a professor of political science at Pennsylvania State University, warned that ethnic polarization could ignite conflict among Serbs, Croats, and Muslims within Bosnia-Herzegovina.[2] The expansion of the war into Bosnia-Herzegovina had been feared for long enough, it had been in preparation for nearly a year, it had been the subject of urgent meetings involving Western mediators, it had been anticipated and predicted,[3] and Radovan Karadžić, the psychiatrist-turned-leader of the Bosnian SDS (Serbian Democratic Party), described by Ivo Žanić as "an ambitious but untalented poet," who had been suspected by his colleagues back in the 1980s of being a police informer,[4] had told the Muslims of Bosnia that they were about to experience hell on earth. Moreover, there had been telltale incidents in various parts of Bosnia-Herzegovina since 1990. But for all that, when the war broke out in earnest in early April 1992, it was, for all who cared about Bosnia-Herzegovina and its people, a great shock. In spite of all the gathering clouds, one could not help but hope that the clouds would somehow blow away. When they did not and when the fighting became truly ugly (already in the course of

413

April), it was clear to many that only a decisive intervention from outside—involving the threatened use of force and most probably also the use of force—held much hope of stopping the violence in the short term. In the absence of a decisive international response, given the ambitions of the parties to the war and their present and prospective military resources—the war was likely to drag on for years. The British magazine *The Economist* summarized UN secretary-general Boutros Boutros-Ghali's advice to the Security Council in a May 1992 article. "If the Council members wanted to intervene," Boutros-Ghali was reported to have told the Security Council, "they should not try to do so on the cheap; they would have to consider sending in tens of thousands of troops equipped with offensive capability. Even if they opted, at this stage, only for armed escorts to protect the relief convoys, they would have to think along similarly expensive lines."[5] But the Western response was muddled, marred by expressions of sympathy for the insurgents,[6] ineffectual, penny-pinching at the wrong time so that over the long run the policy approach embraced ended up being more expensive than a more decisive response would have been, and morally dubious.[7]

While the West Lay Slumbering

In the course of 1989, inter-ethnic relations in Bosnia-Herzegovina began to deteriorate.[8] Relations between Bosnia's Muslims and Serbs became especially strained, and enough Serbs left the republic, complaining about Islamic fundamentalism, that Serbian authorities felt justified in violating Bosnia's limited sovereignty by sending its security police to gather information in the neighboring republic. Serbs also complained that Muslims were attacking their children, maltreating their priests, and so forth.[9] Most of these stories bore all the marks of police-manufactured rumor-mongering—and stirred up panic among Serbs, mutual fear between the two groups, social distance, and gradually also hatred. The sowing of mutual fear was the first step in setting the stage for war; it was, thus, not simply a spontaneous reaction to economic stress or to anything else. It was, on the contrary, the fruit of deliberate policies adopted in Belgrade.

By 1990, Milošević and Jović were ready to take the second step—organizing Serb militias in Croatia and Bosnia. Serbian documents seized by the Bosnian Army show that the JNA began organizing Bosnian Serb civilians into militias and arming them as early as September or October 1990.[10] The lame-duck communist authorities in Sarajevo made no response, however, and it was only in March 1991, several months after the elections which ended the role of the communist party in Bosnia, that the SDA—not the Bosnian government as such—established the "Patriotic League," as a defensive armed force.[11] But by then, the JNA had already distributed nearly 52,000 firearms to Serb volunteer units and individuals in Vogošća, Ilijaš, Hadžići, Breza, Visoko, Doboj, Brčko, Bihać, and other areas, and 23,298 weapons to members of the SDS.[12] By this point, agents of KOS, the Counterintelligence Service of the JNA, were busy in Bosnia, infiltrating religious institutions, cultural institutions, and the media in order to foster pacifism and optimism about the prospects for a peaceful solution.[13] KOS, as an agency of the JNA, was also involved in the distribution of arms to Serbs in Bosnia. Fikret Muslimović was the chief of KOS in Bosnia-Herzegovina with his seat in Sarajevo, at the time that this distribution took place, and yet Izetbegović continued to place his trust in Muslimović. Another mole in the Bosnian apparatus, according to Sefer Halilović, was Dragiša Mihić, who served until April 1992 as head of a branch of the Ministry of Internal Affairs in Bosnia and subsequently as chief of state security services in Serbia; Halilović claims that, together with Dušan Kozić, an SDS deputy in the Bosnian Assembly, Mihić coordinated the shipment of weapons from Montenegro to Bosnia-Herzegovina. Then there was Bakir Alispahić, Bosnia's minister of police, said by Munir Alibabić-Munja to have collaborated with KOS. And again, one of Bosnian president Izetbegović's most trusted ministers was Alija Delimustafić, then minister of the interior, on whose authority the reserve contingents of the police in much of the republic were disbanded around the end of February 1991. As if this were not already sufficiently questionable, Delimustafić also reached an agreement in the second half of 1991 with Petar Gračanin, federal minister of internal affairs, and General Aleksandar Vasiljević, chief of KOS, on the dispatch of about 100 inspectors, who, under the cover of making routine inspections, "completely paralyzed work on defense preparations."[14] The nature of inspection also lent itself very well to espionage, providing Milošević and Karadžić with useful intelligence. It was also at this time that Delimustafić arranged for the transport of about 12,000 rifles to western Herzegovina, on Vasiljević's orders. Izetbegović was informed about this at the time but, strangely, did not stop the transport of these weapons, which eventually ended up in the hands of Bosnian Croat forces.[15] Thanks to the emplacement of the aforementioned and other collaborators in key offices in the Ministry of Defense and the republic TO, KOS was able to do irreparable damage to defense preparations in Bosnia even while preparing local Serbs to launch an insurrection.[16] Milošević and Karadžić were in regular contact by telephone, sometimes talking two or three times a day.[17] Then, in August 1991, Karadžić met with Milošević to discuss the timing of an eventual army attack on Bosnia; in the course of this meeting, Milošević informed Karadžić that he would soon be receiving his next delivery of armaments, from General Nikola Uzelac, commander of the JNA garrison in Banja Luka.[18] This planning meeting came just prior to the imposition of an arms embargo against all the Yugoslav successor states by the UN Security Council (Resolution no. 713), at the suggestion of none other than Belgrade. The Milošević-JNA-Chetnik alliance also made other preparations for war—disarming the Bosnian TO (in 1990), moving artillery pieces into position around the major cities of Bosnia by the end of 1991, and even removing some of the arms factories in Bosnia-Herzegovina to Serbia.[19] Although Izetbegović and some of his close advisers were rather obviously suffering from terminal naïveté, the SDS was playing an obstructionist role from the first days of the coalition government, behaving as a "fifth column."

Among the Bosnian Serbs, the key players, besides Karadžić, who would serve as president of the Bosnian Serb republic, were Momčilo Krajišnik, who would become president of the Bosnian Serb Assembly, and Nikola Koljević, one of two Bosnian Serb vice presidents, who at one time had taught Shakespeare at Nottingham University. Collectively, these three came to be known as "the KKK."[20] The other vice president was Biljana Plavšić, who had been dean of the Faculty of Natural Sciences at the University of Sarajevo and who, in July 1992, was given responsibility for refugees, humanitarian aid, contacts with the Serbian Orthodox Church and other religious communities, and contacts with UNPROFOR (the UN Protection Force) except for questions relating to war or combat.[21] Prior to their resignation in April 1992, Koljević and Plavšić had been Serb representatives in the collective presidency of Bosnia-Herzegovina.

By July 1991, according to Tanjug, Milošević and the JNA were stepping up the smuggling of armaments to Bosnian Serbs,[22] and Colonel-General Drago Vukosavljević, commander of the Territorial Defense Headquarters of Bosnia, ordered the mobilization of police reservists in the ten municipalities of the Bosnian Krajina. This order was issued in defiance of instructions by the Bosnian government, leading the MBO (the Muslim Bosniak Organization), the SDA, the HDZ of Bosnia-Herzegovina, and the Social Democratic Party to issue a joint statement warning that a de facto coup was being carried out in Bosnia under Serbian sponsorship.[23] In August, Nikola Koljević and Biljana Plavšić, members of Karadžić's SDS sitting on the collective Bosnian presidency, announced that they would not be attending any further meetings of that body. In September, Bosnian Serbs appealed to the JNA for "protection," and on 20 September 1991, the JNA moved troops into Bosnia, in a move which would allow the army to cut across that republic's territory and open a new, southern front against the beleaguered Croatian town of Vukovar.[24] Local Croatian and Bosniak residents erected barricades and set up machine-gun nests; they succeeded in bringing a column of 60 Serbian tanks to a standstill in the vicinity of Višegrad. The following morning, the JNA units opened fire on Muslim and Croatian positions, and more than a thousand Bosniaks and Croats fled the area; the clash resulted in the first casualties on the Bosnian front.[25] Five days later, Yugoslav Army units destroyed the Bosnian village of Ravno, which was inhabited mostly by Croats.[26]

Eventually, in mid-October, the Bosnian parliament held a marathon session to discuss the question of sovereignty. The 73 Serbian delegates walked out, declaring the session illegal. Thereupon, the remaining parliamentary deputies (Bosniaks and Croats) adopted a memorandum, preparing the way for self-government and underlining that Bosnia would under no circumstances allow itself to be conjoined to either Croatia or Serbia. Radovan Karadžić, who was not a parliamentary deputy and had no business attending the session in the first place, reacted fiercely, warning that the memorandum set Bosnia "on the same road to hell as Croatia and Slovenia."[27] The SDS established illegal links with the government of Slobodan Milošević, pulling more than 50 municipalities into its illegal para-state network by November 1991.[28] Five Serbian Autonomous Districts were organized—in effect, seceding from Bosnia-Herzegovina even before the republic held its referendum on independence.

At this point, the SDS organized an illegal plebiscite on 9–10 November, asking Serbs to choose between an independent Bosnia and continued association with Yugoslavia, and "then, *on the basis of falsified results,* announced that the majority had voted for the second option."[29] On 21 December 1991, the "Assembly of the Serbian People," a body having no clear constitutional basis, announced the establishment of a Serbian state within the Republic of Bosnia-Herzegovina; this assembly consisted of Serbian deputies elected to the Bosnian parliament. The SDS then pushed forward with the proclamation of a "sovereign" Serb Republic of Bosnia-Herzegovina in early January 1992.

In the meantime, the Bosnian government had approached the EU to ask for international recognition of Bosnia-Herzegovina. The EU appointed a commission, headed by French diplomat Robert Badinter, to review the claims of Slovenia, Croatia, Macedonia, and Bosnia-Herzegovina for international recognition. Concluding that Yugoslavia was "in the process of dissolution," the Badinter Commission recommended the immediate recognition of Slovenia and Macedonia, recognition of Croatia after legislation had been passed in Zagreb to protect Serbs and other non-Croat minorities, and recognition of Bosnia-Herzegovina if a majority of its citizens endorsed independence in a referendum.[30] The referendum was duly scheduled for 29 February–1 March 1992. The SDS wanted to assure a Serb boycott and, as far as possible, prevented those Serbs who might have wanted to vote from doing so; in spite of this coercive boycott, 99.7% of those voting endorsed independence, amounting to 63.4% of the total number of eligible voters in the republic.[31] On this basis, the Sarajevo government now requested international recognition. Bosnian Serb leader Karadžić, however, declared that the Serbs would not allow themselves to become a minority, thereby rejecting the democratic principle of majority rule.[32]

But the international community—by which is meant, in practice, the United States, Russia, Germany, Great Britain, France, the UN General Secretary, NATO, the EU, and sometimes also Italy and Spain—was not confident that Bosnian independence as such would provide a peaceful solution.[33] Thus, in February 1992, José Cutilheiro, a Portuguese diplomat serving as UN special envoy for human rights, conducted talks with representatives of the parliamentary parties in Sarajevo. After a subsequent meeting in Lisbon at the end of the month, attended by Izetbegović, Bosnian foreign minister Haris Silajdžić, Bosnian minister for special-purpose production Rusmir Mahmutćehajić, Karadžić, and Bosnian Croat leader Mate Boban, Cutilheiro presented a revised plan to the three sides in mid-March. The plan was described (in the press) as a recipe for the "cantonization" of Bosnia-Herzegovina and would have created a patchwork quilt of ethnic districts; under this plan, the Serbs and Bosniaks (Muslims) would have been assigned 44% of Bosnia's territory each, leaving 12% of the land to the Croats.[34] None of the three parties were satisfied with this proposal, however—the Serbs because they hoped to annex about two-thirds of the republic to Serbia; the Croats because, with more than 17% of the population, they felt that this plan "cheated" them by 5%; and the Bosniaks because they did not want to agree to a partition of their republic.[35]

Within Bosnia, the coalition government had proven so dysfunctional that, by September 1991, many firms in that republic were paying taxes, not to the Bosnian state, but to one or another nationalist political party.[36] The economy itself was near collapse, with exports stagnant, depleted foreign exchange reserves, the Port of Ploče blockaded, several major plants facing the prospect of bankruptcy, and increasing concerns about food supplies. Moreover, by the end of 1991, the infusion and dissemination of weapons had reached the point that, according to information collected by the secret police, an estimated 301,500 civilians in the republic had firearms (significantly more than had been the case two years earlier): some 157,200 Serb civilians were now armed, as were 92,500 Muslim civilians, and 51,800 Croat civilians.[37] In spite of this, Izetbegović, whose government would proclaim Bosnia's independence on 3 March 1992, remained blithely optimistic, telling a radio interviewer in December that he did not expect the Yugoslav Army to attack Bosnia's population and reiterating his conviction, as late as mid-March 1992, that "[t]here will be no war in Bosnia, [neither] local, nor imported."[38] It was only later—on 9 April 1992—after the conflict had broken out, that the Bosnian presidency would declare the unification of the sundry armed units in the republic into the Armed Forces of the Republic of Bosnia-Herzegovina, later renamed the Army of the Republic of Bosnia-Herzegovina (ARBiH).[39]

Competing Ideologies

It has become commonplace in much of the literature concerning the war, and most especially in works written in North America, to reduce the competing ideologies in the War of Yugoslav Succession to three: Serbian, Croatian, and Bosniak/Muslim. This is, regrettably, a serious oversimplification, insofar as it ignores the presence of a liberal-pacifist current among all three national groupings, not to mention the inconsistent pacifism and incoherent monarchism of Vuk Drašković in Serbia and the differences between (1) the power-hungry Milošević, who embraced nationalism but connected it to socialist ideology, (2) the nationalist expansionism represented by Karadžić, Plavšić, Krajišnik, and the Serbian Orthodox Church,[40] and (3) the racist fascism espoused by Vojislav Šešelj and others—to mention only permutations on the Serbian political landscape. Again, one could differentiate among pacifists coming out of the rock scene and lacking an articulated liberal understanding, pacifists coming out of feminist circles and articulating a feminist-liberal critique, and nonfeminist liberal pacifists. A detailed account of all the permutations at play is beyond the scope of this book. What follows is an effort to distinguish among the four principal competing ideologies having an impact in Bosnia: Serbian nationalist expansionism, Croatian nationalist expansionism, Izetbegović's inconsistent blend of Islamic principle and secular politics, and the liberal opposition, as represented by Žarana Papić, Ivo Banac, and Adil Zulfikarpašić.

Serbian Nationalist Expansionism

The Serbian nationalist program, as articulated by Karadžić and others, represented a revival of the Chetnik dream—in terms of territorial aspirations, ideological content, and the means to which these nationalists were prepared to go. It is not without significance that many Serb nationalists chose to call themselves "Chetniks." If we bear this in mind and bear in mind also the fact that many Serbs were completely opposed to this self-declared "Chetnik" program, it will prove to be more useful, at least some of the time, to refer to the Serb nationalists as "Chetniks," rather than as "Serbs."

What, then, did the Chetniks claim? First of all, they claimed the right of all Serbs to live in Serbia. In so saying, they were not offering an invitation to Serbs to move to Serbia, on the model of postwar Germany, but, quite the contrary, they were advertising their claim that Serbs living anywhere in the lands which had earlier been attached to the SFRY had the right (and, in practice, in their view, also the obligation) to attach their lands to the emerging Serbian state, even if they were a distinct minority (as the Serbs in Croatia, constituting 12% of the population, clearly were). Insofar as this claim entailed a rejection of majority rule, it comes as no surprise that, in Bosnia-Herzegovina, when discussions took place during 1991–1992 concerning the future of that republic, the Chetniks denied that the Bosniaks and Croats had the right to make any decisions without the assent of the Serbs; instead of majority rule, thus, they asserted the principle of ethnic condominium, in which each national grouping would enjoy a veto over decisions being taken. Yet even this principle was not asserted consistently, since the Chetniks wanted to be able to veto independence for a Bosnian state retaining its pre-existing borders but were not prepared to allow the Bosniaks, for example, to veto the partition of the republic.

In spite of the foregoing, the Chetniks claimed to want to build a democratic state with freedom for its citizens.[41] The catch was that once the process of "ethnic cleansing" (involving the wholesale murder or expulsion of locals and the destruction of their cultural monuments) was complete, the resulting state would be a state consisting almost entirely of Serbs. In the Chetnik concept, thus, nationalism, even in its most chauvinistic interpretation, and democracy are construed as compatible. There were other claims developed for foreign audiences, specifically that Serbs owned 60%–65% of Bosnian land prior to the war and that this entitled the Serbs to annex two-thirds of Bosnia, and that, in any event, the conflict between Serbs and non-Serbs had to be traced back over centuries. Neither of these claims had any merit. For one thing, Bosnian Serbs owned not 60%–65% of Bosnian land but 42.6% (less than the 44.8% owned by Bosniaks) at the beginning of the 1990s.[42] For another, there is no *modern* ideology which ties political rights of self-determination to land ownership. At best, this concept is a throwback to the Middle Ages, when references to "the Nation" were intended to be understood to mean the land-owning nobility. But such a state could not be described as a democracy in *any* sense of the word. Nor is it customary to simply divide states up just because they are multi-ethnic, though if it were customary, then it would be relevant to note that the Serbs constituted, according to the 1991 census, only 31.46% of the population of Bosnia-Herzegovina, with Muslims accounting for 43.77% and Croats for 17.34%.[43] As for the claim that the conflicts among Serbs, Croats, and Bosniaks have long historical roots, no serious scholar has been prepared to trace these conflicts any further back than the 1870s, and most argue, as I do, that it makes the most sense to take the winter of 1918–1919 as marking the beginning of the problems. But the importance of the Chetnik claim has nothing to do with the particulars of one century versus another, but with the Chetnik argument that the conflict is not about specific issues, or even about the legacy of grievances from the interwar kingdom, World War Two, and the years since, but is, rather, a matter of incompatible civilizational alternatives.

The Chetniks also fed on the myth of encirclement fostered by the SANU Memorandum, in which Serbs were portrayed as the great victims of socialist Yugoslavia,[44] embraced the morbid characterization of Croatian Serbs as "remnants of a slaughtered people," congratulated themselves on allegedly enjoying superior capacities for sexual performance, and contrasted their "holy Serbia" with "rotten Western Europe," thus offering their state as a "guardian of authentic European values"[45] and as fulfilling a sacred duty, even while perpetrating atrocities against non-Serbs. Moreover, "just as Christ had to die on the cross, in order to rise again after three days, to claim his place in the Kingdom of Heaven, so too Serbia, whose tsar, Lazar, had renounced the earthly kingdom for a heavenly one in 1389, had to wait six centuries before rising again, to claim its earthly kingdom, earned through long suffering."[46]

The Milošević regime, which made a decisive contribution to launching the Chetnik insurrection in 1990–1992 and to funding it thereafter, benefited from and used its propaganda apparatus to reinforce tendencies toward collective paranoia, exaggerated perceptions of conspiracy, sinister attribution error, and dysphoric rumination ("the tendency for individuals to unhappily reimagine, rethink, and relive pleasant or unpleasant events . . . [resulting in an] increase in negative thinking about those events"[47]) in order to induce in Serbs a psychological state in which they would be prepared to commit atrocities.[48] Although all three sides did this, the Serbian side did this more systematically and over a longer period. Inconsistently, Milošević demanded that Serbs in Croatia and Bosnia enjoy the right of self-determination, including also the right to secede from their respective republics, while denying the same right to Albanians in

Kosovo or to Bosniaks in the Sandžak. Indeed, to the extent that one may speak of Serbian propaganda emphasizing the threat posed by one group in particular, that group would be Muslims, whether the Muslims of Bosnia or the Muslims of Albania. This theme was particularly associated with Biljana Plavšić, who was quoted as saying that "Muslims are degenerated Slavs. As a biologist, I know this."[49]

Croatian Nationalist Expansionism

Franjo Tudjman, alone among the presidents of the three republics at war, viewed himself as the benevolent father of his people and, much more than either Milošević or Izetbegović, linked his nationalism with a demand for the retraditionalization of society and of the family in particular.[50] For the HDZ, in Tudjman's time, there was no room in Croatian society for gays and lesbians, and every Croatian family had an obligation to produce children for the *Domovina* (the Homeland). The Croatian national revival of the 1990s, thus, was backward looking, rather than progressive, with the invention of tourist-pleasing pseudo-renaissance uniforms for the palace guards and the proliferation of statue renovations and of street renamings figuring as symptoms of this larger syndrome. Tudjman and his hangers-on loved every historical Croat— whether Starčević, who wanted to subsume Serbs within the Croatian nation, or Strossmayer, who wanted Serbs and Croats to come together as equals, or Stepinac, who saw Serbs as separated from Croats by an unbridgeable cultural and spiritual gulf, or Radić, the anti-clerical Peasant Party leader, or Maček, who did not share Radić's anti-clericalism, or Budak and, albeit less openly, also Pavelić, who destroyed the legacy of Radić and Maček, or Tito, whose Partisans fought against Pavelić and Budak and who would gladly have put Maček on trial if he had had the chance, or Hebrang, who had broken with Tito and supported Stalin in 1948, or, for that matter, Jelačić, who had fought for the Habsburgs, Croatia's foreign masters. Inevitably, the nationalism promoted by the HDZ, although riddled with intolerance and attractive to Croats with neo-fascist political profiles,[51] was—at least during Tudjman's years—too much of a jumble to be considered simply a revival of Ustašism.

Like Milošević, Tudjman founded his national program on a fundamental inconsistency. In Tudjman's case the inconsistency lay in his insistence that, with the collapse of the SFRY, Bosnia's borders were open to negotiation, even while insisting that the inviolability of Croatia's borders had to be respected. But the "solution" to this paradoxical thinking lay in Tudjman's embrace of a thesis first promulgated by Starčević and later picked up by the Ustaše, viz., that the Bosniaks, i.e., the Muslims of Bosnia-Herzegovina, were Croats of Islamic faith. Tudjman was so convinced of this that he insisted, in a conversation with Stjepan Kljuić in late 1989 or early 1990, that the HDZ would win 70% of the votes in the Bosnian elections because, he was convinced, "all the Muslims felt as Croats."[52] It followed, as Petar Vučić put it in a book published in 1995, that

"Bosnia and Herzegovina are Croatian lands which should be integrated into Croatia. Croatia in its current borders should be understood as being merely the heartland, which in the course of time should be widened until the concepts of Croatia and of Croatian territory coincide both in concept and in fact."[53]

In spite of their territorial ambitions vis-à-vis Bosnia, Croatian nationalists tend to reject the Balkans as alien. And again, in spite of their association with Serbs, Bosniaks, Macedonians, and Montenegrins in a common state for much of 70 years, Croatian nationalists prefer to see themselves as "part of Europe"— though, of course, the Balkan peninsula is in Europe and nowhere else—and more Western than any of their former fellow citizens, except for the Slovenes. During the war years, even at the height of the conflict with the Bosniaks, Croatian war propaganda made it clear that the Serbs were the Croats' principal foe, while internal critics of Croatian efforts to annex portions of Bosnia-Herzegovina were denounced, in the press—often by name—as "Yugo-nostalgics" or "spiritual fifth-columnists."[54]

The war itself was inevitably cast as the *Domovinski rat*—the Homeland War—and although the Croatian government displayed the "politically correct" version of the checkerboard emblem (red square first, as in the socialist era), the veterans' organization displayed (and still does today) the Ustaša version (white square first); moreover, in Tudjman's era, the Croatian government did, in fact, fulfill a modified version of the Ustaša program by removing Serbs from the *Domovina* and, for this reason, dragged its feet when it came to allowing Serbs expelled from Croatia during the war to return to their homes.

Izetbegović's Pepper Pot

To this day there is disagreement as to the nature of Izetbegović's political program; this is, apparently, no coincidence. His incongruous "pepper pot" included appeals to secular values as well as to Islamic values ostensibly incompatible with those same secular values. Izetbegović—imprisoned by the communists in 1946 for his involvement with the anti-regime "Young Muslims" and again in 1983 on charges of Islamic fundamentalism—portrays himself (in his reminiscences) as a liberal, committed to "the equality of people and citizens, without regard to religion, nation, race, language, sex, or social position and political conviction." In a speech delivered in Velika Kladuša on 15 September 1990, Izetbegović rejected the concept of a *nacionalna država* (a state privileging one national group—the concept advocated by Radovan Karadžić and Franjo Tudjman, for example) and called for the establishment of citizens' equality in Bosnia-Herzegovina (a *gradjanska država*, or citizens' state) and, by extension, the abandonment of the concept of constituent nations, established under the communists, with its privileging of the three dominant groups. To Izetbegović's mind, the debate in Yugoslavia about whether to adopt a confederal arrangement or stick to some version of federalism, which flared during 1990–1991, was a false dilemma, because, he said, the essential issue was democracy, not the allocation of jurisdiction. Izetbegović admitted, in an interview with the weekly magazine *Dani* (11 December 1994), that there were at least two currents within the SDA: one more religious in orientation, even radical, and the other more liberal and cosmopolitan in orientation. Izetbegović maintains that he was aligned with the liberal-cosmopolitan orientation; in token of this, he told *Dani*, in a subsequent interview (March 1998), that women should not be asked (let alone required) to wear veils, and declared himself opposed to this practice.[55]

Some observers have offered an entirely different interpretation of Izetbegović, however. Hrvoje Šarinić, chief counselor to Tudjman 1992–1993, for example, writes that Izetbegović wanted to strengthen the influence of Islamic principles in Bosnia in such a way as to lean toward fundamentalism.[56] Or again, Vjekoslav Perica, a lecturer at the University of Utah, claims that the Bosnian leader's controversial "Islamic Declaration," which he wrote in 1970, took the partition of India (into Muslim Pakistan and Hindu India) as a model for Muslims worldwide and describes him as a "Sarajevo radical"—not as a liberal or a cosmopolitan.[57] Significantly, in the "Declaration," Izetbegović took it for granted that Islamic and non-Islamic systems are "incompatible" and that Islamic systems should prevail, arguing that "once Muslims become a majority in one country (thanks to their relatively high population growth), they should demand a state of their own, organized according to Islamic laws and norms."[58] Moreover, although the SDA adopted a declaration on religious liberty and religious pluralism at the time of its founding, the Muslim ulema were involved in that party's founding and played a dominant role in the logistics for that party's campaign in 1990, giving some of its campaign rallies a strongly religious character; the ulema also did their best to reinforce the fundamentalist wing in Izetbegović's party. In the course of the war, the SDA gravitated steadily toward clericalism and undertook steps (such as introducing Islamic teaching in the army and "allowing" Muslim women to wear veils) which have been interpreted as "launch[ing] an Islamic revolution aimed at creating an Islamic republic in Bosnia-Herzegovina."[59]

But there may be some truth to both of these images of Izetbegović; i.e., he may have been using both liberal-secular rhetoric, for local urban elites and Western audiences, and religious rhetoric, for the more clerically oriented locals as well as for foreign Islamic audiences. Sefer Halilović, who served as commander of the Bosnian Army from 1992 to 1993, describes the Bosnian president as Machiavellian, charging him with "the misuse of religion for political purposes" and alleging that the smaller the territory of the Bosnian state became, the greater Izetbegović's authority became. There is some truth to that charge, though it does not follow, as Halilović concludes, that Izetbegović was actually pleased to see Bosnia shrink. What it suggests, rather, is that Izetbegović was, in the first place, a political opportunist, prepared to make incompatible appeals to different audiences and, when it seemed to be politically useful, to allow Islamic principles to encroach on the legal sphere of his supposedly secular state. It was in this same spirit that Izetbegović indicated, as early as November 1992, a readiness to trade eastern Herzegovina to the Serbs, in exchange for the Sandžak—in spite of his professions of commitment to the territorial integrity of Bosnia-Herzegovina.[60] The program of the SDA was, thus, not Islamic fundamentalism as such, nor can it be described as liberal cosmopolitanism—it was, rather, an opportunistic mix of both of these, together with some other disconnected ad hoc notions, blended into an incongruous "pepper pot" into which so many spices had been added, to please the diverse tastes of different constituencies, as to yield what can best be described as a very spicy dish, indeed all but indigestible!

The Liberal Opposition

Liberal pacifists were active throughout the war in all three republics, though in none of the republics did they command a large following. But they acted as the conscience for their respective communities and were important in making it plain that the nationalists could not speak for the nation as a whole. For purposes of this discussion, I highlight the activity of three brave individuals of great integrity—Žarana Papić in Serbia, Ivo Banac in Croatia, and Adil Zulfikarpašić in Bosnia.

Žarana Papić, who died in September 2002, was an associate professor of sociology at the University of Belgrade, co-founder of the Women's Studies Center in Belgrade, and co-founder in 1990 (with Lina Vušković) of the Women's Party, a party dedicated to promoting democratic principles and emphasizing provisions for education, environmental protection, and free medical care.[61] She played an instrumental role in setting up the opposition "Women's Parliament" on 8 March 1991 and joined other pacifists in protesting against the war on the streets of Belgrade on 9 October 1991. That protest was, in fact, the first act of the opposition group Women in Black, in which Papić was a leading figure. Women in Black was possibly the most vocal pacifist group in Serbia during the war years, protesting on the streets, pamphleteering, and, above all, maintaining an independent standpoint in an atmosphere dense with nationalistic propaganda.[62]

Papić took the existence of "universal moral values" as her starting point and charged Milošević with having had the "primary responsibility . . . for having relativized" those values.[63] Espousing values of tolerance, equality, and human rights, and rejecting clericalism,[64] she argued that "hegemonist nationalism, national separation, chauvinist and racist exclusion or marginalization of (old and new) minority groups are, as a rule, closely connected with patriarchal, discriminatory, and violent policies against women, policies subversive of women's social and civil rights." Moreover, in her analysis, the cultural "retraditionalization" pursued by the Milošević regime had resulted in "civic disempowerment" in which both women and men lost power.[65] Recalling that the interwar fascists had also promoted "retraditionalization," marginalized women, promoted the cult of the leader and the cult of violence, and orchestrated a nationalist frenzy in which those designated as "Others" became targets of physical attack, Papić did not hesitate to characterize the Milošević regime as fascistic and openly described the war of 1991–1995 as "the Serbian Hegemonic War."[66]

Ivo Banac (b. 1947), a professor of history at Yale University and, during 2003–2005, also head of Croatia's Liberal Party, was a columnist for the independent weekly *Feral Tribune* for a number of years, using that forum to criticize Tudjman, the HDZ, Croatian efforts to annex portions of Bosnia-Herzegovina, nationalists in general, and corruption, among other things. Banac even devoted one of his columns to criticizing Croatian intellectuals, as a class, for "intellectual laziness and cowardice, cynicism, and corruption," characterizing them as "a comatose elite, entirely incapable of competing globally."[67] He has also criticized clericalist tendencies on the part of the Catholic Church[68] and, in the face of considerable anti-Serb sentiment among ordinary Croats, has embraced the cause of the return of expelled Serbs to their homes, arguing that the "presence of minorities promotes tolerance and democracy."[69] These views have made him enemies on the right, and at one point, the demented right-wing newspaper *Hrvatsko slovo* called on its readers to kill the distinguished human rights activist.[70] During the war years, Banac was one of the most outspoken critics of Tudjman's policies in Bosnia, repeatedly espousing the principle of respect for the territorial integrity of that republic. Against Serb nationalists who denounced the Bosnian referendum on independence *because* it referred the decision to the outcome of a majority vote, Banac traced the occasional Western sympathy for the Chetnik position on this question to "great—at times, willful—ignorance," emphasizing that Bosnia was not an artificial creation but "a historical entity which has its own identity and its own history."[71]

Banac's position is grounded in liberal values, so that, in a 1992 publication in Zagreb, he both condemned the Chetnik aggression against Croatia and upheld the territorial integrity of Bosnia-Herzegovina against its would-be partitioners.[72] What Banac envisioned was the preservation of a multi-ethnic Bosnia, within the borders it had inherited from the Habsburgs and from the socialist era; thus, in January 1991, Banac warned against dangerous "solutions" which nationalists were fantasizing for Bosnia, urging that the republic belonged to all three of its peoples, who would do best to avoid partition schemes.[73] The fact that Banac has refused to sacrifice principle to convenience has earned him a sobriquet as Croatia's Don Quixote from *Novi list,* a newspaper more or less sympathetic to Banac's views.[74]

Adil Zulfikarpašić (b. 1921) began his political life as a communist, but by the 1990s he had embraced anti-nationalist liberalism and a commitment to the principle of human equality.[75] Already during World War Two, as a communist and Partisan fighter, he mobilized fellow Muslims to protest Ustaša terror against Serbs in his native town of Foča and tried, with less success, to organize Serb opposition to the Chetnik massacres of Muslims.[76] Instead of remaining in Yugoslavia after the end of that conflict, however, Zulfikarpašić drove to Rome in February 1946; in emigration, Zulfikarpašić went into business; with the money he made, he launched a journal, *Bosanski pogledi,* in the 1960s and set up a Bosnian Institute in Zürich, eventually collecting between 30,000 and 40,000 books dealing with the history, culture, and politics of Bosnia, as well as archival material. His objective, where *Bosanski pogledi* was concerned, was to use the journal to foster liberal-democratic principles.[77] Zulfikarpašić returned to Yugoslavia at the end of March 1990 and 11 months later agreed with Izetbegović, who had visited him in Zurich several times before 1990, to establish a political party (what became the SDA). The two men soon became rivals, with Zulfikarpašić, supported by Muhamed Filipović and others,[78] urging that the SDA be fashioned into a modern, liberal party, while Izetbegović indulged in the cult of his own personality and exploited religious sentiments to build his own power. Zulfikarpašić recalls a meeting at Velika Kladuša attended by an estimated 300,000 persons. "I had been at Tito's rallies in Belgrade," Zulfikarpašić told Milovan Djilas and Nadežda Gaće,

> but I had never seen one like this. When people breathed it was like the roar of a tank, it was unbelievable. There were slogans, green flags, shouts, signs saying "We'll kill Vuk!" and "Long live Saddam Hussein!" Saddam Hussein? There were pictures of Saddam Hussein, people wearing Arab dress, hundreds of green flags. . . . People were screaming, raving, falling into a delirium at the words of a crazy professor from Cazin. . . . In the depths of my soul I felt that this was not my party.[79]

Zulfikarpašić called a press conference at the Holiday Inn and announced that he was breaking with Izetbegović because he objected to the infusion of Islamic fundamentalism into the party. He subsequently founded the Muslim Bosniak Organization (MBO), but this party made its appearance so late in the election campaign that its chances were slight; the MBO won only two seats in the new Bosnian parliament. In spite of this split, Zulfikarpašić and Filipović, vice president of the MBO, met with Karadžić in mid-July 1991 and outlined a proposal for a "historic agreement" between the two sides.[80] On 27 July, as the Bosnian president was preparing for a short trip to the U.S., Zulfikarpašić and Filipović came to his office and presented the draft agreement, which they hoped could avert war in Bosnia. The plan called for a Serb-Muslim understanding, which could only be premised on Bosnia's remaining in union with Serbia and Montenegro; Bosnia was to have been granted wide autonomy, while, as a concession to Bosniak sensitivities, the Sandžak, which had been a part of Bosnia-Herzegovina until 1878, would have been granted cultural and administrative autonomy.[81] At first Izetbegović welcomed this initiative. But Stjepan Kljuić, at that time head of the HDZ's Bosnian branch organization, denounced the agreement as an anti-Croat pact, while Ivo Komšić, then vice president of the SDP, described the agreement as "a betrayal and surrender of Bosnia-Herzegovina to Greater Serbia."[82] Izetbegović now distanced himself from the agreement, which rapidly became a dead letter.

Silber and Little say that even if his initiative had borne fruit, it would, at the most, have only postponed the war for a while, because it did not address the fundamental roots of the waxing conflict.[83] Zulfikarpašić was not prepared to accept an unequal position to Bosnia, as Silber and Little say would have been the result of any agreement which might have been reached, but insists that a confederal union could have both preserved the peace and respected the interests of the respective peoples.[84] Perhaps Zulfikarpašić's project was too idealistic to have any real chances, but if so, it was because his was one of the few pleas for rationality, at a time when increasing numbers were giving in to frenzied, emotional appeals.

Into the Mouth of Hell (March–November 1992)

During the night of 1 March 1992, immediately after the Bosnian referendum on independence, nationalist Serbs erected barricades in Sarajevo, the villages of Bravsko and Vrtoće near Bosanski Petrovac, Cajnice, and elsewhere. The barricades paralyzed traffic both within cities and between communities. On 2 March, one person was killed in Sarajevo, two persons were killed in Doboj, and shooting from automatic weapons could be heard in Zvornik. There were armed clashes in Sarajevo during the night of 3 March, while shooting in the northern Bosnian town of Bosanski Brod left several persons dead.[85] Local Serbs also erected barricades in Mostar, though by 20 March, these had been taken down.[86] In Goražde, Serbs covered barricades with gasoline and set fire to them, contributing to an atmosphere of fear and anxiety.[87] In downtown Mostar, Čapljina, and Bosanski Brod, tempers flared, while Serbian state television (in Belgrade) reported that war could break out, especially in and around Mostar, "at any time."[88] Even while tensions mounted, Bosnia's leading political figures continued to negotiate, with the SDS demanding 64% of Bosnian territory for their "cantons," Croats expressing outrage at the SDS demand and demanding that their 12% share be increased to 35%, and the three sides signing what would prove to be a stillborn agreement on the constitutional arrangement for the republic.[89] At the end of March, the conflict escalated when Bosnian Serb guerrillas intensified heavy artillery fire at the border town of Bosanski Brod, killing at least 10 persons, with the Croatian 108th brigade crossing the border in response and entering the Serb-inhabited village of Sjekovac; across Bosnia as a whole, about 30 persons were killed during the last week of March.[90]

On 1 April 1992, the Serbian Voluntary Guard "Tigers," commanded by Željko Ražnatović "Arkan," the owner of an ice-cream parlor in downtown Belgrade wanted by Interpol on charges of murder of émigré Croats and of armed robbery in several West European countries, attacked the northeastern Bosnian town of Bijeljina (with an ethnically mixed population of 36,000), quickly overrunning it.[91] The Tigers were directly subordinate to Milošević, and Ražnatović reported directly to the Serbian president.[92] After his forces had entered Bijeljina, Ražnatović briefly held Fikret Abdić in custody, but Plavšić came to

Bijeljina and was able to secure his release.[93] As the JNA and Chetnik irregulars began shelling Sarajevo and its suburbs on 4 April, Izetbegović ordered a general mobilization; that same day, Bosnian Serb irregulars seized the Republic Police Academy strategically situated on a key hill overlooking downtown Sarajevo.[94] As the war began, the Bosnian government had only one tank at its disposal, and that tank was not even in Sarajevo at the time.[95] Gunfire and explosions were heard in Sarajevo on 5 April, while fighting in Kupres left "at least a hundred" people dead as a result of mortar and artillery battles between Bosnian Serb paramilitaries and the HVO (the Croatian Defense Council, i.e., Bosnian Croat forces).[96] Up to now, the fighting had been localized, and many communities still hoped to avoid warfare. But on 6 April, the JNA and the Chetniks attacked Bijeljina and Foča, continuing against Bratunac and Višegrad, and the fighting exploded into a republic-wide conflict.[97] Three days later, guerrillas of Ražnatović's Serbian Voluntary Guard, backed up by Vojislav Šešelj's "Serbian Chetnik Movement," Serbian security force special units, and regular JNA troops, pounded Zvornik (a town of 15,000 residents, 60% of them Muslims) into submission. After taking control of the town, the Serb forces ordered all Muslims to surrender their weapons; thousands of locals fled the town. In the next four months, Serb militias would kill or expel all of Zvornik's native Muslims and destroy all of the town's mosques, as well as any other evidence of interconfessional coexistence.[98]

Although the "Assembly of the Serbian People" had declared the formation of their own republic three months earlier, they had not yet declared their secession from Bosnia. They did so only on 7 April 1992, changing the name of their republic from the Serbian Republic of Bosnia-Herzegovina to simply the Serbian Republic (*Republika Srpska*) in August 1992.[99] The well-armed Serb irregulars, backed by the JNA, continued their advance and, within less than two weeks, had overrun a number of other cities and towns, among them Bratunac, Srebrenica, Višegrad, Derventa, and Foča.[100] On 8–10 May 1992, however, "local Muslim forces," led by Naser Orić, pushed Serb forces out of Srebrenica.[101]

In the meantime, after having been recognized by the United States and the major European powers, Bosnia-Herzegovina was admitted to the United Nations, along with Slovenia and Croatia. Under the UN charter, all member states are guaranteed the right of self-defense, which of necessity includes the right to procure such weaponry as they may deem suitable; moreover, under the UN charter, an arms embargo could be imposed on a state only by request of its recognized government. Accordingly, it could be argued (as it was by Sarajevo's advocates) that while the arms embargo was technically legal as long as the independence of Slovenia, Croatia, Bosnia-Herzegovina (and for that matter Macedonia) was not recognized, once these states were recognized and admitted to the community of states, the embargo requested by Belgrade could no longer be considered legally valid. It was maintained all the same, basically because Britain and France believed (wrongly, as it turned out) that keeping the embargo in place would serve their interests.

In mid-May, the Serb insurgents established the Army of the Serbian Republic (*Vojska Republike Srpske,* or VRS), appointing Colonel Ratko Mladić, the erstwhile commander of the Zadar artillery training center, as VRS commander. Milošević announced that he was ordering the JNA to withdraw from Bosnia, but this took the form of the transfer of about 55,000 Bosnian Serb soldiers from the JNA to the VRS; moreover, although now under Karadžić's authority, these troops continued to be paid out of Belgrade's budget.[102] In fact, the VRS was also dependent upon Belgrade for military vehicles, weaponry and other supplies, and some of its fuel.[103] (The VRS also received some of its fuel from UNPROFOR, in spite of the UN embargo.) According to CIA estimates, the VRS initially had more than 250,000 troops, while Jovan Divjak, brigadier general of the ARBiH and deputy chief of staff of the General Staff of the ARBiH from 1993 to 1995, has estimated the initial strength of the VRS at 90,000– 100,000.[104] Whatever the original strength, the VRS was to be depleted by massive desertions in the course of the war.[105] That same month, the Bosnian TO was converted into the ARBiH; Sefer Halilović, who had been commander of the TO, now became commander of the ARBiH.

The Milošević-Karadžić game plan, in which Chetnik forces loyal to Ražnatović and Šešelj figured as subordinate units, was to drive out the non-Serb population from those parts of Bosnia to be annexed to "Greater Serbia." This game plan was to be realized through a combination of ethnic cleansing, general terror, demoralization, and the elimination of all traces of multicultural cosmopolitanism. The policy of "ethnic cleansing" (*etničko čišćenje),* according to a report issued by the International Society for Human Rights in July 1992, "almost invariably entail[ed] expelling people from their homes, either by rounding them up and forcing them to leave, or by driving them away with a campaign of terror."[106] Inhabitants of villages to be "cleansed" were routinely given 20 minutes to leave town or be killed; needless to say, with such short notice, the terrified refugees could take very little with them. While the international community watched in apparent uncertainty as to whether Bosnia was worth the bother, the ethnic composition of entire areas of Bosnia-Herzegovina changed rapidly, as is illustrated in Table 15.1.[107] In the West, politicians and scholars debated the question whether "ethnic cleansing" was tantamount to genocide or not.[108] While the question might seem academic at first glance, it had a very practical aspect since, if the policies being carried out by the VRS and the Serb paramilitaries were judged to constitute genocide, then all states which had signed the Genocide Convention would be bound, under international law, to take all necessary measures to stop the genocide. Although some scholars were prepared to describe what was happening as "genocide,"[109] Western politicians were not prepared to do more than send in humanitarian assistance and deploy a limited force to protect the humanitarian convoys.

The second instrument used to promote ethnic homogenization was general terror. The brutal killing of civilians, involving the gouging out of their eyes and the cutting off of male genitals, was intended, in the first place, to instigate ter-

Table 15.1. **Ethnic Composition of Bosanska Krajina
(1991, 1994)**

	1991	1994
Serbs	625,000	875,000
Croats and Muslims	550,000	50,000

Source: "War Crimes in Bosnia-Hercegovina: U.N. Cease-Fire Won't Help Banja Luka," *Human Rights Watch Helsinki*, vol. 6, no. 8 (June 1994): 5.

ror, though, as Marie-Janine Calić has noted, it is also true that about 20% of paramilitary volunteers had had problems with the law before 1991, that a large portion of the paramilitary forces came either from the countryside or from a low urban caste, and that some perpetrators of atrocities had a history of patho-logical problems.[110] But these considerations relate to individual motivation, telling us something about the motivations of those who supported the Bel-grade regime's plans for a "Greater Serbia." They should *not* lead us to conclude that the terror or, for that matter, the military campaign was anything but the realization of a calculated plan with clearly defined objectives.

Other policies also served to instill terror in the local population, especially rape. As two activists connected with Human Rights Watch concluded in a study first published in 1994,

rape is neither incidental nor private. It routinely serves a strategic function in war and acts as an integral tool for achieving particular military objectives. In the former Yugo-slavia, rape and other grave abuses committed by Serbian forces were intended to drive the non-Serb population into flight.[111]

According to a report published by the Institute for War & Peace Reporting, about 40,000 women were raped in the Yugoslav region in the course of the war.[112] Resentment of the success of others also played a role. A Muslim civil-ian identified only as 004 JF testified as follows:

Omarska extermination camp was a place where Serbs were executing so-called "revenge" killings. Serbs would accuse doctors of choking to death Serb children, profes-sors and teachers of being unfair to Serb students, and killed them immediately for these "crimes." . . . Omarska extermination camp had women prisoners as well. Daily, Serb sol-diers would take girls and bring 5–6 men per girl, Serb soldiers, to rape them. . . . They were raped constantly, non-stop every day. They raped older women, Croats, 60–65 years of age. One named Diviš was raped by 12 men. There were many young girls, around 16 years [of age] that were being raped daily. . . . Serbs would also shove bottles (mostly half-liter beer bottles) up the Muslim girls' vaginas. . . . Serbs would stick a bottle inside Mus-lim women's vaginas and then break them inside them.[113]

United Nations analysts identified altogether some 715 detention camps in Bosnia-Herzegovina, of which 237 were identified as Serb-operated, 89 as Bosniak-operated, and 77 as operated by Croatian forces; four were operated by

Croats and Bosniaks jointly; in the cases of the remaining 308, the analysts did not have enough information to be able to identify which warring parties were operating which camps.[114]

The third instrument used by the VRS to further its campaign for a "Greater Serbia" involved the use of detention camps in which not just enemy combatants but also civilians (Bosniaks, Croats) were incarcerated. The Serb troops put the prisoners to work digging trenches and performing other tasks for the Serbian war effort. Among the best known Serb-run camps were those at Omarska, Keraterm, Trnopolje, and Sušica by Vlasenica. Camp regime was designed to degrade, humiliate, intimidate, and demoralize the inmates, crushing their spirits. Rapes played a role in this, but there were other techniques as well. As James Gow recounts,

New prisoners were ordinarily greeted by beatings administered by the prison guards, while camp commanders looked on. Prisoners frequently were not fed for several days after arrival, and then they received meager rations once a day. At the height of summer, water was often withheld and when provided was visibly contaminated. Toilet and hygiene facilities were inadequate. Prisoners were forced to sing, and listen to, Serbian nationalist songs; at Omarska, the song "Ko kaže, ko laže, da je Srbija mala?" ("Who says, who lies, that Serbia is small?") was played repeatedly. Beatings were routine, especially at mealtime and at night. Almost every night, some prisoners were killed. Corpses were stacked up most mornings, waiting to be removed by truck. At each camp there was at least one mass killing.[115]

The fourth instrument used to promote ethnic homogenization was the delegitimation of the very idea of multi-ethnic and multi-confessional coexistence. Or, to put it another way, the war could be understood, in part, as a war waged by the countryside—in which Serbs, Croats, and Muslims often lived in ethnically homogeneous villages—against the ethnically mixed, cosmopolitan cities. The destruction of many of Sarajevo's libraries, including the National Library and the Library of the University of Sarajevo, represented the quintessential expression of the hatred which Karadžić's and Mladić's country folk bore toward the city. In the course of four years of war, the population of Sarajevo declined from 500,000 to 300,000, and half of the latter were not locals at all, but refugees from villages which had been "cleansed" by Serb forces. The objective was to destroy the belief in the possibility for different peoples to live together, and to establish the new faith in the primacy of the ethnic community. When Islamic enthusiasts tried to insinuate elements of traditional Islam into the public life of the country, local urbanites rebelled. Some young Muslims took to greeting each other with the neologism "lamsa," transposing the syllables in the traditional Muslim greeting "salam," in order to suggest that they disapproved of Islamic fundamentalism, much as members of an earlier generation had greeted each other, in communist times, with "vozdra," in open mockery of the communist-promoted greeting "zdravo" (hello).[116] When Islamic fundamentalists tried, in 1995, to push through a bill banning confessionally mixed marriages, people took to the streets of Sarajevo and the bill failed.

On 30 May 1992, the UN Security Council imposed trade sanctions on Serbia; but the arms embargo, which froze the Bosniaks into a position of military inferiority vis-à-vis the Serbs, was left in place. This was only superficially inconsistent. What the U.S., British, and French governments hoped to achieve with this combination of policies was to simultaneously assure their voting publics that they were doing "something" about the war in Bosnia, without committing their own economic or military resources beyond what they hoped would remain a politically acceptable level, while allowing the Serbs—so at least some of the policymakers in these states hoped—to finish the job as quickly as possible. This was apparently what Douglas Hurd, the British foreign secretary during the first part of John Major's term as prime minister, meant when, in opposing any lifting of the arms embargo, he argued that allowing the Bosniaks to obtain armaments and thereby equalizing the military balance would "only prolong the fighting."[117]

Meanwhile, Lord Carrington, "an urbane and likeable English aristocrat"[118] who, in semi-retirement, had been working as chair of Christie's, the London art auction house, had been asked in September 1991 to serve as chair of the conference on Yugoslavia, with responsibility to bring peace to the region. Carrington did not want to take leave from his job at Christie's and therefore shuttled back and forth between London and The Hague. On 17 July 1992, Carrington brought representatives of the Bosnian Serbs, Croats, and Muslims to Christie's, where they reached an agreement on a ceasefire and for the stowing of heavy weaponry with international supervision. Carrington had in mind that UN "peacekeepers" could take responsibility to carry out this task, but although Boutros Boutros-Ghali, the UN secretary-general, called the agreement "ridiculous," the Security Council was prepared to go along with Carrington's agreement. As Boutros-Ghali recalled later,

I reported to the Security Council on July 21, 1992, that the United Nations had neither the mandate nor the means to carry out [this] request. Despite the "cease-fire" signed at Christie's, the fighting had not stopped. The parties were not cooperating. In fact, they were relocating their heavy weapons to places where they could not be monitored. Moreover, no peacekeepers were available for the job.[119]

Boutros-Ghali now submitted a letter to the president of the Security Council, expressing his dismay that the UN Security Council had made commitments without first obtaining an expert opinion on the technical requirements for enforcement of the ceasefire. The nub of the problem, in Boutros-Ghali's view, was that the Security Council was unwilling "to provide UN forces with the weapons and mandates they would need to operate effectively in the middle of a bitter and bloody war."[120]

Continued diplomatic efforts within the framework of the London conference (convened on 26 August 1992) got nowhere, though it was perhaps symptomatic of the international community's incipient grasp of the gravity of the situation that Boutros-Ghali told the London conference that the crisis in

Bosnia met his three criteria for an international response, insofar as it threatened security, involved the flouting of basic universal moral standards, and, if not checked, could subvert the very foundations of the international system.[121] But for the time being, the U.S., Britain, and France could not reach a determination that their interests were threatened, let alone harmed, by the war in Bosnia. The problem, as Daniel Eisermann has noted, was that "[t]he longer the war lasted and the West declined to undertake a limited military intervention in pursuit of a political solution, the greater were the obstacles on the road to a calibrated peace settlement."[122]

Large battles pitting more than 50,000 troops on both sides took place during 1992, for example, in the strategic Posavina corridor. In early June, the VRS First Krajina Corps, commanded by General Momir Talić, initiated operations to open a gap between Doboj and Derventa. By 20 June, the VRS First Corps had taken Kotorsko and Johovac and, four days later, launched Operation "Corridor 92," designed to break through to troops northeast of Gradačac. The VRS achieved success within two days, taking the town of Modrica on 28 June. The VRS scored further victories during that summer and autumn, pushing the forces of the HV (Croatian Army) and HVO out of the territory between Bosanski Brod and Bosanski Šamac in July and capturing Bosanski Brod itself on 6 October. The VRS captured the historic town of Jajce on 29 October 1992, causing at least 40,000 defenders and civilians to flee to Travnik, but the Serbs failed to take Bihać or Orasje.[123] By the end of 1992, Bosnian Serb forces were in control of about 70% of Bosnia-Herzegovina, with HV/HVO forces controlling another 20% (in the southwest and in the north); the rump Bosnian government's effective jurisdiction was limited to a handful of cities and towns—among them, Sarajevo, Bihać, Goražde, Srebrenica, Tuzla, and Žepa—together with some nearby villages.[124] By then, more than 100,000 persons were dead—more than 90% of them civilians.[125] About 2 to 2.5 million persons were homeless.

The Croat-Muslim War (October 1992–February 1994)

It is often argued that the fighting between Croat and Muslim forces started only after Cyrus Vance (the UN peace negotiator) and David Lord Owen (the EU peace negotiator) had presented their plan to partition Bosnia in January 1993. According to some accounts, the fighting began only as late as April 1993, with some accounts blaming the Croats for starting the fighting, others blaming the Muslims, and one fanciful account even casting blame on the British for having allegedly staged a duplicitous provocation! In fact, conflict between Croatian and Muslim forces broke out as early as October 1992.[126] There had been some clashes even earlier between Croatian and Muslim paramilitaries, especially in and around Sarajevo, apparently sparked by disagreements concerning the division of black-market goods, but it was only in October that there was sustained artillery fire between these two sides. The HVO (Bosnian Croat forces) had a strength of about 45,000 at that time (up from 37,000 in April), while the Bosnian Army had a strength of 80,500 troops at the time; the Bosnian Army was, however, seriously under-equipped and even at the end of 1993 could outfit only 44,000 of these with firearms.[127]

The outbreak of Muslim-Croat fighting was overdetermined. It was, thus, simultaneously anticipated and spontaneous, driven by President Tudjman's territorial appetite and sparked by local tempers. What were the elements, then, which contributed to the violence between these two communities?

The first factor which will occur to most observers is the fact that Tudjman had sat down with Milošević in March 1991 in order to discuss a plan which, among other things, would have restored the borders Croatia had had in 1939–1941. It is well known, too, that Tudjman repeatedly returned to the theme of Bosnia's "Croatianness"—for example, in a February 1990 speech to the HDZ's general assembly in Zagreb, when he declared that Bosnia-Herzegovina was a "national state of the Croatian nation."[128] Or again, for example, at a meeting with a visiting Bosnian Croat delegation on 27 December 1991, Tudjman argued that the conditions were ripe for an agreement to redraw the boundaries of Bosnia-Herzegovina—indeed, that he considered that Bosnia-Herzegovina was "finished."[129] When Stjepan Kljuić, president of the Bosnian branch of the HDZ and vice president of Bosnia-Herzegovina, protested that Croats should loyally support the elected government of Alija Izetbegović and the territorial integrity of the republic, Tudjman saw to it that Kljuić was removed (in January 1992) and replaced by Mate Boban, a Herzegovinan Croat infused with "Greater Croatian" notions. And again, when the HOS, the paramilitary forces set up by Dobroslav Paraga, leader of the Croatian Party of Right, in late 1991, embraced the cause of Bosnia's territorial integrity and made common cause with the Bosniaks, it came into conflict with the Bosnian HDZ's military arm, the HVO, soon after Boban had pushed Kljuić aside; this situation was resolved to Tudjman's satisfaction on 9 August 1992, when HOS commander Blaž Kraljević and eight of his staff were assassinated by HVO troops under the command of Mladen Naletilić Tuta, a shady character who was compared, in the Croatian press, with the American outlaw Jesse James.[130] But Tudjman tried, largely in vain, to confuse foreign audiences about his intentions and to justify himself in the eyes of both the Croatian public and the world public, and for this reason, it is possible to find statements from the Croatian president which appear to indicate an intention to respect Bosnian sovereignty.[131]

A second factor, according to Charles Shrader, was that the arms-poor ARBiH was "[t]oo weak to seize the arms and equipment it needed from the far more powerful Bosnian Serb army," but was strong enough to score some victories at the expense of its erstwhile Croatian ally.[132] In other words, the UN-imposed arms embargo contributed directly to igniting Muslim attacks on Croatian forces.

A third factor contributing to the outbreak of conflict was the arrival of *mujahedin* volunteers from various Islamic countries including Iran and Afghanistan and military instructors from Iran; one unit was actually called "El Mudžahid" and was placed under the command of the Third Corps of the Army of Bosnia-Herzegovina (ARBiH).[133] The *mujahedin* had not lived side by side with Croatian neighbors in Bosnia's cities and had not been raised on a political diet of "brotherhood and unity"; the *mujahedin* soon gained a reputation for ruthlessness after some of their number seemed to be making a practice of decapitating their prisoners.

Fourth, both Bosniak and Croatian television played their parts in stoking tensions. In May 1992, for example, Sarajevo Television broadcast what it described as footage of (Bosnian) TO soldiers being killed by HVO troops in the village of Lješće; Bosniaks were outraged. But the footage had been misrepresented and actually showed HVO troops from Travnik who had been massacred in Vlašić on 15 May—by Chetniks![134] Croatian Television made its own contribution to the growing mutual fear, so that by June 1993, no one was surprised when a soldier of the HVO appeared on television declaring that "there never was an alliance between the Croats and [the] Muslims, nor could there ever be, [because] the Muslims want to destroy everything that is Christian, be it Croatian or Serbian."[135] Irresponsible reportage certainly played a part, though group fear quickly acquires a momentum of its own.

A fifth factor contributing to Muslim-Croat tensions was the rapid change in the ethnic structure of many municipalities, as a direct result of expulsions from areas being seized by the Chetniks. The refugees often came from small, ethnically homogeneous villages and were not used to living side by side with Croats. Moreover, having lost their homes and possessions and, in many cases, also their loved ones, and having been reduced to poverty and dependence, they were psychologically ill prepared to adapt to their new circumstances.

Yet another problem (a sixth problem), usually neglected, was that the newly established Bosnian Army included former JNA officers (such as General Sead Delić, who had become commander of the Second Corps of the Bosnian Army), who had fought in Croatia in 1991 *against the Croats,* while within the HVO, "part of the officer corps also had experience in the war in Croatia, naturally on the other side. Both sides, unsurprisingly, were suspicious towards each other."[136]

And finally, a seventh factor is that the HVO and the ARBiH constituted parallel military structures operating in the same environment but owing allegiance to rival authorities. Tudjman and Izetbegović themselves recognized the problem—which is why, on 21 July 1992, they signed a military agreement under which the HVO was supposed to be subordinated to the command of the Bosnian TO (the embryo of the future ARBiH).[137] It may be relevant, on this point, that when the Croatian Community of Herceg-Bosna had been proclaimed in November 1991 as a self-governing autonomous unit, the decision authorizing its establishment noted that the intent was not to secede from Sarajevo's jurisdiction but to assert autonomy within that jurisdiction; the decision also vowed that the new self-governing body would respect the government headed by President Izetbegović as long as it remained independent "of the former and every kind of a future Yugoslavia."[138] Moreover, after Bosnian Croats set up the HVO in early 1992 as a defensive paramilitary force, Muslims were involved in both the civilian and the military structures of the HVO until spring 1993. But even if one were to concede that Tudjman's intentions as regards Bosnia were honorable[139]—and most observers are not prepared to make that concession—the mere fact of rival military organizations already constituted yet another factor contributing to ethnic polarization and conflict. An early indication that this last-mentioned factor was a problem came in May 1992 when Major General Ante Ros issued a statement declaring that the HVO was the only legal military force in Herceg-Bosna (as the area controlled by the HVO was already being called) and that "all orders from the TO [Territorial Defense] command (of Bosnia-Hercegovina) are invalid, and are to be considered illegal on this territory."[140]

By July 1992, as a result of a combination of the seven factors enumerated above—but above all as a result of Croatian irredentism and growing Croatian desires to take steps to assure their own security—Boban and his nationalist-minded associates proclaimed the establishment of the Croatian Republic of Herceg-Bosna, ironically about two weeks before the stillborn military agreement signed by Tudjman and Izetbegović. In spite of this false start, Presidents Tudjman and Izetbegović sat down at the end of September to discuss the prospects for establishment of military coordination against Bosnian Serb forces.[141] But the Muslim-Croat alliance had already come under strain even before it was formalized on paper. In the municipality of Kakanj, ethnic tensions rose as Croats complained of petty harassment at the hands of local Muslims and even unjustified arrests. By June, at the same time that HVO forces and the Bosnian Army combined their resources to break a Serbian siege of Mostar, the two sides clashed in the district of Novi Travnik. After six days of fighting, local officials negotiated a ceasefire, but in October of that year, fighting erupted again in the villages surrounding Novi Travnik.[142] Fighting escalated in October, when Bosnian Army troops successfully asserted control of a (disputed) part of Novi Travnik. Meanwhile, HVO-TO joint action against the VRS at Jajce foundered by September, and on 9 October, local Bosnian Croats signed a separate cease-fire with the VRS in exchange for a Serbian pledge to supply the Croats with electricity. That reversal notwithstanding, the Croatian forces seemed to have the upper hand at this point, and by early November, they were consolidating their military control of about 20% of Bosnia-Herzegovina. As the conflict escalated, the government in Zagreb deployed Croatian Army (HV) units in Bosnia, as well as MUP (Ministry of Internal Affairs) special forces.[143] Božo Rajić, minister of defense of Bosnia-Herzegovina, blamed Belgrade (or, more specifically, KOS) for having fomented the Muslim-Croat rift, and called on the former allies to "sober up."[144] Rajić, a Bosnian Croat, had a solution in mind and, on 15 January 1993, ordered all ARBiH units to place themselves under the command of the HVO.[145] Soon thereafter, Rajić's authority was whittled down; he remained at his post but had little effective authority over the Bosnian Army after this.[146] Tempers were running high, and efforts in February and May 1993 to effect a rapprochement between the Bosniaks and the Bosnian Croats came to naught.[147]

Izetbegović, elected to a two-year term as president in 1990, presented himself as the legitimate head of a legitimate government, but it was a government in disarray, a government which some, though not all, of its Serbian members had abandoned, indeed a rump government which Izetbegović was increasingly transforming into his private dominion. Thus, for example, when Izetbegović's term expired in late 1992, he declined to step down, and Stjepan Kljuić, who was supposed to succeed Izetbegović as president, was excluded from the succession in the name of wartime exigencies. Meanwhile, in January 1993, Cyrus Vance and David Lord Owen, co-chairs of the International Conference on the Former Yugoslavia and international mediators in the Bosnian conflict, presented their peace plan, which proposed to set up 10 provinces constituted on an ethnic basis. The Croats quickly accepted the plan, which satisfied all of their war aims. But the plan did not bring the parties together. On the contrary, Mile Akmadžić, a Croat who had originally been appointed prime minister of Bosnia, told Lord Owen at a meeting on 20 January that "the Bosnian Croats were no longer going to subscribe to the idea that decisions taken alone by Izetbegović or with his inner clique were the decisions of the Government of Bosnia-Herzegovina or its [collective] presidency."[148] The flare-up in Muslim-Croat fighting in April 1993 was fanned by the Vance-Owen Plan, as the HVO moved in to claim its allotted portions. On 14 April, ARBiH forces attacked the Croatian villages of Bušćak and Buturović Polje. Two days later, HVO forces, commanded by General Tihomir Blaškić, advanced against the village of Ahmići, situated at a strategic point on the main route in the Lasva Valley, linking Travnik, Vitez, Busovača, Zenica, and Kiseljak. The HVO attack on Ahmići came on the order of Dario Kordić, then vice president of Herceg-Bosna, and began at 5 A.M.; by the end of the day, 116 Muslim villagers (including women and children) lay dead, 24 were wounded, and all 169 houses owned by Muslims and two mosques had been destroyed.[149] Buildings owned by Croats were not touched. Nearly a decade later, a team of CIA analysts summed up the importance of the Ahmići massacre by noting that "The images from this small central Bosnian town—the Guernica of the Bosnian conflict—would shock and outrage the world."[150] But the HVO had no monopoly on atrocities; Izetbegović himself admits, in his memoirs, that Bosnian Army troops massacred 27 Croat civilians in the village of Grabovica on 8 September 1993 in the course of Operation Neretva.[151]

During the following months, fighting between the ARBiH and the HVO raged across Bosnia, while the HV supplied the HVO and intervened directly in the conflict; by January 1994 there would be about 30,000 HV troops deployed in Bosnia.[152] While Tudjman publicly promoted the idea of a tri-partite division of Bosnia, Karadžić and Boban met privately in Njivice (near Herceg Novi) to discuss the future map of Bosnia, and Lord Owen was sounding increasingly reconciled to the eventual partition of the republic.[153] Back in Croatia, Vlado Gotovac, the distinguished human rights activist, Zagreb archbishop Franjo Kuharić, prominent HDZ members Stipe Mesić and Josip Manolić, Ivo Banac, and others criticized Tudjman for authorizing Croatia's direct intervention in the Bosnian conflict in pursuit of the annexation of portions of Herzegovina to Croatia; Mesić and Manolić left the HDZ in protest. Bosnian Franciscan Luka Markesić told an anti-war rally in July that "[t]he entire Catholic Church, ranging from the pope to Bosnia's Franciscans, favors a united Bosnia-Herzegovina."[154]

During the months following the Ahmići massacre, ARBiH and HVO forces clashed around Kiseljak, Busovaća, Novi Travnik, Žepce, Maglaj, Tesanj, Fojnica, Vinište, Gornji Vakuf, Dubravica, Lukavica, Bugojno, and other locations, while the ARBiH launched an abortive attack, in July, on the village of Gornja Papratnica near Žepce. On 23 October 1993, HVO forces commanded by General Ivica Rajić attacked the village of Stupni Do in central Bosnia; as *Nacional* reported much later, "dozens of unarmed Muslim civilians were massacred, and the entire village was then systematically looted and destroyed."[155] In retaliation, the ARBiH mounted an offensive against the Croatian town of Vareš, driving its inhabitants to flight. Fighting was particularly fierce in Mostar where HVO forces eventually asserted their dominance in mid-July, incarcerating about 22,000 Muslims in a converted helicopter aerodrome.[156] On 9 November 1993, in symbolic affirmation of their victory, HVO troops, acting on orders from General Slobodan Praljak, commander of the HVO, blew up the world-famous old bridge in Mostar. But the HVO victory in Mostar notwithstanding, the tides of war were, in fact, turning against the Croats, and on 12 November 1993, Mate Boban, in his capacity as head of the Bosnian HDZ organization and head of Herceg-Bosna, removed General Praljak from command of the HVO, appointing General Ante Roso in his place. By February 1994, the Bosnian Croats had lost 40% of the land they had held in April 1993—some of it to the VRS, but most of it to the Bosnian Army.[157] As the tide turned against Tudjman, he ordered HV forces to cooperate with the VRS in fighting against the ARBiH.

In the meantime, at the height of Muslim-Croat fighting in 1993, Fikret Abdić, a highly popular businessman who had built up an agricultural and food-processing concern in Velika Kladuša known as Agrokomerc (the focus of the 1987 finance scandal) and who was by then a member of Bosnia's collective presidency, had returned to Velika Kladuša from Sarajevo and, on 26 September 1993, proclaimed the "Autonomous Province of Western Bosnia" in the Bihać enclave in northwestern Bosnia. Abdić may well have been involved in an abortive conspiracy to depose Izetbegović the previous year when the Bosnian president was briefly in the hands of Serb captors.[158] In any event, Abdić was a rival of Izetbegović's, having criticized the Bosnian president publicly in June. The Bihać enclave was strategically located, which gave Belgrade and Zagreb sufficient reason to support its secession. Thus, when Abdić went to Milošević with a request for support, the Serbian leader happily agreed.[159] Tudjman also welcomed Abdić's secession, and soon Abdić's enclave was cooperating with both Bosnian Serb and Bosnian Croat forces and benefiting from trade with both of Izetbegović's foes.[160] Abdić processed foodstuffs for the Krajina Serbs, bought oil and other goods from Croatia, resold much of the oil to the Serbs of the Krajina and Bosnia, as well as to Serbia itself, and for a while, seemed to have assured his local supporters of peace and prosperity.[161] In August 1994, the Sarajevo government sent its Fifth Corps against Velika Kladuša, capturing it on the 20th of that month. Abdić and some 30,000 of his adherents fled to the safety of Bosnian Serb lines.[162]

In August 1993, Charles Redman, U.S. president Clinton's personal envoy, sat down for dinner with Haris Silajdžić, by then Bosnian prime minister, and Mate Granić, prime minister of Croatia. What became apparent in the course of this meal was that both parties to this conflict wanted to resolve it and to make a common front against the Bosnian Serb forces. Redman took the lead in the effort to bring the Muslim-Croat conflict to an end, though fighting continued at a high level of intensity for some months yet. An agreement on 14 September 1993 envisaged the creation of a Croat-Bosniak federation; it was subsequently revised to frame a confederation, before dying on the table. Then, on 16 February 1994, Redman and U.S. ambassador Peter Galbraith met with Tudjman and urged him to give up his dreams of a "Greater Croatia." They suggested instead that Tudjman think in terms of a confederal union with Bosnia-Herzegovina, offering Croatia an accelerated economic, political, and military integration into Western alliances and organizations. By the end of the month, Bosnian and Croatian officials were sitting across the table from each other in Washington, D.C., to hammer out an agreement. Signed, finally, in March 1994, it came to be known as the Washington Agreement and restored the military partnership between the Bosnian government and the Croatian government. The agreement did not bring a complete end to Muslim-Croat frictions.[163] Indeed, Croatia, which had already been selling fuel directly to the VRS, continued to supply Bosnian Serb forces with fuel "long after the Federation was founded."[164] But the agreement ended the large-scale military campaigns which the Croats and the Bosniaks had fought against each other, created an atmosphere in which arms from Islamic states could flow more easily through Croatia into government-controlled parts of Bosnia (the Croats, of course, skimmed what they wanted off the top), and laid the foundation for eventual military cooperation against the VRS. In May 1994, the reconciled partners formulated common war objectives, demanding that 58% of the territory of Bosnia-Herzegovina be allocated to the Croat-Bosniak federation.[165] From the perspective of that time, this was a huge concession, because it signified Croat-Bosniak assent to the notion that the Serbs would be allowed to keep a larger proportion of Bosnian territory than was consistent with their population, and because Izetbegović, who had long resisted any notion of partition, was finally embracing that remedy as his own.

Serb Ambitions and Failed Peace Plans
(December 1992–March 1995)

Meeting in a small stuccoed building perched amid pine trees and commanding an extraordinary view of the mountains above Sarajevo—in what had been a psychiatric sanitarium before the outbreak of war—the Bosnian Serb parliament issued a statement on 17 December 1992, declaring that the war was over. The declaration noted that "the Serb nation" had achieved its territorial objectives in Bosnia and that "the borders which from today at 1200 are guarded by the Army of the Serb Republic are the provisional borders of the Serb Republic."[166] It was an extraordinary act of hubris since, as was obvious at the time, the Bosnian Croats and Bosniaks were by no means reconciled to the existing territorial arrangement and had not yet been militarily depleted; indeed, time would show that, as of December 1992, neither the Croatian side (HV and HVO) nor the Bosnian Army had reached their full military potential. Scarcely a week later, Karadžić, whose parliament had just announced the end of the war, warned that if the Albanians of Kosovo staged an uprising in spring and if Croatia were to launch an offensive against Chetnik positions in Knin and Krajina, then Albania, Turkey, and Russia might intervene, which, he claimed, would "mean the beginning of World War III."[167] But Karadžić loved hyperbole, bluster, and the language of war. It was, after all, this same Karadžić who, in a poetic moment a decade earlier, had penned these lines:

When you put on your hard shoes,
Your brave boots,
Your manly shoes,
Your war boots,
You just automatically
Reach for your gun
And set out
Down muddy roads.

When the time comes for gun barrels to speak,
For heroic days, valorous nights,
When a foreign army floods your country,
And wreaks havoc and causes damage in it,
That condition must be righted:
Then you roam your homeland on foot,
And your boots fight side by side with you.[168]

Now Karadžić—the psychiatrist, the poet, the lobbyist for better food labeling, the aficionado of Mexican songs,[169] the hyperbolic nationalist whose parliament had just announced that the Bosnian Serb forces planned to keep what they had conquered—was being asked by Cyrus Vance and David Lord Owen to give up some of the land his forces had captured, to pull his forces back, to compromise. The Vance-Owen Plan was presented to Ćosić, Izetbegović, Tudjman, Boban, and Karadžić on 2 January 1993. In addition to the creation of a 10-

province structure, the plan also called for the cessation of all hostilities within 72 hours, the immediate demilitarization of Sarajevo and subsequently of the entire republic, the dismantlement of all states within the state, the return of refugees to their prewar homes, freedom of movement for all Bosnians, democratically elected local and national governments, and internationally monitored human rights protection.[170] Because of the compact concentration of Croats in southwestern Herzegovina—the principal objective of the Bosnian Croat forces loyal to Boban and Tudjman—any partition plan was certain to grant the Croats' primary objective. Bosnian Croat assent was therefore not a problem, and both Croatian representatives quickly agreed to the cessation of hostilities, the constitutional principles, and the map. Izetbegović accepted the 10 constitutional principles drafted by Vance and Owen but asked for further negotiations on the map, and he agreed to the cessation of hostilities. Karadžić objected to both the constitutional principles and the map, but he was prepared to sign the clause relating to the cessation of hostilities—a more or less empty gesture. While Karadžić dragged his feet, the foreign ministers of the European Community states adopted a declaration on 6 April, threatening the FRY with long-term international isolation in the event that the Vance-Owen Plan was not accepted by Karadžić. Milošević had been paying the salaries of all officers in the VRS,[171] as well as the salaries of those assigned to the Special Operations Unit of the Serbian Interior Ministry which operated in Bosnia, under his direct command, during the war.[172] The Serbian leader now felt motivated, as a result of EU threats, to put pressure on Karadžić to sign the agreement, knowing that Karadžić could not continue the war without his support. But by this point Karadžić was rejecting the plan outright. Eventually, in Athens, under heavy pressure from Milošević and Greek prime minister Konstantin Mitsotakis, who said that they would not let Karadžić leave the city until he had signed the plan, the Bosnian Serb leader accommodated his hosts, attaching the proviso, however, that the Bosnian Serb parliament would have to ratify the plan. Four days later, on 6 May 1993, the Bosnian Serb parliament rejected the plan; Milošević now announced that he would cut off shipments of arms and ammunition to Karadžić's forces (thereby admitting what he had denied up to this point, viz., that Belgrade had been supplying the VRS all along). But Milošević continued to pay the salaries of the VRS officer corps, without interruption, and later resumed arms shipments to the VRS. Within the month, Cyrus Vance stepped down as UN special envoy, being replaced in this post by Norwegian diplomat Thorvald Stoltenberg. That same month, the UN Security Council announced that it had decided to establish a war crimes court to try war criminals from the War of Yugoslav Succession.

Other Peace Plans

The abortive Vance-Owen plan would be followed by the Karadžić-Boban plan of June 1993, the Owen-Stoltenberg Plan of August 1993, the EU Action Plan of

December 1993, and the Contact Group Plan of July 1994. The first of these was a nonstarter, among other reasons because it was premised on the partition of Sarajevo and, apparently, on a coup aimed at replacing Izetbegović with the maverick businessman Fikret Abdić; the principal logistical problem with that idea was that the Bosnian Army remained loyal to Izetbegović.[173] Perhaps it is no coincidence that rumors circulated the following month claiming that Fikret Muslimović, by then security chief in the Bosnian Army, and Bakir Alispahić, chief of police, had worked out a plan, on Izetbegović's behalf, to assassinate Abdić.[174] The Owen-Stoltenberg Plan was largely based on a map developed by Tudjman and Milošević during talks in Geneva but was immediately and vociferously rejected by Izetbegović. The plan envisaged Bosnia as a union of three ethnic republics, with each constituent republic enjoying the right of secession; the plan was transparently intended to provide a cover for the *Republika Srpska* and Herceg-Bosna to attach themselves to Serbia and Croatia respectively. The EU Action Plan, hammered out during the latter months of 1993, offered the Muslims 33.5% of the republic, the Croats 17.5%, and the Serbs the lion's share—49%. Negotiations concerning this plan lasted during February 1994 before dying on the table. And finally, the Contact Group Plan, prepared under the leadership of Russia and Britain and presented on 18 July 1994, retained the EU Action plan formula awarding 49% of Bosnia-Herzegovina to the Serbian side and 51% to the Croat-Bosniak federation and proposed placing Sarajevo and Mostar under international protectorates; although the plan was not accepted, the percentages offered in the EU Action plan and again in the 1994 plan would later be enshrined in the Dayton Peace Accords.

The Bosnian Serbs may well have been encouraged, in their defiance, by Russian support. In January 1993, for instance, the Russian representative at the UN proposed sanctions against Croatia in the event that Croatia continued combat operations against the insurgents in the Krajina.[175] More significantly, the Russian Army and intelligence service signed a secret agreement about the same time, under which military hardware, including sophisticated missiles, began to arrive in Serbia and in Serb-controlled areas of Bosnia and Croatia.[176] The British newspaper *The Observer* reported that the Russians had "already sent their own technicians and soldiers to operate the missile batteries and that some of these have been positioned in Serbian-held Krajina. . . . The Serbs . . . agreed to buy $360 million (250m pounds sterling) of weaponry, including the small, mobile Soviet T-55 tank and an array of antiaircraft and antimissile missiles capable of destroying targets up to 375 miles away."[177] Emboldened by their rapid territorial gains during the previous year, by warm support from NATO member Greece,[178] by Russia's diplomatic and military support, and by the ineffectual diplomatic efforts on the part of the international community, Momčilo Krajišnik, speaker of the Assembly of the Serbian Republic, declared on 9 April that the insurgent Serbian zones in Croatia and Bosnia-Herzegovina would "in the nearest future start implementing the declaration on unification of the two Serb states, adopted at the end of October last year in Prijedor."[179]

Setting up "Safe Havens"; Stalemate

In April 1993, the VRS attacked Srebrenica once again, shelling it relentlessly. On 6 May, the UN Security Council took a controversial step by adopting Resolution 824, declaring the establishment of six "safe havens," which were supposed to be free from attack or any other hostile action; the hope was that the VRS would respect the special status of these six cities. The UN Security Council followed this up on 4 June 1993 with Resolution 836, which authorized UNPROFOR, the UN Protection Force which had been protecting the humanitarian convoys, to use force to protect these "havens."[180] With this step, the Security Council hoped that it had provided some security for the inhabitants of the six designated "safe havens": Sarajevo, Tuzla, Goražde, Foča, Srebrenica, Žepa, and Bihać. Critics compared the "safe havens" to Indian reservations and noted that Srebrenica, encircled and largely cut off from the outside, was degenerating into lawless violence, as prostitution among young girls, theft, and black marketeering proliferated.[181] Ratko Mladić, the Bosnian Serb general, expressed his opposition to the plan, and the VRS showed its contempt for the "safe havens" by immediately blasting a makeshift stadium in Sarajevo, killing at least 15 persons, and by reviving its attacks on Goražde, killing 59 persons in a single day.[182] Efforts by German chancellor Kohl and, albeit inconsistently, U.S. president Clinton to build a consensus that the arms embargo should be lifted ran aground, and when, at the end of the year, the UN General Assembly passed a resolution in favor of lifting the arms embargo against Bosnia, Britain and France used their veto powers in the Security Council to keep the embargo in place.[183] Nor was NATO prepared to adopt any military measures to stop the fighting, in spite of periodic calls for a military response.[184]

The big surprise of 1993 was the ability of the Bosnian Army to fight a two-front war, holding the line against the Bosnian Serb forces and rolling back Bosnian Croat forces. No one had expected this result. Most observers had expected or feared that with the arms embargo in place, the Bosnian Army would simply be crushed. But instead, although diplomatic efforts were stalemated and although the VRS continued to hold onto 70% of Bosnian territory, the ARBiH had held its own; this provided a tremendous boost to its morale,[185] while the rank-and-file in the Bosnian Serb forces, armed to the teeth and yet unable to make an end to the war, were gradually becoming demoralized. The ARBiH was also gaining battle experience and becoming steadily more battle-worthy. With the Muslim-Croat conflict raging through all of 1993, the Bosnian Serbs gloated and did what they could to aggravate that conflict; what they did *not* manage to do was to destroy the Bosnian Army. According to a publication prepared for the CIA,

The VRS ignored opportunities to crush the Tuzla and Zenica areas—the heart of Muslim-held Bosnia—with the major operations needed, and the operations the VRS launched late in the year failed to achieve their objectives. The Serbs in 1993 had had a last chance to win the war for Bosnia outright, and they failed to take advantage of it. . . .

The Bosnian Serb Army's failure to exploit the Muslim-Croat war and knock out the Bosnian Army in 1993 would haunt the Serbs for the remainder of the war.[186]

NATO as the Military Arm of the UN?

The international presence in Croatia and Bosnia was under UN auspices. This created a context in which it was expected that any international involvement, for example by NATO, would operate within the framework and under the authority of the UN. Indeed, it had been established through a number of UN Security Council resolutions that any use of air power had to be approved, in advance, by Boutros Boutros-Ghali, the UN secretary-general. During the latter months of 1993, there had been some controversy concerning Boutros-Ghali's apparent reluctance to approve air strikes against Bosnian Serb positions. In an effort to calm the discontented, Boutros-Ghali appointed a special envoy (in fact as a successor to Thorvald Stoltenberg, who had stepped down); Boutros-Ghali's choice was Yasushi Akashi, a Japanese diplomat who had been responsible for a successful UN operation in Cambodia and who was now authorized to approve or disapprove air strikes in the secretary-general's name. It was a fateful decision. Given the end of the Cold War and the dissolution of the Warsaw Pact, NATO was operating in a new security field, and some observers felt that NATO could serve as the military arm of the UN. Akashi brought in Susan Woodward, a scholar at the Brookings Institution, as his adviser; Woodward was soon viewed as pro-Serb and came to be known locally as "Mrs. Mladić."[187] Akashi, too, would be accused of being pro-Serb in orientation,[188] especially after he repeatedly turned down local requests from UNPROFOR for air strikes against the Bosnian Serbs.

Whatever may have been the intentions of the players, when one adds up Akashi's vetoing of air strikes against the Bosnian Serbs, the UN arms embargo, and the fact (to which I alluded above) that UNPROFOR was allowing the Bosnian Serbs "to skim off nearly 50% of all food brought in for 'humanitarian' purposes and nearly 40% of all UNPROFOR fuel,"[189] it is hard to avoid the conclusion that, without the UN's assistance, conscious or not, the Bosnian Serbs could not have continued the war for as long as they did. Douglas Hurd's protests notwithstanding, the actions of the UN Security Council as well as those of Boutros-Ghali and Akashi served to *prolong* the war, not to bring it to a speedy resolution. When, in July 1995, the UN failed to approve air strikes to protect the "safe havens" of Srebrenica and Žepa from being overrun by Mladić's forces and those forces massacred thousands of unarmed civilians (details below), the entire notion of placing NATO under UN authority was completely de-legitimated; the rather palpable failure of the UN in Bosnia in turn set the stage for NATO's military unilateralism in Kosovo in 1999 and for George W. Bush's military unilateralism beginning in 2001.

As 1994 opened, the U.S. and its European allies (except for Germany) were divided over what to do about the Bosnian war. The British, French, and Russians feared that the war might spread and, in the interests of damming it, wanted to get a peace agreement in place as quickly as possible; since they had no intention of going to war, their position was that a peace plan should take the existing lines of separation as the starting point. The American position was that the Bosniaks were victims of aggression—above all by the VRS—and that they had the right under international law to fight for the recovery of their lost lands. France and Russia pressed the government of Izetbegović to sign on the dotted line and asked the U.S. to put pressure on him to do so. Clinton continued to advocate a strategy of "lift and strike"—lift the arms embargo against the Bosniaks and strike the Serbian forces using NATO air power—while the British and French, with more than 9,000 "peacekeepers" on the ground, protested that air strikes would endanger their "peacekeepers." Rather than pulling out their "peacekeepers," however, Britain, France, Spain, and the Netherlands demanded that the U.S. also send its troops to "keep the peace" in the Balkans. The U.S. rejected both of these demands; nor did Izetbegović express any desire to see American troops on the ground in Bosnia. What he *did* want, as he signaled on 21 January 1994, after "relentless bombing" of Sarajevo by the VRS had provoked only verbal chastisement from the Security Council, was for NATO to launch air strikes against the Bosnian Serb forces. NATO officials replied that UN secretary-general Boutros-Ghali had to authorize any such strikes, while Alvaro DeSoto, a senior aide to Boutros-Ghali, said that the secretary-general would do so "if the need arises."[190] Apparently, the need had not yet arisen.

The need arose two weeks later after Bosnian Serbs fired a shell into the Markala marketplace in downtown Sarajevo on 5 February, killing 68 persons and wounding more than 200.[191] The attack produced a tidal change in international public opinion and persuaded Boutros-Ghali, Major, Hurd, and others who had been reluctant to bomb that it was time for a tougher approach.[192] While Akashi dithered,[193] Boutros-Ghali wrote to NATO general secretary Manfred Woerner to ask NATO to make a determination whether to respond with air power. As a result, on 9 February, NATO issued an ultimatum to the Bosnian Serbs to pull their heavy weapons back to a distance of 20 kilometers from Sarajevo or face air strikes. At first the Serbs did not seem inclined to cooperate. VRS spokesperson Miroslav Toholj, for example, replied to the ultimatum with bluster, charging that NATO had become "an international terrorist organization and we will consider it as such until it changes its stance with regard to us," adding that any strike against Serb positions would immediately ignite World War Three and induce the VRS to use weapons "never before used by the Serbs."[194]

Karadžić was also defiant and threatened that his artillery would inflict heavy losses on any NATO aircraft sent against VRS positions.[195] But on 12 February, two days into the ultimatum period, the Serbs indicated a willingness to withdraw their heavy weapons, provided that the Bosnian Army would pull back its infantry. A compromise was reached under which both sides would surrender some heavy weapons to UN control, with the Serbs to pull their armor back beyond the exclusion zone; indeed, some weapons were turned in that same day. On the following day, however, the VRS stopped turning in weapons, and the Bosnian Army did likewise. The Serbs seemed to be hardening their position once again. Krajišnik, in a tone of unadulterated braggadocio, used the occasion of the opening of a sporting event on Mt. Jahorina to declare that

[t]he international community . . . is threatening us, without any reason. It is threatening us because we are to blame for opposing denigration and destruction. We are guilty because we wanted, like all other peoples of the former Yugoslavia, to preserve our freedom and state. We will reply to their ultimatums in the same way as our forebears did. We do not accept the ultimatum. We want freedom and peace. We have opted for freedom and are resolved to defend the honor of the Serb nation with all available means.[196]

But there were reasons to suspect that NATO meant business, and on 14 February the surrender of heavy weaponry was resumed, and the withdrawal of Serb forces likewise resumed. By 21 February, the Bosnian Serbs had withdrawn or surrendered most but not all of their big guns. Izetbegović wanted NATO to hold the Serbs to the letter of the ultimatum and demanded that air strikes against VRS positions begin; but Yasushi Akashi decided that the level of compliance was sufficient and announced that he had "decided that it is not necessary at this stage for me to request NATO to use air power."[197] The victory was only apparent—first, because the weapons pulled back could be either brought back within firing range of Sarajevo or transferred to other zones coveted by the Bosnian Serbs; and second, because along the way, the definition of what constituted "UN control" had changed, and the weapons surrendered by the Serbs were deposited in "concentration points" where UNPROFOR could inspect them but from which the VRS could easily withdraw them, if the need were to arise.[198]

The Bosnian government would have preferred air strikes but recognized that the withdrawal had given Sarajevo some breathing space. The German government and UNPROFOR commander General Sir Michael Rose wanted to apply the same model (threaten air strikes in order to obtain Serb withdrawals) to relieve sieges elsewhere, and Rose, in fact, requested that the UN authorize such an approach in the case of Tuzla, where Swedish peacekeepers had been attacked by the VRS. The request was turned down by Akashi, while a request from Izetbegović for relief for Bihać, where Bosnian Army troops were engaged in combat with VRS forces, was simply ignored.[199]

Showdown at Goražde

The Bosnian Serbs remained defiant and showed their defiance by launching three rocket-propelled grenades at ARBiH troops in Sarajevo on 3 March and by blockading seven aid convoys on 6 March. When the UN aid convoy headed for Maglaj was finally allowed to go through, people ran onto the streets shouting, "Food! Food!"[200] But the international community was also getting tougher, and after months of non-enforcement of the UN-declared no-fly zone, two American F-16 fighter jets shot down four Bosnian Serb Soko G-3 Super Galeb light attack aircraft flying in the vicinity of Banja Luka on 28 February.

Meanwhile, the VRS's strategic offensive, launched against the Bosnian Army at the beginning of 1994, was foiled by the capable ARBiH commander General Rasim Delić, who succeeded in throwing the VRS on the defensive by the end of March. Then, on 16 March, the Bosnian Army launched a strike against Serb-held Donji Vakuf, capturing the peak at Mala Suljaga; although the ARBiH failed to retake the town, it mounted its first assault on Serb-held Mt. Vlasić at the end of the month and, in the Tesanj area north of Maglaj, succeeded in denting Serb lines.[201] But the VRS was still a force to be reckoned with, and on 29 March, it launched an attack on Goražde, an east Bosnian town (population before the war: 40,000) commanding key strategic routes coveted by the Bosnian Serb command. On 5 April, the VRS penetrated the outer perimeter around the town, capturing several villages and forcing the villagers to flee to Goražde in hope of finding safety; in the first eight days of bombardment, the VRS had taken at least 49 lives.[202] In response, U.S. defense secretary William Perry declared that the U.S. would "not enter the war" to prevent Goražde from falling to the VRS, with General John Shalikashvili, chairman of the Joint Chiefs of Staff, adding that, in his view, air strikes would be ineffective at Goražde.[203] On 10 April, a VRS tank began firing directly into Goražde, provoking General Rose to request authorization for air strikes. Approval was granted, and two US F-16 fighter aircraft (based at Aviano Air Base) struck Serb targets around Goražde the evening of the same day.[204] Serb forces opened fire against the NATO aircraft, but after renewed strikes by NATO warplanes the following day, in which at least one VRS tank was destroyed, Bosnian Serb artillery and tank fire into the town abated.[205] By then, the death toll among the residents and refugees in Goražde had risen to 156, with at least 646 wounded.[206] Bosnian Serb Television broadcast old footage of the bodies of U.S. servicemen being hauled through the streets of Mogadishu in 1993 by a Somali mob.

The air strikes of 10–11 April had been limited in scope, and when General Mladić "made good on his threats and took about 200 blue helmets in Bosnia as hostages, the UN special envoy for Bosnia-Herzegovina, Yasushi Akashi, refused to authorize further air strikes."[207] Mladić also issued a threat to NATO on 12 April: if any more NATO aircraft attempted to fly missions against his forces, he would have them shot down.[208] While President Clinton spoke of expanding the air campaign to other UN-designated "safe havens," Bosnian Serb forces seized some 58 UN peacekeepers and aid workers in various locations, many of them at gunpoint, by 13 April and sealed off two UN compounds outside Sarajevo, trapping the UN peacekeepers posted there. Counting also those UN peacekeepers placed under house arrest by the Serbs, more than 200 peacekeepers had been detained by the Serbs by mid-month.[209] By that point, the VRS had captured several strategic sites in the Goražde enclave, while UN peacekeepers assigned to protect the enclave retreated toward the city center. On 21

April, General Shalikashvili contacted General Michael Rose, who was serving at the time as commander of the UN Protection Force in Bosnia. Shalikashvili told Rose that the U.S. was entertaining the possibility of launching air strikes against Serb forces. Rose felt that NATO did not have the requisite force on hand to back up air strikes and advised against any such action.[210] But NATO was growing impatient. Finally, on 22 April, having cleared its announcement with the UN, NATO issued an ultimatum to the VRS to cease all hostilities against Goražde immediately, to pull its forces back to an outer perimeter of 3 kilometers within 48 hours, and to pull its heavy weaponry back to a perimeter of 20 kilometers. The VRS ignored the ultimatum and continued artillery fire. When NATO presented what it considered a routine request to Akashi for authorization to initiate air strikes against the VRS the next day, however, Akashi rejected the request, on the argument that there should be no air strikes until the 48-hour deadline had expired.[211] Eventually, over the next few days, the VRS complied with the terms of the ultimatum (removing its heavy weapons from around Goražde by 27 April), but the enclave had been whittled down by the offensive, and there was no move to reverse the shrinkage. The VRS offensive against Goražde had lasted 26 days, during which time 716 civilians or defenders had lost their lives, while an additional 2,000 had been wounded.[212]

Arms from Iran

Some arms began to flow to Croatia and Bosnia from Iran soon after the outbreak of the conflict in Bosnia in spring 1992, with Saudi Arabia, Malaysia, Brunei, and Pakistan covering some of the costs. In a separate channel, Argentina and South Africa also had become involved in a covert arms smuggling operation to Croatia.[213] During 1993, during the Muslim-Croat conflict, Croatia did not allow arms to pass through its territory to Bosnia. But the Washington Agreement signed in March 1994 reopened the possibility of arms transshipments through Croatia. Accordingly, at the end of March 1994, in the wake of the Washington Agreement, Croatian president Tudjman asked U.S. ambassador Galbraith if the U.S. had any objections to the shipment of arms through Croatia to Bosnia. Since arms had flowed from Iran earlier, the fact that Tudjman approached Galbraith with this question suggests that Tudjman envisaged a much more significant flow of arms than what had taken place heretofore. Galbraith consulted with the State Department and was told to advise Tudjman that he had "no instructions" and to make sure that Tudjman understood that he was being given a green light. The first shipment arrived soon thereafter, delivering assault rifles, rocket launchers, grenades, and ammunition.[214] The financing of this operation was coordinated through the Third World Relief Agency, a humanitarian agency headed by Sudanese citizen Elfatih Hassanein, which opened an office in Sarajevo and opened an account at *Die Erste Österreichische Bank* in Vienna. Between 1992 and 1995 about $350 million was deposited into this account to finance the arms flow to Croatia and Bosnia; the funds were deposited by Saudi Arabia, Iran, Sudan, Turkey, Brunei, Malaysia, and Pakistan, more than half of it going to defray the costs of the arms-smuggling operation.[215] In addition, Iran also shipped weapons to Croatia and Bosnia on its own account; all told, the value of weapons smuggling into Bosnia during 1994–1995 alone amounted to between $500 million and $800 million. The purpose of the operation was to arm the Bosnian Army, but by general agreement, the Croatian Army set aside one-third of all shipments for its own use. Iranian personnel followed, in order to train the ARBiH in the use of the arms.[216]

Croatia also benefited from this arms flow, as already noted, and it has been estimated that the value of the arms smuggled into Croatia during the years 1993–1995 amounted to about $308 million.[217] By November 1994, the combined troop strengths of the Bosnian Army and the HVO were more than a match for the VRS (as is clear from Table 15.2); thanks to the infusion of arms, the ARBiH and the HVO were gradually building their strength (see Table 15.3). But data from August 1995 for the Croatian Army show that by the time of Operation Storm, the Croatian Army was more than a match for the Krajina Serb Army (see Table 15.4).

The European Union "Action" Plan of July 1994

As a direct result of the Goražde crisis and the realization that the use of international peace mediators had failed to bring about a peace settlement, the U.S., Russia, Germany, Britain, and France decided to return to the Metternichean model and to see if direct pressure from the Great Powers would produce faster results. Accordingly, these five powers constituted themselves as a "Contact Group" (the term was coined by Pauline Neville-Jones, political director in Whitehall's Foreign Office) and appointed representatives to undertake the work of peace plan development. During the following weeks they conducted

Table 15.2. Troop Strengths of Rival Forces in Bosnia (November 1994)

Source of estimate	Bosnian Serbs	Bosnian Muslims	Bosnian Croats
McNeil-Lehrer News	80,000	100,000	50,000
Die Welt	60,000	210,000	n/a
Jane's Defence Weekly	102,000	164,000	50,000[a]
Nedjeljna Dalmacija	80,000	120,000	n/a

Sources: McNeil-Lehrer News Hour, 4 November 1994; *Die Welt* (Bonn), 4 November 1994, p. 4; *Jane's Defence Weekly,* as cited in the *Baltimore Sun,* 6 November 1994, p. 11A; International Institute for Strategic Studies, *The Military Balance, 1993–1994* (London: Brassey's, October 1993), p. 74; and *Nedjeljna Dalmacija* (Split), 4 November 1994, p. 21.

a. 1993, from *The Military Balance*

Table 15.3. Armaments Possessed by the Combatants in Bosnia (November 1994)

	Bosnian Serbs	Bosnian Muslims	Bosnian Croats
Tanks	330	40	75
Artillery pieces	800	a few[a]	200
Armored personnel carriers	400	30	n/a
Aircraft	37	0	0

Sources: *McNeil-Lehrer News Hour,* 4 November 1994; and International Institute for Strategic Studies, *The Military Balance, 1993–1994* (London: Brassey's, October 1993), pp. 74–75.

a. 1993

talks with the various sides and, on 5 July 1994, announced their plan. This plan retained the formula of 51% for the federation, 49% for the Bosnian Serbs, and called for the surrender of Bosanski Brod and Derventa to the federation and a narrowing (at the Serbs' expense) of the Posavina Corridor. The plan was presented on a "take it or leave it" basis, but although the Croats and the Bosniaks accepted the plan, Karadžić, speaking as president of the *Republika Srpska,* attached so many conditions to his "yes" ("yes, but . . . ") that his response was universally interpreted as a rejection of the plan.[218] Milošević, who had tried to persuade Karadžić to accept the plan, now criticized the Bosnian Serb leader in a front-page interview for *Politika.* On 4 August, Milošević announced that Serbia's border with the Bosnian Serb republic would be closed to all traffic except humanitarian shipments, for which he was rewarded with an easing of the UN economic embargo, and on 9 September, he presented a speech underlining the

Table 15.4. Military Strengths of the Croatian Forces and the Krajina Serb Army at the Time of Operation Storm (August 1995)

	HV/HVO	Krajina Serb Army
Troops	160,000	20,000–30,000
Brigades/regiments	51	20
Tanks	320–705	385–430
Armored personnel carriers	240	195–210
Artillery pieces	812–1,400	440–570
Aircraft	36	20–25
Helicopters	12	10–13

Sources: Ozren Žunec, "Operations Flash and Storm," in Branka Magaš and Ivo Žanić (eds.), *The War in Croatia and Bosnia-Herzegovina, 1991–1995* (London: Frank Cass, 2001), p. 78; *Welt am Sonntag* (Hamburg), 16 July 1995, p. 23; Daniel Eisermann, *Der lange Weg nach Dayton: Die westliche Politik und der Krieg im ehemaligen Jugoslawien 1991 bis 1995* (Baden-Baden: Nomos Verlagsgesellschaft, 2000), p. 327; *Neue Zürcher Zeitung* (31 July 1995), p. 1; and *The Economist* (London), 5 August 1995, p. 47.

fairness of the Contact Group plan. But, as Louis Sell has noted, "[a]lthough Milošević's anger with the Pale leadership was real, there were limits to the extent he was prepared to pressure the Bosnian Serbs. The 'Drina blockade' was never a formidable barrier to the Bosnian Serbs' obtaining the supplies they needed. After he was ousted from power, Milošević portrayed the barrier as 'a clever political maneuver so as to reduce the severity of the sanctions' and said it was 'never a real blockade.'"[219]

Within the U.S., the Senate and House of Representatives passed resolutions urging Clinton to declare that the U.S. would no longer respect the arms embargo against the Muslims. But thanks to the infusion of arms from Iran, still more or less secret at the time, the ARBiH was gaining in strength and launched four offensives against VRS positions in the second half of 1994. The second of these, involving an effort by Bosnian forces in the Bihać enclave to break out, was successful at first and resulted in the capture of four tanks and numerous mortars by the ARBiH,[220] but then a VRS counteroffensive drove the ARBiH back to the outskirts of that town. There were reports that the VRS was brandishing new air defense equipment at Bihać—equipment which it could only have received from Belgrade, blockade or no blockade.[221] But ARBiH units held onto strategically important hills surrounding Otoka and blunted the Bosnian Serb advance; ARBiH sabotage units managed to infiltrate VRS lines and undermined the VRS from within when the main body of the Bosnian Army's Fifth Corps, spearheaded by the 505th Buzim Motorized Brigade, launched a counteroffensive, pushing panicked VRS troops back and nearly capturing Mladić.[222]

The Fifth Corps now went on the offensive and, by 27 October, had captured 100–150 square kilometers of territory and was pushing toward Bosanski Petrovac. Along the way, the Bosnian Army had taken the town of Kulen Vakuf, 30 kilometers south of Bihać.[223] The ARBiH was not able to hold that town for long, however, and by 1 November it had changed hands once again. The VRS objective in the northwest was to eviscerate the Bosnian Army Fifth Corps and to reestablish Fikret Abdić in Velika Kladuša, where he could preside as a Serb marionette. Abdić was, in fact, commanding about 4,000–5,000 troops of his own and participating in the campaign on the Serb side. On 8 November, a Krajina Serb Orao fighter-bomber took off from Udbina Air Base and, in violation of the "no-fly" zone around Bihać, approached the city and destroyed an ammunition storage facility. In reprisal, NATO war planes were belatedly (on 21 November) sent to bomb the Serbs' air base at Udbina near Bihać. The damage inflicted at Udbina was slight, but Mladić responded by taking 165 UN peacekeepers hostage. It was neither the first nor the last humiliation inflicted on the UN by the VRS.

On 7–8 December, the VRS took control of Bihać's water treatment plant, but that was as far as the VRS was able to push in that direction. The Bosnian Army held its ground at Bihać, though the VRS, with the participation of Abdić's forces, retook Velika Kladuša. The VRS's failure to take Bihać itself owed something to the Croatian Army's entry into this theater, on 29 November, in an effort to relieve the pressure on the embattled Muslim town. For the Croats, Bihać was of vital strategic importance, and it was critical, from their perspective, that Bihać not fall to Serb forces. Croatian defense minister Šušak declared utterly explicitly on 1 December that the Croatian Army would under no circumstances permit Bihać to fall to the VRS.

Finally, in the ARBiH's fourth offensive, it had taken control of strategically important Kupres in November. The VRS was also losing territory southwest of Tesanj, southeast of Konjić, and in the Livno-Glamoč valley. As a distinguished group of analysts concluded in a work published in May 2002, "These losses were not rapid or especially serious as individual cases. Cumulatively, however, they led to the irrefutable conclusion that the VRS could not sustain its war indefinitely and that its losses of troops and territory were almost sure to increase."[224]

The Changing Military Balance

The sustained deliveries of armaments to the Croatian and Bosnian forces beginning in 1991–1992 (including, in the Bosnian Army's case, from Slovenia[225]) gradually produced a shift in the military balance. By February 1995, the Krajina Croatian-Serb Army was thought to be able to arm at most 50,000 troops, with the VRS capable of fielding at most about 80,000 soldiers. Against this force, the Croatian Army, HVO, and Bosnian Army could field a combined force of 250,000 and command a fleet of 570 tanks.[226] A "Memorandum of Cooperation on Defense and Military Relations" signed on 29 November 1994 by U.S. defense secretary William J. Perry and his Croatian counterpart provided for an expansion of defense contacts and for American military training for Croatian forces and left no doubt but that Croatia's military prospects would continue to improve.[227]

While the Croatian and Bosnian forces were growing in strength, the Yugoslav Army, the VRS, and the Krajina Serb Army were growing weaker. Part of the problem had to do with the very nature of the Serbian war strategy, which was to finish the war quickly, using plunder to motivate the troops. VRS soldiers were not paid at all between the end of March and the end of July 1994, leaving plunder as the sole means for the army to support itself. As the war dragged on and as what there had been to loot was looted, morale in the VRS began to decline. The VRS also had problems obtaining good intelligence about the ARBiH, poor coordination, and difficulties in obtaining spare parts for military machinery. Colonel Vladimir Arsić, commander of the VRS defense unit at Doboj, prepared a "highly confidential" report dated 17 August 1994, in which he complained that "[VRS] units are unfit . . . [;] instead of fighting, they flee in panic, leaving behind their personal weapons and other combat equipment as well as their wounded comrades in an attempt to save their own lives, which can be most easily lost in this way."[228] Arsić and his fellow officers were unable to rectify the situation, however, which only deteriorated in the succeeding months, so that by March 1995, large numbers of troops in the Doboj region were reported to be "abandoning their combat positions."[229] Nor were the VRS's problems confined to Doboj: a report written by the VRS Sixth Sanska Brigade, defeated by the Bosnian Army near Gradačac, revealed that about 10% of the brigade's recruits had been interned for disciplinary problems while another 10% were AWOL.[230]

Nor was the situation much better with the Yugoslav Army (VJ), supposedly the VRS's ultimate guarantor. As early as September 1994, Tim Judah, the respected journalist for *The Times* of London, reported that the VJ was nearly bankrupt, that even its officers were simply leaving, and that VJ aircraft were crashing because resources were lacking to keep them airworthy.[231] A lengthy report written for *Globus* by Denis Kuljiš five months later noted that Yugoslavia's military budget was only half the size of Croatia's, that the VJ lacked money to equip itself with modern tanks, that its anti-armor technology was antiquated, and that it no longer had funds for the procurement of new weaponry or for the modernization of its arsenal.[232] Desperate for assistance, Yugoslav defense minister Pavle Bulatović flew to Moscow in late February 1995 for talks with his Russian counterpart, Pavel Grachev. The visit resulted in the signing of an agreement on military cooperation on 28 February, though the exact nature of that agreement was kept vague, probably because of the arms embargo which Belgrade now had reportedly come to regret was still in place.[233] *Krasnaya Zvezda*, the Russian Army newspaper, commented, "[S]ince the United States and Croatia can conclude an agreement on military cooperation, why cannot Russia and Yugoslavia do the same?"[234]

Getting Tough: The Tide Turns (March–August 1995)

Neither the UN arms embargo nor either of Milošević's self-declared embargoes of shipments to the Bosnian Serbs prevented arms from flowing to the warring parties. Indeed, in the case of Milošević's second alleged embargo against the Bosnian Serbs, it was reported that the VJ used bulldozers to clear a new detour road for the shipment of arms, while international observers continued to monitor the old road.[235] In addition to Argentina, South Africa, and the Islamic states, both Russia and the United States were increasingly becoming involved— the U.S. quite directly, in spite of official denials. Indeed, there were confirmed reports of the presence of military advisers from Military Professional Resources, Inc. (MPRI) of Alexandria, Virginia, working with both the Croatian Army and the Bosnian Army; insofar as MPRI made use of former U.S. generals, it would seem to be beyond question that the organization's involvement in the war zone must have been authorized at the highest levels of the U.S. government. The MPRI team in Bosnia was headed by General John Galvin (retired) until April 1995, when Major General John Sewall, the former deputy chief of strategic planning and military policy at the U.S. General Staff, took over. The MPRI team working in Croatia included General Carl Vuono, the former chief of staff of the U.S. Army, General Crosbie "Butch" Saint, the former commander of the U.S. Army in Europe, and Lieutenant-General Ed Soyster, the former chief of the Defense Intelligence Agency. The Italian newspaper *Il Giornale* also reported that the CIA had set up a base on the Croatian island of Krk, from which Predator spy planes were taking off. [236] Americans were said to have played a part in the building of a secret airfield between Visoko and Kakanj for use for weapons shipments to the ARBiH.[237] American-made C-130 cargo planes were also seen landing at Tuzla in February, and it was generally believed that Turkey was operating these flights with U.S. approval as "part of a covert operation by the Central Intelligence Agency to re-arm the Muslims."[238] The CIA also began using Gjadër Air Base in Albania in March 1994 to fly unmanned spy missions over Bosnia and Serbia, using Gnat-750 pilotless drones.[239]

Where the UN-imposed embargoes were concerned (arms embargo against everyone, economic embargo against the FRY), the Albanian and Macedonian borders proved to be completely porous, with goods flowing in both directions; Greek oil companies were said to be shipping fuel to Yugoslavia through Albania. In addition, Russian soldiers in the UN peacekeeping contingent in Croatia sold fuel to Serb insurgents, with Major-General Alexander Perelyakin being accused of having allowed rebel Serb forces to cross into Croatia, of having allowed heavy weapons to pass from Serbia to the area around Knin, and of black marketeering with rebel Serbs: his assignment with the UN peacekeeping contingent was terminated in April 1995.[240] There were also instances of commercial transactions between ARBiH soldiers and VRS soldiers. In March 1994, for example, *NIN* published a report concerning an open-air market at Vučja Planina where Serbian and Muslim soldiers bought and sold various wares, including artillery shells and even mortars. The VRS soldiers were reportedly even willing to deliver munitions to ARBiH soldiers by truck, for the right price.[241] The open-air market at Vučja Planina was only one example of the disjunction between the private and the collective: in collective terms, the two sides were at war; but in private terms, deals could be made, profit could be made, past friendship could be remembered.

In December 1995, Zebulan Pinkas (age 42), incarcerated in a mental ward in Tuzla where he passed the time reading philosophy, reminisced about survival on the front lines:

For months along the front, he said, he and his buddies shouted conversations with Serbs on the other side.

"Once I recognized the voice of a man I knew and I reminded him how we all used to sing together," Pinkas said, "and I begged him to sing a funny song he knew about mothers-in-law."

The Serb sang it, and everyone laughed.

"And then," Pinkas concluded, "everyone started shooting [again]."[242]

NATO Wants to Get Tough

In March 1995, in spite of a three-month old ceasefire, fighting resumed in Bosnia when an envigorated ARBiH launched offensives in the Majevica Mountains east of Tuzla and at Mt. Vlasić. VRS forces withdrew heavy weapons which they had surrendered to a "concentration point" near Sarajevo, while the struggle continued. In early April, the ARBiH scored a strategic victory when its troops drove the VRS off Mt. Vlasić, overlooking the central Bosnian town of Travnik. In the midst of these battles, Karadžić made a public plea for peace.[243]

In NATO councils it was increasingly acknowledged that the limitation of UNPROFOR's mandate to protecting the humanitarian convoys and to protecting itself had not contributed in any perceptible way to a resolution of the conflict; on the contrary, the Anglo-French approach had failed to achieve anyone's objectives. The result was that, as of April 1995, NATO commanders were talking about getting "tough" with the VRS, by sending in about 40,000 alliance troops to evacuate the roughly 24,000 UN "peacekeepers" on the ground and following that up with what was vaguely described as "decisive military action" to resolve the conflict.[244] But for the time being, the VRS seemed to have the upper hand, with the UN having to request permission from the Bosnian Serb Army in order to deliver food to Dutch soldiers serving in the area.

Croatia Gets Tough in "Sector West": Operation Flash

In mid-December 1994, Hrvoje Šarinić, chief adviser to President Tudjman, met with Slobodan Milošević in Belgrade. Milošević told Šarinić on this occasion that he was prepared to recognize Croatia within its internationally recognized borders; this was the first time that the Serbian president had admitted the defeat of the "Greater Serbia" project to a Croatian diplomat. It could also be read as a signal that Milošević would not object to any steps which Croatia might take to reestablish its control in the areas under insurgent control. A month later, Milošević repeated that he was prepared to recognize Croatia within its internationally recognized borders; it was agreed that Croatian foreign minister Mate Granić would visit Belgrade on 15 February with the opening of embassies on the same day and that full mutual recognition would follow on 1 May.[245] Ironically, at the very time when Belgrade's commitment to the Croatian Serbs was flagging, the international community pressed Croatia to agree to the so-called Z-4 plan, which would have provided a legal basis for a permanent Serbian para-state within Croatia.[246] Under pressure, the Croatian government reluctantly agreed to an extension of the UN "peacekeeping" mandate in Croatia, but on condition that its designation be changed from UNPROFOR to UNCRO (United Nations Confidence Restoration Operation in Croatia). Meanwhile, the Croatian Army was engaged in intense preparations for a decisive blow against the insurgents.[247]

The target of the impending campaign was western Slavonia, or "Sector West," as it was called in UN jargon. It was Šarinić's assignment to telephone

General Crabbe, commander of the military component of UNCRO, just before the initiation of hostilities and advise him that the Croatian campaign would begin at 5 A.M. sharp. He called General Crabbe at 3:58 A.M., rousing him from his nocturnal repose. Crabbe became hysterical, according to Šarinić, and tried to object, but eventually he realized that Šarinić was merely conveying information to him and had no authority to call off the operation, even if he had been so disposed. The purpose of the call was not to give Crabbe a chance to talk the Croats out of their campaign, but to allow him to make sure that UNCRO troops stayed out of the line of fire.[248] In fact, the operation began at 5:30, involving some 7,500 HV troops, who quickly overcame the 4,500 Croatian Serb troops in "Sector West." The Croatian troops captured Pakrac, taking control of a 27-kilometer stretch of the "brotherhood and unity" highway. By 5 P.M. on 2 May, the Croatian forces had asserted their dominance in western Slavonia, and by 4 May, they had taken control of all of western Slavonia. Two-thirds of the region's 14,000 Serbs fled immediately; another 2,000 more were evacuated to Bosnia at their own request within the month.[249] By late June, at most 1,500 Serbs remained in western Slavonia.[250]

Serb forces fought back by firing cluster bombs into downtown Zagreb on 2 and 3 May. The attack on 2 May killed at least 10 persons, wounding about 200 persons, and destroying 150 cars as well as one tram; the attack on 3 May killed one person, injuring another 53.[251] The VRS also "responded," in a manner of speaking, by intensifying heavy artillery fire on the Bosnian "safe haven," Bihać.[252] There were also attacks on Croatian Army positions southeast of Osijek the evening of 10 May. According to Croatian defense minister Gojko Šušak, Operation Flash itself took the lives of 188 Serbs—whether civilians or combatants—while 33 Croatian soldiers lost their lives.[253] Subsequently, there were UN reports of HV shelling of Serb refugees fleeing the sector and of looting by Croatian forces. The UN Security Council issued a statement on 4 May condemning the operation and demanding, for the record, that the Croatian Army withdraw from western Slavonia; the Security Council also condemned the bombardment of Zagreb and other population centers by Serb forces. As for Milošević, he made no public statement about Operation Flash, and TV Belgrade reported only very briefly, and even then only after a delay, about the events in "Sector West." Meanwhile, those Serb refugees arriving in Serbia who were judged to be "able-bodied" were force-recruited into the VRS and sent back to the front.[254]

Mladić Gets Tough with the UN

On 7 May, a VRS grenade was fired into Butmir, a Sarajevo suburb, killing 10 persons and wounding about 30. The Bosnian government demanded air strikes against the VRS. British General Rupert Smith, General Rose's successor as UNPROFOR commander in Bosnia, agreed with the Bosnian government and called for air strikes, bombing a VRS ammunition dump at Pale. The VRS replied by firing a grenade into Tuzla, killing 71 mostly younger people and wounding about 150 persons. NATO in turn replied with an air attack on several VRS bunkers. Now, on 26 May, the VRS apprehended between 350 and 400 UN "peacekeepers" and shackled them to bridges and other potential targets of NATO attacks. An angry UNPROFOR spokesperson now condemned the VRS as a "terrorist organization."[255] This single act had demonstrated, for all the world to see, that Karadžić, Mladić, and their adherents were willing to defy the whole world.[256] But Milošević was not amused, and sent Jovica Stanišić, his security chief, to Bosnia to talk with Karadžić. Milošević told Ivor Roberts, the British chargé d'affaires in Belgrade, "Stanišić will tell Karadžić that I will have him killed if he doesn't release the hostages. He knows that I can do it."[257] But the price of their release was Milošević's agreement to send the VRS some urgently needed spare parts for its military machine.[258] There were also rumors floating at the time that France may have promised Mladić to veto any future efforts to launch NATO air strikes against VRS positions and facilities.[259] These rumors proved to lack any real foundation.

Dangerous Escalation

All four parties to the conflict—the Serbs (Belgrade, the VRS, and the Krajina Serbs), the Croats (Zagreb, the HVO), the Bosnian government (and its army), and the international community—were getting impatient. After the UN hostage crisis, Whitehall was also getting fed up and, in the course of a special three-hour cabinet meeting late on Sunday, 28 May, decided on a tangible strengthening of the British contingent in Bosnia, announcing that an additional 1,200 soldiers would be sent to reinforce the 3,380 British soldiers already assigned to UNPROFOR.[260] Additional heavy artillery and tanks would also be sent. On the following day, however, Karadžić declared, in his capacity as supreme commander of the VRS, that the sundry resolutions of the UN were no longer binding on the *Republika Srpska,* which was thereby affirming its sovereignty "over its entire territory and airspace."[261] Implicit in this declaration was Karadžić's indication that UNPROFOR was no longer welcome in Bosnia, at least as far as he was concerned, and that he would henceforth treat the UN mission as a hostile force. Karadžić showed that he meant business when, on 18 June, a VRS tank destroyed a French armored personnel carrier, wounding a French UN "peacekeeper."[262] The following day a French soldier serving with UNPROFOR was shot in the head by a Bosnian Serb sniper.[263]

But Karadžić had to reckon with a general hardening of the line against his posture. French policy vis-à-vis the Bosnian war had changed abruptly after Jacques Chirac assumed the presidency on 17 May 1995 and, already in his first month in office, blasted the Serbs as "an unscrupulous people, terrorists."[264] In Germany, Defense Minister Volker Rühe criticized the UN for its impotence in the face of aggression and declared that the formula of placing NATO forces under the authority of the UN, with the timid Akashi vetoing many requests for air strikes, had failed. Nor was there any reason, Rühe declared, why NATO should ever place itself under UN command in the future.[265] In the U.S., former ambassador to Yugoslavia Warren Zimmermann demanded the lifting of the arms embargo against the Bosnian government and asserted that "Serbs understand only the language of force."[266] For its part, Russia denounced the hostage-taking of UN personnel and emphasized that it would support any measures which would protect UNPROFOR troops from attack.[267] Moscow offered no objections when the Western allies decided to dispatch a "rapid reaction force" of about 14,000 troops.[268] Yasushi Akashi hastened to announce, however, that the Anglo-French-Dutch rapid reaction force "would abide by the tight rules of engagement that have rendered the more than 22,000 UN troops already in Bosnia largely ineffective."[269]

Meanwhile, the fighting continued, with an unprecedented massing of ARBiH troops, up to 30,000, north and northwest of Sarajevo, around the towns of Breza and Visoko. The purpose of the operation was to break through the VRS encirclement of the city, but given the 3-to-1 Serb advantage in tanks and artillery—a result of the UN arms embargo—the ARBiH could not afford a head-on collision with the VRS and instead concentrated its efforts on taking control of supply routes. The ARBiH broke through at several points and, at one point, took control of a key supply route, but shortly thereafter, the VRS reasserted its control of that route.[270] As the battle to break the encirclement raged, VRS gunners fired into Sarajevo's city center, hitting the city's main hospital, killing two patients in their beds; the ARBiH, for its part, fired artillery grenades at Pale for the first time in the war.[271] As the fighting continued, the Bosnian Army became concerned that the "peacekeepers" might be a source of intelligence to the VRS and, therefore, as a precautionary measure, confined them to their compounds; this measure provoked an outcry from UN officials, but no meaningful response.[272] Through it all, the Bosnian government continued to plead for a lifting of the illegal arms embargo, but as ever to no avail.[273]

Potentially the most significant development during June took place not on the battlefield but in inter-Serb relations: specifically, Borislav Mikelić, Milošević's hand-picked prime minister for the Croatian Krajina, was fired by Milan Martić, who proceeded to push for the unification of the Krajina with the *Republika Srpska*. Mikelić worried that unification would strip the Krajina of such international guarantees as it had and would open it to a Croatian military campaign.[274] Then, on 30 June, the Serbs fired a grenade into downtown Sarajevo; given that Sarajevo had been designated a "safe haven," the Bosnian government was disappointed that there was no immediate response from the UN and NATO. The following day, Hasan Muratović, the Bosnian government official responsible for contacts with the UN, announced that his government would have nothing further to do with Akashi.[275] Toward the end of the month, Silajdžić came to Washington, D.C., to plead for a lifting of the arms embargo, either multilaterally or unilaterally by the U.S. Silajdžić met with Vice President Al Gore since President Clinton refused to receive him; Gore told Silajdžić that it was not a good idea to lift the arms embargo because, in the administration's view, "lifting the arms embargo would cause the Serbs to attack the eastern enclaves of Žepa, Goražde, and Srebrenica."[276]

The Serbs Attack Srebrenica and Žepa

Mladić had stood up to the world, had shackled UN "peacekeepers" to bridges, had violated the UN-declared "no-fly" zones, had made a mockery of the "safe havens." By summer 1995 he was strutting around like the new Achilles, experiencing "a perpetual high," indulging in vaporous gasconade in interviews with Western journalists, and issuing threats on a weekly basis.[277] "He is a god," an admirer said of him, "I would follow him anywhere, through the woods or across rivers. He is our savior and the greatest man in the world."[278] Now, in July, this new Achilles was getting ready to take Troy by storm.

In fact, Mladić's forces had maintained a siege of the "safe havens" throughout the war, stepping up the bombardment of one or the other from time to time. In May 1995 he had tried for the second time to overrun Goražde but had once more been stopped. The Bosnian government suspected that Mladić would turn on Srebrenica and Žepa, and the Bosnian Army actually drew up plans to break the Serbian blockade of these two cities, but it was ultimately decided to devote ARBiH resources to an effort to break the siege of Sarajevo instead.[279] But Belgrade had been reinforcing Mladić's troops over the previous several weeks, sending in not its demoralized and poorly paid VJ troops but rather the more highly motivated and better paid MUP special units.[280] About the same time, Milošević sent VJ General Mile Mrkšić, a veteran of the siege of Vukovar, to take command of Krajina Serb forces in the Croatian Krajina; Mrkšić arrived with a fleet of new tanks from Serbia.[281]

Of the six "safe havens," only Sarajevo was guarded by a more or less serious UNPROFOR contingent, as the figures in Table 15.5 make clear. During the first week of July, the VRS stepped up the pressure on four of the "safe havens," with artillery bombardment of Sarajevo, heavy pressure on Goražde, and VRS air strikes against both Bihać in the northwest and Srebrenica in the east.[282] Srebrenica was, because of its geographic situation, among other reasons, the most vulnerable of the six "havens," but until the last minute, foreign observers could not be entirely sure just what Mladić's intentions were. It seemed unlikely that he meant to take all four of these "safe havens" at once, and he had been playing cat-and-mouse with UNPROFOR for so long that UNPROFOR was no longer able—if it had ever been—to judge the seriousness of any potential threat. Mladić's forces subjected Srebrenica to heavy bombardment and then paused, to see if UNPROFOR or NATO would respond. But in the three weeks beginning on 15 June, VRS shelling of Srebrenica killed 95 civilians and wounded 436 in a supposed "*safe* haven," and UNPROFOR did nothing.[283] The Dutch battalion ("Dutchbat") had been equipped with TOW missiles which could be used to destroy tanks, but Dutchbat needed spare parts to keep the missiles operable;

when they tried to bring the spare parts into the enclave, the VRS confiscated them, leaving the missiles inoperable.[284] There was no response from UNPRO-FOR. Mladić began his assault on Srebrenica on 6 July with his trademark strike-and-wait tactics which left the small Dutch force uncertain as to whether there was a real threat or not.[285] In the evening of 9 July, the staff of Lieutenant General Bernard Janvier, who had by then succeeded Rupert Smith as UNPROFOR commander, recommended to the general that there be close air support for Dutchbat; Janvier refused, however. As late as 10 July, the UN officials assessed that the VRS's objectives at Srebrenica were "limited," and limited themselves to uttering threats of air strikes.[286] Mladić, quite obviously, was not impressed. Only at the last minute—at 8 A.M. on 11 July—did the Dutch contingent request air strikes. Janvier turned down the request, but by noon the VRS forces were already walking into Srebrenica. The Dutch made a second request at that point, and Janvier now changed his mind and ordered air strikes. Four U.S. F-16 fighter aircraft were sent in and destroyed one VRS tank. Mladić now threatened to have the Dutch "peacekeepers" executed if there were any further air strikes; this threat was conveyed to Akashi, who ordered that air strikes be terminated.[287] Back in New York, the UN Security Council passed a resolution demanding that Bosnian Serb forces leave Srebrenica—to which RS president Karadžić declared, "Srebrenica is our land!"[288] On 12 July, Mladić's forces separated able-bodied men from women, children, and elderly men, removing the men for slaughter. Many witnesses heard screams during the night of 12 July.[289] By the end of the following day, Mladić's forces had killed more than 7,000 men; troops who showed any reluctance to shoot the unarmed civilians were told that if they did not want to kill, they could join the civilians and be executed.[290] By May 2003, the bodies of more than 5,000 victims of the massacre at Srebrenica had been exhumed by UN authorities.[291]

On 12 July, Bosnian Serb troops surrounded the Dutchbat camp at Potočari, a village just outside Srebrenica. The Dutch were forced to strip; the VRS soldiers took their uniforms and put them on. In the meantime, the women, children, and elderly had been driven to Potočari, from which they were told they would be evacuated. The evacuations began on 13 July, but were temporarily halted that same evening. VRS soldiers now came into the area where the civilians had been brought and picked out about 30 boys, saying that they wanted to talk to them; shortly after that, witnesses heard terrible screams, and the boys were never seen again.[292] About 50 buses were made available to transport the women, children, and elderly from Potočari to the border of VRS-held territory near Tišća. The drive took approximately two and a half hours. The displaced then had to walk six to eight kilometers in order to reach government-held territory. During the drive, Bosnian Serb soldiers stopped the buses several times to demand money and jewelry. Men of military age who had tried to ride the buses were caught during these stops and pulled off the buses.

Some residents of Srebrenica had fled the town during the night of 11 July; the number has been estimated at 12,000–15,000.[293] The VRS was not unaware

Table 15.5. The UN Safe Havens (1 July 1995)

City	Population	UN Blue Helmets
Bihać	227,000	1,244
Tuzla	446,000	1,139
Srebrenica	40,000	400
Žepa	15,000	69
Goražde	60,000	300
Sarajevo	430,000	6,690

Source: Der Spiegel (Hamburg), no. 29/1995, p. 113; and *Scotland on Sunday,* 16
July 1995, p. 1.

of the attempted escape by this 10-kilometer-long column of people and harassed the refugees as they tried to make their escape. One survivor, identified only as I.N., recalled a month later:

On July 12, around 11 A.M., I left Srebrenica with approximately 6,000 to 7,000 men. Our scouts told us to leave by walking in two columns because everything in the area was mined. We were so vulnerable to ambushes—walking in two long columns like that— but it was the only thing we could do to avoid getting blown up [by mines]. . . . After about three kilometers, we encountered our first ambush at a stream. The center of our column was hit by anti-aircraft machine guns (PAMs) and mortars; around 200 people died just from that. The Chetniks then came down from the hills, and about 2,000 men from the middle of the column got caught in the line of fire. The people at the front and back of the columns scattered everywhere. I was in the middle and saw how the Serbs were shooting everyone and slaughtering us with bayonets.[294]

When night fell, Bosnian Serb soldiers in civilian clothes infiltrated the column, spreading disinformation, trying to lead people in the wrong direction, passing around poisoned water, and injecting the wounded with hallucinatory drugs. I.N.'s account continues:

As night fell, we saw groups of men merging into our column. I saw unfamiliar faces; one of them started saying, "Hurry up with the wounded! Hurry up with the wounded!" All of a sudden we realized that the unfamiliar men were Chetniks who had infiltrated our column. There [were] a lot of them, about 300. They ordered us to leave the injured and wounded at the side of the road, while their men started giving them injections and making them swallow some kind of pills. Later, people who were at the end of our column said that the injured and wounded people looked like they were dying after they were injected or forced to swallow the pills.

All of a sudden, in all that chaos, we noticed that the Chetniks had suddenly disappeared; panic erupted. We were all in a meadow, when shooting suddenly erupted from a hill behind us. I ran for the woods right away. The Chetniks came out into the meadow and started to kill and slaughter everyone they could. I ran about 500 meters with about twenty guys towards a creek when suddenly three grenades emitting red fire and smoke dropped in front of us. My eyes, nose, and mouth started stinging. I thought it was some kind of poison, and for the first time, I became really frightened that I was going to die.

Fortunately, a wind started carrying the smoke up the hill, so I turned downhill with about five guys. The stinging lasted for about half an hour. We descended to a creek where we heard running water. We wanted to go in, but we saw about twenty massacred bodies floating in it, some decapitated.[295]

In some cases, the VRS soldiers, wearing blue helmets and driving the white jeeps they had confiscated from the Dutch, lured even the women and children into traps. The entire operation, in which unarmed civilians, refugees fleeing for their lives, were ambushed, picked off, given lethal injections, shot and mutilated, had no conceivable military value.[296] It was motivated by a combination of desire to terrorize the Bosniaks, hatred, sheer brutality, and, arguably, the pressure of "group think"; it is reasonable to suspect that Mladić personally organized the ambushes of the fleeing refugees.

Instead of mobilizing the "rapid reaction force" or calling for air strikes against the Serbs or making some other convincing response to this butchery, the UN reacted in the weakest way imaginable. Boutros-Ghali, for example, declared after the fall of Srebrenica, "In spite of the aggression, negotiation is for the time being the only way to find a solution."[297] French president Chirac noted that if the major democracies proved unwilling to respond to such a massive atrocity, then they would discredit themselves,[298] while in Washington, D.C., President Clinton issued a threat of immediate NATO air strikes if the VRS were to attack Goražde. But the VRS was turning against Žepa, not Goražde, and, on 17–18 July 1995, ratcheted up the pressure on this town of now 15,000 inhabitants, with its nominal UNPROFOR presence of 69 troops.[299] The VRS took the local Ukrainian UNPROFOR "peacekeepers" into custody on 17 July and threatened to kill them if any NATO warplanes appeared in the sky. Žepa is situated on top of a hill and, on the face of it, should have been defensible, given the will and the military resources. But NATO/UNPROFOR, which had the resources, lacked the will. On 19 July came the announcement that Žepa's political representatives had negotiated terms of surrender with the VRS; in exchange for guarantees of safety, they surrendered the town.[300] The VRS honored its word this time, and by the beginning of August, the civilian population had been successfully evacuated to safety. The Serb troops now looted Žepa and torched it.[301]

By this point, many in the West were prepared to agree with Jonathan Clarke, a former member of the British diplomatic service, who, in an opinion piece for the *Los Angeles Times,* declared,

The fact of the matter is that . . . the Serbs have won the war in Bosnia. . . . [It would be best] to tell the Bosnians that the West is not coming to their aid, that half-baked proposals like lifting the arms embargo will only make their defeat more complete and, therefore, they should cut the best deal they can today. Because tomorrow the deal will be worse. It is all too easy to savage a proposal of this kind. The victim is indeed being punished. But preference for the easy option has been the cancer at the heart of American policy toward Bosnia.[302]

But this opinion was offered under the influence of the VRS's conquest of the undefended city of Srebrenica, in which the small Dutch force possessed inoperable missile systems and with NATO unwilling, not unable, to come to its defense. Moreover, although the arms embargo had not been formally lifted, it had been violated during the entire war, and the Iranian arms flow since April 1994 had already contributed to transforming the military effectiveness of both the Croatian Army and the Bosnian Army. Moreover, elsewhere in Bosnia, where actual military conflict was taking place, the ARBiH was making territorial gains at the expense of the VRS.[303]

By the end of the month, the International Criminal Tribunal for the former Yugoslavia (ICTY) had drawn the obvious conclusions from the massacres at Srebrenica and indicted Karadžić and Mladić for war crimes, also indicting Karadžić for genocide. Meanwhile, in Paris, government spokespersons were sounding a more belligerent tone than heretofore. But while the U.S. Senate voted, 69 to 29, to lift the arms embargo against the Bosnian Muslims, a Russian foreign affairs expert serving as a member of Russia's presidential council warned against any such action, adding that if the U.S. took such an action for the Muslims, Russia would consider doing the same for the Serbs.[304] Perversely, Russian prime minister Viktor Chernomyrdin chose this moment to say that he favored "the lifting of sanctions against Yugoslavia and categorically opposed the bombing of Bosnian Serb positions that would possibly be carried out by NATO."[305] NATO councils limited themselves to a pledge to defend Goražde (though NATO's defense of Sarajevo could be taken for granted), while General Bernard Janvier offered his opinion that it was not UNPROFOR's assignment to protect the locals and that it was not in a position to defend Bihać, in the event of a Serb attack on that city.[306] But if UNPROFOR was not in a position to defend Bihać, the Croatian Army was.

Operation Storm

As is well known, after taking control of the Krajina, the Krajina Serbs had expelled some 117,000 Croats from the region.[307] Croatia had been preparing for a strike against the Krajina for weeks, and these preparations were well known to the Croatian Serb insurgents in the Krajina. In fact, on 22 July 1995, Presidents Tudjman and Izetbegović met in Split and signed a declaration in which Tudjman agreed to the formal request of the Bosnian president to provide emergency military assistance, especially in the Bihać region.[308] In the days immediately preceding "Operation Storm," as the Croatian Army's thrust into the Krajina would be called, Croatian Army personnel, tanks, and heavy artillery were being concentrated along the border with the Krajina and Bihać, while the Krajina Serb and Bosnian Serb authorities declared a general mobilization.[309] As these preparations were underway, UN deputy secretary-general Kofi Annan and UNPROFOR commander General Janvier gave a press conference in Brussels in which they announced that they were readying air strikes against the Bosnian Serbs in the event that they were needed to protect Bihać.[310]

By the end of July, the Croats had mobilized some 160,000 well-trained and well-armed troops ready to throw against the Krajina Serbs' 20,000–30,000 troops, among whom discipline had broken down and whose arms stock was failing for lack of spare parts.[311] After some preliminary artillery exchanges around the village of Srmica, near Knin, the Croatian offensive started on 4 August; approximately 100,000 HV troops, commanded by General Ante Gotovina, and special units of the police were involved in the assault, giving the Croats a massive numerical advantage over the defenders.[312] Given the Croats' overwhelming advantage both in quantitative terms and in qualitative terms, and given the failure of either the VRS or the VJ to come to the Krajina Serbs' rescue, the operation was swift. By 7 August, the Croatian forces had taken control of the entire Krajina, with the last battle between the Krajina Serb forces and the Croatian Army taking place on 11 August in the city of Dvor on the border with Bosnia.[313] Martić's frantic appeals to Milošević to provide assistance got him nowhere.[314] Some 150,000 Krajina Serbs fled eastward, heading for Bosnia and Serbia.[315] According to preliminary figures cited by James Sadkovich, the total number of casualties in Operation Storm came to 750 Serbs and 174 Croats killed.[316] Revised figures were provided by Human Rights Watch/Helsinki a year later; according to these revised figures, a total of 526 Serbs were killed during the operation, i.e., fewer than originally thought, while 211 Croatian soldiers and police officers, alongside 42 Croatian civilians, lost their lives at that time. There were confirmed reports of looting by Croatian troops, as well as burning of Serbian property, continuing for months after the offensive; according to Human Rights Watch, Bosnian Army soldiers from the Bihać enclave crossed into the Krajina in order to join in some of the looting of Serb homes.[317] The looting was so excessive that after reviewing the evidence, Archbishop Franjo Kuharić felt constrained to raise his voice in protest.[318] Meanwhile, Tudjman donned his smartest military uniform—apparently modeled on Tito's uniforms—and struck a grand pose for the camera, right hand stretched across his chest as if to pull a handkerchief from his pocket. The pose inspired the British weekly *The Economist* to dub him "Napoleon Tudjman."[319]

Bosnian Serbs, who had been expelling Croats and Muslims from Banja Luka, Bosanska Krajina, and Bijeljina throughout the war, replied by expelling additional Croats from Banja Luka, a city in which there had been no combat whatsoever during the entire war, bringing the number of Croats down from a prewar presence of about 300,000 to fewer than 15,000.[320] In Serbia, Yugoslav authorities rounded up men of military age among the Krajina Serb refugees in order to send them to Bosnia to join the VRS. As for Serbia's entering the war, however, this was out of question for economic, political, military, logistical, and diplomatic reasons. Indeed, an opinion poll conducted by the Partner Agency among 1,000 citizens of Yugoslavia found that only 24.4% of those surveyed thought that the FRY should enter the war, while 37.1% opposed this; some 38.5% either had not made up their minds or had no opinion.[321]

NATO Air Strikes and After

On 28 August 1995, a mortar shell struck Sarajevo's central market, killing at least 37 persons and wounding more than 80.[322] Coming just after the fatal attack on three high-ranking diplomats who had been driving on the Mount Igman road to Sarajevo, this was the proverbial last straw. In spite of Serb nationalist protests that the Bosnian government was behind the attack, experts quickly established beyond any reasonable doubt that the shell had been fired from VRS positions. Even the Russians, up to now staunch allies of the Serbs, had had enough and condemned the shelling.[323] When, on 30 August, 60 NATO aircraft initiated the bombing of VRS missile sites, radar sites, communications facilities, heavy artillery, ammunitions dumps, and other targets, a senior member of the Russian foreign ministry issued a statement calling NATO's response justified and explaining, "There are certain limits beyond which actions by the parties involved in the conflict in Bosnia cannot be left without answer. The Serbs overstepped those limits."[324] After two days of bombing, NATO paused, resuming the bombing on 5 September and continuing it for more than 10 days. Although the Russians and the Greeks eventually began to suggest that the air strikes should be brought to an end as soon as possible, NATO continued to bomb until the VRS had pulled its heavy weapons out of the UN weapons exclusion zones and gave some signs, judged convincing, of a willingness to abide by UN resolutions. Meanwhile, under the cover of the NATO air strikes, Bosnian and Croatian forces pushed into western Bosnia, rolling the Serbs out of Jajce and coming within striking distance of Banja Luka. U.S. assistant secretary of state Richard Holbrooke was sent in as peacemaker and presented a draft agreement to Milošević, Karadžić, and Mladić on 13 September, calling for the cessation of all offensive operations in the Sarajevo environs within the week. Holbrooke also met with Tudjman on 14 September and 17 September, and with Holbrooke's encouragement, Croatian forces swept into Sanski Most, Prijedor, and Bosanski Novi; Holbrooke indicated that their conquest would strengthen Croatia's bargaining hand at the eventual peace talks.[325] The Croatian advance continued until 19 September, when the HV was stopped by the VRS at the Una River. The last major operation of the ARBiH was conducted 13 September–12 October 1995, with the engagement of about 16,000 troops; in this operation, the Bosnian Army took back Kulen Vakuf, Bosanska Krupa, Otoka, Bosanski Petrovac, Ključ, and Sanica, and participated in the Croatian liberation of Sanski Most. Bosnian Army casualties were 178 dead, 588 wounded, and 41 captured; VRS losses came to more than 900 soldiers killed and more than 1,000 wounded during this operation.[326] By this point, not only Milošević but also Karadžić, Mladić, Tudjman, and Izetbegović were more than ready to sit down for peace talks; in the meantime, Milošević had accepted an agreement on the peaceful reintegration of eastern Slavonia into Croatia on Croatia's terms, i.e., without a referendum. The Croatian reconquest of the Krajina and the NATO bombing of VRS positions during August–September had succeeded in bringing the Bosnian Serbs to the negotiating table. The Americans arranged that Milošević would negotiate on behalf of the Bosnian Serbs and Tudjman on behalf of the Bosnian Croats, and brought those two men, together with Bosnian president Izetbegović, to Dayton, Ohio, on 1 November to begin peace talks. Two principles were established from the beginning: (1) that two entities (one Serb, one Croat-Muslim) would enjoy wide-ranging autonomy within the framework of a unified Bosnian state, and (2) that the division of land between the two sides would be handled in such a way as to assign 51% of the land to the Croat-Muslim federation and 49% to the *Republika Srpska*. The negotiations dragged on because of disagreements concerning the details, with Milošević entertaining the staff by playing at the piano and singing show tunes. Finally, on 21 November 1995 the three sides reached an agreement.[327] The war had ended, and a stop had been put to the worst of the atrocities.

Tallying Up the Costs of War

In 1998, the distinguished Croatian demographer Vladimir Žerjavić estimated the number of casualties in the Bosnian War. His estimate was that some 215,000 persons had died as a direct result of the fighting (see Table 15.6). According to his estimates, Muslims accounted for most of the casualties (160,000), while Serbs were responsible for most of the deaths (by his estimates, for 186,000 of the dead). The CIA offered a slightly higher estimate, suggesting that as many as 237,500 (156,000 civilians and 81,500 military personnel) had lost their lives in the war, all but 10,000 of the civilians in parts of the country held by the Bosnian government or HVO.[328] Some 2.7 million persons had been displaced from their homes.[329] In Sarajevo alone, at least 10,500 persons were killed and about 50,000 wounded.[330] By November 1992, "more than 70% of the historical buildings, places of worship, cemeteries, libraries, and archives had already been destroyed."[331] The National and University Library of Sarajevo had been bombed by Bosnian Serb forces on 25 August 1992, resulting in the destruction of more than 600,000 books constituting nearly 40% of the collection.[332]

Then there were the economic costs. All told, the estimated cost of the damage to Bosnia's economy, 1992–1995, came to about $115 billion—a staggering amount. As of 1996, the GNP of Bosnia-Herzegovina was less than one-fourth of its 1991 GNP; industrial production stood at 10% of the 1991 level; as of 1996, 60% of Bosnia's inhabitants lived below the poverty line.[333] Sarajevo had emerged from World War Two with less than 5% of its buildings damaged, and as of May 1945, 100 percent of its public utilities were in operation.[334] The story 50 years later was very different. Across Bosnia as a whole, about 60% of all

Table 15.6. **War Dead in Bosnia-Herzegovina, 1992–1995**

	Killed by Muslims	Killed by Croats	Killed by Serbs	Total killed
Muslims	—	2,000	158,000	160,000
Croats	2,000	—	28,000	30,000
Serbs	12,500	12,500	—	25,000
Totals	14,500	14,500	186,000	215,000

Source: Estimates provided by the Croatian demographer Vladimir Žerjavić in Dražen Rajković, "Tragična bilansa," *Globus* (Zagreb), 9 January 1998, p. 24.

homes were damaged or destroyed; Rory O'Sullivan, a World Bank official, estimated the cost of rebuilding at $25 billion.[335] The war had also provided conditions in which ordinary criminals could get rich quickly and in which organized crime grew rapidly, subverting the legitimate economy and retaining the potential to impede the development of a truly free economy.[336] In addition, the brain drain during the war years, affecting especially Serbia and Bosnia-Herzegovina, threatened to have a long-term impact not only in cultural and scientific terms, but also in economic terms.[337]

The war has also had effects on the physical and mental health of locals. In 1993, for example, *Vreme* and *Politika* reported the outbreak of tuberculosis, malaria, and typhus, alongside other diseases which had supposedly been conquered.[338] The psychological health of the residents of Croatia, Bosnia, and Serbia was damaged, too, with an ongoing rash of cases of depression, deep stress and post-traumatic stress disorder (PTSD), sleeping problems, nightmares, schizophrenia, startle reactions, withdrawal, alcoholism, and fear of places or situations which remind the person of a traumatic event.[339] In Croatia, for example, about 400,000 persons, accounting for nearly 10% of the population, sought psychiatric help in 2000—in 38% of the cases for schizophrenia and in 9% for deep stress and PTSD.[340] In Bosnia, some 1,700,000 citizens experienced psychological problems after the war (among them, one out of every three children), according to Muhamed Sestanović, a scientific associate of the Sarajevo Institute for Investigating Crimes against Humanity and International Law;[341] moreover, up to 60% of the population may be suffering from PTSD, and psychiatrists say that in some cases entire towns or regions may be affected by the disorder.[342] According to *Nova Bosna,* a huge number of Serbs (of Bosnia) participated in atrocities or witnessed them passively.[343] Whether any of them will ever recover their prewar innocence and psychological serenity may be doubted. Nor is time guaranteed to "heal all wounds": Dr. Richard Mollica, head of a research team from Harvard University studying trauma victims, said that "people who experience mass violence or torture are unable to recover good mental health, irrespective of the passage of time."[344]

The increase in reported domestic violence is a related phenomenon and is widely believed to be, at least in part, a result of war-induced stress. Domestic violence has been found to be "more prevalent in conflict-torn societies," and in Bosnia-Herzegovina, one in every three women has been a victim of domestic violence.[345] While the phenomenon usually involves women being beaten by their husbands and boyfriends, in Mostar an SOS hotline reported a sharp increase in the number of mothers being beaten by their sons—a phenomenon largely unknown before the war.[346] Still, some of the increase in the reportage of domestic violence may be due to the significant increase in the number of women's centers and SOS hotlines since 1991, to increased awareness that domestic violence is not "tradition," and to an increased willingness, since the war, to speak out about violence.

Nor were people the only ones to suffer. When Bosnian Serb forces began to subject Sarajevo to systematic bombardment, zookeepers were afraid to expose themselves to danger and did not feed the animals; after some weeks during which the animals could be heard crying out from hunger, the zoo went silent—the animals had died. Nor did animals elsewhere in Bosnia fare much better.

The trauma of the war is also likely to affect the next generation. As unpublished work by Robert Pynoos (as summarized by Jeffrey Prager) has shown, traumatic experience "yields thoughts and actions that continually re-create in [the] mind the experience of danger and helplessness. Such experiences result in altered schematizations of 'safety, security, risk, injury, loss, protection and intervention.' . . . [The resulting traumatic] expectations become transmitted to the next generation 'verbally, through unusual anxious behavior, and by means of imposed behavioral avoidance that limits developmental opportunities.'"[347]

And finally, there are the lessons learned, or perhaps better, relearned. Here one may speak not only about lessons concerning the fallacy of a delayed response to serious crisis, about the dangers of chauvinism and intolerance, or about the readiness of foreign publics and foreign statesmen to find it "impossible" to believe reports of atrocities.[348] One may also speak of lessons about the primacy of human rights over sovereignty, lessons which are already impacting international law, driving further evolution in international law and in international understandings of universal moral standards. The work of Norman Cigar, Thomas Cushman, James Gow, Andreas Hasenclever, James Sadkovich, and Michael J. Smith in presenting the war as a moral problem and in judging the international response as morally bankrupt may be highlighted.[349] W. Michael Reisman and Rasmus Tenbergen, the former casting his net more widely and the latter focusing primarily on the lessons to be drawn from the case of Kosovo, have incontrovertibly advanced the state of knowledge about international norms.[350] Jean Baudrillard, a French academic known for his theory that advertising has created "an implosion of meaning," believes that intellectuals are "an endangered species" whose "ability to intervene in international events is over," so that their role is "reduced to that of commentators."[351] But commentary is not necessarily nugatory; informed commentary may, on the contrary, have both immediate and delayed impact. One immediate impact of the rethinking provoked by the Bosnian war is that rape, sexual slavery, and forced prostitution in conditions of armed conflict have now been classified as war crimes.[352] Another impact is a growing consensus that, under appropriate conditions, humanitarian intervention may be not merely legitimate but obligatory. This growing consensus reflects what Andreas Hasenclever has called "a transformation in the moral structure of the problem field," reflecting a change in how we understand the scope of human rights and how we understand our duties when human rights are systematically violated.[353]

CHAPTER 16

A Flawed Peace: Post-Dayton Bosnia

Since the signing of the Dayton Peace Accords at Versailles on 14 December 1995, a debate has raged between advocates of what we might call the "Kemalist" model and advocates of what could be termed the "Weimar" model. "Kemalists," like Kemal Ataturk, believe that the successful construction of a democratic system requires that there already be some progress toward the development of a liberal political culture before locals are allowed to run their own system—in other words, that there are circumstances in which stable liberal democracy can only be built from above, according to a plan which prioritizes education for tolerance over the holding of elections. Advocates of a "Kemalist" approach include Marie-Janine Calic and Jack Snyder. Calic, for example, writes that "in and of themselves, elections are . . . no guarantee for the stabilization of peace." While she does not trivialize the need to build democratic institutions and include citizens in the political process, she emphasizes "national reconciliation, which will guarantee the members of the several nationalities a life in security," underlines the importance of "the development of an educational and cultural policy oriented toward tolerance," and urges that "the political pressure "from above" must be complemented by the promotion of civil society structures 'from below.'"[1] What marks her as a "Kemalist" is her fear that locals in Bosnia-Herzegovina cannot do this for themselves and must, therefore, rely on international authorities to assist them. Along similar lines, Snyder argues that in building a civic state in a multi-ethnic setting, one should delay the expansion of political participation until liberal norms and practices have been successfully promulgated and warns of the dangers entailed in expanding freedom of speech in illiberal settings. He also warns that "factionalism in politics during . . . democratization [in multi-ethnic states] often follows ethnic lines. And given that starting point, effective institutions for channeling social cleavages in other directions need to be well developed before democratization can be part of the solution rather than part of the problem."[2] The "Kemalist" point of view entails the acceptance of the principle, argued by Fareed Zakaria, that liberalism may exist apart from democracy and democracy apart from liberalism, and that, therefore, in the quest for liberal democracy, it may be prudential to begin with the development of liberalism before undertaking democratization.[3]

I have called the alternative point of view a "Weimarist" viewpoint *not* because I want the reader to believe that some form of rightwing extremism is inevitable when democratic institutions are set up before a liberal culture has been nurtured, but because the underlying supposition is that when it comes to liberalism and democracy, "you can't have one without the other," as Marc Plattner has put it,[4] and that therefore the only sensible strategy to build democracy is to push ahead with elections as quickly as possible and allow locals to build democracy their own way. This was the approach taken in the case of Weimar Germany, which built its system with minimal external support or involvement (unless one counts the temporary French occupation of the Saarland and the heavy reparations as manifestations of foreign "involvement"). The leading advocates of this approach are David Chandler, Elizabeth Cousens, and Charles Cater. Chandler argues that the delay in surrendering full authority for Bosnia to those living there serves no useful purpose and only delays the process of democratization; to his mind, what residents of Bosnia have been offered by the Office of the High Representative (OHR) and other international bodies is at best a "fake" democracy.[5] Along similar lines, Cousens and Cater, in a collaborative work, warn that "To attempt to implement democratic reforms through what are viewed as nondemocratic methods is inherently contradictory."[6] Moreover, in their view, the empowerment of the OHR, in late 1997, to dismiss public officials and to issue binding decrees is "a troubling precedent . . . , not least because resort to OHR power may undermine both indigenous democratization and the legitimacy of the international community's presence in Bosnia."[7] The challenge inherent in pushing for rapid democratization in a society with little or no experience with liberal democracy and divided by the resentments stoked up by intercommunal warfare is that people's electoral choices will be guided by illiberal motivations. As Sumantra Bose has noted of the officials dismissed by High Representatives Carlos Westendorp (1996–1999) and Wolfgang Petrisch (1999–2002),

it is stretching credulity to claim that [these officials] had "failed the voters who elected them." The voters who elected these persons to their offices generally did not do so in the hope and expectation that they would toil to promote inter-ethnic harmony and coexistence. To the contrary, in many instances it is likely that these individuals won election because their voters believed that they would strive towards just the opposite once elected.[8]

The "Weimar" approach did not work in postwar Germany in the interwar era. Could it work in postwar Bosnia? The question has both theoretical and practical dimensions. On the theoretical side, it is not just a matter of looking for counterexamples, unless one also takes note of which factors are the same and which are different from one case to another. On the practical side, one needs to keep in mind that these two approaches have been presented as ideal types, and that actual practice need not stick strictly to either one; it is, for example, possible to encourage the development of grass roots civic organizations and to actively promote local democracy, while retaining, for an interim period, a firm rudder where national politics are concerned.

The Dayton Structure

The Dayton Accords simultaneously established an overarching government for Bosnia-Herzegovina, with a constitution vesting sovereignty in that government alone, and sanctioned the continuance of separate administrative authorities for two constituent "entities"—the Croat-Bosniak Federation and the *Republika Srpska*. Within the Federation, although the Croatian Republic of Herceg-Bosna had been officially dissolved at Dayton, the Bosnian Croats continued to assert considerable independence, to a degree in violation of the constitutional order. The HVO was, in theory, converted into a Croatian Corps and integrated into the ARBiH, but in practice there continued to be close ties between the Croatian Corps and the Croatian Army, as well as between the Bosnian Croat political authorities (all of them HDZ) and authorities in the Republic of Croatia.[9] This close relationship ended only with the death of Tudjman at the end of 1999 and the election of a non-HDZ government. The *Republika Srpska* (literally, the Serbian Republic) was so-named in order to affirm that the ruling SDS remained committed to integrating Serb-controlled areas into the Republic of Serbia. Miloš Milinčić, president of the municipal committee of Sarajevo and member of the SDS ruling committee, openly declared that from the point of view of his party, "[t]he *sole* value of the Dayton agreement is that the Serb Republic was recognized as an *independent* entity in relation to the Muslim-Croat Federation, which means that *we can proceed with creating an independent Serb state* and realizing the final Serb national interest."[10]

The Dayton Accords provided that the government for Bosnia-Herzegovina as a whole would have effective power, exercised through a collective presidency, a bicameral legislature, and a constitutional court, one third of whose members would be selected by the European Court of Human Rights. Annex 6 of the Dayton Accords provided for the establishment of a 14-member Human Rights Chamber, empowered to hear human rights cases and complaints brought to its attention, and an independent human rights ombudsman. These bodies were established only after a delay; Gret Haller of Switzerland was appointed to serve as Bosnia's first ombudsman, while a majority of the members of the Human Rights Chamber were appointed by the Council of Europe. The Dayton Accords also provided for the establishment of *a secure environment* (to be realized through partial disarmament, the integration of paramilitary forces into the armed forces of the two entities, and the dispatch of some 60,000 Implementation Force (IFOR) peacekeepers), the restoration of freedom of movement, the return of internally displaced persons and refugees to their prewar homes, the arrest of persons indicted for war crimes, and the creation of "conditions in which free elections can be held, by protecting the right to vote without fear of intimidation and ensuring freedom of speech, the press and association."[11] The Organization for Security and Cooperation in Europe (OSCE) was placed under obligation to certify when conditions appropriate for the holding of free elections existed. The Dayton Accords also placed Serbia, Croatia, and all three governments in Bosnia-Herzegovina under obligation to cooperate with the International Criminal Tribunal for the former Yugoslavia (ICTY) in The Hague, by arresting and turning over those indicted for war crimes. Among these were Radovan Karadžić, then still serving as president of the *Republika Srpska* (RS), and General Ratko Mladić, still serving as commander of the VRS. IFOR was authorized "to detain indicted war criminals and hand them over to the International Tribunal if they are encountered by IFOR personnel during the normal course of their duties and [if] the tactical situation permits. IFOR, however, has no mandate from the North Atlantic Council, which provides its policy guidance, to actually seek out and hunt down indicted war criminals."[12] But critics later charged that IFOR had had "many chances" to arrest Karadžić and Mladić during the year it was in place (before being replaced by the Stabilization Force, SFOR) but preferred to turn a blind eye—perhaps for fear of provoking a reaction from nationalistic Serbs.[13]

The international community's formula for Bosnia has been neither "Kemalist" nor "Weimarist" but a mixture of the two. The leading "Kemalists" to date have been High Representatives Carlos Westendorp and Wolfgang Petritsch; asserting their preemptory powers, these High Representatives removed various officeholders from office, including Nikola Poplašen of the SDS, a former commander in the VRS, from the office of RS president, in March 1999, and Ante Jelavić, HDZ-Bosnian president, from the presidency of Bosnia-Herzegovina in spring 2002. The leading "Weimarists" have been the Americans, with their blind faith in the ballot box. Secretary of State Madeleine K. Albright gave an optimistic assessment from a "Weimarist" point of view when she told the House National Security Committee in March 1998 that "far from finding ourselves Bosnia's permanent administrators, we are handing more and more responsibility back to multi-ethnic institutions."[14] Haris Silajdžić, the former prime minister of Bosnia-Herzegovina, criticized the international pressure to hold elections before the return of the refugees. In his view, holding elections in the RS in the absence of 750,000 of its prewar residents was unconscionable and could scarcely be reconciled with customary notions of democratic life.[15] Indeed, the key to understanding why the nationalist parties which were trying to block the return of refugees kept winning—including in the parliamentary elections of October 2002—has lain precisely in the vested interest of those who are on hand to vote. In other words, by rushing to hold elections before the majority of refugees wanting to return had been able to do so, the international community assured that the local voters, in many cases occupying houses belonging to would-be returnees, would keep voting for the nationalist parties which do not, in fact, want to see a complete fulfillment of the conditions specified at Dayton.

Off to a Rocky Start

On the occasion of the signing of the Dayton Peace Accords, Karadžić declared the abolition of the state of war; ominously, he converted it only into "a state of immediate war danger."[16] Under the circumstances, it was not surprising that, throughout 1996, the *Republika Srpska* continued to operate on the basis of regulations adopted for a state of war, regulations which resulted in a curtailment of certain human rights.[17] As of the end of 1995, unemployment was estimated at about 90%, the GDP had contracted by an estimated 75% since 1991, an estimated 3 million landmines had been planted, making Bosnia "one of the most heavily mined places in the world," and about 70% of the adult population was female, as a result of both the killing of mostly male soldiers and the flight of draft-age men abroad.[18] Depleted uranium from weapons used in 1994 and 1995 had contaminated local supplies of drinking water as well as the air, and by the beginning of 2001, sharp increases in the incidence of leukemia and cancer among the local population were being reported.[19] Prostitution and the trafficking of women both into Bosnia and out of Bosnia quickly became a problem, and, in the context of "the high levels of mental disorder and the high levels of depression, anxiety, and aggression" already outlined in the previous chapter, suicides rose dramatically, especially in the RS, where mental health services were poorer than in the Federation.[20] Then there were those who remained unaccounted for—presumed dead—for whose last remains the search continued; by July 2003, more than 15,000 bodies had been exhumed, while authorities are still searching, at this writing, for the bodies of more than 20,000 Bosnian citizens who are presumed to be lying in mass graves.[21] In March 1997, the first UN expert on missing persons in the former Yugoslavia—Manfred Nowak—resigned his post because of inadequate international support for his mandate.

In institutional terms, the structure sanctioned at Dayton was completely dysfunctional. To begin with, the peace accords sanctioned the existence of two entirely different and even incompatible legal systems, with subsidiary legal systems which sometimes overlapped and sometimes contradicted the overarching legal systems.[22] Strangely, "the constitution of Bosnia and Herzegovina contained provisions which," according to the International Helsinki Federation for Human Rights (IHF-HR), "encouraged discrimination, and subordinated basic rights to ethnic principles."[23] Judicial bodies functioned poorly, with judges susceptible to bribery (in part because of low salaries), often influenced by the dominant political parties, and with political connections counting too much in the selection of judges and prosecutors.[24] Even when a judge did hand down a fair ruling, local officials sometimes ignored it. Academic freedom was also restricted, with favoritism shown toward SDA members in faculty hiring and promotion at the University of Sarajevo, and with a Serbs-only hiring policy at the University of Banja Luka.[25] The two entities maintained separate armed forces and, as of January 1997, had still not restored telephone and fax links between the two entities. Many of Bosnia's problems were symbolically represented in the fact that the constitution of the *Republika Srpska* described the RS as fully sovereign—a claim incompatible with the constitution of Bosnia-Herzegovina as a whole.

But before the first steps could be taken in the direction of restoring peace and something akin to normal life in Bosnia, there had to be an exchange of POWs and an exchange of territory, since the territorial apportionment reached at Dayton necessitated some adjustments. Even the exchange of prisoners did not proceed without "haggling and suspicion,"[26] while the exchange of territory saw ample manifestations of the hatred stirred up by four years of warfare. In Sarajevo, the Serbs were required to yield the suburbs of Grbavica, Vogošća, and Ilidža to the Federation, but this transfer of jurisdiction excited intense emotions among the Serbs of those districts. Bosnian Serb authorities in Sarajevo requested UN aid to disinter thousands of coffins holding the last remains of Serbian dead, so that they might take their departed back behind Serbian lines.[27] Some 20,000 Serbs left the city by late February, rather than live under Federal authority.[28] By mid-March, on the eve of the transfer (on 19 March 1996) of jurisdiction, chaos and anarchy were reigning in the Serb districts of Sarajevo, with Serb nationalists threatening to set up to 200 houses on fire.[29] By then, some 60,000 Serbs had abandoned Sarajevo.[30] Where Croatian-held territory was slated to be turned over to Serb authority, the HVO looted and set fire to the houses in villages to be surrendered. The HVO also completely razed the village of Podrdo and incinerated about a third of the houses in Mrkonjić Grad, a larger town. UN officials expressed fears that the HVO troops may have laid land mines in some villages as well.[31]

UN, NATO, and Western officials were optimistic that, if given a choice among candidates in free elections, locals would view the choice as it was viewed in the West, would want to distance themselves from nationalist projects, would reject the rhetoric of hatred, and would vote for anti-nationalist candidates ("moderates"). "Expectations were too high," Christopher Bird, a spokesperson for the Office of the High Representative, admitted five years later. "After the huge political changes which brought democracy to Croatia and Yugoslavia, this was a chance for Bosnian voters to catch the tide in the Balkans, and we thought they would take it. To some extent they did, but the pace of change is frustratingly slow."[32] Under the Dayton Peace Accords, indicted war criminals were barred from holding office, and under considerable pressure from the West, Karadžić finally stepped down as president of the RS in July 1996; Ratko Mladić was also compelled to step down. With Karadžić out of the way, Predrag Radić, the mayor of Banja Luka and head of the Democratic Patriotic Bloc, Miodrag Živanović, a professor of philosophy at the University of Banja Luka and head of the Liberal Party, and other moderates hoped for change.[33] But local elections, held on 13–14 September 1997, were pushed forward in spite of warnings from the IHF-HR secretariat and Helsinki committees in Bosnia and Herzegovina that the preconditions for the elections had not been fulfilled, insofar as

freedom of movement remained restricted; opposition parties had little or no chance to conduct their election campaigns and had unequal access to media; and most indicted war criminals remained at large. They [also] criticized the decision of the OSCE to reinstate a number of candidates who had been removed from the lists for disrespecting electoral rules.[34]

Many persons who had registered to vote were excluded from the voters' lists, many refugees and displaced persons were unable to vote in the districts where they had lived before the war, and political propaganda was conducted at polling stations, especially in the RS. Then came the November 1996 extraordinary elections held in the RS for the People's Assembly, at which the SDS captured 24 seats, making it the strongest party in the Assembly. One seasoned observer, writing at about this time, reached the conclusion that Bosnia was "an example of failed democratization."[35]

Among the challenges with which Bosnia has found itself confronted have been: reestablishing security in the country, assuring refugees and displaced persons of the possibility to exercise their right to return to their prewar homes, combating xenophobia and nationalist intolerance, fighting corruption and organized crime, rounding up the war criminals, and building democracy and protecting human rights. These will be discussed seriatim.

Peace and Security

The dispatch of the 60,000-strong IFOR (among whom 27,000 were Americans) was considered a transitional expedient, and in the United States, people were encouraged to believe that after a year, the peacekeeping mission could end and American troops could come home. By January 1998, the strength of the by-now-renamed peacekeeping contingent (SFOR) had been reduced to 36,000, and by December 2001, it was down to 18,400, among whom 3,100 were Americans. With American president George W. Bush pushing for American disen-

gagement from Bosnia altogether, the EU prepared itself to take over full responsibility for the mission in Bosnia, even as U.S. defense secretary Donald Rums-
feld complained that "[c]ivil security . . . is not an effective use of NATO's valuable military assets." The EU did so at the end of 2004, establishing a new
EUFOR contingent to take the place of SFOR. As of March 2005, EUFOR's
strength stood at 6,300 troops.[36]

In June 1996, representatives of the Federation and the RS agreed, in Florence, on strict limits on the arms which each of their armies would retain. These
limits are shown in Table 16.1. By 31 October 1996, some 6,700 heavy weapons
had been destroyed.[37]

But disarmament was not the whole story. The U.S. also felt that it was necessary to bring the Federation Army (ARBiH) up to the level of the VRS. To
accomplish this, the U.S. launched the "Train and Equip" program, allowing the
Federation to enter into a contract with Military Professional Resources, Inc.
(MPRI), the same organization which had assisted the ARBiH during the war
itself. Under the contract with MPRI, some 170 former leaders of the U.S. Army
would come to Bosnia in order to build the Federation Army into an effective,
professional fighting force. Before the program could begin, President Clinton
was required to certify that the Bosnian government had terminated its military
and intelligence relationship with Iran; on 26 June of that year, President Clinton did so.[38] Shortly thereafter, shipments of tanks, artillery, and other weapons
started arriving.[39] But in disunified Bosnia, these separate armed forces were
intended chiefly to defend against each other—a rather unique arrangement in
what was, after all, supposed to be a single state. Inevitably, there have been calls
to unite the two armies into a single force—both for reasons of security and for
reasons of the budget. These reasons were, for the time being, rejected by the
Serbian side.[40] But on both sides of the divide there had been an interest in joining the EU, Partnership for Peace, and NATO, and Bosnia could only manage
that if it could forge a unified military organization; as a result, pressure for a
military merger only increased.[41] The difficulty was that the Serb nationalists of

Table 16.1. **Maximum Strength Limits on the Armed Forces of the
Croat-Bosniak Federation and the Republika Srpska, as Agreed at
Florence (June 1996)**

	The Federation	Republika Srpska
Tanks	273	137
Artillery pieces over 75 mm. caliber	1,000	500
Armoured combat vehicles	227	113
Combat aircraft	0	0
Attack helicopters	0	0

Source: Nedeljni Telegraf (Belgrade), 3 July 1996, p. 39, trans. in FBIS, *Daily Report* (Eastern Europe), EEU-
96-142, 23 July 1996, p. 73.

the SDS and SRS (Serbian Radical Party) remained committed to the goal of eventual unification with the Republic of Serbia, and when they dreamed of entry into the EU and NATO, it was as part of the Republic of Serbia. This difficulty may not be insuperable, however: in April 2003, Paddy Ashdown, Petritsch's successor as High Representative, issued a series of decisions abolishing the Supreme Defense Council of the *Republika Srpska* and amending the provisions of the constitutions of the two entities, the RS laws on defense and the army, and the Federation law on defense to delete references declaring or implying that the entities should be viewed as states in their own right, rather than parts of the state of Bosnia-Herzegovina. Ashdown also decreed the removal, from the constitution of the RS, of all references to that entity's statehood, independence, or sovereignty.[42]

Security requires a certain level of economic well-being, since, in conditions of widespread poverty, hopelessness can give rise to anomic behavior and violence, and when widespread poverty exists among people who have been stoked into a state of intense ethnic hatred, the combination can be incendiary. After a furious economic growth rate of 80% in the first year after Dayton, the growth rate sank dramatically, coasting at an annual rate of 2.3% during 2001–2002, hardly enough to drive a postwar recovery. But foreign direct investment, viewed by many as the key to Bosnia's economic recovery, was the lowest in southeast Europe as of 2001, even lower than for Albania and Moldova; in the meantime, the public debt was expected to reach 71% of the GDP by the end of 2003.[43] The Federation has looked to Saudi businesspeople in hopes of investments.[44] In the meantime, an estimated 60% of the Bosnian population still lived in poverty as of 2000, with unemployment estimated at 60% for Bosnia-Herzegovina as a whole as of October 2002.[45] As of mid-2002, the Bosnian government stood at the brink of bankruptcy.[46]

Going Home—A Slow Process

In the first months after Dayton, not only was it all but impossible for refugees and internally displaced persons to return to their homes, but, in some areas, the processes of ethnic cleansing continued, as if by momentum. One example was Teslić in central Bosnia, where some 200 Bosniaks fled during summer 1996 as a result of beatings, stone throwing, bombings, and verbal harassment by local Bosnian Serbs.[47] Violent incidents flared, especially during the years 1996–1998, when members of one nationality group attempted to return to villages or towns in which another nationality group was now dominant; such incidents took place between Croats and Bosniaks, Bosniaks and Serbs, and Serbs and Croats.[48] In some cases, local figures (among them—allegedly—Alija Izetbegović, Ejup Ganić, Zlatko Lagumdžija, Ivo Komšić, more than 30 ministers, deputies, and party dignitaries from both entities, journalists and editors, and local power-mongers together with their chauffeurs and secretaries) had taken advantage of the war to move into more luxurious homes being vacated by those fleeing for their lives.[49] Under these conditions, it comes as no surprise that officials did their best to stay put in their new homes. From the beginning, bureaucrats in both entities created obstacles to the return of refugees; in Sarajevo, for example, it was reported in 1998 that many citizens were unable to file claims for the return of their prewar apartments because the functionaries with whom the claims were supposed to be filed simply refused to accept the claim forms or, in some cases, demanded the submission of documents which were not required by law.[50] In late 1999, the Temporary Electoral Commission, a body associated with OSCE, issued a directive barring persons illegally residing in apartments or houses belonging to other people from running for election or reelection.[51] Another approach taken locally was to change the law so that returns would no longer be construed as imperative. In 1999, for example, RS prime minister Milorad Dodik met with Federation prime minister Edhem Bičakčić to discuss a bill in which refugees from one entity would swap their residences with refugees from the other entity, in this way giving legal sanction to some of the results of "ethnic cleansing."[52] In 2000, High Representative Petritsch annulled the RS Law on Return of Confiscated Property and Compensation, the RS Law on Return of Seized Real Property, and the RS Law on Return of Seized Land, on the grounds that the laws obliged the RS to provide financial compensation to claimants "whose property could not be returned"; the problem, as Petritsch saw it, was that the RS lacked both the funds required for such compensation and the funds to establish new administrative bodies to process such compensations.[53] But in addition to fear of violence and bureaucratic obstacles, there has been a third important factor contributing to the slowness in refugee returns, viz., the fact that many of the houses in which the refugees had lived prior to the war had been destroyed during that war, and that international funding to assist with reconstruction is limited. But some refugees have been determined to return to their native villages, regardless of the circumstances; as of late 2000, thus, UNHCR estimated that there were about 1,000 Bosniaks living in tent settlements in eastern Bosnia, pitching their tents on the edge of the villages where they used to live.[54]

In 2000, thanks to a lowering of local tensions and to sustained international assistance, refugee returns bounded upward, leading UNHCR officials to speak of a "breakthrough." The trick has been to assure "minority returns," i.e., the return of persons to an area in which their nationality group is now in the minority. In 2000, there were 67,445 minority returns in Bosnia-Herzegovina, representing an increase of 64.5% over 1999.[55] With many native Bosnians still outside their republic, the population of Bosnia as of January 2001 was estimated at just over 3 million—a decline of more than a million since the 1991 census (see Table 16.2). As of June 2003, some 949,257 refugees and displaced persons had returned to their prewar villages and municipalities; of this number, 430,370 had been refugees (i.e., had fled abroad during the war) and 518,887 had been internally displaced.[56] More than a third of these were minor-

Table 16.2. **Population of Bosnia-Herzegovina (2001),
by Nationality**

Bosniaks	1,400,000
Serbs	980,000
Croats	440,000
Others	250,000
TOTAL	3,070,000

Source: Vjesnik (Zagreb), 19 January 2001, at www.vjesnik.hr.

ity returns. The minority returns, needless to say, have affected voting patterns, eroding the strength of nationalist parties.[57]

Putting the Genie Back in the Bottle: The Struggle against Hate

As I have stressed elsewhere, the ethnic hatred which fueled the war was *manufactured artificially,* through skillful use of the media, propaganda, secret-police rumor-mongering, and the rehabilitation of nationalistically inclined agents, such as the Serbian Orthodox Church, most of whose bishops and clergy remain nationalistic.[58] But once the genie has been summoned, how does one get it to go away? The question is not of purely academic interest, since hatreds can lead to violent incidents, which in turn can sow the seeds of resentment and rage which, if associated with a large proportion of the members of a nationality group, can result in a (further) escalation of ethnic hatred. It is, in part at least, because the hatreds manufactured in the late 1980s and reinforced during the war years have not yet dissipated that international observers have worried about a fresh outbreak of war in Bosnia. Certainly, the popularity of Croatian pop music in Serb-dominated Banja Luka four years after Dayton signified that at least one marker of ethnic distance had come down.[59] But the cultural barriers between the Christian Croats and Serbs, on the one side, and the Muslim Bosniaks, on the other, seem to be higher than between Croats and Serbs. One finds, for example, Catholic bishop Ratko Perić of Mostar drawing a parallel (in a sermon delivered in 2001) between the Jews living in ancient Egypt as "twenty-second class citizens" deprived of the right to keep even their own male children and Croatian Catholics during four centuries of Ottoman (Muslim) rule in Bosnia, concluding that the Croatian people "does not want to be in anyone's, either domestic or foreign, chains, but wants to be a nation on its own land, with human dignity, self-respect and respect of others."[60] Apparently, in the bishop's view, the Croats could not find dignity in a multi-ethnic (or at least not in a multi-confessional) setting. There were also reports of both Bosnian Serb and Bosnian Croat authorities raising obstacles to the rebuilding of mosques destroyed during the war.

The nationalist-controlled media have also played a role in sustaining prejudice and xenophobia, especially in the first two to three years. One example was Serb Television in Banja Luka, where Nikola Deretić, editor of a cultural and entertainment program, used the occasion of Catholic Christmas 1997 to broadcast a program originally broadcast on Belgrade Television, in which viewers were informed that "Tudjman is the same as Pavelić," "all Croats are *Ustaše*," and "Muslims [are] fascists and fundamentalists."[61] In 1997, SFOR dealt with a Serb station broadcasting inflammatory material by simply seizing its transmitters.[62] OHR eventually took up the issue by drafting a law on information in June 2000 and by issuing a decision on restructuring of the public broadcasting system later that year.[63]

One of the most disturbing signs, however, of the potential for inter-ethnic bitterness to lead to continuing distance was to be found in the schoolbooks. Not only did Bosnian Serb children have their own schools with their own distinct curricula and textbooks, but Bosnian Croat children and Bosnian Muslim children also attended separate schools with distinct curricula and textbooks—and all of this within what was held to be a single state. In the textbooks in use in the late 1990s, Serb pupils learned that Gavrilo Princip, the young man who murdered Archduke Franz Ferdinand in Sarajevo in 1914, was "a hero and a poet," that the interwar kingdom was "an open, tolerant democracy," while Croats committed themselves to "the destruction of Yugoslavia," and that Croatian and Muslim fascists committed war crimes against the Serbs during World War Two, while learning nothing about the atrocities committed by the Serb Chetniks or about the Chetniks' collaboration with the Axis. Croat pupils learned that Princip was an "assassin trained and instructed by the Serbs to commit this act of terrorism," that the interwar kingdom was a "dictatorship" which the Croats heroically resisted, and that both the Ustaše and the Chetniks committed terrible misdeeds during World War Two. And Bosniak pupils learned that Princip was a "nationalist whose assassination [of Franz Ferdinand] sparked anti-Serbian rioting that was only stopped by the police from all three ethnic groups," that the interwar kingdom was a harsh political environment for Bosniaks, with separate chapters devoted to "Evictions and Violence Directed against the Muslims in Sandžak" and "The Abolition of the Autonomy of the Islamic Community in Bosnia." Bosniak pupils learned nothing about the Muslim Handžar Division which fought alongside the Ustaša forces during World War Two.[64]

Bitterness and resentment were also reflected and stoked in grammar books. In a grammar book in use in the Federation, the following sentences were used to illustrate the use of certain grammatical cases:

"She fled from Brčko."
"They will pay for their crime."
"We were banished from our home."
"We found ourselves between life and death."

"Black clouds hung over our homeland."
"Free us, O God, from this evil."[65]

But the OHR and other international bodies were not unaware of the cultural apartheid being promoted in the schoolbooks. Accordingly, an Education Working Group was established in 1998 to study the educational systems operating in Bosnia-Herzegovina; this group in turn established a Sub-Group on Textbooks which, in the space of less than a year, reviewed the textbooks in use and made recommendations designed to make the textbooks less polemical and less incendiary.[66] Then, in February 2000, Matei Hoffmann, senior deputy High Representative, announced that educational "apartheid" would no longer be tolerated and, summarizing the recommendations drafted at a symposium on curriculum reform held on 7–8 February in Sarajevo, urged the embrace of the Swiss model, involving "parallel curricula with a high level of coordination between the authorities of the Entities" and with pedagogical representatives of each constituent nation developing "curricular modules to be integrated in the curriculum of others, especially in the areas of culture and language."[67] Subsequently, the OHR also pressed successfully for an agreement under which all school pupils would learn both the Latin and the Cyrillic script, and pressed forward with a project to add a class in "The Culture of Religion," in which pupils would learn about all of Bosnia's religions, in all the schools of the republic.[68] In addition, the OHR launched an "education for peace" project in June 2000; financed by the Luxemburg government and implemented by the Suiss Landegg Academy, which specializes in education for tolerance and peace, the project is intended to sow the seeds of trust, tolerance, and mutual acceptance among the peoples of Bosnia.[69]

Summer 2000 also saw important symbolic gestures on the part of the Bosnian Croats and Bosnian Serbs. On 13 July 2000, the HDZ-Bosnian branch issued a statement in which it acknowledged "mistakes . . . made in the past and asks for understanding and forgiveness for all [its] failures," and also "expresse[d] sorrow for all victims, and it particularly apologize[d] to the families of victims [who were affected] by transgression of [the] ethics of war and violations of international humanitarian norms and the law of war committed by individuals from the Croat [side]."[70] A week later, RS prime minister Dodik reciprocated with an apology to the Bosniak and Croat nations, on behalf of the Bosnian Serbs.[71]

The Fight against Corruption

In addition to the illicit confiscation of other people's housing and the writing of legislation to further one's own interests, as mentioned above, corruption in postwar Bosnia-Herzegovina has also taken the form of electoral fraud, stripping the assets of state firms, favoritism toward cronies during the privatization process, customs fraud, embezzlement of international aid, and the complicity of both local and international officials in allowing a prostitution network to flourish, in which Bosnian police allegedly forged documents to facilitate the trafficking in women and girls.[72] Where the RS is concerned, Biljana Plavšić's brief term as president of that "entity" (1996–1998) was a halcyon period from the standpoint of the OHR. During her term as RS president, Plavšić conducted a vigorous campaign against organized crime and corruption. In particular, the intelligence services of the RS uncovered illegal trafficking in cigarettes, oil, and other commodities on the part of two local companies—Centrex and Select Impex—both of them owned by indicted war criminal Radovan Karadžić. Thanks to Plavšić's commitment to the campaign against corruption and smuggling, intelligence services also uncovered illegal activities on the part of the Pale-based company Javnost, owned by Ljiljana Zelen-Karadžić, Radovan Karadžić's wife, as well as of firms in Zvornik and Banja Luka which were owned and operated by some of Karadžić's closest collaborators. These firms had been obtained, in the first place, by graft or outright theft, and during the war years had even traded weapons and oil to the Bosnian Serbs' foes![73]

In November 1997, there were parliamentary elections in the RS, as a result of which 39-year-old Milorad Dodik, a Social Democrat who had spoken out against the war during the first half of the decade, became prime minister. Dodik worked hand in glove with Plavšić to fight corruption, and one mark of their success was a tangible improvement in the economy, which lasted as long as they were in power.[74] Plavšić enjoyed a very positive profile in the West in these years, and the Plavšić-Dodik team was widely considered the best guarantee of progress toward accomplishing the tasks set forth at Dayton. But Dodik, a member of the small Independent Social Democratic Party, and Plavšić, founder and president of the relatively new Serbian People's Alliance (founded in August 1997), lacked a significant power base, and in elections held on 12–13 September 1998, Plavšić was swept out of office by Nikola Poplašen, candidate of the Serbian Radical Party (SRS), by a vote of 322,117 to 285,921.[75] With this, the fight against corruption in the RS ground to a halt, because corruption there was largely the monopoly of Karadžić's SDS, to which the SRS was allied, while Plavšić herself reviled Karadžić and had been pleased to do whatever she could to weaken the SDS.[76]

Corruption was, of course, not restricted to the RS. In the Croatian sector, for example, the Herzegovinan Bank (Hercegovačka banka) was set up in 1998 with the nominal goal of providing assistance to the Croatian community in Herzegovina. In actual fact, however, the largest part of the money was pilfered, ending up in the pockets of Ante Jelavić, then-president of the HDZ-Bosnia and member of the Bosnian presidency, then-defense minister of the federation Miroslav Prce, and then-director of Herzegovina Insurance Miroslav Rupčić.[77] And there were problems of corruption in Bosniak circles as well. Although the sudden wealth of Bakir Izetbegović, the son of Bosnia's president, did not go unnoticed,[78] it was the removal of Edhem Bičakčić, the former prime minister of Bosnia-Herzegovina, from his subsequent post as director of Elektroprivreda which proved to be the noisiest corruption scandal. In removing him from the directorship, Petritsch charged Bičakčić with having abused the office of prime minister by redirecting public revenues, "through a complex and corrupt system of financial diversions," into the coffers of his own political party, the SDA.[79] It is no wonder that, upon being appointed High Representative at the end of May 2002, Ashdown identified the fight against political corruption and organized crime as his number one priority.[80]

Corruption is, thus, a particular preserve of the nationalist parties, who have used corruption and illicit sources of cash to fund their organizations. In spite of various declarations of determination to fight corruption on the part of sundry politicians, the problem has remained ubiquitous in Bosnia.[81]

Rounding Up the War Criminals

When the ICTY was established in 1993, with no apparent ability to actually round up the people it would indict for war crimes, there was widespread skepticism as to whether it would prove to be more than a fig leaf for general Western and international incompetence in the face of atrocities. But in no small measure due to the hard work of chief prosecutors Louise Arbour and Carla Del Ponte, the ICTY has been able to wield the "sword of justice" and lock up at least some of the worst offenders. In its first 10 years of operation, the ICTY, working methodically and paying scrupulous attention to evidentiary matters, indicted 134 persons, with another 30 expected to be indicted by 2004.[82] Among those brought to The Hague to stand trial (whether taken into custody or surrendering on their own initiative) are the following (not a complete list):

Yugoslav government: Slobodan Milošević, former president of Serbia and the FRY; Milan Milutinović, former president of Serbia; General Dragoljub Ojdanić, former defense minister; Nikola Šainović, former deputy prime minister; Vojislav Šešelj, former deputy prime minister; and Jovica Stanišić, former chief of the State Security Service.

Yugoslav Army/Navy and special forces: Admiral Miodrag Jokić; General Pavle Strugar; General Mile Mrkšić; General Vladimir Lazarević; General Momčilo Perišić; General Nebojša Pavković; Colonel Veselin Sljivančanin; Captain Miroslav Radić; and Frenki Simatović.

Croatian Army and Croatian paramilitary: General Rahim Ademi; General Mirko Norac; Mladen "Tuta" Naletilić; Vinko "Stela" Martinović; General Ivan Čermak; and General Mladen Markač.

Bosnian Army (ARBiH): General Sefer Halilović; General Mehmed Alagić (who died of a heart attack while in detention); General Enver Hadžihasanović; Colonel Amir Kubura; Hažim Delić, deputy commander of the Ćelebići camp; Enes Sakrak; and General Naser Orić, who led the defense of Srebrenica in 1995; (Zejnil Delalić was acquitted).

Bosnian Serb government and military: Momčilo Krajišnik, former president of the Bosnian Serb Assembly; Biljana Plavšić, vice president of the *Republika Srpska* during the war (and its president for two years after the war), sentenced to 11 years in prison;

Radoslav Brdjanin, former deputy prime minister; General Radislav Krstić (who received a prison sentence of 46 years); Milomir Stakić (who, at the end of July 2003, received a life sentence, the first such sentence meted out in connection with the Yugoslav War); General Momir Talić; General Milan Gvero; General Stanislav Galić, former commander of the Romanija corps; army commander Dragan Obrenović; Blagoje Šimić, mayor of Bosanski Šamac; Radivoje Miletić, acting chief of staff of the VRS main staff; Zvornik Brigade commander Vinko Pandurević; Zvornik Brigade security chief Drago Nikolić and his assistant, Milorad Trbić; military police general Ljubomir Borovčanin; VRS commanders Vidoje Blagojević and Dragan Jokić; Mitar Vasiljević, a paramilitary commander; Steven Todorović, police chief; Dražen Erdemović; Ranko Ćesić; Gojko Janković; and policemen Miroslav Deronjić and Darko Mrdja.

Bosnian Serb camp directors, deputy directors, and staff: Nenad Banović; Predrag Banović; Ljubiša Beara; Damir Dosen; Momčilo Gruban; Goran "Adolf" Jelišić; Dragan Kolundžija; Milojica Kos; Radomir Kovač; Milorad Krnojelac; Dragoljub Kunarac; Miroslav Kvočka; Željko Meakić; Rade Mikanović; Dragan "Yankee" Nikolić; Vujadin Popović; Dragoljub Prčac; Mlado Radić; Duško Sikirica; Milan Šimić; Radovan Stanković; Dušan Tadić (sentenced to 45 years in prison); Miroslav Tadić; Nikola Vučković; Zoran Vuković; Šimo Žarić; and Zoran Zigić.

Bosnian Croat government and military: Dario Kordić; General Ivica Rajić; General Tihomir Blaškić (initially given a 45-year prison sentence, reduced on appeal in 2004 to 9 years); Mario Čerkez; Anto Furundžija; Mirjan Kupreškić; Paško Ljubičić; Vladimir Santi; and Pero Skopljak.

Bosnian Croat prison commandants: Zlatko Aleksovski; and Zdravko Mučić.

Croatian Serb leaders: Milan Babić (sentenced to 17 years in prison); and Milan Martić.

Vlajko Stojiljković, former FRY interior minister, and Janko Janjić, a Bosnian Serb fighter, committed suicide rather than face arrest. Bosnian Serbs Simo Drljača (a prison camp commander) and Dragan Gagović were killed while resisting arrest. Slavko Dokmanović, a former Yugoslav Army officer, committed suicide in prison, while Bosnian Serb Milan Kovačević died in detention. Nikola Koljević, a Shakespeare scholar and Bosnian Serb leader, committed suicide in 1997, perhaps recalling Shakespeare's warning in *Macbeth*, "Unnatural deeds do breed unnatural troubles" (act 5, scene 1). And Goran Hadžić, at one time president of the Republic of Serbian Krajina, was indicted for war crimes in July 2004.[83]

The foregoing list of persons brought to The Hague to stand trial underlines the fact that the longer the ICTY has been in operation, the more it has proven its value—to the extent that an apparently worried George W. Bush saw the necessity of obtaining an exemption from prosecution for all American service personnel and other American citizens before launching his long-delayed attack on Iraq in March 2003. The ICTY was preparing indictments against Franjo Tudjman, Alija Izetbegović, and Croatian general Janko Bobetko when they died.[84] At this writing, the ICTY's "most wanted" list is topped by the names Radovan Karadžić, Ratko Mladić, and Croatian general Ante Gotovina.[85] All three men went into hiding, although there continued to be credible reports of sightings of Mladić in prominent restaurants in Belgrade.[86] For its part, the government in Belgrade repeatedly denied that Mladić is in Belgrade.[87] Rumors continued to circulate concerning Mladić, and in July 2003 the prestigious German newspaper, *Frankfurter Rundschau,* published a provocative report in which it was claimed that French President Jacques Chirac had promised Mladić that he would never be brought to justice, in exchange for the release of two French pilots whose aircraft had been shot down over Bosnia and who, as of December 1995, were in Bosnian Serb hands.[88]

According to General Heinrich, deputy commander of IFOR, the reason that Karadžić and Mladić were not apprehended by IFOR in 1996 was because "the Americans were not at all keen on arresting them."[89] But there were other opportunities to arrest the two men. Until February 2002, Mladić enjoyed protection from elite Yugoslav Army units, but during the early months of 2002, SFOR reportedly had at least three opportunities to take Mladić into custody.[90] Karadžić, thought to be protected by paramilitary troops financed by organized crime, left his home in Pale in winter 1997 and went into hiding.[91] At various times he has been reported to be hiding at the Mt. Athos monastery in Greece, at the Ostrog monastery in Montenegro, in Belgrade, and inside Bosnia somewhere, though he is generally thought to have been hiding in the mountainous region in eastern Bosnia, close to the border with Montenegro.[92] There have been repeated raids on suspected sanctuaries: for example, on 28 February 2002, some 40 American troops swept into Ćelebići, a small village with just 30 houses, on a tip that Karadžić could be found there. Indeed, the Bosnian Serb leader *had* been there but had escaped, allegedly thanks to a tip from a French officer who had been apprised of the plan.[93] Later, Paddy Ashdown came up with the idea of cutting off Karadžić's financial lifeline; thus, on 8 March 2003, Ashdown ordered that Karadžić's bank account and assets be frozen, along with the bank accounts and assets of two alleged associates of his.[94] Karadžić is held responsible for the deaths of some 75,000 civilians, for 417 massacres and 93 mass graves, and for the establishment and operation of 378 detention camps. In October 2003, Miroslav Deronjić, himself charged with war crimes, testified that Karadžić had personally ordered the killing of Muslim men and boys at Srebrenica—an act which, in April 2004, the ICTY found to have constituted genocide.[95] One of the reasons that it has proven so difficult to apprehend Karadžić is that he may have continued to enjoy financial support from the SDS, according to Petritsch's successor as High Commissioner, Paddy Ashdown.[96]

But after the apprehension of fallen Iraqi dictator Saddam Hussein, SFOR decided to try to apply the same tactics which had proven successful in Saddam's case to the effort to capture Karadžić, viz., to apprehend former bodyguards in the hope that they might lead SFOR to the former leader of the Bosnian Serbs. But renewed raids in August 2003, January 2004, and April 2004 failed to achieve their goal, though, in July 2004, SFOR apprehended Rajko Banduka, Mladić's secretary during the war years.[97] Meanwhile, officials of the RS Ministry of Internal Affairs maintained regular contact with Karadžć's family. Even in hiding, Karadžić has remained defiant. In 1999, for example, the former Bosnian Serb leader gave a speech in Srebrenica in which he praised the "heroism" of Serbian forces and advised Serbs not to move out from the town "where the most glorious pages of Serbian history have been written."[98] Three years later, Karadžić launched his new play, "Sitovacija: A Light Comedy," which mocked the international community's role in Bosnia, bringing out a semi-autobiographical novel, *Miraculous Chronicle of the Night,* in 2004; the 416-page novel portrays a Serb psychiatrist who has a love affair.[99]

The ICTY continues, at this writing, to issue new indictments. In October 2003, for example, Carla Del Ponte announced the indictments of the former chief of staff of the Yugoslav Army, General Nebojša Pavković; the chief of staff of the Serbian Third Army, General Vlastimir Lasarević; and the former deputy minister of internal affairs for Serbia, Sreten Lukić.[100] In March 2004, she turned once again to Croats suspected of war crimes and issued indictments against Jadranko Prlić, at one time prime minister of Herceg-Bosna; Bruno Stojić, former defense chief of Herceg-Bosna; Valentin Ćorić, former commander of the HVO military police; Milivoj Petković, former chief of staff of the HVO General Staff; and General Slobodan Praljak, former chief of staff of the HVO. The accused were specifically charged with having perpetrated ethnic cleansing in Herzegovina. As she issued these indictments, the ICTY chief prosecutor said that she had documentation of secret lines of communication, during the war years, between the HVO and the Tudjman-government—thus giving the lie to official denials by Zagreb—and announced further that the court was in possession of documentary evidence that HV units had disguised themselves as HVO units in order to take part in military operations in Bosnia.[101] The following month, the authoritative daily *Oslobodjenje* claimed that the ICTY was preparing to indict also Rasim Delić, wartime commander of the ARBiH; Sakib Mahmuljin, commander of the Third Group of the ARBiH; and Ejup Ganić, wartime member of the Bosnian presidency.[102]

In July 2004, in the wake of the Serbian presidential elections, the U.S. Congress put renewed pressure on Belgrade to produce Mladić, threatening to cut off some $57 million in aid unless Mladić were delivered into custody.[103] Vesna Pešić, the prominent Serbian liberal then serving as Serbian ambassador to Mexico, expressed a growing consensus in telling *Glas javnosti* that it was only a matter of time before both Mladić and Karadžić would be taken into custody.[104]

Inevitably, the ICTY has excited outrage and protest among both Serbs and Croats. Many Serbs and Croats feel that the work of the ICTY serves to propagate the myth of collective guilt, even though Croatian president Stipe Mesić has emphasized that the effect of its work is, in fact, quite the opposite. But this is too simple. When popular leaders and popular generals are convicted, the societies are ipso facto implicated in their crimes, at least as regards those who voted for the leaders in question and who continue to report their approval of the indictees in opinion polls. The burden of guilt on the part of past supporters of a regime which perpetrates atrocities is lifted (only partially) when those who supported the regime repudiate the excesses of that regime and the past actions and decisions of its leaders. As for the Bosniaks, it was reported in *Slobodna*

Bosna in 2000 that Izetbegović had ordered the destruction of all documentation relevant to the prosecution of war crimes committed in Bosnia-Herzegovina.[105]

The work of the Tribunal has been vital in giving the victims an opportunity to face their former tormentors, in giving victims some sense of retributive justice, in bringing the people of Bosnia one step closer to reconciliation, and in strengthening international law. In addition, the testimony of eyewitnesses helps to clarify some previously disputed aspects of the war, thus serving the cause of truth.

From Petritsch to Ashdown

In seeking to promote the development of liberal democracy in Bosnia, Petritsch endeavored to marginalize nationalist discourse and, as already seen, removed nationalist politicians from their posts when he felt they were not acting responsibly.[106] His successor as High Representative, the veteran British diplomat Paddy Ashdown, assumed his new responsibilities on 27 May 2002 and immediately issued a series of statements radiant with optimism for the future. Less than five months later, elections were to be held in Bosnia, and Ashdown let it be known that he was prepared to work on a collaborative basis with whosoever might emerge victorious. When the nationalist parties—the SDS, HDZ, and SDA—won the elections, Ashdown looked to them as partners for reform and lent them his support. He courted, and obtained, the support of *Dnevni avaz,* a widely read daily newspaper close to the Bosniak SDA.[107]

Ashdown could, to be sure, note some achievements during his term of office. By May 2003, for example, 85% of property claims in the federation were said to have been "resolved," one way or the other, with 77% of property claims in the RS described as having been "resolved."[108] The OHR's strategy has been to use cash compensation to resolve at least some of the claims—which is to say, to accept the results of at least some of the wartime seizures of property. That same year, parliamentary deputy Nikola Špirić (Social Democrat) introduced a bill in the Bosnian parliament to return to their original owners all properties confiscated after 1 January 1945; the leading political parties were said to be quietly supporting the bill, but the OHR continued to advocate that cash payments to former owners be used to redeem domiciles for their present occupants.[109]

Ashdown could also point to the establishment of a joint intelligence agency for Bosnia, the agreement (in early 2004) on the part of the RS to demobilize 2,200 members of the VRS and 621 police officers, gradual improvement in the quality of local journalism, and, in the Brčko district, significant reform in primary and secondary education.[110] Indeed, in a briefing to the UN Security Council in early March 2004, Ashdown cited progress in the implementation of reform not only in the aforementioned areas, but also in customs, indirect tax, and the reintegration of the city of Mostar.

In order to be treated as a candidate for membership in the EU, Bosnia was supposed to adopt 44 new laws and 46 ordinances and establish 25 new institutions, within the framework of 16 reforms—all by the end of June 2004. Yet, according to an article published in the weekly magazine *Dani* at the end of April, Bosnia had made only "superficial" progress in this regard, so that "it finds itself on the brink of isolation together with Serbia and Montenegro."[111] Moreover, in the absence of completion of even one of the 16 reforms, claims of "progress" sounded hollow and self-serving.[112]

Problems extend over the entire range of policy areas and are often reflections of the Dayton formula under which Bosnia was fashioned along lines which recalled the dysfunctional and unstable *Ausgleich* model tried in Austria-Hungary during the years 1867–1918. There have been what one might call institutional problems, such as the lack of a uniform television network, thereby reinforcing the division of the country, and the continued politicization of education.[113] There have also been problems with crime of various kinds, ranging from organized crime to sporadic looting to extensive drug abuse resulting in a rising number of drug-related deaths to embezzlement at high echelons.[114] Then there have been problems of obstruction, which have included the alleged obstruction of the return of expelled Croats to their homes in the Banja Luka region, the involvement of high-ranking Bosnian Serbs in extending support to fugitive Karadžić, foot-dragging in educational reform and other policy spheres as well as in realizing the reintegration of Mostar, continued discrimination against Bosniaks and Croats in the RS administration, and systematic obstruction, on the part of RS government and military authorities, of SFOR efforts to apprehend Serbs indicted for war crimes, and the withholding of documents sought by the Commission for Investigation of Events in and around Srebrenica.[115] Indeed, so serious has the obstruction on the part of RS authorities been (since the departure of Biljana Plavšić from office) that, in May 2004, Robert Beecraft, head of the OSCE mission to Bosnia, issued a warning that "Republika Srpska's lack of cooperation with the Hague-based international war crimes tribunal could prove an obstacle to Bosnia's entry into NATO's Partnership for Peace program."[116]

By March 2004, Ashdown decided that his strategy of looking to the nationalists as potential partners had been a mistake, indeed that it may have contributed to the marginalization of civic moderates, without winning the nationalists over to the path of reform. Zlatko Lagumdžija, the Social Democratic leader, commented that locals call the attempt to combine nationalism and reform a "wooden stove"—i.e., certain to burn up.[117]

Ashdown's strategy was neither Kemalist nor Weimarist, though it could be said to have been highly optimistic. With that strategy in shambles, Slavko Kukić, a professor of sociology at the University of Sarajevo, suggested that Ashdown could embrace any of three alternatives: to assert his "Bonn powers" and simply ram through the reforms his office considers vital (a pure Kemalist approach), draw closer to moderate civic parties and give them every encouragement, or call for early parliamentary elections and hope for the best.[118] And then there is always the "pure Weimarist" approach, recently embraced by Zdravko Grebo, a professor of law at the University of Sarajevo, viz., for the international community to pull out of Bosnia-Herzegovina and allow the Bosnians to solve their own problems for themselves.[119]

Lord Ashdown seems to have been converted, belatedly, to a more Kemalist approach. Among Ashdown's moves during spring and summer 2004 which suggest a more robust approach were his decisions to block all state financing of the SDS until it could account for how it had been spending such funds as had been allocated, and to press authorities in both entities to agree to a unified educational system and a unified police force.[120] Indeed, Bosnia's failure to pass a key education law, thanks to obstruction by Bosnian Croat deputies, cost the country $12 million in World Bank funding for the reform of secondary and higher education.[121]

Then, on 30 June 2004, following the publication of a report to the UN Security Council concerning Bosnian Serb sheltering of indicted war criminal Karadžić, Ashdown removed some 60 Bosnian Serb officials from their posts— among them, SDS leader and speaker of the Bosnian Serb parliament Dragan Kalinić and Bosnian Serb police chief Zoran Djerić—froze their bank accounts, and issued travel bans.[122] The following day, the OHR published a report on the financial activities of the SDS, finding, in Lord Ashdown's words,

a catalogue of abuse, corruption, and tax evasion at all levels of the SDS. There is a complete, even criminal absence of proper control designed to ensure the observance of the law and to prevent the passage of funds to and from criminal and war criminal networks and support structures; the financial review also reveals substantial evidence of illegal transactions by SDS subsidiaries with enterprises and public bodies, and, prima facie, clear indications of repeated, multiple and flagrant breaches of electoral law.[123]

Rather than buckling, however, the RS leadership responded, in a spirit of defiance, by demanding that the RS parliament exclude three Bosnian Muslim ministers from its benches.[124]

Building Democracy

Although the Weimarists believe that holding elections and turning over responsibility to local authorities as quickly as possible is the best course of action for the international community to take, no Weimarist has ever counseled, or would ever counsel, the holding of elections in conditions of "widespread fraud in voter registration," "ballot counting irregularities," control by the local ruling party "of the media and security apparatus" in such a way as to preclude "citizen participation without intimidation," "disruptions of [opposition] meetings," and acts of violence against independent journalists and editors.[125] Yet, in the case of Bosnia, so eager were the international administrators of Bosnia and so convinced of the universality of their political formulas, regardless of local conditions, that they pushed ahead with elections, in the presence of all of the aforementioned factors. Such an approach, however well meaning, was not Weimarist, but Jacobin. Had it not been for the strong-arm methods taken by the various High Representatives, corruption would be far more widespread in Bosnia than it is today, and far more accepted.

For all that, international observers allowed themselves to indulge in a degree of optimism and even self-congratulation during the years 1997–2002.[126] This occurred first because of the role of moderates Biljana Plavšić in the RS presidency and Milorad Dodik in the RS prime ministership, and later because of the electoral victory, in the November 2000 parliamentary elections, of the non-nationalist Alliance for Change, consisting of Zlatko Lagumdžija's Social Democratic Party and Haris Silajdžić's Party for Bosnia-Herzegovina. Observers did not mind too much when the Helsinki Committee for Human Rights reported that the pre-election campaign for the November 2000 elections had been "the dirtiest one so far,"[127] and they were apparently surprised when, after two years of intra-coalition brawling and policy stagnation, with unemployment still running at 60%, voters, perhaps also resenting open Western pressure on them to vote "correctly," rejected the "correct" choices and brought the nationalists back to power. This result probably also owed something to the unusually low turnout for the October 2002 elections—a record-low of 55%.[128]

But at least some international observers paid insufficient attention to the problems plaguing the system even during the years 1997–2002. If one recalls that the liberal project entails and requires rule of law, a culture of tolerance, and equal treatment of all citizens, among other things, then it is a matter of no small interest that there have been repeated instances of violations of the rule of law, including at the ballot box itself, open hate propaganda and tendencies toward blaming various other national groups within the country or the international community for the tribulations suffered by one's own group, an inability to think in terms of the Bosnian community as a whole, mockery of the principle of ethnic equality as a return to the Tito-era model of "brotherhood and unity,"[129] and complaints from spokesmen of all three groups of victimization: the HDZ-Bosnian branch, for example, complained that "Croats are not enjoying equality in politics, culture, education and media representation,"[130] and that the SDA was taking unilateral steps designed to change the Dayton structure at the expense of Croats;[131] the SDA complained that the erosion of its electoral base in the April 2000 local elections was the result of "a horrible media campaign against the SDA and its staff" as well as a "one-sided attitude [on the part] of the international community";[132] and the Serbs were told that Croatian leaders Ivica Račan, Tonino Picula, and Dražen Budiša were plotting to eliminate the *Republika Srpska* and allegedly had already held a secret meeting with allies in Bosnia for the purpose of putting their conspiracy into action.[133] Moreover, in order to have a stable democracy, it is necessary to have a broad consensus on the basic rules of the game, so that the political debates between the major political parties concern policy rather than framework. In post-Dayton

Bosnia, however, this has not been the case. On the contrary, there have been interminable efforts to change the framework, either in the direction of concentrating power in the center even to the extent of abolishing the separate "entities" or in the direction of granting the two entities even greater self-governing authority than they already enjoy. Moreover, the hard-line nationalists in the RS still hope for annexation to the Republic of Serbia, while the HDZ under Ante Jelavić, at the time the Croatian member of the Bosnian collective presidency, told his adherents that "the Dayton accord had been implemented in such a way that it excluded the Croat nation from [meaningful representation in] the federation."[134] Jelavić reportedly organized a referendum on Bosnian Croat separation in which voting cards for dead persons were distributed among the party faithful, who, using these cards, were able to vote two or three times.[135] Finally he repudiated the Dayton framework altogether in what appeared to be an incipient putsch designed to pull the supposedly dismantled "Herceg-Bosna" out of Bosnia-Herzegovina altogether.[136] High Representative Petritsch wasted no time in removing Jelavić from both his governmental post and his party post, barring him for running for elective office in the future.[137] Croatian president Mesić also criticized Jelavić for his maverick politics, declaring, "We recognize the independence and territorial integrity of Bosnia-Herzegovina and we encourage the Bosnian Croats to seek the solutions to their problems within the institutions of the system in Bosnia."[138] Jelavić and the HDZ do not, however, speak for all Bosnian Croats. Krešimir Zubak, president of the New Croat Initiative (NHI), has denied Jelavić's thesis that the Croats are threatened in Bosnia, while Miljenko Brkić, president of the Croat People's Union (HNZ), has declared himself against secession from Bosnia-Herzegovina.[139]

Conclusion: Revising Dayton?

In April 2004, after lengthy discussion, it was officially announced that the EU would take over responsibility for the peacekeeping mission in Bosnia from NATO by the end of 2004,[140] though American spokespersons quickly offered reassurances that American troops would remain in Bosnia even after the EU assumed primary responsibility.[141] Nearly a decade after Dayton, it would be an oversimplification to describe the Dayton process as either a "success" or a "failure." Bosnia-Herzegovina is rather obviously not yet a stable, liberal democracy, but, as Victor Bojkov wisely stated, it may be considered a "controlled democracy" facing "correctable" problems.[142] Where political culture is concerned, the most vital tasks, as Patrick Joseph O'Halloran has argued, continue to be to adopt and carry out "measures designed to encourage tolerance, to promote active citizenship, to develop shared commitments to fellow citizens and respect for diversity, and to promote compatible conceptualizations of nation and homeland."[143]

There has been a tendency in some quarters to treat the Dayton Peace Accords as if they were Holy Writ, so that it would be some sort of sacrilege to change even one word of this Scripture.[144] Against this notion, High Representative Paddy Ashdown emphasized in July 2004 that it was entirely within the authority of existing Bosnian authorities to rewrite the Dayton Peace Accords and negotiate a new modus vivendi, if they wished to do so.[145] Indeed, it should be recalled that the Dayton Accords were the product of wrangling among Izetbegović, Milošević, and Tudjman, who had their own short-term political interests and the short-term political interests of their states in mind. The Dayton structure has proven to be dysfunctional in many ways and has so far failed to generate fully legitimate sovereign institutions. Thus, alongside repeated demands for a wholesale revision of the framework, there have also been elements of creeping de facto revision, as shown, for example, in the constitutional revision concerning "constituent peoples," the military reforms, and the OHR-imposed changes to the media laws in the RS. As Ivan Lovrenović noted in a column originally written for *Feral Tribune,*

An irreducible and discriminatory difference was built into the constitution[s] of the two entities. The Federation of Bosnia-Herzegovina . . . is divided into ten cantons, i.e., ten self-contained administrative entities, leaving it quite unclear whether it is a federation of the cantons or of the Bosniak and Croat ethnic groups.[146]

Not unrelated in Lovrenović's view is the fact that the SDA and HDZ were able to establish virtual political monopolies in their respective spheres, controlling media, patronage, and investment. But the heart of the problem, as Lovrenović quite rightly emphasizes, is

the organic symbiosis between the institutions run by the nationalists and the criminal and corrupt system that prevails in the country. These two vitally depend on each other, indeed so much so that one can safely say that nationalism, corruption and crime are synonymous terms in Bosnia-Herzegovina.[147]

Whether Bosnia can deal with this twin problem will determine when it can move forward toward some stable solution based on consensus, mutual respect among its peoples, rule of law, and a politics of tolerance.

In this respect, the agreement of Bosnia's Muslim, Serb, and Croat leaders in November 2005, under pressure from the U.S., to create a stronger national government is an important and, indeed, promising step. In recognition of the importance of this agreement, the European Union invited Bosnia to start accession talks that same month.[148]

CHAPTER 17

The Third Yugoslavia and After, 1992–2005

The record of Serbian opposition to Milošević is striking both for its tenacity and, until 2000, for its ineffectiveness. One need but remember the anti-Milošević protests of 9 March 1991, the anti-regime procession led by the Serbian Orthodox patriarch on 14 June 1992, the anti-regime demonstrations led by Vuk and Danica Drašković in early June 1993, the protests by Women in Black and other Serbian pacifist groups during the war years, the 78-day protests in several cities in the winter of 1996–1997, the wildfire of anti-Milošević rallies in a number of Serbian cities in June–August 1999 (where demands were raised for Milošević's resignation), the energetic anti-regime activities by the student resistance group Otpor during 2000, and the repeated efforts by courageous journalists to revive independent media throughout the years of Milošević's rule to see the point. There *was* public willingness to resist the Milošević regime. The difficulty was that, among Serbs, such opposition to Milošević was largely concentrated in the larger cities, especially Belgrade, Niš, and Kragujevac. On the other hand, Milošević had his base of support in Serbia's small towns and villages. Indeed, Milošević's rule opened a chasm between city and countryside and deepened the mutual distrust between them. Moreover, as Eric Gordy notes, Milošević's support was strongest among persons over 45 years of age, especially those with less education. At the same time, between 300,000 and 600,000 young university graduates emigrated during the Milošević years, confirming the alienation of the educated classes from the regime.[1]

If, as has been argued, political legitimacy hinges on the observance of routinized, legal, and accepted procedures for political succession, then much depends on the origins of the given regime. Accordingly, to understand the nature of the Milošević regime and the roots of its present crisis, one must return to its origins in 1987. Slobodan Milošević did not come to power through either popular election or normal party procedures: he seized power through an internal party coup, embracing the waxing anti-Albanian and anti-Muslim phobias which were then spreading among rural Serbs in particular as the core of his ideology. The Milošević regime built its ideological foundations on hatred, rapidly expanding that hatred to include also Croats, Hungarians (in the Vojvodina), Germans, Austrians, the Vatican, and, of course, the U.S.—and expanded its power through a series of unconstitutional and illegal measures. These included the mobilization of protesters to destabilize and topple the elected governments in Novi Sad, Titograd (Podgorica), and Priština, the arrest of Kosovar Albanians who had signed a petition supporting the 1974 SFRY constitution, the installation by Belgrade of Momir Bulatović and Rahman Morina (in 1989) as the party chiefs in Montenegro and Kosovo, respectively, the amendments to the Serbian constitution adopted in 1989 (which bypassed the federal constitution), the suppression of the provincial autonomy of Kosovo and Vojvodina in March 1989, the subsequent suppression of the provincial Assembly in Kosovo, the use of official channels to declare a boycott of Slovenian goods (in December 1989), the Serbian bank swindle of December 1990, the conduct of local Serbian referenda in Croatia in summer 1990 without the approval of Croatian authorities, the unilateral establishment of Serb autonomous regions in Croatia and Bosnia between August 1990 and April 1991, and the establishment and arming of Serb militias in Croatia, beginning in summer 1990. And this is only a partial list of unconstitutional and illegal measures taken by Serb authorities between 1988 and 1991.[2] That said, it is clear that the Milošević regime was illegitimate both objectively (in terms of its political system, economic system, and general disregard for human rights) and contextually (in terms of its failure to comply with the laws of the land). It is no coincidence that among his few close allies Milošević could count Iraq's Saddam Hussein, who in early 2000 promised to send troops to Serbia to shore up Milošević's regime in the event of any future conflict with NATO.[3]

The third Yugoslavia was born on 27 April 1992 when Serbia and Montenegro proclaimed the establishment of the Federal Republic of Yugoslavia (FRY). From the beginning, it was a curious construction: Serbia and Montenegro were nominally equal, but, in fact, Serbia clearly dominated the union; the FRY president would seem to have to be the superior of the Serbian president, but Serbian president Milošević was clearly in charge and even (illegally) arranged for the removal of FRY president Dobrica Ćosić in June 1993; and though its officials constantly reiterated that the country was "at peace," Yugoslav Army troops and war materiel were simply transferred outright to Bosnian Serb command in 1992, crucial supplies were diverted to Bosnian Serb forces, and the economy itself was put on war footing (partly, though not exclusively, under the duress of UN economic sanctions). Then there was the spectacle of Serbian parliamentary deputy Milan Paroški proposing, in May 1992, that the newly established FRY seek affiliation with the post-Soviet Commonwealth of Independent States.[4] It was no wonder, then, that Serbs' strategies of coping in conditions of Milošević's despotic rule have been compared with strategies adopted by patients in mental asylums.[5]

Milošević's Strategy of Control

Milošević built his power through the control of three key institutions: financial institutions and large industrial concerns (controlled directly or by his trusted cronies), the secret police and regular police, and the media.[6] Of the three, it was the media which proved the hardest to keep under control, in spite of the clear priority Milošević assigned to its control.

The combination of the war and the sanctions created conditions which facilitated the subversion of the economy. Already on 9 July 1992, barely three months after the outbreak of hostilities in Bosnia-Herzegovina, the Serbian Assembly adopted legislation which granted Milošević emergency powers over every facet of the economy. Some 15,000 students marched through the streets of Belgrade in protest, as the Assembly considered the measure—but to no avail. Milan Paroški, president of the opposition Serbian People's Party and a presidential candidate in the December 1992 elections, summed up his despair, declaring, "Lenin-style war communism has been introduced without a single, positive governmental measure to safeguard production."[7] Milošević's brand of "war communism" meant that ordinary citizens became steadily poorer and poorer, until 60% of Serbs lived below the poverty line, while Milošević and his wife, and the members of their inner circle, became egregiously wealthy, spiriting funds clandestinely into bank accounts in Russia, China, Cyprus, and elsewhere.[8] At the same time, organized crime spread its activity throughout Serbian society, some of it benefiting from regime protection; among its operations were smuggling of fuel, arms smuggling, and drug smuggling.[9]

The economy shrank by 6.6% in 1990, by another 8.2% in 1991, by a further 26.2% in 1992, and by a catastrophic 30.3% relative to the previous year in 1993.[10] Skyrocketing inflation wiped out ordinary citizens' savings overnight,[11] annihilated pensions, and accelerated the widening gap between Serbia's new kleptocrats and the growing mass of impoverished Serbs, as prices rose an average of 62% *per day* as of late 1993.[12] During these same years, industrial production also plummeted: by 12.9% in 1990, by 15.9% in 1991, by 21.4% in 1992, and by 37.3% in 1993. The modest reversal of these trends in 1994–1995, when economic growth was recorded at 6.5% for 1994 and 6.0% for 1995 (with industrial growth rates of 1.3% and 3.8%, respectively), could scarcely begin to compensate for the dramatic contraction of the preceding four years.[13] During the winter of 1994–1995, there were shortages of electric energy, with intervals of no electricity lasting up to six hours at a stretch.

Where the police are concerned, by 1993, the regular police had been built up to an 80,000-strong, heavily militarized force, most of them recruited from among the Serbian populations of Croatia and Bosnia or from rural parts of Serbia itself; these recruits had little sympathy for urban intellectuals in Belgrade.[14] Some 25,000 police were stationed in Belgrade alone. But, as important as their loyalty was, Milošević ultimately depended much more on the security police, the so-called "secret police," who could carry out "dirty jobs" such as the murder, in March 1999, of independent journalist Slavko Ćuruvija.[15]

The third foundation of Milošević's power was his control of the media. In the war years, Milošević's strategy was to control Radio-Television Serbia and the newspapers *Politika* and *Politika ekspres,* while circumscribing the influence of other media outlets. Among leading weekly magazines, *Duga* was under clear regime influence, too, while *NIN,* the prestigious Belgrade weekly, espoused a clear Serb nationalist line. *Borba* (Struggle), an independent Belgrade newspaper dating back to the interwar years, was critical of Milošević's rule; it experienced difficulties in obtaining newsprint and, in December 1993, missed an issue because of newsprint supply problems.[16] Later, on 23 December 1994, the regime seized control of the wayward newspaper, installing Yugoslav information minister Dragutin Brčin as its new director and chief editor. All but 15 of *Borba'*s 120 journalists refused to go along with the new management and launched a rival newspaper, *Naša borba* (Our Struggle), which maintained its integrity and continued to publish until 15 October 1998, when it, too, was finally brought down by the regime.[17] Independent-minded journalists purged from Tanjug, the state news agency, adopted a similar approach, establishing the independent Beta news agency, which has maintained high professional standards to this day.[18] The independent media struggled to maintain balance in their reportage of the war. But in the regime-controlled media, which, in addition to RTV Belgrade, included also Radio NTV-Studio B (after its takeover), the newspapers *Politika,* *Politika ekspres,* and, after Christmas 1994, *Borba* too, as well as some provincial newspapers, the Serbs were always and everywhere innocent victims, while Croats and Muslims were the aggressors. Even the siege of Sarajevo was inverted, so that the Muslims were said to be "holding Sarajevo under siege from within," while the Serbs were described as "defend[ing] their centuries-old hills around Sarajevo."[19] And if the siege of Sarajevo could be turned upside down, then it followed for *Politika* that the bread-line massacre in Sarajevo on 27 May 1992 could "only" be the work of the Muslims themselves, in an effort to make the Serbs look bad! Not surprisingly, opinion polls found Serbs to be often quite ignorant concerning the most basic facts about the war in Bosnia.[20]

Yet the media proved adept at shaping most Serbs' views of the world and, with the media constantly harping on the alleged hostility of Croats, Bosnian Muslims, Albanians, Hungarians, the U.S., Germany, Austria, Italy, the Vatican, and perhaps other states and groups as well, it is not surprising that xenophobia and nationalist chauvinism among Serbs grew steadily in these years (though they had been present at lower levels before Milošević's rise of power, of course).[21] The media were also able to change Serbs' views rather rapidly, at least on occasion. Thus, in March 1993, for instance, Belgrade's main evening news program was severely critical of the Vance-Owen Peace Plan, which, it said, would lead to the "ethnic cleansing" of Bosnian Serbs and thus be tantamount to "national suicide." An opinion poll conducted on 9 April 1993 found that 70% of Serbs were opposed to the Vance-Owen plan. But then Milošević became convinced that a Serbian rejection of the plan might lead to Western military intervention against the Bosnian Serb forces, and the regime-controlled media switched tracks and began to endorse the plan as a reasonable compromise. After this reversal, a second opinion poll, taken on 27 April, found that only 20% of Serbs were still opposed to the plan, while 39% declared themselves in favor.[22] When Serbian journalists stepped out of line, they ran the risk of being harassed or beaten by police, as happened to three journalists who covered the 1 June 1993 anti-regime demonstrations in Belgrade.

Serbia at War

On 9 March 1992, on the first anniversary of the 1991 demonstrations, 50,000 anti-Milošević protesters attended a rally held outside St. Sava's Cathedral. Patriarch Pavle, defying the authorities, spoke to the protesters, advising them that Milošević's government had failed to acknowledge "the truth that out of such evil no good can come."[23] As the war spread to Bosnia, a groundswell of anti-war feeling rocked Belgrade, where, on 4 June, university students initiated anti-government demonstrations running for 40 days. It was in the course of these demonstrations that, on 14 June, Patriarch Pavle led a procession of several thousand people through Belgrade's streets to demand that Milošević resign.[24] Subsequently, on 28 June 1992, the opposition coalition DEPOS began a series of anti-regime demonstrations running through 5 July.

Seeking to enlist useful allies, Milošević saw to it that novelist Dobrica Ćosić, author of *A Time of Death,* was elected the first FRY president by the federal Skupština (on 15 June 1992) and recruited Milan Panić, a Serbian-American pharmaceuticals entrepreneur, to serve as prime minister. Ćosić's nationalist credentials could be expected to appeal to the nationalist right, while Panić, Milošević hoped, could be useful in relations with the U.S. and Europe. But Panić and Ćosić were against the war and wanted to seek a negotiated settlement. During October 1992, Milan Panić met several times with Života Panić, chief-of-staff of the Yugoslav Army. With presidential elections scheduled for December, Prime Minister Panić decided to challenge Milošević for the office and brought Ćosić on board as a political ally. Milošević's supporters countered by calling for a vote of no confidence in Panić on 4 November, but the Montenegrin deputies rallied to Panić's defense, and the prime minister survived the vote.

Meanwhile, bureaucratic obstacles were created to obstruct Panić's candidacy for the Serbian presidency. Until his candidacy had been approved, he could not campaign, and his candidacy was, in fact, held up on a technicality. But on 9 December 1992, the constitutional court ruled that the electoral commission's refusal to accept Panić's candidacy was illegal and ordered the commission to register Panić as a candidate. On the following day, Vuk Drašković withdrew from the race in order to encourage the opposition to unite behind Panić. Milošević employed a number of questionable devices, including arranging for university registration to be held the same day as the elections, in order to assure his election,[25] and when the elections were held on 20 December, irregularities were reported at 86 polling stations. The final results gave Milošević 56.32% of the vote, against 34.02% for Milan Panić, and 3.31% for Milan Paroški, with the remaining votes divided among four other candidates.[26] In the parliamentary race, Milošević's Socialist Party and Šešelj's Radical Party were the big winners, garnering 101 seats and 73 seats, respectively.[27] The postscript came on 29 December 1992, when Panić's Montenegrin allies abandoned him, and the prime minister lost a no-confidence vote 95 to 2 with 12 abstentions.[28]

FRY president Ćosić continued to hope for a negotiated settlement to the conflict. On 27 May 1993, Ćosić held a meeting with Chief-of-Staff Života Panić and other high-ranking officers. News of the meeting spread quickly; it was rumored that Ćosić wanted to enlist the army's help to remove Milošević from power. Four days later, Vojislav Šešelj's Serbian Radical Party introduced a no-confidence motion against Ćosić in the federal Skupština, alleging that he had been conspiring to organize a military coup against Serbian president Milošević. The Socialist Party backed the motion, with Socialist MP Nedeljko Sipovac accusing Ćosić of having "contested the current constitution and expressing doubts about the ability of federal Yugoslavia to function" in the course of his meeting with General Panić.[29] The bicameral legislature thereupon voted on 1 June (by 22 to 10 with four blank votes in the Chamber of Republics and by 75 to 34 in the Chamber of Citizens) to remove Ćosić from the presidency. The next day, some 1,500 persons, led by Vuk Drašković and his wife Danica, staged a protest rally in downtown Belgrade, alleging that Ćosić's removal from office was unconstitutional. Riot police flooded into the city center, fired tear gas at the protesters, and beat them with batons. One policeman was killed, dozens of persons were injured, and 121 were arrested. Vuk Drašković, addressing reporters in an ad hoc news conference in front of the federal Skupština, announced that the opposition was now in "a state of war" with the regime. That same night, police visited SPO headquarters, where they arrested the Draškovićes, beating them severely. The Draškovićes were detained in prison and charged, under article 114 of the constitution, with having carried out "a criminal attack against the constitutional order" (maximum penalty, 10 years in prison) and, under article 24 of the law on public order, with "preventing officials from carrying out security duties and maintaining law and order." They were finally released from prison, with charges dropped, only after appeals from the governments of France, Greece, and Russia.[30] At the height of the crisis, as

Milošević considered the possibility of banning the SPO, the leadership of the opposition coalition DEPOS issued a statement (published by the still-independent *Borba*) warning that such a move "not only would be illegal but would lead to the introduction of dictatorship and the outbreak of civil war" in Serbia.[31]

In the meantime, the war had its reverberations within the FRY—in Vojvodina, in the Sandžak, and in Kosovo. In Vojvodina, purges were carried out during 1992 in the police, customs service, and, reportedly, the judiciary as well. By December 1992, there were almost no Croats or Hungarians still working in the police force or customs service of Vojvodina, and not a single judge in Subotica of Croatian nationality.[32] Altogether, in the years 1991–1999, between 50,000 and 100,000 Hungarians were driven from their homes in Vojvodina, together with some 45,000 Croats.[33] In the Sandžak, more than 100,000 Muslims were driven from their homes in the years 1991–2000.[34] This was to a considerable extent the work of Serbian paramilitary formations which were active in the Sandžak in the years 1992–1994 and which played a dominant role in these years in creating an atmosphere of terror in the region.[35] In addition, in the first half of the 1990s, numerous physicians, educators, army officers, and police officers of Bosniak-Muslim ethnicity were dismissed from their positions in the public sector in the Sandžak.[36] And in Kosovo, conditions were, by some measures, even worse. The situation in Kosovo in the Milošević era will be discussed later in this chapter.

If the stoking of nationalism by the Serbian (and later also by the Croatian) media helped to prepare the people for war, the war, in turn, fed the flames of ravenous nationalism and fantasies of a Great Serbian state to be built on the corpses of non-Serbs. In July 1991, Mihalj Kertes, who had helped to organize some of the famous "meetings for truth" in 1988–1989, promised that Serbs would soon see "a great Serbian state [stretching] from Montenegro to the left bank of the Neretva River with Dubrovnik as the capital city."[37] Kertes even promised that Dubrovnik would be renamed Nikšić-on-Sea. Then there was the figure of Radovan Karadžić, leader of the Bosnian Serbs, whose poetry was largely unnoticed until his forces began killing non-Serbs, but who was now decorated with Russian and Montenegrin prizes for poetry. But probably no one could exceed Ratko Mladić for sheer hubris. Mladić boasted in 1993, "Through the war I have broken away from Communism and Yugoslavia and have become the greatest Serb. Sooner or later I will liberate the Serbian city of Zadar. . . . Trieste is an old Serbian city, too, and will be ours in the end. The Serbian army will finish this war, just like the previous two, on the Trieste-Vienna line."[38] It was symptomatic of the psychological state of Serbian society that, in those years, Mladić was the single most popular Serb among Serbs.

The nationalist sickness penetrated even into the Church, whose clergy, however, were divided about the war. Metropolitan Amfilohije embraced the "Serbian cause" fully and spoke of his hope that all lands inhabited by Serbs would be integrated into what he called "the United States of Serbia,"[39] though he surely realized that in some of the areas inhabited by Serbs, Serbs were, in fact, in the minority. Patriarch Pavle, on the other hand, was unambiguously opposed to the prosecution of the war. Milovan Djilas, the aging *enfant terrible* who had earned a reputation as the conscience of the nation, spoke out against Serbian nationalism and the war in Bosnia. In recompense, he was demonized as anti-Serb. Yet Djilas had understood these processes for a long time. Political thieves, he had warned in *The New Class* in 1957, "elevate the pygmies and destroy the great, especially the great of their own time."[40]

Pseudo-heroic Escapism and the Wages of War

The war years also saw the rising popularity of so-called turbo-folk, which blended synthesized pop music with traditional Serbian folk conventions. Among its divas were Svetlana (Ceca) Veličković, who toured the Croatian front attired in combat fatigues, and Simonida Stanković, whose stage wardrobe included mock peasant garb, the habit of an Orthodox nun, and tight black leather pants, and who likened the Serbs to "modern Mohicans defending their land."[41] Sponsored by the regime, turbo-folk purveyed a strong nationalist message, while serving up images of a glamorous life—a blend one might call "pseudo-heroic escapism." The recurrent theme in turbo lyrics was that Serbs were strong and would defeat their enemies.

But in August 1994, even as Milošević embraced the Contact Group peace plan for Bosnia-Herzegovina, in a reversal of his previous position, Nada Popović-Perišić, Belgrade's minister of culture, declared the inception of "a war on all forms of 'cultural kitsch.'"[42] State patronage of turbo now largely vanished, as television commercials and posters declared that 1995 would be "the Year of Culture" and urged the public to visit museums and galleries and attend classical symphonic concerts.[43] State television also changed its fare, giving more air time to symphonic concerts and even to documentaries about Yugoslav rock groups of the 1980s. Turbo fans could nonetheless celebrate one last time in February 1995 when 42-year-old paramilitary leader Željko "Arkan" Ražnatović married 21-year-old "Ceca" Veličković, the buxom queen of turbo. For many Serbs, it seemed a marriage ordained by destiny.

In spite of the efforts made on behalf of the "Serbian cause," whether on the battlefield or via turbo, Serbia did not expand by even one square kilometer. Meanwhile, the combination of war, sanctions, and the greed of Belgrade's kleptocrats bled Serbia dry. Economic sanctions were first imposed on Serbia on 30 May 1992; these sanctions were expanded on 26 April 1993. As state coffers (though not the bank accounts of Milošević and his cronies) emptied, the Milošević regime simply printed the money it needed, thereby fueling horrific rates of inflation, possibly without precedent, which, in turn, enabled them to pay off at huge discounts the bank loans they had contracted to purchase various "privatized" enterprises. The Serbian economy was strained to the breaking point. Meanwhile, Vuk Drašković, who had earlier sponsored a Serbian paramilitary unit in Croatia but who had subsequently adopted an anti-war stance, threw his support behind the Vance-Owen plan.[44]

By July 1993, inflation was roaring at a *monthly* rate of 500%, with the black market offering an exchange of 7 million dinars to the dollar (as compared with 300 dinars to the dollar a year earlier). A 5-million dinar note was in circulation. But the government did nothing to slow the inflation and printed 6.9 trillion dinars in unbacked currency to purchase wheat from private farmers.[45] In December 1993, in an effort to head off complete economic disaster, Milošević appointed respected economist Dragoslav Avramović to put together an economic reform package. Avramović launched a "new" dinar on 1 January 1994, pegging it to the German mark, and reduced inflation to minus 0.6%.[46] But these measures did not hold, and by October 1994, the dinar was sliding against the mark, and inflation was returning in force. Later, after the Dayton Peace Accords, the FRY would make ends meet by shipping arms clandestinely to Libya;[47] demobilized Serb soldiers and paramilitaries would sell their services as mercenaries to President Mobutu of Zaire.[48]

As the economy continued its downward hurtle, Mirjana Marković, Milošević's neo-Marxist wife, took the initiative in establishing a new political party, the Yugoslav United Left (JUL). The new party held its first congress on 24–25 March 1995, at Belgrade's plush Sava Center, where JUL leaders declared their unanimous rejection of nationalism. A few months later, Marković explained that JUL was "opposed to the terrible, primitive, Četnik nationalism at work in Bosnia and personified by Radovan Karadžić."[49] But in spite of this ostensibly principled declaration, JUL had not at all been created for the purpose of promoting legitimate politics and economics. On the contrary, JUL's leaders, including Marković, believed that the sun had set on parliamentary democracy and that the future lay with one-party systems such as communist China.

Mirjana Marković was unmistakably an ideologue. But Milošević, as many observers have noted, not only was not an ideologue but, in fact, had no programmatic vision to offer, beyond fantasizing about a Greater Serbia and stealing from the public. Although he imagined himself as Serbia's greatest ruler— the sight of his followers carrying his portrait alongside the portraits of St. Sava, Tsar Lazar, and Draža Mihailović was symptomatic of his megalomania—who would expand the state in accordance with the Chetnik vision, he was prepared to scuttle the Chetnik project when his own personal political survival was at stake. Indeed, this became patently clear to Serbs when he made no response to the Croatian Army's reconquest of western Slavonia in May 1995 and when, as the Croatian Army moved into the Krajina on 4 August, he reportedly ordered the Krajina Serbs to withdraw from the Krajina rather than fight.[50] About 20,000 persons demonstrated in Belgrade on 10 August 1995 to protest Milošević's failure to come to the defense of the Krajina Serbs, accusing him of "betrayal" and "complicity."[51] The final straw, for Serb nationalists, was Milošević's signing of the Dayton Peace Accords, which effectively jettisoned the project to establish a Greater Serbia.

A Victory for the Opposition

At the end of 1995, after more than four years of war, per capita income in the FRY was less than $1,500 per year, or less than half of what it had been in 1991. The standard of living was officially reported to be 25% lower in December 1995 than it had been a year earlier. Inflation, though modest by comparison with the rates of 1993, was still strong at 119%.[52] The formal economy lay in ruins, and economic life had been effectively criminalized.

It was in this context that in January 1996, the SPO (Serbian Renewal Movement, Vuk Drašković's party), the DS (the Democratic Party, headed by Zoran Djindjić), and the DSS (the Democratic Party of Serbia, headed by Vojislav Koštunica) formed an alliance on the local level in Kragujevac. Two months later, the three parties collaborated in staging a rally on the fifth anniversary of the 9 March 1991 demonstrations which Milošević had suppressed. The rally was attended by about 30,000 opposition supporters. Vuk Drašković and Zoran Djindjić (1952–2003) temporarily mended fences, and although they were later spurned by DSS president Vojislav Koštunica (born 1944), who now complained that Drašković and Djindjić were turning their backs on Serbs living outside Serbia, they built bridges with Vesna Pešić's Civic Alliance of Serbia (GSS). That same month, the SPO, DS, and GSS staged a rally under the banner of "Zajedno" (Together). But it was not until 2 September 1996 that the Zajedno coalition was formally established, with an agreement on the allocation of such seats as they might win in the local elections scheduled for November 1996.

Elections were scheduled for 3 November 1996, with the second round scheduled for 17 November. International observers were on hand for the 3 November elections but left immediately after they were finished, much to the disgust of the Serbian opposition parties. Already in the first round, Zajedno candidates took the lead in 14 of Serbia's largest towns, including Belgrade, Niš, Kragujevac, Novi Sad, Čačak, Kraljevo, Pirot, and Užice. After the votes had been counted on 17 November, Zajednjo's victories in these towns were confirmed; in the Assembly of the city of Belgrade, Zajedno won a particularly resounding victory, capturing 70 of its 110 seats (with Milošević's Socialists winning 23 seats there and Šešelj's Radicals taking 15). On 18 November, the Zajedno coalition held a victory celebration on Belgrade's Square of the Republic.[53] Then, however, the electoral commission refused to confirm the results, citing "irregularities." Authorities subsequently annulled the opposition victories in Niš, Jagodina, and Kraljevo. This sparked protests in the cities affected. Further annulments were announced soon thereafter.

On 24 November, authorities announced the annulment of the victories of

33 Zajedno candidates for offices in and around Belgrade and declared that a third round of elections would be held on 27 November. Meanwhile, the mass protests which had begun the evening of 19 November spread, drawing tens of thousands, in some cases as many as 100,000–200,000, participants.[54] Then, on 26 November, the Supreme Court of the Republic of Serbia confirmed the cancellation of several election results, while 30,000 persons (among them, 15,000 students) protested. On the following day, the third round of voting was held but was boycotted by the opposition. The official results now gave the ruling Socialist Party a resounding victory, though the opposition still won in seven cities, in spite of the announced boycott.[55]

Milošević counted on four things: first, that the opposition would simply get tired of the protests and give up; second, that the combination of Belgrade's icy winter and constant police harassment would prove too much for the protesters; third, that he could establish and maintain control of information, so that most Serbs would remain unaware of the demonstrations or of their true character; and fourth, that he could rely on the army as his *ultima ratio*. Milošević proved to be mistaken in all four calculations. First, the protesters showed a resilience which the Serbian strongman had not anticipated. In fact, as days wore into weeks, Belgrade's daily protests (involving 150,000–200,000 persons on 30 November, more than 150,000 persons on 4 December, 100,000 persons on 6 December, and 100,000 persons on 15 December[56]) increasingly took on a festive character, with protesters marching on one day with their pets (some grinning protesters carrying their fish tanks through town) or on another day holding their noses for the camera, to signal their belief that Radio-Television Belgrade's news broadcasts (in which the strictly nonviolent protests were being characterized as aggressive and violent) stank. A huge effigy of Milošević dressed in striped convict garb was carried aloft as the opposition demanded that Milošević resign. To emphasize their commitment to nonviolence, the opposition protesters threw eggs at government buildings, while shouting, "Slobo is Saddam!"[57]

Since the protesters were neither tiring nor finding the winter too cold to continue, Milošević tried threats and force. On 2 December, the regime banned all public meetings in Belgrade and brought several hundred specially trained riot police to the city center. While the police applied force, protesters shouted back Milošević's famous pledge of 1987: "No one will ever beat you again!"[58] But Milošević was not yet ready to give up, and as December drew to a close, riot police cordoned off Belgrade's streets and beat protesters with their batons, killing one man, named Predrag Starčević, thereby giving the Zajedno opposition its first martyr.[59]

Milošević also had counted on being able to control the information system, and when, on 1 December, Serbian Assembly Speaker Dragan Tomić accused the opposition of "deliberately provoking unrest with destructive, violent, and pro-fascist demonstrations" and of resorting "to certain undemocratic moves," this was supposed to be the view which Serbs would adopt.[60] But an opinion poll taken in early December showed that Milošević's popularity rating had dropped to a slender 16.5%, while Djindjić's had risen from a nearly nullibici- tous 2% to 10%.[61] Then, on 2 December, five Serbian Supreme Court justices issued an open letter to the government, declaring their opposition to "the changing of election results."[62] The following day, the authorities shut down Radio B-92, began jamming the broadcasts of a small student radio station operating in Belgrade, arrested 32 student activists, and blocked busloads of would-be protesters from reaching Belgrade's main bus station.[63] But B-92 was not to be silenced. First, Voice of America agreed to carry its transmissions. Then, before the week was out, Radio B-92 began digital broadcasts in Serbo- Croatian and English over audio Internet links.[64]

Finally, Milošević had hoped that the loyalty of the army and in particular of the respected 63rd Parachute Brigade, highly regarded for its high standards of recruitment and training, could, if necessary, be used as had been done on 9 March 1991. But on 29 December, opposition leaders read to crowds of sup- porters a letter described as representing the views of the commanding officers and troops of several military units including the 63rd Brigade, which declared that the army would not allow its weapons to be used against the people of Ser- bia.[65] Milošević had struck out.

As the protests continued, the state-run Theater T prepared to stage an adap- tation of Shakespeare's *Hamlet*. In what Chris Hedges of the *New York Times* called a "vast perversion of the play," Prince Fortinbras was dressed as Bosnia's High Representative Carl Bildt and walked onstage to the sound of a Nazi marching song. Horatio, an intellectual and usually a positive character, was recast as the villain of the piece. As for Hamlet himself, he was painted as gripped by "the steely drive to seize power," wrote Hedges. "Here is a Hamlet for our time," director Dejan Krstović explained. "Because of Hamlet, the bodies pile up on the altar of authority and the system collapses. Because of Hamlet, the foreign prince, Fortinbras, who for us represents the new world order, comes in from the outside and seizes control, as has happened to the Serbs throughout their history."[66]

Milošević now resorted to a risky gambit: he invited the Organization for Security and Cooperation in Europe (OSCE) to send a team to Belgrade to study the facts and make recommendations. Perhaps he hoped that he could pull the wool over the eyes of the OSCE mediators. Or perhaps he believed that once the demonstrators knew OSCE representatives were involved, they would go home. Whatever Milošević's calculations, when the OSCE mission, led by former Spanish prime minister Felipe Gonzalez, finished its research, it submit- ted a report urging Belgrade to accept opposition victories in all 14 disputed towns, including Belgrade, where opposition victories in 9 districts had been overturned.[67] By this point, Zajedno had been endorsed by former FRY presi- dent Dobrica Ćosić, 30 members of the Serbian Academy of Sciences and Art, the Serbian Association of Writers, the pretender to the Serbian/Yugoslav throne

Crown Prince Aleksandar, the Montenegrin opposition coalition, and even Adem Demaqi, the Albanian human rights activist in Kosovo.[68]

On 2 January 1997, the Serbian Orthodox Synod held an emergency session to discuss the crisis produced by Milošević's effort to deny the opposition its electoral successes. Characterizing the regime as "Communist, godless, and satanic," the Assembly condemned the "falsification of the people's votes, the elimination of political and religious freedom, and particularly the beating and killing of people on the streets of Belgrade. . . . [Milošević] has already set us against the whole world and now he wants to pit us against each other and trigger bloodshed in order to preserve his power."[69] On 7 December 1996, when approached by a delegation from Belgrade's protesting students who were seeking his blessing, Patriarch Pavle had declined to give it, averring that it would not be proper for the Church to take sides in the dispute. But on 27 January 1997, Patriarch Pavle led a huge procession through town in honor of St. Sava's day and, addressing the more than 100,000 persons who had joined in the procession, offered implicit support to the opposition. By that point, moreover, Milošević's minister of information, as well as the Socialist mayors of Belgrade and Niš, had resigned, in what could only be interpreted as tacit votes of no confidence in Milošević's handling of the situation. Finally, on 4 February, noting that "great damage" had been done to Serbia's reputation, both domestically and internationally, Milošević ordered the reinstatement of the opposition victories in all 14 local elections.[70] It had taken 78 days of protests and demonstrations to persuade Milošević to respect the law.[71]

The Unraveling, March 1997–May 1998

Among those who gained political office as a result of the November 1996 elections were Zoran Djindjić, who became mayor of Belgrade, and Vojislav Šešelj, who was elected mayor of Zemun. Šešelj predictably waded into controversy, targeting local Croats for harassment but also creating anxiety for the 170 Jews inhabiting Zemun, as well as for all those who cherish historical and cultural treasures. Specifically, the summer following his election, Šešelj confiscated the Jewish community's 147-year-old synagogue, which had been designated a state-protected historical monument, and had it converted into a nightclub.[72]

In mid-March 1997, Milošević regained his balance and pushed through a new law on the media which imposed new restrictions on privately owned newspapers and set down an "anti-monopoly" clause stipulating that no privately owned radio or television station would henceforth be permitted to broadcast to more than 25% of the country's population.[73] Subsequently, in July 1997, Serbian authorities shut down 55 small radio and television stations. That same month, Milošević, whose five-year term as president of Serbia was about to end, engineered his election, by the Skupština, as president of the FRY.

Zoran Lilić, the erstwhile FRY president (since the ouster of Ćosić), was now nominated by the Socialist Party to run as its candidate for the office of president of Serbia.

Combined presidential and parliamentary elections were scheduled for 21 September. The Socialists calculated, correctly, that the principal challenge to Lilić would come not from the SPO's Vuk Drašković but from the neo-fascist Vojislav Šešelj;[74] accordingly, they granted candidate Drašković a generous amount of time on state television.[75] Although the Socialists felt confident that Drašković had no prospects of winning the presidency, Drašković himself believed that he could emerge as the electoral victor. But Djindjić and Drašković were vying for leadership of the opposition, and Djindjić knew that if Drašković were to win the presidency, his position as leader of the opposition would be unassailable.[76] Accordingly, Djindjić joined Vesna Pešić and Vojislav Koštunica in calling for a boycott of the elections, bringing their rivalry into the open. The growing animosity between the two men was given aggressive expression in mid-August when a group of SPO members barged into a 3,000-strong anti-election rally in Kraljevo being held by the Democratic Party and pelted Djindjić with eggs. Curiously, while most of the rest of the opposition understood the problem in Serbia in terms of a lack of democracy, for Drašković, the problem was the abolition of the monarchy in 1945—an abolition which he wanted to repeal.[77] In a transparent reference to Crown Prince Aleksandar, who had repeatedly cited the Spanish example, Drašković offered that "Serbia needs a Serbian Juan Carlos."[78]

In the parliamentary returns, 110 seats were won by Milošević's Socialists, JUL, and the satellite Nova Demokratija, 82 seats by the Serbian Radical Party, 45 seats by Drašković's Serbian Renewal Movement, and the remaining 13 seats by five smaller parties, representing ethnic Hungarians, Sandžak Muslims, and Serbian oppositionists from Vojvodina.[79] In the presidential race, the Socialist candidate Lilić obtained 35.9% of the vote, with Šešelj securing 28.6%, and Drašković finishing third, with 22% of the vote.[80] Convinced that the boycott had cost him the presidency, Drašković had his deputies in the Belgrade City Assembly join the Socialist and Radical deputies in ousting Djindjić from his post as mayor of Belgrade on 30 September. Drašković and Djindjić had fallen out soon after their victory in January, but after this ouster, a reconciliation between the two men became, in practice, impossible. Although Drašković urged his supporters to abstain from voting in the second round (on 5 October), most of those who had voted for Drašković in round one gave their support to Šešelj in round two. The result was that Šešelj finished slightly ahead of Lilić, collecting 49.9% of the vote, according to the official results, against 46.9% for the Socialist contender.[81] But according to official rules, this result was inconclusive, because voter turnout did not reach the 50% threshold required for a presidential contest. (Officials said that the turnout was 49%.)

A third round was now scheduled for 7 December. Since this was, in theory, a replay of the "runoff," one would normally have expected to see Lilić once more facing Šešelj in an electoral duel. But in the topsy-turvy world of Serbian politics, anything was possible. Accordingly, Lilić pulled out of the race, and Yugoslav foreign minister Milan Milutinović, regarded as the quintessential "yes man" for Milošević, took his place as the Socialist contender. Moreover, under the electoral law of that time, Drašković was allowed to reenter the race, rendering it less a runoff than a completely fresh election. In another curiosity, a 90-minute televised debate, broadcast on 29 November, included only Drašković and Šešelj, while Milutinović, who would ultimately win the election, did not take part. In this debate, Drašković and Šešelj accused each other of being Croats, Drašković accused Šešelj of having friends such as Russian ultra-nationalist Vladimir Zhirinovsky and French ultra-nationalist Jean-Marie Le Pen, Šešelj accused Drašković of having no friends at all, and neither of them discussed any real issues.[82] Although Milutinović surged ahead in this third round, picking up 43.7%, he did not break the 50% barrier, thanks to Drašković's reentry into the "runoff." Šešelj finished second with 32.2%, while Drašković attracted only about 17% of the vote. The remaining 7% of the ballots were, presumably, invalid.[83]

Accordingly, a fourth round of voting was held on 21 December, in which, amid "widespread evidence of election fraud,"[84] Milan Milutinović, a protégé of Milošević, was declared the winner. According to the official results, Milutinović won 2,185,218 votes (59.68%), against Šešelj's 1,363,577 (37.24%).[85] SRS deputy Dragan Todorović brought diagrams to the Skupština, in an effort to demonstrate that, given the Albanians' well-established practice of boycotting all elections, it was impossible for Milutinović to have collected as many votes as he was said to have garnered in Kosovo. But his protests were waved aside, on the grounds that the electoral commission had already certified the result.[86] Besides, staging yet another round of voting would have risked turning Serbia into an international laughing stock.

As 1998 opened, the Socialists found themselves, for the first time, faced with the necessity of forming a coalition government. They approached Drašković who, to the horror of many in the opposition, proved receptive to Socialist courting. After weeks of negotiations, Drašković agreed on 17 February to enter the government; he was now named deputy prime minister (one of five), and let it slip that he hoped to see the double-headed eagle (a symbol used by several European states, including Albania) reinstated as the national symbol.[87] Mirko Marjanović, prime minister since 1994, was chosen for another four-year term. The SPO, which had demanded 10 cabinet ministries as well as the prime ministership, was advised that it would have to be content with eight cabinet ministries (though not the most important ones) and a deputy prime ministership. The SPO's demand for the post of director of *Politika* was also rebuffed.[88]

By this point, tensions in Kosovo were escalating rapidly, and Milošević had decided to hit the Albanians hard. Drašković was not prepared to support a hard line in Kosovo and "told Milutinović that the Kosovo Albanians should be urgently offered agreement on a democratic solution to the Kosovo problem and that, if they fail to accept it, they will be held responsible."[89] As late as 23 March 1998, Milutinović said that he was still trying to come to an agreement with the SPO and ruled out the possibility of a "red-brown" coalition, which would bring Šešelj's Radicals into the government. But the same day, discussions between the Socialists and the Radicals were begun in earnest. On the following day, it was announced that the left-wing parties (the Socialists, JUL, and New Democracy) would form a coalition government with the Radicals, with Marjanović staying on as prime minister. The Socialists retained 15 ministerial posts, JUL was awarded five, and the Radicals were given 15.[90] Nicknamed "the Titanic" and "honored" by the issuance of a rock album (by Rambo Amadeus) bearing that title, the new government quickly passed a new university law (on 26 May), resulting in the purge of certain academics unfriendly toward the regime, and, on 30 September, suspended 10 professors from the Faculty of Law, under the provisions of the same law which, inter alia, required professors to swear their loyalty to the regime and to submit their research plans for approval by state-appointed functionaries.[91] It was with this "red-brown" coalition in the government that Milošević would take up the challenges being presented in Kosovo.

Tensions in Kosovo, 1991–1999

As of 1991, there were some 1.6 million Albanians in Kosovo, according to official statistics, or 2 million, according to Albanian estimates; Albanians constituted about 90% of the population of the province.[92] Yet, in August 1990, the Serbian parliament had introduced a new uniform school curriculum for the republic, under which the teaching of Albanian language, history, literature, songs, and even dances was severely curtailed, while instruction in Serbian language, history, culture, songs, and dances was expanded.[93] Albanian teachers and students refused to accept the new curriculum and withdrew from the school system, setting up a parallel education system operating out of ordinary citizens' homes. The following year, all Albanian students were expelled from the University of Priština, and registration was restricted to non-Albanians, which, in practice, meant mainly Serbs together with a few Greeks. And in spite of their strong demographic presence, Kosovo's Albanians became the target of discrimination in other spheres as well.

After the abolition of Kosovo's autonomy in 1989, five policy spheres— police, economic planning, justice, territorial defense, and international relations—had been placed under Belgrade's direct administration.[94] Milošević now began a multi-pronged campaign designed, in the short run, to reduce the Albanians to second-class citizens and, in the long run, to drive them from the province. Albanians were fired from their jobs only because they were Albanians, and then were expelled from their state-owned apartments because the apartments were linked with the jobs they had now lost. In the years 1990–1995, about 130,000 Albanians were dismissed from their posts in this way; among them were judges, university rectors, factory directors, physicians, and police officers. Their jobs were taken by Serbs who, in many cases, were brought to Kosovo from outside the province.[95] In spring 1991, there were reports that the Yugoslav National Army had been distributing firearms among Serb and Montenegrin civilians in Kosovo; meanwhile, authorities were confiscating arms from local Albanians, even where they were able to produce valid licenses. After the war broke out in Croatia, many young Albanian men were drafted into the army and sent off to fight Croats. Thousands of Albanian men went into hiding or fled abroad, rather than be drafted to do service for Greater Serbia.[96]

In frustration, deputies of the suppressed provincial parliament approved a resolution on 22 September 1991 to put the option of independence before the public, via a clandestine referendum to be conducted 26–30 September. According to Albanian opposition sources, some 87% of eligible voters in Kosovo took part in the referendum (which is to say, essentially all the Albanians), with 99.87% declaring themselves in favor of independence. Only 164 votes were recorded against independence, with 933 invalid ballots.[97] The suppressed parliament thereupon declared the independence of Kosovo on 19 October 1991, naming Dr. Bujar Bukoshi as prime minister. Subsequently, on 24 May 1992, the Kosovar Albanians staged clandestine presidential elections, electing Dr. Ibrahim Rugova, president of the local writers association and president of the Democratic League of Kosovo (LDK), as president of the Republic of Kosovo. From the 1970s until the late 1980s, as Predrag Tasic has noted, separatism had been a minority view among the Albanians of Kosovo; it was Milošević's repressive policies, his complete disregard of rule of law, his embrace of naked intolerance, and his scorn for the harm principle which made separatism mainstream among the province's Albanians.[98]

In the latter half of 1992, Serbian authorities renamed the streets and squares of Priština, removing references to Albanian heroes and cultural figures and emblazoning signs with the names of Serbian heroes and cultural figures instead.[99] The Serbian authorities also engaged, in the years after 1990, in frequent harassment and beatings of local Albanians, in the ejection of Albanian civilians from their homes, in the plundering of Albanian-run businesses, and in raids of Albanian homes on the pretext of searching for weapons.[100] Toward the end of 1994, Serbian police arrested some 200 former police of Albanian nationality, subsequently bringing 159 of them to trial on charges of seeking to bring about the secession of Kosovo from the FRY.[101] On 13 January 1995, Belgrade issued a decree offering free land to Serbs who would settle in Kosovo, promising them 40-year loans so that they could build new houses on the properties they would receive. The land was to be obtained through forcible confiscations from Albanian landowners.[102]

In the meantime, the Kosovo problem was already being quietly "internationalized." In October 1992, Kosovar prime minister Bukoshi came to Washington, D.C., and, in a news briefing at the National Press Club, alerted those present to what he called "an alarming and very dangerous situation in Kosova," noting that "life in Kosova is unbearable, the repression is increasing every day." He added, probably more presciently than he realized, that, unless some effective prophylactic measures were taken, in time "there would be a massacre of [the] Albanian population in Kosova. And also almost one million refugees would seek shelter in the neighboring countries."[103] Six and a half years later, Bukoshi's forebodings would be borne out, when 855,000 Albanians would flee the province to escape ravaging Serb forces, taking refuge primarily in neighboring Albania and Macedonia.[104]

The year 1993 saw the issuance of what came to be known as the Minnesota Plan. Drafted by the Organization of Independent Attorneys for the Promotion and Protection of Human Rights, based in Minnesota, the plan called for the restoration of Kosovo's autonomy by June of that year or, failing that, for the UN Security Council to establish a protectorate in the province, under Articles 75–91 of the UN Charter.[105] Between the end of 1987 and the end of 1989, an estimated 400,000 Albanians fled from Kosovo.[106]

In March 1994, as the West considered lifting some of the economic sanctions imposed on Serbia, President Sali Berisha of Albania called on Western states to hold off on such a move and to make any lifting of sanctions contingent upon a settlement in Kosovo. Berisha also requested that UN monitors be dispatched to Kosovo, so that there would be at least a symbolic international presence in the province.[107] Berisha's advice was ignored, and the sanctions were eased. Later that year, Bukoshi submitted testimony to the House Foreign Affairs Committee. He took the opportunity to scold the U.S. and the West for undue equanimity about Milošević's politics in Bosnia and for having ignored developments in Kosovo.[108] This, and similar pleading from Rugova himself as the Dayton peace talks were being organized, were ignored. Kosovo was "peaceful," Western "realists" calculated: so why get involved? For all that, the Council of Foreign Ministers of the European Union did call on Belgrade, on 30 October 1995, to restore wide-ranging autonomy to Kosovo, but the suggestion was not backed up with either carrots or sticks. Subsequently, on 24 January 1996, the Parliamentary Assembly of the Council of Europe adopted Resolution 1077, noting its concern in connection with "systematic human rights violations against the Albanian population in Kosovo, including torture, police brutality, violent house searches, arbitrary arrests, political trials, and irregularities in legal proceedings."[109]

But Belgrade did not even blink. Indeed, in the mid-1990s, thousands of Albanian-language books were confiscated from the National and University Library of Kosovo and pulped.[110] The Yugoslav Army and the police were reportedly harassing Albanians "frequently," and some Albanian civilians were fatally shot.[111] In February 1996 alone, the Priština-based Council for the Defense of Human Rights and Freedoms recorded 580 cases of human rights abuses in Kosovo, noting that women and children had not been exempted from the systematic abuse.[112] Serbian police demolished Albanian-owned shops, raided Albanian homes, and raided video-cassette shops across the province, confiscating copies of the film *Nje Pallto per Babain tim ne Burg* (A Coat for My Convicted Father).[113] Directed by Adem Mikullovci and edited by Ekrem Dobercani and Ergyn Dobercani, the film was said to portray "the life of children in Kosova under Serbian occupation and the Serbian police practices against the Albanian children."[114]

In the meantime, radical militant groups had begun organizing themselves among Kosovar Albanians in spring 1993, purchasing weapons in Albania or on the international arms black market. When the Albanians saw themselves once more sidelined and ignored at Dayton, their patience snapped.[115] Albanians knew instinctively that the time for armed struggle had arrived. Then, in April 1996, a Serb shot a young Albanian in Priština, because he thought that the Albanian was stealing his car. Some 10,000 people turned out for the young Albanian's funeral. In the following days, five Serbs were shot in different towns across Kosovo, and a policeman was wounded. Another Serbian policeman lost his life in a shooting attack in June, when three police were wounded.[116] Before the end of 1996, rumors began to circulate that an armed resistance group calling itself the Kosova Liberation Army (KLA) had been formed, and some actions were already being attributed to this body. But many observers remained uncertain, at the time, as to whether the KLA, which can trace its birth back to 1982 (albeit under a different name),[117] was more than a phantasm of Albanian wishful thinking. These doubts were laid to rest in mid-January 1997, when the KLA carried out a bombing attack on the rector of the University of Priština, Radivoje Papović, leaving him wounded.[118] In the meantime, the KLA was building up a small arsenal rather quickly, thanks to an uprising in southern Albania during December 1996–March 1997 in which arms depots throughout Albania were looted, with the booty often being put up for sale at bargain prices.[119]

Meanwhile, Albanians failed to make any headway in obtaining their reintegration into the educational system. Although they had set up an underground educational system, embracing all levels from elementary to university education, and could count about two-thirds of Kosovo's 450,000 school-age Albanian youngsters as enrolled in the underground system as of 1994, the Albanian side wanted to see an opening of the state schools to Albanian pupils and students and the restoration of Albanian-language instruction.[120] In September 1996, Rugova and Milošević had signed an agreement to such an effect, but the agreement was stillborn. On 1 October 1997, there were demonstrations by Albanian students in Priština and several other cities in Kosovo. The students demanded implementation of the 1996 agreement between Milošević and Rugova on the reopening of schools to Albanians and the resumption of Albanian-language instruction. Serbian police suppressed the demonstrations with force, arresting dozens and putting them on trial on charges of membership in the KLA.[121] On 30 December there were renewed protests by Albanian students, who demanded unconditional access to university facilities. Once again, the police forced them to disburse. But after this second incident, Patriarch Pavle wrote a conciliatory letter to the leadership of the Albanian Students' Union, criticizing the use of violence by the police and noting that both Serbian students (in winter 1996–1997) and Albanian students had been subjected to police violence under the Milošević regime.[122]

About this time (specifically, on 20 November 1997), the UN General Assembly passed a resolution which was critical of Belgrade for human rights violations in Kosovo, including the closure of Albanian schools there and the use of force by Serbian police against the peaceful Albanian student protests on 1 October. But the Serbian people were less sympathetic to the Albanians. Poisoned by ten years of chauvinistic propaganda, 41.8% of Serbs surveyed told pollsters in November 1997 that the solution to the problems in Kosovo lay in the expulsion, whether peacefully or by force, of the Albanian population of the province. Only 27.2% felt that a policy combining tolerance and cultural autonomy would be the best approach.[123]

In spite of some misunderstanding in Western capitals concerning the depth and seriousness of the crisis in Kosovo,[124] NATO ambassadors meeting in Brussels on 7 January 1998 expressed "great concern" about developments in Kosovo. Subsequently, after the repression of Albanians in the Drenica region and in Priština in the period 28 February–2 March, EU external relations commissioner Van den Broek called on Milošević on 3 March to press the FRY president to enter into dialogue in good faith with Kosovo's Albanians and to restore their autonomy. Two days later, the North Atlantic Council issued a statement about Kosovo in which it condemned "unreservedly the violent repression of [the] non-violent expression of political views."[125]

By this point, however, the KLA had declared an insurrection and, by late July 1998, controlled about 40% of the countryside, including some important towns.[126] But Serbia fought back with tanks, helicopter gunships, and a strategy of terror. The Albanian resistance was quickly put on the defensive and sent reeling, and by mid-September, there were more than 700 dead on the Albanian side and more than 265,000 Albanians were homeless, many of them camping in the woods.[127] In the course of this counteroffensive, Serbian forces were said to have carried out massacres in Likoshan, Qirez, Prekaz, Lybeniq, Poklek, Rahovec, Goluboc, Galica, and Abria.[128] When some brave Serbian broadcasters for private radio and television stations dared to raise their voices in criticism of Milošević's policies, they found themselves taken off the air; some 20 independent radio stations and 10 independent television stations were shut down by Belgrade in May 1998 alone.[129]

NATO councils issued a series of threats and "last warnings." But the more NATO ministers threatened, the more they seemed to confirm Stefan Troebst's suspicion, voiced about this time, that "swift and robust Western intervention is unlikely."[130] Even after an 11th-hour agreement between Milošević and U.S. special envoy Richard Holbrooke on 13 October 1998, in which the Serbian leader promised to cease military operations in the province, to grant Kosovo autonomy of some sort, to reduce his military presence in the province, and to allow some 2,000 international "compliance verifiers" freedom of movement in Kosovo, Milošević did not deviate from his dangerous course. In fact, Yugoslav troop strength was actually *reinforced* after this agreement with Holbrooke, rising from 18,000 at the time of the agreement to 23,500 as of 23 December, and to 29,000 on the eve of the initiation of NATO aerial strikes on 24 March 1999.[131] According to Louis Sell, the build-up was part of a Serbian plan known as Operation Horseshoe, which was designed to drive the Albanians out of Kosovo.[132] General Momčilo Perišić, chief-of-staff of the Yugoslav Army, considered Milošević's plans to be complete folly and told him so. Perišić went further and, addressing a group of political leaders in Gornji Milanovac in October 1998, warned them that Milošević's plans for Kosovo would take the country to war with NATO.[133] Perišić was thereupon fired from his post, and a military campaign against Albanians in Kosovo was set in motion on 24 December 1998.[134] In addition to regular troops, authorities also enlisted Serbian paramilitaries recruited from within Serbia proper and also reportedly recruited an unknown number of thugs from Serbian jails, offering these criminal elements amnesty, high incentive pay, the chance to engage in wanton violence without accountability, and the "right" to keep whatever they plundered from Kosovo's Albanians.[135]

Although the Albanians who had been camping in the woods as of July–September 1998, for fear of Serb reprisals, had been encouraged after the October 1998 agreement to return to their houses, which in many cases were damaged, and although some, in fact, did return, the renewed military campaign launched on 24 December drove some 20,000 Albanians from their homes by the end of January 1999. Combined with those who had remained homeless since the previous year, the total number of displaced persons was estimated at about 200,000 as of the end of January 1999.[136] Then, after the massacre of 45 persons, including young children—all thought, at the time, to be Albanians—in the town of Račak on 15 January, the international community once more roused itself and summoned Serbs and Albanians to a peace conference at Rambouillet, France, on 6 February. (Five years later, Finnish pathologist Helena Ranta revealed that only 40 of the 45 bodies were delivered to the Priština Forensic Institute for examination, and that some of the dead were members of Serbian forces and others were members of the KLA.[137]) The Albanians sent a high-level delegation to Rambouillet with the earnest desire to find a solution. Milošević was concerned that if he went to Rambouillet, he could be forced into a corner. He therefore sent Milan Milutinović, the Serbian president, at the head of the Yugoslav delegation. But, as Tim Judah has pointed out, the members of the FRY delegation kept "much of the rest of the chateau awake by late-night carousing and the singing of Serbian songs, which induced the [other] negotiators to complain."[138] The Yugoslav delegation objected, among other things, to NATO's intention to send a peacekeeping force which would be exempt from Yugoslav law, but the more basic problem was that while the Albanians wanted independence, the Serbs were completely opposed and did not even want to restore Kosovar autonomy. The Yugoslav side therefore ultimately rejected the compromise offered by Western mediators, even though the draft endeavored to find a middle ground between the Serbian and Albanian positions. At one point in the proceedings, however, Milutinović asked Chris Hill, the American ambassador to Macedonia and a key member of the U.S. team, to meet him at the piano bar at the Hotel Bristol. There, Milutinović revealed what had been a secret fantasy of Milošević's for several years and proposed that Yugoslavia be admitted into NATO, offering the use of bases at commercial rates. Hill could not believe what he was hearing and had to point out that the eve of a possible NATO attack on Yugoslavia was not the best time to discuss Yugoslavia's desire to join the North Atlantic alliance.[139] Meanwhile, even as the conference at Rambouillet continued its deliberations, Colonel M. Marković, a special unit commander, gave orders for the summary liquidation of 66 pro-independence Albanians, while Serbian tanks and artillery continued to pound Albanian villages, and the Yugoslav Army even reinforced its strength in the province.[140] The death toll for the period March 1998 through mid-March 1999 stood at more than 2,000, while the number of Albanians driven from their homes by Serbian forces by the eve of the NATO attack (i.e., by the of week 16–23 March 1999) has been estimated at about 459,000 (260,000 displaced within Kosovo and 199,000 having fled abroad).[141]

NATO secretary general Javier Solana had indicated, in unambiguous terms, the alliance's readiness to make good on its many threats if Belgrade did not come to some agreement at Rambouillet.[142] NATO set a deadline of 24 March for Belgrade to acquiesce, and as the deadline approached, British foreign secretary George Lord Robertson and the Supreme Allied Commander, Europe, General Wesley Clark flew to Belgrade for talks with Milošević. However, the CIA allegedly feared that the Serbs were planning to use shoulder-launched SAMs to shoot down the helicopter bearing Lord Robertson and General Clark; as a result, their itinerary was changed, delaying their arrival by more than five hours.[143] In any event, Milošević refused to budge, and when Holbrooke visited Belgrade on 23 March, for a "last chance" offer, Milošević received him but sent him home empty-handed. By that point, Milošević had brought additional troops close to the border with Kosovo and had sent an unspecified number of heavy M-84 tanks into Kosovo, in overt violation of the October 1998 agreement.[144] Since tanks are not used in defense against aerial attacks, the only conceivable purpose of this buildup was to use the impending attack by NATO as a "cover" to intensify the drive against Albanian civilians.

'Til Great Birnam Wood to High Dunsinane Hill Shall Come . . .[145]

At 2 P.M., EST, 24 March 1999, after seemingly endless threats and hesitations, NATO began a campaign of aerial strikes against targets in Serbia, Kosovo, and, initially, Montenegro.[146] Instead of backing down, however, Serbian forces on the ground intensified their "scorched earth" attacks on the noncombatant Albanian civilians, torching villages, driving the Albanians out, and even confiscating the documents from the fleeing Albanians. At peak, some 855,000 Albanians fled Kosovo to neighboring countries, fulfilling the horrific prediction made by Bukoshi in 1992.[147] At first, Serbs rallied around their government, holding outdoor anti-NATO rock concerts in Belgrade, while anti-war activists took to the streets in many European cities. But NATO remained united and conducted some 12,575 strike sorties against the FRY, over a period of 78 days.[148] On 28 May 1999, a day after the International War Crimes Tribunal announced its indictment of FRY president Slobodan Milošević and four other high-ranking Yugoslav officials on three counts of crimes against humanity and one count of violation of the laws or customs of war, for their role in the terror being perpetrated by Serbian forces in Kosovo, the FRY government announced its acceptance, in principle, of the peace resolution drafted by the Group of 8.[149] Russian envoy Viktor Chernomyrdin and Finnish president Martti Ahtisaari flew to Belgrade at the beginning of June for discussions with Milošević, but the latter stalled, haggling over details, while Yugoslav forces shelled several locations in neighboring Albania on 6 June.[150] Finally, on 9 June, Belgrade signed a military-technical agreement with NATO, effectively establishing an international protectorate in Kosovo (details in the next chapter), and the NATO aerial campaign was brought to an end. In the course of the preceding 78 days, NATO bombs had killed an estimated 500 Serb and Albanian civilians in 90 separate incidents, according to Human Rights Watch Helsinki, while Serbian forces killed between 10,000 and 12,000 Albanian civilians, according to American governmental and private sources.[151]

As KFOR troops entered Kosovo, GSS chair Vesna Pešić commented, "People are beginning to draw the conclusion that there is no future with Milošević."[152] Momčilo Trajković, head of an anti-regime grouping of Serbs in Kosovo, was even more explicit: "The Milošević policy [has been] catastrophic, and he is most responsible for the situation in which we have found ourselves. His policy regarding the national issue is traitorous."[153]

Milošević's Last Stand

As early as 1993, there were reports that increasing numbers of Montenegrins favored separation from Serbia.[154] By 1996, when Milošević's ally Momir Bulatović was still Montenegro's president, the gulf between Serbia and Montenegro seemed to some observers to have grown wider.[155] Later, when Milošević had himself elected FRY president in July 1997, Montenegrin authorities protested vociferously.[156] Belgrade rejected a Montenegrin plan to convert Yugoslavia into a confederation, in which Montenegro would have had its own currency, its own foreign ministry, and its own defense system.[157] But by September 1999,

43.9% of Montenegrin citizens favored Montenegrin independence (vs. 38.9% opposed, 9% having no opinion, and 8.2% declaring that they would not vote in any eventual referendum on the question).[158] By late May 2000, 65% of Montenegrins were reported to be in favor of independence.[159]

In fact, the Montenegrin government introduced the German DM as its official currency (alongside the Yugoslav dinar) on 2 November 1999, later declaring the DM, and in 2002, the euro, its sole currency.[160] Within the republic, elites polarized, with Momir Bulatović setting up his own battalion of military police. Then, in early March 2000, as Serb authorities imposed a blockade of supplies of medicine to Montenegro, and a total blockade "on the import of raw materials and semi-finished goods for Montenegrin industry and the export of industrial products from Montenegro." Montenegrin president Djukanović began to express concerns that war could break out in Montenegro between advocates and opponents of independence.[161] Yugoslav Army officers and soldiers began defecting to the Montenegrin police, while Belgrade took steps to organize a new military police battalion inside Montenegro.[162] At the same time, Montenegrin authorities tightened security in the republic, appointing three dismissed Yugoslav Army generals to serve as advisers for security and defense.[163]

Milošević adopted a series of measures which seemed to constitute preparations for a fifth war, against Montenegro. In a telling signal of his intentions, Milošević omitted Montenegrin officers from a list of 17 senior officers being appointed to new posts in mid-March 2000.[164] The regime also called for "loyal forces" to volunteer for military service, organized paramilitary units within Montenegro (as already mentioned), set up an "illegal" television station inside Montenegro, using military equipment to broadcast programs prepared in Belgrade, and initiated verbal attacks on the Montenegrin government, charging that it "had 'massively' armed the local police with anti-aircraft and anti-tank weapons, had armed trusted civilians, and had employed foreign experts to provide training in 'terrorism and sabotage.'"[165] These steps replicated the pattern of events which had preceded the outbreak of hostilities in Croatia and Bosnia a decade before.[166]

In addition, making use of repressive legislation on the media passed in October 1998,[167] the Milošević regime moved decisively to quash or suffocate independent media across a broad range, confiscating equipment, imposing fines, and, on occasion, simply taking control of an outlet. Authorities also shut down a number of television and radio stations in the course of March 1999. The Independent Association of Journalists of Serbia (NUNS) demanded the retraction of the 1998 Law on Public Information and the cessation of all repression against independent media and journalists, but in vain.[168] The repression of the media continued until Milošević's removal from power. On 17 May, in a particularly important blow, government authorities seized control of the broadcasting facilities shared by Studio B television and Radio B2-92, simultaneously assuming control of Radio Index, an erstwhile independent Belgrade radio station located in the same building.

Then, in midsummer 2000, Slobodan Cekić, the director of Radio Index, died in a mysterious water sports accident at the Adriatic resort town of Herceg Novi. Montenegrin police considered the circumstances suspicious and immediately launched an investigation.[169] Meanwhile, Radio B2-92, banned by Belgrade authorities in May 2000, made arrangements to broadcast from Kosovo (via Radio Kontakt in Priština) and from Hungary (via Radio Tilos), inter alia.[170] Reviewing this dismal record, Veran Matić, the editor-in-chief of Radio B2-92, noted, in June 2000, that over the preceding two years, 26 employees of broadcast or print media had been killed, at least 60 journalists had been taken into custody, and six had been given prison terms.[171]

In late March 2000, Milošević arranged for the government to propose a new law to the federal government. Under the provisions of this law, the composition of the deputations sent by the Serbian and Montenegrin legislatures to the Chamber of the Republics, the upper house of parliament, would be changed in such a way that Djukanović would be constrained to include also delegates from Momir Bulatović's Socialist People's Party. This, in turn, promised to give Milošević the two-thirds majority he would need in that house in order to change the constitution. In spite of opposition from Djukanović's party, the law was passed by the Serbian parliament on 11 April.[172] The law also provided that only a political party with at least 12 deputies in the republic's legislature could send deputies to the Chamber of Republics. Dragan Veselinov, chair of the Vojvodinan Coalition, characterized the passage of this law as "an internal coup in the Serbian Assembly."[173]

Three days after the passage of this law, between 100,000 and 200,000 persons turned out for a protest rally in downtown Belgrade.[174] The sheer size of the turnout raised opposition spirits, but the regime responded in force;[175] throughout April and May, police repeatedly beat protesters with batons, inflicting wounds on them, and used tear gas to break up peaceful gatherings. Even so, more than 50,000 persons demonstrated against the regime in several Serbian cities on 19 May, with some 15,000 persons turning out for an anti-regime rally in Belgrade on 27 May.[176] The regime responded to these latter protests by arresting opposition activists in Čačak, Novi Sad, Užice, and other cities, and by accusing opposition leaders of trying to break up what remained of the country.[177] On 23 May, masked men attacked a sit-in protest at the university, beating up several dozen students; three days later, Jevrem Janjić, the Serbian minister of education, ordered the immediate closure of all universities and colleges, a week ahead of schedule, and declared that all university premises would remain out-of-bounds to professors and students until further notice.[178] As students marched in protest, Serbian Patriarch Pavle lent his support to the students, even as authorities showed their contempt for world public opinion by characterizing the ICTY as a criminal organization.[179] Finally, at month's end, with the opposition parties still unable to formulate an effective strategy, the 25,000-strong "Otpor" (Resistance) student movement announced its transformation into a broader citizens' association, to be called the Popular Resistance Movement (Narodni Pokret Otpor, or NPO).[180]

Predictably, the restructured Chamber of Republics played the role assigned to it by Milošević, and on 6 July, the bicameral legislature adopted amendments to the constitution, prescribing the direct popular vote of both the president of the Federal Republic of Yugoslavia and the deputies to the Chamber of Republics.[181] This move allowed citizens of Serbia to outvote citizens of Montenegro, thereby nullifying Montenegro's constitutionally guaranteed equality with Serbia. Montenegro's government repudiated the amendments, which, it said, had been adopted by "an illegal and illegitimate federal parliament."[182]

With the constitution "fixed," Milošević now called for elections on 24 September 2000. Djukanović, calculating as many did that Milošević would fix the elections, declared that his republic would boycott the elections.[183] Djindjić, however, contacted Vojislav Koštunica, the president of the Democratic Party of Serbia (DSS) and suggested that he run for president as the candidate of a coalition of opposition parties. This move threatened to marginalize Drašković, who now offered his own candidate for the presidency: Mayor of Belgrade Vojislav Mihailović, grandson of the Chetnik commander Draža Mihailović.

As the election campaign got underway, Ivan Stambolić, whom Milošević had removed from office in 1987, gave several interviews to Montenegrin television. In these interviews, he described the Serbian leader as a "master of consuming and reproducing chaos," a "Frankenstein's monster," and declared that "At the end, he must be destroyed, most people are against him and they will get him. He will never go in peace."[184] On 25 August, the 64-year-old Stambolić, who had maintained contact with opposition circles, was kidnapped in broad daylight in the Banovo Brdo area of Belgrade on 25 August 2000.[185] Radio 2-B92 adopted Stambolić's case as its own cause and frequently reminded its listeners of the kidnapping. Nearly three years later, when Stambolić's body was finally found, a police investigation reached the conclusion that Stambolić had been killed "by members of an elite paramilitary police unit loyal to Milošević."[186]

Milošević had increasingly been surrounding himself with sycophants, who told him what he wanted to hear. When independent opinion polls indicated that about three out of every four Serbs disapproved of his performance in office, his sycophants told him that this was Western propaganda. When rumors reached him that the Yugoslav economy was not doing well, his trusted associates assured him that Yugoslavia was recovering, that citizens were facing only a few shortages, and that postwar reconstruction was proceeding at a satisfactory pace.[187] Gorica Gajević, general-secretary of the Socialist Party, and other close aides assured Milošević that his electoral victory in September was "certain," and when Zoran Lilić, the party's vice president, dared to level with Milošević and described the holding of an election as "an adventure," Milošević rejected Lilić's analysis out of hand. In August, Lilić resigned from the Socialist Party in frustration. Indeed, as late as August 2000, it seemed likely that Milošević would simply have himself declared the winner in the 24 September elections. Had Milošević achieved his objectives, it is likely that he would have moved quickly to execute his plans—already drawn up by then—to have Montenegrin president Djukanović arrested.[188] But as election day approached and as the tangible strength of the opposition became all too obvious, foreign observers began to speculate that Milošević would "concede" the need for a run-off election and then set his sights on stealing the run-off. This was, apparently, Milošević's strategy when the Federal Electoral Commission released its official results, holding that 56-year-old Vojislav Koštunica, candidate of the Democratic Opposition of Serbia (DOS) coalition, had won 48.22% of the votes, versus 40.23% for Milošević, with the remainder of the votes spread among three other candidates (Drašković's candidate, Mihailović, for example, received 2.95% of the vote).[189] The opposition, on the other hand, had been monitoring the voting independently and claimed that Koštunica had won 54.6% of the vote, against 35.01% for Milošević.[190] Under FRY election rules, a run-off was required if no candidate garnered more than 50% of the votes. The Federal Election Commission now set the run-off elections for 8 October, even as the U.S. and West European states announced their recognition of Koštuncia's first-round victory.

The Fall

Refusing to participate in the run-off election, Koštunica announced that he had already won. The opposition charged the regime with fraud, while hundreds of riot police were deployed in downtown Belgrade. Even as Milošević was pressing the opposition to agree to a run-off, tens of thousands of opposition supporters crowded Belgrade's streets on 25 September to celebrate their victory, chanting, "Kill yourself, Slobodan, and save Serbia!"[191] But in spite of his failure with this tactic in 1996, Milošević held fast to the notion of holding a run-off and, at 2 A.M. on 28 September, confirmed his intention to stage a run-off election on 8 October. That same day (28 September), Vuk Obradović, a former Yugoslav Army general and now leading opposition figure, met with other opposition leaders to plan protest actions. Massive street demonstrations involving 100,000 or more continued, and on 2 October, the opposition announced a general strike, to bring down the government.[192] Roads and railways were blockaded, and miners at the Kolubara mines, who had hitherto been a bulwark of support for Milošević, now turned against him and went on strike. By this point, Milošević's friend Vladimir Putin had also endorsed Koštunica's victory.[193] As the strike spread, two television stations in provincial cities were taken over by opposition supporters. But the regime drew its wagons in a circle, as it were, and there were reports of police beatings in at least two locations. On 3 October, a government statement was read over state television, warning that protesters risked reprisals of an unspecified nature. But the opposition had taken the precaution of organizing its own armed units, recruiting about a thousand military veterans, including former members of the famed 63rd Parachute Brigade, special anti-terrorist units, and paramilitaries; these forces were equipped with automatic rifles, pistols, and anti-tank weapons.[194] In the meantime, many of the police were defecting to the opposition, while the army had already begun to distance itself from the Milošević regime.[195] At this point, riot police were sent to crush the strike at the Kolubara mines and to arrest 13 of the strike's organizers. When the police arrived, they ordered the miners to leave the mine. But when the miners refused, and some 20,000 working people rallied in support of the miners, police forces simply melted away.[196] This was a turning point. Meanwhile, about 40,000 people rallied in support of Koštunica in the industrial town of Kragujevac.

Velimir Ilić, mayor of Čačak, played a key role in these days, organizing a caravan of protesters who streamed into Belgrade from the Čačak district. Some 25 busloads of protesters from Novi Sad also arrived in Belgrade by mid-day 5 October.[197] Protesters quickly took control of the facilities of leading media outlets in Belgrade and Novi Sad.

At this point, Milošević sent the army general staff a list of 50 DOS leaders who, in his view, should be arrested or liquidated. Six of the names on the list were for "liquidations"; these included Koštunica, Djindjić, DOS coordinator Vladan Batić, Nebojša Ćović, Čačak mayor Velimir Ilić, and former general Momčilo Perišić, now head of the Movement for a Democratic Serbia.[198] The army refused to act. Milošević, by now ensconced in a presidential hunting lodge in the village of Garešnica in eastern Serbia, picked up the phone and ordered army chief-of-staff Nebojša Pavković to bring tanks onto Belgrade's streets and to shoot protesters who were storming the Skupština and other critical buildings, such as Radio-Television Serbia; Pavković refused. Milošević then called Vlajko Stojiljković, the Serbian minister of internal affairs, and ordered him to send helicopters to spray protesters with tear gas and other chemical agents. Stojiljković passed along Milošević's orders, but his subordinates refused to obey.[199] By this point, crowds of angry Serbs, estimated in the hundreds of thousands, had taken over the Skupština which caught fire.[200] Milošević finally resigned, and Koštunica was officially declared the FRY's new president.[201]

Koštunica enjoyed moral authority, but under the constitution, his prescribed powers were actually rather limited. In addition, the Socialist Party was still the strongest bloc in the Skupština. Thus, for DOS, the first order of business was to set legislative elections, in order to clean the Socialists out of office. Elections were set for 23 December. In the meantime, FRY prime minister Bulatović and Serbian interior minister Stojiljković resigned, and a transitional government was named, consisting of, among others, FRY prime minister Zoran Djindjić, Serbian prime minister Milomir Minić, FRY foreign minister Goran Svilanović, FRY defense minister Slobodan Krapović, FRY interior minister Zoran Živković, and FRY finance minister Dragiša Pešić.[202] Yet, until the new elections would be held, DOS's power was too limited, and Serbia remained in a state of political suspended animation, in which relatively little could be done.[203] DOS was unable, for example, to prevent state security police from shredding important files containing incriminating information.[204] Moreover, in spite of firm indications from the ICTY that the arrest of Milošević remained a high priority,[205] no action was taken to restrict Milošević's freedom of movement, and the former strongman even attended his party's congress, where he was reelected party president. Indeed, even as late as early January 2001, some 39 of Milošević's closest associates retained automatic and sniper rifles and other armaments; Interior Minister Živković set a deadline of 10 January for the return of these weapons to the ministry's arsenal.[206]

Koštunica visited Montenegro as early as 17 October, in an endeavor to find a common ground with Montenegrin president Djukanović. But Djukanović felt that Montenegro's fate had been tied to Serbian political uncertainty for too long and insisted that Montenegro would settle for nothing less than full independence, while suggesting a confederal union with limited shared activities.[207] On 1 November, the Montenegrin parliament approved legislation establishing a central bank of Montenegro, and on 11 November, the German DM became Montenegro's sole legal tender, in a clear signal of Djukanović's determination to stay on an independence course. His political nemesis, Momir Bulatović, leader of Montenegro's Socialist National Party and former FRY prime minister, declared his party's opposition to this course, however, and promised to wage "a decisive and wide anti-referendum campaign . . . by way of citizens' peaceful protests."[208] Koštunica, a former law professor, worried, for his part, that if Montenegro were to secede from the FRY, then the FRY would cease to exist; under the circumstances, the UN Security Council 1244, which guaranteed FRY sovereignty but not Serbian sovereignty as such over Kosovo, would become a dead letter; a Montenegrin secession, thus, could make Kosovo's secession unavoidable.[209] But even the collapse of the Montenegrin government at the end of December 2000, when a small coalition partner withdrew its support, seemed unlikely to abort the momentum toward at least a Montenegrin referendum on independence, if not independence itself.[210] At a minimum, Montenegro's self-assertion promised to bring about significant changes to the FRY constitution, an option endorsed by FRY prime minister Zoran Djindjić in January 2001.[211] Indeed, after the failure of talks between Koštunica and Djukanović on 19 January, the Montenegrin parliament agreed to hold legislative elections on 22 April, which President Djukanović promised would be followed by a referendum on Montenegro's future relationship with Serbia.[212]

EU and American criticism of Djukanović's aspirations for independence may have dampened the support for Djukanović, at least temporarily. Be that as it may, the margin of victory won by Djukanović's party on 22 April—a plurality of 42.05%, against 40.67% captured by Predrag Bulatović's pro-Yugoslav coalition, "Together with Yugoslavia"—was razor thin.[213] The result came as a surprise for Djukanović, who had expected a more decisive victory, as opinion polls had suggested he might anticipate. In February 2001, for example, some 58% of Montenegrins were said to favor independence for their republic.[214]

For his part, Djukanović continued to insist that a referendum would provide the best means of resolving the issue, even while entering into negotiations with Serbian politicians concerning a possible revamping of the federal state. Montenegrin secessionism was having repercussions elsewhere in the FRY. In Vojvodina, Miodrag Isakov, chair of the Vojvodina Reformist Party, lent his support to Montenegro's confederalist platform, while calls for a restoration of Vojvodina's autonomy became more insistent.[215] As of April 2001, only 5% of Vojvodinans wanted to see a complete severing of relations with Serbia, while some 8% supported the notion of a confederal union with Serbia.[216] But support for a restoration of Vojvodina's autonomy—snuffed out in early 1989— was widespread. Within Serbia itself, a new, rather anomalous organization now made an appearance; calling itself the State-Forming Movement of Serbia (Državnotvorni Pokret Srbije), the organization was founded by journalist Ratko Dmitrović, television broadcaster Dina Čolić, and political scientist Vinko Djurić.[217] If Montenegro could secede from Serbia, then Serbia, in Dmitrović's view, could also secede from Montenegro!

With the fall of Milošević, the FRY was rapidly reintegrated into the international family of states, being admitted to the UN and the Balkan Stability Pact, and readmitted to the OSCE. Belgrade's new government also moved expeditiously to normalize relations with the other Yugoslav successor states.[218] The international community moved quickly with pledges of financial assistance, supplies of gas and electricity, emergency food supplies, and pharmaceuticals. President Clinton promised to support a rapid lifting of all sanctions against the FRY. Yugoslavia also filed for membership in the Council of Europe, admission into which was likely to be a more involved process, insofar as the council requires that domestic legislation meet certain uniform standards.

The arrest of corrupt and otherwise culpable officials internally was a slower process, by contrast, though Mihalj Kertes who, as director of the Yugoslav Customs Bureau, had supervised a massive smuggling operation designed to evade UN sanctions, was arrested on 15 December.[219] The new government also reopened an investigation of former Tanjug director Zoran Jevdjović and several other employees of Tanjug on charges of corruption.[220] But the new government was, in fact, moving very slowly until the elections of 23 December would not only confirm its mandate but also consolidate its strength.

The 23 December elections fully lived up to DOS's expectations. The coalition won about 65% of the votes (garnering 178 of the 250 seats in the Serbian Assembly), while the Socialists won only 13.35% (for 36 seats), the Radicals 8.51% (22 seats), and the SSJ (Party of Serb Unity) 5.13% (14 seats). Drašković's SPO, like JUL, failed to win any seats in the Serbian Assembly.[221] To almost no one's surprise, Zoran Djindjić was now named Serbian prime minister.

In the wake of this electoral victory, the new government now announced further arrests and investigations. Among the first to be arrested were the members of the Federal Electoral Commission, who had initially wanted to deny Koštunica his first-round victory; they were brought before the court on charges of electoral fraud.[222] In the meantime, Koštunica also fired many of the military's top brass, though not Chief-of-Staff Nebojša Pavković. On 26 January 2001, the new Serbian parliament removed the controversial Rade Marković as head of the State Security Forces, appointing Goran Petrović, a police official fired during the Milošević era, in his stead. The government also promised to arrest Milošević in January, later deferring this to March. But although the new authorities conceded that Milošević had committed crimes against humanity, Koštunica in particular was unwilling to remand the fallen dictator to the ICTY. Instead, the authorities floated the alternative that Milošević be put on trial in Belgrade. Meanwhile, international pressure for the arrest of Milošević and for his remand to The Hague continued. Then, on 24 January, Carla Del Ponte, the UN war crimes chief prosecutor, was rebuffed by Koštunica and left the presidential office fuming. Koštunica argued that Milošević had to be tried under Yugoslav law, not under international law; in effect, Koštunica was insisting that Yugoslavia was above international law. This, in turn, suggested that while Koštunica and his DOS partners might enjoy the mantle of political legitimacy, they had yet to come to grips with the necessity of abiding by international law, or to realize the incompatibility of narrow nationalism with the cosmopolitan imperatives of the liberal project.[223]

The West, however, kept up its pressure on Belgrade to arrest Milošević. On 10 March, in a significant move, Washington advised Belgrade that if it wished to continue to receive American assistance (nonrelief aid amounting to $100 million for the 2000–2001 fiscal year), Milošević should be under arrest by the end of March. Belgrade, desperate for every bit of assistance it could obtain, took the threat seriously and, in the early hours of 31 March, sent 100–150 police to Milošević's villa in Dedinje, to place him under arrest. But the handful of hard-core Milošević loyalists guarding the villa exchanged gunfire with the police, who withdrew in confusion.[224] Negotiations were now undertaken with Milošević, lasting deep into the following night. Finally, at 4:50 A.M. on 1 April, after several police deadlines had passed and after five final gunshots from his residence, Milošević surrendered and was taken into custody.[225] The UN war crimes tribunal wasted no time in delivering a warrant for the surrender of former president Milošević to international authorities.[226] Indicted by Yugoslav authorities on charges of corruption and ostensibly protected by a Yugoslav law prohibiting the extradition of Yugoslav citizens to foreign or international authorities, Milošević hoped at least to be able to stay in Yugoslavia. But Serbian prime minister Djindjić increasingly felt it was imperative to meet this demand of the international community, fueling frictions with Koštunica, who insisted on the primacy of Yugoslav law over international law. But in May 2001, officials at the Serbian Ministry of the Interior presented evidence that Milošević had ordered Interior Minister Vlajko Stojiljković in March 1999 to remove evidence of crimes committed against Kosovar Albanians from Kosovo; this concerned, in particular, the removal and reinterment (or dumping) of the bodies of dead Albanians.[227] The following month, the government introduced legislation in the Skupština to legalize the extradition of Yugoslav citizens who were wanted for trial by international authorities. When members of the Socialist People's Party (SNP) from Montenegro, opposed to Djukanović and still loyal to Milošević, declared that they would refuse to vote in support of this legislation, the government simply bypassed the Skupština by issuing a decree, on 23 June, committing itself to extradite all persons indicted by international authorities, including Milošević.[228] The Serbian public was almost equally divided, with an estimated 37% of citizens favoring Milošević's extradition, and 43% of citizens opposed, according to the report of an opinion poll conducted by the Institute of Social Sciences in Belgrade, released in June 2001.[229]

In mid-June, Mira Marković, Milošević's wife, tried to organize a national uprising in order to save her husband from extradition.[230] The rally on 26 June, attended by some 20,000 adherents of the Socialist Party of Serbia, fell far short of realizing her goal. Then, on 28 June, known to Serbs as Vidovdan (originally named for the pre-Christian god, Vid, but identified, by the Orthodox Church, with St. Vitus) and having a special resonance with Serbs as the day on which the Battle of Kosovo took place in 1389, the day on which a Serb assassin killed Habsburg archduke Franz Ferdinand (in 1914), setting off World War One, the day on which the interwar constitution had been adopted (in 1921), and the day on which communist Yugoslavia was expelled from the Cominform (in 1948), Yugoslav authorities remanded Milošević to the custody of the international tribunal. As he boarded the helicopter which would carry him to The Hague, Milošević turned to those present and asked them, "Do you know that today is Vidovdan?"[231]

But even with Milošević's extradition, there remained, for the interim, little change in Serbs' willingness, or perhaps ability, to confront their own recent past honesty. Part of the problem is that many Serbs are simply ignorant about some of the most basic facts of the war, or choose to deny them. A poll conducted in April 2001, among 2,200 Serbs, for example, found that most Serbs could talk at length about the sufferings of Serbs at the hands of Croats, Bosniaks, and Albanians, but that about half of those polled could not (or would not) cite even a single crime committed by Serbian forces anywhere. A plurality among respondents also blamed Croatian nationalism for the breakup of the SFRY, seemingly unaware that the SANU Memorandum, the rise to power of Milošević, the quashing of the autonomy of Kosovo and Vojvodina, and the Serbian media campaign against Croats (e.g., for "stealing" Serbian factories after 28 June 1948, when Tito decided to move factories exposed to possible Soviet invasion to more mountainous areas), all *preceded* the wave of Croatian nationalism which carried retired general Franjo Tudjman into the office of president of Croatia.[232]

From Precarious Duumvirate to a Fresh Hope

With Koštunica in the Yugoslav presidency and Djindjić as Serbian prime minister, Serbs hoped for better times. But, in the short term at least, things seemed to get worse, not better. Most of the major problems confronting the Koštunica-Djindjić duumvirate—such as endemic organized crime, rampant petty crime, widespread lawlessness and corruption, widespread poverty, high unemployment, Albanian secessionism in Kosovo, Montenegrin separatism, and Vojvodinan resentment at the loss of autonomy—were parts of Milošević's legacy. But what they added was a division of power at the top and intramural squabbling which seemed to have the potential to paralyze policymaking. Where Milošević had kept politicians, criminals—those two categories involving some of the same people—police, and army in his pocket, Koštunica and Djindjić were at war with each other, vying for control of the police, and targeting each other's protégés.[233] The main points of contention came down to three: the first was that Djindjić wanted to extradite Milošević to The Hague and to establish a relationship of cooperation with the ICTY so that Serbia might be restored to good favor with the West, while Koštunica was intent on courting nationalists and therefore adopted a posture of defiance of the ICTY, insisting that Milošević be tried, if anywhere, in Serbia; the second was that while Djindjić wanted to uproot organized crime in Serbia, which of necessity meant confronting the Red Berets' links with organized crime, Koštunica maintained close connections with the Red Berets, viewing them as allies against Djindjić; and the third was that Djindjić wanted to move Serbia closer to the West, which meant abandoning the kind of "blood and soil" nationalism with which Koštunica continued to identify himself.[234]

But there were also points of agreement between the two men. Both of them were in agreement that Kosovo should remain part of Serbia, and that friendly relations with the United States should be exploited for the purpose of making sure that the referendum on independence, which the Albanians had been led to believe would be held, would never take place. Both of them also believed, as Koštunica put it on the occasion of an election rally on 7 September 2002, that the *Republika Srpska* was "a part of the family that is dear to us, near, temporarily split off, but always in our heart." Although Djindjić avoided such openly provocative language, he tellingly linked the fate of the RS with the fate of Kosovo, in January 2003, suggesting that if Serbia had to give up land in Kosovo, by partition, then it should be compensated by being allowed to annex the RS.[235] And in spite of everything, both men agreed that it was politically impossible to extradite Mladić, with both men claiming, rather unbelievably, that Mladić was not in Serbia at all![236]

But while Koštunica and Djindjić continued to squabble, tempers were rising in Vojvodina, Albanians in Kosovo remained intent on independence, Muslims in the Sandžak were becoming steadily more assertive, and in Montenegro, the growing movement for independence was only pulled back from the brink by the intervention of Javier Solana, the high representative of the European Union, who intervened to broker an agreement on 14 March 2002 to bury the Federal Republic of Yugoslavia and fashion a new, looser union, to be called simply Serbia and Montenegro.[237] As if those problems were not enough, the Albanians of Preševo, Bujanovac, and Medvedja in southern Serbia, adjacent to Kosovo, were stirring and demanding to be annexed to Kosovo. A new guerrilla force called the Albanian National Army portrayed itself as more militant than the KLA and promised to fight to achieve this objective.[238]

Heavily dependent upon the West in both financial and political terms, Serbia seemed to have little alternative but to cooperate with the ICTY—the West's chief condition for continued support and assistance. But within Serbia, there continued to be opposition to cooperation with the ICTY. One center of such opposition was the Red Berets. Established as a paramilitary force in 1991 on the initiative of Mihalj Kertes, the Red Berets under their first commander, Franko "Frenki" Simatović, earned notoriety for their brutality and viciousness in Bosnia but were incorporated into the State Security Service in 1996, under the rubric Special Operations Forces (Jedinice za specijalne operacije, JSO). Since the JSO was determined not to cooperate in arresting persons indicted by the ICTY, thus taking the same position as Koštunica, and since Interior Minister Dušan Mihajlović was determined to use them for that purpose, a showdown was perhaps inevitable. In early November 2001, Mihajlović ordered the JSO to arrest brothers Predrag and Nenad Banović on ordinary criminal charges. The Red Berets soon discovered the real reason for the arrest, viz., that the brothers "were wanted for torturing and killing prisoners in the Keraterm concentration camp in Bosnia in 1992."[239] The following day, 9 November, the Red Berets set up roadblocks and demanded the release of the two brothers, passage of a law "regulating" cooperation with the tribunal, and the removal of Mihajlović from the post of minister of internal affairs. Koštunica characterized the Red Berets' revolt as a legitimate protest, betraying the depth of his rivalry with Djindjić.[240] In some circles, the mutiny was being described as a putsch.[241] The confrontation continued for a week, and at one point, Mihajlović tendered his resignation to Djindjić. Djindjić refused to accept his loyal adjutant's resignation, however, but only too gladly extracted the resignations of Goran Petrović, chief of state security, and his deputy, Zoran Mijatović, both of whom had supported the Red Berets. In declining Mihajlović's resignation, Djindjić declared that he had no intention of allowing any "interest group" to dictate to him who could or could not serve as a minister.[242]

But the revolt involved more than a mere disagreement about cooperation with The Hague. The JSO had ties to organized crime, specifically with the so-called Zemun clan, which reportedly controlled 80% of the illegal drug trade in Serbia. One of the Zemun clan's leaders was Milorad Luković, aka Milorad Ulemek aka "Legija," while Dušan Maričić, commander of the JSO, was also said to have links with the Zemun clan, described as part of one of the world's largest networks of heroin and cocaine trade.[243] The JSO was, thus, intimately tied to organized crime, while Djindjić and Mihajlović had committed themselves to a campaign to uproot organized crime in Serbia.[244] The JSO would also be implicated, later, in the abduction and murder of Ivan Stambolić in August 2000.[245] Koštunica may well have been unaware of the JSO's involvement in the murder of Stambolić, but he must surely have been aware of its murky past and shady connections.

Since the office of Yugoslav president was dissolving around him, Koštunica decided to run for president of Serbia. The first round of the 2002 Serbian presidential elections was scheduled for 29 September. Among the 11 candidates contesting for the office were Miroljub Labus, a highly popular deputy prime minister, General Nebojša Pavković, and SRS leader Vojislav Šešelj. Labus was the favorite among Belgrade's liberal intellectuals; recognized for his cosmopolitan views, Labus was known to prioritize cooperation with the international community and the integration of Yugoslavia into European institutions as quickly as possible. In the first round of the presidential elections, Koštunica placed first with 1,123,420 votes (30.89%), with Labus close behind with 995,200 votes (27.36). Šešelj came third, with 845,308 votes (23.24%).[246]

Koštunica and Labus now faced each other in a run-off election, held on 13 October 2002. Many of those who had voted for other candidates now rallied behind Koštunica, boosting his tally to 1,991,947 votes (66.86%), while support for Labus actually declined slightly to 921,094 (30.92%). But Šešelj had spitefully called on his supporters to boycott the second round, and only 45.46% of eligible voters actually voted, failing thus to cross the 50% threshold required under the Serbian constitution for the election to be valid.[247]

A third round was accordingly deemed necessary. Labus conceded defeat and withdrew from the race, but Šešelj, taking advantage of Serbia's unique electoral law, reentered the contest. Koštunica won some 1,695,000 votes in the 8 December polling (57.50%) to Šešelj's 1,068,000 (36.30%), but since only 45.20% of the electorate had participated in this third round, the election was judged to have "failed."[248] It might have been possible to hold yet a fourth round, as had been done in 1997, but the political parties could not come to an agreement on adopting that expedient. Nor was there sufficient support for Justice Minister Vladan Batić's proposal to allow the Serbian president to be elected by the Serbian parliament. Meanwhile, Milutinović's mandate was to expire on 29 December. Under the constitution of Serbia, the president of the Serbian parliament was authorized to succeed to the presidency of the Republic in the event that the president was indisposed; exercising this constitutional mandate, Nataša Mićić now assumed the post of president of Serbia.

In January 2003, the U.S. offered to drop its demand for the extradition of several war crimes suspects to The Hague, provided that the Serbian government extradite Ratko Mladić, Veselin Šljivančanin, and Miroslav Radić—the latter two wanted in connection with war crimes in Vukovar—by 31 March 2003. The West hoped that Djindjić, who had already remanded Milošević to The

Hague and who had played a role in obtaining Biljana Plavšić's surrender to the ICTY, would respond positively to this pressure. Indeed, Šljivančanin and Radić were shortly extradited.[249] And on 24 February 2003, Šešelj more or less voluntarily surrendered to the ICTY in The Hague, where he immediately began to protest that he could not understand the interpreter, who was apparently speaking in Croatian, which Šešelj described as a "foreign language."

But in late February, a well-known Serbian gangster drove a truck in front of Djindjić's speeding vehicle, in an attempt to cause a fatal traffic collision. Tellingly, the gangster in question was released by a Belgrade court within four days.[250] The release raised eyebrows. Less than three weeks later, on 12 March 2003, Djindjić was gunned down by Zvezdan Jovanović, deputy commander of the JSO.[251] Apparently, the assassination of Djindjić was intended as only the first in a series of killings aimed at paralyzing the government and paving the way for the JSO "to step in to establish order, while the 'patriotic forces' would return to power."[252] But the government not only succeeded in apprehending the assassin on the spot but also declared martial law and moved resolutely to round up those responsible. Within a day, Serbian police had arrested 70 suspects, including Jovica Stanišić, once head of Milošević's internal security network, and "Frenki" Simatović.[253] By 4 April, more than 7,000 persons had been detained, with more than 1,000 of them being sent to prison, among them Jovanović and Milorad "Legija" Luković himself. Others were arrested subsequently, including two of Koštunica's senior security aides.[254] There were also suspicions that Milošević, Koštunica, and Arkan's widow may have been involved in the conspiracy.[255] Legija finally turned himself in to the police in early May 2004 and reportedly offered to provide information concerning the whereabouts of Mladić and Karadžić in exchange for immunity, protection, and a new identity.[256]

On 29 March, the newly sworn-in Serbian prime minister, Zoran Živković, who had been one of Djindjić's closest confidants, triumphantly announced that "the criminal group which organised and carried out the murder of Prime Minister Zoran Djindjić no longer exists," adding that, "The crackdown on organised crime is drawing to a close."[257] Even as the campaign against organized crime was still underway, the Serbian parliament voted to dismiss 35 judges on charges that they had failed to prosecute underworld gangsters who were ultimately responsible for the assassination of Djindjić. The hard-line security chief, General Aco Tomić, was also fired—on 21 March; Tomić had been appointed by Koštunica in mid-2001 and had been seen as an obstacle to the country's cooperation with the war crimes tribunal in The Hague. On 26 March, the JSO itself was dissolved.[258]

But the assassination of Djindjić, whose funeral was attended by half a million persons, including dignitaries from more than 70 countries, raised questions about the future of Serbia. Dušan Janjić, a Belgrade sociologist, and Djordje Vukadinović, editor of *Nova srpska politička misao*, warned that the assassination was profoundly destabilizing, at least in the short term, while the

Swiss newspaper, *Neue Zürcher Zeitung*, fretted that the assassination would open up a power vacuum in Serbia.[259] On the other hand, the resolve with which the new government rounded up the leading figures in the criminal underworld, the support given by Svetozar Marović, the newly elected president of the new union of Serbia and Montenegro, to cooperate with the ICTY, and the ratification by the parliament of Serbia and Montenegro of a state for entry into the Council of Europe seemed to be good omens. The optimism which Živković's anti-crime campaign inspired was short-lived, however. The difficulty was that institutional structures were not invested with the real power in the system, which was concentrated in informal groupings cutting across police, organized crime, big business, and certain figures in or behind the executive branch.

Koštunica's Return

On 17 February 2003, the federal parliament adopted a new constitutional charter for the country, burying the third Yugoslavia and giving birth to Serbia and Montenegro. Then, in mid-November, Belgrade announced that parliamentary elections would be held a year earlier than required. About 80% of eligible voters took part, handing a victory to Šešelj's Serbian Radical Party (SRS), now headed by Tomislav Nikolić. Capturing 27.7% of the vote, the SRS won 82 seats in the 250-member Assembly, with Koštunica's DSS picking up 18% for a second-place finish and 53 seats in the Assembly. The DS (headed, since the death of Djindjić, by Boris Tadić) won 37 seats (12.6% of the vote), the G17 Plus (headed by Miroljub Labus) won 34 seats (11.7% of the vote), the Socialist Party won 22 seats, as did also a coalition of Drašković's SPO and the New Serbia party headed by Velimir Ilić.[260] Given the general reluctance of other political leaders to enter into a coalition with the SRS, it fell to second-place Koštunica to put together a government. Eschewing the party associated with his now deceased foe, Djindjić, Koštunica put together a minority government by entering into an alliance with the SPO-NS a(Narodna Stranka, or People's Party) coalition and Labus's G-17 Plus; this government could, thus, count on the support of 109 deputies in the Assembly.[261] Vuk Drašković now assumed the post of foreign minister.

Koštunica soon made some bold moves—halting certain economic reforms, revoking certain reforms in the educational and justice systems, downgrading most of the principal figures in charge of Operation Saber, the police action against organized crime launched after the assassination of Djindjić, and taking steps which provoked the Hungarians of Vojvodina to demand autonomy.[262] In an equally controversial move, the Assembly adopted a bill to cover the costs of legal defense for indicted war criminals, to provide pensions for their families, and even to defray the cost of telephone calls on the part of families having members on trial in The Hague.[263] Perhaps most controversial of all, Koštunica declared, in February 2004, that the extradition of persons indicted of war crimes would not be a top priority for his government, though, after the American government froze $25 million in aid because of "insufficient" cooperation with the ICTY, the new prime minister modified that statement, telling *Politika* that cooperation with the ICTY was "unavoidable," while insisting that it should be done "in a way which will not destabilize [Serbian] institutions."[264] Meanwhile, even while admitting that there was still a lot of work to do to combat organized crime and corruption, Belgrade bungled the trial of Djindjić's assassin, appointing a judge whom the defense attorneys characterized as a member of an "underworld gang" and allowing a key witness to be killed.[265] Then there was the fact that, even before Koštunica took office, the official version of the Djindjić assassination had been called into question.[266]

Montenegro has been an unwilling partner in the new state, and in April 2004, bucking EU pressure, the government in Podgorica announced its intention to hold a referendum on independence in March 2005, only to back away from this plan the following month, under renewed pressure from the EU.[267] Meanwhile, with Serbian presidential elections scheduled for 13 June 2004, speculation centered on whether Tomislav Nikolić would be able to capitalize on the recent electoral victory of the SRS and what that might mean.[268] As was largely expected, Nikolić emerged as the frontrunner in the first round, having won some 30.1% of the vote, with Boris Tadić, by then head of the Democratic Party (Djindjić's DS) close behind with 27.3%.[269] But Tadić won the second round later that month, capturing 52.1% of the vote, trumping Nikolić's 46.5%.[270] Tadić accordingly took office, pledging full cooperation with the ICTY, including in the apprehension of war crimes fugitive Ratko Mladić, who was said to be somewhere in Serbia or Montenegro.[271]

In an opinion poll conducted among 617 Serbs between 23 February and 4 March 2004, Tito was considered, by a plurality of respondents, to have been the person to have contributed the most to the prestige of Serbia, with Nikola Tesla, a Serb from Croatia, in second place and Djindjić in third place. More than half of respondents said that Milošević had done the most to damage Serbia's prestige.[272] Yet Serbia, like most if not all countries, consists of several competing political cultures. In Serbia, the chief competitors are secular intolerant nationalism, traditionalist clerico-nationalism, cosmopolitan liberalism, and what might be called atavistic socialism, looking back with nostalgia to a past that never was. The Serbian Orthodox Church is, on the whole, a force for reaction, not for liberalism, and "seems to be increasingly and openly tied to ultra-conservative and nationalist groups, particularly those with ideologies emanating from the period of Serbia's World War Two fascist government."[273] In fact, the culture of nationalism—whether secular or clerical—is, at this writing, still dominant, while liberal culture remains underdeveloped.[274] Nor should one be too sanguine about the prospects for the growth of liberal culture in a democratic setting in the absence of an educational and media policy which is consciously tailored to move toward liberalism. In Serbia, the educational and media system are pushing in precisely the *opposite* direction. For example, a new history textbook written by Kosta Nikolić, Nikola Žutić, and Momčilo Pavlović and published in 2002 glorifies the Chetniks, Serb nationalists, generals, and wars, plays down culture, demeans women, treats Vojvodinan Croats, Bosnian Muslims, and Bosnian Catholics as Serbs, and defends Milan Nedić, leading its young readers in the direction of "rejecting cultural pluralism . . . [and the] rehabilitation of nationalism."[275] Or again, in September 2004, controversy flared when Ljiljana Čolić, the minister of education, approved a science curriculum for the eighth grade from which any mention of Charles Darwin's theory of evolution had been removed; the minister explained that children enrolled in Orthodox religious instruction learned that God created the world, including humankind, and therefore found the theory of evolution confusing. Serbian biologists demanded that the minister resign, which she did before the end of the month.[276] Or again, on the TV evening news, the weather map does not show Novi Pazar, a city of 100,000 with a Muslim majority; instead, the map shows "Ras," the name of a medieval settlement which once existed close to where Novi Pazar is now located.[277] These are just three small examples from a society dominated by nationalist culture. The difficulty is that nationalist culture is not compatible with liberal democracy. It is compatible with *illiberal* democracy, however, and for as long as nationalism is ascendant in Serbia, it would appear that, as Fareed Zakaria has argued at the level of theory, what is needed "is not more democracy but less."[278] An illiberal, nationalist public in a democratic setting will use democratic institutions to promote the politics of intolerance, to erode individual rights, to glorify the Nation, and to create the Heavenly Kingdom on earth. In a word, it will turn democracy on its head, fashioning a "tyranny of the saints." The most successful liberal democracies developed liberal cultures long before they became truly democratic in anything like the modern sense of the word. To reverse the process and endeavor to build democracy first and defer the development of liberal culture to sometime in the future is, at best, to undertake a risky political experiment. In the Bosnian setting, the OHR creates the possibility to emphasize the development of liberal culture "first" as it were, while setting up the facade of democratic institutions. In Serbia, if there is to be any hope of fashioning a liberal democracy, the two tasks need to be undertaken *at the same time*.

The 13-year record of the Milošević regime (1987–2000) fully confirms propositions 2, 3, 4, 7, and 13. These asserted the distinctive internal and external behavior of illegitimate states (proposition 2), the inability of illegitimate systems to attain stable equilibrium (proposition 3), the tendency of unstable equilibrium to generate pressure for change (proposition 4), the correlation between system illegitimacy and popular disaffection (proposition 7), and the connection between public awareness of the problematic nature of the system and public willingness to oppose the system (proposition 13).

These propositions have also been confirmed in the case of post-Milošević

Serbia, although less overtly. To begin with, there is no consensus on the question of Serbia's borders, with continued efforts to block Albanian self-determination in Kosovo and even a revival, albeit outside government circles, of revanchism vis-à-vis the Krajina.[279] Second, corruption remains at high levels. Commenting on the problem in April 2005, a representative of the Friedrich Ebert Stiftung, Germany, commented that while the level of corruption in Serbia had been reduced since 2002, it remained unacceptably high. Among those sectors in need of reform (including depoliticization and separation from criminal influence) were the police, the judiciary, and the legal system more generally.[280] Third, there is the question of cooperation with the ICTY, which may be taken as a measure of Serbia and Montenegro's readiness to accept international law and to play by international rules. The government in Belgrade has recognized that cooperation with the ICTY is the key to eventual accession into the EU,[281] but as recently as April 2005, the Army of Serbia and Montenegro was said to be protecting indicted war criminal Ratko Mladić.[282] For that matter, Djindjić himself has been said to have been killed as part of an operation called "Stop the Hague."[283]

A fourth problem is the nature of the nationalism which is being kept alive in Serbia. Through the erection of a monument to Axis collaborator Draža Mihailović, the promulgation in school textbooks of a myth of the Chetniks as liberators and freedom fighters, and the passage of a law in January 2005 equating the wartime role of the Chetniks and the Partisans, the Koštunica government has sought to rehabilitate the Chetnik movement.[284] In the context of recurrent disparagement of Tito and the Partisans, this law in fact signified the embrace of the Chetnik tradition as such—a tradition which, as seen in chapter 4, embraces a program of national expansionism and ethnic cleansing. When this Chetnik revivalism is placed alongside troubling signals concerning Belgrade's attitude toward Serbia's borders with Croatia and Bosnia, it comes as no surprise that the EU demanded that Serbia break with nationalism as one of its conditions for admission into its ranks.[285]

The EU's other conditions are, of course, cooperation with the ICTY and the adjustment of Serbian and Montenegrin laws to accord with European standards. Thus, the fifth challenge for the dual state is to adapt its legal structure in accord with EU and Council of Europe standards. As of April 2005, this was said to involve the passage of some 55 laws and roughly 25,000 new or revised regulations.[286] As daunting as this challenge may seem, the government in Belgrade committed itself to this legislative program, which was seen by some as having the potential to reinforce tendencies toward liberalization in Serbia and Montenegro.[287] But if Serbs are to wrest themselves out of their dysfunctional nationalist syndrome and embark on a path to legitimate politics, passing laws and transforming institutions will not be enough. As the EU has noted, a break with Chetnik nationalism and an embrace of liberal principles will also be necessary. Thus, the fact that a school textbook introduced in Serbian elementary schools at the end of the 1990s offered the wildly inflated figure of 700,000 Serbs dead at Jasenovac camp alone[288] is a matter for concern, as is the fact that in new textbooks introduced in Serb elementary schools in 2001, Chetnik leader Draža Mihailović was portrayed as the leader of an anti-Axis resistance movement with nothing said about his collaboration with the Axis.[289] In general, school textbooks have portrayed Serbian history as one of constant struggle and suffering, Serbs as innocent victims of foreign conspiracies, and the expulsion of non-Serbs from Serb lands as a "logical" course of action. The importance of textbooks in shaping the political attitudes of people should not be underestimated.[290] To ignore the moral component (liberalism versus nationalism) in legitimate politics, would be to condemn the project of building a legitimate state to certain failure. Or, to put it another way, democracy without liberalism is unstable at best, tyrannical (in the sense intended by John Stuart Mill) at worst.

CHAPTER 18

UNMIK, KFOR, and the Future of Kosovo

The undeclared war between NATO and the Federal Republic of Yugo-slavia, initiated by NATO on 24 March 1999, was formally ended on 9 June 1999, with the signing of a military technical agreement under which the Kosovo International Security Force (KFOR) obtained a legal foundation. Confirming the document tendered to Belgrade by Finnish president Martti Ahtisaari and approved by the Yugoslav Skupština on 3 June, the military technical agreement provided for the phased withdrawal within 11 days of all FRY forces from Kosovo and the deployment of KFOR with the mandate "to take all necessary action to establish and maintain a secure environment for all citizens of Kosovo and otherwise carry out its mission." In a key passage, Article 5 provided that "the international security force (KFOR) commander is the final authority regarding interpretation of this agreement and the security aspects of the peace settlement it supports. His determinations are binding on all parties and persons."[1] On 10 June 1999, the UN Security Council adopted Resolution 1244, which "reconfirms the commitment of all member states to the sovereignty and territorial integrity of the Federal Republic of Yugoslavia," even while pledging to secure "substantial autonomy and self-government" for Kosovo.[2]

The challenges for Kosovo's would-be protectors were staggering. Belgrade's security forces had, in the course of 1998–1999, scorched the province with a thoroughness reminiscent of William Tecumseh Sherman's march to the sea, while NATO's bombardment had caused further damage.[3] According to UN food agencies, Kosovo lost 65% of its agricultural produce and livestock as a result of the war in spring 1999, with wheat production in 1999 adequate to meet only 30% of the province's needs.[4] In addition, some 120,000 houses had been destroyed or damaged by Serbian forces. Estimates of the cost to rebuild the province's economy ranged from $2 billion to $5 billion.[5] Thus, the first challenge confronting the international peacekeepers was to deal with the province's complex economic problems. As a first step, the UN mission set up a task force to identify commercial opportunities for the reconstruction of Kosovo.[6]

Another of the mission's first decisions, aimed at stabilizing the local currency, was to introduce the German mark as the official currency.[7] In spite of some bottlenecks in terms of aid transfusion, and in spite of the stoppage of work at Kosovo's mineral-rich mines (because of an unresolved dispute concerning ownership), small commerce gradually began to revive, with some 51,000 private businesses in operation as of September 2002.[8] Even so, the province continued to be plagued by high unemployment even though, according to the preliminary results of a survey conducted by the UN Population Fund, some 25% of Kosovars between the ages of 25 and 40 lived abroad as of April 2000.[9] As of June 2004, unemployment in Kosovo was set at more than 60%.[10]

A second challenge, quite apart from the confirmed deaths of some 12,000 Kosovar Albanians between February 1998 and June 1999, was the displacement and disappearance of locals.[11] By early August 1999, nearly 90% of the Albanians who had fled the province between 1998 and 1999 had returned (700,000 from neighboring countries and 30,000 from countries outside the region).[12] On the other hand, roughly 2,000 Kosovar Albanians remained incarcerated in Serbian prisons, having been taken hostage by Serbian forces in spring 1999, while more than 80,000 of the roughly 200,000 Serbs living in the province as of March 1999 had fled Kosovo, under Albanian pressure, by the end of July 1999.[13] By late 2001, the number of Serbs and other non-Albanians who had fled the province had risen to about 200,000; during the same time frame, nearly 100,000 Serb-owned houses and apartments were usurped. More than 15,000 Serbs or Serb families sold their property in despair of any firm guarantees of their security in the foreseeable future.[14] As of May 2003, moreover, non-Albanians were still said to "face security problems and . . . lack access to education, health services, and equitable employment," according to a report filed jointly by the UN High Commissioner for Refugees and the OSCE.[15]

A third challenge has had to do with infrastructure, in particular as regards education and the legal system. Kosovo's Albanians had relied for a decade on an underground educational system operating out of people's homes, in conditions of extreme scarcity of books of any kind. In addition, in the mid-1990s, Serbian authorities had pulped Albanian-language books from the Priština National Library in an effort to erase the cultural memory. But the damage was not limited to the National Library of Kosovo: on the contrary, some two-thirds of Kosovo's 180 libraries were said to have been "annihilated" between 1990 and 1999, during which period Serbian authorities destroyed more than 900,000 books, almost half of all library books in Kosovo.[16] An additional 263,322 books were destroyed by fire during NATO's aerial campaign in spring 1999.[17] The International Federation of Library Associations estimated that it would require the infusion of at least $6.7 million to rehabilitate Kosovo's libraries.[18] Where school books are concerned, the international community was still arranging for the printing of some 3.2 million copies of more than 200 different textbooks, even as the school year approached.

With the legal system also in disarray and widely held in contempt, the UN Mission in Kosovo (UNMIK) set about drafting a penal code, setting up 47 courts, training judges, and establishing a detention system. The Kosovo Law Center, established by the Organization for Security and Cooperation in Europe (OSCE) in June 2000 as a nonpartisan center for legal research and publisher of all laws, regulations, and decrees, is seen as a building block for establishing the rule of law in the province.[19] UNMIK also undertook to train local recruits to serve in a new Kosovo Police Service (KPS). The first 200 graduates—Serbian and Albanian women and men—received their diplomas in ceremonies on 7 September 1999.[20] As of 30 October 2000, there were 4,130 UNMIK police officers stationed in Kosovo, alongside 2,549 KPS officers.[21] But in October 2000, the OSCE Legal Systems Monitoring Service, having completed a six-month review of the judicial system, concluded that Kosovo's criminal justice system was below international standards and that there was "compelling evidence" of judicial bias against Kosovo Serb defendants.[22]

The fourth challenge, criminality, is closely associated with the aforementioned need to develop respected legal institutions and enforcement agencies. UNMIK initially made a number of mistakes. One of the more serious mistakes was the delay in granting the UNMIK police authority to conduct undercover surveillance until January 2001; as a result, there were "serious inefficiencies in intelligence." On the other hand, the arrest by KFOR troops of hundreds of suspected criminals in the first months of the peacekeeping operation, together with the confiscations of weapons, contributed to improved stability and security.[23] The murder rate, for example, declined from more than 50 per week in June 1999 to about three per week in September 2000. The incidence of arson also declined from an average of 14 per week during the period January–March 2000 to seven per week during the period July-mid-September 2000. On the other hand, the incidence of kidnapping increased from 2.5 per week to 3.5 per week over the same period, while the frequency of assaults edged gradually upward, peaking at 82 per week in early July and mid-August.[24] Organized crime is also a major problem, especially in the areas of trafficking in women and drugs.[25]

Fifth, the Kosovo conflict left many locals with mental health problems. A study published in the *Journal of the American Medical Association* in summer 2000 found that 43% of 1,358 Kosovar Albanians surveyed displayed signs of "nonspecific psychiatric morbidity." Another 17.1% of Kosovar Albanians were found to manifest symptoms of post-traumatic stress disorder. The study also found that more than 88% of both women and men expressed "strong feelings" of hatred toward Serbs, while 35% of men and 23% of women admitted to fantasizing "all the time" about taking revenge against Serbs.[26]

Sixth, there was the most immediate challenge of confiscating the weapons held by paramilitaries in the province and establishing KFOR's unchallenged ability to assure a secure environment. Although paramilitaries were not permitted under the military technical agreement signed by Belgrade and the NATO alliance, the Albanians were quick to point out that they had not been signatories to the agreement, and for a few days there was some uncertainty as to the willingness of the leadership of the Kosova Liberation Army (KLA) to comply with this requirement.[27] By 19 June, however, NATO commanders had reached a tentative agreement with KLA leaders that the rebel force would be disbanded and that it would surrender its arms.[28] But compliance has been incomplete, and confiscations of small firearms, grenades, and the like remained a daily occurrence well into 2000, with continued confiscations during 2001–2003.[29] Although most of these confiscations have involved Albanian-held weaponry, KFOR peacekeeping troops reported that they had found 13 AK-47 assault rifles, one light anti-tank weapon, and various other armaments in a search of two Serbian villages in Kosovo on 1 November 2000.[30] That same month, NATO peacekeepers seized a truckload of weapons intended for Albanian guerrillas in Serbia's Preševo valley.[31] In addition, there were problems connected with the establishment (in 2002) of the hard-line Albanian National Army, operating not only in Serbia but also in Kosovo and Macedonia, as already mentioned in the previous chapter.

FRY uniformed personnel met the 20 June deadline for withdrawal from the province with 12 hours to spare, and as early as 2 July, a KFOR spokesperson was able to report that there had been "broad compliance" on the part of the KLA, noting that "in one area seven truckloads of weapons" were collected from the KLA.[32]

KFOR entered Kosovo on 12 June 1999, under a UN mandate; its strength was steadily increased, reaching 29,000 troops in Kosovo as of 5 July (with 36,000 troops in theater) and 32,400 troops in Kosovo as of 14 July 1999 (with 42,400 in theater, the 10,000 being stationed in Macedonia).[33] All 19 NATO nations alongside 18 non-NATO nations have contributed troops to KFOR. At peak, KFOR numbered 42,500 troops in Kosovo itself, backed up by an additional 7,500 stationed in Macedonia, Albania, and Greece, adding up to a total of 50,000. Of this total, 7,000 were American, 492 were Russian, 3,900 were British, 4,700 were French, 5,800 were German, and 940 were Turkish, according to official KFOR data.[34] Among the relevant contingents outside Kosovo is COMQUEST, a 1,200-strong unit stationed in Durrës, Albania, and tasked to secure communications and transport links through Albania to Kosovo and Macedonia. The command of COMQUEST was entrusted to an Italian general.[35] According to a report published in the *Los Angeles Times* in October 2000, there were some 39,900 KFOR troops in the province as of midmonth, of whom 5,700 were Americans.[36] The U.S. contribution to KFOR, thus, came to about

14%, regardless of which set of figures one prefers. As of June 2005, KFOR strength stood at 17,000 troops.[37]

The U.S. contribution to humanitarian and reconstruction assistance has been at a comparable level. Providing $3 billion for civilian assistance during 1999–2000, the European Union picked up 75% of the tab for the province's operational budget. The U.S. contributed $900 million for civilian assistance over the same period, covering 13% of the provincial budget.[38]

Although Bernard Kouchner, UNMIK's first civilian head of mission, was given broad administrative authority in the province, he quickly established an advisory council, appointing the following as members: Hashim Thaqi, erstwhile leader of the KLA and founder of the Party of Democratic Progress;[39] Ibrahim Rugova, president of the Democratic League of Kosova (LDK); Rexhep Qosja, head of the United Democratic Movement; journalist Veton Surroi and Blerim Shalja as independent members; Momčilo Trajković of the anti-Milošević Serb National Council of Kosovo; Serbian Orthodox bishop Artemije Radosavljević of the Raška-Prizren diocese; Numan Balić of the Party of Democratic Action for Kosovo; and Sezair Shaipi of the local Turkish minority party.[40] The council held its first meeting on 16 July in Rugova's absence: Rugova was reported to be piqued that his party had not been allocated more ample representation in the council.[41]

Subsequently, in December 1999, Kouchner signed a power-sharing agreement, establishing an Interim Administrative Council consisting of Thaqi, Rugova, and Qosja and inviting the local Serbian community to put forth a Serb representative. Local Serbs, however, denounced the agreement, claiming that it put Serbs in a "humiliating and unacceptable position."[42] The Serb National Council elaborated on its rejection of the council, indicating that Serbs would participate only if they were assigned self-governing cantons in Kosovo.[43] However, local Albanians and international authorities had rejected this demand four months earlier and were not inclined to reconsider their position.[44] Four months later, however, Bishop Artemije and Sava Jančić of the Serb National Council relented and agreed to cooperate with the UN-sponsored Administrative Council.[45]

Inter-ethnic Frictions

In spite of frustrations in their quest for republic status and in spite of Ranković's tough line in the first two decades of communist rule, Kosovo's Albanians and Serbs maintained civil and often friendly relations with each other well into the 1980s. Indeed, until the end of the 1980s, many Muslim Albanians joined Orthodox Serbs in making the annual pilgrimage to the Orthodox shrine at Zočiste, four kilometers southeast of Orahovac.[46]

Today all that is left of the Zočiste shrine is a heap of rubble. It is one of at least 60 Serbian Orthodox churches and other religious sites to have been destroyed, damaged, or looted by local Albanians between mid-June and early September 1999.[47] There was also a rash of often fatal attacks on local Serbs by vengeance-minded Albanians, who remembered how local Serbs had jeered at them when they had fled before Serbian security forces in March 1999. For example, the first week of July 1999 saw the kidnapping of the Serb mayor of Kosovska Mitrovica and an assault on 10 Kosovar Serb physicians and nurses inside Lipljan's medical clinic by four Kosovar Albanians.[48] In October 1999, Albanians attacked a UN convoy carrying 150 Serbs out of the province to Montenegro; four persons were reported missing after the attack.[49] A spontaneous campaign of verbal harassment also contributed to an atmosphere of terror, in which Serbs felt as unsafe as Albanians had felt earlier.[50] Local Albanians also attacked Kosovo's Roma, accusing them of collaboration in Belgrade's war crimes. By early September, some 90,000 of the 150,000 Roma who had inhabited the province as of March 1999 had fled.[51] Senior leaders of the KLA, including Thaqi, condemned the attacks on Serbs and Roma but were powerless to defuse the anger which had built up over more than a decade of repression by Milošević's agents.

Local Serb difficulties were compounded by the role reversal occurring at the workplace. In the early 1990s, Serbs had taken over managerial positions from Albanians; local Albanians had been fired and their jobs reassigned to Serbs. Now, with the FRY's sovereignty reduced to little more than a nominal title, Albanians took over the managerial posts, informing Serbs that "if they had been hired after 1990 they are not legally employed."[52]

As inter-ethnic tensions continued, escalating dangerously in Kosovska Mitrovica in March 2000, extremists on both sides targeted their own moderates, thereby revealing their complete disinterest in reconciliation. On the Serbian side, there was the case of Momčilo Trajković, a moderate Serb hostile to the Milošević regime, on whose life there were four attempts by November 1999; the Belgrade daily *Borba* made it clear who was behind these attempts by publishing a column two days after the fourth attempt on Trajković's life, in which the opposition activist was derided as "a 'quisling', a man who got rich from the misfortune of his compatriots in Kosovo . . . , naturally a traitor, the KLA collaborator Thaqi's friend." *Borba* also accused Trajković of staging the assassination attempt and concluded that "together with his spiritual father, Artemije, Trajković has been caught in a camouflaged treason."[53] Kosovar Serbs who were prepared to cooperate with international officials feared that the Trajković case was not unique. On 6 August 2000, Father Sava Janjić, a leading figure in the anti-regime Serb National Council (SRC), told UNMIK officials that the SRC had received a tip from a reliable source that SRC members should be on guard against attacks and even further assassination attempts.[54]

On the Albanian side, young Albanian men, as a rule clad in black and claiming to be acting on behalf of the "Ministry of Order," attacked the offices and members of Rugova's LDK, targeting prominent LDK figures. Veton Surroi, the distinguished journalist and newspaper publisher, who, in summer 1999, had sharply criticized the attacks on Serbs as reflecting "fascist" attitudes, was later the subject of a long and vicious commentary in the local Albanian nationalist press.[55]

There were also problems between KFOR troops and locals. In September 1999, for example, there were violent confrontations in Kosovska Mitrovica between local Albanians wanting to cross into the Serb-held part of the divided city and French KFOR troops, who were tasked to keep the sides apart.[56] Or again, in May 2000, two Russian KFOR troops were wounded when Kosovar Albanians attacked their encampment near Kijevo in the middle of the night.[57] On other occasions, KFOR troops allegedly initiated the trouble. According to an article first published in the *Los Angeles Times*, U.S. soldiers attached to Alpha Company, 3rd Battalion, 504th Parachute Infantry Regiment, allegedly "followed the motto 'Get Ugly Early' to make sure people in Kosovo knew who was [the] boss." The *Times* reported that "sometimes these U.S. soldiers also kidnapped people, threatened them with knives and guns, beat them and spat on them. Sometimes they made them lie on the icy ground and stepped on them if they complained." U.S. Army high command was reported to have been outraged by what it had heard about Alpha Company and reportedly issued a statement to the effect that the unit "had violated basic standards of conduct, human decency and the Army['s] values."[58] Six months earlier, in March 2000, Amnesty International had issued a statement accusing NATO and the United Nations "of failing to observe high human rights standards in Kosovo" and specifically of detaining 49 persons "in inhumane, cold and unsanitary conditions."[59]

Finally, the Milošević regime pursued a policy of actively obstructing the work of the International Criminal Tribunal for the former Yugoslavia (ICTY), though KFOR troops reportedly apprehended three Serbs for questioning in August 1999. Six months later, two Kosovar Serbs were arrested by UNMIK police in the town of Hoca Madhe in southwestern Kosovo on charges of war crimes. This brought the total number of Kosovar Serbs arrested since June 1999 on suspicion of war crimes to "at least" seven, the others having been arrested by KFOR troops.[60] But even without Belgrade's cooperation, forensics experts and tribunal investigators exhumed bodies from some 195 mass graves out of 529 identified grave sites between June and early November 1999, exhuming about 2,100 bodies.[61] By August 2000, the bodies of nearly 3,000 Kosovar Albanians had been exhumed, and by February 2003, some 4,200 bodies had been exhumed in Kosovo, most of them identified as Albanians.[62]

Barely Holding?

In the short term, it has seemed, for the most part, that the KFOR-enforced peace has been barely holding. In March 2000, for instance, amid escalating provocations against Serbs in Kosovska Mitrovica, U.S. secretary of state Madeleine Albright told a congressional panel that Kosovo's Albanians were in danger of losing Western support if the provocations continued.[63] About the same time, American troops in Kosovo staged raids across eastern Kosovo, confiscating bombs, other armaments, ammunition, and uniforms held by recalcitrant ethnic Albanian guerrillas.[64] Albanian leaders got the message and, the following month, joined local moderate Serbs in a joint statement calling on their adherents to renounce the violence which had plagued the province. Subsequently, on 9 September, some 30,000 persons assembled on Priština's Mother Teresa Square under the motto "Kosova without Violence Is Our Future."

Meanwhile, battle lines were being drawn over the limits of legitimate press freedom. In one corner was the Albanian-language newspaper *Dita,* which, in April 2000, published an article accusing a Serb translator for the UN of membership in a Serbian paramilitary unit which had committed atrocities against Albanian civilians in spring 1999. In the other corner was chief UN administrator Kouchner who, after the murder of that translator in mid-May, imposed an eight-day ban on the publication of *Dita,* on the grounds that the paper's article had likely contributed to the translator's death. Kouchner also ordered *Dita* to pay a DM 25,000 fine. Returning to the stands on 4 July, *Dita* defiantly published the names and photos of 15 more Serbs who, it alleged, had committed war crimes against Albanians. Meanwhile, Blerim Stavileci, chief editor of *Dita,* started court proceedings against the UN administrator, seeking $489,000 in damages.[65] Given *Dita*'s recalictrant stance and its refusal to pay the DM 25,000 fine, UNMIK authorities ordered the newspaper to terminate operations on 28 July.[66]

In the midst of this controversy, the Kosovo Administrative Council passed a law, on 16 June, regulating newspapers, spelling out the code of ethics to which newspapers and other periodicals would be expected to adhere.[67] As their counterparts in Bosnia had already discovered, UNMIK officials were finding that in the absence of general respect for the harm principle and of a tolerant atmosphere, old-fashioned "administrative measures" afforded the most obvious shortcut to liberal results, thus confirming Herbert Marcuse's thoughts on the subject.[68]

In an effort to provide balanced broadcasting, the OSCE and UN launched Radio-Television Kosovo in September 1999, with programming in both Albanian and Serbian; soon after, Britain, France, Germany, Canada, and the United States agreed to co-finance a Serbian-language radio station in Kosovo to provide unbiased reportage of local developments.

The KFOR mission could also draw encouragement from the failure of a Republican-sponsored bill to set a deadline for the withdrawal of American ground troops from Kosovo. The measure, which would have cut off funding for American KFOR troops by 1 July 2001 unless specifically extended by Congress, failed in the Senate by a vote of 53 to 47.[69]

The Impact of Milošević's Fall

As late as April 2000, Ibrahim Rugova warned that war would break out once again in the event that the international community should attempt to place Kosovo once more under Yugoslav authority.[70] Indeed, there was a clear consensus among all of Kosovo's Albanian politicians that independence for Kosovo, within its established borders, was the only acceptable option.

Then came Milošević's ouster on 5 October. Vojislav Koštunica, the new FRY president, had a reputation for legalism to the point of fastidiousness, integrity, and honesty. And despite repeated vague allusions to his being a "nationalist," the international community was eager to show its readiness to rebuild diplomatic and economic ties with post-Milošević Yugoslavia, as already noted in the previous chapter. Kosovo's Albanians worried that their best chance for independence may have passed, and they rejected Koštunica to the man. "Nothing has changed in Serbia," said Baton Haxhiu, editor-in-chief of *Koha Ditore,* a widely respected Albanian-language newspaper in the province. "It's just the transfer of power from one nationalist side to another nationalist side."[71]

An AP report released on 15 October only further fueled Albanian fears. According to this report, the U.S. government was backing a formula under which Kosovo would obtain republic status within the Yugoslav federation, alongside Serbia and Montenegro.[72] To counter the fears stirred up by this report, U.S. special envoy to the Balkans Jim O'Brien met with the National Albanian American Council on 17 October and denied that the U.S. was supporting any such plan. O'Brien left the final resolution of the question open, though he referred to the need for respect for the procedures outlined in UNSC Resolution 1244.[73]

Russia's president Vladimir Putin entered into the discourse at the end of October, receiving Koštunica in Moscow and joining him in issuing a joint declaration underlining that independence for Kosovo should be excluded in advance.[74] About the same time, Zoran Djindjić, Koštunica's right-hand man, viewed by some as "the power behind the throne," announced that Belgrade wanted to station Yugoslav Army troops and police officers in Serb-populated areas in Kosovo.[75] This announcement met with an immediate rebuff from Albania's foreign minister, Paskal Milo.

In the meantime, municipal elections throughout Kosovo had been scheduled for 28 October. The vote was widely interpreted as a choice between militant radicalism (Thaqi's party) and pacifist moderation (Rugova's party), though both parties are committed to Kosovar independence. In the event, the roughly 900,000 voters who turned out on election day cast their ballots, by a large margin, for Rugova's ticket. Rugova's LDK won 58% of the vote, against 27% for Thaqi's Party of Democratic Progress, sweeping 21 of the 27 contested municipal races.[76] And even though virtually all of Kosovo's remaining Serbs boycotted the election, the vote was interpreted as affording a chance to "avert a

[fresh] crisis in relations with Serbia," if not also as a commitment to a negotiated settlement.[77]

Serb leaders in Kosovo described the elections as a "catastrophic mistake."
Trajković alleged that the elections catered only to the Albanian community and
that they were, by that virtue, undemocratic.[78] The Koštunica government con-
curred, issuing a statement to the effect that in the absence of freedom of movement, the "conditions for a free expression of political views had not been created" in the province.[79]

For his part, Koštunica sent out mixed signals, repeatedly avowing that
Kosovo cannot be allowed to go its own way, leaving Serbia behind, but also
averring that he could imagine Serbia whether with Kosovo or without Kosovo,
expressing his interest in meeting with Rugova, releasing Kosovo pediatrician
Flora Brovina from prison, and hinting that the remaining Albanians still in
Serbia's prisons might soon be released.[80]

But just as would be the case with later American-led interventions in
Afghanistan and Iraq, the NATO intervention left Kosovo in chaos, breaking
down existing institutions and leaving international peacekeepers unable to
restore stability. Indeed, in at least one respect, the arrival of 45,000 mostly male
international peacekeepers actually contributed to a worsening of local conditions, viz., in the sudden and explosive growth of the sex industry, for which the
peacekeepers have allegedly been the principal customers.[81]

The intervention also allowed Albanians to introduce significant changes in
the school curriculum, though not always of the sort likely to promote reconciliation. For example, in autumn 2003, EU and UN officials expressed their
concern that history schoolbooks in use in Albanian schools were so one-sided
that they were almost certain to reinforce sentiments of hatred and resentment.
Or again, one might mention efforts by local Islamic clerics to introduce the
Koran in the classroom, for Muslim schoolchildren; those efforts have provoked
concern and even alarm among local Albanian Catholics, who fear a rise in religious intolerance, as well as among liberal Muslims.[82]

Alternative Futures

In spite of the no doubt transient honeymoon in relations between Western
leaders and Koštunica and in spite of Russian opposition to the idea, Kosovar
independence continued to gain momentum, with numerous Western scholars
and public figures endorsing the concept. A key development was the filing of
an independent commission's report on Kosovo with UN secretary-general Kofi
Anan on 23 October 2000. Entitled "The Kosovo Report: Conflict, International
Responses, Lessons Learned," the report was the product of a commission
chaired by Justice Richard Goldstone of South Africa and Carl Tham, secretary-
general of the Olaf Palme International Center in Stockholm; the report recommended independence for the long-troubled province.[83] While some Serbs

remain adamant that they will never give up Kosovo, other Serbs are coming around to the idea that the best conceivable solution would be to partition Kosovo at the town of Kosovska Mitrovica, with areas north of the Ibar River falling to Serbia.[84] To say that Albanian leaders resist any form of partition would be an understatement.

But, in fact, the question of Kosovo's future involves four interlocking questions: whether Kosovo should be partitioned or remain integral; whether Kosovo should become independent or remain under Yugoslav sovereignty, or whether there is some third option, as hinted by Carl Bildt's advocacy of "layered sovereignty" for Kosovo;[85] whether Serb and Romany refugees from Kosovo should be encouraged to return, in hopes of reviving the multi-ethnic Kosovo of times past; and how long and in what role the international community should maintain its presence in the area.

On the last of these points, a proposal by presidential candidate George W. Bush, floated by his prospective national security adviser, Condoleeza Rice in late October 2000, to pull American troops out of the Balkans, provoked such alarm in European capitals, even to the extent of calling into question the continued existence of NATO, that Bush was compelled to retract his proposal.[86] But in September 2002, NATO councils adopted a plan to reduce their contingent in Kosovo, foreseeing the replacement of KFOR by an EU force by 2006 at the latest.[87]

Partition is probably the most slippery of these points, insofar as eventual independence for at least part of Kosovo is all but a foregone conclusion. But if partition is to be considered, what would be the criteria for partition? Current population dispersal? The location of such Serbian holy shrines as have not yet been destroyed? The distribution of mineral wealth? Some other criteria? Or a combination of these? Whatever the formula proposed, it is certain to encounter impassioned Albanian opposition.

In January 2003, Serbian prime minister Djindjić called for the opening of talks concerning the final status of Kosovo, admitting that he feared that further delay would allow the Albanians to present Belgrade with a fait accompli. Then, at the end of February, just two weeks before he was gunned down in Belgrade, Djindjić revived an earlier proposal to partition Kosovo along ethnic lines.[88] Djindjić did not intend for the Albanian sector to become independent, however, but rather for its reinclusion in what had, in the meantime, been renamed Serbia and Montenegro. But Djindjić remained uncertain about UNMIK chief Michael Steiner's notion of a multi-ethnic Kosovo and proposed a "civilized and peaceful transfer of populations" between the two sectors of Kosovo.[89] Rejecting Djindjić's proposal, a group of 42 Kosovar legislators offered their own plan—to proclaim the independence of Kosovo. Although UNMIK officials were not prepared to put independence on the agenda at that time, they nonetheless gave encouragement to the Albanians, suggesting that a formal secession from Serbia would be supported once certain standards defined by UNMIK had been met.[90]

Moving toward Independence

Nebojša Čović, Serbian deputy prime minister and head of the Coordinating Center for Kosovo and Metohija, tried throughout 2002 to win concessions for Serbian jurisdiction over Kosovo—but to no avail. Indeed, in March 2002, Steiner advised Čović that "Belgrade authorities have no right to interfere in Kosova's affairs."[91] In the meantime, on 17 November 2001, Kosovar (Albanians and Serbs) went to the polls to elect a parliament with legislative powers. Serbs rallied behind the *Povratak* (Return) coalition headed by Rada Trajković and won 22 of the 120 seats at stake.[92] With some 65% of registered voters taking part in the elections, Ibrahim Rugova's LDK captured 46% of the vote, with 25.54% going to Hashim Thaqi's Democratic Party of Kosovo (DPK) and 10.96% to the Serbian *Povratak* coalition. Under the procedures established by law, the parliament was required to elect the president of Kosova within three rounds of voting. But Rugova's party had obtained only 47 seats in the parliament, and Rugova was, at first, unwilling to make any bargains with the other parties. Thus, it was not until March 2002 that the parliament managed to reach an agreement to elect Rugova president, even though he had been the only candidate for the post, and only after Rugova agreed to accept Bajram Rexhepi, a moderate in Thaqi's DPK, as his prime minister.[93] On 4 March, In his first public address as president, Rugova affirmed his commitment to "build a society of tolerance, understanding, reconciliation among the people and respect for each other," as well as of the "rule of law," but at the same time called for international recognition of Kosovo's independence.[94]

The international community has felt, for a number of reasons, that Kosovo is not yet ready for independence. First of all, Albanians unprepared to accept Serbs in their future state ("radicals") continued to murder Albanian politicians committed to work with Serbs toward a multi-ethnic Kosova ("moderates"); indeed, 28 Albanian moderates—20 of them adherents of Rugova—were murdered between 2002 and late February 2003.[95] Certainly, if President Rugova is not able to protect legally elected officeholders and high party officials, then it is not apparent that his government is ready to operate independently.

Second, arrests of KLA figures suspected of having committed war crimes against Serb *and Albanian* civilians have provoked protests among ordinary Albanians and demands for their release, while a key witness in a case involving atrocities allegedly committed by a five-man KLA unit was murdered near Peja in western Kosovo in April 2003.[96] Under the circumstances, one is entitled to doubt whether a young Kosovar state, with no international forces present, would consider itself in a position to cooperate with the ICTY.

Third, the newly elected Kosovar parliament showed surprising immaturity and naïveté in May 2002 when it adopted a resolution invalidating the border agreement between Macedonia and the FRY. This resolution was "immediately denounced"—not only by the Macedonian parliament but also by U.S. officials, by UNMIK chief Steiner, and even by the UN Security Council.[97]

Fourth, attacks on non-Albanians, especially Serbs, continued to be commonplace, even four years after the conclusion of the NATO campaign, prompting Čović to complain in early 2003 that "there is still no rule of law and freedom of movement for Serbs in the province."[98] The situation remained sufficiently serious that Marek Nowiczki, the internationally appointed ombudsman for Kosovo, tasked to protect human rights, admitted to *Glas javnosti* in March 2003 that it was unrealistic to hold out hope for the return of more than a few thousand Serbs.[99] Indeed, just a month earlier, local Albanians stoned the houses of Serb returnees in the village of Bića, near Klina.[100] Then, in May, following the murder of Zoran Mirković, a teacher of Russian, the Serbian parliament declared that the security situation, for which UNMIK and KFOR were responsible, was "at the lowest level possible."[101] Another murder followed, this time of an elderly Serb couple and their son, in the town of Obilić in early June.[102] Five Serbs were reported killed in 2002, while at least 12 more Serbs were said to have been killed during 2003.[103] Dejan Sahović, the Serbian and Montenegrin ambassador to the UN, brought Serbian concerns about security in Kosovo before the UN Security Council on 10 June; in response, Steiner proposed the creation of a specialized UNMIK police unit in charge of protecting Serbs and other non-Albanians.

Fifth, distrust between Albanian and Serb parliamentarians runs so deep that on at least two occasions Serb deputies boycotted sessions of the parliament. This distrust was also reflected in a declaration adopted in Mitrovica on 25 February 2003 vowing that "anyone who tries to break the territorial integrity of Serbia must know that it will be defended by all available means."[104]

To this list may be added unresolved property disputes, as well as claims arising from local debts repaid by Serbia, the continued operations of the Albanian National Army, and Kosovo's continued dependence on foreign grants just to stay afloat. Yet, for all that, Steiner pledged to transfer many governmental responsibilities to Kosovar institutions and agencies during 2003, and within Kosovo, eventual independence is increasingly taken for granted, with attention already beginning to shift to questions of admission to the EU and NATO.[105]

The pain experienced by both Albanians and Serbs is still fresh, but already some efforts toward reconciliation are being made. At Lillehammer, in Norway, Professor Steinar Bryn has been hosting reconciliation meetings for Albanians and Serbs for several years. And while those coming to these meetings initially want only to hurl accusations at each other, by the start of the second day, constructive dialogue begins, and a foundation for mutual understanding begins to be laid, according to Bryn.

Moreover, even a partial reconciliation typically involves a recognition of the pain suffered by the other side and an acknowledgment of the culpability of one's own side in causing that pain. On this point, Deputy Prime Minister Čović took an important step forward, declaring in April 2003,

Serbia has the strength to say that it is truly sorry, but also the right to say that this does not mean that now things should be better only for the Albanians, and worse for the Serbs.

Is this so difficult to say? Well, I don't find it difficult and I am ready to say it, but the Albanian representatives should also open up their souls and admit just how cruel the vengeance of Albanian extremists has been.

I want to say that we, who represent the Serb people today, and those who represent the Albanian people today, have a lot of reasons to feel ashamed and to repent.[106]

The Failure of Reconciliation

What the international community hoped to achieve in Kosovo was to promote sentiments of multiculturalism, in which Serbs and Albanians would treat each other with respect, form friendships across ethnic lines, and appreciate each other's cultures and histories as fully legitimate. Not everyone accepts that this vision can be realized, however. For example, Rasim Ljajić, the minister for human rights and national minorities in Serbia and Montenegro, told the Sarajevo weekly magazine *Ljiljan* in spring 2004,

the development of a multi-ethnic society in Kosovo along the lines which the international community wants to realize is simply impossible. . . . If you look at the history of Albanian-Serb relations, it is clear that Serbs and Albanians lived side by side . . . [but in] parallel worlds, and that such coexistence was possible [only] in conditions when a repressive regime, which is to say the communist regime, created the illusion of that coexistence.[107]

Indeed, in the course of 2003–2004, there were signs of an escalation of violence, with at least four explosions in the divided town of Mitrovica in August 2003 alone, the murder of two Serbian young people that same month, and a spontaneous stone-throwing attack on Bajram Rexhepi, the prime minister of Kosovo, in December of that year. There were also continued attacks on Serbian Orthodox Church facilities and cemeteries. Some of the violence was the work of the rejectionist Albanian National Army, which, in April 2003, was characterized by then-UN chief of mission Michael Steiner as "a terrorist group."[108]

By March 2004, Koštunica, who had failed to be elected president of Serbia in 2002, was the prime minister–designate for Serbia.[109] In his first address to the Skupština, Koštunica outlined his government's program, declaring the resolution of the status of Kosovo to be one of his highest priorities. In Koštunica's view, the best solution, where Kosovo was concerned, was to allow Kosovo wide-ranging autonomy within Serbia and to allow designated Serb "cantons" wide-ranging autonomy with Kosovo.[110]

Two weeks later, to the day, there was renewed violence in Kosovo, when Albanians rioted and attacked local Serbs. Albanians claimed that the disturbances came as a spontaneous response to the drowning of two Albanian children, but Chris Patten, the EU's foreign minister, said that there was evidence "that prominent Albanian politicians in the crisis province had plotted the attacks on Serbs, Roma, and KFOR troops" in advance.[111] After two days of violence, at least 19 persons were dead, more than 900 were wounded (among them, at least 55 KFOR troops and 61 police officers), 800 houses had been incinerated, and some 35 Serbian Orthodox churches and monasteries had been destroyed.[112] A UNESCO expert mission estimated that it would cost about $30 million to repair and rebuild the ecclesiastical facilities alone.[113] KFOR declared a curfew and rushed in additional troops. Dušan Janjić, a political moderate and head of the Forum for Ethnic Relations in Belgrade, commented that the fresh violence signaled the "final collapse of the ideology of a multicultural society in Kosovo."[114]

In response, Koštunica redoubled his efforts to promote his cantonization scheme, in spite of initial EU resistance to the concept, and told the Serbian Assembly that the notion that Serbs and Albanians could live together in peace was "utopian" and that a "multiethnic heaven" was simply not realizable.[115] A commission was appointed to develop a plan to assure "equal rights for all citizens in Kosovo-Metohija," and in early May 2004, the Serbian Skupština reviewed and adopted the resulting plan, by unanimous vote.[116] The plan, promptly endorsed by Russia, reflected continued Serbian unwillingness to give up Kosovo and, as such, only prolonged the dangerous stalemate.[117] In a key passage, the plan charges,

> The nationalist intolerance demonstrated by the majority population is so powerful that it literally threatens the physical existence of local Serbs on the territory they have inhabited continually for more than ten centuries. . . . Consequently, it is necessary to change the institutional framework and the policy supposed to create conditions for a peaceful and normal life for all Serbs and other non-Albanians in Kosovo and to ensure their safe and unimpeded return to the territory of Kosovo and Metohija, from which they were forcibly expelled. Likewise, it is necessary to provide for efficient protection and promotion of human rights in accordance with European norms and standards. . . . The "autonomy-within-autonomy" principle does not mean that the fundamentals of a multiethnic and multicultural society will be abandoned. Quite the contrary, this is the only way to make it possible.[118]

The plan calls for the creation of five autonomous districts for Serbs, to be known collectively as the Autonomous Serb Community in Kosovo and Metohija, for a combination of territorial, cultural, and personal autonomy, for the protection of both individual and collective rights, and for the protection of those Serbian cultural monuments and artifacts which still survive. The plan also calls on the UN to "make it possible for two thirds of the Kosovo Serb population (around 220,000) expelled to central Serbia to return to their homes in Kosovo."[119]

Kosovo is a paradigmatic case of failed legitimation and its consequences. As repression escalated in the Milošević years, so too did resistance, with the appearance, first, of a parallel infrastructure set up by the Albanians and later with the establishment of the KLA. This confirms the prognosis given in proposition 3 ("Stable equilibrium in a political system hinges on that system's legitimacy"—with violations of human rights constituting an important factor for de-legitimation). By the same virtue, these phenomena confirm proposition 7 ("The more illegitimate the system is, the more likely it is that people will organize to overthrow it"). Again, proposition 8 ("The greater the correlation between political-programmatic preferences and ethnic affiliation, the greater the ethnic polarization") fits the case of Kosovo just as well as it fit the interwar kingdom. At this time, it appears inevitable that the Albanians of Kosovo will get their independence. Whether they shall succeed in establishing the rule of law, in assuring social justice, and in building and sustaining a legitimate state remains to be seen.

Talking with Serbs and Albanians over the years, and reading such literature as has been available to me, I have been impressed with the degree to which Serbs and Albanians alike have seen themselves as victims and each other as oppressors.[120] Yet, casting an eye over their history over the past century, I am impressed by the extent to which the role of victim has switched back and forth between these two groups. In the years 1878–1913, it would be fair to characterize the Serbs as largely victims, but in the years 1913–1915, it was the Albanians who were the victims of Serbian repression. The relationship was reversed during World War One, but in 1918, the victorious Serb Army returned to Kosovo, and once again the Albanians felt that they were the victims of Belgrade's oppression. During World War Two, the relationship was once more inverted, with the Albanians of Kosovo conjoined to a Greater Albania under Italian occupation; during these years, it was the Serbs who suffered the most. But after that war ended, it was the Serbs who were dominant from 1945 until 1966. By 1968, the Albanians were once more acquiring a position of dominance, which they lost some two decades later, only to regain it once more in 1999, as a result of NATO's intervention. Since 1878, thus, there have been four periods during which the Albanians were dominated or repressed by the Serbs and five periods during which the Serbs have been dominated or persecuted by the Albanians. Thus, if a sense of victimization seems to be particularly acute in this part of the world, it is not without some reason. And yet, what the Serbs and Albanians have not yet tried in the years since 1878, up to now, is to live together as equal citizens, in a civic state structured on liberal principles, in which the Serbian and Albanian languages would enjoy equal status in government, administration, and education, in which the common history of Serbs and Albanians would be celebrated, rather than made the object of contestation, and in which the rule of law is so well honored that it can be taken for granted. It is in such a concept that the keys to harmony and stability could be found—to be built not all at once, but gradually, over time. Hence, too, from the standpoint of human rights, the moral law, harmony, and stability, the construction of a state founded on liberal principles—by which I mean, the rule of law, individual (and societal) rights, tolerance, respect for the harm principle, equality, and the neutrality of the state (including the public schools) in matters of religion—is far more important than questions of borders and jurisdictions for the long-term stability of the region.

CHAPTER 19

Separate Paths: Slovenia, Macedonia, Croatia

Where post-Dayton Bosnia has operated, in part (and only in part, because the situation in Bosnia remains, at this writing, highly complex), on the principle that the fostering of liberal culture needs to be accomplished before democratic institutions can be allowed free rein, and where Serbia in the first months of the Koštunica presidency was operating on the premise that democracy comes first, and even that nationalism may have a legitimate place in the political culture of the society, the other Yugoslav successor states—Slovenia, Croatia, and Macedonia—offer other paths. Slovenia, under President Kučan and Prime Minister Drnovšek, undertook to build both liberal culture and democratic institutions simultaneously, building on the foundation of incipient liberalization and democratization in the republic already during the years 1986–1990. Croatia, under Tudjman, adopted a formula broadly comparable with the Serbian formula, albeit in a more moderate variation, with its own local versions of nepotism and cronyism. And Macedonia has opted to try to offer something to everyone: declaring a national state, providing guarantees more appropriate to a civic (i.e., liberal) state, building democracy, but proving to be porous, at least to some extent, to organized corruption.

These cases fully confirm propositions 1, 3, 4, 8, 11, 12, and 14. Proposition 1, which affirms the interrelatedness of political, moral, and economic legitimacy, is confirmed in the case of Tudjman's Croatia, where his endeavors to partition Bosnia with Milošević (a violation of moral legitimacy) and his indulgence in forms of economic corruption, including even nepotism, eroded his political legitimacy (as reflected, for example, in the resignation of Stipe Mesić from the HDZ and the persistent criticism of Tudjman by a number of intellectuals and journalists). Proposition 3, which hinges stability on legitimacy, obtains confirmation from all three cases. A skeptic might conjecture that Slovenian stability could be reduced to economic prosperity rather than to legitimacy. But in Macedonia, about one in every five citizens is below the poverty line and economic trends have been largely downward, and yet, until the Albanian insurrection of spring 2001, the state seemed to be relatively stable, even surviving a failed assassination attempt on President Kiro Gligorov in October 1995. Proposition 4, which notes that instability provides a constant pressure toward change, is confirmed best, among these three cases, in Croatia, where Tudjman's cronyist proclivities remained intolerable for certain sectors of the population. Proposition 8, which postulates that the greater the correlation between political-programmatic preferences and ethnic affiliation, the greater the ethnic polarization, is confirmed by the secession of Serbs from Croatia in 1990–1991, while in Macedonia, the divisions among the Albanian parties prevented ethnic polarization from escalating to the threshold of danger, until battles in neighboring Kosovo radicalized those Albanians from Macedonia who volunteered into the KLA. Proposition 11, which postulates that the greater the correlation between economic class and ethnic affiliation, the greater the potential for ethnic mobilization, obtains some confirmation from the Macedonian case, while proposition 12, which links lack of consensus on symbols of legitimation with an awareness of the problematic nature of the system, is best revealed in the Croatian case, in the early 1990s, while the Slovenian system revealed some internal divisions in summer 2000, when members of the short-lived Bajuk government sang Domobrani (quisling) songs from World War Two and spoke against the wartime Partisan movement. Finally, proposition 14, which links the tendency of different nationality groups to have competing legitimating symbols with ethnic polarization and the erosion of system legitimacy is confirmed, up to a point, in the relations between the Macedonians and Albanians of Macedonia.

General Observations

Of all of the Yugoslav successor states, Slovenia has recorded the smoothest and least problematic transition toward liberal democracy and has maintained the highest level of system stability, as measured by several conventional indicators.[1] What accounts for this relative success?

It is fashionable in some quarters to attribute Slovenia's smoother transition variously to the country's high degree of ethnic homogeneity or to its greater prosperity.[2] While it may be that these factors are not entirely irrelevant, I would prefer to place the stress on two rather different factors, viz., the fact that the LC Slovenia already embarked on the transition to a pluralist system in the mid-1980s, building bridges with the Slovenian opposition and in the process beginning the transition to legitimate government; and the fact that liberal political culture was planting its seeds in Slovenia already in the 1980s, if not before.[3] Indeed, the activities of pacifist, environmentalist, punk, and lesbian and gay associations at that time helped to lay the foundations for a tolerant liberal culture in Slovenia, at a time when Serbia was sinking ever deeper into a thoroughly nationalist culture. Seymour Martin Lipset and R. J. Dalton are among those who have emphasized the importance of transformations of political culture in transitions from authoritarianism.[4] In their view, attitudes and values appropriate to an authoritarian setting may be problematic in a democratic setting and may risk deflecting a society from a liberal course. Thus, there are two factors at work in a successful transition from authoritarianism: the construction of a legitimate system and the development of a liberal culture. Without the latter, the former is at risk.

A comparison of the post-1987 transitions in Slovenia, Serbia, Macedonia, and Croatia illustrates this clearly. In Slovenia, liberal culture was already sprouting at the time that the system was converted to a pluralist model. Moreover, Ljubljana intellectuals such as Slavoj Žižek, Slavko Gaber, Rudi Rizman, and Rastko Močnik, among others, have been actively involved in fostering a dialogue about the content of liberalism and in promoting liberal values in the educational system, as well as in the society more broadly.

In Serbia, by contrast, the exponents of liberal culture were, for the most part, concentrated in Belgrade and were, in any case, dwarfed in influence by the more vocal exponents of nationalist culture, at least some of whom looked back nostalgically to the Chetnik movement of Draža Mihailović. And where the Slovene communists built bridges with the liberals and gradually assimilated liberal-democratic values as their own, in Serbia, Milošević and his allies built bridges with the nationalists and, adopting nationalist rhetoric, touted nationalist values and objectives. Such consistent liberals as continued to speak out in Milošević's Serbia, such as the members of Women in Black and Nebojša Popov with his journal *Republika,* were confined to the absolute margins of the Serbian political landscape; the leading figures in the opposition, with the sole exception of Vesna Pešić, all spoke the language of nationalism.

In Macedonia, both liberal culture and nationalist culture were weak at the onset of the 1990s, and the will to independence was correspondingly weak and derivative. And yet, with the help of NGOs, such as the American Bar Association's CEELI (Central European and Eurasian Law Initiative) program and Search for Common Ground (directed locally by Oran Fraenkel), Macedonian elites charted a wobbly course, with some figures (such as Ljupčo Georgievski) trying to pull the country toward a more nationalist course and others (such as Boris Trajkovski and Branko Crvenkovski) endeavoring to hold Macedonia on a more moderate path steady course.

And in Croatia, Franjo Tudjman and the HDZ came to power with an inchoate grab bag of underdeveloped and sometimes incompatible notions, not even realizing the threat that nationalism posed to liberal culture.[5] Tudjman could be better described as a "traditionalist" than as an "ideologue," and his intolerance of gays and lesbians, for example, reflected not so much an elaborated political strategy as old-fashioned prejudices which Tudjman had assimilated earlier in his life, having no essential connection with his political program as such.[6] Moreover, Croatian society had had its liberal period in the late 1960s and early 1970s, though, by contrast with Slovenian liberalism, Croatian liberalism had been more penetrated by nationalist values and also had been much more mercilessly crushed by the communist authorities than had been the case in Slovenia. In the Tudjman era, however, democratization was undermined by corruption in both the political sphere and the economic sphere, while liberal culture developed largely in opposition to the government. The Croatian, Slovenia, Serbian, and Macedonian political trajectories have, thus, been diverse and distinct from each other.

The Slovenian Model

The adoption of 82 amendments (nos. 9–90) to the 1974 Slovenian constitution in September 1989, together with the passage of two laws in December 1989 (regulating the status of political parties and reforming the election system) laid the foundation for a pluralist system in Slovenia and provided a legal basis for the holding of free elections in April 1990. Shortly before these legislative acts, a group of deputies in the Slovenian Assembly discovered that there were secret federal laws and regulations in force, prompting an investigation which culminated in a report to the Assembly on 21 June 1989 and to loud protests from Slovenian citizens.[7]

In the elections of April 1990, the two biggest vote getters were the Liberal Democratic Party (which had developed out of the former youth organization) and the Party of Democratic Renewal (the former League of Communists of Slovenia). These parties did not come to power, however, because seven noncommunist parties had formed a coalition called Demos which, collectively, outpolled any of their rivals. Altogether, in the new Assembly, Demos parties controlled 127 out of 240 seats.[8] But Demos was riddled with internal controversies, and by the beginning of 1992, the coalition had been formally dissolved. Subsequently, Lojze Peterle, the Christian Democratic prime minister whose tenure in office had been rocked by controversies over privatization, abortion, religious instruction in public schools, and supervision of the media, was ousted by a coalition of parties in mid-April 1992. Janez Drnovšek, the former member of the Yugoslav collective presidency and new head of the LDS, was now entrusted with the prime ministership. Except for a few months in 2000, Drnovšek served as prime minister from then until winning the presidency in 2002. A new constitution was adopted on 23 December 1991, establishing a 90-member State Assembly, which exercises legislative competence, and a 40-member Council of State, which has an advisory role. The Slovenian constitution provides special protection for the Italian and Hungarian minorities living in the republic as well as for the Romany community. The Italian and Hungarian minorities are guaranteed one representative each in the Slovenian parliament, and all three groups enjoy representation on local municipal councils.[9]

Democratization

As Danica Fink-Hafner has noted, crediting Juan Linz, "that political system is consolidated in which: a) no major political performer, party, force or institution studies the possibility of an alternative democratic process for the purpose of the assumption of power and b) no political institution or group demands a veto on the activity [or decisions] of the democratically elected decision-makers."[10] Or, to put it another way, a political system is consolidated when there is a broad agreement on the rules of the game.

In this regard, post-communist Slovenia's one serious internal disagreement concerning the rules of the game had to do with a dispute between those favoring the adoption of a majority-vote system (led by Janez Janša, president of the Social Democratic Party, or SDS) and those favoring the retention in some form of a system of proportional representation (led by Janez Drnovšek and vociferously seconded by Zmago Jelinčič, president of the Slovenian National Party, or SNS). The dispute began in early 1996, months before the elections scheduled for later that year, when Janša's Social Democratic Party proposed that the system of proportional representation being used be replaced with a two-round majority system modeled on the French example. It was generally understood that the majority system would wipe out the smaller parties, leaving only two clearly defined blocs: a progressive, center-left bloc and a traditionalist, center-right bloc. Since there was insufficient support for this change within the Assembly (by now, a 90-seat body), Janša pressed for a popular referendum on the question.

After various skirmishes and delays, a referendum on amending the electoral law was put before voters on 8 December 1996, a month after the elections had been held. What followed was confusing to all concerned. Voters had been offered three alternatives, and only 44% favored the two-round majority system proposed by Janša's SDS; 26% supported an amended proportional system as proposed by a group of 35 Assembly deputies; and 14% voted for a mixed electoral system, an alternative drafted by the State Council (Slovenia's largely advisory upper house).[11] Since none of the three alternatives had garnered more than 50% of the vote, it was generally understood that all three alternatives had failed and that the system should remain as it was.

Nearly two years later, however—on 8 October 1998—the Constitutional Court reviewed the vote and concluded that since the SDS proposal had attracted more "yes" votes than "no" votes, while the other two proposals had attracted a greater number of rejections than approvals, the majority system had won. This decision was handed down on the basis of a 5 to 3 vote, in which the outvoted judges wrote dissenting opinions, arguing "that the Court should not have ruled on the issue at all, since the referendum results were already final and the petitioners had not sought to exhaust proper legal remedies immediately after the results were initially declared."[12]

But with the Assembly still deeply divided on this issue, the cause of election reform quickly became bogged down, and by spring 2000, opponents of the majority system were talking of amending the constitution in order to provide a constitutional anchor for the proportional representation system. Ironically, the issue came to a head during the brief prime ministership of Andrej Bajuk (April–November 2000), when the SLS+SKD (formed in spring 2000, under the influence of the Catholic hierarchy, through the merger of Marjan Podobnik's SLS and Lojze Peterle's SKD, the Slovenian Christian Democrats) abandoned its center-right coalition partners and voted with the left to reject the majority model and amend the constitution. Janša mocked SLS+SKD chair Franc Zagožen by telling a news conference that Zagožen's party "does not even know whether it is in the government or [in] the opposition."[13] At the same time, Bajuk and Peterle resigned as deputy chairs of the SLS+SKD, leaving the party altogether and founding a new party—New Slovenia–Christian People's Party (NS-KLS). Meanwhile, the 25 July 2000 vote amended Article 80 of the constitution to provide for the election of the National Assembly by a system of proportional representation, with a 4% threshold.

But as stormy as the fight over majority model vs. proportional representation had been, its conclusion brought new clarity to the system and potentially settled the issue with sufficient finality to enable the system to move forward.

Rule of Law

Slovenia has been ranked among the least corrupt countries in the world. But for all that, it has had its share of problems, though it should be emphasized that corruption in Slovenia has been due to individual dereliction rather than being rooted in the system itself. In the first decade of independence, the two "noisiest" scandals related to the participation of certain high-ranking Slovenian officials in arms smuggling to Bosnian Muslim forces during the War of Yugoslav Succession, and to the inappropriate allocation of certain funds by SLS chair Marjan Podobnik (as revealed in September 1999).[14] The smuggling scandal presaged Janša's eventual dismissal from the post of minister of defense in April 1994, while a series of scandals touching Marjan Podobnik led to his eventual ouster as leader of the SLS.

There have also been accusations of cronyism and "clannish" behavior hurled across the barricades between left and right. President Kučan and Prime Minister Drnovšek were accused, for years, of dispensing favors on members of their "clans," while Janša was also accused, in connection with his first term as minister of defense, of subverting the resources of the ministry to advance his own private political ambitions.[15] The Liberal Democrats also denounced the extensive personnel changes in the administration carried out by Bajuk's government, in a 1 August 2000 statement, as "significantly harsher than announced by even the greatest pessimists,"[16] implying that only political orientation counted for the short-lived center-right government. In January 2001, a fresh corruption scandal flared when Marjan Glavar, head of the district state prosecutor's office in Ptuj, was incarcerated on suspicion of corruption and of links to Josip Lončarič's transport operations, in which illegal immigrants had been smuggled across the Slovenian border.[17] Ironically, the public prosecutor never filed the indictment against Glavar, with the result that the case never came to court.

In spite of these and other cases of corruption, Slovenia seemed, at first, to be so much of an oasis for the rule of law in the East-Central European region that, as of the beginning of 2001, Slovenia still had not established any special body to fight corruption.[18] Indeed, a GRECO evaluation team reported, after a three-day visit to Ljubljana in September 2000, that Slovenia's crime rates were safely below European standards and that Slovenia was, according to an index prepared by the Economist Intelligence Unit, "the least corrupt country in Central and Eastern Europe." Yet, about the same time, research conducted by the Slovenian Institute of Social Sciences of the University of Ljubljana found that 38% of Slovenes believed that "almost all or the majority" of government officials were engaged in some form of corruption, while 60% of those polled felt the corruption and the abuse of public office had been rising in recent years.[19]

Corruption is apparently the most serious in healthcare, where patients sometimes bribe their physicians in order to get faster treatment, and tax collection, although there have been reports of corruption in some police stations, as well as in the public prosecutor's office.[20] Among the problems underlying corruption in Slovenia have been "a lack of [a] regulatory framework and/or reform, especially at a local level," and serious levels of conflict of interest among officeholders.[21] In 2000, Slovenia was ranked 28th out of 90 states in level of corruption, but slid to 34th place in 2001, with Finland, Denmark, and New Zealand holding onto the top three places.[22] But in 2002, Slovenia's ranking improved: among 102 countries rated, Slovenia placed 27th—ahead of Italy (ranked 31st), Greece (44th), and all other countries in the East-Central European area, including Poland (tied for 45th place with four other countries).[23]

Since 2001, Slovenia has established an anti-corruption unit, has developed a strong anti-money-laundering regime, has intensified its cooperation with Interpol, and has agreed to cooperate with neighbors Croatia, Italy, and Hungary in a joint campaign against organized crime.[24] But even though the incidence of street crime and burglaries is, within the East-Central European region, lowest in Slovenia,[25] many Slovenes fear that their way of life is gradually being eroded and that their country is neither as safe nor as rule-abiding as in the past. The brutal beating in 2001 of Miro Petek, a respected journalist for the daily newspaper *Večer,* after he had written about corruption in local business in the town of Slovenj Gradec, did nothing to allay such fears.[26] Nor was Petek's case unique. On the contrary, other journalists have also been beaten or intimidated in other ways, in an effort to persuade them to keep silent about corruption.[27]

Equality

There have been three salient vectors along which issues of inequality have been manifested: confessionality (to be discussed obliquely below, in the subsection on "Education and Values"), nationality, and gender. Where nationality is concerned, Slovenian law distinguishes between "autochthonous groups" (Italians, Hungarians, Roma, Germans or "Old Austrians," and Jews) and "new minorities" (Serbs, Croats, Kosovar Albanians, and non-autochthonous Roma from Kosovo and Albania). Members of the former groups enjoy special protection under the constitution, with the Italians and Hungarians enjoying guaranteed representation in the Assembly. In the case of the "new minorities," there was a six-month window in 1991–1992 during which non-Slovene citizens of the defunct SFRY were granted the option to assume Slovenian citizenship, provided that they registered their wish to do so. But most of the non-Slovene Yugoslavs failed to do so, apparently because the requirement to register was not well publicized.[28] The International Helsinki Federation for Human Rights reported in 1999 that some 130,000 former permanent residents of Slovenia had been "erased from the register of permanent residents due to their non-Slovene or mixed ethnic origin" following the collapse of the SFRY in June 1991, which had the consequence that their names were erased from the public records. By 1998, about 90,000 of these former permanent residents had left Slovenia, while those who remained existed in a kind of legal limbo, in which social and health insurance and pensions became uncertain and in which other rights were denied.[29] By 2003, some 18,000 "erased" persons remained in Slovenia. But in April 2003, the Constitutional Court of Slovenia ruled that the previous legislation regulating the legal status of former citizens of the SFRY was unconstitutional, setting the stage for those affected to apply for Slovenian citizenship.[30] A group of 33 legislators asked the court to reconsider its ruling, but when the court refused to do so, the issue was put to a vote via a national referendum held on 5 April 2004. Only about one-third of Slovenia's 1.6 million eligible voters took part in the referendum, but among these, 95% voted their disapproval of the court's willingness to reinstate the 18,000 "erased" persons—mostly Bosniaks, Croats, and Serbs.[31] Tanja Rener, a noted sociologist at the University of Ljubljana, described the outcome as a victory for "racism, intolerance, and extreme nationalism."[32] It served also as a reminder of the fact that Slovenia, too, is home to xenophobic tendencies.

A discriminatory law on military pensions was adopted in summer 1998 which terminated pension payments to some 200 non-Slovene military pensioners. There was also an unsuccessful attempt by the Ministry of the Interior to prohibit the use of the letters *ć* and *dj*, which are common in Croatian, Bosnian, and Serbian names.

Where gender equality is concerned, although some 69.2% of Slovenes polled in December 1991 felt that democracy entails, of necessity, equal rights for women, women have remained, in Slovenia as in most other countries, very much "second-class" citizens.[33] There are, to be sure, guarantees of full gender equality in Articles 14 and 53 of the constitution. But in spite of these guarantees, there is discrimination against women in promotions, in vulnerability to dismissal from employment, in the media, and in political offices.[34] Indeed, the Christian Democrats, People's Party, and Social Democrats have actively discouraged women from becoming actively involved in party politics.[35] In its day, the Demos coalition, in particular, promoted the notion that women should stay at home and care for their husbands and children, on the old concept of "Kinder, Küche, Kirche." Perhaps as a result of such pressures, women constituted only 12% of the deputies in the Slovenian Assembly as of 2003, just barely over 50% of the EU average.[36] The Christian Democrats actually introduced legislation at the end of 1994 which would have provided for three years of paid maternity leave; functionaries at the Office for Women's Policy fought this measure, in the conviction that its passage would have generated a tangible pressure on mothers to take full advantage of the provision, whether they wanted to or not, lest they be viewed as "bad mothers."[37]

In addition, there have been problems of violence in the family. It is estimated that 20% of Slovenian families are afflicted with this problem; women are the victims in about 60% of the cases reported.[38] The Office for Women's Policy (established in mid-1992) has been active in organizing seminars on this problem. The first shelter for women victims of domestic violence was opened in Krško in 1991 by the Center for Social Work; today there are nine such shelters in Slovenia.

Tolerance/Intolerance

Without tolerance, the liberal project withers and dies. Without tolerance, there is no such thing as civilized society. And yet, intolerance continues to reassert itself in societies which profess to be civilized. Part of the explanation of this phenomenon, as Mitja Hafner-Fink has noted, is the co-existence of traditional and modern values, in which Slovenianness, for example, is assumed to mean Slovene by birth and in which low levels of spatial mobility reinforce provincial orientations.[39]

Gays, lesbians, transsexuals, and transvestites constitute the least accepted group in Slovenia, with higher ratings for homophobia and transophobia than for phobias about Roma or Muslims, for example. Prejudice is manufactured in a number of ways, including via religious associations, but in Slovenia, the media has also contributed to homophobia by spreading stereotypes.[40] In 1994, some 56.2% of Slovenes said that they would not want to have a homosexual for a neighbor, though 95.4% of the total sample admitted that they had had no contact or experience with homosexuals. By 2002, however, in spite of annual

gay festivals and the steady dissemination of information, the proportion of
Slovenes fearing the prospect of having a homosexual neighbor remained more
or less steady at 55.1%.[41] In spite of that, when *Delo* conducted an opinion poll
in July 2001, of the 43% who felt that Slovenian society was not tolerant enough,
60% would not accept a homosexual as a babysitter for their children—a figure
which reveals some strange notions about what homosexuality is.[42]

Given these attitudes, it is scarcely surprising that a bill on registered partnerships (establishing a legal basis for same-sex bonds), prepared in 1998, was
never introduced in the parliament. Still, advocates of sexual tolerance can take
comfort in the fact that current legislation outlaws discrimination on the basis
of sexual orientation (though subtle and not-so-subtle forms of discrimination
continue). A law granting gay and lesbian couples full legal equality with heterosexual couples, except in adoption, was scheduled to be introduced in the
parliament in autumn 2003, but the Slovenian People's Party registered its
opposition and managed to delay discussion of the bill.[43] Where xenophobia is
concerned, prejudicial attitudes have focused on immigrants from other Yugoslav successor states (including Roma), Muslims, and Jews. While some measures show a decline in xenophobia, there is a "hard core" of about 12% of the
population who continue to reject all three groups.[44]

Tonči Kuzmanić, a professor of theoretical political science at the University
of Ljubljana, has offered a telling commentary on the phenomenon of social
intolerance among Slovenes, taking as his specimen the weekly column "Night-
watch" written by columnist M.S. and featured in the Sunday edition of *Delo*.
Kuzmanić found that the column figured as "one of the most systematic and
constant sources of 'intolerance towards foreigners and the different in general
(including women) expressed through the media." In M.S.'s usage, as Kuzmanić
notes, the terms "bar flies," "men," "honest folk," and "Slovenes" become inter-
changeable. Xenophobia, homophobia, and a simplistic faith that the "problems" posed by those who are in some way *different* can be solved by violence
and repression—these are the ideas smuggled into the discourse of M.S.'s
columns, via the vehicle of the "bar flies" of Slovenia. In their concept, Slobodan
Milošević, even though a Serb, commanded respect "because he is the man of
mettle, he is 'cunning' and 'understands', and knows how to handle the most significant things . . . [and] because he knows how to 'screw' properly." The danger,
as Kuzmanić notes, is not so much that the "bar flies" will come to power as
"that the bar-fly style of discourse will prevail and . . . that the state apparatus,
which is among other things the single legal and legitimate protagonist and exe-
cutioner of the use of violence, takes over their style of perceiving, arranging,
concluding, reasoning and action."[45]

Education and Values

The dominant political culture has, to some extent, lagged behind changes in
institutions and in the system as a whole.[46] Insofar as the transition from

authoritarianism is still at an early stage, it is perhaps inevitable that there have been struggles over the direction in which society will evolve, struggles over, in a word, values. In this regard, battle lines have been drawn between the Roman Catholic Church and its political advocates, who favor Catholic influence in education and in state policies (the Christian Democrats, the People's Party, and the Social Democrats) and those who champion a secular state (above all, the LDS and the former communist United List or ZLDS). At the center of the battle was the insistence on the part of Archbishop Franc Rode, who assumed the archepiscopal office on 6 April 1997, that Catholic religious instruction be incorporated into the curriculum of state elementary schools as an optional subject.[47] In order to secure this prize, the Church pressed for an agreement to be negotiated between the Holy See and the Republic of Slovenia. There had been a huge debate in the parliament on this subject already in 1995–1996, but under Article 72 of the Basic Law on Education, no confessional activity is permitted on public school premises from elementary school to university.[48] But Archbishop Rode made this his priority, and finally, the Slovenian government agreed to negotiations, appointing to its team Peter Tos from the Foreign Ministry; Nina Čoz, the director of the Government Office for Religious Communities; Janez Pogorelić, spokesperson for the Government Office for Legislation; and Peter Kastelič, state undersecretary for the Foreign Ministry. The Holy See appointed to its negotiating team Edmund Farhat, the apostolic nuncio in Ljubljana; Bishop Franc Kramberger of Maribor; Dr. Anton Stres, dean of the Theological Faculty; and Dr. Borut Kosir, professor of theology. On 11 November 1999, the Slovenian government accepted the text of the agreement drawn up by the negotiating teams as the basis for discussion, and presumably ratification, in the State Assembly (Državni Zbor). Article 2 declared that "The Republic of Slovenia recognizes the legal character of the Catholic Church. The Republic of Slovenia also recognizes the legal character of all Church institutions . . . in the Republic of Slovenia, which possess this character in accordance with the norms of canon law."[49] Article 10 guaranteed the Church's right to establish and operate educational facilities and declared that other questions pertaining to education would be handled via mutual consultation between authorized representatives of Church and state.

It did not take long for controversy to flare. In the forefront was Matevž Krivic, a former justice of the Constitutional Court, who protested that Article 10 opened the door for the Church to meddle in the Slovenian educational system. He was soon joined in this criticism by Dr. Borut Bohte, director of the Department of International Law in the Faculty of Law.[50] Under pressure from various quarters, the Holy See agreed to a revision of Article 10, but a disputed section of Article 2, which stipulated that the Republic of Slovenia and the Holy See "are obligated to endeavor to resolve open questions which are not included in the agreement," remained intact.[51] By this point, however, Ivan Kristan, president of the Society for Constitutional Law, was declaring "constitutionally impermissible any agreement which would empower the Holy See and put pressure on and undermine the status of state legislation," while the Associated List warned grimly that, if ratified, the agreement "would legitimate the encroachment of the Roman Catholic Church in the sovereignty of Slovenia."[52]

Addressing an audience in Maribor, Archbishop Rode stated his position flatly: "When they made these schools, they ignored us, as if we did not exist."[53] He went on to complain that, quite apart from the exclusion of religious instruction from the schools, the textbooks currently in use for other subjects were "atheistic" and needed to be replaced. Shortly thereafter, Rode, who had initially speculated that the realization of the Church's goals vis-à-vis the Slovenian educational system might take 50 years, sounded impatient, declaring that "This school is not our school," and that his Church would never accept secular education.[54] In response, Tomaž Mastnak, the noted Slovenian sociologist, observed that the destruction of secular schooling would be tantamount to the destruction of the secular state, which is to say, of the liberal project itself.[55] As for the charge that the textbooks were "atheistic" in content, this charge was rebuffed by Alojzi Pluška, state secretary for middle school education, who added that the textbooks met the "highest professional standards."[56]

After long-drawn-out negotiations, Slovenia and the Vatican finally signed the bilateral agreement on 14 December 2001, under which ecclesiastical law would be brought into line with Slovenian law, while the Holy See's rights were catalogued.[57] Although the Church's demand that it be allowed to introduce Catholic religious instruction in the public schools remains unsatisfied, the government has provided the Church with money to operate private Catholic schools. But Church conservatives complain that the Church does not have adequate facilities and other resources to develop an adequate educational network of its own and speak of wanting Slovenia to become a "full democracy," by which they mean a democracy in which the Church's voice is decisive.[58] The agreement was ratified by the Assembly more than two years later.[59]

The Church has also maintained vigilance in sexual matters in general. In April 2001, parliament enacted a law allowing single women to obtain in vitro fertilization. The Catholic Church immediately marshaled its forces against this newly recognized right, which runs contrary to traditional notions of the family. With the support of 34 deputies in the parliament, the Church succeeded in putting the law to a referendum vote just two months after its passage.[60] As a result of this vote, the law was struck down, and in vitro fertilization was once more limited to women in heterosexual unions unable to conceive by intercourse.

But in February 1998, a curious polemic ensued after the release, by the hitherto relatively undistinguished rock group Strelnikoff, of an album, *Bitchcraft,* with an altered version of Slovenia's most famous depiction of the Blessed Virgin Mary, the "Madonna of Brezje," on its cover. In Strelnikoff's version, the Christ-child was replaced with a giant rat, who was still being lovingly embraced by the Queen of Heaven. The opening song on the album, "Bitchcraft (Radio Vatikan edit)," included the following provocative lines (sung in English): Why did you kill your unborn baby?

Why did you flush foetus down the drain?
Where did you hide your knitting needle?
You are the poison in our nation's vein!
Bitchcraft! Bitchcraft! Bitchcraft!
Someone's gotta stop it!
Don't you know that the life is sacred? . . .
You live to breed and not to question![61]

Many Slovenian Catholics were deeply offended by this album, and Archbishop Rode publicly denounced the CD, organizing a special mass, which was attended by 7,000 people, to beg for forgiveness from the Virgin Mary. Petitions were also circulated in the churches, calling for the criminal prosecution of the members of Strelnikoff, while police in their hometown of Celje interrogated the band members. In addition, the Young Christian Democrats organized a boycott of stores which put the CD on sale.[62] The dispute concerning *Bitchcraft* became one of Slovenia's noisiest polemics of 1998, making the album an overnight best seller. One could argue, of course, that the issuance of the album violated the liberal precept of respect for the harm principle. But what is significant here is that the Church, predictably, did not appeal to the secular notion of a harm principle, but rather to ecclesiastical notions of sin and forgiveness.

Archbishop Rode's engagement against abortion, for religious instruction in state schools, and against local rock groups Strelnikoff and Laibach cast him as the nemesis of the center-left, who viewed him as a polarizing factor.[63] When, in February 2004, the Vatican announced that he would be brought back to the Curia the following July, in what was cast as a promotion, the Slovenian daily *Delo* surmised that the archbishop was, in fact, being kicked upstairs, in order to remove him from the scene of his "numerous failures and errors."[64]

Controversies over the Past

Andrej Bajuk came to the prime ministership not as a result of an election but as a result of coalition shifts within the parliament. The center-right coalition which put him in power left office seven months later as a result of an electoral defeat. One of the factors which contributed to the resounding defeat of the center-right coalition was the participation of several leading members of the coalition in June 2000 in a ceremony honoring those who had collaborated with the Nazis during World War Two and rejecting as "absurd" the Partisan resistance against Axis occupation.[65] Among those attending the ceremony, where the anthems of the collaborationist Home Guards was sung, were Prime Minister Andrej Bajuk, Assembly Speaker Janez Podobnik, Defense Minister Janez Janša, Foreign Minister Lojze Peterle, and Archbishop Franc Rode. The event suggested that the coalition was not so much a "center-right" coalition as a "right-wing" coalition. The event sent shock waves through Slovenian society. President Milan Kučan sent a letter to Prime Minister Bajuk subsequently, asking him to explain his views on the importance of AVNOJ and its decisions

regarding Slovene statehood, and indicating that he was undertaking unspecified international initiatives—presumably to undo the damage done to Slovenia's reputation in European circles.[66] Meanwhile, Assembly deputy Zmago
Jelinčič declared clearly, "Collaborationism can by no means be a part of Slovenian identity, because those who betrayed their own people and joined the foreigners in the destruction of their own people are worse even than the occu-
piers."[67] Yet the mere fact that the prime minister and other notables could
consider it appropriate to honor fascist collaborators calls into question the
ability of the right wing of the Slovenian political spectrum to comprehend even
the minimal preconditions of liberal democracy.

The Future of Slovenian Politics

On 15 October 2000, Slovenes went to the polls for the third time since independence and handed the left-of-center Liberal Democrats their largest victory
ever. Capturing 36.2% of the vote, the LDS won 34 seats in the Assembly; its
most natural ally, the ZLDS, took 12.2% of the vote, for 11 seats. Together with
their frequent partner, the Pensioners' Party (DeSUS), which won 5.1% of the
vote, for 4 seats, the left could control 49 of the 90 seats in the Assembly.[68] However, Drnovšek wanted to put together a "grand coalition." Drnovšek and Janša
had ruled out any coalitions with each other in advance, and speculation centered on the SLS+SKD Party, which had been straddling the barricades.[69]
Finally, on 10 November, after nearly a month of negotiations, the LDS reached
an agreement with the ZLDS, DeSUS, and Franc Zagožen's SLS+SKD and
announced a four-party center-left coalition. The coalition controlled 58 of the
Assembly's 90 seats.[70] The remaining seats were distributed among Janša's
Social Democrats (14 seats), Bajuk's New Slovenia Party (8 seats), Jelinčič's
Slovenian National Party (4 seats), and the Party of Youth (4 seats).[71]

Upon the expiration of Milan Kučan's third term as president—he was first
elected in 1990, and then reelected in 1992 and again in 1997—Janez Drnovšek
succeeded him in that office, after securing 56.4% of the vote in a run-off election held on 1 December 2002.[72] Anton Ropp (LDS) succeeded him as prime
minister. Already in October 2002, the European Commission endorsed Slovenia's application for admission into the EU, and in January 2003, Slovenia was
invited to join NATO; these two admissions fulfilled a decade-long ambition of
Slovenia's political establishment; subsequently, on 23 March 2003, Slovenes
endorsed their country's entry into these organizations in a double referendum
(with 89.6% endorsing EU membership and 66% supporting membership in
NATO).[73] Slovenia's political transformation has been facilitated by its robust
economy, with GDP growth rates of 3.5% in 1997, 3.9% in 1998, 4.0% in 1999,
4.9% in 2000, 3.0% in 2001, 3.3% in 2002, 2.5% in 2003, 3.9% in 2004, and 4%
projected for 2005, and by inflation below 10% annually since 1995 (8.4% in
2001, 7.2% in 2002, 4.6% in 2003, 3.2% in 2004, and 2.5% projected for 2005).
Unemployment in the first quarter of 2005 was 6.9%.[74] Only about 1% of

Slovenes were said to be below the poverty line; Slovenia's per capita income of $11,000 (as of November 2002) has been described as comparable to that of Portugal or Greece.[75]

Slovenia was among those countries formally admitted into the EU in May 2004. But bitter controversies over the rights of non-Slovenes who had been living in Slovenia and over Muslim hopes to build a mosque in Ljubljana, plus a general sense that perhaps the left had not done as well as they might have done, contributed to an upset victory for the right in elections held on 3 October of that year. The largest gain was recorded by Janez Janša's Social Democratic Party, which increased its share of the vote to 29.13% (winning 29 seats in the parliament, more than doubling its representation there); the largest loss was recorded by the LDS, which held onto 22.78% of the vote (retaining 23 seats, down from 34 in the previous parliament). Janša was, thus, invited to put together a coalition and, given the results obtained by the New Slovenia Party and the Slovenian People's Party, could already count on 45 out of 90 votes in the parliament.[76] Janša was subsequently sworn in as prime minister.

Macedonia: Stable but Impoverished

By contrast with Slovenia, Macedonia's economic prospects have remained bleak, in spite of some Western assistance. As of July 2000, about 21% of the Macedonian population was living in "extreme poverty"; by 2002, this proportion had risen to an estimated 22.7%.[77] Indeed, according to *AIM Press,* as of 2000, 74% of employed persons were not able to afford more than one meal per day.[78] Unemployment was recorded at 36.7% in 2003, edging upward to 37.2% in 2004, while the country was still coping with the effects of the plummeting of industrial production in the early 1990s.[79] In 2004, the industrial sector contracted, with 78% of Macedonians reporting that losing their jobs was their greatest fear.[80] Meanwhile, after making some headway in bringing down the foreign debt, Skopje saw its debt rise again in early 2000, reaching $1.46 billion, nearly what it had been in 1991. A November 2000 government report revealed that Macedonia's level of indebtedness placed it in the middle category of debtor states.[81] There was some good news in the economic sector in 2000, however; viz., industrial production rose 3.5% that year over the previous year's level, but by 2002, industrial production was once more contracting—by 5%, though inflation was held to a manageable 4% (for consumer prices) in 2002, dipping to a deflationary -0.4% in 2004. GDP real growth rate in 2002 was estimated at 3.8%, dipping to 3.1% the following year and staying even at 3.1% in 2004. Growth is expected to accelerate to 5% in 2005.[82]

Independent Macedonia passed its first constitution in 1991, declaring Macedonia the national state of the Macedonian people. The Albanians of Macedonia considered this discriminatory, and a decade later, after a six-month insurgency by Albanian guerrillas, the Macedonian parliament adopted a new constitution (in November 2001), in which, among other things, Albanian was declared an official language of the republic, alongside Macedonian, and the constitutional status of the Albanians was equalized with that of the Macedonians.[83]

The country was seriously shaken when, on 3 October 1995, an attempt was made on the life of Kiro Gligorov, the country's popular president. Stojan Andov, president of the Sobranie (the Assembly) assumed the duties of the presidency until Gligorov was able to return to work in January 1996. Although he lost sight in one eye, Gligorov was able to serve out the remainder of his term.

For the first five years of its existence as an independent republic, there were constant worries about the possibility that the war might spread to Macedonia, about possible Greco-Serbian collusion in a partition of the republic, about surviving the two Greek economic embargoes, and about Greek insistence that Macedonia change its name.[84] Border provocations by FRY forces in 1994 may have been the opening gambit in a renewed effort to destabilize Macedonia and perhaps to initiate hostilities.[85] This remains speculative, however, since after the introduction of UNPROFOR (UN Protection Force) troops into Macedonia, there were no further provocations on the border.

From 1991 to 1998, Macedonia was governed by a coalition headed by the Social Democratic Party of Macedonia (the former League of Communists of Macedonia) led by Prime Minister Branko Crvenkovski (b. 1962); in late 1998, this coalition was unseated through parliamentary elections, which propelled the vaguely populist IMRO-DPMNU (Internal Macedonian Revolutionary Organization–Democratic Party of Macedonia National Unity) to power, in a coalition with Vasil Tupurkovski's Democratic Alternative and Arben Xhaferi's Democratic Party of Albanians (DPA). Ljupčo Georgievski, the head of IMRO-DPMNU, thereupon became prime minister. A little more than a year later, IMRO-DPMNU's candidate for president, the affable Boris Trajkovski, triumphed over the Social Democrats' Tito Petkovski thanks, in no small measure, to the support he won from the country's Albanian minority. In elections held in September 2002, however, Georgievski's party went down to defeat, capturing only 23% of the vote, against the 40.8% captured by the "Together for Macedonia" coalition, led by the Social Democratic Party. Branko Crvenkovski forged a coalition with the leading Albanian party and returned to the prime minister's office.[86]

Democratization

The controversy concerning the constitution has already been mentioned. On this point, three alternative views were advocated as of 1990–1991: the IMRO-DPMNU preferred to see Macedonia declared to be "the national state of the Macedonian people" with sovereignty derived from the Macedonian nation as such; the Albanian parties wanted to see themselves included on an equal basis with the Macedonians, so that the republic might be described, for example, as "the national state of the Macedonian and Albanian peoples," with sovereignty derived from the Macedonian and Albanian nations living within the republic; parties on the left wanted to see Macedonia described as a "citizens' state," with sovereignty derived from the citizens of the republic. The eventual constitution, adopted in November 1991, was actually a compromise and was therefore confusing to some uninitiated observers. The preamble appeared to want to have it both ways (i.e., to establish the republic as both a national state and a citizens' state), declaring that "Macedonia is established as a national state of the Macedonian people, in which full equality as citizens and permanent coexistence with the Macedonian people is provided for Albanians, Turks, Vlachs, Romanies, and other nationalities living in the Republic of Macedonia." But almost immediately thereafter, Article 2 affirms, "Sovereignty in the Republic of Macedonia derives from the citizens and belongs to the citizens," while Article 48 provides that "Members of nationalities have a right freely to express, foster, and develop their identity and national attributes. . . . Members of the nationalities have the right to establish institutions for culture and art, as well as scholarly and other associations for the expression, fostering, and development of their identity."[87] What was involved here, however, was not the expression of confusion but the assertion of a civic concept of state, while providing, in the spirit of compromise, some protections for national minorities. Thus, on balance, as Aleksandar Soljakovski notes, the constitution "enthrines civil, not national values."[88] Be that as it may, the Albanians continued to demand that they be mentioned alongside the Macedonians, in the preamble, as co-sovereign. Under the circumstances, when then Serbian President Milošević suggested in 1993 that the republic call itself Slavo-Macedonia, offering himself as a "mediator" between Skopje and Athens, the Albanians immediately rejected the name, pointing out that neither they nor a number of other minorities living in Macedonia are Slavic.[89]

A second controversy flared over allegations of electoral fraud and "irregularities" over the years beginning in 1994. At that time, the first round of parliamentary and presidential elections, on 16 October, yielded a clear victory for the Alliance for Macedonia, as the three-party coalition headed by President Kiro Gligorov of the Social Democrats was called, and a second round was scheduled for 30 October. On 22 October, however, Aleksandar Dinevski, member of the Election Commission of the Republic of Macedonia, resigned his position to protest what he called "the flagrant violations by the Republican Election Commission of the Constitution, and the laws of the Republic of Macedonia before, during, and after the 16 October presidential elections; the direct involvement of the Republican Election Commission in falsifying the election results and the concealment of the actual ones; the undefined position, rights and duties, as well as the incompetence, of the Republican Election Commission in conducting its activities; the lack of responsibility . . . of the REC's President, Mr. Petar Najdenov, and the majority of the REC's members; and the purposeful misrepresentation of the election results to the domestic and foreign publics."[90] Both IMRO-DPMNU and Petar Gosev's Democratic Party protested the results and called for their adherents to boycott the second round of elections. The result was that only 57.5% of the eligible electorate voted. Even so, Gligorov's margin of victory over the IMRO-DPMNU's candidate for the presidency, theater director Ljubiša Georgievski (no relation to the then underage head of the party, Ljupčo Georgievski), was narrow; even with the opposition sitting out the second round, Gligorov won only 52.4% of the vote. In the parliamentary races, however, the Alliance for Macedonia captured 95 seats out of the 120 in the Assembly. But the opposition continued to grumble about alleged electoral fraud.[91] The IMRO-DPMNU issued a statement on 28 December 1994, signed by Ljupčo Georgievski, alleging "forgery" in the elections and denouncing what it called "this illegitimate and illegal establishment."[92] Party chief Georgievski told me, in 1995, "The main problem is that Macedonia is still a totalitarian system. This is basically a one-party system. There exists practically no opposition. The censorship system still exists, and there is no possibility for us to reach a broad audience through the press. The censorship is worse now than it was earlier [in communist times]."[93]

Later, with the positions now reversed, there were allegations of intimidation and fraud during the September 2000 elections. Vlado Bučkovski, spokesperson for the joint opposition, claimed that there had been "incidents and irregularities" at many polling stations and that, in Ohrid, a member of the local election board was held at gunpoint while "racketeers" hired by the IMRO-DPMNU and the Democratic Alternative stuffed ballot boxes with pre-prepared ballots.[94] *Start,* a publication which has consistently criticized the IMRO-DPMNU government, alleged, in its 15 September 2000 issue, that on election day, western Macedonia "closely resembled the Macedonia from one hundred years ago when all sorts of criminal gangs terrorized Macedonians, Albanians, and Turks," claiming that "the storm troopers of Xhaferi and Georgievski" were conducting a campaign of "violence and terror" against members of the Party for Democratic Prosperity (a rival Albanian party).[95] The relative freedom which the press enjoys is measured in the hyperbolic vocabulary which it employs with evident impunity.

For that matter, the second round of the 1999 presidential elections had been disputed by the Social Democrats. That had resulted in the calling of a partial third round, under international supervision, which duplicated the results of the second round.[96] Subsequently, in 2002, when the Social Democrats emerged victorious, Ljube Boskovski of the IMRO-DPMNU cried foul.[97]

What these recurrent allegations of fraud from both left and right suggest is that Macedonia has not, at this writing, succeeded in establishing valued and fully legitimate institutions of state, which may be presumed to be stable. Whether future elections will enjoy greater credibility remains to be seen.

Rule of Law

The Macedonian state was slow to dismantle the inheritance of socialist law, and even in 1995, the main part of the country's criminal law had been preserved from SFRY law, including provisions still in place which had been designed to protect self-managing organs (though these organs had quickly disappeared).[98] The government moved slowly to draft new legislation regulating the functioning of the courts, and in the meantime, various socialist-era practices were maintained, such as the prerogative of the prosecuting attorney to provide evidence to the judge which the defender was not allowed to see, the prerogative of the judge to filter any questions from the defender, and the practice of not allowing the defending attorney to gather evidence on her or his own, to interview witnesses or talk to witnesses before the trial, or to introduce witnesses for the defense.[99] Even then, when drafting the legislation, the government did not consult with the Macedonian Bar Association to obtain any input, so that one MBA member complained that the government was treating the association as a kind of opposition. As for legislation to regulate the practice of law, nothing had been done in this field as of spring 1995, with the result that a kind of juristic chaos reigned, with various persons practicing law even though they lacked either legal training or any suitable credentials.[100]

Corruption and crime have presented challenges to the rule of law as well, and though the government gave the struggle against these two plagues a high priority from the very beginning, progress has been slow and uncertain. On the other hand, in Macedonia as in some neighboring countries, trafficking in women and girls for prostitution and pornography has presented a special challenge.[101] Where the honesty of the government is concerned, there was a considerable uproar in 1993, when Pavle Trajanov, then undersecretary in the Ministry of Internal Affairs, alleged that high government officials were knee-deep in corruption and cooperation with organized crime. The government rejected this charge with Prime Minister Branko Crvenkovski later explaining that such inconsistencies in figures as had emerged could be traced to "subjective lapses on the part of some counter clerks at the ministries, without any major government predators involved in the whole mess."[102] Later, however, in August 1995, the government announced the adoption of several programs designed to curtail or prevent corruption in the administration and to combat organized crime, including in drug trade and money laundering.[103] Commenting on the announcement, *Nova Makedonija* noted that "The problem of crime and corruption seriously endangers the democratic processes in the state," adding that "if the institutions of the system had worked the way they should have, is it now necessary to make a campaign in the struggle against organized crime and form special bodies and commissions that will discover it?"[104] Although Macedonian corruption does not make news in Western countries, it has remained a problem. A major concern as of 2000 was the takeover of local governments by organized crime; indeed, this was the topic of a discussion between Thomas Pickering, the U.S. undersecretary for political affairs, and Prime Minister Georgievski in early February 2000.[105] Two years later, the International Crisis Group (ICG) released a report finding that corruption was pandemic in Macedonia, "especially at high levels of government." Edward Joseph, the ICG project director for Macedonia, offered that "In effect, the state has come to function in important respects as a 'racket' and the racketeers thrive in a culture of impunity." The areas most affected by corruption were said to be the customs office and its agents, the Health Insurance Fund, the privatization processes of several companies including Makedonija Telekon and the OKTA oil refinery, and a number of ministers and heads of state institutions. Although Prime Minister Georgievski pledged to fight corruption, his best-known comment on the problem was his yawn, "Corruption is present in every country in transition."[106]

In general, Macedonia's record in moving toward rule of law has been mixed. The Helsinki Committee in Macedonia has reported repeated occurrences of police beatings of detainees and of other forms of police brutality, attributing these problems, however, not to political deformities at the highest levels but rather to "the irresponsible behavior by individuals or the lack of [a professional] police culture."[107] The Helsinki Committee also reported in 1998 that individuals were being held for longer periods than justified under the law before their cases were heard, including in cases where detention was not mandatory, and that persons being detained were often not informed as to the reasons for their detention.[108] Regulations regulating police behavior adopted in March 1999 reportedly "did not come close to meeting international standards." While police violence cut across ethnic and socio-economic lines, police violence was reported to be more common against persons active in the political opposition, of low socio-economic status, or of Albanian or Roma ethnicity.[109]

There were repeated problems in the first seven years with confirming the independence of the judiciary in practice; in 1996, for instance, only candidates supported by the ruling coalition were elected. After the adoption of a package of laws reorganizing the judicial system in June 1997, the judiciary remained in a state of confusion for some months, and the quality of the work of the courts was judged to be "very low," though many verdicts were overturned on appeal.[110]

Finally, in January 2001, Macedonian and Bulgarian media were awash with news about a wiretapping scandal allegedly involving Bulgarian special services, in which the telephones of 102 leading Macedonian politicians and prominent public figures were tapped.[111] The "wiretapping affair" began with a press conference involving Social Democratic Party of Macedonia (SDSM) president Branko Crvenkovski, the former prime minister, who announced that he was in possession of transcripts of phone conversations of more than 100 eminent public figures in the country, including both governmental officeholders and journalists.[112] Some of these transcripts were subsequently authenticated, as the parliament set its supervisory commission to work on tracking down what had happened. The SDSM alleged that Interior Minister Dosta Dimovska had arranged for the wiretaps on orders from Prime Minister Georgievski, but Crvenkovski would not reveal how he had come into possession of the transcripts; the ruling coalition, in turn, noted that it was Crvenkovski who was in possession of the transcripts, alleging that it was he who had arranged for the wiretaps and tracing this to Crvenkovski's alleged "pathological craving for power."[113]

Crvenkovski's insinuations that the Macedonian Intelligence Agency had conducted the wiretapping were denied by spokespersons for the government and for that agency, whereas Slobodan Bogoevski, former undersecretary for Macedonia's State Security Service, claimed that the secret services of Bulgaria and Albania were implicated in the affair.[114] The story of a "Bulgarian connection" was enriched on 28 January, when *Mediapool online magazine* published a report to the effect that Crvenkovski had visited Sofia on 15 January in order to hand over to Tsvyatko Tsvetkov, member of the Bulgarian Socialist Party Supreme Board, excerpts of the transcripts of tapped telephone conversations.[115] Crvenkovski denied any such involvement, as did Bulgarian government spokespersons. Meanwhile, allusions to "a parallel wiretapping system" were intended to implicate the SDSM in illegal para-governmental intelligence gathering.[116]

As if this was not already bad enough, Crvenkovski made another sensational revelation at a follow-up press conference on 6 February, when he announced that he had been given additional transcripts of taped phone conversations involving the president, members of the president's cabinet, leaders and members of political parties, businessmen and journalists, "by an anonymous 'source or sources.'"[117] Subsequently, criminal proceedings were initiated against Crvenkovski on the grounds that he had maligned the Ministry of Internal Affairs, the chief of the Department of Operational Techniques, and the chief of the Sector of Exploitation by implicating them in activities in which they had supposedly played no role.[118]

Prime Minister Georgievski continued to blame the Social Democrats themselves for the wiretapping, alleging, in mid-February 2001, that "this is a continuation of the SDSM tendency to destroy everything in this country" and that "the SDSM remains the main organizer of the wiretapping, . . . [and] has its own structures in the state administration."[119] Even so, Dosta Dimovska tendered her resignation as minister of the interior on 16 February, even while continuing to insist that she had never authorized the wiretapping of the persons mentioned in this case or behaved in any way inconsistent with the constitution and laws of the land. About halfway through her brief resignation speech, however, she made accusations of her own, which raised the question (which has been raised throughout post-communist Europe) as to the extent to which the country continues to be penetrated by the old communist nomenklatura. "What is most scary," said Dimovska in her letter of resignation,

> is the fact that physical force is being used against certain citizens, which is only one proof of the old manner of behavior by the officers who . . . seriously disturb the reputation of the security structures in the country. Unfortunately, the old structures in these departments are politically instrumentalized by the SDSM and seriously obstruct the security system in the Republic of Macedonia, by revealing methods of the security bodies and by revealing state secrets. If this situation is not changed with

fundamental reforms, there is a serious threat for future political manipulations with the security structures.[120]

While the SDSM welcomed Dimovska's resignation, the ruling coalition was not prepared to see her step down and refused to accept her resignation. Dimovska stayed on for the time being. A year later, Dimovska was forced to resign by her erstwhile defender, Georgievski, after she had spoken in favor of making concessions to the country's Albanian minority.[121]

Belatedly, in April 2002, the government established the Office for Struggle Against Corruption, in which experts from the Ministry of Internal Affairs and the Ministry of Finance would also play a role. In June 2003, the Macedonian Sobranie identified the need to pass or amend more than 40 laws in the fight against corruption.[122] Organized crime also remains a problem, especially in the areas of drug trafficking and trafficking in women and children, and in this connection, Macedonia has signed cooperation agreements with its neighbors.[123]

Ethnic Inequalities and Tensions

According to the second census of 1994, conducted under international supervision, Macedonians constitute 66.5% of the population of the republic, Albanians 22.9%, Turks 4%, Sinti and Roma 2.3%, and Serbs 2%, with some 2,200 Croats living in Macedonia.[124] These data were disputed by both the Albanians and the Serbs: the Albanians, who boycotted both censuses of 1994, claim that they represent about 40% of the republic's population; Serb leaders in Macedonia claimed that there were 250,000 Serbs living in Macedonia, rather than the 39,000 recorded in June 1994.[125] Macedonia's Albanians, Serbs, and Turks all complained that they were "second-class citizens," basing this claim on constitutional provisions and on alleged inadequacies in the educational system and in cultural amenities, while Mirko Jović, chair of the Serbian Renewal Party (in Serbia), urged in 1993 that "currently the most threatened part of the Serb people lives on the territory of the Former Yugoslav Republic of Macedonia."[126]

Members of national minorities represent only 8.7% of law enforcement officers; even in the largely Albanian towns of Tetovo and Gostivar, Albanians constituted only 17% and 12% of the local police forces, respectively (as of 1999). Albanians have also been underrepresented in the officer corps of the military and in university enrollments, though as the U.S. Department of State reported in 1999, "the traditional nature of parts of Albanian society leads many families in rural areas to see no need to educate their children, particularly girls, beyond the eighth grade."[127] An important step in the direction of rectifying the ethnic imbalance in the army NCO ranks, at least, was taken in May 2002, with the launching of a (new) course, training 60 Albanians to serve as NCOs.[128]

In January 1992, Albanians of Macedonia organized an illegal referendum on autonomy, reporting that 90% of those eligible to vote did so and that of that number, 99% voted in favor of autonomy. A little over two months later, some

40,000 Albanians demonstrated in Skopje, demanding autonomy and calling on the international community to withhold recognition until such time as Skopje should grant the Albanians an autonomous region in the western part of the country. Later that year, the Ministry of Internal Affairs confiscated about 2,000 leaflets calling on the country's Albanians to launch an insurrectionary war in order to assert their right to self-determination; these leaflets were found in three Albanian-majority villages south of Skopje and were signed by the Ilirida Albanian Youth Movement. One source suggested that the leaflets may have originated with the Milošević regime, but this cannot be proven.[129]

In August 1994, the Party for Democratic Prosperity (PDP), then headed by Abdurrahman Haliti, announced that it was no longer seeking to obtain an autonomous zone for Albanians but would seek to obtain proportional representation of Albanians throughout the political and administrative system. Albanians achieved a breakthrough on 26 January 1995, when the Ministry of Justice recognized Albanian as the second official language of the Republic of Macedonia.[130]

In spite of that, there continued to be a number of issues and incidents, including the furor over the Albanian initiative to establish an "Albanian university" in Tetovo (discussed in the next subsection), allegations of poisoning of a group of students of the Nikola Stajn Medical High School of Tetovo, violent disturbances following the arrest and incarceration of the (Albanian) mayors of Gostivar and Tetovo in 1997 on charges of flying the Albanian flag over their city halls without due authorization and, indeed, after they had been informed that this would not be permitted, and the mobilization of special Macedonian police units around the village of Aračinovo (near Skopje) in January 2000, after protests following the arrest of 10 Albanians suspected of having killed three policemen on 11 January.[131] By January 2001, moreover, there seemed to be at least some spillover effect from Albanian insurgency in southern Serbia. Macedonian police arrested four Albanians on suspicion of carrying out a grenade attack on a police post in Tearce, on 22 January, killing one policeman; the following month, crew members of the Skopje-based A-1 Television Station were detained by members of the Albanian National Liberation Army in the village of Tanuševci, and stripped of their camera and cell-phones before being released.[132] Dragiša Miletić, the head of Macedonia's Democratic Party of Serbs, perhaps eager to attract Macedonia to the Serbian banner, warned ominously that "ethnic Albanian terrorist activities in southern Serbia and Macedonia are synchronized," claiming that the Albanians sought to take control of the Belgrade-Skopje-Athens arterial road. Speaking rather cautiously to the press on 29 January, Prime Minister Georgievski nonetheless conceded that "the events that have and are taking place in southern Serbia . . . are indeed a cause for immense and profound concern."[133]

Some observers were worried as of early 2001 that Macedonia was about to explode into inter-ethnic violence and often expressed concern about the alleged mafia connections of Menduh Thaqi, thought by many to be the most likely successor to the moderate Arben Xhaferi to head the Democratic Party of Albanians (DPA).[134] But others attached greater significance to the fact that the DPA, by far the most important political party among Macedonia's Albanians, had joined the government in autumn 1998, holding six ministerial posts as of the end of 2000. Optimists also speculated that Bedredin Ibrahimi, general secretary of the DPA, rather than Menduh Thaqi, would succeed to the helm of the DPA.[135] Ibrahimi, holding the post of deputy prime minister in Georgievski's government, was thought to see greater benefits for Macedonia's Albanians in continuing to support the Macedonian state within its recognized boundaries than in seeking to attach portions of western Macedonia to a patchwork Greater Albanian state with uncertain prospects.[136]

Education and Values

In the field of education, the most significant controversy concerned the demand registered by the leading Albanian political parties and asserted by Albanian educators that there be a state-supported University of Tetovo with instruction in Albanian. The values in dispute embrace not only the Albanian language itself but also Albanian history and culture, to which the Macedonian school curriculum has allocated less time than the more vocal Albanians would like. The controversy began in December 1994, when Macedonian authorities rejected an application by Albanians of Tetovo (Tetova in Albanian) for permission to establish a university with instruction in Albanian. The grounds for rejection were twofold. First, under the constitution, all citizens are guaranteed the right to study in their native language in elementary and secondary school, but there is no guaranteed right to study in any language other than Macedonian at the university level; therefore, the Albanians did not have a "right" to the university. Second, under Macedonian law, a state university could be established only according to certain fixed procedures and not on popular initiative; therefore, the university initiative in Tetovo was illegal.[137] The Albanians, however, proceeded as if they had obtained permission, outfitting facilities in Tetovo for the future university. Authorities responded by sending in bulldozers on 14 December to demolish the building, while 200 armed special deployment police watched.[138]

Talks between the two sides continued, inconclusively, but in mid-February, the Albanians made a second attempt to open the university, which was to have consisted of six faculties initially. Once again police and bulldozers were sent to Tetovo, but this time there was violence, and one Albanian was shot dead during the confrontation.[139] And once again, the facilities which the Albanians had proposed to use for the university were bulldozed. These actions left deep bitterness among the Albanians, who had difficulty comprehending why the authorities were not prepared to turn a blind eye to their initiative until the constitution and laws could be changed. Two months later, Macedonian police closed down the only Albanian private high school in Macedonia, the Hajdar Dushi School in Ladorisht, Struge.[140]

Authorities also imprisoned university rector Fadilj Sulejmani and his colleagues Miljaim Fejziu, Musli Halili, Nevzad Halimi, and Ardun Rusi; Sulejmani, accused of having incited violent resistance to the police, would spend two years in prison. In spite of this, the Albanians were allowed, ultimately, to proceed to organize university classes and instruction in Tetova; the hitch was that the degrees and credentials granted by the University of Tetova would not be recognized anywhere in Macedonia. In an interview which reflected the thinking of the Alliance for Macedonia coalition, Macedonian president Kiro Gligorov told the *Frankfurter Allgemeine* in May 1996 that the University of Tetova was "an institution planned and realized by separatists."[141]

Matters remained at an impasse until July 2000, when the Macedonian parliament passed legislation which simultaneously approved an OSCE initiative to set up an internationally funded, multi-lingual Tetovo University (with instruction in Albanian, Macedonian, and English) to open in autumn 2001 and granted formal approval for the hitherto underground University of Tetova to operate as a private educational institution. Arben Xhaferi's Democratic Party of Albanians welcomed the bill, which it said would lay to rest the controversies in the educational sector. But the rival Party for Democratic Prosperity denounced the bill, leaving parliament before it came to a vote; the PDP insisted that there should be a *state-funded* university in Tetovo, with Albanian as the *exclusive* language of instruction.[142] For cash-strapped Macedonia, this was a tough demand.

Tetovo University (to be known officially as the Southeast European University of Tetova) was the brainchild of OSCE High Commissioner Max van der Stoel, whose proposal called for the institution to be funded in its initial stages by foreign donors; it was to begin modestly with two departments, one for teacher training and the other for business management and public administration.[143] Yet, in spite of this modest beginning, it was promised that the "Max van der Stoel University," as it has been called by some, would be "committed to the [nurturing of] Albanian language and culture."[144] Although Sulejmani, rector of the rival University of Tetova, dismissed this development by claiming that "Nothing has changed here,"[145] others were clearly more positive, describing the OSCE initiative as a "breakthrough."[146] In spite of the Albanian insurgency in 2001 (discussed below) and continued incidents thereafter, the Southeast European University officially opened in November 2001, with classes in law, business administration, public administration, teacher training, communications, and computer studies.[147]

Gender Inequality, Religious Equality

Under the constitution, women are guaranteed the same legal rights as men; legislation on primary, secondary, and higher education is also completely nondiscriminatory. In practice, the gap between women and men in Macedonia is greatest among the Albanians, Turks, and Roma, and least among the Macedonians and Vlachs. Gender inequality has been manifested in all areas of public and private life from the severe underrepresentation of women in political offices and in positions of managerial responsibility in the private sector to persistent problems of violence in the family (with no specific legal regulations on domestic violence) to social ostracism in the villages of women bearing children out of wedlock.[148]

Ethnicity is a significant factor where gender inequality is concerned. For example, in 1993 there were 2,022 ethnic Macedonians who received university degrees, alongside 38 Albanians. Among the Macedonians, the larger proportion (1,141) were women, while among the Albanians, the larger proportion (26) were men. When it came to dropout rates in elementary education, the figures (for the 1996–1997 academic year) were reversed. Among Macedonians, only 36.6% of dropouts were girls, while among Albanians 82.4% were girls. The figures for Turks and Serbs were 61% and 7%, respectively. Finally, where secondary education was concerned, the same trend could be observed: 50.6% of Macedonian secondary school pupils were female, alongside 37.3% of Albanian pupils, 33.5% of Turkish pupils, 40.4% of Serbs, 30.4% of ethnic Muslims (Bosniaks), 32.5% of Roma, and 83% of Vlachs.[149] Even the so-called League of Albanian Women places its emphasis on *Albanian* complaints, rather than on *women's* complaints, even though there have been several Albanian political parties to press the case for the former.[150]

Macedonian legislation on gender equality is progressive, with guarantees of equal treatment at the workplace in terms of promotion and remuneration, of equal property rights in the family, of access to abortion, etc. But women's advocacy groups, such as the Humanitarian Association for the Emancipation, Solidarity, and Equality of Women and the Union of Associations of Macedonian Women have been trying to raise public consciousness about certain problems, such as that of violence in the family.

Where religious equality is concerned, a 1997 law on religious communities and groups recognized the Macedonian Orthodox Church, the Islamic Community, and the Roman Catholic Church as "religious communities" and other religious associations, including the Methodist Church, of which President Trajkovski was a member, as "religious groups." This appeared to imply some legal distinction, but in fact, "communities" and "groups" enjoy the same rights and protections under the law, according to the U.S. Department of State.[151] Macedonian authorities have refused to recognize an Orthodox Church of the Vlach minority on the argument that there was already one Orthodox Church in the country and that they should join that one. Yet, if there is some basis for asserting religious equality, it is also clear that the Macedonian Orthodox Church enjoys a far greater prominence in Macedonian public life than any other religious organization. One example of this greater prominence comes from September 1999, when Orthodox priests and Islamic hodjas were brought to the public elementary schools on the first day of school in order to hold religious ceremonies to launch the school year. Minister of Education Nenad Novkovski indicated, at the time, that he planned to introduce religious instruction into the elementary schools as a regular subject the following school year.[152]

Prospects for Macedonian Stability and Integration into Europe

In February 2001, President Boris Trajkovski paid a visit to Washington, D.C. In the course of his visit, he addressed an audience at the Center for Strategic and International Studies, where he admitted his bitterness that Macedonia had been receiving less money in aid and less attention than "some neighboring countries which were involved in the recent wars" (code for post-Milošević Federal Republic of Yugoslavia). At the same time, he underlined his government's clear interest in fostering cooperation with NATO and in eventual membership in the alliance and signaled his conversance with the classics of the liberal tradition by asserting that Macedonian foreign policy was based on the principles spelled out by Immanuel Kant in his *Perpetual Peace*.[153] Determined to play a positive role in southeastern Europe, Trajkovski had hosted a conference of nine heads of state from the region in October 2000, so that they might discuss how to foster political and economic cooperation and work, where appropriate, toward reconciliation. Trajkovski had already planned to host a follow-up conference of southeast European heads of state in Skopje in March 2001.

On the face of it, Macedonia's Albanians would seem to have had much reason for satisfaction with the progress registered in post-1990 Macedonia. As of 2001, there were 25 Albanians in the 120-member national parliament (11 of them representing the Democratic Party of Albanians), and five of the 15 cabinet ministers were Albanian as well as two deputy ministers (the deputy ministers of defense and of internal affairs). Ethnic Albanians had been elected to serve as mayor in 26 municipalities (among a total of 123) in elections in 2000. And, as already indicated, preparations for an officially recognized and internationally funded Tetovo University were already underway by the beginning of 2001. Moreover, where only 3% of employees in public administration in 1993 had been Albanians, by 2001 this figure had risen to 10%; and while there had been no Albanian four-star generals as late as 1998, by early 2001, three of the seven four-star generals in the Macedonian Army were Albanians.[154]

But in late February 2001 a series of skirmishes and incidents along the border region with Kosovo signaled a deterioration in security.[155] NATO councils offered the Macedonian government its sympathy but ruled out the deployment of any NATO troops in Macedonia.[156] By mid-March, Albanian rebels had seized control of several villages above Tetovo, and Macedonian security forces were mobilized in a forceful response, literally blasting the rebels from their toeholds. Although the Macedonian Army was ill-equipped to deal with this insurgency, it seemed to make headway against the rebels in late March.[157] There was a lull in the fighting in April, and talks were initiated between the Macedonian and Albanian political parties. But spokespersons for the two leading Albanian political parties (spokesman Zahir Bekteshi for the PDP, party leader Arben

Xhaferi for the DPA) were soon charging that the talks lacked substance and seemed to be designed more to impress foreign audiences than to address the real concerns of local Albanians.[158] About this time, the European Commission Against Racism and Intolerance issued a report that described ethnic discrimination in Macedonia as "widespread" and requiring "urgent action."[159] To some, the solution might seem to have been an effort to move beyond the confines of guarantees extended to ethnic collectivities and the movement toward a completely consistent concept of a "civic state." But in an interview with the Albanian émigré newspaper *Illyria,* Xhaferi expressly rejected such a solution: "multi-ethnic states cannot be pure civic states. In the end you must pose the question: who is civic? In which language is he talking? If the Macedonians want to create a civic society, but the civilian is Macedonian, speaking [the] Macedonian language, we must again ask the question, who is he?"[160] By the end of the month, Albanian rebels fired at a Macedonian Army patrol, signaling the resumption of the insurrection.[161] In a show of unity, the Party for Democratic Prosperity joined the government coalition, alongside the Democratic Party of Albanians, reflecting the refusal of the major Albanian parties to endorse the insurrection. At the same time, neither Albanian party gave the government a carte blanche; indeed, in mid-May 2001, the PDP pointedly demanded that the government call a total halt to all shelling of Albanian towns.[162] By this point, more than 10,000 Macedonian Albanians had fled the conflict zone to seek refuge in Kosovo, as the Macedonian Army bombarded villages in an effort to smoke out the rebels.[163]

The Ohrid Agreement and After

In early June 2001, Albanian insurgents took control of Aračinovo, a Skopje suburb, and issued an ultimatum to the Macedonian government. Within less than two weeks, however, Macedonian forces had driven the insurgents out of Aračinovo, thanks in part to indirect assistance from NATO.[164] Amid rising pressure from both the local population in Skopje and the international community, the Macedonian government agreed to negotiate, even as the fighting continued.[165] While negotiations continued, the fighting escalated, with rebels ambushing a government convoy (on 8 August), killing 10 Macedonian soldiers, and Macedonian Sukhoi SU-25 jets bombing rebel positions near Tetovo (on 10 August).[166] By mid-August 2001, about 100 people lay dead.[167] In the meantime, interior minister Ljube Boskovski had created a paramilitary group called the Lions. But the fighting ended before the Lions saw any action.[168]

On 13 August 2001, an agreement was signed in Ohrid, in which the government promised to recognize Albanian as the (second) official language in areas where at least 20% of the local population is Albanian, to extend state support to the university in Tetova which the Albanians had established, to recruit 1,000 Albanians into the police force, and to provide for an amnesty for all the insurgents.[169] For their part, the insurgents of the National Liberation Army agreed to surrender their arms and to end their insurgency. An advance team of 400 British soldiers was rushed to Macedonia within days, as the first contingent in a 3,500-strong force mandated to collect the weapons.[170] The difficulty lay in establishing just how many weapons the insurgents had. The Macedonian Ministry of Defense estimated that the insurgents had at least 8,000 weapons, since they had fielded between 7,000 and 8,000 fighters; but the insurgents said that they disposed of only around 2,000 weapons. Meanwhile, Macedonian Prime Minister Georgievski claimed that the insurgents possessed as many as 80–85,000 weapons![171] *Jane's Defence Weekly* estimated their weapons arsenal at 8,700 pieces. But NATO contentedly spoke of collecting only 3,300 weapons.[172] Most observers took it for granted that the insurgents had surrendered only a small part of their stock. This supposition seemed to be confirmed by the Macedonian government's continued preoccupation with the proliferation of illegal weapons, some of them in the hands of ordinary criminal gangs.[173] More significantly, while the National Liberation Army, which had been commanded by Ali Ahmeti, cooperated in turning in at least some weapons and by declaring its own self-dissolution, a rival group calling itself the Albanian National Army vowed to continue to fight, presumably aiming at the annexation of western Macedonia to Albania. Almost exactly a year after the signing of the Ohrid Agreement, Macedonian police authorities confirmed the existence of a newly established paramilitary group called the Army of the Republic of Ilirida, described as a wing of a larger organization called the National Front for the Liberation and Unity of All Albanian Territories, alongside the militant Albanian National Army (ANA).[174] Repeated incidents involving gunfire in villages on the Sar Mountain, in the vicinity of Tetovo, and in the villages of Lipkovo, Slupčane, and Vaksince, continuing into 2003, culminated in major clashes between the ANA and the Macedonian Army in September 2003, in which the Macedonian Defense Ministry claimed to have neutralized the armed groups in the region of the village of Brest.[175]

As tensions escalated, Georgievski, who in September 2002 had been voted out of office, poured oil on the fires of discontent by publishing a lengthy editorial in the daily newspaper *Dnevnk,* in which he accused Albanians of carrying out the "ethnic cleansing" of Macedonia, demanded that the republic be partitioned, with all Albanians to be expelled from rump Macedonia, and warned that, if nothing were done, there would be another "bloodbath" within three years.[176] The Albanian newspaper *Fakti* replied the following day with a resolute repudiation of Georgievski's proposal.[177] More strikingly, Ali Ahmeti, the former leader of the National Liberation Army who had, in the meantime, taken a seat in the ruling coalition, had already expressed his abhorrence of partition proposals; the whole point of the rebellion, Ahmeti underlined, was to win equality for the Albanians *within* Macedonia, not to split off a portion of Macedonian territory.[178] That, at any rate, was his position on the subject. And yet, in spite of these complications, some progress has been recorded. Among the factors for progress in moving toward ethnic harmony, one may mention the new constitution, elevating the status of the Albanian minority, the passage of a law concerning local self-government, the adoption of laws authorizing that the IDs of Albanians be trilingual (Macedonian, English, and Albanian), etc.[179] On the other hand, there continued to be considerable distrust between the two communities, and as Edward Joseph told an audience at the Wilson Center in September 2003, "Albanians do not aid their cause by failing to respect the authority of the state—by sometimes dodging taxes and utility bills or resisting even well conducted police operations. Likewise, Macedonians drag their feet on key Ohrid Agreement obligations."[180]

The Future of Macedonia

In addition to the challenges already described in some detail, there are others, such as threats to the independence of the press during Georgievski's term as prime minister, a trade war with Serbia which broke out in early 2002, pandemic insolvency among those state-owned enterprises still in place as of 2003, and controversies concerning the supposedly dissolved "Lions," blessed by the head of the Macedonian Orthodox Church in January 2002.[181] In fact, the Lions refused to dissolve peacefully, and in January 2003, some 800 members of the Lions used trucks and jeeps to set up a blockade 20 kilometers north of Skopje; several hundred riot police were rushed to the location, while negotiators tried to defuse the situation.[182] Eventually, a compromise was found, under which some of the demobilized Lions were kept on the state payroll.[183]

On the other hand, there are also positive factors, including significant investments by Greek businessmen, generous donations arranged by the EU and the World Bank as well as from the U.S., a decrease in the foreign debt by U.S. $59.4 million between 2000 and 2001, and budgetary cuts suggesting fiscal responsibility.[184] In addition, Macedonia has been given some encouragement (by the U.S.) in its application to join NATO—especially after Skopje's strong support for the Bush administration in its wars against the Taliban regime in Afghanistan and against the regime of Saddam Hussein in Iraq—and hopes to be admitted to NATO as a full member. Moreover, the results of the elections of September 2002 were also encouraging to many, who felt that Georgievski's style was too mercurial, too headstrong, even too unprofessional. Crvenkovski, returning to the prime ministership after four years, forged a coalition with Ali Ahmeti's Democratic Union of Integration, which had overtaken Xhaferi's Democratic Party among Albanian voters. Ahmeti, who now assumed a seat in the parliament, called for the development of "new values" in the society.[185] But values, such as trust, tolerance, and mutual respect—as Kant knew—do not develop spontaneously; on the contrary, they require a fertile bed of liberal institutions, civic-oriented education, and an economic structure in which dignified work is available for all.

In December 2003, the Western military mission in Macedonia came to an end; in its place, the EU set up a 200-strong police mission. Javier Solana, the coordinator of EU foreign policy, explained that in the view of the EU, criminality, rather than armed conflict, now constituted the principal threat to Macedonia's stability.[186] Then, in February 2004, Macedonian president Boris Trajkovski and his entourage were killed when their plane crashed in Bosnia, while en route to an international investment conference. The incumbent prime minister, Branko Crvenkovski, candidate of the Social Democratic Party, was elected to succeed Trajkovski, in special elections held the following month, defeating three other candidates.[187] Hari Kostov (SDP) assumed the office of prime minister, carrying over all but one of the ministers from Crvenkovski's cabinet. The smoothness of the transition seemed to demonstrate that in spite of all the challenges it had faced since obtaining independence, Macedonia had, as it were, come of age.

Under the Ohrid Agreement, the government in Skopje had agreed to give the Albanians greater autonomy in areas where they constituted a local majority. In fulfillment of this pledge, the coalition headed by the SDP pushed through a package of three laws, in July 2004, redistricting the country, granting local authorities greater control in education, health services, economic policy, and other spheres, declaring Skopje a dual-language zone, and giving the Albanians the right to use their native language in administration in certain districts.[188] Various intellectuals and other citizens, as well as representatives of the Macedonian Orthodox Church, the Macedonian Academy of Sciences and Art, and the political opposition protested the decision, and there were sharp protests across the country, prompting the police to close all roads into Skopje.[189] After at least 17 people were injured in rioting in clashes in the lakeside town of Struga in the southwestern region of the country, Prime Minister Kostov offered to resign, though his government survived a vote of no confidence. By late August, however, opponents of the legislative package had gathered enough signatures to force the government to put it up to a public referendum, which was duly scheduled for 7 November 2004. The referendum failed to attract the necessary 50% participation, however, with the result that the effort to repeal the Ohrid Framework Agreement failed.

Croatia since 1990

By contrast with Slovenia and Macedonia, Croatia has seen three distinct phases since 1990: the years of escalation and war, 1990–November 1995 (actually this phase had begun in earnest in summer 1989 with the "Opačić affair"); the late Tudjman era, December 1995–December 1999; and the post-Tudjman era, since December 1999. Each of these phases has had its own specific tasks, challenges, and context, and the policies in each of these phases must be assessed within the context of the time. Thus, the Tudjman government's desire to control the principal media meant one thing during the years of war, for most of which time 30% of the country was controlled by Serbian paramilitaries who denied

Zagreb's sovereignty; but once Dayton was signed and Croatia returned to peace, it was harder for Tudjman to plead extenuating circumstances or the needs of warfare to justify his continued desire to see his party's preferred interpretation dominant in the key media.

Tudjman's rule has been compared with old-fashioned caudillo politics in Latin America. Tudjman used the levers of power to aggrandize himself and his family, his cronies, and his party, used computers to falsify election returns, and used the security and intelligence services to carry out "a secret war against the liberal fraction within the HDZ, and also against opposition parties, non-governmental organizations, and similar [organizations]."[190]

In December 1999, Tudjman died, after having served nine and a half years in office. In the wake of his death, Ivica Račan, the former chief of the LC Croatia and now head of the Social Democratic Party, was elected prime minister at the head of a six-party coalition government. Stipe Mesić, head of the Croatian People's Party and considered a long-shot candidate by most people, won the presidency in a runoff, edging out Social Liberal Dražen Budiša, with a solid 56% of the vote.[191] Within a year, secret tape recordings made by Tudjman, recording conversations at the Pantov presidential palace, had been released, proving that Tudjman had masterminded Croatia's intervention in the war in Bosnia, had known about atrocities, and had hoped even in 1999 to divide Bosnia with Milošević.[192] These tapes did much to undercut Tudjman's reputation among Croats. Finally, by spring 2001, Carla Del Ponte admitted that, but for his death in late 1999, Tudjman would have found his name on the list of persons indicted for war crimes by the International War Crimes Tribunal in The Hague.[193]

In June 2002, the State Statistical Office released the final figures from its most recent census, showing that Croatia had 4,437,460 inhabitants as of April 2001. This represented a decline of 200,000 since 1991, reflecting both outright casualties and the flight of Croats and Serbs alike (alongside smaller numbers from other nationality groups) from the republic.[194] Some 89.3% of the population was Croat. There were 369,786 unemployed persons in Croatia, as of November 2002, representing a slight decline from two years earlier.[195]

Rule of Law, Opening Volleys

Tudjman began his term of office with an ill-considered and insensitive move to rectify, at one fell swoop, the heavy representation of Serbs in the police forces and administration of Croatia. Imagine, for a moment, an American president taking office and deciding to correct, at one fell swoop, the heavy representation of men in university faculties (especially among deans and provosts) and among corporate upper management, and then using all the force at his disposal to remove these men and replace them with women. He would immediately be charged with sexism and would face massive resentment on the part of the newly dismissed men. He would also, most likely, be charged with having

violated the principle of rule of law, and no doubt with having caused unnecessary harm, and it would immediately be noticed that the president was treating
men not as individuals with individual merits and achievements but as members of a category. The same was true of Croatia in 1990. Tudjman's action
against the Serbs was not merely foolish, but harmful in an illiberal sense. It was
a blow against liberal democracy. On the other hand, with Milošević and Jović
already mobilizing Croatia's Serbs for war, Tudjman had reasons to want to
remove Serbs from the police force.

Nor did it stop there. In the course of the early 1990s, Serbs were expelled
from their apartments, merely for being Serbs; some of them went to the FRY,
others moved in with relatives in Croatia. (The expulsions were always legal, in
formal terms, according to Josip Manolić, president of the Croatian Independent Democratic Party, though not necessarily in the spirit of the laws.[196])
Zagreb was one of the hardest hit, in this regard, according to Milorad Pupovac.
Pupovac himself, president of the Serbian Democratic Forum, which preached
and practiced loyalty to the Croatian constitutional order, was prosecuted in
1992 for spreading lies and misinformation about Croatia. The prosecutor was
Vladimir Šeks, a prominent figure in the HDZ, who prosecuted thousands of
Serbs, according to Pupovac.[197]

Controversies about Symbols

In May 1994, Franjo Tudjman restored the kuna, the currency used by the
medieval Kingdom of Croatia; it was also the currency used by the Croatian fascist NDH during World War Two, and some persons, including many local
Serbs, objected that the kuna evoked too many bad memories to be acceptable
as the national currency. Tudjman's government also preserved the checkerboard coat of arms, with the red square in the upper left-hand corner, which
had been used throughout the communist era. Oddly, some local Serbs began
to complain that this was the Ustaša coat of arms and that, again, it was unacceptable. Yet they surely knew that the Ustaša had "inverted" the coat of arms,
starting with a white square in the upper left-hand corner; the communists
restored the authentic medieval coat of arms, which Tudjman merely carried
over. Viktor Meier has suggested that, at least on these two points, there has been
more fuss than necessary. As Meier put it in 1996, "The number of national
symbols which a nation has at its disposal is limited. The Ustaše had adopted
much that had comprised old Croatian tradition or folklore. It would have been
unusual if these symbols had not been embraced also by today's Croatian state.
Even in Germany, today's national anthem and the name of the currency (until
Germany switched to the Euro) had been used by the Nazis, but no one has ever
suggested that this signified that the Federal Republic was associating itself with
Nazi tradition."[198] On the other hand, the rehabilitation of prominent Ustaša
figures, including the renaming of streets after them, could only be characterized as offensive, while the reemergence of the old Ustaša song "Evo Zora, evo

dana, evo Jure i Bobana," was deeply troubling to Serbs, as was the headlong language reform, which left Croatian citizens scrambling to keep up with the torrent of restorations and neologisms.[199] While Tudjman tried to "square the circle," simultaneously emulating Tito, rehabilitating Pavelić, dancing around NDH atrocities, praising Croats as anti-fascists, and celebrating an exclusivist, expansionist nationalism, many of his supporters embraced Ustaša mythology openly and without qualification. When I traveled around Croatia in 1997, I saw the letter *U* scrawled on public buildings in a number of towns: the *U* stood for *Ustaša.*

At issue is the attitude which Croatia should take toward its most recent history, with Mile Budak, minister of education and religious affairs in the NDH, and Josip Broz Tito serving as symbols of rival fascist and Partisan-communist models of Croatia's past. As of August 2004, some 17 cities across Croatia had streets named for Budak.[200] Then an initiative got underway, financed by Croatian émigrés, to install a plaque to Budak in the town of Sveti Rok. The installation of a public plaque seemed to all concerned to be a much bigger step than merely naming a street after him, with critics rejecting the notion that "the Croatian Goebbels" was being honored only as a literary figure, or that his literary accomplishments somehow outweighed his war crimes.[201] When Church circles declared that they had no objection to the erection of such a monument, the Rijeka daily *Novi list* accused the Church's news organ, *Glas koncila*, of having adopted fascist views.[202] Finally, on 3 September 2004, President Mesić entered the fray, declaring that, in his view, honoring Budak on the pretext that he was "a good writer" was comparable to honoring Adolf Hitler on the pretext that he was "a good painter."[203] However, a parallel initiative by a group of right-wing intellectuals to restage, posthumously, the trial of Mile Budak suggested that, at least for some Croats, the meaning of World War Two is still an unresolved question.[204] But it should be stressed that both the Budak plaque and another plaque to Jure Francetić, another Ustaša from World War Two, were financed by Croats abroad and did not win any significant support within Croatia. Moreover, these two plaques were both removed and prompted Prime Minister Ivo Sanader to send a letter to all Croatian organizations abroad, advising them that the country's fascist past is nothing of which anyone should be proud and that they should put the past behind them.

About the same time, a right-wing citizens' initiative group calling itself "Enough ideological tyranny" filed a petition to change the name of Zagreb's Marshal Tito Square to Square of the Victims of Communism and to remove the monument to Tito from his hometown, Kumrovec.[205] This initiative did not go unchallenged, however, with Vesna Teršelić, a prominent peace activist, protesting the petition and underlining that "Tito is the undisputed symbol of antifascism." Indeed, that seemed to be the general sentiment among Croats.

Still, it is remarkable that in the years since 1990, no new monuments to Stjepan Radić have been erected and, even at this writing (December 2005), there are apparently no monuments to Vladko Maček to be found anywhere in Croatia. Since Radić and Maček could serve as inspirations for the building of liberal democracy, this omission is remarkable.

Democratization and the Problem of Corruption

When I met with Vlado Gotovac for the second and, as it turned out, last time (in 1997), he seemed to have distanced himself from his earlier belief that liberalism and nationalism could be reconciled. He spoke critically of Tudjman's HDZ and complained that, under Tudjman, Croatia had become a one-movement system, in which the HDZ controlled the army, the police, the judiciary, scientific institutions, the educational system, economic administration, and television.[206] While he recognized that the HDZ was not a classical party, as such, he clearly felt that the authoritarian elements in Tudjman's Croatia were salient and corrosive of democracy.

Corruption is a problem for democracy because it chews away at the rule of law, undermines procedural predictability, compromises the neutrality of the state, and erodes the autonomy of the economic sector. As already indicated, corruption became a huge problem in the Tudjman era. Indeed, in 1999, Transparency International ranked Croatia 74th in terms of the control and curtailment of corruption among 99 countries, which is to say that Croatia was considered by TI to be the 15th most corrupt country among those it ranked. In 2000, however, Croatia was ranked 51st, with a score of 3.7, still far below first-place Finland's perfect score of 10.[207] Corruption was manifested in diverse forms ranging from the appropriation of news media for political control to automobile smuggling with the assistance of the Croatian Intelligence Service to drug smuggling with army complicity to outright embezzlement to police corruption to the siphoning of funds into an Irish bank for use in HDZ election campaigns to outright graft on the part of the Tudjman family.[208] As early as April 2000, in drawing up a balance sheet on the Tudjman regime, *Nacional* described the system as a "gangster state."[209] Even the Church was drawn into the morass, according to Vjeko Perica, who describes how the Church affiliated itself with the HDZ, benefiting from financial subsidies doled out to its parishes and winning pensions for its clergy.[210] The Račan/Mesić government, which took office in winter 1999–2000 pledged to fight against corruption and has reportedly made some progress. In his first year in office, Račan took steps to set up an agency to fight corruption and crime, known by its acronym—USKOK (which, as a word, means "fugitive" or "resistance fighter").[211] Two years later, however, Beta news agency (in Belgrade) reported that the Croatian state's campaign against corruption remained "ineffective" and noted that only 10% of Croats polled believed that the government was capable of combating corruption at all.[212] A Gallup poll conducted in 2001 found that 89% of Zagreb residents who were polled believed that there was at least some corruption in the companies where they worked, while 42% thought that the government authorities were corrupt.[213] Corruption has cost Croatia dearly, with millions of dollars in lost foreign investments.

Ethnic Relations and Tolerance

During the war, the Krajina Serbs talked of erecting a "Chinese wall" (Great Wall of China) to separate themselves from the Croats and frequently repeated the refrain that all Serbs should live in one state.[214] Yet there were always some Serbs who professed their loyalty to Zagreb and preferred to remain within the territory under Zagreb's jurisdiction. In May 1993, it was estimated that only about 300,000 Croatian Serbs were living in the insurgent-controlled krajinas; between 120,000 and 150,000 Serbs continued to live in the part of Croatia still under the control of Croatian authorities. This adds up to a maximum of 450,000 Serbs then living in one or the other part of the Republic of Croatia—a decline from the 580,000 Serbs living in Croatia as of 1991.[215] Already by 1994, dreams of an eventual union of the Croatian krajina with the Republic of Serbia were starting to fade among Serbs, but even after the Croatian military campaigns of May and August 1995 put an end to such programs, local Serbs continued to talk of wanting regional autonomy from Zagreb.[216]

Under pressure from the international community, the Tudjman regime promised to encourage Serb refugees wanting to return to Croatia to do so, and to make accommodations to reintegrate them into Croatian society. The two most basic elements in this process are housing and employment; yet there have been continued delays in finding housing for the returnees, since the houses which the returnees had owned have generally been turned over to Croatian refugees from Bosnia and Vojvodina. Both Tudjman and Stipe Mesić, elected president after Tudjman's death in November 1999, promised to accelerate the construction of new housing, in order to accommodate Serb returnees, but as of February 2001, only 97,000 of the 300,000 Serbs thought to have left Croatia under duress had returned to Croatia (77,000 officially, 20,000 "unofficially"); *Globus* estimated that only about 130,000 total would ever return to Croatia.[217] Milorad Pupovac had made contact with the highest functionaries of the state in 2000 and had been promised action, but several months later he complained that not a single concrete step had been taken toward resolving the housing issue for Serbs.[218]

Aside from the issue of refugee returns and housing, local Serbs have complained of discrimination, especially in the job sector, have faced long delays in the processing of their pensions, and continued to confront overt forms of ethnic hatred, such as the poster campaign in Karlovac, Petrinja, and Sisak in 2000, accusing certain local Serbs by name of having committed war crimes, the demolition of 300 damaged Serb homes in Gospić on 5 June 2000 by local authorities, and the scrawling of "Srbi van!" ("Serbs out!") on a Serb Orthodox church in downtown Split in 2002.[219] In this connection, too, the destruction in the years 1991–2001 of nearly 3,000 monuments to Croatia's anti-fascist struggle and the erection of the aforementioned memorial plaque to Ustaša leader Jure Francetić in Slunj figure not merely as rejections of the Partisan and communist legacy but also as an embrace, by those responsible, of the NDH and, in consequence, of ethnic hatred.[220]

During the years 1991–2001, more than 2,100 persons were murdered "privately" (i.e., not in connection with combat) in Croatia. As of January 2002, 543 of those cases remained unsolved, with the majority of these victims being Serbs or self-declared "Yugoslavs."[221] Given all of the above, it is generally thought that the latest census underreports the number of Serbs still living in Croatia, which is to say that some Serbs consider it wiser to declare themselves Croats.[222] Officially, there were just over 200,000 Serbs living in Croatia as of April 2001 (representing 4.54% of the population), but the real figure may be between 250,000 and 300,000.

Gender Inequality and Sexual Intolerance

During the decade of HDZ rule, the regime actively propounded so-called traditional values, both directly and indirectly, through agencies supported by government money. One of the agencies supported in this way was Don Anto Baković's Croatian Population Movement, a xenophobic, homophobic organization dedicated to encouraging Croatian Catholics to have as many children as possible. Baković, a vocal exponent of his cause, cannot be accused of subtlety. In an interview with the weekly magazine *Globus* in 1994, for instance, he described himself as "a huge opponent of religious sects" since "they destroy the unity of the Croatian people," telling that same magazine on another occasion that "AIDS is the product of moral degeneration and sin . . . [and] homosexuals should suffer the consequences of their sins."[223] Baković is also opposed to sex education, with its information about contraception; sex education, Baković has claimed, is "poisoning Croatian youth."[224] The prominence enjoyed by Baković, a retired priest, was symptomatic of the character of Croatian society in the Tudjman era.

Although the notion of what an "ideal" family looks like lies at the heart of both homophobia and contempt for women, these are, of course, distinct phenomena, with different dynamics. Where sexual minorities are concerned, "queer festivals" have recently become an annual event, challenging traditional perceptions of sexuality and gender roles.[225] *Feral Tribune,* the irreverent weekly magazine from Split, has also played a constructive role in overcoming sexual phobias—among other things, by publicizing the harm inflicted on gays and lesbians by skinheads and other intolerant persons and by running an article explaining transsexuality and exploding seven myths about transsexuals.[226]

Dorino Manzin, a leader of the gay rights group Iskorak, which organized the 2003 gay pride parade in Zagreb, has estimated that one out of every 10 Croats is gay.[227] Gays are allowed to serve in the Croatian Army but were not being allowed to marry, to adopt children, or to keep the possessions accumulated in the course of a lifelong relationship when one partner dies. In July 2003, however, the Sabor passed a law regulating property rights for same-sex couples; subsequently, laws were adopted banning discrimination on the basis of sexual orientation in education, the workplace, and representations in the media.[228] But legal changes alone will not solve the problems of inequality—as is clear from the fact that schoolbooks used in Catholic religious instruction during the 2003–2004 school year equate homosexuals and transvestites, on the one hand, with prostitutes and perpetrators of incest, on the other hand.[229] Indeed, the Catholic Church has not only taken steps to remove gays from its seminaries but also, during the autumn 2003 elections, advised Croats to vote against political parties favoring the legalization of gay/lesbian marriage or of abortion.[230] So far only two or three political parties on the left have endorsed gay/lesbian marriage.[231] Meanwhile, an analysis of 11 major Croatian periodicals, carried out by the Rijeka-based lesbian organization Lori, found that there was a general trend away from mockery of homosexuals and toward treating the subject seriously, even though there continued to be a tendency among most of these periodicals to place homosexuality in a negative context; only *Feral Tribune* was found to treat homosexuality "in a serious and positive way."[232] The work of activist groups such as Lori, which in April 2003 staged a public exhibit titled "Against Homophobia," is no doubt contributing to a change in local attitudes regarding same-sex partnerships.[233]

There have been problems also where gender inequality is concerned. As in the case of Slovenia and Macedonia, legal guarantees are one thing, reality is another. For example, Article 82 of the Labor Code specifies that women and men shall obtain equal pay for equal work. But in practice, women are generally excluded from managerial positions and generally hold lesser-paying jobs.[234] Or again, while sexual harassment is strictly illegal under the terms of the penal code, women often put up with forms of sexual harassment rather than risk losing their jobs. Moreover, while violence within the family used to be included in the category of crimes to be prosecuted automatically by the state prosecutor, a 1998 legal reform removed intra-family violence from that category.[235] Research conducted by Diana Otrošak, a professor of sociology at the University of Zagreb, among 1,000 Croatian women aged 18 to 65, found that 24% of them had been raped by their husbands, and 21% had been beaten by them.[236] Between 1996 and 1998, according to police records, 1,066 Croatian women sought police assistance because of domestic violence. Moreover, research conducted by NGOs found that 84.6% of Croats felt that women did not receive adequate protection from violence and 63.6% agreed that women were most vulnerable to violence within their own homes, whereas, on the other hand, 25.8% of respondents felt that there were situations in which it was "acceptable" for the husband to hit his wife. Some 44.2% of respondents said that they knew at least one woman who had been beaten at home.[237]

Women are also underrepresented in political office, though the parliamentary elections of 3 January 2000 brought about a tangible improvement in women's representation in the ranks of the Sabor.[238] At the same time, among members of the government, only 13% were women (in 2000). However, more than half of all judges in municipal courts are women, and nearly half of judges in county courts are women. But there are no women in the Constitutional Court, and no woman has ever served as president of the Croatian bar association, though 76% of students at the Faculty of Law in Zagreb were women as of 2000.[239]

Women may look to any of a number of organizations to advocate change. These include B.a.B.e. (Be active, Be emancipated), Biser, Kareta, NONA Multimedia Women's Center, Ženska Infoteka, and the Network Women's Program.

Education and Values

One of the earliest controversies in the field of education in Croatia concerned the introduction of Catholic religious instruction in public schools in 1991. At that time, only 76% of the inhabitants of Croatia were Catholics; among the other 24%, and especially among Serb families, there were complaints of discrimination. Technically, the classes were optional, but in practice the pressure from both teachers and fellow students was often too difficult to resist. Tempers became so inflamed that in November 1994, Franjo Cardinal Kuharić, archbishop of Zagreb, sent a letter to parishes to inquire about the attendance of non-Catholic children at Catholic religion classes and about allegations of baptisms of Serbian Orthodox children into the Catholic Church. That all of this stirred memories, among Croatia's Serbs, of the forced baptisms and other forms of religious pressure in the days of the NDH goes without saying.[240] By 1997, with the end of the war, the pressure on Serbian children subsided, and in the 1996–1997 school year, some 60–70 Serbian children opted for Orthodox religious instruction in Zagreb's schools. But an estimated 3,000 Serbian children continued to be enrolled in Catholic religious instruction, and it was generally conceded that this was due to pressure, not free consent.[241] By the 1999–2000 academic year, 75% of school-age children were enrolled in religious instruction; by the following academic year, the proportion had risen to 77%.[242]

The controversy remains unresolved at this writing. Although the government supports the principle that non-Catholic as well as Catholic religious instruction should be available in public schools where there is a demand, the small number of non-Catholic pupils and a shortage of qualified teachers result in there often being only Catholic religious instruction available. Conservatives defend the presence of Catholic religious instruction by urging that it is important for the development of values. But in 2001, the Jewish community brought a suit before the Croatian Constitutional Court and also before the Council of Europe, charging that the agreement between the Holy See and the Republic of

Croatia, under which Catholic religious instruction was introduced into the public schools, is unconstitutional and discriminatory.[243]

Curriculum reform has been even more controversial. In the early 1990s, as the political pendulum swung rightward, with Croatian officials concerned to provide an anchor for Croatian independence in the minds of the young, textbooks, and especially history textbooks, were revised for all grades from elementary through university level. Marxist ideology was systematically removed, emphasis was placed on Croatia, Yugoslavia was de-emphasized, and the communist legacy was selectively, but not totally, de-legitimated.[244] At the center was the affirmation of the Croatian national project. As Vjeran Pavlaković has pointed out, school textbooks in the Tudjman era sought to portray Croats during World War Two as simultaneously anti-fascist and pro-NDH, construing the NDH, thus, as a legitimate expression of the Croatian people's yearning for an independent state.[245]

With the passing of the Tudjman era, there has been a serious review of the school textbooks. A study authorized by Vladimir Strugar, Croatian minister of education, assessed the majority of history textbooks negatively, characterizing Draga Pavlicevic's textbook for the third year of high school, for example, as "unacceptable" and criticizing Iva Perić's textbook for the fourth year of high school for a "superficial" treatment of the liquidation of Croats by the Partisans at the end of World War Two.[246] Already in the waning months of Tudjman's presidency, an experimental class in Fundamentals of Civic Education and Democracy was introduced as an elective subject in all Croatian primary and secondary schools. In reference to this new class, Nevenka Lončarić-Jelačić, then adviser for human rights and civic education, explained that "Young people should be taught that it is very important to fight for a common and general cause, since there is no citizen who can live exclusively for his or her own sake."[247] About the same time, Vlatko Pavletić, president of the Croatian Sabor, promised that classes in tolerance and human rights would soon be part of the school curriculum.[248] But since Tudjman's death, calls for curriculum reform have intensified, and an overhaul of the treatment of Croatian history was placed at the center of attention.[249]

Toward the end of 2001, the Sabor adopted a law on textbooks, prescribing the establishment of the Council for Textbooks, which would draw up basic standards for textbooks. By spring 2002, the council had begun work.[250] But the standards have allowed for considerable variation. Thus, while a recent textbook by Snježana Koren presents alternative points of view, takes up controversial issues in an open way, and is designed in such a way as to encourage critical thinking, a textbook for the eighth grade written by Josip Jurčević and Marija Raić and published in 2004 is, according to Magdalena Najbar-Agičić and Damir Agičić, "a step back in many respects—emphases, interpretation, and methodological approach."[251] Moreover, in the current syllabus, much attention is paid to Croats living in neighboring countries, while Serbs and other minorities who have lived in Croatia "are mentioned only in the context of conflicts."[252] As for the role that history classes and history textbooks might play in civic education, this "is completely neglected in Croatia," according to Najbar-Agičić and Agičić.

As a consequence, we have citizens who are not able to estimate the credibility of information. Throughout the history education in schools, students are taught that "we" have always been right, that "we" are victims, while the others are simply negative . . . and hostile toward "us."[253]

Cooperation with the ICTY

Croatian moderates have argued that cooperation with the International Criminal Tribunal for the former Yugoslavia in The Hague is both an obligation under international law and a moral obligation. In addition, the Croatian government, which hopes to enter the EU in 2007, has been told that cooperation with the ICTY is a prerequisite for admission to that body.[254] But conservatives in the HDZ and in Miroslav Tudjman's HIP, in the Catholic Church, and on the editorial board of *Globus* opposed Croatian cooperation with The Hague. One casualty of the right wing was Milan Levar, a war veteran, who was cooperating with the ICTY in an effort to identify some of those responsible for war crimes; he was gunned down by extremists in late summer 2000. The conservatives have behaved irresponsibly, even rewriting the texts of ICTY advocates in their self-righteous determination to erect a "Fortress Croatia," alone with its own unique "moral" law. *AIM Press,* the independent news service based in Paris, characterized the Church's response to the ICTY indictments as "completely mad."[255] However, the post-Tudjman governments prioritized cooperation with the ICTY and by early 2005 had met all the preconditions for EU accession except the arrest of Gotovina.

In November 2003, a revived HDZ, now led by Ivo Sanader, emerged as the victor in parliamentary elections in Croatia. Sanader put together a coalition government and immediately made some symbolic gestures designed to reassure local Serbs and Italians of his good will.[256] Sanader also underlined his government's commitment to cooperate with the ICTY—a commitment which he was soon able to demonstrate when, in March 2004, he remanded indicted Croatian generals Ivan Čermak and Mladen Markač to the custody of The Hague—and reconfirmed Croatia's commitment to joining the EU, which it hopes to do by 2007, and NATO.[257] Meanwhile, among Croats, support for membership in the EU continued to grow, reaching 72.4% by December 2003.[258] Prime Minister Sanader indicated that he hoped that Croatia would be admitted to the EU by 2007.[259] By the beginning of 2005, Croatia stood literally at the EU portal and was advised that all that remained for Zagreb to do was to turn over Ante Gotovina, the general who had commanded Croatian forces in Operation Storm, to the ICTY. The complication was that, although Carla Del

Ponte was convinced that Gotovina was still in Croatia, Croatian sources insisted that Gotovina had fled Croatia in 2001.[260] The EU had set a deadline of 17 March 2005 for Gotovina to be remanded, if EU accession talks with Croatia were to begin on time. The deadline passed, and the talks were postponed. But even though EU accession was temporarily put on hold, by the end of May NATO was declaring itself "satisfied with Croatia's progress and the pace at which Croatia is fulfilling criteria for joining the alliance."[261] Croatia was subsequently given the green light to begin EU accession talks.

But Croatia still faces serious economic challenges. While real GDP growth and inflation for 2004 were recorded at 3.7% and 2.5%, respectively, the gross foreign debt accounted for some 56.3% of the GDP in 2004, with unemployment declining from 19.5% in 2003 to 13.8% by the end of 2004.[262] According to research conducted by the Economic Institute in Zagreb, more than 80% of Croats consider themselves to be "poor," but according to figures provided by the Central Intelligence Agency, only 11% of Croats actually lived below the poverty line as of 2003.[263]

All three states discussed in this chapter had to deal with disagreements over national symbols. But in Slovenia, the disagreement was of a purely internal nature, had little to do with ethnic polarization or rival views of history, and was generally so amicably resolved that it can scarcely be called a "controversy." It was, at the most, a contest of rival ideas. The selection of Mt. Triglav to adorn the national flag and of the *tolar* as the new currency did not inflame any tempers. In Macedonia, the controversies which emerged, most prominently over Macedonia's desire to use the Star of Vergina as its national symbol, were purely international, involving a feud with neighboring Greece. These controversies did not, therefore, divide the Macedonian population, even if the symbols did not refer to Albanian history and traditions as such. Only in Croatia did the disagreements take on the character of a controversy between ethnic communities—in this case, between Croats and Serbs. This was why the controversy over symbols in Croatia was politically explosive.

All three states faced disagreements over privatization and challenges in erecting a new constitutional-legal system and regularizing a new system of education. Yet, beyond that, the differences are striking. In Slovenia, the noisiest controversies have had to do with religion and values, above all the Roman Catholic Church's desire to introduce Catholic religious instruction in the public schools. In Macedonia and Croatia, by contrast, the most troublesome issue has involved the treatment of numerical minorities: Albanians in Macedonia, Serbs in Croatia. Only in the case of Tudjman-era Croatia have there been serious allegations of authoritarianism and of the corruption of the rule of law. An assessment by Transparency International, an international organization, released in late October 1999 (while Tudjman was still in office), provided a ranking of 99 countries in the world according to their level of corruption. Denmark was ranked the least corrupt, with a perfect score of 10. Cameroon obtained the lowest rating, a 1.5. On this scale, Slovenia was ranked 25th from the top (an index of 6.0), ahead of Hungary, the Czech Republic, Poland, and Slovakia; Macedonia was somewhat lower (an index of 3.3, the same as for Romania and Bulgaria); and Croatia placed 74th of the list with a 2.7, below India and Colombia (2.9), Argentina (3.0), and Nicaragua (3.1), but ahead of Cote d'Ivoire, Moldova, Ukraine, Venezuela, and Vietnam (all assigned an index of 2.6).[264] All three countries have signed the Criminal Law Convention on Corruption, sponsored by the Council of Europe.[265] Five years later, by which point Slovenia had slipped to 31st place, Croatia, by contrast, had risen to 67th place, with a composite score of 3.5 (as compared with Slovenia's 6.0 and Finland's first-place 9.7). Macedonia was ranked 97th among the 146 countries rated in 2004, tied with Serbia and Montenegro, Algeria, Lebanon, and Nicaragua.[266]

In terms of democratization and press freedom, the country ratings issued by Freedom House are telling. Slovenia has been ranked as "free" the entire time since 1991, with scores of 2.3 and 2.2 in 1991–1992 and 1992–1993, respectively, and a score of 1.2 since then. Macedonia and Croatia both started with a score of 3.4 ("partially free"), and both sank in the years 1994–1998 (to 4.3 for Macedonia, 4.4 for Croatia); but for the period 1998–2000, Macedonia's rating improved to 3.3, while Croatia's score remained a 4.4 even in 1999–2000.[267] By 2002, Slovenia ranked 14th on the press freedom index, ahead of Switzerland (15th), the United States (17th), and Italy (40th). Finland, Iceland, and Norway topped the list.[268]

Finally, by December 2005, Slovenia had been admitted to the EU, negotiations on Croatia's accession had been agreed, and the European Commission had announced that it would recommend that Macedonia be accorded candidate status for EU membership. Indeed, Macedonia was being praised for having set "a good example for resolving multiethnic problems."[269]

CHAPTER 20

Conclusion

In accounting for the triple failure of the effort to build a Yugoslav state, some writers have conjured up mystical notions of "ancient hatreds," although those doing so have been completely unable to cite even one violent instance involving Serbs, Croats, or Bosniaks in "ancient times." Other writers, having nationalist axes to grind, have blamed perfidious Croats or wicked Serbs for the complications which developed along the way, as if all Croats and all Serbs were the same. That such an assumption is utterly preposterous must surely be obvious to any reader of this book. Still others have had recourse to theories of historical determinism, arguing, in one example, that "the illiberal facets in the Serbian political legacy were reinforced by the long period of Ottoman rule," so that Serbia became trapped in a self-replicating pattern, with the result that Milošević could be seen as embodying (or reincarnating) the behavior of Karadjordje or Prince Miloš, and even suggesting that in some societies (Serbia being indicated), "collectivist nationalism . . . is rooted in the mythic lore passed from one generation to another"—so that any given generation is somehow seen as trapped in the complexes developed by previous generations.[1] If this futilitarian concept were true, then humankind would perhaps never have evolved beyond primitive tribal folk politics. But nationalism and politics alike are more complex phenomena than historical determinism would have us believe. Yet another writer, in considering the collapse of the third Yugoslavia, traced problems to a combination of constitutional "blueprints," the ambitions of Milošević, and the egoism of "the Slovenes."[2] If these had actually been the sole factors at work, then how is it that the communist system was not robust enough to contain their effects?

By contrast with these intellectual dead-ends, there is much to be said for Jasna Dragović-Soso's argument that the growth of nationalism (and, I would add, the development of political syndromes) should be seen as "context-specific and relational, rather than historically immutable and isolated," with contingent factors interacting with each other to produce results which could have been avoided in many, perhaps even most, instances.[3] One may, then, differentiate between *factor* and *agency.* By *factor,* I mean any fundamental problem which is seen as leading to the result to be explained—what social scientists often call the "independent variable" or "explicans" (that which explains). That which is to be explained is the "explicandum," also called the "dependent variable," insofar as it is seen as changing in accordance with changes to the "independent variable." In this book, the "explicandum" has been system failure, and the "explicans" (the independent variable) has been the failure of legitimation. But the failure of legitimation was ultimately only one factor, even if, as I have argued, the most important factor in producing system failure. Other relevant factors have included economic deterioration, system design (bearing in mind, for example, the way that the quasi-confederal design of the SFRY contributed to creating fissures in the Yugoslav power structure), and external involvement (such as the Axis attack on Yugoslavia in April 1941).

But such factors do not soar out of the sky like comets or meteors. All of them, even economic deterioration, are the result of or are shaped by the specific choices and behaviors of *agents.* Thus, in order to complete the explanation as to why each of the three Yugoslavias failed, one must make at least a preliminary assessment as to which agents were responsible for the strategies and policies which failed to ensure the survival of the system. Political leaders enjoy resources which position them to exert influence on a society; but cultural figures (such as Dobrica Ćosić), religious leaders (such as Patriarch German), economic tycoons, and persons of profound integrity may also influence developments in a society. In the Yugoslav case, as I have tried to suggest in the foregoing chapters, one may highlight the primary role played by Nikola Pašić and King Aleksandar in the failure of the first Yugoslavia, and the secondary role played by Svetozar Pribićević in the early years, alongside other persons. Had Dragoljub Jovanović been king, instead of Aleksandar Karadjordjević, and had Jaša Prodanović been the leading voice in the fashioning of the first constitution, rather than Pašić, the first Yugoslavia would most likely have taken a very different course—at least until 1941, when the country might still have fallen victim to attack by the Axis. In the second Yugoslavia, to speak of "agency" is to speak, in the first place, of Josip Broz Tito and his closest collaborators—Ranković until 1966, Kardelj, Bakarić, and Dolanc. Later, after the deaths of Kardelj (in 1979) and Tito (in 1980), the political establishment consisted of such people as Petar Stambolić, Draža Marković, Mitja Ribičič, France Popit, Lazar Koliševski, Milka Planinc, Branko Mikulić, and others. But by the late 1980s, people such as Dragiša Pavlović (Belgrade party chief) and Tahir Hasanović (member of the presidency of the LC of Serbia) were coming around to the view that "Yugoslavia needed to move towards social democracy and political liberalisation."[4] For that matter, Dobrica Ćosić, in spite of his contributions to the gathering nationalist storm, recognized the importance of system legitimacy; he put it this way in 1989:

If we had a state based on the rule of law and a democratic approach to the Kosovo question and the situation of the Serbs, if our national oligarchies had had political sense . . . and [had] call[ed] upon the Yugoslav government . . . to guarantee fundamental civil rights, if this question had not been perceived as purely a Serbian one, but as a democratic and Yugoslav one, I am sure that Yugoslavia would not have sunk into the agony in which it is today.[5]

The second Yugoslavia was untenable because it was essentially illegitimate. Fans of Tito sometimes claim that Tito enjoyed widespread "legitimacy," but in so saying they confuse acceptance and his mythic status as a powerful leader with legitimacy. These are not the same. Moreover, if legitimacy is treated as a purely subjective matter, then any despotic government with a highly effective system of propaganda may claim to be "legitimate."[6] Yet despotic governments tend to be significantly less stable, and markedly less capable of generating system continuity, than systems which are objectively more legitimate. Indeed, the very term *despotism* includes a notion of objective illegitimacy, which is why no one speaks of "legitimate despotisms." Objective illegitimacy abides in illegitimacy in the triadic sense outlined in chapter 1, as well as more specifically in a failure to maintain the rule of law.

In that regard, the complete contempt for the rule of law displayed by the Milošević regime was an early symptom of the illegitimacy and inherent instability awaiting the third Yugoslavia. Milošević himself promised, "We Serbs will act in the interest of Serbia whether we do it in compliance with the constitution or not, whether we do it in compliance with the law or not, whether we do it in compliance with party statutes or not."[7] Among the *many* unconstitutional and illegal moves undertaken by Milošević and his collaborators one may mention the use of antigovernment protestors to topple the governments in Novi Sad, Titograd, and Priština in rallies which "were highly planned and organised by Milošević and the Serbian secret service" and coordinated through Miroslav Šolević's Organizing Committee, the arrest of Albanians who signed a petition in 1988 in support of the existing (1974) constitution, the suppression of the autonomy of the provinces of Kosovo and Vojvodina in 1989, the pocketing by Serbia of control of Kosovo's and Vojvodina's votes in the collective presidency (which they had enjoyed by virtue of their autonomy) after the suppression of their autonomy, the Serbian bank swindle of December 1990, and the establishment and arming of Serb militias in Croatia and Bosnia-Herzegovina.[8]

In fact, of the five states to emerge out of the carcass of the SFRY, only Slovenia quickly succeeded in charting a smooth course toward erecting a legitimate system. Croatia under Tudjman developed a corrupt populist system inspired by an often chauvinistic nationalism, while the post-Tudjman leadership of Ivica Račan and Stipe Mesić failed to resolve the vitally important issue of corruption or to create conditions in which those Serbs who fled the country earlier and who had not been indicted for war crimes could return to their homes. But the nationalism whipped up by Tudjman and the HDZ, deepened by the war and sustained by various conservative nationalist ideologues and their followers, remains a problem in Croatia a decade after the war ended.

Where Macedonia is concerned, local politicians acted as if the Albanians living in the western part of the country had no special interests or concerns which needed to be addressed. By spring 2001, this formula had reached a dead-end, with the Albanian insurrection confirming the vulnerability of illegitimate states to destabilization, with ethnic lines often proving to be lines of fracture.

The same dynamic which tore apart the SFRY was also played out in the FRY, with rival elites in Montenegro (Djukanović and his associates) and Kosovo (Rugova and his associates) advocating the separation of their respective zones from the FRY. What was not always understood, and understood perhaps least of all by those trying to hold the FRY together, was that the persistent manifestations of separatism were the epiphenomenon of the crisis of the system, rather than the cause of it.[9] While it may seem a bit idealistic to argue, as Lionel Curtis has done, that "[t]he end and object of human society is to increase in men their sense of duty, one to another"[10]—a claim fully in the spirit of John Stuart Mill's *Considerations concerning Government*—if one considers what a government would look like which would fail to develop in its citizens any sense of mutual duty or of solidarity, one might well agree that such a government could at best be seen as derelict and delinquent in the performance of its own duties. And if one considers, further, what kind of government it is which stirs up the darker passions of ethnic hatred and fosters sentiments of "self-pity and bitterness,"[11] then one might agree with Plato's comment in *Gorgias,* when he recorded Socrates' criticism of Pericles for having made the citizens of Athens "wilder" than he had found them. This, for Socrates and Plato, was one of the worst sins a head of state could commit. In this connection, one may note that whereas, in spite of the sufferings on both sides since 1878 (or possibly earlier), Albanians and Serbs of Kosovo had developed patterns of mutual respect and mutual cooperation over the years, even accompanying each other to local shrines, so that an Orthodox shrine valued by local Serbs was also shown respect by local Albanian Muslims.[12] But once the Milošević regime began stoking Serb hatred of Albanians, suppressed the autonomy of Kosovo, arrested leading figures in the Kosovar Albanian community, and undertook measures of discrimination against and persecution of local Albanians, Serb-Albanian relations were poisoned beyond easy repair, and the traditions of mutual cooperation disappeared. And once the damage is done, it is exceeding difficult to reverse the process: while it takes legitimate (or at least partially legitimate) government— an illegitimate government is unlikely to manage this—to undertake the process of "decontamination," it is also more difficult for a people contaminated with various hatreds and prejudices to erect legitimate government in the first place without outside assistance, or—for that matter—even to sustain it, so that processes of subversion or erosion are always a danger in such cases (as Plato understood). And this is, in turn, why the challenge of state-building in post-Dayton Bosnia has proven so treacherously difficult.

The First Yugoslavia

That the interwar kingdom failed politically requires no special proof. The Vidovdan constitution lasted barely a decade, the river-based regional organization was stillborn, the 1931 constitution was widely rejected across ethnic lines, and the Sporazum of 1939 provoked resentment in Serbia and Bosnia and even divided Croats (some of whom rejected it as a "capitulation"). The question, then, is *why* did it fail? Or perhaps: could it have succeeded?

The kingdom got off to a bad start, with the State of Slovenes, Croats, and Serbs, and the Kingdom of Serbia lacking an agreement on political arrangement prior to unification and rushing into a "shotgun marriage" under the pressure of fears of Italian military incursions; indeed, the delegation from the National Council in Zagreb actually exceeded its authority in agreeing to unification without conditions, so that the unification was, one could say, unauthorized.

There was, as noted in chapter 2, lack of consensus on the state itself. In Macedonia (annexed by force in 1912–1913), pro-Bulgarian sentiment resurfaced, and there was local resistance to the Belgrade government. Some 50,000 Serbian Army troops and police, as well as *četas,* patrolled the region, and there were murders and disappearances. In Montenegro, unification sparked civil war between the pro-independence "greens" and pro-union "whites" lasting until the mid-1920s. In Kosovo, *kaçaks* (outlaws) mounted armed resistance, and local violence continued until 1924; the authorities shut down Albanian-language schools and promoted Serb colonization of the province. In Bosnia, about 2,000 Muslims were killed by Serbs between December 1918 and September 1920, as a result of hate propaganda in the Serbian press. And in Croatia, the Croatian Peasant Party leadership drafted a letter to the Paris peace conference calling for a neutral Croat Peasant Republic, and there was violence in the Croatian countryside in the years 1918–1920. One may safely say, thus, that there was no consensus at all outside of core Serbia on the establishment of the state.

There was also lack of consensus on the principles of state, with autonomism widespread among the Croats and Bosniaks. There were five basic orientations at the inception: centralism combined with subscription to the theory of the "tri-named people" (the Democrats, the Agrarians); centralism combined with a rejection of the theory of the "tri-named people" (the Radicals, except for Protić); decentralization combined with a belief in the amalgamation of the peoples of the kingdom (the Republicans); decentralization and rejection of the theory of the "tri-named people" (the SLS, the Croatian Peasants, the Montenegrin federalists, and the Croatian Community); and advocacy of federalism (Dragoljub Jovanović and the Left Agrarians). The Vidovdan constitution itself was the product of majority vote, with significant abstentions, but not of consensus, and the Croatian Peasant Party was never entirely reconciled to it.

In addition, there were fundamental problems of inequality, ethnic hegemonism, ethnic politics, extralegal activity (on the part of ORJUNA, HANAO, SRNAO, Chetniks, Ustaše, and the Croatian Peasant Defense), obstruction of parliament by the king and other instances of contempt for the rule of law, major assassinations in 1928 and 1934, and the disintegration of the social fabric as manifested in the spread of civil strife in Croatia in the 1930s. In proclaiming a royal dictatorship on 6 January 1929, the king had hoped to bring some order to the system, but all the major political parties rejected the dictatorship, and violence only escalated after 6 January. And finally, the interwar kingdom failed to build a sense of community, so that, as noted in chapter 3, Maček could tell the newspaper *Le petit Parisien* in 1933 that Serbs and Croats inhabited "two different worlds" and should separate as much as possible. The state's prejudicial religious policy only contributed to this last-mentioned failure.

The central problem in the interwar kingdom, thus, was the failure to establish a legitimate system, a failure for which King Aleksandar and Nikola Pašić shared a particular responsibility, as manifested in the failure to establish the rule of law, to protect individual rights, to build an atmosphere of tolerance and fair play, to support real equality, and to guarantee the neutrality of the state in matters of religion, language, and national culture. The first Yugoslavia had largely failed, thus, even before the Axis attack on the country in April 1941, though the *Sporazum* of 1939 had opened up some new possibilities which were never fully explored. Still, where the *Sporazum* is concerned, one should not forget that most politically active Serbs resented it, Slovenes and Bosnians felt that they, too, were entitled to autonomy (with Bosnians resenting the assignment of land historically part of Bosnia-Herzegovina to the Banovina of Croatia), Albanians remained unreconciled to the system, and even among Croats, those committed to a program of secession and independence were utterly opposed to the banovina, which they viewed as a halfway measure.

Wartime Fascism and the Second Yugoslavia

What fascists would have us believe is that an ideology of anti-liberalism—an ideology based on the advocacy of rule of the leader (rather than of law), collective rights (rather than individual rights), intolerance, the right of the state to harm individuals and entire groups at will, inequality, and state endorsement of one or another religion, possibly even including the subversion of the chosen religion for political purposes—can provide the basis for consolidation of a stable state. The record of fascist states, including those in wartime Croatia and

Serbia, shows that there have always been large sections of the population who have been so totally opposed to fascism that they have been prepared to abandon their work, take up arms, and join partisan resistance.

The second Yugoslavia, dominated by the communist party, lasted from 1945 until 1991, though to be entirely accurate one should note that the communists were already setting up their state in those areas which they controlled from 1943 onward. The communists understood the importance of ethnic equality and gender equality, they understood the bitterness which could be stirred up by dwelling on grievances from the interwar and wartime periods, they understood that mutual tolerance (which they translated as "brotherhood and unity") was essential to civil peace, and they adopted a version of confessional neutrality, albeit one which treated all religious belief as equally dangerous and equally false.

But such insights did not enable the Yugoslav communists to fashion a workable, legitimate system. Their greatest failures were their refusal to give up their political monopoly and allow the creation of a multi-party system (in spite of repeated proposals to that effect), their refusal to allow an open and frank discussion of the bloodletting of World War Two or even, for that matter, of the sundry grievances stirred up in the interwar kingdom, and their failure to fashion a shared Yugoslav political culture, in spite of endless talk about the virtue of "Yugoslav socialist patriotism." The communists were fond of repeating that "every nationalism is dangerous," but their policies did not serve to defuse nationalism; on the contrary, the decision to devolve extensive powers to republics established along ethnic lines backfired and actually resulted in an increase of inter-ethnic bickering. Devolution also created lines of fracture, along which the system could fall apart, if the unresolved crisis of state should reach the point of no return.

Economic deterioration, which received a powerful impetus from the oil price shock of 1974, had its roots in uncontrolled borrowing, wasteful duplication of services, and general economic inefficiency. These problems had been only partially remedied in the course of the reforms of 1962–1965, and soon after Tito died, leading figures in the party began to admit that the country was engulfed in a deep economic and political crisis. The commissions headed by Sergej Kraigher and Tihomir Vlaškalić, devoted respectively to the study of the economic and political systems, prepared lengthy reports proposing various reforms, changes, and adjustments, but their recommendations were never implemented. In any event, it is doubtful that these recommendations would have been sufficient to remedy the problems which by the early 1980s included not only lack of legitimacy but inefficiency, dysfunctionality, and incipient deterioration in both the economy and the political sphere. More radical solutions, proposed by Svetozar Stojanović, as well as by the aforementioned Pavlović and Hasanović, fell on deaf ears. The result was that problems grew steadily worse, until the Serbian and Croatian publics became increasingly receptive to the beguiling promises of populist demagogues. As Jack Snyder has shown, political elites in authoritarian states undergoing democratization sometimes embrace nationalist programs in an effort to retain power. Indeed, both Milošević and Tudjman used ethnic nationalism as an instrument to build (and, in Milošević's case, retain) power. But a comparison of Yugoslavia with other countries abandoning communism at the end of the 1980s and beginning of the 1990s shows that Yugoslavia had the highest rate of illiteracy among seven states (Bulgaria, Czechoslovakia, Hungary, Poland, Romania, the USSR, and Yugoslavia), the highest infant mortality of the seven, the second highest proportion of its population engaged in agriculture (after Romania), and the lowest rate of urbanization.[13] These considerations, in turn, suggest that even among states with illegitimate systems, there are additional factors which serve to make a state more or less susceptible to civil strife and violence.

The Third Yugoslavia

The third Yugoslavia, declared in April 1992 on the basis of the union of Serbia and Montenegro, was born in a time of war, seeking legitimacy through the achievement of an illegitimate goal—the creation of a Greater Serbia in which all Serbs would live in one state, to be realized by driving non-Serbs from lands sought by Serbia. Serb nationalists never allowed that that principle might have universal application, because to have done so would have been to expose the implicit assumption of Serbian territorial expansionism to self-contradiction. But a principle which cannot be universalized is an indefensible principle. The battlefield failures, swamping of Serbia by refugees, rampant violations of the harm principle (including in "peaceful" Vojvodina, Sandžak, and lands held by the Bosnian Serbs), hate-mongering by the Serbian press, and the creation of a criminal elite which flagrantly flouted both domestic laws and the UN-imposed embargoes are all well-known. The core of the problem with the third Yugoslavia lay in its nature as a criminalized oligarchy built on a foundation of institutional and legal chaos. This dual chaos was the result both of the aforementioned unconstitutional and illegal actions taken by Milošević and his cronies and of the regime's more general disinterest in procedural regularity. It is procedural regularity which lays the foundation for rule of law, and although Milošević used elections and the independent press to signal his regime's alleged respect for democracy, he subverted the elections when it suited his purposes, and he shut down the independent media when they offended him. What counted for Milošević was obtaining the results he desired, not maintaining procedural regularity. But the emphasis on getting what one wants is the hallmark of authoritarianism, not of democracy, not even of "soft democracy," as one optimist described the Milošević regime.

At this writing, Milošević is in the dock at The Hague, standing trial for war crimes in Croatia, Bosnia, and Kosovo, while Montenegro and Kosovo continue to press for full, internationally recognized independence.[14]

A Summing Up

There are several conclusions which may be drawn from this study. First, ethnicity as such is not a problem. In Yugoslavia, it was made into a problem through a combination of discriminatory policies, scorn for regional interests, and the phenomenon of ethnic politics (as defined in chapter 1). Second, problems between the South Slavs before 1878 were nothing unusual; indeed, collaboration and cooperation were at least as important as conflict. In the years 1878–1918, such conflicts as developed were not exceptional by European standards. Inter-ethnic problems did increase after 1918, but as an epiphenomenon of system illegitimacy. Third, not all principles of legitimation work equally well. The socialist triad (self-management, brotherhood and unity, nonalignment) and the Greater Serbian program alike were flawed and were incapable of generating stable equilibria. Fourth, the role of specific individuals cannot be ignored. Social and political problems do not come out of the heavens; they are the result of strategic and policy choices taken by identifiable individuals and parties. And fifth, contemporary regimes violate human rights at their own risk. Practices common at the time that the Egyptian pyramids were built or at the height of the Inquisition are no longer accepted as proper; indeed, in the 21st century, people are increasingly disinclined to accept violations or infringements of human rights except under conditions of siege (the possibility of such an exception being made clear in the current debate about the torture of suspected terrorists, though, as *The Economist* put it, "democracies break the taboo at their [own] peril"[15]). Indeed, there is a growing consensus that human rights trump sovereignty, thus returning to the arguments of Jean Bodin (1529/30–1596).[16] Moreover, it was Bodin who suggested that "as long as rulers practised impiety and injustice . . . their only reward would be disorder and change," but that "by following the principles of the divine and natural order rulers could secure a lasting harmony and order in their republics."[17]

Beyond that, this book has provided some confirmation of the hypotheses stated at the outset. Among them, the following bear recapitulation. First, only a legitimate system can enjoy stable equilibrium, while the more illegitimate a system, the more unstable is its equilibrium.[18] Second, as repeatedly shown in Yugoslavia's history, an unstable equilibrium is no guarantee of transformation toward legitimate politics, even though an unstable equilibrium provides incessant pressure for change (and hence conjures up the ever-present sense of crisis).[19] Third, the greater the correlation between political-programmatic preferences and ethnic affiliation, the greater the ethnic polarization.[20] This, in fact, defines the dangerous syndrome of ethnic politics. But economic variables may also reinforce polarization, and hence, fourth, the greater the correlation between economic class and ethnic affiliation, the greater the potential for ethnic mobilization.[21] Moreover, as the sense of discrimination rises, members of victimized groups become more prepared to resort to violence to change the system, as the example of the interwar paramilitary groups makes clear.[22]

Symbols are also important in the calculus. Indeed, the less the consensus on symbols of legitimation, the greater the awareness of the problematic nature of the system,[23] and in turn, the greater and the more widespread the willingness to oppose the system.[24] In a related phenomenon, one finds, further, that the greater the tendency of different ethnic or nationality groups to have *competing* legitimation symbols, the greater the ethnic polarization and the less the legitimacy of the regime.[25]

Yugoslavia was not doomed to fail. The first Yugoslavia's chances of consolidation were undermined by the insensitive choices taken by the dominant political actors, discriminatory policies, contempt for the rule of law at the highest levels, and growing tendencies to resort to violence on the part of various actors. The experiences of the kingdom left perhaps all of Yugoslavia's peoples bitter and resentful; this bitterness and these resentments were only deepened in the course of World War Two. By the end of that war, nationalist hatreds had, rather obviously, been stirred to a fever pitch, and bitterness ran deep. With time, the bitterness might have healed, but the strategies adopted by the SFRY were not conducive to this end, and nationalism, manifesting itself as an unhealthy riveting of collective attention on the identity, culture, and destiny of the nation, claiming hegemonic rights for one's own nation over others, increasingly became the currency of exchange in Yugoslavia in the course of the 1980s, with tragic results. Some writers would have us believe that the use of force to achieve ethnic homogeneity within a given area may be "an essential element in the program of many state builders and national liberation(?) movements" and that "violence may be most required to break up populations that have long been living intermingled, such as those of Croatia and Bosnia in 1941 and 1991–92."[26] But research conducted in Germany in the 1990s found that people exposed to members of other racial, ethnic, and religious groups are likely to be *more* tolerant than people who do not enjoy much contact with members of other groups.[27] In other words, partition and separation tend to *increase* prejudice and ethnic bigotry, rather than the reverse. And this, in turn, provides yet another reason why the four waves of homogenization in southeastern Europe which began with the Balkan Wars of 1912–1913 have failed to achieve their nominal object, as spelled out in the 1923 Treaty of Lausanne (which sanctioned involuntary population exchanges among Greece, Turkey, and Bulgaria), viz., to end inter-ethnic conflict and bring peace to the region.[28] The more fundamental reason why ethnic homogenization has proven unavailing in the quest for stability is, of course, that it is the wrong means. If the problem is illegitimate politics, then the solution is to foster legitimate politics.

Abbreviations and Acronyms Used in the
Notes and Bibliography

/B	at the US Embassy in Belgrade
C	Confidential
CIA	Central Intelligence Agency
CIC/S	Counter Intelligence Corps, 430th CC Detachment, Salzburg Sub-Detachment
D	Dispatch
DoD	Department of Defense
Decl.	declassified
ED	Enclosure to dispatch
FBIS	Foreign Broadcast Information Service
FIA	Freedom of Information Act
GRECO	Groupe d'Etats contre la corruption (Group of States against corruption)
HT	Hrvatski tjednik
IM	Incoming Message
IT	Incoming Telegram
JPRS	Joint Publications Research Service
JPRS/EER	Joint Publications Research Service, East Europe Report
LOU	limited official use
/M	at the US Embassy, Madrid
MA	Military Attaché
MC	Memorandum of Conversation
NA	National Archives II, College Park, Maryland
NIE	National Intelligence Estimates
NYT	New York Times
/O	at the US Embassy, Oslo
OA	Outgoing Airgram
OACS	Office of the Assistant Chief of Staff
ORE	Office of Research Evaluation
OT	Outgoing Telegram
OUO	Official Use Only
OUSCCWC	Office of the U.S. Chief of Counsel for War Crimes APO 696A
R	Restricted
/R	at U.S. Embassy, Rome
RAOOH	Records of the Allied Operational and Occupation Headquarters
RFE/RL	Radio Free Europe/Radio Liberty
RG	Research Group
RIRR	Records of the Investigative Records Repository

ROACS	Records of the Office of the Assistant Chief of Staff
S	Secret
S/A	Special Agent
SAL	Suzzallo-Allen Library of the University of Washington
SHAEF	Supreme Headquarters Allied Expeditionary Forces
SKFVOH	Staatliche Kommission zur Feststellung der Verbrechen der Okkupation und ihrer Helfershelfer
State	Department of State
T	Telegram
TS	Top Secret
UNMIK	United Nations Interim Administration Mission in Kosovo
UNRRA	United Nations Rescue and Relief Agency

Notes

Material cited from Web sites was accessed during the years 1999–2005. I have provided date of access for those sites for which I felt such information would hold some interest. Some Web sites accessible on one computer may not be accessible on another computer. Moreover, since Web sites have use-by dates and since Web addresses change from time to time, it is possible that some URLs might no longer function. In that event, a reader might use a Web browser such as Google to search for key words and click on the "cached" virtual button. Another possibility is to look for a cached copy at the Internet Archive, www.archive.org/.

Introduction

1. Matjaž Klemenčič and Mitja Žagar, *The Former Yugoslavia's Diverse Peoples: A Reference Sourcebook* (Santa Barbara, Calif.: ABC-Clio, 2004), pp. 12–13.

2. Ludwig Steindorff, *Kroatien. Vom Mittelalter bis zur Gegenwart* (Regensburg/Munich: Verlag Friedrich Pustet and Südosteuropa-Gesellschaft, 2001), pp. 33–38.

3. Mitja Velikonja, *Religious Separation and Political Intolerance in Bosnia-Herzegovina*, trans. from Slovenian by Rang'ichi Ng'inja (College Station: Texas A&M University Press, 2003), pp. 22–26, 32–33.

4. L. S. Stavrianos, *The Balkans since 1453* (New York: Holt, Rinehart, & Winston, 1958), p. 28.

5. Zeev Sternhell, with Mario Sznajder and Maia Asheri, *The Birth of Fascist Ideology*, trans. from French by David Maisel (Princeton, N.J.: Princeton University Press, 1994), introduction; and Roger Griffin, *The Nature of Fascism* (New York: St. Martin's Press, 1991).

6. See Elizabeth Wiskemann, *Europe of the Dictators 1919–1945* (Ithaca, N.Y.: Cornell University Press, 1966).

7. See Vojislav Koštunica and Kosta Čavoški, *Party Pluralism or Monism: Social Movements and the Political System in Yugoslavia, 1944–1949* (Boulder, Colo.: East European Monographs, 1985).

8. See Ildiko Erdei, "'The Happy Child' as an Icon of Socialist Transformation: Yugoslavia's Pioneer Organization," in John Lampe and Mark Mazower (eds.), *Ideologies and National Identities: The Case of Twentieth-Century Southeastern Europe* (Budapest and London: Central European University Press, 2004), pp. 154–179.

9. Klemenčič and Žagar, *Former Yugoslavia's Diverse Peoples*, p. 204.

10. On this era, see Ante Čuvalo, *The Croatian National Movement, 1966–1972* (Boulder, Colo.: East European Monographs, 1990).

11. See Jozo Tomasevich, *War and Revolution in Yugoslavia, 1941–1945: Occupation and Collaboration* (Stanford, Calif.: Stanford University Press, 2001), pp. 187–189, 183, 194–195.

12. For an estimate of 49,602, see Meho Visočak and Bejdo Sobica, *Jasenovac: Žrtve rada prema podacima statističkog zavoda Jugoslavije* (1998), as summarized in a review by Norman Cigar, in *Journal of Croatian Studies*, vol. 39 (1998): 146–148. For an estimate of 100,000, see Vladimir Žerjavić, *Population Losses in Yugoslavia, 1941–1945* (Zagreb: Dom i Svijet, 1997), p. 89.

13. For details, see Sabrina P. Ramet, *Balkan Babel: The Disintegration of Yugoslavia from the Death of Tito to the Fall of Milošević*, 4th ed. (Boulder, Colo.: Westview Press, 2004), chap. 3.

14. John Major, *The Autobiography* (New York: HarperCollins, 1999), pp. 533–534.

15. See, for example, Charles R. Shrader, *The Muslim-Croat Civil War in Central Bosnia: A Military History, 1992–1994* (College Station: Texas A&M University Press, 2003).

1. A Theory of System Legitimacy

1. See the following writings: Charles Beitz, *Political Theory and International Relations* (Princeton, N.J.: Princeton University Press, 1979); John Finnis, *Natural Law and Natural Rights* (Oxford: Clarendon Press, 1980); Samuel P. Huntington, *Political Order in Changing Societies* (New Haven, Conn.: Yale University Press, 1968); Russell Hardin, *Morality within the Limits of Reason* (Chicago: University of Chicago Press, 1988); L. W. Sumner, *The Moral Foundation of Rights* (Oxford: Clarendon Press, 1987); Amitai Etzioni, "Particularistic Obligations: A Communitarian Examination," in *The Responsive Community*, vol. 14, no. 1 (Winter 2003/2004): 38–48; Michael Sandel, *Liberalism and the Limits of Justice*, 2nd ed. (Cambridge: Cambridge University Press, 1998).

2. On this point, see W. Michael Reisman, "Sovereignty and Human Rights in Contemporary International Law," *American Journal of International Law*, vol. 84, no. 4 (October 1990); Michael J. Smith, "Ethics and Intervention," in *Ethics and International Affairs*, vol. 3 (1990); and Michael J. Smith, "Humanitarian Intervention: An Overview of the Ethical Issues," in *Ethics and International Affairs*, vol. 12 (1998).

3. Perhaps the boldest statement of this argument is advanced by Steven R. David in a 1986 article in *International Security*, in which he argued that through a combination of security assistance, the promotion of the establishment of Leninist-style vanguard parties, and the use of proxy armies (especially from Cuba and the German Democratic Republic), the Soviets had "largely succeeded in eliminating the threat of a pro-Western coup against its Third World friends. . . . The Soviet record of deterring or preventing 'reactionary' coups in countries where they wish to maintain their influence is nothing short of remarkable." S. R. David, "Soviet Involvement in Third World Coups," *International Security*, vol. 11, no. 1 (Summer 1986): 29, 31. But the same idea may also be found in Samuel P. Huntington's *Political Order*, where he argued that Leninist regimes had solved the problem of political institutionalization and were therefore likely to prove durable.

4. My summary of the consequentialist position, in Sabrina P. Ramet, "The Classical Liberal Tradition: Versions, Subversions, Aversions, Traversions, Reversions," in Oto Luthar, Keith A. McLeod, and Mitja Žagar (eds.), *Liberal Democracy, Citizenship and Education* (Niagara Falls, N.Y.: Mosaic Press, 2001), p. 52.

5. Colin Farrelly, *An Introduction to Contemporary Political Theory* (London: Sage Publications, 2004), p. 97, summarizing Sandel.

6. Ibid., summarizing the consequentialist position broadly.

7. Henry Tam, *Communitarianism: A New Agenda for Politics and Citizenship* (Houndmills: Macmillan, 1998), p. 14.

8. See David Miller, *On Nationality* (Oxford: Clarendon Press, 1995), especially chaps. 3–4; see also pp. 11, 184, 195. For a critique of Miller's approach, see Andreas Follesdal, "The Future Soul of Europe: Nationalism or Just Patriotism? A Critique of David Miller's Defence of Nationality," *Journal of Peace Research*, vol. 37, no. 4 (July 2000): 503–518.

9. Tam, *Communitarianism*, p. 7.

10. Immanuel Kant, "On the Common Saying: 'This May Be True in Theory, but It Does Not Apply in Practice'" (1793), in I. Kant, *Political Writings*, 2nd enlarged ed., trans. by H. B. Nisbet, ed. by Hans Reiss (Cambridge: Cambridge University Press, 1991), pp. 73–74, 79–84; and Immanuel Kant, "Perpetual Peace" (1795), in ibid., p. 101.

11. Thomas Hobbes, *On the Citizen*, ed. and trans. by Richard Tuck (Cambridge: Cam-

bridge University Press, 1998). Indeed, the Hobbesian endeavor to place self-interest at the center of his system, while rationally coherent, has an essential connection with his supposition that people are naturally asocial and naturally more disposed toward conflict with each other than toward cooperation. Rousseau, who also feared that people, left to their own devices, might prove to be asocial and conflict oriented, looked to education to remedy this feature of life. Civic education, which was also stressed by Plato, Locke, and Kant, among others, did not occupy Hobbes's attention. This in turn tells us something about the Hobbesian project as a whole.

12. Kant, "Perpetual Peace," pp. 124, 125.

13. David Hume, *Treatise of Human Nature* (Buffalo and New York: Prometheus Books, 1992 [1739]), p. 543.

14. Plato, *The Laws*, trans. by Trevor J. Saunders (London: Penguin Books, 1970).

15. Jean Bodin, *De Republica* (1591), as cited in Max Adams Shepard, "Sovereignty at the Crossroads: A Study of Bodin," in *Political Science Quarterly*, vol. 45, no. 4 (December 1930): 587.

16. For a discussion of equality, see Joseph Raz, *The Morality of Freedom* (Oxford: Clarendon Press, 1986), chap. 9 (pp. 217–244).

17. St. Thomas Aquinas, *Summa theologiae*, in St. Thomas Aquinas, *Political Writings*, ed. and trans. by R. W. Dyson (Cambridge: Cambridge University Press, 2002), p. 123.

18. Ibid., p. 124.

19. Given the breadth of disputes about Rousseau, any coherent interpretation of Rousseau's political thought will inevitably be controversial. Leaving aside Rousseau's ideas about the relationship of Church and state, I would argue that Rousseau accepts and incorporates, in one way or another, all of the other five principles which I have identified as central to the liberal project.

20. For a discussion of the harm principle, see Raz, *Morality of Freedom*, pp. 412–424.

21. Finnis, *Natural Law and Natural Rights*, p. 217.

22. Robert P. George, *Making Men Moral: Civil Liberties and Public Morality* (Oxford: Clarendon Press, 1993).

23. Since homosexual marriage is now available in more than a dozen countries, as well as in some parts of the United States, the characterization of homosexual "sex acts" as necessarily "nonmarital" is no longer accurate. Later in the same essay, the authors make clear that they object at least as much to homosexuality as such as to nonmarital sex. See Robert P. George and Christopher Wolf, "Natural Law and Public Reason," in Robert P. George and Christopher Wolfe (eds.), *Natural Law and Public Reason* (Washington, D.C.: Georgetown University Press, 2000), p. 58; also p. 66. See also Robert P. George (ed.), *Natural Law, Liberalism, and Morality: Contemporary Essays* (Oxford: Clarendon Press, 1996).

24. John Rawls, *Political Liberalism* (New York: Columbia University Press, 1993, 1996), p. 110.

25. See F. Clark Power, Ann Higgins, and Lawrence Kohlberg, *Lawrence Kohlberg's Approach to Moral Education* (New York: Columbia University Press, 1989), especially chapters 1 and 4.

26. See Charles Edwards, "The Law of Nature in the Thought of Huge Grotius," *Journal of Politics*, vol. 32, no. 4 (November 1970): 784–807.

27. Ted Robert Gurr, *Why Men Rebel* (Princeton, N.J.: Princeton University Press, 1970), p. 185.

28. Seymour Martin Lipset, "Social Conflict, Legitimacy, and Democracy" [an extract from *Political Man: The Social Bases of Politics*, rev. ed. (1981)], in William Connolly (ed.), *Legitimacy and the State* (Oxford: Basil Blackwell, 1984), p. 88.

29. In fact, Lipset does not seem to have taken violations of human rights seriously as an impediment to either legitimacy or stability, which explains his admitted surprise when the communist systems in Eastern Europe collapsed. Indeed, in spite of published predictions of the imminent collapse of East European communism more than a year in advance by Anneli Gabanyi, Ivan Volgyes, Zbigniew Brzezinski, and Francis Fukuyama and more than five years in advance of that date by Ernst Kux and George Schöpflin, Lipset, who apparently was not keeping up with publications dealing with Eastern Europe, saw fit to declare, in one publication, that no one had anticipated the collapse of communism. This prediction, by a celebrated figure in the field of political science, stands as a warning against those who, without having read *everything* written on a given subject, see fit to pontificate on what has *not* been said on that subject.

30. Peter G. Stillman, "The Concept of Legitimacy," in *Polity,* vol. 7, no. 1 (Fall 1974): 43.

31. Rodney Barker, *Political Legitimacy and the State* (Oxford: Clarendon Press, 1990), p. 11.

32. Richard M. Merelman, "Learning and Legitimacy," in *The American Political Science Review,* vol. 60, no. 3 (September 1966): 548, my emphasis.

33. Andreas Hasenclever, *Die Macht der Moral in der internationalen Politik: Militärische Interventionen westlicher Staaten in Somalia, Ruanda und Bosnien-Herzegowina* (Frankfurt: Campus Verlag, 2001), p. 117.

34. John H. Schaar, "Legitimacy in the Modern State," in Connolly, *Legitimacy and the State,* pp. 108, 109.

35. Ibid., p. 109. James S. Fishkin, *Tyranny and Legitimacy: A Critique of Political Theories* (Baltimore and London: Johns Hopkins University Press, 1979), pp. 4–5.

36. Rawls, *Political Liberalism,* p. 428.

37. Cited in Bernhard Blanke, "Gesellschaftliche Ungleichheit und politische Gleichheit als Legitimationsproblem," in Wolfgang Fach and Ulrich Degen (eds.), *Politische Legitimität* (Frankfurt: Campus Verlag, 1978), pp. 238–239.

38. Fishkin, *Tyranny and Legitimacy,* p. 5.

39. Ibid., p. 7. This is a point also made by John Stuart Mill in his *On Liberty.*

40. Ibid., p. 90.

41. John Stuart Mill, *Considerations on Representative Government* (1861), in J. S. Mill, *Utilitarianism, On Liberty, Considerations on Representative Government* (London: Everyman's Library, 1972), p. 207.

42. For an explanation of the perfect moral commonwealth, see J. C. Davis, *Utopia and the Ideal State: A Study of English Utopian Writing, 1516–1700* (Cambridge: Cambridge University Press, 1981). For my own previous ruminations on this issue, see Sabrina P. Ramet, *Balkan Babel: The Disintegration of Yugoslavia from the Death of Tito to the Fall of Milošević,* 4th ed. (Boulder, Colo.: Westview Press, 2002), chap. 12.

43. Kant, "Perpetual Peace," p. 113.

44. Gabriel Almond and Sidney Verba, *The Civic Culture: Political Attitudes and Democracy in Five Nations* (Boston: Little, Brown, 1965).

45. Here I shall anticipate a possible objection: when, in the foregoing passage, I write "to the degree," I mean to suggest that system legitimacy (in this case, in the objective sense) is a matter of degree and not of absolutes, and that not that all systems can be categorized as either "legitimate" or "illegitimate" but rather that there may be multiple axes along which a system's practices may be plotted as more or less legitimate than those of another system, at least, as per Barker, in the eyes of the society itself. Thus, when angry citizens took to the streets of Los Angeles to protest the police beating of Rodney King some years ago, they were not declaring that the entire American system was "illegitimate," and they were also not merely registering

a merely subjective opinion about something they did not "like"—they were rejecting the unprovoked beating for what it was, viz., a practice which they believed should be seen as illegitimate in any system. Subjectivity enters into the calculus, however, not as the ultimate measure of legitimacy but as popular assessment of the extent to which a system measures up to certain criteria. Some of these criteria, such as the belief that a legitimate government will respect certain basic human rights, are fairly universal, even if some skeptics show their contempt for non-Western peoples by arrogantly rejecting human rights as mere Western conceit.

46. It would thus be a serious mistake to believe that the understanding of rights which fuels outrage at such practices is merely an invention of the past 30 years or so, let alone an understanding found only in America and Western Europe.

47. This is not to say that people always think clearly. Some of U.S. president George W. Bush's fans, who like his style and approve of his aggressivity toward critics, if given a choice between Bush, with his deficit spending, and a Bush clone who would be fiscally responsible, might well reject the deficit-spending Bush in a voluble clamor.

48. Jürgen Habermas, *The Inclusion of the Other: Studies in Political Theory*, trans. from German by Ciaran Cronin et al., ed. by Ciaran Cronin and Pablo De Greiff (Cambridge and Oxford: Polity Press and Blackwell, 1999), p. 12.

49. Yves R. Simon, *Philosophy of Democratic Government* (Chicago: University of Chicago Press, 1951), p. 147.

50. Ibid., pp. 158–159. Aquinas, of course, did not use the term "popular sovereignty."

51. Quoted in ibid., p. 165.

52. Ibid., pp. 169–175.

53. Ibid., pp. 177, 186.

54. Jean Bethke Elshtain, *Democracy on Trial* (New York: BasicBooks, 1995), p. 2.

55. Hume, *Treatise of Human Nature*, p. 564.

56. See, for example, Milovan Djilas, *The New Class: An Analysis of the Communist State* (New York: Praeger, 1957).

57. See Danica Fink-Hafner and John R. Robbins (eds.), *Making a New Nation: The Formation of Slovenia* (Aldershot, England: Dartmouth, 1997).

58. Owen Ulph, "Jean Bodin and the Estates-General of 1576," *Journal of Modern History*, vol. 19, no. 4 (December 1947): 289–290; and Robert P. Kraynak, "John Locke: From Absolutism to Toleration," *American Political Science Review*, vol. 74, no. 1 (March 1980): 53–69.

59. See Ivo Banac, *The National Question in Yugoslavia: Origins, History, Politics* (Ithaca, N.Y.: Cornell University Press, 1984).

60. See Pedro Ramet, "Women, Work, and Self-Management in Yugoslavia," in *East European Quarterly*, vol. 17, no. 4 (January 1984): 459–468; and Sabrina P. Ramet, "In Tito's Time," in Sabrina P. Ramet (ed.), *Gender Politics in the Western Balkans: Women and Society in Yugoslavia and the Yugoslav Successor States* (University Park: Pennsylvania State University Press, 1999).

61. Stella Alexander, in conversation with the author, Bromley, UK, August 1982. See also Stella Alexander, *Church and State in Yugoslavia since 1945* (Cambridge: Cambridge University Press, 1971).

62. Bishop Djuro Kokša, in interview with the author, Zagreb, July 1982.

63. Quoted in Rusmir Mahmutćehajić, *The Denial of Bosnia*, trans. from Bosnian by Francis R. Jones and Marina Bowder (University Park: Pennsylvania State University Press, 2000), pp. 43–44.

64. *Dnevni avaz* (Sarajevo), 27 December 1997, p. 5, cited in Mahmutćehajić, *Denial of Bosnia*, p. 63.

65. Quoted in Mahmutćehajić, *Denial of Bosnia*, p. 45, from *Tjednik* (Zagreb), 11 July 1997, p. 7.

66. See, for example, Yael Tamir, *Liberal Nationalism* (Princeton, N.J.: Princeton University Press, 1993); and Liah Greenfeld, *Nationalism: Five Roads to Modernity* (Cambridge, Mass.: Harvard University Press, 1992).

67. See also the intelligent discussion in Dan Smith, "Ethical Uncertainties of Nationalism," *Journal of Peace Research*, vol. 37, no. 4 (July 2000): 489–502.

68. *Civic-mindedness* is the term I have used in my *Whose Democracy* to refer to an orientation toward one's community or society *as opposed to* an orientation toward one's national group. See Sabrina P. Ramet, *Whose Democracy? Nationalism, Religion, and the Doctrine of Collective Rights in Post-1989 Eastern Europe* (Lanham, Md.: Rowman & Littlefield, 1997), introduction, chap. 3, conclusion.

69. Kant, "On the Common Saying," p. 74.

70. See Hanna Arendt, *The Origins of Totalitarianism*, new ed. (San Diego: Harcourt Brace Jovanovich, 1973).

71. Seymour Martin Lipset, "Some Social Requisites of Democracy: Economic Development and Political Legitimacy," *American Political Science Review*, vol. 53, no. 1 (March 1959): 86.

72. Ekkehart Krippendorff, "Legitimität als Problem der Politikwissenschaft," in Fach and Degen (eds.), *Politische Legitimitat*, p. 26, 31.

73. Gurr, *Why Men Rebel;* Crane Brinton, *The Anatomy of a Revolution*, rev. ed. (New York: Vintage Books, 1965); and James C. Davies, "Toward a Theory of Revolution," in Barry McLaughlin (ed.), *Studies in Social Movements: A Social Psychological Perspective* (New York: Free Press, 1969).

74. Ronald Rogowski, *Rational Legitimacy: A Theory of Political Support* (Princeton, N.J.: Princeton University Press, 1974), p. 45.

75. Lipset, "Some Social Requisites," p. 87.

76. Gurr, *Why Men Rebel*, p. 170.

77. Mill, *Considerations on Representative Government*, p. 392.

2. The First Yugoslavia, Part 1

1. J. Peter Burgess, *Culture and Rationality: European Frameworks of Norwegian Identity* (Kristiansand, Norway: Høyskoleforlaget AS, 2001), p. 30.

2. See my essay "The So-Called Right of National Self-Determination and Other Myths," *Human Rights Review*, vol. 2, no. 1 (October–December 2000): 84–103.

3. On this issue, see John R. Searle, "How to Derive 'Ought' from 'Is,'" *Philosophical Review*, vol. 73, no. 1 (January 1964): 43–58; James Thomson and Judith Thomson, "How Not to Derive 'Ought' from 'Is,'" *Philosophical Review*, vol. 73, no. 4 (October 1964): 512–516; Robert V. Hannaford, "You Ought to Derive 'Ought' from 'Is,'" *Ethics*, vol. 82, no. 2 (January 1972): 155–162; and Warren J. Samuels, "You Cannot Derive 'Ought' from 'Is,'" *Ethics*, vol. 83, no. 2 (January 1973): 159–162.

4. The argument here is Kantian, not Hobbesian. See Immanuel Kant, *The Metaphysics of Morals*, trans. from German by Mary Gregor (Cambridge: Cambridge University Press, 1991), 130–133, 176–177; Sven Arntzen, "Kant's Denial of Absolute Sovereignty," *Pacific Philosophical Quarterly*, vol. 76, no. 1 (March 1995): 1–16; and Peter Nicholson, "Kant on the Duty Never to Resist the Sovereign," *Ethics*, vol. 86, no. 3 (April 1976): 214–230.

5. Bernard Yack, "Popular Sovereignty and Nationalism," *Political Theory*, vol. 29, no. 4 (August 2001): 530.

6. Mark Biondich, *Stjepan Radic, the Croat Peasant Party, and the Politics of Mass Mobilization, 1904–1928* (Toronto: University of Toronto Press, 2000), pp. 143–148, 154–155; and Ivo Perić, *Stjepan Radić 1871,–1928.* (Zagreb: Dom i Svijet, 2003), pp. 291–375.

7. Clifford Geertz, "After the Revolution," in Geertz (ed.), *The Interpretation of Cultures* (New York: Basic Books, 1973), p. 245, as quoted in Helmut Walser Smith, *German Nationalism and Religious Conflict: Culture, Ideology, Politics, 1870–1914* (Princeton, N.J.: Princeton University Press, 1995), p. 239.

8. The *Načertanije,* a program for a Greater Serbian state, was drafted in 1844 but kept secret; it was first revealed in 1902.

9. John Lampe, *Yugoslavia as History: Twice There Was a Country* (Cambridge: Cambridge University Press, 1996), p. 52.

10. For discussion, see Milada Paulová, *Jugoslavenski odbor (Povijest Jugoslavenske emigracije za svjetskog rata od 1914.–1918.)* (Zagreb: Prosvjetna Nakladna Zadruga, n.d. [1924]), pp. 41–56.

11. Šerbo Rastoder, "A Short Review of the History of Montenegro," in Florian Bieber (ed.), *Montenegro in Transition: Problems of Identity and Statehood* (Baden-Baden: Nomos Verlagsgesellschaft, 2003), p. 129.

12. Regarding Montenegrin unification with Serbia, see Branislav Gligorijević, *Kralj Aleksandar Karadjordjević,* vol. 1: *Ujedinjenje Srpskih zemalja* (Belgrade: Beogradski izdavačkografički zavod, 1996), pp. 421–423.

13. Quoted in Mark Thompson, *A Paper House: The Ending of Yugoslavia* (New York: Pantheon Books, 1992), p. 259.

14. Šaćir Filandra, *Bošnjačka politika u XX. stoljeću* (Sarajevo: Sejtarija, 1998), pp. 33–42.

15. Thompson, *Paper House,* p. 201.

16. See discussion in Wolf Dietrich Behschnitt, *Nationalismus bei Serben und Kroaten, 1830–1914* (Munich: R. Oldenbourg Verlag, 1980), pp. 65–82. See also *Vuk Karadžić. Spomenica 1864–1964* (Belgrade: Vukov i Dositejev muzej and Nolit, 1966); Miljana Radovanović, *Vuk Karadžić, etnograf i folklorist* (Belgrade: Srpska akademija nauka i umetnosti, 1973); and Mirko Skakić, *Vuk Karadžić u svom i današnnjem vremenu, ili Uočavanja sa vremenske distance* (Belgrade: NB "Vuk Karadžić," 1998).

17. See Ferdo Šišić, *Biskup Strosmajer i južnoslovenska misao* (Belgrade and Novi Sad: Štamparsko poduzeće 'Zastava,' 1922); Charles Joseph Slovak III, "Josip Juraj Strossmayer, a Balkan Bishop: The Early Years, 1815–1854" (Ph.D. dissertation, University of Illinois at Urbana-Champaign, 1974); Kosta Milutinović, *Strosmajer i jugoslovensko pitanje* (Novi Sad: Institut za izučavanje istorije Vojvodine, 1976); Pedro Ramet, "From Strossmayer to Stepinac: Croatian National Ideology and Catholicism," *Canadian Review of Studies in Nationalism,* vol. 12, no. 1 (Spring 1985); and Ivo Padovan (ed.), *Zbornik radova o Josipu Jurju Strossmayeru* (Zagreb: Hrvatska akademija znanosti i umjetnosti, 1997).

18. Sabrina P. Ramet, "Ante Starčević: Liberal Champion of a 'Citizens' State,'" in Sabrina P. Ramet, James R. Felak, and Herbert J. Ellison (eds.), *Nations and Nationalisms in East-Central Europe, 1806–1948: A Festschrift for Peter F. Sugar* (Bloomington, Ind.: Slavica Publishers, 2003), p. 138. See also V. Bogdanov, *Ante Starčević i Hrvatska politika* (Zagreb: Biblioteka Nezavisnih Pisaca, 1937); Vaso Bogdanov, *Starčević i Stranka prava prema Srbima i prema jedinstvenu Južnoslavenskih naroda* (Zagreb: Naklada 'Školska knjiga', 1951); and Pavo Barišić, "Staat und Nation bei Ante Starčević," *Zeitschrift für Politik,* vol. 43, no. 3 (September 1996).

19. On Frank, see Mirjana Gross and Agneza Szabo, *Prema hrvatskome gradjanskom društnvu* (Zagreb: Globus, 1992), passim; and Mirjana Gross, *Izvorno pravašntvo: Ideologija, agitacija, pokret* (Zagreb: Golden Marketing, 2000), pp. 688–722. See also Stjepan Matković, *Čista stranka prava 1895.–1903* (Zagreb: Hrvatski Institut za Povijest, 2001).

20. See L. Südland [Ivo Pilar], *Die Südslawische Frage und der Weltkrieg* (Vienna: Manzsche K.u.K. Hofs-u. Universitäts-Buchhandlung, 1918).

21. Branimir Anzulović, *Heavenly Serbia: From Myth to Genocide* (London: Hurst, 1999), p. 30.

22. Quoted in Branko Petranović, *Istorija Jugoslavije, 1918–1988*, vol. 1: *Kraljevina Jugoslavija 1914–1941* (Belgrade: Nolit, 1988), p. 11.

23. Dunja Melčić, "Der Jugoslawismus und sein Ende," in D. Melčić (ed.), *Der Jugoslaw-ien-Krieg. Handbuch zu Vorgeschichte, Verlauf und Konsequenzen* (Opladen/Wiesbaden: Westdeutscher Verlag, 1999), p. 209. See also Behschnitt, *Nationalismus bei Serben und Kroaten*, pp. 60, 66, 133, 140–147; Ferdo Šišić, *Pregled povijesti Hrvatskoga naroda* (Zagreb: Nakladni Zavod MH, 1975), pp. 401–412; and Elinor Murray Despalatović, *Ljudevit Gaj and the Illyrian Movement* (Boulder, Colo.: East European Monographs, 1975).

24. Quoted in Zlatko Matijević, *Slom politike katoličkog jugoslavenstva: Hrvatska pučka stranka u političkom životu Kraljevine SHS (1919.–1929.)* (Zagreb: Hrvatski institut za povijest, 1998), p. 33.

25. Zlatko Matijević, "Odjeci Svibanjske deklaracije Jugoslavenskog kluba u Hrvatskoj, te Bosni i Hercegovini (1917.–1918. Godine)," in *Spomenica Ljube Bobana* (Zagreb, 1996), pp. 245–249; and Mustafa Imamović, *Historija Bošnjaka*, 2nd ed. (Sarajevo: Bošnjacka zajednica kulture, 1998), p. 476.

26. Matijević, *Slom politike katoličkog jugoslavenstva*, p. 61.

27. Svetozar Pribićević, *Diktatura Kralja Aleksandra*, trans. from French by Andra Milosavljević (Belgrade: Prosveta, 1952), p. 51.

28. Mahnič was a Slovene by birth. In Croatian publications, his name is usually spelled "Mahnić."

29. Quoted in Matijević, *Slom politike katoličkog jugoslavenstva*, p. 65.

30. Petranović, *Istorija Jugoslavije*, vol. 1, p. 13.

31. Paulová, *Jugoslavenski odbor*, p. 32.

32. Ibid., pp. 331–333, 340–341.

33. The text of the Korfu Declaration is given in ibid., pp. 342–345.

34. Nedim Šarac, *Uspostavljanje šestojanuarskog režima 1929. godine, sa posebnim osvrtom na Bosnu i Hercegovinu* (Sarajevo: Svjetlost, 1975), p. 25.

35. *Vojvoda* is usually translated as "duke," as if it were a royal title and as if the wife of the "*Vojvoda*" would be a "duchess." In fact, the conventional translation is completely misleading. The title *Vojvoda* could be better translated as "commander."

36. Imamović, *Historija Bošnjaka*, p. 480.

37. Ferdo Čulinović, *Jugoslavija izmedju dva rata* (Zagreb: Jugoslavenska akademija znanosti i umjetnosti, 1961), vol. 1, pp. 105–107.

38. Janko Šimrak, theologian and later director of the Catholic daily newspaper *Hrvatska Straža* from 1929 to 1941, was among the members of the delegation. He felt strongly that the future state community should assume a federal form, with internal borders coinciding with ethnic (and historical) boundaries. See Matijević, *Slom politike katoličkog jugoslavenstva*, p. 73.

39. Regarding Vojvodina, see Čulinović, *Jugoslavija izmedju dva rata*, vol. 1, pp. 119–128; regarding Montenegro, see pp. 129–138.

40. Regarding local reactions to Italian encroachment, see Gligorijević, *Kralj Aleksandar Karadjordjević*, vol. 1, pp. 438–439.

41. Noel Malcolm, *Kosovo: A Short History* (London: Macmillan, 1998), p. 268.

42. Dušan Bilandžić, *Hrvatska moderna povijest* (Zagreb: Golden Marketing, 1999), pp. 68–

69. For a general expostulation of Radić's ideas about federalism and the state structure, see Tihomir Cipek, *Ideja hrvatske države u političkoj misli Stjepana Radića* (Zagreb: Alinea, 2001).

43. Branislav Gligorijević, *Parlament i političke stranke u Jugoslaviji, 1919–1929* (Belgrade: Narodna knjiga, 1979), p. 39; and Petranović, *Istorija Jugoslavije, 1918–1988*, vol. 1, pp. 124–125.

44. Imamović, *Historija Bošnnjaka*, p. 486.

45. Quoted in ibid., p. 486.

46. Ibid., p. 487.

47. Dodge, American Mission/B to State, 3 August 1919, decl. 8 January 1958, in *Records of the Department of State Relating to Internal Affairs of Yugoslavia 1910–1929*, RG-5, 860h.00/0-159, M-358 [hereafter, *Records 1910–29*], Roll 2, frame 0008, at NA; and Šarac, *Uspostavljanje šnestojanuarskog režima*, p. 25.

48. Šarac, *Uspostavljanje šnestojanuarskog režima*, p. 25.

49. For a discussion of the Bulgarian identity of Macedonians at this time and of their desire to be attached to Bulgaria, see Albert Howe Lybyer, *Macedonia at the Paris Peace Conference* (Indianapolis: Central Committee of the Macedonian Political Organization of the United States and Canada, 1944), pp. 5–8.

50. Regarding murders and disappearances, Ivo Banac, *The National Question in Yugoslavia: Origins, History, Politics* (Ithaca, N.Y.: Cornell University Press, 1984), p. 319; regarding administrative acts, "Macedonia in the Kingdom of the Serbs, Croats and Slovenes," *MI-AN Publishing*, at www.unet.com.mk/mian/shs.htm [accessed 10 August 2000], p. 1. Regarding the way in which Macedonia figured in the kingdom's foreign policy, see Vladan Jovanović, *Jugoslovenska država i južna Srbija, 1918–1929* (Belgrade: INIS, 2002), pp. 147–226.

51. Banac, *National Question*, p. 320. Regarding Chetnik operations in Macedonia 1921–23, see also Nusret Šehić, *Četništvo u Bosni i Hercegovini (1918–1941): Politička uloga i oblici djelatnosti četničkih udruženja* (Sarajevo: Akademija nauka i umjetnosti, 1971), pp. 164–166.

52. "Macedonia in the Kingdom," pp. 1–3.

53. Cited in Banac, *National Question*, p. 319.

54. Regarding the IMRO's operations in the Kingdom, see Stefan Troebst, *Mussolini, Makedonien und die Mächte, 1922–1930* (Cologne and Vienna: Böhlau Verlag, 1987), pp. 120–126, 289–307.

55. Banac, *National Question*, pp. 319–320.

56. Details in Čulinović, *Jugoslavija izmedju dva rata*, vol. 1, pp. 129–138.

57. Rastoder, "Short Review of the History of Montenegro," pp. 131–133. For more extensive discussion of this period in Montenegro's history, see Dragoljub P. Živojinović, *Kraj Kraljevine Crne Gore: Mirovna konferencija i posle, 1918–1921* (Belgrade: Javno preduzeće/Službeni list SRJ, 2002).

58. Banac, *National Question*, pp. 286, 288–289. For more extensive discussion of this period in Montenegro's history, see Dragoljub P. Živojinović, *Kraj Kraljevine Crne Gore: Mirovna konferencija i posle, 1918–1921* (Belgrade: Javno preduzeće/Službeni list SRJ, 2002).

59. Djoko Slijepčević, *Istorija Srpske pravoslavne crkve*, vol. 2: *Od početka XIX veka do kraja drugog svetskog rata* (Belgrade: Beogradski izdavački-grafički zavod, 1991), pp. 558–559; and Rastoder, "Short Review of the History of Montenegro," p. 124, citing Živko Andrijašević, *Kratka istorija Crne Gore 1496–1918* (Bar: Conteco, 2000), pp. 171–172.

60. Milija Šćepanović, "The Exodus of Serbs and Montenegrins 1878–1988," in *Kosovo: Past and Present* (Belgrade: Review of International Affairs, 1989), p. 146; the figure is confirmed (but for the years 1876–1912) in Slavenko Terzić, "Old Serbia in the Eyes of the 'Merciful Angel': The Phenomenon of Historian as a Destructionist," in Slavenko Terzić (ed.), *Response to Noel Malcolm's Book, "Kosovo: A Short History"* (Belgrade: Serbian Academy of Sciences & Arts, 1999), at www.decani.yunet.com/nmalk.html [accessed 6 May 2002], p. 5.

61. Malcolm, *Kosovo,* p. 274.

62. Ibid., pp. 273, 254.

63. Banac, *National Question,* p. 298.

64. Ibid., pp. 303–305.

65. Ibid., p. 299.

66. Miranda Vickers, *Between Serb and Albanian: A History of Kosovo* (New York: Columbia University Press, 1998), p. 105.

67. Imamović, *Historija Bošnnjaka,* p. 490.

68. Noel Malcolm, *Bosnia: A Short History* (Washington Square: New York University Press, 1994), p. 163.

69. Imamović, *Historija Bošnnjaka,* pp. 490–492.

70. Malcolm, *Bosnia,* p. 163.

71. Imamović, *Historija Bošnnjaka,* p. 510.

72. Bosiljka Janjatović, "Karadjordjevićevska centralizacija i položaj Hrvatske u Kraljevstvu (Kraljevini) SHS," *Časopis za suvremenu povijest,* vol. 27, no. 1 (1995): 56–57.

73. Hrvoje Matković, *Povijest Hrvatske seljačke stranke* (Zagreb: Naklada P.I.P. Pavičić, 1999), pp. 75–76.

74. Banac, *National Question,* pp. 248–260; and Zvonimir Kulundžić, *Atentat na Stjepana Radića* (Zagreb: Biblioteka Vremeplov, 1967), pp. 156–59. See also Čulinović, *Jugoslavija izmedju dva rata,* vol. 1, pp. 181–190.

75. T. Karayovonoff, *Les causes de la crise yougoslave* (Budapest: Imprimerie de la Société Anonyme Atheneum, 1929), pp. 11–12.

76. Damjan Guštin, "1.IX.1918—Maister prevzame oblast v Mariboru," in Marjan Drnovšek and Drago Bajt (eds.), *Slovenska kronika XX. stoletja,* vol. 1: *1900–1941* (Ljubljana: Nova revija, 1995), pp. 210–211; and "Maister, Rudolf," in *Enciklopedija Slovenije* (Ljubljana: Mladinska knjiga, 1992), vol. 6, pp. 365–366.

77. Čulinović, *Jugoslavija izmedju dva rata,* vol. 1, pp. 300–301; and Gligorijević, *Parlament i političke stranke,* p. 60.

78. Two of these eventually reopened.

79. Hugh Seton-Watson, *Eastern Europe between the Wars, 1918–1941,* 3rd ed. (Hamden, Conn.: Archon Books, 1962), p. 345. Concerning the expulsion of Hungarians, see also *Aftenposten* (Oslo), 7 December 1934, morning ed., p. 7.

80. Bilandžić, *Hrvatska moderna povijest,* p. 77.

81. Quoted in Charles Jelavich, "Education, Textbooks and South Slav Nationalisms in the Interwar Era," in Norbert Reiter and Holm Sundhausen (eds.), *Allgemeinbildung als Modernisierungsfaktor: Zur Geschichte der Elementarbildung in Südosteuropa von der Aufklärung bis zum Zweiten Weltkrieg* (Berlin and Wiesbaden: Harrassowitz Verlag, 1994), p. 134.

82. Ibid., p. 135.

83. Janjatović, "Karadjordjevićevska centralizacija," p. 58.

84. Ibid., p. 64.

85. Gligorijević, *Parlament i političke stranke,* pp. 74–78; and Banac, *National Question,* pp. 193, 195.

86. Vlasta Jalušić, "Women in Interwar Slovenia," in Sabrina P. Ramet (ed.), *Gender Politics in the Western Balkans: Women and Society in Yugoslavia and the Yugoslav Successor States* (University Park: Pennsylvania State University Press, 1999), p. 57.

87. Thomas Emmert, "Ženski pokret: The Feminist Movement in Serbia in the 1920s," in Ramet, ed., *Gender Politics in the Western Balkans,* pp. 43–44.

88. In spite of Starčević's championing of women's suffrage!

89. Gligorijević, *Parlament i političke stranke,* pp. 68–69; and Bilandžić, *Hrvatska moderna povijest,* p. 73.

90. Matković, *Povijest Hrvatske seljačke stranke,* . p. 87.

91. From the Croatian: Hrvatska republikanska seljačka stranka.

92. Gligorijević, *Parlament i političke stranke,* pp. 90–91; and Matković, *Povijest Hrvatske seljačke stranke,* pp. 88–89.

93. Quoted in Gligorijević, *Parlament i političke stranke,* p. 99. See also Matković, *Povijest Hrvatske seljačke stranke,* pp. 89–91.

94. Gligorijević, *Parlament i političke stranke,* p. 101; and Momčilo Zečević, *Slovenska ljudska stranka i jugoslovensko ujedinjenje, 1917–1921* (Belgrade: Institut za savremenu istoriju i NIP export-press, 1973), pp. 429–443.

95. Quoted in Gligorijević, *Parlament i političke stranke,* p. 101.

96. Imamović, *Historija Bošnnjaka,* p. 501.

97. Regarding the communists, Gligorijević, *Parlament i političke stranke,* p. 299; regarding the HRSS, Biondich, *Stjepan Radić,* p. 176.

98. Čulinović, *Jugoslavija izmedju dva rata,* vol. 1, pp. 360–362.

99. Šarac, *Uspostavljanje šnestojanuarskog režima,* p. 46.

100. From the Serbian, *Organizacija Jugoslovenskih Nacionalista.*

101. Petranović, *Istorija Jugoslavije 1918–1988,* vol. 1, pp. 161–162.

102. Ante Čuvalo, "Persecution of Croats in the First Yugoslavia and Its Political Consequences," *Croatian Studies,* at homepage.altavista.com/croatianstudies/files/hist_pers.html [accessed 23 June 2000], pp. 9–10.

103. Ivan Avakumović, "Yugoslavia's Fascist Movements," in Peter F. Sugar (ed.), *Native Fascism in the Successor States, 1918–1945* (Santa Barbara, Calif.: ABC-Clio, 1971), pp. 136–137; and Čulinović, *Jugoslavija izmedju dva rata,* vol. 1, pp. 388–389.

104. Čulinović, *Jugoslavija izmedju dva rata,* vol. 1, p. 389.

105. From the Serbian, *Srpska Nacionalna Omladina.*

106. Quoted in Čuvalo, "Persecution of Croats," p. 10.

107. From the Croatian, Hrvatska Nacionalna Omladina.

108. Šehić, *Četnišntvo u Bosni i Hercegovini,* p. 65.

109. Šarac, *Uspostavljanje šestojanuarskog režima,* p. 25; and Čuvalo, "Persecution of Croats," p. 8.

110. Čulinović, *Jugoslavija izmedju dva rata,* vol. 1, p. 388.

111. Šehić, *Četništvo u Bosni i Hercegovini,* pp. 63–64.

112. Quoted in Bilandžić, *Hrvatska moderna povijest,* p. 78.

113. Gligorijević, *Parlament i političke stranke,* pp. 123–124; and Šarac, *Uspostavljanje šestojanuarskog režima,* p. 40.

114. Quoted in Gligorijević, *Parlament i političke stranke,* p. 150.

115. Quoted in Atif Purivatra, *Jugoslavenska Muslimanska Organizacija u političkom životu Kraljevine Srba, Hrvata i Slovenaca,* 2nd ed. (Sarajevo: Svjetlost, 1977), p. 147.

116. Gligorijević, *Parlament i političke stranke,* p. 154.

117. Quoted in Jože Pirjevec, *Il giorno di San Vito: Jugoslavia, 1918–1992—Storia di una tragedia* (Torino: Nuova Eri Edizioni Rai, 1993), p. 51.

118. Purivatra, *Jugoslavenska Muslimanska Organizacija,* p. 161; and Gligorijević, *Parlament i političke stranke,* p. 155.

119. Quoted in Gligorijević, *Parlament i političke stranke*, p. 155.

120. Biondich, *Stjepan Radić*, p. 194.

121. Quoted in Gligorijević, *Parlament i političke stranke*, p. 162.

122. Ibid., p. 165.

123. Matković, *Povijest Hrvatske seljačke stranke*, p. 165.

124. Biondich, *Stjepan Radic*, p. 199.

125. Matković, *Povijest Hrvatske seljacke stranke*, p. 179.

126. Čulinović, *Jugoslavija izmedju dva rata*, vol. 1, p. 442.

127. Gligorijević, *Parlament i političke stranke*, p. 181.

128. Nada Boškovska, "Jugoslawisch-Makedonien in der Zwischenkriegszeit: Eine Randregion zwischen Repression und Integration" (Habilitationsschrift, Universität Zürich, 2001), pp. 52–54, 66.

129. Purivatra, *Jugoslavenska Muslimanska Organizacija*, p. 189.

130. Gligorijević, *Parlament i političke stranke*, p. 188.

131. The figures which follow are derived from ibid., pp. 188–195, and Matković, *Povijest Hrvatske seljačke stranke*, p. 185.

132. Gligorijević, *Parlament i političke stranke*, p. 199.

133. Quoted in ibid., p. 201.

134. Biondich, *Stjepan Radić*, p. 203.

135. Ibid., pp. 214–215.

136. Ibid., p. 216.

137. Čulinović, *Jugslavija izmedju dva rata*, vol. 1, p. 485.

138. Gligorijević, *Parlament i političke stranke*, p. 210.

139. Matković, *Povijest Hrvatske seljačke stranke*, pp. 210–211.

140. Gligorijević, *Parlament i političke stranke*, p. 223.

141. Čulinović, *Jugoslavija izmedju dva rata*, vol. 1, pp. 496–497.

142. Details in Purivatra, *Jugoslavenska Muslimanska Organizacija*, pp. 254–258.

143. The Democratic Party and the JMO had, in the meantime, formed a bloc of their own, the "Democratic community," and the proposal was, in fact, sent to the presidency of this bloc.

144. From the Croatian, Seljačko-demokratska koalicija.

145. Nadežda Jovanović, *Politički sukobi u Jugoslaviji 1925–1928* (Belgrade: Izdavačko preduzeće "Rad," 1974), p. 277.

146. Gligorijević, *Parlament i političke stranke*, pp. 245–246.

147. Ibid., p. 250.

148. Quoted in ibid., p. 252.

149. Kulundžić, *Atentat na Stjepana Radića*, pp. 212–213.

150. Jozo Tomasevich, *War and Revolution in Yugoslavia, 1941–1945: Occupation and Collaboration* (Stanford, Calif.: Stanford University Press, 2001), p. 24; confirmed in Josip Horvat, *Politička povijest Hrvatske*, vol. 2 (Zagreb: August Cesarec, 1990), pp. 347–348.

151. *Chicago Tribune*, 21 June 1928, p. 3.

152. Quoted in Matković, *Povijest Hrvatske seljačke stranke*, p. 251.

153. Kulundžić, *Atentat na Stjepana Radica*, p. 211. On 24 July 1928, S. Radić told a group of people that he considered it possible that Ninko Perić, the president of the Assembly, and Prime Minister Vukićević had personally authorized the attempt on his life on 29 June. See Šarac, *Uspostavljanje šestojanuarskog režima*, p. 162, n. 2. *Dom*, the HSS organ, directly accused

members of the Radical and Democratic Parties of complicity in the shootings, and Radić himself demanded that indictments be brought against Assembly president Perić, Prime Minister Vukičević, and 21 Serbian deputies. See James J. Sadkovich, *Italian Support for Croatian Separatism, 1927–1937* (New York and London: Garland, 1987), p. 53; and Hrvoje Matković, *Povijest Jugoslavije*, 2nd enlarged ed. (Zagreb: Naklada P. I. P. Pavičić, 2003), p. 166.

154. *Chicago Tribune*, 21 June 1928, p. 3.

155. Jovanović, *Politički sukobi*, p. 280.

156. *Chicago Tribune*, 22 June 1928, p. 3.

157. Matković, *Povijest Hrvatske seljačke stranke*, pp. 255–256; and Gligorijević, *Parlament i političke stranke*, pp. 260–261.

158. Gligorijević, *Parlament i političke stranke*, p. 264.

159. Bilandžić, *Hrvatska moderna povijest*, p. 85.

160. Quoted in Ljubo Boban, *Maček i politika Hrvatske seljačke stranke, 1928–1941: Iz povijesti hrvatskog pitanja* (Zagreb: Liber, 1974), vol. 1, p. 30.

161. Quoted in Karayovonoff, *Les causes de la crise*, p. 4.

162. Quoted in Biondich, *Stjepan Radić*, p. 207.

163. Bilandžić, *Hrvatska moderna povijest*, p. 105.

164. Petranović, *Istorija Jugoslavije*, vol. 1, pp. 61, 67; and Seton-Watson, *Eastern Europe between the Wars*, p. 75.

3. The First Yugoslavia, Part 2

1. Todor Stojkov, *Opozicija u vreme šestojanuarske diktature, 1929–1935* (Belgrade: Prosveta, 1969), p. 340. Regarding the Croatian economic establishment, confirmed in Dušan Bilandžić, *Hrvatska moderna povijest* (Zagreb: Golden Marketing, 1999), p. 89. Regarding French understanding, confirmed in François Broche, *Assassinat de Alexandre Ier et Louis Barthou: Marseille, le 9 Octobre 1934* (Paris: Balland, 1977), pp. 21–22.

2. Nedim Šarac, *Uspostavljanje šestojanuarskog režima 1929. godine, sa posebnim osvrtom na Bosnu i Hercegovinu* (Sarajevo: Svjetlost, 1975), p. 197.

3. Ibid., p. 201.

4. Ibid., p. 207. For Jovanović's views, see Dragoljub Jovanović, *Sloboda od straha. Izabrane političke rasprave*, ed. Nadežda Jovanović and Božidar Jakšić (Belgrade: Filip Višnjić and Naučna Knjiga, 1991).

5. Šarac, Uspostavljanje, pp. 198, 199, 219 n. 51.

6. Jože Pirjevec, *Il giorno di San Vito: Jugoslavia 1918–1992—Storia di una Tragedia* Torino: Nuova Era Edizioni, 1993), p. 90.

7. Mentioned in HQ. IV Army District to the Ban, Pov. B. br. 2611 (7 June 1936), in *Savska Banovina, Državna zaštita: Strogo povjerljivi spisi 1929–1933. g.*, Kutije 1152–1320, at *Hrvatski Državni Arhiv* (Zagreb) [hereafter, SBDZ–SPS], Box 21, Strogo pov. Spisi br. 94–626 / 1936. g. The boxes in this collection of materials were renumbered after the title was assigned; although the title indicates that the collection includes materials from 1929 to 1933, in fact the collection includes materials up through 1939.

8. See, for example, Uprava policije u Zagreb [hereafter, UPZ], predsednički ured, br. 1 (1 January 1931), br. 20 (2 January 1931), br. 90 (3 January 1931), br. 130 (4 January 1931), br. 200 (5 January 1931), br. 300 (6 January 1931), br. 350 (7 January 1931), br. 380 (8 January 1931), and br. 500 (9 January 1931), in SBDZ-SPS, Box 3, br. 1-259 / 1931. g.

9. Rothschild says that the assassins "apparently enjoyed police protection." Joseph Rothschild, *East Central Europe between the Two World Wars* (Seattle: University of Washington Press, 1974), p. 240.

10. The defectors were Stanko Šibenik, Nikola Preka, Mirko Najdorfer, and Ivan Švegl. Hrvoje Matković, *Povijest Hrvatske seljačke stranke* (Zagreb: Naklada P.I.P. Pavičić, 1999), p. 297.

11. Ivo Goldstein, *Croatia: A History,* trans. from Croatian by Nikolina Jovanović (McGill-Queen's University Press, 1999), p. 124.

12. Fikreta Jelić-Butić, *Ustaše i Nezavisna Država Hrvatska 1941–1945* [hereafter, *Ustaše i NDH*] (Zagreb: S.N. Liber & Školska knjiga, 1977), p. 16.

13. Ibid., pp. 18–19.

14. James J. Sadkovich, *Italian Support for Croatian Separatism, 1927–1937* (New York and London: Garland, 1987), p. 135. See also the photo of Košutić with Pavelić, taken in Livorno, Italy, in 1929, reproduced in Matković, *Povijest,* p. 293.

15. Jelić-Butić, *Ustaše i NDH,* p. 21.

16. On the glorification of violence, see Sadkovich, *Italian Support,* p. 158; on the characteristics of fascism, see Roger D. Griffin, *The Nature of Fascism* (New York: St. Martin's Press, 1991).

17. Jelić-Butić, *Ustaša i NDH,* p. 23.

18. Sresko načelstvo [hereafter, SN] (Koprivnica) to K-ODZ, Pov. Br. 496 (20 April 1932), in SBDZ-SPS, Box 70, Pov. Spisi, 1932, br. 9406-9857.

19. Sadkovich, *Italian Support,* pp. 169, 176, 179.

20. *The Times* (London), 8 October 1932, p. 11, and 10 October 1932, p. 13.

21. K-ODZ to all county administrators and to all city police chiefs, Pov. II br. 28187 (28 October 1932), in SBDZ-SPS, Box 99, Pov. II Spisi, 1932, br. 28117-28990.

22. "Optužnica" br. 580-34/12, signed by the public prosecutor (Belgrade, 17 June 1934), in SBDZ-SPS, Box 98, Pov. II Spisi 1932, 26853-28116.

23. Stojkov, *Opozicija u vreme,* pp. 91–92.

24. Pirjevec, *Il giorno di San Vito,* pp. 90–91; and Matković, *Povijest,* pp. 297–299. Šufflay was the author of the highly regarded book *Srbi i Arbanaši* [Serbs and Albanians], published in 1925.

25. Dragoš Jevtić, "O ustavnim pravima gradjana po ustavu Kraljevine Jugoslavije od 3. Septembra 1931. godine," in *Istorijski glasnik* (Belgrade), no. 1–2 (1975): 52, 57, 62.

26. Stojkov, *Opozicija u vreme,* pp. 135, 159–162, 170–173.

27. See examples in SBDZ-SPS, Box 70, Pov. spisi, 1932, br. 9406-9857.

28. Matković, *Povijest,* p. 304.

29. *The Times,* 2 June 1932, p. 9.

30. *The Times,* 28 January 1932, p. 9; my emphasis.

31. Matković, *Povijest,* p. 308; and Ljubo Boban, *Maček i politika Hrvatske seljačke stranke 1928–1941,* vol. 1 (Zagreb: Liber, 1974), pp. 82–83.

32. Quoted in Matković, *Povijest,* p. 312.

33. Ibid., p. 313.

34. Quoted in Vladko Maček, *In the Struggle for Freedom,* trans. from Croatian by Elizabeth and Stjepan Gazi (University Park: Pennsylvania State University Press, 1957), p. 139.

35. Pirjevec, *Il giorno di San Vito,* pp. 98–99.

36. Matković, *Povijest,* p. 324.

37. Regarding the Belgrade trial, *The Times,* 29 April 1931, p. 13; 25 May 1931, p. 9; and 2 June 1931, p. 13; regarding the Zagreb trial, *The Times,* 7 May 1931, p. 13, and 24 June 1931, p. 15; regarding the Maribor trial, *The Times,* 2 June 1932, p. 9, and 17 June 1932, p. 13; regarding the Pernar trial, *The Times,* 7 March 1933, p. 13.

38. Sadkovich, *Italian Support*, p. 207.

39. The government did not appreciate Korošec's suggestions and, accordingly, interned him, in early 1933, in Vrnjačka banja, moving him later to Tuzla, and eventually to internment on the island of Hvar.

40. Komandant-pukovnik, Savski žandarmeriski puk to K-ODZ, Pov. OB, br. 2502 (13 December 1932), in SBDZ-SPS, Box 104, Pov. Spisi, 1932, br. 33171-35702.

41. Stojkov, *Opozicija u vreme*, pp. 190, 219, 220–221.

42. Ibid., pp. 181–182.

43. *The Times*, 2 June 1932, p. 9.

44. Stojkov, *Opozicija u vreme*, pp. 183–184.

45. Ibid., pp. 242–244.

46. Regarding Sunj and Orahovica, SN (Petrinja) to K-ODZ, Pov. Br. 1024 (23 December 1929), and SN (Našice) to K-ODZ, II. pov. br. 16796 (9 January 1930), in SBDZ-SPS, Box 99, Pov. II Spisi, 1932, br. 28117-28990; regarding Rajić, SN (Novska) to K-ODZ, Pov. br. 1230 (29 December 1929), in ibid.

47. See *Pravila udruženenja četnika 'Petar Mrkonjić' Kraljevine Srba, Hrvata i Slovenaca za Kralja i Otadžbinu, sa izmenama i dopunama od 29. Juna 1928. godine* (Belgrade: M. Erlenvajn, 1928).

48. *Student*, no. 1 (1934), attached to Upravnik policije UPZ pretsednički ured to Kraljevska Banska Uprava Savske Banovine u Zagrebu [hereafter KBUSBZ], Otsek za državnu zaštitu [hereafter, ODZ], Str. pov. br. 46/1934 (15 May 1934); and Pomoćnik za Upravnika policije to KBUSBZ, ODZ, Pov. br. 20.638/1934 (13 September 1934)—both in SBDZ-SPS, Box 10, br. 118-292/1934. g.

49. According to Ferdo Čulinović, *Jugoslavija izmedju dva rata*, vol. 2 (Zagreb: Jugoslavenska Akademija Znanosti i Umjetnosti, 1961), p. 60.

50. Ibid., p. 56.

51. Bilandžić, *Hrvatska moderna povijest*, p. 88.

52. Ministarstvo Unutrašnjih Poslova [hereafter, MUP] (Belgrade), ODZ to K-ODZ, Pov. I br. 46455 (14 December 1932), in SBDZ-SPS, Box 104, Pov. Spisi, 1932, br. 33171-35702.

53. Ibid.

54. For example, the anti-regime demonstrations in Rijeka in December 1932. On this point, see Pretstojništvo gradske policije u Susaku VII. granični sektor to K-ODZ, Str. pov. br. 119 (20 December 1932); and Komandant-pukovnik, Savski žandarmeriski puk to K-ODZ, Pov. JB br. 1303 (20 December 1932)—both in SBDZ-SPS, Box 104, Pov. Spisi, 1932, br. 33171-35702.

55. *Grič*, European supplement to *Hrvatski domobran* (Buenos Aires), 21 May 1932, p. 3.

56. *Grič*, 4 June 1932, p. 3.

57. SN (Ludbreg) to K-ODZ, Pov. br. 337 (20 April 1932), in SBDZ-SPS, Box 70, Pov. spisi, 1932, br. 9406-9857.

58. Very loosely translated, taking full "poetic" license, from: "Tamo dolje oko Niša / krv se lije kano kiša, / Kad je prva kugla pala, / Od Račića radikala. / U kugli je tvrdo gvoždje, / Tak su pali naše vodje. / Oj Hrvatska majko mila, / Sve si tuge prepatila / O Srbine, neka neka, / I tebe tvoja sudba čeka. / Aleksandru kralju 'mili' / Sav hrvatski narod cvili. / Aleksandru neka, neka, / I tebe tvoja sudba čeka." *Grič*, 20 August 1932, p. 4.

59. Broche, *Assassinat de Alexandre Ier*, pp. 47–48, 52–53. See also the commentary in *Aftenposten*, 21 March 1934, evening ed., p. 3.

60. HQ Intelligence Center, 6825 HQ & HQS Company, Military Intelligence Service in Austria, APO SH, U.S. Army, *Special Investigation and Interrogation Report: The Croatian*

National Independence Movement, 9 April 1946, C, decl. 29 January 1986, auth. Para 1-603 DoD 5200, I-R, in Records of the Army Staff, ROACS, G-2, Intelligence RIRR, *Security Classified Intelligence and Investigative Dossiers, 1939–76,* IRR Impersonal File, RG 319, Stack Area 270, Row A, Box 107, file ZF010183 (Ustashi), at NA.

61. Broche, *Assassinat de Alexandre Ier,* pp. 58–59.

62. Ibid., pp. 75, 116, 135, and 155; Croatian grief confirmed in KBUSBZ, ODZ, Str. Pov. br. 469/1934 (20 October 1934), in SBDZ-SPS, Box 11, br. 308-703/1934. g. The king's ability to exploit royal mystique and his own personal charm to win over many Croats, in spite of the harshness of his rule, is also confirmed in *Aftenposten,* 11 October 1934, morning ed., p. 1.

63. UPZ, Otsek opšte policije to KBUSBZ, ODZ, Pov. br. 26486/1934 (2 November 1934), in SBDZ-SPS, Box 11, br. 308-703/1934. g.

64. Details in *Aftenposten,* 10 October 1934, morning ed., p. 1; and *Aftenposten,* 12 October 1934, morning ed., p. 6.

65. *Aftenposten,* 15 October 1934, morning ed., p. 6.

66. *Aftenposten,* 16 October 1934, morning ed., p. 6; and *Aftenposten,* 7 December 1934, morning ed., p. 7.

67. *Aftenposten,* 16 November 1934, morning ed., p. 1.

68. Sadkovich, *Italian Support,* pp. 251–252, 261, 255.

69. See, for example, SN (Jastrebarsko) to KBUSBZ-ODZ, Str. Pov. 46/1935 (14 May 1935), in SBDZ-SPS, Box 18, br. 578-691/1935. Regarding Maček's release, see also Matković, *Povijest,* p. 336; and Boban, *Maček i politika,* vol. 1, pp. 167–169.

70. Stojkov, *Opozicija u vreme,* pp. 299–301.

71. SNN (Sl. Požega) to KBU-II.-ODZ, Str. Pov. br. 42/1935 (17 May 1935), in SBDZ-SPS, Box 18, br. 578-691/1935.

72. SN (Karlovac) to KBUSBZ-ODZ, Str. Pov. br. 32/1935 (17 May 1935), in SBDZ-SPS, Box 18, br. 578-691/1935.

73. SN (Vukovar) to KBUSBZ-ODZ, Str. Pov. br. 44/1935 (17 May 1935), in SBDZ-SPS, Box 18, br. 578-691/1935.

74. SN (Zagreb) to KBUSBZ-ODZ, Pov. br. 817 (19 May 1935), in SBDZ-SPS, Box 18, br. 578-691/1935.

75. SN (Petrinja) to KBU-ODZ, Strogo Pov. br. 31/1935 (16 May 1935), in SBDZ-SPS, Box 18, br. 578-691/1935.

76. SN (Gospić) to KBU-ODZ, Str. Pov. br. 43/1935 (17 May 1935), in SBDZ-SPS, Box 18, br. 578-691/1935.

77. SN (Prelog) to KBUSBZ-ODZ, Str. Pov. br. 42/1935 (11 May 1935), in SBDZ-SPS, Box 18, br. 578-691/1935.

78. Čulinović, *Jugoslavija izmedju dva rata,* vol. 2, p. 132.

79. Stojkov, *Opozicija u vreme,* pp. 311–312.

80. Quoted in ibid., p. 315.

81. Mustafa Imamović, *Historija Bošnjaka,* 2nd ed. (Sarajevo: Bošnjačka zajednica kulture, 1998), pp. 508–509.

82. Sadkovich, *Italian Support,* p. 203. On 4 December 1927, the Ministry of Faiths of the Kingdom of the SHS actually acknowledged that the organs of state were actively involved in promoting Orthodox and Old Catholic proselytism at the expense of Catholicism. See Roko Rogošić, *Stanje Kat. Crkve u Jugoslaviji do sporazuma* (Šibenik: Pučka tiskara, 1940), p. 14. As of 1933, there were some persons in Sušak agitating for the withdrawal of the Catholic Church from papal authority, thus setting up an autocephalous "Yugoslav Catholic Church" (*Jugoslavenska katolička crkva*). See Marohnić v.r., Biskupski ordinarijat (Senj) to Martin Bubaj,

administrator of the Church of St. Križa, 7 February 1933, in SBDZ-SPS, Box 121, Pov. Spisi, 1933, br. 2131-2686.

83. Jerzy Kloczowski, "Katholiken und Protestanten in Ostmitteleuropa," in Jean-Marie Mayeur (ed.), *Die Geschichte des Christentums—Religion ! Politik ! Kultur,* vol. 12: *Erster und Zweiter Weltkrieg, Demokratien und Totalitäre Systeme (1914–1958),* trans. from French by Kurt Meier (Freiburg/Basel/Vienna: Herder Verlag, 1992), p. 892.

84. Rogošić, *Stanje Kat. Crkve,* pp. 24–25.

85. Ibid., pp. 17–19.

86. Ante Ciliga, in interview with *Il Popolo Lombardo* (Milano), 17 March 1951, encl. no. 1 to dispatch 2977 (11 April 1951), U, Outerbridge Horsey, Counselor/Rome to State, 768.00/4-1151, in *Records of the U. S. Department of State Relating to the International Affairs of Yugoslavia 1950–1954,* Decimal file 768 (RG-59, LM77), at NA.

87. *Glasnik* (Belgrade), July 1924), as quoted in Rogošić, *Stanje Kat. Crkve,* p. 11.

88. Regarding Bauer, ibid., p. 204; regarding Stepinac and the Croatian Union, report quoted in memorandum from the Office of His Royal Highness, Pov. br. 10204 to KBUSBZ (Belgrade, 25 August 1934), in SBDZ-SPS, Box 11, br. 308-703/1934. g.

89. *Vesnik* (1931), 1054–1064, quoted in *Katolički list* (Zagreb), 30 June 1932, p. 317.

90. *Glasnik,* no. 9 (Belgrade, 1932), quoted in *Katolički list,* 30 June 1932, p. 317.

91. *Glasnik* (Belgrade, 1931), 161–166, as quoted in Rogošić, *Stanje Kat. Crkve,* p. 40.

92. Kloczowski, "Katholiken und Protestanten," p. 892.

93. Rogošić, *Stanje Kat. Crkve,* p. 70.

94. Miloš Mišović, *Srpska crkva i konkordatska kriza* (Belgrade: Sloboda, 1983), p. 29.

95. Ibid., p. 41.

96. Ibid., p. 48.

97. Ibid., p. 49.

98. Anonymous [Bishop Platon], *Primedbe i prigovori na projekat Konkordata izmedju naše države i Vatikana* (Sremski Karlovci: Patrijaršija štamparija, 1936).

99. Mišović, *Srpska crkva i konkordatska,* p. 56.

100. *The Times,* 5 January 1937, p. 11.

101. *The Times,* 8 July 1937, p. 15.

102. *Hrvatska straža* (Zagreb), 9 July 1937, p. 3.

103. *Hrvatska straža,* 16 July 1937, p. 3.

104. *The Times,* 20 July 1937, p. 16; and *Hrvatska straža,* 21 July 1937, p. 3.

105. Quoted in *The Times,* 20 July 1937, p. 16.

106. Quoted in *The Times,* 20 July 1937, p. 16. In fact, the bishop of Šabac subsequently recovered. See *The Times,* 27 July 1937, p. 13; also *Katolički list,* 29 July 1937, pp. 365–369.

107. *Hrvatska straža,* 22 July 1937, p. 3.

108. *Hrvatska straža,* 25 July 1937, p. 3.

109. Known popularly as the minister of war.

110. *The Times,* 3 August 1937, p. 9; 9 August 1937, p. 9; and 8 October 1937, p. 13.

111. Mišović, *Srpska crkva i konkordatska,* pp. 145, 147–148.

112. Stella Alexander, *The Triple Myth: A Life of Archbishop Alojzije Stepinac* (Boulder, Colo.: East European Monographs, 1987), p. 36.

113. Branko Petranović, *Istorija Jugoslavije 1918–1988,* vol. 1: *Kraljevina Jugoslavija 1914–1941* (Belgrade: Nolit, 1988), p. 98.

114. The 45,000 and 60,000 figures are derived from Christine von Kohl and Wolfgang

Libal, *Kosovo: Gordischer Knoten des Balkan* (Vienna and Zürich: Europaverlag, 1992), pp. 42–43, 44. Elez Biberaj estimates the number of Serb and Montenegrin "colonists" who settled in Kosovo in 1918–41 at 40,000, while Tim Judah sets the figure at 70,000. See E. Biberaj, *Albania: A Socialist Maverick* (Boulder, Colo.: Westview Press, 1990), p. 113; and T. Judah, *Kosovo: War and Revenge* (New Haven, Conn.: Yale University Press, 2000), p. 22. Dušan Janjić sets the number of Albanians displaced in these years at about 40,000. See Dušan Janjić, "National Identities, Movements and Nationalism of Serbs and Albanians," *Balkan Forum,* vol. 3, no. 1 (March 1995): 69, n. 48.

115. Ivo Banac, *The National Question in Yugoslavia: Origins, History, Politics* (Ithaca, N.Y.: Cornell University Press, 1984), pp. 299–301.

116. Excerpted in Judah, *Kosovo,* pp. 23–24.

117. Noel Malcolm, *Kosovo: A Short History* (London: Macmillan, 1998), pp. 285–286; confirmed in Judah, *Kosovo,* pp. 22–23; reconfirmed in Miranda Vickers, *Between Serb and Albanian: A History of Kosovo* (New York: Columbia University Press, 1998), p. 118.

118. Vickers, *Between Serb and Albanian,* p. 119.

119. Quoted in Matkovic, *Povijest,* pp. 345–346.

120. Petranović, *Istorija Jugoslavije 1918–1988,* vol. 1, p. 280.

121. Philip J. Cohen, *Serbia's Secret War: Propaganda and the Deceit of History* (College Station: Texas A&M University Press, 1996), p. 14.

122. Inspector, MUP to KBUSBZ, Str. Pov. br. 396 (5 April 1935), in SBDZ-SPS, Box 15, br. 120-196/1935. g.

123. KBUSBZ, ODZ to all district authorities and all city police chiefs et al., Str. Pov. br. 139/1935. god. (26 February 1935), in SBDZ-SPS, Box 15, br. 120-196/1935. g.

124. KBUSBZ-SPS to city police chiefs et al., Str. Pov. br. 1312/35 (4 September 1935), in SBDZ-SPS, Box 15, br. 120-196/1935. g.

125. From the Croatian, *Hrvatska seljačka zaštita.*

126. SN (Samobor) to KBUSBZ-ODZ, Pov. broj 1049 (7 August 1936), in SBDZ-SPS, Box 20, Strogo pov. br. 1-94/1936. g.

127. From the Croatian, Seljačka gospodarska sloga.

128. SGS founding, SN (Slavonski Brod) to KBUSBZ-ODZ, Str. Pov. 12 (17 October 1936), in SBDZ-SPS, Box 20, Strogo pov. br. 1-94/1936. g.; fears of local authorities, SN (Virovitica) to KBU-ODZ, Str. Pov. br. 24 (5 November 1936), in SBDZ-SPS, Box 20, Strogo pov. br. 1-94/1936. g.

129. SN (Kutina) to KBUSBZ-ODZ, Pov. broj 893 (31 August 1936), in SBDZ-SPS, Box 20, Strogo pov. br.oj 1-94/1936. g.

130. Komandir, Zagrebačka žandarm. četa to KBUSBZ, Pov. br. 434 (24 June 1936), in SBDZ-SPS, Box 21, Strogo pov. spisi, br. 94-626/1936. g.

131. Izveštaj stanice Vrapce Pov. br. 372 (24 June 1936), in SBDZ-SPS, Box 21, Strogo pov. spisi, br. 94-626/1936. g.

132. SN (Zagreb) to KBUSBZ-ODZ, II. Pov., Str. Pov. br. 1 (17 June 1936), in SBDZ-SPS, Box 21, Strogo pov. spisi br. 94-626/1936. g.

133. SN (Pregrada) to K-ODZ, Str. Pov. br. 20 (3 November 1937), in SBDZ-SPS, Box 22, Str. pov. 1937, br. 1-1016.

134. Potpukovnik, Savski žandarmeriski puk to K-ODZ, Pov. JB. br. 1085 (6 December 1937), in SBDZ-SPS, Str. pov. 1937, br. 1-1016.

135. SN (Sisak) to K-ODZ, Str. Pov. II (11 June 1937), in SBDZ-SPS, Str. pov. 1937, br. 1-1016.

136. Spreading, K-ODZ to UPZ-OOP, all county administrators, and all city police chiefs,

Str. Pov. br. 669 (5 March 1938); weaponry, UPZ, Otsek opšte policije to K-ODZ, Str. Pov. br. 161 (3 January 1939); department for military affairs, K-ODZ to UPZ, Str. Pov. br. 1791 (24 December 1938); uniforms, SN (Vojnic) to K-ODZ, Pov. br. 285 (11 February 1939); *Hrvatski list,* as summarized in *Bilten,* Odeljenja za državnu zaštitu, Strogo poverljivo (April 1939), p. 6—all in SBDZ-SPS, Box 27, Str. Pov. 1939.

137. Frank C. Littlefield, *Germany and Yugoslavia, 1933–1941: The German Conquest of Yugoslavia* (Boulder, Colo.: East European Monographs, 1988), p. 10.

138. Quoted in Čulinović, *Jugoslavija izmedju dva rata,* vol. 2, p. 114.

139. Ibid., pp. 114–117.

140. Littlefield, *Germany and Yugoslavia,* pp. 30–32.

141. Ibid., p. 34–35.

142. Čulinović, *Jugoslavija izmedju dva rata,* vol. 2, pp. 132, 130.

143. J. B. Hoptner, *Yugoslavia in Crisis, 1934–1941* (New York: Columbia University Press, 1962), p. 123; confirmed in Srdjan Trifković, "Yugoslavia in Crisis: Europe and the Croat Question, 1939–41," *European History Quarterly,* vol. 23, no. 4 (October 1993): 536.

144. Hoptner, *Yugoslavia in Crisis,* p. 124.

145. Trifković, "Yugoslavia in Crisis," p. 536.

146. Hoptner, *Yugoslavia in Crisis,* p. 128.

147. Regarding contacts with the Italians, see Čulinović, *Jugoslavija izmedju dva rata,* vol. 2, pp. 136–147; Ljubo Boban, *Maček i politika Hrvatske Seljačke Stranke 1928–1941,* vol. 2 (Zagreb: Liber, 1974), pp. 87–90; and Hoptner, *Yugoslavia in Crisis,* pp. 138–139.

148. Trifković, "Yugoslavia in Crisis," pp. 538–539; and Čulinović, *Jugoslavija izmedju dva rata,* vol. 2, pp. 137–139.

149. Petranović, *Istorija Jugoslavije,* vol. 1, pp. 291–292.

150. Matković, *Povijest,* pp. 395–396.

151. Ibid., p. 396; and Čulinović, *Jugoslavija izmedju dva rata,* vol. 2, p. 141.

152. Text of the ordinance in Čulinović, *Jugoslavija izmedju dva rata,* vol. 2, pp. 148–150. See also Ivo Perić, *Vladko Maček: Politički portret* (Zagreb: Golden Marketing, 2003), pp. 223–228.

153. Čulinović, *Jugoslavija izmedju dva rata,* vol. 2, pp. 168–169.

154. Matković, *Povijest,* p. 405.

155. Quoted in Šaćir Filandra, *Bosnjačka politika u XX. stoljecu* (Sarajevo: Sejtarija, 1998), p. 107.

156. Quoted in ibid., p. 111.

157. Ibid., pp. 113–126.

158. *Muslimanski ogranak* in Bosnian.

159. *Nezavisna hrvatska država* (May 1939), in *Bilten,* ODZ, Strogo poverljivo (May 1939), pp. 6–7, in SBDZ-SPS, Box 27, Str. Pov. 1939.

160. Čulinović, *Jugoslavija izmedju dva rata,* vol. 2, pp. 156, 158.

161. More details in ibid., pp. 176–177.

162. Littlefield, *Germany and Yugoslavia,* p. 75.

163. Ibid., p. 78.

164. Boban, *Maček i politika,* vol. 2, pp. 370–373.

165. Littlefield, *Germany and Yugoslavia,* p. 100.

166. Matteo J. Milazzo, *The Chetnik Movement and The Yugoslav Resistance* (Baltimore and London: Johns Hopkins University Press, 1975), p. 2.

167. Boban, *Maček i politika*, vol. 2, pp. 398–399.

168. Maček, *In the Struggle for Freedom*, pp. 220–222; Jozo Tomasevich, *War and Revolution in Yugoslavia, 1941–1945: Occupation and Collaboration* (Stanford, Calif.: Stanford University Press, 2001), pp. 49–50; and Bogdan Krizman, *Ante Pavelić i Ustaše* (Zagreb: Globus, 1978), pp. 356–361.

169. Quoted in Tomasevich, *War and Revolution: Occupation and Collaboration*, p. 51.

170. Perica M. Višnjić, "Nemački okupacioni sistem u Srbiji 1941 godine," *Istoriski glasnik* (Belgrade), vol. 9, no. 3–4 (1956): 84. The figure for the number of soldiers captured is confirmed in P. Cohen, *Serbia's Secret War*, p. 29.

4. World War Two and the Partisan Struggle, 1941–1945

1. Bernd J. Fischer, *Albania at War, 1939–1945* (London: C. Hurst & Co., 1999), pp. 85–86.

2. Regarding the Partisans, see Ivan Jelić, *Jugoslavenska socijalistička revolucija (1941–1945)* (Zagreb: Školska knjiga, 1979). Regarding the Chetniks, see Jozo Tomasevich, *War and Revolution in Yugoslavia, 1941–1945: The Chetniks* (Stanford, Calif.: Stanford University Press, 1975).

3. Helga H. Harriman, *Slovenia under Nazi Occupation, 1941–1945* (New York and Washington: Studia Slovenica, 1977), p. 36.

4. Ibid., p. 42.

5. Svein Mønnesland, *Før Jugoslavija, og etter,* 4th ed. (Oslo: Sypress forlag, 1999), p. 193.

6. Fischer, *Albania at War,* p. 87.

7. Quoted in Jozo Tomasevich, *War and Revolution in Yugoslavia, 1941–1945: Occupation and Collaboration* (Stanford, Calif.: Stanford University Press, 2001), p. 338.

8. Holm Sundhaussen, "Der Ustascha-Staat: Anatomie eines Herrschaftssystems," in *Österreichische Osthefte,* vol. 37, no. 2 (1995): 499.

9. Ladislaus Hory and Martin Broszat, *Der kroatische Ustascha-Staat 1941–1945* (Stuttgart: Deutsche Verlags-Anstalt, 1964), p. 67.

10. This is the NDH population according to ibid., p. 69. Sundhaussen estimates the NDH's population at 6.5 million. See Sundhaussen, "Der Ustasche-Staat," p. 500. The breakdown of population by nationality is according to Hory and Broszat, *Der kroatische Ustascha-Staat,* p. 69.

11. Fikreta Jelić-Butić, *Ustaše i NDH / Ustaše i Nezavisna Država Hrvatska 1941–1945* (Zagreb: S.N. Liber and Školska knjiga, 1977), p. 80.

12. Sundhaussen, "Der Ustascha-Staat," p. 503.

13. Ibid., p. 504.

14. Jelić-Butić, *Ustaše i NDH,* pp. 82–83; and Hrvoje Matković, *Povijest Nezavisne Države Hrvatske* [hereafter, *Povijest NDH*], 2nd, expanded ed. (Zagreb: Naklada P.I.P. Pavičić, 2002), p. 63.

15. Holm Sundhaussen, "Jugoslawien," in Wolfgang Benz (ed.), *Dimension des Völkermords: Die Zahl der jüdischen Opfer des Nationalsozialismus* (Munich: R. Oldenbourg Verlag, 1991), pp. 321–322.

16. 49,602 according to Meho Visočak and Bejdo Sobica, *Jasenovac: Žrtve rada prema podacima statističkog zavoda Jugoslavije* (1998), as summarized in a review by Norman Cigar, in *Journal of Croatian Studies,* vol. 39 (1998), pp. 146–148. 100,000 according to Vladimir Žerjavić, *Population Losses in Yugoslavia, 1941–1945* (Zagreb: Dom i Svijet & Hrvatski Institut za Povijest, 1997). p. 89. István Deák, in a review essay for *New York Review of Books,* accepts a figure of 60,000 persons killed at Jasenovac. See his essay "Jews and Catholics," *New York Review of Books,* 19 December 2002, p. 42. Finally, Ivo Goldstein and Slavko Goldstein con-

clude, on the basis of exhaustive analysis, that some 80,000–90,000 persons were killed at Jasenovac. See Ivo Goldstein with Slavko Goldstein, *Holokaust u Zagrebu* (Zagreb: Novi Liber & Židovska općina Zagreb, 2001), p. 342.

17. Žerjavić, *Population Losses,* p. 79.

18. Quoted in Dušan Bilandžić, *Hrvatska moderna povijest* (Zagreb: Golden Marketing, 1999), pp. 124–125, from *Die Deutsche Zeitung in Kroatien* (Zagreb), 22 April 1941.

19. Bilandžić, *Hrvatska moderna povijest,* p. 125. Regarding the fate of the Jews in Croatia, see Jure Krišto, *Sukob simbola: Politika, vjere i ideologije u Nezavisnoj Drvavi Hrvatskoj* (Zagreb: Globus, 2001), pp. 265–322.

20. HQ Intelligence Center, 6825 HQ & HQS Company, Military Intelligence Service in Austria, APO S41, U.S. Army, *Special Investigation and Interrogation Report: The Croatian National Independence Movement* (9 April 1946), C, decl. 29 January 1986, Auth. Para. 1-603 DoD 5200, I-R, in Records of the Army Staff, ROACS, G-2, Intelligence RIRR, *Security Classified Intelligence and Investigative Dossiers, 1939–76* (Ustashi), IRR, Impersonal File, RG 319, Stack Area 270, Row A, Box 107, file ZF-010183, on deposit at NA [hereafter, HQ Intelligence Center, *Special Investigation and Interrogation Report* (Ustashi), at NA].

21. Tomasevich, *War and Revolution: Occupation and Collaboration,* p. 384.

22. The Youth Organization's news organ, *Ustaška mladež,* began publication in January 1942. See the report in *Hrvatski narod* (Zagreb), 25 January 1942, p. 3.

23. Tomasevich, *War and Revolution: Occupation and Collaboration,* p. 341.

24. *Hrvatski narod,* 28 January 1942, p. 1.

25. *Hrvatski narod,* 11 June 1942, p. 1.

26. *Hrvatski narod,* 13 January 1942, p. 3, and 27 January 1942, p. 7.

27. For more accurate accounts of Starčević, see V. Bogdanov, *Ante Starčević i Hrvatska politika* (Zagreb: Biblioteka Nezavisnih Pisaca, 1937); Vaso Bogdanov, *Starčević i Stranka prava prema Srbima i prema jedinstvu Južnoslavenskih naroda* (Zagreb: Naklaka 'Školska knjiga,' 1951); and Mirjana Gross, *Izvorno pravaštvo: Ideologija, agitacija, pokret* (Zagreb: Golden Marketing, 2000).

28. *Hrvatski narod,* 18 February 1942, p. 3.

29. *Hrvatski narod,* 10 January 1942, p. 3.

30. *Hrvatski narod,* 26 March 1942, p. 1.

31. *Ustaša,* 13 June 1941, as quoted in Jelić-Butić, *Ustaše i NDH,* p. 17.

32. *Hrvatski narod,* 13 February 1942, p. 5.

33. *Hrvatski narod,* 12 February 1942, p. 7, and 1 January 1943, p. 1.

34. Jelić-Butić, *Ustaše i NDH,* p. 158.

35. Quoted in HG Intelligence Center, *Special Investigation and Interrogation Report* (Ustashi), at NA.

36. *Hrvatski narod,* 22 January 1943, p. 2.

37. Jelić-Butić, *Ustaše i NDH,* pp. 164–165.

38. *Hrvatski narod,* 11 January 1942, p. 3.

39. *Hrvatski narod,* 26 February 1942, p. 2.

40. Sundhaussen, "Der Ustascha-Staat," p. 530.

41. Vladimir Žerjavić, *Gubici stanovništva Jugoslavije u drugom svjetskom ratu* (Zagreb: Jugoslavensko Viktimološko Društvo, 1989), pp. 61–66.

42. Toward the end of 1942, Mussolini personally made the decision to take Croatian Jews into protective custody, in order to protect them from the Nazis and the Ustaše. See Jelić-Butić, *Ustaše i NDH,* p. 180; and Jonathan Steinberg, *All or Nothing: The Axis and the Holo-*

caust 1941–1943 (London and New York: Routledge, 1990), p. 133. See also Zvi Loker, "The Testimony of Dr. Edo Neufeld: The Italians and the Jews of Croatia," *Holocaust and Genocide Studies,* vol. 7, no. 1 (Spring 1993): 67–76.

43. Goldstein and Goldstein, *Holokaust u Zagrebu,* pp. 155–156.

44. Ivo Goldstein, *Croatia: A History,* trans. from Croatian by Nikolina Jovanović (Montreal: McGill–Queen's University Press, 1999), p. 137.

45. Jelić-Butić, *Ustaše i NDH,* p. 166.

46. Ibid., p. 167.

47. Ibid., pp. 168–172.

48. Martin Conway, *Catholic Politics in Europe, 1918–1945* (London and New York: Routledge, 1997), p. 61.

49. "Mit Brennender Sorge: Rundschreiben des Papstes Pius XI über die Lage der katholischen Kirche im Deutschen Reich, vom 14. März 1937," in *Mit Brennender Sorge, Das Christliche Deutschland 1933 bis 1945,* ed. by Simon Hirt, Katholische Reihe vol. 1 (Freiburg-im-Breisgau: Verlag Herder, 1946), p. 16

50. Ibid., p. 5.

51. "Schreiben des Vorsitzenden der Fuldauer Bischofskonferenzen an den Reichs- und Preussischen Minister für die Kirchlichen Angelegenheiten" (Breslau), 27 April 1939, signed by A. Card. Bertram, Archbishop of Breslau, in ibid., p. 41.

52. Pope Pius XII, *Selected Encyclicals and Addresses* (Harrison, N.Y.: Roman Catholic Books, N.D.): re anti-Semitism, pp. 20–21; re idolatry of the state, p. 28; quotation re state worship, p. 28.

53. Ibid., p. 12.

54. José M. Sánchez, *Pius XII and the Holocaust: Understanding the Controversy* (Washington, D.C.: Catholic University of America Press, 2002), p. 50.

55. For that matter, the French also considered it obvious that the condemnations in *Summi Pontificatus* were directed at the Third Reich and, for that reason, dropped 88,000 copies of the encyclical on Germany from the air. See Sánchez, *Pius XII and the Holocaust,* pp. 50–51.

56. Ibid., pp. 51–52, 55.

57. Pope Pius XII, *Selected Encyclicals:* quotation, p. 284; role of the state, p. 282.

58. Pinchas Lapide, *Three Popes and the Jews* (1967), as quoted in David G. Dalin, "Pius XII and the Jews," in *The Weekly Standard,* 26 February 2001, at www.weeklystandard.com/magazine [last accessed 7 September 2001], p. 2. See also Rabbi David G. Dalin, *The Myth of Hitler's Pope: How Pope Pius XII Rescued Jews from the Nazis* (Washington D.C.: Regnery Publishing, 2005), chap. 4.

59. Re Pius's "silence," see Carlo Falconi, *The Silence of Pius XII,* trans. by Bernard Wall (Boston: Little, Brown, 1970). Re intelligence, see Michael Phayer, *The Catholic Church and the Holocaust, 1930–1965* (Bloomington: Indiana University Press, 2000), p. 43.

60. Phayer, *Catholic Church and the Holocaust,* pp. 44–45.

61. Dalin, "Pius XII and the Jews," p. 4.

62. Ronald J. Rychlak, *Hitler, the War, and the Pope* (Columbus, Miss.: Genesis Press, 2000), p. 167.

63. Dalin, "Pius XII and the Jews," pp. 6, 7.

64. "Vatican Directives to Clergy in the Independent State of Croatia," 24 July 1941, originally published in *Glas koncila* (Zagreb), 19 February 1989, and trans. in *South Slav Journal,* vol. 11, no. 4 (Winter 1988–89): 56.

65. Tomasevich, *War and Revolution: Occupation and Collaboration,* p. 369. See also Hory and Broszat, *Der kroatische Ustascha-Staat,* p. 72.

66. Tomasevich, *War and Revolution: Occupation and Collaboration,* p. 401 n. 51.

67. Jahn Otto Johansen, *Ustasja* (Oslo: J. W. Cappelens Forlag, 1984), p. 32.

68. Re priests, see Jelić-Butić, *Ustaše i NDH,* p. 218–219. Guberina, quoted in Menachem Shelah, "The Catholic Church in Croatia, the Vatican and the Murder of the Croatian Jews," in *Holocaust and Genocide Studies,* vol. 4, no. 3 (1989): 327.

69. Ćiril Petešić, *Katoličko svećenstvo u NOB-u 1941–1945* (Zagreb: VPA, 1982), p. 55.

70. See ibid., pp. 63–70, 84–87, 130, 200–205.

71. Srećko M. Džaja, *Die politische Realität des Jugoslawismus (1918–1991). Mit besonderer Berücksichtigung Bosnien-Herzegowinas* (Munich: R. Oldenbourg Verlag, 2002), p. 101.

72. Jelić-Butić, *Ustaše iNDH.,* 217–218. See also Klaus Buchenau, *Orthodoxie und Katholizismus in Jugoslawien 1945–1991* (Wiesbaden: Harrassowitz, 2004), pp. 65–66.

73. Petešić, *Katoličko svećenstvo,* p. 95.

74. Theresa Marie Ursić, *Religious Freedom in Post–World War II Yugoslavia: The Case of Roman Catholic Nuns in Croatia and Bosnia-Herzegovina 1945–1960* (Lanham, Md.: International Scholars, 2001), p. 7.

75. Nada Kisić Kolanović, *NDH i Italija. Političke veze i diplomatiski odnosi* (Zagreb: Naklada Ljevak, 2001), p. 109.

76. Quoted in speech by Dr. Ivo Politeo before the Supreme Court of Croatia, 8 October 1946, trans. as ED4, 31 October 1946, American Consulate/Z to State in U.S. Department of State, *Records of the U.S. Department of State Relating to the Internal Affairs of Yugoslavia 1945–1949,* Decimal file 860h, at SAL, Reel 3 (files 00/10-1146 to 00/1-2747), substituting "motivating" for "moving" [hereafter, *Records 1945–1949*].

77. Quoted in Shelah, "Catholic Church in Croatia," p. 331.

78. Richard Pattee, *The Case of Cardinal Aloysius Stepinac* (Milwaukee: Bruce., 1953), pp. 114, 276–281, 300–305. See also Ivan Mužić, *Pavelić i Stepinac* (Split: Logos, 1991); O. Aleksa Benigar, *Alojzije Stepinac, Hrvatski Kardinal* (Rome: Ziral, 1974); J. Batelja and C. Tomić (eds.), *Alojzije Kardinal Stepinac, Nadbiskup Zagrebački: Propovijedi, govori, poruke (1941–1946)* (Zagreb: AGM, 1996); and Marina Stambuk-Skalić, Josip Kolanović, and Stjepan Razum (eds.), *Proces Alojziju Stepincu: Dokumenti* (Zagreb: Kršćanka sadašnjost, 1997).

79. Stella Alexander, *The Triple Myth: A Life of Archbishop Alojzije Stepinac* (Boulder, Colo.: East European Monographs, 1987), p. 91; confirmed in Tomasevich, *War and Revolution: Occupation and Collaboration,* p. 400.

80. Quoted in Alexander, *Triple Myth,* pp. 74, 75.

81. Ibid., pp. 75, 76.

82. Vatican regulation of 18 October 1941, as quoted in Tomasevich, *War and Revolution: Occupation and Collaboration,* pp. 535–536.

83. Quoted in ibid., p. 537.

84. Matteo J. Milazzo, *The Chetnik Movment and the Yugoslav Resistance* (Baltimore and London: Johns Hopkins University Press, 1975), p. 49.

85. Djoko Slijepčević, *Istorija Srpske pravoslavne crkve,* vol. 2: *Od početka XIX veka do kraja drugog svetskog rata* (Belgrade: Beogradski izdavačko-grafički zavod, 1991), pp. 618–619.

86. Jure Krišto, "Crkva i država: Slučaj vjerskih prijelaza u Nezavisnoj Državi Hrvatskoj," in Hans-Georg Fleck and Igor Graovac (eds.), *Dijalog povjesničara-istoričara 1* (Zagreb: Zaklada Friedrich-Naumann, 2000), pp. 191, 198.

87. Quoted in Pattee, *Case of Cardinal Aloysius Stepinac,* pp. 384–387, emphases as given in Pattee. In December 1945, the Catholic newspaper *Il Quotidiano* carried a report about this conference, noting that on 20 November 1941 the Croatian bishops wrote to Pavelić avowing, among other things, that "no one can deny that acts of violence have been committed and that frightful atrocities were found to have been perpetrated. . . . By virtue of its evangelical teach-

ings the Church must indeed condemn the crimes and abuses committed by irresponsible elements and immature youths, and demand full respect for human beings, irrespective of age, sex, creed, nationality or race." *Il Quotidiano* (Rome), 23 December 1945, p. 1, trans. by Marta Christener, trans. attached as ED no. 486 (28 December 1945), American Mission/Holy See to State, in *Records 1945–1949*.

88. Tomasevich, *War and Revolution: Occupation and Collaboration*, p. 539.

89. Re forced conversions, see Krišto, "Crkva i država," p. 205; re estimate, see Vejko Dj. Djurić, "Josif (Cvijović), mitropolit Skopljanski, i Alojzije Stepinac, nadbiskup Zagrebački, prvosveštenci: Srpske pravoslavne i Rimo-katoličke Crkve i prekrštavanje 1941–1945. godine," in Hans-Georg Fleck and Igor Graovac (eds.), *Dijalog povjesničara-istoričara 4* (Zagreb: Zaklada Friedrich-Naumann, 2001), p. 462.

90. Ursić, *Religious Freedom*, p. 9.

91. Regarding the Croatian Orthodox Church, see Krišto, *Sukob simbola*, pp. 247–262.

92. Tomasevich, *War and Revolution: Occupation and Collaboration*, p. 539.

93. Phayer, *Catholic Church*, pp. 46–47. Quote on p. 47.

94. See, for example, Jakov Blažević, *Mać a ne mir: Za pravnu sigurnost gradjana* [vol. 3 of Memoirs, 4 vols.] (Zagreb/Belgrade/Sarajevo: Mladost/Prosveta/Svjetlost, 1980), pp. 208–209, 211, 234–238.

95. Ivo Goldstein, in interview with Zoran Daškalović, "Crkva zatvara vatra Europe," in *Feral Tribune* (Split), no. 853 (19 January 2002): 22.

96. Quoted in Ivo Goldstein, with Slavko Goldstein, *Holokaust u Zagrebu* (Zagreb: Novi liber & Židovska općina Zagreb, 2001), p. 567.

97. Quoted in Shelah, "Catholic Church in Croatia," p. 331, my emphasis.

98. Goldstein, "Crkva zatvara vatra," p. 23.

99. Quoted in ibid., pp. 23–24. Concerning Stepinac's early visit to Slavko Kvaternik and the Vatican's de facto recognition of the NDH, see Matković, *Povijest NDH*, pp. 125–126.

100. Milazzo, *Chetnik Movement*, pp. 48–49.

101. See *Hrvatski narod*, 19 February 1942, p. 1, and 20 February 1942, p. 2.

102. Kolanović, *NDH i Italija*, pp. 133–136.

103. Tomasevich, *War and Revolution: Occupation and Collaboration*, p. 243.

104. Re German dismay, see Hory and Broszat, *Der Kroatische Ustascha-Staat*, p. 85; re Glaise von Horstenau, see Steinberg, *All or Nothing*, p. 174.

105. Kolanović, *NDH i Italija*, pp. 113, 424.

106. In this connection, see Bogdan Krizman, *NDH izmedju Hitlera i Mussolinija*, 3rd ed. (Zagreb: Globus, 1986).

107. Fikreta Jelić-Butić, *Četnici u Hrvatskoj 1941–1945* (Zagreb: Globus, 1986), pp. 103–119.

108. For an argument along this line, see Walter Manoschek, *'Serbien ist judenfrei': Militärische Besatzungspolitik und Judenvernichtung in Serbien 1941/42* (Munich: R. Oldenbourg Verlag, 1995).

109. Milan Ristović, "Rat i razaranje društva u Srbiji 1941–1945. godine: Skica za jednu društvenu istoriju," in Hans-Georg Fleck and Igor Graovac (eds.), *Dijalog povjesničara-istoričara 3* (Zagreb: Zaklada Friedrich-Naumann, 2001), p. 205.

110. Quoted in Philip J. Cohen, *Serbia's Secret War: Propaganda and the Deceit of History* (College Station: Texas A&M University Press, 1996), p. 33.

111. Czesław Madajczyk, "Restserbien unter Deutscher Militärverwaltung," in Anonymous, eds., *The Third Reich and Yugoslavia, 1933–1945* (Belgrade: Institute for Contemporary History and Narodna knjiga, 1977), p. 460.

112. Milan Borković, *Milan Nedić* (Zagreb: Centar za Informacije i Publicitet, 1985), pp. 31–32.

113. Ibid., p. 33.

114. "In France, Marshal Petain has repudiated the democratic illusion about equality and political rights, and in their place he has put the family as the foundation . . . of social and national life, from which naturally radiate all rights and all duties." M. Spalajković, preface to Milan Dj. Nedić, *Govori Generala Milana Nedića pretsednika Srpske vlade* (Belgrade, 1943), p. 7.

115. Malajczyk, "Restserbien," p. 461.

116. Milan Ristović, "General M. Nedić—Diktatur, Kollaboration und die patriarchalische Gesellschaft Serbiens 1941–1944," in Erwin Oberländer (ed.), *Autoritäre Regime in Ostmittel- und Südosteuropa 1919–1944* (Paderborn: Ferdinand Schöningh, 2001), p. 638.

117. Malajczyk, "Restserbien," p. 461.

118. Manoschek, '*Serbien ist judenfrei*,' pp. 35–39; also "Report from Staatsrat Dr. Turner and Commander SE Löhr," 29 August 1942, OUSCCWC, U.S. Army, Roll 20 (1472–1550), NOKW-1486, *Records 1945–1949*.

119. Venčeslav Glišić, "Concentration Camps in Serbia (1941–1944)," in Anonymous, eds., *Third Reich and Yugoslavia*, pp. 694, 695, 700–701.

120. Ibid., pp. 702, 708. See also the discussion in Menachem Shelach, "Sajmište—An Extermination Camp in Serbia," in *Holocaust and Genocide Studies*, vol. 2, no. 2 (1987): 243–260.

121. Glišić, "Concentration Camps in Serbia," p. 715.

122. Milan Dj. Nedić, *Reći Generala Milana Nedića Srpskom narodu i omladini* (Belgrade: Nacionalni spisi, 1941), pp. 9–10 (speech of 2 September 1941). Even today, there are those who are inclined to give a positive assessment of Nedić's wartime role, sometimes representing him as having endeavored to "save" the Serbian people. See, for example, Lazo M. Kostić, *Armijski General Milan Nedić: Njegova uloga i delovanje* (Novi Sad: Dobrica knjiga, 2000 [1976]), especially pp. 10–16.

123. Branko Petranović, *Srbija u drugom svetskom ratu 1939–1945* (Belgrade: Vojnoizdavački i novinski centar, 1992), pp. 220–221. See also Roger Griffin, *The Nature of Fascism* (New York: St. Martin's Press, 1991); and Zeev Sternhell with Mario Sznajder and Maia Asheri, *The Birth of Fascist Ideology: From Cultural Rebellion to Political Revolution*, trans. from French by David Maisel (Princeton, N.J.: Princeton University Press, 1994).

124. Spalajković, preface to Nedić, *Govori*, p. 6.

125. Nedić, *Govori*, pp. 45–47 (speech of 2 November 1941) and p. 70 (speech of 8 February 1942).

126. Nedić, *Govori*, pp. 75, 80 (speech of 8 March 1942) and p. 96 (speech of 25 March 1942).

127. Nedić, *Govori*, p. 153 (speech of 8 November 1942).

128. P. Cohen, *Serbia's Secret War*, p. 81.

129. Ibid., p. 73; and Ljubica Štefan, *Srpska pravoslavna crkva i fašizam* (Zagreb: Globus, 1996), pp. 47–49.

130. Quoted in P. Cohen, *Serbia's Secret War*, p. 81.

131. Ibid., p. 84.

132. A German report on the arrest of Patriarch Gavrilo is included in "Report of the Commander of the Ersatz Kommando, Security Service," 6 May 1941, OUSCCWC, U.S. Army, NO NOKW-1061, in *Records of the U.S. Nuernberg War Crimes Trials*, NOKW Series, 1933–47, RG-238, T1119, on deposit at NA [hereafter, *Records of Nuernberg Trials*].

133. Tomasevich, *War and Revolution: Occupation and Collaboration,* p. 513.

134. Ibid., pp. 513–514.

135. Manoschek, '*Serbien ist judenfrei,*' pp. 145–146.

136. Tomasevich, *War and Revolution: Occupation and Collaboration,* p. 215.

137. Manoschek, '*Serbien ist judenfrei,*' p. 145.

138. Tomasevich, *War and Revolution: Occupation and Collaboration,* pp. 216–217.

139. Kirk Ford Jr., *OSS and the Yugoslav Resistance, 1943–1945* (College Station: Texas A&M University Press, 1992), p. 47. For additional, extensive documentation concerning Chetnik collaboration with the Axis, see *Tajna i javna saradnja Četnika i okupatora 1941–1944* (Belgrade: Arhivski pregled, 1976); and Branko Latas (comp.), *Saradnja Četnika Draže Mihailovića sa okupatorima i Ustašama (1941–1945)* (Belgrade: Društvo za istinu o antifašističkoj narodnooslobodilačkoj borbi 1941–1945, 1999).

140. Jovan Marjanović, "The Neubacher Plan and Practical Schemes for the Establishment of a Greater Serbian Federation (1943–1944)," in Anonymous, eds., *Third Reich and Yugoslavia,* pp. 489–490.

141. *Novo vreme* (Belgrade), 16 September 1941, 19 October 1941, and 4 November 1941—all trans. into German by SKFVOH, in OUSCCUS, U.S. Army, Inv. Nr. 387, L-15, Roll 22 (1630–1685), NOKW-1637, in *Records of Nuernberg Trials.*

142. Hermann Neubacher, *Sonderauftrag Südost: Bericht eines fliegenden Diplomaten,* 2nd ed. (Göttingen: Musterschmidt Verlag, 1957), p. 155.

143. Ibid., pp. 158–160; and Marjanović, "Neubacher Plan," pp. 490–491.

144. Neubacher, *Sonderauftrag Südost,* p. 156.

145. Marjanović, "Neubacher Plan," p. 493.

146. The agreement was renewed on 17 January 1944. Ibid., p. 495.

147. Neubacher, *Sonderauftrag Südost,* pp. 163–164; and Tomašević, *War and Revolution: Chetniks,* p. 260.

148. Tomasevich, *War and Revolution: Occupation and Collaboration,* pp. 777–778.

149. Ferdo Čulinović, *Okupatorska podjela Jugoslavije* (Belgrade: Vojnoizdavački zavod, 1970), pp. 91, 131; Harriman, *Slovenia under Nazi occupation,* p. 32; and Tomasevich, *War and Revolution: Occupation and Collaboration,* p. 83.

150. Harriman, *Slovenia under Nazi Occupation,* p. 36; confirmed in Tone Ferenc, "Die Kollaboration in Slowenien," in Werner Röhr (ed.), *Okkupation und Kollaboration (1938–1945): Beiträge zu Konzepten und Praxis der Kollaboration in der deutschen Okkupationspolitik* (Berlin and Heidelberg: Hüthig Verlagsgemeinschaft, 1994), p. 338.

151. Čulinović, *Okupatorska podjela,* pp. 109–110; Harriman, *Slovenia under Nazi Occupation,* pp. 35–36; and Helga H. Harriman, "Slovenia as an Outpost of the Third Reich," *East European Quarterly,* vol. 5, no. 2 (1971): 224.

152. Harriman, "Slovenia as an Outpost," pp. 226–227; and Harriman, *Slovenia under Nazi Occupation,* p. 40.

153. Harriman, "Slovenia as an Outpost," p. 230; and Harriman, *Slovenia under Nazi Occupation,* p. 46.

154. Tomasevich, *War and Revolution: Occupation and Collaboration,* pp. 89–90. Harriman provides a different estimate, reporting that about 55,000 Slovenes were expelled from the German zone of occupation during the war. See Harriman, *Slovenia under Nazi Occupation,* p. 42.

155. Ferenc, "Die Kollaboration in Slowenien," pp. 338, 341.

156. Tamara Griesser-Pečar and France Martin Dolinar, '*Rožmanov proces*' (Ljubljana, 1996).

157. Tamara Griesser-Pečar, *Das zerrissene Volk—Slowenien 1941–1946. Okkupation, Kollaboration, Bürgerkrieg, Revolution* (Vienna and Cologne: Böhlau Verlag, 2003), p. 181, also pp. 179–180.

158. Ibid., pp. 188, 189–190.

159. Ferenc, "Die Kollaboration in Slowenien," p. 343.

160. Dimitrije Boarov, *Politička istorija Vojvodine* (Novi Sad: Europanon consulting, 2001), p. 166; and Tomasevich, *War and Revolution: Occupation and Collaboration,* p. 169.

161. Tomasevich, *War and Revolution: Occupation and Collaboration,* p. 170.

162. Boarov, *Politička istorija Vojvodine,* pp. 166–167.

163. Čulinović, *Okupatorska podjela,* pp. 565, 575.

164. Josip Mirnić, "The Enlistment of Volksdeutschers from the Bačka Region in the Waffen SS," in Anonymous, eds., *Third Reich and Yugoslavia,* p. 624–625.

165. Ibid., p. 653.

166. Tomasevich, *War and Revolution: Occupation and Collaboration,* p. 205.

167. Marshall Lee Miller, *Bulgaria during the Second World War* (Stanford, Calif.: Stanford University Press, 1975), p. 54.

168. Ibid., p. 123.

169. Dimitrije Kulić, *Bugarska okupacija 1941–1944,* vol. 1 (Niš: Prosveta, 1970), pp. 68, 72, 76.

170. Čulinović, *Okupatorska podjela,* pp. 600–602.

171. Fischer, *Albania at War,* p. 85.

172. Svetozar Vukmanović(-Tempo), *Struggle for the Balkans,* trans. by Charles Bartlett (London: Merlin Press, 1990), pp. 22, 29.

173. Miller, *Bulgaria during the Second World War,* p. 133.

174. Čulinović, *Okupatorska podjela,* pp. 625–633; and Tomasevich, *War and Revolution: Occupation and Collaboration,* pp. 138–139.

175. Tomasevich, *War and Revolution: Occupation and Collaboration,* p. 139.

176. Fischer, *Albania at War,* pp. 85–86.

177. Nenad Antonijević, "Arhivska gradja o ljudskim gubicima na Kosovu i Metohiji u Drugome svetskom ratu," in Hans-Georg Fleck and Igor Graovac (eds.), *Dijalog povjesničara-istoričara 5* (Zagreb: Zaklada Friedrich-Naumann, 2002), pp. 470–471; Fabian Schmidt, "Im Griff der grossen Mächte: Das Kosovo in der wechselvollen Geschichte des Balkans," in Thomas Schmid (ed.), *Krieg im Kosovo* (Reinbek-bei-Hamburg: Rowohlt Taschenbuch Verlag, 1999), pp. 94–95; Miranda Vickers, *Between Serb and Albanian: A History of Kosovo* (New York: Columbia University Press, 1998), p. 122; and Milija Šćepanović, "The Exodus of Serbs and Montenegrins 1878–1988," in Anonymous, eds., *Kosovo: Past and Present* (Belgrade: Review of International Affairs, 1989), pp. 147–148.

178. Antonijević, "Arhivska gradja," pp. 478–479. The same figure is given in Šćepanović, "Exodus of Serbs and Montenegrins," p. 147.

179. Vickers, *Between Serb and Albanian,* p. 123.

180. Šćepanović, "Exodus of Serbs and Montenegrins," p. 154.

181. Fischer, *Albania at War,* pp. 133–134.

182. Walter R. Roberts, *Tito, Mihailović and the Allies, 1941–1945* (New Brunswick, N.J.: Rutgers University Press, 1973), pp. 20–21; and Milazzo, *Chetnik Movement,* p. 12, 48.

183. Petranović, *Srbija u drugom svetskom ratu,* p. 179.

184. Milazzo, *Chetnik Movement,* p. 20.

185. Manoschek, *'Serbien ist judenfrei,'* pp. 124–125.

186. See the discussion in Klaus Schmider, *Partisanenkrieg in Jugoslawien 1941–1944* (Hamburg and Berlin: Verlag E. S. Mittler & Sohn GmbH, 2002), pp. 54–85.

187. Milazzo, *Chetnik Movement,* p. 22.

188. Manoschek, *'Serbien ist judenfrei,'* p. 143.

189. Regarding OKW, ibid., p. 131; regarding German loss of patience, Proclamation addressed "to the Serbian people" and signed only by "the German Commandant" (October 1941), OUSCCWC, U.S. Army, no. NOKW-1202, Roll 17, in *Records of Nuernberg Trials.*

190. Dančo Zografski, "Macedonia and the Third Reich's Balkan Policy," in Anonymous, eds., *Third Reich and Yugoslavia,* p. 394.

191. Vickers, *Between Serb and Albanian,* p. 126.

192. Of the captured Partisans, 389 were murdered on the spot. Manoschek, *'Serbien ist judenfrei,'* p. 150.

193. Ibid., pp. 152–153.

194. Petranović, *Srbija u drugom svetskom ratu,* p. 214.

195. Davorin Rudolf, *Rat koji nismo htjeli: Hrvatska 1991* (Zagreb: Nakladni zavod Globus, 1999), p. 44.

196. Manoschek, *'Serbien ist judenfrei,'* pp. 114–115. These figures are confirmed in P. Cohen, *Serbia's Secret War,* p. 44; and reconfirmed in Rudolf, *Rat koji nismo htjeli,* p. 44.

197. Zdravko Dizdar and Mihael Sobolevski, *Prešučivani Četnicki zlocini u Hrvatskoj i u Bosni i Hercegovini 1941.–1945* (Zagreb: Hrvatski institut za povijest & Dom i svijet, 1999), p. 39.

198. Jelić-Butić, *Četnici u Hrvatskoj,* p. 162.

199. Ibid., pp.149–150, 160–161.

200. Quoted in ibid., p. 162.

201. As cited in Dizdar and Sobolevski, *Prešučivani Četnički zločini,* p. 146; see also p. 147.

202. Attila Hoare, "The People's Liberation Movement in Bosnia and Hercegovina, 1941–45: What Did It Mean to Fight for a Multi-National State?" in *Nationalism & Ethnic Politics,* vol. 2, no. 3 (Autumn 1996): 419.

203. Tomaševich, War and Revolution: *Chetniks,* p. 188.

204. Roberts, *Tito, Mihailović and the Allies,* p. 41.

205. Jelić-Butić, *Četnici u Hrvatskoj,* pp. 35, 54–55.

206. Ibid., pp. 64–65; and Milazzo, *Chetnik Movement,* pp. 71–73.

207. Milazzo, *Chetnik Movement,* p. 56.

208. Ibid., p. 72.

209. Ibid., pp. 62, 72; and Tomaševich, *War and Revolution: Chetniks,* p. 213.

210. Milazzo, *Chetnik Movement,* pp. 73, 75, 76, 77.

211. Ibid., pp. 94, 97; and Jelić-Butić, *Četnici u Hrvatskoj,* pp. 105–107.

212. Milazzo, *Chetnik Movement,* p. 101.

213. Ibid., pp. 106, 110.

214. Quoted in ibid., p. 112.

215. Roberts, *Tito, Mihailović and the Allies,* p. 102.

216. Ibid., pp. 100, 102. Under the Cavallero-Löhr agreement signed in early January 1943, the Italians had promised to terminate all weapons deliveries to the Chetniks and to make a break with the Chetnik movement. In flagrant disregard of this agreement, however, the Italians delivered even greater quantities of arms to the Chetniks at this time. On this point, see Milazzo, *Chetnik Movement,* p.115.

217. Quoted in Roberts, *Tito, Mihailović and the Allies*, p. 93.

218. Ann Lane, *Britain, the Cold War and Yugoslav Unity, 1941–1949* (Brighton: Sussex University Press, 1996), pp. 31, 37.

219. Roberts, *Tito, Mihailović and the Allies*, p. 105–106.

220. Milazzo, *Chetnik Movement*, pp. 143–145, 147.

221. Ibid., pp. 149, 150–151. Regarding the deterioration of relations between the Italians and the Chetniks in 1943, see Slobodan D. Milošević, *Nemačko-Italijanski odnosi na teritoriji okupirane Jugoslavije 1941–1943* (Belgrade: Institut za savremenu istoriju, 1991), pp. 174–207.

222. Diego De Castro, *Trieste. Cenni riassuntivi sul problema Giulano nell'ultimo decennio* (Bologna: Cappelli, 1953), p. 24.

223. For discussion, see Barbara Jancar-Webster, "Women in the Yugoslav National Liberation Movement," in Sabrina P. Ramet (ed.), *Gender Politics in the Western Balkans: Women and Society in Yugoslavia and the Yugoslav Successor States* (University Park: Pennsylvania State University Press, 1999).

224. Mønnesland, *Før Jugoslavia og etter*, 4th ed., p. 196.

225. See the discussion in Branko Petranović, *Istorija Jugoslavije 1918–1988*, vol. 2: *Narodnooslobodilački rat i revolucija 1941–1945* (Belgrade: Nolit, 1988), pp. 193–200; and Nada Kisić Kolanović, "Neki aspekti razvoja prava na oslobodjenom teritoriju Hrvatske 1943–1945. godine: U povodu 45. godišnjice ZAVNOH-a," *Časopis za suvremenu povijest* (Zagreb), vol. 19, no. 3 (1987): 1–24.

226. Quoted in Lane, *Britain, the Cold War*, p. 36.

227. For further details concerning Tito's life, see Phyllis Auty, *Tito* (London: Longmans, 1970); and Milovan Djilas, *Tito: The Story from Inside*, trans. by Vasilije Kojić and Richard Hayes (New York: Harcourt Brace Jovanovich, 1980).

228. Quoted in Milovan Djilas, *Wartime*, trans. by Michael B. Petrovich (New York: Harcourt Brace Jovanovich, 1977), p. 79, from *Zbornik dokumenata*, vol. 3, book I (1950), p. 68.

229. Edvard Kardelj, *Reminiscences—The Struggle for Recognition and Independence: The New Yugoslavia, 1944–1957*, trans. by David Norris (London: Summerfield Press, 1982), p. 22; and Alexander Dallin and F. I. Firsov (eds.), *Dimitrov and Stalin 1934–1943: Letters from the Soviet Archives*, Russian documents, trans. by Vadim A. Staklo (New Haven, Conn.: Yale University Press, 2000), pp. 217–218..

230. Djilas, *Wartime*, pp. 97–98.

231. Džaja, *Die politische Realität*, pp. 86, 88; and Tomaševich, *Chetniks*, p. 161.

232. From the Serbo-Croatian, *Antifašističko Vjeće Narodnog Oslobodjenja Jugoslavije*.

233. Dallin and Firsov, eds., *Dimitrov and Stalin*, pp. 209, 211–212.

234. Bilandžić, *Hrvatska moderna povijest*, p. 182.

235. Marko Attila Hoare, "The Bosnian Serb Identity and the Chetnik-Partisan Conflict," *South Slav Journal*, vol. 21, no. 3–4 (Autumn–Winter 2000): 10–11.

236. Cited in Džaja, *Die politische Realität*, p. 88. For a discussion of later disputes concerning the ethnic composition and legacy of the Partisan struggle, see Marko Attila Hoare, "Whose Is the Partisan Movement? Serbs, Croats and the Legacy of a Shared Resistance," *Journal of Slavic Military Studies*, vol. 15, no. 4 (December 2002): 24–41.

237. Vukmanović(-Tempo), *Struggle for the Balkans*, p. 40; Dragoicheva, as cited in ibid., pp. 188–189.

238. Ibid., pp. 198–200, 203–204.

239. Quoted in ibid., p. 210.

240. Ibid., pp. 213, 217.

241. Elizabeth Barker, *British Policy in South-east Europe in the Second World War* (Lon-

don: Macmillan, 1976), pp. 196–197, as cited in Vukmanović(-Tempo), *Struggle for the Balkans*, pp. 220, 223.

242. Zografski, "Macedonia and the Third Reich," pp. 396–397.

243. Stefan Troebst, "'Führer—befehl!'—Adolf Hitler und die Proklamation eines unabhängigen Makedonien (September 1944): Eine archivalische Miszelle," *Osteuropa*, vol. 52, no. 4 (April 2002): 495–499.

244. Fischer, *Albania at War*, p. 123; and Anton Logoreci, *The Albanians: Europe's Forgotten Survivors* (London: Victor Gollancz, 1977), p. 71.

245. Vickers, *Between Serb and Albanian*, pp. 130, 140.

246. Quoted in Branko Petranović, "AVNOJ and the Bujan Conference," in Anonymous, eds., *Kosovo—Past and Present* (Belgrade: Review of International Affairs, 1989), p. 143.

247. Petranović, *Srbija u drugom svetskom ratu*, pp. 550, 557.

248. Vickers, *Between Serb and Albanian*, p. 143.

249. Petranović, *Srbija u drugom svetskom ratu*, p. 691.

250. Logoreci, *Albanians*, p. 86.

251. Giacomo Scotti, *Ventimila caduti: Gli italiani in Jugoslavia dal 1943 al 1945* (Milan: Mursia, 1970), pp. 13, 33, 145.

252. Tomašević, *War and Revolution: Chetniks*, p. 413.

253. Roberts, *Tito, Mihailović and the Allies*, p. 157.

254. CIA, *National Intelligence Survey*, Section 53, Chap. V, NIS 21: "Yugoslavia—Political Dynamics," 1 August 1960), vol. 17, C, decl. 22 November 2000, under the FIA, by the authority of NND 011144 by SDT/SL, p. 10, on deposit at NA.

255. Vlado Strugar, *Der jugoslawische Volksbefreiungskrieg 1941 bis 1945*, trans. from Serbo-Croatian by Martin Zöller (Berlin: Deutscher Militärverlag, 1969), p. 168.

256. Jože Pirjevec, *Il giorno di San Vito. Jugoslavia 1918–1992—Storia di una tragedia* (Torino: Nuova Eri Edizioni, 1993), p. 187.

257. Quoted in Roberts, *Tito, Mihailović and the Allies*, p. 182.

256. *The Times* (London), 5 January 1944, p. 4.

259. P. Cohen, *Serbia's Secret War*, pp. 119–120.

260. For one account of these developments, see Ahmet Djonlagić, Žarko Atanacković, and Dušan Plenča, *Jugoslawien im Zweiten Weltkrieg*, trans. from Serbo-Croatian by Zoran Konstantinović (Belgrade: Medjunarodna štampa, 1967), pp. 183–189.

261. Roberts, *Tito, Mihailović and the Allies*, p. 260.

262. According to one source, the Partisans lost 2,953 men in the battle for Belgrade, while the Soviets lost about 1,000 men. As cited in Jozo Tomasevich, "Yugoslavia during the Second World War," in Wayne S. Vucinich (ed.), *Contemporary Yugoslavia* (Berkeley and Los Angeles: University of California Press, 1969), p. 106. Regarding Tito's visit to Moscow, see Scotti, *Ventimila caduti*, pp. 230–231.

263. Vladimir Geiger, "Sudbina njemačke manjine u Jugoslaviji potkraj i nakon Drugoga svjetskog rata u hrvatskim udžbenicima povijesti," in Fleck and Graovac (eds.), *Dijalog povjesničara-istoričara 5*, p. 518.

264. Alfred-Maurice de Zayas, *A Terrible Revenge: The Ethnic Cleansing of the East European Germans, 1944–1950*, trans. from German by John A. Koehler (New York: St. Martin's Press, 1994), pp. 95–96; Geiger, "Sudbina njemačke manjine," p. 519; and Bilandžić, *Hrvatska moderna povijest*, p. 223. See also Edit Petrović and Andrei Simić, "Montenegrin Colonists in Vojvodina: Objective and Subjective Measures of Ethnicity," *Serbian Studies*, vol. 5, no. 4 (Fall 1990): 5–20.

265. Partisan strength as given in Strugar, *Der jugoslawische Volksbefreiungskrieg*, pp. 298–

300; figure for Partisan strength confirmed in Džaja, *Die politische Realität*, p. 88; figures for the strength of NDH and German armed forces, Zdenko Radelić, *Križari gerila u Hrvatskoj 1945.–1950* (Zagreb: Hrvatski institut za povijest & Dom i svijet, 2002), p. 177.

266. See Ingomar Pust, *Titostern über Kärnten 1942–1945. Totgeschwiegene Tragödien*, 2nd enlarged ed. (Klagenfurt: Kärntner Abwehrkämpferbund, 1984), pp. 10–12, 130–247.

267. IM No. FX-77382, 17 May 1945, TS, from AFHQ signed Alexander to AGWAR for Combined Chiefs of Staff, AMSSO for British Chiefs of Staff, in *Records of the Allied Operational and Occupation Headquarters, World War II*, SHAEF, Office of the Chief of Staff, Decimal file MAY 1943–AUG 1945, RG 331, NND 760174, HM 1999, Stack Area 290, Row 7, Box 70, on deposit at NA (hereafter, *RAOOH*).

268. IM No. FX-78667, 20 May 1945, TS, from AFHQ signed Alexander to AGWAR for Combined Chiefs of Staff, AMSSO for British Chiefs of Staff, in *RAOOH*.

269. IM No. WX-85593, 21 May 1945, TS, from AGWAR/Combined Chiefs of Staff to SHAEF fwd for Eisenhower, AFHQ for Alexander, in *RAOOH*.

270. IM No. FX-79634, 21 May 1945, TS, from AFHQ signed Alexander to AGWAR for Combined Chiefs of Staff, AMSSO for British Chiefs of Staff, in *RAOOH*.

271. Griesser-Pečar, *Das zerrissene Volk*, p. 485.

272. Nikolai Tolstoy, "The Klagenfurt Conspiracy: War Crimes and Diplomatic Secrets," *Encounter*, vol. 60, no. 5 (May 1983): 27; and Žerjavić, *Opsesije i megalomanije*, p. 77.

273. Quoted in Nikolai Tolstoy, *The Minister and the Massacres* (London: Century Hutchinson, 1986), p. 199.

274. Tomasevich, *War and Revolution: Occupation and Collaboration*, p. 723 n. 7.

275. Vladimir Žerjavić, *Population Losses in Yugoslavia, 1941–1945* (Zagreb: Dom i svijet & Hrvatski institut za povijest, 1997), p. 55.

276. Žerjavić, *Gubici stanovništva Jugoslavije*, pp. 61–66.

277. For losses due to reduced natality, Lah estimated 338,000; Kočović estimated 333,000; Žerjavić estimated 326,000. See Tomasevich, *War and Revolution: Occupation and Collaboration*, p. 730. Emigration losses are as cited in ibid., p. 731.

278. Hannah Arendt, *Totalitarianism* [Part Three of *The Origins of Totalitarianism*] (New York and London: Harcourt Brace Jovanovich, 1951), pp. 160, 42.

279. According to Arendt, this claim of functionalism is, in any event, self-contradictory to the extent that fascist parties reject the entire concept of utility and utilitarianism—a rejection which undermines any functionalist claims. See Arendt, *Totalitarianism*, pp. 9, 45.

5. Happy Comrades?

1. Srećko M. Džaja, *Die politische Realität des Jugoslawismus (1918–1991): Mit besonderer Berücksichtigung Bosnien-Herzegowinas* (Munich: R. Oldenbourg Verlag, 2002), pp. 211–212.

2. Dimitrije Boarov, *Politička istorija Vojvodine* (Novi Sad: Europanon consulting, 2001), p. 176.

3. Ivo Goldstein, *Croatia: A History*, trans. from Croatian by Nikolina Jovanović (Montreal: McGill-Queen's University Press, 1999), p. 159. See also Ludwig Steindorff, *Kroatien. Vom Mittelalter bis zur Gegenwart* (Munich and Regensburg: Südosteuropa-Gesellschaft and Verlag Friedrich Pustet, 2001), pp. 191–192.

4. See Miloš Mišović, *Ko je tražio republiku. Kosovo 1945–1985* (Belgrade: Narodna knjiga, 1987), chaps. 1–2.

5. Tim Judah, *The Serbs: History, Myth and the Destruction of Yugoslavia* (New Haven, Conn.: Yale University Press, 1997), p. 150.

6. Stefan Troebst, "Yugoslav Macedonia, 1943–1953: Building the Party, the State, and the

Nation," in Melissa K. Bokovoy, Jill A. Irvine, and Carol S. Lilly (eds.), *State-Society Relations in Yugoslavia, 1945–1992* (New York: St. Martin's Press, 1997), pp. 252–253.

7. John Micgiel, "'Bandits and Reactionaries': The Suppression of the Opposition in Poland, 1944–1946," in Norman Naimark and Leonid Gibianskii (eds.), *The Establishment of Communist Regimes in Eastern Europe, 1944–1949* (Boulder, Colo.: Westview Press, 1997), p. 103.

8. Georgi M. Dimitrov was no relation to Bulgarian communist leader Georgi Dimitrov.

9. In a speech delivered in Zagreb on 31 October 1946, Tito branded Maček "public enemy no. 1." D530, 4 November 1946, S, T. A. Hickok, Chargés d'Affairs/B to State, in U. S. Department of State, *Records Relating to the Internal Affairs of Yugoslavia 1945–1949*, Decimal file 860h, at SAL [hereafter, *Records 1945–1949*], Reel 3 (files 00/10–10-1146 to 00/1-2747). Re Maček's cooperation, see D817, 27 June 1950, R, George V. Allen, Ambassador/B to State, 768.00/6-2750 in *Records of the U.S. Department of State Relating to the Internal Affairs of Yugoslavia 1950–1954*, Decimal file 768 (RG59, LM77), at NA [hereafter, *Records 1950–1954*], Reel 1 (files 00/3-2150 to 00/4-2852); and MC, by Mr. Marcy (EE/State), 9 May 1952, R, 768.00/5-952, in *Records 1950–1954*, Reel 2 (files 00/5-652 to 00/1-1554).

10. Letter from C. Fotić, former Yugoslav ambassador, to State (21 July 1945), in *Records 1945–1949*, Reel 1 (files 00/1-245 to 00/4-246).

11. D389 (18 June 1946), S, Harold Shantz/B to State, in *Records 1945–1949*, Reel 2 (files 00/4-346 to 00/10-1046); and Jožo Tomaševich, *War and Revolution in Yugoslavia, 1941–1945: The Chetniks* (Stanford, Calif.: Stanford University Press, 1975), pp. 458–460.

12. Lester C. Houck, chairman of the Reporting Board of the Strategic Services Unit of the War Department, memo, 12 April 1946, to Samuel Beber, Division of Southern European Affairs (State), in *Records 1945–1949*, Reel 1.

13. T, 15 June 1946, S, Shantz/B to State via War, in *Records 1945–1949*, Reel 2. See also *The Trial of Dragoljub-Draža Mihailović*, Stenographic Record and Documents from the Trial of Dragoljub-Draža Mihailović (Salisbury, N.C.: Documentary Publications, 1977; reprint of Belgrade, 1946), pp. 17–19, 24, 27–28, 34, 41–44, 47, 50, 54–59.

14. Denial of collaboration with occupation forces, reported in T, 16 June 1946, R, Shantz/B to State, in *Records 1945–1949*, Reel 2; denial of collaboration with Nedić, T, 26 June 1946, S, Shantz/B to State, in *Records 1945–1949*, Reel 2.

15. *Trial of Dragoljub-Draža Mihailović*, p. 136.

16. O. Aleksa Benigar, *Alojzije Stepinac, Hrvatski Kardinal* (Rome: Ziral, 1974), p. 639; confirmed in *Polet* (Zagreb), 8 and 15 February 1985, as cited in *Glas koncila* (Zagreb), 24 February 1985, p. 3.

17. ED 2427, 9 October 1945, American Embassy/R to State, in *Records 1945–1949*, Reel 1.

18. Benigar, *Alojzije Stepinac*, pp. 519, 542–543.

19. For Stepinac's indictment, see Jakov Blažević, Public Prosecutor of the People's Republic of Croatia, *Act of Indictment* (Zagreb, 23 September 1946), trans. as ED2 (14 October 1946), American Consulate/Z to State, in *Records 1945–1949*, Reel 3.

20. Verdict, ED2, 14 October 1946, American Consulate/Z to State, in *Records 1945–1949*, Reel 3.

21. In 1998, Cardinal Stepinac was beatified by Pope John Paul II. Beatification is the first step toward eventual canonization. See *Slobodna Dalmacija* (Split), 2 October 1998, pp. 1–3; and *Večernji list* (Zagreb), 2 October 1998, pp. 1–3.

22. Quoted in a memorandum from the Italian minister of foreign affairs, 19 June 1945, forwarded from Alexander Kirk, US Embassy/R to State, 21 June 1945, p. 1, in *Records 1945–1949*, Reel 1.

23. See Tito's talks with Winston Churchill in Naples, 12 August 1944, as summarized in the public records of the War Office, Great Britain, as cited in Vojislav Koštunica and Kosta Čavoški, *Party Pluralism or Monism: Social Movements and the Political System in Yugoslavia, 1944–1949* (Boulder, Colo.: East European Monographs, 1985), p. 48.

24. Quoted in Koštunica and Čavoški, *Party Pluralism or Monism*, p. 59.

25. T, 27 July 1945, S, Shantz/B to State via War, in *Records 1945–1949*, Reel 1; and D, 29 July 1945, S, Shantz/B to State via War, in *Records 1945–1949*, Reel 1.

26. T, 21 August 1945, Shantz/B to State via War, in *Records 1945–1949*, Reel 1; and Vojislav Koštunica and Kosta Čavoški, *Party Pluralism or Monism: Social Movements and the Political System in Yugoslavia, 1944–1949* (Boulder, Colo.: East European Monographs, 1985), p. 27.

27. Koštunica and Čavoški, *Party Pluralism or Monism*, p. 63.

28. T, 13 November 1945, Richard C. Patterson, Jr., Ambassador/B to State, in *Records 1945–1949*, Reel 1.

29. T, 16 November 1945, Patterson/B to State via War, in *Records 1945–1949*, Reel 1.

30. Regarding a trial of six students from Smederevo on charges of criticizing the November 1945 elections, refusing to perform "volunteer" work or to take part in communist demonstrations, and smashing pictures of Tito and former education minister Ribnikar, see D380, 10 June 1946, C, Shantz/B to State, in *Records 1945–1949*, Reel 2. Kardelj, quoted in Koštunica and Čavoški, *Party Pluralism or Monism*, p. 151.

31. ED2427, 9 October 1945, John A. Blatnk, Capt. Air Corps/R to State, in *Records 1945–1949*, Reel 1; and Sgt. Mirko Dominis, "An account of my 7-day visit to Jugoslavia," forwarded by Alfred T. Nester, Rep. of the U.S. Political Adviser, HQ 13th Corps, Trieste, to U.S. Embassy/R, 16 October 1945, TS, in *Records 1945–1949*, Reel 1.

32. See Ildiko Erdei, "'The Happy Child' as an Icon of Socialist Transformation: Yugoslavia's Pioneer Organization," in John Lampe and Mark Mazower (eds.), *Ideologies and National Identities: The Case of Twentieth-Century Southeastern Europe* (Budapest and New York: Central European University Press, 2004), especially pp. 154, 159–160, 166–171.

33. Carol S. Lilly, *Power and Persuasion: Ideology and Rhetoric in Communist Yugoslavia, 1944–1953* (Boulder, Colo.: Westview Press, 2001), p. 121.

34. Koštunica and Čavoški, *Party Pluralism or Monism*, p. 208.

35. Airgram, 2 May 1946, U.S. Embassy/B to State, in *Records 1945–1949*, Reel 2.

36. *The Times* (London), 1 January 1947, p. 3, and 7 January 1947, p. 4.

37. *Vjesnik* (Zagreb), 27 February 1947, trans. in ED33 (12 March 1947), American Consulate/Z to State, in *Records 1945–1949*, Reel 4 (files 00/1-2847 to 00/12–3047), emphasis as given.

38. *Vjesnik*, 28 February 1947, trans. in ED33, in ibid., my emphasis.

39. Koštunica and Čavoški, *Party Pluralism or Monism*, p. 117.

40. Quoted in ibid., p. 117.

41. T335, Control 517, 1 April 1947, C, John M. Cabot, Chargé d'Affaires/B to State, in *Records 1945–1949*, Reel 4.

42. T525, Control 5851, 19 May 1947, R, Cabot/B to State, in *Records 1945–1949*, Reel 4.

43. T536, Control 6458, 20 May 1947, Cabot/B to State, in *Records 1945–1949*, Reel 4.

44. T2037, Control 419, 2 October 1947, C, Cavendish W. Cannon/B to State; and T2076, Control 2512, 8 October 1947, C, Cannon/B to State—both in *Records 1945–1949*, Reel 4.

45. D576, 22 October 1956, C, Niles W. Bond, Counselor/R to State, 768.00/10–2256 HBS, in *Records of the U.S. Department of State Relating to the Internal Affairs of Yugoslavia, 1955–1959*, Decimal file 768 (RG59, C0034), at NA, Reel 2 (files .00/9-2756 to .00/1-2758).

46. The Times, 24 February 1948, p. 3.

47. D427, Control 5543, 14 April 1948, Cannon/B to State; D473, Control 7870, 21 April 1948, Cannon/B to State; and D483, Control 8605, 23 April 1948, Cannon/B to State—all in Records 1945–1949, Reel 5 (files 00/1-248 to 00/7-2948).

48. Vjesnik, 25 June 1948, trans. in ED91, 30 June 1948, S, Consul Theodore J. Hohenthal/Z to State, in Records 1945–1949, Reel 5. Tartaglia had also worked, in the interwar years, for an accord between Croats and Serbs.

49. Quoted in Koštunica and Čavoški, Party Pluralism or Monism, p. 176.

50. Diego De Castro, Trieste: Cenni riassuntivi sul problema Giuliana nell'ultimo decennio (Bologna: Cappelli, 1953), pp. 38, 41–43; and Robert Lee Wolff, The Balkans in Our Time (Cambridge, Mass.: Harvard University Press, 1956), pp. 305–309.

51. Tito's speech (1 June 1945), as reported in Borba, 4 June 1945, and quoted in D, 4 June 1945, Patterson/B to State via Army, in Records 1945–1949, Reel 1, Borba's emphasis.

52. Demanded by General Velebit, deputy foreign minister, in talks with U.S. Embassy officials, as reported in D 549, 27 November 1946, C, US Embassy/B to State, in Records 1945–1949, Reel 3.

53. Edvard Kardelj, Reminiscences: The Struggle for Recognition and Independence— The New Yugoslavia, 1944–1957, trans. by David Norris (London: Summerfield Press, 1982), pp. 80–81; and De Castro, Trieste, p. 127.

54. C. M. Woodhouse, Modern Greece: A Short History, 5th ed. (London and Boston: Faber & Faber, 1991), pp. 244–247; and Risto Kiriazovski, Narodnoosloboditelniot Front i Drugite Organisatsi na Makedontsite og Egliaska Makedoniia, 1945–1949 (Skopje: Kultura, 1985), p. 116.

55. Kiriazovski, Narodnoosloboditelniot Front, p. 176.

56. Jasper Ridley, Tito (London: Constable, 1994), p. 264; and Kiriazovski, Narodnoosloboditelniot Front, pp. 237–238.

57. Kiriazovski, Narodnoosloboditelniot Front, pp. 176–177; confirmed in Ann Lane, Britain, the Cold War and Yugoslav Unity, 1941–1949 (Brighton: Sussex Academic Press, 1996), p. 112.

58. Andrew Rossos, "Incompatible Allies: Greek Communism and Macedonian Nationalism in the Civil War in Greece, 1943–1949," Journal of Modern History, vol. 69, no. 1 (March 1997): 42.

59. Kiriazovski, Narodnoosloboditelniot Front, pp. 233–234, 247–248.

60. Georgi Dimitrov, Georgi Dimitrov, Dnevnik 1933–1949, ed. by Dimitŭr Sirkov (Sofia: Universitetsko Izdatelstvo "Sv. Kliment Ohridski," 1997), p. 460.

61. Slobodan Nešović, Bledski sporazumi: Tito-Dimitrov (1947) (Zagreb: Globus & Školska knjiga, 1979), pp. 52, 57, 64; and Dimitrov, Georgi Dimitrov, p. 554.

62. Nešović, Bledski sporazumi, pp. 126, 132–133.

63. Milovan Djilas, Fall of the New Class: A History of Communism's Self-Destruction, trans. from Serbo-Croatian by John Loud, ed. by Vasilije Kalezić (New York: Alfred A. Knopf, 1998), pp. 71, 72.

64. Pravda, 29 January 1948, as cited in Nešović, Bledski sporazumi, p. 170.

65. R. J. Crampton, The Balkans since the Second World War (London: Pearson Education, 2002), p. 27. See also The Times (London), 21 March 1947, p. 3, and 28 March 1947, p. 3.

66. Quoted in Djilas, Fall of the New Class, p. 64.

67. Quoted in ibid., p. 65, from Savo Kržavac and Dragan Marković, Informbiro—šta je to? Jugoslavija je rekla ne (Belgrade, 1976), p. 95.

68. D 1017, 7 September 1947, R, Cavendish W. Cannon/B to State, in Records 1945–1949, Reel 4.

69. Robert Owen Freedman, *Economic Warfare in the Communist Bloc: A Study of Soviet Economic Pressure against Yugoslavia, Albania, and Communist China* (New York: Praeger, 1970), p. 19.

70. For discussion, see Jill A. Irvine, "Tito, Hebrang, and the Croat Question," *East European Politics and Societies,* vol. 5, no. 2 (Spring 1991): 306–340.

71. Stjepan Djureković, *Ja, Josip Broz-Tito* (International Books–USA, 1982), pp. 38–39; and Vladimir Dedijer, *The Battle Stalin Lost: Memoirs of Yugoslavia, 1948–1953* (New York: Viking Press, 1971), p. 141.

72. Djureković, *Ja, Josip Broz-Tito,* pp. 35–37.

73. Ivo Banac, *With Stalin, against Tito: Cominformist Splits in Yugoslav Communism* (Ithaca, N.Y.: Cornell University Press, 1988), p. 111.

74. "Resolution of the Information Bureau on the Situation of the Communist Party of Yugoslavia," 28 June 1948, trans. as ED 384, 1 July 1948, U, Rudolf E. Schoenfeld/US Legation in Bucharest to State, pp. 2–3, 9, in *Records 1945–1949,* Reel 5 (files 00/1-124 to 00/7-2948).

75. Petričević and Dapčević were put on trial on charges of treason, espionage, and subversion in Belgrade on 1–7 June 1950. They were convicted on 7 June and sentenced to 20 years imprisonment at hard labor and confiscation of their property. See D 630, 20 June 1950, R, Fowler/B to State, 768.00/6-2050; and D 737, 12 June 1950, C, Allen/B to State, 768.00/6-1250—both in *Records 1950–1954,* Reel 1.

76. Duncan Wilson, *Tito's Yugoslavia* (Cambridge: Cambridge University Press, 1979), pp. 61–62.

77. "Yugoslavia—Political Dynamics" (1 August 1960), C, de-cl. 22 November 2000 under the FIA, by the authority of NND 0011144, by SDT/SL, vol. 17, in CIA, *National Intelligence Survey,* Section 53, chap. V, NIS #21, RG 273, Box 92, on deposit at NA.

78. Cited in Banac, *With Stalin, against Tito,* pp. 148–149, 150–151.

79. Ibid., p. 177.

80. Ibid., pp. 234–235.

81. This section draws upon a section of my earlier article "Gradualism in International Confrontation: The Soviet-Yugoslav Crisis of 1947–51," *Ukrainian Quarterly,* vol. 44, no. 3–4 (Fall–Winter 1988): 238–252.

82. Vladimir Dedijer (ed.), *Dokumenti 1948,* vol. 3 (Belgrade: Rad, 1979), Document 279, p. 290; and Vladimir Dedijer, *Novi prilozi za biografiju Josipa Broza Tita,* vol. 3 (Belgrade: Rad, 1984), p. 428.

83. TURAR 2011, 17 July 1950, S, USAIRA Ankara to CSAF Washington D.C., 768.00/7-1750 in *Records 1950–1954,* Reel 1.

84. Kržavac and Marković, *Informbiro—šta je to,* p. 317, as quoted in Ivo Banac, "Yugoslav Cominformist Organizations and Insurgent Activity: 1948–1954," in Wayne S. Vucinich (ed.), *At the Brink of War and Peace: The Tito-Stalin Split in a Historic Perspective* (New York: Brooklyn College Press, 1982), p. 244.

85. Banac, "Yugoslav Cominformist Organizations," pp. 242–243, 241, 247–248.

86. Veljko Mićunović, *Moskovske godine 1956/1958* (Zagreb: S. N. Liber, 1977), p. 19.

87. Quoted in Dedijer, *Novi prilozi,* vol. 3, p. 428.

88. Stephen Clissold (ed.), *Yugoslavia and the Soviet Union, 1939–1973* (London: Oxford University Press, 1975), Document no. 133, 31 May 1949, pp. 216–217.

89. Banac, "Yugoslav Cominformist Organizations," p. 245.

90. Dedijer, *Battle Stalin Lost,* p. 212.

91. Dedijer, *Novi prilozi,* vol. 3, pp. 432–433.

92. Béla K. Király, "The Aborted Soviet Military Plans against Tito's Yugoslavia," in Vucinich (ed.), *At the Brink of War and Peace*, pp. 274–275, 278, 279.

93. Ibid., pp. 285–286.

94. Dedijer, *Novi prilozi*, vol. 3, p. 418.

95. Király, "Aborted Soviet Military Plans," pp. 286–287.

96. Freedman, *Economic Warfare*, p. 35; and Djureković, *Ja, Josip Broz-Tito*, p. 68.

97. *Borba*, 9 August 1950, summarized in D 121, 10 August 1950, R, R. Borden Reams, Counselor/B to State, Control no. 4628, 768.00/8-1050 in *Records 1950–1954*, Reel 1.

98. T, 14 February 1951, R, Acheson/State to London, 768.00/2-1451 in *Records 1950–1954*, Reel 1.

99. Dedijer, *Dokumenti 1948*, vol. 3, Document no. 274, pp. 237, 246.

100. IT YUG 358, 13 April 1951, S, MA/B to State, 768.00 (W)/4-1351; IT YUG 378, 20 April 1951, S, MA/B to State, 768.00 (W)/4-2051; IT YUG 400, 4 May 1951, S, MA/B to State, 768.00 (W)/5-451; Message no. 101630Z, 10 August 1951, S, MA/B to State et al., 768.00 (W)/8-1051; M no. 171655Z, 17 August 1951, S, MA/B to State et al., 768.00 (W)/8-1751; M no. 241725Z, 24 August 1951, S, MA/B to State et al., 768.00 (W)/8-2451; and IT "Unnumbered," 8 September 1951, S, Beam/B to State, 768.00 (W)/9-851—all in *Records 1950–1954*, Reel 3.

101. Dedijer, *Dokumenti 1948*, vol. 3, Document no. 278, pp. 274–277.

102. Ibid., vol. 3, Document no. 279, p. 334; and Kiraly, "Aborted Soviet Military Plans," pp. 287–288.

103. D 290, 31 October 1950, S, Reams/B to State, 768.00/10–3150, in *Records 1950–1954*, Reel 1.

104. T 645, 18 May 1950, priority, Allen/B to State, Control no. 9252, 768.00/5-1850 in *Records 1950–1954*, Reel 1.

105. D 1211, 11 May 1954, S, Riddleberger/B to State, 768.00/5-1154 in *Records 1950–1954*, Reel 3 (files 00/1-1854 to 00 (W)/5-2952).

106. Woodhouse, *Modern Greece*, p. 281.

107. D 386, 30 November 1950, C, Fowler/B to State, 768.00/11-3050 in *Records 1950–1954*, Reel 1.

108. Edvard Kardelj, *The Communist Party of Yugoslavia in the Struggle for New Yugoslavia, for People's Authority and for Socialism: Report Delivered at the V Congress of the CPY* (Belgrade, 1948), p. 51.

109. Edvard Kardelj, *Deset godina narodne revolucije* (1951), as quoted in Ivo Lapenna, *State and Law: Soviet and Yugoslav Theory* (London: University of London Press, 1964), p. 45.

110. Rodoljub Čolaković, "Socialism and Democracy," in *Review of International Affairs* (Belgrade), vol. 3, no. 22 (16 November 1952): 11.

111. Edvard Kardelj, "The Role and Tasks of the Socialist Alliance of the Working People of Yugoslavia," report submitted to the Fourth Congress of the People's Front in Belgrade, 23 February 1953, ED 666, 24 February 1953, Woodruff Wallner, Counselor/B to State, 768.00/2-2453, in *Records 1950–1954*, Reel 2.

6. Dreaming a New Dream, 1950–1962

1. From *Politika*, 12 March 1951, quoted in ED677, 15 March 1951, R, William A. Fowler, Charges d'Affaires/B to State, 768.00/3-1551, in *Records of the U.S. Department of State Relating to the Internal Affairs of Yugoslavia 1950–1954*, Decimal file 768 (RG59, LM77), at NA [hereafter, *Records 1950–1954*], Reel 1.

2. Dušan Bilandžić, *Management of Yugoslav Economy (1945–1966)*, trans. by Jelena Hercog, rev. Betty Popovic, ed. Milorad Marković (Novi Sad: Dnevnik, 1967), pp. 17–18.

3. D280, 18 October 1952, R. Jacob D. Beam, Charges d'Affaires/B to State, 768.00/10-1352, in *Records 1950–1954*, Reel 2; and *The Times* (London), 23 April 1957, p. 11.

4. CIC/S: Report by Robert Clayton Mudd, S/A, 12 February 1947, S, decl. 14 January 1986, Auth Para 1-603 DoD 5200.1-R, in *Records of the Army Staff*, ROACS, G-2, Intelligence RIIR, *Security Classified Intelligence and Investigative Dossiers, 1939–1976*, IRR Impersonal File, RG 319, Stack Area 270, Row A, Box 107, file ZF010183 (Ustashi), at NA [hereafter, *Records of the Army Staff—Ustaše*].

5. CIC/S: Report from Steve Daich, S/A, no. 3-18961, 20 August 1953, classification not clear (presumably S), decl. 29 January 1986, in *Records of the Army Staff—Ustaše*.

6. See Milo Bošković, *Antijugoslavenska fašistička emigracija* (Belgrade and Novi Sad: Sloboda and Dnevnik, 1980).

7. Report from Daniel Radell, S/A, CIC Badgastein Field Office, 4 April 1950, Ref. X-7021, to CIC/S, classification not clear (presumably S), decl. 29 January 1986, in *Records of the Army Staff—Ustaše*.

8. CIC/S: Report by Special Agents George Milovanovich, Jack E. Heibler, Kurt A. Meitner, and Ralph A. Peavey, no. S-767, 11 December 1947, S, decl. 29 January 1986, in *Records of the Army Staff—Ustaše*. The meeting took place on 25 November 1947.

9. Report from John L. Spiegler, S/A, 970th Counter Intelligence Corps Detachment, 16 February 1948, C, decl. 1 September 1978 by Dep Cdr USAINSCOM FOIC, Auth Para 1-603 DoD 5200, in *Records of the Army Staff—Ustaše*.

10. D678, 20 December 1950, C, Milton C. Rewinkel, Second Secretary/M to State, 768.00/12-2050 in *Records 1950–1954*, Reel 1.

11. MC, 16 May 1950, C, John C. Campbell to Mssrs. Yost & Joyce, Balkan Affairs, 768.00/4-1750, in *Records 1950–1954*, Reel 1. A dispatch dated 24 June 1952 suggested, however, that Šokić was "fundamentally out of touch with post-war economic life" and had "no very clear view of how to put [his projects] into action." D13, 24 June 1952, S, Boland More, American Consul/Benghazi, Libya to State, 768.00/8-1852, in *Records 1950–1954*, Reel 2.

12. D807, 27 June 1952, S, Villard/Tripoli, Libya to State, 768.00/6-2752, in *Records 1950–1954*, Reel 2.

13. D13, 24 June 1952, S, Bolard More, American Consul/Benghazi, Libya to State, 768.00/8-1852, in *Records 1950–1954*, Reel 2.

14. Quoted in MC, by Mr. Marcy (EE/State), 9 May 1952, R, 768.00/5-952, in *Records 1950–1954*, Reel 2.

15. IT, YUG 616, 10 February 1950, S, MA/B to State, 768.00 (W)/2-1050; and IT, YUG 623, 18 February 1950, S, MA/B to State, 768.00 (W)/2-1850—both in *Records 1950–1954*, Reel 3.

16. D995, 29 January 1951, C, George V. Allen, Ambassador/B to State, 768.00/1-2951, in *Records 1950–1954*, Reel 1.

17. IT, YUG 236, 26 January 1951, S, MA/B to State, 768.00 (W)/1-2651; IT, YUG 243, 2 February 1951, S, MA/B to State, 768.00 (W)/2-251; and IT, YUG 257, 9 February 1951, S, MA/B to State, 768.00 (W)/2-951—all in *Records 1950–1954*, Reel 3.

18. *The Times*, 5 February 1951, p. 5.

19. Kocebu was sentenced to 15 years at hard labor. See D810, 11 May 1951, Cloyce K. Huston, Acting Officer in Charge of Balkan Affairs (State) to Mr. Chadbourne, 768.00/4-2651, in *Records 1950–1954*, Reel 1.

20. Report from Ronald J. Wenner, S/A, 66th CIC Det, Reg VII, 12 January 1951, Ref. VVI-2790, C, decl. 16 January 1998, in *Records of the Army Staff—Ustaše*.

21. D118, 6 November 1952, C, Bernard C. Connelly, American Consul/Z to State, 768.5/11-652, in *Records 1950–1954,* Reel 2.

22. Re. Chetniks, D1682, 7 June 1957, OUO, Riddleberger/B to State, 768.00/6-757 HBS, in *Records 1955–1959,* Reel 2; re. Ustaše, D61, 20 December 1957, C, Stephen E. Palmer, Jr., American Consul/Sarajevo to State, 768.00/12-2057, in *Records 1955–1959,* Reel 2.

23. Quoted in *The Times,* 7 January 1958, p. 7; also D1114, 21 January 1958, C, Elim O'Shaughnessy/B to State, 768.00/1-2158, in *Records 1955–1959,* Reel 2; and D1154, 31 January 1958, C, O'Shaughnessy/B to State, 768.00/1-3158, in *Records 1955–1959,* Reel 2.

24. Pavlović was given eight and a half years in prison, Krekić seven years, and Žujović four years. See *The Times,* 4 February 1958, p. 8, and 5 February 1958, p. 6.

25. D1158, 1 February 1958, C, O'Shaughnessy/B to State, 768.00/2-158, in *Records 1955–1959,* Reel 2.

26. *The Times,* 1 April 1959, p. 8, and 6 April 1959, p. 7.

27. *The Times,* 18 January 1960, p. 11.

28. *The Times,* 23 January 1960, p. 7, and 30 January 1960, p. 7.

29. Franz Goedhart, columnist for the Dutch newspaper, *Het Parol,* as quoted in D104, 18 July 1950, C, William T. Nunley, Attache/The Hague to State, 768.00/7-1850, in *Records 1950–1954,* Reel 1.

30. D441, 17 April 1950, C, Fowler/B to State, 768.00/4-1750, in *Records 1950–1954,* Reel 1.

31. The elections were held on 18 March 1951. D713, 22 March 1951, R. John J. Haggerty, First Secretary/B to State, 768.00/3-2251, in *Records 1950–1954,* Reel 1.

32. ED485, 14 September 1950, U, Oslo to State: Article by Sigurd Evensmo for *Arbeiderbladet,* 26 August 1950, trans. by R. Askeroi, 768.00/9-1450, in *Records 1950–1954,* Reel 1.

33. T1019, 3 February 1951, C, Allen/B to State, 768.00/2-351, in *Records 1950–1954,* Reel 1.

34. *Borba,* 15 April 1951, extracted in D769, 12 April 1951, C, Haggerty/B to State, 768.02/4-1751, in *Records 1950–1954,* Reel 5.

35. D29, 11 July 1952, C, Richard F. Allen, Counselor for Economic Affairs/B to State, 768.00/7-1152, in *Records 1950–1954,* Reel 2.

36. D1767, 26 May 1951, S, George Allen/B to State, 768.00/5-2651, in *Records 1950–1954,* Reel 3.

37. Ilija Jukić, as reported in an MC of 6 October 1956, attached to Counselor/Rome to State, 768.00/10-2256 HBS, in *Records of the U.S. Department of State Relating to the Internal Affairs of Yugoslavia 1955–1959,* Decimal file 768 (RG259, C0034), at NA [hereafter, *Records 1955–1959*], Reel 2.

38. *Borba,* 23 March 1952, trans. as E1 to D917, 27 March 1952, Jacob D. Beam, Charge d'Affaires/B to State, 768.00/3-2752, in *Records 1950–1954,* Reel 3.

39. The proposal to change the "party" to a "league" originated with Milovan Djilas. See Milovan Djilas, *Rise and Fall* (San Diego and New York: Harcourt Brace Jovanovich, 1983), p. 292.

40. Paul Shoup, "Problems of Party Reform in Yugoslavia," *American Slavic and East European Review,* vol. 18, no. 3 (October 1959): 339–340.

41. Quoted in George W. Hoffman and Fred Warner Neal, *Yugoslavia and the New Communism* (New York: Twentieth Century Fund, 1962), p. 213.

42. D501, 1 February 1954, C, Edwin M. I. Kretzmann, First Secretary/B to State, 768.00/2-154, in *Records 1950–1954,* Reel 3.

43. D1038, 29 June 1953, R, Turner C. Cameron, Jr., First Secretary/B to State, 768.00/6-2953, in *Records 1950–1954,* Reel 2.

44. *Komunist,* as quoted in D67, 21 July 1953, R, Wallner/B to State, 768.00/8-2053, in *Records 1950–1954,* Reel 2.

45. D TOUST 10, 2 November 1953, C, John E. McGowan, Acting Public Affairs Office USIS/B to USIA, 768.00/11-253, in *Records 1950–1954,* Reel 2.

46. Stephen Clissold, *Djilas: The Progress of a Revolutionary* (Hounslow, Middlesex: Maurice Temple Smith, 1983), pp. 233–235, 240.

47. Quoted in ibid., p. 240.

48. Quoted in A. Ross Johnson, *The Transformation of Communist Ideology: The Yugoslav Case, 1945–1953* (Cambridge, Mass.: MIT Press, 1972), p. 217; Thomas Taylor Hammond, "The Djilas Affair and Jugoslav Communism," *Foreign Affairs,* vol. 33, no. 2 (January 1955): 306.

49. Quoted from *Oslobodjenje,* 19 January 1954, in D174, 11 February 1954, C, Connelly/Z to State, 768.00/2-1154, in *Records 1950–1954,* Reel 3; regarding Slovenia and Croatia, D841, 16 June 1954, C, Kretzmann/B to State, 768.00/6-1654, in *Records 1950–1954,* Reel 3; regarding Macedonia, *Komunist,* no. 4 (April 1954), E1 to D767, 12 May 1954, U, Kretzmann/B to State, 768.00/5-1254, in *Records 1950–1954,* Reel 3.

50. D521, 8 February 1954, C, Kretzmann/B to State, 768.00/2-854, in *Records 1950–1954,* Reel 3.

51. Quoted in Clissold, *Djilas,* p. 244.

52. D525, 14 or 24 February 1954 (date partly obscured by stamp), C, Kretzmann/B to State, 768.00/2-2454, in *Records 1950–1954,* Reel 3.

53. *Borba,* 18 January 1954, trans. as ED490, 25 January 1954, C, Kretzmann/B to State, 768.00/1-2554, in *Records 1950–1954,* Reel 3.

54. D483, 19 January 1954, U, Kretzmann/B to State, 768.00/1-1954, in *Records 1950–1954,* Reel 3.

55. Quoted from *Borba,* 18 January 1954, in D480, 18 January 1954, C, Kretzmann/B to State, 768.00/1-1954, in *Records 1950–1954,* Reel 3.

56. According to a speech by Aleksandar Ranković, minister of the interior, at the Fourth Plenum of the CC, 29 March 1954, as summarized in D660, 30 March 1954, C, Kretzmann/B to State, 768.00/3-3054, in *Records 1950–1954,* Reel 3.

57. D174, 11 February 1954, C, Connelly/Z to State, 768.00/2-1154, in *Records 1950–1954,* Reel 3.

58. D841, 16 June 1954, C, Kretzmann/B to State, 768.00/6-1654, in *Records 1950–1954,* Reel 3.

59. *Borba,* 31 March 1954, trans. as E2 to D767, 12 May 1954, U, Kretzmann/B to State, 768.00/5-1254, in *Records 1950–1954,* Reel 3.

60. XIR No. 0539, 21 August 1957, C, Rome, SP 103 MARS, Evaluation: B-F-6, in *Records of the Army Staff,* ROACS, G-2, Intelligence, RIRR, *Security Classified Intelligence and Investigative Dossiers, 1939–1976,* IRR Personal Name File, RG319, Stack Area 270, Row A, Box 10A, file AE 517838 (Bakarić), at NA [hereafter, *Records of the Army Staff—Bakarić*].

61. Robert Lee Wolff, *The Balkans in Our Time* (Cambridge, Mass.: Harvard University Press, 1956), pp. 430–431.

62. Melissa K. Bokovoy, *Peasants and Communists: Politics and Ideology in the Yugoslav Countryside, 1941–1953* (Pittsburgh: University of Pittsburgh Press, 1998), pp. 103, 116–117, 119, 136–137. See also Vera Kržišnik-Bukić, *Cazinska buna* (Sarajevo: Svjetlost, 1991).

63. IT, YUG 768, 9 June 1950, S, MA/B to State, 768.00 (W)/6-950, *Records 1950–1954,* Reel 3.

64. IT, YUG 93, 29 September 1950, S, MA/B to State, 768.00 (W)/9-2950, in *Records 1950–1954,* Reel 3.

65. *The Times,* 15 January 1951, p. 3.

66. *The Times,* 7 May 1951, p. 3.

67. *The Times,* 12 June 1951, p. 7.

68. *The Times,* 19 August 1952, p. 4; and Wolff, *Balkans in Our Time,* p. 433.

69. Wolff, *Balkans in Our Time,* p. 435.

70. D1169, 29 April 1954, OUO, Riddleberger/B to State, 768.00/4-2954, in *Records 1950–1954,* Reel 3.

71. See Ćiril Petešić, *Katoličko svećenstvo u NOB-u 1941–1945* (Zagreb: VPA, 1982).

72. *New York Times,* 3 February 1950, p. 4, and 5 February 1950, p. 16.

73. *New York Times,* 4 March 1950, p. 8.

74. *New York Times,* 7 March 1950, p. 5.

75. *New York Times,* 14 September 1950, p. 22.

76. *New York Times,* 27 September 1950, p. 17, and 7 October 1950, p. 5.

77. *New York Times,* 20 February 1952, p. 11.

78. Quoted in *The Times,* 26 January 1952, p. 3.

79. *Slovenski poročebalec,* 13 September 1952, as reported in *Il Quotidiano,* 21 September 1952, as summarized in D1349, 25 September 1952, C, Durbrow/Rome to State, 768.00/9-2552, in *Records 1950–1954,* Reel 2.

80. *New York Times,* 18 December 1952, pp. 1, 14, and 19 December 1952, pp. 6.

81. D634, 23 June 1950, C, Fowler/B to State, 768.00/6-2350, in *Records 1950–1954,* Reel 1.

82. *New York Times,* 2 July 1950, p. 8.

83. *Borba,* 12 May 1952, attached as ED1045, 12 May 1952, from Turner C. Cameron, Jr., First Secretary/B to State, 768.00/5-1252, in *Records 1950–1954,* Reel 2.

84. *The Times,* 30 July 1954, pp. 8, 9. See also Klaus Buchenau, *Orthodoxie und Katholizismus in Jugoslawien 1945–1991* (Wiesbaden: Harrassowitz Verlag 2004), pp. 129–130, 254–255.

85. *New York Times,* 27 June 1950, p. 13, and 4 July 1951, p. 9; and *The Times,* 26 July 1954, p. 6.

86. Quoted from *New York Times,* 8 October 1950, p. 44.

87. *New York Times,* 10 February 1952, p. 10.

88. *The Times,* 25 August 1953, p. 9.

89. *The Times,* 28 September 1953, p. 4.

90. D519, 22 April 1958, Oliver M. Marcy, First Secretary/B to State, 768.00/4-2253, in *Records of the U.S. Department of State Relating to the Internal Affairs of Yugoslavia, 1955–1959,* Decimal file 768 (RG59, C0034), at NA [hereafter, *Records 1955–1959*], Reel 2.

91. *The Times,* 17 May 1955, p. 8.

92. D281, 8 November 1956, C, Edward W. Burgess, Second Secretary/B to State, 768.11/11–856 HBS, in *Records 1955–1959,* Reel 2.

93. See, for example, IT YUG 378, 20 April 1951, S, MA/B to State, 768.00 (W)/4-2051; IT YUG 400, 4 May 1951, S, MA/B to State, 768.00 (W)/5-451; IM no. 031610Z, 3 August 1951, S, MA/B to State et al., 768.00 (W)/8-1051; Message no. 171655Z, 17 August 1951, S, MA/B to State et al., 768.00 (W)/8-1751; and IT "Unnumbered," 8 September 1951, S, Beam/S to State, 768.00 (W)/9-851—all in *Records 1950–1954,* Reel 3.

94. UPI, 10 June 1993, and AP, 11 June 1993, in *Lexis-Nexis Academic Universe,* citing archival sources unearthed by Russian historian Dmitry Volkogonov.

95. AFP, 11 June 1993, in *Lexis-Nexis Academic Universe.* See also *Japan Times,* 12 June 1993, p. 4.

96. Robert F. Byrnes, "The Dispute: Historical Background," in Václav L. Beneš, Robert F. Byrnes, and Nicolas Spulber (eds.), *The Second Soviet-Yugoslav Dispute: Full Text of Main Documents* (Bloomington: Indiana University Press, n.d. [1958?]), p. xvi; Pierre Maurer, *La reconciliation Sovieto-Yougoslave, 1954–1958. Illusions et disillusions de Tito* (Fribourg, Switz.: Editions Delvar, 1991), p. 66.

97. "Statement by Soviet First Party Secretary Nikita S. Khrushchev on Arrival at Belgrade Airport, May 26, 1955," in Robert Bass and Elizabeth Marbury (eds.), *The Soviet-Yugoslav Controversy, 1948–58: A Documentary Record* (New York: Prospect Books, 1959), p. 53.

98. Maurer, *La reconciliation Sovieto-Yougoslave,* p. 79.

99. "Joint Soviet-Yugoslav Declaration, Belgrade, June 2, 1955," in Bass and Marbury, eds., *Soviet-Yugoslav Controversy,* p. 57; and *The Times,* 3 June 1955, p. 6.

100. *The Times,* 28 June 1955, p. 9.

101. D88, 9 February 1956, C, Robert C. Martindale, American Consul/Z to State, 768.00/2-956, in *Records 1955–1959,* Reel 1.

102. Quoted in *The Times* 21 June 1956, p. 8.

103. *The Times,* 20 September 1956, p. 9.

104. *The Times,* 19 September 1956, p. 6, and 1 October 1956, p. 8.

105. *The Times,* 2 October 1956, p. 8.

106. *The Times,* 16 October 1956, p. 8.

107. "Marshal Tito's speech at Pula, November 11, 1956," in Bass and Marbury, *Soviet-Yugslav Controversy,* p. 73. See also interview with Tito conducted by Edward R. Murrow (26 June 1957), S, attached to a missing D, 768.11/6-2657, in *Records 1955–1959,* Reel 7.

108. D307, 23 November 1956, C, Burgess/B to State, 768.00/11—2356 HBS, in *Records 1955–1959,* Reel 7.

109. "Pravda Article of November 23, 1956, in reply to Tito's speech at Pula," in Bass and Marbury eds., *Soviet-Yugoslav Controversy,* p. 78.

110. "Vice-President Kardelj's speech to the Federal People's Assembly of Yugoslavia, December 6, 1956," in Bass and Marbury, *Soviet-Yugoslav Controversy,* pp. 90, 91.

111. Quoted in *The Times,* 12 August 1957, p. 6.

112. *The Times,* 13 December 1956, p. 9; 27 July 1957, p. 6; 12 August 1957, p. 6; 6 September 1957, p. 9; and 7 October 1957, p. 6.

113. *The Times,* 20 January 1961, p. 12, and 21 January 1961, p. 6.

114. P. Fedoseev, I. Pomelov, and V. Cherpakov, "On the Draft Program of the League of Communists of Yugoslavia," from *Kommunist,* 15 April 1958, trans. in Benes, Byrnes, and Spulber, *Second Soviet-Yugoslav Dispute,* p. 96.

115. "The Unity and Solidarity of Marxist-Leninist Parties—Guarantee of Further Victories of the World Socialist System (*Pravda,* May 9, 1958)," trans. in Benes, Byrnes, and Spulber, eds., *Second Soviet-Yugoslav Dispute,* pp. 139, 142, 151, 154.

116. "Reply to the Moscow *Pravda* Article on the Seventh Congress of the League of Communists of Yugoslavia and Questions of Cooperation (*Borba,* May 17, 1958)," trans. in Benes, Byrnes, and Spulber, *Second Soviet-Yugoslav Dispute,* pp. 235, 244.

117. *Yugoslavia's Way: The Program of the League of the Communists of Yugoslavia,* trans. by Stoyan Pribechevich (New York: All Nations Press, 1958), pp. 24, 48, 111–120, 188–197, 252–253.

118. For a report about problems of internal party discipline, see *The Times,* 12 February 1952, p. 4.

119. *Komunist,* 28 February 1958, trans. as ED428, 6 March 1958, C, Oliver M. Marcy, First Secretary/B to State, 768.00/3-658 HBS, in *Records 1955–1959,* Reel 3.

120. Quoted in *The Times,* 1 March 1958, p. 5.

121. Quoted in Hoffman and Neal, *Yugoslavia and the New Communism,* p. 201.

122. Ibid., p. 203.

123. Quoted in *The Times,* 24 November 1959, p. 10.

124. *The Times,* 22 April 1960, p. 13. See also Hoffman and Neal, *Yugoslavia and the New Communism,* p. 209.

125. Dušan Bilandžić, *Historija Socijalističke Federativne Republike Jugoslavije: Glavni procesi* (Zagreb: Školska knjiga, 1978), pp. 247–250.

7. The Reform Crisis, 1962–1970

1. Dušan Bilandžić, "Šok nakon buma," *Start,* no. 479 (30 May 1987): 40.

2. Dušan Bilandžić, "Tajno pismo pred javnošću," *Start,* no. 478 (16 May 1987): 35; and Dušan Bilandžić, "Pet važnih koraka," *Start,* no. 481 (27 June 1987): 46.

3. Bilandžić, "Pet važnih," p. 46.

4. Božo Repe, "Slovenians and the Federal Yugoslavia," in *Balkan Forum* (Skopje), vol. 3, no. 1 (March 1995): 145–146.

5. Fritz W. Hondius, *The Yugoslav Community of Nations* (The Hague: Mouton, 1968), p. 294.

6. Quoted in ibid., p. 242.

7. CIA, "Outlook for Yugoslavia," NIE, HRP 92-4, NNR-263-94-008, 23 May 1961, S, decl. 2/15/95, on deposit at NA, RG 263, Box 8, folder 5, p. 7.

8. *The Times* (London), 9 April 1962, p. 7.

9. Deborah D. Milenkovitch, *Plan and Market in Yugoslav Economic Thought* (New Haven, Conn.: Yale University Press, 1971), p. 177.

10. Stipe Šuvar, "Radnička klasa i samoupravni sistem," in *Naše teme,* vol. 5 (1968), as quoted in Slaven Letica, "O privrednoj reformi deset godina kasnije," *Pitanja,* vol. 7, no. 7–8 (1978): 60.

11. Šime Djodan, "Gospodarska reforma i izbor optimalnog modela rasta," *Kolo,* vol. 6, no. 4 (April 1968): 303.

12. Repe, "Slovenians," p. 148. These views were expressed by Kardelj at the November 1965 session of the Executive Bureau of the CC LCY.

13. See Othmar Nikola Haberl, *Parteiorganisation und nationale Frage in Jugoslawien* (Berlin: Otto Harassowitz, 1976), pp. 24–28; and Stipe Šuvar, *Nacionalno i nacionalisticko* (Split: Marksistički Centar, 1974), pp. 127–134.

14. See Pedro Ramet, "Political Struggle and Institutional Reorganization in Yugoslavia," *Political Science Quarterly,* vol. 99, no. 2 (Summer 1984): 289–301.

15. Laszlo Sekelj may be correct in suggesting that I had deemphasized (underestimated?) the complexity of the Yugoslav political landscape in my decision to emphasize the polarization at this time, in my *Nationalism and Federalism,* 1st ed. But, by the same virtue, Sekelj is probably guilty of having deemphasized (underestimated?) the degree of polarization in the LCY at that time. On this point, see Laslo Sekelj, *Yugoslavia: The Process of Disintegration,* trans. from Serbo-Croatian by Vera Vukelić (Boulder, Colo.: Social Science Monographs, 1993), pp. 28–29.

16. Interviews, Belgrade, Zagreb, and Ljubljana, July 1982.

17. World Bank, *Yugoslavia: Self-Management, Socialism and the Challenges of Development,* Report No. 1615a-YU, 21 March 1978, p. I-41.

18. See Leon Geršković, "Istorijski razvoj društveno-političkog sistema Jugoslavije," in *Društveno-politički sistem SFRJ* (Belgrade: Radnička štampa, 1975), p. 99.

19. See Crane Brinton, *The Anatomy of a Revolution,* rev. and enlarged ed. (New York: Vintage Books, 1965).

20. *Borba,* 17 February 1970, p. 5.

21. Dennison I. Rusinow, *The Yugoslav Experiment, 1948–1974* (Berkeley and Los Angeles: University of California Press, 1977), pp. 112, 126, 130–131; and Paul Shoup, *Communism and the Yugoslav National Question* (New York: Columbia University Pess, 1968), p. 240.

22. Kosta Mihailović, "Regionalni aspekt privrednog razvoja," in *Ekonomist,* no. 1 (1962), as cited in Šime Djodan, "Pred kritičnom barijerom," in *Dometi,* vol. 2, no. 3 (March 1969): 5.

23. Milenkovitch, *Plan and Market,* p. 185.

24. Detailed figures on labor efficiency are given in Momir Ćećez, "O efikasnosti društvenih sredstava u privredno nedovoljno razvijenim područjima," *Pregled,* vol. 70, no. 1 (January 1980): 27–40.

25. "Another concept of development, originating in Slovenia, is that the leading areas should be the most developed area in the country, which by its fast development can accumulate resources for investment in the development of other areas, which should follow the lead of the most industrially advanced part." Rudolf Bičanić, *Economic Policy in Socialist Yugoslavia* (Cambridge: Cambridge University Press, 1973), p. 201.

26. Djodan, "Pred kritičnom barijerom," p. 6.

27. Šime Djodan, "Robno-novčani privredni model i regionalni razvoj u našim uvjetima," *Kolo,* vol. 6, no. 10 (October 1968): 363. Djodan is inconsistent when it comes to Bosnia—he sometimes claims that it had "benefited" from investment in "political factories" and at other times argues that Bosnia, like Croatia, was exploited by the "East." My guess, based on a reading of many of Djodan's writings and on a lengthy interview with him in 1989, is that Djodan probably thought of the Serbian-inhabited areas of Bosnia as benefiting from the disbursement of funds, and of Croatian-inhabited areas of Bosnia-Herzegovina as being exploited.

28. Djodan, "Pred kritičnom barijerom," p. 6.

29. Edvard Kardelj, *Raskršća u razvitku našeg socijalističkog društva* (Belgrade: Komunist, 1969), p. 42, as quoted in Šuvar, *Nacionalno i nacionalističko,* p. 284.

30. Rusinow, *Yugoslav Experiment,* pp. 158–159.

31. Shoup, *Communism and the Yugoslav National Question,* p. 192.

32. Ibid., pp. 251, 222.

33. See Haberl, *Parteiorganisation,* pp. 28–29, 41–43. On Vojvodina's association, see Steven L. Burg, "Decision-making in Yugoslavia," *Problems of Communism,* vol. 29, no. 2 (March–April 1980): 4.

34. Dennison I. Rusinow, "The Price of Pluralism," in *American Universities Field Staff Reports,* Southeast Europe Series, vol. 18, no. 1 (July 1971): 9.

35. See Voja Jovanović, "Otkloniti sve što smeta saradnji i boljem razumevanju," *Komunist,* 24 March 1966, p. 2.

36. Boro Krivokapić, *Jugoslavija i komunisti: Adresa Jovana Djordjevića* (Belgrade: Mladost, 1988), p. 55.

37. Branko Petranović, *Istorija Jugoslavije, 1918–1988* (Belgrade: Nolit, 1988), vol. 3, p. 387.

38. Vojin Lukić, *Sećanja i saznanja: Aleksandar Ranković i Brionski plenum* (Titograd: Novica Jovović, 1989), p. 25.

39. Ibid., pp. 23, 43–44, 93, 34.

40. *Nova Makedonija* (Skopje), 3 July 1966, p. 3.

41. J. B. Tito, *Govori i članci,* as quoted in Haberl, *Parteiorganisation,* p. 32.

42. Petranović, *Istorija Jugoslavije,* vol. 3, p. 383; and Zoran Sekulić, *Pad i ćutnja Aleksandra Rankovića* (Belgrade: Dositej, 1989), p. 15.

43. The plenum was informed that, on the basis of materials assembled by the public prosecutor, it was apparent that both Ranković and Stefanović were guilty of "anti-constitutional activity." However, bearing in mind Ranković's past contributions and the fact that their alleged conspiracy never had any chance of success, it was decided not to initiate criminal procedures against them. See Sekulić, *Pad i ćutnja,* pp. 316–320. In the wake of the dismissal of Ranković and his associates, various party organizations and enterprises issued statements of support for the party's decision. See *Nova Makedonija,* 8 July 1966, p. 2.

44. Duncan Wilson, *Tito's Yugoslavia* (Cambridge: Cambridge University Press, 1979), pp. 163, 173–174; and Dušan Bilandžić, *Historija Socijalističke Federativne Republike Jugoslavije: Glavni procesi* (Zagreb: Školska knjiga, 1978), pp. 323–324.

45. *Politika,* 13 September 1969, p. 5. For a further discussion of the "Žanko affair," see Mihailo Blečić and Ivica Dolenc (eds.), *Slučaj Žanko* (Belgrade: Kosmos, 1986).

46. Stevan Vračar, "Partijski monopolizam i politička moć društvenih grupa," *Gledišta,* nos. 8–9 (1967), summarized in "Jugoslawischer Theoretiker für Zweiparteiensystem," *Osteuropäische Rundschau,* vol. 13, no. 12 (December 1967): 19–21.

47. See the report by Jure Bilić in *Deseti Kongres Saveza Komunista Jugoslavije (Beograd, 27–30 maja 1974)—Stenografske beleške* (Belgrade: Komunist, 1975), vol. 2, p. 369.

48. April Carter, *Democratic Reform in Yugoslavia: The Changing Role of the Party* (Princeton, N.J.: Princeton University Press, 1982), pp. 97–98.

49. Ibid., p. 75.

50. Haberl, *Parteiorganisation,* p. 60.

51. Ibid., p. 59.

52. Ibid., p. 94.

53. Ibid., p. 58.

54. See the reports by Avdo Humo (a liberal) and Milentije Popović (a conservative), in *Deveti Kongres Saveza Komunista Jugoslavije (Beograd, 11–13 III 1969)—Stenografske beleške* (Belgrade: Komunist, 1970), vol. 3, pp. 344, 306.

55. *Deveti Kongres,* vol. 6, p. 406.

56. Quoted in Haberl, *Parteiorganisation,* p. 105.

57. *Treća sednica predsedništva SKJ* (Belgrade: Komunist, 1969), as cited in Martin C. Sletzinger, "The Reform and Reorganization of the League of Communists of Yugoslavia, 1966–1973" (Ph.D. dissertation, Harvard University, 1976), pp. 81–83.

58. *Delo,* 1 August 1969, p. 1.

59. *Vjesnik,* 1 August 1969, p. 2; and *Vjesnik,* 2 August 1969, p. 2.

60. Bilandžić, *Historija SFRJ,* p. 360.

61. See Haberl, *Parteiorganisation,* p. 105.

62. Božo Repe, *"Liberalizem" v Sloveniji* (Ljubljana: CIP Kataložni zapis o publikaciji Narodna in univerzitetna knjižnica, 1992), p. 89.

63. See *Borba,* 3 September 1969), as cited in Haberl, *Parteiorganisation,* p. 106.

64. Interviews, Ljubljana, July 1982. See also Stevo Govedarica, "Economic Development, 1971–1975," *Yugoslav Survey,* vol. 17, no. 3 (August 1976).

65. Miko Tripalo, "Osnovni problemi i pravci dalje idejno-političke akcije na preobražaju SKJ," *Socijalizam,* vol. 12, no. 11 (November 1969): 1392–1393.

66. See Bilandžić, *Historija SFRJ,* pp. 366–367.

8. The Rise and Fall of Yugoslav Liberalism, 1967–1973

1. Branko Petranović, *Istorija Jugoslavije 1918–1988* (Belgrade: Nolit, 1988), vol. 3, p. 382.

2. Šime Djodan, "Gospodarska reforma i izbor optimalnog modela rasta," *Kolo,* vol. 6, no. 4 (April 1968): 306.

3. Šime Djodan, "Gdje dr Stipe Šuvar 'pronalazi' nacionalizam, a gdje ga ne vidi," *Kolo,* vol. 7, no. 7 (July 1969): 702–703.

4. See *Hrvatski tjednik* (hereafter, cited as *HT*), 26 November 1971, p. 7.

5. *HT,* 12 November 1971, p. 7.

6. *HT,* 5 November 1971, p. 7, and 19 November 1971, p. 7.

7. Paul Shoup, "The National Question in Yugoslavia," in *Problems of Communism,* vol. 21, no. 1 (January–February 1972): 21.

8. See Šime Djodan, "Jedinstveno tržište, razvijenost republika i kompenzacije," *HT,* 14 May 1971, pp. 4–5.

9. Šime Djodan, "The Evolution of the Economic System of Yugoslavia and the Economic Position of Croatia," *Journal of Croatian Studies,* vol. 13 (1972): 11.

10. Ante Čuvalo, *The Croatian National Movement, 1966–1972* (Boulder, Colo.: East European Monographs, 1990), pp. 105, 106.

11. Vlatko Pavletić, in *HT,* 9 July 1971, as quoted in ibid., p. 106.

12. "Die Sprachenstreit in Jugoslawien," *Osteuropa,* vol. 21, no. 10 (October 1971): A602.

13. The complete text of the declaration appears in German translation in "Der jugoslawische Sprachenkonflikt," *Wissenschaftlicher Dienst Südosteuropa,* vol. 16, no. 3 (March 1967): 41–43.

14. *Airgram* A-164, 30 March 1967, LOU, R. Owen/Z to State, in *General Records of the Department of State,* Central Foreign Policy Files 1967–1969, Political & Defense, decl. 1996, RG59, Stack Area 150, Row 64/65 [hereafter, *General Records 1967–1969*], Box 2842, at NA.

15. *Airgram* A-166, 5 April 1967, LOU, Owen/Z to State, in *General Records 1967–1969,* Box 2842, at NA; and *Airgram* A-176, 19 April 1967, LOU, Owen/Z to State, in *General Records 1967–1969,* Box 2842, at NA. Regarding reactions to the declaration, see Čuvalo, *Croatian National Movement,* pp. 60–64.

16. *Airgram* A-181, 25 April 1967, LOU, Owen/Z to State, in *General Records 1967–1969,* Box 2842, at NA, p. 1.

17. *NIN* (Belgrade), no. 1082 (3 October 1971): 36.

18. Cited in *Politika* (Belgrade), 13 November 1968, as given in ibid.

19. "Saopštenje Matice srpske o pitanjima oko izrade Rečnika srpskohrvatskog književnog jezika," *Komunist,* 21 January 1971, trans. into German in "Die Sprachenstreit," p. A603.

20. "Novosadski dogovor je zastario," *Komunist,* 21 January 1971, trans. into German in "Die Sprachenstreit," p. A606.

21. *NIN,* no. 1082 (3 October 1971): 35.

22. *The Population of Yugoslavia* (Belgrade: Institute of Social Sciences, 1974), appendixes, Tables 2, 9–10.

23. Slobodan Stanković, "Preliminary Report on Yugoslavia's Census," *Radio Free Europe Research,* 18 May 1981, p. 2.

24. *Population of Yugoslavia,* appendixes, Table 6.

25. Djodan, "Evolution of the Economic System," p. 81.

26. M. Rendulić, "Demografska kretanja u Hrvatskoj," as cited in Djodan, " Evolution of the Economic System," pp. 80–81.

27. *Statiskički godišnjak Jugoslavije 1979* (Belgrade: Savezni zavod za statistiku, July 1979),

pp. 112, 413; Tanjug, 13 February 1982, in Foreign Broadcast Information Service (FBIS), *Daily Report* (Eastern Europe), 18 February 1982; and *Statistički godišnjak Jugoslavije 1982* (Belgrade: Savezni zavod za statistiku, February 1982), p. 37.

28. Quoted in Ivan Perić, *Suvremeni hrvatski nacionalizam* (Zagreb: August Cesarec, 1976), p. 185. The letter was dated 6 July 1967.

29. Stijepo Obad, "Geneza autonomaštva," *Vidik*, vol. 18, no. 32/33 (July–August 1971): 15.

30. Tomislav Slavica, "Krivnja autonomaštva," *Vidik*, vol. 18, no. 32/33 (July–August 1971): 15, 17.

31. See *Vesnik: Organ Saveza udruženog Pravoslavnog sveštenstva Jugoslavije* (Belgrade), 1–15 October 1971, p. 6.

32. *Borba* (Belgrade), 29 May 1970, p. 7; *Politika*, 2 June 1970, p. 8; and *Borba*, 3 June 1970, p. 7.

33. *Politika*, 31 December 1971–2 January 1972, p. 4.

34. Tomislav Slavica, "Unitarizam recidiva autonomaštva," *HT*, 7 May 1971, p. 7.

35. *Vjesnik u srijedu*, 28 January 1970, p. 4.

36. Vlado Gotovac, "Mogućnost izdaje," *Vidik*, vol. 18, no. 32/33 (July–August 1971): 22.

37. Slavica, "Krivnja autonomaštva," p. 18.

38. As summarized in Šuvar, *Nacionalno i nacionalističko*, p. 222.

39. George Schöpflin, "The Ideology of Croatian Nationalism," *Survey*, vol. 19, no. 1 (Winter 1973): 133, 136–137.

40. Othmar Nikola Haberl, *Parteiorganisation und nationale Frage in Jugoslawien* (Berlin: Otto Harrassowitz, 1976), p. 115. Concerning *Hrvatski književni list*, see also *Airgram* A-49, 20 May 1969, LOU, Owen/Z to State, in *General Records 1967–1969*, Box 2842, at NA; and *Airgram* A-80, 5 August 1969, LOU, Owen/Z to State, in *General Records 1967–1969*, Box 2842, at NA.

41. Perić, *Suvremeni hrvatski nacionalizam*, p. 20.

42. Cited in Haberl, *Parteiorganisation*, p. 115.

43. Petranović, *Istorija Jugoslavije 1918–1988*, vol. 3, p. 400.

44. See *Politika*, 13 September 1969, p. 5.

45. Haberl, *Parteiorganisation*, p. 118.

46. Savez komunista Hrvatske, *Izvještaj o stanju SKH u odnosu na prodor nacionalizma u njegove redove*, 28th session, 8 May 1972 (Zagreb: Informativna služba CK SKH, 1972), p. 132.

47. Cited by Vladimir Košćak, "Što je nacija," *Kritika*, vol. 3, no. 15 (November–December 1970): 872.

48. As quoted in Haberl, *Parteiorganisation*, p. 143.

49. For various references to Radić, see *HT*, 28 May 1971, p. 10; 11 June 1971, pp. 1, 11–13; 8 June 1971, p. 23; and 25 June 1971, p. 5.

50. *HT*, 3 September 1971, p. 23, and 12 November 1971, p. 22; and *Borba*, 13 February 1972, p. 5.

51. *Politika*, 3 January 1972, p. 6.

52. Zvonimir Kulundžić, "Spomenik Banu Jelačiću," in *HT*, 4 June 1971, p. 10.

53. Miko Tripalo, former secretary of the League of Communists of Croatia, in interview with the author, Zagreb, 8 September 1989.

54. Regarding Vice Vukov, see Gordan Malić, "Razumljivo mi kad ljudi kaže da sam ih kao nacionalist razočarao" [An interview with Vice Vukov], *Globus* (Zagreb), 7 January 2000: 80–81.

55. *HT,* 25 June 1971, p. 23.

56. Yugoslav Railways had, however, done little by mid-August to bring that any closer to fruition. See *HT,* 20 August 1971, p. 14.

57. *HT,* 12 November 1971, p. 24.

58. Dalibor Brozović, "Eskalacija rasprave o jeziku Srba u Hrvatskoj," *HT,* 5 November 1971, p. 3.

59. Djurić also called for similar guarantees from Macedonia, Bosnia-Herzegovina, and Montenegro. See Dušan Bilandžić, *Ideje i praksa društvenog razvoja Jugoslavije, 1945–1973* (Belgrade: Komunist 1973), p. 287.

60. *Ustav Socijalističke Republike Hrvatske* (1963), in *Ustav Socijalističke Federativne Republike Jugoslavije sa Ustavima Socijalističkih Republika i statutima Autonomnih Pokrajina* (Belgrade: Službeni list, 1963), Article 1, pp. 272, 265.

61. Italics added. Quoted in *HT,* 10 September 1971, p. 1.

62. Tim Judah, *The Serbs: History, Myth and the Destruction of Yugoslavia* (New Haven, Conn.: Yale University Press, 1997), p. 149.

63. *HT,* 10 September 1971, p. 3.

64. Jovan Stefanović, *Ustavno pravo FNR Jugoslavije i komparativno,* 2nd ed. (1956), pp. 85–86, as quoted in ibid.

65. "Srbo-Hrvatska," in *HT,* 12 November 1971, p. 2, as reported in *Izvještaj o stanju u Savezu komunista Hrvatske,* p. 197.

66. *HT,* 24 September 1971, p. 1.

67. As quoted in *NIN,* no. 1082 (3 October 1971): 11.

68. *HT,* 5 November 1971, p. 12.

69. Veljko Mratović, "Prva faza ustavnih promjena u Socijalističkoj Republici Hrvatskoj," *Arhiv za pravne i društvene nauke,* vol. 58, no. 1 (January–March 1972): 4; and *Constitutional System of Yugoslavia* (Belgrade: Jugoslovenska stvarnost, 1980), p. 85.

70. Andrew Ludanyi, "Titoist Integration of Yugoslavia: The Partisan Myth and the Hungarians of the Vojvodina, 1945–1975," *Polity,* vol. 12, no. 2 (Winter 1979): 251; *Borba,* 18 December 1971, p. 5; *Politika,* 19 December 1971, p. 10; and *Borba,* 22 February 1972, p. 6.

71. Dragan Vukčević, "Od vere do politike i natrag," *NIN,* no. 1016 (28 June 1970): 17.

72. Quoted in Fred Singleton, *Twentieth Century Yugoslavia* (New York: Columbia University Press, 1976), p. 229.

73. Vukčević, "Od vere do politike," p. 17.

74. Hans Hartl, *Nationalismus in Rot* (Stuttgart: Seewald Verlag, 1968), pp. 93–95.

75. The films were, of course, in Slovenian. See ibid., pp. 96–97.

76. Carl Gustaf Stroehm, *Ohne Tito* (Graz: Verlag Styria, 1976), pp. 236–237.

77. Tanjug, 13 April 1967.

78. Report by Alojz Vindiš, in *Deseti Kongres Saveza Komunista Jugoslavije (Beograd, 27–30 maja 1974)—Stenografske beleške* (Belgrade: Komunist, 1975), vol. 2, p. 392.

79. *Komunist,* 3 February 1966, p. 2.

80. For a short history of the Croatian Serbs, 1522–1995, see Sabrina P. Ramet, *Whose Democracy? Nationalism, Religion, and the Doctrine of Collective Rights in Post-1989 Eastern Europe* (Lanham, Md.: Rowman & Littlefield, 1997), pp. 82–90. See also Drago Roksandić, *Srbi u Hrvatskoj, od 15. Stoljeća do naših dana* (Zagreb: Vjesnik, 1991); Gunther E. Rothenberg, *The Military Border in Croatia, 1740–1881: A Study of an Imperial Institution* (Chicago: University of Chicago Press, 1966); Wayne S. Vucinich, "The Serbs in Austria-Hungary," in *Austrian History Yearbook,* vol. 3, pt. 2 (1967); Ivo Banac (ed.), *Srbi u Hrvatskoj: Jučer, danas, sutra* (Zagreb:

Hrvatski Helsinski Odbor za ljudska prava, 1998); and Vjeran Pavlakovic, "Minorities in Croatia since Independence," in Vjeran Pavlakovic (ed.), *Nationalism, Culture, and Religion in Croatia since 1990,* Donald W. Treadgold Papers in Russian, East European, and Central Asian Studies no. 32 (Seattle: Henry M. Jackson School of International Studies of the University of Washington, November 2001), esp. pp. 20–28.

81. *Izvještaj o stanju u Savezu komunista Hrvatske,* pp. 62, 234, 61–63, 233. "Certain members of the Initiative Committee *(Inicijativni odbor)* from Zadar, at a plenum of the Main Committee in Zagreb in 1970, demanded the political autonomy of the Serbs in Croatia, and more especially 'the convocation of a Congress of Croatian Serbs.'" Ibid., p. 234.

82. Ibid., pp. 235–236.

83. Stroehm, *Ohne Tito,* p. 257.

84. *Airgram* A-397, 18 December 1967, LOU, C. B. Elbrick/B to State, in *General Records 1967–1969,* Box 2842, at NA, pp. 3–4.

85. *Airgram* A-217, 2 October 1967, LOU, Elbrick/B to State, in *General Records 1967–1969,* Box 2842, at NA, pp. 1–2; *Airgram* A-241, 9 October 1967, C, Elbrick/B to State, in *General Records 1967–1969,* Box 2841, at NA, p. 2; *Airgram* A-377, 8 December 1967, C, Elbrick/B to State, in *General Records 1967–1969,* Box 2841, at NA, pp. 2–3; and *Airgram* A-396, 18 December 1967, C, Elbrick/B to State, in *General Records 1967–1969,* Box 2841, at NA, p. 2.

86. *Airgram* A-377, 8 December 1967, C, Elbrick/B to State, in *General Records 1967–1969,* Box 2841, at NA, p. 2.

87. *Airgram* A-1137, 12 December 1968, LOU, I. M. Tobin/B to State, in *General Records 1967–1969,* Box 2842, at NA, pp. 2, 5.

88. Jože Pirjevec, *Il giorno di San Vito: Jugoslavia 1918–1992—Storia di una tragedia* (Torino: Nuova Eri Edizioni, 1993), pp. 375, 396.

89. Vesna Pešić, "The War for Ethnic States," in Nebojša Popov (ed.), *The Road to War in Serbia: Trauma and Catharsis,* English version by Drinka Gojković (Budapest: Central European University Press, 2000), p. 26.

90. Pirjevec, *Il giorno di San Vito,* p. 373; and Raif Dizdarević, *Od smrti Tita do smrti Jugoslavije: Svjedocenja* (Sarajevo: Svjedok, 1999), p. 332.

91. Quoted in John R. Lampe, *Yugoslavia as History: Twice There Was a Country* (Cambridge: Cambridge University Press, 1996), p. 303. For Nikezić's own account of these years, see Marko Nikezić, *Srpska krhka vertikala,* with a preface by Latinka Perović (Belgrade: Helsinški odbor za ljudska prava u Srbiji, 2003).

92. Slavoljub Djukić, *Slom srpskih liberala: Tehnologija političkih obračuna Josipa Broza* (Belgrade: Filip Višnjić, 1990), p. 97.

93. Raif Dizdarević, former president of the presidency of Bosnia-Herzegovina, former foreign minister, and former president of the SFRY presidency, in interview with the author, Sarajevo, 18 July 2004.

94. In March 1967 it was reported that the liberal wing of the Serbian party had wanted to see Dragoslav Marković, then Yugoslav ambassador to Bulgaria, appointed chair of the Serbian Executive Council. See *Airgram* A-607, 17 March 1967, C, Elbrick/B to State, in *General Records 1967–1969,* Box 2842, at p. 1.

95. Djukić, *Slom srpskih liberala,* pp. 106–107, 116–117.

96. Božo Repe, *"Liberalizem" v Sloveniji* (Ljubljana: CIP Kataložni zapis o publikaciji Narodna in univerzitetna knjižnica, 1992), pp. 108–109, 110.

97. Stane Kavčič, *Dnevnik in spomini, 1972–1987,* 3rd ed., ed. by Igor Bavčar and Janez Janša (Ljubljana: Časopis za kritiko znanosti, 1988), p. 36.

98. Pirjevec, *Il giorno di San Vito,* p. 379.

99. *Intelligence Note* 656 (21 August 1968), LOU, Thomas L. Hughes, director of intelli-

gence and research, to the U.S. secretary of state, in *General Records 1967–1969,* Box 2842, at NA.

100. Repe, *"Liberalizem,"* pp. 190–192.

101. Peter Vokopivec, "Slowenien," in Dunja Melčić (ed.), *Der Jugoslawien-Krieg. Handbuch zu Vorgeschichte, Verlauf und Konsequenzen* (Opladen/Wiesbaden: Westdeutscher Verlag, 1999), p. 35.

102. Repe, *"Liberalizem,"* p. 159.

103. *Airgram* A-75, 12 December 1967, LOU, R. I. Owen/Z to State, in *General Records 1967–1969,* Box 2841, at NA, p. 1.

104. Repe, *"Liberalizem,"* pp. 208–209.

105. Petranović, *Istorija Jugoslavije,* vol. 3, p. 383.

106. Repe, *"Liberalizem,"* pp. 244–248.

107. *Airgram* A-1129, 9 December 1968, C, Tobin/B to State, in *General Records 1967–1969,* Box 2842, at NA, pp. 2–3.

108. *Airgram* A-552, 25 February 1967, LOU, Elbrick/B to State, in *General Records 1967–1969,* Box 2842, at NA, p. 2.

109. See *Politika,* 14 May 1971.

110. Interviews, Belgrade, February 1980.

111. Quoted in Petar Vujić, "Kako rade 'komiteti devetorice,'" *Komunist,* 30 March 1972, p. 15.

112. *Borba,* 24 July 1972, p. 9.

113. Vujić, "Kako rade 'komiteti devetorice,'" p. 16. The Coordination Commission did not decide issues but performed a function often as important—drafting the proposals, which were turned over to the appropriate interrepublican committee.

114. *Borba,* 21 August 1972, p. 5.

115. *Izvještaj o stanju u Savezu komunista Hrvatske,* p. 152.

116. The two articles are reprinted in *HT,* 21 May 1971, pp. 1, 22–23.

117. *Borba,* 30 May 1971, p. 5; and *HT,* 11 June 1971, p. 5.

118. See the discussion in Jonke, "Slovo o Matici hrvatskoj," *HT,* 20 August 1971, p. 3; and Vlado Gotovac, "Letak za Maticu hrvatsku," *HT,* 4 June 1971, p. 1.

119. Milan Kangrga, "Fenomenologija ideološko-političkog nastupanja jugoslavenske srednje klase," *Praxis,* vol. 8, no. 3–4 (May–August 1971): 425–426, 437, 444–445; and Gerson S. Sher, *Praxis* (Bloomington: Indiana University Press, 1977), pp. 219, 311n.

120. Sher, *Praxis,* p. 220.

121. Šime Djodan, then adviser at the Institute for Public Finances (later briefly Croatian minister of defense in 1991), in interview with the author, Zagreb, 12 September 1989.

122. "Govor Druga Tita u Labinu," from *Politika,* 3 May 1971, reprinted in *Kako ostvarujemo dogovor: Posle XVII Sednice Predsedništva SKJ* (Belgrade: Komunist, 1971), p. 17.

123. *Izvještaj o stanju u Savezu komunista Hrvatske,* pp. 83, 84.

124. Ibid., pp. 90, 92.

125. *Borba,* 16 September 1971, as quoted in Slobodan Stanković, "Die kroatische Krise—Triebkrafte und Perspektiven," *Osteuropa,* vol. 22, no. 6 (June 1972): 413.

126. Cvijetin Mijatović, president of the SFRY presidency in 1980, had admitted in the late 1960s that "in the postwar period, it was difficult to be a Croat [in Bosnia]." Quoted in Djodan, "Gdje dr Stipe Šuvar," p. 695.

127. *Politika,* 20 August 1971, p. 5; and *Borba,* 2 December 1971, p. 5.

128. See *Izvještaj o stanju u Savezu komunista Hrvatske,* p. 157.

129. See *Oslobodjenje,* 20 August 1971, as cited in *HT,* 10 September 1971, p. 8.

130. "Nacionalne strukture u Bosni i Hercegovini," *HT,* 19 November 1971, pp. 10–11.

131. Hamdija Pozderac, *Nacionalni odnosi i socijalističko zajedništvo* (Sarajevo: Svjetlost, 1978), p. 96.

132. Calculated from figures in Tanjug, 16 February 1982, in FBIS, *Daily Report* (Eastern Europe), 17 February 1982. See also Haberl, *Parteiorganisation,* p. 209; *Oslobodjenje,* 17 May 1982, p. 5; and *Oslobodjenje,* 20 March 1984, pp. 2–3.

133. Fuad Muhić, in interview with Mirko Galić in *Start,* no. 283 (28 November–12 December 1979): 13.

134. *HT,* 18 June 1971, p. 6.

135. Stroehm, *Ohne Tito,* p. 192.

136. See Schöpflin, "Ideology of Croatian Nationalism," p. 143; and Dennison I. Rusinow, *The Yugoslav Experiment, 1948–1974* (Berkeley and Los Angeles: University of California Press, 1977), p. 305.

137. *Izvještaj o stanju u Savezu komunista Hrvatske,* pp. 135, 204–205.

138. *Ekonomska politika,* no. 1023 (8 November 1971): 12.

139. *HT,* 4 June 1971, p. 9, cited in *Izvještaj o stanju u Savezu komunista Hrvatske,* p. 205.

140. Mahmut Mujačić, *Nova dimenzija jugoslovenskog federalizma* (Sarajevo: Oslobodjenje, 1981), p. 76.

141. Rusinow, *Yugoslav Experiment,* p. 298.

142. *New York Times,* 25 May 1972, p. 45. See also *Der Spiegel,* 2 July 1973, pp. 72–73.

143. *Borba,* 1 December 1971, as quoted in *Izvještaj o stanju u Savezu komunista Hrvatske,* pp. 118–119.

144. Rusinow, *Yugoslav Experiment,* p. 306.

145. *Borba* claimed that only about 2,000 students attended, but *HT* numbered attendance at more than 3,000. See *Borba,* 23 November 1971, p. 5; and *HT,* 3 December 1971, pp. 10–11.

146. *Borba,* 23 November 1971, p. 5.

147. *Vjesnik u srijedu,* 8 September 1971, as quoted in *Izvještaj o stanju u Savezu komunista Hrvatske,* p. 107.

148. "Memoari Dr. Savke Dabčević Kučar (2)," *Globus* (Zagreb), 31 October 1997, p. 83.

149. As quoted in *Izvještaj o stanju u Savezu komunista Hrvatske,* p. 58.

150. *HT,* 3 December 1971, pp. 10–11.

151. *Izvještaj o stanju u Savezu komunista Hrvatske,* p. 169.

152. Alvin G. Rubinstein, "The Yugoslav Succession Crisis in Perspective," *World Affairs,* vol. 135, no. 2 (Fall 1972): 112. Apparently Matica Hrvatska maintained some 36 branches abroad, which afforded the organization some contact with Croatian émigrés, especially in West Germany. On this point, see Duncan Wilson, *Tito's Yugoslavia* (Cambridge: Cambridge University Press, 1979), p. 207n.

153. "Memoari Dr. Savke Dabčević Kučar (1)," *Globus,* 24 October 1997, p. 87.

154. Dušan Bilandžić, *Historija Socijalističke Federativne Republike Jugoslavije* (Zagreb: Školska knjiga, 1978), pp. 427–428.

155. *Borba,* 6 December 1971, p. 5, emphasis added.

156. *Izvještaj o stanju u Savezu komunista Hrvatske,* pp. 114–115. Bijelić himself lost his job shortly thereafter.

157. Ibid., pp. 12, 116–117.

158. "Programme of Action Adopted by the Second Conference of the LCY" (Belgrade, 25–27 January 1972), *Review of International Affairs,* vol. 23, nos. 524–525 (5–20 February 1972): 16.

159. *Izvještaj o stanju u Savezu komunista Hrvatske*, pp. 127–128.

160. Djodan, arrested in January 1972, was one of the very first to be apprehended. See "Memoari Dr. Savke Dabčević Kučar (2)," pp. 84–85.

161. Viktor Meier, *Yugoslavia: A History of Its Demise*, trans. from German by Sabrina P. Ramet (London: Routledge, 1999), p. 19. Regarding the 1972 trial of Tudjman (not a "show trial" but a trial nonetheless), see Darko Hudelist, *Tuđman; Biografija* (Zagreb: PROFIL, 2004), pp. 484–491.

162. These figures were provided to me by Miko Tripalo (see note 53 in this chapter) and confirmed by Dušan Bilandžić, professor of political science, in interview with the author, Zagreb, 29 August 1989.

163. K. F. Cviić, "Yugoslavia," in *Britannica Book of the Year 1974* (Chicago: Encyclopedia Britannica, 1974), p. 732.

164. Rubinstein, "Yugoslav Succession Crisis," p. 109.

165. *Ekonomska politika*, no. 1040 (6 March 1972): 12.

166. Ivan Kampus and Igor Karaman, *Zagreb through a Thousand Years: From Ancient Settlements to Modern City* (Zagreb: Školska knjiga, 1995), p. 338.

167. *Politika*, 12 September 1972, p. 6.

168. Latinka Perović, former secretary of the League of Communists of Serbia, in conversation with the author, Belgrade, 12 June 2004.

169. Božo Kovačević, "Hrvatska snovi i stvarnost," *Tjednik* (Zagreb), 21 November 1997, p. 35.

9. Controversies in the Economic Sector, 1965–1990

1. Hamdija Pozderac, *Nacionalni odnosi i socijalističko zajedništvo* (Sarajevo: Svjetlost, 1978), p. 135.

2. Kosta Mihailović, *Nerazvijena područja Jugoslavije*, 2nd ed. (Belgrade: Ekonomski Institut, 1970), p. 87.

3. Dennison I. Rusinow, "The Other Albanians," *American Universities Field Staff Reports*, Southeast Europe Series, vol. 12, no. 2 (November 1965): 19.

4. Edvard Kardelj, *Speech at the Plenary Session, Fifth Congress of the Socialist Alliance of Working People* (Belgrade, 1960), p. 162, as quoted in F. E. Ian Hamilton, *Yugoslavia: Patterns of Economic Activity* (New York: Praeger, 1968), p. 148.

5. Paul Shoup, *Communism and the Yugoslav National Question* (New York: Columbia University Press, 1968), p. 241n.

6. R. V. Burks, *The National Problem and the Future of Yugoslavia* (Santa Monica, Calif.: Rand Corporation, October 1971), p. 54.

7. Šime Djodan, "Economic Position of Croatia," *Croatia Press*, vol. 26, no. 2 (April–June 1973): 14.

8. Joseph T. Bombelles, *Economic Development of Communist Yugoslavia, 1947–1964* (Stanford, Calif.: Hoover Institution on War, Revolution, and Peace, 1968), p. 148.

9. Borisav Srebrić, "Neki problemi usavršavanja metoda i mehanizma razvoja nerazvijenih područja u Jugoslaviji," *Ekonomist*, vol. 22, no. 1 (1969): 156. See also Branko Čolanović, *Development of the Underdeveloped Areas in Yugoslavia* (Belgrade: Medjunarodna politika, 1966), p. 19.

10. Bosnia had succeeded in having certain *opštinas* classified as "underdeveloped" in 1959. See Pozderac, *Nacionalni odnosi*, pp. 129–130.

11. Mihailović, *Nerazvijena područja Jugoslavije*, pp. 34, 103.

12. Kiril Miljovski, "Nedovoljno razvijena područja i sedmogodišnji plan," *Ekonomist*, vol. 16, no. 3–4 (1963): 673.

13. Vinod Dubey et al., *Yugoslavia: Development with Decentralization* (Baltimore, Md.: Johns Hopkins University Press, 1975), p. 193.

14. Veselin Djuranović, "Socio-Economic Development of Montenegro," *Socialist Thought and Practice*, vol. 16, no. 11 (November 1976): 81–82; and Tanjug, 24 April 1978, trans. in FBIS, *Daily Report* (Eastern Europe), 26 April 1978.

15. *Nova Makedonija* (Skopje), 21 January 1987, p. 2.

16. Ksente Bogoev, "The Policy of More Rapid Development of the Undeveloped Republics and Provinces" (from *Ekonomist*, no. 2–3 [1970]), trans. in *Eastern European Economics*, vol. 10, no. 4 (Summer 1972): 407.

17. Ragnar Nurkse, *Problems of Capital Formation in Underdeveloped Countries* (Oxford: Basil Blackwell, 1957), p. 10.

18. *Statistical Pocketbook of Yugoslavia*, 19th issue (Belgrade: Federal Institute for Statistics, April 1973), pp. 30–31, 103, 112–114.

19. Nicholas R. Lang, "The Dialectics of Decentralization," *World Politics*, vol. 27, no. 3 (April 1975): 332.

20. Hivši Islami, "Kretanje nepismenosti u Albanaca u Jugoslaviji," *Sociologija*, vol. 20, no. 2–3 (1978): 316.

21. Ivan Stojanović, "Problemi zapošljavanja i medjunacionalni odnosi," *Gledišta*, vol. 15, no. 7–8 (July–August 1974): 746.

22. *Ekonomska politika* (Belgrade), no. 1465/66 (28 April 1980): 20.

23. See, for example, the proceedings at the Fifth Congress of the LC Bosnia-Herzegovina, as reported in Airgram A-66 (3 February 1969), LOU, Elbrick/Z to State, Pol. 12 Yugo, in *General Records of the Department of State*, Central Foreign Policy Files 1967–1969, Political & Defense, decl. 1996 (RG59, Box 2841–2842), on deposit at NA.

24. *Borba* (Belgrade), 4 June 1980, p. 3.

25. Marijan Korošić, *Jugoslavenska kriza* (Zagreb: Naprijed, 1989), p. 133.

26. "Rates of Employment and Unemployment, 1980–1987," *Yugoslav Survey*, vol. 29, no. 4 (1988): 35.

27. Jelica Karačić, "Ekonomski aspekti ravnopravnosti naroda," in Milan Petrović and Kasim Suljević (eds.), *Nacionalni odnosi danas* (Sarajevo: Univerzal, 1971), p. 88.

28. Robert K. Furtak, *Jugoslawien* (Hamburg: Hoffmann and Campe Verlag, 1975), p. 158.

29. Calculated in 1962 prices: Mihailo Vuković, "Neka pitanja razvoja privredno nedovoljno razvijenih republika i krajeva," in *Godišnjak Pravnog Fakulteta u Sarajevu*, vols. 16–17 (2968–69), p. 346.

30. *Komunist*, 4 January 1980, p. 17.

31. *Osmi kongres Saveza komunista Bosne i Hercegovine, 18–20 maja 1982* (Sarajevo: Oslobodjenje, 1982), p. 59.

32. *Komunist*, 4 January 1980, p. 17; *Borba*, 18 January 1980, p. 5; and *Vjesnik—Sedam dana*, 24 April 1982, p. 6.

33. Karačić, "Ekonomski aspekti," pp. 90–91.

34. *Borba*, 7 April 1980, p. 5.

35. "Rates of Employment," pp. 31, 35.

36. Djuranović, "Socio-Economic Development of Montenegro," pp. 81–83; and *Statistički godišnjak Jugoslavije 1979* (Belgrade: Savezni zavod za statistiku, July 1979), p. 414.

37. *Ekonomska politika*, no. 1390 (20 November 1978): 12.

38. "Rates of Employment," pp. 31, 35.

39. *Večernje novosti* (Belgrade), 19 September 1989, p. 4; and *Politika*, 4 December 1989, p. 1.

40. Miodrag Nikolić, *Autonomous Province of Kosovo and Metohija* (Belgrade: Medjunarodna politika, 1965), p. 15.

41. D 469, 27 March 1958, Oliver M. Marcy, First Secretary/B to State, 768.00/3-2758 in *Records of the Department of State Relating to the Internal Affairs of Yugoslavia 1955–1959*, Decimal file 768 (RG59, C0034), at NA, Reel 3.

42. Predrag Cučkić, "Neki ekonomsko-politički aspekti dalje izgradnje sistema za podsticanja razvoja privredno nedovoljno razvijenih republika i SAP Kosova," *Obeležja* (Priština), vol. 5, no. 2 (March–April 1975): 25.

43. Dušan Ristić, "Kosovo i Savez Komunista Kosova izmedju dva kongresa i dve konferencije," *Obeležja* (Priština), vol. 8, no. 2 (March–April 1978): 9.

44. *Statistički godišnjak Jugoslavije 1979*, pp. 474, 500.

45. Ristić, "Kosovo," p. 12.

46. Ibid., p. 10; Nuri Basota, "Problemi ubržanijeg razvoja Kosova kao nedovoljno razvijenog područja," in *Obeležja*, vol. 9, no. 5 (September–October 1979): 41; and *Komunist*, 11 July 1980, p. 17.

47. *Yugoslav Life*, April 1990, p. 2.

48. *Zakon o fondu federacije za kreditiranje privrednog razvoja privredno nedovoljno razvijenih republika i krajeva* (17 February 1965), in *Službeni list SFRJ*, vol. 21, no. 8 (24 February 1965): 181–184.

49. Mihajlo Vuković, *Sistemski okviri podsticanja bržeg razvoja nerazvijenih područja Jugoslavije* (Sarajevo: Svjetlost, 1978), p. 59.

50. *Borba*, 28 December 1969, p. 9.

51. Mihailović, *Nerazvijena područja*, pp. 92, 93, 100, 60.

52. Agim Paca, "Fond federacije za kreditiranje privrednog razvoja privredno nedovoljno razvijenih republika i pokrajina, s osvrtom na SAP Kosovo u periodu od 1966. do 1975. godine," *Obeležja*, vol. 7, no. 3 (May–June 1977): 571; and *Zakon o fondu federacije za kreditiranje bržeg razvoja privredno nedovoljno razvijenih republika i autonomnih pokrajina* (29 July 1971), in *Službeni list SFRJ*, vol. 27, no. 33 (30 July 1971): Article 25, p. 643.

53. *Zakon o raspodeli sredstava fonda federacije za kreditiranje bržeg razvoja privredno nedovoljno razvijenih republika i autonomnih pokrajina u periodu od 1976. do 1980. godine"* (20 July 1976), in *Službeni list SFRJ*, vol. 32, no. 33 (23 July 1976): Article 1.

54. *Društveni plan Jugoslavije za period od 1976. do 1980. godine* (20 July 1976), in *Službeni list SFRJ*, vol. 32, no. 33 (23 July 1976): 806.

55. Croats, *Vjesnik*, 25 April 1980, p. 5; Slovenes, *Borba*, 28 April 1980, p. 9.

56. See, for example, *Vjesnik—Sedam dana*, 23 March 1980, p. 28.

57. *Borba*, 27 February 1980, p. 4.

58. *Borba*, 20 March 1980, p. 12.

59. *Borba*, 22 May 1980, p. 7.

60. *Politika*, 10 July 1980, p. 5; *Oslobodjenje*, 10 July 1980, p. 7; and *Borba*, 13 July 1980, p. 4.

61. Dubey, *Yugoslavia*, p. 192. See also Dijana Pleština, *Regional Development in Communist Yugoslavia: Success, Failure, and Consequences* (Boulder, Colo.: Westview Press, 1992).

62. Belgrade Domestic Service, 5 September 1985, in FBIS, *Daily Report* (Eastern Europe), 9 September 1985, p. 12; Tanjug, 2 October 1985, in FBIS, *Daily Report* (Eastern Europe), 4 October 1985, p. 110; *Politika*, 4 April 1986, p. 5; *NIN*, no. 1978 (27 November 1988): 12; and *Yugoslav Life*, April 1990, p. 2.

63. Tanjug, 23 January 1990, in FBIS, *Daily Report* (Eastern Europe), 24 January 1990, p. 83; *Politika*, 25 January 1990, p. 8; and *Narodna armija*, as cited in *Yugoslav Life*, April 1990, p. 2.

64. Tanjug, 28 February 1990, in FBIS, *Daily Report* (Eastern Europe), 2 March 1990, p. 77; *Borba*, 13 March 1990, p. 4; and *Vjesnik*, 7 July 1990, p. 2.

65. *Borba*, 4 July 1990, p. 1, and 20 July 1990, p. 1.

66. *Borba*, 21/22 July 1990, p. 5.

67. Djuranović, "Socio-Economic Development of Montenegro," p. 82; and Manojlo Stanković, "Transport and Communications," *Yugoslav Survey*, vol. 16, no. 4 (November 1975): 99.

68. Borislav Nikolić, "Development of Transport Service," *Yugoslav Survey*, vol. 7, no. 26 (July–September 1966): 3813.

69. Dennison I. Rusinow, "Ports and Politics in Yugoslavia," *American Universities Field Staff Reports*, Southeast Europe Series, vol. 11, no. 3 (April 1964): 5–6.

70. *Vjesnik*, 27 November 1979, p. 16.

71. Mirko Dokić, *Ekonomika, organizacija i razvoj saobraćaja SFRJ* (Belgrade: Institut Ekonomskih Nauka, 1977), pp. 617–618.

72. F. E. Ian Hamilton, *Yugoslavia: Patterns of Economic Activity* (New York: Praeger, 1968), pp. 282, 293.

73. *Novi list* (Rijeka), 20 October 1974, p. 3.

74. Report by Marin Bakica, in *Osmi kongres Saveza komunista Hrvatske: Zagreb, 24–26, travnja 1978—Stenografske bilješke* (Zagreb: Zrinski, 1978), vol. 2, pp. 239–240.

75. Mirko Dokić, "Društveno-ekonomska uloga i saobraćanji znacaj pruge Beograd–Bar, luke Bar i priključnih pruga, i osnove razvoja turizma u užem gravitacionom području ove pruge," *Železnice*, vol. 32, no. 5 (May 1976): 45.

76. "Tunnel Construction," *Yugoslav Survey*, vol. 3, no. 8 (January–March 1962): 1163; Hamilton, *Yugoslavia*, p. 282; and Gordon C. McDonald et al., *Area Handbook for Yugoslavia* (Washington, D.C.: U.S. Government, 1970), pp. 478–479, 482.

77. See Tihomir Babić, "Značaj pruge Beograd-Bar sa stanovišta saobraćajnog sistema SFRJ," *Železnice*, vol. 32, no. 5 (May 1976): 38–39.

78. *NIN*, no. 1529 (27 April 1980): 12.

79. Viktor Meier, *Wie Jugoslawien verspielt wurde*, 2nd ed. (Munich: Verlag C. H. Beck, 1996), pp. 183, 191.

80. *Süddeutsche Zeitung* (Munich), 21–22 November 1987, p. 8.

81. *NIN*, no. 1925 (22 November 1987): 12–13; and *New York Times*, 5 October 1988, p. 3.

82. *Intervju* (Belgrade), no. 215 (1 September 1989): 19–21.

83. *NIN*, 1290 (18 October 1987), p. 9; and *Večernje novosti* (Belgrade), 14 September 1989, p. 3.

84. *Financial Times*, 16 May 1988, p. 2.

85. Meier, *Wie Jugoslawien*, pp. 189–192.

86. Ljubljana Domestic Service, 19 December 1989, trans. in FBIS, *Daily Report* (Eastern Europe), 20 December 1989, p. 77.

87. Tanjug, 19 December 1989, in FBIS, *Daily Report* (Eastern Europe), 20 December 1989, p. 77.

88. *Vjesnik—Panorama subotom*, 23 July 1988, p. 14.

89. *Politika*, 12 September 1990, p. 14.

90. Tanjug, 15 October 1988, in FBIS, *Daily Report* (Eastern Europe), 17 October 1988, pp. 52–53.

91. *Borba,* 1 June 1989, p. 7.

10. Nationalist Tensions, 1968–1990

1. See Noel Malcolm, *Bosnia: A Short History* (New York: New York University Press, 1994).

2. For example, Ivo Pilar, *Die südslawische Frage und der Weltkrieg* (Vienna: Manzsche k. u. k. Hof-, Verlags u. Universitats-Buchhandlung, 1918), pp. 170, 185, 195, 213.

3. See Viktor Meier, *Yugoslavia: A History of Its Demise,* trans. by Sabrina P. Ramet (London and New York: Routledge, 1999), p. 209; and Franjo Tudjman, *Nationalism in Contemporary Europe* (Boulder, Colo.: East European Monographs, 1981), pp. 113–114.

4. The Serbophile theories are discussed in Kasim Suljević, *Nacionalnost Muslimana* (Rijeka: Otokar Keršovani, 1981). A more recent example of this approach is Mile Nedeljković's *Krst i polumesec* (Belgrade, 1993), as cited in Rusmir Mahmutćehajić, *Bosnia the Good: Tolerance and Tradition,* trans. from Bosnian by Marina Bowder (Budapest: Central European University Press, 2000), p. 203.

5. Milovan Djilas and Nadežda Gaće, *Adil Zulfikarpašić: Eine politische Biographie aus dem heutigen Bosnien,* trans. from Bosnian into German by Jens Reuter (Munich: R. Oldenbourg Verlag, 1996), p. 202.

6. Carl Gustaf Ströhm, *Ohne Tito* (Graz: Verlag Styria, 1976), pp. 243–244; and Hamdija Pozderac, *Nacionalni odnosi i socijalističko zajedništvo* (Sarajevo: Svjetlost, 1978), p. 66. According to Purivatra, no more than 2 or 3% of the Muslim population in Bosnia-Herzegovina is ethnically non-Slavic (that small portion consisting mainly of a Turkish, Arab, Persian, and Caucasian admixture). See Atif Purivatra, "The National Phenomenon of the Moslems of Bosnia-Herzegovina," *Socialist Thought and Practice,* vol. 12, no. 12 (December 1974): 36n. Perhaps the most sophisticated treatment of the Bogomils in English is John V. A. Fine Jr., *The Bosnian Church: A New Interpretation* (Boulder, Colo.: East European Monographs, 1975).

7. Interview with Fuad Muhic, Sarajevo, June 1980.

8. R. V. Burks, *The National Problem and the Future of Yugoslavia* (Santa Monica, Calif.: Rand Corporation, October 1971), p. 26; confirmed in Tim Judah, *The Serbs: History, Myth and the Destruction of Yugoslavia* (New Haven, Conn.: Yale University Press, 1997), pp. 155–156.

9. Pozderac, *Nacionalni odnosi,* p. 44.

10. See *Zadaci SK Srbije u razvoju medjunacionalnih odnosa i borbi protiv nacionalizma* (Belgrade: Komunist, 1978), pp. 122–125; and Branko Petranović, *Istorija Jugoslavije 1918–1988,* vol. 3 (Belgrade: Nolit, 1988), p. 389.

11. But see the admission of inter-ethnic difficulties in the republic in Airgram A66 (3 February 1969), LOU, Elbrick/B to State, Pol 12 Yugo, in *General Records of the Department of State, Central Foreign Policy Files 1967–1969,* Political & Defense, decl. 1996, RG 59, Stack Area 150, at NA [hereafter, *Records 1967–1969*], Box 2842, p. 3. For further discussion of these processes, see Mitja Velikonja, *Religious Separation and Political Intolerance in Bosnia-Herzegovina,* trans. from Slovenian by Rang'ichi Ng'inja (College Station: Texas A&M University Press, 2003), pp. 222–225.

12. Compare the 1953 census figures given in Paul Shoup, *Communism and the Yugoslav National Question* (New York: Columbia University Press, 1968), p. 267, with *Statistički godišnjak Jugoslavije 1979,* p. 112.

13. "Staat und Nationalität in Jugoslawien," *Wissenschaftlicher Dienst Südosteuropa,* vol. 19, no. 8 (August 1970): 119.

14. As quoted in "Muslimani: Nacija ili vera," *NIN*, no. 1048 (7 February 1971): 29.

15. Milan Bulajić, "Problemi samoopredeljenja nacija i čovjeka i jugoslovenski federalizam," in *Federalizam i nacionalno pitanje* (Belgrade: Savez udruženja za političke nauke Jugoslavije, 1971), pp. 267–268.

16. "Muslimani: nacija ili vera," p. 29.

17. Vječeslav Holjevac, in his book *Hrvati izvan domovine: Zapis rodnog grada* (Zagreb: Matica Hrvatska, 1967).

18. *Rilindja*, 7 March 1981, as quoted in Louis Zanga, "Kosovar-Macedonian Quarrel over Nationality Issue," *Radio Free Europe Research*, 27 March 1981, p. 2.

19. Todo Kurtović, *Crkva i religija u socijalističkom samoupravnom društvu* (Belgrade: Rad, 1978), p. 64; and Fuad Muhić, in interview in *Start*, no. 283 (28 November–12 December 1979): 13–14.

20. *Constitutional System of Yugoslavia* (Belgrade: Jugoslovenska stvarnost, 1980), p. 85.

21. *Borba*, 26 April 1970, p. 5, trans. in *Joint Translation Service*, no. 5616.

22. *Oslobodjenje*, 18 October 1973, p.6; and Tanjug, 23 October 1973, trans. in FBIS, *Daily Report* (Eastern Europe), 26 October 1973.

23. *New York Times*, 8 April 1974, p. 2.

24. Aziz Hadžihasanović, "Muslimanski nacionalizam, šta je to?" *Oslobodjenje*, 19 February 1974, p. 5.

25. As quoted in *Borba*, 10 May 1972, p. 5.

26. Kurtović, *Crkva i religija*, p. 63.

27. *Delo*, 28 May 1983, trans. in FBIS, *Daily Report* (Eastern Europe), 9 June 1983; *Vjesnik*, 16 July 1983, p. 8; *Archiv der Gegenwart*, 20 August 1983, p. 26903; and *Christian Science Monitor*, 28 September 1983, p. 7. See also Hamža Bakšić, "Nesudjeni neimari 'Islamistana,'" *Komunist*, 5 August 1983, p. 7; and Nijaz Duraković, "Od 'Mladih muslimana' do panislamizma," *Komunist*, 23 September 1983, p. 20.

28. During his second term in prison, Izetbegović kept notes which he entrusted to the care of a fellow inmate. These were later published in book form. See Alija Izetbegović, *Izetbegović of Bosnia and Herzegovina: Notes from Prison, 1983–1988*, translator not identified (Westport, Conn.: Praeger, 2002).

29. *Vjesnik*, 27 November 1979, p. 1.

30. Edvard Kardelj, *Razvoj slovenačkog pitanja*, 2nd ed. (Belgrade: Kultura, 1958), excepted in *Nacionalno pitanje*, p. 405.

31. Miloš Mišović, *Ko je tražio republiku: Kosovo 1945–1985* (Belgade: Narodna knjiga, 1987), p. 36.

32. Branko Horvat, *Kosovsko pitanje* (Zagreb: Globus, 1988), p. 62.

33. Ljiljana Bulatović, *Prizrenski proces* (Novi Sad: Književna zajednica, 1988), esp. pp. 9–27.

34. *Borba*, 6 January 1953, summarized in D511, 8 January 1953, R, Woodruff Wallner, Counselor/B to State, 768.00/1-853, in *Records of the U.S. Department of State Relating to the Internal Affairs of Yugoslavia, 1950–1954*, Decimal file 768 (RG59, LM77), at NA, Reel 2.

35. Jens Reuter, *Die Albaner in Jugoslawien* (Munich: R. Oldenbourg Verlag, 1982), p. 45; also D676, 21 June 1956, C, Oliver M. Marcy, First Secretary/B to State, 768.00/6-2156, in *Records of the Department of State Relating to the Internal Affairs of Yugoslavia, 1955–1959*, Decimal file 768 (RG59, C0034), at NA, Reel 1.

36. *The Times* (London), 12 March 1962, p. 10, and 13 March 1962, p. 11.

37. Hirzi Islami, "Kretanje nepismenosti u Albanaca u Jugoslaviji," *Sociologija*, vol. 20, nos. 2–3 (1978): 315–316.

38. See the documents in *Nacionalno pitanje*, pp. 500–503.

39. *Sedma sednica pokrajinskog komiteta SKJ na Kosovu i Metohiji* (1966), in *Zadaci SK Srbije*, p. 114.

40. Radio Belgrade, 10 February 1968.

41. Mišović, *Ko je tražio repjubliku*, pp. 133, 134–135, 136.

42. Ibid.; and *New York Times*, 28 November 1968, p. 19.

43. *Borba*, 28 October 1968.

44. Enver Hoxha ruled Albania from the end of World War Two until his death in 1985. See report by Dušan Mugoša, in *Deveti Kongres Saveza Komunista Jugoslavije (Beograd, 11–13 III 1969)—Stenografske beleške* (Belgrade: Komunist, 1970), vol. 3, p. 367; also *New York Times*, 28 November 1968, p. 19.

45. Airgram A130, 20 March 1969, LOU, Elbrick/B to State, Pol. 12 YUGO, in *Records 1967–1969*, Box 2842.

46. Deva on discontents, Airgram A38, 20 January 1969, LOU, O.E. Eskin/B to State, POL 13-3 YUGO, in *Records 1967–1969*, Box 2842; Perović, Airgram A09, 6 January 1969, C, R.O. Mudd/B to State, POL 13-2 YUGO, in *Records 1967–1969*, Box 2842; pre-disturbance report, Airgram A18, 9 January 1969, LOU, Elbrick/B to State, POL 12 YUGO, in *Records 1967–1969*, Box 2842.

47. Sami Repishti, "The Evolution of Kosova's Autonomy within the Yugoslav Constitutional Framework," in Arshi Pipa and Sami Repishti (eds.), *Studies on Kosova* (Boulder, Colo.: East European Monographs, 1984), pp. 210–211, 214–215.

48. *New York Times*, 16 January 1975, p. 8.

49. Sensing that a natural ally against Serbia was under fire, Croatian nationalists sprang to Kosovo's defense, accusing Stanić of manipulating the figures from the various postwar censuses in order to hoodwink *NIN*'s readers and accepting the official results as accurate and legitimate. See Bruno Bušić, "Čudne kosovske brojidbe," in *HT*, 3 September 1971, p. 3.

50. *Sednica predsedništva CK SK Srbije* (17 May 1976), in *Zadaci SK Srbije*, p. 165; Ivan Stojanović, "Problemi zapošljavanja i medjunacionalni odnosi," *Gledišta*, vol. 15, no. 7–8 (July–August 1974): 747; and *Oslobodjenje*, 14 May 1981, p. 20.

51. *Bilten pokrajinskog zavoda za statistiku SAPK* (1975), cited by Nebi Gaši, "Nacionalna ravnopravnost na Kosovu i politika zapošljavanja," in *Udruženi rad i medjunacionalni odnosi* (Belgrade: Komunist, 1978), p. 158.

52. Tanjug, 10 March 1982, trans. in FBIS, *Daily Report* (Eastern Europe), 11 March 1982.

53. *Politika*, 4 March 1971, p. 6; and *Borba*, 5 April 1971, p. 6.

54. *Süddeutsche Zeitung*, 17 and 24–26 December 1971.

55. Radio Belgrade, 18 March 1976, trans. in FBIS, *Daily Report* (Eastern Europe), 18 March 1976; Tanjug, 5, 7, and 12 May 1981, trans. respectively in FBIS, *Daily Report* (Eastern Europe), 6, 8, and 14 May; *The Times* (London), 13 May 1981; and Nikola Milovanović, *Kroz tajni Arhiv UDBe*, vol. 2 (Belgrade: Sloboda, 1986), pp. 252–253. See also Dušan Ristić, "Kosovo i Savez komunista Kosova izmedju dva kongresa i dve konferencije," *Obeležja*, vol. 8, no. 2 (March–April 1978).

56. Tanjug, 12 May 1981, trans. in FBIS, *Daily Report* (Eastern Europe), 14 May 1981.

57. *NIN*, no. 1588 (7 June 1981): 11–12; and *NIN*, no. 1590 (21 June 1981): 13.

58. *Rilindja* (8 November 1975), summarized in Radio Belgrade (7 November 1975), trans. in FBIS, *Daily Report* (Eastern Europe), 10 November 1975.

59. Tanjug, 15 July 1975), trans. in FBIS, *Daily Report* (Eastern Europe), 16 July 1975.

60. *Politika*, 30 March 1980, p. 8.

61. Živorad Z. Igić, "SK Kosova i unutarpartijsko informisanje," *Obeležja,* vol. 9, no. 1 (January–February 1979): 30.

62. Tanjug, 1 November 1980), trans. in FBIS, *Daily Report* (Eastern Europe), 3 November 1980; *Politika,* 12 February 1981, p. 1; and *Komunist,* 20 February 1981.

63. *Financial Times* (London), 13 March 1981, p. 18; *The Times,* 14 March 1981, p. 5; and *New York Times,* 7 April 1981, p. A3.

64. See *Frankfurter Allgemeine,* 24 April 1981, p. 3.

65. *The Times,* 4 April 1981, p. 4; *New York Times,* 7 April 1981, p. A3; *Frankfurter Allgemeine,* 27 April 1981, p. 3; Radio Belgrade, 3 and 24 April 1981, and *Deutsche Presse-Agentur* (Hamburg), 3 April 1981, trans. respectively in FBIS, *Daily Report* (Eastern Europe), 3, 27, and 6 April 1981; and Reuter, *Die Albaner in Jugoslawien,* p. 82.

66. See *Vjesnik,* 7 April 1981, trans. in FBIS, *Daily Report* (Eastern Europe), 13 April 1981.

67. See *Frankfurter Allgemeine,* 4 April 1981, pp. 1, 3.

68. *Vjesnik,* 11 June 1981, p. 12; *Frankfurter Allgemeine,* 14 May 1981, p. 1; Tanjug, 6 June 1981; and *Vjesnik—Sedam dana,* 6 June 1981, trans. respectively in JPRS/EE, 24 June 1981 and 1 July 1981.

69. *Frankfurter Allgemeine,* 12 May 1981, p. 1; and *Politika,* 8 January 1982, p. 7.

70. Tanjug, 26 June 1981, trans. in FBIS, *Daily Report* (Eastern Europe), 30 June 1981; and Tanjug, 14 July 1981, in FBIS, *Daily Report* (Eastern Europe), 15 July 1981.

71. *Nova Makedonija,* 9 June 1981, p. 3; Tanjug, 7 and 9 July 1981, and Radio Belgrade, 24 August 1981, trans. respectively in FBIS, *Daily Report* (Eastern Europe), 7 and 9 July 1981, and 25 August 1981.

72. Radio Belgrade, 5 June and 12 November 1981, and Tanjug, 18 July 1981, trans. respectively in FBIS, *Daily Report* (Eastern Europe), 9 June, 13 November, and 22 July 1981; and *Frankfurter Allgemeine,* 26 June 1981, p. 3.

73. *Agence France Presse* (Paris), 17 November 1981, and Radio Belgrade (24 November 1981), trans. respectively in FBIS, *Daily Report* (Eastern Europe), 18 and 25 November 1981.

74. *Frankfurter Allgemeine,* 29 July 1981, p. 3, and 16 February 1982, p. 1; *Neue Zürcher Zeitung,* 17 February 1982, p. 1; 21–22 February 1982, p. 3; and 14–15 March 1982, p. 4; Radio Belgrade, 7 January, 11 March, and 1 April 1982, and Tanjug, 30 September and 27 October 1982, trans. respectively in FBIS, *Daily Report* (Eastern Europe), 7 January, 12 March, 5 April, 1 October, and 28 October 1982.

75. *Vjesnik,* 7 April 1981, and Tanjug, 17 April, 14 May, and 3 June 1981, trans. respectively in FBIS, *Daily Report* (Eastern Europe), 13 and 20 April, 15 May, and 4 June 1981; Tanjug, 30 March 1982, in FBIS, *Daily Report* (Eastern Europe), 31 March 1982; *Vjesnik,* 26 July 1982, p. 4; and *Christian Science Monitor,* 27 July 1982, p. 8.

76. *Frankfurter Allgemeine,* 12 May 1982, p. 6.

77. Tanjug, 29 May 1981 and 6 June 1983, trans. in FBIS, *Daily Report* (Eastern Europe), 1 June 1981 and 9 June 1983.

78. "Zakljuci 20. Sednice Centralnog komiteta Saveza komunista Jugoslavije," *Socijalizam,* vol. 24, no. 4 (1981): 570–572. See also Lazar Mojsov, "O neprijateljskoj i kontrarevolucionarnoj aktivnosti u SAP Kosovu," and Ali Šukrija, "Nacionalizam i iredentizam na Kosovu," *Socijalizam,* vol. 24, no. 4 (1981).

79. *Borba,* 4 June 1981, p. 4; Tanjug, 5 and 15 June, 23 July, and 17 September 1981, and Radio Priština, 6 August 1981, trans. respectively in FBIS, *Daily Report* (Eastern Europe), 9 and 17 June, 24 July, 18 September, and 7 August 1981; and *Neue Zürcher Zeitung,* 27–28 September 1981, p. 1.

80. *Politika,* 2 June 1981, p. 5; and *Christian Science Monitor,* 2 September 1981, p. 7.

81. See *Frankfurter Allgemeine,* 23 September 1981, p. 2.

82. Radio Budapest, 15 April 1981, trans. in FBIS, *Daily Report* (Eastern Europe), 17 April 1981.

83. *Politika,* 27 October 1981, p. 7.

84. Reuter, *Die Albaner in Jugoslawien,* p. 93.

85. *Borba,* 21 May 1981, trans. in FBIS, *Daily Report* (Eastern Europe), 4 June 1981; and Tanjug, 10 December 1981, trans. in FBIS, *Daily Report* (Eastern Europe), 16 December 1981.

86. For details about these organizations, see Sabrina P. Ramet, *Social Currents in Eastern Europe: The Sources and Consequences of the Great Transformation,* 2nd ed. (Durham, N.C.: Duke University Press, 1995), chap. 8.

87. *New York Times,* 1 November 1987, p. 6.

88. *Večernji list* (Zagreb), 26 June 1987, p. 5. For a complete transcript of the proceedings of 26 June (the first day of the session), see *Borba,* 28 June 1987, special supplement.

89. Tanjug, 7 September 1988, in FBIS, *Daily Report* (Eastern Europe), 13 September 1988, p. 51.

90. *Danas,* no. 278 (16 June 1987): 30; and *Borba,* 20 November 1987, p. 3.

91. For further discussion of the Serbian Orthodox Church, see Sabrina P. Ramet, *Balkan Babel: The Disintegration of Yugoslavia from the Death of Tito to the Fall of Milošević,* 4th ed. (Boulder, Colo.: Westview Press, 2002), chap. 5.

92. Quoted in *New York Times,* 24 October 1986, p. A8. See also *NIN,* no. 1869 (26 October 1986): 14–15.

93. *Književne novine,* 15 June 1987, reprinted in *Pravoslavlje,* 15 June 1987, p. 2.

94. *Duga,* 13–26 June 1987, p. 18. For an example of a poem, see *Reporter,* no. 984 (1 June 1987): 3.

95. *NIN,* no. 1939 (28 February 1988): 8.

96. Quoted in Belgrade Domestic Service, 5 September 1988, trans. in FBIS, *Daily Report* (Eastern Europe), 12 September 1988, p. 65.

97. *New York Times,* 19 November 1998, p. 4.

98. Šime Djodan, adviser at the Institute for Public Finances, in interview with the author, Zagreb, 12 September 1989.

99. *Süddeutsche Zeitung* (Munich), 17 December 1980.

100. Ibid., vol. 28, no. 1–2 (April–June 1975): 4; and *New York Times,* 18 February 1975, p. 6.

101. *Die Welt* (Bonn), 25 November 1980; *Süddeutsche Zeitung,* 5 August 1980, p. 5. A separate group of Serbian intellectuals subsequently submitted a similar petition to the federal government, likewise requesting a blanket amnesty for all political prisoners in Yugoslavia.

102. *Süddeutsche Zeitung,* 26 July 1978, p. 3, trans. in JPRS/EER, 29 August 1978.

103. Viktor Meier, *Yugoslavia: A History of Its Demise,* trans. by Sabrina P. Ramet (London and New York: Routledge, 1999), p. 19.

104. See Franjo Tudjman, *The Case of the Croatian Historian Dr. F. Tudjman: Croatia on Trial,* trans. by Zdenka Palić-Kušan (London: United Publishers, 1981).

105. *Frankfurter Allgemeine,* 24 March 1980.

106. Franjo Tudjman, retired general and president of the HDZ, in interview with the author, Zagreb, 11 September 1989.

107. See Dobroslav Paraga, *Goli otok. Istočni grijeh zapada* (Zagreb: Self-Published by author, 1995).

108. *NIN,* no. 1538 (22 June 1980): 36–37.

109. Interviews, Zagreb, July 1982.

110. Vjekoslav Perica, "The Catholic Church and the Making of the Croatian Nation, 1970–84," *East European Politics and Societies*, vol. 14, no. 3 (Fall 2000): 543–544.

111. *Frankfurter Allgemeine*, 22 May 1981, p. 7.

112. As reported by *Svijet* (Sarajevo), 17 August 1981, as quoted in *Glas koncila* (Zagreb), 30 August 1981, p. 2, and trans. in JPRS/EE, 13 October 1981.

113. Kurtović, *Crkva i religija*, pp. 137, 139.

114. Cited by Zdenko Antić, "Catholic Clergy in Croatia under Sharp Attack," *Radio Free Europe Research*, 29 July 1977, p. 4.

115. *Süddeutsche Zeitung*, 5 August 1980, p. 5, trans. in JPRS/EE, 9 September 1980.

116. *Frankfurter Allgemeine*, 29 July 1981, p. 3. The campaign began with attacks on the character and memory of Cardinal Stepinac, broadened by criticizing current Church leaders for their defense of Stepinac, and finally assumed the form of a campaign against the Church per se. A particularly striking development was the arrest late in the year of the parish priest in the village of Straževan, who allegedly had authorized the inclusion of a likeness of Stepinac in a mosaic in his refurbished church. See Tanjug, 17 and 26 October 1981, trans. respectively in FBIS, *Daily Report* (Eastern Europe), 22 and 27 October 1981.

117. Tanjug, 8 April 1985, trans. in FBIS, *Daily Report* (Eastern Europe), 9 April 1985, pp. 17–18; *Neue Zürcher Zeitung*, 10 April 1985, p. 4; *The Times*, 11 April 1985, p. 4; *Neue Züurcher Zeitung*, 11 April 1985, p. 2; Tanjug, 11 April 1985, trans. in FBIS, *Daily Report* (Eastern Europe), 12 April 1985, pp. 12–14; Tanjug, 12 April 1985, trans. in FBIS, *Daily Report* (Eastern Europe), 15 April 1985, pp. 11–12; *Neue Zürcher Zeitung*, 14–15 April 1985, p. 3; Tanjug, 16 April 1985, trans. in FBIS, *Daily Report* (Eastern Europe), 17 April 1985, p. 16; Tanjug, 19 April 1985, trans. in FBIS, *Daily Report* (Eastern Europe), 23 April 1985, pp. 114–115; Tanjug, 29 April 1985, trans. in FBIS, *Daily Report* (Eastern Europe), 30 April 1985, pp. 121–122; Tanjug, 10 May 1985, trans. in FBIS, *Daily Report* (Eastern Europe), 13 May 1985, p. 15; and *Vjesnik*, 11 May 1985, p. 12.

118. *The Economist* (London), 14 September 1985, p. 57.

119. Quoted in *NIN*, no. 1805 (4 August 1985), trans. in JPRS, *East Europe Report*, no. EPS-85-102 (15 October 1985): 132.

120. *The Economist*, 14 September 1985, p. 57.

121. Gunther E. Rothenberg, *The Military Border in Croatia, 1740–1881: A Study of an Imperial Institution* (Chicago: University of Chicago Press, 1966), pp. 4, 10–11, 13, 18–19, 29, 122, 166; Ferdo Šišić, *Pregled povijesti Hrvatskog naroda* (Zagreb: Nakladni Zavod M.H., 1975), p. 310; and Wayne S. Vucinich, "The Serbs in Austria-Hungary," *Austrian History Yearbook*, vol. 3, pt. 2 (1967): 10, 14, 21.

122. Interview, Zagreb, 30 August 1989.

123. The Latin alphabet made its appearance in Serbian schools only in 1914. Charles Jelavich, "South Slav Education: Was There Yugoslavism?" in Norman M. Naimark and Holly Case (eds.), *Yugoslavia and Its Historians: Understanding the Balkan Wars of the 1990s* (Stanford, Calif.: Stanford University Press, 2003), p. 97.

124. Ivo Banac, *With Stalin, against Tito: Cominformist Splits in Yugoslav Communism* (Ithaca, N.Y.: Cornell University Press, 1988), p. 106.

125. *Danas*, 16 July 1985, pp. 15–16, trans. in JPRS, *East Europe Report*, no. EPS-85-102 (15 October 1985): 132.

126. Airgram A165, 5 April 1967, LOU, Thompson/Owen/B to State, POL 2 YUGO, in *Records 1967–1969*, Box 2842.

127. Airgram A149, 17 April 1968, LOU, Trinka/Owen/B to State, POL 12 YUGO, in *Records 1967–1969*, Box 2842.

128. Ales Gabrič, "Cultural Activities as Political Action," in Leopoldina Plut-Pregelj et al.,

The Repluralization of Slovenia in the 1980s: New Revelations from Archival Records, Donald W. Treadgold Papers in Russian, East European, and Central Asian Studies no. 24 (Seattle: The HMJ School of International Studies of the University of Washington, February 2000), p. 22.

129. "Laibach History Part 2," at www.gla.ac.uk/~dc4w/laibach/hpart2.html.

130. See Aleš Erjavec and Marina Gržinić, *Ljubljana, Ljubljana: The Eighties in Slovene Art and Culture* (Ljubljana: Založba Mladinska knjiga, 1991).

131. The issue is summarized in *Svet* (Belgrade), September 1989, pp. 50–51. See also *Frankfurter Allgemeine,* 12 June 1987, p. 7. For an elaborate discussion of the special issue of *Nova revija,* see Mirjana Kasapović, "O slovenskom nacionalnom programu," *Naše teme,* vol. 32, no. 4 (1988): 771–786.

132. Meier, *Yugoslavia,* p. 62.

133. Ibid., pp. 62–63.

134. Božo Repe, "The Introduction of Political Parties and Their Role in Achieving Independence," in Plut-Pregelj et al., *Repluralization of Slovenia,* p. 45.

135. Janez Janša, *The Making of the Slovenian State, 1988–1992: The Collapse of Yugoslavia* (Ljubljana: Založba Mladinska knjiga, 1994), p. 15.

136. Sabrina Petra Ramet, "Democratization in Slovenia—the Second Stage," in Karen Dawisha and Bruce Parrott (eds.), *Politics, Power, and the Struggle for Democracy in South-east Europe* (Cambridge: Cambridge University Press, 1997), p. 194.

137. Tanjug, 31 May 1988, in FBIS, *Daily Report* (Eastern Europe), 1 June 1988, p. 51.

138. *The Times,* 28 July 1988. See also *Borba,* 18 July 1988, p. 12.

139. Ljubljana Domestic Service, 29 June 1988 and 8 July 1988, trans. respectively in FBIS, *Daily Report* (Eastern Europe), 15 July 1988, pp. 60 and 59; Tanjug, 19 July 1988, trans. in FBIS, *Daily Report* (Eastern Europe), 20 July 1988, p. 61; *Danas,* no. 354 (29 November 1988): 13; and *Delo* (Ljubljana), 26 July 1988, p. 1.

140. *Borba,* 29 July 1988, p. 16.

141. Tanjug, 28 July 1988, in FBIS, *Daily Report* (Eastern Europe), 28 July 1988, p. 32.

142. Meier, *Yugoslavia,* p. 69.

143. *Frankfurter Allgemeine,* 21 June 1988, p. 4.

144. Tanjug, 17 December 1988, in FBIS, *Daily Report* (Eastern Europe), 28 July 1988, p. 32.

145. *Mladina* (Ljubljana), 1 September 1989, p. 4.

146. On the concept of ethnogenesis, see *8 Novosti* (Belgrade), 3 July 1982, p. 33.

147. Nikola Vukčević, *Etničko porijeklo crnogoraca* (Belgrade: Sava Mihić, 1981).

148. Marko Špadijer, "Nacionalizam u Crnoj Gori," *Socializam,* vol. 29, no. 4 (April 1986): 112, 113.

149. *Borba,* 28–29 July 1990, p. 13. See also *Vjesnik,* 23 July 1990, p. 3.

150. *Politika,* 30 August 1990, p. 10.

151. Tanjug, 23 August 1990, trans. in FBIS, *Daily Report* (Eastern Europe), 24 August 1990, p. 43.

152. For a useful examination of the question of Macedonian ethnicity, see John D. Bell, "The 'Ilindentsi'—Does Bulgaria Have a Macedonian Minority?" in John D. Bell (ed.), *Bulgaria in Transition: Politics, Economics, Society and Culture after Communism* (Boulder, Colo.: Westview Press, 1998).

153. For discussion, see Sabrina Petra Ramet, "All Quiet on the Southern Front? Macedonia Between the Hammer and the Anvil," in *Problems of Post-Communism,* vol. 42, no. 6 (November–December 1995).

154. These measures were adopted in July 1981. See Hugh Poulton, *Who Are the Macedonians?* (Bloomington: Indiana University Press, 1995), p. 127.

155. Ibid., pp. 127–128, 130–131.

156. Ibid., p. 128.

157. Ibid., p. 133.

158. Vojin Dimitrijević, "The 1974 Constitution as a Factor in the Collapse of Yugoslavia, or as a Sign of Decaying Totalitarianism," in Nebojša Popov (ed.), *The Road to War in Serbia: Trauma and Catharsis,* English version by Drinka Gojković (Budapest: Central European University Press, 2000), p. 407.

159. This list is taken from Slavoljub Djukić, *Izmedju slave i anateme: Politička biografija Slobodana Miloševića* (Belgrade: Filip Višnjić, 1994), p. 44.

160. Jasna Dragović-Soso, *"Saviours of the Nation": Serbia's Intellectual Opposition and the Revival of Nationalism* (London: Hurst, 2002), p. 185.

161. *Memorandum of the Serbian Academy of Sciences and Art* (1986), trans. by Dennison Rusinow with Aleksandar and Sarah Nikolić and reprinted in Dennison Rusinow, "The Yugoslav Peoples," in Peter F. Sugar (ed.), *Eastern European Nationalism in the Twentieth Century* (Washington, D.C.: American University Press, 1995), pp. 335–336, 338, 341, 336. Regarding the Memorandum's "huge influence on the shaping of the political and social climate in Serbia," see Sonja Biserko, "Nacija protiv pojedinca," in *Helsinška povelja* (Belgrade), vol. 10, nos. 81–82 (March –April 2005): 19.

162. Ibid., p. 342.

163. Laura Silber and Allan Little, *The Death of Yugoslavia* (London: Penguin Books and BBC Books, 1995), pp. 31–32.

164. Milošević, quoted in Judah, *Serbs,* p. 160.

165. Karadžić, quoted in ibid., p. 166.

166. On this phase of Šešelj's career, see Ognjen Pribićević, *Vlast i opozicija u Srbiji* (Belgrade: Radio B92, 1997), pp. 52–69.

167. Christine von Kohl and Wolfgang Libal, *Kosovo: Gordischer Knoten des Balkan* (Vienna and Zurich: Europaverlag, 1992), pp. 96–97.

168. Ivo Banac, "The Dissolution of Yugoslav Historiography," in Sabrina Petra Ramet and Ljubiša S. Adamovich (eds.), *Beyond Yugoslavia: Politics, Economics, and Culture in a Shattered Community* (Boulder, Colo.: Westview Press, 1995), p. 48.

169. This paragraph is based on ibid., pp. 42, 49, 52, 55–56.

170. Susan L. Woodward, "Genocide or Partition: Two Faces of the Same Coin?" *Slavic Review,* vol. 55, no. 4 (Winter 1996): 755.

171. On the moral responsibility of intellectuals, see Carol S. Lilly, "Amoral Realism or Immoral Obfuscation?" *Slavic Review,* vol. 55, no. 4 (Winter 1996): 749–754.

172. "Interview/Miha Kovač: The Slovene Spring," *New Left Review,* no. 171 (September–October 1988): 115.

11. A Crisis of Legitimacy, 1974–1989

1. Gisbert Flanz, introduction to *The Constitution of the Socialist Federal Republic of Yugoslavia* (Issued December 1974), in Albert P. Blaustein and Gisbert H. Flanz (eds.), *Constitutions of the World,* vol. 15 (Dobbs Ferry, N.Y.: Oceana), p. 4.

2. Miranda Vickers, *Between Serb and Albanian: A History of Kosovo* (New York: Columbia University Press, 1998), p. 178.

3. Viktor Meier, *Yugoslavia: A History of Its Demise,* trans. by Sabrina P. Ramet (London and New York: Routledge, 1999), p. 6.

4. *The Constitution of the SFRY.,* p. 197.

5. Božo Repe, "Slovenians and the Federal Yugoslavia," *Balkan Forum,* vol. 3, no. 1 (March 1995): 148.

6. *The Constitution of the SFRY,* p. 33.

7. The original title is *Pravci razvoja političkog sistema socijalističkog samoupravljanja* (Belgrade: Komunist, 1978).

8. Edvard Kardelj, *Democracy and Socialism,* trans. by Margot and Boško Milosavljević (London: Summerfield Press, 1978), p. 18.

9. Ibid., p. 27.

10. Ibid., pp. 185–186, 192.

11. Raif Dizdarević, *Od smrti Tita do smrti Jugoslavije: Svjedočenja* (Sarajevo: Svjedok, 1999), pp. 99–100.

12. Dušan Bilandžić, *Jugoslavija poslije Tita (1980–1985)* (Zagreb: Globus, 1986), p. 9. See also Ivica Josipović, "Geneza krize savremenog jugoslovenskog društva," *Socijalizam,* vol. 30, no. 10 (October 1987).

13. As I noted in my earlier article, "Yugoslavia 1982: Political Ritual, Political Drift, and the Fetishization of the Past," *South Slav Journal,* vol. 5, no. 3 (Autumn 1982): 20.

14. For preexisting problems see Paul Garde, *Život i smrt Jugoslavije,* trans. from French by Živan Filippi (Zagreb: Ceres, 1996), p. 101; and Svein Mønnesland, *Før Jugoslavia, og etter,* 4th ed. (Oslo: Sypress Forlag, 1999), pp. 229–232. For Tito's performance see John B. Allcock, *Explaining Yugoslavia* (London: Hurst, 2000), p. 78.

15. *Oslobodjenje* (Sarajevo), 27 September 1980 and 26 July 1981, p. 4; *Politika,* Belgrade), 25 May 1981; and *Start,* no. 327 (1 August 1981): 19.

16. See Institut za Uporedno Pravo, *Podela zajedničke nadležnosti izmedju federacije i federalnih jedinica* (Belgrade: Savremena Administracija, 1978), p. 27; and Mahmut Mujačić, "O dogovoranju republika i pokrajina," *Ideje,* vol. 10, no. 2 (March–April 1979): 19. See also Mahmut Mujačić, *Nova dimenzija jugoslovenskog federalizma* (Sarajevo: Oslobodjenje, 1981). For the state presidency see *Komunist,* 24 July 1981, p. 8.

17. *Danas* (Zagreb), 22 June 1982, p. 14.

18. *Politika,* 2 February 1982, p. 6.

19. *NIN,* no. 1594 (19 July 1981): 8.

20. *Komunist,* 9 October 1981; and *Politika,* 17 March 1982.

21. *Borba,* 20 October 1981.

22. *NIN,* no. 1596 (2 August 1981): 15–16.

23. *NIN,* no. 1601 (15 November 1981): 9.

24. *Novosti* (Belgrade), 3 July 1982, p. 9.

25. *NIN,* no. 1645 (11 July 1982): 10.

26. Dizdarević, *Od smrti Tita do smrti Jugoslavije,* p. 88.

27. Ibid., pp. 89, 90–91.

28. *Komunist,* 23 July 1982, pp. 12–13.

29. *Borba,* 24 September 1982; and *NIN,* no. 1656 (26 September 1982).

30. Dizdarević, *Od smrti Tita do smrti Jugoslavije,* pp. 116–118.

31. *Politika,* 30 March 1983, p. 8.

32. See the report by Slobodanka Gaćanović, in *Trinaesti kongres Saveza Komunista Jugoslavije, Beograd, 25–28. jun 1986. magnetofonske beleške,* vol. 2 (Belgrade Izdavački Centar Komunist, 1988), pp. 420–422.

33. See Boro Krivokapić, *Jugoslavija i komunisti: Adresa Jovana Djordjevića* (Belgrade: Mladost, 1988), p. 133.

34. No one was arguing for the confederalization of the system at that stage. I have argued this point and provided documentation in my *Balkan Babel: The Disintegration of Yugoslavia from the Death of Tito to the Fall of Milošević,* 4th ed. (Boulder, Colo.: Westview Press, 2002), chap. 1.

35. For further discussion of the Serbian reform proposal, see Wolfang Höpken, "Party Monopoly and Political Change: The League of Communists since Tito's Death," in Pedro Ramet (ed.), *Yugoslavia in the 1980s* (Boulder, Colo.: Westview Press, 1985).

36. Tanjug, 22 September 1985, trans. in FBIS, *Daily Report* (Eastern Europe), 25 September 1985, p. 14.

37. *Politika,* 23 November 1988, p. 10.

38. For details, see Pedro Ramet, "Yugoslavia's Debate Over Democratization," *Survey,* vol. 25, no. 3 (Summer 1980): 43–48.

39. *Borba,* 12–15 October 1984, summarized in an editorial report for JPRS, *East Europe Report,* no. EPS-84-135 (1 November 1984): 120.

40. See, for example, the resolutions of the party's Twenty-First Session, 31 October 1985, as reported in Tanjug, 2 November 1985, trans. in FBIS, *Daily Report* (Eastern Europe), 13 November 1985, pp. 11–127.

41. *New York Times,* 8 December 1985, p. 12.

42. *Danas,* no. 127 (24 July 1984): 22–24; *Borba,* 18 March 1985, p. 3; and *Politika,* 25 December 1981, pp. 1–4.

43. *Reuters,* 22 August 1983, on *Lexis-Nexis Academic Universe* (hereafter, LNAU); *Yugoslav News Agency,* 22 August 1983, in *BBC Summary of World Broadcasts,* 24 August 1983, on LNAU; and *Danas,* 30 August 1983, trans. in *BBC Summary of World Broadcasts,* 5 September 1983, on LNAU.

44. Belgrade home service, 11 July 1985, trans. in *BBC Summary of World Broadcasts,* 23 July 1985, on LNAU.

45. Tanjug, 18 November 1985, trans. in FBIS, *Daily Report* (Eastern Europe), 26 November 1985, pp. 11–19.

46. *Narodna armija,* 14 August 1986, p. 3, trans. in FBIS, *Daily Report* (Eastern Europe), 21 August 1986, p. 14.

47. *Vjesnik,* 25 June 1986, pp. 4–5.

48. *Vjesnik,* 30 June 1986, p. 2; and *Borba,* 24 November 1986, p. 2.

49. Dizdarević, *Od smrti Tita do smrti Jugoslavije,* pp. 188–189.

50. Tanjug, 6 July 1988, trans. in FBIS, *Daily Report* (Eastern Europe), 12 July 1988, p. 57.

51. Branko Horvat, *Politička ekonomija socijalizma* (Zagreb, 1984), as summarized (and criticized) in Miladin Korač, "Branko Horvat: 'Politička ekonomija socijalizma'—kritička analiza trećeg dela knjige," *Socijalizam,* vol. 27, no. 10 (October 1984).

52. See, for example, Hamdija Pozderac, "Bespartijska demokratija kao politički ideal," *Socijalizam,* vol. 30, no. 6 (June 1987).

53. Neven Andjelić, *Bosnia-Herzegovina: The End of a Legacy* (London: Frank Cass, 2003), pp. 56–61; and Meier, *Yugoslavia,* pp. 41–42.

54. *NIN,* no. 1883 (1 February 1987): 9, 11.

55. *Politika,* 20 March 1987, p. 1.

56. Rupel, quoted in *Politika,* 18 March 1987, p. 10, trans. in FBIS, *Daily Report* (Eastern Europe), 7 April 1987, p. 17.

57. *Danas,* 28 July 1987, pp. 12–14, trans. in JPRS, *East Europe Report,* no. EER-87-149 (28 October 1987): 28–29.

58. Vojislav Vučković, president of the Commission for Constitutional Reforms of SAWP-Croatia, in interview with the author, Zagreb, 11 September 1989.

59. *Borba,* 16 August 1988, p. 1.

60. Čiril Ribičič and Zdravko Tomac, *Federalizam po mjeri budućnosti* (Zagreb: Globus, 1989), p. 322.

61. Zdravko Tomac, member of the Commission for Constitutional Reforms of SAWP-Croatia, in interview with the author, Zagreb, 12 September 1989.

62. Ribičič and Tomac, *Federalizam,* p. 48.

63. Ibid., p. 66.

64. The draft amendments are listed in ibid., pp. 89–90.

65. *Borba,* 1 June 1989, p. 7. See also Ramet, *Balkan Babel,* 4th ed., p. 34.

66. Tanjug, 6 July 1989, in FBIS, *Daily Report* (Eastern Europe), 11 July 1989, p. 67.

67. Interview with Marijan Korošić, in *NIN,* no. 1959 (17 July 1988): 16–18.

68. Quoted in Tanjug, 19 April 1989, in FBIS, *Daily Report* (Eastern Europe), 20 April 1989, p. 49.

69. Belgrade Domestic Service, 5 May 1989, trans. in FBIS, *Daily Report* (Eastern Europe), 8 May 1989, p. 51.

12. Hail Caesar!

1. I expressed some skepticism about the long-term viability of Yugoslavia's political formulae in Pedro Ramet, "Yugoslavia and the Threat of Internal and External Discontents," *Orbis,* vol. 28, no. 1 (Spring 1984); and Pedro Ramet, "Apocalypse Culture and Social Change in Yugoslavia," in Pedro Ramet (ed.), *Yugoslavia in the 1980s* (Boulder, Colo.: Westview Press, 1985).

2. For further discussion, see Sabrina P. Ramet, *Balkan Babel: The Disintegration of Yugoslavia from the Death of Tito to the Fall of Milošević,* 4th ed. (Boulder, Colo.: Westview Press, 2002), chap. 5.

3. *Danas,* no. 354 (29 November 1988): 18. The best English-language biographies of Milošević of which I am aware are Adam LeBor, *Milošević: A Biography* (Polmont, Stirlingshire: Bloomsbury, 2002), and Louis Sell, *Slobodan Milošević and the Destruction of Yugoslavia* (Durham, N.C.: Duke University Press, 2002).

4. For details, see Sabrina P. Ramet, *Social Currents in Eastern Europe: The Sources and Consequences of the Great Transformation,* 2nd ed. (Durham, N.C.: Duke University Press, 1995), pp. 205–207.

5. Ivan Stambolić, *Rasprave o SR Srbiji 1979–1987* (Zagreb: Globus, 1988), pp. 201–202. See also Čiril Ribičič and Zdravko Tomac, *Federalizam po mjeri budućnosti* (Zagreb: Globus, 1989).

6. Milošević, quoted in Slavoljub Djukić, *Izmedju slave i anateme: Politička biografija Slobodana Miloševića* (Belgrade: Filip Višnjić, 1994), p. 51.

7. Quoted in *Washington Post,* 4 February 1990, p. A33.

8. Laura Silber and Allan Little, *The Death of Yugoslavia* (London: Penguin Books and BBC Books, 1995), pp. 36–38.

9. Djukić, *Izmedju slave i anateme,* pp. 53, 54–55.

10. Silber and Little, *The Death of Yugoslavia,* p. 40; and Julie A. Mertus, *Kosovo: How*

Myths and Truths Started a War (Berkeley and Los Angeles: University of California Press, 1999), pp. 145, 147, 40–42.

11. Branko Mamula, *Slučaj Jugoslavija* (Podgorica: CID, 2000), p. 115.

12. Ibid., pp. 115, 120.

13. Ibid., pp. 118, 120.

14. *Pravoslavlje,* 1 July 1990, pp. 1, 3.

15. *Duga,* no. 406 (16 September 1989): 82–83; and *Intervju,* no. 215 (1 September 1989): 29.

16. Tanjug, 3 May 1988, in *BBC Summary of World Broadcasts,*10 May 1988, on LNAU.

17. *Facts on File World News Report,* 11 May 1990, on LNAU.

18. Radio Ljubljana, 13 April 1990, in *BBC Summary of World Broadcasts,* 18 April 1990, on LNAU.

19. *Vjesnik* (Zagreb), 13 August 1990, p. 3, trans. in FBIS, *Daily Report* (Eastern Europe), 22 August 1990, p. 56.

20. Re P. Stambolić, D. Marković, Minić, and Vlaškalić, Yugoslav News Agency, 8 September 1988, and Belgrade home service, 8 September 1988, both trans. in *BBC Summary of World Broadcasts,* 12 September 1988, on LNAU; re Ranković, Yugoslav News Agency, 15 December 1989, 16 December 1989, 17 December 1989—trans. in *BBC Summary of World Broadcasts,* 30 December 1989, on LNAU; re D. Marković's counterattack, Tanjug, 8 September 1988, in *BBC Summary of World Broadcasts,* 12 September 1988, on LNAU.

21. Wolgfang Höpken, "Party Monopoly and Political Change: The League of Communists since Tito's Death," in P. Ramet, *Yugoslavia in the 1980s,* pp. 39, 40.

22. Details in S. P. Ramet, *Balkan Babel,* pp. 71–72.

23. Quoted in *New York Times,* 14 October 1988, p. 7.

24. Belgrade Domestic Service, 19 November 1988, trans. in FBIS, *Daily Report* (Eastern Europe), 21 November 1988, pp. 72–73.

25. *Eastern Europe Newsletter,* vol. 2, no. 20 (12 October 1988): 3; and *Chicago Tribune,* 17 October 1988, p. 2. See also Mirjana Kasapović, "Srpski nacionalizam i desni radikalizam," *Naše teme,* vol. 33, no. 1–2 (1989).

26. See also *Borba* (Belgrade), 9 May 1989, p. 3, and 14 June 1989, p. 13; also Boro Krivokapić, *Jugoslavija i komunisti: Adresa Jovana Djordjevića* (Belgrade: Mladost, 1988), pp. 91–106.

27. Vladimir Dedijer, *Vatikan i Jasenovac* (Belgrade: Izdavačka radna organizacija 'Rad,' 1987); re Jasenovac, as reported in *Glas koncila* (Zagreb), 11 December 1988, p. 3.

28. *Eastern Europe Newsletter,* vol. 2, no. 19 (28 September 1988): 7, and confirmed in many sources.

29. Milorad Tomanić, *Srpska crkva u ratu i ratovi u njoj* (Belgrade: Medijska knjižara krug, 2001), pp. 40, 43.

30. *Le Monde* (Paris), 12 July 1989, trans. in FBIS, *Daily Report* (Eastern Europe), 17 July 1989, p. 53.

31. Quoted in *New York Times,* 6 August 1989, p. 12.

32. Šolević, quoted in *Profil* (Vienna), 24 October 1988, p. 42.

33. Stipe Šuvar, *Nezavršeni mandat,* vol. 2: *Na udaru 'Antibirokratske revolucije'* (Zagreb: Globus, 1989), p. 125.

34. Raif Dizdarević, *Od smrti Tita do smrti Jugoslavije: Svjedočenja* (Sarajevo: Svjedok, 1999), p. 194.

35. *The Economist* (London), 23 July 1988, p. 44.

36. Tanjug, 24 September 1988, in FBIS, *Daily Report* (Eastern Europe), 27 September 1988, p. 51.

37. Raif Dizdarević, former president of the SFRY presidency, in interview with the author, Sarajevo, 18 July 2004.

38. Dizdarević, *Od smrti Tita do smrti Jugoslavije,* pp. 198–200.

39. Ibid., p. 202.

40. *Vjesnik* (Zagreb), 21 August 1988, p. 3.

41. Dizdarević, *Od smrti Tita do smrti Jugoslavije,* pp. 205, 213.

42. Djukić, *Izmedju slave i anateme,* p. 105.

43. *Frankfurter Allgemeine,* 8 October 1988, p. 5; and *Süddeutsche Zeitung* (Munich), 8–9 October 1988, p. 6.

44. Viktor Meier, *Yugoslavia: A History of Its Demise,* trans. from German by Sabrina P. Ramet (London and New York: Routledge, 1999), p. 72.

45. Ibid., p. 78.

46. Dizdarević, *Od smrti Tita do smrti Jugoslavije,* pp. 213–214.

47. Slobodan Milošević, *Godine raspleta,* 2nd ed. (Belgrade: Beogradski izdavačko-grafički zavod, 1989), p. 264.

48. Šuvar, *Nezavršeni mandat,* vol. 2, p. 131.

49. Meier, *Yugoslavia,* pp. 80–93; also Sabrina P. Ramet, *Whose Democracy? Nationalism, Religion, and the Doctrine of Collective Rights in Post-1989 Eastern Europe* (Lanham, Md.: Rowman & Littlefield, 1997), chap. 6.

50. Concerning the arrest of Vllasi and the inception of his trial, see *Start,* no. 539 (16 September 1989): 32–35; and *Politika* (Belgrade), 30 October 1989, p. 6.

51. *Politika ekspres* (Belgrade), 31 August 1989, p. 3.

52. Dizdarević, *Od smrti Tita do smrti Jugoslavije,* p. 294.

53. *Financial Times,* 11 January 1989, p. 2; *New York Times,* 12 January 1989, p. 6; and *Frankfurter Allgemeine,* 13 January 1989, p. 6.

54. For example, academician Vlado Strugar in the Montenegrin Academy of Sciences and Art, as reported in *Borba,* 19–20 November 1988, p. 5, trans. in FBIS, *Daily Report* (Eastern Europe), 5 December 1988, p. 57.

55. The illegal activities of the Serbian security service became known in October 1989; this revelation led to an immediate crisis in relations between Bosnia and Serbia. See the report in *Danas,* no. 401 (24 October 1989): 15–16. See also Tanjug, 30 October 1989, trans. in FBIS, *Daily Report* (Eastern Europe), 1 November 1989, p. 68.

56. Neven Andjelić, *Bosnia-Herzegovina: The End of a Legacy* (London: Frank Cass, 2003), p. 115.

57. *Borba,* 9 May 1989, p. 1.

58. Stipe Mesić, *Kako je srušena Jugoslavija,* 2nd ed. (Zagreb: Mislav Press, 1994), p. 11.

59. Šuvar collected many of his writings and speeches into a two-volume work published in 1988. See Stipe Šuvar, *Socijalizam i nacije,* 2 vols. (Zagreb: Globus, 1988).

60. Dizdarević, *Od smrti Tita do smrti Jugoslavije,* pp. 303, 307.

61. See Milošević's speech to the 1988 conference of the League of Communists of Serbia, reported in *Vjesnik,* 22 November 1988, p. 4. For an elaborate articulation of Milošević's program, see Radoslav Stojanović, *Jugoslavija, nacije i politika* (Belgrade: Nova knjiga, 1988). See also *Borba,* 5 July 1990, p. 3.

62. *Borba,* 19 July 1989, p. 4, trans. in FBIS, *Daily Report* (Eastern Europe), 25 July 1989, p. 45. *Politika* cited a report of the Serbian security service that Serbs were emigrating from

Bosnia in large numbers and blamed poor inter-ethnic relations for the migratory movement. See *Politika,* 27 October 1989, p. 6.

63. *Nova Makedonija,* as summarized in Tanjug, 15 March 1989, in FBIS, *Daily Report* (Eastern Europe), 16 March 1989, p. 58.

64. *Borba,* 28 February 1989, p. 2, trans. in FBIS, *Daily Report* (Eastern Europe), 3 March 1989, p. 71.

65. Meier, *Yugoslavia,* pp. 106–107.

66. This was a remarkable achievement considering the demands of the job and the fact that his predecessor, Branko Mikulić, had ended up one of the most unpopular politicians in Yugoslavia in the entire post–World War Two period. See *The Economist,* 30 June 1990, p. 49.

67. *New York Times,* 14 June 1990, p. A8.

68. Franjo Tudjman, retired general and future president of Croatia, in interview with the author, Zagreb, 11 September 1989.

69. Dušan Bilandžić, *Hrvatska moderna povijest* (Zagreb: Golden Marketing, 1999), pp. 775–776. See also Ivan Grdešić, et al., *Hrvatska u izborima '90* (Zagreb: Naprijed, 1991); and Darko Hudelist, *Banket u Hrvatskoj: Prilozi povijesti hrvatskog višestranacja 1989–1990,* 2nd ed. (Zagreb: Globus, 1999).

70. *Süddeutsche Zeitung,* 23–24 June 1990, p. 8; and *Süddeutsche Zeitung,* 7–8 July 1990, p. 4. For more detailed discussion of Slovenia's transition, see Danica Fink-Hafner and John R. Robbins (eds.), *Making a New Nation: The Formation of Slovenia* (Aldershot: Dartmouth,1997), especially chapters 1–3 and 10.

71. *Helsinki.Watch–Croatia* (17 November 1992), pp. 17–18, at www.bosnet.org/archive .bosnet.w3archive/9211/msg00121.html [accessed 21 September 2001].

72. Risto Lazarev, editor of *Balkan Forum* and former director-general of Tanjug, in interview with the author, Skopje, 21 March 1995.

73. *Frankfurter Allgemeine,* 2 August 1990, p. 1.

74. Meier, *Yugoslavia,* p. 199.

75. Mirko Pejanović, *Through Bosnian Eyes: The Political Memoirs of a Bosnian Serb,* trans. from Serbo-Croatian by Marina Bowder (Sarajevo: TKD Šahinpašić, 2002), pp. 23, 25.

76. Paul Garde, *Život i smrt Jugoslavije,* trans. from French by Živan Filippi (Zagreb: Ceres, 1996), p. 284.

77. Robert Thomas, *Serbia under Milošević: Politics in the 1990s* (London: Hurst, 1999), pp. 53–55.

78. Belgrade Domestic Service, 6 January 1990, trans. in FBIS, *Daily Report* (Eastern Europe), 12 January 1990, p. 65. See also the interview with Drašković in *Borba,* 16 January 1990, p. 6, excerpted in FBIS, *Daily Report* (Eastern Europe), 22 January 1990, p. 102; and *Danas,* no. 414 (23 January 1990): 7–9.

79. Drašković, quoted in Thomas, *Serbia under Milošević,* p. 55.

80. See Ognjen Pribićević, "Changing Fortunes of the Serbian Radical Right," in Sabrina P. Ramet (ed.), *The Radical Right in Central and Eastern Europe since 1989* (University Park: Pennsylvania State University Press, 1999), pp. 192–211.

81. *Frankfurter Allgemeine,* 29 June 1990, p. 6. This was transparently a reversal of his earlier stance, as stated in October 1988. See also *Vjesnik,* 26 June 1990, p. 5.

82. *Frankfurter Allgemeine,* 3 August 1990, p. 6.

83. *Vjesnik,* 3 July 1990, p. 1. See also *Süddeutsche Zeitung,* 23–24 June 1990, p. 8.

84. *Neue Zürcher Zeitung,* 5 September 1990, p. 3; and *New York Times,* 14 September 1990, p. A8.

85. *Frankfurter Allgemeine,* 15 June 1990, p. 8.

86. For discussion of Kosovo's *apartheid* conditions, see Ramet, *Whose Democracy,* chap. 6; also Meier, *Yugoslavia,* chap. 3.

87. See the report in *Vjesnik,* 3 July 1990, p. 8.

88. *Vjesnik,* 28 August 1989, p. 5; *NIN,* no. 2018 (3 September 1989): 17–23; *Slobodna Dalmacija* (Split), 11 September 1989, p. 4; and *NIN,* no. 2020 (17 September 1989): 18–20.

89. *Večernje novosti* (Belgrade), 2 September 1989, p. 18; *Večernje novosti,* 9 September 1989, p. 6; *Slobodna Dalmacija,* 10 September 1989, p. 20; *Nedjeljna Dalmacija,* 10 September 1989, p. 6; *Slobodna Dalmacija,* 12 September 1989, p. 17; *Start,* no. 539 (16 September 1989): 28–29; *Politika ekspres,* 22 September 1989, p. 10; and *Večernji list* (Zagreb), 23 September 1989, p. 39.

90. *Slobodna Dalmacija,* 12 September 1989, p. 3; *Večernji list,* 15 September 1989, p. 2; and *Večernje novosti,* 23 September 1989, p. 4.

91. Rašković, quoted in *International Herald Tribune* (Paris), 8 August 1990, p. 2.

92. Mønnesland, *Før og etter Jugoslavia,* 4th ed., p. 256; *Los Angeles Times,* 18 August 1990, p. A4; *New York Times,* 19 August 1990, p. 3; *La Opinion* (Los Angeles), 19 August 1990, p. 7; and *New York Times,* 20 August 1990, p. A2.

93. *Politika,* 19 August 1990, pp. 7, 10.

94. Tanjug, 1 October 1990, trans. in FBIS, *Daily Report* (Eastern Europe), 1 October 1990.

95. For details and documentation of arms shipments see Ramet, *Balkan Babel,* pp. 58–59.

96. Tanjug, 1 October 1990, trans. in FBIS, *Daily Report* (Eastern Europe), 2 October 1990.

97. For elaboration, see my "Yugoslavia 1987: Stirrings from Below," *South Slav Journal,* vol. 10, no. 3 (Autumn 1987).

98. For discussion of Milošević's affinities for state capitalism, see Meier, *Yugoslavia,* p. 105.

99. Plato, *Gorgias,* trans. by Robin Waterfield (Oxford and New York: Oxford University Press, 1994), p. 119.

100. Obrad Kesić, *Slavic Review,* vol. 54, no. 2 (Summer 1995): 517.

13. The Road to War

1. Jože Smole, president of the Republic Conference of SAWP-Slovenia, as cited in *Politika,* Belgrade), 21 September 1988, p. 12.

2. Stanovnik, quoted in *New York Times,* 15 October 1988, p. 4.

3. *Borba* (Belgrade), 31 May 1989, p. 5.

4. *Borba,* 7 November 1988, p. 11, and 8 March 1989, p. 2.

5. *Süddeutsche Zeitung* (Munich), 1–2 April 1989, p. 8.

6. Raif Dizdarević, *Od smrti Tita do smrti Jugoslavije: Svjedočenja* (Sarajevo: Svjedok, 1999), pp. 376–378.

7. The full text of the telegram is published in *Politika,* 1 March 1989, p. 17. See also *NIN,* no. 1992 (5 March 1989): 32, and no. 1993 (12 March 1989): 39–40.

8. Interview with Rudi Šeligo, president of the Slovenian Association of Writers, Ljubljana, 4 September 1989.

9. *Glas koncila* (Zagreb), 5 March 1989, p. 1.

10. See Tanjug, 27 February 1989, trans. in FBIS, *Daily Report* (Eastern Europe), 2 March 1989, p. 56.

11. See *Borba*, 24 May 1989, p. 3; also *Delo* (Ljubljana), 24 May 1989, p. 3.

12. Quoted in Ljubljana Domestic Service, 2 June 1989, trans. in FBIS, *Daily Report* (Eastern Europe), 5 June 1989, p. 50.

13. *Delo*, 6 July 1989, p. 3, trans. in FBIS, *Daily Report* (Eastern Europe), 12 July 1989, p. 56.

14. *Oslobodjenje*, as summarized in Tanjug, 5 June 1989, in FBIS, *Daily Report* (Eastern Europe), 6 June 1989, p. 44.

15. *Svet* (Belgrade), September 1989, special edition, p. 7.

16. For example, *Politika*, 20 September 1989, p. 8.

17. *Delo*, 21 November 1989, p. 5.

18. Tanjug, 24 November 1989, trans. in FBIS, *Daily Report* (Eastern Europe), 27 November 1989, p. 99.

19. Belgrade Domestic Service, 25 November 1989, and Ljubljana Domestic Service, 25 November 1989, trans. consecutively in FBIS, *Daily Report* (Eastern Europe), 27 November 1989, p. 99.

20. Tanjug, 4 December 1989, trans. in FBIS, *Daily Report* (Eastern Europe), 7 December 1989, pp. 115, 117.

21. Belgrade Domestic Service, 29 November 1989, trans. in FBIS, *Daily Report* (Eastern Europe), 30 November 1989, p. 84; and Belgrade Domestic Service, 13 December 1989, trans. in FBIS, *Daily Report* (Eastern Europe), 15 December 1989, p. 81.

22. *Borba*, 22 December 1989, p. 5.

23. Tanjug, 22 February 1990, trans. in FBIS, *Daily Report* (Eastern Europe), 23 February 1990, pp. 85–86.

24. *Kosovo, 1389–1989*, special edition of the *Serbian Literary Quarterly*, nos. 1–3 (1989): 45.

25. *Danas*, no. 394 (5 September 1989): 33; and Tanjug, 7 December 1989, trans. in FBIS, *Daily Report* (Eastern Europe), 15 December 1989, p. 87.

26. Specifically, Novak Kilibarda, president of the pro-Serbian Montenegrin People's Party, said that in the event of the confederalization of Yugoslavia, Montenegro should annex the "eastern parts" of Bosnia-Herzegovina. *Borba*, 1 November 1990, p. 4.

27. *Borba*, 16 July 1990, p. 3.

28. Tanjug, 5 March 1990, trans. in FBIS, *Daily Report* (Eastern Europe), 6 March 1990, p. 64.

29. Milošević's comments are cited in chapter 11; Tudjman's comments are cited in *Borba*, 22 June 1990, p. 4.

30. Alija Izetbegović, *Sjećanja: Autobiografski zapis* (Sarajevo: TKD Šahinpašic, 2001), pp. 66, 79.

31. *Borba*, 10 May 1989, p. 3.

32. Belgrade Domestic Service, 17 May 1989, trans. in FBIS, *Daily Report* (Eastern Europe), 18 May 1989, p. 60.

33. See, for instance, *NIN*, no. 1885 (15 February 1987): 16–19.

34. *Borba*, 16 July 1990, p. 4.

35. See Dennison Rusinow, "Nationalities Policy and the 'National Question,'" in Pedro Ramet, *Yugoslavia in the 1980s* (Boulder, Colo.: Westview Press, 1985), p. 141.

36. See discussions from a Croatian point of view, in *Danas*, no. 359 (3 January 1989): 29; and *Glas koncila*, 30 July 1989, p. 5; 24 September 1989, p. 3; and 8 October 1989, p. 2.

37. The complete text was published in *Glas koncila*, 19 February 1989. An English translation was published in *South Slav Journal*, vol. 11, no. 4 (Winter 1988/89): 56.

38. The text of the Ćosić interview was republished in many places, including in *Večernje novosti* (Belgrade), 7 September 1989, p. 19.

39. For relevant reports, see *Večernji list* (Zagreb), 11 September 1989, p. 4; *Slobodna Dalmacija* (Split), 12 September 1989, p. 2; *Slobodna Dalmacija,* 13 September 1989, p. 4; and *Večernji list,* 14 September 1989, p. 4.

40. *Slobodna Dalmacija,* 12 September 1989, p. 3.

41. *Večernji list,* 15 September 1989, p. 5; and *Večernje novosti,* 23 September 1989, p. 4.

42. *Nedjeljna Dalmacija,* 6–7 September 1989, reprinted in *Borba,* 8 September 1989, p. 13, trans. in FBIS, *Daily Report* (Eastern Europe), 21 September 1989, pp. 56–57.

43. *Nedjeljna Dalmacija,* 17 September 1989, pp. 11–12.

44. *Pravoslavlje* (Belgrade), 15 March 1989, p. 5, and 15 April 1989, pp. 12–13.

45. *Vjesnik,* 10 September 1989, p. 5; *Večernje novosti,* 21 September 1989, p. 2; and *Slobodna Dalmacija,* 22 September 1989, p. 16.

46. *Slobodna Dalmacija,* 11 September 1989, p. 32.

47. *Večernje novosti,* 11 September 1989, p. 12; and *Večernji list,* 11 September 1989, p. 17. See also Ivan Čolović, "Football, Hooligans and War," in Nebojša Popov (ed.), *The Road to War in Serbia: Trauma and Catharsis,* English ed. by Drinka Gojković (Budapest: Central European University Press, 2000), pp. 373–396.

48. Janez Janša, *The Making of the Slovenian State, 1988–1992: The Collapse of Yugoslavia,* trans. from Slovenian by AMIDAS d.o.o., ed. by Aleksandar Zorn (Ljubljana: Mladinska, 1994), p. 46.

49. Tanjug, 19 July 1989, in FBIS, *Daily Report* (Eastern Europe), 19 July 1989, p. 52.

50. Viktor Meier said 60%; France Tomšič said 70%. See Viktor Meier, "Jugoslawiens Krise wird politisch," in *Schweizer Monatshefte,* vol. 68, no. 2 (February 1988): 101; and interview with France Tomšič, chair of the Slovenian Social Democratic Union, in *Wiener Zeitung,* 14 March 1989, p. 3, trans. in FBIS, *Daily Report* (Eastern Europe), 15 March 1989, p. 74.

51. *Vjesnik,* 26 June 1986, p. 2; and Tanjug, 26 October 1989, trans. in FBIS, *Daily Report* (Eastern Europe), 1 November 1989, p. 74.

52. Branko Mamula, *Slučaj Jugoslavija* (Podgorica: CID, 2000), pp. 158, 167.

53. *Frankfurter Allgemeine,* 17 July 1989, p. 2; and *Narodna armija,* as reprinted in *Večernji list,* 8 September 1989, p. 2.

54. Krstan Milošević, executive secretary of the presidency of the Committee OCK JNA, as reported in *Večernje novosti,* 26 September 1989, p. 6. Also *Politika ekspres* (Belgrade), 26 September 1989, p. 4.

55. Tanjug, 26 October 1989, in FBIS, *Daily Report* (Eastern Europe), 1 November 1989, p. 74.

56. Tanjug, December 1989, trans. in FBIS, *Daily Report* (Eastern Europe), 11 January 1990, p. 87.

57. Janša, *Making of the Slovenian State,* pp. 44–45.

58. Laura Silber and Allan Little, *The Death of Yugoslavia* (London: Penguin Books and BBC Books, 1995), p. 115.

59. *Vjesnik,* 5 July 1990, p. 1.

60. Tanjug, 22 December 1989, trans. in FBIS, *Daily Report* (Eastern Europe), 22 December 1989, p. 85.

61. Tanjug, 25 March 1990, trans. in FBIS, *Daily Report* (Eastern Europe), 27 March 1990, p. 62.

62. See, for instance, Belgrade Domestic Service, 9 March 1990, trans. in FBIS, *Daily Report* (Eastern Europe), 23 March 1990, p. 95.

63. Čavoški, quoted in *New York Times,* 23 September 1990, p. 15.

64. Pedro Ramet [Sabrina P. Ramet], "Apocalypse Culture and Social Change in Yugo-slavia," in Pedro Ramet (ed.), *Yugoslavia in the 1980s* (Boulder, Colo.: Westview Press, 1985), pp. 3–4.

65. See Pedro Ramet, "Yugoslavia's Debate over Democratization," *Survey,* vol. 25, no. 3 (Summer 1980): 43–48.

66. Tanjug, 8 October 1989, trans. in FBIS, *Daily Report* (Eastern Europe), 11 October 1989, p. 27.

67. See *Borba,* 29 June 1990, p. 4; 3 July 1990, p. 3; and 10 July 1990, p. 1.

68. *Neue Zürcher Zeitung,* 1 September 1990, p. 3.

69. See Radoslav Stojanović, *Jugoslavija, nacije i politika* (Belgrade: Nova knjiga, 1988); and Slobodan Samardžić, *Jugoslavija pred iskušenjem federalizma* (Belgrade: Stručna knjiga, 1990).

70. Martin Špegelj, *Sjećanja vojnika,* ed. by Ivo Žanić (Zagreb: Znanje, 2001), pp. 126–131.

71. Sabrina P. Ramet, "Martyr in His Own Mind: The Trial and Tribulations of Slobodan Milošević," in *Totalitarian Movements and Political Religions,* vol. 5, no. 1 (Summer 2004): 121, confirmed in the testimony of Milan Babić, Stipe Mesić, and several other prosecution witnesses.

72. See Zagreb Domestic Service, 17 October 1990, trans. in FBIS, *Daily Report* (Eastern Europe), 18 October 1990, p. 58; and Tanjug, 19 October 1990, trans. in FBIS, *Daily Report* (Eastern Europe), 22 October 1990, p. 53.

73. Viktor Meier, *Yugoslavia: A History of Its Demise,* trans. from German by Sabrina P. Ramet (London and New York: Routledge, 1999), p. 150.

74. *Frankfurter Allgemeine,* 7 January 1991, p. 1.

75. *Vjesnik,* 23 October 1990, p. 2; and *Süddeutsche Zeitung,* 10/11 November 1990, p. 9.

76. Details in Sabrina P. Ramet, *Balkan Babel: The Disintegration of Yugoslavia from the Death of Tito to the Fall of Milošević,* 4th ed. (Boulder, Colo.: Westview Press, 2002), chap. 3.

77. Janez Drnovšek, *Der Jugoslawien-Krieg. Meine Wahrheit,* trans. from Slovenian by Doris Debeniak (Kilchberg: SmartBooks, 1998), p. 233.

78. Meier, *Yugoslavia,* p. 158.

79. Text in *Vjesnik,* 12 October 1990, p. 5.

80. Drnovšek, *Der Jugoslawien-Krieg,* pp. 234–238.

81. Meier, *Yugoslavia,* p. 158.

82. Zdravko Tomac, *The Struggle for the Croatian State . . . through Hell to Democracy,* trans. from Croatian by Profikon (Zagreb: Profikon, 1993), pp. 32–33.

83. Kadijević, quoted in *Croatian Democracy Project,* news release, 12 December 1990.

84. *Oslobodjenje* (Sarajevo), 12 November 1990, p. 1.

85. Tanjug, 27 November 1990, trans. in FBIS, *Daily Report* (Eastern Europe), 29 November 1990, p. 75.

86. Meier, *Yugoslavia,* pp. 161–162; and *The Economist* (London), 2 February 1991, p. 44.

87. Former defense minister Branko Mamula, for example, believed that it was a mistake for the LC Croatia to have endorsed political pluralism at its Ninth Congress in December 1989. See Mamula, *Slučaj Jugoslavija,* p. 198.

88. *Daily Telegraph* (London), 4 December 1990, p. 11; and *New York Times,* 20 January 1991, p. 7.

89. *Süddeutsche Zeitung,* 19/20 January 1991, p. 9; confirmed in *Daily Telegraph,* 23 January 1991, p. 13; reconfirmed in *Neue Zürcher Zeitung,* 23 January 1991, p. 4.

90. Janez Janša, former defense minister of Slovenia, in interview with the author, Ljubl-

jana, 31 August 1999; Konrad Kolšek, *Spomini za začetek oborozenega spopada v Jugoslaviji 1991* (Maribor: Založba Obzorja, 2001), p. 90; and Janša, *Making of the Slovenian State,* p. 150.

91. Borisav Jović, *Posledni dani SFRJ—izvodi iz dnevnika* (Belgrade: Beogradski izdavačko-grafički zavod, 1989), pp. 227–228 (entry for 23 November 1990).

92. Meier, *Yugoslavia,* p. 163.

93. Drnovšek, *Der Jugoslawien Krieg,* pp. 247–257; Silber and Little, *Death of Yugoslavia,* pp. 120–121; and Meier, *Yugoslavia,* pp. 163–164.

94. See Špegelj, *Sjećanja vojnika,* pp. 162–164; Drnovšek, *Der Jugoslawien-Krieg,* pp. 252–254; and Mamula, *Slučaj Jugoslavija,* p. 197.

95. *Il Messaggero* (Rome), 27 January 1991, p. 8.

96. *Süddeutsche Zeitung,* 26/27 January 1991, p. 11.

97. *Neue Zürcher Zeitung,* 29 January 1991, p. 4.

98. *Seattle Times,* 9 February 1991, p. A5; and *Neue Zürcher Zeitung,* 5 February 1991, p. 1.

99. The application of the term *secular theocracy* to communist systems was first made by Zbigniew Brzezinski.

100. Dunja Melčić has argued that while Tudjman certainly returned from Karadjordjevo thinking he had reached an understanding with Milošević, there was, in fact, no agreement. See her paper, "Croatia's Discourse about the Past and Some Problems of Croatian-Bosnian Understanding" (unpublished, 2005).

14. The War of Yugoslav Succession, Phase 1 (1991)

1. See the references in Pedro Ramet, "Yugoslavia and the Threat of Internal and External Discontents," *Orbis,* vol. 28, no. 1 (Spring 1984): 103–121.

2. Olivera Milosavljević, "Yugoslavia as a Mistake," in Nebojša Popov (ed.), *The Road to War in Serbia: Trauma and Catharsis,* English version by Drinka Gojković (Budapest: Central European University Press, 2000), pp. 72–73.

3. Raif Dizdarević, *Od smrti Tita do smrti Jugoslavije: Svjedočenja* (Sarajevo: Svjedok, 1999), pp. 279–280.

4. Zdravko Tomac, *The Struggle for the Croatian State . . . through Hell to Democracy,* trans. by Profikon (Zagreb: Profikon, 1993), p. 181.

5. Tim Judah, *The Serbs: History, Myth and the Destruction of Yugoslavia* (New Haven, Conn.: Yale University Press, 1997), p. 168.

6. Branko Mamula, *Slučaj Jugoslavija* (Podgorica: CID, 2000), p. 197.

7. Reneo Lukić and Allen Lynch, *Europe from the Balkans to the Urals: The Disintegration of Yugoslavia and the Soviet Union* (Oxford: Oxford University Press, 1996), p. 151.

8. Tomac, *Struggle for the Croatian State,* p. 185.

9. Judah, *Serbs,* p. 169; and Dizdarević, *Od smrti Tita do smrti Jugoslavije,* p. 291.

10. Judah, *Serbs,* pp. 170–171; and testimony of Dragan Vasiljković in the trial of Slobodan Miloševic, as reported in *Slobodna Dalmacija* (Split), 20 February 2003, at www.slobodnadalmacija.hr.

11. Sabrina P. Ramet, "Martyr in His Own Mind: The Trial and Tribulations of Slobodan Milošević," in *Totalitarian Movements and Political Religions,* vol. 5, no. 1 (Summer 2004): 121; and Smilja Avramov, *Postherojski rat Zapada protiv Jugoslavije* (Novi Sad: Biblioteka Matice srpske, 1997), p. 160, as cited in Davorin Rudolf, *Rat koji nismo htjeli: Hrvatska 1991* (Zagreb-Globus, 1999), p. 67. See also the summary of the testimony of General Aleksandar Vasiljević, former chief of KOS (the JNA counterintelligence service), in the trial of Slobodan Miloševic, provided in *Frankfurter Rundschau,* 15 February 2003, at www.fr-aktuell.de.

12. According to the testimony of witness C-061 (Milan Babić) in the trial of Slobodan Milošević, as reported in *Glas javnosti* (Belgrade), 22 November 2002, at arhiva.glas-javnosti .co.yu; also Ramet, "Martyr in His Own Mind," p. 127.

13. Rudolf, *Rat koji nismo htjeli*, p. 66.

14. According to the testimony of Milan Babić in the trial of Slobodan Milošević, as reported in *Vjesnik* (Zagreb), 7 December 2002, at www.vjesnik.hr.

15. Viktor Meier, *Yugoslavia: A History of Its Demise*, trans. from German by Sabrina P. Ramet (London: Routledge, 1999), pp. 148–149.

16. See Rudolf, *Rat koji nismo htjeli*, pp. 130–157.

17. Borisav Jović, *Poslednji dani SFRJ—Izvodi iz dnevnika* (Belgrade: Politika, 1995), pp. 257–258 (entry for 23 January 1991).

18. Quoted in Branko Mamula, *Slučaj Jugoslavija* (Podgorica: CID, 2000), p. 178.

19. *The Independent* (London), 10 March 1991, p. 15, on LNAU.

20. Ibid.; and Associated Press, 13 March 1991, on LNAU.

21. Drnovšek, *Der Jugoslawien Krieg*, pp. 271–272; and Meier, *Yugoslavia*, pp. 165–166.

22. As summarized in Meier, *Yugoslavia*, p. 166.

23. Omer Karabeg, "Logika protiv povijesnih silnica," *zarež* (Zagreb), 5 July 2001, p. 8.

24. Drnovšek, *Der Jugoslawien Krieg*, pp. 274–276.

25. I am drawing here upon Meier, *Yugoslavia*, p. 166–167.

26. Quoted in *The Times* (London), 14 March 1991, on LNAU.

27. Quoted in UPI, 27 March 1991, on LNAU.

28. *Yugoslav News Agency*, 12 April 1991, trans. in *BBC Summary of World Broadcasts*, 12 April 1991, on LNAU.

29. *Agence France Presse*, 9 May 1991, on LNAU.

30. Associated Press, 9 May 1991, on LNAU.

31. Tanjug, Belgrade, 16 July 1991, trans. in *BBC Summary of World Broadcasts*, 18 July 1991, on LNAU.

32. Ivo Žanić, *Prevarena povijest* (Zagreb: Durieux, 1998), pp. 41–42, n. 15.

33. See also *Yugoslav News Agency*, 10 April 1991, trans. in *BBC Summary of World Broadcasts*, 13 April 1991, on LNAU; and Sejo Omeragić, *Dogovoreni rat*, 3rd ed. (Sarajevo: Proton, 2002), pp. 7–36.

34. *OÖNachrichten*, 3 April 1991, at www1.oon.at; and Svein Mønnesland, *Før Jugoslavia, og etter*, 3rd ed. (Oslo: Sypress Forlag, 1995), p. 266.

35. Silber and Little, *Yugoslavia*, p. 153.

36. Michael Montgomery, "Spreading the National Virus," *Boston Review*, April/May 1996, at bostonreview.net/BR21.2/montgomery.html); Drago Held, "Just a Small Murder," in *AIM Press*, 21 June 1997, at www.aimpress.ch; Goran Flaunder, "Political Activism of the Widow of Josip Reihl-Kir," *Nacional*, 12 September 1999, trans. on 3/24/00 and posted at www.cdsp.neu .edu/info/students/marko/nacional/naciona14.html; *Vjesnik* (Zagreb), 23 March 2001, at www.vjesnik.hr/html; and *Globus* (Zagreb), no. 545 (18 May 2001): 36–37.

37. Tanjug Domestic Service, 20 February 1991, trans. in FBIS, *Daily Report* (Eastern Europe), 21 February 1991, p. 52.

38. Rudolf, *Rat koji nismo htjeli*, p. 162; and Hannes Hofbauer, "Neue Staaten, neue Kriege," in Hannes Hofbauer (ed.), *Balkan Krieg: Die Zerstörung Jugoslawiens* (Vienna: Promedia, 1999), p. 75.

39. *NIN* (Belgrade), no. 2106 (10 May 1991): 14–15.

40. *The Guardian* (London), 16 May 1991, on LNAU.

41. *Daily Telegraph* (London), 16 May 1991, p. 8, on LNAU.

42. Stipe Mesić, *Kako je srušena Jugoslavija. Politički memoari,* 2nd ed. (Zagreb: Mislav Press, 1994), pp. 11–12.

43. Meier, *Yugoslavia,* p. 98.

44. Mesić, *Kako je srušena,* pp. 13, 14.

45. Alija Izetbegović, *Sjećanja: Autobiografski zapis* (Sarajevo: TKD Sahinpašić, 2001), p. 93.

46. See the transcript of a conversation between President Tudjman and leading figures among Bosnian Croats in Ciril Ribičič, *Geneza jedne zablude: Ustavnopravna analiza nastanka i djelovanja Hrvatske zajednice Herceg-Bosne* (Zagreb: Naklada Jesenski i Turk, 2000), pp. 118–129, 131, 134–135.

47. Yugoslav News Agency, 26 April 1991, in *BBC Summary of World Broadcasts,* 30 April 1991, on LNAU; and *The Times* (London), 30 April 1991, on LNAU.

48. *Politika* (Belgrade), 15 May 1992, p. 9; and *NIN,* no. 2148 (28 February 1992): 28–29.

49. Quoted in Branimir Anzulović, *Heavenly Serbia: From Myth to Genocide* (London: Hurst, 1999), p. 139.

50. Robert L. Hutchings, *American Diplomacy and the End of the Cold War: An Insider's Account of U.S. Policy in Europe, 1989–1992* (Washington D.C. and Baltimore: Woodrow Wilson Center Press and Johns Hopkins University Press, 1997), p. 310.

51. Drago Hedl, "Living in the Past: Franjo Tudjman's Croatia," *Current History,* vol. 99, no. 635 (March 2000): 106.

52. In the coat of arms used by the NDH in 1941–1945, the upper left square in the checkerboard was white; in the coat of arms used since 1945, the upper left square is red. For an extremely helpful account, see Slavko Granić, "The Croatian Coat of Arms: Historical Emblem or Controversial Symbol?" *Journal of Croatian Studies,* vol. 34–35 (1993–1994): 5–28.

53. Ivan Grdešić, "The Radical Right and Its Constituency," in Sabrina P. Ramet (ed.), *The Radical Right in Central and Eastern Europe since 1989* (University Park: Pennsylvania State University Press, 1999), p. 177.

54. Paolo Rumiz, *Masken für ein Massaker: Der manipulierte Krieg: Spurensuche auf dem Balkan,* trans. from Italian by Friederike Hausmann and Gesa Schröder (Munich: Verlag Antje Kunstmann, 2000), pp. 102–103, 107, 113.

55. Milan Kučan, president of Slovenia, in interview with the author, Ljubljana, 6 September 1999.

56. Rudolf, *Rat koji nismo htjeli,* pp. 228, 230.

57. Konrad Kolšek, *Spomini: Na začetek oborozenega spopada v Jugoslaviji 1991* (Maribor: Založba Obzorja, 2001), p. 165.

58. Janez Janša, *The Making of the Slovenian State 1988–1992: The Collapse of Yugoslavia* (Ljubljana: Založba Mladinska knjiga, 1994), pp. 141–142.

59. The date of 26 June had been publicly announced, for example, in an open letter to the SFRY Skupština from the Slovenian Assembly, published in *Neodvisni dnevnik* (Ljubljana), 9 May 1991, p. 4, trans. in FBIS, *Daily Report* (Eastern Europe), 23 May 1991, p. 27.

60. Janša, *Making of the Slovenian State,* p. 147.

61. Quoted in Hutchings, *American Diplomacy,* p. 311.

62. While interpretations of Baker's visit have varied, Zdravko Tomac probably spoke for many Croats when he wrote that, in his view, "James Baker . . . actively encouraged the federal government, Serbia and the Yugoslav Federal Army. By insisting on the territorial integrity of Yugoslavia, he agreed with Milošević's policy and [endorsed] the JNA's threat to Slovenia." Tomac, *Struggle for the Croatian State,* p. 126. The JNA did, to be sure, favor the use of force to crush Slovenia's bid for independence, but Milošević had decided months earlier that "Slovenia should be left in peace." Jović, *Poslednji dani,* p. 281 (entr   for 28 February 1991).

63. Kučan, in interview with the author, Ljubljana, 6 September 1999.

64. Mamula, *Slucaj Jugoslavija,* p. 177.

65. Janša, *Making of the Slovenian State,* p. 148.

66. Mamula, *Slucaj Jugoslavija,* p. 178.

67. Adam LeBor, *Milosevic: A Biography* (London: Bloomsbury, 2002), p. 137.

68. Janša, *Making of the Slovenian State,* pp. 167, 194.

69. Dimitrij Rupel, then Slovenian ambassador to the U.S. and former and future foreign minister of Slovenia, in interview with the author, Ljubljana, 1 September 1999.

70. Janša, *Making of the Slovenian State,* p. 150.

71. Tomac, *Struggle for the Croatian State,* p. 87; and Rudolf, *Rat koji nismo htjeli,* p. 261. See also Kolšek, *Spomini,* p. 180.

72. Kolšek, *Spomini,* p. 180.

73. Martin Špegelj, *Sjećanja vojnika,* ed. by Ivo Zanić (Zagreb: Znanje, 2001), pp. 219, 375, 292.

74. The locations of the barracks in and around Zagreb are given in Božidar Javorović, *Narodna zaštita grada Zagreba u domovinskom ratu* (Zagreb: Defimi, 1999).

75. Slavko Goldstein, editor of *Erasmus,* in interview with the author, Zagreb, 1 August 1997.

76. Quoted in Janša, *Making of the Slovenian State,* pp. 158, 150–151.

77. Kolšek, *Spomini,* p. 183; and Janša, *Making of the Slovenian State,* p. 185.

78. Silber and Little, *Death of Yugoslavia,* p. 177.

79. Janša, *Making of the Slovenian State,* pp. 197, 199.

80. Reuter, 3 July 1991, on LNAU; and *Chicago Tribune,* 4 July 1991, p. 5.

81. *Neue Zürcher Zeitung,* 7/8 July 1991, p. 1.

82. Adžić, quoted in Janša, *Making of the Slovenian State,* p. 216.

83. Meier, *Yugoslavia,* p. 222.

84. Rupel, in interview with the author, Ljubljana, 1 September 1999.

85. Meier, *Yugoslavia,* p. 224.

86. Tomac, *Struggle for the Croatian State,* p. 121.

87. Drnovšek, *Der Jugoslawien Krieg,* pp. 319–321.

88. Rudolf, *Rat koji nismo htjeli,* p. 266.

89. Van den Broek, quoted in Kolšek, *Spomini,* p. 260.

90. Radio Belgrade Network, 26 June 1991, trans. in FBIS, *Daily Report* (Eastern Europe), 27 June 1991, p. 56.

91. Gligorov, quoted in Tanjug, 30 June 1991, in FBIS, *Daily Report* (Eastern Europe), 2 July 1991, p. 71.

92. Radio Slovenia Network, 6 July 1991, in FBIS, *Daily Report* (Eastern Europe), 8 July 1991, p. 56.

93. Rudolf, *Rat koji nismo htjeli,* pp. 167–168.

94. Veljko Kadijević, *Moje vidjenje raspada* (Belgrade: Politika, 1993), p. 134.

95. Stipe Mesić, former SFRY president and future president of Croatia, in interview with the author, Zagreb, 30 July 1997.

96. Tudjman, quoted in *Pravda* (Moscow), 12 July 1991, p. 4, trans. in CDSP, vol. 43, no. 28 (14 August 1991): 20.

97. Špegelj, *Sjećanja vojnika,* p. 241.

98. Tomac, *Struggle for the Croatian State,* p. 86.

99. *Neue Zürcher Zeitung,* 12 July 1991, p. 1.

100. Kossuth Radio Network (Budapest), 24 July 1991, trans. in FBIS, *Daily Report* (East-

ern Europe), 25 July 1991, p. 55; also MTV Television Network (Budapest), 9 July 1991, trans. in FBIS, *Daily Report* (Eastern Europe), 11 July 1991, p. 38.

 101. This latter attack occurred in August. Radio Croatia Network, 22 August 1991, trans. in FBIS, *Daily Report* (Eastern Europe), 23 August 1991, p. 38.

 102. Tanjug, 13 July 1991, trans. in FBIS, *Daily Report* (Eastern Europe), 15 July 1991, p. 50.

 103. Tanjug, 2 July 1991, in FBIS, *Daily Report* (Eastern Europe), 3 July 1991, p. 36.

 104. Foreign Press Bureau, Republic of Croatia (hereafter FPB/RC), Press release 10 (19 September 1991).

 105. Tomac, *Struggle for the Croatian State,* pp. 338–339.

 106. Anton Tus, "Rat u Sloveniji i Hrvatskoj do Sarajevskog primirja," in Branka Magaš and Ivo Žanić (eds.), *Rat u Hrvatskoj i Bosni i Hercegovini 1991–1995* (Zagreb/Sarajevo/London: Naklada Jesenski i Turk, Dani, and the Bosnian Institute, 1999), pp. 81–82.

 107. Jože Pirjevec, *Le guerre jugoslave 1991–1999* (Torino: Giulio Einaudi editore, 2001), pp. 95–96; *Večernji list* (Zagreb), 8 December 2001, at www.vecernji-list.hr [accessed 13 December 2001]; and *Vjesnik,* 12 December 2001, at www.vjesnik.hr/html [accessed 17 December 2001].

 108. Croatian Casualties, Davor Marijan, *Bitka za Vukovar* (Zagreb/Slavonski Brod: Hrvatski institut za povijest & Podružnica za povijest, 2004), p. 284; JNA, Slavko Goldstein, in interview with the author, Zagreb, 1 August 1997.

 109. Aleksandar Fira, former president of the SFRY Constitutional Court, in interview with the author, Tallahassee, Florida, 14 October 1996.

 110. Jović, *Poslednji dani,* p. 387 (entry for 24 September 1991).

 111. Tomac, *Struggle for the Croatian State,* p. 125.

 112. Jović, *Poslednji dani,* pp. 402–403 (entry for 25 October 1991).

 113. *Pravoslavlje* (Belgrade), 15 July 1991, p. 8. See also discussion in Sabrina P. Ramet, "The Serbian Church and the Serbian Nation," in Sabrina P. Ramet and Donald W. Treadgold (eds.), *Render unto Caesar: The Religious Sphere in World Politics* (Washington, D.C.: American University Press, 1995), pp. 301–323.

 114. *Pravoslavlje,* 1 July 1991, p. 9; 15 July 1991, p. 9; 1–15 August 1991, p. 14; and 1 September 1991, p. 9.

 115. *Pravoslavlje,* 1–15 August 1990, p. 3; 1 October 1990, p. 10; and 15 November 1990, p. 3.

 116. *Pravoslavlje,* 1–15 August 1991, p. 18.

 117. Milorad Tomanić makes this argument even more strongly in his book, *Srpska crkva u ratu i ratovi u njoj* (Belgrade: Medijska knjižara krug, 2001).

 118. *Danas,* 18 June 1991, p. 64.

 119. For a detailed account of the destruction of both Catholic and Orthodox churches in Croatia during the years 1991–1995, see *The Wounded Church in Croatia: The Destruction of the Sacral Heritage of Croatia (1991–1995),* trans. from Croatian by Margaret Casman-Vuko (Zagreb: Croatian Conference of Bishops, Croatian Heritage Foundation, Republican Bureau for the Preservation of the Cultural and Natural Heritage of Croatia, and the Croatian War Documentation Center, 1996).

 120. *New York Times,* 22 September 1991, p. 16.

 121. Radio Belgrade Network, 26 August 1991, trans. in FBIS, *Daily Report* (Eastern Europe), 27 August 1991, p. 40.

 122. Regarding atrocities committed by Croatian forces, see *Helsinki.Watch–Croatia,* 17 November 1992, at www.bosnet.org/archive/bosnet.w3archive/9211/msg00121.html [accessed 21 September 2001].

 123. Christopher Bennett, *Yugoslavia's Bloody Collapse: Causes, Course and Consequences* (New York: New York University Press, 1995), p. 166.

124. Tomac, *Struggle for the Croatian State,* p. 131.

125. Reprinted in *Politika,* 17 August 1991, p. 10.

126. Tomac, *Struggle for the Croatian State,* p. 175.

127. Letter signed by Dragutin Zelenović, reprinted in its entirety in ibid., p. 417.

128. Excerpt on CNN Headline News, 4 October 1991.

129. Tomac, *Struggle for the Croatian State,* p. 427.

130. *Politika ekspres* (Belgrade), 2 August 1991, as summarized in Tanjug, 2 August 1991, in FBIS, *Daily Report* (Eastern Europe), 5 August 1991, p. 53. Belgrade was no doubt aware that, at a meeting of EC ministers already in November 1990, Germany had argued that assuring respect for human rights in the Yugoslav area was more important than preserving Yugoslav unity. See Norbert Both, *From Indifference to Entrapment: The Netherlands and the Yugoslav Crisis, 1990-1995* (Amsterdam: Amsterdam University Press, 2000), p. 90.

131. In an interview with RTV Belgrade, 3 July 1991, trans. in FBIS, *Daily Report* (Eastern Europe), 1 August 1991, p. 31.

132. Vienna ORF Television Network, 12 August 1991, trans. in FBIS, *Daily Report* (Eastern Europe), 13 August 1991, p. 34.

133. MTI (Budapest), 28 August 1991, in FBIS, *Daily Report* (Eastern Europe), 29 August 1991, p. 9.

134. AFP (Paris), 5 July 1991, in FBIS, *Daily Report* (Eastern Europe), 5 July 1991, p. 1.

135. BTA (Sofia), 5 July 1991, in FBIS, *Daily Report* (Eastern Europe), 8 July 1991, p. 2.

136. Regarding Bulgaria's role in the Yugoslav war, see Ekaterina Nikova, "Bulgaria in the Balkans," in John D. Bell (ed.), *Bulgaria in Transition: Politics, Economics, Society, and Culture after Communism* (Boulder, Colo.: Westview Press, 1998), pp. 290–298.

137. On British, German, and Russian responses, see Mark Gardner, "A Relationship Both Special and Mundane: The Politics of Power, Party, and Leadership in U.S.–British Relations"; Patricia J. Smith, "The Impact of Post-Cold War Changes on the U.S.–German Relationship"; and Mikhail A. Alexseev, "From the Cold War to the 'Cold Peace': U.S.–Russian Interactions from Gorbachev to the Present"—all in Sabrina P. Ramet and Christine Ingebritsen (eds.), *Coming in from the Cold War: Changes in U.S.–European Interactions since 1980* (Boulder, Colo.: Westview Press, 2002), pp. 60–64, 111–115, and 158, 163–168. On the U.S. response, see Sabrina P. Ramet, "American Policy toward Serbia/Yugoslavia: The Record of Congressional Debates, 1989–2000," forthcoming. On the French response, see Renéo Lukić, "The Anti-Americanism in France during the War in Kosovo." in Renéo Lukić and Michael Brint (eds.), *Culture, Politics, and Nationalism in the Age of Globalization* (Aldershot, UK: Ashgate, 2001).

138. Hans-Dietrich Genscher, *Rebuilding a House Divided: A Memoir by the Architect of Germany's Reunification,* trans. from German by Thomas Thornton (New York: Broadway Books, 1995), p. 499.

139. Bush, quoted in Reneo Lukić and Allen Lynch, "U.S. Policy towards Yugoslavia: From Differentiation to Disintegration," in Raju G. C. Thomas and H. Richard Friman (eds.), *The South Slav Conflict: History, Religion, Ethnicity, and Nationalism* (New York and London: Garland, 1996), p. 266.

140. Regarding Milošević's hostility to privatization, see Meier, *Yugoslavia,* p. 105.

141. Lukić and Lynch, "U.S. Policy," pp. 267–268.

142. Silber and Little, *Death of Yugoslavia,* pp. 209–210.

143. See Sabrina P. Ramet and Letty Coffin, "German Foreign Policy toward the Yugoslav Successor States, 1991–1999," in *Problems of Post-Communism,* vol. 48, no. 1 (January–February 2001): 49–52. Regarding France, see Genscher, *Rebuilding a House Divided,* p. 505. Regarding Britain, see John Major, *The Autobiography* (New York: HarperCollins, 1999), pp. 533–534.

144. Javier Pérez de Cuéllar, *Pilgrimage for Peace: A Secretary-General's Memoir* (Houndmills, Basingstoke: Macmillan Press, 1997), pp. 480–484.

145. Genscher, *Rebuilding a House Divided,* p. 512.

146. Ibid., p. 515.

147. For an effective rebuttal of Germanophobic myths in connection with Yugoslavia, see Daniele Conversi, *German-Bashing and the Breakup of Yugoslavia,* Donald W. Treadgold Papers in Russian, East European, and Central Asian Studies no. 16 (Seattle: Henry M. Jackson School of International Studies, University of Washington, March 1998). See also Ramet and Coffin, "German Foreign Policy," pp. 48–64.

148. Among the most lucid observers at the time was Milan Andrejevich, then working as a researcher for Radio Free Europe, Munich.

149. Radio Belgrade Network, 10 May 1991, trans. in FBIS, *Daily Report* (Eastern Europe), 13 May 1991, p. 56; and Tanjug, 11 June 1991, in FBIS, *Daily Report* (Eastern Europe), 13 June 1991, p. 42.

150. Tanjug, 18 June 1991, in FBIS, *Daily Report* (Eastern Europe), 20 June 1991, p. 43.

151. *Politika* (Belgrade), 31 July 1991, as summarized in Tanjug, 31 July 1991, in FBIS, *Daily Report* (Eastern Europe), 1 August 1991, p. 33.

152. Tanjug, 12 August 1991, in FBIS, *Daily Report* (Eastern Europe), 13 August 1991, p. 33.

153. *Večernji list,* as summarized in Tanjug, 12 August 1991, in FBIS, *Daily Report* (Eastern Europe), 14 August 1991, p. 34.

154. For details, see *Danas* (Zagreb), 11 June 1991, pp. 26–27.

155. As summarized in Tanjug, 31 July 1991, in FBIS, *Daily Report* (Eastern Europe), 1 August 1991, p. 35.

156. Radio Belgrade Network, 6 August 1991, trans. in FBIS, *Daily Report* (Eastern Europe), 7 August 1991, p. 43.

157. *Nova Makedonija* (Skopje), 14 August 1991, summarized in Tanjug, 15 August 1991, in FBIS, *Daily Report* (Eastern Europe), 15 August 1991, p. 45.

158. *Nova Makedonija,* 15 August 1991, summarized in Tanjug, 15 August 1991, in FBIS, *Daily Report* (Eastern Europe), 16 August 1991, p. 45.

159. Tanjug, 22 August 1991, in FBIS, *Daily Report* (Eastern Europe), 22 August 1991, p. 29.

160. *Financial Times,* 14 October 1991, p. 2.

161. Šešelj, in interview with *Der Spiegel* (Hamburg), 5 August 1991, pp. 124–126, trans. in FBIS, *Daily Report* (Eastern Europe), 8 August 1991, pp. 51–52. For further discussion of Šešelj, see Ognjen Pribićević, "Changing Fortunes of the Serbian Radical Right," in S. P. Ramet, *Radical Right in Central and Eastern Europe,* pp. 193–211.

162. For details, see Ramet, *Balkan Babel,* chap. 11.

163. See Robert Thomas, *Serbia under Milošević: Politics in the 1990s* (London: Hurst, 1999), passim; also Vuk Drašković, foreign minister of Serbia and Montenegro, in interview with the author, Belgrade, 11 June 2004.

164. Radio Slovenia Network, 20 August 1991, trans. in FBIS, *Daily Report* (Eastern Europe), 21 August 1991, p. 33.

165. *Borba,* 12 August 1991, quoted in Tanjug, 12 August 1991, in FBIS, *Daily Report* (Eastern Europe), 14 August 1991, p. 39.

166. *NIN,* no. 2117 (26 July 1991): 14.

167. Tanjug, 7 August 1991, in FBIS, *Daily Report* (Eastern Europe), 8 August 1991, p. 40. I have substituted "dictatorial" for Tanjug's "dictatorship."

168. *Neue Zürcher Zeitung,* 4 October 1991, p. 4.

169. *Danas,* 9 July 1991, pp. 36–37.

170. *Neue Zürcher Zeitung,* 4 October 1991, p. 3.

171. *Wall Street Journal,* 26 September 1991, p. A1.

172. *NIN,* no. 2116 (19 July 1991): 29.

173. *Daily Telegraph,* 2 October 1991, p. 13.

174. FPB/RC, 20 September 1991, p. 1.

175. *Neue Zürcher Zeitung,* 6/7 October 1991, p. 1.

176. U.S. State Department, quoted in *New York Times,* 5 October 1991, p. 2.

177. *Neue Zürcher Zeitung,* 6/7 October 1991, p. 2. See also Mesić, *Kako je srušena,* p. 222.

178. Tomac, *Struggle for the Croatian State,* pp. 155, 156–157.

179. *Neue Zürcher Zeitung,* 13/14 October 1991, p. 2; confirmed in *Süddeutsche Zeitung,* 12/13 October 1991, p. 1.

180. Tomac, *Struggle for the Croatian State,* p. 303.

181. *Il Messaggero* (Rome), 18 October 1991, p. 4; and *New York Times,* 25 October 1991), p. A7.

182. Milošević, quoted in *New York Times,* 26 October 1991, p. 5.

183. Tudjman, quoted in *Süddeutsche Zeitung,* 7 August 1991, p. 10.

184. EC statement, quoted in *New York Times,* 28 October 1991, p. A5.

185. Silber and Little, *Death of Yugoslavia,* p. 207.

186. Dusko Doder and Louise Branson, *Milosevic: Portrait of a Tyrant* (New York: Free Press, 1999), pp. 113–114.

187. These figures are drawn from my *Balkan Babel,* p. 163.

188. In this connection, see the responses of eight prominent persons to the question "Is civil war inevitable?" in "*NIN* pita: da li je gradjanski rat neizbežan," in *NIN,* no. 2106 (10 May 1991): 14–15.

189. On this point, see James Gow, *Triumph of the Lack of Will: International Diplomacy and the Yugoslav War* (New York: Columbia University Press, 1997); and Brendan Simms, *Unfinest Hour: Britain and the Destruction of Bosnia* (London: Penguin Books, 2002).

190. Tomac, *Struggle for the Croatian State,* p. 410.

15. The War of Yugoslav Succession, Phase 2 (1992–1995)

1. My re-editing of a Chetnik song, on the basis of a text quoted in Ivan Čolović, *The Politics of Symbol in Serbia,* trans. from Serbian by Celia Hawkesworth (London: C. Hurst, 2002), p. 53.

2. Zachary T. Irwin, "The Fate of Islam in the Balkans: A Comparison of Four State Policies," in Pedro Ramet (ed.), *Religion and Nationalism in Soviet and East European Politics* (Durham, N.C.: Duke University Press, 1984), p. 218.

3. See, for example, Sefer Halilović, *Lukava strategija,* 3rd expanded ed. (Sarajevo: Matica, 1998), pp. 68–70.

4. Ivo Žanić, *Prevarena povijest: Guslarska estrada, kult hajduka i rat u Hrvatskoj i Bosni i Hercegovini 1990.–1995. godine* (Zagreb: Durieux, 1998), p. 275.

5. *The Economist* (London), 23 May 1992, as quoted in Boutros Boutros-Ghali, *Unvanquished: A U.S.–U.N. Saga* (New York: Random House, 1999), p. 40.

6. See Carole Hodge, *The Serb Lobby in the United Kingdom,* Donald W. Treadgold Papers in Russian, East European, and Central Asian Studies no. 22 (Seattle: HMJ School of International Studies of the University of Washington, September 1999).

7. One of the toughest indictments of Western policy in Bosnia is Brendan Simms, *Unfinest Hour: Britain and the Destruction of Bosnia,* rev. ed. (London: Penguin, 2002).

8. For discussion, see Sabrina P. Ramet, *Balkan Babel: The Disintegration of Yugoslavia from the Death of Tito to the Fall of Milošević*, 4th ed. (Boulder, Colo.: Westview Press, 2002), chapter 3.

9. *Borba* (Belgrade), 18–19 November 1989, p. 4; and *Danas* (Zagreb), 24 October 1989, pp. 15–16.

10. Originally reported in *Vjesnik* (Zagreb), 15 October 1990, p. 14; confirmed in Jovan Divjak, "The First Phase, 1992–1993: Struggle for Survival and Genesis of the Army of Bosnia-Herzegovina," in Branka Magaš and Ivo Žanić (eds.), *The War in Croatia and Bosnia-Herzegovina, 1991–1995* (London and Portland: Frank Cass, 2001), p. 154.

11. Marko Attila Hoare, "Civilian-Military Relations in Bosnia-Herzegovina, 1992–1995," in Magaš and Žanić, *War in Croatia and Bosnia-Herzegovina*, p. 179.

12. Divjak, "First Phase," p. 154. In January 1992, the JNA felt confident enough to admit to having armed Serb "volunteers" in Bosnia-Herzegovina. See *Vjesnik*, 1 February 1992, p. 7.

13. Halilović, *Lukava strategija*, p. 83.

14. Ibid., p. 74.

15. The weapons were undoubtedly intended for the newly created Bosnian Serb militias, not for the HVO. See ibid., pp. 75 and 87.

16. Ibid., pp. 91–93; and Munir Alibabić-Manja, *Bosna u kandžama KOS-a* (Sarajevo: Behar, 1996), p. 35.

17. Ana Uzelac, "Milošević wire tap revelations," *The Guardian* (London), 14 February 2004, at www.guardian.co.uk. On 8 July 1991, in a key conversation intercepted by the Ministry of the Interior of Bosnia-Herzegovina, Milošević told Karadžić about Belgrade's "Ram" plan to use military force to expand Serbia's territory. The transcript of this conversation was published in *NIN* (Belgrade), no. 2720 (13 February 2003)—as cited in Renéo Lukić, *L'Agonie Yougoslave (1986–2003): Les États-Unis et l'Europe face aux guerres balkanique* (Quebec: Les Presses de l'Université Laval, 2003), p. 208.

18. *Vreme* (Belgrade), 30 September 1991, p. 5; and Mark Thompson, *Forging War: The Media in Serbia, Croatia, Bosnia and Herzegovina*, rev. and expanded ed. (Luton, U.K.: University of Luton Press, 1999), p. 246.

19. According to Gen. Zlatko Binenfeld, a Croatian general, the JNA had an advanced chemical weapons program which had been developed beginning in the 1960s. By the time the SFRY broke up, the Yugoslav chemical arms program had produced the nerve agent sarin, mustard gas, phosgene (a choking agent), BZ (a hallucinogenic incapacitant), and tear gas. "These toxic chemicals were put into a variety of munitions, including artillery shells, aerial bombs, rockets and chemical mines. . . . Three of the four known chemical weapons production facilities in the former Yugoslavia were on Serbian territory, and equipment from the fourth such plant, near Mostar, Bosnia, was reportedly dismantled by Yugoslav troops and moved to Serbia in 1992." William C. Potter and Jonathan B. Tucker, "Well-Armed and Very Dangerous," *Los Angeles Times*, 4 April 1999, at www.latimes.com.

20. General Sir Michael Rose, *Fighting for Peace: Lessons from Bosnia* (London: Warner Books, 1998), p. 46.

21. *Zapisnik, sa 15. sjednice Predsjedništva Srpske Republike Bosne i Hercegovine u neposrednoj ratnoj opasnosti održane 06. jula 1992. godine*, strogo povjerljivo.

22. Tanjug (Belgrade), 10 July 1991, in FBIS, *Daily Report* (Eastern Europe), 11 July 1991, p. 42.

23. Tanjug, 10–11 July 1991, in FBIS, *Daily Report* (Eastern Europe), 11 July 1991, pp. 42–43.

24. See Lukić, *L'Agonie Yougoslave*, p. 208.

25. Alija Izetbegović, *Sjećanja: Autobiografski zapis* (Sarajevo: TKD Sahinpašić, 2001), p. 110.

26. Reneo Lukić and Allen Lynch, *Europe from the Balkans to the Urals: The Disintegration of Yugoslavia and the Soviet Union* (Oxford: Oxford University Press, 1996), p. 203.

27. Quoted in *Financial Times,* 16 October 1991, p. 16.

28. Divjak, " First Phase," p. 153.

29. Ibid., p. 154, my emphasis.

30. Pirjevec, *Le guerre jugoslave,* pp. 101–102.

31. "Aggression against Bosnia-Hercegovina and Conditioning U.S. Recognition of Serbia," S. Res. 290, 102nd Cong., 2nd sess., *Congressional Record 138* (29 April 1992): S 5823, at thomas.loc.gov; *Kronologija rata: Agresija na Hrvatsku i Bosnu i Hercegovinu (s naglaskom na stradanja Hrvata u BiH)* (Zagreb: Hrvatski Informativni Centar, 1998), p. 144.

32. *Salzburger Nachrichten,* 28 March 1992, p. 4.

33. Among those books with which I am familiar, I would rank Lukić and Lynch's *Europe from the Balkans to the Urals* as the most detailed and the most useful work for understanding the role of the UN and the Great Powers during the Yugoslav War.

34. Esad Hećunović, "Cutilierov plan za Bosnu: Povratak u budućnost," *Dani* (Sarajevo), no. 215 (20 July 2001), at www.bhdani.com/arhiva/215/t21511.shtml; and Svein Mønnesland, *Før Jugoslavia, og etter,* 4th ed. (Oslo: Sypress Forlag, 1999), pp. 289–290. See also James Gow, *Triumph of the Lack of Will: International Diplomacy and the Yugoslav War* (London: Hurst, 1997), pp. 80–82.

35. See Milan Jajčinović, "Svi izgubili—a zadovolnji?," *Večernji list* (Zagreb), 24 March 1992, p. 2.

36. Marie-Janine Calic, *Krieg und Frieden in Bosnien-Hercegovina,* expanded ed. (Frankfurt-am-Main: Suhrkamp, 1996), pp. 88.

37. Ibid., p. 89.

38. Alija Izetbegović, in interview with Mirza Delibegović, as broadcast by Radio Sarajevo Network, 20 December 1991, trans. in FBIS, *Daily Report* (Eastern Europe), EEU-91-246, 23 December 1991, p. 34; and Alija Izetbegović, in interview with Jelena Lovrić, in *Danas,* 17 March 1992, pp. 29–30, trans. in FBIS, *Daily Report* (Eastern Europe), EEU-92-057, 24 March 1992, p. 39. For a comparative analysis of the background and sources of the wars in Lebanon and Bosnia-Herzegovina, see Florian Bieber, *Bosnien-Herzegowina und der Lebanon im Vergleich: Historische Entwicklung und Politisches System vor dem Bürgerkrieg* (Sinzheim: Pro Universitate Verlag, 1999).

39. For details and discussion, see Marko Attila Hoare, *How Bosnia Armed* (London: Saqi Books in association with the Bosnian Institute, 2004), especially chap. 2.

40. See Milorad Tomanić, *Srpska crkva u ratu i ratovi u njoj* (Belgrade: Medijska knjižara krug, 2001).

41. See Norman Cigar, "Serb War Effort and Termination of the War," in Magaš and Žanić (eds.), *War in Croatia and Bosnia-Herzegovina,* p. 208, n. 26.

42. Divjak, "First Phase," p. 170.

43. *Popis stanovništva domaćinstva, stanova i poljoprivrednih gazdinstava 1991: Prvi rezultati za republiku i po opštinama,* S. R. Bosna i Hercegovina, Statistički bilten no. 219 (Sarajevo: Republički Zavod za Statistiku, May 1991), p. 11.

44. See chapter 10 of this book; see also Jasna Dragović-Soso, *"Saviours of the Nation": Serbia's Intellectual Opposition and the Revival of Nationalism* (London: Hurst, 2002), chap. 4.

45. Čolović, *Politics of Symbol,* pp. 92 n, 41.

46. Sabrina P. Ramet, "Under the Holy Lime Tree: The Inculcation of Neurotic and Psychotic Syndromes as a Serbian Wartime Strategy, 1986–1995," in *Polemos* (Zagreb), vol. 5, no. 1–2 (December 2002): p. 89, reprinted in Sabrina P. Ramet and Vjeran Pavlaković (eds.),

Serbia since 1989: Politics and Society under Milošević and After (Seattle: University of Washington Press, 2005).

47. Roderick M. Kramer and David M. Messick, "Getting By with a Little Help from Our Enemies: Collective Paranoia and Its Role in Intergroup Relations," in Constantine Sedikides, John Schopler, and Chester A. Insko (eds.), *Intergroup Cognition and Intergroup Behavior* (Mahwah, N.J.: Lawrence Erlbaum, 1998), p. 246.

48. For further discussion, see Ramet, "Under the Holy Lime Tree," pp. 83–97. See also N. T. Feather, "Deservingness, Entitlement, and Reactions to Outcomes," in Michael Ross and Dale T. Miller (eds.), *The Justice Motive in Everyday Life* (Cambridge: Cambridge University Press, 2002); Albert Bandura, "Moral Disengagement in the Perpetuation of Inhumanities," *Personality and Social Psychology Review,* vol. 3, no. 3 (1999); Herbert C. Kelman, "Violence without Moral Restraint: Reflections on the Dehumanization of Victims and Victimizers," *Journal of Social Issues,* vol. 29, no. 4 (1973); and David M. Bersoff, "Why Good People Sometimes Do Bad Things: Motivated Reasoning and Unethical Behavior," *Personality and Social Psychology Bulletin,* vol. 25, no. 1 (January 1999).

49. Quoted in Vidosav Stevanović, *Milošević, jedan epitaf* (Belgrade: Montena, 2002), p. 122.

50. See Tatjana Pavlović, "Women in Croatia: Feminists, Nationalists, and Homosexuals," in Sabrina P. Ramet (ed.), *Gender Politics in the Western Balkans: Women and Society in Yugoslavia and the Yugoslav Successor States* (University Park: Pennsylvania State University Press, 1999).

51. See Ivan Grdešić, "The Radical Right in Croatia and Its Constituency," in Sabrina P. Ramet (ed.), *The Radical Right in Central and Eastern Europe since 1989* (University Park: Pennsylvania State University Press, 1999), pp. 176–177, 180–184, 188–189.

52. Viktor Meier, *Yugoslavia: A History of Its Demise,* trans. from German by Sabrina Ramet (London and New York: Routledge, 1999), p. 209.

53. Petar Vučić, *Politička sudbina Hrvatske: Geopolitičke, geostrateške karakteristike Hrvatske* (Zagreb, 1995), p. 419, as quoted in Rusmir Mahmutcehajić, *The Denial of Bosnia,* trans. from Bosnian by Francis R. Jones and Marina Bowder (University Park: Pennsylvania State University Press, 2000), p. 30.

54. Jasmina Kuzmanović, "Media: The Extension of Politics by Other Means," in Sabrina Petra Ramet and Ljubiša S. Adamovich (eds.), *Beyond Yugoslavia: Politics, Economics, and Culture in a Shattered Community* (Boulder, Colo.: Westview Press, 1995), p. 97.

55. Extract from a text read by Izetbegović at a press conference at Sarajevo's Holiday Inn on 27 March 1990, as quoted in Izetbegović, *Sjećanja,* pp. 70, 82, 86, 440, 446.

56. Hrvoje Šarinić, *Svi moji tajni pregovori sa Slobodanom Miloševićem 1993–95 (98)* (Zagreb: Globus, 1999), p. 140.

57. Vjekoslav Perica, *Balkan Idols: Religion and Nationalism in Yugoslav States* (Oxford and New York: Oxford University Press, 2002), p. 77.

58. Perica's paraphrase, in ibid., p. 77.

59. Ibid., pp. 87, 142, 169.

60. Halilović, *Lukava strategija,* pp. 154, 156, 20.

61. See Cynthia Cockburn, "A Women's Political Party for Yugoslavia: Introduction to the Serbian Feminist Manifesto," *Feminist Review,* no. 39 (Winter 1991): 155, 157.

62. See the manifesto issued on the seventh anniversary of the founding of Women in Black, quoted in full in Žarana Papić, "Kosovo War, Feminists and Fascism in Serbia" (Belgrade, 1999), at k.mihalec.tripod.com/fem_in_serbia.htm.

63. Žarana Papić, "Women in Serbia: Post-Communism, War, and Nationalist Mutations," in S. P. Ramet, *Gender Politics in the Western Balkans,* p. 159.

64. Clericalism is the endeavor or aspiration on the part of a religious organization to dictate, control, or influence the political agenda or policies of a state.

65. Papić, "Women in Serbia," pp. 154, 158. See also pp. 164, 166–167, and Žarana Papić, "Nationalism, Patriarchy and War in ex-Yugoslavia," *Women's History Review,* vol. 3, no. 1 (1994): 115–117.

66. Papić, "Women in Serbia," p. 155.

67. Ivo Banac, "Protiv Močvare—Uvjetna inteligencija," *Feral Tribune* (Split), no. 875 (22 June 2002): 39.

68. Ivo Banac, "Rat protiv represije," talk presented at the Liberal Center in Zagreb (8 June 2000), reprinted in *Feral Tribune*—posted at store.feral.hr/feral/2000/770/banac.html.

69. Quoted in Jelena Lovrić, "Serbs in Croatia," *AIM Press,* 23 October 1996, at www.aim-press.ch, p. 2.

70. *Hrvatsko Slovo* has continued to dog Banac over the years. In 1997, for example, *Hrvatsko Slovo* described Banac as "a lunatic" and as "a man blinded by hate," who "takes [it] upon himself to pronounce judgments on everything." *Hrvatsko Slovo* (Zagreb), 14 February 1997, translation posted at www.cdsp.neu.edu/info/students/marko/hrslovo/hrslovo9.html. More recently, *Hrvatsko Slovo* has mocked Banac as "the Saviour from America." See Zoran Vukman, "Spasitelj iz Amerike," in *Hrvatsko Slovo,* 7 February 2003, posted at www.hkz.hr/Hrvatsko_slovo/2003/407/raskrizje.htm.

71. Ivo Banac, "Separating History from Myth" [in interview with Rabia Ali], in Rabia Ali and Lawrence Lifschulz (eds.), *Why Bosnia? Writings on the Balkan War* (Stony Creek, Conn.: Pamphleteer's Press, 1993), pp. 137, 138.

72. Ivo Banac, *Protiv straha* (Zagreb: Slon, 1992), pp. 144–148, 169–174, 212–215.

73. "Ima jedna Bosna" [Ivo Banac in interview with Enes Karić], *Danas,* 22 January 1991, reprinted in Banac, *Protiv straha,* p. 78.

74. Neven Šantić, "Banac kao Don Kihot," *Novi list* (Rijeka), 7 May 2003, at www.novilist.hr.

75. For a brief account of Zulfikarpašić's life, see *Neue Zürcher Zeitung,* 29 June 1990. For an expostulation of his ideas, see *Bosanski Muslimani: Čimbenik mira izmedju Srba i Hrvata; Interview Adila Zulfikarpašića* (Zürich: Bosanski Institut, 1986); and Fahrudi Djapo and Tihomir Luza, *Povratak u Bosnu: Razgovori sa Adilom Zulfikarpašićem* (Ljubjlana: Karantanija, 1990).

76. Ivo Banac, introduction to Adil Zulfikarpašić, in dialogue with Milovan Djilas and Nadežda Gaće, *The Bosniak* (London: Hurst, 1998), p. x.

77. Zulfikarpašić, *Bosniak,* p. 110.

78. Several are named in ibid., p. 137.

79. Ibid., p. 141.

80. Tanjug, 31 July 1991, in FBIS, *Daily Report* (Eastern Europe), 1 August 1991, p. 41.

81. Adil Zulfikarpašić, Vlado Gotovac, Miko Tripalo, and Ivo Banac, *Okovana Bosna—Razgovor,* ed. by Vlado Pavlinić (Zürich: Bosnjački Institut, 1995), pp. 103–108.

82. Izetbegović, *Sjećanja,* p. 96.

83. Laura Silber and Allan Little, *The Death of Yugoslavia* (London: Penguin Books and BBC Books, 1995), p. 236.

84. Zulfikarpašić, *Bosniak,* p. 180.

85. *Neue Zürcher Zeitung,* 6 March 1992, p. 1.

86. *Večernji list,* 20 March 1992, p. 8.

87. *Slobodna Dalmacija* (Split), 22 March 1992, p. 32.

88. *Neue Zürcher Zeitung,* 19 March 1992, p. 2.

89. *Vjesnik,* 20 March 1992, p. 9; *Večernji list,* 26 March 1992, p. 7; *Politika ekspres* (Bel-

grade), 18 March 1992, p. 2; *Večernji list,* 19 March 1992, p. 9; *Dnevnik* (Ljubljana), 19 March 1992, p. 9; *Večernji list,* 21 March 1992, p. 6; and *Politika ekspres,* 22 March 1992, p. 5.

90. *Salzburger Nachrichten,* 28 March 1992, p. 4; *Die Presse* (Vienna), 28–29 March 1992, p. 1; *Welt am Sonntag* (Berlin), 29 March 1992, p. 6; and Biljana Plavšić, former vice president (1992–1996) and former president (1996–1998) of the Republika Srpska, in interview with the author, Hinsenberg Prison (Frövi, Sweden), 6 April 2004.

91. See *Corriere della Sera* (Milano), 2 April 1992, p. 8.

92. Sabrina P. Ramet, "Martyr in His Own Mind: The Trial and Tribulations of Slobodan Milošević," in *Totalitarian Movements and Political Religions,* vol. 5, no. 1 (Summer 2004): 134.

93. Biljana Plavšić in interview with the author [note 90].

94. *Balkan Battlegrounds: A Military History of the Yugoslav Conflict, 1990–1995,* 2 vols. (Washington, D.C.: Central Intelligence Agency, Office of Russian and European Analysis, May 2002), vol. 1, p. 136.

95. Divjak, "First Phase," p. 164.

96. *The Independent* (London), 6 April 1992, p. 1.

97. Ibrahim Pašić, *Od hajduka do četnika: Stradanje i genocid nad glasinačkim bošnjacima od najstarijih vremena do 1994* (Sarajevo: Dokumenti, 2000), p. 141; regarding the involvement of the JNA in the initial assaults, see pp. 175–176.

98. See Michael A. Sells, *The Bridge Betrayed: Religion and Genocide in Bosnia* (Berkeley and Los Angeles: University of California Press, 1996), pp. 68–70.

99. Calic, *Krieg und Frieden,* p. 93. See also *Il Messaggero* (Rome), 29 March 1992, p. 7.

100. Pirjevec, *Le guerre jugoslave,* pp. 153–154.

101. *Balkan Battlegrounds,* vol. 1, p. 151.

102. Adam LeBor, *Milošević: A Biography* (Polmont, Stirlingshire: Bloomsbury, 2002), p. 177.

103. *VOA News,* 25 June 2003, at www.voanews.com; *Aftenposten* (Oslo), 2 September 2003, at www.aftenposten.no; and *Scotsman,* 7 February 2003, at www.news.scotsman.com.

104. CIA estimate, *Balkan Battlegrounds,* vol. 1, p. 141; Divjak estimate, Divjak, "First Phase, 1992–1993," p. 155.

105. According to Norman Cigar, the VRS suffered a hemorrhaging of 120,000–150,000 deserters and draft dodgers. See Cigar, "Serb War Effort," p. 213.

106. Quoted in *Financial Times,* 4–5 July 1992, p. 2.

107. On 18 August 1992, British prime minister John Major held an emergency meeting with the British military chiefs of staff and asked them how many Western troops would be required to impose peace in Bosnia; the reply was 400,000, i.e., nearly three times as large as the British Army. The chiefs also felt that any NATO commitment of peacekeeping forces would perforce be long-term in nature. But as Major notes in his autobiography, the Conservatives were split into four camps—some arguing for bombing the Serbs and deploying ground troops, others for bombing only, still others for delivering humanitarian aid only, and still others insisting that no British interests were at stake and that Her Majesty's government should therefore stay out of the Bosnian conflict as much as possible. See John Major, *The Autobiography* (New York: HarperCollins, 1999), pp. 535–536.

108. For powerful indictments of relativism and cynicism, see Thomas Cushman and Stjepan G. Meštrović (eds.), *This Time We Knew: Western Responses to Genocide in Bosnia* (New York and London: New York University Press, 1996); and Keith Doubt, *Sociology after Bosnia and Kosovo: Recovering Justice* (Lanham, Md.: Rowman & Littlefield, 2000).

109. See, for example, Norman Cigar, *Genocide in Bosnia: The Policy of 'Ethnic Cleansing'* (College Station: Texas A&M University Press, 1995).

110. Calic, *Krieg und Frieden,* pp. 141–146.

111. Dorothy Q. Thomas and Regan E. Ralph, "Rape in War: The Case of Bosnia," originally published under a different title in *SAIS Review,* vol. 14, no. 1 (Winter–Spring 1994), and reprinted in S. P. Ramet, *Gender Politics in the Western Balkans,* p. 206.

112. Sanela Hajdarhodžić, "Bosnia's Traumatised Citizens," *Institute of War and Peace Reporting,* BCR no. 306 (21 December 2001), at www.iwpr.net. Although most of the women who were raped were Muslim women, Croatian and Serbian women were also raped. See Vesna Nikolić-Ristanović (ed.), *Women, Violence and War: Wartime Victimization of Refugees in the Balkans* (Budapest: Central European University Press, 2000).

113. Quoted in Francis A. Boyle, *The Bosnian People Charge Genocide: Proceedings at the International Court of Justice Concerning Bosnia v. Serbia on the Prevention and Punishment of the Crime of Genocide* (Amherst, Mass.: Aletheia Press, 1996), pp. 21–22.

114. Calic, *Krieg und Frieden,* p. 134.

115. James Gow, *The Serbian Project and Its Adversaries: A Strategy of War Crimes* (London: Hurst, 2003), p. 136.

116. Paolo Rumiz, *Masken für ein Massaker: Der manipulierte Krieg: Spurensuche auf dem Balkan,* expanded ed., trans. from Italian by Friederike Hausmann and Gesa Schröder (Munich: Verlag Antje Kunstmann, 2000), pp. 129, 139, 190.

117. Hurd, quoted in Noel Malcolm, *Bosnia: A Short History* (Washington Square, N.Y.: New York University Press, 1994), p. 244. In his memoirs, Hurd denies that Whitehall was pro-Serb and lashes out at opponents of the arms embargo, claiming that what they really wanted was to arm locals to the teeth so that genocidal massacres could continue for years on end. See Douglas Hurd, *Memoirs* (London: Little, Brown, 2003), pp. 452, 460.

118. Silber and Little, *Death of Yugoslavia,* p. 209.

119. Boutros-Ghali, *Unvanquished,* p. 43.

120. Ibid., p. 44.

121. Ibid., p. 47.

122. Daniel Eisermann, *Der lange Weg nach Dayton: Die westliche Politik und der Krieg im ehemaligen Jugoslawien 1991 bis 1995* (Baden-Baden: Nomos Verlagsgesellschaft, 2000), p. 158.

123. *Balkan Battlegrounds,* vol. 1, pp. 146–150.

124. Sabrina P. Ramet, *Social Currents in Eastern Europe: The Sources and Consequences of the Great Transformation,* 2nd ed. (Durham, N.C.: Duke University Press, 1995), pp. 407–408.

125. Mønnesland, *Før Jugoslavia og etter,* 4th ed., p. 292.

126. Ivana Nizich, *War Crimes in Bosnia-Hercegovina,* vol. 2 (New York: Human Rights Watch, 1993), p. 379.

127. Calic, *Krieg und Frieden,* pp. 99–100.

128. Tudjman, quoted in Letty Coffin, "Tudjman and Bosnian-Croat Relations," *South Slav Journal,* vol. 18, no. 3–4 (Autumn–Winter 1997): 27.

129. Ciril Ribičič, *Geneza jedne zablude. Ustavnopravna analiza nastanka i djelovanja Hrvatske zajednice Herceg-Bosne* (Zagreb/Sarajevo/Idrija: Naklada Jesenski i Turk, Šejtarija, and Založba Bogataj, 2000)—Supplement: "Zapisnik sa sastanka predsjednika Republike Hrvatske dr. Franja Tudjmana s delegacijom HDZ-a BiH (Zagreb, 27. prosinca 1991.)," pp. 131, 168.

130. *Balkan Battlegrounds,* vol. 1, pp. 133–134; and *Nacional,* no. 284 (26 April 2001), at www.nacional.hr. Regarding the comparison with Jesse James, see Žanić, *Prevarena povijest,* p. 367. See also Elirija Hadžiahmetović, "Kraljević je priznavao samo Aliju za predsjednika," *Ljiljan* (Sarajevo), no. 586 (9–16 April 2004): 31–32; and Darko Hudelist, "Gojko Šušak znao je za plan o ubojstvu zapovjednika HOS-a Blaža Kraljevića," *Globus* (Zagreb), no. 476 (21 January 2000): 62–65.

131. One example: "Right from the beginning we advocated the preservation of a single

Bosnia-Herzegovina. . . . Our policy has been consistent. We favored the preservation of Bosnia. We advised Croats there to take part in the referendum on Bosnia's independence. We were willing to accept the cantonal, confederal organization that was proposed by Ambassador Cutilheiro. We were also willing to accept a division of Bosnia into provinces, i.e., the Vance-Owen plan, and finally a proposal on the union of Bosnia-Herzegovina republics, hoping to develop cooperation with the Muslims. We exerted special efforts by signing agreements—the ones known to the public and even those yet to be revealed when the right time comes." Franjo Tudjman in interview with Mirjana Radić, Denis Latin, and Darko Herceg on Radio Croatia Network (Zagreb), 30 December 1993, trans. in FBIS, *Daily Report* (Eastern Europe), EEU-94-002, 4 January 1994, p. 21.

132. Charles R. Shrader, *The Muslim-Croat Civil War in Central Bosnia: A Military History, 1992–1994* (College Station: Texas A&M University Press, 2003), p. 71.

133. *Vjesnik,* 24 July 1996), article by Marko Barišić, trans. in FBIS EEU-96-150 (26 July 1996), AFS No. AU2907191996.

134. Davor Marijan, "The War in Bosnia and Herzegovina, or the Unacceptable Lightness of 'Historicism,'" *National Security and the Future* (Zagreb), vol. 1, no. 1 (Spring 2000): 167.

135. Quoted in *Danas,* 25 June 1993, p. 32, trans. in FBIS, *Daily Report* (Eastern Europe), EEU-93-133 (14 July 1993), p. 40.

136. Marijan, "War in Bosnia and Herzegovina," p. 170 and p. 182, n. 77.

137. Attila Hoare, "The Croatian Project to Partition Bosnia-Hercegovina, 1990–1994," *East European Quarterly,* vol. 31, no. 1 (March 1997): 131.

138. *Dossier: Crimes of Muslim Units against the Croats in BiH 1992–1994* (Mostar: Centre for Investigation and Documentation, 1994), p. 10.

139. See James J. Sadkovich, "Argument, Persuasion, and Anecdote: The Usefulness of History to Understanding Conflict," *Polemos* (Zagreb), vol. 5, no. 1–2 (December 2002): 45–48.

140. Ros, quoted in *Borba,* 22 May 1992, p. 2, trans. in FBIS, *Daily Report* (Eastern Europe), EEU-92-108 (4 June 1992), p. 58.

141. Tanjug, 30 September 1992, in FBIS, *Daily Report* (Eastern Europe), EEU-92-190 (30 September 1992), p. 25.

142. *Dossier: Crimes of Muslim Units,* pp. 75, 116.

143. *Balkan Battlegrounds,* vol. 1, pp. 147, 144.

144. Rajić, quoted on Croatian Television (Zagreb), 3 November 1992, trans. in *BBC Summary of World Broadcasts,* 5 November 1992, on *Lexis-Nexis,* at www.nexis.com. See also Croatian Radio (Zagreb), 20 January 1993, trans. in *BBC Summary of World Broadcasts,* 22 January 1993, on *Lexis-Nexis,* at www.nexis.com.

145. Jože Pirjevec, *Le guerre jugoslave 1991–1999* (Torino: Giulio Einaudi editore, 2001), p. 282.

146. Croatian Radio, 24 April 1993, trans. in *BBC Summary of World Broadcasts,* 26 April 1993, on *Lexis-Nexis,* at www.nexis.com.

147. Regarding February, see Radio Bosnia-Hercegovina Network (Sarajevo), 3 February 1993, trans. in FBIS, *Daily Report* (Eastern Europe), EEU-93-022 (4 February 1993), p. 43; regarding a ceasefire in May 1993, see Radio Croatia Network (Zagreb), 19 May 1993, trans. in FBIS, *Daily Report* (Eastern Europe), EEU-93-096 (20 May 1993), p. 26.

148. David Owen, *Balkan Odyssey* (London: Victor Gollancz, 1995), p. 99.

149. Ines Sabalić, "Ahmići," *Globus* (Zagreb), no. 476 (21 January 2000): 17; and Pirjevec, *Le guerre jugoslave,* 283–284.

150. *Balkan Battlegrounds,* vol. 1, p. 192.

151. Izetbegović, *Sjećanja,* p. 151.

152. Silber and Little, *Death of Yugoslavia,* p. 355. In early February 1994, Tanjug reported that the UN was estimating that there were "between 3,000 and 5,000 regularly Croatian Army troops" in Bosnia-Herzegovina, fighting alongside the HVO against the ARBiH. See Tanjug, 5 February 1994, in FBIS, *Daily Report* (Eastern Europe), EEU-94-025 (7 February 1994), p. 2.

153. Tudjman, AFP (Paris), 16 June 1993, in FBIS, *Daily Report* (Eastern Europe), EEU-93-115 (17 June 1993), p. 24; Karadžić and Boban, Tanjug Domestic Service (20 June 1993), trans. in FBIS, *Daily Report* (Eastern Europe), EEU-93-117 (21 June 1993), p. 26; and Owen, Tanjug, 17 June 1993, in FBIS, *Daily Report* (Eastern Europe), EEU-93-116, p. 1.

154. Radio Croatia Network (10 July 1993), trans. in FBIS, *Daily Report* (Eastern Europe), EEU-93-131 (12 July 1993), p. 40.

155. *Nacional,* no. 284 (26 April 2001), at www.nacional.hr.

156. Regarding the prisoners: AFP, 13 August 1993, in FBIS, *Daily Report* (Eastern Europe), EEU-93-156 (16 August 1993), p. 33.

157. Coffin, "Tudjman and Bosnian-Croat Relations," p. 31.

158. For details, see Silber and Little, *Death of Yugoslavia,* pp. 262–263.

159. Milisav Sekulić, *Knin je pao u Beogradu* (Bad Vilbel: Nidda Verlag, 2001), p. 90.

160. Branko Mamula, *Slučaj Jugoslavija* (Podgorica: CID, 2000), p. 250.

161. Tim Judah, *The Serbs: History, Myth and the Destruction of Yugoslavia* (New Haven, Conn.: Yale University Press, 1997), p. 245.

162. Eisermann, *Der lange Weg,* p. 266.

163. Between March 1994 and February 1995, an estimated 40,000 Bosnian Croats were forced by Bosnian Muslim authorities to abandon their homes, according to Dario Kordić, a general in the HVO, as cited by the Belgrade newspaper *Borba.* In March 1995, Croats and Bosniaks hurled accusations at each other, with Ejup Ganić, a member of the Bosnian collective presidency and vice president of the Croat-Bosniak federation, accusing the Croats of having given up any thought of cooperation within the federal framework agreed upon in Washington, and with Ivan Bender, chair of the chamber of deputies of the Croatian Republic of Herceg-Bosna, accusing the Bosniaks of trying to set up a Jamahiriyah (Islamic republic) in Bosnia. See *Borba,* 16 February 1995, p. 2, trans. in FBIS, *Daily Report* (Eastern Europe), EEU-95-049 (14 March 1995), p. 40; SRNA (Belgrade), 17 March 1995, trans. in FBIS, *Daily Report* (Eastern Europe), EEU-95-053 (20 March 1995), p. 25; and Radio Croatia Network, 29 March 1995, trans. in FBIS, *Daily Report* (Eastern Europe), EEU-95-060 (29 March 1995), p. 45.

164. *The Guardian* (London), 18 March 1996, p. 8, on *Lexis-Nexis,* at www.nexis.com.

165. *Neue Zürcher Zeitung,* 14 May 1994, p. 3.

166. Tanjug Domestic Service, 17 December 1992, trans. in FBIS, *Daily Report* (Eastern Europe), EEU-92-244 (18 December 1992), p. 22.

167. Radovan Karadžić, in interview with the Greek political weekly *Pondiki,* quoted in Tanjug, 25 December 1992, in FBIS, *Daily Report* (Eastern Europe), EEU-92-249 (28 December 1992), p. 22.

168. Radovan Karadžić, *Ima čuda—Nema čuda* (Sarajevo: Svjetlost, 1982), trans. by Omer Hadžiselimović for *Christian Science Monitor,* 19 July 1995, p. 19.

169. Karadžić: "We have always loved Mexico for its songs, which we sing here. We love Mexico because of Pancho Villa and other national heroes." Karadžić in interview with Kasia Wyderk (in Pale), on *XEW Television Network* (Mexico City), 11 February 1995, trans. in FBIS, *Daily Report* (Eastern Europe), 13 February 1995, p. 27.

170. Owen, *Balkan Odyssey,* pp. 89–90.

171. *ABC News,* 13 May 1999, summarized in *Serbia Watch* no. 83 (24 May 1999).

172. Testimony of witness K-2 in the trial of Slobodan Milošević, as reported in *The Guardian* (London), 9 January 2003, at www.guardian.co.uk.

173. Plan, AFP (Paris), 29 June 1993, in FBIS, *Daily Report* (Eastern Europe), EEU-93-124 (30 June 1993), p. 36; partition of Sarajevo, Tanjug Domestic Service (24 June 1993), trans. in FBIS, *Daily Report* (Eastern Europe), EEU-93-121 (25 June 1993), p. 27; coup, AFP (21 June 1993), in FBIS, *Daily Report* (Eastern Europe), EEU-93-117 (21 June 1993), p. 24; Army's loyalty, Radio Bosnia-Herzegovina, 20 June 1995, trans. in FBIS, *Daily Report* (Eastern Europe), EEU-93-117 (21 June 1993), p. 24.

174. Tanjug, 7 July 1993, citing *Vjesnik,* in FBIS, *Daily Report* (Eastern Europe), EEU-93-128 (7 July 1993), p. 35.

175. *ITAR-TASS World Service* (Moscow), 28 January 1993, trans. in FBIS, *Daily Report* (Central Eurasia), SOV-93-017 (28 January 1993), p. 15.

176. *The Observer* (London), 28 February 1993, p. 1, in FBIS, *Daily Report* (Eastern Europe), EEU-93-039 (2 March 1993), p. 1; confirmed in Meier, *Yugoslavia,* p. 169.

177. *The Observer,* 28 February 1993, p. 1.

178. Details in Takis Michas, *Unholy Alliance: Greece and Milošević's Serbia* (College Station: Texas A&M University Press, 2002), pp. 22–30; see also the photos on pp. 24–27.

179. Tanjug Domestic Service, 9 April 1993, trans. in FBIS, *Daily Report* (Eastern Europe), EEU-93-068 (12 April 1993), p. 40.

180. *Frankfurter Allgemeine,* 12 April 1994, p. 7. See also James Gow, *Triumph of the Lack of Will: International Diplomacy and the Yugoslav War* (New York: Columbia University Press, 1997), pp. 141–145.

181. *The Guardian,* 25 May 1993, p. 10.

182. Sarajevo, *The Times* (London), 2 June 1993, in *Lexis-Nexis,* at www.nexis.com; Goražde, Radio Bosnia-Herzegovina Network, 13 June 1993, trans. in FBIS, *Daily Report* (Eastern Europe), EEU-93-112 (14 June 1993), p. 28.

183. *The Times,* 29 December 1993, p. 9.

184. See, for example, Sabrina P. Ramet, "War in the Balkans," *Foreign Affairs,* vol. 71, no. 4 (Autumn 1992): 79–98.

185. In January 1994, General Rasim Delić, commander of the Bosnian Army, broached the possibility of an eventual Muslim victory, claiming to have some 200,000 well-disciplined troops under his command. See *The Times,* 26 January 1994, p. 10.

186. *Balkan Battlegrounds,* vol. 1, pp. 207, 219.

187. Attila Hoare, review of Susan Woodward's *Balkan Tragedy,* in *Bosnian Institute,* at www.bosnia.org.uk/bosrep/report_format.cfm?articleID=1766&reportid=114 [accessed 29 June 2005].

188. "Akashi paktiert mit den Serben" [An interview with Ejup Ganić], *Focus* (Munich), 21 May 1994, 218.

189. S. P. Ramet, *Balkan Babel,* p. 226, summarizing *Christian Science Monitor,* 20 December 1994, p. 5.

190. "Relentless," *Japan Times,* 9 January 1994, p. 1; "need arises," *Mainichi Daily News* (Tokyo), 22 January 1994, p. 3.

191. Andreas Hasenclever, *Die Macht der Moral in der internationalen Politik: Militärische Interventionen westlicher Staaten in Somalia, Ruanda und Bosnien-Herzegowina* (Frankfurt: Campus Verlag, 2001), p. 356. The VRS denied that it was responsible for the shell which hit the Markala marketplace, but a crater analysis carried out by UN monitors showed that the mortars came from Serbian lines. For the Serbian denial, see Tanjug Domestic Service (5 February 1994), trans. in FBIS, *Daily Report* (Eastern Europe), EEU-94-025 (7 February 1994),

p. 26. For the UN assessment, see *Japan Times,* 6 February 1994, p. 1; also Silber and Little, *Death of Yugoslavia,* pp. 344–345.

192. Regarding Major and Hurd, *The Times,* 8 February 1994, p. 1.

193. Akashi was quoted in *Mainichi Daily News,* 8 February 1994, p. 1, as saying: "This is a single mortar attack and air strikes are a major instrument of full-scale warfare."

194. Toholj, quoted in AFP, 10 February 1994, in FBIS, *Daily Report* (Eastern Europe), EEU-94-028 (10 February 1994), p. 27.

195. Silber and Little, *Death of Yugoslavia,* p. 350.

196. Momčilo Krajišnik, on Radio-Televizija Srpske Studio S (Pale), 14 February 1994, trans. in FBIS, *Daily Report* (Eastern Europe), EEU-94-031 (15 February 1994), p. 43.

197. Akashi, quoted in *Japan Times,* 22 February 1994, p. 1.

198. Silber and Little, *Death of Yugoslavia,* p. 352.

199. In early May, Akashi granted permission to the VRS to move seven tanks into the NATO exclusion zone around Sarajevo; after vociferous protests from the Bosnian government, the UN overruled Akashi and ordered the three tanks which had already crossed into the exclusion zone to leave. See *Daily Telegraph* (London), 6 May 1994, p. 18. At the end of the same month, Bosnian Serbs shelled an airfield located within a UN "safe area" a few minutes after a UN plane had landed there, but when local command asked for permission to proceed with retaliatory air strikes, Akashi turned down the request, while "express[ing] his deep concern over the shelling," according to an official statement. See *Globe and Mail* (Toronto), 1 June 1994, p. A7. The *Wall Street Journal,* 13 June 1994, added to the chorus of criticism of Akashi by writing: "Yasushi Akashi, the U.N.'s limp-wristed vicar in Bosnia, even seems willing to spare the Serbs from embargo hardships. An article in London's *Daily Telegraph* last month said that quantities of imports, including oil and material for armaments, are flowing into Serbia across its border with Macedonia. An anonymous U.N. official was quoted as saying that Mr. Akashi had termed this violation an 'external' matter having nothing to do with him." Article by George Melloan for the *Wall Street Journal,* inserted into the *Congressional Record,* by Congressman Gerald B. H. Solomon: "Bosnia—(by George Melloan) (Extension of Remarks—June 15, 1994)," 103rd Cong., 2nd sess., *Congressional Record* 140 (15 June 1994): E1220, at thomas.loc.gov.

200. As reported in *International Herald Tribune* (Hong Kong ed.), 21 March 1994, p. 1.

201. *Balkan Battlegrounds,* vol. 1, pp. 219, 230–231.

202. *Die Welt* (Bonn), 6 April 1994, p. 1.

203. Boutros-Ghali, *Unvanquished,* p. 147.

204. *La Stampa* (Torino), 11 April 1994, pp. 1, 2.

205. *The Times,* 11 April 1994, p. 1.

206. *International Herald Tribune* (Tokyo ed.), 12 April 1994, p. 1.

207. Hasenclever, *Die Macht der Moral in der internationalen Politik,* p. 357.

208. *International Herald Tribune* (Tokyo ed.), 13 April 1994, p. 1.

209. At gunpoint, *The European* (London), 15–21 April 1994, p. 1; more than 200, *Asahi Evening News* (Tokyo), 15 April 1994, p. 3.

210. Rose, *Fighting for Peace,* pp. 173–174.

211. Hasenclever, *Die Macht der Moral in der internationalen Politik,* pp. 357–358.

212. Pirjevec, *Le guerre jugoslave,* p. 381.

213. "Establishing Select Subcommittee to Investigate United States Role in Iranian Arms Transfers to Croatia and Bosnia," HR Res. 416, 104th Cong., 2nd sess., *Congressional Record* 140 (8 May 1996), at thomas.loc.gov; *Bosnia Update,* 1–15 May 1996, p. 2; and *Glas javnosti* (Belgrade), 28 April 2002, at arhiva.glas-javnosti.co.yu.

214. "Hearing of the House International Relations Committee, Subject: Iranian Arms Transfers to Bosnia," chaired by Representative Benjamin Gilman (R, N.Y.), on *Federal News Service,* 30 May 1996, on *Lexis.Nexis,* at www.nexis.com; and Mark Danner, "Bosnia: Breaking the Machine," in *New York Review of Books,* 19 February 1998, at journalism.berkeley.edu/faculty/MarkDanner?wnyrbosniabreaking.html. See also Pirjevec, *Le guerre jugoslave,* pp. 383–387, 444.

215. "Politically Correct Contraband: The Emergence of Balkan Smuggling Channels in the Context of Yugoslav Wars and International Sanctions," *CSD Reports,* no. 10: 10.

216. "Senate Select Committee Report on Iran/Bosnia Arms Transfers," U.S. Actions Regarding Iranian and Other Arms Transfers to the Bosnian Army, 1994–1995 of the Select Committee on Intelligence, United States Senate (November 1996), at www.parascope.com/articles/0197/bosnia.htm, pp. 11, 16.

217. "Politically Correct Contraband," pp. 9–10.

218. Eisermann, *Der lange Weg,* pp. 243–250.

219. Louis Sell, *Slobodan Milošević and the Destruction of Yugoslavia* (Durham, N.C.: Duke University Press, 2002), p. 218.

220. *Globe and Mail* (Toronto), 28 October 1994, p. A7.

221. Sell, *Slobodan Milošević and the Destruction,* p. 221.

222. *Balkan Battlegrounds,* vol. 1, p. 247.

223. See the discussion in Lukić, *L'Agonie Yougoslave,* pp. 246–247.

224. *Balkan Battlegrounds,* vol. 2, p. 251.

225. The operation, once discovered, resulted in a scandal in Slovenia. See Tanjug, 17 February 1995, in FBIS, *Daily Report* (Eastern Europe), EEU-95-034 (21 February 1995), p. 63.

226. *Slobodna Dalmacija* (Split), 25 February 1995, p. 8, trans. in FBIS, *Daily Report* (Eastern Europe), EEU-95-044 (7 March 1995), pp. 40–41.

227. From the authentic English text, courtesy of the Embassy of the Republic of Croatia, Washington D.C.

228. *Ljiljan* (Sarajevo), 9 November 1994, p. 15, trans. in FBIS, *Daily Report* (Eastern Europe), 23 November 1994, pp. 36, 37.

229. Radio Bosnia-Herzegovina, 10 March 1995, trans. in FBIS, *Daily Report* (Eastern Europe), EEU-95-047 (10 March 1995), p. 23.

230. *Ljiljan,* 9 November 1994, p. 15, trans. in FBIS, *Daily Report* (Eastern Europe), EEU-95-047 (10 March 1995), p. 37.

231. *The Times,* 20 September 1994, on AmeriCast-Post@AmeriCast.com.

232. *Globus,* 17 February 1995, pp. 12–13, trans. in FBIS, *Daily Report* (Eastern Europe), EEU-95-036 (23 February 1995), p. 60.

233. Tanjug Domestic Service, 28 February 1995, trans. in FBIS, *Daily Report* (Central Eurasia), SOV-95-040 (1 March 1995), p. 6. The agreement is also reported in *Die Welt* (2 March 1995), p. 4.

234. *Krasnaya Zvezda* (Moscow), 3 March 1995, p. 3, trans. in FBIS, *Daily Report* (Eastern Europe), SOV-95043 (6 March 1995), pp. 13–14.

235. Radio Bosnia-Herzegovina (9 February 1995), trans. in FBIS, *Daily Report* (Eastern Europe), EEU-95-028 (10 February 1995), p. 26.

236. *Il Giornale* (Milan), 14 April 1995, p. 14, trans. in FBIS, *Daily Report* (Eastern Europe), EEU-95-074 (18 April 1995), p. 25; and *Welt am Sonntag* (Hamburg), 25 June 1995, p. 25.

237. *The European,* 18–24 November 1994, p. 1.

238. *Sunday Times* (London), 5 March 1995, p. 16.

239. *Philadelphia Inquirer,* 15 May 1994, p. A17.

240. *Daily Telegraph,* 12 April 1995, p. 13; confirmed in *The European,* 14–20 April 1995, pp. 1–2.

241. *NIN* (Belgrade), 4 March 1994, pp. 32–33, trans. in FBIS, *Daily Report* (Eastern Europe), EEU-94-061 (30 March 1994), p. 24.

242. *The Gazette* (Montreal), 23 December 1995, p. A22.

243. *Neue Zürcher Zeitung,* 21 March 1995, p. 1; *The Times,* 22 March 1995, p. 8; *Süddeutsche Zeitung* (Munich), 22 March 1995, p. 9; *Die Welt* (Bonn), 25–26 March 1995, pp. 1–3; *Boston Sunday Globe,* 26 March 1995, p. 26; *Neue Zürcher Zeitung,* 3 April 1995, p. 2; *The Times,* 5 April 1995, p. 10; and *Neue Zürcher Zeitung,* 6 April 1995, p. 2.

244. *The Times,* 26 April 1995, p. 11.

245. Šarinić, *Svi moji tajni pregovori,* pp. 188, 198.

246. Eisermann, *Der lange Weg,* pp. 275–279; *Vjesnik,* 4 February 1995, p. 2; and *Narodni list* (Zadar), 3 February 1995, p. 4.

247. As reported at the time in *Naša borba* (Belgrade), 20 March 1995, p. 2.

248. Šarinić, *Svi moji tajni pregovori,* pp. 247–248.

249. Ibid., p. 253; Pirjevec, *Le guerre jugoslave,* pp. 452–453; *Stern* (Hamburg), 11 May 1995, pp. 200–202; *Balkan News and East European Report* (Athens), 28 May–3 June 1995, p. 15; and "Croatia: The Croatian Army Offensive in Western Slavonia and Its Aftermath," *Human Rights Watch / Helsinki,* vol. 7, no. 11 (July 1995): 7.

250. *Neue Zürcher Zeitung,* 22 June 1995, p. 5.

251. *FPB Bulletin,* 4 May 1995.

252. *Welt am Sonntag,* 7 May 1995, pp. 1–2.

253. Cited in "Croatia: The Croatian Army Offensive," p. 8.

254. *Neue Zürcher Zeitung,* 20 June 1995, p. 1; confirmed in *Balkan News and East European Report,* 18–24 June 1995, p. 3.

255. Eisermann, *Der lange Weg,* pp. 298–299; and Sell, *Slobodan Milošević and the Destruction,* p. 230. See also Madeleine Albright, *Madam Secretary: A Memoir* (New York: Hyperion, 2003), pp. 185–186.

256. See "'Serbien ist Gottes Werk,'" in *Der Spiegel* (Hamburg), 5 June 1995, pp. 130–140.

257. Quoted in Sell, *Slobodan Milošević and the Destruction,* p. 230.

258. Their release was accomplished gradually, but as of 7 June, 148 "peacekeepers" were still being held as hostages by the Bosnian Serbs. See *Neue Zürcher Zeitung,* 8 June 1995, p. 1. The last hostages were released on 18 June.

259. Officials denied that there had been any such deal. See *The Guardian* (London), 14 June 1995, on LNAU. See also *Balkan News and East European Report,* 25 June–1 July 1995, p. 11.

260. *Neue Zürcher Zeitung,* 30 May 1995, p. 1.

261. *Neue Zürcher Zeitung,* 31 May 1995, p. 1.

262. *Christian Science Monitor,* 20 June 1995, p. 1.

263. *Agence France Presse,* 19 June 1995, on LNAU.

264. Quoted in Eisermann, *Der lange Weg,* p. 309.

265. *Reuters World Service,* 2 June 1995, on LNAU.

266. Warren Zimmermann, in interview with *BH Eksklusiv* (Sarajevo), 30 June 1995, p. 1.

267. *Balkan News and East European Report,* 18–24 June 1995, p. 35.

268. *Los Angeles Times,* 4 June 1995, on LNAU; *Komsomolskaya pravda* (Moscow), 6 June 1995, pp. 1, 7, trans. in FBIS, *Daily Report* (Eastern Europe), SOV-95-108 (6 June 1995), p. 5;

Balkan News and East European Report, 11–17 June 1995, p. 35; and *Neue Zürcher Zeitung,* 24–25 June 1995, p. 5.

269. *Globe and Mail,* 23 June 1995, p. A8.

270. *Neue Zürcher Zeitung,* 15 June 1995, p. 1; *Christian Science Monitor,* 19 June 1995, p. 6; and *The Times,* 20 June 1995, p. 14.

271. *Irish Times* (Dublin), 17 June 1995, p. 1; and *Welt am Sonntag,* 18 June 1995, p. 6.

272. *Süddeutsche Zeitung,* 24–25 June 1995, p. 8.

273. *Neue Zürcher Zeitung,* 28 June 1995, p. 2.

274. *Balkan News and East European Report,* 11–17 June 1995, p. 15.

275. *OÖNachrichten,* 1 July 1995, p. 004, at www.oon.at.

276. Senator Orrin G. Hatch, recalling a conversation with Haris Silajdžic in testimony on Capitol Hill, 14 April 1999, in *Federal Document Clearing House: Congressional Testimony,* on LNAU.

277. Sell, *Slobodan Milošević and the Destruction,* p. 233.

278. Quoted in Robert Block, "The Madness of General Mladić," *New York Review of Books,* 5 October 1995, p. 7.

279. Brigadier Sead Delić, commander of the 2nd Corps of the ARBiH, in interview with Sefko Hodžić, in *Oslobodjenje* (Sarajevo), 14–21 December 1995, p. 13, trans. in FBIS, *Daily Report* (Eastern Europe), EEU-95-244 (20 December 1995), p. 26.

280. *El Pais* (Madrid), 7 July 1995, p. 2, trans. in FBIS, *Daily Report* (Eastern Europe), EEU-95-131 (10 July 1995), p. 52.

281. *Christian Science Monitor,* 5 July 1995, p. 6.

282. *Neue Zürcher Zeitung,* 3 July 1995, p. 2; 6 July 1995, p. 2; 7 July 1995, pp. 1–2; and 8–9 July 1995, p. 2.

283. *The Economist* (London), 8 July 1995, p. 44.

284. "Bosnia-Hercegovina: The Fall of Srebrenica and the Failure of U.N. Peacekeeping," *Human Rights Watch / Helsinki,* vol. 7, no. 13 (October 1995): 10.

285. Gow, *Serbian Project and Its Adversaries,* p. 187.

286. *Neue Zürcher Zeitung,* 11 July 1995, p. 1.

287. "Bosnia-Hercegovina: The Fall of Srebrenica," pp. 13–14, 21.

288. Quoted in ibid., p. 14.

289. Ibid., p. 21.

290. Eisermann, *Der lange Weg,* p. 306; and Gow, *Serbian Project and Its Adversaries,* p. 188. See also "Srebrenica report: Excerpts"—from the report produced by the Netherlands Institute for War Documentation, commissioned by the Dutch government in 1996, in *BBC News,* 10 April 1992, at news.bbc.co.uk. The number of victims is also confirmed in Albright, *Madam Secretary,* p. 187.

291. *Salt Lake Tribune,* 9 May 2003, at www.sltrib.com.

292. "Bosnia-Hercegovina: The Fall of Srebrenica," pp. 16–19.

293. Ibid., p. 27.

294. Quoted in ibid., p. 31.

295. Quoted in ibid., p. 32.

296. For another detailed eyewitness account of the VRS ambushes, see *La Repubblica,* 24 July 1995, p. 4, trans. in FBIS, *Daily Report* (Eastern Europe), EEU-95-142 (25 July 1995), pp. 18–20.

297. Boutros-Ghali, quoted in *The European,* 14–20 July 1995, p. 1.

298. *Neue Zürcher Zeitung,* 15–16 July 1995, p. 3.

299. According to *Neue Zürcher Zeitung,* 19 July 1995, p. 1, there were actually 16,000 residents in Žepa as of mid-July 1995.

300. *Globe and Mail,* 20 July 1995, p. A1.

301. *Boston Sunday Globe,* 30 July 1995, p. 1.

302. *Los Angeles Times,* 18 July 1995, p. B9.

303. *Balkan News and East European Report,* 23–29 July 1995, p. 3. See also "Ni pad enklava neće slomiti Bošnjački otpor"[An interview with Norman Cigar], in *Ljiljan,* 19 July 1995, pp. 5–6.

304. *Balkan News and East European Report,* 30 July–5 August 1995, p. 35. The expert in question is Professor Sergei Karaganov, who was also serving as deputy director of the Institute of Europe.

305. Tanjug, 25 July 1995, in FBIS, *Daily Report* (Eastern Europe), SOV-95-143 (26 July 1995), p. 7.

306. *Süddeutsche Zeitung,* 29–30 July 1995, p. 2.

307. HINA (Zagreb), 22 August 1995, in *BBC Monitoring Service: Eastern Europe,* 23 August 1995, on LNAU.

308. Tanjug, 23 July 1995, in FBIS, *Daily Report* (Eastern Europe), EEU-95-141 (24 July 1995), p. 54.

309. Croatian preparations, *Interfax* (Moscow), 28 July 1995, in FBIS, *Daily Report* (Central Eurasia), SOV-95-146 (31 July 1995), p. 2; Krajina Serb mobilization, Tanjug Domestic Service, 27 July 1995, trans. in FBIS, *Daily Report* (Eastern Europe), EEU-95-144 (27 July 1995), p. 31; Bosnian Serb mobilization, *Welt am Sonntag,* 30 July 1995, p. 1.

310. *Welt am Sonntag,* 3 July 1995, p. 6.

311. Croatian strength, *Neue Zürcher Zeitung,* 31 July 1995, p. 1, and *The Economist,* 5 August 1995, p. 47; Krajina Serb strength, Eisermann, *Der lange Weg,* p. 327.

312. "Croatia: Impunity for Abuses Committed during 'Operation Storm' and the Denial of the Right of Refugees to Return to the Krajina," *Human Rights Watch / Helsinki,* vol. 8, no. 13 (August 1996): 7. *Süddeutsche Zeitung,* 5–6 August 1995, p. 1, reported that the figure was 120,000.

313. *Neue Zürcher Zeitung,* 12–13 August 1995, p. 1.

314. Sekulić, *Knin je pao,* pp. 172, 178.

315. *Neue Zürcher Zeitung,* 7 August 1995, p. 1; confirmed in *The Economist,* 12 August 1995, p. 13; reconfirmed in *Christian Science Monitor,* 14 August 1995, p. 5; and in Eisermann, *Der lange Weg,* p. 329.

316. James J. Sadkovich, *The U.S. Media and Yugoslavia, 1991–1995* (Westport, Conn.: Praeger, 1998), p. 222.

317. "Croatia: Impunity for Abuses," pp. 7, 16.

318. Archbishop Kuharić protested on 1 October 1995. See Sabrina P. Ramet, "The Croatian Catholic Church since 1990," *Religion, State and Society,* vol. 24, no. 4 (December 1996): 350.

319. See the photo caption on page 47 of *The Economist,* 5 August 1995. There continues to be controversy concerning whether the expulsion of the Serbs was premeditated. In October 2004, ICTY chief prosecutor Carla del Ponte produced an alleged transcript of a conversation purported to have taken place on Brioni on 31 July 1995, with Tudjman urging his generals to make sure that no Serbs remained in the Krajina after the operation. But the authenticity of the transcript was immediately called into question. See *Novi list,* 11 October 2004, at www.novilist.hr.

320. See "Bosnia-Hercegovina: 'Ethnic Cleansing' Continues in Northern Bosnia," *Human Rights Watch / Helsinki,* vol. 6, no. 16 (November 1994): 4–7; Radio Croatia Network, 6 February 1995, trans. in FBIS, *Daily Report* (Eastern Europe), EEU-95-025 (7 February 1995), p. 45; *Welt am Sonntag,* 26 February 1995, p. 2; and AFP, 1 March 1995, in FBIS, *Daily Report* (Eastern Europe), EEU-95-041 (2 March 1995), pp. 30–31. Re the number of Croats: 300,000 before the war, *Oesterreich Eins Radio* (Vienna), 7 July 1995, trans. in FBIS, *Daily Report* (Eastern Europe), EEU-95-130 (7 July 1995), p. 20; 15,000 before the August 1995 expulsions, *Neue Zürcher Zeitung,* 15 August 1995, p. 2.

321. Conscription of refugees, *Chicago Tribune,* 21 August 1995, on LNAU; opinion poll, SRNA (Belgrade), 1 August 1995, trans. in FBIS, *Daily Report* (Eastern Europe), EEU-95-148 (2 August 1995), p. 49.

322. Sell reports 37 dead, as does Eisermann, while Mønnesland reports 38 dead. See Sell, *Slobodan Milošević and the Destruction,* p. 247; Eisermann, *Der lange Weg,* p. 360; and Mønnesland, *Før Jugoslavia og etter,* p. 346. *Neue Zürcher Zeitung,* 31 August 1995, p. 1, also reports 37 dead in the 28 August bombing.

323. *ITAR-TASS World Service* (Moscow), 28 August 1995, trans. in FBIS, *Daily Report* (Central Eurasia), SOV-95-167 (29 August 1995), p. 11.

324. *Interfax,* 31 August 1995, in FBIS, *Daily Report* (Central Eurasia), SOV-95-169 (31 August 1995), p. 11.

325. Richard Holbrooke, *To End a War* (New York: Random House, 1998), p. 284.

326. Izetbegović, *Sjećanja,* p. 206.

327. For further details concerning the talks at Dayton, see Holbrooke, *To End a War;* Izetbegović, *Sjećanja;* Sell, *Slobodan Milošević and the Destruction,* pp. 251–259; Pirjevec, *Le guerre jugoslave,* pp. 520–526; and S. P. Ramet, *Balkan Babel,* pp. 277–280.

328. *Globus* (Zagreb), 9 January 1998, p. 24; and Sell, *Slobodan Milošević and the Destruction,* p. 360.

329. Calic, *Krieg und Frieden,* p. 128.

330. Hasenclever, *Die Macht der Moral in der internationalen Politik,* p. 352.

331. Calic, *Krieg und Frieden,* p. 131. See also *Analysis of Cultural Heritage Damaged by War in Bosnia-Herzegovina,* synopsis of the PRDU Research and Training Project (Institute of Advanced Architectural Studies, University of York: Post-War Reconstruction and Development Unit (PRDU), in *Revival,* no. 8 (August 1997), at www.york.ac.uk/depts/poli/prdu/worksh/oda.pdf.

332. "S.O.S. Sarajevo Library," *CoOL Documents,* 12 May 2000, at palimpsest.stanford.edu.

333. Rusmir Mahmutcehajić, *The Denial of Bosnia,* trans. from Bosnian by Francis R. Jones and Marina Bowder (University Park: Pennsylvania State University Press, 2000), p. 106.

334. M (9 May 1945), Richard C. Patterson Jr., U.S. Ambassador/B to State, in U.S. Department of State, *Records Relating to the Internal Affairs of Yugoslavia, 1945–1949,* Decimal file 860h, at SAL, Reel 1 (files 00/1-245 to 00/4-246).

335. "Balkan War Leaves Devastation Behind," *CNN,* 11 June 1996, at www.cnn.com/WORLD/Bosnia/updates/9606/11/rebuilding.sarajevo/.

336. See especially Norbert Mappes-Niediek, *Balkan-Mafia: Staaten in der Hand des Verbrechens—Eine Gefahr für Europa* (Berlin: Ch. Links, 2003), especially pp. 24–61, 154–157, 160–162.

337. On the brain drain from Serbia, see *Vreme,* 22 March 1993, pp. 47–48, trans. in FBIS, *Daily Report* (Eastern Europe), EEU-93-071 (15 April 1993), pp. 45–46. On the brain drain from Macedonia, see *RFE/RL Newsline,* 11 July 2003, at www.rferl.org.

338. Calic, *Krieg und Frieden,* p. 275.

339. "Civil War Stress," *Journal of the American Medical Association (JAMA)*, vol. 281, no. 6 (10 February 1999): 503.

340. *Nacional*, no. 290 (5 June 2001): 74. See also Sladjana Ivezić, Ante Bagarić, Liliana Oruč, Ninoslav Mimica, and Tajana Ljubin, "Psychotic Symptoms and Co-morbid Psychiatric Disorders in Croatian Combat-Related Post-traumatic Stress Disorder Patients," *Croatian Medical Journal*, vol. 41, no. 2 (2000): 179–183.

341. ONASA (Sarajevo), 6 January 2001, in FBIS, no. EUP-2001-0106-000076.

342. Hajdarhodžić, "Bosnia's Traumatised Citizens."

343. *Nova Bosna* (Neu Isenburg), 23 December 1995, p. 2.

344. Quoted in ibid. In the words of the report, "psychiatric disorders diagnosed in the early stages of a refugee crisis are predictors of chronic psychiatric illnesses and disabilities." Richard F. Mollica, Narcisa Sarajlić, Miriam Chernoff, James Lavelle, Iris Sarajlić Vuković, and Michael P. Massagli, "Longitudinal Study of Psychiatric Symptoms, Disability, Mortality, and Emigration among Bosnian Refugees," in *JAMA*, vol. 286, no. 5 (1 August 2001): 552.

345. Mary Fitzgerald, "From Bosnia to Belfast—Combating Domestic Violence," *Women's News*, at www.womensnews.fsnet.co.uk/RecentArticles/Features/BosniaToBelfast.htm [accessed 22 July 2003].

346. *Refugee Women and Domestic Violence: Country Studies—Bosnia and Herzegovina*, a report by Refugee Women's Resource Project, Asylum Aid, September 2001, updated March 2002, at www.asylumaid.org.uk.

347. Jeffrey Prager, "Lost Childhood, Lost Generations: The Intergenerational Transmission of Trauma," *Journal of Human Rights*, vol. 2, no. 2 (June 2003): 177–178.

348. Concerning this tendency, see Stanley Cohen, *States of Denial: Knowing about Atrocities and Suffering* (Cambridge: Polity, 2001).

349. Cigar, *Genocide in Bosnia;* Thomas Cushman, *Critical Theory and the War in Croatia and Bosnia,* Donald W. Treadgold Papers in Russian, East European, and Central Asian Studies no. 13 (Seattle: Henry M. Jackson School of International Studies of the University of Washington, 2nd printing, December 2000); Gow, *Triumph of the Lack of Will;* Gow, *Serbian Project and Its Adversaries;* Hasenclever, *Die Macht der Moral in der internationalen Politik;* Sadkovich, *U.S. Media and Yugoslavia;* and Michael J. Smith, "Humanitarian Intervention: An Overview of the Ethical Issues," *Ethics and International Affairs*, vol. 12 (1998): 63–79.

350. See W. Michael Reisman, "Sovereignty and Human Rights in Contemporary International Law," *American Journal of International Law*, vol. 84, no. 4 (October 1990): especially pp. 872–873; and Rasmus Tenbergen, *Der Kosovo Krieg: Eine gerechte Intervention?* (ILD Verlag, 2001). For an English summary of the principal points in Tenbergen's book, see Sabrina P. Ramet, "Debates about Intervention: Recent German Books about Bosnia and Kosovo," pt. 1, in *Internationale Politik—Transatlantic Edition*, vol. 4, no. 2 (Summer 2003): 91–100, at 93–94.

351. "Nihilist with Something to Say," in *The European Magazine* (London), 17–23 March 1995, p. 4.

352. William A. Schabas, *An Introduction to the International Criminal Court* (Cambridge: Cambridge University Press, 2001), pp. 286–287.

353. Hasenclever, *Die Macht der Moral in der internationalen Politik*, p. 391.

16. A Flawed Peace

1. Marie-Janine Calic, *Krieg und Frieden in Bosnien-Herzegovina*, expanded ed. (Frankfurt-am-Main: Suhrkamp, 1996), p. 260, 281.

2. Jack Snyder, *From Voting to Violence: Democratization and Nationalist Conflict* (New York: W. W. Norton, 2000), pp. 321–322, 40.

3. Fareed Zakaria, "The Rise of Illiberal Democracy," *Foreign Affairs,* vol. 76, no. 6 (November–December 1997).

4. Marc F. Plattner, "Liberalism and Democracy: Can't Have One without the Other," *Foreign Affairs,* vol. 77, no. 2 (March–April 1998).

5. David Chandler, *Bosnia: Faking Democracy after Dayton,* 2nd ed. (London and Sterling, Va.: Pluto Press, 2000).

6. Elizabeth M. Cousens and Charles K. Cater, *Toward Peace in Bosnia: Implementing the Dayton Accords* (Boulder, Colo.: Lynne Rienner, 2001), pp. 123–124.

7. Ibid., p. 147. Kristine Ann Hermann-De Luca has also adopted a "Weimarist" approach, urging, in 2002, that "The international community's institution-building approach failed because the new institutions exercised no real power—that remained in the hands of the ruling nationalist parties, with their *nomenklature* system and their practice of maintaining rule by stoking ethnic fears." K. A. Hermann-De Luca, "Beyond Elections: Lessons in Democratization Assistance from Post-War Bosnia and Herzegovina," (Ph.D. dissertation, American University, 2002), pp. 241–242.

8. Sumantra Bose, *Bosnia after Dayton: Nationalist Partition and International Intervention* (London: C. Hurst, 2002), pp. 276–277.

9. U.S. Department of State, *Bosnia and Herzegovina—Country Report on Human Rights Practices for 1996* [hereafter, State, *Bosnia-Herzegovina: Country Report 1996*] (Released by the Bureau of Democracy, Human Rights, and Labor, 30 January 1997), at www.state.gov/www/ global/human_rights/1996_hrp_report/bosniahe.html, p. 2.

10. Srpska Televizija (Banja Luka), 4 December 1995, trans. in FBIS, *Daily Report* (Eastern Europe), EEU-95-234 (6 December 1995), p. 29, my emphasis.

11. The Dayton Peace Accords, as summarized by John Shattuck, assistant secretary of state, in testimony before the House Committee on International Relations, 1 February 1996, in *Federal News Service,* on *CIS: Congressional Universe* [a service of *Lexis-Nexis*].

12. Walter B. Slocombe, undersecretary of defense for policy, in testimony before the Senate Armed Services Committee, 1 August 1996, in *Federal Document Clearing House— Congressional Testimony,* on *CIS: Congressional Universe.*

13. International Helsinki Federation for Human Rights (hereafter, IHF-HR), *Annual Report 1997—Bosnia-Herzegovina* (Vienna, 15 July 1997), at www.ihf-hr.org/ar97bos.htm, p. 10.

14. Madeleine K. Albright, secretary of state, in testimony before the House National Security Committee, 18 March 1998, in *Federal Document Clearing House—Congressional Testimony,* on *CIS: Congressional Universe.*

15. Haris Silajdžić, former prime minister of Bosnia-Herzegovina, in testimony before the U.S. House of Representatives Helsinki Commission, "OSCE Hearing on Bosnia's Future under the Dayton Agreement," 13 June 2000, in *FDCH Political Transcripts,* on *CIS: Congressional Universe.*

16. SRNA (Belgrade), 15 December 1995, trans. in FBIS, *Daily Report* (Eastern Europe), EEU-95-241 (15 December 1995), p. 21.

17. IHFHR, *Annual Report 1997,* p. 2.

18. Unemployment, Ambassador Robert Gelbard, special representative of the president and secretary of state, in a news briefing at the Foreign Press Center, 6 January 1998, in *FDCH Political Transcripts,* on *CIS: Congressional Universe;* GDP, State, *Bosnia-Herzegovina: Country Report 1996,* p. 3; mines, *Minneapolis Star Tribune,* 1 September 1996, at www.startribune .com; females, Jan Goodwin, "A Nation of Widows: The Adult Population of Bosnia is Now 70 Percent Female, but Women Are Being Shortchanged in the Reconstruction," *Gender Watch: The Progressive Woman's Quarterly,* vol. 6, no. 2 (30 April 1997), on *Lexis-Nexis Academic Universe* [hereafter, LNAU].

19. Re uranium, "Depleted Uranium Contaminates Bosnia-Herzegovina," *Environment News Service*, 26 March 2003, at ens-news.com/ens/mar2003/2003-03-25-04.asp; and re leukemia, *BH Press* (Sarajevo), 4 January 2001, trans. in FBIS, no. EUP-2001-0104-000190.

20. Re prostitution, Nidžara Ahmetasević, with Julie Poucher Harbin, "Thousands of Women Lured into Bosnian Brothels," *Institute for War and Peace Reporting* [hereafter, IWPR], BCR no. 2 (18 April 2002), at www.iwpr.net; and re mental disorder, Charles Tauber, director of the Coalition for Work with Psycho-trauma and Peace, as quoted in Jennifer Friedlin, "Bosnia: Suicides on the Rise," in IWPR, BCR no. 303 (12 December 2001), at www.iwpr.net.

21. Aneš Alić, "Missing Persons Pioneers," *TOL* (Prague), 11 July 2003, at www.tol.cz.

22. Re incompatible, Selim Beslagić, mayor of Tuzla, in testimony before the U.S. House of Representatives Helsinki Commission, "OSCE Hearing on Bosnia's Future under the Dayton Agreement," 13 June 2000, in *FDCH Political Transcripts*, in *CIS: Congressional Universe*, p. 39; and re subsidiary, Silajdžić, "OSCE Hearing on Bosnia's Future," p. 51.

23. International Helsinki Federation for Human Rights (hereafter IHF-HR), *Annual Report 1998—Bosnia-Herzegovina* (Vienna, 23 October 1998), at www.ihf-hr.org/reports/ar98/ar98bos.htm, p. 4.

24. Re bribery, David B. Dlouhy, in testimony before the House International Relations Committee, 15 September 1999, in *Federal News Service*, on *CIS: Congressional Universe;* and re connections,U.S. Department of State, *Bosnia and Herzegovina—Country Report on Human Rights Practices for 1999* [hereafter, State, *Bosnia-Herzegovina: Country Report 1999*] (Released by the Bureau of Democracy, Human Rights, and Labor, February 2000), at www.state.gov/www/global/human_rights/1999_hrp_report/bosniahe.html [accessed 29 June 2005].

25. Ibid., p. 10.

26. *New York Times*, 28 January 1996, p. 5.

27. *Christian Science Monitor*, 15 December 1995, p. 9.

28. *Die Welt* (Bonn), 24 February 1996, p. 5; and *Neue Zürcher Zeitung*, 13 March 1996, p. 3.

29. *Neue Zürcher Zeitung*, 12 March 1996, p. 1.

30. *Christian Science Monitor*, 18 March 1996, p. 8.

31. *New York Times*, 10 December 1995, p. 4.

32. Bird, quoted in *The Independent* (London), 19 November 2000, p. 20.

33. *New York Times*, 24 July 1996, p. A3.

34. IHF-HR, *Annual Report 1998*, p. 3.

35. Steven L. Burg, "Bosnia Herzegovina: A Case of Failed Democratization," in Karen Dawisha and Bruce Parrott (eds.), *Politics, Power, and the Struggle for Democracy in South-East Europe* (Cambridge: Cambridge University Press, 1997), p. 122.

36. Troop figures of 27,000/36,000, Ambassador Gelbard, news briefing, 6 January 1998 [note 20], p. 3; 19,000, *Daily Telegraph* (London), 3 June 2002, at www.telegraph.co.uk; EU, *Neue Zürcher Zeitung*, 5 July 2002, at www.nzz.ch; quote, *Minneapolis Star Tribune*, 19 December 2001, at www.startribune.com; EUFOR established, *Radio Netherlands Wereldomroep* (2 December 2004), at www2.rnw.nl/rnw/en; 6,300 troops, *Southeast European Times* (24 March 2005), at www.setimes.com.

37. Ambassador Robert Gelbard, news briefing, 6 January 1998 [note 20], p. 6.

38. James Pardew, special representative on military stabilization in the Balkans, in a special briefing at the State Department, 24 July 1996, in *Federal News Service*, on *CIS: Congressional Universe*.

39. Mark Edmond Clark, "No Military Action Is the Best Action for the Bosnian Federation to Take," *Brown Journal of World Affairs*, vol. 5, no. 1 (Winter–Spring 1998): 297–298.

40. SRNA (Bijeljina), 29 June 2000, trans. in *BBC Summary of World Broadcasts,* 1 July 2000, on LNAU; and Sarajevo TV, 13 December 2000, trans. in FBIS, no. EUP-2000-1213-000446.

41. Habena news agency (Mostar), 6 July 2000, trans. in *BBC Summary of World Broadcasts,* 8 July 2000, on LNAU; and *BH Press,* 16 December 2000, trans. in FBIS, no. EUP-2000-1216-000159.

42. "High Representative Acts to Ensure That Military in BiH Are under Effective Civilian Control," *Office of the High Representative* (Sarajevo), 2 April 2003, at www.ohr.int.

43. *Financial Times* (London), 12 November 2002, p. 1.

44. *Oslobodjenje* (Sarajevo), 16–17 September 2000, p. 3.

45. Re poverty, *Agence France Presse* (Paris), 8 November 2000, on LNAU; and re unemployment, *Minneapolis Star Tribune,* 7 October 2002, at www.startribune.com.

46. *Vjesnik* (Zagreb), 20 July 2002, at www.vjesnik.hr.

47. "Bosnia-Hercegovina—Update: Non-Compliance with the Dayton Accords: Ongoing Ethnically-Motivated Expulsions and Harassment in Bosnia," *Human Rights Watch,* vol. 8, no. 12 (August 1996): 5.

48. For some examples, see AFP (Paris), 1 May 1996, in FBIS, *Daily Report* (Eastern Europe), EEU-96-086 (2 May 1996), p. 27; AFP, 20 May 1996, in FBIS, no. EEU-96-101; and Sabrina P. Ramet, *Balkan Babel: The Disintegration of Yugoslavia from the Death of Tito to the Fall of Milošević,* 4th ed. (Boulder, Colo.: Westview Press, 2002), pp. 282–283.

49. Other names are also mentioned in Hana Bajraktarević, "New Step towards Reintegration of B&H: Everybody out of Other People's Homes," *AIM Press,* 1 May 1999, at www.aimpress.ch, p. 1.

50. AFP, 3 March 1996, in FBIS, *Daily Report* (Eastern Europe), EEU-96-044 (5 March 1996), p. 25; and AFP, 30 April 1998, in FBIS, no. AU-3004-152-998.

51. *Croatia Weekly* (Zagreb), 3 December 1999, p. 10.

52. *Croatia Weekly,* 10 December 1999, p. 10.

53. "The High Representative Annuls RS Restitution Laws," *Office of the High Representative,* 31 August 2000, at www.ohr.int.

54. *San Diego Union–Tribune,* 26 November 2000, p. A26, on *Lexis-Nexis* (www.nexis.com).

55. ONASA (Sarajevo), 6 February 2001, in FBIS, no. EUP-2001-0206-000324.

56. "Mine Accidents Impede the Return Process," at *UNHCR: Representative in Bosnia and Herzegovina,* 5 June 2003, at www.unhcr.ba/press/2003pr/050603.htm.

57. *The Continuing Challenge of Refugee Return in Bosnia and Herzegovina* (Sarajevo/Brussels: International Crisis Group, 13 December 2002), p. 5.

58. S. P. Ramet, *Balkan Babel,* chaps. 1–3, epilogue.

59. *Croatia Weekly,* 29 July 1999, p. 10.

60. *Hrvatska Riječ* (Sarajevo), 10 March 2001, trans. posted 10 May 2001 at www.ex-yupress.com/ hrvrijec/hrvrijec29.html [accessed 29 June 2005]. server1.cdsp.neu.edu/info/students/marko/hrvrijec/hrvrijec29.html, pp. 3–4.

61. Rade Rastanin, "Who Are the People in Banja Luka Studio of Serb Television?" *AIM Press,* 31 January 1998, at www.aimpress.ch, p. 2.

62. Cousens and Cater, *Toward Peace in Bosnia,* p. 121.

63. "Draft Freedom of Information Act for Bosnia and Herzegovina," *Office of the High Representative,* 21 June 2000, at www.ohr.int; and "Second Decision on Restructuring the Public Broadcasting System in BiH," *Office of the High Representative,* 23 October 2000, at www.ohr.int.

64. These examples are taken from an invaluable article written by Chris Hedges for the

New York Times and reprinted in *Dallas Morning News,* 28 November 1997, p. 57A, on *Lexis-Nexis* (www.nexis.com).

65. All these examples are taken from Robert J. Donia, "The Quest for Tolerance in Sarajevo's Textbooks," *Human Rights Review,* vol. 1, no. 2 (January–March 2000): 43.

66. See ibid., pp. 38–39, 45–48.

67. "Symposium on School Curricula: Conclusions," *Office of the High Representative,* 10 February 2000, at www.ohr.int.

68. "All BiH Pupils to Learn Both Scripts," *Office of the High Representative,* 27 September 2000, at www.ohr.int; and "Inter-Religious Council Will Help Draft Curriculum for New School Subject," *Office of the High Representative,* 20 February 2001, at www.ohr.int.

69. AFP, 28 June 2000, on *Lexis-Nexis* (www.nexis.com).

70. HINA news agency (Zagreb), 13 July 2000, in *BBC Summary of World Broadcasts,* 15 July 2000, on LNAU.

71. Radio Montenegro (Podgorica), 20 July 2000, trans. in *BBC Monitoring Europe—Political,* 20 July 2000, on LNAU.

72. *Deutsche Presse-Agentur* (Hamburg), 22 October 1997, on *Lexis-Nexis* (www.nexis .com); HINA, 3 November 1998, in *BBC Summary of World Broadcasts,* 5 November 1998, on *Lexis-Nexis* (www.nexis.com); *New York Times,* 8 July 2000, p. A7, in *Lexis-Nexis* (www .nexis.com); *Human Rights Network News,* 26 November 2002; and *Continuing Challenge of Refugee Return,* p. 15. See also "ABECEDA korupcije," in *Dani* (Sarajevo), no. 117 (27 August 1999): 16–23. Regarding the complicity of UN personnel in the Bosnian sex trade, see *Scotland on Sunday,* 9 February 2003, at www.news.scotsman.com.

73. *Slobodna Bosna* (Sarajevo), no. 384 (25 March 2004): 30–32. Karadžić himself embezzled some 36 million German marks after the war. On this point, see *Večernji list* (31 March 2005), at www.vecernji-list.hr.

74. Wolfgang Petrisch, *Bosnien und Herzegowina. Fünf Jahre nach Dayton: Hat der Friede eine Chance?* (Klagenfurt: Wieser Verlag, 2001), pp. 98–101.

75. Petritsch, *Bosnien und Herzegowina,* pp. 115–116.

76. Biljana Plavšić, former RS president, in interview with the author, Hinseberg Prison, Frövi, Sweden, 5–6 April 2004.

77. Željko Rogošić, "Bosanski HDZ zgranut akcijom uhićenja Jelavića i kompanije," *Nacional* (Zagreb), no. 428 (27 January 2004): 17; and Berislav Jelinić, "Istraga oko Hercegovačke banke širi se na Hrvatsku," *Nacional,* no. 429 (3 February 2004): 18–19.

78. See *Die Woche,* 27 August 1999, p. 20.

79. "High Representative Removes Former Prime Minister Edhem Bičakčić," *Office of the High Representative,* 23 February 2001, at www.ohr.int. For details of this case, see *Washington Post,* 1 March 2001, p. A14, in *Lexis-Nexis* (www.nexis.com).

80. *The Independent* (London), 28 May 2002, at news.independent.co.uk. Regarding the local campaign against organized crime, see *Oslobodjenje,* 15 July 2004, p. 7.

81. See Ivan Lovrenović, "Etnički čista korupcija," in *Feral Tribune,* no. 870 (18 May 2002): 30–32.

82. *Scotsman,* 1 July 2003, at www.news.scotsman.com.

83. *Vjesnik,* 17 July 2004, at www.vjesnik.hr.

84. Regarding Izetbegović, see "Pedeset kila dokaza protiv Izetbegovića," *Glas javnosti* (Belgrade), 6 November 2001, at www.glas-javnosti.co.yu; "Proširena optužnica protiv Izetbegovića predata Hagu," *Vijesti on-line* (Podgorica), 9 November 2001, at www.vijesti.cg.yu; "Optužnica protiv Izetbegovića," *Nezavisna Svetlost* (Kragujevac), 10–17 November 2001, at www.svetlost.co.yu; and Alenko Zornija, "Izetbegović bio pod istragom zbog zločina pripadnika Armije BiH nad Hrvatima i Srbima," *Vjesnik,* 24 October 2003, at www.vjesnik.hr.

85. There have been reported "sightings" of Gotovina at some 500 locations—in France, Italy, Croatia, and out at sea. See *Novi list,* 15 October 2003, at www.novilist.hr.

86. See, for example, *Glas javnosti,* 6 December 2001, at arhiva.glas-javnosti.co.yu; also *Novi list* (5 October 2004) at www.novilist.hr.

87. *Oslobodjenje,* 3–4 April 2004, p. 6.

88. *Frankfurter Rundschau,* 11 July 2003, at www.frankfurterrundschau.de.

89. AFP, 8 February 2001, trans. in FBIS, no. EUP-2001-0208-000258.

90. Re protection, *RFE/RL Newsline,* 15 February 2002, at www.rferl.org, and *Scotsman,* 27 March 2002, at news.scotsman.com; and re opportunities, *Novi list* (Rijeka), 6 March 2002, at www.novilist.hr.

91. Željko Cvijanović, "Serbia: Mandić Arrest Threatens Karadžić," in IWPR, BCR no. 428 (9 May 2003), at www.iwpr.net, p. 1.

92. "Interview—High Representative in BiH, Wolfgang Petritsch: 'Bosnia Envoy Sees New Will to Grab Karadžić,'" *Office of the High Representative,* 24 January 2002, at www.ohr.int.

93. *Berlingske Tidende* (Copenhagen), 28 February 2002 and 6 March 2002—both at www.berlingske.dk; *Berliner Zeitung,* 4 March 2002, at www.berlinonline.de; and Željko Cvijanović, "Regional Report: Karadžić Cornered?" in IWPR, TU no. 256 (25 February–2 March 2002), at www.iwpr.net.

94. *Scotsman,* 8 March 2003, at news.scotsman.com.

95. Held responsible, *Süddeutsche Zeitung* (Munich), 28 February 2002, at www.sueddeutsche.de; ordered the killing, *Vjesnik,* 30 October 2003, at www.vjesnik.hr; and constituted genocide, *Večernji list,* 20 April 2004, at www.vecernji-list.hr.

96. *Dnevni avaz* (Sarajevo), 5 April 2004, pp. 1, 3.

97. Hugh Griffiths, "Karadžićev specijalac i Arkanov tjelohranitelj na platnom spisku Atini!" in *Dani,* no. 347 (6 February 2004): 24; and *Dnevni avaz,* 26 July 2004, p. 8.

98. Contact with family, *Večernji* list (4 February 2005), at www.vecernji-list.hr; Karadžić, quoted in *RFE/RL Newsline,* 15 September 1999, at www.rferl.org.

99. *Scotsman,* 24 April 2002, at news.scotsman.com; *Novi list* (19 October 2004), at www.novilist.hr; and *The Guardian* (20 October 2004), at www.guardian.co.uk.

100. *Frankfurter Rundschau,* 22 October 2003, at www.fr-aktuell.de.

101. Eduard Šoštarić, "Sanader i Žužul mogli bi zbog Praljka biti svjedoci u Haagu," *Nacional,* no. 436 (23 March 2004): 26–28.

102. *Oslobodjenje,* 3–4 April 2004, p. 1.

103. *Glas javnosti,* 18 July 2004, at www.glas-javnosti.co.yu.

104. *Glas javnosti,* 29 July 2004, at www.glas-javnosti.co.yu.

105. *Slobodna Bosna,* as summarized in *Croatia Weekly,* 31 March 2000, p. 10.

106. Petritsch, *Bosnien und Herzegowina,* p. 123.

107. Mirsad Bajtarević and Nerma Jelačić, "Ashdown Celebrates Lonely Anniversary," *IWPR,* BCR no. 490 (2 April 2004), at www.iwpr.net.

108. "PLIP Statistics for May 2003," *OHR Releases,* 3 July 2003, at www.ohr.int.

109. Ermin Čengić, "Stanovi korisnicima zgrade vlasnicima," *Dani,* no. 323 (22 August 2003): 20.

110. Re intelligence, Sead Numanović, "Bosnian Spooks," *IWPR,* BCR no. 432 (23 May 2003), at www.iwpr.net; and re demobilize, *RFE/RL Newsline,* 3 February 2004, at www.rferl.org; journalism, "Bosnia Media Conference," *IWPR* (4 March 2004), at www.iwpr.net; Brčko, "Deadline Set for Harmonized Primary and Secondary School Legislation," *OHR Press Releases,* 29 March 2004, at www.ohr.int.

111. Emir Suljagić, "Država na rubu izolacije?" *Dani,* no. 359 (30 April 2004): 20.

112. See Nerma Jelačić, "Bosnia & Herzegovina: The Dysfunctional State," *IWPR,* BCR no. 493 (22 April 2004), at www.iwpr.net, specifically p. 3.

113. Re television network, see Zekerijah Smajić, "Državanje vode do odlaska 'Majstora,'" *Dani,* no. 336 (21 November 2003): 32; and re politicization of education, "Politicisation of Federation Schools Must End," *OHR Press Releases,* 24 February 2004, at www.ohr.int; confirmed in "Politicisation of Education Reform Damages BiH's EU Prospects," *OHR Press Releases,* 22 March 2004, at www.ohr.int; reconfirmed in *Oslobodjenje,* 3–4 April 2004, p. 2.

114. Re organized crime, *Oslobodjenje,* 3–4 April 2004, p. 6, and *Dnevni avaz,* 5 April 2004, p. 11; re sporadic looting, "Looting Remains a Serious Problem," *OHR Press Releases,* 31 July 2003, at www.ohr.int; and re drug abuse, Dženana Karup-Druško and Cvijeta Arsenić, "Domaće tržište drogom kontroliraju srpska i crnogorska mafija'"" *Dani,* no. 324 (29 August 2003): 26.

115. Re obstruction, Saša Kosanović, "Vlast RS-a perfidnim metodama sprečava povratak Hrvata," in *Nacional,* no. 439 (13 April 2004): 28; Karadžić, *Večernji list,* 10 February 2004, at www.vecernji-list.hr; re discrimination, *Oslobodjenje,* 5 April 2004, p. 4; re war crimes, "Decision Removing Mr. Dragan Basevic from His Position as Police Official in Srpsko Sarajevo," OHR, *Removals and Suspensions from Office,* 10 February 2004, at www.ohr.int; and re withholding of documents, "Srebrenica Report," in *OHR Weekend Media Brief, 17–18/4/2004,* 18 April 2004, at www.ohr.int; and "Decision removing General Cvetko Savic from his position as Chief of the General Staff of Republika Srpska and from the Army of Republika Srpska," OHR, *Removals and Suspensions from Office,* 20 April 2004, at www.ohr.int.

116. *RFE/RL Newsline,* 14 May 2004, at www.rfrerl.org.

117. Bajtarević and Jelačić, "Ashdown Celebrates Lonely Anniversary."

118. Ibid.

119. Emir Suljagić, "Vrijeme je da se medjunarodna zajednica pakuje!" [An interview with Zdravko Grebo], *Dani,* no. 344 (16 January 2004): 12–14.

120. Gordana Katana, "SDS Shrugs Off Ashdown's Financial Squeeze," in IWPR, BCR no. 492 (16 April 2004), at www.iwpr.net; Marija Arnautović, "Bosnia: Call for End to Sectarian Education," in IWPR, BCR no. 501 (3 June 2004), at www.iwpr.net; and *Vjesnik,* 4 July 2004, at www.vjesnik.hr.

121. Elmira Bayrasli, "Comment: Bosnia's Education Law Fiasco," in IWPR, BCR no. 498 (20 May 2004), at www.iwpr.net.

122. *Vjesnik,* 1 July 2004, at www.vjesnik.hr.

123. "Financial Review Reveals Abuse, Corruption, Tax Evasion in SDS," *Office of the High Representative,* 1 July 2004, at www.ohr.int.

124. For details, see Gordana Katana, "Bosnia: Serbs Threaten Constitutional Crisis," in IWPR, BCR no. 507 (15 July 2004), at www.iwpr.net.

125. Re "widespread fraud," IHF-HR, *Annual Report 1998,* p. 2; re "irregularities," ONASA, 19 November 2000, in FBIS, no. EUP-2000-1119-00066; re "citizen participation" and "disruptions," State, *Bosnia-Herzegovina: Country Report 1996,* p. 13; and re acts of violence, IHR-HR, *Annual Report 1998,* p. 4; and State, *Bosnia-Herzegovina: Country Report 1999,* p. 8.

126. For example, Ambassador Gelbard in 1998: "Our policy owes its success to a number of key factors. . . . Political change in the Republika Srpska was key to our success in further reinvigorating Dayton implementation. . . . Recent progress demonstrates that our approach is sound and will lead to further progress if we stay the course." Ambassador Robert Gelbard, special representative of the president and the secretary of state for the implementation of the Dayton Peace Accords, in testimony before the House International Relations Committee, 12 March 1998, in *FDCH Political Transcripts,* in *CIS: Congressional Universe,* p. 6.

127. ONASA, 8 November 2000, in FBIS, no. EUP-2000-1108-000264.

128. *Vjesnik,* 6 October 2002, at www.vjesnik.hr; and *The Guardian* (London), 7 October 2002, at www.guardian.co.uk. These charges were repeated by Dragan Čović, member of the presidency of Bosnia-Herzegovina, in May 2004. See *Oslobodjenje,* 24 May 2004, p. 3.

129. Branko Perić, "Striving for Equality," *AIM Press,* 3 January 2002, at www.aimpress.ch, p. 1.

130. *Croatia Weekly* (11 March 1999), p. 10, summarizing the views of Ante Jelavić, HDZ president in Bosnia.

131. *BH Press,* 15 October 2000, trans. in FBIS, no. EUP-2000-1015-000176; and ONASA, 13 February 2001, in FBIS, no. EUP-2001-0213-000393.

132. Sulejman Tihić, president of the SDA main election headquarters, as quoted in ONASA, 9 April 2000, in *BBC Monitoring Europe—Political,* 9 April 2000, on *Lexis-Nexis* (www.nexis.com).

133. Slavoljub Bogić, "Planiraju da ukinu Republiku Srpsku," in *revija 92* (Belgrade), 13 April 2001, p. 11.

134. TV Bosnia-Herzegovina (Sarajevo), 28 February 2001, trans. in FBIS, no. EUP-2001-0228-000490. See also the discussion of possible division of Bosnia into three states in *Novi list* (12 August 2004), at www.novilist.hr.

135. ONASA, 11 November 2000, in FBIS, no. EUP-2000-1111-000158; and ONASA, 13 November 2000, in FBIS, no. EUP-20000-1113-000205.

136. *Vjesnik,* 1 March 2001, 3 March 2001, 4 March 2001, and 6 March 2001—at www.vjesnik.hr; and *Oslobodjenje,* 10–11 March 2001, pp. 1, 3–4, and 17–18 March 2001, pp. 1, 3–5.

137. *Večernji list* (Zagreb), 8 March 2001, at www.vecernji-list.hr; *Slobodna Dalmacija* (Split), 8 March 2001, at arhiv.slobodnadalmacija.hr; and *Slobodna Bosna,* 19 April 2001, p. 13.

138. Mesić, quoted in *Boston Globe,* 7 March 2001, at www.boston.com/news/globe.

139. Zubak, *BH Press,* 2 February 2001, trans. in FBIS, no. EUP-2001-0203-000055; and Brkić, *BH Press,* 17 October 2000, trans. in FBIS, no. EUP-2000-1017-000187.

140. *Frankfurter Rundschau,* 27 April 2004, at www.frankfurterrundschau.de.

141. *Nezavisne novine* (Banja Luka), 5 May 2004, at www.nezavisne.com. See also *Oslobodjenje,* 16 July 2004, p. 8.

142. Victor D. Bojkov, "Democracy in Bosnia and Herzegovina: Post-1995 Political System and Its Functioning," *Southeast European Politics,* vol. 4, no. 1 (May 2003): 61.

143. Patrick Joseph O'Halloran, "The Role of Identity in Post-Conflict State-Building: The Case of Bosnia-Herzegovina and the Dayton Agreement" (Ph.D. dissertation, York University, November 2001), pp. 289–290.

144. But there have also been recurrent calls to revise the Dayton Peace Accords, with Bosniaks typically demanding that the RS be abolished altogether and with leading figures in the SDS holding that "The preservation of Republika Srpska is a holy task, not only for the SDS and the future Bosnian Serb president but also for all our (Serb) people in general." Dragan Cavić, member of the SDS and then vice president of the RS, as quoted in *OHR BiH Media Round-up, 3/10/2002,* 3 October 2002, at www.ohr.int, p. 3. See also A. O., "Republika Srpska mora nestati," *Dani,* no. 347 (6 February 2004): 11.

145. *Dnevni avaz,* 26 July 2004, p. 11.

146. Ivan Lovrenović, "Who Actually Governs Bosnia-Herzegovina?" *Bosnia Report,* n.s. no. 32–34 (December 2002–July 2003): 1–2.

147. Ibid., p. 2.

148. *Guardian* (10 November 2005), at www.guardian.co.uk [accessed on 3 December 2005]; *Die Presse* (Vienna), 24 November 2005, p. 8; *International Herald Tribune* (22 November 2005), at www.iht.com [accessed on 4 December 2005]; and *The Times* (25 November 2005), at www.timesonline.co.uk [accessed on 29 November 2005].

17. The Third Yugoslavia and After, 1992–2005

1. Eric Gordy, "Why Milošević Still?" *Current History,* vol. 99, no. 635 (March 2000): 100–101. For a discussion of the cultural and political gulf between city and countryside in Serbia, see Sabrina P. Ramet, "Nationalism and the 'Idiocy' of the Countryside: The Case of Serbia," *Ethnic and Racial Studies,* vol. 19, no. 1 (January 1996).

2. For a more complete list, see Sabrina Petra Ramet, *Balkan Babel: The Disintegration of Yugoslavia from the Death of Tito to the Fall of Milošević,* 4th ed. (Boulder, Colo.: Westview Press, 2002), pp. 71–72.

3. *Agence France Presse,* 6 March 2000, on *Lexis-Nexis Academic Universe* (hereafter LNAU); and *Beta news agency,* Belgrade), 5 March 2000, in *BBC Summary of World Broadcasts,* 7 March 2000, on LNAU. See also *Minneapolis Star Tribune,* 12 May 2000, at www.star tribune.com.

4. Itar-TASS (Moscow), 21 May 1992, on nexis.com.

5. Eric D. Gordy, *The Culture of Power in Serbia: Nationalism and the Destruction of Alternatives* (University Park: Pennsylvania State University Press, 1999), p. 98.

6. "Testimony of Nebojša Čović, Coordinator of the Alliance for Change," in *The Milošević Regime versus Serbian Democracy and Balkan Stability,* Hearing before the Commission on Security and Cooperation in Europe, 105th Congress, 2nd session, 10 December 1998 (Washington, D.C.: U.S. Government Printing Office, 1999), p. 6.

7. Paroški, quoted in UPI, 9 July 1992, on nexis.com.

8. Details and documentation in S. P. Ramet, *Balkan Babel,* chap. 14.

9. Re arms smuggling, see *Politika* (Belgrade), 19 May 1993, p. 13, trans. in FBIS, *Daily Report* (Eastern Europe), 18 June 1993, p. 44.

10. Herbert Buschenfeld, "Die wirtschaftliche Lage der Nachfolgestaaten Jugoslawiens vor dem Kosovokrieg," in Dunja Melčić (ed.), *Der Jugoslawien-Krieg: Handbuch zu Vorgeschichte, Verlauf und Konsequenzen* (Opladen/Wiesbaden: Westdeutscher Verlag, 1999), p. 513.

11. At one point, hyperinflation had so distorted the Serbian economy that, at least in theory, a bunch of carrots cost a year's salary. Tim Judah, *The Serbs: History, Myth and the Destruction of Yugoslavia* (New Haven, Conn.: Yale University Press, 1997), p. 259.

12. Vidosav Stevanović, *Milošević, jedan epitaf* (Belgrade: Montena, 2002), p. 143.

13. Buschenfeld, "Die wirtschaftliche Lage," p. 513.

14. Robert Thomas, *Serbia under Milošević: Politics in the 1990s* (London: Hurst, 1999), p. 161.

15. *Glas javnosti* (Belgrade), 31 October 2000, at www.glas-javnosti.co.yu; and "Ko je pratio Ćuruviju?" in *Nezavisna Svetlost* (Kragujevac), no. 267 (5–12 November 2000), at www .svetlost.co.yu/arhiva.

16. AP Worldstream, 15 December 1993, on nexis.com.

17. *Deutsche Presse-Agentur,* 19 February 1995, on nexis.com; *The Guardian* (London), 7 August 1995, p. T13, on nexis.com; and "Yugoslav Independent Press: Naša Borba" (12/2/99), at server1.cdsp.neu.edu/students/marko/nasaborba/nasaborbaindex.html.

18. For discussion, see *Financial Times,* 29 April 1995, p. III, on nexis.com.

19. *Borba* (Belgrade), 28 December 1992, as quoted in Mark Thompson, *Forging War: The Media in Serbia, Croatia, Bosnia and Herzegovina,* completely revised and expanded ed. (Luton: University of Luton Press, 1999), p. 90.

20. For details and examples, see S. P. Ramet, *Balkan Babel,* pp. 340–341.

21. Interview with Dr. Bora Kuzmanović, in *Duga* (Belgrade), 28 October–10 November 1995, pp. 23–25, trans. in FBIS, *Daily Report* (East Europe), 23 April 1996, pp. 66–70.

22. Thompson, *Forging War,* pp. 85, 108.

23. Pavle, quoted in Thomas, *Serbia under Milošević,* p. 112.

24. See Sabrina Petra Ramet, "The Serbian Church and the Serbian Nation," in Sabrina Petra Ramet and Donald W. Treadgold (eds.), *Render unto Caesar: The Religious Sphere in World Politics* (Washington, D.C.: American University Press, 1995), pp. 317–318.

25. For details, see Douglas E. Schoen, "How Milošević Stole the Elections," in *New York Times Magazine,* 14 February 1993; and *Neue Zürcher Zeitung,* 19 December 1992, p. 5.

26. *Agence France Presse,* 25 December 1992, on nexis.com.

27. *Daily Telegraph* (London), 28 December 1992, p. 8, on nexis.com.

28. *Agence France Presse,* 29 December 1992, on nexis.com.

29. Sipovac, quoted in *Agence France Presse,* 1 June 1993, on nexis.com. See also *Vjesnik* (Zagreb), 2 June 1993, p. 9; and *Glas istre* (Pula), 2 June 1993, p. 16.

30. *Agence France Presse,* 1 June 1993, on nexis.com; Associated Press, 1 June 1993, on nexis.com; Inter Press Service, 2 June 1993, on nexis.com; *The Independent* (London), 3 June 1993, p. 10, on nexis.com; *Agence France Presse,* 3 June 1993, on nexis.com; *Vjesnik,* 4 June 1993, p. 9; *Glas Istre,* 6 June 1993, p. 5; *The Independent,* 7 June 1993, p. 8, on nexis.com; Inter Press Service, 8 June 1993, on nexis.com; *Chicago Tribune,* 8 June 1993, p. 7, on nexis.com; and Associated Press, 9 June 1993, on nexis.com.

31. Quoted in *Agence France Presse,* 5 June 1993, on nexis.com. I have corrected the incorrect syntax in the original translation.

32. Radio Croatia Network (Zagreb), 8 December 1992, trans. in FBIS, *Daily Report* (Eastern Europe), 10 December 1992, p. 59.

33. 50,000 Hungarians according to the Hungarian news agency MTI (Budapest), 29 July 1999, on LNAU; 100,000 Hungarians according to MTI, 13 September 1999, in *BBC Monitoring Europe: Political,* 14 September 1999, on LNAU; and 45,000 Croats according to Larisa Inić, "Lutanje po državi pravnih iluzija," in *Nezavisni* (Novi Sad), 11 February 2000, at www.nezavisni.co.yu/327/htm/327subotica.htm, p. 2.

34. Miroslav Filipović, "The Sandžak Dilemma" (BCR no. 125, 17 March 2000), published by *The Institute for War and Peace Reporting,* 1 August 2000, at www.iwpr.net/index.p15? archive/bcr/bcr_2000317_2_eng.txt.

35. For details, see *Christian Science Monitor,* 11 April 1994, p. 2, on LNAU; *Washington Post,* 29 May 1993, p. A2, on LNAU; and Serbian Radio (Belgrade), 20 February 1993, in *BBC Summary of World Broadcasts,* 22 February 1993, on LNAU. See also "Sandžak: Calm for Now," in *International Crisis Group,* 9 November 1998, at www.crisisweb.org/projects/sbalkans/ reports/yu04rep.htm.

36. International Helsinki Federation for Human Rights, *Annual Report 1997: Federal Republic of Yugoslavia (Serbia and Montenegro)* (Vienna, 15 July 1997), at www.ihf-hr.org/ ar97yug.htm, p. 12 of 21.

37. Kertes, quoted in Sreten Vujović, "An Uneasy View of the City," in Nebojša Popov (ed.), *The Road to War in Serbia: Trauma and Catharsis,* English version by Drinka Gojković (Budapest: Central European University Press, 2000), p. 131.

38. Mladić, quoted in Vujović, "Uneasy View," p. 138.

39. Amfilohije, quoted in Radmila Radić, "The Church and the 'Serbian Question,'" in Popov (ed.), *The Road to War,* p. 263.

40. Djilas, quoted in *New York Times,* 19 January 1997, p. 46.

41. Re wardrobe, see *Sunday Times* (London), 2 July 1995, on nexis.com.; and Stanković, quoted in Thomas, *Serbia under Milošević,* p. 173.

42. *The Independent,* 25 September 1994, p. 16, on nexis.com.

43. *The Guardian,* 24 March 1995, p. 14, on nexis.com.

44. Drašković later distanced himself from the "Serbian Guard" which he had helped to create. On this point, see Florian Bieber, *Nationalismus in Serbien vom Tode Titos bis zum Ende der Ära Milošević* (Vienna-Wiener Osteuropa Studien, 2005), pp. 275–276. Re. Vance-Owen plan, Vuk Drašković, president of the SPO and Foreign Minister of Serbia and Montenegro, in interview with the author, Belgrade, 11 June 2004.

45. Associated Press, 13 July 1993, on nexis.com.

46. *Agence France Presse,* 3 January 1994), on nexis.com; and *Japan Times,* 6 March 1994, p. 10.

47. *Illyria,* 9–11 November 1996, p. 3.

48. *The Times* (London), 4 March 1997, on AmeriCast.com.

49. Marković, quoted in Thomas, *Serbia under Milošević,* p. 227.

50. Ibid., pp. 238–239.

51. *taz* (Berlin), 11 August 1995, p. 8, on nexis.com.

52. *Deutsche Presse-Agentur,* 22 December 1995, on nexis.com.

53. *Neue Zürcher Zeitung,* 19 November 1996, p. 1. See also *Vreme* (Belgrade), 16 November 1996, pp. 16–17.

54. *Neue Zürcher Zeitung,* 21 November 1996, p. 5; 23/24 November 1996, p. 3; 25 November 1996, p. 3; 26 November 1996, p. 2; and 2 December 1996, p. 2; SRNA (Bosnian Serb news agency), 30 November 1996, trans. in *BBC Summary of World Broadcasts,* 2 December 1996, on Nexis; and *New York Times,* 16 December 1996, p. A4.

55. See the chronology for 17 November–2 December 1996 in *Agence France Presse,* 2 December 1996, on Nexis.

56. Re 150,000 on 30 November, SRNA, 30 November 1996, trans. in *BBC Summary of World Broadcasts,* 2 December 1996, on Nexis; re 200,000 on 30 November, *Neue Zürcher Zeitung,* 2 December 1996, p. 2; re more than 150,000 on 4 December, *Christian Science Monitor,* 6 December 1996, p. 5; re 100,000 on 6 December, *Neue Zürcher Zeitung,* 7/8 December 1996, p. 1; and re 100,000 on 15 December, *New York Times,* 16 December 1996, p. A4.

57. *Sunday Telegraph,* 1 December 1996, p. 23.

58. Radio B92 (Belgrade), 2 December 1996, trans. in *BBC Monitoring Service: Eastern Europe,* 3 December 1996, on Nexis; SRNA, 2 December 1996, trans. in *BBC Monitoring Service: Eastern Europe,* 3 December 1996, on Nexis; and *Neue Zürcher Zeitung,* 4 December 1996, p. 1.

59. *Illyria* (The Bronx), 28–30 December 1996, p. 1; and *New York Times,* 29 December 1996, p. 6.

60. Serbian TV (Belgrade), 1 December 1996, trans. in *BBC Monitoring Service: Eastern Europe,* 3 December 1996, on Nexis.

61. *Illyria,* 7–9 December 1996, p. 2.

62. Quoted in AFX News, 3 December 1996, on Nexis.

63. *New York Times,* 4 December 1996, p. A1.

64. *New York Times,* 8 December 1996, p. 1.

65. *New York Times,* 30 December 1996, p. A3.

66. *New York Times,* 17 December 1996, p. A6.

67. *New Europe* (Athens), 22–28 December 1996, p. 4; and *New York Times,* 28 December 1996, pp. 1, 5.

68. Thomas, *Serbia under Milošević,* pp. 295–297.

69. Quoted in ibid., p. 308.

70. *Christian Science Monitor,* 5 February 1997, p. 2.

71. *New York Times,* 6 February 1997, p. A1.

72. *Jerusalem Post,* 19 September 1997, p. 10, on nexis.com.

73. *New Europe,* 16–22 March 1997, p. 32.

74. Šešelj, of course, denied that he was a fascist. As the *Los Angeles Times* reported at the time, "Asked once if he was bothered that many people fear his fascist tendencies, Šešelj responded: 'I've been accused of being a homosexual and of being a Croat. Those are far worse accusations. . . . We are chauvinists. We hate Croats. What is fascist about that?'" *Los Angeles Times,* 20 September 1997, p. A2, on nexis.com. See also *New York Times,* 7 December 1997, p. 9, on nexis.com.

75. Sonja Biserko and Seška Stanojlović (eds.), *Radicalisation of the Serbian Society: Collection of Documents,* trans. by Mirka Janković and Ivana Damjanović (Belgrade: Helsinki Committee for Human Rights in Serbia, December 1997), p. 22.

76. Dušan Pavlović, *Akteri i modeli: Ogledi o politici u Srbiji pod Miloševićem* (Belgrade: Samizdat B92, 2001), pp. 111–117.

77. Biserko and Stanojlović (eds.), *Radicalisation of the Serbian Society,* pp. 41, 42.

78. Quoted in *The Times* (London), 27 February 1997, on AmeriCast.com.

79. Inter Press Service, 26 September 1997, on nexis.com.

80. Thomas, *Serbia under Milošević,* pp. 347–349.

81. *Il Sole 24 Ore,* 7 October 1997, on nexis.com.

82. Serbian TV (Belgrade), 29 November 1997, trans. in *BBC Summary of World Broadcasts,* 2 December 1997, on nexis.com.

83. *Deutsche Presse-Agentur,* 8 December 1997, on nexis.com; and *La Stampa* (Torino), 8 December 1997, p. 6, on nexis.com.

84. AP Worldstream, 23 December 1997, on nexis.com.

85. *Agence France Presse,* 22 December 1997, on nexis.com; and *Der Tagesspiegel* (Berlin), 23 December 1997, p. 2.

86. *Agence France Presse,* 29 December 1997, on nexis.com.

87. *Agence France Presse,* 17 February 1998, on nexis.com; and *The Times,* 18 February 1998, on nexis.com.

88. Re 8 cabinet ministries, *Beta news agency,* Belgrade), 18 February 1998, trans. in FBIS-EEU-98-049; and *Beta news agency,* 19 February 1998, in FBIS-EEU-98-050. Re *Politika, Beta news agency,* 22 January 1998, trans. in FBIS-EEU-98-022. Re negotiations, see also *Beta news agency,* 5 March 1998, in FBIS-EEU-98-064; and *Beta news agency,* 17 February 1998, trans. in FBIS-EEU-98-048.

89. *Beta news agency,* 16 February 1998, trans. in FBIS-EEU-98-047.

90. Thomas, *Serbia under Milošević,* p. 415; and *Beta news agency,* 26 March 1998, in FBIS-EEU-98-085.

91. Jens Reuter, "Die innere Situation Serbiens 1998—Politische Säuberungen im Windschaften der Kosovo-Krise," *Sudost-Europa,* vol. 48, no. 1–2 (January–February 1999): 1; and *Duga* (Belgrade), no. 1702 (10–23 October 1998): 14–15.

92. Elez Biberaj, *Albania in Transition: The Rocky Road to Democracy* (Boulder, Colo.: Westview Press, 1998), p. 14.

93. Miranda Vickers, *Between Serb and Albanian: A History of Kosovo* (New York: Columbia University Press, 1998), p. 247.

94. *What the Kosovars Say and Demand* (Tirana: 8 Nentori Publishing House, 1990), p. 25.

95. *Rilindja* (Tirana), 22 February 1995, p. 5, trans. in FBIS, *Daily Report* (East Europe), 24 February 1995, p. 43; and Radio Tirana Network, 27 October 1992, trans. in FBIS, *Daily Report* (East Europe), 28 October 1992, p. 30.

96. Vickers, *Between Serb and Albanian,* pp. 250, 256–259.

97. Ibid., p. 251.

98. Predrag Tasić, *Kako je ubijena druga Jugoslavija* (Skopje: Self-published by the author, 1994), p. 69.

99. *Agence France Presse,* 23 September 1992, in FBIS, *Daily Report* (East Europe), 24 September 1992, p. 44.

100. See, inter alia, Radio Croatia in Albanian, 14 May 1991, trans. in FBIS, *Daily Report* (East Europe), 15 May 1991, p. 40; TVSH Television Network, 28 February 1994, trans. in FBIS, *Daily Report* (East Europe), 1 March 1994, p. 42; TVSH Television Network, 22 June 1994, trans. in FBIS, *Daily Report* (East Europe), 23 June 1994, p. 30; TVSH Television Network, 15 October 1994, trans. in FBIS, *Daily Report* (East Europe), 17 October 1994, p. 75; TVSH Television Network, 16 February 1995, trans. in FBIS, *Daily Report* (East Europe), 17 February 1995, p. 58; *Rilindja* (Tirana), 22 February 1995, p. 5, trans. in FBIS, *Daily Report* (East Europe), 24 February 1995, p. 43; ATA, 20 May 1995, trans. in *BBC Summary of World Broadcasts,* 24 May 1995, on Nexis; *Kosova Daily Report* (Priština), 4 October 1995, in FBIS, *Daily Report* (East Europe), 12 October 1995, p. 71; and Julie Mertus and Vlatka Mihelić, *Open Wounds: Human Rights Abuses in Kosovo* (New York: Human Rights Watch/Helinski, March 1993), pp. xiv–xv, 2–17, 31–37, 98–99.

101. Details in Fabian Schmidt, "Menschenrechte, Politik und Krieg in Kosovo 1989 bis 1999," in Konrad Clewing and Jens Reuter (eds.), *Der Kosovo-Konflikt: Ursachen—Akteure—Verlauf* (Munich: Bayerische Landeszentrale für politische Bildungsarbeit, 2000), p. 197.

102. Tanjug Domestic Service, 16 January 1995, trans. in FBIS, *Daily Report* (East Europe), 18 January 1995, p. 60; *Večernji list* (Zagreb), 1 April 1995, p. 24; and Fabian Schmidt, "Kosovo: The Time Bomb That Has Not Gone Off," *RFE/RL Research Report,* 6 February 1995, p. 56.

103. "News Briefing with Bujar Bukoshi, Prime Minister, Republic of Kosova, National Press Club, Washington D.C.," in *Federal News Service,* 21 October 1992, on *Lexis-Nexis Congressional Universe* (hereafter *LNCU*).

104. *Miami Herald,* 3 June 1999, at www.herald.com.

105. *Borba,* 20 April 1993, p. 8, trans. in FBIS, *Daily Report* (East Europe), 7 May 1993, p. 44.

106. Louis Sell, *Slobodan Milošević and the Destruction of Yugoslavia* (Durham, N.C.: Duke University Press, 2002), p. 270.

107. *The Times,* 31 March 1994, p. 15.

108. "Testimony October 5, 1994 Dr. Bujar Bukoshi on behalf of the Government of Kosova, House Foreign Affairs Committee," *Federal Document Clearing House Congressional Testimony,* 5 October 1994, on *LNCU*.

109. Quoted in Stefan Troebst, *Conflict in Kosovo: Failure of Prevention? An Analytical Documentation, 1992–1998,* ECMI Working Paper no. 1 (Flensburg: European Centre for Minority Issues, 1998), p. 33.

110. *Kosova Daily Report* (Priština), 19 March 1996, in FBIS, *Daily Report* (Eastern Europe), 20 March 1996, pp. 60–61.

111. See Sabrina P. Ramet, *Whose Democracy? Nationalism, Religion, and the Doctrine of Collective Rights in Post-1989 Eastern Europe* (Lanham, Md.: Rowman & Littlefield, 1997), p. 152.

112. *Kosova Daily Report,* 11 March 1996, in FBIS, *Daily Report* (Eastern Europe), 14 March 1996, pp. 60–61.

113. Re shops, *Kosova Daily Report,* 21 March 1996, in FBIS, *Daily Report* (Eastern Europe), 25 March 1996, p. 56; and re homes, *Kosova Daily Report,* 22 March 1996, in FBIS, *Daily Report* (Eastern Europe), 25 March 1996, p. 57.

114. *Kosova Daily Report,* 18 and 19 March 1996, in FBIS, *Daily Report* (Eastern Europe),

21 March 1996, p. 58; see also *Kosova Daily Report,* 21 March 1996, in FBIS, *Daily Report* (Eastern Europe), 25 March 1996, p. 58.

115. See the discussion in *Bota Sot* (Zurich), 16 December 1995, p. 2, trans. in FBIS, *Daily Report* (East Europe), 19 December 1995, pp. 58–59.

116. Matthas Rüb, "'Phoenix aus der Asche'. Die UCK: Von der Terrororganisation zur Bodentruppe der Nato?" in Thomas Schmid (ed.), *Krieg im Kosovo* (Reinbek bei Hamburg: Rowohlt Taschenbuch Verlag, 1999), pp. 50–51.

117. Jens Reuter, "Zur Geschichte der UCK," in Clewing and Reuter, *Der Kosovo-Konflikt,* pp. 171ff.

118. Rub, "'Phoenix aus der Asche,'" p. 53.

119. Fabian Schmidt, "Upheaval in Albania," *Current History,* vol. 97, no. 617 (March 1998): 129.

120. Vickers, *Between Serb and Albanian,* p. 275.

121. Biberaj, *Albania in Transition,* p. 330.

122. Thomas, *Serbia under Milošević,* pp. 403–404.

123. Troebst, *Conflict in Kosovo,* pp. 11, 23.

124. Pointed out in James Pettifer, "Kosova and Its Neighbours—Perspectives after the Catastrophe," *Südosteuropa Mitteilungen,* vol. 39 (1999): 88.

125. Quoted in Troebst, *Conflict in Kosovo,* p. 46.

126. *The Australian,* 22 July 1998, p. 9.

127. Re tanks and helicopter gunships, *The Times,* 8 June 1998, p. 11. Re deaths and homeless, *International Herald Tribune* (Tokyo ed.), 30 June 1998, p. 1; and *Daily Yomiuri,* 13 September 1998, p. 3.

128. International Helsinki Federation for Human Rights, *Annual Report 1999: Federal Republic of Yugoslavia (Serbia, Montenegro, Kosovo)* (Vienna, 5 July 1999), at www.ihf-hr .org/viewbinary/viewdocument.php?doc_id=6049 [accessed 29 June 2005].

129. *Frankfurter Rundschau,* 18 May 1998, p. 1.

130. Troebst, *Conflict in Kosovo,* p. 16.

131. *New York Times,* 26 February 1999, p. A7, and 14 April 1999, p. A12. This is broadly confirmed in General Wesley K. Clark, *Modern War: Bosnia, Kosovo, and the Future of Combat* (New York: PublicAffairs, 2001), p. 165.

132. Sell, *Slobodan Milošević and the Destruction of Yugoslavia,* pp. 304–305, 320. Jürgen Elsässer, editor of *Konkret* magazine, by contrast, claims that Operation Horseshoe was an invention of the German secret service. See Jürgen Elsässer, *Kriegsverbrechen: Die tödlichen Lügen der Bundesregierung und ihre Opfer im Kosovo-Konflikt,* 4th ed. (Hamburg: Konkret, 2001), pp. 67–77.

133. "Conflict with NATO Would Bring Survival of Both the Country and the People into Question, We Clearly Told the State Leadership," in *Nedeljni telegraf* (Belgrade), 4 August 1999, trans. by Snežana Lazović and posted at www.ex-yupress.com/telegraf/telegraf4.html [accessed 29 June 2005].

134. For details and documentation, see *Kosova Daily Report,* no. 1697 (19 February 1999), at www.kosova.com; and *Washington Post,* 11 April 1999, p. A26. For more details and documentation, see *Los Angeles Times,* 8 August 1999, p. A1, on LNAU.

135. Tim Judah, *Kosovo: War and Revenge* (New Haven, Conn.: Yale University Press, 2000), pp. 245–246.

136. *Illyria,* 27 January–3 February 1999, p. 1.

137. *B-92 News* (Belgrade), 20 January 2004, at www.b92.net/english/news.

138. Judah, *Kosovo,* p. 205. This account is confirmed in Sell, *Slobodan Milošević and the Destruction,* p. 297.

139. According to the recollections of Milan Milutinović, former Serbian president, and Chris Hill, U.S. ambassador to Macedonia, for "The Fall of Milošević," *BBC* (2003), aired in Norway on NRK 1 on 29 July 2003 and on NRK 2 on 30 July 2003.

140. Document signed by Col. M. Markovic, presented by Halit Barani, human rights activist and member of the Democratic League of Kosovo, to accompany his testimony at the trial of Slobodan Milošević in The Hague, as reported in *Calgary Herald,* 27 February 2002, at www.canada.com/news.

141. Re pounding of villages, *Kosova Daily Report* no. 1681 (2 February 1999), no. 1698 (20 February 1999), no. 1700 (22 February 1999), no. 1702 (24 February 1999), no. 1703 (25 February 1999), no. 1704 (26 February 1999), and no. 1707 (1 March 1999)—all at www.kosova .com. Re reinforcements, *Washington Post,* 11 April 1999, p. A26; and *Sunday Oregonian* (Portland), 18 April 1999, p. A13. Re death toll, *Frankfurter Allgemeine,* 16 March 1999, p. 1. The figure for the number of homeless is an official UN figure, taken from United Nations High Commissioner for Refugees (UNHCR), *Kosovo Crisis Update* (Geneva: UNHCR, 1999), as cited in Barbara Lopes Cardozo, Alfredo Vergara, Ferid Agani, and Carol A. Gotway, "Mental Health, Social Functioning, and Attitudes of Kosovar Albanians Following the War in Kosovo," *Journal of the American Medical Association (JAMA),* vol. 284, no. 5 (2 August 2000): 569. The *New York Times,* 17 March 1999, p. A8, offered a preliminary estimate of 200,000 on the eve of the NATO intervention, while, about the same time, the number of Albanian homeless was estimated at 450,000 by U.S. Representative Christopher Smith (R–N.J.), in "Hearing of Commission on Security and Cooperation in Europe (Helsinki Commission)," 2172 Rayburn House Office Building, Washington D.C., 6 April 1999, in *Federal News Service,* 6 April 1999, on *LNC.*

142. *Agence France Presse,* 18 February 1999, in FBIS-EEU-1999-0218.

143. *Illyria,* 31 March–3 April 2000, p. 3.

144. *New York Times,* 17 March 1999, p. A1.

145. From William Shakespeare's *Macbeth,* act 4, scene 1, lines 104–6.

146. The NATO campaign provoked a lively debate concerning its rectitude. Among those scholarly contributions to deal with this subject are Alex J. Bellamy, *Kosovo and International Society* (Houndmills: Palgrave Macmillan, 2002); Joachim Hösler, Norman Paech, and Gerhard Stuby, *Der gerechte Krieg? Neue Nato-Strategie, Völkerrecht und Westeuropäisierung des Balkans* (Bremen: Donat Verlag, 2000); Reinhard Merkel (ed.), *Der Kosovo-Krieg und das Völkerrecht* (Frankfurt-am-Main: Suhrkamp, 2000); Julie Mertus, "Beyond Borders: The Human Rights Imperative for Intervention in Kosovo," *Human Rights Review,* vol. 1, no. 2 (January–March 2000): 78–87; Markus Spillmann, "Der Westen und Kosovo: Ein leidvoller Erfahrungsprozess," and Wolfgang Ischinger, "Keine Sommerpause der deutschen Aussenpolitik: Zwischenbilanz nach dem Kosovo-Krieg," both in Angelika Volle and Werner Weidenfeld (eds.), *Der Balkan Zwischen Krise und Stabilität* (Bielefeld: W. Bertelsmann Verlag, 2002); and Rasmus Tenbergen, *Der Kosovo-Krieg: Eine gerechte Intervention?* (ILD Verlag, 2001).

147. *Miami Herald,* 3 June 1999, at www.herald.com. Tim Judah gives a slightly lower figure, reporting 848,000 Kosovar Albanians leaving the province by early June 1999. See Judah, *Kosovo,* p. 250.

148. *Wall Street Journal,* 4 June 1999, p. A7.

149. Press release from the International War Crimes Tribunal for the Former Yugoslavia, 27 May 1999, at www.latimes.com.

150. Re haggling, *Frankfurter Rundschau,* 8 June 1999, trans. in FBIS-EEU-1999-0608. Re shelling Albania, *CNN Headline News,* 6 June 1999.

151. 500, as reported in *Minneapolis Star Tribune,* 7 February 2000, at www.startribune .com: 152,000 deaths, according to a U.S. government report dated December 1999, cited in

Illyria, 14–16 December 1999, p. 1; and 12,000 deaths, according to a report prepared by Paul Spiegel and Peter Salama of the Center for Disease Control and Prevention, Atlanta, Georgia, dated June 2000, cited in *Illyria,* 27–29 June 2000, p. 2. As early as August 1999, Pajazit Nushi, chair of Kosovo's oldest human rights group, the Council for the Defense of Human Rights and Freedoms, claimed to have a register of more than 10,000 names of persons confirmed to have been killed by Serbian forces and said that the list continued to grow longer. Re Nushi's list, see *Los Angeles Times,* 8 August 1999, p. A1, on LNAU.

152. Vesna Pešić, in interview with *Le Monde* (Paris), 17 June 1999, trans. in FBIS-EEU-1999-0617.

153. Trajković, quoted in *Beta news agency,* 11 August 1999, trans. in FBIS-EEU-1999-0811. Among the many books to have been published about Kosovo in the wake of NATO's aerial campaign, one may mention Jens Reuter and Konrad Clewing (eds.), *Der Kosovo Konflikt. Ursachen, Verlauf, Perspektiven* (Klagenfurt: Wieser Verlag, 2000); Tony Weymouth and Stanley Henig (eds.), *The Kosovo Crisis: The Last American War in Europe?* (London: Reuters, 2001); and Mary Buckley and Sally N. Cummings (eds.), *Kosovo: Perceptions of War and Its Aftermath* (London: Continuum, 2001).

154. *Vreme,* 8 March 1993, pp. 22–24, trans. in FBIS, *Daily Report* (Eastern Europe), 6 April 1993, p.51.

155. *Agence France Presse,* 3 May 1996, in FBIS, *Daily Report* (Eastern Europe), 3 May 1996, p. 25.

156. The remainder of this section follows closely, albeit in abbreviated form, the text in my *Balkan Babel,* chap. 14.

157. "Montenegrin Government Adopts Platform Redefining Relations with Serbia," *Tanjug,* 6 August 1999, at www.freeserbia.net/News.html. See also Olja Obradović, "Čekajući demokratsku Srbiju," *Helsinška povelja,* vol. 4, no. 20–21 (September–October 1999): 11–12.

158. Zoran Radulović, "Montenegrin Public Opinion at a Turning Point," *AIM-Press,* 4 October 1999, at www.aimpress.ch, p. 1.

159. *Volksblatt* (Würzburg), 25 May 2000, at www.volksblatt-wuerzburg.de. For background, see Zoran Radulović, "Život na klačkalići," *Monitor* (Podgorica), no. 500, at www.monitor.cg.yu/.

160. *Die Welt,* 3 November 1999, at www.welt.de/daten; and Montena-fax news agency (Podgorica), 27 March 2000, in *BBC Monitoring Europe—Political,* 27 March 2000, on LNAU.

161. Re blockade of medicine, *Agence France Presse,* 8 March 2000, on LNAU; also *OÖNachrichten,* 7 March 2000, p. 4, at www.nachrichten.at [accessed 29 June 2005]. Re total blockade, Montena-fax news agency, 8 March 2000, in *BBC Summary of World Broadcasts,* 10 March 2000, on LNAU. Re Djukanović's concerns, *Der Standard* (Vienna), 20 March 2000, in *BBC Monitoring Europe—Political,* 20 March 2000, on LNAU.

162. Re defecting, *BH Press news agency* (Sarajevo), 5 April 2000, trans. in *BBC Summary of World Broadcasts,* 7 April 2000, on LNAU. Re new military police, *Agence France Presse,* 8 April 2000, on LNAU.

163. UPI, 1 April 2000, on LNAU. See also *Die Presse,* 31 March 2000, at www.diepresse.at.

164. TV Crna Gora (Podgorica), 13 March 2000, in *BBC Monitoring Europe—Political,* 13 March 2000, on LNAU.

165. Re "loyal forces," *Frankfurter Rundschau,* 16 March 2000, at www.fr-aktuell.de/english/401/t401013.htm. Re "illegal" television station, *Deutsche Presse-Agentur,* 14 March 2000, on LNAU. Re verbal attacks, *Deutsche Presse-Agentur,* 16 March 2000, on LNAU.

166. The opposition has taken the threat seriously. See "Režim spreman za dramatične sukobe," *Blic,* 6 March 2000, at www.blic.co.yu [accessed 6 March 2000]. For an extended dis-

cussion of Montenegro's situation in the late Milošević era, see Milan Popović, *Crnogorska alternativa: Neizvesnost promene* (Podgorica: Vijesti, 2000).

167. See text of the law in *Politika,* 22 October 1998, pp. 21–22.

168. Beta news agency, 31 January 2000, trans. in *BBC Summary of World Broadcasts,* 2 February 2000, on LNAU.

169. *Deutsche Presse Agentur,* 6 August 2000, on LNAU.

170. Re Kosovo, *FoNet news agency,* 26 July 2000, trans. in *BBC Summary of World Broadcasts,* 28 July 2000, on LNAU. Re Hungary, Hungarian TV2 satellite service (Budapest), 29 July 2000, trans. in *BBC Summary of World Broadcasts,* 1 August 2000, on LNAU.

171. Veran Matić, "Independent Serbian Media Should be Supported," *International Herald Tribune* (Tel Aviv ed.), 16 June 2000, p. 6.

172. *Beta news agency,* 30 March 2000, trans. in *BBC Monitoring Europe—Political,* 30 March 2000, on LNAU; and *Agence France Presse,* 11 April 2000, on *LNAU.*

173. Radio B2-92, 11 April 2000, trans. in *BBC Summary of World Broadcasts,* 13 April 2000, on *LNAU.*

174. State radio claimed that only 30,000 persons took part. *Radio Belgrade,* 14 April 2000, trans. in *BBC Summary of World Broadcasts,* 17 April 2000, on LNAU. Re "at least 100,000," Radio B2-92, 14 April 2000, trans. in *BBC Summary of World Broadcasts,* 17 April 2000, on LNAU. Re "nearly 200,000," *Beta news agency,* 14 April 2000, trans. in *BBC Summary of World Broadcasts,* 17 April 2000, on LNAU. AFP reported that "more than 70,000 people" took part in the protest: see *Agence France Presse,* 14 April 2000, on LNAU. DPA accepted the opposition figure and reported attendance at "more than 100,000 people": see *Deutsche Presse Agentur,* 14 April 2000, on LNAU. The *New York Times* reported "at least 100,000 people" in attendance. See *New York Times,* 15 April 2000, p. A3.

175. "Dobar dan za srpsku opoziciju," in *Vreme,* no. 485 (22 April 2000): 6–8.

176. *taz* (Berlin), 12 May 2000, p. 10, at www.taz.de/tpl/2000/05/12/a0195.fr; *Die Presse,* 19 May 2000, at www.diepresse.at; *Main Post newsline,* 19 May 2000, at www.mainpost.de; *Holsteiner Courier,* 19 May 2000, on Powerball; *tirol online,* 19 May 2000, at www.tirol.com; *Berliner Zeitung,* 20 May 2000, at www.berlinonline.de; *Holsteiner Courier,* 20 May 2000, on Powerball; *Süddeutsche Zeitung* (Munich), 20 May 2000, at www.sueddeutsche.de; *taz,* 22 May 2000, at www.taz.de; *Beta news agency,* 24 May 2000, trans. in *BBC Summary of World Broadcasts,* 27 May 2000, on LNAU; *Beta news agency,* 25 May 2000, trans. in *BBC Summary of World Broadcasts,* 27 May 2000, on LNAU; "Srbi skloni pobuni," in *NIN* (Belgrade), 25 May 2000, at www.nin.co.yu/2000-05/25/12882.html; and *Financial Times,* 27 May 2000, p. 6, on LNAU.

177. Re arresting opposition activists, *Berliner Zeitung,* 19 May 2000, at www.berlinonline.de/aktuelles; *SonntagsZeitung,* 21 May 2000, at www.sonntagszeitung.ch; and *Die Presse,* 23 May 2000, at www.diepresse.at. Re accusing opposition leaders, *Minneapolis Star Tribune,* 19 May 2000, at www.startribune.com.

178. Re the beating, *Minneapolis Star Tribune,* 24 May 2000, at www.startribune.com; and *Süddeutsche Zeitung,* 25 May 2000, at www.sueddeutsche.de. Re the closure, UPI, 26 May 2000, on LNAU; Radio B2-92, 25 May 2000, trans. in *BBC Summary of World Broadcasts,* 27 May 2000, on LNAU; and "Profesori Beogradskog univerziteta o odluci da se okonče nastava," in *Blic-online,* 27 May 2000, at blic.gates9696.com/danas/broj/strane/drustvo.htm [accessed 27 May 2000]. For background, see also "Za 26. Maj najavljen studentski miting," in *Pobjeda* (Podgorica), 24 May 2000, at www.pobjeda.co.yu/arhiva/maj_00/2405/rubrike/politika/politika_13.htm.

179. Re Pavle's support, Radio B2-92, 25 May 2000, trans. in *BBC Summary of World Broadcasts,* 27 May 2000, on LNAU. Re contempt for tribunal, *Tanjug* (Belgrade), 24 May 2000, trans. in *BBC Summary of World Broadcasts,* 26 May 2000, on LNAU.

180. *Beta news agency,* 25 May 2000, trans. in *BBC Summary of World Broadcasts,* 27 May 2000, on LNAU; and UPI, 14 June 2000, on LNAU.

181. Tanjug, 5 July 2000, trans. in *BBC Summary of World Broadcasts,* 7 July 2000, on LNAU; *Beta news agency,* 6 July 2000, trans. in *BBC Summary of World Broadcasts,* 8 July 2000; and Tanjug, 6 July 2000, in *BBC Summary of World Broadcasts,* 8 July 2000, on LNAU.

182. Governmental draft submitted to the Montenegrin parliament on 7 July, as quoted in *Agence France Presse,* 7 July 2000, on LNAU. See also *Stuttgarter Zeitung,* 11 July 2000, at www.stuttgarter-zeitung.de.

183. *Vjesnik,* 22 August 2000, at www.vjesnik.hr/html/2000/08/22/.

184. Stambolić, quoted in *Sunday Times* (London), 27 August 2000, on LNAU.

185. "Nastavlja se istraga povodom nestanka Ivana Stambolića," *Politika,* 1 September 2000, at www.politika.co.yu; *Christian Science Monitor,* 29 August 2000, p. 7, on LNAU; and UPI, 30 August 2000, on LNAU.

186. *Baltimore Sun,* 25 April 2003, at www.sunspot.net. Police arrested four JSO members and brought charges against Milošević, by then already standing trial in The Hague, as well as certain associates of his. See also *Scotsman,* 29 March 2003, at news.scotsman.com; *The Guardian,* 29 March 2003, at www.guardian.co.uk; Batić Bačević, "Prva i poslednja žrtva," *NIN,* no. 2727 (3 April 2003): 10–11; and *Glas javnosti,* 24 April 2003, at www.glas-javnosti.co.yu.

187. *Washington Post,* 15 October 2000, p. A30.

188. See the report in *Aftenposten* (Oslo), 9 September 2000, at www.aftenposten.no.

189. Pavlović, *Akteri i modeli,* p. 227.

190. Official results in *Borba,* 27 September 2000, at www.borba.co.yu; opposition figures as reported in *Monitor* (Podgorica), no. 519 (29 September 2000), at www.monitor.cg.yu.

191. Quoted in *Star Tribune,* 25 September 2000, at www.startribune.com. See also *Oslobodjenje* (Sarajevo), 23/24 September 2000, p. 9.

192. *La Repubblica* (Rome), 25 September 2000, at www.repubblica.it; *Baltimore Sun,* 28 September 2000, p. 1A; *Washington Post,* 29 September 2000, p. A22; *Glas javnosti,* 2 October 2000, at www.glas-javnosti.co.yu; and *Die Presse,* 2 October 2000, at www.diepresse.at.

193. *Glas javnosti,* 1 October 2000, at arhiva.glas-javnosti.co.yu.

194. *Washington Post,* 15 October 2000, p. A30.

195. Re the police, *New York Times,* 5 October 2000, p. A1; re the army, *Süddeutsche Zeitung* (Munich), 22 September 2000, at www.sueddeutsche.de.

196. CWI Statement (Committee for a Workers' International), October 2000, at www.slp.at/cwi/statement_servien.html [accessed 29 June 2005]; and *The Militant,* vol. 64, no. 39 (16 October 2000), at www.ilor.com.

197. *Beta news agency,* 5 October 2000, trans. in FBIS-EEU-2000-1005, on *World News Connection.*

198. Re the strike leader, *Minneapolis Star Tribune,* 3 October 2000, at www.startribune.com. Re the list of 50, UPI, 1 November 2000, on nexis.com.

199. *Washington Post,* 15 October 2000, p. A30.

200. See the detailed account in *New York Times,* 6 October 2000, pp. A1, A14–A15.

201. The Federal Election Commission "admitted its error," as *Glas javnosti* put it. See *Glas javnosti,* 6 October 2000, at arhiva.glas-javnosti.co.yu.

202. *Deutsche Presse-Agentur,* 3 November 2000, on nexis.com.

203. See "Demokratski haos," in *Nezavisna Svetlost,* no. 265 (22–29 October 2000), at www.svetlost.co.yu.

204. Details in *Agence France Presse,* 6 November 2000, on nexis.com.

205. Božo Nikolić, "Milošević kao prioritet," *Monitor* (Podgorica), no. 530 (15 December 2000), at www.monitor.cg.yu.

206. *Los Angeles Times,* 5 January 2001, at www.latimes.com.

207. *Agence France Presse,* 22 October 2000, on nexis.com.

208. Bulatović, quoted in *Beta news agency,* 15 December 2000, trans. in FBIS-EEU-2000-1215.

209. *The Observer* (London), 31 December 2000, p. 19, on nexis.com; and *Glas javnosti,* 9 January 2001, at arhiva.glas-javnosti.co.yu.

210. Re collapse of the Montenegrin government, *Netzeitung,* 28 December 2000, at www.netzeitung.de; and UPI, 31 December 2000, on nexis.com. Re Montenegrin referendum, see the comments by Dragan Šoć, leader of the People's Party, in *Glas javnosti,* 5 January 2001, at arhiva.glas-javnosti.co.yu.

211. *Večernje novosti* (Belgrade), 4 January 2001, trans. in FBIS-EEU-2001-0104.

212. *Pobjeda* (Podgorica), 25 January 2001, at www.pobjeda.co.yu; and *Vijesti on-line* (Podgorica), 26 January 2001, at www.vijesti.cg.yu.

213. *Telegraf* (Belgrade), 24 April 2001, p. 3. See also *Die Presse* (Vienna), 24 April 2001, pp. 1, 4. For further discussion of Serb-Montenegrin relations, see Reneo Lukić, "From the Federal Republic of Yugoslavia to the Union of Serbia and Montenegro," in Sabrina P. Ramet and Vjeran Pavlaković (eds.), *Serbia since 1989: Politics and Society under Milošević and After* (Seattle and London: University of Washington Press, 2005), pp. 54–94.

214. *Agence France Presse,* 19 February 2001, on nexis.com.

215. Re Isakov, *Beta news agency,* 8 January 2001, trans. in FBIS-EEU-2001-0108. Re autonomy, *Neue Zürcher Zeitung,* 21 October 2000, p. 7, in nexis.com.

216. *Nedeljni telegraf* (Belgrade), 18 April 2001, p. 7.

217. *Beta news agency,* 13 December 2000, trans. in FBIS-EEU-2000-1213.

218. On Bosnia, see *Glas javnosti,* 16 December 2000, at www.glas-javnosti.co.yu.

219. *Washington Post,* 29 November 2000, p. A32, on nexis.com; and *Glas javnosti,* 20 December 2000, at www.glas-javnosti.co.yu.

220. *Beta news agency,* 11 December 2000, on FBIS-EEU-2000-1211.

221. *Glas javnosti,* 24 December 2000, at arhiva.glas-javnosti.co.yu; *Washington Post,* 25 December 2000, p. A30; and *Vjesnik,* 27 December 2000, at www.vjesnik.hr/html.

222. *Glas javnosti,* 19 January 2001, at arhiva.glas-javnosti.co.yu.

223. Re military purges, *Agence France Presse,* 30 December 2000, on nexis.com. Re arrest of Milošević in January, *Glas javnosti,* 27 January 2000, at arhiva.glas-javnosti.co.yu, and *Ostsee-Zeitung,* 29 December 2000, at www.ostsee-zeitung.de. Re arrest of Milošević in March, *Vjesnik,* 23 January 2001, at www.vjesnik.hr/html. Re crimes against humanity, *Beta news agency,* 19 December 2000, on FBIS-EEU-2000-1218. Re trial in Belgrade, *Glas javnosti,* 4 January 2001, at arhiva.glas-javnosti.co.yu. Re pressures for the arrest of Milošević, "Uhapsite Miloševića," in *Nezavisna Svetlost,* no. 273 (16–23 December 2000), at www.svetlost.co.yu, and *Agence France Presse,* 6 January 2001, on nexis.com. Re visit by Del Ponte, *Glas javnosti,* 25 January 2001, at www.glas-javnosti.co.yu, *International Herald Tribune* (Paris), 25 January 2001, p. 5, and *Chicago Tribune,* 25 January 2001, at www.chicagotribune.com/news. See also the editorial in the *Washington Post,* 26 January 2001, p. A22.

224. Re handful, *Beta news agency,* 1 March 2001, trans. in FBIS-EEU-2001-0301. Re the failed siege, *Boston Globe,* 31 March 2001, pp. A1, A10; *New York Times,* 31 March 2001, pp. A1, A6; and *Washington Post,* 31 March 2001, pp. A1, A16.

225. *New York Times,* 1 April 2001, pp. 1, 6.

226. *Aftenposten,* 5 April 2001, at www.aftenposten.no.

227. BBC News, 25 May 2001, 14:31 GMT, 15:31 UK, at news.bbc.co.uk/hi/english/world/europe/newsid_1351000/1351317.stm; and Maroje Mihovlović, "Puć protiv Koštunice," *Nacional* (Zagreb), no. 292 (19 June 2001): 32–34.

228. *Jutarnji list* (Zagreb), 23 June 2001, p. 12; *Slobodna Dalmacija* (Split), 23 June 2001, p. 6; and *Jutarnji list,* 25 June 2001, p. 9.

229. *Jutarnji list,* 20 June 2001, p. 12.

230. *Vjesnik,* 25 June 2001, p. 1, citing a report in the London *Sunday Times.*

231. Milošević, quoted in *Glas javnosti,* 29 June 2001, at www.glas-javnosti.co.yu.

232. Poll results reported in *Beta news agency,* 17 May 2001, trans. in FBIS-EEU-2001-0517, on *World News Connection.*

233. See Željko Cvijanović, "Rat za policiju," *Dani* (Sarajevo), 17 August 2001, pp. 32–33. For more details concerning the Koštunica-Djindjić rivalry, see Obrad Kesić, "An Airplane with Eighteen Pilots: Serbia after Milošević," in Ramet and Pavlaković, *Serbia since 1989*), pp. 95–121.

234. On Koštunica, see Norman Cigar, *Vojislav Koštunica and Serbia's Future* (London: Saqi Books, 2001).

235. International Crisis Group (ICG), "Serbia after Djindjić," in *Bosnia Report* (London), n. s. no. 32–34 (December 2002–July 2003): 42.

236. For Djindjić's denial, see *Novi list* (Rijeka), 24 February 2002, at www.novilist.hr.

237. For details concerning all of these regional challenges, see Sabrina P. Ramet and Philip W. Lyon, "Discord, Denial, Dysfunction: The Serbian-Montenegrin-Kosovar Triangle," *Problems of Post-Communism,* vol. 49, no. 5 (September–October 2002): especially pp. 1–2, 12–16.

238. *Glas javnosti,* 20 September 2001 and 15 February 2003—both at arhiva.glas-javnosti.co.yu.

239. *The Scotsman,* 12 November 2001, at news.scotsman.com.

240. Davor Pašalić, "Ratko Mladić živi u ulici Blagoja Parovića u Beogradu," *Nacional,* no. 316 (4 December 2001): 36.

241. *Magyar Nemzet* (Budapest), as summarized in *Glas javnosti,* 13 November 2001, at arhiva.glas-javnosti.co.yu.

242. Dragan Bujošević, "Crvenkape i vukovi," *NIN,* no. 2655 (15 November 2001): 12–13; and *Glas javnosti,* 15 November 2001, at www.glas-javnosti.co.yu. See also *Bosanska pošta—Bosnisk post* (Mysen), 16 November 2001, p. 4.

243. *Glas javnosti,* 19 November 2001, at arhiva.glas-javnosti.co.yu; and *The Independent,* 26 March 2003, 28 March 2003, and 29 March 2003—all at news.independent.co.uk. See also *The Guardian,* 28 March 2003, at www.guardian.co.uk.

244. For discussion of organized crime in the Balkans, see Norbert Mappes-Niediek, *Balkan Mafia. Staaten in der Hand des Verbrechens—Eine Gefahr für Europa* (Berlin: Ch. Links Verlag, 2003), especially pp. 24–66.

245. *The Independent,* 29 March 2003, at news.independent.co.uk. According to a statement by Serbian deputy prime minister Žarko Korač, Stambolić's assassins were paid 100,000 DM to liquidate the retired politician and dispose of his remains. On this point, see *Novi list* (Rijeka), 31 March 2003, at www.novilist.hr.

246. Reinhold Vetter, "Kuda ideš Srbijo? Serbien nach dem erfolglosen Präsidentenwahl und dem Mord an Djindjić," *Osteuropa,* vol. 53, no. 4 (April 2003): 483–484.

247. Ibid., p. 484; and *Glas javnosti,* 15 October 2002, at www.glas-javnosti.co.yu.

248. Vetter, "Kuda ideš Srbijo?" p. 484.

249. Regarding Šljivančanin, see *Večernji list,* 14 June 2003, at www.vecernji-list.hr.

250. *BBC News,* 24 February 2003, at news.bbc.co.uk; and *The Guardian,* 13 March 2003, at www.guardian.co.uk.

251. *Frankfurter Rundschau,* 12 March 2003, at www.frankfurterrundschau.de; *la Repubblica* (Rome), 12 March 2003, at www.repubblica,it; *Berlingske Tidende* (Copenhagen), 12 March 2003, at www.berlingske.dk; *Novi list,* 13 March 2003, at www.novilist.hr; and *Blic online* (Belgrade), 13 March 2003, at www.blic.co.yu. Re Jovanović, see *Glas javnosti,* 26 March 2003, at www.glas-javnosti.co.yu.

252. *The Independent,* 9 April 2003, at news.independent.co.uk.

253. Simatović was subsequently turned over to the ICTY. See *Glas javnosti,* 3 June 2003, at www.glas-javnosti.co.yu .

254. *The Guardian,* 10 April 2003, p. 6.

255. *Vjesnik,* 18 March 2003, at www.vjesnik.hr; *Glas javnosti,* 18 March 2003, at www.glas-javnosti.co.yu; *Frankfurter Rundschau,* 26 March 2003, at www.frankfurterrundschau.de; "Zemun Gang Leaders Dušan 'Šiptar' Spasojević, Mile 'Kum' Luković Killed during Arrest," 27 March 2003, at www.serbia.sr.gov.yu; *Glas javnosti,* 28 March 2003), at arhiva.glas-javnosti.co.yu; *Glas javnosti,* 30 March 2003, 1 April 2003, and 2 April 2003—all at www.glas-javnosti.co.yu; and "Serbian Police have taken in 7,000 during state of emergency," 4 April 2003, at www.serbia.sr.gov.yu.

256. Re custody, *Berlingske Tidende,* 3 May 2004, at www.berlingske.dk. Re providing information, *Beta news agency,* carried by B-92, 31 March 2003, at www.b92.net/english.

257. "Crackdown on Organised Crime Drawing to a Close," 29 March 2003, at www.serbia.sr.gov/yu.

258. *Adresseavisen* (Trondheim), 27 March 2003, p. 6.

259. Re destabilizing, Slobodan Ćuparić, "Srbija posle Djindjića—Obnova institucija," *Nezavisna Svetlost,* no. 391 (22–29 March 2003), at www.svetlost.co.yu. Re power vacuum, "Gefährliches Machtvakuum in Serbien," *Neue Zürcher Zeitung,* 13 March 2003, at www.nzz.ch.

260. *Glas javnosti,* 29 December 2003, at www.glas-javnosti.co.yu; *Jutarnji list* (Zagreb), 29 December 2003, p. 9; and Željko Cvijanović, "Serbia: New Regime Faces Instability from Start," *IWPR,* BCR no. 475 (8 January 2004), at www.iwpr.net, p. 1.

261. *Frankfurter Rundschau,* 20 February 2004, at www.fr-aktuell.de.

262. Sonja Biserko, "Comment: Backsliding in Serbia," *IWPR,* BCR no. 491 (8 April 2004), at www.iwpr.net, pp. 1–2. Re political currents in Vojvodina, see Emil Kerenji, "Vojvodina since 1988," in Ramet and Pavlaković, *Serbia since 1989,* pp. 350–380.

263. *Oslobodjenje* (Sarajevo), 3–4 April 2004, p. 9. Within two weeks, the Constitutional Court suspended the law, pending a review of its constitutionality. On this point, see *Glas javnosti,* 16 April 2004, at arhiva.glas-javnosti.co.yu.

264. *Associated Press,* 21 February 2004, at , www.washingtonpost.com; Saša Grubanović, "Serbia and Montenegro: Helping and Unhelpful," *Transitions Online–TOL* (Prague), 5 April 2004, at www.tol.cz, p. 1; and *Dnevni avaz* (Sarajevo), 5 April 2004, p. 14.

265. Re combating organized crime, *Dnevnik* (Novi Sad), 27 April 2004, at www.dnevnik.co.yu. Re "underworld gang," *The Independent,* 10 February 2004, at news.independent.co.uk. Re killing of key witness, *Nezavisne novine* (Banja Luka), 9 March 2004, at www.nezavisne.com.

266. *Vjesnik* (Zagreb), 9 December 2003, at www.vjesnik.hr.

267. Nedjeljko Rudović, "Montenegro Plans Independence Vote," *IWPR,* BCR no. 492 (16 April 2004), at www.iwpr.net; and Nedjeljko Rudović, "Montenegro Backs Off Separation Vote," *IWPR,* BCR no. 497 (14 May 2004), at www.iwpr.net.

268. *Politika,* 16 March 2004, at www.politika.co.yu; Vladimir Sudar, "Serbia May Return Right-Wing President," *IWPR,* BCR no. 491 (8 April 2004), at www.iwpr.net; Slobodan

Vučetić, "Comment: Far-Right President No Threat to Serbia," *IWPR*, BCR no. 491 (8 April 2004), at www.iwpr.net; and *Glas javnosti*, 9 April 2004, at arhiva.glas-javnosti.co.yu.

269. *Glas javnosti*, 14 June 2004, at www.glas-javnosti.co.yu.

270. Srboljub Bogdanović, "Centlmeni u Srbiji," *NIN*, no. 2792 (1 July 2004): 10–11. Regarding Boris Tadić's popularity, see *Večernje novosti*, 24 July 2004, p. 2.

271. According to Michael Polt, the American ambassador in Belgrade, as reported in *Glas javnosti*, 2 September 2004, at arhiva.glas-javnosti.co.yu.

272. *Vjesnik*, 9 March 2004, at www.vjesnik.hr.

273. ICG, "Serbia after Djindjić," p. 42.

274. On the continuing strength of nationalist culture, see the commemoration of the first anniversary of Arkan's death, as reported in *Glas javnosti*, 13 January 2001, at arhiva.glas-javnosti.co.yu.

275. Dubravka Stojanović, "The New History Text Books," *Bosnia Report*, n. s. no. 32–34 (December 2002–July 2003): 40.

276. *Glas javnosti*, 7 September 2004; 10 September 2004; and 12 September 2004—all at arhiva.glas-javnosti.co.yu; and "'Anti-Darwin' Serb Minister Quits," *BBC News*, 16 September 2004, at newsvote.bbc.co.uk. See also "Serb Schools Told to Drop Darwin," *BBC News*, 7 September 2004, at newsvote.bbc.co.uk.

277. ICG, "Serbia after Djindjic," pp. 43–44.

278. Fareed Zakaria, *The Future of Freedom: Illiberal Democracy at Home and Abroad* (New York: W. W. Norton, 2003), p. 248.

279. Re Kosovo, see *Glas javnosti* (2 March 2005), at arhiva.glas-javnosti.co.yu, *Dnevnik* (Novi Sad), 3 March 2005, at www.dnevnik.co.yu, and *Glas javnosti* (30 April–2 May 2005), at www.glas-javnosti.co.yu. Re the Krajina, see Davor Pašalić, "Povratak Velike Srbije: Obnova Krajine po Šešeljevu scenariju," *Nacional*, no. 485 (1 March 2005), pp. 12–17.

280. *Danas* (Belgrade), 11 April 2005, p. 5; *International Herald Tribune* (Paris), 14 September 2004, p. 3; and Nebojša Milosavljević, "Srbija nepravna država," *Republika*, vol. 17, nos. 348–349 (1–31 January 2005), at www.republika.co.yu/348-349/16.html [accessed 1 February 2005], pp. 1–7.

281. "Hag je ključ," *Politika* (1 February 2005), at www.politika.co.yu [accessed 1 February 2005].

282. *The Independent* (12 April 2005), at news.independent.co.uk. See also *Glas javnosti* (28 February 2005), at arhiva.glas-javnosti.co.yu.

283. *Novi list* (12 April 2005), at www.novilist.hr.

284. Re the law, see *Glas javnosti* (11 December 2004), at arhiva.glas-javnosti.co.yu; and "Četnički zakon," *Republika*, vol. 17, nos. 348–349 (1–31 January 2005), at www.republika.co.yu/348-349/09.html [accessed 1 February 2005].

285. *Večernji list* (25 January 2005), at www.vecernji-list.hr.

286. *Glas javnosti* (22 April 2005), at www.glas-javnosti.co.yu.

287. For example, by Željko Cvijanović, in "Serbia: EU Green Light Would Secure Wobbly Government," in *IWPR*, BCR no. 548 (March 2005), at www.iwpr.net [accessed 29 March 2005].

288. Boško Blahović and Bogoljub Mihajlović, *Priroda i društvo, za 3. razred osnovne škole* (Belgrade: Zavod za udžbenike i nastavna sredstva, 1997), p. 57.

289. *Vjesnik* (Zagreb), 17 September 2001, at www.vjesnik.hr..

290. See Wolfgang Höpken, "Between Civic Identity and Nationalism: History Textbooks in East-Central and Southeastern Europe," in Sabrina P. Ramet and Davorka Matić (eds.),

Democratic Transition in Croatia: Value Transformation, Education, Media (manuscript under review).

18. UNMIK, KFOR, and the Future of Kosovo

1. "Text of Kosovo Military Technical Agreement," posted at 12:01 A.M., EDT Thursday, 10 June 1999, at www.herald.com/herald/content/archive/news/kosovo/docs/071148.htm.

2. As quoted in *International Herald Tribune* (Paris), 30 October 2000, p. 9.

3. Michael Steiner, the chief foreign policy adviser to German chancellor Gerhard Schroeder, citing the written blueprint for the campaign drawn up by Serbian authorities in late 1999 and known as Operation Horseshoe, a copy of which was said to be in the possession of the German government, pointed to indications that the Yugoslav Army and Interior Ministry police were moving forces into position in mid-March 1999, in preparation for using the expected NATO attack as a cover for carrying the plans to fruition. See *Los Angeles Times,* 8 August 1999, on *Lexis-Nexis Academic Universe* (LNAU). Some German observers have questioned whether there was actually an Operation Horseshoe, although they do not deny that Serb forces were brought into position on the eve of NATO's deadline, with the precise intention of using the NATO campaign as a pretext to attack the Albanians. See Heinz Loquai, "Dichtung und Wahrheit in der NATO-Kriegsführung: Der Hufeisenplan" (Amselfeld.com, May 2000); and Franz-Josef Hutsch, "Kritische Töne. Zum Hufeisenplan," *Hamburger Abendblatt,* 21 March 2000, reprinted in *Friedenspolitischer Ratschlag,* at www.uni-kassel.de/fb10/frieden/aktuell/Hufeisen.html.

4. *Illyria* (The Bronx), 14–16 September 1999, p. 3.

5. $2 billion according to the European Commission, as cited in ibid.; $5 billion according to the *Wall Street Journal,* 21 June 1999, p. A21.

6. *Scotland on Sunday,* 8 October 2000, at news.scotsman.com.

7. *Sächsische Zeitung* (Dresden), 9 September 1999, p. 4.

8. Re bottlenecks, *Croatia Weekly* (Zagreb), 28 January 2000, p. 10. Re private businesses, Robert Muharremi, Lulzim Peci, Leon Malazogu, Verena Knaus, and Teuta Murati, *Administration and Governance in Kosovo: Lessons Learned and Lessons to Be Learned* (Priština/Geneva: Center for Applied Studies in International Negotiations, January 2003), p. 42.

9. The study was released at the end of April 2000. See *Illyria,* 28 April–1 May 2000, p. 3.

10. Krenare Kurtishi and Mevlyde Salihu, "Jobless Kosovars Head Abroad," *Institute for War and Peace Reporting (IWPR),* BCR no. 501 (3 June 2004), at www.iwpr.net; confirmed in *The Guardian* (London), 22 June 2004, at www.guardian.co.uk.

11. Confirmed deaths according to Paul Spiegel and Peter Salama of the Center for Disease Control and Prevention in Atlanta, Georgia, as cited in RFE/RL, *Newsline,* 23 June 2000, at www.rferl.org/newsline, p. 14. For a Serbian commentary on the numbers of victims, see Roksanda Ninčić, "Zločini na Kosovu: U potrazi za pravdom," *Vreme* (Belgrade), 20 November 1999, pp. 9–13.

12. *Illyria,* 6–9 August 1999, p. 1.

13. Re Albanian hostages, *International Herald Tribune,* 1 September 1999, p. 6, on LNAU. Re Serbs fleeing Kosovo, *New York Times,* 25 July 1999, p. 1; and *Politika* (Belgrade), 30 August 1999, pp. 1, 15. About 100,000 Serbs were thought to remain in Kosovo as of January 2000, according to a UN source. See *Illyria,* 14–17 January 2000, p. 3.

14. Fled, *Minneapolis Star Tribune,* 14 November 2001, at www.startribune.com; usurped, *Borba* (Belgrade), 20 December 2001, at www.borba.co.yu; and sold, *Borba,* 6 March 2003, at www.borba.co.yu.

15. *UNMIK News Coverage,* 11 March 2003, at www.unmikonline.org.

16. Jolyon Naegele, "Kosovo's Libraries Cleansed of Albanian Books," *Bosnia Report,* n.s. no. 19/20 (October–December 2000), at www.bosnia.org.uk. See also the report in *Kosova Daily Report,* 19 March 1996, in FBIS, *Daily Report* (Eastern Europe), 20 March 1996, pp. 60–61.

17. *Illyria,* 3–6 December 1999, p. 3.

18. Naegele, "Kosovo's Libraries Cleansed."

19. Llazar Semini, "News from Kosovo," *Central Europe Review,* vol. 2, no. 24 (19 June 2000), at www.ce-review.org/00/22/Kosovonews24.html, p. 4. See also *Revija 92* (Belgrade), 20 August 1999, p. 5.

20. *Leipziger Volkszeitung,* 8 September 1999, p. 2.

21. *UNMIK Police—United Nations Mission in Kosovo,* "Facts & Figures—Police Strength" (updated 31 October 2000), at www.civpol.org/unmik/strength.htm.

22. "Kosovo Justice System Falls Short of International Standards," 18 October 2000, in *Bringing Peace to Kosovo—News Reports,* at www.un.org/peace/kosovo/news/kosovo2.htm.

23. Muharremi et al., *Administration and Governance in Kosovo,* pp. 22, 20.

24. *UNMIK Police—Crime Statistics* (updated 23 September 2000), at www.civpol.org/ummik/statistics.htm. Between 200 and 400 Serb civilians are thought to have been killed in Kosovo between June and December 1999. See Peter Salama, Paul Spiegel, Marci Van Dyke, Laura Phelps, and Caroline Wilkinson, "Mental Health and Nutritional Status among the Adult Serbian Minority in Kosovo," *JAMA,* vol. 284, no. 5 (2 August 2000): 578.

25. See Norbert Mappes-Niedliek, *Balkan-Mafia: Staaten in der Hand des Verbrechens—Eine Gefahr für Europa* (Berlin: Ch. Links Verlag, 2003), especially pp. 83–103, 158–162.

26. Barbara Lopes Cardozo, Alfredo Vergara, Ferid Agani, and Carol A. Gotway, "Mental Health, Social Functioning, and Attitudes of Kosovar Albanians Following the War in Kosovo," *JAMA,* vol. 284, no. 5 (2 August 2000), pp. 577, 572.

27. Re paramilitaries not being permitted, see remarks by Gen. Wesley Clark in "KFOR Press Conference" (Priština, 24 June 1999), at www.nato.int/kosovo/press/1999/b990624p.htm. Re Albanians not being signatories to the agreement, *Wall Street Journal,* 6 July 1999, p. A11.

28. *New York Times,* 20 June 1999, pp. 1, 10.

29. See "KFOR Press Update" for 22 October, 23 October, 24 October, 25 October, 26 October, 28 October, 31 October, and 1 November 2000—all at www.nato.int/kfor/ [accessed autumn 2000]; "Joint UNMIK Police/KFOR Operation," 14 October 2000, at *UNMIK Police,* Daily Press Update, at www.civpol.org/unmik/PressUpdateArchi/news/141000.htm; "New Weapons and Ammunition Destruction Programme," 12 February 2002, and "KFOR Press Release," 18 March 2002—both at *KFOR Online* homepage, www.nato.int/kfor; and *Glas javnosti* (Belgrade), 12 February 2003, at www.glas-javnosti.co.yu.

30. *Illyria,* 3–6 November 2000, pp. 1, 3.

31. *Daily Telegraph* (London), 30 November 2000, at www.telegraph.co.uk. See also *Daily Telegraph,* 21 December 2000, at www.telegraph.co.uk.

32. Re deadline, "Transcript of Press Conference by Lt Col Robin Clifford, KFOR," 18 June 1999, at www.nato.int/kosovo/press/1999/b990618p.htm; and "KFOR News Conference by Lt. Col. Robert Clifford," 20 June 1999, at www.nato.int/kosovo/press/1999/b990620p.htm. (The KFOR press office seems to have been confused as to whether Colonel Clifford's first name was Robin or Robert. It is Robin.) Re "broad compliance," "KFOR Press Statement by Major Jan Joosten," 2 July 1999, at www.nato.int/kosovo/press/1999/k990702a.htm.

33. "KFOR Press Statement Delivered by Lieutenant-Commander Louis Garneau, KFOR Spokesman," 5 July 1999, at www.nato.int/kosovo/press/1999/k990705a.htm; and "KFOR

Press Statement by Maj. Jan Joosten," 14 July 1999, at www.nato.int/kosovo/press/1999/k990714a.htm.

34. *KFOR Online*, "Structure Objectives MNBs: Nations Contributing to KFOR" and associated links; also *KFOR Online*, "Structure Objectives MNBs: KFOR Structure," both at www.nato.int/kfor [accessed autumn 2000].

35. "KFOR at Its Western Front," *AIM Press*, 11 May 2000, at www.aimpress.ch.

36. *Los Angeles Times*, 17 October 2000, p. A7.

37. "6th Anniversary of KFOR Ceremony," *Kosovo Force (KFOR)*, 13 June 2005, at www.nato.int/kfor/inside/2005/06/i050613a_htm [accessed on 3 December 2005].

38. Ivo H. Daalder and Michael E. O'Hanlon, "The United States in the Balkans: There to Stay," *Washington Quarterly*, vol. 23, no. 4 (Autumn 2000): 166–167.

39. See *Die Presse* (Vienna), 18 October 1999, at www.diepresse.at. Regarding Thaqi, see also "Hašim Tači: Ja sam Majka Teresa," in *NIN*, no. 2540 (2 September 1999), cover story.

40. *Jutarnji list* (Zagreb), 6 September 1999, p. 11. Regarding the political parties currently operating in Kosovo, see Stephan Lipsius, "Kosovo: Politische Führung zerstritten," *Südost Europa*, vol. 48, no. 7/8 (July–August 1999): 359–372.

41. *Minneapolis Star Tribune*, 17 July 1999, at www.startribune.com.

42. Quoted in *Minneapolis Star Tribune*, 15 December 1999, at www.startribune.com; see also *Illyria*, 17–20 December 1999, pp. 1, 3.

43. Z. V. Vlaškalić and N. Žejak, "Serb National Council of Mitrovica Rejected New Kouchner's Proposal," *Blic* (Belgrade), 2 February 2000, trans. posted at free.freespeech.org/ex-yupress/blic/blic14.html.

44. ATA news agency (Tirana), 25 August 1999, in *BBC Summary of World Broadcasts*, 27 August 1999, on LNAU. See also *Jutarnji list*, 31 August 1999, p. 10.

45. "Secretary-General Praises 'Courageous' Decision of Serb National Council of Gračanica to Participate in Kosovo Bodies," *Press Release SG/SM/7348*, 4 April 2000, at www.scienceblog.com/community/older/archives/L/2000/A/un000522.html [accessed 29 June 2005].

46. Ger Duijzings, *Religion and the Politics of Identity in Kosovo* (London: Hurst, 2000), p. 71.

47. According to the *Los Angeles Times*, 22 September 1999, at www.latimes.com.

48. "KFOR Press Statement, Delivered by Lieutenant-Commander Louis Garneau, KFOR Spokesman" (hereafter "KFOR Garneau 1"), 5 July 1999, at www.nato.int/kosovo/press/1999/k990705a.htm; and "KFOR Press Statement, by Lieutenant-Commander Louis Garneau," 7 July 1999, at www.nato.int/kosovo/press/1999/k990707a.htm.

49. *New York Times*, 28 October 1999, p. A8.

50. See *Politika*, 20 November 1999, 23 November 1999, 24 November 1999, 4 December 1999, 10 January 2000, 2 February 2000, and 17 June 2000—all at www.politika.co.yu; *Minneapolis Star Tribune*, 4 October 1999, at www.startribune.com; and Sabrina P. Ramet, "The Kingdom of God or the Kingdom of Ends: Kosovo in Serbian Perception," in Mary Buckley and Sally N. Cummings (eds.), *The Kosovo Crisis: International Perceptions* (London: Continuum Press, 2002).

51. *Politika*, 31 August 1999, p. 3; Tanjug, 8 September 1999, in *BBC Summary of World Broadcasts*, 10 September 1999, on LNAU; and *Süddeutsche Zeitung* (Munich), 8 September 1999, p. 7. See also Stephen Muller, "Zur Situation der Roma in Kosovo," *Südost Europa*, vol. 48, nos. 9–10 (September–October 1999).

52. "KFOR Garneau 1."

53. Quoted in Biserka Matić, "Background of the Attempt on Trajković's Life in Kosovo," *AIM Press*, 13 November 1999, at www.aimpress.ch, p. 2.

54. *Illyria,* 8–10 August 2000, p. 4.

55. *Los Angeles Times,* 20 November 1999, at www.latimes.com; and *Mittelbayerische Zeitung,* 6 November 2000, at www.donau.de [accessed 29 June 2005]. See also Kosova press agency web site, 25 September 1999, trans. in *BBC Monitoring Europe—Political,* 27 September 1999, on LNAU.

56. *Der Standard* (Vienna), 11/12 September 1999, p. 3; also *Salzburger Nachrichten,* 11 September 1999, p. 6.

57. *Die Presse,* 25 May 2000, at www.diepresse.at. Regarding frictions between Russian peacekeepers and local Albanians, see also *Vjesnik* (Zagreb), 30 August 1999, pp. 1–2.

58. Paul Richter, "U.S. Troops Violated Rights in Kosovo," *Los Angeles Times,* reprinted in *Seattle Times,* 19 September 2000, p. A7.

59. *Baltimore Sun,* 14 March 2000, at www.baltimoresun.com.

60. *Illyria,* 4–7 February 2000, p. 3.

61. *The Guardian,* 11 November 1999, at www.guardian.co.uk. See also *Süddeutsche Zeitung,* 15 June 2000, p. 8.

62. Re 3,000 bodies, *The Guardian,* 18 August 2000, at www.guardian.co.uk. Re 4,200 bodies, *Radio B92* (Belgrade), 2 February 2003, on "News from the Neighborhood."

63. *Star Tribune,* 15 March 2000, at www.startribune.com.

64. *New York Times,* 16 March 2000, pp. A1, A12; and *Los Angeles Times,* 16 March 2000, at www.latimes.com.

65. Oliver Vujović, "Kosovo," *Medienhilfe Ex-Jugoslawien* (2000), at archiv.medienhilfe .ch/Reports/ipi2000/kos.htm; and Semini, "News from Kosovo," p. 5, n. 22.

66. Danica Kirka, "Kosovo Media Practice Targeted," *Associated Press,* 30 May 2000, posted at www.balkanpeace.org/hed/archive/may00/hed168.shtml; and Ana Bardhi, "Is the Press Turning into a Judge?" *AIM Press,* 16 June 2000, at www.aimpress.ch.

67. UPI, 16 June 2000, on LNAU.

68. Herbert Marcuse, "Repressive Toleranz," in Wolfgang Fach and Ulrich Degen (eds.), *Politische Legitimität* (Frankfurt-am-Main: Campus Verlag, 1978).

69. *New York Times,* 19 May 2000, pp. A1, A10.

70. UPI, 17 April 2000, on LNAU.

71. Haxhiu, quoted in *Los Angeles Times,* 17 October 2000, p. A7.

72. AP report published in *Minneapolis Star Tribune,* 15 October 2000, at www.star tribune.com.

73. *Illyria,* 20–23 October 2000, p. 2. This is also reported in "US Denies Backing Republic Status for Kosova," *National Albanian American Council,* 18 October 2000, at www .naac.org/pr/2000/10-18-00.html. At month's end, *The Guardian* published a report by Ewen MacAskill alleging that U.S. government lawyers had been studying UNSC Resolution 1244 and had concluded that although the resolution affirmed the "territorial integrity" of Yugoslavia, it did not rule out eventual independence for Kosovo. See *The Guardian,* 30 October 2000, p. 14, on LNAU; and also *The Future of Kosovo,* Hearing before the Committee on International Relations, House of Representatives, 108th Cong., 1st sess., 21 May 2003 (Washington, D.C.: U.S. Government Printing Office, 2003).

74. *Kölnische Rundschau,* 30 October 2000, at www.rundschau-online.de.

75. *Prague Post,* 18 October 2000, at www.praguepost.cz/news101800g.htm; and *Illyria,* 17–19 October 2000, p. 3.

76. *Washington Post,* 29 October 2000, p. A33; *Die Presse,* 30 October 2000, at www .diepresse.at; *Westfaelische Rundschau,* 30 October 2000, at www.westfaelische-rundschau.de; and *New York Times,* 31 October 2000, p. A15.

77. *Washington Post,* 31 October 2000, p. A22.

78. AP Worldstream, 27 October 2000, on LNAU; and *Agence France Presse,* 28 October 2000, on LNAU.

79. Quoted in UPI, 29 October 2000, on LNAU.

80. Re allowing Kosovo to go its own way, *Washington Post,* 16 October 2000, p. A18. Re Brovina, see *Minneapolis Star Tribune,* 29 November 1999, at www.startribune.com. Re releasing remaining Albanian prisoners, see *Washington Post,* 31 October 2000, p. A16.

81. Jeta Xharra, "Kosovo Sex Industry," *IWPR,* BCR no. 2 (10 October 2003), at www .iwpr.net.

82. Alma Lama, "Kosovo: History Revision Call Sparks Anger," *IWPR,* BCR no. 471 (3 December 2003), at www.iwpr.net, pp. 1–2; and Alma Lama, "Kosovo: Religious Tuition Calls Spark Concern," *IWPR,* BCR no. 430 (16 May 2003), at www.iwpr.net, pp. 1–2.

83. UPI, 23 October 2000, on LNAU.

84. Re not giving up Kosovo, see the report in *Philadelphia Inquirer,* 22 October 2000, on LNAU. Re partitioning Kosovo, see the report in *Los Angeles Times,* 12 October 2000, at www.latimes.com.

85. Carl Bildt, "Towards Self-Sustaining Stability in the Balkans," Remarks at the South-East Europe High Level Conference (Tokyo, 15 May 2000), at www.bildt.net/index.asp? artid=170, p. 5.

86. *Washington Post,* 24 October 2000, p. A7; and *International Herald Tribune,* 3 November 2000, p. 12.

87. *Glas javnosti,* 7 February 2003, at arhiva.glas-javnosti.co.yu. See also *Süddeutsche Zeitung,* 8 May 2002, at www.sueddeutsche.de.

88. "Time Is Now for Opening Talks on Kosovo Status," 20 January 2003, at www.serbia.sr.gov/yu; *Glas javnosti,* 2 February 2003, at arhiva.glas-javnosti.co.yu; and *Borba,* 27 February 2003, at www.borba.co.yu.

89. Michael Steiner became chief of UNMIK in January 2002, following Hans Haekkerup, who had succeeded Bernard Kouchner. Re "transfer of populations," see Arben Qirezi, "Kosovo Talks Stall after Djindjić Murder," in IWPR, 25 March 2002, at www.iwpr.net.

90. *Radio-televizioni 21* (Prishtina), 5 February 2003 and 25 March 2003—both at www.radio21.net/english/index.htm; *B92 News,* 30 April 2003, at www.b92.net/english/news; and *Borba,* 20 June 2003, at www.borba.co.yu.

91. *RFE/RL Newsline,* 7 March 2002, at www.rferl.org.

92. *Glas javnosti,* 20 November 2001, at arhiva.glas-javnosti.co.yu.

93. *OÖNachrichten,* 20 November 2001, at www.nachrichten.at/archiv; *The Independent* (London), 14 December 2001, p. 12; "Parliament to Appoint Kosovo President on Jan. 10," *Web site of Serbian Government,* 22 December 2001, at www.serbia.sr.gov.yu/news; *Kölnische Rundschau,* 10 January 2002, at www.rundschau-online.de; *Kurier* (Vienna), 4 March 2002, at intern.telekurier.at; and *Die Welt* (Berlin), 5 March 2002, p. 6.

94. Quotations from *International Herald Tribune* (Paris), 5 March 2002, p. 5. Re independence call, "Kosovo: New President Calls for Independence," *RFE/RL,* 4 March 2002, at www.rferl.org/nca.

95. *Frankfurter Rundschau,* 3 April 2003, at www.frankfurterrundschau.de.

96. Re arrests of KLA figures, "Two KLA Members Suspected of War Crimes Arrested in Kosovo," 28 January 2002, at www.serbia.sr.gov.yu/news; Arbnora Berisha, "Demonstrations against the Rule of Law," *AIM Press* (Paris), 20 February 2002, at www.aimpress.ch; and *The Guardian,* 15 August 2002, p. 6. Re murder of key witness, Arben Qirezi, "Kosovo: Witness Protection Fears Grow," in IWPR, BCR no. 426 (29 April 2003), at www.iwpr.net.

97. Macedonian Information Center, *Daily News Service,* 24 May 2002 and 30 May 2002—both at www.makedonija.com/mic; Republic of Macedonia, *Agency of Information: News,* 24 May 2002 and 27 May 2002—both at www.sinf.gov.mk; *Macedonian Information Agency* (29 May 2002), at www.mia.com.mk; and *UNMIK News Coverage,* 30 May 2002, at www.unmikonline.org/news.htm.

98. Re attacks on non-Albanians, *Frankfurter Rundschau,* 2 May 2003, at www.frank-furterrundschau.de. Re Covic's comment, see "There is no rule of law and freedom of movement for Serbs in Kosovo: Čović," 24 April 2003, at www.serbia.sr.gov.yu.

99. *Glas javnosti,* 11 March 2003, at www.glas-javnosti.co.yu.

100. "Extremists Stone Serb Homes in Kosovo-Metohija," 19 February 2003, at www.serbia.sr.gov.yu.

101. "Security in Kosovo-Metohija at Lowest Level Possible," 19 May 2003, at www.serbia.sr.gov.yu.

102. *Aftenposten* (Oslo), 4 June 2003, at www.aftenposten.no.

103. *UNMIK News Coverage,* 24 August 2004, at www.unmikonline.org.

104. Quoted in "Bosnia Model for Kosovo?" *TOL* (Prague), 3 March 2003, at www.tol.cz.

105. Re transferring governmental responsibilities, *radio-televizioni 21,* 20 January 2003, at www.radio21.net/english/index.htm. Re eventual independence, see the comments by Prime Minister Rexhepi, as quoted in *Glas javnosti,* 29 August 2002, at arhiva.glas-javnosti.co.yu.

106. Čović, quoted in *radio-televizioni 21,* 24 April 2003, at www.radio21.net/english/index.htm.

107. Anes Džunuzović, "Kosovo je problem, a BiH je nezavisna država" [An interview with Rasim Ljajić], *Ljiljan* (Sarajevo), no. 584 (26 March–2 April 2004): 19.

108. *Aftenposten,* 17 April 2003, at www.aftenposten.no.

109. For a discussion of the background to the election, see Sabrina P. Ramet and Philip W. Lyon, "Discord, Denial, Dysfunction: The Serbian-Montenegrin-Kosovar Triangle," in *Problems of Post-Communism,* vol. 49, no. 5 (September–October 2002): 3–19.

110. *Glas javnosti,* 3 March 2004 and 4 March 2004, at www.glas-javnosti.co.yu.

111. *Spiegel Online* (Hamburg), 28 April 2004, at www.spiegel.de; confirmed in *The Scotsman,* 18 March 2004, at the scotsman.scotsman.com. See also *Dagbladet* (Oslo), 25 March 2004, at www.dagbladet.no.

112. *CNN,* 17 March 2004, at www.cnn.com/world; *Aftenposten,* 18 March 2004, at www.aftenposten.no; *Politika,* 18 March 2004, at www.politika.co.yu; *CNN,* 18 March 2004, at www.cnn.com/world; *Berlingske Tidende* (Copenhagen), 25 March 2004, at www.berlingske.dk; *Glas javnosti,* 28 March 2004, at arhiva.glas-javnosti.co.yu; and *Spiegel Online,* 28 April 2004, at www.spiegel.de. The Danish newspaper *Berlingske Tidende* reported that 28 persons lost their lives in the mid-March unrest. See *Berlingske Tidende,* 20 March 2004, at www.berlingske.dk.

113. "Damage to Serbian Orthodox Churches Estimated at $30 Mln," 4 May 2004, at www.srbija.sr.gov.yu.

114. Janjić, quoted in *The Economist* (London), 20 March 2004, p. 32.

115. Re EU resistance, *Glas javnosti,* 23 March 2004, at www.glas-javnosti.co.yu; *Berlingske Tidende,* 23 March 2004, at www.berlingske.dk; and *The Independent,* 24 March 2004, at news.independent.co.uk. Re "multiethnic heaven," *Novi list* (Zagreb), 27 March 2004, at www.novilist.hr.

116. "Serbian, Serbia-Montenegrin Governments Call for Strict Adherence to Resolution 1244," 11 May 2004, at www.serbia.sr.gov.yu.

117. *Glas javnosti,* 4 June 2004, at www.glas-javnosti.co.yu.

118. "A Plan for the Political Solution to the Situation in Kosovo and Metohija" (Belgrade, May 2004), attachment to "Serbian, Serbia-Montenegrin," p. 2.

119. Ibid., pp. 4–5, 8, 10–11, 14.

120. See Sabrina P. Ramet, "Competing Narratives of Resentment and Blame: Historical Memory, Revitalization, and the Causes of the Yugoslav Meltdown" (Trondheim, March 2004), draft chapter for Charles Ingrao and Thomas Emmert (eds.), *Resolving the Yugoslav Controversies: A Scholars' Initiative* (project in progress).

19. Separate Paths

1. Government turnover, political violence, unconventional political activity, and democratic deficit. See Danica Fink-Hafner, "Slovenia in a Process of Transition to Political Democracy," in Adolf Bibič and Gigi Graziano (eds.), *Civil Society Political Society Democracy* (Ljubljana: Slovenian Political Science Association, 1994), pp. 390–401.

2. For an argument tying Slovenia's stability to its ethnic homogeneity, see Thomas Friedman's op/ed piece for the *New York Times,* 23 January 2001, p. A21, on nexis.com.

3. See Leopoldina Plut-Pregelj et al., *The Repluralization of Slovenia in the 1980s: New Revelations from Archival Material,* Donald W. Treadgold Papers no. 24 (Seattle: HMJ School of International Studies of the University of Washington, 2000).

4. As cited in Ivan Bernik, Brina Malnar, and Niko Toš, "Slovenian Political Culture: Paradoxes of Democratization," in Danica Fink-Hafner and John R. Robbins (eds.), *Making a New Nation: The Formation of Slovenia* (Aldershot, UK: Dartmouth, 1997), p. 57.

5. I am basing this assessment in part on a two-hour interview I had with Franjo Tudjman in Zagreb, September 1989.

6. See Tatjana Pavlović, "Women in Croatia: Feminists, Nationalists, and Homosexuals," in Sabrina P. Ramet (ed.), *Gender Politics in the Western Balkans: Women and Society in Yugoslavia and the Yugoslav Successor States* (University Park: Pennsylvania State University Press, 1999).

7. Drago Zajc, "The Changing Political System," in Fink-Hafner and Robbins, *Making a New Nation,* pp. 162 and 170n.

8. For more details, see Sabrina Petra Ramet, "Slovenia's Road to Democracy," *Europe-Asia Studies,* vol. 45, no. 3 (1993): 871–872.

9. *Slovenia News,* 3 December 2002, at slonews.sta.si.

10. Fink-Hafner, "Slovenia in a Process," p. 389.

11. Andrej Auersperger Matić, "Electoral Reform as a Constitutional Dilemma," *East European Constitutional Review,* vol. 9, no. 3 (Summer 2000): 78–79.

12. Ibid., p. 79.

13. Janša, quoted in *Delo* (Ljubljana–Internet version), 10 October 2000, trans. in FBIS-EEU-20001010.

14. See *Dnevnik* (Ljubljana), 4 September 1999, 7 September 1999, 14 September 1999, and 15 September 1999, at www.dnevnik.si.

15. Re Kučan and Drnovšek, see, for example, *Mladina* (Ljubljana), 18 June 1996, pp. 20–23, trans. in FBIS, *Daily Report* (Eastern Europe), 1 July 1996, pp. 44–46. Re Janša, see Rudolf M. Rizman, "Radical Right Politics in Slovenia," in Sabrina P. Ramet (ed.), *The Radical Right in Central and Eastern Europe since 1989* (University Park: Pennsylvania State University Press, 1999).

16. Radio Slovenia 1 (Ljubljana), 1 August 2000, trans. in FBIS-EEU-2000-0801.

17. Radio Slovenia 1, 23 January 2001, trans. in FBIS-EEU-2001-0123.

18. Re cases of corruption, see, for example, those involving Boris Suštar, the former state undersecretary in the Ministry of the Economy, and Zdenko Kodrič, the mayor of Koper. See Igor Mekina, "Slovenia: Far from Its Southern Neighbours," *AIM Press*, 29 November 2001, at www.aimpress.ch. Re Slovenia not fighting corruption, GRECO, *Evaluation Report on Slovenia*, adopted by the GRECO at its 4th Plenary Meeting, 12–15 December 2000, Greco Eval I Rep (2000) 3E Final (Strasbourg, 15 December 2000), p. 19; and "Slovenia's Experience with Fighting Corruption: A Virtually Powerless Anti-corruption Bureau," *Beta agency* (Belgrade), 13 November 2002, at www. beta.co.yu.

19. GRECO, *Evaluation Report*, pp. 3–4.

20. On 17 July 2003, Dr. Ali Nassib, an immigrant, was sentenced to four months in prison on charges of having taken a bribe from a patient. Re healthcare and tax collection, Susanne W. Stetzer (International Action Commissions), "Corruption and Anti-Corruption Policy in Central and Eastern Europe," *Action Commission for an Enlarged Euro-Atlantic Community* (n.d.); and "The Media Do Not Prevent Corruption," *Slovenia Business Week* (n.d.), at www .einnews.com/slovenia/newsfeed-SloveniaBusiness. Re police stations and the public prosecutor's office, "Corruption in Slovenia (European Perspectives)," posted at www.geocities.com/slocorruption/.

21. Stetzer, "Corruption and Anti-Corruption," p. 1; and *Corruption and Anti-corruption Policy in Slovenia*, EU Accession Monitoring Program (Open Society Institute, 2002), p. 580.

22. Mekina, "Slovenia: Far from," p. 1.

23. *Transparency International Corruption Perceptions Index 2002* (Berlin: Transparency International Secretariat, 2002), p. 4: see www.transparency.org [last accessed 6 June 2005].

24. "First Evaluation Report on Slovenia," *Council of Europe* (Strasbourg, 5 June 1998), at www.coe.int/; "Slovenia to Upgrade Cooperation with Interpol," *Slovenia News*, 10 September 2002, at slonews.sta.si; and "Slovenian-Croatian Relations High on Agenda," *Slovenia News*, 21 January 2003, at slonews.sta.si. See also "Government Passes Anti-Corruption Resolution," *Slovenia News*, 23 March 2004, at slonews.sta.si.

25. Richard Rose, "How Free from Fear Are Citizens in Transition Societies?" in *Transition Newsletter*, May/June 2002, at www.worldbank.org/transitionnewsletter/.

26. "Corruption in Slovenia," p. 2; and *Transparency International Corruption Perceptions Index 2004* (Berlin: Transparency International Secretariat, 2004), at www.transparency.org [accessed 6 June 2005].

27. Sandra Bašić-Hrvatin, "The Media and Values," paper presented on her behalf by Danica Fink-Hafner at a conference on *Democratic Transition in Slovenia: Value Transformation, Education, Media,* sponsored by the Norwegian University of Science and Technology, Trondheim, 13–14 June 2003.

28. *The Independent* (London), 2 April 2004, at news.independent.co.uk.

29. International Helsinki Federation for Human Rights, *Annual Report 1999: Slovenia* (Vienna, 5 July 1999), pp. 1, 2.

30. "Erased Citizens Prove Their Right," *Slovenia News*, 15 April 2003, at slonews.sta.si.

31. *Tallahassee Democrat*, 5 April 2004, at www.tallahassee.com; and *Taipei Times*, 6 April 2004, p. 7, at www.taipeitimes.com.

32. Rener, quoted in *Taipei Times*, 6 April 2004, p. 7.

33. Re poll, Fink-Hafner, "Slovenia in a Process," p. 401. For a development and discussion of women as "second-class" citizens, see Vlasta Jalušič, "Women in Post-Socialist Slovenia: Socially Adapted, Politically Marginalized," in S. P. Ramet (ed.). *Gender Politics in the Western Balkans;* and Sabrina P. Ramet, "Democratization in Slovenia—the Second Stage," in Karen Dawisha and Bruce Parrott (eds.), *Politics, Power, and the Struggle for Democracy in South-east Europe* (Cambridge: Cambridge University Press, 1997), pp. 202–204.

34. *Women 2000: An Investigation into the Status of Women's Rights in Central and South-eastern Europe and the Newly Independent States* (Vienna: International Helsinki Federation for Human Rights, 2000), chapter on "Slovenia," pp. 414–415, 418–420.

35. Zmago Jelinčič, president of the Slovenian National Party and deputy in the Assembly, in interview with the author, Ljubljana, 7 September 1999.

36. The average representation of women in parliaments in EU countries as of 2003 was 23%. See STA news agency (Ljubljana), 10 September 2003, in *BBC Monitoring Europe—Political,* 11 September 2003, on *Lexis-Nexis* (www.nexis.com).

37. Milica Antić-Gaber, assistant professor at the Faculty of Arts; Vera Kozmik, director of the Office for Women's Policy; Dragica Bač, executive director of Institute for the Study of the Humanities; and Mojca Dobnika, assistant professor at the Faculty of Arts—in interview with the author, Ljubljana, 6 September 1999.

38. *Women 2000,* p. 421.

39. Mitja Hafner-Fink, "Social Structure and Cleavages: Changing Patterns," in Fink-Hafner and Robbins, *Making a New Nation,* p. 265.

40. See Roman Kuhar, *Media Representations of Homosexuality: An Analysis of the Print Media in Slovenia, 1970–2000* (Ljubljana: Mirovni Inštitut, 2003), pp. 47–56.

41. Roman Kuhar, "Sexual Minorities in Slovenia," paper presented at a conference on *Democratic Transition in Slovenia: Value Transformation, Education, Media,* sponsored by the Norwegian University of Science and Technology, Trondheim, 13–14 June 2003.

42. *Delo* (Ljubljana), 15 July 2001, as cited in ibid. For fuller discussion of the gay and lesbian scene in Slovenia and problems of discrimination, see Brane Možetić, "Once upon a Time There Was a Tolerant Country . . . ," *Kinoeye,* vol. 1, no. 8 (10 December 2001), at www.kinoeye.org/01/08/pozun08.html; and Tatjana Greif and Nataša Velikonja, *Anketa o diskriminaciji na osnovi spolne usmerjenosti* (Ljubljana: ŠKUC-LL, 2001).

43. I am grateful to Roman Kuhar for providing me with this update (e-mail, 18 May 2004).

44. The proportion rejecting all three groups remained stable at 12% for opinion polls conducted in 1994, 1998, 2000, and 2002. No data for 1996 are available. Mitja Hafner-Fink, "Values of the Slovenian Population: Local and Collective or Global and Individual?" paper presented at a conference on *Democratic Transition in Slovenia: Value Transformation, Education, Media,* sponsored by the Norwegian University of Science and Technology, Trondheim, 13–14 June 2003.

45. Tonči Kuzmanić, *Hate-Speech in Slovenia: Slovenian Racism, Sexism and Chauvinism* (Ljubljana: Open Society Institute, 1999), pp. 15, 22, 56, 66.

46. Fink-Hafner, "Slovenia in a Process," p. 396.

47. *Dnevnik,* 6 November 2000, at www.dnevnik.si.

48. Slavko Gaber, former minister of education, in interview with the author, Ljubljana, 1 September 1999.

49. *Dnevnik,* 16 November 1999, at www.dnevnik.si.

50. *Dnevnik,* 4 December 1999 and 14 December 1999, at www.dnevnik.si.

51. *Dnevnik,* 10 March 2000, at www.dnevnik.si.

52. Re Kristan, letter to the editor from Ivan Kristan, in *Dnevnik,* 9 March 2000, at www.dnevnik.si. Re Associated List, *Dnevnik,* 13 March 2000, at www.dnevnik.si.

53. Rode, quoted in *Dnevnik,* 18 March 2000, at www.dnevnik.si.

54. Rode, quoted in *Dnevnik,* 29 March 2000, at www.dnevnik.si.

55. Mastnak, in ibid.

56. Pluška, in *Dnevnik,* 18 March 2000, at www.dnevnik.si.

57. *Deutsche Presse-Agentur,* 11 December 2001, on *Lexis-Nexis* (www.nexis.com); and *Associated Press Worldstream,* 14 December 2001, on *Lexis-Nexis* (www.nexis.com).

58. See the comments by Dr. Anton Stress, suffragan bishop of Maribor, in *Frankfurter Allgemeine* 27 February 2002, p. 4.

59. "Vatican Agreement Finally Wrapped Up," *Slovenia News,* 3 February 2004, at slonews .sta.si.

60. *Associated Press Worldstream,* 17 June 2001, on *Lexis-Nexis* (www.nexis.com).

61. Strelnikoff, *Bitchcraft,* Law & Auder Records, 001 (1998).

62. AP Worldstream, 2 March 1998, on nexis.com; and "Slovenia's Holy Civil War: Rock Group Strelnikoff and [the] Virgin Mary," on *Telepolis,* 9 April 1998, at www.heise.de/tp/english/inhalt/te/1440/1.html [accessed 29 June 2005].

63. Archbishop Rode judged that Laibach's album *WAT,* released at the end of 2003, was disrespectful of the Church.

64. Re promotion, "Ljubljana Archbishop to Assume Senior Vatican Post," *Slovenia News,* 17 February 2004, at slonews.sta.si; re kicked upstairs, *Delo,* as summarized in *Večernji list* (Zagreb), 13 February 2004, at www.vecernji-list.hr.

65. Igor Mekina, "Support to Former Collaborationists of Hitler," *AIM Press,* 12 July 2000, at www.aimpress.ch.

66. Radio Slovenia (Ljubljana), 25 August 2000, trans. in *BBC Summary of World Broadcasts,* 29 August 2000, in *Lexis-Nexis Academic Universe* (hereafter LNAU).

67. Jelinčič, quoted in Mekina, "Support to Former Collaborationists," p. 2 of 3.

68. "Slowenien: Gute Chancen auf eine stabile Regierung," in *OÖNachrichten,* 17 October 2000, at www.nachrichten.at/archiv.

69. *Delo* (Ljubljana—Internet version), 18 October 2000, trans. in FBIS-EEU-2000-1018.

70. *Deutsche Presse-Agentur,* 10 November 2000, on nexis.com.

71. *Deutsche Presse-Agentur,* 16 October 2000, on nexis.com.

72. "Drnovšek Elected President," *Slovenia News,* 3 December 2002, at slonews.sta.si. For further discussion, see Danica Fink-Hafner and Tomaž Boh (eds.), *Predsedniške volitve 2002* (Ljubljana: Fakulteta za družbene vede, 2003).

73. *Agence France Presse,* 9 October 2002, on *Lexis-Nexis* (www.nexis.com); "NATO Invites Slovenia to Join in 2004," *Slovenia News,* 7 January 2003, at slonews.sta.si; and *die tageszeitung* (Berlin), 25 March 2003, at www.taz.de.

74. Re GDP growth rates, *Agence France Presse,* 30 September 2002, on *Lexis-Nexis* (www.nexis.com); "Slovenian Economy Strong," 8 October 2002, at slonews.sta.si; "Slovenia's 2003 GDP Growth at 2.3 Percent," *Slovenia News,* 23 March 2004, at slonews.sta.si; and *International Monetary Fund* (21 March 2005), at www.imf.org/external/np/ms/2005032105.htm [accessed 6 June 2005]. Re inflation rates, *ČTK National News Wire* (Prague), 13 November 2002, on *Lexis-Nexis* (www.nexis.com); "Inflation to Be Curbed in 2003," *Slovenia News,* 5 November 2002, at slonews.sta.si; "Inflation at Acceptable Level," *Slovenia News,* 11 February 2003, at slonews.sta.si; and "February Inflation at 0.1%," *Slovenia News,* 2 March 2004, at slonews.sta.si. Re industrial output, *OECD Economic Surveys: Slovenia 1997* (Paris: Organisation for Economic Cooperation and Development, 1997), p. 38; *New Europe* (Athens), 9–15 January 2000, p. 41; *New Europe,* 16–22 January 2000, p. 41; and "Slovenia in 1999, Outlook for 2000," in *About Slovenia* (SKB Banka dd., June 2000), at www.skb.si; and *Statistical Office of the Republic of Slovenia,* "Inflation in December 2004" (30 December 2004), at www.stat.si/eng/novice_poglej.asp?ID=416 [accessed 6 June 2005].

75. *Associated Press Worldstream,* 9 November 2002 on *Lexis-Nexis* (www.nexis.com); *Agence France Presse,* 18 November 2002, on *Lexis-Nexis* (www.nexis.com); *Deutsche Presse-Agentur,* 2 September 2003, on *Lexis-Nexis* (www.nexis.com); and Republic of Slovenia, *Sta-*

tistical Office of the Republic of Slovenia, at www.stat.si/eng/iskanje_novo.asp [accessed 18 May 2004].

76. *Dnevnik,* 4 October 2004, at www.dnevnik.si.

77. Branka Nanevska, "Macedonia—Africa in the Balkans," *AIM Press,* 16 July 2000, at www.aimpress.ch; and "FYR Macedonia Country Brief 2004," *The World Bank Group,* at www.worldbank.org.mk [accessed 6 June 2005].

78. Branka Nanevska, "The Life of the Poor in Macedonia," *AIM Press,* 9 October 2000, at www.aimpress.ch.

79. Production, *The European* (London), 18–21 February 1993, p. 39; unemployment 2003, U.S. Department of State, *Background Note: Macedonia* (Bureau of European and Eurasian Affairs, May 2004), at www.state.gov/r/pa/ei/bgn/26759.htm, p. 2; unemployment 2004, Republic of Macedonia, *State Statistical Office* (6 June 2005), at www.stat.gov.mk/english/glavna_eng.asp [accessed 6 June 2005].

80. Re unemployment, *BBC Monitoring International Reports,* 25 June 2003, on *Lexis-Nexis* (www.nexis.com). Re losing jobs, *Deutsche Presse-Agentur,* 27 May 2003, on *Lexis-Nexis* (www.nexis.com).

81. MIC (Skopje), 8 November 2000, in FBIS-EEU-2000-1108.

82. Re rise in industrial production, MIA (Skopje), 29 January 2001, in FBIS-EEU-2001-0129. Re GDP real growth rate, *Financial Times,* 19 February 2001; *Survey,* p. 11, on nexis.com; CIA, *The World Factbook 2002; Background Note: Macedonia* (2004), p. 2; and U.S. Department of State, *Background Note: Macedonia* (May 2005), at www.state.gov/r/pa/ei/bgn/26759.htm [accessed on 6 June 2005].

83. "Macedonia Adopts New Constitution," *BBC News,* 16 November 2001, at news.bbc.co.uk.

84. Re war, *Republika* (a Macedonian independent daily newspaper), as cited in Radio Croatia Network (Zagreb), 30 December 1991, trans. in FBIS, *Daily Report* (Eastern Europe), 31 December 1991, p. 44, and *The Times* (London), 6 April 1994, p. 16. Re partition, Radio Belgrade Network, 22 February 1992, trans. in FBIS, *Daily Report* (Eastern Europe), 24 February 1992, p. 40, and *Agence France Presse,* 13 November 1992, in FBIS, *Daily Report* (Eastern Europe), 16 November 1992, p. 44. Re partition and embargo, Sabrina P. Ramet, "The Macedonian Enigma," in Sabrina P. Ramet and Ljubisa S. Adamovich (eds.), *Beyond Yugoslavia: Politics, Economics, and Culture in a Shattered Community* (Boulder, Colo.: Westview Press, 1995); re. the name, Vladimir Milčin, "A Little Miracle in the Balkans," in *War Report* (London), September 1992, p. 14. Re partition and the name, Sabrina P. Ramet, "All Quiet on the Southern Front? Macedonia between the Hammer and the Anvil," *Problems of Post-Communism,* vol. 42, no. 6 (November–December 1995).

85. Re the withdrawal of Yugoslav Army units from Čupino Brdo in Macedonia, see MILS-NEWS (Skopje), 4 July 1994, in FBIS, *Daily Report* (Eastern Europe), 5 July 1994, p. 49. Re earlier efforts, see S. P. Ramet, "Macedonian Enigma," pp. 221–225.

86. *Neue Zürcher Zeitung,* 12 September 2002, at www.nzz.ch; *The Times* (London), 17 September 2002, at www.timesonline.co.uk; *Frankfurter Rundschau,* 17 September 2002, at www.fr-aktuell.de; and *Fuldaer Zeitung,* 19 September 2002, at www.parzeller.de.

87. *Constitution of the Republic of Macedonia,* trans. into English by Dimitar Mirchev (Skopje: NIP MAK Pablik 21, 1994), pp. 3, 5, 17.

88. Aleksandar Šoljakovski, "An Education in Ethnic Complexity," in *War Report* (London), October 1992, p. 5.

89. *Kosova Daily Report* (Priština), no. 114 (8 June 1993), in FBIS, *Daily Report* (Eastern Europe), 10 June 1993, p. 43.

90. English text of Aleksandar Dinevski's letter of resignation, provided to me by Georgi Avramčev and Jovan Manasievski, members of the executive board of the Democratic Party,

in the course of an interview, Skopje, 23 March 1995. I have made two small corrections to the syntax, which do not affect the meaning.

91. Georgi Avramčev, Jovan Manasievski, and journalist Mirče Donevski, members of the Executive Board of the Democratic Party, in an interview with the author, Skopje, 23 March 1995; Natasha Gaber and Klime Babunski, researchers at the Institute for Social-Political and Legal Research, in interview with the author, Skopje, 16 March 1995; and Duncan M. Perry, "The Republic of Macedonia: Finding Its Way," in Karen Dawisha and Bruce Parrott (eds.), *Politics, Power, and the Struggle for Democracy in South-east Europe* (Cambridge: Cambridge University Press, 1997), pp. 235–236.

92. English text of the IMRO-DPMNU statement, given to me by Ljupčo Georgievski in Skopje, 16 March 1995.

93. Ljupčo Georgievski, head of the IMRO-DPMNU, in interview with the author, Skopje, 16 March 1995.

94. MIC (Skopje), 27 September 2000, in FBIS-EEU-2000-0927.

95. *Start* (Skopje), 15 September 2000, trans. on 23 October 2000, posted at www.cdsp.neu.edu/info/students/marko/mkstart/mkstart5.html.

96. *Illyria* (The Bronx), 2–4 November 1999, p. 1; *OÖNachrichten,* 16 November 1999, at www.nachrichten.at; and *Illyria,* 7–9 December 1999, pp. 1, 4.

97. *Fuldaer Zeitung,* 19 September 2002, at www.parzeller.de.

98. Savo Kosharov, in the course of a meeting with Slavko Petrov (president of the Macedonian Bar Association), Blažo Muratovski (MBA member), Milorad Martinovski (MBA member), Savo Kosharov (MBA member), Jim Peterson of CEELI, and American jurists, which I was permitted to attend, Skopje, 20 March 1995 (hereafter, cited as "Skopje Meeting").

99. S. Petrov, M. Martinovski, and S. Kosharov, at "Skopje Meeting."

100. M. Martinovski, S. Kosharov, S. Petrov, and Blazo Muratovski, at "Skopje Meeting."

101. U. S. Department of State, *1999 Country Reports—Macedonia,* p. 11 of 16.

102. *Puls* (Skopje), 22 July 1994, pp. 17–18, trans. in FBIS, *Daily Report* (Eastern Europe), 16 August 1994, p. 25.

103. MIC, 9 August 1995, in FBIS, *Daily Report* (Eastern Europe), 10 August 1995, p. 49.

104. *Nova Makedonija* (Skopje), 10 August 1995, p. 2, trans. in FBIS, *Daily Report* (Eastern Europe), 11 August 1995, p. 46.

105. AP Worldstream, 1 February 2000, on nexis.com.

106. Report summarized in "Corruption 'Endemic' Ahead of Macedonian Elections," in *TOL* (Prague), 13–19 August 2002, at www.tol.cz, pp. 1, 2.

107. Helsinki Committee for Human Rights (Skopje), *Newsletter,* Year 3, no. 9 (October 1996) [hereafter, HCHR, *Newsletter*], p. 4. See also International Helsinki Federation for Human Rights (IHF-HR), *Annual Report 1998: Macedonia* (Vienna, 23 October 1998), at www.ihf-hr.org/index.php, pp. 3–4; and IHF-HR, *Annual Report 1999: Macedonia* (Vienna, 5 July 1999), at www.ihf-hr.org/index.php, pp. 5–6.

108. IHF-HR, *Annual Report 1998: Macedonia,* p. 3.

109. IHF-HR, *Annual Report 1999: Macedonia,* pp. 4, 5 .

110. HCHR, *Newsletter* (October 1996), p. 4; and IHRF, *Annual Report 1998: Macedonia,* p. 3 of 8.

111. BTA (Sofia), 28 January 2001, in FBIS-EEU-2001-0128.

112. Radio Makedonija (Skopje), 17 January 2001, trans. in FBIS-EEU-2001-0117.

113. Radio Makedonija, 23 January 2001, trans. in FBIS-EEU-2001-0123; MIA (Skopje), 29 January 2001, in FBIS-EEU-2001-0130; MIA, 7 February 2001, in FBIS-EEU-2001-0207; Radio Makedonija, 7 February 2001, trans. in FBIS-EEU-2001-0207; MIA, 8 February 2001,

in FBIS-EEU-2001-0208; and Radio Makedonija, 16 February 2001, trans. in FBIS-EEU-2001-0216.

114. Re Macedonian Intelligence Agency denials, Radio Makedonija, 24 January 2001, trans. in FBIS-EEU-2001-0124; MIA, 24 January 2001), in FBIS-EEU-2001-0125; MIC (29 January 2001), in FBIS-EEU-2001-0129; and MIA, 31 January 2001), in FBIS-EEU-2001-0131. Re Bogoevski's claim, BTA (Sofia), 22 January 2001, in FBIS-EEU-2001-0122.

115. BTA, 28 January 2001, in FBIS-EEU-2001-0128, citing *Dnevnik* (Skopje), 20–21 January 2001, and MIA (Skopje), 25 January 2001.

116. Re "a parallel wiretapping system," see MIA, 14 February 2001, in FBIS-EEU-2001-0214.

117. MIA, 6 February 2001, in FBIS-EEU-2001-0206.

118. MIA, 7 February 2001, in FBIS-EEU-2001-0208.

119. Georgievski, quoted in MIA, 11 February 2001, in FBIS-EEU-2001-0212, syntax in the first extract modified to accord with standard English usage.

120. From the full text of her letter of resignation, in MIA, 16 February 2001, in FBIS-EEU-2001-0216.

121. Borjan Jovanovski, "Macedonia: Dimovska Exit Sparks Political Turmoil," in *Institute for War and Peace Reporting* (IWPR), BCR no. 312 (25 January 2002), at www.iwpr.net.

122. Republic of Macedonia, *Agency of Information: News* [hereafter, *Macedonia Agency News*], 3 April 2002 and 18 June 2003—at www.sinf.gov.mk.

123. *Macedonia Agency News,* 7 February 2003, 11 June 2003, and 13 June 2003—all at www.sinf.gov.mk.

124. *Neue Zürcher Zeitung,* 17 November 1994, p. 2; and *Croatia Weekly* (Zagreb), 3 March 2000, p. 10.

125. Re Albanian claims, Xheladin Murati, MP, and Enver Shala, journalist for *Flaka ë vellazerimit,* in interview with the author, Tetovo, 20 March 1995. Re Serb claims, Tanjug (Belgrade), 15 November 1994, trans. in FBIS, *Daily Report* (Eastern Europe), 16 November 1994, p. 45.

126. Re "second-class citizens," Arben Xhaferi, head of the radical wing of the Party for Democratic Prosperity (and future head of the Democratic Party of Albanians), in interview with the author, Tetovo, 20 March 1995; Tanjug (Belgrade), 30 March 1992, in FBIS, *Daily Report* (Eastern Europe), 31 March 1992, p. 39; Tanjug, 31 October 1992, in FBIS, *Daily Report* (Eastern Europe), 2 November 1992, p. 42; *Beta news agency,* 5 March 1995, trans. in FBIS, *Daily Report* (Eastern Europe), 7 March 1995, p. 45; and *Večer* (Skopje), 30 March 1995, p. 8, trans. in FBIS, *Daily Report* (Eastern Europe), 3 April 1995, p. 26.Tanjug Domestic Service (Belgrade), 10 April 1993, trans. in FBIS, *Daily Report* (Eastern Europe), 12 April 1993, p. 59.

127. U. S. Department of State, *1999 Country Reports on Human Rights Practices—Former Yugoslav Republic of Macedonia,* Released by the Bureau of Democracy, Human Rights, and Labor, 25 February 2000, at www.state.gov/www/global/human_rights/1999_hrp_report/macedoni.html, pp. 12, 13.

128. *Macedonia Agency News,* 16 May 2002, at www.sinf.gov.mk. See also *Macedonia Agency News,* 12 February 2003, at www.sinf.gov.mk.

129. Bruce Fekrat, "Albanians in Macedonia," Minority at Risk Project, University of Maryland, College of Behavioral and Social Sciences (1994).

130. BBC, 17 August 1994, as cited in "Update" by Jonathan Fox (no. 106), 12/25/95, to Fekrat, "Albanians in Macedonia," pp. 10, 11.

131. Re allegations of poisoning, MIC, 7 June 1996, and MIC, 10 June 1996, both in FBIS, *Daily Report* (Eastern Europe), 12 June 1996, p. 50; and FBIS report based on *Koha Jone* (Tirana), 14 June 1996, in FBIS, *Daily Report* (Eastern Europe), 17 June 1996, p. 43. Re incar-

ceration of Albanian mayors, *OÖNachrichten,* 11 July 1997 and 15 July 1997, both at www1.oon.at; and Ducan Perry, "Destiny on Hold: Macedonia and the Dangers of Ethnic Discord," *Current History,* vol. 97, no. 617 (March 1998): 124. See also Sabrina P. Ramet, *Balkan Babel: The Disintegration of Yugoslavia from the Death of Tito to the Fall of Milošević,* 4th ed. (Boulder, Colo.: Westview Press, 2002), p. 191. Re mobilization of Macedonian police units, SRNA news agency (Bijeljina), 28 January 2000, trans. in *BBC Summary of World Broadcasts,* 31 January 2000, on LNAU.

132. Tearce, Nexhbedin Shaqiri, "Raketiranje policijske stanice u selu Tearce," *AIM Press,* 26 January 2001, at www.aimpress.ch; and *Neue Zürcher Zeitung,* 3 February 2001, p. 5, on nexis.com. Tanuševci, *Beta news agency* (Belgrade), 17 February 2001, trans. in FBIS-EEU-2001-0217.

133. Miletić's comments, Tanjug, 31 January 2001, in FBIS-EEU-2001-0131; Georgievski's comments, MTV1 Televizija (Skopje), 29 January 2001, trans. in FBIS-EEU-2001-0129.

134. For an expostulation of his views, see Arben Xhaferi, "Makedonien zwischen Ethnozentrismus und Multiethnie," in Walter Kolbow and Heinrich Quaden (eds.), *Krieg und Frieden auf dem Balkan—Makedonien am Scheideweg?* (Baden-Baden: Nomos Verlagsgesellschaft, 2001), pp. 36–43.

135. *Illyria,* 20–22 February 2001, p. 5.

136. *Financial Times,* 19 February 2001: *Survey,* p. 4, on nexis.com.

137. MIC (Skopje), 13 December 1994, in FBIS, *Daily Report* (Eastern Europe), 14 December 1994, p. 65; Radio Tirana Network, 17 December 1994, trans. in FBIS, *Daily Report* (Eastern Europe), 19 December 1994, p. 47; and Ilenka Mitreva, MP from the Social Democratic Party and chair of the Foreign Policy Committee of the Sobranie, in interview with the author, Skopje, 24 March 1995.

138. Tanjug, 14 December 1994, and *Agence France Presse,* 14 December 1994—both in FBIS, *Daily Report* (Eastern Europe), 15 December 1994, p. 34; and *Rilindja* (Tirana), 15 December 1994, p. 1, trans. in FBIS, *Daily Report* (Eastern Europe), 16 December 1994, p. 27.

139. *Neue Zürcher Zeitung,* 22 February 1995, p. 5; and *Boston Sunday Globe,* 5 March 1995, p. 15.

140. TVSH Television Network (Tirana), 21 April 1995, trans. in FBIS, *Daily Report* (Eastern Europe), 24 April 1995, p. 36.

141. Gligorov, quoted in MIC (Skopje), 7 May 1996, in FBIS, *Daily Report* (Eastern Europe), 8 May 1996, p. 50.

142. MIC (Skopje), 26 July 2000, in *BBC Summary of World Broadcasts,* 28 July 2000, on LNAU; *Illyria,* 28–31 July 2000, p. 5; *Utrinski Vesnik* (Skopje), 27 July 2000, p. 4, trans. in *BBC Summary of World Broadcasts,* 1 August 2000, on LNAU; *Illyria,* 1–3 August 2000, p. 4; and Kosova news agency Web site, 9 August 2000, in *BBC Summary of World Broadcasts,* 12 August 2000, on LNAU.

143. Iso Rusi, "University of Tetovo," *AIM Press,* 13 May 2000, at www.aimpress.ch.

144. *Illyria,* 8–11 December 2000, p. 4.

145. MIC (Skopje), 9 August 2000, in *BBC Summary of World Broadcasts,* 12 August 2000, on LNAU.

146. Prof. Alajdin Abazi, an electrical engineer, as quoted in *Financial Times,* 1 August 2000, p. 6, in LNAU.

147. "South East European University Opens in Tetovo," *OSCE in Focus,* at www.osce .org/news [accessed 8 May 2002].

148. *Women 2000,* chapter on "Macedonia," pp. 298–300, 303–304; and U.S. Department of State, *1999 Country Reports—Macedonia,* p. 11.

149. *Women 2000,* pp. 299–300.

150. Mekerem Rusi, president of the League of Albanian Women, in interview with the author, Tetovo, 20 March 1995.

151. U.S. Department of State, *1999 Country Reports—Macedonia,* pp. 7–8. But for an alternative point of view, see IHF-HR, "Religious Discrimination and Related Violations of Helsinki Commitments: Macedonia" (Vienna, 16 March 1999), at www.ihf-hr.org/index.php.

152. Goran Mihajlovski, "Religion in School: Churches and Mosques Moved to Schools," *AIM Press,* 11 September 1999, at www.aimpress.ch/dyn/trae/archive/data/199909/90911-002-trae-sko.htm.

153. Boris Trajkovski, president of the Republic of Macedonia, in an address to CSIS, Washington D.C., 1 February 2001.

154. *Washington Post,* 4 April 2001, p. A16.

155. See, for example, MIA (Skopje), 28 February 2001, in FBIS-EEU-2001-0228.

156. *Oslobodjenje* (Sarajevo), 17/18 March 2001, p. 8.

157. *Aftenposten* (Oslo), 22 March 2001, at www.aftenposten.no.

158. PDP, *Illyria,* 3–5 April 2001, pp. 1, 3; DPA, *Illyria,* 6–9 April 2001, pp. 1, 3.

159. *Illyria,* 6–9 April 2001, p. 2.

160. *Illyria,* 10–12 April 2001, p. 6.

161. *Süddeutsche Zeitung,* 30 April/1 May 2001, p. 8; and *Glas javnosti,* 29 April 2001, at arhiva.glas-javnosti.co.yu.

162. *Illyria,* 11–14 May 2001, p. 1.

163. *Vjesnik* (Zagreb), 7 May 2001, at www.vjesnik.hr/html.

164. *Jutarnji list* (Zagreb), 10 June 2001, p. 11; *Večernji list,* 11 June 2001, p. 8; *Jutarnji list,* 25 June 2001, p. 10; and *Vjesnik,* 28 June 2001, p. 3.

165. Re rising pressure, *Dagbladet* (Oslo), 26 June 1001, at www.dagbladet.no. Re agreeing to negotiate, *Dagbladet,* 24 July 2001, at www.dagbladet.no.

166. Re the fighting around Skopje, see *Dagbladet,* 12 August 2001, at www.dagbladet.no.

167. *Washington Post,* 14 August 2001, p. A1.

168. *Washington Post,* 28 January 2003, p. A16.

169. The full text of the Ohrid agreement is reprinted in Wolf Oschlies, *Makedonien 2001–2004. Kriegstagebuch aus einem friedlichen Land* (Berlin: Xenomos, 2004), pp. 117–134.

170. *Aftenposten,* 15 August 2001, at www.aftenposten.no; and *Vjesnik,* 16 August 2001, at www.vjesnik.hr.

171. *Dagbladet,* 19 August 2001 and 24 August 2001, at www.dagbladet.no. See also *Vjesnik,* 17 August 2001, at www.vjesnik.hr.

172. *Dagbladet,* 26 August 2001 and 29 August 2001, at www.dagbladet.no.

173. *Macedonia Agency News,* 31 January 2003 and 20 March 2003, at www.sinf.gov.mk.

174. *Dagbladet,* 15 August 2001, at www.dagbladet.no; *Netzeitung,* 1 October 2001, at www.netzeitung.de; and *Macedonian Agency News,* 9 August 2002, at www.sinf.gov.mk.

175. Re incidents involving gunfire, see *Macedonian Information Agency,* 20 March 2002, 8 May 2002, 29 May 2002, 28 June 2002, 19 August 2002, and 18 March 203, at www.mia .com.mk/ang; and *Macedonia Agency News,* 17 February 2003, at www.sinf.gov.mk. Re neutralizing the armed groups, Radio Netherlands Wereldomroep, 4 September 2003, at www .rnw.nl/hotspots; and MIA Macedonian Information Agency, 9 September 2003, at www .mia.co.mk.

176. *Dnevnik* (Skopje), 18 April 2003, pp. 6–7, trans. in *BBC Monitoring Europe—Political,* 21 April 2003, on *Lexis-Nexis* (www.nexis.com).

177. *Fakti* (Skopje), 19 April 2003, p. 4, trans. in *BBC Monitoring Europe—Political*, 21 April 2003, on *Lexis-Nexis* (www.nexis.com).

178. Boris Pavelić, "Nismo se borili za podjelu Makedonije" [An interview with Ali Ahmeti], in *Novi list* (Rijeka), 13 December 2002, at www.novilist.hr.

179. *Nezavisni dnevnik Vijesti* (Podgorica), 23 January 2002, at www.vijesti.cg.yu; and Macedonian Information Centar, *Daily News Service* (Skopje), 31 May 2002, at www.makedonija.com/mic.

180. Edward P. Joseph, "Macedonia: The Risks of Complacency," at the Woodrow Wilson International Center for Scholars, 24 September 2003, in *EES News*, November–December 2003, p. 2.

181. Re independence of the press, *Medienhilfe Ex-Jugoslawien* (Zürich, 2001), at archiv.medienhilfe.ch/Projekte/2001/MAC2001.htm; "Media Complaints and Advisory Commission," in IWPR, 2–6 March 2002, at www.iwpr.net; "Macedonian Editors Face Arrest," in IWPR, BCR no. 365 (6 September 2002), at www.iwpr.net; and *Amnesty International* (9 September 2002), sent by e-mail from hrnetnews@u.washington.edu. Re trade war with Serbia, Sabina Fakić, "Macedonia: Trade War with Serbia Erupts," in IWPR, BCR no. 336 (15 May 2002), at www.iwpr.net. Re pandemic insolvency, *Macedonia Agency News*, 25 March 2003, at www.sinf.gov.mk. Re controversies concerning "Lions," Vladimir Jovanovski, "Macedonia: Church Enrages Albanians," in IWPR, BCR no. 309 (16 January 2002), at www.iwpr.net.

182. *Aftenposten*, 22 January 2003, at www.aftenposten.no.

183. *Die Welt* (Berlin), 24 January 2003, at www.welt.de; and *Washington Post*, 28 January 2003, p. A16.

184. Re Greek investments, *Macedonia Agency News*, 19 April 2002, at www.sinf.gov.mk. Re generous donations, *RFE/RL Newsline*, 13 March 2002, at www.rferl.org; and *Macedonia Agency News*, 7 March 2003, at www.sinf.gov.mk. Re decrease in foreign debt, *Macedonian Information Agency*, 14 March 2002, at www.mia.com.mk/ang. Re budgetary cuts, *Macedonia Agency News*, 25 March 2003, at www.sinf.gov.mk.

185. *International Herald Tribune* (Paris), 15–16 June 2002, p. 5.

186. *Frankfurter Rundschau*, 22 December 2003, at www.frankfurterrundschau.de.

187. For details, see *Novi list*, 14 April 2004, at www.novilist.hr; and *Frankfurter Rundschau*, 30 April 2004, at www.frankfurterrundschau.de.

188. *Oslobodjenje* (Sarajevo), 16 July 2004, p. 19; and *International Herald Tribune*, 24/25 July 2004, p. 3. For further details, see Ana Petruševa, "Fury over Decentralization Forces Poll Delay," IWPR, BCR no. 510 (5 August 2004), at www.iwpr.net.

189. *Oslobodjenje*, 19 July 2004, p. 20; and *Der Standard* (Vienna), 27 July 2004, p. 4. For further details, see Tamara Causidis, "Macedonians Threaten Revolt over Decentralization," IWPR, BCR no. 509 (30 July 2004), at www.iwpr.net.

190. Re falsifying election returns, *Nacional*, no. 215 (30 December 1999), at www.nacional.hr. Re "secret war," Hrvatski Helsinski Odbor za Ljudska Prava, *CHC Statement No. 81* (Zagreb, 13 November 1998), at www.open.hr, quoted in Vjeran Pavlaković, "Between Balkans and the West: Liberal Democracy in Croatia," in *Modern Greek Studies Yearbook*, vol. 16/17 (2000/2001), p. 364. For a recent biography of Tudjman, see Zdravko Tomac, *Predsjednik: Protiv Krivotvorina i zaborava*, rev. ed. (Zagreb: Slovo M, 2004).

191. *Globus*, no. 479 (11 February 2000): 6–11; and *Aftenposten*, 8 February 2000, at www.aftenposten.no.

192. *The Independent*, 1 November 2000, p. 16, on LNAU; and *Nacional*, no. 269 (11 January 2001), at www.nacional.hr. See also Mirna Solić, "The Tudjman Tapes," in *TOL* (Prague), 10 July 2000, at archive.tol.cz/itowa/ju100cro.htm.

193. *Večernji list*, 29 April 2001, p. 2; and *Slobodna Dalmacija* (Split), 29 April 2001, p. 2.

194. *Večernji list,* 18 June 2002, at www.vecernji-list.hr.

195. *Jutarnji list,* 10 December 2002, p. 7. See also *Vjesnik,* 16 December 2000, at www .vjesnik.hr/html.

196. Josip Manolić, president of the Croatian Independent Democratic Party, in interview with the author, Zagreb, 4 August 1997.

197. Milorad Pupovac, president of the Serbian Democratic Forum, in interview with the author, Zagreb, 29 July 1997.

198. Viktor Meier, *Wie Jugoslawien verspielt wurde,* 2nd ed. (Munich: C. H. Beck'sche Buchdruckerei, 1996), p. 241.

199. Milorad Pupovac, in interview with the author, Zagreb, 1 August 1997.

200. *Novi list,* 25 August 2004, at www.novilist.hr.

201. Re "the Croatian Goebbels," *Novi list,* 9 August 2004, at www.novilist.hr. Re Budak's literary accomplishments, Petar Strčić, a Croatian academic, said, "The literary work of Mile Budak is average and does not have a lasting value. The major part of his life was [his] political life." Quoted in *Novi list,* 14 August 2004, at www.novilist.hr.

202. Re no objection, *Novi list,* 8 August 2004, at www.novilist.hr; accused the Church, *Novi list,* 22 August 2004, at www.novilist.hr.

203. *Vjesnik,* 4 September 2004, at www.vjesnik.hr.

204. See *Novi list,* 30 August 2004, at www.novilist.hr.

205. *Vjesnik,* 9 September 2004, at www.vjesnik.hr.

206. Vlado Gotovac, president of the Croatian Social-Liberal Party, in interview with the author, Zagreb, 31 July 1997. I had met Gotovac previously in 1989.

207. HINA (Zagreb), 13 September 2000, in FBIS-EEU-2000-0913.

208. Re the appropriation of news, see, for example, the discussion in *Nacional,* no. 233 (4 May 2000), at www.nacional.hr. Re automobile smuggling, see the report in *Nacional,* no. 261 (16 November 2000), at www.nacional.hr. Re drug smuggling, see *Nacional,* no. 258 (26 October 2000), at www.nacional.hr. Re embezzlement, see *Croatia Weekly,* 24 June 1999, p. 7; and *Agence France Presse,* 19 June 2000, on LNAU. Re police corruption, see *Nacional,* no. 278 (15 March 2001), and *Nacional,* no. 282 (12 April 2001)—both at www.nacional.hr. Re graft by the Tudjman family, see *Irish Times,* 1 November 2000, p. 7, on LNAU; *Nacional,* no. 260 (9 November 2000), at www.nacional.hr; and *TOL* (Prague), 15–21 October 2002, at www.tol.cz.

209. "Tudjmanova gangsterska država," in *Nacional,* 5 April 2000, pp. 8–9.

210. Vjekoslav Perica, "The Catholic Church and Croatian Statehood," in Vjeran Pavlaković (ed.), *Nationalism, Religion, and Culture in Post-Communist Croatia,* Donald W. Treadgold Papers no. 32 (Seattle: Henry M. Jackson School of International Studies of the University of Washington, November 2001), pp. 58–61.

211. Milivoj Djilas, "The Government Plans to Create an Anti-Organized Crime Bureau," *AIM Press,* 16 November 2000, at www.aimpress.ch, p. 1.

212. The poll was commissioned by the BBC and conducted by Prizma among 400 persons across Croatia. See Ivan Lovreček, "A Culture of Corruption," *Beta news agency,* 22 November 2002, at www.beta.co.yu/korupcija/eng, p. 2.

213. Ivica Djikić, "Corruption, Croatia's Tragedy," *AIM Press,* 29 November 2001, at www .aimpress.ch, p. 2. For further discussion, see Zoran Malenica, "Corruption in the Judiciary and the State Administration in the Republic of Croatia," in Dragica Vujadinović, Lino Veljak, Vladimir Goati, and Veselin Pavićević (eds.), *Between Authoritarianism and Democracy: Serbia, Montenegro, Croatia,,* vol. 2 (Belgrade: CEDET, 2005), pp. 455–469.

214. See, for example, *Borba,* 4 April 1993, p. 4, trans. in FBIS, *Daily Report* (Eastern Europe), 14 April 1993, pp. 32–3.

215. *Globus,* 14 May 1993, pp. 9–10, trans. in FBIS, *Daily Report* (Eastern Europe), 3 June 1993, p. 36.

216. Re dreams of union, *International Herald Tribune* (Tokyo ed.), 5 April 1994, p. 2. Re regional autonomy, *Vesti* (Bad Vilbel), 24 May 1996, p. 13, trans. in FBIS, *Daily Report* (Eastern Europe), 30 May 1996, p. 37; and *Croatia Weekly,* 7 April 2000, p. 3.

217. *Globus,* no. 526 (5 January 2001): 24–25. In Split, the number of "Orthodox" (i.e., Serb) residents dropped precipitously from 5,409 in 1991 to just 9 in 2002. Viktor Ivančić, "Posljednji Pravoslavci," *Feral Tribune,* no. 875 (22 June 2002): 59–60. See also Vjeran Pavlaković, "Minorities in Croatia since Independence," in Pavlaković (ed.), *Nationalism, Religion, and Culture.* See also *Vjesnik,* 9 February 2001, at www.vjesnik.hr/html.

218. *Vjesnik,* 23 November 2000, at www.vjesnik.hr/html; and HINA (Zagreb), 13 December 2002, in FBIS No. EUP-2000-1213-000369. See also *Frankfurter Rundschau,* 4 September 2003, p. 1.

219. Re job discrimination, *Vjesnik,* 22 June 2002, at www.vjesnik.hr; and *Agence France Presse,* 23 June 2002, on *Lexis-Nexis,* at www.nexis.com. Re delays in pensions, *Vukovarske novine,* 6 December 2002, p. 4. Re overt forms of ethnic hatred, *Human Rights Watch—World Report 2001: Croatia,* at www.hrw.org/wr2k; and *Vjesnik,* 30 October 2002, at www.vjesnik.hr.

220. Re destruction of monuments, HINA, 2 February 2001, in FBIS no. EUP-2001-0202-000349. Re erection of plaque to Francetić, *Vjesnik,* 7 February 2001, at www.vjesnik.hr.

221. *Nacional,* no. 321 (10 January 2002), at www.nacional.hr. *Nacional* adds: "[T]hese murders took place primarily in three police districts: Sisak, Osijek, and Vukovar, which at that time were under the control of HDZ military dilettantes, enjoying their roles as macho military leaders."

222. *Klik Magazin* (Zagreb), 28 May 2002, at www.klik.hr/naslovnica/politika; and *Agence France Presse,* 23 June 2002, at www.reliefweb.int.

223. Re "opponent of religious sects," *Globus,* 14 January 1994, quoted in Zlatko Gall, "Pit-Bull in Court," *Vijenac* (Zagreb), 5 June 1997, trans. on 11/55/99, at www.ex-yupress .com/vijenac/vijenac6.html, p. 2. Re AIDS, *Globus,* 14 July 1994, quoted in ibid., p. 3.

224. Baković, quoted in "Croatian Pro-Lifers Attacking Women's Rights—Update," 3 November 1998, *B.a.B.e., Women's Human Rights Group (Zagreb),* at www.babe.hr/eng/statements/anti-choice-98.htm.

225. See, for example, Aleksandra Žarak, "Homo kultura osvaja Zagreb," *Globus,* 25 April 2003, pp. 66–68; *Novi list,* 3 April 2003, at www.novilist.hr; and *Vjesnik,* 29 June 2003, at www.vjesnik.hr.

226. Re intolerance, see Ivana Erceg, "Hrvatska—Gay pod zemljom," *Feral Tribune,* no. 852 (12 January 2002): 21–23. Re transsexuality, Ivana Erceg, "Tijelo ne čini čovjeka," *Feral Tribune,* no. 855 (2 February 2002): 68–71.

227. Zoran Radosavljević, "Some Pride but Mainly Prejudice for Gays in Balkans," *Reuters,* 10 July 2002, at www.womenngo.org.yu. Regarding the 2003 gay pride parade in Zagreb, see *Novi list,* 29 June 2003, p. 2.

228. *Jutarnji list,* 14 June 2003, p. 8; and Dean Vuletić, "Gay Men and Lesbians in Croatia," paper presented at a conference on *Croatia after the War,* supported by the Friedrich Naumann Stiftung, held at the Inter-University Centre, Dubrovnik, 10–11 June 2005. For further discussion of the situation of gays and lesbians in Croatia, see Ivana Erceg, "Kako će glasati homoseksualci u Saboru," *Feral Tribune,* no. 876 (29 June 2002): 34–35.

229. *Novi list,* 8 November 2003, at www.novilist.hr.

230. *Jutarnji list,* 6 November 2002, p. 7, and 31 October/1 November 2003, p. 5.

231. One of these is Vesna Pusić's Croatian People's Party. See *Jutarnji list,* 3 November 2003, p. 3.

232. V. Matijanić, "Mediji i homoseksualizam," *Feral Tribune,* 22 November 2003, p. 22. It is my impression, however, that the same could be said of the Rijeka-based daily, *Novi list.*

233. *Novi list,* 12 April 2003, at www.novilist.hr.

234. *Women 2000,* chapter on "Croatia," p. 123; and U.S. Department of State, *1999 Country Reports on Human Rights Practices,* released by the Bureau of Democracy, Human Rights, and Labor, 25 February 2000—*Croatia,* at www.state.gov/www/global/human_rights/1999_hrp_report/croatia.html, p. 23 of 31.

235. U.S. Department of State, *1999 Country Reports—Croatia,* p. 23 of 31.

236. *Jutarnji list,* 3 November 2003, p. 8.

237. *Women 2000,* p. 129.

238. "Elektorine: Percentage of Women in Croatian Parliament after Elections," 11 January 2000, *B.a.B.e., Women's Human Rights Group* (Zagreb), at www.babe.hr/eng/research/elektorine4.htm, p. 1 of 2.

239. *Women 2000,* p. 12.

240. For more details, see Sabrina P. Ramet, "The Croatian Catholic Church since 1990," in *Religion, State and Society,* vol. 24, no. 4 (1996): 346–347.

241. Žarko Puhovski, vice president of the Croatian Helsinki Committee for Human Rights, in interview with the author, Zagreb, 4 August 1997.

242. *Večernji list,* 25 February 2001, at www.vecernji-list.hr.

243. *Jutarnji list,* 28 October 2001, p. 5; *Novi list,* 28 April 2002, at www.novilist.hr; *Vjesnik,* 26 November 2001, at www.vjesnik.hr; and *Nacional,* no. 314 (22 November 2001), at www.nacional.hr.

244. Damir Agičić, "Nastava povijesti u Hrvatskoj," *Povijest u nastavi,* vol. 1, no. 2 (2003): 141.

245. Vjeran Pavlaković, "From Saints to Sinners: Reinterpretations of the Partisans in Yugoslavia" (unpublished paper, Seattle, 2000), pp. 14–15.

246. *Večernji list,* 9 March 2001, at www.vecernji-list.hr.

247. Lončarić-Jelačiv, quoted in *Croatia Weekly,* 10 June 1999, p. 2.

248. *Croatia Weekly,* 24 June 1999, p. 3.

249. *Jutarnji list* (27 May 2000), p. 35.

250. Agičić, "Nastava povijesti," p. 145.

251. Re Koren's eighth-grade text, Snježana Koren, *Povijest 8, udžbenik za 8. razred osnovne škole,* 5th ed. (Zagreb: Profil International, 2004). See also, for the seventh grade, Damir Agičić, Snježana Koren, and Magdalena Najbar-Agičić, *Povijest 7, udžbenik povijesti za sedmi razred osnovne škole,* 4th ed. (Zagreb: Profil International, 2004). Re Jurčević and Marija Raić's eighth-grade text, Magdalena Najbar-Agičić and Damir Agičić, "The Use and Misuse of History Teaching in 1990's Croatia," paper presented at a conference on *Democratic Transition in Croatia: Value Transformation, Education, Media,* sponsored by the Norwegian Research Council, Trondheim, 3–4 September 2004, p. 16.

252. Najbar-Agičić and Agičić, "Use and Misuse of History," p. 16. See also Snježana Koren, "Manjine u hrvatskim udžbenicima povijesti i zemljopisa," *Povijest u nastavi,* vol. 1, no. 1 (2003): especially pp. 18–27.

253. Najbar-Agičić and Agičić, "Use and Misuse of History," p. 17.

254. Re entering the EU, *Vjesnik,* 23 June 2003, at www.vjesnik.hr. Re cooperating with the ICTY, *Vjesnik,* 22 June 2002, at www.vjesnik.hr.

255. Jelena Lovrić, "Church against Tribunal," *AIM Press,* 10 August 2001, at www.aimpress.ch.

256. Drago Hedl, "Croatia: HDZ Makes Astonishing U-turn," in *IWPR,* BCR no. 475 (9 January 2004), at www.iwpr.net.

257. Re Čermak and Markač, *Vjesnik,* 9 March 2004, at www.vjesnik.hr. Re joining the EU, *Vjesnik,* 22 April 2004, at www.vjesnik.hr.

258. *Slobodna Dalmacija,* 29 January 2004, at www.slobodnadalmacija.hr.

259. *Vjesnik,* 7 September 2004, at www.vjesnik.hr.

260. *Hrvatski Informativni Centar* [hereafter, HIC] (Zagreb), 3 May 2005, at www.hic.hr/ english [accessed 3 May 2005].

261. HIC (30 May 2005), at www.hic.hr/english [accessed 30 May 2005].

262. *Croatia Economic—Update 2003/2004,* at www.moit.gov.il.; and Central Intelligence Agency, *The World Factbook,* last updated on 17 May 2005, at www.cia.gov/cia/publication/ factbook/geos/hr.html Econ [accessed on 6 June 2005].

263. *Novi list,* 16 July 2003, at www.novilist.hr.

264. HINA news agency (Zagreb), 26 October 1999, in *BBC Monitoring Europe—Political,* 27 October 1999, on nexis.com.

265. Ankara Anatolia, 26 January 2001, in FBIS-WEU-2001-0126.

266. *Transparency International Corruption Perceptions Index 2002,* pp. 4–5.

267. Scores as posted at www.freedomhouse.org/ratings/congo.htm.

268. "Slovenia Places 14th in Press Freedom Index," *Slovenia News,* 29 October 2002, at slonews.sta.si.

269. *Macedonian Agency of Information* (Skopje), 28 November 2005, at www.inf.gov.mk/ english [accessed on 29 November 2005].

20. Conclusion

1. Lenard J. Cohen, *Serpent in the Bosom: The Rise and Fall of Slobodan Milošević* (Boulder, Colo.: Westview Press, 2001), pp. 82, 85, 398.

2. Robert M. Hayden, *Blueprints for a House Divided: The Constitutional Logic of the Yugoslav Conflicts* (Ann Arbor: University of Michigan Press, 1999), passim. For a useful review of Hayden's book, see Thomas Cushman's review in *Slavic Review,* vol. 60, no. 1 (Spring 2001): 172–173. For an effective rebuttal of some of Hayden's ideas, see Thomas Cushman, *Critical Theory and the War in Croatia and Bosnia,* Donald W. Treadgold Papers in Russian, East European, and Central Asian Studies no. 13 (Seattle: Henry M. Jackson School of International Studies of the University of Washington, 1997).

3. Jasna Dragović-Soso, *"Saviours of the Nation": Serbia's Intellectual Opposition and the Revival of Nationalism* (London: C. Hurst, 2002), pp. 256–257.

4. Adam LeBor, *Milošević: A Biography* (Polmont, Stirlingshire: Bloomsbury, 2002), p. 94, also p. 154.

5. Ćosić, quoted in Dragović-Soso, *"Saviours of the Nation,"* pp. 122–123.

6. On the other hand, the subjective orientations of people should not be considered irrelevant, since it is people who are interpreting the actions of the regime and holding them up to judgment. For further discussion, see Edward N. Muller, "Correlates and Consequences of Beliefs in the Legitimacy of Regime Structures," *Midwest Journal of Political Science,* vol. 14, no. 3 (August 1970): 392–412.

7. Milošević, as recalled by Slovenian president Milan Kučan and quoted in LeBor, *Milošević,* p. 116.

8. Unconstitutional and illegal moves are detailed and documented in Sabrina P. Ramet, *Balkan Babel: The Disintegration of Yugoslavia from the Death of Tito to the Fall of Milošević,*

4th ed. (Boulder, Colo.: Westview Press, 2002), pp. 71–72. Re Organizing Committee, LeBor, *Milošević*, pp. 107, 109.

9. For a fuller development of this argument, see Sabrina P. Ramet and Philip W. Lyon, "Discord, Denial, Dysfunction: The Serbia-Montenegro-Kosovo Triangle," in *Problems of Post-Communism*, vol. 49, no. 5 (September/October 2002): 3–19.

10. Lionel Curtis, *Civitas Dei* (London, 1950), p. 655, as quoted in Tiziana Stella, "Federalismo e Atlantismo nella politica estera degli Stati Uniti: Il contributo di Clarence Streit" (Ph.D. dissertation, University of Pavia, 1999), p. 156.

11. LeBor, *Milošević*, p. 103.

12. Detailed and documented in Ger Duijzings, *Religion and the Politics of Identity in Kosovo* (London: C. Hurst, 2000).

13. Jack Snyder, *From Voting to Violence: Democratization and Nationalist Conflict* (New York: W. W. Norton, 2000), pp. 200–201.

14. Re Montenegro, see *Glas Slavonije* (Osijek), 16 September 2005, at www.glas-slavonije.hr [accessed on 17 September 2005]; *Glas javnosti* (21 September 2005), at www.glas-javnosti.co.yu [accessed on 21 September 2005]; and *Dagens Nyheter* (Stockholm), 20 November 2005 [accessed on 20 November 2005]. Re Kosovo, see *Glas javnosti* (15 November 2005), at www.glas-javnosti.co.yu; *Večernje novosti* (Belgrade), 18 November 2005, at www.novosti.co.yu [accessed on 18 November 2005]; and *Glas javnosti* (20 November 2005), at www.glas-javnosti.co.yu [accessed on 20 November 2005].

15. "Is Torture Ever Justified?" *The Economist* (London), 11 January 2003, p. 11.

16. See, for example, Michael J. Smith, "Humanitarian Intervention: An Overview of the Ethical Issues," *Ethics & International Affairs*, vol. 12 (1998): 63–79; and W. Michael Reisman, "Sovereignty and Human Rights in Contemporary International Law," *American Journal of International Law*, vol. 84, no. 4 (October 1990): 866–876.

17. D. Engster, "Jean Bodin, Scepticism and Absolute Sovereignty," *History of Political Thought*, vol. 17, no. 4 (Winter 1996), p. 476.

18. Corollaries 3a and 3b to Proposition 3.

19. Proposition 4 and corollary 4a.

20. Proposition 8.

21. Proposition 11.

22. Corollary 11b.

23. Proposition 12.

24. Proposition 13.

25. Proposition 14.

26. Robert M. Hayden, "Schindler's Fate: Genocide, Ethnic Cleansing, and Population Transfers," *Slavic Review*, vol. 55, no. 4 (Winter 1996): 733, 736.

27. See Sabrina P. Ramet, "The Radical Right in Germany," in Sabrina P. Ramet (ed.), *The Radical Right in Central and Eastern Europe since 1989* (University Park: Pennsylvania State University Press, 1999).

28. Joachim Hösler, "'Balkanisierung'—'Europäisierung'? Zu Südosteuropas historischer Spezifik und den Folgen westeuropäischen 'Zivilisations- und Stabilitätsexports,'" in Joachim Hösler, Norman Paech, and Gerhard Stuby, *Der gerechte Krieg? Neue Nato-Strategie, Völkerrecht und Westeuropäisierung des Balkans* (Bremen: Donat Verlag, 2000), pp. 26–32.

Selected Bibliography

Archival Materials

CIA, *National Intelligence Estimate,* HRP 92-4 (RG263, Box 8): "Outlook for Yugoslavia," NNR-263-94-008, 23 May 1961, folder 5, S, decl. 2/15/95, on deposit at NA.

CIA, *National Intelligence Survey,* Section 50, Chap. V, NIS 21 (RG273, Box 92): three reports, on deposit at NA.

CIA, *National Intelligence Survey,* Section 53, Chap. V, NIS 21 (RG273, Box 92): "Yugoslavia—Political Dynamics," 1 August 1960, vol. 17, C, decl. 22 November 2000, under the FIA, by the authority of NND 0011144, by SDT/SL, on deposit at NA.

CIA, *National Intelligence Survey,* Section 57, Chap. V, NIS 21 (RG273, Box 92): "Yugoslavia—Subversive," 1 August 1951, vol. 29, S, decl. 22 November 2000, under the FIA, by the authority of NND 0011144, by SDT/SL, on deposit at NA.

CIA, *Records of the Central Intelligence Agency, Estimates of the ORE, 1946–1950,* Intelligence Publication File HRP 92-4/001 (RG263, Box 3): three reports, on deposit at NA.

CIA, *Record of the Central Intelligence Agency, National Intelligence Estimates Concerning the Soviet Union, 1950–1961,* Intelligence Publication File HRP 92-4/001 (RG263, Box 1): three reports, on deposit at NA.

General Records of the Department of State, Central Foreign Policy Files 1967–1969, Political & Defense, decl. 1996 (RG59, Box 2841–2842), on deposit at NA.

Records of the Allied Operational and Occupation Headquarters, World War II, SHAEF, Office of the Chief of Staff, Decimal file MAY 1943–AUG 1945, NND 760174, HM 1999 (RG331, Box 70), on deposit at NA.

Records of the Army Staff, OACS, RIRR, Security Classified Intelligence and Investigative Dossiers—IRR Impersonal File, 1939–1976, NND 007034 (RG319, Boxes 142–143), on deposit at NA.

Records of the Army Staff, OACS, G-2, RIIR—NND 853125 (RG319), on deposit at NA.

Records of the Army Staff, OACS, G-2, RIIR—NND 983021 (RG319), on deposit at NA.

Records of the Army Staff, ROACS, G-2, RIRR, Security Classified Intelligence and Investigative Dossiers, 1939–1976—IRR Personal Name File (RG319, Boxes 10a, 107), on deposit at NA.

Records of the Department of State Relating to the Internal Affairs of Yugoslavia 1930–1939, Decimal file 860H (RG59, M-1203), on deposit at NA.

Records of the U.S. Department of State Relating to the Internal Affairs of Yugoslavia 1945–1949, Decimal file 860h, on deposit at SAL—reels 1–3.

Records of the U.S. Department of State Relating to the Internal Affairs of Yugoslavia 1950–1954, Decimal file 768 (RG59, LM77), on deposit at NA—reels 1–3, 5.

Records of the U.S. Department of State Relating to the Internal Affairs of Yugoslavia 1955–1959, Decimal file 768 (RG59, C0034), on deposit at NA—reels 1–3, 7.

Records of the U.S. Nuernberg War Crimes Trials, NOKW Series, 1933–47, RG 238, T1119, on deposit at NA.

Savska Banovina—Državna zaštita, *Strogo povjerlivi spisi 1929–1939 g.,* Boxes 1–121—at HDA (Zagreb).

Dallin, Alexander, and F. I. Firsov (eds.). *Dimitrov and Stalin, 1934–1943: Letters from the Soviet Archives.* Russian documents trans. by Vadim A. Staklo. New Haven, Conn.: Yale University Press, 2000.

Memoirs, Diaries, Autobiographies

Bildt, Carl. *Peace Journey: The Struggle for Peace in Bosnia.* London: Weidenfeld and Nicolson, 1998.

Boutros-Ghali, Boutros. *Unvanquished: A U.S.–U.N. Saga.* New York: Random House, 1999.

Clark, General Wesley K. *Waging Modern War: Bosnia, Kosovo, and the Future of Combat.* New York: PublicAffairs, 2001.

Dimitrov, Georgi. *Georgi Dimitrov: Dnevnik, 1933–1949.* Ed. by Dimitŭr Sirkov. Sofia: Universitetsko Izdatelstvo 'Sv. Kliment' Ohridski, 1997.

Dizdarević, Raif. *Od smrti Tita do smrti Jugoslavije: Svjedočenja.* Sarajevo: Svjedok, 1999.

Djilas, Milovan. *Conversations with Stalin.* Trans. from Serbo-Croatian by Michael B. Petrovich. New York: Harcourt, Brace, & World, 1962.

———. *Fall of the New Class: A History of Communism's Self-Destruction.* Trans. from Serbo-Croatian by John Loud, ed. by Vasilije Kalezić. New York: Alfred A. Knopf, 1998.

———. *Wartime.* Trans. by Michael B. Petrovich. New York: Harcourt Brace Jovanovich, 1977.

Drnovšek, Janez. *Der Jugoslawien-Krieg. Meine Wahrheit.* Trans. from Slovenian by Doris Debeniak. Kilchberg: SmartBooks Publishing AG, 1998.

Genscher, Hans-Dietrich. *Rebuilding a House Divided: A Memoir by the Architect of Germany's Reunification.* Trans. from German by Thomas Thornton. New York: Broadway Books, 1995.

Halilović, Sefer. *Lukava strategija.* 3rd enlarged ed. Sarajevo: Matica, 1998.

Holbrooke, Richard. *To End a War.* New York: Random House, 1998.

Hurd, Douglas. *Memoirs.* London: Little, Brown, 2003.

Hutchings, Robert L. *American Diplomacy and the End of the Cold War: An Insider's Account of U.S. Policy in Europe, 1989–1992.* Washington, D.C.: Woodrow Wilson Center Press and Johns Hopkins University Press, 1997.

Izetbegović, Alija. *Izetbegović of Bosnia and Herzegovina: Notes from Prison, 1983–1988.* Translator not identified. Westport, Conn.: Praeger, 2002.

———. *Sjećanja: Autobiografski zapis.* Sarajevo: TDK Sahinpašic, 2001.

Janša, Janez. *The Making of the Slovenian State, 1988–1992: The Collapse of Yugoslavia.* Trans. by AMIDAS d.o.o., ed. by Aleksander Zorn. Ljubljana: Založba Mladinska knjiga, 1994.

Jović, Borisav. *Posledni dani SFRJ—izvodi iz dnevnika.* Belgrade: Politika, 1995.

Kadijević, Veljko. *Moje vidjenje raspada.* Belgrade: Politika, 1993.

Kardelj, Edvard. *Reminiscences: The Struggle for Recognition and Independence—The New Yugoslavia, 1944–1957.* Trans. by David Norris. London: Summerfield Press, 1982.

Kavčič, Stane. *Dnevnik in spomini, 1972–1987.* Ed. By Igor Bavčar and Janez Janša. Ljubljana: Casopis za kritiko znanosti, 1988.

Kolšek, Konrad. *Spomini na začetek oborozenega spopada v Jugoslaviji 1991.* Trans. from Croatian by Maja Novak. Maribor: Založba Obzorja, 2001.

Letica, Slaven. *Obećana zemlja—politički antimemoari.* Zagreb: Biblioteka Ex Ungue Leonem, n.d. [1992].

Lukić, Vojin. *Sećanja i saznanja: Aleksandar Ranković i brionski plenum.* Titograd: Novica Jovović, 1989.

Maček, Vladko. *In the Struggle for Freedom*. Trans. by Elizabeth and Stjepan Gazi. University Park: Pennsylvania State University Press, 1959.

Major, John. *The Autobiography*. New York: HarperCollins, 1999.

Mamula, Branko. *Slučaj Jugoslavija*. Podgorica: CID, 2000.

Mesić, Stipe. *Kako je srušena Jugoslavija: Politički memoari*. 2nd ed. Zagreb: Mislav Press, 1994.

Neubacher, Hermann. *Sonderauftrag Südost 1940–1945: Bericht eines fliegenden Diplomaten*. 2nd ed. Göttingen: Musterschmidt Verlag, 1957.

Nikezić, Marko. *Srpska krhka vertikala*. Belgrade: Helsinški odbor za ljudska prava u Srbiji, 2003.

Paraga, Dobroslav. *Goli otok: Istočni grijeh zapada*. Zagreb: Grafikon, 1995.

Pejanović, Mirko. *Through Bosnian Eyes: The Political Memoirs of a Bosnian Serb*. Trans. from Serbo-Croatian by Marina Bowder. Sarajevo: TKD Šahinpašić, 2002.

Pérez de Cuéllar, Javier. *Pilgrimage for Peace: A Secretary General's Memoir*. Houndmills, Basingstoke, UK: Macmillan, 1997.

Petritsch, Wolfgang. *Bosnien und Herzegowina Fünf Jahre nach Dayton: Hat der Friede eine Chance?* Klagenfurt and Vienna: Wieser Verlag, 2001.

Rose, General Sir Michael. *Fighting for Peace: Lessons from Bosnia*. London: Warner Books, 1999.

Rudolf, Davorin. *Rat koji nismo htjeli. Hrvatska 1991*. Zagreb: Globus, 1999.

Šarinić, Hrvoje. *Svi moji tajni pregovori sa Slobodanom Miloševićem: Izmedju rata i diplomacije 1993–95 (98)*. Zagreb: Globus, 1999.

Špegelj, Martin. *Sjećanja vojnika*. Ed. by Ivo Zanić. Zagreb: Znanje, 2001.

Tomac, Zdravko. *The Struggle for the Croatian State . . . through Hell to Democracy*. Trans. by Profikon. Zagreb: Profikon, 1993.

Tripalo, Miko. *Hrvatsko proljeće*. Zagreb: Globus, 1989.

Vukmanović[-Tempo], Svetozar. *Struggle for the Balkans*. Trans. by Charles Bartlett. London: Merlin Press, 1990.

Zimmermann, Warren. *Origins of a Catastrophe: Yugoslavia and Its Destroyers*. Updated ed. New York: Times Books, 1999.

Official Documents / Party (in chronological order)

The Trial of Dragoljub-Draža Mihailović. Stenographic Record and Documents from the Trial of Dragoljub-Draža Mihailović. Reprint, Salisbury, N.C.: Documentary Publications, 1977. Belgrade: Union of the Journalists Associations of . . . Yugoslavia, 1946.

The White Book on Aggressive Activities by the Governments of the USSR, Poland, Czechoslovakia, Hungary, Rumania, Bulgaria and Albania towards Yugoslavia. Belgrade: Ministry of Foreign Affairs of the FPRY, 1951.

Yugoslavia's Way: The Program of the League of Communists of Yugoslavia [adopted by the Seventh Congress]. Trans. by Stoyan Pribechevich. New York: All Nations Press, 1958.

Treći plenum CK SK Srbije, januar 1966. Belgrade: Sedma sila, 1966.

"Thesenentwurf zur Reorganisation des Bundes der Kommunisten Jugoslawiens" (27 April 1967). *Osteuropaische Rundschau*, vol. 13, no. 6 (June 1967): 37–40.

Šesti kongres Saveza komunista Srbije. Belgrade: Komunist, 1968.

Peti kongres Saveza komunista Bosne i Hercegovine (Sarajevo: 9–11 januar 1969). Sarajevo: Oslobodjenje, 1969.

Nacrti dokumenata za Deveti kongres SKJ. Belgrade: Komunist, 1969.

Deseta konferencija Saveza komunista Srbije za Kosovo i Metohiju. Priština: Rilindja, 1969.

Deveti kongres Saveza komunista Jugoslavije (Beograd, 11–13 III, 1969)—Stenografske beleške. 6 vols. Belgrade: Komunist, 1970.

Sedma sednica Predsedništva Saveza komunista Jugoslavije. Belgrade: Komunist, 1970.

Reforma Saveza komunista Bosne i Hercegovine. Sarajevo: Studijski centar gradske konferencije SK BiH, 1971.

Dalji razvoj i idejnopolitičko delovanje Saveza komunista SAP Vojvodina. 2 vols. Novi Sad, December 1971.

Aktivnost Saveza komunista Srbije u borbi protiv nacionalizma i šovinizma u SR Srbiji. Belgrade: Komunist, 1972.

Savez komunista Hrvatske, Centralni komitet. *Izvještaj o stanju u Savezu komunista Hrvatske u odnosu na prodor nacionalizma u njegove redove.* Zagreb: Informativna služba CK SKH, 1972.

Razgovori o platformi za deseti kongres SKJ. Belgrade: Komunist, 1973.

Sedmi kongres Saveza komunista Hrvatske (Zagreb, 7–9 IV 1974)—Stenografske bilješke. 3 vols. Zagreb: Centralni Komitet Saveza Komunista Hrvatske, 1974.

Deseti kongres Saveza komunista Jugoslavije (Beograd, 27–30 V, 1974)—Stenografske beleške. 4 vols. Belgrade: Komunist, 1975.

Savez komunista Srbije, Centralni komitet. *Savez komunista i aktuelna pitanja idejne borbe.* Belgrade: Komunist, 1976.

Deveta sjednica CK SK Bosne i Hercegovine. Sarajevo: Mala politička biblioteka, 1977.

Osnovne teze za pripremu stavova i dokumenata jedanaestog kongresa Saveza komunista Jugoslavije. Belgrade: Komunist, February 1978.

Osmi kongres Saveza komunista Hrvatske (Zagreb, 24–26 travnja 1978)—Stenografske bilješke. 4 vols. Zagreb: Zrinski, 1978.

Osmi kongres Saveza komunista Srbije. Belgrade: Komunist, 1978.

Jedanaesti kongres Saveza komunista Jugoslavije (Beograd, 20–23 juna 1978)—Magnetofonske beleške. 5 vols. Belgrade: Komunist, 1981.

Osmi kongres SK BiH. Sarajevo: Oslobodjenje, 1982.

5. Sednica CKSKJ. Aktuelni idejno-politički problemi i zadaci Saveza komunista Jugoslavije. Belgrade: Komunist, 1983.

15. Sednica CKSKJ. Obeležavanje Pedesetogodisnjice Četvrte zemaljske konferencije KPJ. Donošenje Odluke o pripremama 13. Kongresa SKJ. Belgrade: Komunist, 1984.

19. Sednica CKSKJ. Razmatranje Predloga platforma za pripremu 13. Kongresa SKJ. Odluke CKSKJ o primprei 13. Kkongresa SKJ. Belgrade: Komunist, 1985.

Official Documents/Government

SAP Kosova. *Ustav Socijalističke Autonomne Pokrajine Kosova.* Belgrade: Savremena administracija, 1974.

SAP Vojvodina. *Ustav Socijalističke Autonomne Pokrajine Vojvodine.* Belgrade: Savremena administracija, 1974.

SFRY. *The Constitution of the Socialist Federal Republic of Yugoslavia.* Trans. by Marko Pavičić. Belgrade and Ljubljana: Dopisna Delavska Univerza, 1974.

———. *Constitutional System of Yugoslavia.* Trans. by Marko Pavičić. Belgrade: Jugoslovenska stvarnost, 1980.

SR Hrvatske. *Ustav Socijalističke Republike Hrvatske.* Belgrade: Službeni list, 1963.

———. *Ustav Socijalističke Republike Hrvatske.* Zagreb: Političke teme, 1974.

SR Srbija. *Ustav Socijalističke Republike Srbije.* Belgrade: Savremena administracija, 1974.

Review Essays

Andrees, Beate, and Christian Boulanger. "Protektorat oder Demokratie 'von unten'? Zur Debatte über die externe Demokratieforderung in Südosteuropa." *Südost Europa,* vol. 49, no. 11/12 (November–December 2000): 629–635.

Aulette, Judy. "Transition in the Balkans and Eastern Europe: How Are Women Faring?" *Feminist Collections,* vol. 21, no. 24 (Summer 2000): 1–3.

Banac, Ivo. "Misreading the Balkans." *Foreign Policy,* no. 93 (Winter 1993/94): 173–182.

———. "Sorting Out the Balkans: Three New Looks at a Troubled Region." *Foreign Affairs,* vol. 79, no. 3 (May/June 2000): 152–157.

Crampton, Richard. "Myths of the Balkans." *New York Review of Books,* 11 January 2001, at www.nybooks.com/nyrev/WWWarchdisplay.cgi?20010111014R [accessed 10 January 2005].

Cviic, Christopher. "Review Article: Perceptions of Former Yugoslavia—An Interpretive Reflection." *International Affairs,* vol. 71, no. 4 (October 1995): 819–826.

Cviic, Christopher. "Review Article: The Serbian Exception." *International Affairs,* vol. 75, no. 3 (July 1999): 635–641.

Dalin, David G. "Pius XII and the Jews." *The Weekly Standard Magazine,* vol. 6, no. 23 (26 February 2001), at www.weeklystandard.com/magazine/mag_6_23_01/dalin_bkart_6_23_01 .asp [accessed 7 September 2001; reprinted in *Catholic Educator's Resource Center,* at www.catholiceducation.org/articles/persecution/pch0024.html [acessed 27 May 2005].

Danner, Mark. "The US and the Yugoslav Catastrophe." In *New York Review of Books,* 20 November 1997, at www.nybooks.com/nyrev/WWWarchdisplay.cgi?19971120056R [accessed 10 January 2005].

Emmert, Thomas. "Greece's Northern Neighbor: Yugoslavia in Recent Bibliography." *Modern Greek Studies Yearbook,* vol. 2 (1986): 287–295.

Glenny, Misha. "Yugoslavia: The Great Fall." In *New York Review of Books,* 23 March 1995, at www.nybooks.com/nyrev/WWWarchdisplay.cgi?19950323056R [accessed 10 January 2005].

Kent, Sarah A. "Writing the Yugoslav Wars: English-Language Books on Bosnia (1992–1996) and the Challenges of Analyzing Contemporary History." *American Historical Review,* vol. 102, no. 4 (October 1997): 1085–1114.

Krokar, James P. "Insiders and Outsiders on the Former and Present Yugoslavia." *Nationalities Papers,* vol. 28, no. 4 (December 2000): 723–735.

Mertus, Julie A. "Legitimizing the Use of Force in Kosovo." *Ethics & International Affairs,* vol. 15, no. 1 (2001): 133–150.

Ramet, Sabrina P. "Can a Society Be Sick? The Case of Serbia." *Journal of Human Rights,* vol. 1, no. 4 (December 2002): 615–620.

———. "Debates about Intervention: Recent German Books about Bosnia and Kosovo." *Internationale Politik—Transatlantic Edition,* vol. 4, no. 2 (Summer 2003): 91–100; vol. 4, no. 3 (Fall 2003): 101–106.

———. "In Search of the 'Real' Milošević: New Books about the Rise and Fall of Serbia's Strongman." *Journal of Human Rights,* vol. 2, no. 3 (September 2003): 455–466.

———. "Kuga nacionalizma in zapuščina vojne" [The Scourge of Nationalism and the Legacy of War: Recent Books about Serbia and Bosnia]. *Teorija in praksa* (Ljubljana), 4/2003: 759–770.

———. "Revisiting the Horrors of Bosnia: New Books about the War." *East European Politics and Societies,* vol. 14, no. 2 (Spring 2000): 475–486.

————. "The Sources of Discord, the Making of Harmony: Books about Yugoslav Violence: A Review Article." *Europe-Asia Studies,* vol. 53, no. 2 (2001): 351–356.

————. "Tracing the Roots of the Collapse of Yugoslavia." *Modern Greek Studies Yearbook,* vol. 9 (1993): 479–487.

————. "Views from Inside: Memoirs concerning the Yugoslav Breakup and War." *Slavic Review,* vol. 61, no. 3 (Fall 2002): 558–580.

Ramet, Sabrina P., and Angelo Georgakis. "Milošević and Kosovo through Western Eyes: A Review Essay." *Modern Greek Studies Yearbook,* vol. 16/17 (2000/2001): 591–602.

Simmons, Cynthia. "Baedeker Barbarism: Rebecca West's *Black Lamb and Grey Falcon* and Robert Kaplan's *Balkan Ghosts.*" *Human Rights Review,* vol. 2, no. 1 (October–December 2000): 109–124.

Stokes, Gale, John Lampe, and Dennison Rusinow, with Julie Mostov. "Instant History: Understanding the Wars of Yugoslav Succession." *Slavic Review,* vol. 55, no. 1 (Spring 1996): 136–160.

van Heuven, Martin. "Understanding the Balkan Breakup." *Foreign Policy,* no. 103 (Summer 1996): 175–188.

Williams, Ian. "The Butcher Shop." *Nation* (12–19 January 1998): 28–31.

Other Published Materials

Aleksić, Mihailo. *Koncepcija dugoročnog razvoja saobraćaja Jugoslavije.* Belgrade: Ekonomski institut, 1975.

Alexander, Stella. *The Triple Myth: A Life of Archbishop Alojzije Stepinac.* Boulder, Colo.: East European Monographs, 1987.

Ali, Rabia, and Lawrence Lifschultz (eds.). *Why Bosnia? Writings on the Balkan War.* Stony Creek, Conn.: Pamphleteer's Press, 1993.

Allcock, John B., John J. Horton, and Marko Milivojevic (eds.). *Yugoslavia in Transition: Choices and Constraints—Essays in Honour of Fred Singleton.* Oxford: Berg, 1992.

Anderson, Kenneth. *Yugoslavia: Crisis in Kosovo.* New York: Helsinki Watch, March 1990.

Andjelić, Neven. *Bosnia-Herzegovina: The End of a Legacy.* London: Frank Cass, 2003.

Anić, Nikola. *Njemačka vojska u Hrvatskoj 1941.–1945.* Zagreb: Hrvatski Institut za Povijest, 2002.

Anzulović, Branimir. *Heavenly Serbia: From Myth to Genocide.* London: Hurst, 1999.

Banac, Ivo. "The Fearful Asymmetry of War: The Causes and Consequences of Yugoslavia's Demise." *Daedalus,* vol. 121, no. 2 (Spring 1992): 143–174.

————. *The National Question in Yugoslavia: Origins, History, Politics.* Ithaca, N.Y.: Cornell University Press, 1984.

————. *With Stalin against Tito: Cominformist Splits in Yugoslav Communism.* Ithaca, N.Y.: Cornell University Press, 1988.

Barić, Nikica. *Srpska pobuna u Hrvatskoj 1990–1995.* Zagreb: Golden Marketing-Tehnička Knjiga, 2005.

Barker, Rodney. *Political Legitimacy and the State.* Oxford: Clarendon Press, 1990.

Basota, Nuri. "Problemi ubrzanijeg razvoja Kosova kao nedovoljno razvijenog područja." *Obeležja,* vol. 9, no. 5 (September–October 1979): 37–50.

Bass, Robert, and Elizabeth Marbury (eds.). *The Soviet-Yugoslav Controversy, 1948–58: A Documentary Record.* New York: Prospect Books, 1959.

Batelja, J., and C. Tomić (eds.). *Alojzije Kardinal Stepinac, Nadbiskup Zagrebački: Propovijedi, govori, poruke (1941–1946).* Zagreb: AGM, 1996.

Bates, Drago. *Ekonomika saobraćaja*. Belgrade: Naučna knjiga, 1979.

Bax, Mart. "Mass Graves, Stagnating Identification, and Violence: A Case Study in the Local Sources of 'the War' in Bosnia Hercegovina." *Anthropological Quarterly*, vol. 70, no. 1 (January 1997): 11–19.

Becker, Jens, and Achim Engelberg (eds.). *Montenegro im Umbruch. Reportagen und Essays.* Münster: Verlag Westfälisches Dampfboot, 2003.

Behschnitt, Wolf Dietrich. *Nationalismus bei Serben und Kroaten 1830–1914.* Munich: R. Oldenbourg Verlag, 1980.

Bellamy, Alex J. *Kosovo and International Society.* Houndmills: Palgrave Macmillan, 2002.

Benderly, Jill, and Evan Kraft (eds.). *Independent Slovenia: Origins, Movements, Prospects.* New York: St. Martin's Press, 1994.

Beneš, Václav L., Robert F. Byrnes, and Nicolas Spulber (eds.). *The Second Soviet-Yugoslav Dispute: Full Text of Main Documents, April–June 1958.* Bloomington: Indiana University Press, 1959.

Benigar, O. Aleksa. *Alojzije Stepinac, Hrvatski Kardinal.* Rome: Ziral, 1974.

Bennett, Christopher. *Yugoslavia's Bloody Collapse: Causes, Course and Consequences.* New York: New York University Press, 1995.

Bertsch, Gary K., and M. George Zaninovich. "A Factor-Analytic Method of Identifying Different Political Cultures: The Multinational Yugoslav Case." *Comparative Politics*, vol. 6, no. 2 (January 1974): 219–244.

Bieber, Florian. *Nationalismus in Serbien vom Tode Titos bis zum Ende der Ära Milošević.* Vienna: Wiener Osteuropa Studien, 2005.

Bieber, Florian (ed.). *Montenegro in Transition: Problems of Identity and Statehood.* Baden-Baden: Nomos Verlagsgesellschaft, 2003.

Bilandžić, Dušan. *Historija socijalističke federativne republike Jugoslavije.* Zagreb: Školska knjiga, 1978.

———. *Hrvatska moderna povijest.* Zagreb: Golden Marketing, 1999.

———. *Ideje i praksa društvenog razvoja Jugoslavije, 1945–1973.* Belgrade: Komunist, 1973.

———. *Jugoslavija poslije Tita, 1980–1985.* Zagreb: Globus, 1986.

Biondich, Mark. *Stjepan Radić, the Croat Peasant Party, and the Politics of Mass Mobilization, 1904–1928.* Toronto: University of Toronto Press, 2000.

Biserko, Sonja, and Seška Stanojlović (eds.). *Radicalisation of the Serbian Society.* Belgrade: Helsinki Committee for Human Rights in Serbia, December 1997.

Bjelajac, Mile. "Military Elites: Continuity and Discontinuities—The Case of Yugoslavia, 1918–1980." *Association for Social History* (Belgrade). Posted at www.udi.org.yu/Founders/Bjelajac/Military-elite.htm [accessed 6 May 2002].

Blet, Pierre, S.J. *Pius XII and the Second World War: According to the Archives of the Vatican.* New York and Mahwah, N.J.: Paulist Press, 1997.

Boarov, Dimitrije. *Politička istorija Vojvodine.* Novi Sad: Europanon consulting, 2001.

Boban, Ljubo. *Maček i politika Hrvatske seljačke stranke 1928–1941. Iz povijesti hrvatskog pitanja.* 2 vols. Zagreb: Liber, 1974.

Bogdanov, Vaso. *Ante Starčević i Hrvatska politika.* Zagreb: Biblioteka Nezavisnih Pisaca, 1937.

———. *Starčević i Stranka prava prema Srbima i prema jedinstvenu Južnoslavenskih naroda.* Zagreb: Naklada 'Školska knjiga,' 1951.

Bogdanović, Dimitrije. *Knjiga o Kosovu.* Belgrade: Srpska Akademija Nauka i Umetnosti, 1985.

Bogovac, Tomislav. *Reforma obrazovanja—šta je to.* 2 vols. Belgrade: Novinska Ustanova Prosvetni Pregled, 1976, 1977.

Bokovoy, Melissa K. *Peasants and Communists: Politics and Ideology in the Yugoslav Country-side, 1941–1953.* Pittsburgh: University of Pittsburgh Press, 1998.

Bokovoy, Melissa K., Jill A. Irvine, and Carol S. Lilly (eds.). *State-Society Relations in Yugoslavia, 1945–1992.* New York: St. Martin's Press, 1997.

Bombelles, Joseph T. *Economic Development of Communist Yugoslavia, 1947–1964.* Stanford, Calif.: Hoover Institution on War, Revolution, and Peace, 1968.

Borković, Milan. *Milan Nedić.* Zagreb: Centar za Informacije i Publicitet, 1985.

Bose, Sumantra. *Bosnia after Dayton: Nationalist Partition and International Intervention.* London: C. Hurst, 2002.

Both, Norbert. *From Indifference to Entrapment: The Netherlands and the Yugoslav Crisis, 1990–1995.* Amsterdam: Amsterdam University Press, 2000.

Boyle, Francis A. *The Bosnian People Charge Genocide: Proceedings at the International Court of Justice Concerning Bosnia v. Serbia on the Prevention and Punishment of the Crime of Genocide.* Amherst, Mass.: Aletheia Press, 1996.

Broche, François. *Assassinat de Alexandre Ier et Louis Barthou—Marseilles, le 9 Octobre 1934.* Paris: Bolland, 1977.

Buchenau, Klaus. *Orthodoxie und Katholizismus in Jugoslawien 1945–1991.* Wiesbaden: Harrassowitz Verlag, 2004.

Buckley, Mary, and Sally N. Cummings (eds.). *Kosovo: Perceptions of War and Its Aftermath.* London: Continuum, 2001.

Bulatović, Ljiljana. *Prizrenski proces.* Novi Sad: Književna zajednica, 1988.

Burg, Steven L. "Elite Conflict in Post-Tito Yugoslavia." *Soviet Studies,* vol. 38, no. 2 (April 1986): 170–193.

Burg, Steven L., and Michael L. Berbaum. "Community, Integration, and Stability in Multinational Yugoslavia." *Amercan Political Science Review,* vol. 83, no. 2 (June 1989): 535–554.

Burg, Steven L., and Paul S. Shoup. *The War in Bosnia-Herzegovina: Ethnic Conflict and International Intervention.* Armonk, N.Y.: M.E. Sharpe, 1999.

Burks, R. V. *The National Problem and the Future of Yugoslavia.* Santa Monica, Calif.: Rand Corporation, October 1971.

Calic, Marie-Janine. *Krieg und Frieden in Bosnien-Hercegowina.* Expanded ed. Frankfurt-am-Main: Suhrkamp, 1996.

Canapa, Marie-Paule. *Reforme economique et socialisme en Yougoslavia.* Paris: Armand Colin, 1970.

Carter, April. *Democratic Reform in Yugoslavia: The Changing Role of the Party.* Princeton, N.J.: Princeton University Press, 1982.

Čemerlić, Hamdija. "Državnost republika u jugoslovenskom federativnom sistemu." *Godišnjak Fakulteta u Sarajevu 1976,* vol. 24 (1977): 15–32.

Chandler, David. *Bosnia: Faking Democracy after Dayton.* 2nd ed. London and Sterling, Va.: Pluto Press, 2000.

Cigar, Norman. "Croatia's War of Independence: The Parameters of War Termination." *Journal of Slavic Military Studies,* vol. 10, no. 2 (June 1997): 34–70.

———. *Genocide in Bosnia: The Policy of "Ethnic Cleansing."* College Station: Texas A&M University Press, 1995.

———. *The Right to Defence: Thoughts on the Bosnian Arms Embargo.* London: Institute for European Defence & Strategic Studies, 1995.

———. *Vojislav Koštunica and Serbia's Future.* London: Saqi Books, with the Bosnian Institute, 2001.

Cigar, Norman, and Paul Williams. *Indictment at The Hague: The Milošević Regime and Crimes of the Balkan War.* New York: New York University Press, with Pamphleteer's Press, 2002.

Cipek, Tihomir. *Ideja hrvatske države u političkoj misli Stjepana Radića.* Zagreb: Alinea, 2001.

Clissold, Stephen. *Djilas: The Progress of a Revolutionary.* Hounslow, Middlesex: Maurice Temple Smith, 1983.

Coffin, Letty. "Tudjman and Bosnian-Croat Relations." *South Slav Journal,* vol. 18, no. 3–4 (Autumn/Winter 1997): 24–41.

Cohen, Lenard J. *Broken Bonds: Yugoslavia's Disintegration and Balkan Politics in Transition.* 2nd ed. Boulder, Colo.: Westview Press, 1995.

———. *Serpent in the Bosom: The Rise and Fall of Slobodan Milošević.* Boulder, Colo.: Westview Press, 2001.

Cohen, Philip J. *Serbia's Secret War: Propaganda and the Deceit of History.* College Station: Texas A&M University Press, 1996.

Čolanović, Branko. *Development of the Underdeveloped Areas in Yugoslavia.* Belgrade: Medjunarodna Politika, 1966.

Colić, Mladen. "Oružane formacije NDH u Slavoniji 1941–1945. godine." *Zbornik. Historijski Institut Slavonije i Baranje* (Slavonski Brod), vol. 13 (1976): 209–243.

Čolović, Ivan. *The Politics of Symbol in Serbia: Essays in Political Anthropology.* Trans. from Serbian by Celia Hawkesworth. London: C. Hurst, 2002.

———. "The Renewal of the Past: Time and Space in Contemporary Political Mythology." *Other Voices,* vol. 2, no. 1 (February 2000), at www.othervoices.org/2.1/colovic/past.html [accessed 10 January 2005].

Connolly, William (ed.). *Legitimacy and the State.* Oxford: Basil Blackwell, 1984.

Conversi, Daniele. *German-Bashing and the Breakup of Yugoslavia.* Donald W. Treadgold Papers in Russian, East European, and Central Asian Studies, no. 16. Seattle: Henry M. Jackson School of International Studies, University of Washington, March 1998.

Ćosić, Dobrica. *This Land, This Time.* Trans. from Serbian by Muriel Heppell. [Original title: *Vreme smrti,* or *A Time of Death.*] San Diego, Calif.: Harcourt Brace Jovanovich, 1981.

———. *Stvarno i moguće: Članci i ogledi.* 2nd ed. Ljubljana and Zagreb: Cankarjeva založba, 1988.

Cousens, Elizabeth M., and Charles K. Cater. *Toward Peace in Bosnia: Implementing the Dayton Accords.* Boulder, Colo.: Lynne Rienner, 2001.

Cowan, Jane K. (ed.). *Macedonia: The Politics of Identity and Difference.* London & Sterling, Va.: Pluto Press, 2000.

Crvenkovski, Krste. *Medjunacionalni odnosi u samoupravnom društvu.* Belgrade: Sedma sila, 1967.

Čulinović, Ferdo. *Jugoslavija izmedju dva rata.* 2 vols. Zagreb: Historijski Institut Jugoslavenske Akademije Znanosti i Umjetnosti u Zagrebu, 1961.

———. *Okupatorska podjela Jugoslavije.* Belgrade: Vojnoizdavački zavod, 1970.

Cushman, Thomas. *Critical Theory and the War in Croatia and Bosnia.* Donald W. Treadgold Papers in Russian, East European, and Central Asian Studies, no. 13. Seattle: Henry M. Jackson School of International Studies, University of Washington, 2nd printing, December 2000.

Cushman, Thomas, and Stjepan G. Meštrović (eds.). *This Time We Knew: Western Responses to Genocide in Bosnia.* New York and London: New York University Press, 1996.

Čuvalo, Ante. *The Croatian National Movement, 1966–1972.* Boulder, Colo.: East European Monographs, 1990.

Danforth, Loring M. *The Macedonian Conflict: Ethnic Transnationalism in a Transnational World.* Princeton, N.J.: Princeton University Press, 1995.

Dawisha, Karen, and Bruce Parrott (eds.). *Politics, Power, and the Struggle for Democracy in South-East Europe.* Cambridge: Cambridge University Press, 1997.

De Castro, Diego. *Trieste: Cenni Riassuntivi sul Problema Giuliano nell-Ultimo Decennio.* Bologna: Cappelli, 1953.

Dedijer, Vladimir. *The Battle Stalin Lost: Memoirs of Yugoslavia, 1948–1953.* New York: Viking Press, 1971.

———. *Novi prilozi za biografiju Josipa Broza Tita.* Vol. 3. Belgrade: Rad, 1984.

——— (ed.). *Dokumenti 1948.* 3 vols. Belgrade: Rad, 1979.

Degan, Vladimir-Djuro. "Yugoslavia in Dissolution: Opinion No. 1 of the Arbitration Commission of 7 December 1991." *Croatian Political Science Review,* vol. 1, no. 1 (1992): 20–32.

de Zayas, Alfred-Maurice. *A Terrible Revenge: The Ethnic Cleansing of the East European Germans, 1944–1950.* Trans. from German by John A. Koehler. New York: St. Martin's Press, 1994.

Djilas, Aleksa. *The Contested Country: Yugoslav Unity and Communist Revolution, 1919–1953.* Cambridge, Mass.: Harvard University Press, 1991.

———. "A Profile of Slobodan Milošević." In *Foreign Affairs,* vol. 72, no. 3 (Summer 1993): 81–96.

Djilas, Milovan. *Anatomy of a Moral.* Ed. by Abraham Rothberg. New York: Frederick A. Praeger, 1959.

———. *The New Class: An Analysis of the Communist System.* New York: Praeger, 1957.

———. *Tito: The Story from Inside.* Trans. by Vasilije Kojić and Richard Hayes. New York: Harcourt Brace Jovanovich, 1980.

Djilas, Milovan, and Nadežda Gaće. *Adil Zulfikarpašić: Eine politische Biographie aus dem heutigen Bosnien.* Trans. from Bosnian by Jens Reuter. Munich: R. Oldenbourg Verlag, 1996.

Djodan, Šime. "Autonomaštvo kao recidiva unitarizma." *Vidik,* vol. 18, no. 32/33 (July–August 1971): 33–41.

———. "Gdje dr Stipe Šuvar 'pronalazi' nacionalizam, a gdje ga ne vidi." *Kolo,* vol. 7, no. 7 (July 1969): 686–713.

———. "Gospodarski položaj Hrvatske." *Kritika,* vol. 4, no. 17 (March–April 1971): 348–352.

———. "Pred kritičnom barijerom." *Dometi,* vol. 2, no. 3 (March 1969): 4–13.

———. "Prilog raspravi o regionalnom razvoju u SFRJ." *Kolo,* vol. 6, no. 11 (November 1968): 471–473.

———. "Robno-novčani privredni model i regionalni razvoj u našim uvjetima." *Kolo,* vol. 6, no. 10 (October 1968): 379–387.

Djordjević, Jovan et al. *Federalizam i nacionalno pitanje.* Belgrade: Savez udruženja za političke nauke Jugoslavije, 1971.

Djukić, Slavoljub. *Izmedju slave i anateme: Politička biografija Slobodana Miloševića.* Belgrade: Filip Višnjic, 1994.

———. *Milošević and Marković: A Lust for Power.* Trans. from Serbian by Alex Dubinsky. Montreal: McGill–Queen's University Press, 2001.

———. *Slom srpskih liberala. Tehnologija političkih obračuna Josipa Broza.* Belgrade: Filip Višnjic, 1990.

Djureković, Stjepan. *Ja, Josip Broz-Tito.* Zagreb: International Books–USA, 1982.

Doder, Dusko. *The Yugoslavs.* New York: Random House, 1978.

Doder, Dusko, and Louise Branson. *Milosevic: Portrait of a Tyrant.* New York: Free Press, 1999.

Dodić, Mirko. *Ekonomika, organizacija i razvoj saobraćaja SFRJ.* Belgrade: Institut Ekonomskih Nauka, 1977.

Donia, Robert J. "The Quest for Tolerance in Sarajevo's Textbooks." *Human Rights Review,* vol. 1, no. 2 (January–March 2000): 38–55.

Donia, Robert J., and John V. A. Fine, Jr. *Bosnia and Hercegovina: A Tradition Betrayed.* New York: Columbia University Press, 1994.

Doubt, Keith. *Sociology after Bosnia and Kosovo: Recovering Justice.* Lanham, Md.: Rowman & Littlefield, 2000.

Dragnich, Alex N. *The First Yugoslavia: Search for a Viable Political System.* Stanford, Calif.: Hoover Institution Press, 1983.

———. *Serbia, Nikola Pašić, and Yugoslavia.* New Brunswick, N.J.: Rutgers University Press, 1974.

Dragnich, Alex N., and Slavko Todorovich. *The Saga of Kosovo.* Boulder, Colo.: East European Monographs, 1984.

Dragović-Soso, Jasna. *"Saviours of the Nation": Serbia's Intellectual Opposition and the Revival of Nationalism.* London: C. Hurst, 2002.

Dubey, Vinod, et al. *Yugoslavia: Development with Decentralization.* Baltimore: Johns Hopkins University Press, 1975.

Dugandžija, Nikola. *Religija i nacija: Istraživanja u zagrebačkoj regiji.* Zagreb: Stvarnost, 1986.

Duijzings, Ger. *Religion and the Politics of Identity in Kosovo.* London: Hurst, 2000.

Džaja, Srećko M. *Die politische Realität des Jugoslawiens (1918–1991). Mit besonderer Berücksichtigung Bosnien-Herzegowinas.* Munich: R. Oldenbourg Verlag, 2002.

Eckstein, Harry. "On the Etiology of Internal Wars." *History and Theory,* vol. 4 (1965), no. 2: 133–163.

Eisermann, Daniel. *Der lange Weg nach Dayton: Die Westliche Politik und der Krieg im ehemaligen Jugoslawien 1991 bis 1995.* Baden-Baden: Nomos Verlagsgesellschaft, 2000.

Emmert, Thomas A. *Serbian Golgotha: Kosovo, 1389.* Boulder, Colo.: East European Monographs, 1990.

Emmert, Thomas A., and Wayne S. Vucinich (eds.). *Kosovo: Legacy of a Medieval Battle.* Minneapolis: University of Minnesota Press, 1991.

Fach, Wolfgang, and Ulrich Degen (eds.). *Politische Legitimität.* Frankfurt: Campus Verlag, 1978.

Falconi, Carlo. *The Silence of Pius XII.* Trans. from Italian by Bernard Wall. Boston: Little, Brown, 1970.

Farley, Brigit. *Ethnic Conflict and European Affairs Revisited: The Serb-Croat Quarrel and French Diplomacy, 1929–1935.* Donald W. Treadgold Papers in Russian, East European, and Central Asian Studies, no. 25. Seattle: Henry M. Jackson School of International Studies, University of Washington, April 2000.

Filandra, Saćir. *Bosnjačka politika u XX. stoljeću.* Sarajevo: Sejtarija, 1998.

Fink-Hafner, Danica. "The Case of Slovenia." In Henriette Riegler (ed.), *Transformation Processes in the Yugoslav Successor States between Marginalization and European Integration,* pp. 11–43. Baden-Baden: Nomos Verlagsgesellschaft, 2000.

———. "The Disintegration of Yugoslavia." *Canadian Slavonic Papers,* vol. 37, nos. 3–4 (September–December 1995): 339–356.

———. "The Left in Slovenia." In Charles Bukowski and Barnabas Racz (eds.), *The Return of the Left in Post-communist States: Current Trends and Future Prospects,* pp. 107–128. Cheltenham, UK: Edward Elgar, 1998.

———. *Nova družbena gibanja—Subjekti politične inovacije.* Ljubljana: Znanstvena Knjižnica, Fakulteta za družbene vede, 1992.

———. "Political Culture in a Context of Democratic Transition: Slovenia in Comparison with other Post-Socialist Countries." In Fritz Plasser and Andreas Pribersky (eds.), *Political Culture in East Central Europe,* pp. 71–89. Aldershot, UK: Avebury, 1996.

————. "Political Modernization in Slovenia in the 1980s and the Early 1990s." *Journal of Communist Studies*, vol. 8, no. 4 (December 1992): 210–226.

————. "Slovenia in a Process of Transition to Political Democracy." In Adolf Bibič and Gigi Graziano (eds.), *Civil Society, Political Society, Democracy*, pp. 387–407. Ljubljana: Narodna in univerzitetna knjižnica, 1994.

Fink-Hafner, Danica, and Terry Cox (eds.). *Into Europe? Perspectives from Britain and Slovenia*. Ljubljana: Faculty of Social Sciences, 1996.

Fink-Hafner, Danica, and John R. Robbins (eds.). *Making a New Nation: The Formation of Slovenia*. Aldershot, UK: Dartmouth, 1997.

Fischer, Bernd J. *Albania at War, 1939–1945*. London: C. Hurst, 1999.

————. "Resistance in Albania during the Second World War: Partisans, Nationalists and the S.O.E." *East European Quarterly*, vol. 25, no. 1 (March 1991): 21–47.

Fischkin, James S. *Tyranny and Legitimacy: A Critique of Political Theories*. Baltimore and London: Johns Hopkins University Press, 1979.

Fleck, Hans-Georg, and Igor Graovac (eds.). *Dijalog povjesničara-istoričara.* Vols. 1–5. Zagreb: Zaklada Friedrich-Naumann, 2000–2002.

Francis, E. K. *Interethnic Relations*. New York: Elsevier Scientific Publishing, 1976.

Freedman, Robert O. *Economic Warfare in the Communist Bloc: A Study of Soviet Economic Pressure against Yugoslavia, Albania, and Communist China*. New York: Praeger, 1970.

Friedlander, Saul. *Pius XII and the Third Reich: A Documentation*. Trans. from French and German by Charles Fullman. New York: Alfred A. Knopf, 1966.

Furtak, Robert K. *Jugoslawien*. Hamburg: Hoffmann und Campe Verlag, 1975.

Gaber, Slavko, and Tonči Kuzmanić (eds.). *Kosovo—Srbija—Jugoslavija*. Ljubljana: Krt, 1989.

Gallagher, Tom. *The Balkans after the Cold War: From Tyranny to Tragedy*. London and New York: Routledge, 2003.

Gazi, Stjepan. "Stjepan Radić: His Life and Political Activities (1971–1928)." *Journal of Croatian Studies*, vol. 14/15 (1973–74): 13–73.

Glenny, Misha. *The Balkans: Nationalism, War, and the Great Powers, 1804–1999*. New York: Viking Press, 1999, 2000.

Gligorijević, Branislav. *Parlament i političke stranke u Jugoslaviji, 1919–1929*. Belgrade: Narodna knjiga, 1979.

Goati, Vladimir, Zoran Dj. Slavujević, and Ognjen Pribićević. *Izborne borbe u Jugoslaviji, 1990–1992*. Belgrade: NIP Radnička stampa, 1993.

Goldstein, Ivo. *Croatia: A History*. Trans. from Croatian by Nikolina Jovanović. London: Hurst, 1999.

———— with Slavko Goldstein. *Holokaust u Zagrebu*. Zagreb: Novi Liber & Židovska općina Zagreb, 2001.

Gordy, Eric D. *The Culture of Power in Serbia: Nationalism and the Destruction of Alternatives*. University Park: Pennsylvania State University Press, 1999.

Gow, James. *Legitimacy and the Military: The Yugoslav Crisis*. London: Pinter, 1992.

————. *The Serbian Project and Its Adversaries: A Strategy of War Crimes*. London: Hurst, 2003.

————. *Triumph of the Lack of Will: International Diplomacy and the Yugoslav War*. London: Hurst, 1997.

Gow, James, and Cathie Carmichael. *Slovenia and the Slovenes: A Small State and the New Europe*. Bloomington: Indiana University Press, 2000.

Gow, James, Richard Paterson, and Alison Preston (eds.). *Bosnia by Television*. London: British Film Institute, 1996.

Grafstein, Robert. "The Failure of Weber's Conception of Legitimacy: Its Causes and Implications." *Journal of Politics,* vol. 43, no. 2 (May 1981): 456–472.

Granville, Johanna. "Hungary, 1956: The Yugoslav Connection." *Europe-Asia Studies,* vol. 50, no. 3 (May 1998): 493–517.

Granville, Johanna . "Tito and the Nagy Affair." *East European Quarterly,* vol. 32, no. 1 (Spring 1998): 23–55.

Grbelja, Josip. *Cenzura u Hrvatskom novinstvu 1945.–1990.* Zagreb: Naklada Jurčić, 1998.

Grdešić, Ivan, Mirjana Kasapović, Ivan Šiber, and Nenad Zakošek. *Hrvatska u izborima '90.* Zagreb: Naprijed, 1990.

Greenberg, Robert D. *Language and Identity in the Balkans: Serbo-Croatian.* Oxford: Oxford University Press, 2004.

———. "The Politics of Dialects among Serbs, Croats, and Muslims in the Former Yugoslavia." *East European Politics and Societies,* vol. 10, no. 3 (Fall 1996): 393–415.

Griesser-Pečar, Tamara. *Das zerrisene Volk: Slowenien 1941–1946—Okkupation, Kollaboration, Bürgerkrieg, Revolution.* Vienna: Böhlau Verlag, 2003.

Guttman, Samuel A. "Robert Waelder and the Application of Psychoanalytic Principles to Social and Political Phenomena." *Journal of the American Psychoanalytic Association,* vol. 34, no. 4 (1986): 835–862.

Haberl, Othmar Nikola. *Parteiorganisation und nationale Frage in Jugoslawien.* Berlin: Otto Harrassowitz, 1976.

Hadžijahić, Muhamed. *Od tradicije do identiteta: Geneza nacionalnog pitanja bosanskih muslimana.* Sarajevo: Svjetlost, 1974.

Hafner-Fink, Mitja. *Sociološka razsežja razpada Jugoslavije.* Ljubljana: Znanstvene knjižnica, Fakulteta za družbene vede, 1994.

Hall, Gregory O. "The Politics of Autocracy: Serbia under Slobodan Milošević." *East European Quarterly,* vol. 33, no. 2 (Summer 1999): 233–249.

Hamilton, F. E. Ian. *Yugoslavia: Patterns of Economic Activity.* New York: Praeger, 1968.

Hammond, Thomas Taylor. "The Djilas Affair and Jugoslav Communism." *Foreign Affairs,* vol. 33, no. 2 (January 1955): 298–315.

Harriman, Helga H. *Slovenia under Nazi occupation, 1941–1945.* New York: Studia Slovenica, 1977.

Harris, Erika. *Nationalism and Democratisation: Politics of Slovakia and Slovenia.* Aldershot, UK: Ashgate, 2002.

Hartmann, Ralph. *"Die ehrlichen Makler": Die deutsche Aussenpolitik und der Burgerkrieg in Jugoslawien.* 4th ed. Berlin: Dietz Verlag, 1999.

Hasanbegović, Zlatko. "O pokušajima donošenja Ustava Islamske vjerske zajednice u Nezavisnoj Državi Hrvatskoj." *Časopis za suvremenu povijest,* vol. 33, no. 1 (2001): 75–89.

Hasani, Sinan. *Kosovo—istine i zablude.* Zagreb: Centar za informacije i publicitet, 1986.

Hasenclever, Andreas. *Die Macht der Moral in der internationalen Politik: Militärische Interventionen Westlicher Staaten in Somalia, Ruanda und Bosnien-Herzegowina.* Frankfurt-am-Main: Campus Verlag, 2001.

Hibbert, Reginald. *Albania's National Liberation Struggle: The Bitter Victory.* London: Pinter, 1991.

Hoare, Marko Attila. "The Bosnian Serb Identity and the Chetnik-Partisan Conflict." *South Slav Journal,* vol. 21, no. 3–4 (Autumn–Winter 2000): 7–17.

———. "The Croatian Project to Partition Bosnia-Hercegovina, 1990–1994." *East European Quarterly,* vol. 31, no. 1 (March 1997): 121–138.

———. *How Bosnia Armed*. London: Saqi Books, with the Bosnian Institute, 2004.

———. "The People's Liberation Movement in Bosnia and Hercegovina, 1941–45: What Did It Mean for a Multi-national State?" *Nationalism & Ethnic Politics*, vol. 2, no. 3 (Autumn 1996): 415–445.

———. "Whose Is the Partisan Movement? Serbs, Croats and the Legacy of a Shared Resistance." *Journal of Slavic Military Studies*, vol. 15, no. 4 (December 2002): 24–41.

Hodge, Carole. *The Serb Lobby in the United Kingdom*. Donald W. Treadgold Papers in Russian, East European, and Central Asian Studies, no. 22. Seattle: Henry M. Jackson School of International Studies, University of Washington, 2000.

Hofbauer, Hannes (ed.). *Balkan Krieg: Die Zerstörung Jugoslawiens*. Vienna: ProMedia, 1999.

Hoffman, George W., and Fred Warner Neal. *Yugoslavia and the New Communism*. New York: Twentieth Century Fund, 1962.

Hondius, Frits W. *The Yugoslav Community of Nations*. The Hague: Mouton, 1968.

Hoptner, J. B. *Yugoslavia in Crisis, 1934–1941*. New York: Columbia University Press, 1962.

Horvat, Branko. *Kosovsko pitanje*. Zagreb: Globus, 1988.

Hory, Ladislaus, and Martin Broszat. *Der kroatische Ustascha-Staat, 1941–1945*. Stuttgart: Deutsche Verlags-Anstalt, 1964.

Hösler, Joachim, Norman Paech, and Gerhard Stuby. *Der gerechte Krieg? Neue Nato-Strategie, Völkerrecht und Westeuropäisierung des Balkans*. Ed. by Johannes Klotz. Bremen: Donat Verlag, 2000.

Imamović, Mustafa. *Historija Bošnjaka*. 2nd ed. Sarajevo: Bošnjačka zajednica kulture, 1998.

Institut za ekonomska istraživanja Ekonomskog Fakulteta—Zagreb. *Autoceste i magistralne ceste u SR Hrvatskoj do 2000 godine*. Zagreb: Ekonomski Fakultet, 1978.

Institut za uporedno pravo. *Podela zajedničke nadleznosti izmedju federacije i federalnih jedinica*. Belgrade: Savremena administracija, 1978.

———. *Specifičnosti republičkih i pokrajinskih ustava od 1974*. Belgrade: Savremena administracija, 1976.

Institute of Social Sciences, Demographic Research Center. *The Development of Yugoslavia's Population in the Post-war Period*. Belgrade: Radiša Timotić, 1974.

Irvine, Jill A. "Tito, Hebrang, and the Croat Question, 1943–1944." *East European Politics and Societies*, vol. 5, no. 2 (Spring 1991): 306–340.

Iveković, Rada. *La Balcanizzazione della ragione*. Rome: Manifestolibri, 1995.

Janigro, Nicole. *L'Esplosione delle Nazioni: Il caso Jugoslavo*. Milan: Feltrinelli, 1993.

Janjić, Dušan. "National Identities, Movements and Nationalism of Serbs and Albanians." *Balkan Forum* (Skopje), vol. 3, no. 1 (March 1995): 19–84.

Janjatović, Bosiljka. "Karadjordjevićevska centralizacija i položaj Hrvatske u Kraljevstvu (Kraljevini) SHS." *Časopis za suvremenu povijest*, vol. 27, no. 1 (1995): 55–76.

Jareb, Jere. "Hrvatski narod u Drugom svjetskom ratu 1941.–1945." *Časopis za suvremenu povijest*, vol. 27, no. 3 (1995): 403–423.

Jelavich, Charles. "Education, Textbooks and South Slav Nationalisms in the Interwar Era." In Norbert Reiter and Holm Sundhausen (eds.), *Allgemeinbildung als Modernisierungsfaktor: Zur Geschichte der Elementerbildung in Südosteuropa von der Aufklärung bis zum Zweiten Weltkrieg*, pp. 127–142.Wiesbaden: Harrassowitz Verlag, 1994.

Jelić-Butić, Fikreta. *Četnici u Hrvatskoj 1941–1945*. Zagreb: Globus, 1986.

———. *Ustaše i NDH*. Zagreb: S.N. Liber and Školska knjiga, 1977.

Jelinek, Yeshayahu A. "Bosnia-Herzegovina at War: Relations between Moslems and Non-Moslems." *Holocaust and Genocide Studies*, vol. 5, no. 3 (1990): 275–292.

Jevtić, Dragoš. "O ustavnim pravima gradjana po ustavu Kraljevine Jugoslavije od 3. Septembra 1931. godine." *Istorijski glasnik* (Belgrade), no. 1–2 (1975): 49–74.

Johnson, A. Ross. *The Transformation of Communist Ideology: The Yugoslav Case, 1945–1953.* Cambridge, Mass.: MIT Press, 1972.

Jončić, Koča. *Odnosi izmedju naroda i narodnosti u Jugoslavije.* Belgrade: Mladost, 1988.

Jovanović, Dragoljub. *Ljudi, ljudi. . . .* Ed. Nadežda Jovanović. Belgrade: Filip Višnjić, 2005.

———. *Sloboda od straha: Izabrane političke rasprave.* Ed. Nadežda Jovanović and Božidar Jakšić. Belgrade: Filip Višnjić & Naučna knjiga, 1991.

Jovanović, Vladan. *Jugoslovenska država i južna Srbija 1918–1929.* Belgrade: INIS, 2002.

Jovanovich, Leo M. "The War in the Balkans in 1941." *East European Quarterly,* vol. 28, no. 1 (Spring 1994): 105–129.

Jović, Dejan. *Jugoslavija država koja je odumrla: Uspon, kriza i pad Kardeljeve Jugoslavije (1974–1990).* Zagreb: Prometej, 2003.

Jovičić, Miodrag. *Savremeni federalizam.* Belgrade: Savremena administracija, 1973.

Judah, Tim. *Kosovo: War and Revenge.* New Haven, Conn.: Yale University Press, 2000.

———. *The Serbs: History, Myth and the Destruction of Yugoslavia.* New Haven, Conn.: Yale University Press, 1997.

Jukić, Ilija. "Tito's Legacy." *Survey,* no. 77 (Autumn 1970): 93–108.

Kant, Immanuel. *Groundwork of the Metaphysic of Morals.* Trans. by H. J. Paton. London and New York: Routledge, 1948.

———. *The Metaphysics of Morals.* Trans. by Mary Gregor. Cambridge: Cambridge University Press, 1991.

Karayovonoff, T. *Les causes de la crise Yougoslave.* Budapest: Imprimerie de la Societé Anonyme Atheneum, 1929.

Kardelj, Edvard. *Democracy and Socialism.* Trans. from Serbo-Croatian by Margot and Boško Milosavljević. London: Summerfield Press, 1978.

Kasapović, Mirjana. *Bosna i Hercegovina: podijeljeno društvo i nestabilna država.* Zagreb: Politička Kultura, 2005.

Kecmanović, Dušan. "Psychiatrists in Times of Ethnonationalism." *Australian and New Zealand Journal of Psychiatry,* vol. 33, no. 3 (June 1999): 309–315.

Kesić, Obrad. "Politics, Power, and Decision Making in the Serb Republic." *Problems of Post-Communism,* vol. 43, no. 2 (March–April 1996): 56–64.

King, Robert R. *Minorities under Communism.* Cambridge, Mass.: Harvard University Press, 1973.

Kiriazovski, Risto. *Narodnoosloboditelniot Front i Drugite Organizatsii na Makedontsite od Egeiska Makedoniia, 1945–1949.* Skopje: Kultura, 1985.

Kiš, Danilo. *Garden, Ashes.* Translator not identified. Boston and London: Faber & Faber, 1975.

Kisić Kolanović, Nada. *NDH i Italija: Političke veze i diplomatski odnosi.* Zagreb: Ljevak, 2001.

Koštunica, Vojislav and Kosta Čavoški. *Party Pluralism or Monism: Social Movements and the Political System in Yugoslavia, 1944–1949.* Boulder, Colo.: East European Monographs, 1985.

Kramer, Roderick M., and David M. Messick. "Getting By with a Little Help from Our Enemies: Collective Paranoia and Its Role in Intergroup Relations." In Constantine Sedikides, John Schopler, and Chester A. Insko (eds.), *Intergroup Cognition and Intergroup Behavior,* pp. 233–255. Mahwah, N.J.: Lawrence Erlbaum, 1998.

Krivokapić, Boro. *Jugoslavija i komunisti: Adresa Jovana Djordjevića.* Belgrade: Mladost, 1988.

Krizman, Bogdan. *Ante Pavelić i Ustaše.* Zagreb: Globus, 1978.

Kržišnik-Busić, Vera. *Cazinska buna 1950*. Sarajevo: Svjetlost, 1991.

Kubović, Branko. *Regionalna ekonomika*. Zagreb: Informator, 1974.

Kulić, Dimitrij. *Bugarska okupacija 1941–1944*. Vol. 1. Nis: Prosveta, 1970.

Kulundžić, Zvonimir. *Atentat na Stjepana Radića*. Zagreb: Biblioteka Vremeplov, 1967.

Kumar, Radha. *Divide and Fall? Bosnia in the Annals of Partition*. London and New York: Verso, 1997.

Kuzmanić, Tonči A. *Hate-Speech in Slovenia: Slovenian Racism, Sexism and Chauvinism*. Ljubljana: Open Society, 1999.

Lampe, John R. *Yugoslavia as History: Twice There Was a Country*. Cambridge: Cambridge University Press, 1996.

Lane, Ann. *Britain, the Cold War and Yugoslav Unity, 1941–1949*. Brighton: Sussex Academic Press, 1996.

Lapenna, Ivo. "Main Features of the Yugoslav Constitution, 1946–1971." *International and Comparative Law Quarterly*, 4th series, vol. 21, pt. 2 (April 1972): 209–229.

Latas, Branko (comp.). *Saradnja Četnika Draže Mihailovića sa okupatorima i ustašama (1941–1945): Dokumenti*. Belgrade: Društvo za istinu o antifašističkoj narodnooslobodilačkoj borbi 1941–1945, 1999.

LeBor, Adam. *Milošević: A Biography*. Polmont, Stirlingshire: Bloomsbury, 2002.

Lilly, Carol S. *Power and Persuasion: Ideology and Rhetoric in Communist Yugoslavia, 1944–1953*. Boulder, Colo.: Westview Press, 2001.

———. "Problems of Persuasion: Communist Agitation and Propaganda in Post-war Yugoslavia, 1944–1948." *Slavic Review*, vol. 53, no. 2 (Summer 1994): 395–413.

Lipset, Seymour Martin. "Some Social Requisites of Democracy: Economic Development and Political Legitimacy." *American Political Science Review*, vol. 53, no. 1 (March 1959): 69–105.

Littlefield, Frank C. *Germany and Yugoslavia, 1933–1941: The German Conquest of Yugoslavia*. Boulder, Colo.: East European Monographs, 1988.

Löffler, Berthold. "Konsens und Dissens in der jugoslawischen Politik. Der Kosovo-Krieg und seine Folgen aus Sicht von Regierung und Opposition." *Osteuropa*, vol. 49, no. 11–12 (November–December 1999): 1220–1232.

Logoreci, A. *The Albanians: Europe's Forgotten Survivors*. London: Victor Gollancz, 1977.

Loker, Zvi. "The Testimony of Dr. Edo Neufeld: The Italians and the Jews of Croatia." *Holocaust and Genocide Studies*, vol. 7, no. 1 (Spring 1993): 67–76.

Lukić, Reneo. "The Anti-Americanism in France during the War in Kosovo." In Reneo Lukić and Michael Brint (eds.), *Culture, Politics, and Nationalism in the Age of Globalization*, pp. 145–181. Aldershot, UK: Ashgate, 2001.

———. "Greater Serbia: A New Reality in the Balkans." *Nationalities Papers*, vol. 22, no. 1 (Spring 1994): 49–70.

———. *The Wars of South Slavic Succession: Yugoslavia 1991–1993*. PSIS Occasional Papers no. 2/93. Geneva: Graduate Institute of International Affairs, 1993.

———. "The Withering Away of the Federal Republic of Yugoslavia." *Acta Slavica Iaponica* (Sapporo), vol. 19 (2002): 137–162.

Lukić, Reneo, and Allen Lynch. *Europe from the Balkans to the Urals: The Disintegration of Yugoslavia and the Soviet Union*. Oxford: Oxford University Press, 1996.

Lumsden, Malvern. *Peacebuilding in Macedonia: Searching for Common Ground in Civil Society*. PRIO Report no. 2/97. Oslo: International Peace Research Institute, 1997.

Luthar, Oto, Keith A. McLeod, and Mitja Žagar (eds.). *Liberal Democracy, Citizenship and Education*. Niagara Falls, N.Y.: Mosaic Press, 2001.

Macesich, George. *Yugoslavia: The Theory and Practice of Development Planning.* Charlottesville: University Press of Virginia, 1964.

Magaš, Branka. *The Destruction of Yugoslavia: Tracking the Break-up 1980–92.* London: Verso, 1993.

Magaš, Branka, and Ivo Žanić (eds.). *Rat u Hrvatskoj i Bosni i Hercegovini 1991–1995.* Zagreb/Sarajevo/London: Naklada Jesenski i Turk, Dani, and the Bosnian Institute, 1999.

Mahmutćehajić, Rusmir. *Bosnia the Good: Tolerance and Tradition.* Trans. from Bosnian by Marina Bowder. Budapest: Central European University Press, 2000.

———. *The Denial of Bosnia.* Trans. from Bosnian by Francis R. Jones and Marina Bowder. University Park: Pennsylvania State University Press, 2000.

Malcolm, Noel. *Bosnia: A Short History.* New York: New York University Press, 1994.

———. "Bosnia: A Study in Failure." *National Interest,* no. 39 (Spring 1995): 3–14.

———. *Kosovo: A Short History.* London: Macmillan, 1998.

Manoschek, Walter. *"Serbien ist judenfrei": Militärische Besatzungspolitik und Judenvernichtung in Serbien 1941/42.* Munich: R. Oldenbourg Verlag, 1995.

Mappes-Niediek, Norbert. *Balkan-Mafia: Staaten in der Hand des Verbrechens—Eine Gefahr für Europa.* Berlin: Ch. Links Verlag, 2003.

Marković, Sima. *Ustavno pitanje i radnička klasa Jugoslavije.* Belgrade(?): n.p., n.d. [1923].

Matijević, Zlatko. "Hrvatska pučka stranka i II. parlamentarni izbori u Kraljevini Srba, Hrvata i Slovenaca (1923. god.)." *Časopis za suvremenu povijest,* vol. 28, no. 1–2 (1996): 27–43.

———. "Jugoslavenska povijesna literatura o političkoj djelatnosti katoličke crkve u Hrvatskoj 1918–1945." *Časopis za suvremenu povijest,* vol. 13, no. 2 (1981): 73–103.

———. *Slom politike katoličkog Jugoslavenstva: Hrvatska pučka stranka u političkom životu Kraljevini SHS.* Zagreb: Hrvatski Institut za Povijest, 1998.

Matković, Hrvoje. *Povijest Hrvatske seljačke stranke.* Zagreb: Naklada P.I.P. Pavičić, 1999.

———. *Povijest Nezavisne Države Hrvatske.* 2nd expanded ed. Zagreb: Naklada P.I.P. Pavičić, 2002.

Maurer, Pierre. *La Réconciliation Soviéto-Yougoslave, 1954–1958: Illusions et disillusions de Tito.* Fribourg, Switzerland: Editions Delvar, 1991.

Meier, Viktor. *Jugoslawiens Erben: Die neuen Staaten und die Politik des Westens.* Munich: Verlag C. H. Beck, 2001.

———. *Yugoslavia: A History of Its Demise.* Trans. from German by Sabrina Ramet. London and New York: Routledge, 1999.

———. "Yugoslavia: Worsening Economic and Nationalist Crisis." In William E. Griffith (ed.), *Central and Eastern Europe: The Opening Curtain?* pp. 263–282. Boulder, Colo.: Westview Press, 1989.

Melčić, Dunja (ed.). *Der Jugoslawien-Krieg: Handbuch zu Vorgeschichte, Verlauf und Konsequenzen.* Opladen/Wiesbaden: Westdeutscher Verlag, 1999.

Merelman, Richard M. "Learning and Legitimacy." *American Political Science Review,* vol. 60, no. 3 (September 1966): 548–561.

Merkel, Reinhard (ed.). *Der Kosovo-Krieg und das Völkerrecht.* Frankfurt-am-Main: Suhrkamp Verlag, 2000.

Mertus, Julie A. *Kosovo: How Myths and Truths Started a War.* Berkeley and Los Angeles: University of California Press, 1999.

Michas, Takis. *Unholy Alliance: Greece and Milošević's Serbia.* College Station: Texas A&M University Press, 2002.

Mihailović, Kosta. *Nerazvijena područja Jugoslavije.* 2nd ed. Belgrade: Ekonomski Institut, 1970.

Mijanović, Gaso. "Ustavna reforma i proces jačanja uloge republika i pokrajina u ostvarivanju zajedničkih interesa u Jugoslaviji." *Godišnjak Pravnog Fakulteta u Sarajevu 1976,* vol. 24 (1977): 109–133.

Milanović, Nikola. *Kroz tajni arhiv UDBe.* 2 vols. Belgrade: Sloboda, 1986.

Milazzo, Matteo J. *The Chetnik Movement and the Yugoslav Resistance.* Baltimore and London: Johns Hopkins University Press, 1975.

Milenkovich, Deborah D. *Plan and Market in Yugoslav Economic Thought.* New Haven, Conn.: Yale University Press, 1971.

Miller, Marshall Lee. *Bulgaria during the Second World War.* Stanford, Calif.: Stanford University Press, 1975.

Milošević, Slobodan. *Godine raspleta.* 2nd ed. Belgrade: Beogradski izdavačko-grafički zavod, 1989.

Mirković, Damir. "Victims and Perpetrators in the Yugoslav Genocide, 1941–1945: Some Preliminary Observations." *Holocaust and Genocide Studies,* vol. 7, no. 3 (Winter 1993): 317–332.

Mišović, Miloš. *Ko je tražio republiku: Kosovo, 1945–1985.* Belgrade: Narodna knjiga, 1987.

———. *Srpska crkva i konkordatska kriza.* Belgrade: Sloboda, 1983.

Mojzes, Paul. "The Role of the Religious Communities in the War in Former Yugoslavia." *Religion in Eastern Europe,* vol. 13, no. 3 (June 1993): 13–31.

Mønnesland, Svein. *Før Jugoslavia, og etter.* 4th ed. Oslo: Sypress Forlag, 1999.

Mousset, Albert. *Le Royaume Serbe, Croate, Slovene: Son organisation, sa vie politique et ses institutions.* Paris: Bossard, 1926.

Mujačić, Mahmut. *Nova dimenzija jugoslovenskog federalizma.* Sarajevo: Oslobodjenje, 1981.

Mužić, Ivan. *Katolička crkva, Stepinac i Pavelić.* 2nd ed. Zagreb: Dominović, 1997.

———. *Stjepan Radić u Kraljevini Srba, Hrvata i Slovenaca.* 4th ed. Zagreb: Nakladni Zavod Matice Hrvatske, 1990.

Naimark, Norman M., and Holly Case (eds.). *Yugoslavia and Its Historians: Understanding the Balkan Wars of the 1990s.* Stanford, Calif.: Stanford University Press, 2003.

Nava, Massimo. *Milošević: La tragedia di un popolo.* Milano: Rizzoli, 1999.

Nedić, Milan Dj. *Govori Generala Milana Nedića pretsednika Srpske vlade.* Belgrade: n.p., 1943.

———. *Reći Generala Nedića Srpskom narodu i omladini.* Belgrade: Nacionalni spisi, 1941.

Nešović, Slobodan. *Bledski sporazumi: Tito–Dimitrov (1947).* Zagreb: Globus and Školska knjiga, 1979.

Nikolić, Milenko M. *Ravnopravnost naroda i narodnosti u obrazovanju.* Belgrade: Novinska Ustanova Prosvetni Pregled, 1975.

Nikolić, Miodrag. *Autonomous Province of Kosovo and Metohija.* Belgrade: Medjunarodna Politika, 1965.

Nikolić-Ristanović, Vesna. *Women, Violence and War: Wartime Victimization of Refugees in the Balkans.* Budapest: Central European University Press, 2000.

Nikšić, Stevan. *Oslobodjenje štampe.* Belgrade: Oslobodjenje, 1982.

Oberländer, Erwin (ed.). *Autoritäre Regime in Ostmittel- und Südosteuropa 1919–1944.* Paderborn: Verlag Ferdinand Schöningh GmbH, 2001.

Oschlies, Wolf. *Makedonien 2001–2004: Kriegstagebuch aus einem friedlichen Land.* Berlin: Xenomos, 2004.

Osland, Kari M. "Rettsaken mot Slobodan Milošević—et overblikk." *Nordisk Øst•forum,* vol. 16, no. 1 (2002): 5–18.

Paća, Agim. "Fond federacije za kreditiranje privrednog razvoja privredno nedovoljno razvijenih republika i pokrajina, s osvrtom na SAP Kosovo u periodu od 1966. do 1975. godine." *Obelezja*, vol. 7, no. 3 (May–June 1977): 561–581.

Palmer, Stephen E., Jr., and Robert R. King. *Yugoslav Communism and the Macedonian Question.* Hamden, Conn.: Archon Books, 1971.

Pašić, Najdan, et al. *Društveno-politički sistem SFRJ.* Belgrade: Radnička stampa, 1975.

———. *Nacionalno pitanje u savremenoj epohi.* Belgrade: Radnička stampa, 1973.

———. *Razvoj nacija i medjunacionalnih odnosa u socijalističkom samoupravnom društvu.* Belgrade: Marksističko obrazovanje, 1979.

Pattee, Richard. *The Case of Cardinal Aloysius Stepinac.* Milwaukee: Bruce, 1953.

Pavlaković, Vjeran. "Between the Balkans and the West: Liberal Democracy in Croatia." *Modern Greek Studies Yearbook,* vol. 16/17 (2000–2001): 359–375.

Pavlaković, Vjeran , Sabrina P. Ramet, and Philip Lyon. *Sovereign Law vs. Sovereign Nation: The Cases of Kosovo and Montenegro.* Trondheim Studies on East European Cultures & Societies, no. 11. Trondheim, Norway: Norwegian University of Science and Technology, October 2002.

Pavlović, Dušan. *Akteri i modeli: Ogledi o politici u Srbiji pod Miloševićem.* Belgrade: Samizdat B92, 2001.

Pavlowitch, Stevan K. *A History of the Balkans, 1804–1945.* London: Longman, 1999.

Pejovich, Svetozar. *The Market-Planned Economy of Yugoslavia.* Minneapolis: University of Minnesota Press, 1966.

Pekić, Borislav. *The Houses of Belgrade.* Trans. from Serbian by Bernard Johnson. Evanston, Ill.: Northwestern University Press, 1978.

Peles, Aleksandar. "O postupku zaključenja medjunarodnih ugovora SFRJ, sa posebnim osvrtom na učešće republika i pokrajina." *Godišnjak Pravnog Fakulteta u Sarajevu 1976,* vol. 24 (1977): 169–177.

Perić, Ivan. *Ideje 'Masovnog pokreta' u Hrvatskoj.* Zagreb: Političke teme, 1974.

———. *Suvremeni hrvatski nacionalizam.* Zagreb: August Cesarec, 1976.

———. "Za objektivnu valorizaciju Desete sjednice Centralnog komiteta Saveza komunista Hrvatske." *Naše teme,* vol. 15, no. 10 (October 1971): 1651–1691.

Perić, Ivo. *Stjepan Radić, 1871–1928.* Zagreb: Dom i Svijet, 2003.

———. *Vladko Maček: Politički portret.* Zagreb: Golden Marketing, 2003.

Perić, Tatjana. "On Being Agents of God's Peace: Relationship and Roles of the Roman Catholic Church in Croatia and the Serbian Orthodox Church in Ethnic Conflicts in Former Yugoslavia." *Religion in Eastern Europe,* vol. 18, no. 1 (February 1998): 28–47.

Perica, Vjekoslav. *Balkan Idols: Religion and Nationalism in Yugoslav States.* Oxford: Oxford University Press, 2002.

Pesaković, Milentija. *Autonomous Provinces in Yugoslavia.* Belgrade: Medjunarodna Politika, 1964.

Petešić, Ciril. *Katoličko svećenstvo u NOB-u 1941–1945.* Zagreb: VPA, 1982.

Petranović, Branko. *Istorija Jugoslavije 1918–1988,* 3 vols. Belgrade: Nolit, 1988.

———. *Srbija u drugom svetskom ratu 1939–1945.* Belgrade: Vojnoizdavački i novinski centar, 1992.

Petrinović, Ivo. "Hrvatska kao suverena država i novi smisao republičke državnosti." *Pogledi,* vol. 2, no. 7 (1971): 5–7.

Petrović, Milan, and Kasim Suljević (eds.). *Nacionalni odnosi danas.* Sarajevo: Univerzal, 1971.

Petrović, Ruža. "Etnički mešoviti brakovi u Jugoslaviji." *Sociologija,* vol. 8, no. 3 (1966): 89–104.

————. *Migracije u Jugoslaviji i etnički aspekt.* Novi Beograd: Istrazivačko izdavački centar SSO Srbije, 1987.

Petrović, Ruža, and Marina Blagojević. *The Migration of Serbs and Montenegrins from Kosovo and Metohija: Results of the Survey Conducted in 1985–1986.* Belgrade: Serbian Academy of Sciences and Arts, 1992.

Pettifer, James. "Kosova and Its Neighbours: Perspectives after the Catastrophe." *Südosteuropa Mitteilungen,* vol. 39, no. 2 (1999): 87–91.

———— (ed.). *The New Macedonian Question.* London: Macmillan, 1999.

Pipa, Arshi, and Sami Repishti (eds.). *Studies on Kosova.* Boulder, Colo.: East European Monographs, 1984.

Pirjevec, Jože. *Il giorno di San Vito: Jugoslavia 1918–1992—Storia di una tragedia.* Torino: Nova Eri, 1993.

————. *Le guerre jugoslave 1991–1999.* Torino: Giulio Einaudi editore, 2001.

Pius XII, Pope. *Selected Encyclicals and Addresses.* Harrison, N.Y.: Roman Catholic Books, n.d.

Pleština, Dijana. *Regional Development in Communist Yugoslavia: Success, Failure, and Consequences.* Boulder, Colo.: Westview Press, 1992.

Plut-Pregelj, Leopoldina, et al. *The Repluralization of Slovenia in the 1980s: New Revelations from Archival Records.* Donald W. Treadgold Papers in Russian, East European, and Central Asian Studies, no. 24. Seattle: Henry M. Jackson School of International Studies, University of Washington, February 2000.

Plut-Pregelj, Leopoldina, and Carole Rogel. *Historical Dictionary of Slovenia.* Lanham, Md.: Scarecrow Press, 1996.

Popov, Nebojša (ed.). *The Road to War in Serbia: Trauma and Catharsis.* English version by Drinka Gojković. Budapest: Central European University Press, 2000.

————. "Serbian Populism and the Fall of Yugoslavia." *Uncaptive Minds,* vol. 8, nos. 3–4 (Fall/ Winter 1995–96): 83–111.

Popović, Danko. *Knjiga o Milutinu.* Belgrade: NIRO Književne novine, 1986.

Poulton, Hugh. *Who Are the Macedonians?* Bloomington: Indiana University Press, 1995.

Pozderac, Hamdija. *Nacionalni odnosi i socijalističko zajedništvo.* Sarajevo: Svjetlost, 1978.

Pribićević, Ognjen. *Vlast i opozicija u Srbiji.* Belgrade: Radio B92, 1997.

Pribićević, Svetozar. *Diktatura Kralja Aleksandra.* Trans. from French by Andra Milosavljević. Belgrade: Prosveta, 1952.

Pridham, Geoffrey, and Tom Gallagher (eds.). *Experimenting with Democracy: Regime Change in the Balkans.* London and New York: Routledge, 2000.

Purivatra, Atif. *Jugoslavenska Muslimanska Organizacija u političkom životu Kraljevine Srba, Hrvata i Slovenaca.* 2nd ed. Sarajevo: Svjetlost, 1977.

————. *Nacionalni i politički razvitak muslimana.* Sarajevo: Svjetlost, 1970.

Pusić, Vesna. "A Country by Any Other Name: Transition and Stability in Croatia and Yugoslavia." *East European Politics and Societies,* vol. 6, no. 3 (Fall 1992): 242–259.

Rabushka, Alvin, and Kenneth A. Shepsle. *Politics in Plural Societies.* Columbus, Ohio: Charles E. Merrill, 1972.

Radelić, Zdenko. *Križari gerila u Hrvatskoj 1945.–1950.* Zagreb: Hrvatski institut za povijest and Dom i svijet, 2002.

Radoš, Ivica. *Tuđman izbliza: Svjedočenja suradnika i protivnika.* Zagreb: PROFIL, 2005.

Raičević, Jovan. "Savez komunista Jugoslavije i nacionalno pitanje." In *KPJ–SKJ: Razvoj teorije i prakse socijalizma, 1919–1979.* Belgrade: Savremena administracija, 1979.

Ramet, Pedro (ed.). *Religion and Nationalism in Soviet and East European Politics.* Rev. and expanded ed. Durham, N.C.: Duke University Press, 1989.

———. "Yugoslavia and the Threat of Internal and External Discontents." *Orbis,* vol. 28, no. 1 (Spring 1984): 103–121.

——— (ed.). *Yugoslavia in the 1980s.* Boulder, Colo.: Westview Press, 1985.

———. "Yugoslavia 1982: Political Ritual, Political Drift, and the Fetishization of the Past." *South Slav Journal,* vol. 5, no. 3 (Autumn 1982): 13–21.

———. "Yugoslavia's Troubled Times." *Global Affairs,* vol. 5, no. 1 (Winter 1990): 78–95.

Ramet, Sabrina P. "All Quiet on the Southern Front? Macedonia between the Hammer and the Anvil." *Problems of Post-Communism,* vol. 42, no. 6 (November–December 1995): 29–36.

———. *Balkan Babel: The Disintegration of Yugoslavia from the Death of Tito to the Fall of Milošević.* 4th ed. Boulder, Colo.: Westview Press, 2002.

———. "The Breakup of Yugoslavia." *Global Affairs,* vol. 6, no. 2 (Spring 1991): 93–110.

———. "The Croatian Catholic Church since 1990." *Religion, State, and Society: The Keston Journal,* vol. 24, no. 4 (December 1996): 345–355.

———. "Democratization in Slovenia: The Second Stage." In Karen Dawisha and Bruce Parrott (eds.), *Politics, Power, and the Struggle for Democracy in South-East Europe,* pp. 189–225. Cambridge: Cambridge University Press, 1997.

———. *Eastern Europe and the Natural Law Tradition.* Donald W. Treadgold Papers in Russian, East European, and Central Asian Studies, no. 27. Seattle: Henry M. Jackson School of International Studies, University of Washington, August 2000.

———. "Explaining the Yugoslav Meltdown, 1: 'For a Charm of Pow'rful Trouble, Like a Hellbroth Boil and Bubble': Theories about the Roots of the Yugoslav Troubles." *Nationalities Papers,* vol. 32, no. 4 (December 2004): 731–763.

———. "Explaining the Yugoslav Meltdown, 2: A Theory about the Causes of the Yugoslav Meltdown: The Serbian National Awakening as a 'Revitalization Movement.'" *Nationalities Papers,* vol. 32, no. 4 (December 2004): 765–779.

——— (ed.). *Gender Politics in the Western Balkans: Women and Society in Yugoslavia and the Yugoslav Successor States.* University Park: Pennsylvania State University Press, 1999.

———. "Kosovo: A Liberal Approach." *Society,* vol. 36, no. 6 (September/October 1999): 62–69.

———. "Martyr in His Own Mind: The Trial and Tribulations of Slobodan Milošević." *Totalitarian Movements and Political Religions,* vol. 5, no. 1 (Summer 2004): 112–138.

———. *Nationalism and Federalism in Yugoslavia, 1962–1991.* 2nd ed. Bloomington: Indiana University Press, 1992.

———. "Nationalism and the 'Idiocy' of the Countryside: The Case of Serbia." *Ethnic and Racial Studies,* vol. 19, no. 1 (January 1996): 71–87.

———. *Nihil Obstat: Religion, Politics, and Social Change in Eastern Europe and Russia.* Durham, N.C.: Duke University Press, 1998.

———. "Die politische Strategie der Vereinigten Staaten in der Kosovo Krise: Parteipolitik und nationals Interesse." In Jens Reuter and Konrad Clewing (eds.), *Der Kosovo Konflikt: Ursachen—Verlauf—Perspektiven,* pp. 365–380. Klagenfurt: Wieser Verlag, 2000.

———. "Primordial Ethnicity or Modern Nationalism: The Case of Yugoslavia's Muslims, Reconsidered." In Andreas Kappeler, Gerhard Simon, and Georg Brunner (eds.), *Muslim Communities Reemerge: Historical Perspectives on Nationality, Politics, and Opposition in the Former Soviet Union and Yugoslavia.* Durham, N.C.: Duke University Press, 1994.

——— (ed.). *The Radical Right in Central and Eastern Europe since 1989.* University Park: Pennsylvania State University Press, 1999.

———. "Shake, Rattle, and Self-Management: Rock Music and Politics in Yugoslavia, and

After." In Sabrina P. Ramet and Gordana Crnković (eds.), *Kazaaam! Splat! Ploof! The American Impact on European Popular Culture*. Lanham, Md.: Rowman & Littlefield, 2003.

———. *Social Currents in Eastern Europe: The Sources and Consequences of the Great Transformation*. 2nd ed. Durham, N.C.: Duke University Press, 1995.

———. *Thinking about Yugoslavia: Scholarly Debates about the Yugoslav Breakup and the Wars in Bosnia and Kosovo*. Cambridge: Cambridge University Press, 2005.

———. "Under the Holy Lime Tree: The Inculcation of Neurotic and Psychotic Syndromes as a Serbian Wartime Strategy, 1986–1995." *Polemos* (Zagreb), vol. 5, no. 1–2 (January–December 2002): 83–97.

———. "The United States and Slovenia, 1990–1992." *Acta Histriae* (Koper), vol. 11 (2003), no. 1: 53–71.

———. "War in the Balkans." *Foreign Affairs*, vol. 71, no. 4 (Fall 1992): 79–98.

———. *Whose Democracy? Nationalism, Religion, and the Doctrine of Collective Rights in Post-1989 Eastern Europe*. Lanham, Md.: Rowman & Littlefield, 1997.

———. "The Yugoslav Crisis and the West: Avoiding 'Vietnam' and Blundering into 'Abyssinia.'" *East European Politics and Societies*, vol. 8, no. 1 (Winter 1994): 189–219.

Ramet, Sabrina P., and Letty Coffin. "German Foreign Policy toward the Yugoslav Successor States, 1991–1999." *Problems of Post-Communism*, vol. 48, no. 1 (January–February 2001): 48–64.

Ramet, Sabrina P., and Danica Fink-Hafner (eds.). *Democratic Transition in Slovenia: Value Transformation, Education, Media*. College Station: Texas A&M University Press, forthcoming in 2006.

Ramet, Sabrina P., and Phil Lyon. "Discord, Denial, Dysfunction: The Serbian–Montenegrin–Kosovar Triangle." *Problems of Post-Communism*, vol. 49, no. 5 (September–October 2002): 3–19.

———. "Germany: The Federal Republic, Loyal to NATO." In Tony Weymouth and Stanley Helwig (eds.), *The Kosovo Crisis: The Last American War in Europe?* pp. 83–105. London: Reuters, 2001.

Ramet, Sabrina P., and Vjeran Pavlaković (eds.). *Serbia since 1989: Politics and Society under Milošević and After*. Seattle: University of Washington Press, 2005.

Rawls, John. *Political Liberalism*. New York: Columbia University Press, 1993, 1996.

Razumovsky, Andreas Graf. *Ein Kampf um Belgrad*. Berlin: Ullstein Verlag, 1980.

Redžić, Enver. *Bosna i Hercegovina u drugom svjetskom ratu*. Sarajevo: OKO, 1998.

Reinhartz, Dennis. "Unmarked Graves: The Destruction of the Yugoslav Roma in the Balkan Holocaust, 1941–1945." *Journal of Genocide Research*, vol. 1, no. 1 (1999): 81–89.

Repe, Božo. "The Liberalization of Slovene Society in the Late 1960s." *Slovene Studies*, vol. 16, no. 2 (1994): 49–58.

———. *"Liberalizem" v Sloveniji*. Ljubljana: CIP Kataložni zapis o publikaciji Narodna in univerzitetna knjižnica, 1992.

———. "Slovenians and the Federal Yugoslavia." *Balkan Forum* (Skopje), vol. 3, no. 1 (March 1995): 139–154.

Reuter, Jens. *Die Albaner in Jugoslawien*. Munich: R. Oldenbourg Verlag, 1982.

———. "Die innere Situation Serbiens 1998—Politische Säuberungen im Windschaften der Kosovo-Krise." *Sudost Europa*, vol. 48, no. 1–2 (January–February 1999): 1–15.

———. "Die internationale Gemeinschaft und der Krieg in Kosovo." *Südost Europa*, vol. 47, no. 7–8 (July–August 1998): 281–297.

———. "Die politische Entwicklung in Bosnien-Herzegowina: Zusammenwachsen der Entitäten der nationale Abkapselung?" *Südost Europa*, vol. 47, no. 3–4 (March–April 1998): 97–116.

Reuter, Jens, and Konrad Clewing (eds.). *Der Kosovo Konflikt. Ursachen, Verlauf, Perspektiven.* Klagenfurt and Vienna: WieserVerlag, 2000.

Ribičič, Ciril. *Geneza jedna zablude: Ustavnopravna analiza nastanka i djelovanja Hrvatske zajednice Herceg-Bosne.* Zagreb: Naklada Jesenski i Turk, 2000.

Ribičič, Ciril, and Zdravko Tomac. *Federalizam po mjeri budućnosti.* Zagreb: Globus, 1989.

Ristić, Dušan. "Kosovo i Savez komunista Kosova izmedju dva kongresa i dve konferencije." In *Obeležja,* vol. 8, no. 2 (March–April 1978): 7–26.

Rizman, Rudolf Martin. *(Un)certain Path: The Problems of Democratic Transition and Consolidation in Slovenia.* College Station: Texas A&M University Press, forthcoming in 2006.

Roberts, Walter R. *Tito, Mihailović and the Allies, 1941–1945.* New Brunswick, N.J.: Rutgers University Press, 1973.

Rogošić, Roko. *Stanje Kat. Crkve u Jugoslaviji do sporazuma.* Šibenik: Pučka Tiskara, 1940.

Röhr, Werner (ed.). *Okkupation und Kollaboration (1938–1945): Beiträge zu Konzepten und Praxis der Kollaboration in der deutschen Okkupationspolitik.* Berlin and Heidelberg: Hüthig Verlagsgemeinschaft, 1994.

Roksandić, Drago. *Srbi u Hrvatskoj od 15. stoljeća do naših dana.* Zagreb: Vjesnik, 1991.

Rossos, Andrew. "The British Foreign Office and Macedonian National Identity, 1918–1941." *Slavic Review,* vol. 53, no. 2 (Summer 1994): 369–394.

———. "Incompatible Allies: Greek Communism and Macedonian Nationalism in the Civil War in Greece, 1943–1949." *Journal of Modern History,* vol. 69, no. 1 (March 1997): 42–76.

Rumiz, Paolo. *Masken für ein Massaker: Der manipulierte Krieg; Spurensuche auf dem Balkan.* Trans. from Italian by Friederike Hausmann and Gesa Schröder. Munich: Verlag Antje Kunstmann, 2000.

Rupić, Mate. "Ljudski gubici u Hrvatskoj u Drugom svjetskom ratu prema popisu iz 1950. godine." *Časopis za suvremenu povijest,* vol. 33, no. 1 (2001): 7–18.

Rusinow, Dennison I. *The Yugoslav Experiment, 1948–1974.* Berkeley and Los Angeles: University of California Press, 1977.

Rychlak, Ronald J. *Hitler, the War, and the Pope.* Columbus, Miss.: Genesis Press, 2000.

Sadkovich, James J. "Il regime di Alessandro in Iugoslavia: 1929–1934; Un'interpretazione." *Storea Contemporanea,* vol. 15, no. 1 (February 1984): 5–37.

———. *Italian Support for Croatian Separatism, 1927–1937.* New York and London: Garland, 1987.

———. *The U.S. Media and Yugoslavia, 1991–1995.* Westport, Conn.: Praeger, 1998.

Samardžić, Slobodan. *Jugoslavija pred iskušenjem federalizma.* Belgrade: Stručna knjiga, 1990.

Sánchez, José M. *Pius XII and the Holocaust: Understanding the Controversy.* Washington, D.C.: Catholic University of America Press, 2002.

Šarac, Nedim. *Uspostavljanje šestojanuarskog režima 1929. godine sa posebnim osvrtom na Bosnu i Hercegovinu.* Sarajevo: Svjetlost, 1975.

Schmid, Thomas (ed.). *Krieg im Kosovo.* Reinbek bei Hamburg: Rowohlt Taschenbuch Verlag, 1999.

Schmider, Klaus. *Partisanenkrieg in Jugoslawien 1941–1944* (Hamburg and Berlin: Verlag E. S. Mittler & Sohn GmbH, 2002).

Schöpflin, George. "The Ideology of Croatian Nationalism." *Survey,* vol. 19, no. 1 (Winter 1973): 123–146.

Scotti, Giacomo. *Ventimila caduti: Gli italiani in Jugoslavia dal 1943 al 1945.* Milan: Mursia, 1970.

Šefer, Berislav. *Privredni razvoj Jugoslavije sedamdesetih godina.* Zagreb: Informator, 1976.

Sehić, Nusret. *Četništvo u Bosni i Hercegovini (1918–1941)*. Sarajevo: Akademija Nauka i Umjetnosti Bosne i Hercegovine, 1971.

Sekelj, Laslo. *Yugoslavia: The Process of Disintegration*. Trans. from Serbo-Croatian by Vera Vukelić. Boulder, Colo.: Social Science Monographs, 1993.

Sekulić, Milisav. *Knin je pao u Beogradu*, 2nd ed. Bad Vilbel: Nidda Verlag, 2001.

Sell, Louis. *Slobodan Milošević and the Destruction of Yugoslavia*. Durham, N.C.: Duke University Press, 2002.

Sells, Michael A. *The Bridge Betrayed: Religion and Genocide in Bosnia*. Berkeley and Los Angeles: University of California Press, 1996.

Šetinc, Franc. *Misao i djelo Edvarda Kardelja*. Trans. from Slovenian into Serbo-Croatian by Ivan Brajdic. Zagreb: Globus, 1979.

———. *Što je i za što se bori Savez komunista*. Zagreb: Globus, 1974.

Seton-Watson, Hugh. *Eastern Europe between the Wars, 1918–1941*. 3rd ed. Hamden, Conn.: Archon Books, 1962.

Shelah, Menachem. "The Catholic Church in Croatia, the Vatican and the Murder of the Croatian Jews." *Holocaust and Genocide Studies*, vol. 4, no. 3 (1989): 323–339.

———. "Sajmište: An Extermination Camp in Serbia." *Holocaust and Genocide Studies*, vol. 2, no. 2 (1987): 243–260.

Shepard, Max Adams. "Sovereignty at the Crossroads: A Study of Bodin." *Political Science Quarterly*, vol. 45, no. 4 (December 1930): 580–603.

Shoup, Paul. *Communism and the Yugoslav National Question*. New York: Columbia University Press, 1968.

———. "The League of Communists of Yugoslavia." In Stephen Fischer-Galati (ed.), *The Communist Parties of Eastern Europe*. New York: Columbia University Press, 1976.

———. "The National Question in Yugoslavia." *Problems of Communism*, vol. 21, no. 1 (January–February 1972): 18–29.

———. "Problems of Party Reform in Yugoslavia." *American Slavic and East European Review*, vol. 18, no. 3 (October 1959): 334–350.

Shrader, Charles. *The Muslim-Croat Civil War in Central Bosnia: A Military History, 1992–1994*. College Station: Texas A&M University Press, 2003.

Silber, Laura, and Allan Little. *The Death of Yugoslavia*. London: Penguin Books and BBC Books, 1995.

Simms, Brendan. *Unfinest Hour: Britain and the Destruction of Bosnia*. London: Penguin Books, 2001, 2002.

Simović, Vojislav. *Zakonodavna nadležnost u razvitku jugoslovenske federacije*. Belgrade: Centar za pravna istraživanja Instituta društvenih nauka, 1978.

Singleton, Fred. *Twentieth Century Yugoslavia*. New York: Columbia University Press, 1976.

Skjelsbæk, Inger. "Sexual Violence and War: Mapping Out a Complex Relationship." *European Journal of International Relations*, vol. 7, no. 2 (2001): 211–237.

Skjelsbæk, Inger, and Dan Smith (eds.). *Gender, Peace and Conflict*. Oslo: International Peace Research Institute, 2001.

Slavica, Tomislav. "Krivnja autonomaštva." *Vidik*, vol. 18, no. 32/33 (July–August 1971): 15–20.

Snyder, Jack. *From Voting to Violence: Democratization and Nationalist Conflict*. New York: W. W. Norton, 2000.

Špadijer, Balša. *Federalizam i federalni odnosi u socijalističkoj Jugoslaviji*. Belgrade: Centar za pravna istraživanja Instituta društvenih nauka, 1978.

———. *Federalizam i medjunacionalni odnosi u Jugoslaviji*. Belgrade: Institut za političke studije, 1975.

Sruk, Josip. *Ustavno uredjenje Socijalističke Federativne Republike Jugoslavije.* Zagreb: Informator, 1976.

Stambolić, Ivan. *Rasprave o SR Srbiji, 1979–1989.* Zagreb: Globus, 1988.

Stambuk-Skalić, Marina, Josip Kolanović, and Stjepan Razum (eds.). *Proces Alojziju Stepincu: Dokumenti.* Zagreb: Kršćanska sadašnjost, 1997.

Stankiewicz, W. J. (ed.). *In Defense of Sovereignty.* New York: Oxford University Press, 1969.

Steinberg, Jonathan. *All or Nothing: The Axis and the Holocaust, 1941–1943.* London and New York: Routledge, 1990.

Steindorff, Ludwig. *Kroatien. Vom Mittelalter bis zur Gegenwart.* Regensburg/Munich: Verlag Friedrich Pustet & Südosteuropa-Gesellschaft, 2001.

Stevanović, Vidosav. *Milošević, jedan epitaf.* Belgrade: Montena, 2002.

Stillman, Peter G. "The Concept of Legitimacy." *Polity,* vol. 7, no. 1 (Fall 1974): 32–56.

Stojanović, Radoslav. *Jugoslavija, nacije i politika.* Belgrade: Nova knjiga, 1988.

Stojkov, Todor. *Opozicija u vreme šestojanuarske diktature 1929–1935.* Belgrade: Prosveta, 1969.

Stroehm, Carl Gustaf. *Ohne Tito.* Graz: Verlag Styria, 1976.

Sugar, Peter F. (ed.). *Eastern European Nationalism in the Twentieth Century.* Washington, D.C.: American University Press, 1995.

———— (ed.). *Native Fascism in the Successor States, 1918–1945.* Santa Barbara, Calif.: ABC-Clio, 1971.

Sugar, Peter F., and Ivo John Lederer (eds.). *Nationalism in Eastern Europe.* Seattle: University of Washington Press, 1969; reissued 1994.

Suljević, Kasim. *Nacionalnost Muslimana.* Rijeka: Otokar Keršovani, 1981.

Sundhaussen, Holm. "Der Ustascha-Staat: Anatomie eines Herrschaftssystems." *Österreichische Ostheft,* vol. 37, no. 2 (1995): 497–533.

————. "Jugoslawien." In Wolfgang Benz (ed.), *Dimension des Völkermords: Die Zahl der jüdischen Opfer des Nationalsozialismus,* pp. 311–330. Munich: R. Oldenbourg Verlag, 1991.

————. "Zur Geschichte der Waffen-SS in Kroatien 1941–1945." *Südost-Forschungen* (Munich), vol. 30 (1971): 176–196.

Šuvar, Stipe. *Nacionalno i nacionalističko.* Split: Marksistički Centar, 1974.

————. *Nacionalno pitanje u marksističkoj teoriji i socijalističkoj praksi.* Belgrade: Novinska Ustanova Prosvetni Pregled, 1976.

Szasz, Paul C. "The Protection of Human Rights through the Dayton/Paris Peace Agreement on Bosnia." *American Journal of International Law,* vol. 90, no. 2 (April 1996): 301–316.

Tanner, Marcus. *Croatia: A Nation Forged in War.* New Haven, Conn., and London: Yale University Press, 1997.

Tenbergen, Rasmus. *Der Kosovo-Krieg: Eine gerechte Intervention?* N.p.: ILD Verlag, 2001.

Terzuolo, Eric R. "Nationalism and Communist Resistance: Italy and Yugoslavia, 1941–1945." *Canadian Review of Studies in Nationalism,* vol. 12, no. 1 (Spring 1985): 25–45.

Thomas, Robert. *Serbia under Milošević: Politics in the 1990s.* London: Hurst, 1999.

Thompson, Mark. *Forging War: The Media in Serbia, Croatia, Bosnia and Herzegovina,* Revised and expanded ed. Luton, UK: University of Luton Press, 1999.

Tollefson, James W. "The Language Planning Process and Language Rights in Yugoslavia." *Language Problems and Language Planning,* vol. 4, no. 2 (Summer 1980): 141–156.

Tolstoy, Nikolai. "The Klagenfurt Conspiracy: War Crimes and Diplomatic Secrets." *Encounter,* vol. 60, no. 5 (May 1983): 24–37.

————. *The Minister and the Massacres.* London: Century Hutchinson, 1986.

Tomanić, Milorad. *Srpska crkva u ratu i ratovi u njoj.* Belgrade: Medijska knjižara Krug, 2001.

Tomasevich, Jozo. *War and Revolution in Yugoslavia, 1941–1945: The Chetniks.* Stanford, Calif.: Stanford University Press, 1975.

———. *War and Revolution in Yugoslavia, 1941–1945: Occupation and Collaboration.* Stanford, Calif.: Stanford University Press, 2001.

Tomasi, John. "Kymlicka, Liberalism, and Respect for Cultural Minorities." *Ethics,* vol. 105, no. 3 (April 1995): 580–603.

Troebst, Stefan. "Chronologie einer gescheiterten Prävention: Vom Konflikt zum Krieg im Kosovo 1989–1999." *Osteuropa,* vol. 49, no. 8 (August 1999): 777–795.

———. *Conflict in Kosovo: Failure of Prevention? An Analytical Documentation, 1992–1998.* ECMI Working Paper no. 1. Flensburg, Germany: European Centre for Minority Issues, 1998.

Tudjman, Franjo. *The Case of the Croatian Historian Dr. F. Tudjman: Croatia on Trial.* Trans. from Croatian by Zdenka Palić-Kusan. London: United, 1981.

Udovički, Jasminka, and James Ridgeway (eds.). *Burn This House: The Making and Unmaking of Yugoslavia.* Durham, N.C.: Duke University Press, 1997.

Ule, Mirjana, and Tanja Rener (eds.). *Youth in Slovenia: New Perspectives from the Nineties.* Ljubljana: Youth Department of the Ministry of Education and Sport, 1998.

Ursić, Theresa Marie. *Religious Freedom in Post–World War II Yugoslavia: The Case of Roman Catholic Nuns in Croatia and Bosnia-Hercegovina, 1945–1960.* Lanham, Md.: International Scholars, 2001.

Velikonja, Mitja. *Religious Separation and Political Intolerance in Bosnia-Herzegovina.* Trans. from Slovenian by Rang'ichi Ng'inja. College Station: Texas A&M University Press, 2003.

Veljić, Andjelko. *Od osnovnih organizacija udruženog rada do medjurepubličkih dogovora i sporazuma.* Belgrade: Kultura, 1974.

Vetter, Reinhold. "Bosnien-Herzegowina—vom Protektorat zum Partner." *Osteuropa,* vol. 52, no. 4 (April 2002): 476–490.

———. "Kuda ideš Srbijo? Serbien nach der erfolglosen Präsidentenwahl und dem Mord an Djindjić." *Osteuropa,* vol. 53, no. 4 (April 2003): 483–501.

Vickers, Miranda. *Between Serb and Albanian: A History of Kosovo.* New York: Columbia University Press, 1998.

Vlajčić, Gordana. *KPJ i nacionalno pitanje u Jugoslaviji, 1919–1929.* Zagreb: August Cesarec, 1974.

Volle, Angelika, and Werner Weidenfeld (eds.). *Der Balkan Zwischen Krise und Stabilität.* Bielefeld: W. Bertelsman Verlag, 2002.

Von Kohl, Christine, and Wolfgang Libal. *Kosovo: Gordischer Knoten des Balkan.* Vienna and Zurich: Europaverlag, 1992.

Vucinich, Wayne S. (ed.). *At the Brink of War and Peace: The Tito-Stalin Split in a Historic Perspective.* New York: Brooklyn College Press, 1982.

——— (ed.). *Contemporary Yugoslavia: Twenty Years of Socialist Experiment.* Berkeley and Los Angeles: University of California Press, 1969.

Vujadinović, Dragica, Lino Veljak, Vladimir Goati, and Veselin Pavićević (eds.). *Between Authoritarianism and Democracy: Serbia, Montenegro, Croatia.* 2 vols. Belgrade/Podgorica/Zagreb: CEDET/CEDEM/CTCSR, 2003, 2005.

Vuković, Mihajlo. *Sistemski okviri podsticanja razvoja nerazvijenih područja Jugoslavije.* Sarajevo: Svjetlost, 1978.

Wachtel, Andrew Baruch. *Making a Nation, Breaking a Nation: Literature and Cultural Politics in Yugoslavia.* Stanford, Calif.: Stanford University Press, 1998.

Weymouth, Tony, and Stanley Henig (eds.). *The Kosovo Crisis: The Last American War in Europe?* London: Reuters, 2001.

Wheare, K. C. *Federal Government.* 3rd ed. London: Oxford University Press, 1956.

Wilson, Duncan. *Tito's Yugoslavia.* Cambridge: Cambridge University Press, 1979.

Wolff, Robert Lee. *The Balkans in Our Time.* Cambridge, Mass.: Harvard University Press, 1956.

Woodward, Susan L. *Balkan Tragedy: Chaos and Dissolution after the Cold War.* Washington, D.C.: Brookings Institution, 1995.

———. *Socialist Unemployment: The Political Economy of Yugoslavia, 1945–1990.* Princeton, N.J.: Princeton University Press, 1995.

Žanić, Ivo. *Prevarena povijest: Guslarska estrada, kult hajduka i rat u Hrvatskoj i Bosni i Hercegovini 1990.–1995. godine.* Zagreb: Durieux, 1998.

Zečević, Momčilo. *Slovenska ljudska stranka i jugoslovensko ujedinjenje 1917–1921.* Belgrade: Institut za Savremenu Istoriju i NIP Export-Press, 1973.

Žerjavić, Vladimir. *Gubici stanovništva Jugoslavije u drugom svjetskom ratu.* Zagreb: Jugoslavensko Viktimološko Društvo, 1989.

———. *Opsesije i megalomanije oko Jasenovca i Bleiburga.* Zagreb: Globus, 1992.

Ziherl, Boris. *Komunizam i otadžbina.* Zagreb: Kultura, 1950.

Zulfikarpašić, Adil, Vlado Gotovac, Miko Tripalo, and Ivo Banac. *Okovana Bosna—Razgovor.* Ed. by Vlado Pavlinić. Zurich: Bosnjački Institut, 1995.

Collective or anonymous. *Balkan Battlegrounds: A Military History of the Yugoslav Conflict, 1990–1995.* 2 vols. Washington, D.C.: Central Intelligence Agency, Office of Russian and European Analysis, May 2002.

———. *Dossier: Crimes of Muslim Units against the Croats in BiH 1992–1994.* Mostar: Centre for Investigation and Documentation, 1999.

———. *Kongresi, konferencije: Pedeset godine Saveza komunista Jugoslavije.* Belgrade: Privredni pregled, 1969.

———. *Kosovo 1389–1989.* Special issue, *Serbian Literary Quarterly,* nos. 1–3. Belgrade, 1989.

———. *Kosovo—Past and Present.* Belgrade: Review of International Affairs, n.d. [1989].

———. *The Milošević Regme versus Serbian Democracy and Balkan Stability.* Hearing before the Commission on Security and Cooperation in Europe, 105th Cong., 2nd sess., 10 December 1998. Washington, D.C.: U.S. Government Printing Office, 1999.

———. *Nacionalno pitanje u djelima klasika marksizma i u dokumentima i praksi kpj/skj.* Zagreb: Centar Društvenih Djelatnosti SSOH, 1978.

———. *Primedbe i prigovori na projekat Konkordata izmedju naše države i vatikana.* Sremski Karlovci: Patrijaršija štamparija, 1936.

———. *Slučaj Žanko.* Belgrade: Kosmos, 1986.

———. *Srpska Pravoslavna Crkva 1920–1970: Spomenica u 50-godišnjici vaspostavljanja Srpske Patrijaršije.* Belgrade: Kosmos, 1971.

———. *Sudjenje Dr. Vlatka Mačka.* 64-page pamphlet (no publishing information in the pamphlet).

———. *The Third Reich and Yugoslavia, 1933–1945.* Belgrade: Institute for Contemporary History, 1977.

———. *Udruženi rad i medjunacionalni odnosi.* Belgrade: Komunist, 1978.

———. *Ustav Socijalističke Federativne Republike Jugoslavije: Stručno objašnjenje.* Belgrade: Privredni pregled, 1975.

———. *Zadaci SK Srbije u razvoju medjunacionalnih odnosa i borbi protiv nacionalizma.* Belgrade: Komunist, 1978.

Unpublished Sources

Interviews: Yugoslavia (Belgrade, Zagreb, Ljubljana, Sarajevo, Skopje), October 1979–July 1980, July 1982, July 1987, July 1988, August–September 1989; Croatia, (Zagreb), August–September 1997, July 2001, December 2002; Bosnia-Herzegovina (Sarajevo), July 2004; Macedonia (Skopje and Tetovo), March 1995; Serbia (Belgrade and Novi Sad), June 2004; Slovenia (Ljubljana), March 1992, October 1998, August–September 1999, November 1999; Sweden (Frövi), April 2004; United States (Washington, D.C.), March–April 2001.

Boškovska, Nada. "Jugoslawisch-Makedonien in der Zwischenkriegszeit: Eine Randregion zwischen Repression und Integration." Habitationsschrift, Universität Zürich, 2001.

Emmert, Thomas A. "The Battle of Kosovo: A Reconsideration of Its Significance in the Decline of Medieval Serbia." Ph.D. diss., Stanford University, 1973.

Fogelquist, Alan F. "Politics and Economic Policy in Yugoslavia, 1918–1929." Ph.D. diss., UCLA, 1990.

Hermann-De Luca, Kristine Ann. "Beyond Elections: Lessons in Democratization Assistance from Post-War Bosnia and Herzegovina." Ph.D. diss., American University, 2002.

Jovanović-Ozegović, Jelena. "The Relationship between Ethnic Identity, Collectivism, Psychological Distress, and Secondary Trauma as a Result of an Ethnic Conflict." Ph.D. diss., Loyola University, Chicago, 2002.

O'Halloran, Patrick Joseph. "The Role of Identity in Post-Conflict State-Building: The Case of Bosnia-Herzegovina and the Dayton Agreement." Ph.D. diss., York University, 2002.

Sletzinger, Martin C. "The Reform and Reorganization of the League of Communists of Yugoslavia, 1966–1973." Ph.D. diss., Harvard University, 1976.

Stambolić, Vukašin. "Položaj i odnosi republika u SFRJ." Master's thesis, University of Belgrade, 1968.

Wambold, Alan B. "The National Question and the Evolution of the Yugoslav Constitution, 1971–1974." Ph.D. diss., University of Virginia, 1976.

Zimmermann, William. "Issue Area, International-National Linkages, and Yugoslav Political Processes." Unpublished ms., Ann Arbor, Mich., 1977.

Index

Abdić, Fikret, 336, 357, 389, 427–28, 438–39, 442, 451
Abria (village in Kosovo), 514
absolute rights principles, 20
Acheson, Dean, 182
Ačimović, Milan, 105, 129, 130, 133
Ada, Mikro, 314–15
Ademi, General Rahim, 485
Adžić, Blagoje, 395, 396
Afghanistan, U.S. war in, 546
Agičić, Damir, 592–93
agrarian reform, 50, 166–67
Agrarian Union, 52–53, 57, 59, 63, 65, 74, 88–89, 158
Agrokomerc, 336, 438
Ahmeti, Ali, 581
Ahmići massacre, 438
Ahtisaari, Martti, 517, 537
Ai Dalmati (Tommaseo), 233
aid for underdeveloped regions, 265–67
AIM Press (Macedonian newspaper), 567, 593
air strikes, 444–48, 456–60, 462, 464–66, 515–17
Ajtič, Predrag, 244
Akashi, Yasushi, 444, 445, 446, 447, 448, 457–58
Akmadžić, Mile, 437
Akšamović, Bishop Antun, 123
Alagić, General Mehmed, 485
Albania: aspirations in, 174–75; and Italian Occupation Zone, 140–42; and resistance, 144; Soviet and Yugoslav position on, 175
Albanian National Army, 540, 550
Albanians. *See* Albania; Kosovo; Macedonia
Albanians of Kosovo, 38, 293–307
Albanian Students' Union, 514
Albright, Madeleine K., 474, 544
Aleksandar, Crown Prince, 507
Aleksandar, King: and abolition of monarchy, 508; "amputation" option of, 74–75; assassination of, 3, 51, 80, 83–84, 90–92, 105; confirmation of as king, 60; and constitution, 13, 56; contempt for

political parties by, 46; and dysfunctional system, 76; expectations of, 75; and failure of first Yugoslavia, 598, 602; and Markov protocol, 62; and new government, 60; and opposition, 63; and provincial government, 52; and religion, 94; response to Assembly shootings by, 74–75; royal dictatorship of, 3, 75, 79–82, 84, 86, 602; and Serbia, 99; and suffrage, 53; and unification of Yugoslavia, 43–44. *See also* Karadjordjević dynasty
Alexander, Field Marshal Sir Harold, 159–60
Alexander, Stella, 99
Alibabić-Munja, Munir, 415
Alispahić, Bakir, 415, 442
Alliance for Change, 492
Almond, Gabriel, 21
Alternative Movement, 313
amendments to constitution. *See* constitutional amendments
American Bar Association, 555
American Historical Review, 322
Amfilohije, Metropolitan, 501–2
Amnesty International, 321, 543
"anarcho-liberalism," 186, 210–11
Andres, Ivan, 107
Anić, Vladimir, 309
animals, effect of war on, 468
Ankara (Turkey), 100
Anna Monro Theater, 313
Annan, Kofi, 463–64, 546
Anti-Fascist Council of the National Liberation of Yugoslavia (AVNOJ), 153, 157–58, 164
anti-Semitism, 121, 132–33. *See also* Jews, treatment of
Antonescu, Marshal, 165
apocalypse culture, 373
apologies by Bosnian Serbs and Bosnian Croats, 483
Aquinas, Thomas, 13, 16, 22, 24, 26
Aračinovo (Macedonia), 575, 580

Mojsov, Lazar, 345
Molitva (The Prayer) (Drašković), 389
Moljević, Stevan, 145, 166
Mollica, Richard, 467
Molotov, Vyacheslav, 175, 180
monarchy: abolition of, 508; differences over, 53; hereditary, 22. *See also specific ruler*
Monastery of Prohor Pcinski, 164, 355
Mongol sacking of Budapest, 2
Montenegrin Literary Society, 241
Montenegrin Orthodox Church, 47–48, 94
Montenegro: and birth of second Yugoslavia, 164; Chetniks in, 147; civil war in, 601; and communists, 6; economic sector in, 272–73; elections in, 65–66; independence of, 527–28; and Italian Occupation Zone, 140–45; and Kingdom of SHS, 47–48; and Koštunica, Vojislav, 523; and Milošević, 23, 353–54; and nationalism, 6, 241, 316–17; and NATO air strikes, 516–17; resistance in, 140–45; and Serbia, 517–18, 531, 532, 534; and War of Yugoslav Succession, 408. *See also names of cities*
morality: and legitimacy, 20, 22, 26–27; moral law, 15–16; and war, 468
More, Bolard, 188
Morina, Rahman, 353, 496
Moscow, 63, 65
Moskovljević, Miloš S., 231
Most (Slovenian journal), 242
Mostar (Herzegovina), 124, 125, 427, 436, 438, 489, 490
MPRI. *See* Military Professional Resources, Inc.
Mrkonjić, Petar, 89. *See also* "Petar Mrkonjić" Association of Serbian Chetniks
Mrkonjić Grad (Bosnia), 129, 476
Mrkšić, General Mile, 459, 485
Mršić, Zdravko, 374
Mugoša, Dušan, 155
mujahedin volunteers, 435
multi-ethnic state, 29–30, 32–33, 37, 411, 481, 550
multi-party system, 24, 335, 372, 379, 603
Muratović, Hasan, 458
music: Croatian pop music, 481; Domobrani (quisling) songs, 554; and nationalism, 313; rock, 313, 564–65; turbo-folk, 502

Muslimanska svijest (official organ of Gajret), 108
Muslim Bosniak Organization (MBO), 416, 426
Muslimović, Fikret, 415, 442
Muslims: and Aleksandar, 94; and Chetniks, 146, 148; and constitution of 1963, 208–9; and Croat-Muslim War, 10, 433–39, 448; and cultural barriers, 481; and education, 546; and extremism in Bosnia, 29; fundamentalism, 431; and Izetbegović's "pepper pot," 419, 422–24, 426; and Kingdom of Serbs, Croats, and Slovenes, 44; *mujahedin* volunteers, 435; and nationalism, 285–93; and neutrality, 29; and Orthodox Church, 61; in Sandžak, 527; in Serbia, 368; Turkish schools, 48; and *Ustaše*, 118; and violence in Bosnia, 49; and war against organized religion, 197, 198–99; and War of Yugoslav Succession (1992–1995), 413. *See also* Kingdom of Serbs, Croats, and Slovenes (1918–1929); Yugoslav Muslim Organization (JMO)
Mussolini, Benito, 82, 102–4, 109, 150, 156
Mustać, Zdravko, 345
MVAC. *See* Milizia volontaria anticomunista

Načertanije of 1844, 37, 40
Nacional (Croatian weekly magazine), 438, 587
nacionalna država, 422
Nagodba of 1868, 40
Nagy, Imre, 201
Nahum, Archimandrite of Rousee, 165
Najbar-Agičić, Magdalena, 592–93
Najdenov, Petar, 569
Naletilić, Mladen "Tuta," 485
napalm, allegations of use of, 407
Napoleon, 2–3
Naprijed (newspaper), 194
Narodna armija (army daily newspaper), 279, 335, 401
Narodni glas (newspaper), 168–69, 171
Naša borba (newspaper), 498
Nasir, Gamal abd al, 186
Nastić, Vojislav Varnava, 198
National Committee of Liberation, 157
National Council of the Slovenes, Croats, and Serbs, 42, 43, 44–45, 46, 57
nationalism: Albanian nationalism in Kosovo, 293–307; bureaucratic, 370; and

nationalism (*continued*)
Catholic Church, 259; and Chetniks,
419–21; civic, 30; collectivist, 597; and
Ćosić, 29; and Croatia, 235, 242, 260,
307–12, 421–22; culture of, 532; eclectic,
389, 390; ethnic, 6, 39, 390, 604;
exclusivist, 257; growth of, 598; and
Kingdom of Serbs, Croats, and Slovenes,
36–37; liberalism vs., 533, 535;
Macedonianism, 317–19; and
Montenegro, 6, 241, 316–17; and music,
313; and Muslims, 285–93; in occupied
Serbia, 132–33; and Praxis group, 250;
and road to war, 367–69; Serbian, 243,
295, 319–23, 379, 534; Slovenian, 242,
312–16; and system legitimacy, 29–30;
tensions of (1968–1990), 285–323; Tripalo
on, 214; and Tudjman, 14
nationality on census forms, 9, 287–88
National-Liberal coalition, 217, 219–22
National Liberation Committee, 158
National Liberation Front (NOF), 173, 174
National Liberation Struggle, 152, 177
National Liberation War, 7, 162. *See also*
World War Two and partisan struggle
(1941–1945)
National Library of Kosovo, 538
National Radical Party. *See* Radical Party
NATO: admission to, 549; air strikes,
465–66; and Albanians, 552; and Bosnia,
490, 493; and Bush, George W., 547; and
human rights violations, 543; and Kosovo,
514, 515, 516, 543, 546; and Macedonia,
579; and paramilitaries, 540;
peacekeepers, 515, 540; and post-Dayton
peace, 478–79; and Yugoslav War of
Succession, 443–46, 455, 457–58, 462–63,
465–66, 537. *See also* air strikes
Natural Law, 15–17, 22, 26, 120–21
Nazi Germany. *See* Germany; World War
Two and partisan struggle (1941–1945)
NDH. *See* Independent State of Croatia
Nedeljna borba, 353
Nedić, Milan, 8, 107, 113, 115, 129–30,
132–35, 143, 533
Nedjeljna Dalmacija (Split weekly
newspaper), 369
Negovanović, Marko, 395
Nehru, Jawaharlal, 186
Nemanja, Stefan, 2
Nešković, Blagoje, 142, 191
Neubacher, Hermann, 134–35

Neubacher Plan, 134
Neue Slowenische Kunst (NSK) arts
collective, 313
Neue Zürcher Zeitung (Swiss newspaper),
407, 531
Neurath, Konstantin Baron von, 104
neutrality, 27–29
Neville-Jones, Pauline, 449
The New Class (Djilas), 202, 203–4, 502
New Course, 200
New Croat Initiative (NHI), 493
New Left Review, 323
newspapers: and anti-monopoly law, 507;
censorship of, 81, 166, 192; in Kosovo,
544; and Milošević, 345; and reporting of
corruption in Slovenia, 559–60; and war
against organized religion, 199. *See also*
press, freedom of; *specific papers*
New York Times, 400, 506
NHI (New Croat Initiative), 493
Nikezić, Marko, 5, 211, 243, 244, 245, 253,
260, 319
Nikić, Nikola, 68–69
Nikola, King of Montenegro, 38, 47
Nikolić, Tomislav, 359
Nikolić, Kosta, 533, 535
Nikolić, Tomislav, 531, 532
Nikšic (Montenegro), 47, 85, 179, 351
Nikšic-on-Sea, 501
NIN (Belgrade weekly magazine): on arms
sales, 454; on civil war, 387; on
constitution, 336; on ethnic tensions, 232,
242; and Milošević, 345, 350, 498; and
nationalism, 241–42; on nuclear power
plant, 407; on Serbs, 309; and Stanić, 298
Ninth Congress, 222
Niš, Serbia, 81, 89, 131, 495, 504
Nje Pallto per Babain tim ne Burg (A Coat
for My Convicted Father) (film), 513
Njivice, Bosnia, 438
NOB (People's Liberation Struggle), 185
NOF. *See* National Liberation Front
no-fly zones, 447, 451, 459
nonaligned movement, 8, 186, 605
Norac, General Mirko, 485
North Atlantic Council, 474, 514
North Atlantic Treaty Organisation. *See*
NATO
North Korea, offensive by, 4, 181, 182, 199
Nova Borba (Cominformist newspaper), 179
Nova Gradiška, Croatia, 409
Novaković, Ljubo, 143

About the Author

Sabrina P. Ramet (born in London, England) is professor of political science at the Norwegian University of Science and Technology (NTNU), Trondheim, Norway; a senior research associate of the Centre for the Study of Civil War of the International Peace Research Institute in Oslo (PRIO); a member of the Royal Norwegian Society of Sciences and Letters; and a research associate of the Science and Research Center of the Republic of Slovenia, Koper. She is the author of eight previous books—among them, *Balkan Babel: The Disintegration of Yugoslavia from the Death of Tito to the Fall of Milošević*, 4th ed. (Westview Press, 2002)—and editor or coeditor of 19 books. She studied philosophy at Stanford University and received her Ph.D. in political science from UCLA; she subsequently taught at the University of California at Santa Barbara, UCLA, the University of Washington, and Ritsumeikan University in Kyoto, Japan, before moving to Norway in 2001. Her book *Whose Democracy? Nationalism, Religion, and the Doctrine of Collective Rights in Post-1989 Eastern Europe* (Rowman & Littlefield, 1997) was named an Outstanding Academic Book by *Choice* magazine. Her articles have appeared in *Foreign Affairs, World Politics, Problems of Post-Communism, Orbis,* and other journals.